THE KURDISH QUESTION

The Kurdish Question Revisited

Edited by

GARETH STANSFIELD AND

MOHAMMED SHAREEF

HURST & COMPANY, LONDON

First published in the United Kingdom in 2017 by
C. Hurst & Co. (Publishers) Ltd.,
41 Great Russell Street, London, WC1B 3PL
© Gareth Stansfield, Mohammed Shareef and the Contributors, 2017
All rights reserved.

Printed in the United Kingdom by Bell & Bain Ltd, Glasgow

The right of Gareth Stansfield, Mohammed Shareef and the Contributors to be identified as the authors of this publication is asserted by them in accordance with the Copyright, Designs and Patents Act, 1988.

A Cataloguing-in-Publication data record for this book
is available from the British Library.

9781849045919 paperback

9781849045629 hardback

This book is printed using paper from registered sustainable and managed sources.

www.hurstpublishers.com

To the people of Kurdistan

CONTENTS

Kurdistan

Kurds in Iran

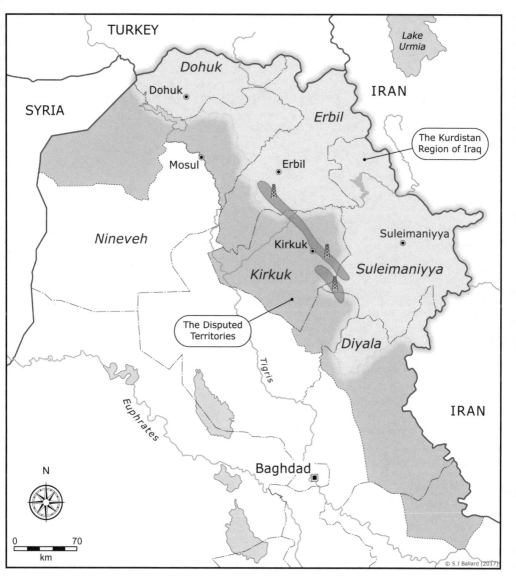

Kurds in Iraq

Kurds in Turkey

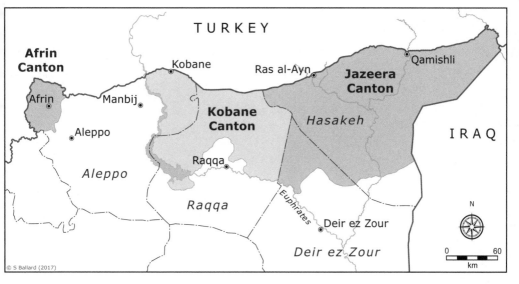

Kurds in Syria: the three cantons of Rojava, 2014–2016

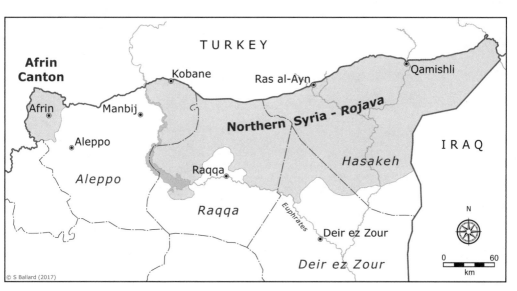

Kurds in Syria: The Democratic Federation of Northern Syria, 2016–

INTRODUCTION

Gareth Stansfield and *Mohammed Shareef*

Even for the most seasoned of observers, the world of Middle East politics has changed in almost unbelievable ways in a very short period of time. As former senior US State Department official and president of the Council on Foreign Relations Richard Haass stated in a *Foreign Affairs* piece about the rapidly changing situation in the region: "The old order in the Middle East is disappearing. The transition is still in its early phases, and what will follow (and when) is uncertain... Some borders are likely to be redrawn, and some new states may even emerge."[1] Echoing these sentiments, former UK Foreign Secretary William Hague warned that "[t]he sad truth is that the disorder and civil war that has erupted in much of the Middle East is probably still in its early stages rather than coming to an end."[2] Swift though they may be today, these changes started slowly, almost imperceptibly, as different social forces waxed and waned since the end of the Second World War, and as the Middle East state system became more consolidated. Currents of different social movements—whether related to religious belief, sectarianism, nationalism, or to traditional social constructs such as tribes, or the structures that were nurtured under the influence of modernity's many agencies—interacted with the forces of the state, coming together to form the difficult and sometimes dangerous world of Middle Eastern political life in the period post-Second World War.

The fundamental problem in the post-war Middle East was the existence of the imposed state system that facilitated the rise of authoritarian regimes and nurtured a powerful dynamic of a dominant Arab nationhood in the Arab states, Turkish nationhood in Turkey, Persian nationhood in Iran, and Zionism in Israel.[3] From this structural problem stemmed many seemingly irresolvable issues. Among these, nothing was more important in policy and academic circles than the Arab-Israeli conflict and the plight of the Palestinians—a state of affairs that has, in the twenty-first century, changed markedly as the relative importance of the Palestinian question seemed to fall down the list of priorities of policy makers, if not in the minds of academics and observers.[4] Of course, other situations also exercised observers of Middle Eastern affairs. The transformation of Iran from monarchy to Islamic Republic sent shock waves throughout the region and gave added impetus to a sectarian divide that had, for most of the twentieth century, been marginalized in importance and effect in Arab states.[5] The effects of oil wealth, too, generated much attention, either in terms of the ossifying effect such wealth had on traditional socio-cultural systems, or on the need to maintain the stability of oil-rich states for reasons related to Western interests.[6] The toppling of pro-Western monarchies and the rise and role of the military in Arab states was also a prevalent feature, and one that came to be viewed as perhaps a lasting, rather than temporary, aspect of the political landscape.[7] And where were the Kurds in this volatile period? In "state" terms, they were nowhere: no Kurdistan existed as an independent state and, as the decades wore on, the Kurds remained marginalized, suppressed, and oppressed in every state in which they found themselves.

During this post-Second World War period, very few observers thought the Kurdish issue would gain any prominence in the politics and international relations of the Middle East. Even fewer would imagine a region in which the military regimes of the Arab world, and the militarist state in Turkey, would be altered. But these unforeseen events did come to pass. The twenty-first century saw the Ba'ath regime of Iraq removed by US-led military forces in 2003; the established republican/military regimes challenged by popular movements in successive uprisings across Arab countries, otherwise known as the Arab Spring, from 2011; and Turkey reworked from the inside out by Recep Tayyib Erdoğan's Justice and Development Party (AKP), mainly from 2008 onwards. In the midst of these sudden and dramatic changes, the once marginalized Kurds became geopolitically central and relevant as their interests aligned with Western powers.[8] Because of these changes, the Kurdish Question, or "Questions", of the twentieth century now need to be reconsidered, as ideas that were once posited as hypothetical questions—such as "could the Kurds be independent?"—are now very much real possibilities, if not probabilities, generating even greater debate and discussion than they did in the post-war period because of the far greater likelihood of them coming to pass.

From maligned proxies to valued allies, and back again?

During this period following the Second World War, the subject of the Kurds was not commonly addressed in academic literature, nor was it a focus of journalists beyond those who sought to portray the story of an isolated people in inaccessible lands.[9] The Kurds were largely seen as an inconvenience by Western powers, who offered little other than sympathy as the Kurdish issue was categorized as a domestic issue with little incentive for any political support. Even at the height of the Cold War, senior US officials made it clear that they had no interest in any involvement in the Kurdish cause; and attempts by the Shah's Iran were largely dismissed within this context until 1972, when the Shah made a personal plea to President Nixon. Even that was short-lived when the Shah signed the Algiers Agreement with Saddam Hussein in 1975.[10] This all changed in 1991 when the Kurds of Iraq were thrust into the international spotlight following Saddam Hussein's invasion of Kuwait in 1990, and the subsequent Kurdish rebellion (*rapareen*) in the north of the country, alongside the Shia uprising (*intifadah*) in the south.[11] The Iraqi Kurds felt that a golden opportunity had presented itself with Saddam Hussein this time on the wrong side of history, in contrast to the favored position he had enjoyed during the war against Ayatollah Khomeini's revolutionary Shia regime in Tehran.[12]

Dating back to the end of the Ottoman Empire and the imposition of international boundaries across the Middle East by competing Western imperial powers, the Kurdish situation had rumbled on throughout the twentieth century and, from the perspective of those Kurds engaged in the several nationalist movements that had emerged, without resolution. The "question" was of critical importance to those states that accommodated, though more accurately subjugated, Kurdish populations—namely Turkey, Iran, Iraq, and Syria—as the presence of a significant ethnic minority in states that were rapidly coalescing around a narrative of a particular dominant nationhood (Turkish, Persian, and Arab) presented an uncomfortable reality and a challenge to them. The Kurdish question(s) would often exercise the judgment and decision-making powers of international actors, including Western powers and the Soviet Union/Russia, as to whether they should acknowledge and recognize atrocities committed against Kurdish populations, or ignore them, or even exploit their effects and use recalcitrant Kurds as proxies to promote their own strategies. It would be a rare occurrence, if it happened at all, that international actors would come to the Kurds' assistance—even when they were systematically targeted in Iran following the rise of the Islamic Republic, subjected to genocide by the Iraqi state during the *Anfal* campaign in the 1980s, or targeted by chemical weapons.[13] And so the Kurds were either ignored as inconvenient and marginalized outliers in Middle Eastern political life, or sometimes supported as conveniently placed fighters to be deployed in the national interests of others, against the countries in which they found themselves.

The perennial Kurdish weakness had always been that their problems were too big to resolve, but not big enough to be of primary concern to an international community that was effectively a club of sovereign states largely acting to preserve the integrity of its members. It would take a series of very significant developments in world politics to begin the process of aligning the Kurds—and the resolution of the various Kurdish questions—with the interests of the most important states in the international community. This process began in 1991, when Iraqi Kurds fled into the mountainous border region of Iraq and Turkey as Saddam Hussein deployed his Republican Guards divisions to the Kurdish populated areas where rebellions had begun in earnest following unintentional statements by US President George H. W. Bush, calling upon the people to rise against the regime. From this critical moment in time key dynamics were established, the legacies of which are evident today. Perhaps most significantly is the way in which the United States established itself in the region, becoming an unrivaled military power in the Middle East. Over the years, US interests and partners would move and change: who could have foreseen the warming of relations between the Obama administration and the Rouhani government of Iran, and the consternation this would invoke in Saudi Arabia and Israel? But the US capability to project power in the region, even during the more cautious Obama presidency, remained impressive. And the Kurds, at least those in Iraq and Syria if not in Iran and Turkey, would make the transition from being regarded with suspicion by the US and her Western partners, to being key allies in the struggle against the Islamic State. This also then saw the US find itself in a difficult position with regard to her NATO ally Turkey, yet sharing many interests, including on the battlefields of Iraq and Syria, with the Islamic Republic of Iran.

A further key legacy to have emerged from 1991 was the emergence of a piece of territory governed by Kurds and called Kurdistan or, more accurately, the Kurdistan Region of Iraq. To be sure, many various "Kurdistans" had existed in different parts of the Middle East over the years, and academics would debate their "Kurdishness" vis-à-vis other forms of pre-modern identities. Many Kurdish nationalists would point to the semi-autonomous Kurdish emirates that existed in the Ottoman and Persian empires as being "Kurdish", which is true, but they did not exist as "Kurdistan" but rather as manifestations of tribal power in the borderlands of empires that saw utility in empowering pliant local rulers.[14] The twentieth century saw entities emerge that were influenced by the nationalist ideas that had restructured Europe and had taken root in the Ottoman and Qajar Empires, as well as other parts of the Middle East. Sheikh Mahmoud Barzinji of Sulaimani in Iraqi Kurdistan may well have been a local power-holder attempting to use the rhetoric of nationalism to further his power and influence, but his attempt to proclaim an independent Kurdistan, against the wishes of the British occupying powers, exemplified the rising nationalist feelings of Kurds.[15] Perhaps the emergence of the Kurdistan Region of Iraq in 1991 mirrored most closely the establishment of the Republic of Kurdistan in the Iranian city of Mahabad, in 1946.[16] The similarities are striking: both appeared in power vacuums that came after conflict ended, with the Mahabad Republic coming about following the end of the Second World War, and the Kurdistan Region following Iraq's defeat in Kuwait; and both saw foreign intervention determine their survival. In the case of 1991, this intervention allowed the Kurdistan Region to survive and then prosper; in the case of 1946, the intervention (which was the US effectively forcing the USSR to end its support of the nascent state), saw the Republic end and its leaders executed, apart from Mullah Mustafa Barzani who managed to escape to the Soviet Union with his followers, leaving with a deeply held mistrust of US motives, and consequently leading Kurdish notables and nationalists almost simultaneously to form the Kurdistan Democratic Party (KDP) in Iraq.[17]

A Kurdistan Autonomous Region of Iraq was also delineated in the March Agreement signed between Mullah Barzani and the vice-president of Iraq, a young Saddam Hussein, in 1970.[18] The March Agreement would never be implemented due to Barzani's demands to include Kirkuk in the Autonomous Region. Instead, the Autonomy Law of 1974 was unilaterally introduced by the government of Iraq, without including Kirkuk, thus prompting a further Kurdish rebellion that would ultimately fail. But the law's outlining of the territorial parameters of the Kurdistan Autonomous Region greatly influenced the spatial extent of the entity that emerged in 1991. And so, after a long and depressing history of failed or abortive attempts to carve out a piece of Kurdish-controlled territory called Kurdistan somewhere in the Middle East, few expected the entity of 1991 to survive for very long. But, for once, Kurdish interests in Iraq matched the interests of Western powers and, for the first time, the plight of the Kurds, albeit from one "part" of Kurdistan, was disseminated to a global audience through print and TV media. Having saved the Kurds of Iraq from slaughter at the hands of the Iraqi Republican Guard, and then from a savage winter in the Zagros mountains, Western powers found themselves the unintended guardians of the fledgling Kurdistan Region of Iraq—an entity created totally by accident, surrounded by states which viewed the development as a threat to their own integrity, and which therefore existed as a geopolitical anomaly maintained by a highly peculiar set of political circumstances. Few expected this region to survive, and it very nearly did not. Riven with internal rivalries, Kurdish parties in Iraq succumbed to the influence of their neighbors and fell into a series of conflicts between 1994 and 1997; yet against all odds, the entity remained. Looking back at this period some twenty years later, it seems clear that this simple act of survival in the dangerous years of the 1990s should be regarded as the Kurds' biggest success story. Now, the KRI has become an institutionalized presence on the map of the Middle East, creating new dynamics among the Kurds of Iran, Turkey, and Syria, many of whom viewed the Kurdistan Region of Iraq as something to emulate. This was to happen in Syria some twenty-five years later, although following the implementation of a centrally organized plan, very different to the haphazard manner in which the KRI unfolded over a much longer period of time.

The Kurds in Iraq now very openly talk about independence; something that would have been deemed impossible even ten years ago. Various regional geopolitical and economic factors have come together to make this life-long dream seem within reach. The most important factor has been the discovery of large oil and gas reserves in the KRI and the involvement of international oil companies (IOCs) in the sector.[19] Managed correctly, the oil and gas sector could indeed provide the Kurds of Iraq the wherewithal to secede and declare an independent republic. Yet many questions need to be addressed, such as the lack of reliable and secure export routes across countries that have not proven to be supportive of any attempts by the Kurds to exist independently in the past. Furthermore, the KRG would need to show its capability in managing its affairs effectively and reducing the risk posed by corruption and the threat posed by having an economy wholly dependent upon oil exports. At the time of writing, the KRG was heavily engaged in facing these problems as the economy of the KRI spiraled into appalling levels of debt, with figures ranging from $18 to $25 billion by mid 2016.[20] On the political side, the KRI again looked strong when viewed from a certain angle. With a history of multi-party elections, what seemed to be a vibrant parliament, and with an emergent, and vocal, civil society, the KRI was increasingly viewed by many Western observers as a democratic beacon in the region. But the reality was different. The transition to democracy had stuttered and stalled since the end of 1990s and, no matter what the leaders of the KDP, PUK, and Lîstî Gorran said about democracy, the fact remained that the same figures that had been in power in 1991 were still contesting it in 2015. More enlightened figures among the leaderships realized that this was not a tenable situation, but few had workable ideas for how the transition could be re-energized, and how the established parties could facilitate a process that could very easily undermine their hegemonies. In addition to the economic and political developments, the KRI became important to Western powers for military reasons. The rise of the Islamic State in Iraq and Syria (ISIS) and the invasion of Mosul in June 2014 altered the nature of the relationship with the KRI, making the Kurdish *peshmerga* key allies in a fight that, for Western powers, was deemed of unparalleled importance.[21] But, as with the problems with oil and gas, and also with regard to the faltering performance of Kurdish democracy in Iraq, the military relationship with the West was also problematic, due to one question: if the alliance was built upon the need to target the Islamic State, what would happen once Islamic State was no more? Would the Western powers once again forget about the Kurds, or would this new relationship prove to be more durable? Independence had certainly become possible, but much work needed to be done in these three areas—the economy, the democratic transition, and Western alliances—to ensure that it could, indeed, come to pass.

Meanwhile Turkey, home to the largest population of Kurds, was also seeing significant changes with regard to its domestic political life, and the impact this would have on its own Kurdish question. An early attempt at a Kurdish entity on Turkish territory, the Kurdish Republic of Ararat, lasting only from 1927 to 1930, was the only political structure they had ever achieved.[22] The 1970s and 1980s had seen a surge in leftist-rightist violence in Turkey, with Kurds as key supporters of the leftist cause.[23] By 1984, the Partiya Karkerên Kurdistanê (PKK) had emerged as a distinctly Kurdish party—although still heavily leftist in its political orientation—and commenced its insurgent attacks against the Turkish state in what has become one of the longest civil wars in the post-Second World War period.[24] This new dynamic of violent Kurdish activism in Turkey combined with the example of the de facto state that had come about in Iraq, made Turkey a critical focal point for the development of the Kurdish nationalist movement.[25] Yet the PKK failed to carve out an enclave in Turkey to mirror the one that had emerged in Iraq. Instead, the Kurdish movement in Turkey was torn between those forces, in the form of the PKK, that saw violent insurrection as being the only way to satisfy Kurdish nationalist demands in Turkey, and those who had hope that the Kurds could be accommodated successfully within the Turkish state through a political strategy that utilized democratic methods.

However, the Kurdish situation in Turkey has fluctuated greatly since the abduction of PKK leader Abdullah Öcalan in 1999.[26] In what was seen as a positive development, the Turkish government adopted a new outward-facing philosophy of "zero problems with neighbors", and Ankara won praise both at home and abroad as Turkey re-engaged with the Middle East following a half century of estrangement.[27] Business and trade links were expanded with Arab states, as well as with Iran; visa restrictions were lifted with neighboring countries; and from 2008, the relationship between Ankara and the KRI began to show marked improvements. Starting in 2004, Turkey showed some flexibility on the Kurdish issue consequence of the Justice and Development Party's (AKP) rapprochement, or at least the impression that it intended to do something to resolve the Kurdish issue. Also, in late 2008 there was some reconciliation between Iraqi Kurds and the Turks; on 14 October 2008 a special envoy from Turkey, Murad Ocalik, visited the President of the Kurdistan Region of Iraq, Masoud Barzani, in Baghdad, to work toward an easing of relations.[28] As regards the US strategic alliance with Turkey and the obstacle this would present to its relations with the KRI, initially the US swung toward the Kurds on some occasions and back to Turkey on others. The US, eventually, came to a point where it could actually have a relationship with both sides, coming to the conclusion that it did not have to be a zero-sum game, and thus giving the Kurds of Iraq heightened legitimacy in international affairs.

From 2008 onwards, Turkey's relations with the KRI grew gradually closer. Financially, Turkey was the biggest investor in Iraqi Kurdistan. By 2013 the volume of trade between the KRI and Turkey had peaked at 8 billion US dollars. Turkey and the KRI, once at odds because of Ankara's fears over Kurdish political aspirations, have also found themselves politically aligned since 2011 in their alarm at the Shia-led government of Iraqi Prime Minister Maliki: particularly its tilt toward Iran, especially after the US withdrawal in December 2011 and Maliki's aggressive attempts at unilateralism and consolidation of power. Following the rise of Islamic State, this tension still exists between President Erdoğan of Turkey and Prime Minister Abadi of Iraq, although the relationship between Erdoğan and the Iraqi Kurds also seems to have suffered in recent years.

Domestically, inside Turkey the pro-Kurdish Peoples' Democratic Party's (HDP) spectacular success in the June 2015 elections was a major turning point.[29] The HDP became the first pro-Kurdish party to surpass the 10 per cent electoral threshold with its gain of 80 seats in the Turkish parliament and 13 per cent electoral support: seen as a major threat by the AKP government. From a Turkish perspective, the allegedly PKK-associated HDP was transferring the violent and bloody struggle to the hall of the Turkish parliament with the significant vote-share giving the cause the legitimacy it had craved, something the Turkish state was unwilling to concede. A transformation to peaceful politics was not something the AKP was willing to allow. Increasing domestic pressure and intimidation in the Kurdish south-east led to a 21-seat decline and a reduced electoral mandate of 10.75 per cent in the second round of elections held just a few months later in November 2015: simultaneously a disappointment and a major relief, as it was just enough to pass the parliamentary threshold.

The situation in Syria and Iran was less well-known, and far less understood.[30] With the Kurds a smaller minority in Syria, the Ba'athist state of Hafez al-Assad found it straightforward to suppress Kurdish political activism. Yet the regime also saw a powerful proxy in the form of Kurdish separatists in Turkey, and encouraged Kurds from Syria—who had been denied Syrian citizenship by the regime—to enrol with the PKK which, in the 1980s, had found in Damascus a strongly supportive patron. With bases made available in the secure Beqaa Valley of Lebanon, the PKK grew its expertise considerably, and saw its ranks swell with a strong and steady stream of recruits emanating from Syria's Kurdish community. But, for those Kurds in Syria who did not want to join the PKK to fight Turkey, but rather sought to find a way to challenge the state system in which they found themselves, the situation was dangerous.

The Kurds in Syria eventually found an opening in the "Arab Spring" of 2011, similar in many ways to the opportunity presented to the Iraqi Kurds after the Iraqi occupation of Kuwait in 1990. The unfolding events of the rebellion allowed the Kurds a historic opportunity unlike any since the establishment of the artificial Kingdom of Syria in 1920, and more recently the suppressed and short-lived uprising of 2004.[31] The Kurds in Syria, in a way not dissimilar to the aftermath of the 1991 uprising in Iraqi Kurdistan, have managed to carve out and establish a de facto entity that has no real recognition, but has within it seeds of a federal system (unilaterally declared in March 2016) that could potentially be applied to the whole country after the dust from the civil war settles. Also similarly to the Iraqi Kurds in the early 1990s, they are serving a political and military purpose immensely important to the West, and the US in particular. Essentially, parallel interests have emerged giving Kurds in Rojava (Syrian Kurdistan/western Kurdistan) an unprecedented opportunity. With this new situation, the Kurds in Syria—namely the Democratic Union Party (PYD) and their armed wings the People's Protection Units (YPG) and Women's Protection Units (YPJ)—have inadvertently become allies of major Western powers, especially the US in the fight against the so-called Islamic State. And due to the sequence of events related to the Arab Spring, Syria has become a very sensitive area for the Kurds. For the first time in contemporary history, as the co-chair of the PYD, Salih Muslim said during an interview: "the Kurds are fighting for themselves, they have become their own soldiers." In essence, the Kurds in Syria are about to build a homeland according to their own cultural, social, political, and self-defence plans in this western region of greater Kurdistan, based on theories of Democratic Confederalism, developed by Öcalan and inspired by the writings of political theorist Murray Bookchin.[32]

The PYD as the main Kurdish party in Syria, and the YPG and YPJ as the principal Kurdish armed forces in Syria, are actively struggling to draw some clear lines between the major powers in Syria, principally themselves, the Syrian Army, and the Syrian opposition forces. Interestingly and tellingly the PYD itself, including the YPG and YPJ, is under the hegemonic umbrella of the PKK's Group of Communities in Kurdistan (KCK). The PYD/YPG organization of Syria is regarded as the third dominant power, alongside that of the state, and the opposition groups such as Islamic State, Jabhat al-Nusra, and the Free Syrian Army. The Kurdish Supreme Committee was created by the PYD and several other smaller Kurdish parties to demonstrate to the public that the PYD does not have, nor intends to have, all the power at its disposal. However, the PYD and YPG remain dominant in Rojava and, since January 2014, they have led in the establishment of three autonomous local governments—known as cantons—in the predominantly Kurdish areas of northern Syria. The mass support the PYD, YPJ, and YPG enjoy among the Kurdish populace can be traced back to the impact of the liberal ideology of the PKK, and the policy of the KCK, on the Kurds of Syria.

On the other hand, in Iran the Kurds had been marginalized and isolated since the early days of the short-lived Kurdish Republic of Mahabad of 1946; following the Islamic Revolution of 1979, they found themselves severely discriminated against, not only as an ethnic minority in a state dominated by the narrative of Persian nationalism, but as a minority confessional group—Sunnis—in a state that was now firmly controlled by the Shia religious establishment. This combination of two forms of exclusionist identity politics in the Islamic Republic would prove to be highly detrimental for the Kurds of Iran.

Currently the Kurdish movement in Iran finds itself largely stagnant as a result of the disunity and continuous fragmentation of the existent traditional political parties. These parties also lack grass-roots political support from the domestic population, mostly a consequence of the relative absence of oppression to enrage and inflame the Kurdish movement in eastern Kurdistan, but also due to the lack of a strong and charismatic leadership. However, now with the rise of the PKK-affiliated Party of Free Life of Kurdistan (PJAK) the political situation may be changing. This organization is emerging as a real threat to the Iranian regime, which has invested significant resources to try to defeat it. Traditionally, the Kurds in Iran have had a slightly different lifestyle from other regional Kurds and thus have gone unnoticed for a long time.

Their cultural and social rights have been respected to some extent, due to various similarities with the other components of multi-ethnic Iran. Interestingly, the land the Kurds now claim as theirs was recognized as such since the time of the Seljuk Empire; the region was governed and administered under the name of Kurdistan for many centuries.[33] Yet, the notion of diversity could not and has not yet brought about some sort of democratic rule throughout Iran's history. For instance, Kurdish language education and political activities remain prohibited. Essentially, since the Sassanid era, the Kurds have been living within an area that literally translates to "the land of Aryans", and under this guise have been greatly mistreated. In the 1990s and especially after the successive assassination of two leaders of the Kurdistan Democratic Party of Iran (KDPI), Qasimlo in 1989 and Sharafkandi in 1992, the Iranian government announced that the Kurdish struggle against the state had collapsed and the Kurds had accepted that they were Iranians, with limited cultural and no special political rights. Iran, the state reasoned, is a land for all Iranians, including the Kurds and other minority ethnic groups. This has long been the discourse of the Iranian authorities. Yet PJAK, as another Kurdish party that is conducting an armed struggle in Iran, has slightly altered the balance of forces in this decades-long Kurdish defeat. In 2002, PJAK began its struggle with a different methodology and discourse. It was linked to the PKK and became an Iranian branch of the Kurdish movement within a broader system, namely the pan-Kurdish KCK. Despite this small yet significant revival, currently Kurds in Iran have been experiencing some of the most brutal repression in living memory. There are still daily detentions and executions of Kurdish and anti-Iranian regime activists. Yet, due to the relative weakness of the Iranian Kurdish movement's social, cultural, and political cohesion, the national struggle, along with other opposition movements in Iran, have had to endure an almost total absence of recognition and acknowledgement throughout the world.

It is now accepted as a truism that the Kurds were dealt a heavy blow after the collapse of the Ottoman Empire. Since then there has been a clear transition from colonial rule in the aftermath of the First World War to post-colonial rule characterized by autocratic revolutionary nationalist regimes, in which the Kurds have for the large part been oppressed, ignored, and subjugated. Following the toppling of Saddam's regime after the US-led invasion of 2003, and primarily as a result of the Arab Spring, early signs of democratic rule can be seen within the Middle East. In this development the Kurds have managed to turn the tables, and what was deemed impossible now seems within reach. The recent astonishing recognition by incumbent and former senior foreign policy and intelligence officials that the Sykes-Picot agreement—1916's secret agreement to divide much of the Middle East between Great Britain and France—is now effectively defunct exactly 100 years after it was signed speaks to the rapidly changing situation in the region.

The Middle East is seeing unmistakable upheaval, and the Kurds, far from being marginal actors, are now very much center-stage. But their current salience in regional and international affairs cannot be taken as a given, and it cannot be guaranteed that the many and significant gains made by the Kurds, in Iraq and Syria in particular, will not be unraveled in the years ahead. Indeed, this poses yet another manifestation of "the Kurdish question", but this time acknowledging that political, economic, and social transitions may not simply be proceeding on a positive and linear trajectory. This new Kurdish question is simply "what happens next?" following a period of profound upheaval in the Middle East. Of course, predicting the future is difficult, and especially so when the future in question relates to developments in the Middle East. This collected volume cannot answer these future questions, but it can at least attempt to provide an understanding of how the current situations have emerged, and how their many underlying and interconnected dynamics may manifest themselves in the years ahead.

The Kurdish Question Revisited

The varying situations of the Kurds in the countries in which they reside have been transformed over the second half of the twentieth century. Of course, the political transformations of the Kurds are often the most well known to observers (especially those from the West), to which the wealth of literature on the subject of Kurdish politics would attest. But there have also been concomitant and equally profound transformations occurring in the social and cultural realms, as Kurdish populations have reacted to the new and complex realities of the world around them. Naturally, there are also interactions across these realms, as social and cultural developments and political transformations meet and thus alter how Kurds engage between themselves, across imposed boundaries, and with the wider world.

These transformations are also evident in the realm of the academic study of the Kurds and Kurdistan, with the significant changes in the status of the Kurds in contemporary affairs being mirrored by the considerable expansion in the study of them, across the full gamut of social science and humanities disciplines. From being the preserve of a select few specialists who had very specific foci, the study of the Kurds has now blossomed into a significant and notable area of research within the multidisciplinary community of those engaged in Middle East Studies in particular, and comparative studies more generally. The result has been astonishing, with the literature on the Kurds and Kurdistan expanding considerably over the last twenty years. What was always a vibrant and active, but small, community of scholars addressing the Kurds has now become a vibrant, active, large, and still growing community from around the globe who have furthered understandings of the Kurds and Kurdistan from a range of disciplinary backgrounds, and through multi- and inter-disciplinary approaches. In addition to many high-quality research monographs, journalistic accounts, and academic journal articles, several excellent edited collections have also been published in recent years on specific and focused aspects of the Kurds and

Kurdistan. But there exists no single volume that attempts to present a comprehensive overview of the multi-faceted Kurdish question, bringing together expertise in an attempt to cover the entirety of the Kurdish-populated areas of the Middle East, and to bring together scholars and specialists from a range of disciplinary backgrounds to provide a snapshot not only of the contemporary situation of the Kurds and Kurdistan, but also to present a state-of-the-art collection of chapters that show the strength of the field of Kurdish studies, broadly defined, today. This is what we have attempted to do, and we stress our over-use of the word "attempt." The field of study of the Kurds and Kurdistan is not only broad, but is also geographically and historically complex and presents those authors and editors embarking upon a "whole of Kurdistan" work with numerous organizational problems that we will discuss. These challenges are then multiplied by attempting to provide a snapshot of the academic field across the many and varied disciplines that exist within the social sciences and humanities. As such, we have aimed for comprehensive coverage in *The Kurdish Question Revisited*, but we have had to accept an end result that may well have to suffice as an admirable failure. We hope, however, that it has managed to tick as many boxes as it possibly could.

Struggling Against Boundaries

As we have seen, since the end of the First World War, the Kurds have been divided between Iraq, Iran, Turkey, and Syria, with a smaller community also present in the Caucasus region. Therefore, until relatively recently, the study of the Kurds has tended to be ordered according to this imposed state framework. Writers on Kurdish politics would tend to address the situation of the Kurds in one particular country, making reference to the plight of Kurds in neighboring states only when doing so was apposite to the primary analysis. This has certainly been the case for subjects of a political nature—whether historical or contemporary—and this method of taxonomy can also be seen, albeit to a lesser extent, in works that focus on humanities and arts disciplines. Such a framework represents a certain reality that not only had to be acknowledged at an intellectual level—as Kurdish polities were increasingly conditioned according to the host countries in which they lived—but also a reality that imposed constraints on what researchers could and could not do. Entering any part of Kurdish-populated regions was difficult enough in the twentieth century; then to undertake cross-boundary research even more so.

In recent years, more research has been undertaken by scholars keen to uncover the intricacies and nuances of the Kurdish world, whether in terms of political development, economic interactions, social engagements, cultural production, or popular movements, to name but a few areas. This research has seen publications appear that are genuinely pan-Kurdish in their approach, and present a new and exciting set of

INTRODUCTION

analyses of the Kurds a century after their division into four regions. Even so, there remain serious weaknesses in the knowledge base of the broader field of Kurdish studies. While there has been a very considerable amount of research undertaken on the subject of the Kurds in Iraq and Turkey, there was, until recently, virtually nothing on the status of the Kurds in Syria, let alone detailed sociological and anthropological work on how Kurdish society operated under a brutally chauvinistic regime. With the commencement of the Syrian civil war in 2011, and as the Syrian Kurds took up arms, the political importance of what were previously referred to as "the forgotten Kurds", and the opening up of some areas of Rojava to academic researchers, has seen a nascent and vibrant new literature emerge.

The same cannot be said of the situation in Rojhelat, or Kurdistan in Iran. With the Iranian state suppressing Kurdish activism with brutal efficiency in western Iran, undertaking academic research, investigative journalism, or think-tank analysis writing on the standing of the Kurds in Iran remains difficult to the point of being impossible, and pursuing work on Kurdish culture and arts activities would be equally problematic. Indeed, most research on the Kurds in Iran would have to be done via secondary sources made available through activists, by meeting with representatives of the myriad political parties of Rojhelat, or by trying to piece together a particular picture from whatever can be gleaned from visiting Iran but without undertaking formal research. Indeed, the inability to access Kurdish-populated areas in Iran in any meaningful way means that, even today, this significant part of the Middle East remains *terra incognita* for even the most informed of experts.

In structuring this book, we thought carefully about how best to arrange the chapters, so as to present a thematic approach to "the Kurdish Question" and try to break away from the intellectual status quo that is in itself a product of the political status quo imposed upon the Kurds. The end result is, however, a compromise; a useful and necessary one, too. While a thoroughly thematic approach would have been an interesting avenue to pursue, it became readily apparent that a purely thematic approach, for such a broadly-based collection, would not in itself be representative either of the reality of the Kurdish situation today, or the manner in which academics and specialists largely continue to structure their research. The boundaries of the Middle East state system—stressed and strained though they may be, and challenged by new political and social forces—remain the organizing feature of political life in the region, and also continue to exert a strong influence on the work of those interested in the Kurds and Kurdistan. It is also the case that Kurds still largely operate within this state framework—whether purposefully or passively—and the legacy of this century-old set of boundaries is deeply rooted in Kurdish societies. Maybe years from now Kurds will have dropped statist prefixes such as "Iraqi" or "Syrian" that define what sort of Kurd they happen to be; but in 2017 these identities remain rooted in the broader Kurdish psyche, as does the notion that the Kurdish question is multi-faceted, still to be resolved within the boundaries of the established states rather than across the divides.

While we had to succumb to the organizational logic provided by the current state system, we were still determined to illustrate the burgeoning cross-region expertise, as scholars recognize the trans-state dynamics that are increasingly being felt across Kurdistan, and also reflect upon subjects that are perhaps not constrained so easily by these artificial boundaries. Part One of *The Kurdish Question Revisited* commences with "Reflections on Identity, Culture, and the Nation": three key areas of discussion for anyone with more than a passing interest in the Kurds. Chapters in this section range far and wide across academic disciplines, with concepts of political mobilization being juxtaposed alongside everyday religion, the international relations of the Kurdish sub-system, the development of the Kurdish novel, and a discussion of Kurdish music in Armenia. Jordi Tejel embarks upon a broad canvas survey of the writing of the Kurds' history in all of their domains, while David Romano further considers the subject of his earlier book on the application of social movement theory to Kurdistan. Two chapters—by Michiel Leezenberg and Diane King—consider the role of religion among the Kurds, with Leezenberg addressing the polar opposites of Sufism and Salafism, and King considering the "everyday" practice of religion. Considering broader notions of identity and memory formation and usage, Hakan Özoğlu addresses the "politics of memory", but instead of the methods and practice of memory accumulation, rather the phenomenon of "collective forgetting." Hamit Bozarslan provides a challenging chapter on the Kurdish quest for the Universal. Nationalism and literature are intimately entwined, yet the extremely well-developed body of Kurdish literature is relatively unknown outside specialist scholars: Hashem Ahmadzadeh—one of the leading figures in the study of the Kurdish novel—focuses upon themes in the Kurdish novel and short story, tying their development to the sociopolitical conditions of Kurdish society at the time of writing. Building on this relationship between story-telling and the nation-building process, Christine Allison looks at the politics of folklore in Kurdistan. Part One finishes with Nahro Zagros looking at Kurdish music in Armenia, with particular reference to the Yezidis.

Part Two moves to northern Kurdistan (in Turkey) and is more political in its focus as it addresses the development of the Kurdish question in the Ottoman Empire and Turkey. Perhaps the most formative moment in the history of the Kurdish nationalist movement was the Sheikh Ubeidullah Rebellion of 1880, the subject of Sabri Ates' contribution, in which he recalls how Ubeidullah planned to end the division of the Kurds between Iran and the Ottoman Empire. Janet Klein then turns her attention to the "first Kurdish gazette" and the role played by the Bedirkhan family in producing the pioneering Kurdish-language newspaper *Kurdistan* at the end of the nineteenth century. We then unapologetically have four chapters that address, roughly, a similar subject: the modern manifestations of the Kurdish question in Turkey, particularly since the 1980s. Cengiz Gunes focuses particularly on the mobilization of the Kurds in the 1980s and 1990s, explaining the growth of the PKK and its use of nationalist symbols and events to generate a "myth of resistance." Bill Park plays with the notion of "Turkey's Kurdish problems" and also considers "the Kurds' Turkish problems", presenting a detailed account of the on-off peace process from 2012 to 2015. Considering this issue further, Henri Barkey investigates the rationale that underpinned the peace process between the Turkish state and the PKK, and the evolution of Turkish thinking. Finally, Michael Gunter provides a *longue durée* overview of the "contrasting Turkey paradigms towards the volatile Kurdish problem", arguing that continuity is as evident as change. Completing Part Two are two chapters that focus principally on the PKK: Joost Jongerden sheds light on the under-studied concept of "democratic autonomy" that has become the cornerstone of the PKK's political discourse, while Clémence Scalbert-Yücel shows how the wider Kurdish movement's cultural policies took shape around a rationale formulated by the leader of the PKK, Abdullah Öcalan.

Parts Three and Four between them present five chapters on the Kurdish question in Syria and in Iran. Clearly an imbalance in a book that presents far more chapters on the situation in Turkey, Iraq, and the "trans-state" aspect, it remains the case that the weight of activity of academics and specialists on the Kurds in Syria, and especially Iran, is very light indeed. However, the quality is thankfully very high and, in these sections, two important issues regarding the case of the Kurds in Syria are addressed: the relationship between the PYD and PKK by Zeynap Kaya and Robert Lowe, and the role of the Kurds in the Syrian uprising against the Assad regime by Harriet Allsopp. It seems that the Kurds in Iran live not only in political, but also academic, isolation, such is the scarcity of scholars who work on this subject. Nader Entessar provides a compelling account of what he refers to as "the Kurdish conundrum" that exercised the Islamic Republic between 1979 and 2003; Olivier Grojean then questions the multi-ethnic and supposedly cosmopolitan nature of the Iranian state, investigating identities and ethnic hierarchy, while Walter Posch delves into how the Iranian government views the Iranian Kurds from its own state-centric and ideological perspectives.

The Kurdish Question and Iraq is then considered in Part Five. Gareth Stansfield provides an overview of the main political trends and developments that have taken place in the post-2003 period, before four chapters address different key issues. The first of these, written by Mohammed Ihsan, considers the Arabization program of Saddam Hussein's government in what are now referred to as Iraq's "disputed territories"; Katherine Ranharter takes stock of the rapid growth of the KRI's higher education perspective, while Greg Shapland provides an assessment of that most critical resource in the KRI, water, and its role in current and future development plans and opportunities. Finally, Kelsey Shanks provides a forward-looking chapter, taking the subject of "peace education" as a means of managing inter-communal tensions by giving younger people the means to understand and empathize with the world around them. Returning to recent political developments, Benjamin Isakhan looks at the Kurdish response to the rise of the Islamic State, and in particular the Kurds' seizing of most of the disputed territories and the manner in which they then used their advantageous position to leverage a much improved relationship with the US and Western powers. Adding further weight to this argument, Renad Mansour delves into the strategy pursued by the KRG leadership as they sought to position themselves favorably with international actors from 2003 onwards. Completing this trilogy of foreign affairs analyses is Mohammed Shareef's chapter: in an erudite analysis, he views the KRI relationship with the US as having undergone a transition since 2003, which after 2014 was subject to a complete paradigm shift in terms of both policy and strategy. Yet, irrespective of the improved relations the Kurds of Iraq have with Western powers, the KRG still needs to generate legitimacy within Kurdistan itself, which in recent years it has very much struggled to achieve. Nicole Watt's powerful chapter on "re-claiming Halabja" investigates the way in which the traumatic memories of the Halabja chemical attack are now contested by the KRG, Kurdish elites, and the local people of Halabja themselves through a febrile set of engagements that have, on occasion, broken down into violence. Recognizing similar dynamics of hegemonic traditional party control, Andrea Fischer-Tahir focuses on the control of the media and political culture in the KRI, asking a series of pointed questions that illustrate how the Kurdish media still have some way to go before they can be considered truly free of state and party influences. A further aspect of Kurdish life in desperate need of change is that of the treatment of women. Nazand Begikhani and Gill Hague present some of their research findings from an extensive research project that focused on honor-based violence (HBV) in the KRI. They note the depressingly slow progress made in eradicating HBV, and the need to establish legal provisions as a matter of urgency. Finally, Francis Owtram broaches the question that many observers ask concerning the Kurds of Iraq: will they declare their independence? Owtram places the discussion within the context of the Iraqi constitution of 2005, concluding that independence may come, but perhaps later rather than sooner, and only if the Kurds manage their political and economic affairs more shrewdly than they have done to date.

The Genealogy of The Kurdish Question Revisited

This collection has had a reasonably long gestation period, perhaps befitting a book of this size and complexity, but being understandably frustrating to those contributors who had the challenge of writing on rapidly moving political events. The initial idea for such a volume came about following the successful creation of a Kurdish Studies programme at the University of Exeter, commencing in 2004. With a range of students, from undergraduates through MA candidates and PhD researchers, all coming together in the green hills of the south-west of England, Exeter's Centre for

INTRODUCTION

Kurdish Studies proved that there was a significant and wide interest in the field, and the University soon became a destination for students worldwide who were interested in furthering their knowledge of the Kurds and Kurdistan. These developments in Exeter were also mirrored by the building and expansion of research clusters across Europe—especially in France and Germany—and the US, and were intimately linked to new and exciting research initiatives unfolding across Kurdistan, in Turkey and Iraq in particular. The growth of this academic community was also matched by the very rapid growth in wider public interest in the Kurdish question, driven by the changes that began to emerge in the Middle East after the invasion of Iraq in 2003, and especially following the commencement of the Syrian civil war in 2011 and the rise and consolidation of Islamic State in Syria and Iraq from 2014 onwards. It was therefore a relatively straightforward notion to conceive of a significant edited collection like this, and it was an idea to which Michael Dwyer of Hurst Publishers enthusiastically lent his support.

An opening research seminar was convened at the Royal Institute for International Affairs, Chatham House, in London in January 2015, which brought together the majority of the contributors to this volume for an eye-opening two days of private presentations and discussions, which then moved into a public event, where those focused upon the contemporary politics of the Kurds engaged in open discussion with London's community of policy analysts. Various other contributors were then invited to join the project in order to ensure that the scope of the collection, and the revisiting of the Kurdish question, would be as comprehensive as possible.

But this book is not only about providing geographically comprehensive coverage of developments in Kurdistan, and ensuring that the range of intellectual disciplines that have interests in Kurdistan and Kurdish society are represented. The book also presents a snapshot of the world of Kurdish studies, bringing together established scholars in the field alongside those specialists who have become engaged in the study of the Kurds from other regional endeavors, and those new scholars who are beginning to make a name for themselves through outstanding and challenging new research. Of course, we could not accommodate everybody that we would ideally have had—although, as the length of the book attests, we certainly did try—but we have attempted to provide a window into who is doing what, and how, in this exciting field, at a critical moment for the affairs of the Middle East in general, and the Kurds in particular. Perhaps a *Revisiting II* should be considered, to ensure that those excellent scholars who were not included, or are in the midst of their studies, may join those presented in this volume. While Middle East politics may be unpredictable, it would seem safe to say that the Kurds and Kurdistan will continue to attract the attention of scholars in the years ahead.

PART 1

REFLECTIONS ON DEBATES OF IDENTITY AND NATION

1.

NEW PERSPECTIVES ON WRITING THE HISTORY OF THE KURDS IN IRAQ, SYRIA AND TURKEY

A HISTORY AND STATE OF THE ART ASSESSMENT[1]

Jordi Tejel

Introduction

During the second international conference on Kurdish Studies held at Exeter during 6-8 September 2012, Djene Bajalan—a colleague and historian—and I were struck by the paucity of panels dealing with Kurdish history. As in previous conferences, an overwhelming majority of papers presented in Exeter focused on issues related to ethnicity, nation, and nationalism, with a near dominance of political science, and to a lesser extent anthropological, lenses. While the field of Kurdish studies, a relative newcomer in social sciences in Western universities, has expanded over the last two decades and continues to do so, it appears still that few academic historians and PhD students are interested in writing Kurdish history.

Prompted by this appraisal, Djene took the lead and organized, with the aid of colleagues at the University of Oxford, a conference entitled *New Perspectives on Writing the History of the Kurds* at St Antony's College (Ertegun House) on 17 May 2013. Bringing together ten junior and senior scholars of different nationalities and from different fields of inquiry—literature, politics, historiography, intellectual history—it was intended that the colloquium would discuss the prevailing narratives and paradigms of interpretation of Kurdish history, society, and culture; thereby contributing to the assessment of areas where research is lacking and, eventually, suggesting new grids of analysis. In particular, the organizers invited us to rethink the way we write Kurdish history in order to avoid falling into the methodological and epistemological "dangers" presented by the nationalist paradigm. In other words, we were asked to reflect on alternative ways to write a history of the Kurds from a non-nationalist perspective, which at the same time would not deny "the Kurdish reality." The papers presented, together with the debates we held, proved that there is in fact a growing awareness of the pitfalls of the nationalist paradigm within the field of Kurdish studies.

In a recent piece, Bajalan pursued this ongoing reflection on an even more positive note for, although "the writing of Kurdish history has not been as prominent among scholars as might have been expected," a new generation of Kurdish and non-Kurdish scholars trained in Western universities have "contributed greatly to our understanding of the Kurdish past."[2] Furthermore, developments in Turkey have led to the "emergence of local historians such as those in the Bogaziçi Performing Arts Ensemble (BGST) [...], as well as the group formed around the popular history journal *Kürt Tarihi* (Kurdish History) [...], who have sought to promote greater understanding of Kurdish history without falling into the nationalistic discourse of earlier generations of Kurdish historians."[3]

Thus, is the glass half empty or half full? In order to provide a comprehensive answer to that question, I shall first address the main question of the workshop convened in Oxford, namely whether or not it is possible to write Kurdish history from a non-nationalist perspective, which at the same time does not deny the aforementioned "Kurdish reality." In the second part of the chapter, I shall provide a quick overview on the origins and development of scholarship on the history of the Kurds in Iraq, Syria, and Turkey in order to improve understanding of the relatively late development of academic history writing within Kurdish studies. I argue that there are enough signs to assess a momentum for academic history writing on Kurds and Kurdistan notwithstanding the need for further research in some of the directions already undertaken, and a number of remaining lacunae.

In that sense, in the third section, I shall point out various alternative approaches that, in my view, deserve further attention from practitioners, as they may offer innovative ways to avoid some of the epistemological pitfalls presented by the national paradigm. Among many potential alternative approaches I shall focus upon only three: comparative history, transnational history, and global history. Although these "alternative" avenues may appear rather obvious, one must bear in mind that within the field of Kurdish studies very few such approaches have been practiced so far. Obviously, the aim of this discussion is not to provide a detailed overview of these methods, but rather to highlight the advantages they offer to historians, as well as their feasibility with regard to the Kurds. Finally, the chapter will develop some methodological issues that are intimately related to the overall discussion.

NEW PERSPECTIVES

National histories

Is it possible to write Kurdish history from a non-nationalist perspective, which at the same time does not deny the Kurdish reality? The answer to that question actually demands some nuance. If the question is whether it is possible to write a Kurdish *national* history without falling into the nationalist paradigm, such prospects seem almost irremediably dismal. First of all, national history writing is an eminently political project where its practitioners see themselves working within the matrix of history, cultural memory, and politics. As such, historians of the nation hold specifically political views of the "imagined community," its past, its present and, more often than not, its future. Put differently, studying the formation and development of a specific national identity is almost more of an academic exercise in "historical teleology" than a search for any actual historical roots of a nation. It is a process that begins from an already known conclusion, whereby the historian selects events and employs them retrospectively in order to provide a given nation with a sense of historical legitimacy.[4]

Historians such as Stefan Berger have underlined the continued strength of national history throughout the world. It persists despite the shortcomings and negative consequences triggered by the Romantic national paradigm adopted by most, yet by no means all,[5] European and Middle Eastern historians throughout the nineteenth and early twentieth centuries: the various forms of discrimination, wars, civil wars, ethnic cleansing, and genocide.[6]

As a matter of fact, national history has been a dominant genre of history writing in Europe for almost two centuries. It is still an important type of historical text outside Europe,[7] with the possible exception of India, where the field of Subaltern Studies has found an important following in the last thirty years.[8] In that respect, "national histories can be described as one of the most successful exports of Europe in the imperial age."[9] More surprisingly, in spite of the emergence of alternative approaches to national history throughout the twentieth century—Marxist, social, transnational, global, and micro-history, etc.—national histories have witnessed a revival in Europe since 1989, for several reasons.

Firstly, the collapse of the former Soviet bloc and the subsequent creation of new states, along with the discourse about a united Europe, has precipitated the unexpected comeback of the nation as a central subject of study in many Eastern European countries.[10] Secondly, and paradoxically, as ethnicity is now automatically understood to be a social construct, it no longer needs to be "denounced" or deconstructed as such. Thus, as Joep Leersen points out, under the proviso of its constructed nature, the concepts of "ethnicity" and "national group"—used interchangeably in many cases—are gaining new legitimacy among scholars as operative factors in history.[11]

Finally, in the Middle East, no less than elsewhere, the nationalist ideal of "one nation, one state" was widely embraced, and the leaders of the post-colonial states were expected and encouraged, both by interested groups and the international community, to engage in nation-building. Thereafter, the nation-state became the self-evident spatial unit for professional historians, without need of any further justification. Furthermore, the burden of three distinct but related dynamics—the Millet system, colonial legacies, and the imperatives of post-colonial nation-building[12]—led local historians both to deny or at least overlook ethnic and religious pluralism within their societies, and to place national history at center stage on the intellectual agenda, thereby neglecting other possible narratives.[13] Sometimes they were moved by genuine enthusiasm; and sometimes they drifted along with the new "forced consensus" and official unanimity.

In the past twenty years, one can certainly identify a growing number of publications focusing on the "forgotten" peoples and groups of the Middle East: Kurds, Alevis in Turkey, Shi'as in Iraq, Copts in Egypt, and so forth, in addition to memoirs written by dissident activists, leftists and Islamists alike. Yet, these works do not seek to put forward the basis of a new approach to history, but rather to contest the dominant national narrative. Against this background, it seems safe to predict that national history writing in general will continue to predominate for a considerable time to come. In that respect, one could argue that the Kurds, as a people, are also entitled to write their *own* national history, especially since Iranian, Turkish, and Arab national narratives continue to neglect the Kurdish reality as the figment of an "imagined nation."

Hence, we as historians in the field of Kurdish studies should try to respond to two broad and non-exclusive questions. First, can we write a different, non-parochial Kurdish national history? Second, can we explore other avenues that would complement the mainstream national narrative? I suggest that, before answering these questions, we need to examine the origins and developments of history writing on Kurds in Iraq, Syria, and Turkey, as well as the constraints this academic activity has traditionally faced.

Where do we come from and where are we going?

In the first place, one must keep in mind that academic history writing should be distinguished from writings by Kurdish political elites and intellectuals attempting to "root" the nation by constructing a nationalist historiography. Throughout most of the twentieth century, the proponents of a Kurdish historiographical discourse in today's Iraq (until the emergence of a generation of university-trained Kurdish scholars in the 1960s), Syria, and Turkey have been multifunctional actors, moving between the political and cultural fields.[14] In that sense, Kurdish historiography, and historiography in general, is "part of the construction of a wide range of cultural and intellectual knowledge and meanings" and, more importantly, it "has meaning only when it is part of a political process."[15]

Thus, unsurprisingly, the pioneers of Kurdish history in the early twentieth century were members of the Kurdish intelligentsia educated in Western countries or in the Westernized schools of the Ottoman Empire. Like their Arab or Turkish counterparts, Kurdish historiographical producers, coming from different parts of Ottoman Kurdistan, chose periodicals as the main vehicle for the writing of Kurdish national history.[16]

Newly created states in the Middle East brought about the physical division of Kurdish groups and the subsequent emergence of distinct national narratives in which the Kurds found no place. In Turkey, where their very existence was denied and Kurdish associations were closed down immediately after the creation/birth of the republic, Kurdish intellectuals were simply unable to produce such a counternarrative. It was in Syria and Lebanon that certain Kurdish intellectuals, previously based in Istanbul and Diyarbakır, found refuge and worked on founding the Khoybun League.[17] This committee laid out the basis for the conceptualization, in Kurmanji Kurdish, of modern Kurdish nationalism in Turkey and Syria. The continuity of Kurdish discourse in the post-Ottoman period manifested itself in the Khoybun's project to lead the Kurds toward Western civilization and the declared necessity of modernizing Kurdish society from the top down.

The Khoybun insisted on these aspects as a reaction to Kemalist propaganda, which claimed to have brought "civilization" to Kurdistan. The process of mimesis also affected the discourse about the *we* group and the *other*. Thus, while the official discourse in Turkey (and partially in Iran) depicted the Kurds as tribal and primitive, traditional and anti-modern, the Kurds sought not only to prove that they were indeed "modern" and "civilized," but also to demonstrate that in fact the Turks were "barbarians" and a model of "uncivilized people." Though carrying a message concerning an *us* (the "Kurdish national community"), Kurdish intellectuals were not independent of state categories: the search for a golden age, the purity of language, the homogeneity of their society, the "civilized" *we* group as opposed to "barbarians," among others.[18]

Despite their pretensions, the brochures published in different languages during the 1920s and 1930s by the League can hardly be considered historical studies. They have to be viewed instead as a nationalist discourse aimed at legitimizing Kurdish claims and deconstructing the Kemalist discourse on Kurds. Interestingly, however, between the 1930s and 1940s, the two main leaders of the Khoybun, Jaladat, and Kamuran Badirkhan published a series of Kurdish periodicals (*Hawar, Ronahî, Roja Nû*) in Damascus and Beirut, in which local history (Kurdish Ottoman emirates, local tribes, Kurdish leaders) was present along with *national* political myths and the anti-Kemalist discourse.

In Iraq, Mohammed Amin Zaki Beg (1880-1948), a former officer of the Ottoman army and a Westernized Kurdish intellectual, during the first half of the twentieth century compiled the most comprehensive studies on Kurdish history and its leading figures.[19] As to the second half of the century, various regimes in Iraq from 1958 onwards did acknowledge the right of the Kurds to create their own Kurdish intellectual platforms. Despite this advance, academic research on Kurdish history remained a sensitive issue in Iraq, compared to research on Kurdish literature and language. In that respect, Kurdish historians had severe difficulty even including "Kurdish history" as a focus of their research agenda. Contrary to common belief, however, scholars took advantage of some spaces of relative academic freedom to publish works on some aspects of Kurdish history. Among the most prestigious Kurdish-Iraqi scholars, one must mention Kamal Mazhar Ahmad (b.1938), lecturer in history in Baghdad for many years and eventually head of the University of Baghdad's department of history until 2003. He was one of the first Kurdish historians to address the Armenian genocide during the First World War from an academic perspective.[20]

In parallel, Orientalists such as Basil Nikitine and Thomas Bois, as well as former Western officials in Kurdistan such as Cecil J. Edmonds and William Eagleton, wrote important contributions on various episodes of Kurdish history until the 1960s.[21] From the 1960s onwards, the renewal of Kurdish nationalism in Kurdistan as a whole piqued the interest of the Western media and research centers in the United States. The Barzani revolt (1961-75), the guerrilla warfare in Iran (1979-83) and in Turkey (1984 until now), and the emergence of an autonomous Kurdish region in northern Iraq in 1992 each contributed to this. International reporters published significant contributions, in particular on the Barzani revolt,[22] and later helped the public become aware of Kurdish suffering during the Anfal campaign in Iraq (1987-8) and the human rights abuses in Turkey.[23] In parallel, the increase of academic studies in Europe and the United States on different aspects of Kurdish society also reflected this new momentum.

Yet, except for some scholars such as Hamit Bozarslan, Nelida Fuccaro, Hans-Lukas Kieser, and Robert Olson,[24] up to the 2000s few works were the product of academic historians. Martin van Bruinessen, a well-known anthropologist, has worked extensively on various aspects of the Kurdish issue, including historical events such as the Shaikh Said rebellion, for the last forty years.[25] Tellingly, he continues to be one of the most-cited authors in studies dealing with Kurdish history. In the same vein, the very helpful *A Modern History of the Kurds* by David McDowall—a respected British author, albeit not a historian—constitutes one of the works of reference for any student or scholar dealing with contemporary Kurdish history.[26]

In addition, as Hamit Bozarslan pointed out, between the 1980s and 1990s most of these endeavors had been the result of individual initiatives and personal interest. Scholars in this field had been forbidden to project long-term research programs.

Further, unlike ancient and medieval studies, modern and contemporary histories of the Middle East "[were] rather poorly developed."[27] And yet, the glass is half full.

An uneven blooming of history of the Kurds and Kurdistan

While practitioners of Kurdish history have faced some trying circumstances in pursuing their work, mainly due to severe political and material constraints, they have also been challenged by broader dynamics that affect academic historians elsewhere. Historians are not, and never have been, the only producers of history writing. Yet, for the last three decades, within the discipline of history, both recent and even present events have imposed themselves on the hegemonic field, both in its academic and popular expressions. As a result, interest in "the very contemporary" has grown exponentially among a wide range of people (journalists, intellectuals, teachers, politicians, and so forth), thereby marginalizing the "academic historian" in favor of the "witness," and subsequently triggering a sort of identity crisis among professional historians.[28]

The Middle East has been no exception. Following a tradition already started in Syria among exiled Kurdish intellectuals and leaders,[29] it is schoolmasters, intellectuals,[30] leading political figures,[31] and journalists who are the most popular and prolific practitioners of history writing in Turkey and Iraqi Kurdistan.

Paradoxically, universities in Iraqi Kurdistan, freed from Ba'athist ideological constraints since 1992, have further developed neither their departments of history, nor any new scientific approaches for dealing with Kurdish history. On the one hand, at the moment Kurdish universities tend to consolidate and even freeze Kurdish history as focusing on the chapters of mass violence experienced by the Kurds throughout the 1980s and/or backs up political claims over disputed territories such as Kirkuk. Tellingly, the first scientific conference of the Department of History at the University of Sulaimani was organized for 15-17 April 2013 in conjunction with the Ministry of Martyrs' Affairs under the title "Kurdish Genocide: Processes in History."[32]

According to Andrea Fischer-Tahir, Kurdish political rulers have been exploiting the Anfal campaign since the 1990s in order to ensure Kurdish unity and strong national feeling, endangered by corruption and maladministration. In that respect, the narrative on the Anfal campaign serves another interrelated aim: "to teach 'the people' what the word genocide basically means, where it comes from, and that in Kurdistan genocide is not only an experience situated in the past but a lasting (and continuing) threat."[33]

On the other hand, history departments are clearly losing ground compared to other disciplines. Koya University, for example, has only one professor of contemporary history, whereas Soran University and the University of Kurdistan (Erbil) have no department of history at all. The situation is slightly better at the universities of

Dohuk and Sulaimani, where history occupies an important position in BA and MA programs. Partial marginalization of history as an academic activity in Iraqi Kurdistan may explain, at least in part, why the writing of the modern history of Kurdistan is mainly a non-academic pursuit. They have dealt with a wide range of genres, topics, and periods, from medieval history to local history and memoirs, as well as national issues such as Anfal or the history of the national movement.

In contrast, the flourishing intellectual activity of "popular historians" in Turkey has intersected with a specific internal dynamic. Since the 1990s, and in particular since the early 2000s, one can observe an increasing interest in Turkey's ethnic and religious diversity. After decades of apparent hegemonic political discourse on the "homogenous identity" of the Turkish citizens, the publication of dozens of books about various "forgotten" or ethnic and religious groups and their histories has allowed many self-made experts to contribute to the revival of (popular) Kurdish history too.

Within this context, Kurdish scholars have launched initiatives to popularize Kurdish history, from a non-nationalist perspective, for a wider public in different ways. The establishment of the popular history journal *Kürt Tarihi* [Kurdish History] in June 2012 is illustrative of this trend. In addition, the relatively new universities in eastern Turkey have played a significant role in awakening the interest of larger sectors of Kurdish society in local and regional history (including the revolts, and Kurdish-Armenian relations) thanks to the organization of seminars and panels, not only at universities such as Hakkari Üniversitesi, but also in cultural centers in cities such as Tatvan or Mardin.[34]

Finally, scholars reunited around private foundations such as the Ismail Beshikci Vakif have created new spaces for historically informed discussions between academic historians and a larger public.[35] In the same vein, Turkish universities outside Kurdish areas have created the conditions for such developments as well. The Middle East Technical University in Ankara and several universities in Istanbul (Bogaziçi, Bilgi, Sabanci) have trained dozens of Kurdish and non-Kurdish students who have produced a significant number of works on different aspects of Kurdish history, which, importantly, have used varying methodologies and sophisticated theoretical approaches. Subsequently, some of them have written their doctoral dissertations in Western universities, paving the way for their publication by prestigious publishing houses in English, thereby reaching a wider readership.[36]

In addition, a new generation of scholars fully or partly trained in Western universities have attempted to study the history of Kurds and Kurdistan through placing local histories in a broader context, considering, for example, relations with ethnic neighbors in different spatial and temporal contexts. In this respect, Uğur Ümit Üngör, Yektan Türkyilmaz, and Seda Altuğ have examined issues related to mass violence and collective memory among Kurdish and non-Kurdish populations during the interwar years in eastern Anatolia.[37] Likewise, the late Ottoman period has inspired a number of important works on social relations, tribal politics, and state-society relations in the same region.[38]

Finally, the revival of interest in the Mandates in Syria and Iraq has opened the door for a series of monographs and articles on the history of Kurds in those countries during the interwar years. Following the pioneering works of Christian Velud on the Syrian Jazira, Syrian Kurds have increasingly been the object of study for authors who have analyzed the formation of contemporary Kurdish nationalism in Syria, urban mobilization in Upper Jazira,[39] the delimitation of the Turkish-Syrian border, and the complexity of identity dynamics among Damascene Kurds.[40] The renewal of mandatory studies in Iraq has allowed for the publication of useful studies on the Yezidis in colonial Iraq, as well as local politics in Sulaimani.[41]

All in all, it seems that the focus on locality—local and regional history—rather than on ethnic groups, thereby placing the Kurds in a broader context, is increasingly seen as a way of avoiding the biases of methodological nationalism in area studies. If these promising endeavors are to be continued, there are also alternative historical approaches available that remain, by and large, unpractised within the field of Kurdish studies.

Alternative approaches

I shall now briefly touch upon the advantages that alternative approaches offer to historians in order both to advance the knowledge of a pluralistic history of the Kurds, and eventually to avoid some of the epistemological dangers presented by the national paradigm: comparative history, transnational history, and global history.

Comparative history should be considered as an alternative to the traditional "national narrative." One should be aware that calls for an explicit comparative history are by no means a novelty. Marc Bloch, a well-known French historian of the interwar era, would even argue that good historians are constantly comparing.[42] In that respect, if history is more than chronology, which I think it is, any attempt to explain and interpret events in a particular place and at a particular time involves comparison with past events and dynamics, or with events and dynamics happening at the same time elsewhere. As a matter of fact, the units of comparison are not reducible to nations. Researchers may compare localities, economic units, laws, borders, and so on. On the other hand, the purpose of the comparison may also vary. In that respect, scholars might seek either to demonstrate the uniqueness of one particular case (individualizing comparisons) by comparing it to others, or to identify similarities. Comparative historians would state that the comparative method presents some essential advantages, among which, first and foremost, is a better knowledge of their own society through comparison. Further, it allows historians to gain a viewpoint outside one particular regional or national history, and makes history a less provincial undertaking. To sum up, comparative history has the potential to equip the historian with new perspectives and new explanations, and ultimately to allow him/her to define new problems.[43]

Yet, according to Stefan Berger, four conditions need to be fulfilled before successful comparisons can be made. First, the historian needs to be very familiar with more than one social context. Second, practitioners of comparative studies must be clear about their geographical and time boundaries. Choices made in terms of geographical and time scope need to be justified. Third, they also need to be clear about the units of comparison that will fit (or not) into their theoretical and conceptual framework. Finally, comparativists must be aware of the linguistic pitfalls in transnational comparisons involving more than one language,[44] especially since comparison may be expanded not only to the closest neighbors (Turks, Arabs, and Iranians in this case), but also to other geographical and cultural areas that might shed light on wider historical dynamics.

Comparative history may be an individual academic initiative, but it can also be undertaken collectively. Besides limited collective projects—edited volumes and special issues—in which the comparative approach is explicitly put forward, scholars dealing with comparative history should consider the possibility of establishing stable international networks that ensure the continuity of such endeavors.

Certainly, comparative history has witnessed a revival of interest among scholars as the process of globalization has dramatically quickened throughout the last decades.[45] Prompted by the latter, historians have become more eager to study the past connections and comparisons between different parts of the world. In that respect, "global history" has taken a step forward in order to study the connections and comparisons across and between world regions.[46] In particular, social and cultural historians are increasingly adopting global frameworks to bring new insights and methods to their research. A first distinction is however necessary. As some authors put it, the terms "international" and "transnational" or "global" overlap, but they are not synonymous. To Helgren and Vasconcellos, the "international" refers to "developments, events, and ideas that are global in scale" whereas the usage of "transnational" addresses "the crossing of boundaries." In so doing, transnational studies "include the penetration or exchange of ideas, reform networks, images, technologies, markets, and goods as well as people."[47]

Although there is no clear-cut boundary between *transnational* and *global* history,[48] global historians are inclined to consider transnational history as exclusively concerned with connections and interpenetration, whereas global history is also concerned with comparisons. From her side, Isabel Hofmeyr argues that the claim of transnational methods is not simply that historical processes occur in different places, but that they are constructed in the movement between places, sites, and regions.[49] In so doing, transnational history may "contribute to the discussions about the *whens* and *wheres* of globalization."[50]

NEW PERSPECTIVES

Regardless of their specificities, both approaches are engaged in a project to reconstruct the aspects of the human past that transcend any one nation-state, empire, or other politically defined territory. Hence, I would argue that both transnational and global histories could allow us to inscribe Kurdish history into a wider, interconnected, and non-nation-state narrative. Thus, global history could prove to be extremely helpful in conducting studies about peasantry and labour in the Middle East, an economic history of the Middle East connected to a larger framework, or the effects of the First World War in the Middle East, using a wide range of documents held not only in the Ottoman archives but also in the British or Russian public records.

African and Asian studies, for example, have greatly benefited from the global and transnational approaches to analyze essential topics for the continent such as slavery, trafficking, and labor.[51] Beyond economic and social issues, global and transnational histories might shed some light on cultural and intellectual processes,[52] such as the emergence of nationalism and modernity in the Middle East as a "transnational enterprise," something which has been partially addressed by practitioners of Kurdish history.

Additionally, practitioners of transnational history have examined the role of international organizations, for example, such as the League of Nations and its different bodies in the promotion of educational, scientific, and cultural exchanges, or the limits to its enshrinement of minority rights in the interwar era.[53] The post-1945 order was marked by a political and administrative landscape with partially overlapping national and supranational assemblies, administrations, and legal orders, as well as a growing role of non-state actors such as NGOs and international youth movements.[54]

While scholars in the field of Kurdish studies have shown a rising interest in transnational dynamics related to the formation of a Kurdish diaspora and the ever-increasing transnational relations between Kurdish communities located outside the Middle East and in the homeland, so far there have been no serious attempts to study historical events or trends pertaining to Kurdish history from a transnational perspective. Thus, the extant academic literature focuses on emerging "transnational spaces," "transnational identities," "refugee problems," or alternatively on Kurdish political activities in Western countries in order to persuade state actors and groups from "civil society" to intervene in favor of a political solution of the "Kurdish issue," in particular in Turkey.[55] Despite the unquestionable contribution of these works to the understanding of current dynamics within the Kurdish transnational space, none of them holds a historically-informed research agenda.

Against this background, any comprehensive research about, for example, the actual role of the Kurdish Student Society in Europe (KSSE) and its transnational connections with a wide array of state and non-state actors (International Union of Students, Henri Curiel's Group of Rome, and so on) to raise understanding of the evolution of the Barzani revolt between 1961 and 1975, for instance, is still missing.[56]

13

While the records of the powerful Confederation of Iranian Students National Union have been examined by Iranian scholars as well as transnational historians,[57] the documents produced by the KSSE remain largely unexplored.[58]

By the same token, paying more attention to the field of international organizations and the impact of their decision-making policies could also shed light on recent essential developments for Iraqi Kurds, and for the region in general: notably an accurate account for the emergence and consolidation of the "safe haven" established in Iraqi Kurdistan between 1991 and 1992, including the interplay between states, international agencies such as the United Nations High Commissioner for Refugees (UNHCR), NGOs, Kurdish political parties and, last but not least, the Kurdish populations.[59]

Some methodological considerations

One may argue that calls for a new research agenda and the enlargement of approaches as well as methodologies are theoretically relevant, yet hardly practicable with regard to the Kurdish case for several reasons. In countries such as Iraq and Syria, which have suffered from invasions, a civil war, or ongoing conflicts, is it possible to write history in keeping with international standards? One must recall that much of the archival material held in Baghdad perished in the aftermath of 2003. Furthermore, in Turkey, Syria, Iraq, and Iran, access to local and national archival materials has been and still is severely restricted. These are, of course, serious obstacles to conducting comprehensive research on Kurdish history.

For historians, written documents and archival materials are essential, although a very wide range of other sources are commonly used today. Consequently, there is a question regarding the proliferation of sources (written and oral), and methodological approaches. In that sense, despite all the above-mentioned obstacles, there are indeed some windows open to scholars. On the one hand, fieldwork, memory studies, and oral history—increasingly practised in Turkey since the 1990s[60]—might be able to provide a new empirical construction of objects of study and analysis closer to the reality of the internal dynamics in contemporary Kurdish society, particularly in Iraq and Turkey, where restrictions on access to the fieldwork have been relaxed in the last two decades. Of course, oral history, memory studies, and ethnographic methods have their own limits; they allow scholars to study only two generations before. Yet, given the material constraints that historians dealing with contemporary events have to face, they cannot be discarded out of hand.

On the other hand, a creative and expansive use of Ottoman and Persian archives, as Sabri Atesh's work proves, may greatly contribute to a better knowledge of modern Kurdish history.[61] Likewise, a closer and non-ethnically specific look at French and British archives may also offer new avenues to social and global historians interested in issues such as colonialism, peasantry, and the expansion of capitalism in the Middle East. Historians need to start by critically assessing the epistemological value of categories used by the producers of written sources, such as state archives. In that respect, French and British archives, as with any other archival material, were constructed subjectively; thereby they can tell us how the colonial powers viewed or aimed to reshape local societies. Consequently, uncritically accepting mandate categories such as Kurd, Christian, Arab, Alawite, and so forth as local and natural social sub-groups is highly problematic for any historical research.

On another level, the establishment of multinational research groups is also a potential response to such challenges, for practitioners of Kurdish history may take advantage of empirical data drawn from other regions and sources—in the same way they would with other languages—that might have remained inaccessible to them. In the same vein, opening a dialogue with bordering disciplines, in particular sociology and anthropology, in the study of Kurdish history and related phenomena proves to be equally essential. Historians and anthropologists alike have been insisting extensively on the constructed and relational character of identities, as well as the need to locate their analyses in given spatial and temporal frameworks.

In so doing, they recognize the possibilities for hybridity and fluidity of religion and language as extremely important for any dynamic understanding of minority-majority relations. Similarly, they have come to acknowledge the importance of liminal positions and how political or other changes may make individuals or groups liminal, where previously they might have had little reason to consider themselves so.[62] In that respect, the religious, linguistic, and clannish fault lines within the Kurdish groups, as well as the hybridity of Kurdish segments, should not be seen as *problems* but rather as the *norm* for many Middle Eastern populations. Making hybridity and liminalities central issues in our history writing may help both to avoid the pitfalls of the nationalist paradigm and to enrich our understanding of the history of Kurdistan and beyond.

There are, of course, other methodological issues at stake here, such as the necessity for a constant combination of both sociological and long-term perspectives in order to identify the continuity and discontinuity of certain social and political dynamics; of different scales of analysis (macro, meso, and micro); and of both structural and subjective factors (including perceptions, emotions, and trauma).

Finally, and from a practical viewpoint, interdisciplinary research programs around particular themes need to be reinforced. Africanist scholars, for example, have launched the African Borderlands Research Network (ABORNE). Besides offering a platform for debate and interdisciplinary exchanges, ABORNE "seeks to develop borderland studies as a sub-field in its own right and to promote research activity, including programmes of study at the postgraduate level."[63] In addition, ABORNE aims to provide a mechanism for promoting collaborative research and dissemination amongst researchers based in and outside Africa. The establishment of the Kurdish Studies Network (KSN) in 2009 was an important step in that direction.[64] Yet, compared to initiatives such as ABORNE, the KSN still has a relatively loose research agenda.

All in all, scholars of Kurdish studies, including practitioners of Kurdish history, have indeed undertaken a huge amount of work so far, yet luckily, from the selfish point of view of one of these scholars, we still have a long way to go. The papers collected on this issue are an attempt to bolster those ongoing endeavors and to contribute, with befitting humility, to filling the glass to the brim.

2.

SOCIAL MOVEMENT THEORY AND POLITICAL MOBILIZATION IN KURDISTAN

David Romano

Introduction: What are social movement theories?

Social movements involve the mobilization of large numbers of people to challenge power and press for (or resist) social change. While social movements can include formal political parties that share their goals as part of the movement, they are larger and more amorphous than a political party and include a vast array of possible strategies—both legal and illegal—designed to press for (or resist) the social changes their participants and leaders desire. Ralph H. Turner and Lewis M. Killian offer the following definition:

> A social movement is a collectivity acting with some continuity to promote or resist a change in the society or organization of which it is a part. As a collectivity a movement is a group with indefinite and shifting membership and with leadership whose position is determined more by informal response of the members than by formal procedures for legitimating authority.[1]

Social movement theories in turn seek to understand social movements—their goals, identities, strategies, impacts, and fortunes. They may do so by focusing on a few specific issues, such as the discourse and ideological framings of a movement,[2] or the networks that movements tap into or create.[3] Alternately, social movement theories may take a broader look at the sociopolitical contexts that stifle movements or

17

allow them to thrive,[4] the general array of choices and mobilisation strategies that movements pursue,[5] or the broad cultural framings and identity-based questions that surround social movements' appeal.[6] Although social movement theorists from these three broad traditions (the "structural" approach, the "strategy" or "agency" approach, and the "culture" or "identity" approach) long sought to demonstrate the superiority of their approach to social movement questions, in the 1990s a growing body of literature emerged about the need to pursue a synthesis of the three broad paradigms in social movement theory.[7] While some social movement theorists pursued such a synthesis, others contented themselves by leaving aside such epistemological macro-questions and focusing instead on some individual aspects of specific social movements they wished to analyze.

The classic modern example first analyzed by social movement theories was the labor movement in the industrialized world. This movement focused on political and economic (e.g. "material") goals. In the 1960s and '70s the rise of "new social movements," such as environmentalist groups, the anti-nuclear movement, the new women's movements, and animal rights groups, spawned "new social movement theories." These new social movement theories were pioneered in Europe and focused on the non-material goals, post-modern context, and often innovative or unorthodox tactics and culture of these new movements.[8] All of these social movement theories sought to produce generalizable approaches and insights, despite arising in and focusing on the experience of the Western industrialized world.

Beginning in the 1980s, a growing number of social movement theorists thus sought to apply the literature's insights to non-Western cases and contexts. Some of the most insightful work focused on the broad Latin American social movements that included opposition political parties, civil society initiatives, and armed guerrilla movements working together to change the prevailing status quo in the region.[9] By the 2000s, social movement theory analysis was being applied to a vast array of cases across the world and continues to provide new insights to contentious politics in a wide variety of contexts.[10]

The first attempt to employ social movement theories in Kurdish studies

The author's *The Kurdish Nationalist Movement: Opportunity, Mobilization and Identity*[11] in 2006 was the first serious attempt to apply social movement theories to the Kurdish case. The book represented an attempt to answer larger questions about how, when, and why significant Kurdish episodes of dissidence and revolt in Turkey, Iraq, and Iran emerged. This work applied various schools of social movement theory to different Kurdish cases, with a special focus on twentieth-century Kurdish uprisings in Turkey.

SOCIAL MOVEMENT THEORY & POLITICAL MOBILIZATION

By first applying social movement theories from the three principle paradigms (opportunity structures, resource mobilization/rational choice agency-based approaches, and cultural identity approaches) in isolation of each other, the study sought to demonstrate the advantages and limitations of each broad school of social movement theory. In this sense it was as much a test of social movement theories as an attempt to explain episodes of Kurdish nationalist dissidence. The structural concept of opportunity structures proved to be good at predicting when serious Kurdish uprisings or significant dissidence would occur (in line with Theda Skocpol's expectations, mostly when central states are weak and when the Kurds have elite allies in the center or internationally[12]) as well as the form that such Kurdish movements would take. The open or closed nature of political systems the Kurds lived under played a key role here as well, as in this example from my analysis of Kurdish dissidence in Turkey:

> When the institutionalized political system appeared more open, movements willing to operate legally within the system arose. Before the closing of the system in 1924, many Kurdish nationalists sought to be a part of and work from within Ankara's National Assembly. With the advent of the more liberal 1960 Constitution in Turkey, Kurdish nationalists (as well as many voters) supported and joined the legalized leftist movements. After 1960, several attempts were made to found legal political parties supportive of Kurdish aspirations, such as DEP and HADEP. All of these openings of the system proved ephemeral, however, with Turkish-Kurdish brotherhood crushed in 1925, leftist movements outlawed in 1971, liberal freedoms further suppressed in 1980, and parties such as DEP and HADEP closed down by the military. The result of such closures in the system were the Kurdish uprisings in the early days of the Republic and the subversive, violent left-wing (Kurdish as well as non-Kurdish) movements that emerged in the 1970s, of which the PKK became the most successful and best known.

It is not only the relative openness or closure of the political system that had a compelling effect on the character of emergent Kurdish movements, however. The other variables may also play an important role. Elites available to support Kurdish nationalist movements in the 1920s and 30s tended to be aghas, tribal leaders and religious sheikhs. Consequently, the movements that arose during this time period were conservative, melding religion, tribal politics and Kurdish nationalism together, but not seeking to transform Kurdish society or modes of economic production. By the 1960s and 70s, however, the majority of the old elites were either gone (killed, exiled or reduced to insignificance and poverty) or co-opted by the state. In their place, leftist union leaders, intellectuals, media figures and members of the professional classes emerged as the allies available to both leftist and Kurdish nationalist projects. Most of the Kurdish movements (such as the PKK) that arose at this time in turn espoused a socialist and revolutionary brand of Kurdish nationalism.[13]

Conversely, the opportunity structures approach did not prove particularly adept at explaining the fate of Kurdish movements, nor their impact on Kurdish identity. What should have turned out to be golden moments for these movements, such as the absolute weakness of the Ottoman Empire and nascent Turkish Republic following the First World War, ended with the crushing of organized Kurdish dissidence in the 1920s and 1930s, along with nearly all forms of particularly Kurdish expression in Turkey. Somewhat similar experiences occurred in Iraq and Iran as well. Finally, the most sustained episode of Kurdish dissidence in Turkey's history emerged at a time that did not seem particularly auspicious from an opportunity structures perspective: the Kurdistan Workers' Party (PKK) insurgency and movement emerged soon after the 1980 military coup in Turkey, when structural opportunity factors such as "the presence of elite allies," "the state's capacity and propensity for repression," and "international influences supportive of the state's opponents" hardly appeared to be in the Kurds' favor.

To explain the PKK's rise and eventual hegemonic status amongst Kurdish nationalists in Turkey, I turned to resource mobilization theories and rational choice analysis. These agency-based approaches focus on the strategies and resources available to social movements, including movements with an armed component such as the PKK. Although space limitations do not permit any reasonable summary of the book's examination of PKK strategies, this manner of posing initial questions about the PKK's rise effectively illustrate how these kinds of social movement theories are applied: When it first emerged in the 1970s, the PKK had a plethora of competing radical groups, including the Turkish Kurdish Socialist Party (TSKP), Kurdistan Conservative Party (KCP), Turkish Communist Party and the Marxist-Leninist Turkish Workers' and Peasants' Army (TKP/ML TIKKO), Kizilordu (a breakaway faction of TKP/ML TIKKO), Revolutionary People's Liberation Party/Front (DHKP/C), Hizbullah, Turkish Revolutionary People's Army (THKO), Marxist-Leninist Maoist Party (MLM), Kurdistan Proletarian Union (KAWA), Kurdistan Islamic Union (PIK), and Raya Zazaistan (Path of Zazaistan), to name but a few from a long list.[14] The PKK proved able to develop into a mass movement in Turkey despite the presence of so many competitors, little in the way of start-up resources, and an extremely large, well-equipped opposing Turkish military and security apparatus. Part of *The Kurdish Nationalist Movement*'s theoretically-informed findings about the PKK's rise centered on the importance of its patient Maoist-style preparatory work before launching the guerrilla war, the initial choice of helping Kurdish peasants oppose unpopular feudal landlords, and the utility of violence to demonstrate PKK militants' credibility and apply disincentives to state collaborators.[15] Resource mobilization insights also point to how the PKK's genesis from the Turkish left helped determine the kinds of strategies, networks, and mobilizing appeals the organization relied upon, all of which significantly differed from Kurdish opposition groups stemming from traditional tribal and religious networks.

If resource mobilization and rational choice agency-based approaches proved good at explaining the relative success of the PKK in Turkey vis-à-vis competitors, as well as how it emerged even under unfavorable conditions, they nonetheless have difficulty accounting for the cultural shift that the PKK engendered amongst Kurds in Turkey, the sacrifices and dangers that many PKK militants and supporters willingly undertook, and the "why" behind Kurdish nationalist goals in the movement.[16] Whereas resource mobilization and rational choice approaches tend to treat movement goals as a given and proceed from there, the PKK and the state repression it engendered clearly changed Kurdish identities in Turkey. Identity precedes the selection of movement goals and objectives, of course. Because identity is clearly dynamic and in fact one of the issues under contention between states and opposition social movements, assuming it and treating it as a static variable seems less than adequate.

This is, of course, the focus of the third broad school of social movement theories: those approaches focused on culture, ideological framing, discourse, and identity in general. As with the other social movement paradigms, my book applied a modified and simplified variant of the approach[17] to examine shifting Kurdish identities and demands in Turkey from the time of the 1919 Koçgiri uprising to the PKK in the 1990s. Because early Kurdish rebels such as those of Koçgiri, the Sheikh Said uprising, and the Mount Ararat revolt made demands upon the state on behalf of Kurds—for things like autonomy and Kurdish language rights—it could be concluded that a politicized Kurdish ethnic identity existed to some extent even at this early stage. If it had not, the Kurdish elites would not in all likelihood have found it useful to frame their demands in a Kurdish nationalist manner.

Throughout the modern period, Kurdish nationalist identities formed one option of many that people could attach varying levels of importance to. Other possible identities that people could favor instead included the dominant ethnic identity of states such as Turkey, religious-based identities, class-based identities, or various hybrids of these. Social movements attempt not only to appeal to the identities of potential members, but also to shift large numbers of people's identity to more closely align with the movement in question. *The Kurdish Nationalist Movement* examined the PKK and other Kurdish movements by looking at the following factors:[18]

1. The cultural tool kits available to would-be insurgents;
2. The strategic framing efforts of movement groups;
3. The frame contests between the movement and other collective actors—principally the state, and counter-movement groups;
4. The structure and role of the media in mediating such contests;
5. The cultural impact of the movement in modifying the available tool kit.

Using these factors, one can analyze the competing cultural framing of Kurdish movements and the Turkish state and the impact this had on Kurdish identity in Turkey. In the case of the PKK, a dissident and very politicized Kurdish identity emerged on a mass scale (or re-emerged, depending on one's perspective on nationalism):

> the PKK has altered the cultural tool kit of Kurds in Turkey. In addition to increasing the number of people who identified themselves as Kurds, and in many cases politicizing such an identity, the PKK provided a vehicle for individuals to express their identity. Because most expressions of Kurdish identity in Turkey have been constrained for so long, joining the movement, supporting it, or simply participating in mass protests could function as a form of catharsis for a frustrated populace. Many Kurds even came to identify so much with the larger Kurdish nation, or in Anderson's parlance the "imagined community," that they value the well-being and status of the group more than their own lives as individuals. Given such changes in attitudes, Ankara's attempts at solving the problem solely through programs of socio-economic development will come too late. The PKK's insurgency has already changed the values and goals of too many Kurds—one need only think of Horowitz' [1985] observation that in situations of ethnic strife, symbols of ethnic inclusion and exclusion are more a source of conflict than economic competition.[19]

If cultural framing and identity approaches provided a good understanding of the "why" of Kurdish dissidence, they were not particularly well suited to explaining the "how" and "when" issues discussed above. How was it that the PKK enjoyed relative success leading the effort in Turkey, rather than any number of other Kurdish-oriented groups that existed in the 1970s, for instance, and why did this occur when it did? These were questions more suited to the aforementioned opportunity structures and resource mobilization approaches.

After relying on the Kurdish case in Turkey to test the three broad social movement paradigms in isolation, I went on to examine what might be offered by a theoretical synthesis of the approaches—as increasingly advocated by leading social movement scholars such as McAdam, McCarthy, Zald, Tarrow, Tilly, Melucci, Meyer, and others beginning in the 1990s. The main task here lay in understanding how the different factors continuously impact, affect, and even mutually constitute each other. As such it was necessary to apply a synthesis of the approaches to Kurdish cases in Turkey (in order to see what additional insights unique to the theoretical synthesis might emerge) and then to Iraq and Iran. Although a satisfying summary of the findings is not possible here, an example of such observations for the case of the Kurds in Turkey provides a good idea of the synthesis:

> In addition to being organized enough to take advantage of political opportunities, challenger movements must use their organization to help their constituents perceive the opportunities in question. In the 1920s and 30s, Kurdish nationalist organizations were

not sufficiently organized to take advantage of auspicious opportunity structures. Although they nonetheless attempted to mobilize for their objectives, the mobilization occurred at different times amongst different Kurdish groups, with the result that Ankara was able to defeat the various rebellions one at a time and one after another. Had Kurdish nationalist organizations at the time effectively reached deeper into general Kurdish society (including many tribal elites, but also the non-tribal peasantry), they might have been able to 1) Affect the identity of the Kurdish masses so that politicized Kurdish ethnicity prevailed more often over regional, tribal, class, or religious identities; 2) Help the masses at large perceive the auspicious opportunity structures for Kurdish self-determination that lay before them between 1919 and 1938; 3) Organize a more unified, coordinated Kurdish mobilization to achieve these objectives, much like the Kemalists had organized a unified and coordinated resistance to Allied, Armenian and Greek encroachments; and 4) Convince outside powers such as France and Britain that providing assistance to Kurdish nationalists would serve their own colonial interests, since the Kurds were a power to be reckoned with.

Crawford Young, writing about ethnicity and politics in 1982, argued that "Most individuals ... have more than one cultural identity. Which has relevance will depend upon the situational context. So also will context determine the saliency and intensity of identities." We might therefore add that in addition to the situational context, the existence of an organized movement that helps them view their context in a certain light is equally important for the saliency and intensity of identities. Hence the argument of some scholars, such as Melucci, that the structural conditions forming opportunity structures are only important for collective action in so far as they are perceived by social movement actors and the population.[20]

Phrased otherwise, structure and identity set parameters and limits within which movements emerge and develop their strategies. Movements can also act to change the structures they exist in (for better or worse), spawn counter-movements, and affect the identities around them.

The study concluded by applying a synthesis of the social movement approaches to a broad examination of Kurdish struggles in Iraq and Iran.[21] In Iraq, for example, the state recognized Kurdish identity from the outset, meaning that Kurdish movements there did not have to work so hard at shifting the identities of their potential constituents.[22] Because the main Kurdish movements of Iraq relied upon pre-existing tribal forces and networks to contest Baghdad's power, however, the Kurdish nationalist movement there maintained a very different, more conservative bent than what emerged in Turkey. The more prominent role of tribes likewise increased the saliency of intra-Kurdish divisions in Iraq. Opportunities provided by the 1990–91 Gulf War and the 2003 invasion of Iraq allowed the Iraqi Kurds to develop a proto-state, however, and begin pursuing the cultural framings necessary for an overarching "South Kurdistani" identity.

The chapter applying a synthesis of approaches to Iran included the observation that the Kurdish movements tried to take advantage of opportunities that emerged in the 1920s, 1940s, and 1979 to challenge a weakened central state. Intra-Kurdish divisions and the smaller relative size of Kurds to the overall populations of Iran weakened these efforts, however, no matter what strategies the Kurdish movements attempted to deploy. The establishment of the short-lived Republic of Kurdistan in Mahabad in December 1945 nonetheless had an enduring effect on Kurdish cultural frames across all the regions of Kurdistan. Presently none of the Iranian Kurdish dissident movements appear able to mount a serious challenge to the government in Tehran, however, no matter what strategies and identity-based framings they deploy.

Subsequent efforts to apply social movement theories to the Kurdish cases

A great many master's degrees and doctoral theses have gone on to employ social movement theories to shed light on the Kurdish case. A non-exhaustive list includes the following in date order:[23]

MA theses:

Alis, Ahmet, 'The Process of the Politicisation of the Kurdish Identity in Turkey: the Kurds and the Turkish Labor Party (1961–1971)', MA thesis, Boğaziçi University, 2009.

Couch, Christopher M., 'Aghas, Sheiks, and Daesh in Iraq: Kurdish robust action in turmoil', MA thesis, Naval Postgraduate School, 2016.

Ercan, Harun, 'Dynamics of Mobilisation and Radicalization of the Kurdish Movement in the 1970s in Turkey', MA thesis, Koç University, Comparative Studies in History and Society, 2010.

Gündoğan, Azat Zana, 'The Kurdish Political Mobilisation in the 1960s: The Case of the "Eastern Meetings"', MA thesis, Middle East Technical University, 2005.

Kavak, Seref, 'The Democratic Society Party as a 'Party for Turkey': Official and Grassroots Politics of a Changing Identity 2005–2009', MA Thesis, Boğaziçi University, 2010.

O'Connor, Francis Patrick, 'Armed Social Movements and Insurgency: The PKK and its communities of support', MA thesis, European University Institute, 2014.

Sornsin, Kristin M., 'Out of the Mountains into Politics: The Kurdish Nationalist Movement of Iraq', MA Thesis, Central European University, 2008.

Toktamis, Kumru, 'From Mobilisation to Nationhood', MA thesis, New School for Social Research, 2007.

Yeleser, Selin, 'A Turning Point in the Formation of the Kurdish Left in Turkey: The Revolutionary Eastern Cultural Hearths (1969–1971)', MA Thesis, Boğaziçi University, 2011.

Doctoral theses:

Dryaz, Massoud Sharifi, 'De la résistance microscopique à l'action collective organisée: engagement et désengagement des militants dans l'espace kurde', PhD thesis, L'École des hautes études en sciences sociales, Paris, 2015.

Saeed, Seevan, 'The Kurdish National Movement in Turkey: From the PKK to the KCK', PhD thesis, University of Exeter, 2014.

Uslu, Emrullah, 'The Transformation of Kurdish Political Identity in Turkey: Impact of Modernisation, Democratisation and Globalisation', PhD Thesis, University of Utah, 2009.

A number of publications likewise indicate the increasing prominence of such approaches within the field of Kurdish studies.

Journal articles and collected editions:

Ceren, Belge, 'State building and the limits of legibility: Kinship networks and Kurdish resistance in Turkey', *International Journal of Middle East Studies* 43:1 (2011), pp. 95-114.

Çicek, Cuma, 'Ulus, din, Sinif: Türkiyede Kürt Mutabakatinin Insasi', *Iletisim* (2015).

Ersanli, Busra, Gunay Goksu Ozdogan, and Nesrin Ucarlar (eds), *Türkiye Siyasetinde Kürtler: Direniş, Hak Arayışı, Katılım* 3rd edn (Istanbul: Iletisim Yayinlari, 2016).

Güneş, Murat Tezcür, 'When Democratization Radicalizes: The Kurdish nationalist movement in Turkey', *Journal of Peace Research* 47:6 (2010), pp. 775-89.

O'Connor, Francis 'Radical political participation and the internal Kurdish diaspora in Turkey', *Kurdish Studies* 3:2 (2015) pp. 151-71.

O'Connor, Francis and Leonidas Oikonomakis, 'Preconflict Mobilization Strategies and Urban-Rural Transition: The Cases of the PKK and the FLN/EZLN', *Mobilization: An International Quarterly* 20:3 (September 2015) pp. 379-99.

Şimşek, Sefa, 'New Social Movements in Turkey Since 1980', *Turkish Studies* 5:2 (2004) pp.111-39.

van den Berge, Wietse, 'Syrian Kurdish Political Activism: A Social Movement Theory Perspective', *Middle East: Topics and Arguments* 4 (2015) pp. 160-69.

Watts, Nicole F., 'Activists in Office: Pro-Kurdish Contentious Politics in Turkey', *Ethnopolitics* 5:2 (2006) pp. 125-44.

After 2006, book-length monographs applying social movement theory to Kurdish topics also began appearing. The aforementioned *The Kurdish Nationalist Movement* of 2006 appeared in Turkish translation in 2010.[24] Other studies frequently began by criticizing the work for failing to include an examination of some issue or factor, or not going into sufficient depth on some matters.[25] In contrast to the broader, "forest-oriented" approach of my first application and test of social movement theories, these authors went on to provide more detailed examinations of the "trees" via a more focused analyses of a number of specific issues, or a single case study. In this sense, *The Kurdish Nationalist Movement* may have succeeded in helping to provide some of the next generation of Kurdish studies scholars with ideas to work on and further develop. A number of in-depth, interesting, and useful social movement oriented contributions to the field have emerged since 2006. Noteworthy recent Kurdish studies books that situate themselves within the social movement theoretical literature include:

Books:
Aydin, Aysegül and Cem Emrence, *Zones of Rebellion: Kurdish Insurgents and the Turkish State*, Ithaca, NY: Cornell University Press, 2015.

Gunes, Cengiz, *The Kurdish National Movement in Turkey: From Protest to Resistance*, New York: Routledge, 2012.

Gürbüz, Mustafa, *Rival Kurdish Movements in Turkey: Transforming Ethnic Conflict*, Amsterdam: Amsterdam University Press, 2016.

Tejel, Jordi, *Syria's Kurds, History, Politics and Society,* London: Routledge, 2008.

Watts, Nicole, *Activists in Office: Kurdish Politics and Protest in Turkey,* Seattle: University of Washington Press, 2010.

Tejel's study of the Syrian Kurds begins by situating itself within social movement studies:

a study of political mobilization during the mandatory period is impossible if its interpretation hinges on a binary minority/majority opposition (Kurd/Arab) when each of the two groups constitutes a hybrid sociopolitical entity. In other words, if the Syrian state was in a construction phase during the French Mandate, the Kurdish "group" was experiencing a transition in its own right.[26]

Although a good portion of the book focuses on providing historical detail about the Kurdish political situation in Syria, Chapter 5 in particular applies a social movement theoretical synthesis to explain very limited (at least until 2004) Kurdish political mobilization in the country:

> The Kurdish movement, like all social movements, must maintain collective action in time and space. Structures of political opportunity, defined as a series of coherent dimensions of the political environment which can both encourage and discourage people from taking political action, take on great importance in this context. Generally speaking, at moments when the elites and their political groups become vulnerable to the opposition, social movements are more likely to be initiated and to inspire collective action. At the same time, such political opportunities can be missed due to the lack of an organized social movement.[27]

In the Syrian case, Tejel describes an "ambiguous space" that the Ba'athist regime created, wherein Kurdish communal political mobilization was repressed but some interaction, collusion, and cooperation between Kurdish nationalist parties and the regime was nonetheless permitted.[28] The regime allowed just enough collusion to delegitimize cooperating Kurdish elites and their parties in the eyes of their Kurdish constituencies, in fact, while harshly repressing those who would not work with the regime at all. This and other factors outlined by Tejel accounted for the dearth of Kurdish political challenges in Syria until very recently (after the publication of Tejel's book), when the unparalleled "political opportunity" of the Syrian civil war finally allowed Kurds in the country to organize and push forward their own national agenda.

Watts' study in contrast chooses to focus on a particular facet of Kurdish social and political mobilization in Turkey: attempts to form legal political parties within the Turkish electoral system. For this analysis Watts deploys an in-depth synthesis of social movement theories, examining how changes in the socio-political opportunity structures within Turkey and some Kurds' decision to try to take advantage of this led to the creation (and subsequent banning) of a number of pro-Kurdish political parties functioning parallel to (but neither completely subservient to nor fully independent from) the armed struggle of the PKK. The way she poses her research question (as well as the nuanced answers she finds to it) offers an outstanding synthesis of opportunity structures, resource mobilization, and identity factors:

> In the 1990s and early 2000s, state authorities detained and tortured pro-Kurdish activists, raided their offices, confiscated their computers and documents, and restricted their freedom to publish, travel, and organize meetings. At least 112 Kurdish party members were murdered in the 1990s. Thousands more were imprisoned, and many were prohibited from

any further participation in political life. Simply moving into conventional institutions, in other words, did not ensure "conventional" treatment or routine political outcomes. Given these decidedly difficult circumstances and the less-than-obvious rewards of working within the system, why did Kurdish activists use formal politics to promote their cause? What opportunities did they find, and what constraints? What impact did their incorporation into the mainstream political framework have on the movement, its supporters, the furthering of its goals, and its relations with the Turkish state?[29]

Part of Watts' answer to this question refers to McAdam, Tarrow, and Tilly's notion of "transgressive contention,"[30] wherein Kurdish activists used their limited access to the legal political system to issue constant challenges to its taboos (often by the very act of representing themselves as Kurds) and to pursue "contentious politics" vis-à-vis the Turkish state. Besides contesting the Turkish state's cultural framings and policies, the Kurdish activists also tried to create a competing zone of governances in municipalities they controlled, complete with divergent norms and notions of what it was to be a citizen there. The result has had and continues to have far-reaching impacts on Kurdish mobilization in Turkey and Turkish politics and society in general.

Cengiz Gunes' *The Kurdish National Movement in Turkey* chooses to rely mostly on the identity-based social movement approaches, examining the discourse, ideology, cultural framings, and myth-creation of the PKK's version of Kurdish nationalism. He does so from a post-structuralist viewpoint, refusing to treat Kurdish identity as primordial and largely static and also rejecting approaches that attempt "objectively" to assess the Kurds' status as a nation.[31] Instead, he turns to discourse theory[32] in order to examine things such as the PKK's efforts to trace Kurdish ancestry back to the Medes civilization and the PKK's reconstruction of the Newroz Kurdish new year. In the case of Newroz, the PKK-aligned Kurdish movement constructed a modified legend behind the holiday (of Kawa the blacksmith's fight against a dictator king) and used Newroz celebrations to help change Kurdish identity, mobilize the population against dominant Turkish representations of identity, and in general to socialize people into the national movement. Gunes' research questions demonstrate his focus in this work:

- How was the category of 'Kurd' produced and reproduced within the two discourses [the 1960s and post-1960s discourse] deployed by the Kurdish nationalists? In particular, how are difference and Kurdish subjectivity being constructed within each discourse?

- What kind of political project is proposed by the Kurdish National Movement? How has it changed over time?

- What is the relationship between the assertion of Kurdish identity and the official Turkish (Kemalist) identity?

- Why and how did the discourse of democracy replace the previous 'secessionist' discourse of national liberation?

- What is the character of this discourse of democracy? How or to what extent does it address questions of pluralism, both within and outside the Kurdish community?

- To what extent has this discourse of democracy challenged the dominant conceptions of democracy in Turkish society at large?[33]

Aysegül Aydin and Cem Emrence's *Zones of Rebellion* takes a somewhat different approach. To answer this question, they rely on quantitative data they sourced from news reports regarding violence in Turkey. The authors ask, "How do insurgents and governments select their targets? Which ideological discourses and organisational policies do they adopt to win civilian loyalties and control territory?"[34] They thus compare the strategies of the PKK and the Turkish state in three kinds of zones, which they categorize as: zones of control (or rebellion for the PKK), zones of contestation, and zones out of reach (the zones obviously differ in a binary manner according to the actor). These strategies are in turn linked to the ideological appeals that both actors attempted to make in what amounts to competing "hearts and minds" campaigns. Neither the state nor the PKK was able to claim victory in the conflict, because ideologies and organizational/institutional factors inherent to both actors limited their strategic choices. Although only a very limited taste of their analysis is possible here, the following provides an example of how they approached these issues:

> we highlight the role of brokers, entrepreneurs that link two previously unconnected social sites, in organizing collective action in support of the insurgency. Brokerage is instrumental in forging common fronts out of local cleavages. While the presence of brokers solves the thorny issues of mass mobilization and legitimacy, the absence of such entrepreneurs means limited civilian support to the rebel cause. In that respect, brokers play a critical role in generating compliance. These "frame-bridgers" can be found only in certain political spaces: It requires a unique type of social capital to bridge the differences among individuals, groups, and regions. The PKK example is instructive. As an intermediary, the Transition Zone legitimated the military struggle with nationalist messages and set an example for the rest of the country with its collective action agenda. However, civilian unrest was hard to come by in other Kurdish areas. The problem was the absence of political brokers in these sites.[35]

Each zone of conflict, and the contested zones in particular, displayed different strategies regarding violence at different times, and various kinds of ideological appeals by the competing actors. In the case of the PKK, the authors argue that:

Once rebels learn to be a closed group of practitioners, they turn first on rival groups. Next is the community, which they seek to transform through violence and other means. Finally, the state emerges on the horizon as a political target—only if the rebel group has been resourceful enough to survive in early stages. In their struggle with the state, rebels calibrate their political independence, autonomy, or some other form of power-sharing arrangement, depending on the extent to which it can challenge the state.[36]

The fifth book on the Kurds relying on social movement theories, Mustafa Gürbüz's *Rival Kurdish Movements in Turkey: Transforming Ethnic Conflict*, was a few weeks short of release at the time of writing. Examples of Gürbüz's approach in the book, with citations and a close examination of his argument, are therefore not possible here. The study sits squarely within the social movement theoretical tradition, employing a theoretical synthesis of opportunities, strategies, and identity to examine competition between three rival movements in Turkey: the Sunni Muslim Gülen movement (which used to enjoy linkages with the Justice and Development Party or AKP government), the PKK-aligned Kurdish movement with its various political parties and associations, and the Hizbullah-aligned Kurdish movement[37] with its Huda-Par legal political arm. One of the more interesting observations coming out of Gürbüz's study[38] explains how Islam itself became a contested field for the three movements. Because the Gülen movement was trying to shift Kurdish identities and mobilize people with a 'de-Kurdified' version of Islam, and Hizbullah was combining Kurdish nationalism with a Salafi (often Jihadi-infused) interpretation of Islam, the formerly secular PKK-aligned movement suddenly rediscovered religion. Given that many Kurds remain Muslims who value their religion, the PKK did so in an attempt to compete for people's loyalties. Islam was recently reintegrated into the movement and "patriotic imams" were recruited to hold prayer services in the street, outside the purview of the state's mosques (which at the time had a heavy Gülen presence in them) or the Hizbullah-aligned prayer groups.

Conclusion: Which way forward for social movement theories and Kurdish studies?

A unified, over-arching synthetic social movement account of Kurdish social movements in Turkey, Iran, Iraq, and Syria—as this author attempted to produce in 2006—was probably never achievable in any truly satisfactory sense. No manuscript of any reasonable length could possibly address the myriad complexities, variations, and diverse history of such a phenomenon. As much as such an attempt simplifies and make intelligible the topic it investigates, it leaves out and distorts innumerable phenomena and nuances.

Instead of pursuing such a chimerical goal, Kurdish studies today seem to be busily producing a wide array of more focused analyses on topics that include Kurdish civil society networks, pro-Kurdish parties within institutionalized politics, efforts at identity construction, diaspora networks, cross-border linkages within Kurdish society, insurgent strategies, and competing cultural framings, among others. These efforts should be viewed as the construction of the various pieces of a vast jigsaw puzzle. Properly fitted together,[39] the component parts of this puzzle form an important part of a wider theoretical literature that helps us understand the Kurds and their efforts to affect the world they inhabit. In other words, advances in the social movement literature in Kurdish studies serve as one more example that the field has finally moved beyond basic description and is rapidly coming into its own. This has been most evident in studies on the Kurds in North Kurdistan/Turkey. There undoubtedly remains a plethora of topics to investigate from a social movement theory perspective, especially as regards Kurdish movements in Rojava/Syria, Bashur/Iraq, and Rojhelat/Iran.

3.

RELIGION AMONG THE KURDS

BETWEEN NAQSHBANDI SUFISM AND IS SALAFISM

Michiel Leezenberg

In 2014, the Kurds once again came to international attention; this time, however, it was not primarily their confrontation with existing states that captured the imagination, but rather their confrontation with a new, and radical, religious movement, the so-called Islamic State (IS), and in particular with its offensives against Sinjar in northern Iraq and Kobanî on the Syrian-Turkish border. In the popular press, images of civilians of the Yezidi minority fleeing the roundly genocidal IS onslaught onto Mount Sinjar acquired almost biblical qualities; likewise, reporting about Kobanî created a Manichaean opposition between "modern" Kurdish guerrillas, many of them women, against "medieval" IS fighters reported to treat captured women as slaves. Behind these reductionist and often overheated headlines, one may legitimately ask why the Kurds, the vast majority of whom are Sunni Muslims, proved impossible to mobilize for the project of an Islamic State, and refused to rally behind IS leader Abu Bakr al-Baghdadi, who had pronounced himself caliph in July 2014. Was it primarily religious, national, or other factors that make the Kurds less open to violent Salafi-Jihadi brands of Islam?

A different but related question is whether there are any varieties of Islam that may be considered specifically Kurdish—or are seen as such by Kurds themselves—and whether one may as a result speak of a "nationalization" of religion among the Kurds. I will address these questions by, first, discussing the current state of studies about religion among the Kurds; second, I trace the early modern rise of specifically

Kurdish articulations of Sunni Islam; third, I discuss the confrontation of Kurdish religiosity with secular nationalism and Salafism in the twentieth century; and fourth, I discuss the rise of politicized forms of religion among the Kurds, some of which might be qualified as Salafi-Jihadi, in the 1980s. I will conclude with a few comments about the present predicament.

The study of religion among the Kurds: the current state

There is surprisingly little academic research on the various formations of Sunni Islam among the Kurds. Until the present, research on religion in Kurdistan has displayed a clear bias toward religious minorities like Christians and Jews, and in particular to heterodox groups like the Yezidis and the Ahl-e Haqq. The former two have attracted attention because of their relevance for Semitic and Biblical studies, while the latter two have the appeal of the exotic, and of seeming to be specifically Kurdish religious formations. Thus, perhaps more studies have appeared on the Yezidis alone than of all other religious groups among the Kurds put together.[1]

It is not my intention to cast doubt on this research, much of which is quite valuable. Taken together, however, this bias has led to a systematic downplaying of more orthodox forms of (Sunni) Islam that play a role in the lives of the vast majority of Kurds.[2] A number of authors have studied the Sufi orders in the region, but generally with less attention to matters of doctrine, and more to Sufi sheikhs as leaders of (nationalist) organizations and rebellions.

The relative dearth of studies on more mainstream forms of Sunni Islamic religiosity among the Kurds may result from a tacit assumption—which one may call "orientalist" if one likes—that orthodox varieties of (Sunni) Islam display relatively fewer local particularities, leave relatively less room for regional identities and nationalist agendas, and are shaped by Arab culture and Arabic-language learning rather than by local customs and vernacular traditions. This assumption, however, is misguided: on closer inspection, it appears that specifically Kurdish forms of Sunni Islamic religiosity did emerge in early modern times. Below, I will therefore focus on articulations and re-articulations of more orthodox forms of Sunni Islamic religiosity in the early modern and modern periods, at the expense of religious minorities like those mentioned above. This is not to say, of course, that the complex interactions of evolving religious minority traditions with the development of a secular Kurdish national identity (and of new forms of politicized fundamentalist Islam) are not worth studying, or are any less important.[3] Lack of space is the only justification I can give for this omission.

RELIGION AMONG THE KURDS

Islam among the Kurds: a short historical sketch

It has long been known that Kurds generally belong to the Shafiʻi *madhhab* (one of the four schools of Islamic law in Sunni Islam), as opposed to their generally Hanafi Turkish and Arab neighbors; more specifically, they also have a significant attachment to Naqshbandism. Below, I will briefly sketch how this identification came about. The creation of a pre- or proto-nationalist Kurdish Islamic tradition appears to have occurred primarily among the smaller rural *madrasas* of northern Kurdistan, which were less susceptible to the influence of the Ottoman authorities and of the state-backed *ulema* (scholars), and to the apparent encouragement of the use of Turkish next to Arabic, than the mosques and *madrasas* in the bigger cities of the region. The seventeenth-century Ottoman travel writer Evliya Çelebi noted that the Kurds were famous for their religious learning in Arabic and Persian; but starting in the late seventeenth century, a number of introductory textbooks came to be written in Kurmanji, the northern Kurdish dialect. These textbooks subsequently became part of the *rêz*, or *madrasa* curriculum, all over northern Kurdistan. The most famous of these textbook authors is, of course, Ehmedê Khanî; he not only composed the *mathnawî* poem *Mem û Zîn*, which appears to have been widely read in *madrasa* circles, but also wrote several short Kurdish-language works of religious learning, like the *Nûbihara piçûkan*, a small rhymed Arabic-Kurdish vocabulary, and the *Eqîdeya Emanê*, a short profession of the Sunni Islamic faith according to the Shafiʻi rite. Next to these rhymed works, which also include an older *Mawlûd* or biography of the prophet by Mullah Bateyî (d.1491), in the eighteenth century a number of prose works for use in local *madrasas* were written, like Elî Teremaxî's *Tesrîf*, on the morphology of Arabic, Persian, and Kurdish; and Mullah Yûnus Khalqatînî's *Terkîb û Zurûf*, a commentary of sorts on Abd al-Qâhir al-Jurjânî's famous short textbook on *nahw* or "syntax," the *Miyyat al-amil*. Soon, all these works would become staple items of the curriculum for the rural *madrasas* in northern Kurdistan; jointly, they embody what one may call the vernacularization of Kurdish *madrasa* learning, i.e. the rise of the northern dialect of Kurdish as a language of written literature and religious learning.[4]

Another specifically Kurdish development in early modern Islamic learning is the emergence of the Khalidiyya branch of the Naqshbandi order in the nineteenth century. Its founder, Mawlana Khalid Naqshbandi (1776-1827), has attracted rather less scholarly attention than such early modern reformers as Muhammad ibn Abd al-Wahhab and Shah Waliullah, but authors like Albert Hourani and Butrus Abu-Manneh emphasized his tremendous importance; as some authors have argued, Mawlana Khalid has been crucial in identifying "Sufism in general, and the Khalidi branch of the Naqshbandiyya-Mujaddidiyya brotherhood in particular, as the leading element of Islamic revivalism in the Ottoman polity of the time."[5] He was born in Qaradagh in the Shahrazoor district, into a family belonging to the Jaf tribe. During a pilgrimage to Mecca, he was intrigued by an Indian saint sitting with his back toward the Kaaba, and was moved to turn to India. In Delhi, he was initiated into the Mujaddidi branch of the Naqshbandi order, which had originally been founded by Ahmad Sirhindi (1564-1624); in agreement with this tradition, he enjoined his followers to abide by the shari'a, to follow the sunna, and to avoid *bid'a* or heretic innovation. In around 1812 he returned to Kurdistan, until his increasing rivalry with local Qadiri Sheikh Ma'ruf Nodê forced him to flee the city. In 1821 he left for Baghdad, and eventually settled in Damascus, from where his deputies spread to various parts of the empire, in particular to its non-Arab parts.

Martin van Bruinessen has explained the rapid rise of the Khalidî Naqshbandî *tarîqa* among the Kurds in the nineteenth century, in part at the expense of the rival Qadiri order, as resulting from the Ottoman abolition of the Kurdish local hereditary kingdoms or emirates as part of their centralizing Tanzimat reforms;[6] but this rise began well before the onset of the Tanzimat in 1839, and appears to be part of a wider early modern religious dynamic. The most important factor in this dynamic was undoubtedly the late-eighteenth-century emergence of the Wahhabi movement in the Arabian peninsula. In 1801, warriors of this movement attacked the Shia shrine cities in southern Iraq, besieging Najaf and sacking Karbala; in 1806 they even captured Mecca. These rapid conquests not only dealt a serious blow to the political prestige and religious legitimacy of the Ottoman authorities; they also provoked the local Shia clergy, who felt increasingly unprotected without the support of loyal local tribes, to initiate a campaign of converting the population of southern Iraq to Shiism.[7] Butrus Abu-Manneh has plausibly argued that the Khalidiyya Naqshbandi reform movement, too, was at least in part a reaction against the Wahhabi onslaught: although there are no explicit statements on Sheikh Khalid's reaction to the Wahhabi conquest, his immediate departure from Wahhabi-held Mecca for Delhi—where he went on to study with Shah Waliullah's followers—may indicate a negative attitude to the Wahhabiyya.[8]

Already in the 1820s, some of Sheikh Khalid's deputies had settled in Istanbul; after his death, the order quickly became more dependent on Ottoman patronage and financial support. Although Sultan Mahmud II initially tried to curb the order's expansion, a number of Sheikh Khalid's followers quickly gained positions of influence in the capital, especially in the wake of the demise of both the Bektashi order associated with the Janissaries and the Greek revolt.[9]

In short, the rapid rise of the Khalidiyya Naqshbandis among the Kurds was due not only to the local effects of the Tanzimat reforms, as van Bruinessen argues, but appears to be part of a broader pattern of Islamic renewal across the Ottoman Empire. Thus, in Iraq, Naqshbandis vied with Wahhabis and Shiites for the favor, or the souls, of the population. If this hypothesis is correct, it goes some way to explaining the Khalidiyya's pronouncedly anti-Shia and—as we shall see—increasingly polemical anti-Wahhabi or anti-Salafi character.

Mawlana Khalid was not only a religious reformer or innovator, but also—alongside and possibly in competition with his great Qadiri rival, Shaykh Ma'ruf Nodê—a pioneer of the written use of the Sulaimaniya dialect of Kurdish. In the early nineteenth century, when the Hawrami dialect was still the major medium of literary expression encouraged by the Baban court in Sulaimaniya, both Nodê and Khalid started writing works in the vernacular of the local population. Shaykh Ma'ruf compiled a short rhymed Arabic-Kurdish vocabulary comparable to Khani's *Nûbihar*, the *Ehmedî*, and Sheikh Khalid wrote a profession of faith, the *Eqîdetname*, in a very simple prose.[10] They thus gave an important impetus to the vernacularization of the Sulaimani dialect, which ultimately came to be known as Sorani, and which started around a century after that of the Kurmanji dialect in northern Kurdistan.[11]

In short, from the late seventeenth century onwards, specifically Kurdish forms of religious learning arose, at first in the northern parts of Kurdistan, but from around 1800 onwards also further south, in the area centered around Sulaimaniya. Although these developments were not themselves nationalist, they contributed to laying the foundations for a modern vernacular and language-based Kurdish national identity.

The twentieth century: Kurdish Islam confronting secular nationalism

In the later nineteenth and early twentieth centuries, this reformist religion increasingly coalesced, or collided, with newly emerging forms of secular nationalism. Thus, in the wake of the 1878 Russo-Ottoman war, the Naqshbandis quickly adopted the novel patriotic, or nationalist, vocabulary of "love for the fatherland" (*hubb-ı vatan*) and defense of the nation.[12] It has also been observed that the Kurdish sheikhs, because they could mediate in the now-increasing tribal conflicts, "became the obvious focal points for nationalist sentiment";[13] thus, a number of revolts interpreted as nationalist or "proto-nationalist" have been led by, in particular, Naqshbandi sheikhs. This is not to say, of course, that the Naqshbandis are the sole or even necessarily the most important Sufi order involved in the Kurdish national movement. The Qadiri order in particular, which was characterized by more ecstatic *dhikr* rituals and more hereditary forms of leadership than the Naqshbandis, played a major role in a number of nineteenth- and twentieth-century revolts in the Kurdish provinces, and more generally in the development of a Kurdish national movement, yielding nationalist leaders like, most famously, Sheikh Mahmood Barzinji; likewise, both the Talabani and the Barzani families have Qadiri backgrounds.[14]

Another doctrinal, or ideological, development of late-nineteenth-century Khalidi Naqshbandi Islam is its increasingly pronounced anti-Wahhabi or anti-Salafi character. In early-twentieth-century publications, Salafis like Rashid Rida, most famously, are generally called *lâ-madhhabiyya* or "no-madhhab." One of the central dogmas of the Naqshbandi conception of faith or *imân* is respect for the madhhabs; this article of faith pits the Naqshbandis directly against the Wahhabis, who—nominally, at least—brandish the adherence to a particular madhhab as a form of *taqlîd* or slavish imitation, or worse, idol worship (*shirk*). In practice, of course, Wahhabis abided by the Hanbali rite; but the ideology of rejecting the legitimacy of madhhabs has proved a powerful and enduring aspect of Wahhabi, and more generally Salafi, reformulations of the Islamic faith. Most famously, in the late nineteenth century, a pamphlet appeared in Ottoman Naqshbandi circles alleging that Muhammad ibn Abd al-Wahhab had been visited by a British spy who taught him to drink whisky and conspired with him to destroy true Islam. Versions of this tale circulated in Naqshbandi circles in the form of both oral traditions and printed pamphlets, even as far afield as Central Asia and sub-Saharan Africa.[15]

In the 1920s, the Naqshbandis in formerly Ottoman lands suffered a number of major setbacks, though not a *coup de grâce*, in their confrontation both with secular nationalism and state-backed Salafism. First, in 1925, the Wahhabi warriors of the Bani Sa'ud conquered Mecca and Medina and ousted the Naqshbandis, for whom these cities had been major centers for transnational organization and mobilization. Second, a series of legal measures taken by the staunchly secular and militantly nationalist Kemalist rulers of the new Republic of Turkey seriously weakened Naqshbandism. Firstly, they ordered all Sufi lodges to be closed; secondly, they ordered the closing down of all *madrasas*; thirdly, they banned the use of Kurdish both in public and in private. Thus, the establishment of the Republic of Turkey dealt a major blow both to Kurdish vernacular learning and to the Naqshbandi networks that gave Kurdish society greater coherence.[16]

In the longer run, however, these measures led to the adaptation of the Naqshbandi order to the new circumstances, and to its transformation from a collective *tarîqa*-based form of religiosity to a more individualized, depoliticized, and print-based faith, which successfully adapted to the demands and constraints imposed by the secular-nationalist Turkish state, and of a more urbanized and increasingly literate society.[17] The most famous example of such adaptation is undoubtedly the career of Said Nursî (1876-1960), author of the voluminous, and widely read, *Risale-i nur*, and famous as the inspiration for the so-called Nurcu movement. It is less well known that in his early years Nursî had been an ardent Kurdish patriot, who moreover saw no contradiction between his Islamic reform agenda and his Kurdish national solidarity.[18] Thus, in his *Divan-ı harbi örfi*, written in 1909, Nursî praises the "patriotic zeal" with which his friend Khalil Khayali of Mutki has "created the basis of our language" through his work on Kurdish orthography, grammar, and syntax; stating that "language is the key to the future of peoples," he concludes with an appeal to the "Kurdish lions" to wake up from their "five hundred-year slumber."[19]

Nursî expressed his admiration for such heroes of vernacular Kurdish learning as Melayê Jezîrî, Ehmedê Khanî, and Mawlana Khalid, and was actively involved in efforts to open Kurdish-language schools in the Ottoman Empire's eastern province, and even proposed a "University of the East" to be built in Van. These efforts were inspired not only by a belief in instruction in one's native tongue as basic to national awakening, but also by a view/project of the Shafi'i madhhab of Sunni Islam as a Kurdish national religion. In the newly formed Republic of Turkey, however, Nursî's national and political projects came to an abrupt halt. After the suppression of the Sheikh Said revolt in 1925, Nursî was sent into domestic exile in Isparta province; in his later years, he carefully abstained from any statement that could be construed as political activism, whether of an Islamic religious or a Kurdish nationalist character.

Thus, Naqshbandism, and more specifically its Khalidiyya branch, underwent a major transformation. In Republican Turkey, although virtually invisible, it ultimately came to constitute what Yavuz calls the "matrix" out of which the major Islamist personalities and movements in twentieth-century Turkey have emerged.[20] Naqshbandi discourse, institutions, practices, and networks, he argues, have decisively shaped the outlook of Islamists like Said Nursî, Fethullah Gülen, Necmettin Erbakan, Turgut Özal, and Recep Tayyıp Erdoğan, even if some of these may hardly, and others not at all, be described as "Sufis" in anything like the conventional sense of the word. Thus, already before the Kemalist ban on Sufi orders, Nursî had dismissed the *tariqa*s as backward.

Furthermore, a good many Naqshbandis displayed a clearly Kurdish consciousness, although they were generally not exclusively, unambiguously, or even explicitly Kurdish. As one Kurdish scholar, himself of Naqshbandi sympathies, recently argued, Kurdistan is actually a "Naqshbandistan."[21] While such sweeping claims are undoubtedly an overstatement, they point to an enduring role for Naqshbandi sympathies and conceptions, even if, as noted above, as an organizational framework or institution, the Naqshbandi *tariqa* is no longer a major force in Kurdish society, whether in Turkey or elsewhere.

Syria and Iraq, the new Arab states with substantial Kurdish minorities, were rather more tolerant of organized forms of religion than the Turkish Republic; although the different branches of the Ba'ath Party that came to power in both countries in 1963 considered themselves secular and socialist, neither of them outlawed the Sufi orders. Rather, it was their Arab nationalist agenda that increasingly clashed with Kurdish aspirations. In Ba'athist Iraq, Sunni Arabs were a minority, and the Muslim Brothers were far weaker than in Egypt or Syria; religion may have played a role in organization or mobilization, but it was hardly turned into an ideological expression of the confrontation between the Kurdish insurgence and the regime, which was generally articulated in secular nationalist, rather than in religious or sectarian, terms. In Syria, Assad's Ba'athist regime leaned heavily on Alawites of rural backgrounds, and consequently marginalized the majority Sunni Arab population, in particular in cities like Aleppo, Homs, and Hama; in these cities, opposition to the regime was increasingly articulated in Salafist terms, and expressed through groups including, most importantly, the Muslim Brotherhood. Hence, the regime integrated significant numbers of Kurds of a Naqshbandi background, who were opposed to Salafism, into the national religious leadership. Most famous among these Kurdish-background *ulema* were Ahmad Kaftaro, who was Syria's grand mufti until his death in 2004, and the reformist cleric Sa'id Ramadan al-Bûtî, who according to local observers appeared on television almost as often as the president, until his assassination in the Iman mosque in Damascus in March 2013. Kaftaro hailed from a traditional Kurdish family from Hayy al-Akrad in the Salihiyya quarter of northern Damascus; al-Butî, by contrast, came from a poor Kurdish family that had fled the establishment of the new Turkish Republic, which was as repressive of organized religion as it was of Kurdish identity. Both clerics openly declared their loyalty to the Ba'athist Syrian state, and publicly condemned the violence committed by Islamist activists. Thus, Kaftaro was quite outspoken in his condemnation of actions of the Muslim Brothers, like the 1979 massacre of army cadets in Aleppo and the 1982 revolt in Hama; al-Bûtî also condemned the increasingly sectarian Islamist revolt against Bashar al-Assad's regime that had started in 2011. Both also hailed from Naqshbandi circles and in part reproduced the—by then traditional—anti-Salafist discourse; thus, al-Butî published a refutation of Salafism under the typically Naqshbandi title *al-lâmadhhabiyya* [The no-madhhab].[22]

In the present-day Turkish setting, the contrast between Naqshbandi-inspired and Salafi varieties of Islam overlaps with the national, or nationalist, distinction between Turks and Arabs, and reinforces the negative stereotypes that a good many ethnic Turks and Kurds have about Arabs. Thus, among Kurds in Turkey, Syria, and Iraq, Naqshbandi ideas and attitudes live on, albeit in rather different institutional settings and developing along rather different lines. Clearly, the modern nation state decisively shapes the development of both organized and individualized religion.

The 1980s and beyond: the rise and decline of Kurdish Salafi-Jihadism

It was only in the 1980s that Salafist ideas, and Salafi-inspired forms of politicized Islam, gained more currency among the Kurds, in particular in Iraq; but even now they remain marginal. The origins of this development, which once again varies significantly between Turkey and Iraq, not to mention Syria and Iran, are still only partially understood. Generally, however, it seems to have been encouraged by the example of the Islamic revolution in Iran and its promise of a more revolutionary, progressive form of Islam; by the jihad in Soviet-occupied Afghanistan, led by Sunni insurgents and supported by networks of the Egyptian Muslim Brotherhood and the Jamaat-i Islami and the Jamiat Ulama-e Islam in Pakistan; and by the Sunni revolt against the Assad regime in Syria in the late 1970s and early 1980s. One cannot assume as a matter of course, however, the Salafi-Jihadi character or connections of these new forms of Kurdish religio-political activism. As to the extent and nature of the links to the wider Salafi-Jihadi movement that had emerged during the 1980s, not much is known at present.[23]

Islamist activism among Kurds in Turkey developed in a distinct way, shaped primarily, it seems, by the national arena of that time. Many, if not most, of these Islamist groups were peaceful: from the early 1990s onwards, a number of Kurdish nationalist organizations of Naqshbandi, and more specifically Nurcu, background had emerged, most importantly the Nûbihar publishing house, which over the years produced not only a magazine, but also an impressive list of Kurdish-language books, among which Kurdish translations of Said Nursî's works loomed large.

The most significant, and most violent, form of politicized Islam to emerge in the south-east of Turkey from the late 1970s came in the form of the so-called Kurdish Hizbullah (KH). It originated in circles around a number of Islamist bookstores, especially in Batman province, and divided into different factions; in the course of the 1980s, the one headed by Hüseyin Velioglu (1952-2000) emerged as the strongest. Although its name suggests otherwise, this group had no links with the (Shia and Iran-backed) Hizbullah in Lebanon; rather, Velioglu and his fellow activists studied writings on revolutionary Islam by lay authors like Sayyid Qutb and Ali Shari'ati, and had been inspired by the Islamic revolution in Iran, the Afghan resistance against the Soviet invasion, and the Muslim Brotherhood revolt in Syria, which had culminated in the 1982 Hama uprising.

Dorronsoro criticizes earlier analyses of KH, for taking for granted the existence of links between KH and the Muslim Brothers or international Salafism; such links, he argues, should be demonstrated rather than assumed. There is no evidence either that Velioglu's radicalization was linked in any way to clandestine *madrasa* circles, or to Naqshbandi networks. Instead, his radicalization appears to have occurred while he was a student of political science in Ankara in the later 1970s, around the same time as the future PKK leader, Abdullah Öcalan. This may be no accident: in the Turkey of the late 1970s, it was the secular environment of the universities and student radicalism, rather than any organized—let alone politicized—form of religion, that shaped different forms of militant or violent activism. This is not to say that political activism during this period was entirely secular: in different settings, the opposition between right and left overlapped with, or was construed as overlapping with, the distinction between Muslims and atheists, or between Sunnis and Alevis. The vocabulary in which such conflicts and oppositions were articulated, however, generally came from secular Marxist and nationalist doctrines, rather than from (politicized) Islam.

It was not until the early 1990s that KH gained broader attention, indeed notoriety: in 1991 it started a campaign of assassination targeting PKK activists and journalists of the pro-Kurdish newspaper Özgür Gündem. Pro-PKK sources dismissed the organization, which they disparagingly called *Hizb-i Kontra*, as merely a death squad set up by Turkish intelligence; but this seems to be an over-simplification.[24] By the late 1990s, Kurdish Hizbullah had largely ceased its activities, due in part to several waves or arrests of its members; in 2000, its leader Velioglu was shot in an Istanbul police raid. After 2004, however, it reappeared in a wholly different guise, as the new political landscape created by the AKP and the then-ongoing rapprochement with the EU, and later by what the AKP called the "Kurdish Opening," creating unprecedented, if still precarious, opportunities for Kurdish self-expression. From 2008 on, KH activists published a weekly, *Dogru Haber*.

In this new atmosphere in which public Islam, too, was given much more room than under earlier Kemalist rule, KH re-emerged, but this time operating through civil society organizations rather than resorting to violent action. KH-affiliated activists started convening mass public gatherings, like celebrations to mark the Prophet's birthday; but also protest demonstrations, like one against the Danish cartoons in 2006, which reportedly drew around half a million people; or against the French satirical magazine *Charlie Hebdo* in January 2015, in which some 100,000 people participated. Such public displays of strength were not, however, translated into electoral terms: in late 2012, a political party, the Free Da'wa Party (*Hür Dava Partisi*, abbreviated as Hüda-Par), was formed, but in the June 2015 general elections this party received only 63,493 votes in the (predominantly Kurdish) nine provinces in which it ran; in the new elections in November of the same year, it did not even participate.[25] The year 2014 saw a serious rise in intra-Kurdish tensions in Turkey. Although not themselves engaging in acts of violence, Hüda-Par supporters openly sympathized with the "Islamic State" (IS) whose fighters were at the time besieging the Kurdish-held town of Kobanî. In October, in the wake of the Kobanî crisis, serious clashes erupted between PKK and Hüda-Par sympathizers; or rather, PKK sympathizers commenced attacks on Hüda-Par offices, which left at least 35 Kurds dead, the majority of them Islamists. In particular, the town of Cizre witnessed an ongoing cycle of violence and the deaths of several activists.[26] Opportunities for violent Islamist activism in Turkey only increased with the escalation of the war in neighboring Syria. Although openly expressing sympathy for Salafi-Jihadi groups, and possibly also maintaining contacts of some sort, Kurdish Islamists in Turkey generally appear to have followed their own trajectory. Increasingly, however, reports came in not only of connection between the Turkish government and the so-called Islamic State (Daesh), but also of local hotbeds of Daesh or pro-Daesh activity in several cities in south-eastern Turkey, most importantly Gaziantep.[27] The Salafi-Jihadi links of the activist Islamist groups that emerged in Iraqi Kurdistan during the 1980s and 1990s are far clearer. During the 1990s, the most important of these groups was the Islamic Movement of Iraqi Kurdistan (IMIK), led by Mullah Othman Abdulaziz. Reportedly, Mullah Othman had joined the Muslim Brotherhood during his studies at al-Azhar University in Cairo; he also had contacts with the Jamaat-i Islami in Pakistan and with the Afghan Mujahedin, in particular Burhaneddin Rabbani. One

IMIK spokesman claimed that, although Mullah Othman had developed his own thinking, he was close in outlook to other Salafi-Jihadi groups.[28]

After Mullah Othman's death in 1999, IMIK split into a number of different factions. The most famous, or notorious, of the new leaders was undoubtedly Mullah Krekar (pseudonym of Najmaddin Faraj), who had connections to Abdullah Azzam's Maktab al-Khidamat in Peshawar, and reportedly also to Usama bin Laden. In 2001 he formed a new group, Jund al-Islam, which subsequently merged with other jihadist groups into Ansar al-Islam; the latter was engaged in a number of violent clashes with Patriotic Union of Kurdistan (PUK) forces. In the wake of the 11 September attacks in the US, the PUK succeeded in convincing leading military figures in the West that Ansar formed the missing link between Saddam Hussein and Usama bin Laden; as a result, Ansar, which had its bulwark in the Iran-Iraq frontier area near Halabja, was crushed with the aid of American air power in the spring of 2003. In September 2002, Krekar, who had refugee status in Norway, was arrested while in transit at Amsterdam airport; narrowly avoiding extradition to the US he returned to Norway, where he was eventually tried and imprisoned for several years, on charges of having uttered death threats against local Norwegian politicians and secular Kurdish activists.[29]

In the longer run, however, it was not Krekar but Ali Bapir, another member of the same circle, who played a lasting, if relatively minor, role in Kurdish politics. A native of Ranya, where he continues to have a large constituency, Bapir founded Komalî Îslamî (Islamic Group) after breaking away from IMIK. As part of the operations against Ansar Islam, Bapir was arrested by American forces in 2003 and imprisoned, but released in 2005; in prison, according to his own account, he succeeded in converting a number of Ba'athist inmates.[30] Since then, Komalî Îslamî has been involved in electoral politics rather than armed action, on occasion forming a list combination with parties like Yekgirtuy Islami and Hama Haji Mahmoud's Socialist Party. As of early 2015, Komalî Îslamî has six seats in the regional parliament.

Conclusion

In the twenty-first century, the Qadiri and Naqshbandi orders may no longer mobilize large parts of the population; but Naqshbandi-inspired discourse, attitudes, practices, and organizational forms continue to shape Islamic, and Islamist, sensibilities among Turks, Kurds, and others. As such, they pose an interesting challenge to a number of currently influential accounts of Muslim fundamentalism. For example, the French scholar Olivier Roy has famously argued that political Islam, understood as the revolutionary project of creating an Islamic state, had failed already by the early 1990s; what he calls "neo-fundamentalism," however, or the drive to Islamicize society, remained as strong as ever. In particular out of this failure, Roy argues, Islamist movements (whether in the Islamic Republic of Iran or in post-Mubarak Egypt) have entered into a stage of "post-Islamism," in which (not necessarily liberal-secularist) Islamist activists recognize that there is a distinct sphere or space of politics that is not, and should not, be driven by religious considerations. In later work, Roy has argued that in the early twenty-first century, a new, globalized Islam has emerged that is deterritorialized, deculturalized, and depoliticized: from a territorially limited political struggle for the control of an existing state, it has turned into a worldwide and never-ending moral struggle between good and evil; on this analysis, al-Qaeda is only the most extreme and most visible embodiment of this wider phenomenon.[31] Roy further argues that twenty-first-century Salafism is the ideal candidate for such a globalized Islam: in its puritan rejection of local customs and traditions as forms of *jahiliyya* (ignorance) or *shirk* (idol worship), it develops a deculturalized form of religion, purged of all culturally specific references, which is particularly attractive for converts in other societies.

Roy's theses, important and thought-provoking as they are, encounter a number of major difficulties when confronted with contemporary articulations of Islam among the Kurds. To begin with, they ignore the distinctly Naqshbandi character of Turkish and Kurdish Islamisms: organizations like the Nurcu and Gülen movements arguably have Naqshbandi genealogy and, in some cases, an explicitly anti-Salafi outlook. Further, Roy's neat analytical distinction between political Islam and neo-fundamentalism as targeting the state and society respectively downplays or overlooks the enormous differences in state-society relations, even between neighboring countries like Turkey and Iraq (both of which, it should be recalled, belonged to the same Ottoman polity barely a century ago). The distinct trajectories of Islam and Islamism in these respective countries, moreover, reflect not only distinct state-society relations, but also different Naqshbandi-Salafi dynamics.[32]

Finally, IS, the so-called Islamic State, which wrought such havoc in post-2011 Iraq and Syria, does not fit in well with the picture of a deterritorialized and depoliticized global Islam that is, in the final instance, nihilistic. Firstly, as its very name indicates, it is engaged in the political project of establishing a state. Secondly, despite its rhetorical boasts about a struggle for the worldwide domination of true Islam, IS's main arena is actually a rather well-defined geographical area: those majority Sunni Arab populated parts of the Arab peninsula, and especially northern Mesopotamia, that are marked by a power vacuum or a strong climate of resistance against the state. The fact that a number of jihadist groups in, among others, Libya and the Sinai desert have pledged allegiance to IS does not appear to mean much in terms of central organization or concrete collaboration. Thirdly, despite the universalist rhetoric of establishing a caliphate for the entire *ummah*, or community of believers, IS mobilizes primarily among Sunni Arabs, generally meeting with indifference or even antagonism from other ethnic—let alone sectarian—groups.

Figures presented by the International Centre for the Study of Radicalisation (ICSR) in early 2015 indicate a total of just over 20,000 fighters, of whom a majority hailed from the Arab world. An estimated 2,500 Mujahedin came from Saudi Arabia alone, more than from all Western and Central European countries combined.[33] Thus, these figures indicate that one should not overstate the globalized character of IS mobilization and recruitment; nor should one necessarily see this globalization of the conflict as something qualitatively novel. The estimated figure of some 20,000 foreign fighters is only slightly higher than the estimated number of foreign Mujahedin in the Afghanistan conflict in the 1980s, and significantly lower than the number of foreigners presumed to have fought in the Spanish Civil War (estimated at some 40,000 in total, although at any one point in time slightly over 20,000 were actually involved in the struggle).[34] Most importantly, however, the ICSR figures are systematically misleading, in that they leave out the local fighters from IS-controlled areas in both Syria and Iraq, who in all likelihood constitute the vast majority of IS's rank and file. In other words, despite all appearances, IS primarily appeals to, and mobilizes among, Sunni Arabs, especially in and from Syria and Iraq.[35] Despite openly expressed sympathies for IS in some Islamist circles (not to mention accumulating evidence of direct Turkish state support), the number of Turks actually joining IS is relatively low. Likewise, only a relatively small number of Kurds from Iraq, Turkey, Syria, and Iran appear to have joined IS. Not much is known about their particular motivations; but the Iraqi Kurdish jihadists appear to hail primarily from the Halabja area, long known as a hotbed of Islamic activism, where much of the population had been disappointed with, or alienated by, the secular Kurdish leadership. Kurdish IS fighters from Turkey appear to come primarily from the Batman area, likewise an area with a long tradition of Islamist activism.

In other words, despite its megalomaniac and universalist Islamist rhetoric (or, one is tempted to say, branding), and despite its boasts of undoing the Sykes-Picot agreement, IS very much reproduces existing sectarian, ethnic, and national fault lines. With some over-simplification, one might say that in the propaganda battle waged by all warring sides, one could see the superimposition of, and mutual reinforcement of, existing distinctions between Kurds and Arabs, between Muslim and Christian, between Sunni and Shia, between orthodox and heterodox, and between Naqshbandi-inspired and Salafi-oriented forms of Sunni Islam. Last but not least, the propagandistic imagery of Kurdish woman guerrillas on the one hand, and of IS markets and manuals for female slaves on the other, both equally and eagerly reproduced in the worldwide media, show to what extent gender and sexuality, too, have become weapons in the ongoing conflict.[36]

4

POLITICS OF MEMORY

KURDISH ETHNIC IDENTITY AND THE ROLE OF COLLECTIVE FORGETTING

Hakan Özoğlu

There should be little doubt that there is a link between ethnic identity and nationalism. Yet, the nature of it has not been convincingly demonstrated. In many cases, Kurdish identity and Kurdish nationalism are confused. A significant distinction must be made here. Kurdish identity and Kurdish nationalism are like two adopted brothers: they are related in the context of their adopted family; however, they do not necessarily have a biological bond with each other. In other words, Kurdish identity and Kurdish nationalism do not share the same genealogy. In this context, we can, with a degree of confidence, state that Kurdish nationalism, like any other nationalisms, has not emerged as a result of a predetermined historical process. However, Kurdish identity or "Kurdishness" does indeed evolve as a result of such a process, albeit not predetermined. In other words, the link with the distant past in determining group identity exists, however, this link is not predestined; on the contrary, its development in a certain direction is accidental, affected by internal and external forces in the course of history. This research will argue that collective forgetting is as significant as collective remembering in the creation of Kurdish ethnic identity, which is based on real or created historical narratives. These narratives that help members of a community establish a bond among themselves are almost always manipulated depending on the political needs of the leadership, be it a state or non-state actors. The "politics of memory" is indeed a powerful force in creating group solidarity.

At this point, let us briefly discuss the politics of memory. In an essay on Palestinian women, Ellen L. Fleischmann points out the thorny relationship between history and memory. Though certainly interrelated, memory, or more particularly collective memory, can freely draw its sources from myths, legends, and mythico-history. Fleischmann states:

> The act of remembering is not necessarily an isolated, individualistic activity but one which takes place in a social and political context, resulting in the construction of memory. Ultimately, the community is defined by the meaning given to the event, rather than the event itself, so that members [...] need to share in the interpretations of its meaning.[1]

One could go even further by stating that collective remembering or the "construction of memory" also involves "collective forgetting," which in turn has its own layers, such as manipulation of memory or wilful forgetting of a traumatic event. Usually a central state can control the mechanisms of creating collective memory, most notably through monopolizing "national education." The question I would like to pose here is the following: what are the mechanisms of creating a collective memory through collective forgetting by nationalists that lack a state structure? More specifically, what are the mechanisms of creating Kurdish identity, in the service of Kurdish nationalism, through collective forgetting by Kurds who lack a national state? In other words, how does the Kurdish nationalist leadership create a collective memory by selectively forgetting or blurring certain facts that could be considered a hindrance for the creation of nationalist discourse?

At this stage, I would like to place another argument on a theoretical basis, so that the reader can appreciate the process by which creation of past through collective forgetting is realized. Let me begin with a debate on a relevant issue. Two champions of the debate on history and nationalism are Anthony Smith and Ernest Gellner, whose theoretical arguments have been used by many scholars dealing with ethnic identity and nationalism. Elsewhere, I referenced their debate at Warwick on the role of the past in nationalism and created-ness of nationalism. I now would like to cite the same debate not in regards to nationalism, but identity formation. Since it is relevant to my argument, I will begin by introducing the role of the past and nationalism in the context of the Kurds.

Let me first go back to the aforementioned stimulating debate on the origin of nationalism that took place on 24 October 1995 on the Warwick University campus. The debaters on the panel were Anthony Smith and Ernest Gellner. Smith, as students of nationalism will be aware, is a noted critic of the modernist school. He was also a student of the late Ernest Gellner, himself a modernist. Gellner is known for his stance against not only the primordialist school of nationalism, but more significantly against the position that categorizes nationalism as a pre-modern concept. The issue discussed at the Warwick Debates is quite relevant to the argument of this paper—that is, the memory of the past and nationalism—and therefore the reader should be introduced to it.

In the Warwick Debates, the two scholars presented their views on the origins of nationalism in a very concise yet eloquent way. In his opening remarks, Anthony Smith pointed to the heart of the issue under consideration, that is, the relationship between nationalisms and the past. Before presenting his view, Smith summarized Gellner's general position on the subject as follows:

> [T]he nation is not only relatively recent; it is also the product of specifically modern conditions — those of early industrialism or its anticipations, social mobility, the need for mass literacy, public education and the like. It is the modern transition from spontaneous, non-literate "low" cultures to highly cultivated, literate and specialised "high" cultures that engenders nationalism and nations.[2]

Acknowledging the validity of this statement, Smith responded by claiming that it tells only half of the story. The connection with the past, according to Smith, was the missing part. In order to demonstrate his point, Smith offered his definition of nationalism: By "nationalism" I shall mean an *ideological movement for the attainment and maintenance of autonomy, unity and identity of a human population, some of whose members conceive it to constitute an actual or potential "nation".* A "nation" in turn I shall define as *a named human population sharing an historic territory, common myths and memories, a mass public culture, a single economy and common rights and duties for all members* [emphasis as in the original].[3]

After this definition, Smith went into describing some modernists as being "materialists" and warned that such a line of thinking should not lead us to categorize nationalism as imagined or fabricated. In fact, suggests Smith, "nations and nationalisms are also the products of pre-existing traditions and heritages which have coalesced over the generations."[4] Hence, Smith's main disagreement with the modernists is in his claim that modernists disregard the role of the past:

> Modern political nationalisms cannot be understood without reference to these earlier ethnic ties and memories, and, in some cases, to pre-modern ethnic identities and communities. I do not wish to assert that every modern nation must be founded on some antecedent ethnic ties, let alone a definite ethnic community; but many such nations have been and are based on these [pre-existing] ties...[5]

Anthony D. Smith bases his claim on the link with the past on *ethnie*, a term that he introduced to modern scholarship. Smith claims that *ethnie* does not carry ethnic or racial connotations; it refers only to such dimensions as a common myth of descent, a shared history, a collective name, and a distinctive shared culture. Hence, nationalists are in fact "political archaeologists" trying to construct a nation by redis-covering and reinterpreting the past in order to reconstitute the community as a modern nation. Smith claims:

> [The task of nationalists] is indeed selective — they forget as well as remember the past — but to succeed in their task they must meet certain criteria. Their interpretations must be consonant not only with the ideological demands of nationalism, but also scientific evidence, popular resonance and patterning of particular ethnohistories.[6]

I have argued against Smith's notion of *ethnie* as a terminology that legitimizes the essentialist nature of ethnicity. However, in this study my aim is to demonstrate how Kurdish identity emerged as a result of collective forgetting as well as collective remembering. Therefore, I mainly focus on how the "political archaeologists" create an ideological sphere where collective forgetting is promoted as a way of "remember-ing" the past.

Collective remembering and forgetting

In designing a shared identity, this research argues that collective forgetting is as sig-nificant as collective remembering. As sociologist Anne Galloway puts it, "memories are understood as relations of power through which we, as individuals and groups, actively negotiate and decide what can be recollected and what can be forgotten. And without being able to decide what we can remember and forget, we are effectively left without hope of becoming different people or creating different worlds."[7] Collective forgetting is necessary for the creation of shared identity.

Collective memory is a variant of autobiographical memory that requires a vol-untary or induced forgetting of certain traits of the past. It is voluntary because through selective memory groups can shape their identity to fit their present needs. (A good example is the Turks who have been asked to collectively forget that Kurds exist.) It is induced through powerful external pressure, such as that from a powerful state (as in Turkey), or an internal need (such as imagining an essence for a Kurdish nation in the modern world).

Can this be reversed? Certainly! Forgetting does not mean erasing. When cir-cumstances stimulate a certain memory, groups can re-emerge from amnesia (again, a pertinent example is the Turks acknowledging the existence of the Kurds as a sepa-rate ethnic group).

Let us address who designs collective remembering or forgetting. In attempts to create modern ethnic identity, nation builders in particular utilize "national" educa-tion to instil a form of group solidarity. The greatest problem, however, is that since no ethnically pure nation-state exists, nationalists invariably delve deep into history

through historical texts to create one. Some examples follow, which have been utilized to create a Kurdish identity and nationalism.

Şerefname of the sixteenth century

We are not certain who introduced the term "Kurd" as a group identity. However, we
know that the earliest available record by a Kurd depicting Kurds as a cohesive group
comes from the sixteenth century. This book, titled *Şerefname*, was written by
Şerefhan, a Kurdish tribal leader, and it clearly shows a perception of Kurds as a
distinct group.[8] Although Şerefhan's understanding of the Kurds does not entirely
match what the term means today, it still is an invaluable source for students of
Kurdish identity and nationalism in that it tells us what the term "Kurd" as a group
identity meant to him.

The reader must be warned that the term Kurd was in circulation centuries before
Şerefhan. The earliest reliable source referring to a group of people as the Kurds
comes with the Arab invasion of the area in the seventh century. Arab travelers and
geographers made use of the term as a group identity without any clear definition. As
such, the term Kurd was in circulation as a group identity 900 years prior to Şerefhan,
but there is no evidence prior to the sixteenth century that Kurds saw themselves as
a distinct group above the tribal level.

In their attempt to introduce Kurdish origin legends, scholars often refer to the
Şerefname, which narrates a dynastic history of the Kurds. The story of Zahhak
contained in it appears to be the most popular legend pertaining to the origin of the
Kurds. According to this legend, the Kurds are the children of the populace who fled
from the tyranny of Zahhak, a well-known figure who also appears in Ferdowsi's
classical epic, the *Shahnama*.[9] Zahhak was the fifth ruler after Jamshid in the mythical
Pishdadi dynasty that governed the lands of both Iran and Turan. He was so tyranni-
cal that some historians referred to him as the Shaddad, an ancient ruler who symbolized violence and evil. Due to his evil nature, God punished him with an open wound
on each of his shoulders, gashes resembling serpents. Because of these wounds,
Zahhak lived in extreme pain. The best and most skillful doctors could not cure him.
Finally one day, Satan himself appeared in Zahhak's court under the guise of a doctor
and stated that the only remedy for Zahhak's unending pain was for the brains of two
youths to be applied daily to these serpent-shaped wounds. Accordingly, it was
decided that every day two youths would be executed and their brains applied to the
wounds. Amazingly, this treatment seemed to work.

The practice of putting two young persons to death every day lasted for some
time. In the end, the cook who was in charge of slaughtering innocent people had
mercy on some of them and allowed one of every two of them to escape into the
mountains. He mixed the brains of a sheep with brains of the remaining human victim and presented the concoction to Zahhak. As a condition for freeing the prison-

ers, the cook required that they reside in inaccessible mountains and hence far away from the tyranny of Zahhak.

So inhabit the mountains they did. In time, these freed people multiplied and filled the mountainous regions, and came to be called the "Kurds." For a long time the Kurds stayed away from other people, forgetting the culture, arts, and civilization they had had before they were freed. They produced a unique language under these unique circumstances. Later they came down to the valleys where they became farmers, shepherds, and traders, and established villages, fortresses, and towns. The legend does not tell us who called these people "Kurds."Although this legend, cited in the *Şerefname*, alleges that Kurds are the amalgamation of diverse groups who invented their own language and civilization as a result of their isolated residence in the mountains, we can clearly see an example of collective forgetting present in that even Kurdish popular legends define Kurdish ethnicity as an "amalgamation of diverse groups."

The legend is better known for the struggle led by one—a mythical character, Kawa—who rebelled against and killed Zahhak, consequently freeing the oppressed people in the region. According to the legend, discontent brewed among those who escaped from the tyranny of Zahhak, and they became united under the leadership of Kawa, a legendary blacksmith. Kawa organized his people into open rebellion and marched into Zahhak's palace, killing him with a hammer and freeing his oppressed subjects. The event was marked for the celebration of Newroz (literally new day/ year). Although the root of the story goes back to ancient Iranian legends, Newroz has become the most celebrated festival in Kurdish culture.[10]

One of the earliest examples of utilizing the Kawa legend in the Kurdish nationalist discourse comes from the writings of Kurdiye Bitlisi in *Jin*.[11] Arguing that Kawa's defeat of Zahhak was part of a uniquely Kurdish mythology, Bitlisi states that "the commemoration ceremonies of this event are a Kurdish holiday and only the Kurds celebrate it."[12] Therefore, it is undeniable that 1) Kurds were the ones who stopped the tyranny of Zahhak, thus, Kurdish history must have predated this event, and 2) Kurds are the oldest Iranian people. What is relevant to my argument here is that in the same essay Bitlisi completely and perhaps purposefully overlooks the fact that different forms of the legend do exist in the region and Newroz has been celebrated by diverse groups of peoples from Central Asia to the Middle East. As will be seen below, the legend clearly does not remark on the ethnic origin of the people who escaped the tyranny of Zahhak. Like their counterparts among Iranians, Turks, and Arabs, Kurdish nationalists too attempt to create a unique ethnic identity by modifying and appropriating ancient myths.

This brings us to the argument between Smith and Gellner on the assumed link between nationalism and the ancient past. As I have argued, the link with the ancient past has indeed always been utilized for nationalism, but is in fact established through group identity, rather than nationalism. It is also significant to reiterate that such identity engineering requires selective memory, or collective forgetting, to forge the grand narrative of Kurdish nationalist discourse. The interpreters of legends set the stage for the readers to buy into the idea of a unique and glorious past.

Another example would be Şerefhan's definition of the genealogy of Kurdish notable families. Speaking of Kurdish dynasties, for example, Şerefhan does not hesitate to trace the origin of many Kurdish families to the Arab Umayyad and Abbasid dynasties. In his mind, this does not constitute a contradiction, despite the fact that Arabs and Kurds belong to separate ethnolinguistic categories. This is very illustrative of pre-twentieth-century traditions of categorizing human groups, and is certainly not unique to Şerefhan. Yet, although the *Şerefname* is considered one of the earliest sources defining Kurdish identity, what is collectively forgotten is that Şerefhan traces that genealogy of great Kurdish notables to Arabs. In other words, what is conveniently omitted in modern readings is that, in the sixteenth century, Kurdish identity was not clearly demarcated vis-à-vis the Arabs. This understanding is extremely out of step with the modern definition of Kurdish identity. In the long journey of Kurdish identity formation, the essential characteristics that defined "the Kurd" were constantly altered, modified, and mutated. Yet in modern times those who are responsible for the creation of shared Kurdish identity understandably encourage their constituency to forget these discrepancies.

When we look at the articles published in the Kurdish newspaper *Jin*, the first publication that openly propagated Kurdish nationalism, we see clear examples of collective forgetting. For example, in examining the *Şerefname* for the origins of Kurdish identity, Kurdiye Bitlisi concludes that Kurds are of Iranian origin.[13] Once again we see a conscious omitting, or forgetting, of the fact that Şerefhan traces Kurdish genealogy back to Arab families.

Ahmed-i Hani in the seventeenth century

A more refined example of Kurdish identity comes a century later. In his epic the *Mem u Zin*, Ahmed-i Hani (Ehmede Xani, b.1651), a Kurdish man of religion and a poet, demonstrates a clear group consciousness by distinguishing the Kurds from Arabs, Turks, and Iranians. In a section titled "Derde Me" [Our ills] in his well-known epic *Mem u Zin*, completed in 1695, Hani writes:

> If only there were harmony among us,
>
> If we were to obey a single one of us,
>
> He would reduce to vassalage
>
> Turks, Arabs and Persians, all of them.
>
> We would perfect our religion, our state,

and would educate ourselves in learning and wisdom...[14]

Look, from the Arabs to the Georgians,

The Kurds have become like towers.

The Turks and Persians are surrounded by them.

The Kurds are on all four corners.

Both sides have made the Kurdish people

Targets for the arrows of fate.

They are said to be keys to the borders,

Each tribe forming a formidable bulwark.

Whenever the Ottoman Sea [Ottomans] and Tajik Sea [Persians]

Flow out and agitate,

The Kurds get soaked in blood.

Separating them [the Turks and Persians] like an isthmus.[15]

Inspired by another epic, the *Meme Alan*, which was transmitted orally in the region, Ahmed-i Hani's epic is in the form of a love story between Mem and Zin, with the exception of the passages mentioned above. By virtue of this section and the fact that the epic is written in the Kurmancî dialect of Kurdish, Ahmed-i Hani's version of *Mem u Zin* is regarded as the "national epic of the Kurds" by present-day Kurdish nationalists. Hani does regard the Kurds as a tribal confederation, and more importantly seeks self-rule for them.

One can find plenty of references to the Kurds in the section titled "Our ills." Hani seems to use the word "Kurd" or its Arabic plural *al-Akrad* interchangeably with Kurmancî, a linguistic subgroup in Kurdish society. This is evidence that Hani regards the Kurmancî speakers as Kurds; yet it is not clear whether he regards other groups—such as the Zazas, Lurs, or Kelhurs—as part of the category. Unlike the *Şerefname*, *Mem u Zin* does not mention any of the other subgroups and categorize them as Kurds. Nor does he explicitly define "Kurdistan." Kurdistan, in Hani's account, is rather implicitly described as a region lying in the middle of Persian (Ajam), Ottoman (Rum), Arab, and Georgian (Gürcü) lands.[16] Did the word "Kurd" mean only the Kurmancî speakers for Hani, living between and among these groups? This is categorically not the understanding of Kurds in the twentieth century, but no available information indicates that Hani's definition is inclusive and incorporates other linguistic groups within the umbrella of "the Kurds," and so one can question whether Ahmed-i Hani's perception of Kurdishness coincides with that of twentieth-century writers.[17]

As such, in the process of creating and instilling modern Kurdish identity in the populace, the strong possibility that Hani considered only Kurmancî speakers as Kurds was omitted. There are plenty of references to Ahmed-i Hani in the twentieth century. Articles published in the Kurdish newspaper *Jîn* (published during 1918-19) attest that *Mem u Zin* was frequently represented and reproduced as Kurdish nationalist literature. However, what is omitted and hence collectively forgotten is Hani's emphasis on the Kurmancî identity in Kurdish nationalism.

Jîn, the first Kurdish nationalist newspaper

Toward the end of the First World War, the Kurds became convinced that the Ottoman Empire would not survive in a meaningful way. Due to nationalistic activities in the Balkans (1912-13) and later the rise of Arab nationalism (especially in 1916), many Kurdish notables had been fully acquainted with the idea of nationalism, and as such their intellectual activities clearly demonstrated the desire for a Kurdish nation-state. The greatest challenge for the Kurdish nationalists was to create as wide a shared Kurdish identity as possible. Articles published in the Kurdish newspaper *Jîn* openly propagated Kurdish nationalism based on a community whose ethnic borders had always been in flux. It is in these articles that we see clear examples of collective forgetting. *Jîn* was a significant project and gives us clues as to the type of intellectual negotiations that went in to engineering a political community. The newspaper is also important for the historian working on identity formation. For the Kurds who did not have the advantages of implementing "national" education through state-endorsed and state-implemented policies, the historian can only access evidence of such intellectual activity through popular press articles. Although the examples below indicate a single author's attempt to craft a society by "voluntary forgetting," we can still see what the audience are being asked to forget.

For example, as mentioned above, when examining the *Şerefname* for the roots of Kurdish identity, Kurdiye Bitlisi concludes that Kurds are of Iranian origin, omitting the fact that Şerefhan traces Kurdish genealogy back to Arab families. It is important to forget that fact in order to create a Kurdish identity independent from surrounding militarily and culturally dominant groups such as the Arabs.

Süleymaniyeli Tevfik puts forward another claim that shows not only collective forgetting, but also a process of negotiation in creating a Kurdish identity. In an essay titled "To my Brother Kurdiye Bitlisi via *Jîn*," Tevfik claims that "Today's ethnology shows us that the Kurd, Armenian, Iranian and Nestorian are of the same race. The time has come [to bridge] the abyss created by the great ignorance shared by most of [the members of these groups]. These people are inseparably one and the same."[18] Clearly, the author wishes to expand the definition of what constitutes Kurdish identity; however, what he asks is that language and religion be omitted from the criteria. In other words, in Tevfik's definition what is forgotten is the role of religion and language. The contrast between Kurdiye Bitlisi's position and that of Süleymaniyeli Tevfik is quite significant, and clear proof of ongoing negotiations to solidify Kurdish identity after the catastrophe of the First World War.

Collective forgetting at present

In a study of Kurdish textbooks in Iraqi Kurdistan, Sherko Kirmanj discusses how the Kurdistan Regional Government (KRG) promoted collective forgetting:

> Forging any national collective memory is deemed an integral part of nation formation and nation building. To this end, the authors of KRG textbooks aim to create a common memory, real or imagined, by linking the present to the past and inducing the younger generations into this creation.[19]

According to these textbooks, Lulubis, Cyrtians, Carduchians, and Gutanias were ancient Kurdish groups who formed the first Kurdish states more than 4,000 years ago in the places where Kurds reside today. Despite modern scholarship indicating reasonable doubt regarding the link between these ancient groups and the modern Kurdish identity, the KRG curriculum promotes collective forgetting of such doubt or willingly ignores it. To be clear, it seems pointless to criticize such attempts, essential as they are for creating a shared group identity and hence igniting modern nationalism. My aim is simply to point out the process.

Kirmanj highlights another disputed issue within Iraq and beyond, and demonstrates how collective forgetting or selective remembering has been used to satisfy present needs. The KRG textbooks:

> emphasise that it was in Kurdistan, in what is today a village called Charmo near Kirkuk, that the first human beings supposedly settled as a result of the invention of agriculture. Frequent mention of Kirkuk in the context of ancient history of Kurdistan is aimed at satisfying another need: Kirkuk has, in the modern history of Kurdistan, been the focus of the Kurds' most important territorial dispute. By arguing that Kirkuk has always been a Kurdish city, the textbook authors aim to strengthen the Kurdistan Region's territorial claim over the area.[20]

This example is significant as the KRG is the only Kurdish government that was heavily involved in creating a Kurdish identity in general, but an Iraqi Kurdish nationalism in particular. Yet, Iraq is the only country where the Kurds have their own government to promote a sense of Kurdish nationalism, however parochial it may be. This begs the question: what are the mechanisms of a promotion of Kurdish identity as a unique form of ethnic politics in places where the Kurds lack a government structure of their own? Turkey, where a majority of the Kurds reside and where the Kurds do not govern themselves, is the obvious example.

Clearly, the PKK is the most active proponent of Kurdish identity and nationalism in Turkey. However, its political ideology and ultimate aims seem to evolve depending on the realities of the present moment and the fast-changing political environment in the Middle East. For example, one of the leaders of the PKK movement at present, Cemil Bayık, hints at a significant evolution of the notion of Kurdish nationalism advocated by the PKK:

> Although the PKK had originally envisaged an independent Kurdish homeland it had always been clear to them that a solution would only be possible as a result of agreement among the various people. Thus it would be possible to develop solutions that would not challenge existing political borders. In this respect the PKK's policy was in contrast to the existing political approach in the Middle East, which relies on collaboration among the regional elites.[21]

Is this a form of promoting collective forgetting?

Let us now look at the following question: what are the mechanisms for promoting a certain identity by nationalists who cannot control the education system? Above, we saw that, like any other government, the Kurdistan Regional Government in Iraq designs the curriculum and promotes a certain collective memory. What mechanisms can an "outlawed" organization, such as the PKK, utilize to alter collective memory? The following example can give us clues to understand this process.

Abdullah Öcalan, the leader of the PKK, has become an icon for many Kurdish nationalists in Turkey for the movement he personally led until his capture in 1999. The PKK movement has been active in Turkey since the late 1970s and has successfully promoted a certain Kurdish identity by accommodating the myth of Kawa within its nationalist discourse. This myth originates from the epic *Shahnama* of Ferdowsi. There are different versions of the story of Kawa, who symbolizes the fight against tyranny in the Middle East. However, according to the version widely accepted among the Kurds, Kawa defeated the Assyrian king Zahhak (a tyrant) by organizing a popular movement. Inspired by this epic, Öcalan's earliest writings relate to the myth of Kawa and appropriate it for the Kurdish national struggle:

> Assyrians were the worst kind of slave-owner imperialists who wished to destroy the desire of the Medes people, our first ancestors, to emerge as a [separate] people. The Medes decided to resist the tyranny of [the Assyrians] who were the nightmare of Middle Eastern peoples of its time by declaring themselves as "people of fire." If they surrendered [...] they would not have been able to become a people in their own right. As the steel hardened under the hammer of Kawa, during the 300-year struggle against the Assyrians, Medes became hardened in the battle of becoming a people and owning a homeland. Consequently, they lay the groundwork for the Kurds to emerge as a separate people [nation]. Medes, who saved all Middle Eastern peoples along with themselves, celebrated

every year this momentous event by lighting fire. The Middle Eastern people have not forgotten the memory of that day [of deliverance] and commemorate it by lighting fire.

Just like the Medes who resisted the destruction [...] Kurds today are resisting it. The enemy is in the rank of Assyrians. [...] Kurds will no doubt reestablish their freedom and national existence. This will only be possible by initiating "a new Medes resistance" appropriate for the needs of the present and by commencing a sacred war of independence, conscious of being "the people of fire."[22]

This theme of martyrdom, borrowed from the Kawa story, has been adjusted to fit the need of their struggle; and the new form of resistance was publicized through speeches and the commemoration of events of national significance. Cengiz Güneş points out how the myth of resistance was disseminated among the Kurdish public: "The story of resistance [of those Kurdish nationalists who were jailed and tortured in the Diyarbakir prison] was narrated and disseminated widely in countless commemoration events and practices held for the leaders of resistance and the earliest martyrs of the PKK's struggle."[23] And yet, the appropriation of Kawa and the Newroz story is collectively forgotten.

Clearly, the appropriation of the myth contributes greatly to the effort of conceiving the unity and homogeneity of the Kurdish nation. This can only be done, however, through promoting a form of collective forgetting as well as collective remembering.

Conclusion

Collective memory provides a substructure for group identity, which in turn serves as the main ingredient of nationalism. Therefore, any manipulation at the collective memory level affects nationalism directly. It seems to me that the ebb and flow of Kurdish identity politics through history revolves around religion, nationalism, and tribalism. Although these identities persist, there is no predictable pattern showing that they evolve into one another. Nationalism is certainly the newcomer to the competition for political loyalty, and for the Kurds it protects itself by continuously altering group memory through collective forgetting. This chapter may raise more questions—for further discussion—than answers. Firstly, what is the real nature of the relationship between group identity and nationalism? As we saw in the debate between Anthony Smith and Ernest Gellner, the role of the past in essentializing an ethnic identity is crucial. Gellner claimed that nationalism's link with the past is invented. It is a modern construct aimed at "imagining a community" that did not exist prior to the nineteenth century. Hence, the link with the past can only be established through forged memories. Smith's argument distinguishes itself with the emphasis it puts on the significance of constructing the past. He claims that nationalists are "political archaeologists" who forget as well as remember the past in order to create a popular memory in the present. In this context, we must ask what the role of memory is in linking modern nationalism to the past?

Beyond the study of collective memory and the role of collective forgetting in Kurdish identity politics, as the research progressed, more questions emerged that certainly require more thorough investigation. For example, how do nationalists access Kurdish popular memory in promoting an interpretation of the past, complementary to their own political orientations? This is easier to do in northern Iraq where there is a Kurdish government, which can implement its own educational policies. However, what are the mechanisms of such access in Turkey, where outlawed popular Kurdish movements such as the PKK have successfully instilled among supporters' minds an interpretation of the past? The legend of Kawa is an example in point. The legend was utilized in the nineteenth century as nationalist propaganda in the articles published in *Jîn*. The PKK, however, was very successful in utilizing it to create a Kurdish collective memory. This work has tried to examine what aspects of the Kawa story and others were omitted, de-emphasized, or forgotten to promote a Kurdish nationalist discourse; however, further research is necessary to examine how this is done by an outlawed organization whose access to the public is supposed to be limited. We know that public rallies, anti-government demonstrations, and even literature and music provide a medium allowing for such access.

The mechanisms of nationalist attempts at collective forgetting as well as remembering the past have proven to be a major task to demonstrate. Therefore, I would like to leave an open-ended question: how do Kurdish nationalists, who lack the monopolizing mechanisms of a government, promote a certain type of past? I believe that cultural anthropologists can examine the ceremonies commemorating certain events of the past, such as Newroz or the resistance of Kawa, to see how non-state actors, such as the PKK, create access to popular memory.

We see that textbooks are useful tools in such attempts to tinker with collective memory, as is seen in the case of the Iraqi Kurdistan curriculum.[24] However, the oral tradition of transmitting history is also an undeniable factor in the creation of collective memory. Therefore, the role of the *Dengbêj* tradition also provides future researchers with useful terrain upon which to conduct solid academic research in answering these questions. All these avenues require substantial research and engaged discussion. The current chapter is only a brief treatment to indicate that although often invisible to the naked eye, the "politics of memory" has always been at work throughout the centuries, and Kurdish identity is surely no exception.

5.

"BEING IN TIME"

THE KURDISH MOVEMENT AND UNIVERSAL QUESTS

Hamit Bozarslan

The Kurdish movement has been active in the Near East for many decades, and has recently acquired a new public visibility thanks to the existence of *de jure* or *de facto* Kurdish entities in Iraq and Syria, and their transformation into the main frontline of resistance against ISIS in 2014-15.

Analyzing such a movement is not an easy task. First of all, as with any society, Kurdish society is historically plural and produces a variety of political, social, and cultural forms of expression, resistance, resilience, and in some cases also accommodation; in reality the term "Kurdish movement", used in this chapter as a generic signifier, also designates a plurality of political and/or military movements. Secondly, though the Kurds are not the only "stateless nation" divided between different countries, they constitute nevertheless, as far as I am aware, the only group to be divided between four countries: Iran, Iraq, Syria, and Turkey. Their historical trajectory is determined by complementariness with, and opposition to, three—Arab, Persian, and Turkish—cultural-linguistic airs, which for more than a millennium have been the dominant components of the Middle East. This complex political map shows that the Kurds, and the Kurdish movement, are simultaneously unified and diverse. To some extent, "Kurdish national unity" was already realized between the 1920s and 1940s, thanks to the elaboration of a communal national narrative, including an integrated historiography of the four parts of Kurdistan, a cartographic imaginary, a flag, a national Pantheon, and a national song; on the other hand, the division of the

Kurds between the states produced distinct political cultures and patterns, specific histories which have been determined by distinct "national powers", and in some cases also antagonistic strategies. Thus, the Kurdish political space is obliged to manage its unity to its best benefit and its divisions at the lowest possible cost. Thirdly, and as a consequence of this dialectic of unity and diversity, one observes simultaneously an intra-Kurdish integration, which could not be stopped by the militarization of inter-state borders, and a second process of integration, this time with Iran, Turkey, Iraq, and Syria, and broadly speaking the Middle East. As a consequence of this double integrative process, the Kurdish movements had to combine their peculiarity, i.e. the "Kurdishness" which constitutes their ultimate *raison d'être*, with broader, universal worldviews, norms, and ideologies. That means that throughout the past hundred years, they had to be in *their time* and in *their world*, a world that kept changing in the explanations it brought to the human condition, and ideologies and utopias it offered in order to change it for the better.

This chapter proposes some hypotheses in order to understand the ideological evolution of the Kurdish space since the end of the Ottoman Empire. The first section of the chapter will offer some comments on the concepts of "minority" and "nationalism" as they are usually applied to the Kurdish case. The second section will be devoted to the period of the 1920s through the 1940s, which were marked by the disruptive effects of the collapse of the Ottoman Empire, the formation of the mandate states in Iraq and Syria, and the "reconstruction" of Iran and Turkey in accordance with what one could call the Westphalian model of states. The third section will analyze the period of the 1960s to 1980s, which was dominated, in Kurdistan as in many other parts of the world, by the spread of left-wing ideas and aspirations. In the fourth section, I will address the reasons why Islamism, which became the dominant political and axiological syntax in the 1980s throughout the Middle East, remained rather marginal in the Kurdish political space. The last section will be dedicated to the present situation, marked by an ideological vacuum in the Middle East where two societies—Syria and Iraq—face the risk of total collapse, Turkey evolves under the hegemony of the AKP (Justice and Development Party), and Iran follows a rather undetermined path. The impossibility to translate these region-wide conflicts and hard facts—that offer neither explanation nor promise for change in the Kurdish condition—into the Kurdish political language has forced the Kurdish space to find new sources of legitimization in the universal ideas and norms advocated elsewhere in the world.

Given the plurality of Kurdish society and the extreme complexity of each period under consideration, this chapter will limit itself to some illustrative examples and mainstream tendencies, leaving aside multiple ideological syntheses and fluidities that have been elaborated upon in Kurdistan as in the rest of Middle East, between Islam and "Westernism", or between nationalism and socialism.

"BEING IN TIME"

"Minorities", "nationalism", and ideologies

Many scholars, including the author of this chapter, have used the concept of "minority nationalism" to define a broad social, cultural, and political contest whose aim is to reach a satisfactory degree of national autonomy, a federative status within the existing state-borders, or full independence and political integration of different parts of Kurdistan. While bearing a heuristic meaning, both concepts of "minority" and "nationalism" are, however, ultimately problematic and require some explanations. The term "minority" is widely rejected by Kurdish political actors, opinion-makers, and intellectuals, on the basis that the Kurds do not constitute a demographic minority, but on the contrary an overwhelming majority in the areas they inhabit. In this chapter I will suggest that from a political and/or juridical perspective, "majorities" and "minorities" are not determined by their demographic weight, but rather by the power relations that create and impose an official "identity", integrating those who can identify themselves with this identity and excluding the others, either by depriving them of equal conditions with the "majors", or by designating them as non-loyal subjects and therefore as potential internal enemies. Political and juridical "minoritization" is a process that always goes hand in hand with mechanisms of domination, subordination, denial, and coercion. This fact also has an impact on broader historical trajectories. Gabriel Martinez-Gros, a French scholar of medieval Islam, commented on Ibn Khaldun to suggest that "the history of the dominated groups belong to the victors" who have subdued them.[1] Therefore, any "national struggle" or any struggle by a "subordinated group" is also a struggle to achieve the right to determine one's own history. This is also true as far as worldviews and ideologies are concerned: as with knowledge generally speaking, these ideologies are not produced by the dominated groups but by the dominant ones, or are first "imported" by them from Western countries; the dominated groups can access knowledge, including dissident ideas, and ideologies, including the most subversive ones, only through the language and the available sources of the dominant groups. But as many cases, including the Kurdish situation, show, they are not only "passive receivers", but also "active users" of what they "receive"[2]; they can radicalize the received models, ideas, and axiological models and transform them into tools and interpretative/legitimizing frameworks for their struggle. Basically all anti-colonial struggles fought colonialism by actively using colonial knowledge only available in the language of the colonial power, or an ideology that first saw light in the colonial society.

The term "nationalism" is equally complex; except for a few historical examples going back to the romantic period of the "re-birth" of the Kurdish movement in the 1950s and 1960s, during which the "Kurdist" elite had rather weak political and cultural capital, the term "nationalism" has not been used by the Kurdish movements themselves. On the contrary, as far as I am aware it has always had a negative connotation in the Kurdish political vocabulary, being associated with states' ideologies and praxes, and was criticized as the product of the "oppressive nations." Abdullah Öcalan, leader of the PKK, has even strongly condemned the variant of Kurdish nationalism that he labels a "primitive nationalism."[3] This does not mean that this concept, which is widely used in the scholarly literature, has no heuristic or analytical meaning. It is obvious that it defines Kurdish aspirations as well as the movements that express them, and can be seen in a set of symbolic resources (history-writing, national song, cartographic imaginary, national pantheon), or discourses that derive ultimate legitimacy from their "Kurdishness."[4] Still, one should admit that, as regards the Kurdish movements, this concept has at best a limited descriptive virtue, in the sense that the Kurdish resistance has never defined itself *exclusively* by such Kurdish-peculiar/"particularistic" demands. It should be said that in the Kurdish case, as well as in the case of many other ethnic minorities or colonized peoples, "particularism" and "universalism" always went hand in hand: universalism constructed particularism as a "national" group entitled to enter into a universal history, and particularism has always sought to legitimize itself as part of a broader humanity.[5] Notwithstanding the denunciation of the processes of "alienation" by nationalist discourses, "becoming the other" through the "universal" has always been the only way to remain oneself. While the first imperative allowed the constitution of a peculiar *'asabiyya* (internal solidarity of a would-be-conquering group), as well as a peculiar subjectivity with a specific historical narrative and symbology, the second enabled justification of the national struggle as a universal struggle, that is, as a struggle fought by the oppressed nation for humankind, broadly speaking.

This is also true in the Kurdish case. Only a universalistic *da'wa* (initially an appeal to accept the uniqueness of God and the prophecy of Muhammad; by extension, ideology) could allow the Kurds to comprehend their condition as the outcome of the unjust condition of *humankind*, that had to be radically changed. This equation and the tensions between the peculiar and universal, between the *'asabiyya* and the *da'wa*, has been well-studied by Ibn Khaldun (1332-1406) and continues to offer a valuable key to understanding many national contests throughout recent history. For instance, many nationalist movements in the Balkans had clear socialist inclinations before the First Balkan War in 1912, becoming exclusivist and even aggressive in their nationalism only thereafter. As Taline Ter Minassian shows convincingly in her work on Middle Eastern left-wing movements,[6] the Armenian movement (among others) was a standard-bearer of socialist ideas in the 1920s; as was the case with the Palestinian movement in the 1960s and 1970s, and to a lesser extent the Kurdish movement during the same decades. For all these groups, the combination of "particularism" and "universalism"—an intra-group *'asabiyya* and a supra-group *da'wa*, which required constant abnegation and enormous sacrifices—was not merely instrumental; on the contrary, it was part of the very fabric of their being.

"BEING IN TIME"

The pre-Second World War Kurdish movement

A genealogical approach can easily show that while the Kurdish movement kept its internal dynamics, which ultimately constituted its *raison d'être*, it was among those who lost out by the dissolution of the Ottoman Empire; and yet it has always been *in time*, i.e. in the Middle East's, or the world's, *ideological time*.

We shall start our genealogical survey with the collapse of the Ottoman Empire, which led to, among other processes, the formation of an extremely fragile, yet long-lasting and pluralist Kurdish movement in former Ottoman lands, as well as in Persia. This is not to say that there had been no Kurdish/Kurdist initiatives prior to this period. Some of the nineteenth-century Kurdish rebellions had a clear awareness of their ethnic distinctions, and Sheikh Ubeydullah, who was the last Kurdish leader to lead an armed struggle in that century (between 1881 and 1883), spoke "on behalf of the Kurds" as an entity both in the Ottoman Empire and in Persia.[7] To some extent these contests, which were influenced by other events in the Balkans or Egypt, were of their time; and Ubeydullah even claimed the right of the Kurds to enjoy an equal status "with the other nations." But these armed contests, which had multiple contributing factors, among them resistance to the Ottoman centralizing ambitions and the preservation of Kurdish/Muslim superiority in the eastern provinces of the Empire,[8] did not aim at the establishment of Kurdish autonomy or a state-like entity. Likewise, the newspaper *Kurdistan* (1898-1902) distinguished itself from the other "Young Turk" periodicals as the bearer of a Kurdish voice in the Ottoman Empire, but did not formulate any other demand than reforms in Kurdistan *and* in the Ottoman Empire, much less any autonomist claims. This is also true as far as the Kurdish uprisings of 1909-14 are concerned: they were clearly radical in their promotion of an "awareness of being Kurdish", but remained by and large reflexively anti-Armenian, and also paradoxically pro-Ottoman, even receiving local support from the Unionist military elite. Many of the leaders of these insurrections were more than happy to negotiate an alliance with the Committee of Union and Progress during the Armenian genocide, and despite the Kurdish deportations of 1916-17, later renewed their "Kurdish-Turkish pact" with the Kemalist forces. It is true that in 1914 three Kurdish uprisings (Barzan, Bidlis, and Soran) expressed what one could define as Kurdish nationalist claims, but they were rather modest in their scale, and more importantly, were not long-lasting episodes. A more or less structured Kurdish political movement emerged only after the collapse of the Ottoman Empire in the autumn of 1918, a national consciousness expressing itself among the Kurdish intelligentsia in Istanbul or through Kurdish clubs across Kurdistan.

This post-1918 Kurdish nationalism is not easy to define, not least because it was largely pluralistic and polysemic: in some cases, as was the case with the Koçgiri (1921) and Simko (1919) rebellions, it could express even locally (and in the latter case, in association with Kemalist forces) "Kurdist demands", as attested by Mahmud

Barzandji's resistance in the 1920s, in what would become Iraqi Kurdistan. It could, in other situations, claim recognition of a distinct Kurdish entity, with the right to exert its own "national sovereignty." Notwithstanding the relations it had with the nascent Kemalist power, Barzandji's short-lived "kingdom" constituted one of the first major landmarks in the history of the Kurdish movement, and within it were published a series of "Kurdist" journals including *Roji Kurdistan*, *Bangê Kurdistan*, and *Diyari Kurdistan*.

The 1925 Kurdish uprising—the first in Republican Turkey—led by a *naqshbandi* leader, Sheikh Said, also constituted an important historical landmark. Sheikh Said's discourses attest that during this period of reinforcement of the central authority in Turkey, which promoted a radical Turkish nationalism and an equally radical "secularist" policy, Kurdish nationalism utilized both Islamic *and* national definitions of Kurdishness and the Kurdish struggle. It is fascinating to see that Sheikh Said explicitly used the concept of Kurdish *'asabiyya (asabiyyet)*,[9] a term which was even by then largely obsolete in the common language, and at the same time presented the Kurds as the new bearers of Islamic *da'wa*. The mobilization of this double semantic repertoire shows that by 1925, Kurdish "particularism" already felt the need to legitimize itself through a broader "universalistic" appeal or cause. In Sheikh Said's discourse, Kurdishness was explicitly understood as *the* force that could and should save Islam, whose flag "has been abandoned" by the Turks, who not only betrayed their promises to the Kurds, but also Islam as a religion, and its *umma*.[10]

The official Turkish historiography made hay of Sheikh Said's *jihad* proclamation in order to present his uprising as a "reactionary" movement; and although contradicted by the proceedings of the tribunal (which condemned him to death solely on the basis of his defence of the Kurdish cause),[11] this interpretation was also widely accepted by historians, both in the West and the Soviet Union. But notwithstanding the wide support he received from Kurdish religious dignitaries, and that Sheikh Said was really the only figure who legitimized the Kurdish struggle in the name of Islam, the short-lived Azadi ('Freedom') Committee, which in reality was the main architect of the uprising of 1925,[12] had a rather Westernizing tendency and its members shared basically the same intellectual background as the Unionists and the Kemalists. Some of the closest collaborators of Sheikh Said, such as Fehmi-ê Bilal or Hasan Serdi, were even known to be unbelievers.[13] Barely two years after the failure of the uprising, the Khoybun Committee ("Being oneself, becoming oneself"),[14] the first well-structured Kurdish political and military organization with two distinct leaderships for each activity, expressed an openly Western-oriented discourse, which was in sharp contrast to the worldview of Sheikh Said. For the committee, whose civilian branch was dominated by the members of the well-known Bedirkhani family, the Turkish government or the "Turks" represented barbarism rather than the "civilization" they presented; the Kurdish movement and the "Kurds", on the contrary, represented civilization and fought for it.[15] In this discourse, one could see an equation between the claim of Kurds fighting for their *own* emancipation, and that of fighting "barbarism" in the name of *universal* civilization. It is true that in facing a strong state which was supported not only by Great Britain, but to a lesser extent also by Iran, the Soviet Union, and France as the mandatory power in Syria, Khoybun was not in the "world time" and was therefore politically and militarily doomed to fail; but ideologically speaking it was in *its time*, and as a weak consolation for this synchronism managed to receive some moral support from French colonial officers in Syria, such as Pierre Rondot.[16]

The hegemony of the left

This adequacy between particularism and universalism became even more explicit after the Second World War, with the formation in 1946 of the Republic of Mahabad and the Kurdistan Democratic Party (KDP).[17] These two structures, which largely overlapped, were not exactly left-wing entities; the KDP was a rather conservative party in its discourses and praxis, and politically speaking the "Kurdish republic" was far more moderate than the neighboring (and also short-lived) Azerbaijan Republic, which in contrast was occupied by the Soviet military and adopted a tough "Soviet model." The Kurdish republic, led by the *Qadi* (religious judge) Muhammad, introduced some social reforms, but did not exclude the tribes from the political system or the state administration, and did not interfere in the religious sphere either. In spite of this conservatism, however, the "Soviet umbrella" that made its existence possible positioned this first Kurdish republic on the left of the Iranian political spectrum. This short-lived republic became a reference for the left-wing Kurdish movements of the 1960s and 1970s. Qadi Muhammad, who surrendered to the Iranian forces in order to avoid bloodshed in Kurdistan, was executed on 19 January 1947. But the future context of general upheaval in Mossadegh's Iran contributed to radicalizing Kurdish militants, such as Ghani Bilurian and some other young intellectuals like Abderrahman Ghassemlou,[18] who adopted Marxist-Leninist ideas. The henceforth left-wing KDP obtained some 80 per cent of the vote in Mahabad during the 1952 elections, before a new period of harsh repression.[19]

Except for some episodes, Kurdish history from the Mahabad republic to Abd al-Karim Qassem's military coup in Iraq in 1958 has not been studied with the requisite care; but perhaps because some "Kurdist" social circles remained active on the ground, no uprising took place during these years, during which the legal space for Kurdish activity was also extremely restrained. Still, we know that during these long years some Kurdish militants such as Zınar Silopi (Kadri Cemilpaşazade) tried to get in touch with Soviet representatives[20] without obtaining any concrete results, and many Kurds in Iraq and Syria have since been attracted to the communist parties of these countries.

Qassem's military coup, however, provoked a radical change in the Kurdish political landscape in Iraq. The head of the Kurdistan Democratic Party, Mustafa Barzani, who was forced to seek asylum in Russia after the defeat of the Mahabad republic in 1946, had already returned by the time of the proclamation of the Iraqi republic in 1958. In spite of many years spent in the "homeland of socialism" (or because of them), Barzani returned home more conservative than ever, with basically a Kurdist agenda; but in sharp contrast to his historical and sociological profile, the new cadres of the party such as Ibrahim Ahmad, the secretary general who was also the author of the well-known novel *Jan-i Gel* [Suffering of the People], and Jalal Talabani, his future son-in-law, were largely influenced by left-wing ideas. Many of Barzani's peshmerga, who launched a long-lasting guerrilla war in 1961, had a rural or even tribal background and probably were not keen on adopting left-wing ideas or realizing a socialist revolution in Kurdistan or Iraq. But those with an urban background or who were descendants of urban notables were at once both Kurdish peshmerga and left-wing militants, some of them belonging to both the KDP and the Kurdish branch of the Iraqi Communist Party. The uprising itself was labelled a *chorech*, a polysemic term designating both uprising and "revolution." The party's representative in Europe, Ismet Cheriff Vanly, also declared that "Kurdish nationalism [was] revolutionary" in its essence.[21] It is true that the Barzani rebellion was supported by both Israel and Iran in the mid-1970s; in spite of this complex (but not necessarily unique) "Cold War configuration", however, broadly speaking Iraqi Kurdistan was a part of what was then known as the "Tri-continental" rebellion of the 1960s, reading its own history in the context of the anti-colonial/anti-imperialist struggles, including those of Indochina and North and sub-Saharan Africa. The situation was similar in Syria, where not only did the Kurds have a significant presence within the Syrian Communist Party, but, as the poetry of Cegerxwin[22] and Osman Sabri attests, the "Kurdist" militants themselves had radical left-wing positions. In Turkey, finally, many Kurds who had left-wing ideas even before the 1960s[23] participated actively in nascent Turkish left-wing organizations before acceding to organizational autonomy. To be sure, Turkey's Kurdish movement also had some "conservative" figures, but even these were obliged to accept a left-wing or at least overtly "democratic" label.[24] The formation of the DDKO (The Revolutionary Eastern Cultural Hearths), which championed a Kurdified version of Turkish left-wing discourses in the early 1970s, constituted an important landmark that would become a template for almost all future Kurdish organizations. For this organization, socialism was not only the solution to the Kurdish national issue, but also a way of combating the feudalism, backwardness, and underdevelopment that had been imposed on Kurdish society.[25] Their slogan was "Only socialism can save the East."[26]

There were many reasons for the popularity of left-wing ideas, symbols, and forms of axiology in Kurdistan in the 1960s. The first was that the world of the 1960s was saturated by left-wing vocabulary, graphics, heroes, legends, and narratives, which were not merely abstract symbols, but closely linked to ongoing struggles in Africa, Asia,

Latin America, and last but not least, Europe. The second reason for this popularity, complementing the first, was that the authoritarian regimes in Iran and Turkey in the 1960s were supported by the United States. In both countries not only the term "socialism", but also "freedom", "liberty", or even "social" were associated with the "imminent communist threat"; thus any meaningful opposition could only formulate itself through "anti-imperialist" discourses and axiological forms. On the contrary in Syria and Iraq, which though not fully subordinated to the Soviet Union were allies of the Eastern Bloc, left-wing ideas occupied almost the entire political terrain, allowing no legitimacy for any right-wing opposition; in these two countries even the opposition had to position themselves as "true" left-wing movements combating the powers that had "perverted" true socialism. The third reason was in the messages that Marxism-Leninism sent to the "oppressed nations": here was the only ideology that promised them the right to determine their own fate. There is no doubt that "actually-existing socialism" was highly oppressive, in some cases even totalitarian, and was in no way less repressive than the "capitalist system" vis-à-vis minorities and "oppressed nations" that submitted to its rule; but it is also obvious that elsewhere in the world, namely under authoritarian pro-Western governments, socialism or communism presented a horizon of emancipation for both oppressed classes and nations. The fact that almost all anti-colonial movements had adopted left-wing discourses and ideologies could only reinforce this perception. As Franz Fanon wrote in his comments on Africa, America could have won the hearts and the minds of the African peoples only if it accepted, as the Communist bloc had, their right to independence.[27] This quest for independence, or at least some degree of genuine autonomy and representation, also explains the attraction that left-wing ideas exerted in Kurdistan. Kurdistan was, once again, in its time and its world's time. Fourthly, the vivacity of Kurdish cultural activities in the Soviet Union (namely a Kurdish radio station, a newspaper, and many publications) were accepted as concrete proof of the sincerity of socialism vis-à-vis the oppressed nations.

Beyond this attractiveness, however, one should also take into account the sociological changes in the Kurdish urban landscape: during the 1960s, the old notables and urban dynasties were still quite strong and continued to monopolize, by and large, political and economic power. But as in the Arab societies, in Kurdistan too the old elite no longer had new ideas for the changing circumstances which their societies faced. A new class of intellectuals, very distinct from the late Ottoman intelligentsia, became the main dynamic actor, proposing an integrated reading of the past, present, and future through a teleological perspective. This category, which to some extent constituted the world's intermediary elite during the 1950s and 1970s, was able to transpose its conceptual and analytical tools from the applied sciences (such as physics, medicine, or chemistry) or from law, to social life, in the process elaborating new axiological forms. More importantly, thanks to its intermediary position, it could exert a double impact: on the upper classes and the lower classes. It obliged the upper-class children to renounce their privileges in the name of the people, the nation, or the cause; and it offered the lower class a discourse as well as a space of expression and action, and therefore the possibility of agency that they had never experienced previously.

The left-wing radicalisation of the 1970s

This intelligentsia, dominant throughout the "Tri-continental" rebellion from the 1950s to the 1970s, left space in the following decades for two other categories: a technocratic elite, whose spread was closely linked to the formation of the middle classes; and the plebeian actors, who were propelled toward the historical scene as a consequence of the rapid urbanization of the 1970s and 1980s. The reason why the plebeian actors emerged in the Kurdish case much earlier than the middle classes, only to rise to prominence in the 2000s, was that the "Kurdish 1970s" were determined mainly by states' coercion, violence, and/or Kurdish uprisings, as well as defeats. The 1971 military coup in Turkey dealt a serious blow to any hope of change through constitutional reforms and democratization. It also destabilized the Kurdish intelligentsia, which had been accused of being far too pacifist by the younger, increasingly politicized generation. Immediately after the military regime, which ended in 1973, the fall of the Barzani rebellion created yet another setback in 1975, leading the younger generations or more radical components of the KDP to accuse not only Barzani, but also the former Kurdish elite of betraying "the national cause." Right before its dramatic end, the rebellion, which had 110,000 active and reservist peshmerga, appeared to have reached its acme through important military successes; but it also largely depended on Iranian support, which was withdrawn after the Algiers Agreement between Iran and Iraq on 5 March 1975. This could only harden the resolve of Kurdish "anti-imperialism", showing, in the reading of the most radical militants of the KDP (including Jalal Talabani, future leader of the Patriotic Union of Kurdistan), that any national resistance movement supported by imperialism and reaction was doomed to fail. Finally, after 1977, Iran became a theatre of revolutionary contest, in which the masses of Kurdish youth were mobilized. Here again, one could see an internal diversity: under the leadership of Abdurrahman Ghasemlou—influenced by the "socialism with a human face" of Alexander Dubček—the KDP of Iran, probably Kurdistan's most influential party, was switching during this period from rigid Marxist-Leninist positions toward a rather more social-democratic stand; but other organizations, among them Komalah, were radicalized partly as a consequence of the failure of the Barzani rebellion, and partly in the wake of the revolution itself.

No wonder, then, that during this decade almost all Kurdish political actors accepted Marxism-Leninism (or one of its multiple varieties, including Maoism, Hoxhaism, and Trotskyism)[28] as the only meaningful doctrine answering to the "ideological availability"[29] of Kurdistan. Even the KDP of Iraq adopted a left-wing/anti-imperialist discourse during its period of re-foundation in the second half of the 1970s, and formulated a rather harsh self-criticism of its past experience.[30] This conversion to Marxism-Leninism was largely an indigenous process and could not be explained simply through any support from the Soviet Union (even less so any support from China and Albania, both of which probably ignored much of what was happening in the Kurdish political scene).

It would be difficult to evaluate the Kurdish elite's knowledge of the classics of Marxism-Leninism, which it could mainly read in Arabic, Persian, or Turkish; but in the context of the defeat and "axiological urgency" of the 1970s, where both the intelligentsia and the plebeian youth felt the necessity to act *hic et nunc*, Marxism-Leninism—as an integrated and complete doctrine with an answer to all major social, political, economic, and national questions—appeared to be the *only* doctrine that could explain to the Kurds the reasons for their past or recent failures, show the opportunities and constraints presented by their present condition, and offer them a broader universal horizon. Most importantly, it could enable "the oppressed Kurdish nation" to envision its emancipation not as an isolated group, but *in alliance* with the "oppressed classes" of "oppressive nations", thus allowing them to negotiate a kind of universal emancipation of humankind. Particularism and universalism thus continued mutually to reinforce, rather than exclude, each other.

With the emergence of the PKK between 1975 and 1978, this radicalization reached an unprecedented degree, and eventually led to a real bifurcation in the Kurdish movement: attracted by neither the Soviet model nor by Maoism, the PKK did not abandon Marxism-Leninism, but redefined and radicalized it with a healthy dose of Fanonism, explaining the enslavement of the Kurds as a result of their lack of resistance, and thus presenting them as sharing responsibility for their condition. As is well known, even as early as his *L'An Cinq de la Révolution Algérienne* [Year Five of the Algerian Revolution], published in 1958, Franz Fanon advocated what could be called a "positive violence" aimed mainly at the emancipation of the colonized world; but he was largely disappointed with the decolonization of Africa, which changed neither the structural inequalities between the former colonial powers and the newly independent states, nor the power relations within the decolonized societies where a new 'indigenous' elite had seized power. Thus, in his famous *Les Damnés de la Terre* [The Wretched of the Earth], completed shortly before his death in 1961, he called for a violence that would not only lead to decolonization, but to the invention of a decolonized human being, potentially a violence that would accept no ultimate limit. Likewise, from the very beginning, Öcalan condemned his people's history as the history of the enslavement of the Kurds, and invited Kurdish youth (and the Kurds more generally) to use violence not only as an instrument or means for liberating Kurdistan, but also for liberating the Kurdish being from his internalized enslavement. Similarly for him, a socialist Middle East could and should be constructed through the Kurds' sacrificial efforts. It is obvious that Öcalan did not use Khaldunian concepts, and probably was not familiar with Ibn Khaldun's work; still, in his perspective, the Kurdish *'asabiyya*, i.e. the dynamic force of an "oppressed people", was to be transformed into the instrument of the realization of a universal *da'wa*. In a sense, although no foundational text of the PKK indicates it explicitly, from the party's perspective the Kurds had to replace the Palestinians as the standard-bearers of the revolution (*thawra/chorech/devrim*) in the entire Middle East. Clearly, the material and subjective conditions brought into place at the dawn of the 1980s could not allow the realization of such an ambitious project, and ultimately the Kurds remained in a subordinated position throughout the decades to come. But for Öcalan, the time came for the Kurds not only to be in *their time*, but to position themselves *ahead* of their time.

1980s–2010s: facing the domination of Islamism

After the major events of 1979 (the Iranian Revolution, the occupation of Afghanistan by the Red Army, the Second Camp David Agreement which formalized Israel's recognition by Egypt, the Islamist uprising of Juhayman al-Utabi in Mecca), left-wing ideas lost their hegemonic position in many parts of the Middle East,[31] but still remained attractive in two supra-territorial or trans-state spaces: Palestine and Kurdistan. Already by the 1980s, however, Abdallah Azzam (d.1989), the well-known theoretician of the Afghan jihad and co-founder of al-Qaeda, played a distant but formative role in Palestinian refugee camps through the diffusion of his radical messages.[32] In Palestine, Islamism easily fit as an ideology of resistance against a non-Muslim enemy, and to some extent overshadowed secular Palestinian movements, even if they did not disappear from the political scene. In the Kurdish case, too, Islamism won some popularity and many organizations, both pacifist and violent, emerged at this time. For instance, Mullah Krekar (an alias of Fattah Najmaddin Faraj), a former student of Azzam, played an important role in the formation of Ansar al-Islam, which after 9/11 became the nucleus of what would become al-Qaeda's branch in Iraq. The infamous Hizbollah organization (not to be confused with the Lebanese Shia group), heavily supported by the Turkish secret services, remains active in Turkish Kurdistan to this day. Nevertheless, Islamism in its various hues could not determine the overall evolution of the Kurdish political space.

This remains true in the mid-2010s, some thirty-five years after the dramatic upheavals of 1979: in Turkey, Hüda-Par (shorthand for the Hür Dava Partisi, or the Free Cause Party), a front for the banned Hizbullah that was founded in 2012, remains electorally marginal even in its strongholds, such as the city of Batman; and Turkey's ruling party, the Islamist AKP, can mobilize some 50 per cent of the Kurdish electorate only thanks to its Kurdist cadres. Although reliable information is scarce, it seems that the Kurdish Muslim Brothers remain weak in Iranian Kurdistan, and certainly in Syria's Kurdish cantons, and the two Kurdish Islamist parties in Iraqi Kurdistan (the Islamic Party of Kurdistan and the Islamic Union of Kurdistan), which do not have radical tendencies and are in coalition with non-Islamic parties, regularly command little more than 15 per cent of the vote.

This weakness can be partly explained by the fact that the non-Islamist actors have dominated the Kurdish political space for decades and tend to capitalize on their legacy as either national resistance movements or "state-founders", successfully negotiating networks of allegiances (and in the Iraqi Kurdish case, clientelistic relationships) and political and military structures. But one could also say that, in contrast with traditional left-wing ideas, Islamism neither presents a universalistic perspective for Kurdish liberation nor contains any promise of "national emancipation"; at best it recognizes ethnic entities as legitimate parts of the larger *umma*, which should be governed according to the principle of unity among Muslims. In contrast with the Palestinian case, Kurdish Islamists actors have thus failed to negotiate their legitimacy both vis-à-vis Kurdish society and vis-à-vis Islamic/Islamist transnational movements.

The vacuum of the 2000s–2010s

Since the 1980s, but particularly in the years after 2000, the Kurdish movement has evolved largely independently from "Middle Eastern time"; however, this does not mean that it can now stand exclusively on its own and create an autarkic universe. It is true that it has very few, if any, counter-partners in the Arab world, Turkey, and Iran (and those who exist are weak), and has had to re-invent itself in a context where universalism itself seems hard to re-invent. In Iraq and Syria not just the left-wing movements have vanished, but the societies themselves are at risk of total destruction. Even fifteen or twenty years ago it was possible to translate the Syrian and Iraqi domestic conflicts into Kurdish political language and establish some bridges between the Kurdish claims of autonomy or federalism and the Iraqi and Syrian Arab opposition groups' fight for democracy in these two countries. The social-Darwinist reconfiguration of the sectarian (Alawite-Sunni or Shia-Sunni) conflict in these two countries in recent years has not only radicalized the process of disintegration of the Arab societies in Syria and Iraq, but has also destroyed any communal Kurdish-Arab political language, thus precluding the possibility that a Kurdish political elite, or even Kurdish public opinion, could make sense of these conflicts.

It is true that the Kurdish movement still has some links with Turkish and Iranian left-wing or democratic opposition movements, and there is some possibility that bridges might be built between Kurdish demands and those formulated by the dissident segments of both societies. But these later links, where they exist, are much weaker than they used to be in the 1970s, and cannot constitute a nationwide political alternative. In Turkey, for instance, in spite of close contacts between the Kurdish movement and left-wing actors, the Kurdish and Turkish process of mobilization and de-mobilization, and radicalization and de-radicalization, have been dissociated for many years. The Kurdish political space—where the "political family" of the PKK and BDT-HDP (Party of Peace and Democracy and Democratic People's Party) enjoys an almost hegemonic position—is differentiated from the Turkish one, which in turn is almost entirely dominated by the AKP. One can expect that any regime crisis in Iran would also lead to such an evolution, bringing to light the silent effects of processes of differentiation between the Kurdish, Azeri, and Balochi political spaces and those that are Persian/Iranian.

The Kurdish movement can deal with this hegemonic but constrained isolation partly by using the plurality of Kurdish society as a resource, and partly by legitimizing itself with new international expectations. The plurality means that the transborder Kurdish political space, which also includes a strong diasporic component, has to accept that it is both unified and divided alongside different political cultures, patterns, and genealogies that past history imposed on it. There is no doubt that since more than a decade, two major actors, the KRG (Kurdistan Regional Government, dominated by the KDP of Masoud Barzani) and PKK (led by Abdullah Öcalan), do play the role of *primus inter pares* in this political space, but without being its sole actors.[33] The PYD (Party of Democratic Unity) and PJAK (Party of the Free Life in Kurdistan), for instance, are not simple "mechanical" continuities of the PKK, but the outcomes of intra-Iranian or intra-Syrian processes of mobilization made possible by PKK's acceptance as a model and as a reference or core organization by some segments of the Iranian and Syrian Kurdish societies.

As far as international expectations are concerned, one should admit that since the fall of the Berlin Wall, which put an end to the socialist bloc as a universal reference, new international loci of power have emerged: Brussels, Washington, and European capitals. In contrast with the protagonists of the rigid Cold War period, the new international regime fixes its horizon on a new universalistic model, but also allows criticism of the norms that they themselves advocate. For instance, there is no doubt that neo-liberalism, or at least some variety of economic liberalism, has became a universal norm; and the Kurdish actors in Iraq, but also in Turkey, have no great quarrel with this reorientation. But at the same time, these new "tablets of stone" outlining the immutable laws of economic liberalism are also criticized in the name of political liberalism or radical universalism, feminism, ecology, or local democracy, each of which is echoed to varying degrees in the program of the PKK and its allies, the PYD and the PJAK.

Thus, as in the 1920s–1930s and in the 1960s–1970s, the Kurdish movement can once again claim to be in *time*, either in the *world's time* or perhaps even *ahead* of this time, not just because it accepts what the world defines as norms, but also criticizes these very norms in the name of a better humanity, and not just for a better or emancipated Kurdish society. To be sure, Kurdish political praxis in the 2000s–2010s has been half-democratic and half-patrimonial in Iraq, and half-representative and half-hegemonic in Turkey and Syria; but Kurdish political parties, beginning with the PKK (and to a lesser extent those in Iraq), have had to accept that their hegemonic or patrimonial constructions can be maintained only on condition that they fulfil what they have promised to Kurdish society, including respect of its internal plurality. They are also aware that they have unleashed new dynamics that they are not necessarily capable of controlling. Compared to the situation that prevailed in the 1980s or even the 1990s, Kurdish society has in fact undergone important changes: with the emergence of middle classes, and also the sociological profile of youth and their expectations. In Turkish Kurdistan, the constant mobilization dating back to the 1960s not only allowed inter-generational continuities and transformations, but propelled young men, and more importantly young women, to the frontline.[34] There is no doubt that these categories (middle classes, youth, women's movements) define themselves as committed to the Kurdish cause and do not deny their sympathy for the PKK; but they are not necessarily linked to the party or the armed struggle through partisan or organic ties, and cannot be transformed into simple soldiers of a "national cause."

In post-2003 Iraqi Kurdistan and post-2012 Syrian Kurdistan, Kurdish actors imagined that they could act in mainly pacified frameworks, allowing them to establish a "national time" and to master their "national space." In spite of the absence of any administrative framework, including either autonomy or genuine decentralization, this was also true in Turkish Kurdistan where a ceasefire was brokered in 2013 in order to give the so-called peace process a chance. The de facto margin of maneuver for Kurdish actors has never been so wide in this country.

Since the ISIS attacks on Kurdish territories in Iraq and Syria during the summer of 2014 (Shingal-Sincar, Kobanî), however, this trust in "timing and spacing", which characterizes state-building processes,[35] has been challenged by the new conditions of the Middle East, where the reintroduction of violence at the heart of these societies, among them the various Kurdish enclaves, has constrained political actors to militarize themselves once again. The context of this re-militarization is entirely new in the sense that in both countries the Kurds are no longer fighting an existing state through guerrilla tactics, but rather are defending a "national territory" as de facto state-entities. The Kurdish space is currently experiencing an accelerated process of internal integration and solidarity; the struggles of summer 2014 have already constituted an important episode of the Kurdish national narrative, and to some extent have redefined the Kurdish cause; but during this process, Kurdish authorities and organizations have also been obliged, all of a sudden, to add a Spartan dimension to their (variously) "neo-liberal" and "feminist/ecological" models of pacified society and once again put military mobilization at the heart of their activity.

Nevertheless, this evolution is itself in complete accordance with international expectations, and can ultimately allow the Kurdish movement to reinforce its claim of being once again *in time*.

6

SEPARATED BUT CONNECTED

THE SYNERGIC EFFECTS IN THE KURDISTAN SUB-SYSTEM

Ofra Bengio

The prevailing image of the Kurds during the twentieth century was that of a people plagued by tribalism, chronic divisions, and internecine fighting. This situation, it was widely held, was the primary cause for their failure to establish a state of their own at the end of the First World War, in contrast to the successes of other ethno-national groups in the Middle East. This chapter takes issue with such an argument: whereas significant divisions were indeed part and parcel of Kurdish society, they were hardly unique to it, as Arab, Turkish, Iranian, and Jewish societies were characterized by many of the same internal fissures. The main difference, I argue, lay in the extant political and international circumstances at the end of the First World War that exacerbated the Kurds' fragmentation, this time in four newly founded nation states. In other words, it is not that tribalism and division did not play a role in the failure of Kurdish nationalists to construct a state of their own successfully. Had the British fulfilled their initial commitment to establish a political framework for the Kurds, such an entity might have been able to survive and be no less viable than any other post-Ottoman entity. Moreover, many tribal leaders actually played a pivotal role in the Kurdish national struggle, a unique phenomenon.[1] In addition, even though Kurdish communities were politically separated from each other by the post-First World War redrawing of boundaries and subsequently evolved along different paths in light of their varying experiences within the new states, the borders between the states were never hermetically sealed, and Kurdish communities remained in contact with one another and were mutually influenced by developments beyond state lines. The changing geostrategic map in the twenty-first century led to an exponential increase in these trans-border exchanges, and a reinforced Kurdish nationalist discourse. Accordingly, one may speak of a Kurdish sub-system that functioned under the radar of the governing authorities.

Imagining Greater Kurdistan

Even though the Kurdish populations have been separated politically, socially, and linguistically throughout their history, they were nonetheless bound together by a number of common denominators. There existed a tacit Kurdish sub-system, which allowed for the development of a certain kind of pan-Kurdism. A case in point was the imagining of Kurdistan, the land of the Kurds, and the nurturing of the discourse around it. The term "Kurdistan" was first introduced by Seljuk Turkic rulers in the twelfth century,[2] and subsequently gained wide currency among the Kurds. In 1597, the historian Sharaf Khan Bidlisi (Şerefxanê Bedlisi) published his monumental book *Şerefname*, in which he described "Kurdistan's different rulers and Emirs", emphasizing that everybody knew the term "Kurdistan."[3] Three hundred years later, the first Kurdish journal to be published was entitled, appropriately, *Kurdistan*.[4]

Throughout the last century, Kurdish nationalists have insisted on employing the term Kurdistan rather than Kurdish or Kurd because it refers to a territorial homeland. For example, the organization that was established at the end of the First World War for "the establishment of a Kurdish state" was named Kürdistan Teali Cemiyeti (Society for the Rise of Kurdistan).[5] Interestingly, in attempting to avoid the connotation of an independent state, Kemal Atatürk, the leader of the newly established Turkish Republic, replaced Kurdistan with Kurds: Kürt Teali Cemiyeti (Society for the Rise of Kurds).[6] Two decades later, in 1938, the clandestine organization Komalay Azadixwazi Kurdistan (Society for the Liberation of Kurdistan) was established in Iran; four years later, another independence-minded party was founded in the country, Komalay Jiyanaway Kurdistan (Society for the Revival of Kurdistan).[7] The latter, known as JK, welcomed cross-border links by inviting a member of the Hiwa party from Iraqi Kurdistan to participate in its inaugural meeting.[8] Employing Kurdish as the language of political and cultural discourse, JK called on delegates from all parts of Kurdistan to join.[9] In August 1944, members from Turkey, Iran, and Iraq met on Mount Dalanpour, where the borders of the three countries meet, and pledged mutual support and sharing of resources.[10] It would be redundant to mention the names of the Kurdish parties that were established in all four parts of Kurdistan, but one point should be stressed: namely, that almost all of them carried the title Kurdistan in their names, and not Kurdish, as was sometimes mistakenly translated into English (e.g. Partiya Demokrat a Kurdistanê, the Kurdistan Democratic Party (KDP), was rendered the Kurdish Democratic Party).

A similar misrepresentation can be seen in the name of the Republic of Mahabad, which was established in Iran in January 1946 but collapsed by the end of that year. This term was coined by non-Kurdish writers and became something like the official designation. However, Kurdish nationalists are now reclaiming the original name, Komari Kurdistan (Kurdistan Republic), because it has national rather than local resonance, and is not limited to one city. Even though this republic was short-lived, it remained a symbol of Kurdish independence, and Kurdish groups commemorate the anniversary of its establishment each year.[11]

Another way in which the existence of Greater Kurdistan is highlighted is through maps distributed by Kurdish nationalists, displaying Kurdistan as a single unit. The maximalists use a map which a Kurdish delegation proposed in the 1945 San Francisco Conference on International Organization (at which the United Nations was established) and which delineated the borders of Kurdistan from Adana in the Mediterranean Sea to Bushehr in the Persian Gulf, including the region inhabited by the Lur peoples.[12] This map is today displayed in children's textbooks in Syrian Kurdistan.[13]

The rise of the new media reinforced the ability to imagine Greater Kurdistan as an interconnected unit, as it enabled the forging of closer ties between the different parts of Kurdistan as well as with the diaspora. It also ushered the way to a more holistic discourse. One of the terms that began circulating in cyberspace and in scholarly and literary writing is Greater Kurdistan (Kurdistan Mezin),[14] a single four-part unit consisting of: Rojava, west Kurdistan, which has now become almost the official name of Kurdistan in Syria;[15] Bakur, north Kurdistan, corresponding to the Kurdish region in Turkey; Bashur, south Kurdistan, the Kurdish area in Iraq;[16] and Rojhelat, east Kurdistan, the Kurdish area of Iran. This new lexicon has become so widespread that even in Turkey, where the very word Kurdistan has been a taboo for many decades, the term Bakur has begun to be circulated openly.[17] It should however be noted that Kurdish discourse at the beginning of the twentieth century also employed such holistic terminology.[18] It was only after the division of the Kurdish-populated region and the state-led campaigns for assimilation and denial of their identity that more partial and fragmented concepts of Kurdistan took root, even among the Kurds themselves.

By contrast, official state discourse employed opposing, state-centric terminology to denote the same geographical regions: Turkey's Kurdish region was referred to as the south-east (*güneydoğu*); Iraq's Kurdish region the north (*shimal*); and Syria's Kurdish Jazira region the north too. Interestingly, the president of the Kurdistan Region in Iraq (KRI) Masoud Barzani in October 2013 prohibited the use of the term northern Iraq.[19]

Another new trend in Kurdish discourse has been an emphasis on the vision of a Kurdish confederation that would comprise all four parts of Kurdistan. Abdullah Öcalan, the founder and long-time leader of the Partiya Karkerên Kurdistanê (PKK), is the architect of this new vision, after having abandoned the idea of an independent Kurdistan.[20] According to this conceptualization, Kurdish populations would have democratic autonomy within existing states while also being part of a larger Kurdish confederation.[21] These ideas have become widespread among Öcalan's supporters in Turkey and the diaspora, as well as in the Democratic Union Party (Partiya Yekitiya Demokrat, PYD) a Syrian offshoot of the PKK.[22]

The new media, allowing for an unprecedented development of trans-border interactions, have carried these ideas to other parts of Kurdistan as well. The idea of Kurdish confederation, with all its inherent ambiguity, is supposed to assuage central governments' fears of Kurdish separatism. Be that as it may, the political elite in the KRI is not supportive of this idea, since their region is already part of a federal system with Baghdad, from which they are trying to maneuver away, toward independence.

On another level, for all the rivalries among the leaderships of the four regions and the different ideological and political paths that each of them has pursued, there has been a noticeable strengthening of pan-Kurdish affinity and solidarity among the Kurdish populations of Greater Kurdistan, as well as in the diaspora. Success achieved by one region was a source of national pride and a model for emulation for Kurds in the other regions. Attachment to common national symbols provided further evidence of increased pan-Kurdish sentiment. For example, Newroz is now celebrated throughout Greater Kurdistan as the Kurds' national holiday, in spite of governments' attempts to block the festivities. A Kurdish source depicts the holiday thus: "Every year on 21 March in all parts, hamlets, villages, towns, cities of Kurdistan as well as by Kurds living in the diaspora, they gather to show their unity, joy as well as cry out their need for freedom and democracy."[23] Similarly, a common national hymn has been adopted throughout Greater Kurdistan: the anthem initially created for the Mahabad Republic.

Trans-border ties in Kurdish history

Trans-border Kurdish ties are of long standing, beginning in the sixteenth century during the epoch of the Ottoman and Persian Empires, continuing throughout the difficult years of the twentieth century. These links were manifested in numerous ways: actions either in support of or against another Kurdish community; attempts to forge pan-Kurdish nationalism; and inspiration which one part in Greater Kurdistan drew from another.

In the period of the Ottoman and Persian empires (between the sixteenth to the twentieth centuries), the borders between the two empires were quite loose, enabling Kurds to move freely from one domain to the other.[24] Certainly tribal ties among Kurds that straddled the two empires made such crisscrossing natural and even imperative.[25] In 1818, for example, the Bilbas uprising was characterized by the alliance between the Kurdish nomadic tribes in the Persian Empire with the Kurds in the Pashalik of Bayazid and Van in the Ottoman Empire.[26] Economically speaking, Kurds traversed the borders in search of places for grazing or in flight from conflict zones. On the political level, a Kurd from one empire might have decided to move to the domain of the other in search of political gains. Cross-border marriages between members of different tribes were also common as a way of forging alliances. One such example was the marriage between Adela Khanum (1847-1924) of the Ardelans in the Persian Empire with Uthman Pasha of the Jaf in the Ottoman Empire. In time Adela Khanum became head of the strong Jaf tribe, making Halabja, which was part of the Ottoman Empire, the center of her ruling domain.[27]

Trans-border ties among Kurds became much more complicated and paradoxical following the establishment of the new states on the debris of the two empires. The four states—Turkey, Iran, Iraq, and Syria—that came to share Kurdistan after 1918 sought to create stronger central governments and thus worked to harden their borders so as to limit trans-border Kurdish ties. Nevertheless, the borders could not be sealed. Even though they were not coordinated, Kurdish uprisings in various parts of Kurdistan and in various periods of Kurdish history reflected the continued trans-border exchanges that were taking place. For example, the common denominator of uprisings in the first half of the 1920s—the Mahmud Barzinji uprisings in Iraq, the Simko Shikak revolt in Iran, and that of Sheikh Said in Turkey—was their attempt to exploit the weakness of the state in order to achieve a degree of independence.

There were also earlier attempts at cooperation: at the end of 1918, Simko approached Sheikh Taha of Shamdinan in Turkish Kurdistan to form "a formidable cross-border (Iran-Turkey) bloc, one that in the absence of any credible alternative could realistically dream of independence."[28] Nothing came out of this cooperation, but still the borders remained porous with Simko crossing several times to Turkish and Iraqi Kurdistan to find asylum or prepare for the next uprising in Iran. Similarly, in spite of the rivalry between Simko and Barzinji, the former did give sanctuary to Barzinji's relatives when they fled to Iran in 1919.[29]

Another example was the establishment of the Khoybun (independence) party in 1927 in Lebanon, which marked an early attempt to enhance pan-Kurdish nationalism, seeking as it did to "establish a strong Kurdish national liberation movement."[30] Khoybun was behind the Agri (Ararat) uprising in Turkey which broke out a year later. Khoybun attempted to include the Kurds of Syria in the uprising as well, but with no great success. Lasting until 1931, it did gain the support of Kurdish tribespeople from Iran who crossed the border to participate, both men and women, in the battle against Turkish forces. An eyewitness described one episode thus: "The Kurds, whose women seemed all to carry babies on their backs and rifles in their hands, appeared to regard the fighting more as an amusement than anything else."[31]

The next substantial trans-border Kurdish endeavor occurred in 1946 with the establishment of the short-lived Kurdistan Republic in Iran. In this case, the traversing of the border was from Iraqi to Iranian Kurdistan. Mullah Mustafa Barzani arrived at Mahabad on the eve of the establishment of the Republic, together with 10,000 people, 3,000 of whom were fighters.[32] In this regard it is important to point out that the influx, which was comprised of entire families, meant both greater friction as well as greater familiarity between the two communities. Second, the contribution of the Barzani fighters to the struggle against the Iranian army was quite substantial. Similarly, in spite of tribal rivalries between the Kurds of Iran and Iraq, there were some positive influences on the Kurdish national level. Thus, for example the Kurdistan Democratic Party (KDP) of Iraq was established in Iran in 1946, with clear inspiration emanating from the Kurdistan Democratic Party of Iran, which had been established two years earlier.

It would take another decade for the synergic effect to reach the Kurds of Syria: in 1957, the Kurdistan Democratic Party of Syria (KDPS) was established.[33] The ripples reached the Kurds of Turkey a decade later. At the end of 1965, the first Kurdish party was established there, the Kurdistan Democratic Party of Turkey (KDPT).[34] However, the KDPT, while inspired by the KDP of Mullah Mustafa Barzani, did not succeed in striking deep roots, as Barzani's party had. Indeed, the latter is the longest surviving Kurdish party; moreover, it now rules a quasi-state, the Kurdistan Region in Iraq.[35]

The pattern whereby Kurds, pushed by wars, moved from one country to a neighboring one was repeated time and again in modern history.[36] The largest waves of Kurdish exodus were from Iraq to Iran after the collapse of their rebellion in 1975, and then following the collapse of their intifada in 1991. Two decades later, it was the turn of the Kurdistan Region in Iraq to welcome a new wave of Syrian Kurdish refugees who fled to the region as a result of the fighting that began in 2012 between Kurdish militias and various Islamist groupings.[37] The potential significance of such trans-border human influx is two-fold and contradictory: it could boost solidarity feelings and strengthen an overarching Kurdish national movement, but also increase friction and deepen rivalries between the political elites.

Synergic effects: the case of Rojava

Evidence of past and present ties between the Kurds of Syria and Kurdish communities beyond their borders was provided, ironically, by a hostile Syrian Arab official, Muhammad Talab Hilal, who raised the specter of the establishment of a Kurdish state in Iraqi Kurdistan that could engulf the Kurds of Syria as well. Accordingly, he suggested the establishment of an Arab belt (*hizam 'Arabi*) along the borders, so as to block such trans-border influences.[38] Hilal based his nightmare scenario on a number of assertions: 1) "for all their conflicting tendencies and the enmities and rivalries between them, the Kurdish tribes in *al-jazira* [the region in north-east Syria in which they are concentrated] are united by ... 'the Kurdish race'...and the dream of national homeland (*watan qawmi*)";[39] 2) the Kurds of Syria were "organically tied to the Kurds of Iraq, Turkey and Iran, since [they have] the same problem and the same goal";[40] 3) the borders between the Kurdish regions were porous, enabling ongoing interactions and the strengthening of ties; and 4) their common religion, Islam, could not be the glue between Arabs and Kurds since for the latter, Kurdish national identity had first priority.[41]

As evidence for his assertions, Hilal stated that many Kurds in Syria had close relationships with Mullah Mustafa Barzani, who had proved victorious in his war against the Iraqi army. Kurdish poets from Syria, he stated, took pride in Mustafa Barzani's achievements in the war against ʿAbd al-Karim Qasim in 1961-3. To prove his point, Hilal quoted a long poem extolling Barzani's feat, describing him as a hero who was fighting to save the homeland of Kurdistan, and whose fame reached through the entire Middle East.[42]

Historically, the Kurds of Syria moved in the orbit of the two "big brothers", in Turkish and Iraqi Kurdistan, owing to their smaller size. Until 2012, the Kurds of Rojava were less active than in the other parts of Kurdistan, but they did identify with the movements there. For example, Kurds from Syria crossed into Iraq to support their brethren in the war against the Ba'ath regime in 1974-5.[43] Ironically, the influences of Kurdish groups from Turkey and Iraq on Rojava's Kurds were strengthened by a decision by the Syrian Ba'ath regime in the 1970s to grant asylum and support to Kurdish parties from Iraq, the KDP, and Patriotic Union of Kurdistan (PUK), and then in the 1980s and the 1990s to the PKK.[44]

Another component of Assad's policy which would boomerang against the Syrian regime was the encouragement he gave to Syrian Kurds to join the PKK. The twofold aim of this strategy was to divert attention from the domestic Kurdish problem in Syria, while at the same time pushing them to fight against Turkey, Syria's adversary at the time. According to a Syrian Kurdish PKK commander, by 1991 PKK leader Abdullah Öcalan had at least 8,000-10,000 "armed supporters" among the Kurds of Syria.[45] These numbers go a long way to explain the speed with which the Kurds managed to take control of Syrian Kurdistan in summer 2012. Concurrently, this development accelerated the rivalry between the KDP and PKK, each of which sought to have influence on Rojava.

Harriett Allsopp maintains that the Kurdish movement in Syria has invested manpower, money, and emotion in support of the Kurdish struggle in other parts of Kurdistan, with the result that "their own political movement has suffered and has been stifled by the interference of external political parties in their affairs."[46] However, this observation is no longer relevant. For one thing, it is Rojava which is now getting support from other parts of Kurdistan. For another, even though Kurdish political groupings from Turkey and Iraq have been trying to gain influence in Rojava, the latter managed to stand on its own feet and even become an inspiration for Kurds in other parts of Kurdistan.

The quantum leap forward

The turn of the twenty-first century marked a quantum leap for Kurdish ethno-nationalism. The four previously separate and relatively unconnected movements were being transformed into a more closely knit trans-border one. Three important turning points, all of which took place in Kurdistan of Iraq, reverberated throughout the rest of Greater Kurdistan: the end of the eight year Iraqi-Iranian war (1980-88), with its catastrophic results for the Kurds; the 1991 Gulf war, which ended up with the establishment of the autonomous Kurdistan Region in Iraq; and finally, the dismantling of the Ba'athist state in 2003, which led to the emergence of the Kurdish quasi-state alongside the central government in Baghdad.

The Iraqi-Iranian war ended with the Iraqi army's chemical attack against the town of Halabja on 16 March 1988, in which 5,000 Kurds were killed, and the regime's brutal Anfal campaign, which lasted from February to September 1988, in which an estimated 182,000 Kurds perished.[47] These events were traumatic not just for the Kurds of Iraq but for Kurds everywhere. Not only did Kurds feel solidarity with their brethren in Iraq, but they regarded these murderous actions as attacks against the entire Kurdish community. These events also helped internationalize the Kurdish conflict as a whole.[48]

Kurds began commemorating these events in Kurdistan, as well as in the Kurdish diaspora, while also demanding that the international community recognize them as constituting genocide. In one such event, which took place in March 2012 in the European Parliament and in which Kurds from different parts of Kurdistan participated, a Kurdish member in the Turkish parliament Demir Çelik stated that "Kurds from the four parts of divided Kurdistan went through legendary sufferings, which continue in many places today." The date of 16 March was symbolic, he said, and the Kurds everywhere had to draw lessons from the past.[49] The Kurds of Syria commemorate the Halabja chemical attack each year with five minutes silence.[50] The Kurds of Iran commemorate Halabja as well. On the cultural level too, Halabja arouses strong feelings of sharing a common fate. For example, the famous Kurdish singer Şiwan Perver, a Kurd from Turkey, wrote a song about the trauma of Halabja, which he likened to Hiroshima. So have many other Kurdish artists.[51]

If Halabja and Anfal symbolized the abyss into which the Kurds sank in the twentieth century, the 1991 Gulf war may be regarded as the beginning of the climb upward. Once again, the Kurds of Iraq ushered the way. The establishment of the autonomous region in 1992 was a catalyst and a model for Kurds in other parts of Greater Kurdistan. The PKK, for instance, took advantage of the vacuum left by the Iraqi army after it had withdrawn its forces from Iraqi Kurdistan to fortify their bases on Qandil Mountain from where they could launch attacks on Turkey. It was the first time in modern history that a Kurdish group from one part of Kurdistan had established permanent military bases in another part. Similarly, for all the friction and at times internal fighting that the PKK's presence caused for the KRI, the latter remained unequivocally the political center for all Kurds.

Little by little, Kurdish groupings from Iran and Syria followed suit by establishing their own bases in the KRI. The two-way traffic in and out of the KRI also had other positive effects. For example, Jalal Talabani, head of the PUK, was involved in early 1993 in attempts to broker a peace agreement between the PKK and the Turkish government, headed by Turgut Özal. However, Özal's sudden death in April 1993 put an end to this experiment. Ideologically speaking, while the other Kurdish movements in Turkey, Syria, and Iran continue wavering in their preferences between autonomy and federal arrangements, certain leaders in the KRI have begun to raise openly the idea of independence.

The dismantling of the Ba'ath regime following the Iraqi war in March 2003 catapulted the KRI into the epicenter of Kurdish nationalism. The participation of the peshmerga in the American-led war against the Ba'ath turned them into an ally of the United States and, no less importantly, granted them economic, political, and military dividends that enabled them to become a quasi-state. The impact on the other Kurdish regions was immediate.

In Turkey, after five years of unilateral ceasefire following the capture of its leader, Abdullah Öcalan, in 1999, the PKK regrouped its forces and resumed fighting. One scholar, Aliza Marcus, opined that "the repercussions of the Iraqi Kurdish ministate—even one that is not officially independent, not yet—are rippling across the region."[52] The butterfly effect reached the Kurds of Syria as well. Long considered a silent minority, on 12 March 2004 they initiated a Kurdish uprising (*serhildan*), which started in Qamishli and spread very quickly to other Kurdish centers in Syria. Even though it was crushed within a few days, its impact was far-reaching. Imitating the destruction of Saddam Hussein's statue in Iraq a year earlier, the Kurds of Syria destroyed several statues of Hafiz al-Assad, indicating that fear of the Ba'ath regime in Syria was no longer preventing them from action. Similarly, "for the first time in history", states Jordi Tejel, "political parties and population groups from other Kurdish regions expressed their solidarity with the Syrian Kurds by means of public declarations and demonstrations in Diyarbakir (Turkey), Erbil, and Sulaymaniyya (Iraq)."[53] No less important, this initial popular uprising laid the infrastructure for the more sustained and far-reaching one of July 2012, which in turn became an energizing force for the other parts of Kurdistan.

To be sure, however, this intertwining had negative effects as well. The fact that various parties and groupings from other parts of Kurdistan had established bases in the Kurdistan Region in Iraq rendered the latter extremely vulnerable to pressure and attacks by neighboring countries. For example, in spite of the close relationship that developed in the last few years between the KRG and Turkey, the latter had no qualms in launching repeated attacks on bases of the PKK, the collateral damage to civilians in the KRI notwithstanding. Similarly, Tehran kept pressurizing the KRG not to allow the Kurdish Iranian groups to carry out attacks against Iran; and when the KRG failed to do so, the Iranian army bombarded areas in the KRI. In a way, the KRI has turned into a hostage for the "good behavior" of Kurds from other parts of Kurdistan vis-à-vis their governments and vice versa. Kurdish opposition parties from other parts had to "behave" well to allow the KRI to prosper. In other words, the success of one region could come at the price of the failure of the other.

The Islamic State as a catalyst

The sudden rise of the Islamic State (IS, also known as ISIS, ISIL, and Daesh) in June 2014 in Iraq and Syria represented an important milestone for the Kurds. In fact, the war which the IS initiated against the Kurds on the Syrian and Iraqi fronts is serving as a catalyst for Kurdish nation-building and state-building, with the resulting changes being reflected in Kurdish dicourse.

In terms of geography, the Islamic State's erasure of the border between Iraq and Syria was a mirror image of what the Kurds had done earlier when they effaced the border between the two countries' Kurdish regions. The erection of Semalka bridge, linking the two regions, highlights the reshaping of the old map. In their dicourse, too, Kurdish nationalists began to challenge the Sykes-Picot agreement of 1916, which had shaped the subsequent internationally recognized borders. Thus, for example, KRG President Barzani stated that the Kurds no longer recognized the Sykes-Picot borders and that the new borders in the Middle East were being redrawn with blood.[54] For his part, Sirwan Barzani, a peshmerga commander and nephew of the president, stated unequivocally that "Our plan is to change the Sykes-Picot agreement" since "Iraq is not real. It exists only on the map."[55]

On the popular level, the life and death war between Kurdish forces and the Islamic State aroused unprecedented solidarity and patriotic feelings among Kurds in all parts of Kurdistan as well as in the diaspora, prompting them to mobilize for the fighting.[56] Similarly, for all the animosity and rivalries between the leaderships of the different regions, when it came to confronting the Islamic State, they temporarily buried the hatchet.

Manifestations of soldarity were numerous. At the end of October 2014, 150 KRG peshmerga fighters crossed Turkish territory on their way to support the Kurdish fighters: Yekîneyên Parastina Gel (People's Protection Unit, YPG) in Kobanî, Syria. On that occasion, many Turkish Kurds came from far away to greet them with Kurdish flags and slogans such as "long live the resistance of Kobanî, long live the resistance of peshmerga."[57] Likewise, when the joint Kurdish forces liberated Kobanî from IS at the end of January 2015, Kurds from all parts of Greater Kurdistan celebrated the occasion. Barzani emphasized the unity between the Kurds, stating that "the martyrdom of Zeravan – a Peshmerga from Southern [Iraqi] Kurdistan killed in Kobanî – and Nechirvan – a guerrilla from Rojava killed in the east Mosul operation – both on the same day, is the symbol of brotherhood, union and unanimity of the Kurdish nation; it showed that the whole Kurdish nation has the same cause." A Kurdish commentator stated that "for the Kurds, Kobanî has become a symbol of the Kurdish struggle for statehood, just like... Halabja."[58]

Politically, the fate of Rojava could no longer be disconnected from that of Bakur (Kurdistan of Turkey) or Bashur (Kurdistan of Iraq). What happenened on one side of the border had immediate impact on the other. For example, Cemil Bayik, the deputy leader of the PKK, set forth in March 2015 six conditions for the PKK to lay down its arms, one of which was that Turkey should change its stance toward Rojava and that President Tayyip Erdoğan should stop saying: "We do not recognize northern Syria."[59] The ripple effect of Kobanî was also reflected in the 7 June 2015 general elections in Turkey that resulted in the pro-Kurdish party, the People's Democratic Party (HDP), succeeding in entering parliament for the first time in Turkish history. It was suggested that "the most critical moment for the Kurdish voters' decisions and preferences came when the [Turkish] government refused to assist the Syrian town of Kobanî while it was besieged by ISIS."[60] The Turkish government itself acknowledged the threat emanating from trans-border influences among Kurds when on 23 July 2015 it began attacking PKK bases in the KRI, with one goal being to cut the ties between the PKK in Turkey and the YPG in Rojava.

The close ideological, political, and military relationship between the Turkish and Syrian regions of Kurdistan complicated the situation for both. There is no doubt that the war unleashed by the Turkish military against the PKK since mid-2015 was partly an act of revenge against the Kurdish achievements in Syria, and partly an attempt to pre-empt possible spill-over effects in Turkey. The PKK's links to Syria's Kurds were also used by Turkey to tarnish the image of the PYD by portraying it as a terrorist group, and by attempting to have it included on the US's and EU's list of terrorist groups, alongside the PKK. However, these attempts have failed because both Russia and the West needed the PYD and its military branch, the YPG, for combating the Islamic State and other jihadist elements.

Alarmed by the advances made by the Kurdish fighters in Syria, Turkey initiated on 24 August 2016 the "Euphrates Shield Operation", which aimed at smashing the Islamic State's strongholds along the Turkish borders and more importantly erasing the Kurdish autonomous entity. Ankara's grand strategic objective behind the operation was spelled out in *Hurriyet*:

> The aim of the Euphrates Shield operation is to restore this area to its demographic situation prior to 2011, namely, to revive the area's character before the Syrian civil war. This entails ensuring that the Turkmen and Arab population that was driven away from this area by the PYD-YPG and ISIS, can return to their villages, towns and cities. We can say that the Euphrates Shield operations will continue until this objective is secured.[61]

Nor were the Bashur-Bakur-Rojava triangle dynamics any less complex. With the establishment of autonomy in Rojava and the war against the Islamic State, the competition between the KDP and the PKK over influence in Rojava became more overt. Each of the parties sought to use local Kurdish groupings to achieve its goal. KRG President Barzani conferred his sponsorship on the Syrian Kurdish National Congress (KNC), a conglomeration of fifteen smaller groups that are generally eclipsed by the PKK's offshoot, the PYD. Barzani has made repeated attempts to broker reconciliation between these rival groupings in order to increase the KRG's influence in Rojava. Accordingly, he sponsored the October 2014 Dohuk accord, which called upon the rival parties to set aside their differences and cooperate politically and militarily against the Islamic State. On that occasion, Barzani stated: "This agreement brings us together, and itself is a significant answer to our enemies who did not intend the Kurds to be united." For his part Salih Muslim, co-chairman of the PYD, warned that "all the Kurdish people are under attack so they should be united."[62] Later in March 2015, representatives of the two factions met in Qamishli to coordinate their activities. On that occasion they published a joint statement emphasizing that the Kurdish region in Syria represented a "geographical and political unity" within a federal state. To reinforce this new vision, they posted a map which shows Kurdistan in Syria reaching the Mediterranean Sea and having geographical contiguity between all the three Kurdish cantons, neither of which actually exists.[63]

While such agreements and declarations are more often than not a camouflage for ongoing animosities between the political elites, there is no denying that a certain degree of interdependence has developed. The PKK needed the legitimation which the KRG could help confer on it in the international arena, while the KRG needed the PKK's military prowess, which was demonstrated in a number of military encounters with the Islamic State in the Iraqi Kurdish region.[64] Similarly, while the KRG sought to gain the recognition of the PYD for the role of Erbil's protégés in Syria, the PYD needed the strategic depth and economic support which the KRG could offer it.[65] According to Harriet Allsopp, "despite imbalances in power relations between the Kurdish parties and although problems remained, all parties have displayed a strong commitment to the unity of the Kurdish political movement."[66] Although the reference is to the Kurds of Syria, it is possible to apply it to other parts of Kurdistan as well.

Crossing borders in the diaspora

The Kurdish diaspora is a transnational actor par excellence. It has played a crucial role in transcending political and geographical borders in Greater Kurdistan and energizing the Kurdish national movement as a whole. Representing a non-state nation, the Kurdish diaspora has served as a cultural, political, and economic lifeline for Kurds in the homeland. This role has been all the more important since Kurdistan is a fragmented and landlocked region with inherent difficulties in developing relations among Kurds of all four parts of the homeland and reaching out to the international arena. Accordingly, Kurds outside Kurdistan have played an indispensable role in enhancing a sense of solidarity among Kurds, as well as internationalizing the Kurdish cause.[67]

Their ability to do so stemmed from a combination of their large numbers, their independence from their states of origin, and their organizational capabilities.[68] On the whole, the Kurdish diaspora community is relatively recent in origin, being a byproduct of the conflicts between states and their Kurdish communities beginning in the middle of the last century.[69] According to Amir Hassanpour, a major feature of this diaspora was that it consisted of a large number of educated Kurds who belonged to the urban middle class and were politically active in the Kurdish nationalist movement.[70] Undoubtedly, these were vital for establishing strong organizations in the diaspora. Kurds from Turkey, however, were drawn primarily from the working class who had moved to Western Europe in the 1960s and were initially less involved in politics.[71] In time, however, diaspora Kurds from all parts of Kurdistan became politicized, thanks to the democratic political systems in their host countries, and because the conflict with states in the Kurdish homeland continued unabated.

Enjoying freedom of association and freedom of speech in their mother tongue, the Kurds in the diaspora could organize and communicate freely with each other without the inhibition of borders. Communication lines were further deepened on occasions of festivals and national days such as Newroz, or the commemoration of special events such as the establishment of Mahabad Republic or the Halabja affair. To be sure, rivalries did exist among the different organizations in the diaspora, a reflection of rivalries among the leaderships in the four regions. Still, this did not prevent overall solidarity activities on certain issues, for example, the lobbying of European governments for recognizing Anfal and Halabja as genocide. Another example was the formation of an important pressure group in the corridors of power in the EU as it debated Turkey's accession or the treatment of Kurds in Iraq or Syria. Kurdish diaspora activists also found new channels of expression for grievances, including the European Court of Human Rights.[72]

Other ways to attempt to influence decision-making and expressing solidarity with the homeland include demonstrations, petitions, and conferences. One of the most important platforms is a yearly conferernce held in the EU parliament in Brussels in which Kurds from the diaspora and the homeland participate and exchange views and ideas. Cultural centers like the Institut Kurde in Paris have also played an important role in promoting trans-border exchanges. Sometimes such meetings and conferences reflect the fragmentation in the homeland, but nevertheless they do not weaken the common feeling of Kurdish identity .

Pan-Kurdish tendencies or movements developed early on among Kurds in the diaspora. One of the first examples was the formation of a Kurdish Student Society in Europe in 1956; another was the Kurdistan National Congress (KNC), formed in London in 1989. Generally speaking, the demands and aspirations of Kurdish activists in the diaspora have been much more far reaching than those in the homeland, primarily because democratic countries afforded them the freedom to think big, while their brethren in the homeland could pay a high price for raising radical slogans. For example, the KNC established "the Western Kurdistan government in exile" in 2004 in London in order "to realize the sovereignty of the Kurdish people in their own historical homeland [and] to create a state of Kurdistan."[73] By contrast, for all their achievements on the ground, KRG leaders have until recently refrained from raising the slogan of independence.

On another level, the social media revolution has contributed immensely to transborder nationalism, linking Kurds in Greater Kurdistan with Kurds in the diaspora, as well as among themselves. For all the endeavors of the central governments in those countries to block contacts, they failed to do so. In the era of the internet, Facebook, and Twitter, the new media also became a tool in the hands of Kurdish intellectuals in the diapora for criticizing certain negative phenomena in Kurdistan itself. In the words of one Kurdish writer:

> In today's high-tech, connected world where blogging, social networking, and online journalism are the norm in the Kurdish diaspora communities in Europe, North America, and elsewhere, we must use these tools available to us to speak out against repression, abuses of freedom of expression, suppression of the Kurdish voice in the media, and harassment of journalists and media outlets in Kurdistan.[74]

In short, relations between the diaspora and the homeland may be described as a two-way street, in which geographical borders have lost their importance and where mutual influences continuously stream back and forth.

Conclusion

Notwithstanding the ongoing endeavors of the central governments in Turkey, Iran, Iraq, and Syria to cut the ties among the Kurds of Greater Kurdistan, these ties have strengthened rather than weakened with time. In fact, the borders have never been hermetically closed due to geographical contiguity, similar historical and ethnocultural background, and common ethos and aspirations for self-determination. This has turned the Kurdish experience in nation-building into a unique case of the proverbial imagined community.[75] It is not only that the common people felt solidarity with their brethren across the borders, but crucial developments in one part were bound to reverberate in the others. Sometimes this reverberation was a positive one from the Kurdish point of view, in the sense that a certain event or achievement in one region could become a model for imitation by others. It could also trigger mutual support among the Kurdish communities. At other times, however, relations could take a negative turn, especially among leaderships and political elites. Past events have shown that proximity and open lines of communication were likely to increase rivalries, enmities, and even fratricide. For example, the fact that various groups from the three regions have had their bases in the Kurdish Region in Iraq increased the friction between the host parties and the KRG. Worse still, at times the success of the nation-building and state-building project in one region could be at the expense of the others. For example, the Kurds of Iraq had to buy the goodwill of the governments in the neighboring states such as Iran or Turkey by turning a blind eye to persecution of their Kurdish brethren in those countries.

To sum up, Greater Kurdistan is a kind of sub-system flowing beneath the existing system of states, one in which each region has shaped itself in its own way but in which relations between them are like a kaleidoscope, which change time and again, with every rotation.

7.

FACT AND FICTION IN MODERN KURDISH NARRATIVE DISCOURSE

Hashem Ahmadzadeh

Modern narrative mediums, i.e. the novel and short story, in contrast to traditional modes of narration (such as fable and legend, built upon collective knowledge and didactic transmission from generation to generation), have their origins in individual experiences and modern epistemological ideas. The rise of modern Kurdish narrative discourse provides excellent examples for research into the relationship between fact and fiction. This chapter examines two early examples of Kurdish fiction, a short story and a novel from the early twentieth century, arguing that they are closely related to the sociopolitical condition of Kurdish society during the same period. The pieces that will be discussed are: *La Khawma* (In my Dream) by Jamil Saib (1887–1951) and *Masalay Wizhdan* (The Question of Conscience) by Ahmad Mukhtar Jaf (1896–1935).

The chapter aims to show how fact feeds fiction in the Kurdish context. With the help of existing literary theory such as New Historicism, which discuss the epistemological and social bases of modern narrative discourse, to modern Kurdish literature, it aims to analyze the interrelationship of fact and fiction in the Kurdish context. Ian Watt's ideas about the particularity of experiences, times, and places in the novel, and Michel Foucault's views on the concept of the "will to knowledge," that contributed to the emergence of realism, provide the theoretical bases for this presentation.[1] The chapter will examine themes, lacunae, and space in two Kurdish modern literary narrations, highlighting particular existing relations between fact and fiction in the world of Kurdish society and culture. These fictional works and their detailed record of Kurdish society of the time can represent Kurdish "reality" as effectively as any non-fiction text. After the post-structuralist turn, literary theory is more interested in literary texts "as a basis for philosophical speculation and ideological polemic" rather than for formal analysis.[2] Some scholars have combined the terms fact and fiction to coin a new concept, "faction." The portmanteau "faction" denotes the use of novelistic techniques in bringing actual historical events to life for the reader; this kind of literary work treads the borderline between fact and fiction.[3] While the works discussed in this article are not "faction" but purely fiction, they undoubtedly reflect the social reality of Kurdistan during the early twentieth century. These fictional stories may even hold more interest for the scholar than factual accounts as they "present us with models of (especially) the social world with which we can empathise, but which we can observe because we are not constrained to act."[4] Through highlighting the sociopolitical situation of southern Kurdistan, from where this fiction emerged, and comparing it to the thematic structure of the pieces, we can examine how fact and fiction interplay. We can also see how the individual and social positions of both authors were crucial factors in enabling them to produce the two stand-out early modern Kurdish fictional works. The main departure point of this chapter compared with previous critical works on Kurdish fiction is simply that it moves away from traditional literary criticism, which focuses on the perceived direct intention of the author.[5]

The Kurdish novel: rise and development

Kurdish novelistic discourse was formed as a result of many political, cultural, and historical factors.[6] It was only during the early years of the twentieth century that the idea of Kurdish identity crystallized, centring around the Kurdish language. This Kurdish "consciousness" was accompanied by the rise of Kurdish nationalism and its "modern tendencies such as the presence of a rising urban nationalist elite, organisation of political parties, and nationalist publications."[7] The social change in Kurdish societies, alongside cultural influences from other nations, contributed to the birth of modern Kurdish narrative literature. It is a textbook example of Hawthorn's work regarding the rise of the novel: "[T]he novel is significantly the product of social change on the national level and cultural influence on the international one."[8]

The history of the rise and development of the Kurdish novel clearly illustrate the complicated and fragmented destiny of Kurdish nationalism.

In the second decade of the third millennium, the list of Kurdish novels numbers approximately three hundred titles. Bearing in mind the sociopolitical condition of the Kurds, this is a relatively good showing. Needless to say, this quantitative growth has also been followed by a qualitative change in the literary and aesthetic features of the Kurdish novel.[9] The dominant theme remains the national question, and the effects of statelessness are easy to find.[10] This runs counter to the major trend in recent developments for the novel in the Western context, where the influence of the consequences of rapid globalization are clear, as has been shown by Elaine Showalter.[11]

Southern Kurdistan (Iraqi Kurdistan) during the early decades of the twentieth century

Toward the end of the First World War, the Kurdish areas of the Ottoman Empire became subject to radical political changes. The decline of the Empire and the strong position of the Allied forces set the stage for a redesign of the region's political map. The southern part of Kurdistan became an area of renewed focus. It was during these years that Ottoman Kurdistan was divided among three new nation-states: Iraq, Turkey, and Syria. The period between 1918 and 1925 was seen as a golden opportunity for Kurdish statehood.[12] In 1919 three schools of thought predominated with regard to Kurdish aspirations: pro-Turkey, pro-Allies, and pro-independence.[13] The treaties of Sèvres and Lausanne led to a complicated situation for the Kurds. While the Treaty of Sèvres in 1920 contained three articles supporting the Kurdish right to statehood, the Treaty of Lausanne, only three years later, bore no mention of the Kurds. In fact, the partition of the Ottoman Empire had already been agreed upon on 16 May 1916 in the secret Sykes-Picot treaty. The allied forces and the newly ascendant Turkish nationalist forces relied upon the Kurds and their loyalty. The British, aiming to gain Kurdish support against the Turks, promised them independence. The Turks instead appealed to a Kurdish sense of Islamic solidarity against British designs for the region.[14]

In December 1918 the British authorities declared Sheikh Mahmud Barzinji (1882–1956) the governor of Silemani. Barzinji, a respected landowner and religious leader, was seen by the newly arrived British forces as a safe option to serve as a figurehead leader in Kurdistan. During the early months of 1919, the British authorities in the region started to undermine Barzinji's authority to the extent that he decided to rebel against the British administration. It did not take long for the British authorities in the region to defeat the sheikh and send him into exile in mid-June 1919. Thanks to internal protests and geopolitical considerations, Barzinji was pardoned in mid-September 1922 and brought back to Kurdistan. Deep mistrust between the sheikh and the British authorities meant that disagreements increased rapidly and the British forces bombarded Silemani in May 1924, forcing Barzinji to leave the city. According to Ahmad Khwaja, referring to Barzinji's speech on 10 November 1922 in the first meeting of Kurdish ministers, he was quite aware of both Turkish and British designs upon the region. Barzinji was determined to fight for the right of the Kurds to freedom and independence. In fact, he had a pragmatist approach toward all actors in the region. In his letters of March 1925 to various regional authorities, he emphasized this stance and said, "the Kurds fight for freedom and do not want to live as slaves. Whoever supports our aim for freedom and independence, will have our support."[15]

La Khawma [In my Dream]

Jamil Saib, the author of this fictional work, was born into an educated family in Silemani. He graduated from religious schools and started writing and publishing from 1919 in the newspaper Peshkawtin [Progress]. Jamil's uncle Piramerd (1867–1950) was an influential writer who returned from Istanbul after the collapse of the empire. He is considered by many as one of the founders of Kurdish cultural nationalism. Saib's La Khawma was first published in two successive magazines issued by Piramerd, demonstrating the importance of family relations in getting afforded a voice in Kurdish society at the time.

Arif Saib, Jamil's brother, was accused of spying for the British and was then assassinated by one of the sheikh's men in 1923. It was reported that when Barzinji heard about Arif's murder, he was shocked and exclaimed, "Arif was one of my most beloved men. I would tell him all my secrets — he was a clever man. Hamay Saida Bichkol [the murderer] must face death for this."[16] In 1923, another intellectual and well-known man of Silemani, Jamal Irfan, who was a close friend of Jamil Saib and his brother-in-law, was killed by Barzinji's men. There is no doubt that this cruelty influenced Jamil's approach toward the sheikh.[17]

The story was first published in twenty-three instalments in Jiyanewe and Jiyan in 1925 and 1926. It is primarily an extended meditation on Kurdistan by an unknown character who, in his dream, observes the fatal defects of the government in southern Kurdistan during the early 1920s. The unknown character, aiming to find a job in "shar," the city—a reference to Silemani, the capital of Barzinji's government—leaves his hometown with a caravan. By narrating his observations on the way to the city, the character informs the reader about the treacherous route and how bandits rob unsuspecting travelers. When he arrives in the city he is arrested by the security forces and taken to a room where he can hear and see "the big man" and his meetings through a window. Among his observations are three episodes, which refer to the sheikh's ambiguous policy toward Turkey, Great Britain, and the wish for an independent Kurdistan.

The arrival of some pro-Turkish politicians at the court of the "big man" and the fact that he accedes to their demand that he swear allegiance to Turkey shows one of the tendencies in Barzinji's policy toward the Turks and his cooperation with them on certain occasions. Another group arrives at the court, apparently advocates of British influence in Kurdistan. They try to persuade the "big man" that British policy in Kurdistan is beneficial, and that it would be in the interest of the Kurds to cooperate with British forces. The "big man" shows his interest in this group's plan as well. The last group to arrive at the court offers propaganda for an independent Kurdistan.

They encourage the "big man" to agree to construct an independent Kurdistan far from the influence of foreigners. The "big man" agrees with their argument as well.

The "big man" has his own justifications for all these positions he takes. The justification for supporting the Turks is that cooperation with them can enable him to continue with his administration in defiance of the British forces.[18] His position toward the Englishmen is justified by the unique power of Great Britain and the fact that no government can survive without British support.[19] His third position justifies his own nationalist desires and predilection against both the Turks and the English.[20] These quick changes in the politics of the "big man" make the character more disappointed. He wonders about the man's weak personality and the fact that he changes his mind three times in three hours.[21]

The imprisoned character hears all these contrasting arguments and the approval by the "big man" of all of them, and then bursts into laughter. His loud laughs draw the attention of the "big man" and his men. The "big man" gets angry on hearing the supposed spy's laughter. He and his men start to beat the spy severely. The character is exhausted with the current situation and hopes to get rid of these "strange people." He tells himself he will leave this "bloody" and "destroyed country" as soon as he is released.[22]

There are two aspects in the story regarding dominant cultural and social paradigms. One can easily see the importance of religious discourse and the influence of the religious personalities on the "big man." The dominant rhetoric of some of the religious authorities who have surrounded the "big man" in the story verges on the fanatic. They refer to the Islamic sharia regarding the punishment of those who in one way or another have in any way wronged the sheikh, the religion, or the country. They explicitly say that these "infidels" should be punished severely by confiscating their properties and taking their wives from them.[23]

The lack of any clear political discourse regarding Kurdish identity and will is clearly visible through the whole discussion between the "big man" and his advisors. The fact is that Barzinji was an inexperienced governor and the sociopolitical situation of Kurdistan did not help him. On the contrary, in many cases the internal situation was deteriorating. Rafiq Hilmi, a prominent politician and intellectual of Barzinji's time, states in his memoirs that the sheikh was inexperienced in politics and in managing the country. He emphasizes that in political questions there was nobody to whom he would turn for advice.[24] He asserts that there were some officers and educated persons who had returned from Turkey and Baghdad and wanted to help. But those people who had surrounded the sheikh to protect their own interests did not allow the well-educated and experienced men to get closer to Barzinji.[25]

The rhetoric of the "big man" reminds the reader of Sheikh Mahmud's political speeches as they were recorded in non-fiction works dealing with his period.[26] The prisoner narrates what he hears from the "big man" while he is sitting in a room from where he can see the meeting:

I have been struggling during recent years and I have suffered from imprisonment and insults. I have faced hard and bitter conditions. I left whatever I had — I started fighting and told myself that this nation should breath safely and live independently and freely, far from the reach of foreigners. I meant that we should also, like other nations, live with dignity in peace and happiness. We should also be rich and proud. Our religion should be at the forefront. I stood against England many times. I broke off my relations with the Turks. I appealed to the Russians and the Bolsheviks. A lot of blood was spilt. I have taken no things for myself. I have done all this for my religion and nation. I have asked that the nation find itself in welfare and good fortune, that our religion be widespread and held in high esteem. Nevertheless, despite all this, we see that many from our nation have deviated and followed the infidels. They have gone to the other countries and they serve the others' thoughts [...].[27]

This which the prisoner quotes from the "big man" is very similar to what Barzinji said upon his return from exile in India. On 22 September 1922, when he arrived in his residence in Silemani after one and half years in exile, while surrounded by thousands of his supporters, he stated:

My brothers, for the sake of our people and country, I did not forgo resistance and armed struggle. While I was injured and had been condemned to be hanged, I was sent to exile in India. As it was for the sake of my nation's freedom and independence, I was not perturbed. It was not the first time. I have now come back and reached you again. Believe me — until we gain our wish, freedom, I will not leave this demand and duty. If they do not give us our rights, we will steel ourselves to obtain them.[28]

From a literary point of view, there is a structural and technical shortage in the whole narration. From the very beginning, the first sentence, the narrator tells us that it is a dream he is narrating. Even the title of the first part of the story, the start of the dream, is a traditional Kurdish quote, *"Khuda bekheri bigere"* (May God bless it), which is common after awakening from a dream and hoping that its interpretation will be a good and pleasant one. Toward the end of the story, the narrator/dreamer is beaten because of his laughter. Logically he must have woken up from this severe beating and informed the reader. He does not do this, but as Baban rightly points out, despite this irrationality in the narration, the message or content of the story is quite clear.[29]

Masalay Wizhdan [The Question of Conscience]

Ahmad Mukhtar Jaf was born in Halabja, a town famous in Kurdish culture. His well-known tribe, and especially his parents, influenced his literary and political character. His mother, Adile Khanim (1859-1924), was a famous woman whose family had earlier, following the defeat of the Baban Emirate in 1851 by the Ottomans, fled to Sine, the capital of Ardalan Emirate in Iranian Kurdistan. She was born there and was educated in the religious schools of the city. After marrying Wasman Pasha, she moved to Halabja, her husband's city. She played a crucial role in administrating the affairs of Halabja alongside her husband. After his death in 1905, she took over all administrational responsibilities in the area of Sharazur.

According to Hawar, the Jaf tribe at the time of Sheikh Mahmud was divided into two groups: one, led by Adila Khanim and her sons, Ahmad and Izzet, supported the English against Sheikh Mahmud; the second group, led by Wasman Pasha's other son, Hamid Bag, from a different mother, supported Sheikh Mahmud's authority.[30] Ahmad spoke Persian, Arabic, Turkish, Kurdish, and English. He is mainly known as a poet and there are many patriotic poems in his published Diwan collection. Ahmad became the governor of Halabja in 1922, and in 1924 was elected as a member of the Iraqi parliament. In 1935 Ahmad Mukhtar Jaf was assassinated by some unknown men at the age of thirty-eight, when he was crossing the Sirwan river in the environs of Halabja. The list of suspects extends from his own men to agents of the Iraqi government and Sheikh Mahmud's loyalists.[31]

Some time before the First World War, the British officer Soane arrived in Halabja, disguised as an Iranian named Mirza Gholam Hossein. He worked for the Jaf tribe, and it seems that Soane very likely had contacts with the young Ahmad and influenced him as far as new literary forms, such as the novel, were concerned. *Masalay Wizhdan* was written in 1927 or 1928. Ihsan Foad published it in 1970 in Baghdad. At the beginning of the story, the narrator informs the reader that he was born in a small town, referring to the name of the town only by its first letter, H. It seems to simply be a reference to Halabja, the author's birthplace, as the other descriptions of the town in the story confirm this allusion. The narrator tells us that his family was poor and his father had been martyred in the Great War. His mother worked hard to help her son to go to the town's only school, but unfortunately after a short while she also passes away.[32] As such, the protagonist of the story is an infant. He grows up and becomes a well-known man. While his curious and sharp character in the beginning make him a critic of the current social and political situation, he later on becomes corrupt and hypocritical. If we consider him, based on his social position, a representative of the petty bourgeois of his time, we can accordingly see how the Kurdish petty bourgeois/middle class has, from its inception, been a weak and handicapped social stratum. Bearing in mind the importance of this social stratum for the rise of nationalism, the flourishing of national consciousness and the task of building the nation state, one can understand the reasons behind the failure of Kurdish nationalism and its bitter destiny in the early decades of the twentieth century. Capitalism as a social formation with its particular mode of production has been one of the necessary conditions for the rise of nationalism. The social structure of Kurdish society during the early twentieth century was far from having the prevalent features of a capitalist society, such as new social classes and modern professions. As Delanty and O'Mahony rightly argue, "[t]he rise of middle classes and the emergence of the modern professions have been important factors in the formation of nationalism."[33]

After the death of his mother, the character Zorab lives with his relatives for a while. Despite working hard, his relatives hardly give him enough food to survive. Later on, with the help of one of his father's old friends, he finds a job as a shop assistant. It is here that he notices how the shopkeeper, aiming to earn more money, frequently commits fraud in the shop. The young man once dares to ask his "master" whether the sharia, i.e. Islamic law, permits one to commit fraud in business. The master answers, "whatever makes living easier and more comfortable is allowed, except for murder and insulting other's honour."[34] When Zorab asks about the question of conscience, the master gets angry and forbids him from speaking. It is from here that the odyssey of the protagonist in a world full of fraud and hypocrisy begins. The fortune of the protagonist toward the end of the story, and the fact that he becomes a well-known, rich, and influential person in the country, shows that notions of "conscience" and "justice" in the context of the story are only the dreams of a child. Zorab refers to this bitter truth at the end of the story when he hears some girls complaining about their fortune, saying that "these things are not accepted by God and conscience." Zorab reacts to this statement by saying that "they [these girls] did not realise that God is very patient and has tolerated thousands of similar things. And conscience is only a word — nobody has seen it."[35] This pessimistic end of the story can be interpreted as a sign of the very sad fortune of modernity and modernization in Kurdistan, where ideas of independence, freedom, and justice are still vague and dreamlike visions.

Through Zorab's observations, we notice traditional ways of managing society's affairs. The early steps of modernization and its encounter with traditionalism are quite visible throughout. In a conversation between the protagonist and one of his employers, who deal in the tobacco trade, one sees how traditional business methods are preferred by the employer. A dialogue between him and Zorab, who suggests that his employer could have established a company with the other traders of tobacco in the region in order to produce cigarettes locally, instead of selling the tobacco at a cheap price, shows the traditional mode of production:

> My dear, it seems to me that you are also like the other mad educated ones. Our ancestors have been doing this for centuries, and we should follow suit.- Sir, our ancestors' wisdom was good for their own time. It is useless now. [...]- Even if you say a thousand similar words, the old wisdom is better than the new.[36]

Another aspect of social life that shows the traditional manner of living is how people perceived disease. The way that one aims to treat diseases, and the dismissal of modern medical knowledge as irrelevant, are good examples of the encounter between modernization and traditionalism. Zorab's argument regarding dirty water and the risks of using it is totally rejected by his employer's wife.[37] The family relations referred to in the story reveal the unenviable situation of the women and the way they are treated by their husbands.

There are some allusions in the story that show the protagonist's awareness of the West and its social structure. When he intends to cheat an owner of some land outside the town in order to take ownership of it, he says:

> I had become very interested in those lands and I wished I could find a way to get them from him. Because as it was the case in the West, especially in France, at that time, that unless one owned land or property, he/she was not called a Conte.[38]

Zorab regularly changes his jobs because he discovers his employers' fraud. His emphasis on conscience and being just in running one's affairs clashed with what his greedy employers wanted. In the field of agriculture, when he works for a businessman, he notices how the agents involved steal one third of the distributed seed for sowing and sell it for their own benefit. When the protagonist talks to someone who has stolen the seed and objects to this conscienceless deed, the man simply says that it is what all farmers do.[39] Throughout the harvest period, Zorab notices how a group of workers and farmers and their appointed observers cooperate to steal the harvested wheat. Having protested this, he becomes the target of a conspiracy and is accused of being a thief. The people surrounding him constantly remind him that there is no use in pointing out ideas of honesty, justice, and conscience.[40]

After experiencing many similar professions in his hometown, he goes to another town and aims to work as a writer of petitions.[41] Having failed at this, he is advised by a friend to bribe the relevant authority. It is from this point that he becomes a professional briber and bribe taker. He is regularly promoted and gets high positions in various offices. As a result he becomes very rich and an owner of much land and property. The formula for reaching such a high position had been prescribed by his friend. According to this advice, in order to be promoted, one should betray and lie. Zorab, loving to be promoted, accepts his friend's advice.[42] Soon, he starts visiting the authorities of the town and tries to praise them. After a while he becomes the head of tax collection. By experience, he learns how to get on well with all social and cultural norms. On one occasion, when he asks a Mullah, a religious authority in the mosque, to explain the quoted Arabic statements in Kurdish, he, being accused of disbelief, is severely beaten by the Mullah and the other praying men.[43] However, he manages to go to the Mullah's home and repent. Due to a competition over revenues among the newly arrived chiefs, Zorab falls in a trap. When one of his tax frauds has been reported to the authorities, he gets fired from his job. Soon he changes his attitude and aims to act as a revolutionary nationalist. Gradually Zorab finds himself in alienated from all society. Indeed, "[d]ue to the disjuncture of expectations and experience that has been central to modernity, many groups, in particular the middle classes, have been alienated from the prevailing social order."[44] Zorab's monologue after being fired from his job, when he has decided to pretend to be a revolutionary patriot, is quite revealing regarding the nationalist discourse of that period in Kurdistan, and his alienation from the existing social order:

> I wandered without any job in the city for a while. I found it shameful and degrading to work as a petition writer again, as I was a powerful man when I was a tax collector. After some contemplation, I concluded that it would be bad to be jobless. I pondered my best option. I decided to deal with the question of the nation and become a nationalist, so I wore a very nice suit and acted as would one who has graduated from a very great school. I carried a nice stick. I carried a bag full of papers and books, many of which I could not read. I started waking in the streets of the town, visiting coffee shops and homes. Wherever I sat I started talking about the country, independence and the pleasure of freedom and dignity. Everyday I sent a sonnet to be published, and sometimes I published an article, though none of them had been written by myself.[45]

This is indeed a good reference to the fact that the idea of an independent Kurdistan from the very beginning was controversial and was not articulated by the relevant social class or stratum. Bearing in mind the tribal origins of the author of the book, and the fact that his tribe was tilted against Sheikh Mahmud, one can see Zorab's conversion to being a nationalist perhaps as a sarcastic jape at Sheikh Mahmud's nationalist rhetoric.

Conclusion

There is a clear relationship between the two early Kurdish narratives and the socio-political situation in Kurdistan. A close reading of these two works contributes to a better understanding of the period under discussion. In both works, a certain degree of defamiliarization is visible. This gives a literary and artistic characteristic to the narrations, classifying them as literary works. The weak Kurdish middle class and its deprivation from the necessary modern social and cultural development can be clearly seen in both narratives. From a literary and narrative point of view, both fictions show the primitive features of the invented fictional worlds. Both fictions are narrated in the first person. None of the characters of *La Khawma* have names, which is a crucial sign of individuality. In *Masalay Wizhdan* it is only the protagonist of the story who is, on a few occasions, addressed by name. Despite the fact that the real time of the novel, i.e. the time that the story refers to, is a crucial period of the formation of Kurdish nationalism, the protagonist, by pretending to be a nationalist, parodies nationalism and represents only a sarcastic facsimile. The fact that for decades neither of these works was published independently in book form also indicates the problematic sociopolitical conditions for the development of the Kurdish novel and thus Kurdish nationalism. The unknown and partly known characters of these pieces of fiction are good representatives of Kurdish reality during the early twentieth century. They serve as proof of Hawthorn's argument: "Even though its characters and actions are imaginary they are in some senses 'representative of real life', as the dictionary definition has it; although fictional they bear an important resemblance to what exists outside its pages."[46] As Hawthorn states, the novel from the very beginning of its rise was associated with "movement and travel — with mobility, both geographical and social."[47] In *La Khawma* the main character leaves his city in order to find a job. In *Masalay Wizhdan*, Zorab's movements are all related to his desire to reach ever-higher social and political positions.

The rise of journalism contributed to the rise of modern Kurdish fiction. Jamil Saib published his short stories in *Peshkawtin* [Progress], which was launched by Major Soane in Silemani. Saib participated in a competition organized by *Peshkawtin* and won the prize for the third best Kurdish literary text. The social positions of both authors had a crucial role in enabling them to be the first writers of modern fiction— the novel and short story. Being the nephew of Piramerd, one of the most famous Kurdish intellectuals in the first half of the twentieth century, and a pioneer of Kurdish cultural nationalism, and furthermore having a close relationship with him, provided Saib with the opportunity to write and publish in Kurdish. The fact that he published his fiction in his uncle's journals shows the importance of such networks in promoting literature. It is worth mentioning that Piramerd knew the art of fiction well and had himself translated and published fictional works from Turkish into Kurdish. One can definitely say that Saib was in many ways influenced by Piramerd's acquaintance with modern literary genres.[48] Similarly, Ahmad Mukhtar Jaf's family background and his influential tribal social position facilitated his devotion to writing in this new literary genre, the novel. The significant position of Lady Adila, who was referred to as "the uncrowned queen" and "Khan Bahadur"[49] by the English, resulted in the continuous presence of the British officers at her court. It seems that the presence of the British officers, and especially Major Soane, at Lady Adila's court resulted in some contacts between him and the young Ahmad Mukhtar. Furthermore, Mukhtar's position as governor of Halabja gave him contacts with various British officers in the region during the early 1920s. Edmonds refers to a number of these kinds of meetings. He mentions that Soane had announced himself as a Persian scribe and merchant, and later assumed the post of Persian secretary for Lady Adila.[50] One can assume that there were discussions about modern European literary genres between Soane and the young and talented Ahmad. The fact that there are clear references to European civilization in *Masalay Wijdan* shows that Ahmad Mukhtar was aware of the modernity of European societies and their achievements.

8.

POLITICAL AND EVERYDAY RELIGION
IN KURDISTAN

Diane E. King[1]

"*Her ek dine xwe et hên*"—"Each one has their religion." This is a phrase that I have heard many times while carrying out ten stints of ethnographic research in the Kurdistan Region of Iraq since 1995, and traveling in the Kurdish-majority areas of Turkey and Syria. Kurdistan, the area spanning four states where ethnic Kurds are the majority and which they recognize as their homeland, is a place of both tremendous religious richness and stunning religious paradoxes. This phrase makes reference to multiple communities; in this rendering (there are variations on the saying), religion belongs to multiple communities. When I asked people in Zakho, a small town in the middle of Kurdistan, what was meant by it, they told me that this was a reference to the three Abrahamic faiths: Islam, Christianity, and Judaism. Until the founding of the state of Israel, Zakho had a significant Jewish population. It remains a majority-Muslim town, and also has significant Christian and Yezidi populations. The saying implies much about pluralism, diversity, and identity in Kurdistan. It suggests that identity is ethnic, but that religion adheres to ethnolinguistic identity: Islam to Kurdishness, Judaism to neo-Aramaic language and identity, and Christianity to neo-Aramaic language and identity as well. It seems to call for tolerance, which is both necessary and telling, given that the region has a history of significant religious conflict.

Kurdistan was controlled by two empires, the Ottoman and Persian, for several hundred years prior to the First World War, and in both cases religion, Sunni Islam in the former and Shia Islam in the latter, was integral to the regime and promoted as a key facet of national identity with which the Kurds at times had problematic relationships. Since the Kurdish homeland was divided into four states—Iraq, Syria, Turkey, and Iran—after the First World War, state approaches to religion have been more complicated. The majority of Kurds are Sunni Muslims, and significant minority faiths are also found in the Kurdish population. Yezidism is an indigenous, monotheistic religion with a unique set of beliefs and practices centering around the Peacock Angel. The Ahl-e Haqq (Kakai) believe in multiple divine incarnations, which is a heterodox idea to most of their neighbors.[2] Alevi beliefs are close to those of Shia Muslims, but with enough difference that they also constitute a religious minority. Eastern and Catholic Christians also constitute a significant religious minority in Kurdistan. In the ideal that I have heard from many people, and that is reflected in numerous practices, cultural conventions, and laws, religious categories are transmitted patrilineally, from fathers to their children. Language and ethnicity are as well. This straightforward system of transmitting religion from one generation to the next renders some groups "ethnic" minorities as well as religious, as in the case of Kurdistani Orthodox and Catholic Christians, even though their co-religionists elsewhere may not constitute an ethnic category.

Members of Kurdistan's varied faiths have lived side-by-side for centuries, although often with a limited understanding of each other's beliefs.[3] Opacity is a problem that has plagued specialists as well. The diversity of forms of religion in Kurdistan is extensive and impressive, defying easy generalizations. While an excellent body of scholarship on Kurdistani religion has already been produced there is a need for much more.[4]

One way to tell part of the religious story of the Kurds is to look at each country individually. I will begin with the two states, Turkey and Iran, where ethnic Kurds have little autonomy, and where many are at odds with the government.

In Turkey, a strong secularizing and nationalizing movement led by ethnic Turkish elites arose after the fall of the Ottoman Empire nearly a century ago. This movement, led by Mustafa Kemal Atatürk, sought to fashion Turkey into a "modern" country that maintained Sunni Islam as the de facto state religion, but in which religion was to recede very significantly. It was to create "[a] new community ... with the erasure of the sacred - the Sultan, the Caliph and Islam - in order for the sovereign state to be claimed in defined territories." While the late Ottoman and early republican Turkish state was at times genocidal toward its non-Muslim minority members, it wanted its non-ethnic-Turkish citizens who were Sunnis, which included much of its Kurdish population, to stop highlighting linguistic and ethnic difference. Sunni Muslim Kurds were implicitly and explicitly called upon to maintain their religious identity but drop their ethnolinguistic identity. Non-Sunni Kurds, most of whom adhered to the Alevi mystical branch of Islam, were pressured to become both Sunnis and Turks. Today, religious practices, belief, and identity among Kurds in Turkey still reflect these state homogenization efforts. As I have heard first-hand from many people in

Turkey, and as is well-documented by rights groups, Turkey is still a difficult place in which to adhere to any faith but Sunni Islam. For example, Human Rights Watch recently noted that the 2014 European Court of Human Rights ruling, Mansur Yalçın and Others vs Turkey regarding compulsory religious instruction in Turkish schools, revealed an "overwhelming emphasis on Sunni Islam."[5] The court ordered Turkey to allow students to be exempted from such classes. For Kurds in Turkey, religious and ethnic identity have long been intertwined or at odds. They are to a great degree inextricable from each other.

In Iran, most Kurds are Sunnis, although a significant number are Shia or members of smaller religious minorities. Most members of the majority Persian ethnic group are Shia. For most of the twentieth century, the state promoted "modernization" similarly to the Kemalists. It continued to affirm Shiism in a reserved way just as the Ottomans did with Sunni Islam, but did not rely on religion as a major aspect of the national identity it tried to build. Since 1979, however, the Iranian state has been a Shia theocratic dictatorship. Many Kurds in Iran are therefore, like Alevi Kurds in Turkey, both ethnic and religious minorities, and many Iranian Kurds have responded to heavy-handed state control by rebelling against the government — so far with virtually no success. Iranian Kurdistan is the area for which the least amount of scholarship exists on religions and religiosity.

Iraq and Syria are now the two states with significant Kurdish populations that have regions administered largely by ethnic Kurds and in the Kurdish language. The Kurdistan Region of Iraq was de facto independent from Baghdad from 1991 to 2003, and has been constitutionally autonomous since then. During my research stints there since 1995, I have observed the region become progressively more organized, and this organization has included religion. Citizens of the region are first Iraqi citizens, but because all Iraqi citizens are required to have an official, recognized place of residence that can only be changed through a bureaucratic process, Kurdistan's citizens are those Iraqi citizens whose official state paperwork – birth certificates, nationality card, and state identity card — affirm their official residence in the Region and, in the case of some official state documents, the individual's religion. Early in the Region's existence following its unofficial founding in 1991, Iraqi Kurdistan (which many United Nations agencies and governments then called "Northern Iraq") functioned like a sectarian state: "The North also has its own family law, which is applied in keeping with individuals' religion. This ensures that Christians are not subject to Islamic law."[6]

In Syria, where a new Kurdish-majority entity has been largely sovereign on the ground since 2012 with the tacit approval of the embattled Assad regime, a religious experiment can be said to be taking place within a grander set of social and political experiments. This entity, known as Rojava, is governed by the most powerful of several political parties there, *Yekîneyên Parastina Gel*, the People's Protection Units (PYD). The PYD claims to be religiously egalitarian, allowing those under its control to choose their own approach, or lack thereof, to religion.[7] The PYD's experiment is new, and it is also fragile because it is in many ways an outgrowth of the Syrian civil war, which is ongoing. As a visitor to the region several times in the late 1990s and early 2000s, I observed many signs of religious practice, such as mosque attendance by large numbers of men. There were also many signs of peaceful coexistence: in the town of Qamishli, for example, Sunni Muslim Kurdish and Syriac Orthodox people lived side by side as neighbors and friends. Such scenes are now a thing of the past in most of war-torn Syria. Even though the PYD has been accused of human rights abuses, Rojava still has a reputation as a place of refuge for religious minorities.[8] Although the PYD's ideology, rooted as it is in Marxism, leans atheist, it has more recently been influenced by the writings of political theorist Murray Bookchin and now espouses religious tolerance to a greater degree than atheism.

Religious pluralism, rights, and the state in Kurdistan

Kurdistan is a place dripping with the blood of past genocides carried out by a variety of different groups against their neighbors.[9] Kurds have more often been victims in recent decades, but they have also been perpetrators, especially in the late nineteenth and early centuries, such as when some tribes collaborated with the Ottomans in the Armenian genocide.[10] However, I would like to argue that at this moment in its history, Kurdistan has a legitimate claim as a place of impressive religious tolerance when one considers the high degrees of religious intolerance found among its neighbors. Especially in Rojava and the Kurdistan Region of Iraq, members of religious minorities from the surrounding area have found refuge. Many fled the horrors of the Islamic State (known locally as Daesh), which since 2014 has had a "caliphate" in eastern Syria and western Iraq. As of this writing, Daesh territory includes the significant city of Mosul, which has a large Kurdish population. Others fled other types of sectarian and scorched-earth violence. While many of the refuge-seekers remain in desperate economic straits, many people representing diverse collective identity categories have found relief from violence in Kurdistan.

Moreover, in at least two of Kurdistan's quadrants, religious conversion is tolerated to a greater degree than in nearby places. In Muslim-majority states, it is well-known that conversion from Islam is often frowned upon at best, and punishable by death at worst (as in Saudi Arabia), which is in violation of Article 18 of the Universal Declaration of Human Rights (United Nations General Assembly 1949). However, I have visited several Protestant Christian churches in Turkey and the KRG area in which the congregation largely comprises converts from Islam. Several such congregations meet relatively secretly, but in at least two cases the church has its own building and website, making no attempt to hide its existence. Even in those cases, I learned from affiliates of the churches that some in their ranks felt under threat by various members of the community or their families. However, they did feel comfortable enough to worship openly rather than in secret. Churches comprising converts are rare in Muslim-majority parts of the world, and I think it is significant that at least two exist relatively openly in Kurdistan.

Additionally, various groups that initially organized themselves around a sectarian or ethnic identity have been forming voluntary alliances and moving away from exclusively ethnic or religious labels. To name an early example, the political alliance formed between disparate political parties in 2004 called itself the "Kurdistani Alliance," not the "Kurdish Alliance" or the "Kurdistan Alliance." The alliance included the two largest and oldest parties in Kurdistan, the Patriotic Union of Kurdistan and the Kurdistan Democratic Party. It also included sectarian parties such as the Chaldean Democratic Union, Assyrian National Party, and Kurdistan Islamic Union, but also ideologically-based parties such as the Kurdistan Laborers Party, and the Movement of Kurdistan Oppressed and Farmers.

This relative openness is all the more remarkable given that the religious legalities in all four parts of Kurdistan are still restrictive. All Middle Eastern states record their citizens' ethnic and religious identity on at least some official state documents, and in Iran, Iraq, and Syria an infant's categories are taken directly from its father when the child's birth and citizenship are recorded and registered. State-recognized ethnic and religious categories are therefore not freely chosen or abandoned, but assigned at birth. They may have been freely chosen by the original male who first registered (or was registered) for citizenship, but they are not chosen by his patrilineal descendants. They are seen both by bureaucratic entities and by many individuals who have expressed as much to me as fixed and virtually immutable. In Iraq, for example, every citizen is legally assigned to one of the religions recognized by the state, which includes Islam, Christianity, Yezidism, and some other faiths with smaller numbers of adherents. Recent changes to the Iraqi Constitution, which took place in a context of occupation and war, have rendered the role of religious sects such as Shia, Sunni, Assyrian in personal status vague and inconclusive in terms of the law, but no legislation has overridden the assumption that has existed in the law since the 1920s: that all citizens belong to one of Iraq's recognized religions.[11] The Iraqi state, and by extension the Kurdistan Region, issues several required citizenship documents to its citizens. Following the birth certificate, an Iraqi citizen is required to obtain a nationality certificate, civil status identity card, and a residence card. In addition, in the 1990s the United Nations performed the basic functions of a census agency when it registered (in theory) all Iraqis in the Oil-for-Food program, which was part of the international sanctions regime against Saddam Hussein's Iraq. Each registrant was issued a food ration card, and this has come to constitute a fourth state identity document. Patrilineal religious descent is ratified in several ways by these documents. Iraq's Guide to Consular Affairs Abroad states flatly: "The Civil Status information for the child will reflect the Civil Status identity of the father."[12] The state assigns a religion (and sect in some cases) to the child based on the father's documentation. The state thus supports, in bureaucratic form, the broader set of notions and conventions that comprise "patriliny," a way of understanding descent and kin relationships that heavily favors male lines and downplays mothers' contributions to their children's identity. In patriliny, especially in its relatively restrictive form as found in Kurdistan, a patrilineage has a religion to a greater extent than an individual does. In my view, this goes a great deal of the distance toward explaining the lack of religious options and freedom seen in the region as a whole.

Theologically, religion in Kurdistan has long been patrilineal as well, more so than perhaps anywhere in the world. In Kurdistan, both Christians and Sufi Muslims, two groups that might be expected to emphasize spiritual over biological succession, have a long history of recognizing biological male succession in their leadership. I regard this as a remarkable innovation in both faiths. In the Christianity practiced in the Kurdistani mountains by Nestorian Christians (today called "Assyrians"), a priestly succession line was passed down within a patrilineage. Christianity has a long and elaborate history of dealing with the problem of priestly succession, but in the vast majority of times and places succession was considered to be spiritual rather than biological. However, in the priestly line of the Assyrian Patriarch (Mar Shimun), the spiritual and biological were conflated for centuries.[13] In Islam there is a similar example in Kurdistan. Sufi Islam is mystical, placing great emphasis on spiritualized practices and personalities and what they are seen to reveal of the divine. This would seem to point away from biological patriliny. However, as van Bruinessen notes, "Whereas the Naqshbandiyya-Khalidiyya rapidly spread across all of Kurdistan in the 19th century due to the practice of appointing locally influential ulama as khalîfa, the networks of the Qadiri shaykhs (especially the Barzinjis) remained family networks, with branches of the family established in different places acting as the chief spiritual authorities and with few or no outsiders in positions of importance."[14] As religious authority figures, sheikhs (Sufi leaders) represented power that was deeply embedded in social structure, but they could also be innovators. Almost by definition, a Sufi leader is a theological innovator or is descended from one. Therefore, sheikhs already occupied a social role that could easily be transferred to another arena, such as a tribal or nationalist movement, another twist on what could have remained a purely spiritual role.

Everyday religion in Kurdistan

Kurdistan is a place where for many people a relationship to and posture toward the divine is a strong element in their daily lives. I found that many, women especially, believed in the *jin*, spirts that can inhabit parts of a home or other locations. I have heard many conversations about what the *jin* can do, where they tend to congregate (such as in toilets), and the like. Many of these same women performed the Muslim prayers faithfully, up to five times per day. My research for the past two decades has mainly taken place in households in both rural and urban settings. Although Kurdistan has many religious leaders, it has seemed to me that beliefs about the divine are as much "bottom up" as promoted by people of influence. On encounter in a shop in Zakho illustrates some of the complexities of religion in Kurdistan. In 2008 I was shopping with a woman in whose home I was staying, and we went to a store that sold stationery supplies. As I bought a map there, my friend turned and said that she did not have a favorable opinion of that particular shop. She related that a few months earlier, she had tried to purchase a particular CD containing Quranic recitation. However, the shop owner told her that the government had banned that particular CD because it had not only recitation, but also interpretation. "They said that it is forbidden to interpret the Quran. This makes me so angry!" she fumed.

This conversation took place while Iraq was occupied by the United States, Britain, and their allies, and while an Islamist movement that eventually became the Islamic State struggled to gain strength. This was mainly taking place outside the Kurdish region, but during my two visits in 2008, I heard frequent references to violent Islamists, whom everyone said they feared, and it was clear from the number of checkpoints, blast walls, and the like that the KRG was taking security very seriously. And yet, my friend did not seem to make the connection between the product she sought to buy and a violent Islamist threat. For her, the government was simply being unnecessarily heavy-handed, quashing her attempt at one form of everyday religious observance.

On another occasion, I was in a village watching several women prepare a freshly-butchered goose for lunch when one of them told me about a past incident with a goose:

> One time we were here in the village and we were very, very hungry. One of the men butchered a goose. But he didn't do it right, so technically it was *haram* [forbidden in Islam] to eat it. All of us females refused to eat it for that reason. But our *pismam*s [father's brother's sons, cousins who are in the same lineage] said that they didn't care, and so we cooked it for them and they ate it. While they were eating they were mocking us, smacking their lips and saying how delicious it was. But we held firm, because we didn't want to break the religious rules like they were. I think we females are more religious than our male kin.

This vignette illustrates a possible difference in women's and men's degrees of religiosity, on which I have elaborated elsewhere.[15] It also illustrates religion's influence on daily practice. As the woman told me the story, the other women present reinforced what she said, emphasizing that they had been truly uncomfortable with hunger. They laughed as they recounted the story to me at a later time, but it seemed clear that the experience itself had not been as humorous.

Religion, exile, and return

Kurdistan's troubled history, a great deal of it having to do with religious conflict, has led to high rates of out-migration. Massive migration flows of Christians — Armenians, Chaldeans, and Assyrians — began in the nineteenth century following aggression by the Ottoman government, local Kurdish tribes, and others. Detroit, Michigan is a major center for Christian migrants from Iraq, including Kurdistan; Christians still in Iraq told me that they refer to Detroit as "New Telkaif," after the town at the edge of the Kurdistan Region of Iraq near Mosul. Kurdish people have been moving to the West, mainly as asylum seekers and refugees, for a shorter time, but early Kurdish migratory aspirations may well have been prompted by the example of the Christian populations around them. Significant Kurdish cities abroad, such as Nashville, Tennessee and San Diego, now have Kurdish mosques.

The phenomenon of refuge-seeking from Kurdistan began with religious conflict, and such conflict is still a major factor causing people to seek a better life elsewhere. Recent history has shown that such seeking ebbs and flows. As I write this, the Iraqi military and its Western partners are closing in on the city of Mosul, preparing to re-take it from the Islamic State. This will likely entail a very bloody series of battles, which will liberate many people who have spent more than two years in subjection and captivity, but also produce a new wave of religious refuge-seekers into Kurdistan and other adjacent areas. They will join thousands who have fled since 2014, many of them Yezidis from Shingal (Sinjar), whom the Islamic State targeted with genocidal ferocity. In 2016 I interviewed Yezidi and Muslim Kurdish survivors of the Islamic State's assaults on Shingal and Mosul in 2014. From safe vantage points in the Kurdistan Region, they described being rounded up, watching as friends and family members were abducted and taken away, and being transported to other locations from which they eventually escaped to the Kurdistan Region. They recounted harrowing experiences. One man, a medical professional, told of being forced to give medical care to Islamic State fighters. Each of them knew people who had not been heard from since their abduction, and it was clear that they feared they were either living a horrible existence, or dead. Their suffering was, their Daesh tormenters asserted, for theological reasons: because they regarded them as infidels.

Recent media reports and opinion expressed in the media and social media suggest that some groups in Kurdistan, particularly the Yezidis and Christians, may soon "go extinct." However, my view is cautiously optimistic. In March 2002, while on a drive through a mountainous area of the Kurdistan Region of Iraq, we stopped our vehicle near a Christian village that had been rebuilt following the Iraqi government's killing spree and campaign of village destruction in the late 1980s, perhaps the darkest period in Kurdistani history to that point. Seeing some children and young adults by the side of the road, we stopped the car, greeted them and asked how they were doing. One young woman smiled broadly as she looked at us, and said in a jubilant tone, "It's good now. Everyone is coming back." "From Baghdad?" I asked. "Not just from Baghdad," she said happily. "From all over the world!"

My hope is that in the short term, countries that are stable and able to accept people fleeing the collective violence in and around Kurdistan will accept increasing numbers of asylum-seekers and refugees. The urgent humanitarian situation calls for this and much more. But in the longer term, despite the terrible waves of violence, much of it religiously framed, my hope is that words such as those of the young woman by the side of the road will again be uttered by return migrants in Kurdistan and the surrounding region, and that the trend toward religious tolerance now seen in parts of Kurdistan will be extended both in scope and geography. Millions of people have now been exposed to a genocidal, exploitive, and dominating form of religion. I predict that when the Islamic State's survivors have the opportunity, and as they reflect on the horrors they have witnessed and seek to honor victims, they will build a society that extends tolerance in new directions.

9.

THE SHIFTING BORDERS OF CONFLICT, DIFFERENCE, AND OPPRESSION

KURDISH FOLKLORE REVISITED[1]

Christine Allison

Why isn't folklore dead yet? Its ability to pull millions of post-modern Westerners into cinemas with fantasy blockbusters and fairy tales redux shows that even now the cultural vocabulary of Grimm's fairy tales and the *Arabian Nights* remains a resource for narrating lives, managing fear, and magical thinking. Through global networks, Kurdish society can share these international riffs on folk culture, but the national folklore is not seen through the European or American-style post-ironic lens. Kurdish folklore is a serious national asset, a primary source for collective memory and Kurdish history. At the same time it is viewed with ambivalence, in true Orientalist style.

Folklore matters in Kurdistan because it became an integral part of the nation-building process of the late Ottoman Empire and its successor states, especially Turkey, which then influenced nation-building in Pahlavi Iran. The European romantic nationalism which inspired the process also drove Soviet formulations of national-ity, which in turn influenced Kurdish intellectuals in the homelands.[2] This chapter will be the first in English to interrogate Kurdish folklore studies, firstly by describing briefly the politics of folklore, not only in the well-studied field of Turkey,[3] but also across the under-studied other homelands.[4] I then consider how these politics affect academic folklore study, considering the issues facing scholars seeking to move beyond the Orientalist legacy of the past, especially if, like myself, they are not writing from within the Kurdish nationalist project. Finally, by considering a previously unpublished text, I will demonstrate briefly how the methodologies of contemporary folkloristics can be used to identify and analyze texts which take us to the heart of discourses of power, oppression, and suffering.

The politics of folklore in Kurdistan

The term "folklore" rightly makes us uncomfortable. We sense its ideological nature as we feel its contradictory forces. Its overtones of positive identity, of belonging and warmth, family hearths and village festivals, mask an inherent "othering": folklore as the province of the ignorant, of old women, unschooled men, and little children. In national terms, "we" celebrate it as our heritage even if we are "modern." This ambivalence is already present in the work of Johann Gottfried Herder in the 1770s, which set out the key notions of romantic nationalism fundamental to Europe's modernity project.[5] Long before 1846, when the English antiquarian Thoms coined the word folklore, Herder had outlined the essential characteristics of the *Volk* which still resound today: the purity of their ancient traditions, their intimate and long-standing relationship with their homeland, the fundamental importance of their unique and authentic language, the unique spirit of each *Volk* which imparts their distinctive character and framework to which "we" as countrymen can all belong. Herder's phrase "one people, one fatherland, one language"[6] strikes a chord with anyone familiar with Kemalism. But the "folk" which Herder considered to be the source of "spirit" were to be distinguished from the "rabble" in the streets,[7] and his followers were apt to make a distinction between worthy and vulgar forms of popular culture.[8] On the gender front, Herder acknowledges the role of mothers in transmitting tradition to children, but assigns women a subordinate, non-intellectual role.[9] Herder was only one of a succession of intellectuals involved in the construction of a worthy "folk" without any interest in the lived lives of non-élite persons.[10]

As the scholarly construct of the "folk" developed, so did this "othering" of its real-life members. Notions of progressive stages of human development were also systematized. By the late nineteenth century Edward Burnett Tylor was arguing that folklore represented remnants of people's savage state, and Andrew Lang was writing that where an anomalous cultural survival existed among the civilized, its explanation could be sought by considering similar practices among more primitive peoples.[11] Despite their timeless knowledge, "the folk"—even the European "folk"—may be grateful for the intellectuals' attention when they come to collect material,[12] since they are incapable of interpreting and evaluating it themselves. Only intellectuals can mediate between past and present and represent the interests of the "folk," who cannot step across the class divide in the same way.[13] Thus, even outside the colonial project, folklore study constitutes a vehicle of hegemonic knowledge production. The inequality inscribed into such constructions of the folk is still palpable despite the revolutions in thought of the late twentieth century, when "history from below" came to the fore and more engaged scholars sought to explore the dynamics of power expressed in subaltern discourse.[14]

Folklore, then, is a polyvalent term: a force for inclusivity but also for othering, the latter directly related to notions of modernity and progress. Since its beginnings, folklore collection has been formulated as a rescue operation because the *Volksgeist* and *Volksdichtung* are in danger due to an event, or process, which ruptures the long-standing status quo of folklife.[15] The Kurds' turn toward folklore during the twentieth century is no exception to this.

Folklore and nation-building in the Kurdish home states

Herder's heritage, mediated from Europe into the late Ottoman Empire and its successor states, and through Russia into the nationalities policy of the Soviet Union,[16] remains palpable in Kurdish talk about folklore today. In both the Kurdish homelands and the Soviet Union, folklore studies were founded on the idea that "folklore" reflects the "soul" of the nation. Contemporary Kurdish nationalist discourse is dominated by two "strands" or traditions, emanating from the movement in Turkey and the quasi-State of Iraqi Kurdistan respectively. Here I will describe the notions of folklore operating in the Kurdish home states (for reasons of space omitting the USSR, which despite its small Kurdish population published the most substantial anthologies),[17] and then outline how they have been taken up since the 1960s by the Kurdish nationalist movements of Turkey and Iraq.

Interest in folklore in the Ottoman Empire had begun in the nineteenth century, with the Tanzimat writers' desire to find a literature couched in the language of the people rather than the speech of the Ottoman élite.[18] Turkism's founding ideologue, Ziya Gökalp, was an enthusiast; he amassed a large collection and identified folk literature as the true Turkish literature.[19] As early as 1919 we see Kurdish complaints, made by Kemal Fevzi in the Kurdish review *Jîn* in 1919, that Gökalp had modified Kurdish tales to make them fit Turkish Dede Korkut models;[20] already the cultural artefacts of folklore could be designated national property and thus susceptible to theft. The early Kurdish nationalists were members of the Ottoman upper classes, as influenced as their Turkish counterparts by prevailing European and Slavic ideas; some had studied in Germany. *Kurdistan*, the newspaper founded by Miqdad Midhat Bedir Khan in 1896, aimed to bring the benighted Kurdish masses into the light of modern civilization. As Ottomanism developed into Kurdish nationalism, however, Herder's concept of folk knowledge became more prevalent; in the pages of the magazine *Jîn* (1919) Kurdish folklore is presented as containing valuable ancient knowledge.[21] The idea that all nations deserve self-determination regardless of their level of "progress" is also linked to President Woodrow Wilson's Fourteen Points.[22]

Among the Kurds' new home states, the Republic of Turkey gave perhaps the most coherent formulation of the place of folklore in the life of the state, using Gökalp's principles.[23] After 1923, folklore, like linguistics and history,[24] was co-opted into the nation-building project. This view of folklore as part of the age-old wisdom of the Turkish people permitted it to be used in the construction of a new civic Turkish identity, where loyalties could henceforth be to the Turkish nation-state rather than to the traditional religious and social structures which had commanded popular allegiance in the Ottoman Empire.[25] The impact of Kemalist policies on Kurdish culture, the denial of Kurds' existence in Turkey and the ban on Kurdish publication until the 1990s have all been well studied elsewhere.[26]

Folklore studies in Turkey took both academic and popular routes. From 1924 it was taught at the Institute of Turcology in the University of Istanbul.[27] Georges Dumézil, invited to teach by Atatürk,[28] profoundly influenced many of his students, including Pertev Naili Boratav.[29] In 1927 the new Folklore Association recruited members nationwide and encouraged them to collect material. Strongly nationalist, it advocated mapping the folkloric cultures with a view to identifying and assimilating non-standard linguistic and cultural forms.[30] Its place was taken in 1932 by the "people's houses" as fora for collection and publication of folklore in many cities.[31] At first academics worked closely with these initiatives, but in the climate of popular nationalism of the late 1940s, the academic approach and European training fell under suspicion. Attempts by Boratav to "de-nationalise folklore," as Öztürkmen says, were seen as a political act and punished as such.[32]

In Iran, the Pahlavi Shahs (1925-79) imitated Atatürk's centralized nation-building model in many respects, especially in the enforcement of Persian as the sole official language, which included a ban on publication in Kurdish,[33] although this was relaxed during periods of government weakness such as 1941-53. Unlike Turkey, of course, Iran has never represented itself as a homogenous state.[34] Interest in Iranian folklore included that of Kurds, seen as an Iranian people. In 1961 Abolqasem Enjavi broadcast a radio appeal for folklore collection;[35] listeners responded with enthusiasm. Their findings were broadcast, and then published in the 1970s in a collection called "The Treasury of Popular Culture".[36] Under the Islamic republic, folklore was apt to be branded *khorafat* or "superstition." Collections were appropriated by state bodies such as the broadcasting agency and Enjavi's program was discontinued, although some cultural publications such as the Kurdish-language magazine *Sirve* included articles about folklore.[37] In 1995, Ayatollah Khamenei spoke in favor of promoting native cultures as a defense against creeping Westernization, after which folklore studies revived considerably.[38] Since Khatami's presidency, Iranian Kurds have begun a new wave of cultural activity; with the advent of new technologies and satellite television the PKK's sister party PJAK has gained ground against older Iranian Kurdish political parties, bringing the PKK's cultural ideology with it.[39]

Syria was a major site of Kurdish ideological production until the mid-1940s. Herder's notions are discernible in the work of the brothers Kamuran (1895-1978) and Celadet Bedir Khan (1893-1951), exiles from Turkey. After the Ararat rebellion in Turkey failed (1927-30), they embarked on cultural nationalism. Their periodical *Hawar* [The Call] (1932-43) published Kurdish folkloric texts, gave scholarly descriptions in the French-language sections, and made explicit its view of folklore as a resource for developing the Kurdish language, since it contained numerous old words not found elsewhere, and unlike more everyday Kurdish, had not been adulterated by foreign words.[40] Commentaries were given on how the folklore displayed Kurdish customs or personal qualities. Despite *Hawar*'s undoubted historical importance, its circulation was very small and, even allowing for the practice of reading it aloud in teahouses and *diwankhanes*, it can only have reached a small proportion of Kurds at large. During the 1940s French diplomatic and military personnel worked closely with the editorial team.[41] Another friend, the priest and teacher Thomas Bois, reflected prevailing attitudes with *The Kurds' Soul Revealed Through Their Folklore*, published in 1946.[42]

Iraq presents a very different case study from Turkey, especially before the declaration of the Republic in 1958. Whilst acknowledging the Kurds' existence, the new Iraqi state embraced a pan-Arab historical discourse foregrounding Sunni identity, though it was always "plagued by the populace's inability to agree upon a set of foundational myths."[43] After 1958, however, folklore was more systematically co-opted into government-controlled mechanisms of state-building. The early Republican period saw an upsurge in journalism, publishing, and broadcasting, where leftist intellectuals working with Abdul Karim Qasim saw the emphasis of folk tradition and its collection and documentation as a way of contacting the culture of the masses. Under the Ba'ath, the attempt to achieve hegemony centered on cultural production: history writing, literature, folkloric studies, or art, particularly as it related to reinterpreting the past.[44] Their efforts during the 1970s suggest that they saw folklore as a site of popular meaning and relevance which needed to be recaptured from the intellectuals linked to the Communist party who had privileged it before them. Not only did many cultural and academic publications feature folkloric material, but the state even took control of all handcraft production in 1970 through the Institute of Popular Handcrafts.[45] By comparison with Turkey, there is relatively little scholarship on folklore methodologies used in Iraq; the folklorist Abd al Hamid al-'Alwaji traced the Iraqi school of folklore to the nineteenth-century German tradition.[46] Some contemporary Kurdish academics were trained in the Soviet Union.[47]

Kurdish folklore and the nationalist movements of Turkey and Iraq

Since the Turkish and Iraqi states made use of folklore for nation-building, it is not surprising that the Kurdish movements emanating from these states have done the same.[48] The 1960s saw many changes in Turkey, notably the reactivation of the People's Houses closed in 1951.[49] Meanwhile some publications incorporating Kurdish material appeared: the leftist journal *Dicle-Firat* included folktales, as did journals produced by Kurdish students in the diaspora.[50] Works on Kurdish studies from elsewhere became more available. In the 1970s many *aşiks* (traditional singers) were part of the flourishing leftist movement.[51] However, Kurdish culture remained low-status; in everyday life, people felt ashamed of outward signs of "Kurdish" culture (such as traditional clothes).[52] In school, children were taught that Turkish was scientifically proven to be beautiful and high-status; this continues today.[53] After the 1980 coup and the new constitution of 1982, draconian restrictions were again imposed on non-Turkish linguistic and cultural expression. Cultural production shifted decisively to the diaspora, especially Sweden, where it remained until the 1990s. In Turkey, recordings of traditional performances continued to circulate illicitly, alongside those of political singers.

The PKK's cultural program began in the mid-1980s, with musical groups called *koms*, which aimed to reach the Kurds of Europe as well as the homeland and "denoted the folk music as the source of unspoilt national identity ... The kom musicians identified their mission as stopping the assimilation of Kurdish folk music by the 'colonists.'"[54] Much of the music was contemporary and political and produced in the diaspora.[55] By the early 1990s the Kurdish movement included some who privileged traditional folk performances and others who considered that it was the revolution itself which should be enshrined in Kurdish art forms. Although the latter predominated, interest in Kurdish folklore and its collection has grown since the 1990s. Under Turgut Özal's presidency, Kurdish publication in Turkey was legalized in 1991, which paved the way for various PKK-linked initiatives, notably the establishment of a *Navenda Çanda Mezopotamya* "Mesopotamia Cultural Centre" and a Kurdish Institute in Istanbul. These spread to other cities, serving as a platform for Kurdish historical and linguistic study. More *koms* were established throughout eastern Turkey and independent Kurdish singers were also popularized.[56] Kurdish parties in local government have devoted considerable resources to cultural activity, such as festivals; indeed their own constituencies have criticized this when times are hard for many constituents.[57] Diyarbakir's *dengbêj* house, established to showcase traditional singing, opened in 2007. Since Turkish state media still associate loaded words such as "tribal" and "developing" with Kurds, valorizing Kurdish culture remains a priority for the movement.[58]

Iraqi Kurdistan, which has exercised de facto autonomy since 1991, presents a very different case from Turkey;[59] since that date, the promotion or enactment of Kurdish folklore is not in itself an act of contestation as it is in Turkey. Moreover the Kurdish region's emergence as a quasi-state since 2003 has led to an evolution of state institutions. As early as 1992 local Kurdish TV stations were established; these moved to satellite and multiplied further.[60] Kurdish magazines and newspapers, mostly (like the TV stations) organs of political parties, became numerous over time (though print runs were small), whilst public education replaced Arabic elements with Kurdish ones as resources became available. The Ministry of Culture presides over much folkloric knowledge production; both public and private museums with folkloric collections exist. *Dengbêjî* or traditional singing is less institutionalized than in Turkey, but much of the performance takes place via TV stations belonging to the two dominant political parties, KDP and PUK. Kawa Morad suggests that through these activities the Kurds of Iraq are articulating their claim to statehood, that the collections and museums established since 1991 are seen as assets which help qualify the Kurds for true nationhood.[61] Thus in both Iraq and Turkey, plus the diasporic spaces dominated by the PKK,[62] Kurdish political parties function as gatekeepers to the popular heritage.

The PKK positions itself as definitive prophetic interpreter, claiming ownership of "art" in Kurdistan. Sarıtaş quotes PKK leader Abullah Öcalan:

> In a Kurdistan without the PKK art is dead, and the remaining cannot be called art. The art of the Turkish Republic is an act of invasion. The art of Turkish Republic is an act of suffocation, assimilation and clearance of the existing traditions and activities of people in Kurdistan by the bourgeois. So, art is dead. Therefore emergence of the PKK is the resurrection of the art. It is the source of art, it is the foundation laid down.[63]

In the same speech, from the early 1990s, he also says that without the party there would be no folk music. Thus the authentic national culture, i.e. folk culture, downplaying regional variation, is the remedy for the act of violence perpetrated by the Turkish state.[64] Through the movement one can learn not only music and dancing but Kurdishness itself.[65]

Hamelink's penetrating discussion discerns an "Orientalism of self" in the movement's acceptance of Western and Turkish categories of thinking and its project of modernization of the Kurdish people. However, she adds:

> By defining Kurdish modernity as a project exceeding the immediate local political conflict and as a solution valid for all humanity, but originating in Kurdish society, the PKK ultimately attempts to de-Orientalise itself.[66]

Thus we see how Kurdish folklore is a space for morality, and why tension exists between *dengbêj* folk singers and party activists, who seek to limit performance of songs about local conflicts between Kurdish groups which frame *aghas* and chieftains as heroes, in favour of less "manly" love songs and songs of resistance against the state.[67]

The politics of Kurdish folklore study

The ambivalent relationship between Kurdish nationalism and folklore touches the smaller world of academic study. Most Western Orientalist representations of Kurdish culture of the nineteenth and early twentieth centuries (Jaba is an exception) foreground "folk" elements.[68] Modern (post-1960s) Kurdish movements were predominantly secular leftists reluctant to privilege the long Kurdish tradition of *medrese* (religious school) learning, considered retrogressive by nationalists since the end of the Ottoman Empire. Currently a strong body of Kurdish literary scholars is stressing the need to work on a wider variety of Kurdish authors and publish texts from recently opened manuscript collections. This expresses not only a need to reclaim Kurdish learned heritage, but is also a reaction against the "folklorization" of Kurdish culture. Such tension between "folklore-as-national-asset" and "folklore-as-primitive" need not be incoherent but is rather a dialectic, reflecting the huge role that Orientalism has played in the evolution of both Turkish and Kurdish national consciousness.

Although we can argue that Kurdish intellectuals, particularly the Bedir Khans, Orientalized the Kurds, it is the Orientalism of hegemonic outsiders which hurts most. Currently significant differences exist between academic studies written from within and without the Kurdish nationalist project. Yüksel 2011, for example, comes from within, examining both folklore and the *medrese* tradition as vectors of survival of Kurdishness. Implicit within the work is a moral stance, of the chronicling of virtuous survival against adversity. The mechanics of this survival are explored in Turgut's 2009 study of folklore and oral history, whose analytical perspective is closer to the "ethnography of speaking" approach. Other Kurdish researchers base their fieldwork in parts of Kurdistan not their own, nuancing their field experience and positionality.[69] Some exemplary studies of Kurdish folk production, especially music (Çakir and Saritaş), are written by Turkish nationals, many not identifying as Kurdish, who form part of the new generation of engaged social science scholars exploring Turkey's hidden past. And there remain the "outsider" non-Kurdish scholars, mostly European, most recently Hamelink's engaged analysis[70] of Turkey's *dengbêj* singers and their ideological context.[71] Given the Orientalism of past outputs on the Kurds by Westerners, it is we outsiders who have the most to prove; and we can hardly complain that some Kurdish scholars consider that non-Kurds should not be studying their culture at all. But the ethnographic ideal seeks diverse positionalities and inclusive study. How then can we take Kurdish folklore studies forward, especially if we are not Kurdish ourselves?

American folklorist Margaret Mills, who has worked in Afghanistan and Tajikistan, puts the position with characteristic clarity:

> Nonfolklorists continue to view folklorists as reactionary champions of the past and anti-liberal opponents of liberal nationalism ... In contrast, folklorists perceive themselves as champions of cultural democracy - of the viability of minority cultural systems within large national or transnational economies.[72]

This aspiration compels Western folklorists to point out how Kurds are "folklorized" by their home states; we also note where Kurdish minorities are "folklorized" by the Kurdish mainstream, which wins us far fewer friends.[73] Kurdish hegemony, which understandably values Kurdish unity above almost all else, takes a dim view of academic reporting of intra-Kurdish tensions. Criticism is inevitable, but the onus is upon us to make sure that our use of data and discussion of positionality are robust enough to make it groundless.

Folklore invites engaged scholarship from insiders and outsiders alike. As early as 1958, Americo Paredes conceptualized folklore as "politically-charged expressive forms that define the shifting borders of conflict, difference, and oppression".[74] This speaks directly to Kurdish studies now. Outsider scholars no longer allow folklore research to be a simple exercise in collection and comparison. Kurdish folklorists working within the Kurdish milieu have more leeway; their audiences already understand socio-political conditions and cultural meanings. Outsiders, however, have a responsibility to show awareness of social context and power dynamics.[75] We are morally obliged to make the producers of the folklore we discuss partners in knowledge production as far as possible. This entails constant striving for mutual comprehension in the field and clarity about end product. Working partnerships between "outsider" and "insider" scholars are one way forward (e.g. Kreyenbroek and Rashow on Yezidi texts), though rarely will all other community members agree with the insider scholar. New communications technologies enable outsider scholars to remain in discussion with partners in the field, who can often see and comment on the end product. Disagreements inevitably ensue; nevertheless, these technologies which encourage us to see our work as an ongoing process of communication, an utterance in an unending, multi-voiced dialogue, may help to liberate Western academics caught in the bind of measuring academic "outputs" as quantifiable end product, which our own state infrastructures impose on us.

Contemporary folkloristics, whether we define it as a separate discipline[76] or see it as a liminal area on the fringe of several disciplines, has much to offer Kurdish studies. Its liminality enables us to engage with various theories in the social sciences, philosophy, and literary studies, since folk genres and indigenous knowledge often play a differing role within the stateless nation from the Eurocentric models suggested by many much-cited theorists. For instance, public discourse in Kurdistan shows a much greater role played by orality than literacy, despite the latter's huge prestige. Folkloristics offers methods of analyzing discourse, in terms of text and practice, which, when applied to Kurdish models, may enable us to scrutinize theorists such as Benedict Anderson or Jürgen Habermas.[77] Young scholars in Kurdish studies are currently somewhat reverential toward the gods of theory, but in the future there will no doubt be more such questioning going on. With this and the closer relationship between academics and research partners in the field, Kurdish folkloristics may come closer to Charles Briggs' aim of developing theory and practice so that we can make a meaningful link between, as he puts it, "theorizing the vernacular" and "vernacular theorizing." [78]

Text in context: "Open the prison gates!"

To conclude, I will apply folkloristics scholar Richard Bauman's "philology of the vernacular" to a text to illustrate some of the politics underlying the act of utterance. Bauman, an influential "ethnographer of speaking" (an approach pioneered by sociolinguist Dell Hymes) who has written much about language ideologies, describes a method which pays close attention to text within context, based on the principle that texts are culturally constituted. This is by no means the only way of studying discourse in detail, but it seems undeservedly little known in Kurdish studies. It is important to note that Bauman's notion of a "text" is a crafted and bounded piece of discourse, marked in some way which enables it to be detached from one context and placed in another.[79] This notion does not demand that the text be written or that different iterations be word for word the same.

I will discuss a woman's lament: an extemporized genre, but definable as a "text" by Bauman's criteria. Although a statement from an individual concerning her feelings in the moment, it is also "folklore," since the woman's lament is melodized in traditional ways and covers established repertoires of language and theme. I will briefly consider the text in a "vertical" perspective, by noting how it relates to previous lamentations (genre conventions), and then in a "horizontal" perspective, by locating it within sociopolitical discourses of its time. Thus, rather than poetics and performative details, I will focus rather on the social and affective politics of the performance. This forms part of what Bauman calls the pragmatics of the text, as opposed to its form and content.

On a hot day in July 1992 in a house in the collective village of Qush Tepe near Erbil, "Samira"[80] laments among family and friends. Only women live in Qush Tepe; all members of the Barzani tribe, they were moved here following deportation to the south of Iraq from their home in Barzan.[81] They weep for husbands, brothers, fathers, sons, never seen since the day in 1983 when Ba'ath government forces removed all males between the ages of 7 and 70 as a punishment for the Barzanis' anti-government activities in the Iran-Iraq war.[82] Samira rocks back and forth as she laments, weeping inconsolably in between, while friends offer comfort; others then take up the lament, voicing their own sorrows, before everyone falls to talking, explaining their situation to their Western visitor. The text below reproduces Samira's performance from the beginning of my recording until a second voice joins her.

Keserdar û birîndarê bêcab u su'alên xwe ne

Wa li dunyayê wê babo wê birayao,

Dayka 'Arif ebdal û birîndar e

Heku berê simbêla lê gîr nebû o dayê

We are grieving, wounded for those who don't have answers or questions [asked about them] in the world, o father, o brother

Arif's mother is wretched and wounded

His moustache was not yet grown, mother,

Ne bo xatira Xodê û sê pêxembera bî

Mezinêd hukumet û dewleta

Me ne gotebit derga zindana wa

Bo me veke wey babo wey birayo

It wouldn't honor God and the three prophets

You world leaders,

If we didn't say, open the prison gates

For us, o father, o brother.

Ebdal û birîndar în dayê

Eva sala dehê di zebirînin xo da o

A tikên û tinalîn dayê o

We are wretched and wounded, mother

This is the tenth year of constant pain, oh,

THE KURDISH QUESTION REVISITED

We sigh and moan, mother.

Barzanî xerîbe e ne xudan
Tu nepenî bi me re wa bike o
Ey Xodê, ey Xodê hawara me tu Xodê

The Barzanis are exiled, lord,
Come and help us secretly
Oh God, oh God, we only have you to help us.

Belê namûsa eshabiya ya li me keftiye o
Sere cada xem mastir e û li derga zindanê wa dayê

Our clan's honor has fallen away from us by the roadside,
This pain is worse than the prison gates, o mother

Ebdal û birîndarîn bo me bi tenê
Yêd berê digo wa dayê wa dayê wa dayê o

Wretched and wounded, this is all we have
The older ones were saying, o mother, mother

Xwişka hingo xerîb e bira o
Wa bira wa bira wa birao wa babo

Your sister said she is an exile, o brother
O brother, o father

Wellah mezinêd hikumet û dewleta o
Daykê lava nebine çi xestexana o
Illa bibine ber derga zindana o

KURDISH FOLKLORE REVISITED

O you world leaders,
Don't take our boys' mothers to any hospital,
Take them instead to the prison gates

Wella daykê lava di birîndar in o
Bi şev û roja di ser birînêd xo
A dikin û dinalîn o

Our boys' mothers are wounded
Day and night we sigh and mourn over our wounds

Talan e û talan e
Talan e mezina û maqwîlan o
Li Barzaniya talan e

This is ruin, ruin
It is ruin, for leaders and important people,
It is ruin for the Barzanis

Hebis û zîndan di bê bace ne, Xurbeta min, xwişkê o
Daikê lava û xwişkê biraya o di bêçare ne o

O Ghurbet, my sister, the prisons cost nothing[83]
Our boys' mothers, our brothers' sisters have no way out

Wellah lavêd me qewî kiçekokan in
Nehatibîne hedê zîndana
O berê simbêla lê gîr bibû o

Our boys are much too young
They shouldn't have gone down into the prisons
Before their mustaches had grown

THE KURDISH QUESTION REVISITED

Wellah melakêd daykê lava kerbibûn
Her bo nalenala binê zîndanê o
Heku dest dihavêtine kelek û tenis̨têd Barzaniya o

The livers of our boys' mothers were slashed
Because of the wailing coming from the depths of the prison
Whenever hands struck the flanks, the ribs of the Barzanis

Her bo xerîba bê cab û soalêd xo me o
Heta dinya li dayka 'Arif xirab dibit o
Destêt wê didane ser'êk dayê o

I am exiled for those who do not have questions and answers
Until death comes for Arif's mother
And [she is laid out] with her hands clasped together

Wellah heçyê xerîbiya bivê
Bila bête nav 'eyalê Barzaniya o
Xerîb im bo Barzaniya o

Whoever wants [to see] sadness
Let him come amongst the children of the Barzanis
I am exiled/bereft for the Barzanis

Wellah heku daikê lava êvariya diçine bin girs̨êd nivînka
Dibên nahêneve li serê sindoqa ye o
Wa dayê wa dayê o

If our boys' mothers go in the evening to the foot of their [children's] beds
They will say that they won't come back in a coffin

KURDISH FOLKLORE REVISITED

Heku daikêd lava gerêd cemedaniyêd sor bilind dikin

Ligel şwitkêd spî wa daye o

Wa dayê mêlak lê dihelweriyên o

Belê Xodê ruha me nabet o

If our boys' mothers hold up the twisted red turbans

With their white sash, o mother

O mother, it makes our hearts crumble away

But God does not take our souls

Dê bila 'ebda te berî xo bideto

Me bi tenê xeribiyê derga zîndanê

Belê nobedarêt zîndana wa li me di xayînin

Wê babo wê bira o

O let your servant go

We only have the grief[34] of the prison gate

The prison guards are surely betraying us

O father, o brother

Nexo ma jîna me bo çi ye

Piştî qafila Barzaniya û

Piştî xodanêt 'elaga li me avêtine di munşe'a da o

So what is our life for?

After the deportation of the Barzanis

After they were herded onto a bus, holding only [a few belongings in] a carrier bag

Allah Xodê dilê hungo nerm bibî

Dergê zîndana yan îskêt Barzaniya nişa me bidin

Da dayikê lava bêhîvî bibin o

May God make your hearts soft

So that you show us the prison doors, or the bones of the Barzanis

So that our boys' mothers can be without hope

Eyalê me xeríbe ye li serê cadê

Heta êvarî bêrka di destî da

Bo Soran û bo Goran o

Our children are strangers on the road

Until the evening they have shovels in their hands

[Working] for the Soran and Goran

Wey xerîbiyê wey xerîbiyê

Wey xerîbiyê wey exsîriyê o

Ez nemînim bo Barzaniya o

O exile and loss

Exile and poverty

I don't want to live for the Barzanis.

In formal terms, it is more accurate to call these lamentations "melodized words" rather than song, as in Amy de la Bretèque's ground-breaking research on Yezidi laments in the Caucasus, which uses methodologies from the ethnography of speaking. The melodic range of these laments is rather limited, well under an octave, which may be a mechanism for controlling the content.[85] Stanzas are short, with a fall in pitch at the end of each verse and a return to the key-note at the end of the stanza. Like the Kurdish *kilam/lawik/stran* songs[86] which eulogize heroes or sing mournfully of battles and love affairs, they are performed in a melancholic musical mode— indeed, there are some shared conventions of imagery. Melodization of such words is powerful; it inspires tears in others and it may be unlucky or dangerous to use it at inauspicious moments or when vulnerable people are present.[87]

In terms of content, we can observe how Samira uses the lamentation form for her own purposes. This is not quite a funeral text, but is in keeping with gendered discourse of affect common across the Kurdish region and beyond, whereby women articulate their feelings of loss, grief, sacrifice, and sometimes blame in melodized form. Into a lament for a dead person they may weave references to previous losses, to sons living far away, to bodily sickness. Samira does not quite admit that the lost menfolk are dead (though some of her neighbors, who were listening, and later joined the lament themselves, did say so in normal speech); mostly she speaks as if they were in prison. This goes beyond the normal idiom of the lamentation genre, where sometimes the dead person is said to be "in exile" or even "wounded." The women of Qush Tepe lament for all their menfolk, though here Samira focuses mostly on her son.

Punctuated with interjections such as "o mother/o brother/o father," emotive formulae typical of the genre, this is not a user-friendly text for outsiders. Samira does not give a step-by-step narrative (that is not part of this speech genre) and she uses oblique references such as "those without questions and answers" for the men whose disappearance has not been investigated. However, she tells us much about lack of agency and feelings of hopelessness: "What is our life for?" Her pain is described largely in physical terms; in keeping with the conventions of the genre, the women are *birîndar*, "wounded," their livers (a seat of emotion as the heart is in the West) cut up or crumbled away. But they do not need hospitals; instead they need to be taken to the prisons (to see what has become of their men). There has been no answer to their questions; she calls at several points on Masoud Barzani as "king of the Kurds" and also as clan leader (*xudan*, "lord") to help, also to *mezinêd hukumet û dewleta*, the world leaders. Prosaic details add pathos: the boy was so young that he didn't even have facial hair yet; the men were taken away with only the belongings they could hold in a carrier bag. Their *namûs*,[88] their honor, has "fallen away" from them, she says, and this is even worse than the grief. This refers to the social impossibility for women of living without men in their households to protect them as heads of families. In Qush Tepe there had been cases of women being raped by security forces, cases that were surrounded by shame, but on an everyday level the lack of male kin in the household made it impossible for the women to be part of normal society. This issue has also been noted in connection with Anfal widows.[89]

Although she takes us into her personal anguish, Samira also speaks as part of a group. She uses the first person plural, "we", more often than singular "I"; and then *daykê lava*, "our boys' mothers" in the third person, are the subject of many of her statements. This is partly to do with her uptake of narrative responsibility in speaking for *daykê lava* as a group; such indirect sentence structures may also be a distancing mechanism, like the limited melodic range of the song (see above). Another such mechanism cited by Amy de la Brèteque is the use of reported speech to frame possibly dangerous utterances such as "our fate has betrayed us."[90] There is far less of this in Samira's lament than in Amy de la Brèteque's examples, which may be attributable to Samira's goal of asking for help in revealing what has happened. This is no ordinary funeral lament with a visible body and a known death.

Let us consider what Bauman calls the "pragmatics" of the text. Bauman speaks of significant texts being organized into corpora, which are then ideologized as cultural heritage.[91] This is not such a text, despite its similarities to the high-status melancholic *kilam*. Women's laments were, until recently, considered not only to be distressing to hear (they are), but also, in many areas, distasteful and low-status.[92] In 1992 I had some difficulty gaining access to funerals to listen to them. Even now, they are not sacralized in the same way as the songs produced by *dengbêj* singers.

Moreover, the practice of such lamentation is not cathartic. Although some of Amy de la Bretèque's Caucasian Yezidi partners said that they even derived some pleasure from it, the Barzani women told me in a later interview that they had had enough of lamentation and wanted to give it up.[93] Their practice has more in common with the containment of trauma and the need to live with it. The link between affect and discourse which they make by their use of embodied imagery (Samira's reference to the slashed hearts of the mothers) recalls Veena Das' remarks on the way that Pakistani women who had been raped during Partition spoke of hiding "poisonous knowledge" inside their bodies.[94]

I was not the first foreigner to hear these women lament: they had also lamented during interviews to Western journalists. For mothers to lament, often showing images of their sons, is an immensely powerful act in Kurdish politics, located as they are at the heart of what is considered homely and familiar. The PKK and its sister organizations have made an enormous political impact by turning women's lamentation on its head and having mothers of martyrs dance and ululate for joy and give speeches at funerals, declaring how happy they are that their child has died for the cause. But the lamentation of Qush Tepe Barzani mothers, for a crime against humanity perpetrated by the Ba'ath regime, is directly linked to wider Kurdish politics of victimhood.

Following Reinhardt Koselleck's prediction that one day history would be written from the point of view of the vanquished rather than the victors, Didier Fassin and Richard Rechtman have traced the evolution of victimhood from the early twentieth century, where victims were seen as cowards, until the present day, when victimhood is a strong moral position from which to speak and bearing witness to human suffering in the face of violence is seen as a virtuous act.[95] Victimhood has become one of the key elements of Kurdish national discourse; narratives of suffering, whether testimonies of humiliations suffered in prison, or the loss of murdered or martyred kinfolk, have moved from the private into the public arena. In Turkey and Iraq, initiatives which collect witness testimonies to atrocities exist alongside commemorations and memorials. Fischer-Tahir has described how the discourse of genocide has developed in Iraqi Kurdistan over the past two decades.[96] By the time "Daesh" actively attacked Kurdish border areas in 2014, the campaign for international acknowledgement of the Anfal campaign[97] as genocide had become a cornerstone of the Kurdistan

Regional Government's foreign policy. I would argue that these demands for international recognition are part of the way in which the KRG is performing statehood.

The utterances of Qush Tepe women, speaking from their position as Barzani widows, constitute important texts in Kurdish politics of victimhood. Journalists and researchers visiting Qush Tepe were channeled there by KDP connections wanting to show us Kurdish suffering; the women were happy to reveal their suffering to outsiders for the sake of discovering the truth about their loved ones. By addressing us, they are convoking new audiences, though in 1992 they were not yet consciously speaking to a developed Kurdish national discourse of suffering, as victims now do. The "we" Samira refers to are the boys' mothers, Barzanis, and not (yet) the whole Kurdish nation; she speaks of the Soran and Goran, Kurds from other regions, as "others" that they work for.

Anfal widows are also evocative figures in these politics, as are the people of Halabja, site of the infamous chemical bombing of 1988. Later, Masoud Barzani's envoy Dr Mohammed Ihsan found mass graves of the Barzani men, and the women of Qush Tepe were rehoused in Barzani ancestral areas.[98] However, prominence in the discourses of victimhood is not always a guarantee of "voice" or agency; Anfal widows asserted that despite their reverential treatment as a symbol of Kurdish suffering, their concerns were not always heard;[99] in 2006 the people of Halabja demonstrated against the KRG, claiming that they were being used for raising international funds but were not seeing the benefits.[100] This recalls Das' argument that the women raped during the Partition of India were felt to embody the nation, but their own voices were effaced.[101] It is within such a charged discursive environment that we should locate utterances by victims such as the Qush Tepe women.

Conclusion

In this chapter I have outlined the continuing political importance of folklore in Kurdistan and the politics surrounding Kurdish folklore studies. I have striven to show that the methodologies of folkloristics scholars, including the ethnography of speaking, constitute a type of discourse analysis which can be applied to texts lying outside the comfort zone of cultural heritage. Such texts show us the evolving negotiations and contestations of subaltern individuals and groups: Paredes' shifting borders of conflict, difference, and oppression. They also reveal how deeply texts are embedded in cultural politics: as Bauman says, texts are culturally constituted. Ultimately, they demonstrate clearly how artificial it would be to make a "Great Divide" between political and cultural studies. As scholars embrace such engaged methodologies, "folklore" moves at last from the polluted backwaters of Orientalism into the mainstream of Kurdish studies.

10.

KURDISH MUSIC IN ARMENIA

THE MUSIC OF THE YEZIDIS

Nahro Zagros

Songs in the Yezidi culture, and in Kurdish generally, are differentiated and divided along practice lines and usage, or the function of the songs in society. There are all kinds of songs and musical genres in Yezidi cultural life, such as the music used in ritualistic performances at funerals and weddings, historical and heroic songs that praise leaders and legends, religious recitation of sacred text of the Yezidi *qewil*, field workers' songs of farmers, lullabies by women, and comic songs at informal gatherings. All of these musical forms, except *qewil* which is religious, are branches of *kilamên cimetî* (folk music). I will be defining folk music of the Yezidis in this research in terms of terminology, melodic and rhythmic structure, performance practice, social and cultural context, and musical instruments. This research is therefore concerned merely with Armenian Yezidi folk and traditional music and the ways in which the Yezidis contemplate the relationship between music in terms of contextual basis and society's comprehension of musical associations. Explanation in this research can consequently be seen as a central approach and a foundation for understanding the Yezidis' ritual gatherings of *kilamên cimetî*. Whilst the findings of this research are based on the music of contemporary Yezidis in Armenia, it should also be noted that it can be seen in its general and broader sense within Kurdish, and specifically the Kûrmancî Kurdish, culture.

The Armenian Yezidis[1]

The Yezidis of Transcaucasia are those who left their homeland in eastern Turkey for Christian Armenia, fleeing from war and persecution at the hands of the Muslim Kurds and Ottoman Turks during the eighteenth century and in the later Armenian genocide in 1915.[2] After a short period in Armenia, some Yezidi tribes and families went further to seek refuge in Christian Georgia in the 1920s and 1930s;[3] "in the latter decades of the twentieth century, Muslim hostility made life unbearable for Yezidis in Turkey and they found refuge in Europe, particularly in Germany".[4]

The exact number of the total Yezidi population is not known, but according to Guest they are believed to number "around 200,000, of whom half live in Iraq" (Guest, 2002: 1056). Xanna Omerxalî, a Yezidi religious leader and academic, believes that the Yezidis actually number "700,000 – 800,000 to one million people worldwide".[5] "In Transcaucasia, the number of Yezidis is estimated at 60,000 souls; most of these live in the Republic of Armenia, with a smaller group in Georgia".[6] In the national census of the Republic of Armenia in 2001, the Yezidi numbers were just above 40,000 people. Although a large number of the Yezidis live in Transcaucasia and some former Soviet republics, most people associate the Yezidis with the Middle East rather than the Caucasus.

Literature review of the music of the Armenian Yezidis

As far as the study of Yezidi music is concerned, Armenian scholars and folklorists were among the first people to show an interest in fieldwork and exploration of Kurdish. "The first substantial efforts to notate and analyze Kurdish music were made by the Armenian composer, singer and scholar Komitas Vardapet (1869–1935)."[7] We do not know exactly how many songs were collected by Komitas, but "according to his contemporaries, Komitas had collected approximately 4,000 pieces of Armenian, Turkish and Kurdish folk music."[8] However, only thirteen pieces of his collection of Kurdish music have been published.[9] Another Armenian academic and scholar, Gasparian, also collected Kurdish music. He published his first twelve songs in 1932, and another ten songs with the Yezidi ethnographer and academic Hacyê Cindi in 1942. Also in 1932, three booklets on Kurdish music were published in Yerevan as part of the Armenian national school curriculum for Kurdish pupils. In the 1970s and 1980s, two female Yezidi music scholars also followed Komitas' method and carried out fieldwork in Yezidi villages in Armenia. Both scholars have published over fifteen books so far on Kurdish/Yezidi music.[10] It has to be said that none of these published materials have any descriptive accounts of compositional characteristics, rhythmic and melodic organizations, and the functionality of music in society. So far, the main emphasis has been on transcription and annotating lyrical components of Yezidi/Kurdish songs.

In the past four decades, Yezidi female musicologists Nûra Cewarî and Cemîla Celîl have collected a number of songs and published them in several books. Although these works are invaluable efforts in preserving and documenting Yezidi songs, there is very little analytical writing on the published materials. So far, an in-depth scholarly approach to compositional, melodic arrangements and rhythmic formations of the music of the Yezidis has not been carried out.

To my knowledge, there are two specific writings that deal with the funeral songs of Armenian Yezidis, both related to poetic organization generally: the first is a book by M. B. Roudenko, published in Russian from Soviet Georgia in 1970; the second is a book-chapter by the Celîl brothers published in 1978 in Moscow. M. B. Roudenko dealt with forty-four funeral songs of the Yezidis; the texts of the songs have been analyzed and translated into Russian from Kûrmancî. Roudenko's work, as has been emphasized by the Celîl brothers, "is among the first publications to deal profoundly with the funerary songs of the Yezidis".[11] Arakelova has also praised Roudenko's work and said: "the author emphasizes the richer variety of genres and colourfulness in Yezidi folk poetry."[12] In their two edited volumes of "*Zargotina K'urda*" (Kurdish Oral Literature), the Celîl brothers have included a chapter that contains ninety-six lyrical abstracts of funeral laments.[13] This work is invaluable if one wants to look at the construction of the poetic genre of funeral songs. Although in the introduction of the book the authors claim that they have collected ninety-six songs, only a passage of each song has been presented. Each passage consists of not more than three poetic lines.[14]

These two essential works are still worthy of great respect, although neither work has shed light on the most profound aspects of music and music making of funeral songs; the works also lack sound recordings of the songs. The other important aspect of Roudenko's book that needs to be mentioned as a critique is the fact that the songs have been provided by only one lamenter and not during either a funeral or burial; they were therefore removed from their natural cultural context. As such, Roudenko has said: "it was not possible to collect laments during funerals because the Kurds were refusing to have their voices recorded."[15] In *Zargotina K'urda*, the Celîl brothers have documented the texts of songs provided by a lamenter named H'zireta H'so from Tiblisi, the capital of Georgia.[16]

Concerning the musical aspect of funeral songs, as far as I am aware, earlier scholars and musicologists have made little effort to study the melodic structure, rhythmic organization, or compositional formula of any song. Detailed study of musical aspects of the ritual of funerals has yet to be carried out.

Definitions

The term that has commonly been used for music making and musical activities among the Yezidis is *kilamên cimetî* (literally meaning "folk narratives" but it more accurately denotes folk songs). First and foremost, the Yezidi musical culture, as well as non-Yezidi Kurdish music culture, is primarily vocal.[17] *Kilamên cimetî* is therefore a vocal form of rendering music, which can be performed by one solo vocalist or more, with or without the accompaniment of instrumental musicians. The origins of the songs of *kilamên cimetî* are not known, but the history of some songs can be obtained through their text and contextual information within the songs' lyrics.[18] *Kilamên cimetî* is an orally transmitted kind of music among the Yezidis in Armenia and elsewhere in the former USSR republics as well as in Kûrmancî-speaking society. *Kilamên cimetî* features the classical and colloquial speech of Kurdish folklore poetry sung by an ordinary member of the public, or a virtuoso singer who is accompanied by a small instrumental ensemble, or even without any instrumentation at all. The term *cimetî* is derived from the Arabic *jama'a* or *al-jama'a*, which means people.[19] Thus, *cimetî* music (*kilamên cimetî*) among the Yezidis can be interpreted as traditional folk music in the sense of a shared practice and understanding between people.

The term *kilamên cimetî* can be generally defined as songs that are frequently heard and practiced in society, and is also the type of music that is orally passed down to future generations. This transmission, however, does not necessarily indicate that the music has to be learned from a professional performer or instructor. Many people have gained the knowledge of their *kilamên cimetî* from members of their families or simply by attending musical gatherings and listening to performers. The attendees at these social gatherings often try to become involved through solo singing or playing, repeating the strophes of a song, by humming or clapping as well as listening to the content of the songs.[20]

Alternative terminology

The Kûrmancî-speaking Kurds in Turkey and Syria use the term *gelêrî* instead of *cimetî*, and Soranî Kurdish speakers in Iraq and Iran have used the term *mill* or *folklorî*.[21] Fascinatingly, *gelêrî* and *milli* provide the same meaning as *cimetî* in terms of understanding the music as a human experience that originated from peoples' perception of their social and cultural world. The term *gelêrî* originated from the Kurdish term *gel*, which means people or nation. In a broader sense, both terms (*cimetî* and *gelêrî*) have the same meaning but they are used in different geographical locations: *cimetî* is used primarily in Armenia and other former Soviet Republics; whilst *gelêrî* has been used by contemporary Kûrmancî-speaking Kurds in Turkey and Syria. The Soranî-speaking Kurds from Iraq and Iran have used the term *milli*, which originated from the Ottoman term *millet* that provides definition for a nation and its members.[22]

Interestingly, the term *mûzik* (the equivalent of the Western term music) has a narrower implication to the sound organization. The term *mûzik* among not just the

Yezidis in Armenia but all Kurds from all over Kurdistan, however, applies to two different aspects of musical form, both of which are entirely instrumental music rather than vocal. Firstly, it refers to all *cimetî* or *gelêrî* (folk) songs that can be performed in the absence of a singer: in other words, the musical formation can be regarded as the instrumental version of the vocal melody. Thus, there are several well-known instrumental pieces whose melodic origins stem from vocal songs of *kilamên cimetî*. Most of these pieces have regular rhythmic patterns. The other type of instrumental music whose rhythmic sequences are not fixed and regular (free rhythmic), and do not render any hint of their lyrics, are also sometimes considered as *mûzik*. Secondly, *mûzik* can also be regarded as composed instrumental or art music as opposed to folk music. As such, a number of virtuoso musicians have composed new pieces of music in accordance with the compositional system of traditional songs. The melodic structure of these kinds of instrumental forms is generally monophonic, but occasionally some part of each piece can be harmonized. Every so often people use the phrase *mûsika gelêrî* (folk music), which provides an interpretation and definition of songs that are put together in an organized way and performed by an instrumentalist, or a group of instrumentalists, without any vocal participation. There are many songs arranged for a solo instrument in which the structure lacks vocals whilst the instrumentalists imitate the melody more or less in the same manner in which the song might have been sung.

Occasionally in improvised musical forms one may also refer to, and use, the Arabic term *miqam* (also spelled *maqam* in Arabic and *mugam* in Azeri). *Miqam* is probably the most extensively employed word by musicians as well as people in the Near and Middle East and surrounding areas to define scale, certain genres, and modes of composed and improvised music.[23] Among the Armenian Yezidis, however, *miqam* (pl. *meqamên or meqamêd*) means free rhythmic songs with a prolonged melodic and narrative recitation.[24] Not only for the Yezidis in Armenia but also elsewhere in former USSR Republics, the term *miqam* has only been used to mean improvised music, whether vocal or instrumental.

Interestingly, the other term for song genres, used as a standard and general term in Kurdish society, and one that has been broadly accepted, is the term *stran*.[25] The Armenian Yezidis occasionally use the term *stranên dilanan* (singular: *stran*) instead of *kilamên dilanan* (dancing songs) to refer to the rhythmic form of songs. This term is common amongst urban and university-educated Yezidis in Yerevan and other cities. *Stran*, generally, is performed by bards whom the Yezidis, as well as other Kûrmancî speakers, call *stranbêj* or *dengbêj*.

Melodic structure of kilamên cimetî

Melodic elements of *kilamên cimetî* of the Yezidis in Armenia can be traced from pre-Islamic and Christian modal music to near contemporary Middle Eastern music. The melodies are mainly monophonic, and traditional music consists essentially of *cimetî* (folk) melodies. The rhythmic patterns vary from one melody to another, but there are specific rhythmic prototypes that comply with certain forms of dancing.[26] Alongside the use of traditional musical instruments, such as the *def*, the *zirne*, and the *mey*,[27] European musical instruments are also occasionally used to accompany a *kilambej* (singer, bard), particularly amongst the urban Yezidis at cultural festivals in Yerevan and other large cities. The exercise of employing European musical instruments has become rather common in recent times among societies in the Middle East and the Caucasus; the Yezidis in Armenia have recently integrated some of these instruments for conveying their musical traditions.

Yezidi musicians, like the musicians from the host communities, have also adapted the synthesizer keyboard for conveying some of their musical genres, in particular at wedding ceremonies. Synthesized keyboard music is now one of the most popular instrumental forms at wedding rituals. The Yezidis in the diasporas, particularly Yezidis in Russia, also frequently use the synthesizer keyboard at cultural festivals and social gatherings.

Every song of *kilamên cimetî* possesses its own emotional character, which is chiefly determined by the construction of its musical core. Performers usually present their piece of music using their own emotions, feelings, and memories as a basis for the construction of melodies rather than following the guidelines and restrictions of a musical score or conductor.[28] The use of Western musical notation is not a common practice among the majority of Yezidis in Armenia, with the exception of a few books and articles in which Yezidis and non-Yezidi scholars have transcribed traditional some songs by using Western staff notation.[29]

In the event of instrumental participation to accompany a *kilambej*, the melody of *kilamên cimetî* is divided into a number of melodic strophes followed by a refrain. The refrain normally consists of the melodic structure and imitation of the vocal verse of the melody, repeated each time after the verse. The melodic formation generally starts with the refrain, which will then be followed by the main melody and finishes either with the refrain or the vocal verse. This formation of melodic presentation in Yezidi music can be found in Kurdish music all over Kurdistan and in the diasporas, from traditional and folk music to pop music.[30]

There are only four musical modes commonly used in *kilamên cimetî* (see Example 1). Local terms for these modes do not exist but Kurdish musicians from other parts in Kurdistan use either Arabic, Turkish, or Persian terminologies. Every *kilamên cimetî* consists of one musical mode; only very rarely does one hear two musical modes in a melody. The majority of *kilamên cimetî* use the first mode in Example 1, which is known as *beyat* amongst Kurds in Iraq and Syria; and *beyati* amongst Kurds in Turkey. The melodic pitch of *kilamên cimetî* is stable and the execution of ornamentation largely depends on the performer. Most songs consist of only one melodic phrase and two motifs, one of which is the general orientation of melodic organization while the other one is the cadential motif (see Example 2).

Example 1: musical modes

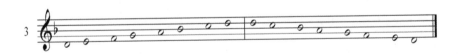

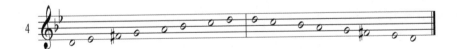

Example 2: typical kilamên cimetî song

Lê Nazikê Nazdarê

Text: Kûrmanc

Lê nazikê nazdarê
Yar, yar, yar eman
Gerden gaze kubarê
Ax lê yeman lê yeman
Lê têr nabim dindarê
Dilo dilo dilo can
Lê têr nabim dindarê
Dilo dilo dilo can

Text: English translation

Oh, sweet and fragile
Oh, sweet and fragile
Love, love, my love
Sensitive soul with your aureate neck
My desire to see her is never satiated
My heart, my heart, my heart and soul

Example 3 is another typical call and response *kilamên cimetî* song, which generally occurs between two singers or a solo singer and a group. The melodic themes of these songs are stable while the *xeber* (text) changes each time the melody is repeated. For example, the lead singer (solo) recites different *xeber* every time she sings, whilst the group repeats more or less the same *xeber*.

Example 3: typical call and response song

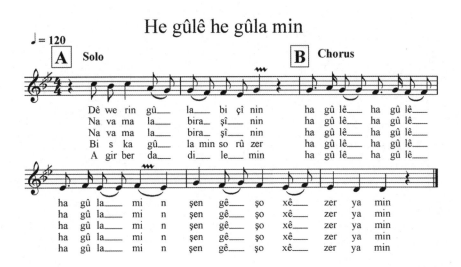

He gûlê he gûla min

Text: Kûrmancî

Solo
Dê werin gûla biçînin

Chorus
Ha gûlê ha gûla min
Şengê şoxê zerya min

Solo
Nava mala biraşînin

Chorus
Ha gûlê ha gûla min
Şengê şoxê zerya min

Solo
Nava mala biraşînin

Chorus
Ha gûlê ha gûla min
Şengê şoxê zerya min

Solo

Biska Gûla min sor û zer

Chorus
Ha gûlê ha gûla min
Şengê şoxê zerya min

Solo
Agir berda dilê min

Chorus
Ha gûlê ha gûla min
Şengê şoxê zerya min

Text: English translation

Solo
Come on all to sow my flowers

Chorus
Oh, flowers, my flowers
Beautiful and elegant my love

Solo
Spread them amongst our homes

Chorus
Oh, flowers, my flowers
Beautiful and elegant my love

Solo
Spread them amongst our homes

Chorus
Oh, flowers, my flowers
Beautiful and elegant my love

Solo
My love's hair is fiery yellow

Chorus
Oh, flowers, my flowers
Beautiful and elegant my love

Solo
My heart is longing for her

Chorus
Oh, flowers, my flowers

Beautiful and elegant my love

The melodies of *kilamên cimetî* are basically monophonic through solo presentations of melodic lines. Although the melodic execution of every melodic phrase varies depending on the performer's singing ability, the melodic structure is usually based on one or two musical phrases that are repeated throughout the song. Generally, the song structure is built around small tonal formations. Most songs tend to be formed of two melodic phrases, such as the opening and closing phrase (cadential). The general intervallic movements of melodic phrases are smooth and diatonic. Melodic phrases of a song are not always of equal length, but as a general rule the majority conform to identical phrase lengths. The direction of the melodies can be assessed based on the ascending and descending movements. The descending movements tend to be formed around the unison and the intervals of the neutral second and the neutral third. Largely, songs are created within the interval of a fourth (D-G). Thus, the first and the fourth degrees have important influences on the direction of the melody. The tonic, however, provides the more stable and central character to the melody.

In free rhythmic forms (see Example 4), the melodic line can be divided into several unequal melodic phrases. The opening of every melodic *mal* (phrase) is similar to that of the beginning of the opening melody, and most verses are to some extent similar to each other through sharing melodic and rhythmic patterns. The melodic presentation of *mal* focuses on the development of only a few tones. Specific similar motifs and melodic patterns recur repeatedly within each *mal*, which characterizes the melodic structure. Thus, most *mal* within the melodic lines of a song appear to be the extensions of one another. The melody also includes a number of short or long pauses.

Example 4: free rhythmic form of kilamên cimetî

Apê Bekir

Rhythmic structure of kilamên cimetî

Kilamên cimetî conveys two rhythmical forms: namely, metered and unmetered (or rhythmic and free rhythmic). This configuration also applies to the music of other parts of Kurdistan. Neither the Yezidis nor the scholars of Yezidi music use localized terms in describing these two rhythmic forms. Sometimes, though, words such as *teqil* and *gef* are used for the word rhythm. Since these two terms are not standardized, I will be using the terms "rhythmic" (designated to all the genres that have a rhythmic formation and rhythmic temporal structure and patterns) and "free rhythmic" (for those melodies that are subject to no definite and regular rhythmic organization).

Most *kilam* of the free rhythmic types are similar in terms of melodic organization, whether the story concerns love or battle and war. For example, *kilamên mêranî* (bravery songs) and the *dîrok* (funeral lamentation) genres are similar in terms of melodic dispositions and internal rhythmic variations. The element that separates these genres, apart from rhythmic organizations, is based on the functionality and the lyrical themes of the songs, rather than the melodic construction. There are also some melodic prototypes used in different songs under different names with different lyrics.

The types of melodies that are formulated with organized rhythmic sequences in Yezidi music and the use of such kinds of rhythmic patterns in a melody are, for example, divided into equal long or short units. All musical genres containing regular rhythmic temporal structures have melodies that hold firm and fixed beats. Amongst such genres, for example, is the form of *kilamên dilanan* (or *dilok*) or *stranên dilanan* (dancing songs). Most wedding songs are based upon a recurring rhythmic pattern and performed by a percussionist or audience participation through clapping. Such kinds of compositions contain a simple and recognizable rhythmic sequence that complies with the patterns of different types of dances. Generally, a fixed rhythmic temporal structure of a melody in *kilamên dilanan* holds equal regular beats in time signatures such as 2/4, 4/4, and 6/8, and occasionally 6/4.

Performance practice

Members of the public will, in general, select recitalists based on an individual's capability in singing and/or playing and the ability to entertain others at a social gathering. Most recitalists who offer this kind of informal performance describe themselves as entertainers, and they may argue that it is a mistake to equate them with professional musicians or *kilambej*. There are three local terms denoting professional musicians, such as *husta* (skillful), *sena't çî* (creator), and *mamhûst* (teacher). None of these terms, however, is clearly defined solely to mean professional musician; but people occasionally use them to refer to a vocalist or instrumental player who has vast knowledge of *kilamên cimetî* and can recite most songs fluently. Although the Yezidis all enjoy taking part in musical activities, nevertheless there are usually two types of performers in the *cimetî* or *kilamên cimetî* performance scene: (a) non-professionals who mainly sing or play for pleasure at both formal and informal gatherings; and (b) professional or semi-professional instrumentalists and singers who usually perform at weddings and funerals.

The appearance of a non-professional singer or musician of *kilamên cimetî* is more common at events involving Yezidi nomads and agricultural farmers. In this respect, these singing performers are typically people who like spending time in congenial company with participants of a similar class and background (equal ranked members of society) singing for *keyf* (pleasure). These social gatherings occur at work places or, more usually, at normal social events. Performers naturally pursue a musical sense that allows them the freedom to articulate elements from various sources in their background and musical culture.[31]

Professional or semi-professional musicians, on the other hand, are rare in today's Yezidi society. They usually provide music at more formal gatherings such as weddings and, occasionally, funerals. The majority of these musicians are rural Yezidis who have other occupations besides music. The amount of money that they receive for their service is minimal.

Social and cultural context

From a cultural and political point of view, *kilamên cimetî* could be regarded as having important sentimental value for the Yezidis. In other words, *kilamên cimetî* brings together classical and folk poetry with singing and improvisation, which will be examined as an emblem of both continuity and existence in relation to the social traditions and political situations which the Yezidis in Armenia may face.

The Yezidis, in general, recognize two different forms of singing that relate to them as a people, each of which can be performed on different social occasions: *dinyayê* (secular) and *ruhaniyê* (sacred) music.[32] Some of these song categories are typical musical forms of folk in Kurdistan, while others are exclusively allied to the Yezidis. Thus, *kilamên cimetî* in its use and function can solely be defined as folk music, not to be confused with religious recitation. This system of definition also applies even when the performer belongs to a religious sect.

During the performance of music at wedding rituals and other less formal social gatherings, various secular musical types may be performed. By contrast, the *qewil* and *beyt* are the main archetypal forms of *stranên ruhaniyê* (sacred songs) performed at sacred meetings and services. While the *beyt* is a form of singing tradition with its lyrical content based on love and heroism that stimulates social values and is known throughout Kurdistan among not only the Yezidis but also Muslim Kurds, the *qewil* is mainly a recital form attached to Yezidi funeral rituals and other sacred events. Although the Yezidis do not consider the recital of a *qewil* and *beyt* to be a form of light-hearted singing, the *qewil* and *beyt* are nevertheless performed vocally. Religious singing carries more gravitas and is regarded as possessing a greater degree of dignity than folk songs.

The context in which the music is performed defines and restricts the musical content that can be used, whether secular or sacred. The Yezidis usually recognize songs by their narrative and its social function, rather than by their melodies and rhythms. For example, the attendees at social gatherings may feel that the crowd requires a song that stimulates social values, and so they may ask the singer to sing a well-known song of *kilamên mêranî* (bravery song). The Yezidis have a perfect understanding of the importance of choosing songs that correspond to the purpose of the event or social occasion; at any social gathering a selection of songs will be presented which match the principle and intention of the event. Since the events of secular music are associated with the variability of *kilamên cimetî*, the *qewil* is more associated with religious ceremonies, such as burial.

At the events where *kilamên cimetî* can be performed, the performers are ordinary members of the local community, and this involves everyone regardless of their religious status. However, as a religious commitment, the performer of the *qewil* should be from the Şêx or Pîr caste.

In summary, there are three accepted terms for these kinds of traditional singing, each of which embraces further repertoires. The terms are (1) *kilamên cimetî*, (2) *qewil*, and (3) *beyt*. These genres can be performed and sung by a single singer, two singers, or a group singing. The choice of selecting the song genre consequently depends on the performance settings and the character of the social event.

Evidently, through analyzing and listening to the songs sung by the Yezidis, it becomes apparent to scholars concerned with cultural studies of Yezidis that the native classifications of songs are crucially based upon the lyrical theme of each song.[33] For example, *kilamên mêranî* (bravery song), *kilamên dila* (love song), and *dîrok* (sometimes called *kilamên şînê*, which means lament, a wake/funeral keening) clearly show the important role of the narrative and textual base of each song. The functionality of these songs is also to link the type of performance and the purpose of the gathering. Thus, the Yezidi's musical performance, as native performers and listeners would describe it, manifests the relationship between music in cultural life and social circumstances. The characteristics of the songs enable the listener to envisage the variety of social and cultural elements of the Yezidi's life in their music.

Equally the role of the musical instruments is important. From the viewpoint of the Yezidis, the *zirne* (double-reed wind instrument) is regarded as the instrument of happy events and happy songs, such as music at weddings. The use of the *zirne* may therefore be regarded as inappropriate to be used in a funeral context. The *def* also equally fits into the category of happy music. The *def* and *zirne* are thus used in wedding gatherings and other cultural festivities of a happy musical nature. At every wedding performance the *zirne* is accompanied by the rhythmic patterns of the *def*. Consequently, the names of these two instruments often appear together in the canon of Yezidis' folk literature, their association regarded as close and interlinked. The *mey*, on the other hand, is a rather more common instrument for professional musicians to use at funerals. The *mey* seldom emerges in musical performances by itself. Frequently, at funeral gatherings for example, two *mey* players perform together: one carries the solo line while the other holds the *dem* (long-drawn note of the tonic in the solo line).

In modern-day musical performances, hardly any women play musical instruments. Several Yezidis told me at a wedding ceremony that this is a cultural phenomenon, women choosing not to play instruments, rather than an institutionalized discriminatory musical requirement. However, it is evident that the art of singing, especially at funerals, is more associated with women. Also, some Yezidi women gained wide-ranging popularity among the Armenians and other ethnic populations during the USSR period. Sûsiyka Simo, who was a Yezidi female singer, achieved widespread recognition and popularity in Armenia through singing with the Armenian State Opera in the 1950s–1970s.[34] She later formed her own musical ensemble which toured within the USSR on numerous occasions. There have also been a number of Yezidi female instrumental players and academics who received musical education at colleges in Armenia and elsewhere in the former USSR. Notable in this group were the two famous music scholars, Cemila Celîl and Mûra Cewarî, who both studied musicology at the Music Department of the State University in Yerevan in the 1960s.

Categorization

Several forms that have been associated with music making and musical activities are embraced by *kilamên cimetî*. Local descriptions, though, may differ considerably from those put forward by academics. There is little agreement whether all the songs performed at musical events can be labeled as *kilamên cimetî*. Overall, by local account, *dîrok* (funeral lamentation) does not meet the criteria to be included in *kilamên cimetî*, since lamentation is associated with mourning and expressing grief. The other forms that are not associated with *kilamên cimetî*, apart from the recitation of *rûhanî* (sacred) texts of *qewil*, are *kilamên lûrandnê* (lullabies) and *kilamên zaroka* (children's songs). Given that wedding music and music for happy occasions can be regarded as *kilamên cimetî*, this brings about a degree of discontent if one attempts to include lamentation within *kilamên cimetî*. Religious recitation such as *qewil* cannot be called *kilamên cimetî* or *mûzik*.

For the purpose of clarity, I have categorized *kilamên cimetî* into two groups (see below). Group A includes all genres which are understood to be *kilamên cimetî* by the overwhelming majority of Yezidis; while group B is a modern classification that includes all genres that are performed in instrumental music and vocal music regardless of local arguments.

Group A

1. *kilamên mêranî* (songs of bravery)

2. *kilamên reqasê/ dawetê/ dîlanan* (wedding songs)

3. *kilamên bengitî/ Evînî* (love songs)

4. *kilamên laqrdîa* (comic songs)

Group B comprises all genres from group A, but also includes the following:

1. *dîrok/ kilamên şînê* (wailing, lamentations)

2. *kilamên şoreşgêrî* (patriotic and nationalistic songs)

3. *kilamên biyanî* (foreign songs)

4. *qewil* (religious chants)

5. *beyt* (folktales)

6. *metelûk* (stories/storytelling)

7. *lûrîn/ kilamên lûrandinê* (lullabies)

8. *Kilamen zaroka* (children's songs)

Musical instruments

The vast majority of Yezidis in the villages and cities do not play musical instruments. There are, however, some instrumentalists among them who have formed small musical ensembles to convey forms of their music at social gatherings, cultural celebrations, and ethnic and religious festivals. These groups are generally made up of a very small number of musicians: ordinary people who usually sing or play a musical instrument at informal gatherings from villages often describe themselves as non-professional singers or players. The instrumentalists who play at weddings or funerals and receive remuneration for their performances, whilst not regarding themselves as professionals, are known as semi-professionals among their fellow villagers. Only musicians who perform on Radio Yerevan and national and international festivals are known as professionals. Most of the professional musicians, although they number very few, are city dwellers. There are several types of instrument employed by the semi-nomadic and urban community players, amongst them the *def*, *zirne*, and *mey*. These three instruments are the most common ones over the past hundred years.

Def

The Yezidis in Armenia use the *def* very often in conveying musical forms such as *kilamên dawetê* (wedding songs). The *def* is a double-headed drum played by professionals using two wooden sticks. Both ends of the *def* are covered with a thin plastic layer (providing the skins) and are fastened with a ribbon to the main body of the instrument (see Figure 10.1). One side of the *def* projects a bass sound while the other side projects a higher-pitched sound. The rhythmic organization of the *def* helps the instrumentalists with a particular recurring rhythmic structure. The *def* is also called *dehol* by some Kûrmancî Kurds and the Armenians; Soranî speakers from Iraq and Iran use this term.[35]

10.1 Photograph of a *def*

Zirne

The *zirne* is an end-blown type of instrument made of apricot wood (see Figure 10.2). The body consists of two parts: the main section, which is the larger piece, has seven regular holes on the upper face and one hole at the bottom, and one on the back face which is intermittently covered by the thumb when played; and the *pik*, which is a double reed that generates the high-pitched sound and is fastened onto the top of the main body. The *zirne* is usually accompanied by the *def* and only used at happy occasions such as the wedding ritual and Eid (see Figure 10.4). Sometimes, two *zirne* players perform together, one of them playing the melodic part while the other plays the drone, mostly the tonic of the main melody.

10.2 Photograph of a *zirne*

Mey

The *mey* is one of the most widely used instruments among the Yezidis in Armenia. The *mey* is also called *dûdûk* (both terms recognized by Armenians, Turk and Kûrmancî Kurds as well), and *balaban* is the term used by Soranî speakers of Iraq and Iran. The *mey* is played chiefly by professional and semi-professional players at cultural festival and social gatherings, and generally with the accompaniment of other instruments. The most renowned Yezidi *mey* player in Armenia is Egîdê Cimo, who became famous through his frequent radio broadcasts in the 1970s and 1980s. Before Egîdê Cimo came to the fore, Şamilê Beko and Xelîlê Evdilene were also well-known players.[36]

The *mey* is an end-blown wooden instrument, open at both ends, made from the wood of mulberry or apricot trees (see Figure 10.3). The *mey* produces a sad and melancholic sound, often used to convey some traditional music of *kilamên cimetî*.[37] It consists of two parts: the first is the main body of the instrument containing eight almost equally spaced finger holes on the upper surface and one thumb hole on the back, located at the higher end toward the second essential part of the instrument; this is the *pik* (reed), made from a thin reed of the bamboo tree. The *pik* should be inserted into the top of the first part of the instrument, near to the thumbhole. The *mey* holds a very important position in Kurdish music and people from mainstream society generally respect and admire skilled players. Like the *zirne*, the *mey* is always played with circular breathing.

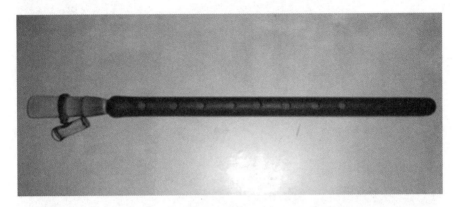

10.3 Photograph of a *mey*

10.4 Photograph of *def zirne* players at a wedding in Avrishat, Armavir

10.5 Photograph of *mey* and *def* players accompanying a singer,
in the Armavir region

Conclusion

Song performance among the Yezidis is based upon its lyrical expression and musical core to render a shared identity. I would further suggest that attending musical performances or listening to *kilamên cimetî* in social gatherings is culturally essential and significant in integrating the individual within society. Therefore, making music in social activities and religious and cultural festivals among the Yezidis can be seen as an explicit symbol of continuity and an emblem of social and ethnic cohesion. I therefore would agree with Martin Stokes "that music is socially meaningful not entirely but largely because it provides the means by which people recognise identities and places, and the boundaries which separate them."[38]

Thus, no activity, cultural festival, or social gathering of the Yezidis can possibly be arranged without including music. The emotional expression of Yezidis can be implicitly observed through song performance. I would also emphasize the important function of music in Yezidi society and would assert that musical activity addresses some indispensable questions regarding the relationship between music in society and the construction of identity among Yezidis in contemporary Armenia. Hence, in all the musical activities with which the Yezidis are associated, their *kilamên cimetî* is responsible for maintaining social integrity and values.

Although a number of books on Yezidi music were published in Armenian during the Soviet era, none of the existing materials have offered any understanding of Yezidi musical culture in terms of melodic and rhythmic organization. So far, mere transcription of songs has been the main characteristic of the published materials and indeed the main focal point of study of Yezidi music by previous scholars and academics. This research should offer a new approach to Yezidi musical culture.

PART 2

THE KURDISH QUESTION IN THE OTTOMAN EMPIRE AND TURKEY

11.

THE SHEIKH UBEIDULLAH REBELLION OF 1880

Sabri Ateş

The Sheikh Ubeidullah rebellion of 1880-81 was a formative step in the history of the Kurdish national movement. A wealth of documents make it clear that Ubeidullah's ultimate goal was to end the division of the Kurds between Iran and the Ottoman Empire and unite them in an autonomous (*mukhtar*) entity that, preferably, he would rule. The *mukhtar* Kurdish domain was to be under the supreme authority of the caliph-sultan. The first part of the sheikh's plan was to liberate the Kurdish regions of Iran from the Qajar "yoke" and unite them with the Ottoman Kurdish regions. However, we lack any concrete information on the sheikh's possible strategy regarding Ottoman Kurdistan. Furthermore, although there is no indication that his ambitions were limited to Sunni Kurds or eastern Kurdistan, we know nothing about his plans for non-Sunni Kurds in Iran or the Ottoman Empire.

Despite these gaps in our direct knowledge of the sheikh's plans, rich archival collections in Iran, Turkey, and England provide an immense amount of data, and no doubt the Russian archives, inaccessible to the author, would provide further details. To the official archival documentation one should add the rich missionary accounts available in archives and libraries of the United States, England, and no doubt the Vatican, France, and Russia. Newspapers of the time, including in the United States, include hundreds of articles about the revolt. Despite this wealth of information, official policies in all countries inhabited by Kurdish populations have effectively silenced Kurdish historical agency and consciousness through academic, judiciary, and security measures. As a result, no thorough monograph or detailed account of this revolt has been published. Nonetheless, this is fast changing, especially in Iran where a large number of related documents and contemporary memoirs have recently been published. Additionally many chronicles, memoirs, and local histories, even though very hostile to the sheikh and the Kurds, describe this revolt in detail.[1]

Among those who have mentioned it in this context, some have treated the revolt as another outburst of savage, tribal, and unruly subjects, defying the "civilizing mission" of the two modernizing states. Others saw the revolt's leaders—as they saw the leaders of all Kurdish revolts—as the puppets of alien powers, and its participants as essentially savage: unable to mobilize themselves, tribal, unruly, ignorant, and easily manipulated. In this context, both the leaders and their followers, therefore, are portrayed as devoid of consciousness and historical agency. Other reports mentioning the revolt portray Sheikh Ubeidullah as a villain, a frontier rebel, a hero, a national liberator, or a new feudal baron, among others. Scholarly works, however, agree on the nationalist character of his rebellion, be it a struggle for autonomy or independence. Following the lead of Wadie Jwaideh, scholars of Kurdish nationalism almost universally trace the origins of Kurdish nationalism to this revolt.[2] The doyen of Kurdish studies, Martin van Bruinessen, concluded that it was the first Kurdish uprising with a clearly nationalist agenda.[3]

Taking into account the archival and scholarly literature briefly sketched above, the present chapter aims to contextualize the Sheikh Ubeidullah Rebellion, highlight the historical agency of its leaders and participants, and tie it to developments taking place in other parts of the Ottoman Empire and Iran, as well as the Ottoman-Iranian borderland where it unfolded. No doubt this revolt is a foundational moment in the formation of the Kurdish nationalist consciousness, but it is not the one true moment from which the Kurdish nationalist movement sprang. Like other similar cases, it was a multi-dimensional phenomenon and various factors contributed to its unfolding.

Prelude

By the time Ubeidullah emerged as its *postnishin* (head), the *taqiyah* (dervish lodge) of Nehri in Shemzinan, Hakkari was a well-established center of the *Naqshbandiyya* (*Jadidi*) order. The sheikh's highly regarded father, Seyyid Taha, had *khalifahs* (representatives) in an area ranging from the Balkans to Egypt and Iran. Aware of his influence, following the demise of the Kurdish Emirates in the 1840s, the Porte was concerned that Taha might emerge as the leader of resistance to the expansion of state power in the Kurdish periphery.[4] Similarly, aware of the influence of Seyyid Taha in his domains, and perhaps due to the encouragement of one of his wives, who was a Kurd from Selmas and a *murid* (follower) of Seyyid Taha, Mohammad Shah Qajar (r.1834-48) rewarded his *taqiyah* with *tuyul* (fiscal immunity) rights to some five or seven villages on the Iranian side.[5] Taha's brother Salih led the order from 1853 to 1873 and Nehri continued to collect the *tuyul* from those villages. With Salih's death in 1873, Taha's charismatic and ambitious son Ubeidullah became the head of the *taqiyah* and took it to unchartered territories.

This is because his tenure, and the revolt he led, coincided with momentous developments taking place in the Ottoman-Iranian borderland and beyond. The first of these was the centralizing regional states' efforts to reorganize and strengthen their administrative functions in ever-larger areas. The long-term effects of this process on the sociopolitical organization of the Kurdish and neighboring peoples were powerful. The disruptions it caused following the elimination of the Kurdish dynasts in the 1840s, as Martin van Bruinessen has noted, "propelled the shaikhs into the role of political leaders."[6] Other developments included Qajar Iran's efforts to make Shia symbols more visible in Kurdistan, and its concomitant oppression of its Sunni subjects; increased imperialist intervention in the region; and the aftershocks of the devastating Russo-Ottoman War of 1877-8, particularly the rise of sectarian affiliations and dynamics. All of these factors contributed to profound socio-economic and environmental changes; and, not coincidentally, they emerged in a particularly potent manner in Urumieh-Hakkari, where the revolt unfolded. It was, for example, the scene of a Russo-British tug-of-war as well as the field on which Ottoman-Iranian rivalries took place. It was also the stage on which sectarian differences were performed; as such, it was an arena in which Kurdish nationalism competed with the better-organized nationalisms of Turks, Persians, and Armenians. Finally, the fierce competition between consuls and missionaries from various countries for the heart and soul of the Nestorian community of the Urumieh-Hakkari region further contributed to the volatile state of affairs, raising local fears that a foreign takeover of the region was imminent. In this context, Ubeidullah emerged as a leader willing to take action and capable of fostering the gradual articulation of a Kurdish nationalist sentiment, albeit informed by sectarian affiliations.

The first incident that brought Ubeidullah to the attention of Tehran and Istanbul took place immediately after he became *postnishin*. In 1873 the governor of Khoi sent agents to collect taxes from the Nehri family's previously mentioned tax-exempt villages on the Iranian side. The villagers resisted. An Ottoman report notes that in the ensuing confrontation some forty men were killed alongside women and children.[7] A joint Ottoman-Iranian Commission of Inquiry failed to resolve the issue, but the incident highlighted Sheikh Ubeidullah's cross-border stature and complicated the issue of land-ownership across boundaries. The Ottoman bureaucrat Necib Ali, a member of the commission, informed Istanbul that "The majority of the inhabitants of Iran in the border region stretching from Beyazid to Suleimanieh are Sunnis, many are the sheikh's followers and he has his agents, *khalifahs*, in these regions. All of them depend and look to the sheikh for protection against harm from the Iranians."[8]

Similar accounts of the sheikh's standing abound in the missionary and consular reports, and are shared by observers like Eskandar Qurians, who wrote a first-hand account of the revolt. Consequently, following the 1873 incident, the sheikh started corresponding with Istanbul. In the meantime, he increasingly drew adherents and entreaties from those who sought justice or intervention in the realms of the sultan and those of the shah,[9] such as Ottoman Kurds complaining about increasing pressure applied by provincial administrators, or Iranian Kurds pleading with the sheikh to stop the oppression (*"zulm ve teaddi"*) of Qajar authorities. The sheikh, in return, appealed to the sultan to intervene on his kinsmen's behalf. We could, with certainty, claim that those appeals fell on deaf ears, and that this played a significant role in motivating the sheikh to lead his people in a quest to establish an administration where they could manage their own affairs.

If the 1873 incident was a local storm that underscored Ubeidullah's regional stature, the 1877-8 Russo-Ottoman War was a tsunami that engulfed the Ottoman Empire, and Kurdistan with it. It also propelled Ubeidullah's career to new heights. The most devastating war the Ottoman Empire had ever waged, it aggravated the economic troubles of a region already suffering from, among other things, locusts, crop failure, and famine. It also stoked the coals of ethnic and religious conflict. It brought a sizeable number of Muslims from the Caucasus and uprooted a considerable number of Armenians from the region. Under Ubeidullah's leadership, Ottoman Kurds joined forces with the Iranian Kurds (despite Iran's attempts to prevent the latter) to rally as auxiliaries to the caliph-sultan's call for jihad. In his later correspondence with Sultan Abdulhmid II, Ubeidullah would remind him that he headed a force of 40,000 to fight the Russians. The Ottoman Commander of the Caucasian and Eastern front, Ahmed Mukhtar Pasha, maintained that the sheikh organized seven *redif* battalions, with battalions coming from other districts as well. In addition to regular troops, he wrote, "Sheikh Abdullah Efendi Hakkari raised 50,000-60,000 irregular soldiers, both infantry and cavalry from his districts of Van province."[10] Even though some others, like Mahmud Celaleddin Pasha, would dispute these numbers and the usefulness of the Kurdish auxiliaries, it was obvious that Ubeidullah played a significant role in raising large numbers of volunteers, some of whom received rifles from Istanbul. He would not hesitate to capitalize on his success.

In fact, post-war volatility and the political vacuum it created would, in a way, force him to rise to the occasion. Thus when the tension between two of the major Iranian tribal groups of the area, the Afshars and the Shekaks, reached boiling point in the summer of 1878, Ubeidullah sent a force of 2,000 cavalry to intervene. In response, Tehran dispatched troops to the Mergever and Tergever districts bordering Nehri and warned Istanbul that it would be held responsible if further complications occurred.[11] To counter the Iranian troop concentration, the governor of Van demanded additional forces, and the Ottoman Council of Ministers inconclusively discussed the issue.

Similarly, when about a year after this incident a dispute arose between the local people and government agents related to the payment of taxes in the Ottoman district of Amadiyah, Ubeidullah dispatched his young son, Abdul Qadir, at the head of a party of nearly a thousand horsemen to intervene on behalf of the local people. Ottoman accounts refer to the small-scale skirmishes that followed as a confrontation or even a rebellion or "*ihtilal*." [12] When an aide-de-camp of the sultan asked about the incident, Ubeidullah accused his enemies of exaggerating, but he did not deny what took place: "His son had only attempted to right the wrongs perpetrated by the local government officials, but he remained a loyal subject of the sultan."[13]

It was due to this loyalty and his emergence as a regional leader that the sheikh sent a letter to Sultan Abdulhamid II raising several concerns and demanding action. Three of the issues he raised stand out. Firstly, he pointed out the depredation and lawlessness of the tribes and the inaction of corrupt officials. Secondly, he noted that under the authority of Mar Shimoon, who had been recalcitrant in delivering the taxes of his community to the imperial treasury, the Nestorians (encouraged by foreigners) were causing considerable distress among the Muslims. Thirdly and perhaps most importantly, the sheikh expressed his displeasure about rumors that foreign powers were planning to create an Armenian state in the vilayet of Van. He informed the sultan that as only one twentieth of the province was Christian, the Muslim majority would fight against such a decision.[14]

As his correspondence indicates, the sheikh was following international developments. The need for administrative reform of the Kurdo-Armenian-inhabited provinces and security of the Armenian people from the Kurds and the newly arrived Circassians was one of the demands of the post 1877-8 war Berlin Congress. The future of the region and the direction it would take were on every political actor's mind. Just as the Kurds did not want to be swallowed up by a possible Armenia, the Armenians did not want to be considered part of a possible Kurdistan. The contention over potential boundaries of these Kurdo-Armenian lands was emerging as a question in need of an answer. Thus the Armenian newspapers of Istanbul protested when the "British Consulate of Kurdistan" was established in 1865.[15] Indeed, due to these protests and other considerations, this consulate soon ceased to exist, but the question of what was to be done with this contentious geography remained. Witnessing these developments and Istanbul's continued inaction, the sheikh and his allies decided to take matters into their own hands and to articulate an answer to the emerging question of Kurdistan.

The rebellion

From the outskirts of Seir Mountain, overlooking the town of Urumieh, the wife of American missionary Dr Joseph Plumb Cochran wrote home on 6 October 1880:

"war is to follow famine. Our friend, the sheikh, is at war with Persia...he wishes to gather all the Kurdish districts lying around Urumieh and form a consolidated Kurdish nation."[16] Indeed, in early September 1880, Ubeidullah, his son Abdul Qadir, and a few other notables coordinated the movement of Ottoman and Iranian Kurdish forces into Iranian territory on two fronts. Different accounts estimate the number of their troops between 10,000 and 30,000 cavalry and infantry. Ottoman and Iranian representatives in the border region hastily wired the same urgent news to their capitals; the Russian, British, and French consuls quickly followed suit.[17] Under the leadership of Ubeidullah and one of his *khalifahs*, a group of rebels marched on the ethnically and religiously mixed Iranian city of Urumieh. A second column marching under his son Abdul Qadir and the chief of the Mangur tribe Hamza Agha tried to extend their conquests beyond the mainly Kurdish towns of the border region and further into Azerbaijan.

The revolt's first military engagement took place on 9 October 1880, when the Kurdish forces defeated the governor of Urumieh at the castle of Badrbud. Ten days after the initial clashes, Sheikh Ubeidullah arrived in Urumieh at the head of a force of about 7,000 (according to other reports 10,000 and even an improbable 60,000).[18] His party camped in the village of San Sergis (Saint Sargis) on the outskirts of Seir Mountain before laying siege to the city.[19] Although rumored to be carrying Henry Martini and Winchester rifles that had been distributed during the Russo-Ottoman war, in reality his troops were poorly armed and trained by the standards of their adversaries. Soon after their arrival negotiations for Urumieh's surrender commenced, and the parties to the confrontation asked the American missionary, Dr Cochran, to be the intermediary. Because Cochran was joined by the British Consul of Tabriz, W. G. Abbott, his role has prompted much speculation, both then and in later historiography: was the Kurdish revolt an instrument of British imperialism? As most Iranian and Turkish historiographies are driven by nationalist ideologies intent on depriving the Kurds of any historical agency, they almost always portray the Kurds as puppets of foreigners and their revolts as foreign incitements rather than conscious responses to the oppression and disenfranchisement they faced. In light of this, it is important to stress that a careful study of the sources shows that, far from being instigated by imperial powers, as both the Qajars and Ottomans feared, this imperial "intervention" was limited to Consul Abbot and Cochran visiting the sheikh while his forces were closing in on Urumieh, and most likely was intended to secure the life of Christian minorities of the region.[20]

An additional argument against the notion that Ubeidullah was acting as a puppet of the Great Powers is that his success would have rendered meaningless at least the northern part of the Ottoman-Iranian boundary that London, St Petersburg, Tehran, and Istanbul had already spent considerable time and money to delimit. Moreover, the region would come under the control of a Sunni religious leader, which would have threatened both the Russian presence in Caucasus and Iranian

Shia domination in north-western Iran, at the same time that it would have challenged the authority of the Sunni Caliph, the Ottoman Sultan. Thus, far from being instigated by them, the rebellion actually renewed the commitment of all parties to making the Ottoman-Iranian boundary that permanently divided the Kurds a reality: without exception they deployed additional troops along the border, and Russia went so far as to offer military assistance to Iran. Indeed, when Cochran and Abbot's appeals convinced the sheikh to postpone his attack on Urumieh, Iranian troops were able to regroup and prepare the city for a confrontation. Thus one could claim that the Anglo-American intervention, far from proving that they were directing events from afar, actually helped prevent the sheikh's ultimate success.

On 9 Zilka'da 1297 (24 October 1880), the deadline given to the city having expired, the sheikh sent a force of 5,000 to Urumieh, led by his older son, Sadiq, and his *khalifah*, Muhammad Sadiq. After three days and nights of intense fighting, the Kurds withdrew to a nearby village. Having assumed a swift victory, the sheikh's forces were poorly provisioned and began plundering this and other villages for food. In the meantime, the city received extra reinforcements.[21] The Kurdish position became untenable, and on 3 November 1880 the Ottoman Tehran Embassy wired Istanbul news of their retreat.[22]

Interpretations of the sheikh's withdrawal vary. The sheikh himself claimed that he withdrew in deference to the caliph-sultan's orders, sent through several representatives. While it is true that he did receive such visitors, attributing the withdrawal to them is questionable at best. Even before his retreat, Ottoman troops had advanced into his country and taken possession of his base of operations at Nehri. In the meantime, Iranian troops, including those of the Khan of Maku, massed at Urumieh, where they not only clashed with Ubeidullah's force but also carried out atrocities against the local people. According to Dr Cochran, the Persian troops did far more damage than the Kurds.[23]

The southern front of the revolt

While the Urumieh front ultimately failed, the southern front of the revolt was different. According to an Ottoman report, in September 1880 the second column of the sheikh's forces, 6,000 very poorly armed men under the command of his son, Abdul Qadir, and the chief of the Mengur tribe, Hamza Aga, descended in a disorderly fashion on the town of Savojbulagh (present-day Mahabad), where the residents welcomed them.[24] On 9 October, Hamza Aga Mengur wrote to the sheikh:

> Four thousand courageous Kurdish cavalry arrived at the plain of Serdesht on the fourth of the month of Zilka'da and the inhabitants of the towns of Tercan, Bukan, Lahijan, Ushnu and Bane came forward to greet us with full respect...we safely arrived at [Savojbolagh] and we participated in the prayer which was read in the name of our master,

the Padishah of Islam, Sultan Abdulhamid Khan, at the seat of the governor... The *imams* and *muezzins* were instructed to call the name of the Khalifah of Islam Sultan Abdulhamid from the pulpits of their mosques, which caused celebration among the people.[25]

After this relatively easy conquest, Abdul Qadir appointed governors to each Kurdish town in the region, even as Ottoman and Iranian troops were fast closing in on his rebel forces. While he wrote letters inviting local notables to join him, news of his troops' lack of discipline and raucous conduct also spread. After securing the Sunni Kurdish towns, they marched toward the majority Shia town of Mianduab. As news of the sheikhzadeh's advance spread, some Sunni villages near Mianduab wrote to him, pleading that if help was not sent promptly, the Ajams would finish them off. In response, Abdul Qadir sent one of his maternal uncles and 200 horsemen to reconnoiter the region. When this small detail ran into a much larger Shia force, they were routed and most were killed, including the sheikhzadeh's uncle, whose head was cut off and publicly displayed. When the sheikhzadeh advanced, the Ajam forces had already departed, leaving severed limbs and cut heads scattered on the battlefield. Appalled at the sight, the young commander ordered retaliation: the massacre of the townspeople of Mianduab. According to the reliable Qurians' account, 800 Muslims, 20 Armenians, and 50 Jews from all walks of life and ages were killed. Widespread pillaging followed.[26] As Qurians observed, it seemed that neither the young Abdul Qadir nor Hamza Aga was in full control of the situation.[27] This bloody event reactivated existing Sunni-Shia sectarian boundaries. It also allowed some of the sheikh's presumed allies to formulate their differences with him and his movement and rethink their identities. Some of the sheikhzadeh's troops, for example, refused to take part in the Mianduab massacre. Mamesh Mamend Aga, who had involuntarily joined the sheikhzadeh's forces, withheld his men from the carnage and helped some inhabitants to escape. Many other Kurdish agas and mullahs also criticized the sheikhzadeh and refused to join him, including the chief of the powerful Dehbokri tribe, Gulabi Agha. Appalled by the Mianduab debacle, he built a successful coalition against the sheikhzadeh. Faced with resistance from his former allies and with the imminent arrival of Iranian troops, Abdul Qadir attempted to lay siege to the town of Benab, but his position was becoming untenable. The flames of the revolt, which started at the end of August 1880, were extinguished by the end of November, when the sheikh returned to his village on the Ottoman side.[28]

No matter how we define it—as a revolt against social and religious oppression, as a rebellion, or as a nationalist insurgency—the sheikh's movement failed to create a unified Kurdish front. The revolt showed that, in a society where nationalist sentiments and an overarching identity were yet to develop, allegiances were determined by the dynamics of sometimes conflicting local power relations, a sense of historical belonging—to the state (either Iranian or Ottoman) or to the shah/sultan—personal or group affiliations, and/or a calculation of cost benefits of loyalty. The sheikh's movement failed to supersede such concerns. But the advancing Iranian army simi-larly failed to exploit the potential benefits of allying with Sunni Kurdish tribes in this moment of upheaval. The Qajar army's scorched-earth tactics and brutality, which far exceeded the scope of Kurdish pillage and plunder, based its logic on a binary division between *us* and *them*, the Kurd-Sunni and the Ajam-Shia.

The response of the Iranian army

While Kurdish forces pillaged the region, their Qajar counterparts directed their violence toward establishing Tehran's supremacy in the Sunni Kurdish territories. They and their allies spread terror in their wake as they beheaded, mutilated, and burned people alive, abducted and raped women and girls, and even cut open the wombs of pregnant women.[29] An estimated 15,000-100,000 families fled into Ottoman lands. Those Sunnis who did not flee the environs of Savojbulagh, Ushnu, Saqqez, and Sinne were put to sword by the Iranian army, villages were burned to the ground, and women and children were led away as captives.[30] Some Shia and Christian villages also suffered at the hands of the Iranian troops. Consul Abbot reported the situation in Urumieh:

> The Sunnis—five thousand families it is said in Oroomiah—are utterly broken up, except a few villages that have changed their faith to Shiah. They are in valleys and hamlets of the mountains in great want and must die of hunger and cold. Many of the men have been killed.[31]

There is no doubt that such atrocities resulted in lasting demographic changes in Urumieh, which became a predominantly Shia city. The Ottoman consul there corroborated Abbot's report, adding that "In Mergevar alone fifteen hundred per-sons were killed, and in the environs of the *nahiyah* of [...Tepe] around Savojbulagh, the inhabitants of twenty villages were killed, youngsters and women were carried off as captives."[32]

Both the sheikh and his adversaries in Istanbul were concerned about the fate of the thousands of families who, fleeing the Iranian army, had crossed the snowy moun-tains in the thick of winter to enter Ottoman domains. While Istanbul pressured Tehran to declare an amnesty in order to alleviate pressure in the region, the Ottoman Council of Ministers concluded that the sheikh was a dangerous figure who should be removed from the frontier.[33] Quoting Ubeidullah's letter to the townspeople of Ercish, which urged them "to be ready by the end of March and unite with those united to attack Iran," the Ottoman Grand Vizier suspected that the leader desired to bring together Christians and Muslims for a new revolt with the possibility of declaring political autonomy.[34] His suspicions were not misplaced. Indeed, the sheikh had sent letters to tribal and religious leaders in Mosul, Van, Bitlis, Urumieh—even to the Taleshi Sunnis in Gilan—inviting them all to rebel. To assuage the fears of Tehran and St Petersburg, Istanbul insisted that the Ottoman troops deployed at the frontier would not allow him to succeed.[35] In the meantime, representatives from London and Paris also began asking for the sheikh's removal from the region.[36] In response, Istanbul sent Suleyman Pasha to Tehran as Envoy Extraordinaire.[37]

At the same time, it sent the sultan's *yaver*, or aide-de-camp, Ahmed Ratib Bey, to Nehri to talk to the refugees and the sheikh himself, who had continued, during all of this time, to pledge his loyalty to the sultan through letters, telegrams, and proxies.[38] Despite these questionable pledges, the Porte felt it to be "dangerous to keep a man capable of calling to arms thirty to forty thousand people in the frontier region [...] he should be expelled." [39] Indeed, Ahmed Ratib witnessed refugees selling their remaining belongings to procure weapons for a rebellion.[40]

Facing resistance from Iranian, Ottoman, and possibly Russian troops, the sheikh relented and on 10 July 1881 arrived in Van.[41] Not wanting him to remain there, Tehran asked Ottoman authorities to treat him as a frontier bandit rather than a political personality, and to banish him from the region.[42] Only after the sheikh's arrival in Istanbul did the Iranians breathe a sigh of relief. Nasr al-Din Shah ordered his Foreign Ministry to send honors to the Ottoman pashas who took part in quelling the rebellion.[43]

Prisoner at the palace: Ubeidullah in Istanbul

A year after the start of the revolt, in the company of a regiment of cavalry and two batteries of artillery, Sheikh Ubeidullah arrived at Constantinople with great pomp.[44] He was given a residence in the Yildiz Palace complex. As he and his sons settled into their palace exile, his other lieutenant, Hamza Agha Mengur, continued a guerrilla war against the Qajar troops. In response, Hasan Ali Khan Garrusi, the high-ranking bureaucrat and governor of Garrus, sent a deputation and a Quran to Hamza Agha, promising him authority over southern Kurdistan if he swore allegiance to the shah. Taking him at his word, Hamza Agha, together with fourteen of his men, went to the governor's tent where they dined together. After dinner, the governor excused himself and the tent was riddled with bullets. He fought the attack and according to Reverend Wilson killed a dozen men before he was slain; his head was cut off and sent to the commander-in-chief at Urumieh.[45] With this last obstacle removed, the Iranian army began "mopping up" the operations that would brutally institutionalize Tehran's supremacy in the borderland.

While in Istanbul, the sheikh, it seemed, had given himself up to religious meditation and even petitioned the sultan to be allowed to make a pilgrimage. Yet, news of Iranian oppression and his people's continued suffering prompted him to develop an ingenious escape plan. Proclaiming that he would pass the month of Ramadan in silent meditation, at the end of July or beginning of August 1882, exactly one year after arriving in Istanbul, he fled. His flight became public when he failed to appear at the Prime Minister's reception for *Eid al-fitr* (Ramadan). His personal attendant and close *khalifah* were interrogated, to no avail.[46] He eluded the frontier authorities of Russia, Iran, and the Ottoman Empire while crisscrossing their frontiers to reach his stronghold. As he approached Nehri, thousands of people met him. He immediately began communicating with possible allies for a revenge attack on Iran. Many tribes informed him that they were with him and preparing for a new revolt.[47] In a letter from this period, the sheikh warned the recipient not to trust the deceiving words of the authorities, maintaining that "Iranians have no refuge but the Ottomans, who are concentrating troops on the border... No doubt Iran and the Ottoman state are united about annihilation and destruction of Kurdistan." If they can, the sheikh wrote, they will get rid of all Kurdish chiefs and leaders including "this humble one." Hence, "from all sides we need to cooperate and there is no way other than the unity of Kurdistan."[48]

Once again, however, the military might of Iran and the Ottoman Empire would frustrate the sheikh's plans to start a new rebellion. The sultan's aide-de-camp, Kamil Bey, delivered an imperial decree for the sheikh's return, and his communication with Istanbul began anew. Nearly two months after his escape became public, he dispatched a letter to the sultan to remind him of his enduring fealty and services to the empire, and to evoke the specter of the Shia-Sunni rivalry.[49] His request to settle in Mosul or Van, however, was firmly rejected. Following a Russo-Iranian memorandum, issued on 11 December 1882, asking for Ubeidullah's removal from the frontier region,[50] the Ottoman troops converged on Nehri. After some small skirmishes, the sheikh agreed to leave for Akra. His son, Abdul Qadir, whom Ottoman authorities were worried would resist, agreed to accompany his father to Mosul. Shortly afterward, Sheikh Ubeidullah and his sons were exiled to Mecca, where he died the following year, in 1883. His death may have put a definitive end to his rebellion; it did not, however, put an end to his family's championing of Kurdistan.

An untimely response to the age of nationalism

How to define the nature of the Sheikh Ubeidullah rebellion is still open to debate. No doubt he was enticed by the dream of forming an autonomous and unified Kurdistan under the umbrella of the Ottoman sultan-caliph, and he was able to rally some tribes and notables to the cause. In his meetings with the American missionary and various British representatives and in the letters to his allies, Ubeidullah did not hide his ultimate goal of uniting the Kurds, and he employed a discourse that invoked a nationalist ideology. In these contexts, he emphasized the distinctiveness of the Kurds and described them as a family of 500,000 needing a state of their own and a ruler who understood them; he lamented their disenfranchisement by the Turks and their "shameful treatment"; and, above all, he decried the tyranny and oppression [*zulm va taaddi*] they had suffered in Iran. While in his letters to Sultan Abdülhamid he took a different tack, complaining about the lawlessness of Kurdistan and the misrule of its governors, he nevertheless appealed to the sultan-caliph's Sunni sensibilities, emphasizing the sectarian nature of Iranian oppression and asking him to intervene on his kinsmen's behalf. It was also the sultan's inaction that prompted him to action. Consequently, when Consul Abbot asked him about his program, he replied: "I want to reorganize Kurdistan."[51] Like any other nation, as he noted elsewhere, they had decided to rule themselves autonomously (*millet-i saire gibi muhtariyeti idare*).[52] This was indeed the fear of some high-ranking Ottoman administrators[53] and of the Porte as well. In its discussion of the sheikh's escape, the Ottoman Council of Ministers concluded:

> While trying to convince that his movement is caused by the calls he received from the Sunnis oppressed by the Iranian government, his words are not enough to disperse the doubts about his illegitimate intention of uniting the Kurds of the two sides in an independent unit under his rule.[54]

Tehran shared similar concerns, as expressed in a wire to the Porte warning that the sheikh wanted to "unite Ottoman and Iranian Kurds and unite them in an independent principality (*eyalet-i mustakile*)."[55]

That unification, it turned out, was easier said than done. It is true that the coming together of nomadic and semi-nomadic tribes, peasants, villagers, and town dwellers required that the participants had a certain notion of unity or possessed categories of affiliation that transcended the tribe, valley, village, or town; otherwise the sheikh's appeals would have fallen on deaf ears. As the ideologue of the movement, the sheikh developed a body of arguments and ideas about a nation, to which the people responded to the extent that they willingly embraced and embodied his political program. To this extent, his revolt should be classified as an early response of the Kurds to the age of nationalism and could be seen as a nationalist attempt per se.

Yet, it should be noted that "nationalism" was not the only medium that brought the revolt's participants together. In the climate of the post Russo-Ottoman War, sectarian differences among the Christian and Muslim inhabitants of the region, and between the Iranian state and its Kurdish subjects, played a significant role in alliance formation. Conversely, however, the activation of sectarian boundaries by the events recounted above, and the resultant violence, diminished the rebels' opportunities to build on traditional socio-religious boundaries in order to articulate an ethnic consciousness. That is to say, the massacre at Mianduab and the Iranian response to it, while sharply activating sectarian boundaries, simultaneously crystallized the inner antagonisms of Kurdish society, thus halting the rebellion and further delaying the molding of various groups into a meaningful whole. Indeed, the rebellion's brevity contributed to its failure to create "ethnic ardour and solidarity," to effect a permanent forgetfulness of internal differences to face a common threat.[56] The old divisions among the Kurds were not left aside, and ethnic fraternity, the nationalist dream par excellence, did not gain even a momentary reality. The sole attempt to end the long division of the Kurds between Iran and the Ottoman Empire thus came to an abrupt end, much to the relief of not only Iran and the Ottoman Empire, but also of England, France, and Russia. The sheikh dreamed of shaping an alternative understanding of identity, space, and leadership—a Kurdistani understanding—that would have deactivated the Ottoman-Iranian boundary. His failure, however, aided and even hastened international efforts to delimit and demarcate the boundary that left the Kurdish people permanently divided.

12.

JOURNALISM BEYOND BORDERS

THE BEDIRKHANS AND THE FIRST KURDISH GAZETTE, 1898-1902[1]

Janet Klein

Until recently, a significant segment of Kurdish print media was produced outside geographic Kurdistan, a phenomenon that found its origins in the very first Kurdish journal, *Kurdistan*, which made its debut in 1898. After the Ottoman Empire was broken apart following the First World War, nation-states emerged and increasingly adopted national identities that excluded and suppressed the Kurdish one and any expressions of it, particularly print media. While Abdurrahman Bedirkhan, his brother Mikdad Midhat, and numerous cohorts turned out their papers with a variety of goals and in a complex context, it is clear that their project is heralded as a significant moment in the development of Kurdish nationalism. Their espousal of a unique Kurdish identity and their commitment to spreading their views in their newspaper were the very identity and activity that the post-Ottoman nation-states later felt compelled to suppress. Ironically, *Kurdistan* was an "exile" gazette not because it was Kurdish, but because it stood in opposition to Ottoman sultan Abdülhamid II and was actually a paper sponsored by the Ottoman Committee of Union and Progress, an umbrella group of diverse Ottomans who wished to, and eventually did, overthrow his regime. This chapter seeks to resurface these complexities to provide a more critical look at the development of early Kurdish nationalism and the various "hats" worn by the Bedirkhan brothers and many of their colleagues, and to view their multiple (and to our eyes, seemingly conflicting) identities and agendas in the context of Ottoman state-building and uncertainties over the empire's future.

Kurdish journalism began with the publication of a gazette called *Kurdistan*—a four-page journal, more like a pamphlet—in 1898.[2] During its four years of publication, 31 issues were printed in such cities as Cairo, Geneva, London, and Folkestone. The gazette carried a few articles on world events as they related to Kurdish and/or Ottoman affairs; several pieces on Kurdish history and literature; a number of petitions to Sultan Abdülhamid II, the reigning sultan of the Ottoman Empire; and an assortment of other clips, in which were included notices of events, obituaries, and letters to the editor. Most articles were printed in Kurdish, but numerous pieces in Ottoman Turkish also appeared, especially in later issues. The paper was printed not in Kurdistan, and not even in the Ottoman Empire "proper," but it was intended, of course, to be read by Kurds "in exile," and also, and perhaps particularly, by Kurds living in the Kurdish provinces of the Ottoman Empire, as well as in Istanbul, which had a sizeable Kurdish population at the time. The head of the paper announced that he would "send two thousand copies of every issue to Kurdistan, to be given to people free of charge." The stated aims of the paper were "to alert the Kurds, and to encourage them to learn industrial arts," and also to "explain the positive aspects of science and knowledge, ... [to] show the Kurds where good education [could] be received and where good schools [could] be found, which wars were being fought and where, what the Great Powers [were] doing and how they conduct[ed] war, [and] how trade [was] conducted."[3]

The publication of an Ottoman-Kurdish gazette near the turn of the twentieth century does not, at first, seem so extraordinary in light of the fact that newspapers had existed in the Ottoman Empire for over a hundred years prior to the publication of *Kurdistan*, and that when the Kurdish newspaper was first published, it seemed to be an insignificant speck in the swarm of journalistic activity taking place during this time both inside the empire as well as outside, by exiled Ottoman intellectuals. However, the newspaper's appearance has since been considered a landmark in Kurdish history—the moment when the Kurdish language entered a new period and could no longer be spoken of as solely a poetic medium, and also when the Kurdish language entered the era of mass communication, as Amir Hassanpour notes.[4] The newspaper has been widely considered a milestone in Kurdish history for other reasons as well, namely in that it represented the first stage of Kurdish nationalism. *Kurdistan* was important for these reasons, but it must also be viewed in the context of late-Ottoman politics. Kurdish nationalism in the late-Ottoman period, by extension, must be seen in all its complexities, as must the careers, outlooks, and agendas of its founders, the Bedirkhan brothers.

Although acclaimed as a landmark in early Kurdish nationalism, the context for the emergence of *Kurdistan* in 1898 was the affiliation of its founders, particularly Abdurrahman Bedirkhan, with the Ottoman Committee of Union and Progress (hereafter, CUP), the central organization of the Young Turk movement during this period.[5] The CUP was founded in Istanbul in 1899 by a group of four students at the Royal Medical Academy who had, since the mid-1880s, taken "an active interest in ways to organize an opposition to the regime of Abdülhamid II."[6] The CUP and the Young Turk movement in general "represented the protest of all those social groups which had been alienated by Hamidian policies and practices."[7] While it may seem strange to contemporary understanding of nationalist politics for a Kurd to belong to the Young *Turk* movement, from its inception the movement "attracted both Muslims and non-Muslims, [and] Turks and non-Turks."[8] In fact, "[u]ntil 1902, the CUP was an umbrella organization composed of loosely affiliated factions ... [with] little in common ... other than the Young Turk *Weltanschauung* [of science and progress], and the wish to dethrone Abdülhamid II."[9]

Although the CUP was founded in Istanbul, the empire's capital, the bulk of the organization's actions took place "in exile," as members found their activities increasingly inhibited and their publications heavily censored by the palace. It was from Cairo, a CUP center abroad, that Mikdad Midhat Bedirkhan founded the newspaper, *Kurdistan*, most likely under CUP auspices. He directed the paper for its first five issues, and all subsequent issues were run by his brother, Abdurrahman, who proceeded to move the paper's publishing location to Geneva, London, and Folkestone, all centers of CUP activity. It is clear that Abdurrahman Bedirkhan was an active member of the CUP, at least during the years in which he published *Kurdistan*,[10] and there is evidence that the Kurdish gazette was published by CUP presses[11] and was read by and written about by other CUP members.[12]

Kurdistan was not simply a CUP organ because its founders were members. The journal itself devoted space to reporting on the activities of the CUP and several of the group's members, particularly in later issues. One such topic that received good press in *Kurdistan* was the First Congress of Ottoman Opposition, organized by the CUP and held in Paris in 1902. This coverage highlighted Abdurrahman Bedirkhan's involvement in empire-wide affairs, and not just those involving his Kurdish compatriots. The last issue of *Kurdistan*, for example, contains a lengthy article that provides rich information on the Congress. In this article, Abdurrahman Bedirkhan discusses plans for the Congress and the problems involved in obtaining permission from the French government to gather; who was present at the meeting; and which factions emerged after disputes arose regarding the group's stance on foreign intervention in Ottoman affairs. Abdurrahman Bedirkhan himself spoke out against the group that favored foreign intervention in implementing the reforms and the re-establishment of the constitutional regime, which was desired by the CUP. However, there is no mention of Kurdish issues in the article; nor is there reference to how events that occurred or decisions made at the Congress might have impacted on the Kurds. This may be due to the fact that while the intention of the Congress was to achieve representation of all elements in Ottoman society, most delegates were invited for their participation in the movement and not for their ethnic origins. Abdurrahman Bedirkhan was one person who was invited for his role in the movement, and not for his Kurdishness, as Hanioğlu notes.[13] Indeed, Abdurrahman Bedirkhan even uses *Kurdistan* as a forum to explain his activities as a result of his need to wake up to the sultan's tyranny and agitate against it. In a petition to the sultan he writes:

> I, your humble servant, upon graduating from secondary school, graduated from the School for Public Administration and was then appointed to an office in the Ministry of Education, which dealt with the secondary schools in the empire, and I worked there for six or seven years. My humble desire was to serve my nation. However, your unbearable suppression prevented me from carrying out my wish. When it became impossible to remain in Istanbul, I sacrificed my position and my salary for my sacred aim, and threw myself into the arms of liberty.[14]

Abdullah Cevdet, a close colleague of Abdurrahman Bedirkhan in the CUP as well as the Kurdish movement, had a similar story. Abdullah Cevdet, who was actually one of the four founders of the CUP, contributed to *Kurdistan* and discussed Kurdish issues, but also published a more general Ottoman opposition journal, *İctihad*, to which Abdurrahman Bedirkhan contributed after the closure of *Kurdistan*. Although interested in the affairs of the Kurds, as is evidenced by their remarks on the pages of *Kurdistan*, these two men, along with others, must also be appreciated in the context of wider Ottoman politics.

Kurdistan must be seen, at least in part, as a CUP organ. However, aside from the lengthy coverage of the Congress of Ottoman Opposition in 1902, the journal preferred to tackle the job of resisting Abdülhamid II's regime in ways other than writing directly about CUP activities. In fact, in many regards the journal's coverage of Kurdish affairs seems to exist for the purpose of attacking the sultan and his policies. Bursting with harsh critiques of Abdülhamid II, his policies, and his sycophantic officials, articles and particularly petitions or open letters to the sultan fill good space in *Kurdistan*. As such the message is twofold: Kurds, by seeing how the sultan's policies negatively affect them, are urged to join the opposition; and second, detailing the sultan's policies that impact on life in Kurdistan can also serve to add to the many examples of the horrors of his reign.

From the first open letter to the last, the Bedirkhan brothers levied increasingly severe criticism against the sultan's neglect of the Kurds and against the despotic policies he enforced in Kurdistan. The petitions to the sultan underscore the importance of Kurdistan's strategic location in the empire as the buffer zone between the two "enemy" states of Russia and Iran and the Ottoman heartland. This point is reiterated throughout the petitions (and in other pieces as well), and the strategic importance of the Kurds is highlighted as a primary reason for the palace to pay better attention to the region and to ensure the well-being of the people. In one such petition, Mikdad Midhat Bedirkhan writes:

My Sultan, As is known by your imperial majesty, the Kurds are the most distinguished of all the peoples [living] under the eternal Ottoman state, and Kurdistan as well, as positioned on the border of two neighboring states, is on account of her unique location the land that inhibits enemy aggression and enemy threats ... Despite [Kurdistan's] occupying an important place, and despite our boasting of Ottoman nationality for a long time, until you, the Sultan, ascended to the throne, the ways and means of improving [our situation] and education has been neglected.[15]

After concluding this passage with a request to the sultan to recognize the importance of allowing the circulation of *Kurdistan*, the author resumes his appeal in the next letter in the same issue, writing, "[T]his Kurdish newspaper will ensure and hasten the necessary reforms in the Kurdish region, and will also act as a primary tool for preventing the oppressive acts exercised by certain officials."[16]

To the uninitiated, these petitions might in themselves seem bizarre: how could opponents of the regime write letters that appear to show confidence that the sultan cares, and is merely unaware of what is happening under "oppressive officials" in his empire? Put plainly, this is simply the style of Ottoman rhetoric: the literary convention of petition to the ruler is one genre of many in the wider body of Ottoman political writing. The real audience, in the minds of these authors, was not the sultan, but the Kurdish people, other CUP members, and any other Ottomans who might read the journal, or listen to its reading in a public or private space. The Bedirkhan brothers and their CUP colleagues were attempting to depose the sultan and to create a new social and political order in the empire. Opposition-movement participants knew that their calls for reform would be ignored by the palace. Their aim was not even for the sultan to acknowledge the need for reforms, but instead they wished to do away with the sultan and his regime altogether and usher in a new era. These appeals were designed to incite readers to become aware of the corrupt nature of the existing regime and the need for change, and to join the opposition movement to enact reforms. It also, as will be discussed below, spoke directly to the Kurds, and urged them to become aware of their identity and importance in the empire, in spite of the paper's alter ego as a medium for Ottoman opposition.

In accomplishing the task of communicating these messages, however, the Bedirkhan brothers faced two obstacles similar to those confronted by their CUP colleagues who published for a different "target audience." First, their publication had been banned in the empire, which is not surprising as censorship was notorious in the Hamidian era. In "letters to the editor," readers wrote what risked arrest if they were caught with *Kurdistan* in their possession.[17] Second, Kurdistan lacked a "reading public."[18] In other words, illiteracy was almost universal in the region. However, in spite of these barriers to dissemination, *Kurdistan*, like other banned publications, was smuggled back into the empire[19] and found a reading (or listening) public. While illiteracy did prevail, the number of readers was slowly growing to include those outside the traditionally literate classes—the nobility and the *ulema*. Most important for dissemination of the content of journals, however, were coffee-house recitations and readings at other public gatherings.[20] Letters to the editor from places like Damascus, Adana, Mardin, and Diyarbakir also reveal that there were readers in diverse parts of the empire.[21]

As I have argued so far, *Kurdistan* must be seen as a publication of the larger Ottoman opposition movement to Sultan Abdülhamid II, and while articles speaking directly to Kurds about issues faced by Kurdistanis (Kurds, Armenians, and others living in the region) continued to serve as a forum to take additional jabs at the sultan and his policies, the journal and its contents must also be seen as a significant moment in *Kurdish* history as well. The title of the journal itself embodies this importance, and was not lost on readers, one of whom wrote that "when this paper of our *mîr* reached Damascus," he found a copy of it, and that when the Kurds there "learned that the newspaper was titled 'Kurdistan,' and that it was the paper of 'our *mîr*,' they kissed the paper, and touched it to their heads and were overjoyed. Then I read it to them."[22]

One Ottoman issue that was particularly relevant to the Kurds was their relationship with neighboring Armenians. Abdurrahman Bedirkhan was, along with others, deeply troubled by recently exacerbated tensions between the two groups and devoted ample space to the topic in *Kurdistan*. In one passage, he denounces Armenian separatist activity, but also reproaches the Kurds for attacking the Armenians, thereby bringing disfavor upon the Kurds in the eyes of Europe. He writes:

> What really irritates me in Europe, because of my nationality of which I am a proud member, is the Europeans' reproachful comments on clashes with Armenians. What are the reasons for these lootings and plunder, making you [Kurds] guilty in the eyes ... of Europe? Believe me, I know all the reasons. I know everything about how Armenians desire to separate this holy land, Kurdistan, from the Ottoman body, and to make it a land for themselves ... However, all these events don't give you the right to clash with Armenians. It is never right to trust the policies of the government.[23]

This article is particularly illustrative of Abdurrahman Bedirkhan's position on the subject. In this article, as in others, he urges the Kurds to treat the Armenians well not simply for humanitarian reasons but also for fear that Kurdish aggression against the Armenians would offer the "Great Powers" of Europe another pretext to meddle in Ottoman affairs, particularly in the region where Kurds lived.[24] Here the blur between Abdurrahman Bedirkhan's Ottomanism and "Kurdism" is clear.

Abdurrahman Bedirkhan's virulent attacks on the sultan's Hamidiye cavalry units also typify his views on this subject. His numerous rants draw attention to how toxic the sultan's policies in the region were, and how they incited increased friction between Kurds and Armenians—"divide and rule," in short. In one piece Abdurrahman Bedirkhan writes, "Greatness is not limited to being a Hamidiye private under the command of Zeki Pasha and those government officials who push you to fight [the Armenians]."[25] After all, he contends in another piece, "The idea of forming the Hamidiye divisions was submitted to the palace by the marshal of the Fourth Army, Zeki Pasha, and such an idea, including the creation of an eternal rivalry between different elements, was accepted by the sultan."[26] He particularly resented the Hamidiye Light Cavalry, because not only did it act as an instrument for "divide and rule" of Kurds against Armenians, but also because it sowed discord among Kurds themselves. A remarkably colorful passage on this topic adds another twist to my suggestion that Abdurrahman Bedirkhan wore several "hats" at the same time, and that while he was at once an Ottomanist and a "Kurdist," he also had a stake in reversing his family's fortunes and reclaiming the leadership role that the Bedirkhans once had in Kurdistan (a topic that will be addressed later in this chapter), and doing this by mocking the tribe (Mîran) that found new fortune under the auspices of Abdülhamid II in the Bedirkhans' former domain of sovereignty:

> Before [Abdülhamid] had ascended to the throne, the Kurds were knowledgeable and civilized people, having brotherly relations with Armenians and avoiding any kind of confrontation. Then what happened? Did [Kurdish] civilization and knowledge turn into barbarity, ignorance, and organized rebellion? Who else carries out the atrocities in Kurdistan but the members of the Hamidiye divisions, who are armed by the sultan and proud of being loyal to him? For example, there is Mustafa Pasha, leader of the Mîran tribe, within the borders of the Diyarbekir province. He used to be a shepherd ten or fifteen years ago in his tribe and was called "Misto the Bald." We don't know what he did to become a favorite of the sultan, but his talent in creating scandals appeased the sultan, who thought that he would assist in bloodshed and hurting people. He made him a pasha and introduced him with the title of Commander of the Hamidiye Division. Now imagine what such a man is capable of doing—a traitor whose own son has even become an enemy to him, and a person who has outraged his daughter-in-law—wouldn't he butcher the Armenians and pillage the Muslims?[27]

While acting as a tool for informing Kurds how the Hamidian regime worked against Kurdish interests and how Hamidian policies were harmful to the Kurds, the authors in *Kurdistan* generally continued to espouse Ottomanist idioms which aimed to protect the empire and create a unity based on a common Ottoman citizenship regardless of religion or ethnicity; however, they did depart from this rhetoric on several occasions. In the first issue that Abdurrahman Bedirkhan released after having taken up the paper's production, he composed a piece that told the Kurds they were an element exploited not only by the sultan, but also by the Turks, thereby departing from the Ottomanist discourse that emphasized a common Ottoman patriotism. In this piece the author declared:

My love for my Kurdish nation drives me to show the Kurds the right path, through this newspaper. Rum [Istanbul, or the Sublime Porte] establishes the great schools in the regions populated by Turks. The government takes money from the Kurds and spends it on the Turks. The poor Kurds are slaves to this government.[28]

Later, he wrote:

After serving the Turks for so many years, what good has come of it? Every time you are decorated or bestowed with ranks you forget all about your suffering under this oppression. This state has killed many Kurds in its wars, but to this day not a single Kurd has fought for his fatherland. It is as if we were created to serve foreigners. Five hundred years ago there was not a single Turk in our country. These Turks all came from Turan [and settled] in our country, and now they rule us in our own land...[29]

Although generally Ottomanist in perspective, Abdurrahman Bedirkhan engaged in bet-hedging, a concept that will be developed below, and recognized that there was a chance that the Ottoman Empire could fall completely apart.

Preparing for that possibility, *Kurdistan* worked to instill in the Kurds a stronger sense of historical uniqueness and national pride by printing pieces on Kurdish history and literature so that Kurds could begin to highlight the Kurdish element of their identity. Additionally, the messages embedded within the pieces published in *Kurdistan*, after establishing the "greatness" of Kurdish historical and literary accomplishments, used these same texts to advance the notion that Kurds should rise in opposition to the existing regime.

The subject of Kurdish history fills many pages of *Kurdistan*. One such article, titled "Kurdistan and the Kurds," traces the history of the Kurds from their descent from the ancient Medes to their present moment as Ottoman subjects. The author underscores the value of studying Kurdish history, and in lamenting the fact that its research has been too long ignored, the author writes:

Despite the fact that Kurds possess special human qualities such as wit and mental acuity, courage and industriousness, are altruistic and sacrificing, and have a love for liberty as if they worshipped it, in world history, their name is not frequently mentioned. And in a century in which civilization has reached its peak, other nations do not really know much about the general history of this noble people.[30]

He proceeds, tracing Kurdish history from ancient times through the Kurds' adoption of Islam and the Islamic dynasties they founded, pausing to comment on the beauty of the Kurdish physiognomy and the qualities of the Kurdish character. Moving on to Kurdish gifts to science and knowledge, he writes:

The Merwanid Dynasty ... gave great services to the Islamic civilization ... [and] many important scholars [contributed] in the fields of science and religion. And as if it wears a black robe of mourning because it longs for those great days, the town of Amed

[Diyarbakir], which was then a center for science and art, today is being annihilated under the oppression of the regime of Abdülhamid II, along with other towns of the country.[31]

In perfect consistency with the stance of the newspaper as an organ of opposition to Abdülhamid II, the history of the Kurds is portrayed here as yet another area that has been damaged by Hamidian rule. This piece, like others, urges the Kurds to react, and to reclaim their "historical greatness." Also in harmony with my suggestion that the Bedirkhan brothers wore multiple "hats" is the way in which they took the opportunity, in the guise of informing Kurds of their history, to advance the history of their own family, a topic that will be treated further below.

Closely related to the publishing of Kurdish history was the decision of the Bedirkhan brothers to feature Kurdish literary works and tributes to famous Kurdish poets in *Kurdistan*. In the third issue, Mikdad Midhat Bedirkhan printed a belated eulogy[32] for the Kurdish poet, Haci Qadirê Koyî, who was, and still is, renowned for his patriotic poetry and his devotion to the Kurdish language.[33] The other Kurdish poet whom the Bedirkhan brothers honored on the pages of *Kurdistan* was Ehmedê Khanî. They paid homage to one of the most famous figures in Kurdish history by reprinting his epic poem (versified in 1694), *Mem û Zîn*, in serial form on the pages of *Kurdistan*.[34] *Mem û Zîn* is the story of two lovers (Mem and Zîn) from rival clans whose union is obstructed by a figure named Bakir, himself of a different clan. After Mem's death, Zîn mourns her lover's passing until she dies of grief, and is buried next to Mem. When Bakir's role in the tragedy is discovered, he fears for his life and takes sanctuary between the two lovers' graves; but he is killed anyway and a thorn-bush springs up from his blood, whose roots separate the lovers even after their death.[35] The theme, adopted by Kurdish nationalists, has been explained by Hassanpour: "Mam and Zin represent the two parts of Kurdistan divided between the Ottoman and Persian empires. Bakir personifies the discord ... and disunity ... of the Kurdish princes which Khani considered to be the main reasons for the Kurdish people to achieve sovereignty."[36] The introduction to the poem expresses this notion more directly:

> Behold: all the country between Arabia and Georgia/ is Kurdish land./ The Kurds live there as in a citadel./ The Turks and Persians are [e]stablished behind them.../ Our nation holds the frontier keys./ She separates both enemies/ strong as a dam./ But when the Turkish sea and the Persian ocean grow rough/ The Kurds are splashed with blood.../ If we were united.../We would be the mightiest.../We would raise the wind.../ We would attain the realm of science and wisdom.[37]

Khanî also blamed the miserable condition of the Kurds on the absence of a Kurdish government, and suggested that if the Kurds were to be unified under one Kurdish king their lot would improve. It is clear that the Bedirkhan brothers were sensitive to the messages conveyed in *Mem û Zîn*. In introducing the reader to the poem, Mikdad

Midhat Bedirkhan writes, "[T]he poem ... appears on the surface to be the story of two lovers, but its ultimate meaning and goals are hidden. For this reason, it is important to read the poem carefully."[38]

As I have mentioned above, in addition to serving as a medium for opposition to the regime of Abdülhamid II and as an instrument to propagate Kurdish nationalist sentiments, *Kurdistan* also served the personal, familial, and tribal/dynastic goals of the Bedirkhan brothers. This suggestion is substantiated by the fact that of the pieces published on Kurdish history, all but one were "historical" passages on the Bedirkhan family and the Botan princes,[39] as if the family's illustrious history was synonymous with the history of the Kurdish people. The Bedirkhan brothers, in drawing upon their family's legendary history and in printing it on the pages of their gazette, surely intended to convey to their readership that they were the natural representatives of the "Kurdish nation in the making," and had claim to its leadership should it emerge as sovereign in the event that the empire fell apart.

Mikdad Midhat and Abdurrahman Bedirkhan were members of one of the most long-lived and powerful ruling families in Kurdistan, which had founded a principality in its name, and which had ruled a major part of Kurdistan for a good part of the Ottoman presence in Kurdistan. While it is likely that the Bedirkhan dynasty conceived of its rule as more dynastic than "national" prior to the nineteenth century, it is clear that the descendants of the famed Bedirkhan Beg who founded *Kurdistan* sought to portray his rule as nationalist, and *Kurdish*. They depicted his uprisings against Ottoman attempts to re-establish control over its far-flung peripheries, here Kurdistan, in the mid-nineteenth century as "nationalist" rebellions. To bolster this picture they drew upon the elements of Bedirkhan Beg's rule and revolt that highlighted his moves toward autonomy beyond his refusal to pay taxes or offer troops to the Ottoman government, or subordinate his authority in general to the Ottoman sultan; they had to push beyond reference to these activities because, after all, these were not so extraordinary given that this was just what local notables *did*. Instead, to illustrate his "nationalist" inclinations, his sons underlined his attempts, from the time he came to power in 1821 to his exile in 1847, to create an "independent Kurdistan" to be ruled by himself and his family. They discussed how he endeavored to mend differences between tribes and to abolish tribal rivalries, as he saw how splits in the Kurdish community would only weaken the chances of achieving independence for Kurdistan. He forged numerous alliances and consolidated his position to the point that he had attained the status of "king of Kurdistan." Tribal chiefs paid taxes to him, he coined his own money, and Friday prayers were recited in his name. Europeans who visited the region also noted the distinctly nationalistic tone in the Emir's political program.[40] In spite of these actions, however, it cannot be denied that his primary aim in revolting and in uniting other tribes under his rule was to protect and further consolidate his own power.[41]

Regardless of this information, what is critical is how Bedirkhan Beg's rule was depicted by his progeny, notably his sons in *Kurdistan*. The story of the battles of Emir Bedirkhan against the Ottoman forces was narrated in *Kurdistan* in a lengthy article titled "Bedirhan Bey." In this piece of writing, Abdurrahman Bedirkhan recalls the devious plots hatched against the Kurds by corrupt Ottoman officials and how his father, Emir Bedirkhan, fought courageously to restore Kurdistan to "just rule." He writes, "Everyone wanted to live within the border of his administration and save themselves from oppression. Thus, the regions in which Bedirhan Bey had power were not limited to Cizre and Botan; they extended to the Hakkari region of the province of Kurdistan."[42] Elsewhere Abdurrahman Bedirkhan laments the condition of Kurdistan in his day and explains how, after his father's rule, the situation worsened:

> Since my father left Kurdistan, the officials dispatched by the government to the towns and villages of Kurdistan are drinking the blood of the Kurdish people like snakes. The patrons do not know who their clients are and nor do the clients know who their patrons are. The Kurdish homeland is exhausted like a wounded body.[43]

Another passage that clearly exhibits how *Kurdistan* at times acted as an avenue for advancing the interests of the Bedirkhan family is the article (mentioned above) in which Abdurrahman Bedirkhan condemns the Hamidiye units and uses the opportunity to vilify Mustafa Pasha of the Mîran tribe. There was clearly a rivalry between the two families. To elaborate on the story begun above, during the Russo-Ottoman war of 1877-8 two of Abdurrahman and Mikdad Midhat's brothers, Osman and Hüseyin, re-established the Botan emirate, and Osman Pasha, the eldest brother, proclaimed himself sovereign. He ruled for around eight months and enjoyed the support of many of the neighboring tribes. However, after Ottoman troops captured Osman Pasha, the emirate disintegrated. The area which had been ruled by the Bedirkhan family fell into the hands of Mustafa Pasha because of his rise in rank upon being appointed commander of a Hamidiye division, and his tribe, the Mîran, came to control the region. Surely this outraged Abdurrahman Bedirkhan, and his remarks ridiculing "Misto the Bald" make more sense once considered in this light.

When grasped in the context of the promotion of the family's interests, an additional motive for printing *Mem û Zîn* also appears. Striking similarities exist between the desires expressed by Ehmedê Khanî in *Mem û Zîn* and by the Bedirkhan brothers in *Kurdistan*. Khanî dreamed of the day when Kurds would "attain the realm of science and wisdom"; the brothers too lamented the "backward" state of the Kurds and how the Kurds lacked education—the newspaper's goal was to remedy this situation by opening up the Kurds to science and knowledge. Khanî grieved for the fact that the Kurds were caught in border politics; the Bedirkhans sought to acquaint the Kurds with their strategic location and to rescue the Kurds from their precarious position on the borderlands of empires. The Bedirkhan brothers agreed with Khanî that changes should be initiated from above, by the princes and nobility, and they did not hide this conviction from their readers. As Abdurrahman Bedirkhan wrote, "It is necessary for the Kurdish elite to teach the little people under your rule science and the arts; then the *beys* and *aghas* will be respected one hundred times over. The warning is up to me and the listening is up to you."[44] However, as if to send a delicate reminder to their readers that only the most enlightened princes should rule (i.e. the Bedirkhan family), they addressed the elite again:

> *Beys, aghas,* and pashas—I am asking you, who among you has done anything for his fatherland, which would let us know that you love your fatherland? Patriotism means preventing enemies from entering the fatherland. Patriotism means making the fatherland prosperous, and patriotism means educating the children of the fatherland and teaching them arts and sciences ... establishing schools and benevolent societies.[45]

The implication here is that while the Kurdish nobility has exerted no effort to bring prosperity to the Kurdish nation, the Bedirkhan family *has*, first by Emir Bedirkhan's attempts to unite the Kurdish tribes and promote security, and second by his sons' later publication of *Kurdistan* on behalf of the Kurds.

On this note, the similarities between Khanî's dream of a valiant Kurdish leader who would unite the Kurds under his benevolent sovereignty and the description in *Kurdistan* of Bedirkhan Beg, the father of Mikdad Midhat and Abdurrahman, becomes even more striking. It may be no coincidence that *Mem û Zîn* and the histories of the Botan emirate were printed together. Perhaps the Bedirkhan brothers envisioned themselves and their family as the heroic figures for which Khanî's epic poem expressed hope. They imagined themselves as the noble leaders who would liberate the Kurds from the plague of backwardness and from their lamentable situation, which stemmed from their geographic location. In drawing indirect references to the parallels between Khanî's king and their own father, the Bedirkhan brothers were, perhaps, also hinting to their Kurdish readership that should there one day be an independent Kurdistan, the Bedirkhan family would be its natural rulers.

It is tough to conclude from the contents of *Kurdistan* alone the extent to which the Bedirkhan brothers were working to advance family/tribal/dynastic interests, were striving to promote Kurdish nationalism, or were operating as Ottomans who wanted to protect the territorial integrity of the empire and spread the Young Turk vision of "science and progress." It may be tempting to choose one ambition as taking precedence, but the evidence at hand does not permit such a claim. Instead, the Bedirkhan brothers and their paper, *Kurdistan*, must be seen as belonging to all three contexts and working to achieve goals presented by all three.

The Bedirkhan brothers and *Kurdistan* were, after all, products of their historical moment, and the situations life brought them were multifarious. The matter of identity was particularly complex for a Kurd living in Ottoman society. All Ottomans had multi-faceted identities that included ties to their religion, region, village, tribe, socio-economic class, and sultan/caliph, and added to this in the nineteenth century was the beginning of a stronger sense of ethnicity. Even for those Kurds who may have felt special loyalty to "family and tribe and to the tribal chieftain," the existence of loyalty to one element, as van Bruinessen notes, "[d]oes not preclude the functioning of other loyalties. Conversely, when new loyalties such as those of nation and class emerge, the primordial ones do not cease to function. It often happens that these different loyalties interact with and mutually modify each other."[46] The Bedirkhan brothers were not exceptional in this regard. Their identity contained all of these components, and their outlook was also guided by the larger Young Turk *Weltanschauung* of science and progress, backed by a heavy dose of elitism. Their gazette, *Kurdistan*, must similarly be understood as being a publication that was informed by these overlapping identities and outlooks. It was a channel for the Bedirkhan brothers to advance their own personal, family, and tribal agendas. They printed laudatory remarks about their own family and spoke disparagingly of rivals. As such, they hoped to campaign for themselves with their pens. But *Kurdistan* was also a CUP newspaper. It reported on the activities of the CUP and the Young Turk movement, and in so doing distinguished itself as a forum for opposing the Hamidian regime; it must therefore be grasped in this framework as well. Additionally, *Kurdistan*'s weight in early Kurdish nationalism is not undercut by the fact that it wore several hats simultaneously. It was the first gazette printed in the Kurdish language and the first paper to devote attention to Kurdish affairs, and is special for these reasons.

Nuancing our understanding of *Kurdistan*, the first Kurdish newspaper, and its contributors, particularly the Bedirkhan brothers, is essential for deconstructing some of the essentialist myths that accounts of Kurdish nationalism have often put forth. It also helps to add a new facet to late-Ottoman politics as well as to stagnant notions of tribalism. *Kurdistan* and its creators were "beyond borders" in many ways. Physically and geographically, the journal was produced outside Kurdistan, and even beyond the borders of the empire, but was nonetheless intended for readers not only in Kurdistan but also for the small diaspora of Kurds living in other parts of the empire and abroad. This has been a key feature of Kurdish journalism ever since, particularly with the growth of the diaspora, and especially because Kurdish print media were largely prohibited inside Kurdistan. This situation has only recently changed, albeit to a measured extent. More essential than physical location, however, are the ways in which the multi-faceted identities, outlooks, and agendas expressed by the Bedirkhan brothers and *Kurdistan* stretched beyond the borders of categories that we have too often taken for granted as fixed, or bounded. For starters, unlike later Kurdish publications that were banned because they were *Kurdish* and stood therefore as threats to the new nationalist regimes that incorporated Kurds following the First World War, *Kurdistan* was banned not because it was Kurdish, but because it was a paper of political opposition to the sultan's administration and was part of the larger movement of subversion identified with the CUP. If a Kurdish journal called "Kurdistan" had been produced by supporters of the Hamidian regime, it is doubtful whether it would have been censored and banned. Noting this helps us to accept the overlapping spheres in which we should situate *Kurdistan* and the Bedirkhans. They all wore several "hats" in their political activities. They agitated as Ottomans, as Kurds, and also as Bedirkhanis who wished to restore their family's dynastic importance, and did so against a backdrop of uncertainty over the empire's future. My contention is that the phenomenon of bet-hedging, or keeping options open on all sides, was acutely important to Kurds, even more so than to other Ottomans who similarly had overlapping identities, because the Kurds had developed the time-honored tradition of hedging bets as a survival tactic for borderlands people. Later accounts have often depicted divisions in Kurdish society as detrimental to their survival, but this is really the case only when one views the continued existence of Kurdish society in strictly nationalist terms. We might perceive some of their apparently conflicting agendas as signs of duplicity or wishy-washiness; but if instead we perceive them as survival strategies, as did the Kurdish-Ottomans themselves, this more nuanced understanding might help us better comprehend not only the twists and turns that Kurdish identity has taken, but also that of other groups, principally those on the margins of empires and states. Studying the careers of the Bedirkhan brothers and their gazette, *Kurdistan*, can help us reconcile those activities that seem self-defeating or contradictory. After all, in an era of deep, anxiety-provoking uncertainty when the empire seemed threatened, they were doing the human thing—quite rational, in fact—of surveying their options and ensuring that they had not only Plan B, but also Plan C, and maybe even Plan D.

13.

MOBILIZATION OF KURDS IN TURKEY DURING THE 1980s AND 1990s

Cengiz Gunes

On 12 September 1980, when the Turkish army carried out a *coup d'état*, very few in its upper echelons would have predicted that Turkey would spend the next two decades fighting the longest and most intense of Kurdish uprisings. The widespread torture that the army inflicted on the Kurdish political activists in prisons, together with the widespread oppressive measures they used to intimidate ordinary Kurds during the subsequent three years that they ruled Turkey, were seen as necessary and sufficient to suppress the rising tide of Kurdish political activism once and for all. So brutal was the army's response that the leader of the military dictatorship and Turkey's seventh president, Kenan Evren, went even a step further than any of the country's previous rulers by effectively banning the use of Kurdish language.[1] The practices associated with the military rule continued long after civilian rule returned on 6 November 1983. However, ultimately the army's iron fist proved ineffective once the guerrilla campaign led by the Kurdistan Workers' Party (PKK in the Kurdish acronym) began to gather pace from the late 1980s onwards.

During the 1970s, the PKK was one of the many new political groups that emerged on the Kurdish political scene in Turkey.[2] Its cadres were influenced by Marxism and the PKK's national liberation discourse, which articulated Kurdish identity and national demands with demands for socio-economic equality. Its guerrilla campaign proved to be a vigorous challenge of the state's rule in Kurdish majority areas. In the late 1980s and early 1990s, the scope and depth of the PKK's guerrilla campaign increased significantly, and through its widespread political consequences the PKK managed to mobilize a large number of Kurds in Turkey, Syria, and amongst the Kurdish diaspora communities in Europe. Through its media and information network, it was able to reach out to many Kurds and evolve into a mass movement, with supporters and sympathizers numbering several millions. By the early 1990s, the PKK had managed to evolve into a transnational mass movement that organized political and cultural activities in Turkey as well as many European countries.[3]

The popular explanation in the existing literature for the PKK's mass mobilization of the Kurds during the 1980s and 1990s highlights the state's excessive use of force and repression and socio-economic regional inequality.[4] The main weakness of such an explanation is that it explains Kurdish mobilization exclusively with reference to the actions of Turkish state and structural factors and at the expense of the actions of the PKK and the wider Kurdish movement as an actor. In contrast, Romano identifies the PKK's strategy to manipulate local politics to its advantage (using the already existing networks and exploiting the conflicts between the landlords and peasants to win the support of and enhance its credibility among the Kurdish peasants) as the key factor for its success: "[w]hat seems to differentiate the PKK from its local competitors is a strategy which would appeal to people who initially cared little for its Marxist–Leninist ideology or a politicised Kurdish ethnic nationalism."[5] Tezcür provides a micro-level perspective looking at individual motivations behind the people's choice in joining the PKK.[6] The study looks at the period before 1980 when mobilization took place in an urban context, and "identifies four causal mechanisms that contributed to the appeal of the PKK among ordinary Kurds in Turkey: credibility, revenge, social mobility, and gender emancipation."[7] It is worth noting that "gender emancipation" was not among the main elements in the PKK's discourse before 1984, and there were serious risks involved with taking part in the PKK's activities—such as detention, torture, and even death—which need to be considered, as they would have offset the benefits gained from social mobility.

The second period under examination in Tezcür's study is the period from 1984 to 1990, which is when the PKK's guerrilla campaign spread across many of the majority Kurdish areas. The army's heavy-handed approach to the insurgency features predominantly in his explanation of the PKK's mass mobilization in this period: "[the army's counter-insurgency] operations victimised and radicalised large segments of the displaced Kurdish peasantry who became the core supporters of the insurgency."[8] Despite being victims of state violence, especially during political crises and military rule, some Kurds chose assimilation instead of resistance; and yet some chose to support Turkish left or Islamist groups. Hence, there were other avenues that were used to channel Kurdish discontent, and what made the Kurdish nationalist movement's interpretation and challenge more appealing than its alternatives needs to be explained. Also, while Romano's and Tezcür's accounts correctly highlight the impact of the PKK's strategy on its credibility with the Kurdish population, more thorough analysis of the representation of the PKK's struggle in its political discourse and through artistic forms are needed to explore the reasons behind its appeal to the Kurds and its hegemony over Kurdish politics in Turkey. We need such an analysis to show how the PKK managed to gain credibility with the Kurds.

In the first part of this chapter, I provide an account of the PKK's growth as an organization during the 1980s and 1990s, the development of its guerrilla campaign, and its political mobilization. In the second part, I analyze the PKK's discourse and the representation of its struggle to its target groups. To complement the military and security operations that the army carried out to contain the PKK's insurgency, the state discourse contested the PKK's representation of its struggle as the embodiment of the Kurds' national struggle by representing it as a case of "terrorism" and a "security threat." To counter the state's representation of its insurgency and enhance its appeal to the Kurdish civilian population, the PKK reactivated the myth of Newroz[9] to construct a contemporary myth of resistance, which was an important symbolic resource that it deployed extensively to represent its struggle; and this played a key role in the PKK's hegemony over the Kurdish national movement in Turkey.[10]

The PKK's organizational growth

Most of the Kurdish political activists and members of the numerous political parties and groups were arrested and incarcerated in numerous prisons during the military rule. In the early 1980s, the prisons became the main site of Kurdish resistance in Turkey, beginning in December 1980 when PKK members and sympathizers in Diyarbakır prison organized a hunger strike to protest against endemic torture and oppression and the violation of their basic human rights. The PKK's resistance in Diyarbakır prison continued throughout 1981 and 1982, and the fact that PKK members were the leading figures of the resistance enabled the PKK in later years to use the resistance practices there to construct a contemporary myth of resistance, which was a significant symbolic resource that it used extensively to represent its struggle. Also, a significant number of PKK members left Turkey for Syria and Lebanon and established the organization's bases there in 1979 and 1980. Its relocation to Lebanon presented the PKK with an opportunity during the early 1980s to form close links with Palestinian organizations and establish guerrilla training camps in preparation for an insurgency.[11]

The PKK's strategy envisaged a protracted "people's war" to overthrow Turkish rule in military, political, and economic terms, and to unify and reconstruct Kurdish society.[12] Furthermore, military struggle was seen as inseparable from political struggle, and the guerrilla insurgency was seen as the first stage of a wider rebellion of the masses and as a tool to accelerate political developments.[13] In this developmental guerrilla strategy, initially small units of guerrillas would carry out attacks against military targets to weaken the army's authority in the majority Kurdish regions and to incite a popular rebellion. In the final phase of the insurgency, the people's army supported by the popular uprising of the masses would overthrow the rule of the state and achieve revolutionary change.

The PKK started its insurgency on 15 August 1984 with two concurrent attacks in the towns of Eruh and Şemdinli. After that, its guerrillas fought the Turkish army and security forces in coordinated attacks predominantly in the rural areas. Initially the PKK's armed forces were organized as the Liberation Forces of Kurdistan (Hêzên Rizgariya Kurdistan, HRK). During 1985 and 1986, the PKK found it difficult to sustain the initial hype generated by its attacks in 1984. As well as lack of experience on its part, this difficulty was caused by the actions that the state took to prevent the development of the PKK's guerrilla campaign. Consequently, the development of its military capacity was the main point of discussion in the PKK's Third Congress held in October 1986, during which a number of significant decisions were taken. One of these was the reorganization of the HRK into the Kurdistan People's Liberation Army (Artêşa Rizgariya Gelê Kurdistan, ARGK). The numbers of ARGK guerrillas together with the resources they had at their disposal ran significantly short of achieving the PKK's ambitious objectives. Thus, the PKK resorted to radical measures in order to increase recruitment, and to this end its Third Congress in 1986 recommended a conscription law to make joining the ARGK compulsory.[14]

As a result, during the late 1980s the numbers of ARGK guerrillas increased significantly and its presence in the region started to grow. During the late 1980s, this led to a gradual increase in the number of attacks against the Turkish security forces and the village guards[15] as well as a widening of the area within which they operated. The mountainous terrain alongside the Turkey–Iraq border provided many hiding places for the guerrillas to shelter, and was particularly suitable for the successful execution of guerrilla war. The guerrillas were able to connect with local populations and establish local militias, who provided the important logistical support and also helped to coordinate the PKK's military activities when needed. The state security forces and village guards were the predominant targets of the guerrillas. The main forms of military activity by the ARGK consisted of raids on gendarme stations and other forms of military installations near the borders with Iraq and Iran, raids on gendarme and army stations in rural areas, ambushes, road checks, raids on villages where the village guards were located, and sabotage against economic facilities or state institutions in the Kurdish regions.

The guerrillas were organized within various levels, from small squads, to teams comprising a number of squads, to larger units equivalent to battalions. Although mainly hit-and-run tactics were deployed, the Turkish army's numerous large-scale operations against the guerrillas and other forms of "hot pursuits" during the early 1990s resulted in large-scale skirmishes that lasted a few days or even weeks. Therefore, the early 1990s were exceptional years in terms of the level of violence, with attacks becoming much more frequent and widespread. The areas in which the guerrilla attacks were carried out also became widespread. The guerrillas were organized extensively in many Kurdish majority regions, though the main conflict zones were the border areas primarily comprising the provinces of Hakkari, Şırnak, and Siirt (the mountainous areas that Kurds popularly refer to as "Botan"). During the mid-1990s, PKK activities expanded to a wider area extending toward southern Turkey to Hatay and Antakya and toward the Black Sea region in north-east Turkey.[16] Turkey found it impossible to eliminate the PKK presence in the region, despite its numerous military campaigns and large-scale operations. From 1992 onwards every year during autumn the Turkish army carried out cross-border operations supported by air strikes against the PKK.

Owing to the early success of the PKK in mobilizing the Kurds, its Fourth Congress held in 1990 hinted at the establishment of a popular government, the creation of "liberated zones," and developing the people's army to take the war to a higher level.[17] Overall, the insurgency proved very practical and the PKK grew in strength and size in a short space of time. Being the only Kurdish organization that challenged the state put the PKK in the leading position to hegemonize Kurdish politics in Turkey. Unlike the other Kurdish political groups—who either ceased to exist or relocated to Europe—the PKK managed to maintain its forces in the region and increased its recruitment throughout the 1980s and early 1990s. Its Turkish socialist rivals, who also drew considerable support, especially from the Alevi Kurds, also began to experience major difficulties during the late 1980s once the signs of the difficulties in the Soviet Union became more apparent.

Consequently, the rival oppositional political organizations in Turkey that the Kurds supported lost their appeal, which created opportunities for the PKK to mobilize a wider section of Kurdish society. Having a presence in the majority Kurdish regions presented the PKK with an opportunity to reach out to many Kurdish rural populations, and through its political work it managed to win the support and cooperation of many villagers. The PKK's popularity also increased because of the state's harsh and heavy-handed approach toward the civilian Kurds. The state's antagonistic and oppressive practices allowed the PKK to galvanize public opinion. From 1990 onwards, the popular expression of Kurdish identity demands and open support for the PKK became much more common-place in Turkey as Kurdish political activism evolved into a vocal social movement. This was demonstrated in a number of popular uprisings (*Serhildan*) between 1990 and 1993, in which large numbers of ordinary Kurds across Kurdish towns participated and often fought with the police and the gendarmeries.

Starting in the early 1980s, the PKK started to build a strong presence in Europe, mainly Germany, through a network of community organizations. In March 1985, the National Liberation Front of Kurdistan (ERNK) was established to carry out the political development and mobilization of the masses.[18] From the mid-1980s onwards much more effort was placed in developing the ERNK, and consequently its activities as well as the organizational network grew rapidly throughout the late 1980s and early 1990s. The ERNK was legally organized through a network of community and cultural centers in Europe. The European activities of the PKK allowed it to draw support from Kurdish communities in Europe, and the funding it collected enabled it to finance and expand its insurgency and political activities. The absence of legal restrictions placed on Kurdish identity and culture in Europe enabled the PKK to organize legally and establish a network of cultural and community organizations to mobilize Kurds in Europe. Throughout the late 1980s and early 1990s in many cities in Europe, the ERNK organized numerous events such as rallies and demonstrations, meetings, protests, hunger strikes, music festivals, cultural activities, the Newroz celebrations, and commemoration events. Such activities attracted large crowds, built the PKK's support base, and helped raise public awareness of the Kurds' struggle.

The PKK's presence in Europe enabled it to establish institutions that produced and disseminated its discourse. Its publication house, Weşanên Serxwebûn, was established in Germany; and both its political magazines, *Serxwebûn* (Independence) and *Berxwedan* (Resistance), were published there and distributed in most European countries. In August 1987, numerous sub-organizations were established within the ERNK to represent women, youth, and workers, and in 1993 more organizations representative of religious groups were established to provide representation for the Muslim, Alevi, and Yezidi religious communities. The existence of such representative organizations enabled the PKK to articulate within its discourse the specific demands of diverse Kurdish social groups and religious communities, and transcend the religious and tribal fragmentation to evolve into a mass movement. Being in Europe offered the space and opportunity for cultural development by enabling the Kurds to establish their own institutions that engaged in and fostered cultural revival. Initially, the PKK's cultural activities included the music group Koma Berxwedan [The Resistance Group], which was formed in 1981 in Germany to communicate the PKK's struggle through music to the Kurds in Europe. Furthermore, the members of the group took a leading role in the establishment, also in Germany, of the PKK's cultural organization, Hunerkom [Association of Artists], in 1983, which had the wider aim of promoting Kurdish cultural development and revival. Music constituted a significant aspect of Kurdish cultural renewal and development and was an important medium to narrate the PKK's resistance practices and communicate its struggle to the Kurds. In fact, Koma Berxwedan established itself as the main vehicle for conveying resistance music, and although it mainly organized performances and musical activities in Europe, its cassettes and CDs managed to reach Kurds in Turkey.

In the early 1990s, the PKK increased its efforts to establish and develop Kurdish national representative organizations in Europe that would provide democratic representation to the Kurds in the international arena. In Europe elections were held in November 1992 for the Kurdistan National Assembly. The elected delegates met in the areas under the control of the PKK guerrillas in Iraqi Kurdistan during the spring of 1993, to engage in meetings and draft laws for a future Kurdish state. The establishment of the Kurdistan Parliament in Exile in 1994 was the highlight of Kurdish political activism in Europe, and although the PKK took an active part in its establishment, numerous other Kurdish organizations and parties as well as numerous leading intellectuals and independent political figures also helped in its establishment and activities. The Kurdistan Parliament in Exile evolved into the Kurdistan National Congress (Kongreya Netawa Kurdistan, KNK) in 1999, which aspires to be a broader representative organization for Kurds from all parts of Kurdistan. The KNK continues its diplomacy activities in Europe from its headquarters in Brussels, and continues to inform the European public about the situation of the Kurds in Turkey and other parts of the Middle East. Additionally, in 1994 an umbrella organization called the Kon-Kurd [Federation of Kurdish Associations in Europe] was established in Belgium. As a representative organization of Kurdish community organizations in Europe, it advocates Kurdish cultural and political rights as well as organizing many Kurdish political activities in Europe. The development of such Kurdish national institutions enabled the Kurds to form and develop stronger relations with the European Left, who have remained perceptive to Turkey's democratization and granting the Kurds their democratic rights.

The myth of Newroz and the PKK's contemporary myth of resistance

My explanation of the PKK's hegemony over the Kurdish national movement in Turkey and its mass mobilization of the Kurds during the 1980s and 1990s pays close attention to the PKK's reactivation of the myth of Newroz to construct and deploy a contemporary myth of resistance that centres on the resistance practices of its leading members in Diyarbakır prison and its struggle in general.[19] From the 1970s onwards, the construction of the relations of difference—and the representation of the alternative Kurdish society—in the discourses of the newly formed Kurdish political parties and groups were done on the basis of the myth of Newroz.[20] The myth allowed the Kurdish national movement to trace the origins of the Kurds to the ancient Medes and re-activated/recreated Newroz and the "legend of Kawa" as the myth of origin. Furthermore, the PKK re-activated the myth of Newroz to construct a contemporary myth of resistance centered primarily on the PKK inmates' resistance in the Diyarbakır prison during the early 1980s and its ongoing struggle. The PKK's construction of a contemporary myth of Kurdish resistance to represent its struggle and the romanticizing of its guerrilla war against the state enhanced its hegemonic appeal by bringing the myth of resistance into reality. The Newroz festival became the most significant day in Kurdish political activism in Turkey, and during the 1990s large crowds were attracted to celebrate and protest on 21 March. The public celebrations and mass protest enhanced Newroz as the day of national resistance, with many individual acts of resistance and self-sacrifice by PKK members taking place on 21 March. The reference to Newroz enabled the PKK to situate its struggle within a historical narrative and represent it as the embodiment of the Kurds' national struggle, which it used in its challenge of the state's hegemonic representation of the insurgency as "separatism" and "terrorism."

In comparison with its rivals, the representation of Kurdish identity and demands in the PKK's discourse were clearer. This was done via establishing a strong association between the Medes and the modern-day Kurds to invoke a historical "golden age" of the Kurdish nation to construct and represent a homogenous notion of Kurdish identity. The deployment of the myth of Newroz in the discourse, especially the construction of the Medean Empire as the "golden age" of the Kurdish nation, was significant for conceiving the unity and homogeneity of the Kurdish nation. Newroz as a symbol of the triumph of the struggle of the Medes was used to construct a benchmark, as something that needed to be recreated and emulated by the contemporary Kurdish national movement. Many of the acts of resistance were committed on the day of the Newroz festival, 21 March, and during the early 1990s organizing mass gatherings during the Newroz festivals and other important days in the Kurdish political calendar in many Kurdish cities and towns, especially in Diyarbakır, created Newroz as a symbol of Kurdish popular resistance.

The PKK's contemporary myth of resistance constituted the performers of resistance practices as "exemplars," and initially the myth was constructed around the performers of the PKK's early resistance in Diyarbakır prison. The significance of the construction of Newroz as a contemporary myth of resistance lay in the fact that it enabled the sedimentation of the PKK's discourse in practice by constructing it as representative of Kurdish struggle in Turkey. Later on, exemplars were broadened and included women. The mobilization of women by the PKK and its effect on the sedimentation of the PKK's discourse helped to embed the notions of "freedom" and "equality" in practice, bringing about an aspect change which in turn reduced the grip of traditional identities and religion and foregrounded the liberation and Kurdish struggle for freedom.[21]

The resistance by the PKK's leading members in Diyarbakır prison has been a mainstay in its contemporary myth. The key events started with the suicide of the leading PKK member Mazlum Doğan on 21 March 1982 in protest at systemic torture. The resistance continued with the self-immolations of four other members (Eşref Anyık, Ferhad Kutay, Necmi Öner, and Mahmut Zengin) on 18 May 1982 and culminated in the hunger strike that started on 14 July 1982 and resulted in the death of four more leading members in September 1982 (Kemal Pir on 7 September, Mehmet Hayri Durmuş on 12 September, Akif Yılmaz on 15 September, and Ali Çiçek on 17 September). Initially the main emphasis was on torture and oppression of political prisoners, and Doğan's death was described in *Serxwebûn* as part of a concerted effort by the Kemalist regime to annihilate all Kurdish political prisoners.[22] However, the statement commemorating the first anniversary of Doğan's death, distributed on 21 March 1983, described him as the "Contemporary Kawa" and his suicide as self-immolation and an act of resistance.[23] In articles published to commemorate the resistance, the significance of the actions of the leading members became the focal point, and their resistance was described as a "conscious political action":

> Since entering the conscious stage of their life, they have taken part at a leadership level in our people's national and social liberation struggle. The prison resistance was conscious political action by people who, if needed, were prepared to consciously sacrifice their life for the sake of developing our struggle. Their actions have created the true measures of our people's national and social liberation struggle under the leadership of the proletariat, and have become the spirit of our struggle. It is its steering and sheltering force and it has left an ineradicable effect that will pull our people into continuous action and organise them.[24]

The historical importance and significance of the resistance in Diyarbakır prison for the Kurds' struggle and their survival as a nation was also emphasized and the resistance was defined as the beginning of a new era:

> To attain an honourable status, human decency, stand on our feet and say a few words or a few sentences in that period of history, we needed to resist. On behalf of a nation and for a section of humanity they said the most significant few words. However, these were such words that if not spoken then our party and our nation would have perished. It would have not made much sense to talk about the other values.[25]

The significance of the resistance lay in the fact that the PKK inmates did not accept the authority of the state, despite continuous unimaginable torture and attempts at subjugation. Their resistance against oppression, the defense of the Kurdish struggle under the harshest conditions, and sacrificing their own lives to defeat the submission imposed on the Kurds were interpreted by the PKK as the "spirit" of its struggle.[26] In numerous articles and books published to commemorate the resistance, the significance of the actions of the leading members became the focal point, and their resistance was described as "conscious political action," the beginning of a "new era" for the struggle and survival of the Kurds as a nation.

With the start of the guerrilla insurgency on 15 August 1984, the PKK's resistance took a new dimension and the insurgency started to take center stage in its contemporary myth of resistance. The start of the guerrilla insurgency was described as the "leap of 15 August" (15 Ağustos Atılımı), and the PKK's activities from 1984 onwards provided ample material that can be used in the construction of its contemporary myth of resistance. The PKK militants who lost their lives in the insurgency were described as "heroes and martyrs of national resistance" and extensive obituaries were published throughout the 1980s and 1990s in each issue of the PKK's magazines, detailing their "bravery" and "heroism."[27]

In addition, numerous acts of self-immolation that took place in the early 1990s also received sustained attention in the PKK's contemporary myth of resistance. They started with Zekiye Alkan, a medical student from Diyarbakır, who set herself alight on the city walls on 21 March 1990; similarly Rahşan Demirel set herself alight in Izmir in 1992; and "Berivan" and "Ronahi," pseudonyms used by Nilgün Yıldırım and Bedriye Taş, respectively, repeated the same practice in Germany in 1994.[28] All the above-mentioned self-immolations occurred on the day of Newroz and were described in numerous articles published in the PKK's magazines as "sacred acts of resistance" and "sacrifice for the sake of the nation's freedom."[29] The crucial difference, however, was that in the early 1990s women were the main performers of the self-immolations and acts of "sacrifice."[30]

Hence, during the early 1990s women started to be the performers of resistance acts and acquired center stage in the PKK's contemporary myth of resistance. From the 1980s onwards, with the gradual increase in the activities of the Kurdish national movement, more and more Kurdish women started to engage in politics. In particular, women participated in large numbers in the numerous popular uprisings. In fact, one of the most significant developments that the PKK initiated, especially in the early 1990s, was the mobilization of women as new political actors, and this had a significant impact on the PKK's overall mobilization. Not only did it significantly increase the PKK's overall support base and fighting force, but also the presence of a significant number of female militants within the PKK ranks lessened the appeal and force of traditional values, such as male domination in society, and helped engrave ideas of equality and freedom in society, which were important elements in the PKK's national liberation discourse.

These members who carried out numerous acts of resistance constituted "exemplars" representing resistance practices in the PKK's discourse. Drawing on Conant's discussion of exemplars in the work of Nietzsche, Norval argues that "the role of the exemplar is to 'unsettle us' and create an impersonal feeling of shame." The importance of exemplars for politics is that their presence "acts as a call, as a reminder of another self, and another state of things, capturing . . . the possibility of another self, another way of doing things."[31] In the commemoration events of the practices of resistance and the statements published on their anniversary, these individual acts of resistance and sacrifice are described by the PKK as the catalyst of a prolonged period of active resistance. For example, the suicide of Mazlum Doğan has been described as the event that activated the resistance in Diyarbakır prison and the PKK's guerrilla war. Similarly, the self-immolation by Zekiye Alkan is described by the PKK as the catalyst of a prolonged period of active resistance and *Serhildans* in the urban centers of the region in which many ordinary Kurds took part.[32] Although it is highly unlikely that a strong casual connection, as emphasized in the PKK's discourse, was present, the importance of such a claim is that the individuals and their resistance practices are constructed as "exemplary" of the PKK's resistance and their actions are used to motivate others to take part in resistance. Given the mobilization of a significant number of women by the PKK and their participation in politics, it is unsurprising that they became performers of resistance practices from the early 1990s onwards, and increasingly began to be seen as exemplars.

Above all, the constitution of the exemplars in the PKK's discourse and the commemoration practices associated with their "resistance" and "sacrifice" had the aim of motivating ordinary Kurds to perform such acts of self-sacrifice for the movement and the Kurdish struggle. The resistance of the leading members has been discussed widely in numerous articles published in *Serxwebûn* and *Berxwedan* throughout the 1980s and 1990s, as well as during meetings and public gatherings that took place on the anniversary of these events to commemorate their resistance. The story of their resistance was narrated and disseminated widely in countless commemoration events and practices held for the leaders of resistance and the earliest "martyrs" of the PKK's struggle. It is standard practice to display pictures of the PKK's leading figures in Kurdish community centers across Europe, especially those of Mazlum Doğan, the performers of resistance practices in Diyarbakır prison, and Mahsum Korkmaz, who was the first commander of the PKK's guerrilla forces and died in March 1986. Extensive obituaries of these leading PKK members, as well as of other militants, frequently appeared in its publications. Remembrance ceremonies were organized in the Kurdish community centers run by the ERNK. These commemoration practices, especially the obituaries and life stories of the PKK militants, romanticized the guerrilla life and were used to disseminate the PKK's contemporary myth of resistance.

The representation of resistance practices was not confined to political discourse, but appeared in other artistic forms, such as music. The stories of resistance practices were narrated in the music of Koma Berxwedan from the early 1980s onwards, and in the music of other groups later in the 1990s. In fact, the contemporary myth of resistance constituted the center of Kurdish cultural revival, as the PKK's resistance was the main theme that the resistance music of Koma Berxwedan and many other groups and musicians narrated. In the early years the resistance was depicted as a celebration or *Dilan* in many popular songs. Songs commemorating specific events, such as the PKK's establishment on 27 November 1978, the start of its war on 15 August 1984, the resistance in Diyarbakır prison in the early 1980s, songs glorifying the guerrilla insurgency, the popular uprisings, and those that commemorated the resistance and sacrifices of the PKK's members, all featured frequently. Through music the story of the PKK's struggle and resistance was narrated and made accessible to many people, and such a representation enabled the PKK to reach out to wider Kurdish communities. The resistance music used and recreated popular folk melodies that many Kurdish people were familiar with, and was used in folk dancing, which added a performative aspect to the commemoration practices.

The PKK's contemporary myth of resistance was used extensively in the mobilization process, and images of the performers of the PKK's resistance practices, including pictures of its women fighters, were widely used in PKK publications. The importance of the contemporary myth of resistance for the PKK's mobilization of the Kurds was that it added force to the PKK's discourse, enhancing its widespread credibility among the Kurds. The guerrilla insurgency and the popular resistance the

PKK organized meant that resistance was something that occurred on a daily basis and convinced many that the PKK was capable of achieving Kurdish independence; this then added force to the PKK's discourse. By representing and interpreting its activities in light of the contemporary resistance myth, the PKK was able to define its struggle as the embodiment of the Kurds' struggle for freedom. Such a representation enabled the sedimentation of the PKK's national liberation discourse in practice and enhanced the PKK's hegemonic appeal by bringing the myth of resistance into reality, which in turn played a key role in its mobilization of the Kurds.

Conclusion

The PKK's political and military activities throughout the 1980s and early 1990s led to the mobilization of a large number of Kurds in Turkey. From the early 1990s onwards, this started to acquire the characteristics of a mass mobilization, with popularly attended demonstrations, protests, and uprisings taking place frequently. The PKK established a well-organized network of community organizations and cultural centers in Europe. The Kurds in Europe played an important role by providing financial support for the PKK and establishing the information and organizational network that forged links with socialist and human rights groups and harnessed diplomatic support.

Additionally, the existence in Europe of institutions that played a key role in Kurdish cultural renewal meant that the restrictions that applied in Turkey could no longer suppress Kurdish cultural production and dissemination and presented the PKK with the opportunity to project Kurdish culture publicly. The Kurdish cultural revival constituted a significant aspect of the PKK's mobilization. Kurdish culture was made available to many people in a variety of contexts, making it part of people's daily life. The fact that music and folk dancing constituted the key components of Kurdish cultural renewal meant that it was accessible to a wide section of Kurdish society and they could easily connect to and consume it.

The PKK's contemporary myth of resistance played a significant role in the mobilization process and the sedimentation of the PKK's national liberation discourse in practice. It added affect and force to its discourse and enabled it to construct and represent resistance acts as the embodiment of the Kurds' long struggle for freedom and independence. In fact, an analysis of the PKK's construction of a contemporary myth of resistance highlights an interesting dimension of the nationalist discourse and shows the importance of the symbolic resources, such as myths, that the nationalist movement uses in its interpellation of the national subject. My analysis has also highlighted the importance of the PKK's reinvigoration of Kurdish culture and music, which played a significant role in the sedimentation of its national liberation discourse in practice.

14.

TURKEY'S KURDISH PROBLEMS, THE KURDS' TURKISH PROBLEMS

Bill Park

In the national elections for the Turkish Grand National Assembly (TGNA) on 7 June 2015, the pro-Kurdish People's Democracy Party (Halklarin Demokratik Partisi, HDP) received 13.1 per cent of the national vote and more than doubled its parliamentary seats to 80. This remarkable lifting of the HDP vote above the 10 per cent threshold was mainly explained by socially conservative Kurdish voters in Turkey's south-east deserting the ruling Justice and Development Party (Adelet ve Kalkinma Partisi, AKP). In previous elections the AKP had been able to match HDP vote levels in Turkey's Kurdish provinces, but in the June 2015 election there were swings of over 30 per cent from the AKP to the HDP, which in some Kurdish provinces won more than 80 per cent of the vote.[1] Largely as a consequence of this transfer of Kurdish votes, the AKP vote fell from over 49 per cent in 2011 to 41 per cent in June 2015 and its parliamentary seat count from 327 to 258, which meant it lost its parliamentary majority.

Rather than form a coalition, the AKP leadership called for a "repeat election" on 1 November. In the run-up to the election, and commencing with the July 2015 Suruc bombing of pro-Kurdish activists on the Turkish border with Syria, Turkey's security forces engaged in a resumption of fighting against the Kurdistan Workers Party (Partiya Karkeren Kurdistane, PKK): infinitely more intense than their more loudly proclaimed campaign against Islamic State (IS), and notably its youth wing. In contrast to the previous pattern of PKK clashes with Turkish security forces, the ensuing violence mainly occurred in the towns and cities of Turkey's south-east and involved prolonged curfews, sniper exchanges, aerial bombing of PKK targets in both Turkey and KRG territory, PKK attacks on soldiers and "village guards", and the like. Whether because they held the PKK responsible at least in part for the resumption of violence, or because they simply wanted peace and stability, this time around the HDP vote dropped to just above the 10 per cent threshold, while the AKP vote leapt back to almost 50 per cent, thereby enabling it form a single-party government once again.[2] However, the violence in the south-east acquired a still greater intensity in the wake of the election, harking back to the worst days of the 1990s and prompting harsh criticism from human rights organizations.[3] Government spokesmen declared that there would be no resumption of peace talks until the PKK was militarily defeated.[4]

Attempts at peace at home...

Both of the 2015 election outcomes and the resort to violence in the second half of the year could be explained in a number of ways,[5] but there was undoubtedly a growing scepticism toward the AKP government's attempts at a so-called "reconciliation process" which aimed to bring to an end the armed struggle against the Turkish state that had been waged by the PKK since 1984. Within weeks of coming to power in November 2002, the AKP government signaled a new approach to Turkey's politically and economically costly Kurdish conflict by lifting the "state of emergency" in the last two remaining provinces where it was still in force. In a speech in Diyarbakir in August 2005, then Prime Minister (and now President) Recep Tayyip Erdoğan conceded that Turkey had a "Kurdish issue" and that "mistakes" had been made in the handling of it. His motivations were several: to appease the European Union, with which accession negotiations began in 2005; to draw Turkey's Kurdish voters away from pro-Kurdish parties and toward the AKP; and to weaken the political influence of the Turkish General Staff (TGS), which had been instrumental in "securitizing" Ankara's approach to its Kurdish problem and which constituted a formidable obstacle to the AKP's ambition to weaken the secular Turkish state's hold over the country's politics.

Erdoğan promised greater economic investment in the impoverished Kurdish provinces, a general democratization of Turkish politics, and specific reforms aimed at addressing Kurdish grievances. A softening of restrictions on the use of the Kurdish language, notably in the media, soon followed. However, the AKP's approach took on a more substantive flavor with the 2009 launch of the so-called "Kurdish opening." Having won a stunning election victory in 2007, the way was paved both for the marginalization of the TGS's political influence and for the so-called Oslo Process, a series of secret talks with Kurdish elements that were led on the Turkish side by Hakan Fidan, who later became head of Turkey's National Intelligence Organisation (Milli Istihbarat Teskilati, MIT) and a close Erdoğan ally.[6] This appeared to represent a sea-change in Ankara's securitized approach to the PKK problem since the conflict began in 1984, and to the exclusive and repressive attitude toward Kurdishness that had been adopted soon after the Republic's establishment in 1923.[7]

However, the government coupled the initiative with the detention of thousands of Kurdish sympathizers, most of whom were members of the Kurdish Communities Union (Koma Civaken Kurdistan, KCK), which had been formed by the PKK in 2007 as an umbrella federation bringing together like-minded and overlapping Kurdish activists and organizations from Turkey, Iraq, Syria, Iran, and the Kurdish diaspora. In late 2009 the Constitutional Court banned the then main Kurdish political party in Turkey, the Democratic Society Party (Demokratik Toplum Partisi, DTP). The period also witnessed a hardening of the government's language, or rather the use of inconsistent and contradictory language that has emerged as a notable feature of the AKP's approach. For example, in April 2011 Erdoğan pronounced that "there is no Kurdish issue in this country, there is a problem of the PKK", a sentiment he repeated in the run-up to the June 2015 vote.[8] Furthermore, the government ruled out talking directly to the PKK or its leader Abdullah Öcalan, and confiscated the roadmap he had made available to it. This mixed messaging reflected the fact that a large segment of the Turkish population, including many AKP voters, was hostile to the initiative. It also suggested that the government had not sufficiently thought the issue through. Turkey's opposition parties, most especially the Nationalist Action Party (Milliyetci Hareket Partisi, MHP) with which the AKP was also in electoral competition, withheld their support, as did the TGS.[9] The government's crackdown and the general absence of substantive progress resulted in 2011 in an intensification of PKK violence. It was estimated that more than seven hundred people were killed in the fourteen months up to August 2012, the highest level of PKK-related violence for thirteen years.[10] All in all, it seemed there were reasons to doubt the good faith of both the government and the Kurdish movement. The objectives of both sides remained obscure, and neither the public nor the political class had been prepared.

However, in November 2012 Öcalan amply demonstrated both his undoubted influence but also his readiness to strike a deal by successfully appealing to around seven hundred imprisoned Kurdish activists to end their two-month hunger strike.[11] After a series of consultations with the PKK leaders in their hideout in northern Iraq's Qandil mountains, Kurdish activists based in Europe, and Kurdish political representatives in Turkey, a message from Öcalan was read out at the Kurdish new year or Newroz gathering on 21 March 2013 in Diyarbakir.[12] In his message he referred to the common past of Turks and Kurds, asserted that they live together under the "flag of Islam", and that they needed to create a common future. In particular, he pronounced that "the period of armed struggle is ending, and the door is opening to democratic politics." He went on to insist that "we have now arrived at the stage of withdrawing our armed forces outside the borders." On 8 May PKK fighters began to withdraw into Iraq in order to implement a ceasefire, although they remained armed. Öcalan's message heralded a second stab at reconciliation, initially dubbed the "Imrali process", named after the prison island to which Öcalan remained confined. One difference between this new "opening" and the previous attempt was that Ankara now recognized Öcalan's centrality to any process aimed at resolving Turkey's domestic Kurdish issue. This looked like progress. However, with respect to the substance of any agreement, the two sides remained far apart.[13] Although some reforms were introduced,[14] the government appeared inactive and increasingly insincere. It was also evident that there were divisions on the Kurdish side. Many PKK fighters and activists were sceptical from the beginning. PKK leader Murat Karayilan openly expressed his doubts regarding Ankara's sincerity, and warned of the possibility of a renewed and even intensified war.[15] At the June 2013 Kurdish gathering in Diyarbakir, senior Kurdish politician Ahmet Turk voiced similar doubts about Ankara's intentions.[16] Kurdish demands were and are extensive, and included Öcalan's release or transfer to house arrest; the winding down of the so-called "village guard" system of government-sponsored and armed Kurdish citizens; the right to maintain a local self-defense force; an amnesty for Kurdish fighters and for imprisoned activists; a reform of Turkey's notorious and wide-ranging anti-terror laws; education in Kurdish; establishing Kurdish as co-equal with Turkish as an official language of the Republic; the replacement of the current ethnic definition of citizenship with a civic one; an end to the 10 per cent electoral hurdle for parliamentary representation; and above all, some kind of devolution, self-determination, or "democratic autonomy" that would, in effect, introduce something tantamount to a federal political system in Turkey.[17] In fact there were few indications that Erdoğan, his party, or the opposition parties were at all ready to concede many, if any, of these demands. Indeed, a case can be made that neither side was in desperate need of a settlement.[18] The PKK remained able to recruit and raise funds, and sensed that time was on its side in light of the wider development in the region. It also refused to meet the government's demand that it disarm before a peace deal could be agreed, insisting instead that Ankara had to make the first moves.[19] Erdoğan appeared to think in terms of an Islamic "brotherhood" between Turkey's Turkish and Kurdish citizens, and did not appreciate the pressure to adopt a pluralistic approach that is inherent in Kurdish ethnic identity demands.[20] Factors such as these contributed to the collapse of the initiative during the second half of 2015.

Although the ceasefire partially held, sporadic violent incidents still occurred. Turkish security forces in the region were increased and their infrastructure improved.[21] Meanwhile the HDP and PKK strengthened their grip on the southeast's local government infrastructure. As the June 2015 elections approached, and the AKP needed both to reassure its nationalistic supporters and to try to keep the HDP vote below the 10 per cent threshold, the rift between the two sides became starker. The AKP targeted a great deal of personal venom against the HDP's leadership, its secularism and leftism, and its links with the PKK. AKP figures responded clumsily to a fatal bomb attack at an HDP rally in Diyarbakir a couple of days before the vote, and HDP leader Demirtas's home was "mistakenly" subjected to a police raid. Clashes in Turkey's south-east between the PKK and Kurdish Islamist groups immediately before and after the election were widely suspected of having been initiated by provocateurs.[22] Clearly Turkey's Kurdish voters had become mistrustful and disillusioned. By the eve of the 7 June vote little headway had been made and little appeared imminent. As the election results suggested, Turkey's Kurds had become more inclined to stress their ethnic identity and more mistrustful of the AKP, while the HDP and PKK hold over Turkey's majority Kurdish south-eastern provinces appeared to have tightened. Indeed, the subsequent downturn in the HDP's electoral fortunes and the return to violence arguably strengthened the PKK at the expense of the HDP as the leading voice of Kurdish disaffection.

Little peace in the world...

As a backcloth to Turkey's stuttering peace process with its own Kurds, and serving as a probable incentive for Ankara to arrive at some kind of understanding, there unfolded dramatic events across the border in Syria.[23] However, developments in Syria and Ankara's reactions to them so angered Turkey's Kurds that they threatened the "peace process" altogether. Turkey's refusal to come to the aid of Kurdish defenders of Kobanî, just across the Syrian border from Turkey, against a four-month onslaught by the *jihadi* forces of IS, and a suspicion by Kurds and others that Turkey was aiding Islamists in Syria in their attacks against Kurds as well as the regime of Bashar al-Assad,[24] led to widespread Kurdish disturbances in Turkey in which over forty people lost their lives. Ankara's demonizing of the Democratic Union Party (Partiya Yekitiya Demokrat, PYD) forces that defended the town added to Kurdish resentment toward Ankara. Turkey also held itself aloof from an anti-IS coalition of Arab and Western countries that Washington had assembled, and even refused to permit access to the NATO air base at Incirlik to US bombers engaged in the campaign. Washington was obliged to air drop military supplies to the People's Protection Units (Yekineyen Parastina Gel, YPG), the PYD's armed wing, and to use non-Turkish military bases from which to conduct air strikes against the IS forces while the Turkish military looked on and Erdoğan loudly criticized Washington's action.[25]

Kobanî eventually fell to the PYD in early 2015, but when within days of the June Turkish election Syrian Kurdish forces attacked and captured (with US help) Tal Abyad, a town on the Turkish border that had been held by IS for two years, President Erdoğan chose to express his concern about the possible "creation of a structure that threatens our borders",[26] a concern he had not expressed while IS had held it. Ankara suspected that the PYD was seeking to claim—or reclaim as the Kurds might have it, in light of the "Arabization" policies pursued by Damascus during the 1960s—these border areas in order to link up the three geographically distinct self-governing majority-Kurdish cantons in Syria's north which it had established in early 2013 and called Rojava. Ankara also accused the PYD of ethnic cleansing of Arabs and Turkmen.[27] Tal Abyad's importance to the PYD was partly related to the fact that it abutted the border crossing with the Turkish town of Akcakale, which had been used by *jihadis* as a crossing point for supplies and recruits.

Turkey's preferences were evident in Erdoğan's comment during the siege of Kobanî that "for us, the PKK is the same as ISIL. It is wrong to consider them as different from each other."[28] Ankara similarly queried the wisdom of US bombing of IS positions during the battle for Tal Abyad. It repeatedly reiterated its position that, for Turkey, Assad and the PKK/PYD were the main problems, rather than the IS threat.[29] Ankara's belief that the PKK and the PYD are one and the same organization provided much of the basis for its opposition to Washington's air drop to Kobanî's Kurdish defenders, as it feared that the arms might fall into the PKK's hands. The symbiotic relationship between the PKK and the PYD troubled Ankara. The PYD was formed by the PKK in 2003 following Damascus's expulsion of the PKK from Syria in 1998; both are affiliated to the KCK; as many as one third of the PKK membership may be of Syrian Kurdish origin;[30] and the PYD's leader, Salih Muslim, spent time with PKK units in northern Iraq's Qandil mountains until he returned to Syria in 2011. The emergence of the PYD as the leading Syrian Kurdish element was unexpected.[31] Syria's Kurds had long been notoriously fractured, but in the chaos that followed the majority-Sunni Arab revolt against the Damascus regime, the PYD emerged as the most organized and militarily most effective of Syria's disparate Kurdish groups.[32] It undoubtedly prospered from its seamless military relationship with the PKK, which provided fighters and arms. Furthermore, many Syrian Kurds are the descendants of Kurds forced to flee Turkey during the repressions of the 1920s and 1930s and have maintained trans-border family and tribal links. To Ankara these developments implied the establishment of PKK-controlled havens on its southern border, and could herald similar initiatives in Turkey's south-east.[33]

Notwithstanding clashes between the PYD and pro-government forces in late 2012 and early 2013,[34] and the PYD's demands for Syrian Kurdish autonomy, Ankara also suspected the PYD of being allied to the Assad regime. Indeed, this formed the basis of Ankara's suggestion made in early 2016 that the PYD could only attend the proposed Geneva talks if it sat with the regime delegation.[35] Turkey also believed that the 2011-12 spike in PKK violence in Turkey had been encouraged by Damascus and Tehran as a counter to Ankara's support for the Syrian opposition to Assad.[36] Syrian regime forces did indeed withdraw from the Kurdish areas soon after the uprisings began, preferring to concentrate on their mainly Sunni Arab opponents and defend Alawite and pro-regime areas, and this effectively handed Syria's largely Kurdish-populated areas over to PYD control. This gesture could yet prove to have consequences as far-reaching as Saddam Hussein's February 1991 withdrawal of the Iraqi state's presence in Kurdish Iraq. Ankara had sought to persuade the PYD to join the anti-Assad Syrian National Council (SNC),[37] despite the fact that most of its constituent elements were opposed to Kurdish self-rule. In the wake of Turkey's shooting down of a Russian air force jet in November 2015, ostensibly because it intruded into Turkish air space, Russia too stepped up its support for Syria's Kurds,[38] who were also regarded by Washington as Syria's most effective anti-IS force. Whatever the legitimacy of Ankara's fears, among the consequences of its mishandling of both its own peace process and of developments in northern Syria was a rise in the status of the PKK and PYD amongst Kurds, Turkey's Western allies, and Russia; a substantial bloc of Kurdish politicians in its parliament; and the establishment of PKK-controlled cantons just across its border with Syria.[39]

The "good Kurds" of the KRG

PYD leader Salih Muslim's condemnation of the Turkish reaction to the PYD's capture of Tal Abyad as "Kurdphobia" was understandable,[40] but overlooked the close relationship Ankara had forged with the Kurdistan Regional Government (KRG), and especially President Massoud Barzani and his party, the Kurdistan Democratic Party (KDP). The AKP government's phobia is towards the secular, leftist and somewhat pan-Kurdish constituent elements of the KCK, and especially its armed units. In Barzani, Turkey saw a socially conservative political leader, one who appreciated the necessity of Ankara's goodwill for the security of his quasi-state, and who shared its distaste for the PKK and PYD, which he regarded as rivals for the leadership of Kurdish nationalism and as a threat to his hold over the KRG. In November 2013 Barzani and Erdoğan even shared a platform in Turkey's overwhelmingly Kurdish city of Diyarbakir, where Barzani expressed his support for Turkey's Kurdish peace process and acclaimed the brotherhood between Turks and Kurds.[41]

Ankara's relationship with the KRG was transformed in the wake of Ahmet Davutoglu's appointment as foreign minister in 2009. His visit to Erbil in October of that year paved the way for the opening of a Turkish consulate there in 2010, and in autumn 2012 Barzani—once scathingly referred to by Erdoğan as a "tribal leader"—was a guest at the AKP's annual convention. Leading figures on both sides were soon using the term "strategic" to describe the Ankara-Erbil relationship. The expanding trade between the two provided a powerful driver to this rapprochement. The KRG was accounting for half or more of Turkey's trade with Iraq, while hundreds of Turkish companies and thousands of Turkish citizens were based there.[42] Energy considerations became increasingly central to this relationship.[43] The KRG's dynamic approach to the development of new energy fields within its boundaries synergized with Ankara's aspiration to develop as an energy "hub." Encouraged by the arrival of major companies such as ExxonMobil in 2011, and frustrated by Baghdad's obstructive approach to the KRG and increasingly sectarian demeanor, Turkey began accepting oil trucked directly from Iraqi Kurdistan in 2012.

In early 2014 Kurdish oil began flowing through a new pipeline that connected the Kurdish oilfields with the existing Kirkuk-Ceyhan pipeline near the Turkish border, for export from the Turkish port of Ceyhan. The first tanker laden with piped Kurdish oil left Ceyhan on 22 May 2014, and by the end of 2015 was flowing at the rate of over 500,000 barrels per day, one seventh of the Iraqi total. This helped Erbil avert the real possibility of a complete financial crash which would have been largely a consequence of its continuing budgetary and oil trade disagreements with Baghdad, and of alleged corruption on a monumental scale. The oil is marketed by the KRG rather than by Iraq's State Oil Marketing Company (SOMO), with the proceeds initially deposited with a Turkish bank pending an agreement between Erbil and Baghdad. In October 2013 the KRG's Natural Resources Minister Ashti Hawrami revealed that a planned second KRG pipeline would enable a KRG export capacity of one billion barrels per day via Turkey,[44] and in early June 2014 KRG Prime Minister Nechirvan Barzani announced the signing of a fifty-year oil export agreement with Ankara.[45] The KRG could also be ready to export natural gas to Turkey before the end of 2016.[46] In light of the financial difficulties for the KRG that resulted from its unresolved oil delivery and payments dispute with Baghdad, in early 2015 Turkey bailed out Erbil with a loan.[47] Such was Turkey's commitment to this oil trade, and to its wider economic and political relationship with Erbil, that it continued with these activities even in the face of Baghdad's insistence that the Kurds had no legal right to export the oil independently of Baghdad, and that Turkey had no right to facilitate it—a position supported heartily from Washington.[48]

Ankara had been hostile to the KRG following its establishment in 1992, largely because it feared the impact of Iraqi Kurdish self-rule on the aspirations of its own Kurds.[49] It was also suspicious of the Iraqi Kurdish unwillingness to tackle the PKK fighters who had taken refuge in the Qandil mountains in the 1980s and had been subjected to numerous Turkish cross-border military raids: throughout the 1990s, as recently as 2008 once Iraq's US occupiers again gave Ankara a green light,[50] and again resuming in the second half of 2015. However, a number of factors contributed to Ankara's shift in its approach to the KRG—or, more accurately, to the KDP. To trade and energy considerations can be added the marginalization of the TGS in Turkish policy-making, the realization that the KRG had become a fixture in the region, Ankara's fracturing and increasingly sectarian relationship with Baghdad, the AKP government's "zero problems" approach to its neighborhood, and the realization that President Barzani especially was a "good Kurd" who shared Ankara's mistrust of the PKK and its affiliates and who might be instrumental in Turkey's desire to marginalize them. Ankara even adopted a relatively passive posture toward Barzani's occasional pronouncements that Iraqi Kurdish independence was inevitable, and toward the KRG's extension of control over the territories it disputed with Baghdad—including Kirkuk—in the wake of Mosul's fall to IS in June 2014.[51] It seemed possible that Turkey was positioning itself in the event of a total collapse of the Iraqi state. On the other hand, Ankara did little to help—in contrast to Tehran—when, a few months later, Erbil found itself under threat from an IS advance. Erbil's disappointment was palpable, and the "strategic" relationship shaken.[52] Barzani shares Ankara's distaste for the PKK and PYD. He is keen to preserve his advantageous relationship with Ankara and to maintain the KRG's economic progress. He is also irritated by the PKK's presence in northern Iraq.[53] His unease about the influence of the PKK and its affiliates mounted in light of the widespread sympathy for the PYD's spirited defense of Kobanî, and the role played by PKK and PYD fighters in Sinjar and Makhmur in Iraqi Kurdistan in the wake of their desertion by Iraqi Kurdish peshmerga.[54] The PYD resisted his attempts to subordinate it to the Kurdish National Council (KNC), a coalition of Syrian Kurdish groups that was formed in 2011 under Barzani's sponsorship,[55] although in 2014 it did enter a power-sharing arrangement with Barzani-sponsored Kurdish groups.[56] Erbil initially offered no assistance to the PYD forces, and even obstructed them from using KRG territory. Indeed, the KRG, like Turkey, closed the KRG-Syrian border even while the PYD was battling *jihadi* elements.[57] However, the siege of Kobanî produced a unanimous vote to support the town's PYD defenders in the KRG's Kurdistan National Assembly (KNA) and, under US pressure,[58] Barzani's and Erdoğan's agreement to the deployment of Kurdish peshmerga units to aid the PYD forces defending the town. Furthermore, they were allowed to transit Turkish territory in order to cross into Syria. Yet this rivalry persisted even as it coexisted with increasing cooperation against IS.[59]

Turks and Kurds; what future together?

Taken together, the developments outlined above led to a rise in pan-Kurdish sentiment across Iraq, Turkey, Syria, and Iran, and of the prestige of the PKK and PYD. The KRG's reputation, or at least that of Barzani, had been punctured and its relationship with Ankara put under scrutiny, but as it won back territory from and remained a steadfast opponent of IS, Erbil gradually won back the respect of the US and its allies, who made increasing quantities of arms and training available. Turkey's stance toward the Syrian Kurds and its general approach to the Syrian crisis led to a loss of trust with its Western allies. The US commitment to a unified Iraq, and therefore its opposition to Iraqi Kurdish independence, did not change, but it was under increasing domestic pressure. Indeed, the readiness of the US and other Western states to train and arm the Kurdish peshmerga in their struggle against IS, although in the US case at least formally channeled via Baghdad, inevitably seemed to many to make more likely the eventual break-up of the Iraqi state. In light of increasing calls in the US and Europe that the proscription of the PKK as a terrorist organization be lifted, the HDP's performance amongst Kurdish voters in both 2015 elections, the continuing military successes against IS of the PYD on the Syrian side of Turkey's southern border, and the identification by the West of both the PYD and the KRG's peshmerga as among the most effective opponents of IS, Ankara found itself confronting a set of interlocking Kurdish developments that were profoundly unsettling.

Fear of a loss of its territorial integrity, bitterness at the PKK's history of violence, and an elemental Turkish nationalism are all hard-wired into Turkish politics and society. For all the AKP government's "openings" toward its own Kurds and the relationship it had established with the neighboring KRG, by the end of 2015 Ankara appeared as committed as ever to opposing Kurdish self-determination in most of the forms in which it presented itself. However, Ankara was now presented with an unprecedented set of circumstances which at least held out the possibility of a transformation in its approach to its Kurdish neighbors. One possible transformation was in the geopolitical arrangements of Turkey's immediate environment. The KRG had already established a level of autonomy from Baghdad that would be difficult, even impossible, to reverse. In and of itself, this did not necessarily mean that full Iraqi Kurdish independence was only a matter of time. However, Baghdad's dysfunctionality and the weakness of its security forces in the face of the challenge posed by IS raised the question of whether Iraq could reasonably be expected to re-establish itself as a more or less functioning state in any foreseeable future. Greater *de facto* if not *de jure* Iraqi Kurdish independence could fall into Erbil's lap as a result of the collapse of Iraq itself. The prospects for Syrian unity and peace looked at least as bad. The PYD had established itself as a formidable opponent to IS, and was valued as such by the US and its allies as well as by Moscow. The best possible outcome for Syria was the country's cantonization: indeed, this, rather than full independence, is the PYD's objective.[60] Syria's Kurds too had had a degree of autonomy thrust upon them, partly by circumstances, and it would not be easy to reverse their gains. These landlocked "Kurdistans" to Turkey's south ultimately have little option but to accept a high degree of dependence on Ankara. Turkey seemed to embrace that advantage with respect to the KRG, and—far-fetched as it might seem—logic suggests it could yet do so with Rojava, notwithstanding the AKP's ideological hostility to the PKK and PYD and the links between them.

Ankara could be encouraged in that approach by the striking internationalization of the Kurdish issue that resulted from the region's chaos, and the gallant stance of the Kurds within it. This was making it ever more difficult for Turkey to persuade its allies to follow its lead with respect to the Kurds. Western countries were under increasing pressure to delist the PKK as a terrorist organization, and to arm both the PYD and the Iraqi peshmerga directly. Turkey's dubious regional policies and its sometimes aggressive denunciation of the West both in detail and in general further undermined Ankara's reputation.[61] Given the West's past behavior toward the Kurds, and especially Iraq's Kurds, one cannot rule out the possibility that they could yet again be deserted by their new-found Western friends. What are presumed to be *realpolitik* considerations will always ensure that the views of Turks, Arabs, and Persians will influence Western thinking, and that the region's map will not be discarded lightly. Even so, the diplomatic and domestic political costs of doing so have been raised significantly, while faith in the value of Turkish friendship, and that of some Arabs, has fallen. Ankara might not only be less advised, but also less able, to manage the region's Kurdish issues according to its own preferences.

Finally, Turkey's domestic politics have changed. At least for the time being, Kurdish political parties are no longer banned, a Kurdish party enjoys strong parliamentary representation, the existence and contours of the Kurdish issue are conceded and discussed openly, and the TGS has lost its capacity to set the agenda. Again, caution must be the watchword, but few in Ankara any longer believe that there can be a military solution to Turkey's Kurdish travails, and most of the country's Kurds would opt for peaceful progress over a return to violence. Some of the PKK's demands would be difficult to meet, but many need not be. In any case, the desire is for the admittedly vague concept of "democratic autonomy" rather than the establishment of an independent state. Furthermore, Ankara would find it increasingly difficult to maintain the status quo internally if it were faced with independent or quasi-independent Kurdish entities on its southern borders; and it would also find it difficult to establish and maintain a *modus vivendi* with any such entities if it reverted to fully repressive policies toward its own Kurds.

Around half of all Kurds live in Turkey. Many are assimilated, and they generally enjoy better economic, political, and social conditions than their ethnic brethren in Iraq, Syria, and Iran. Before the collapse of the Ottoman Empire and the creation of the Middle East's current map, the majority of Kurds were incorporated in it as Ottoman subjects and generally lived harmoniously alongside ethnic Turks. This observation could be interpreted as hinting at the specter of Turkish "neo-Ottoman" revanchism, but it also reminds us that there are alternative ways of conducting this key relationship between these two neighboring and intertwined peoples.

15.

THE TRANSFORMATION OF TURKEY'S KURDISH QUESTION

Henri Barkey

From the moment of the inception of the Turkish republic onwards, successive Turkish governments have had to contend and deal with their Kurdish issue, namely, the presence of an ethnic minority group that, for the most part, proved unwilling to be subjugated or forcefully assimilated into the larger Turkish ethnic entity. After decades of denial and suppression, there has been significant change of late as the Turkish government and much of Turkish society have begun a long (and perhaps painful) process of coming to terms with this Kurdish reality. A peace process between the government and the Kurds had begun but it fell victim to regional developments. Yet, developments such as the 2003 American invasion of Iraq and the onset of the Arab Spring in 2011, especially when it spread to Syria, have complicated the geopolitical environment for Ankara, which is now faced with multiple Kurdish challenges on its borders that reverberate inside Turkey. An internationally recognized Kurdish federal state in northern Iraq, the Kurdistan Regional Government (KRG),[1] and Syrian Kurdish ambitions to carve up a similar entity for themselves in the post-Assad era have muddled Turkey's calculations.

The Justice and Development Party (AKP) government that assumed power in 2002 with an absolute parliamentary majority slowly introduced changes to the traditional approach to both the domestic Kurdish question and to Iraqi Kurds. Although the "peace process" initiated by the AKP government collapsed, its impact has already been significant. A ceasefire in place between the Kurdistan Workers' Party (PKK), fighters, and the Turkish army gave rise to constituencies on both sides that have a genuine stake in its continuation. Even if Turkey is in the midst of one of the most ferocious bouts of strife between the Turkish state and the Kurds, the very fact that the two sides agreed to a ceasefire followed by negotiations, however unsuccessful these may have been, represents the crossing of a major psychological threshold. Having once made progress at the negotiating table and in the absence of a possible military solution, the end to the Kurdish problem will only come through negotiations. The fact remains that Turkey's Kurdish question has been transformed. Decades of denial and an official state policy that refused even to acknowledge the existence of Kurds has been abandoned. Even the Turkish military, which has historically been at the forefront of the struggle against Kurdish identity, has had to relent and reluctantly accept this new reality. A significant development in Turkey's Kurdish political evolution is the success of the pro-Kurdish People's Democracy Party (HDP) which twice in elections in 2015 managed to cross the 10 per cent threshold needed to get its representatives elected into parliament.

Although Kurds have from the beginning of the new Turkish republic resisted Ankara's domination by availing themselves of all the tools of both violent and peaceful politics, the discrepancy in power relations has meant that the Turkish state has almost always been in the driver's seat. It may have been on the defensive at times, but it has nonetheless maintained a steadfast front in the face of Kurdish demands. Even in the heyday of Kurdish rebellions, the state remained far too powerful and immune to a drastic alteration of its boundaries or of its political system by Kurdish action. Change has nevertheless come and it has come at the initiation of the state. Still, this chapter will argue that for the first time the Kurds have gained a certain degree of control over their fate, helped not just by the cumulative impact of their actions but also by international developments ranging from the end of the Cold War, to regional wars, to the Arab Spring.

After a brief contextual retrospective outlying the Kurdish question in Turkey, this chapter will focus on the evolution of Turkish thinking, the role of the AKP, and specifically that of Prime Minister and now President Recep Tayyip Erdoğan. Second, what motivates the primary actors' behavior? Third, how did external variables alter the geopolitical context of Turkey's Kurdish question. The chapter concludes with an analysis of the future potential course of the Kurdish question in Turkey.

From the republic to the AKP

Turkey's Kurds who constitute roughly up to 20 per cent of the population were part of a multi-ethnic Ottoman Empire where religious affiliation trumped other considerations. Being Muslim guaranteed first-class citizenship. Still, the imperial center worried about the Kurdish periphery's affinities and devised institutions and structures to keep the Kurds loyal. One such structure was the notorious *Hamidiye* battalions, which were deployed against Armenians and would re-emerge as anti-PKK village guards.[2] With the weakening of the empire at the end of the nineteenth century, its ability to exercise control over peripheral borderlands diminished. When convenient, Kurdish tribes and their chiefs made their own deals with the imperial capital, Istanbul, which was caught between the competing demands of Kurds, Armenians, and intrusive Russians.[3] The occupation of Ottoman lands at the end of the First World War by the victors galvanized many Kurds to participate in the struggle led by Mustafa Kemal's incipient Turkish forces. Kurds assumed that their support in defeating the invaders would translate some form of power-sharing or autonomy as the defunct 1920 Sèvres Treaty had recommended.

Far from recognizing the Kurdish efforts in this struggle, Turkey's new leaders perceived them and eastern Anatolia with suspicion. In a land already suffering from a century of decline, the Kurdish regions were particularly underprivileged. They were poor, uneducated, far more religiously conservative, and prone to rebellion and banditry. Atatürk and his colleagues, in a rush to modernize the country and consolidate their hold, could not afford to repeat Ottoman mistakes of letting their periphery remain ungoverned. The Kurds constituted a danger to the territorial unity of the new state, a fact made more acute by neighboring Kurdish populations in Iraq, Iran, and Syria.

As Martin van Bruinessen argues, Ankara quickly moved to expropriate large landholdings controlled by tribal sheikhs, and instead of distributing them to local Kurdish landless peasants they gave them to Turks, and especially to immigrants from the Balkans. This was followed by restrictions on using the Kurdish language, its disappearance from school curricula, and even the banishment of the word Kurdistan, hitherto a commonly used geographical term.[4]

Soon after independence, a charismatic religious leader, upset at both the new state's decision to abolish the caliphate and its anti-Kurdish policies, led the 1925 Sheikh Said rebellion. The rebellion was suppressed, but not before large swaths of land fell into the hands of the rebels. Its leader Sheikh Said was executed along with other fellow rebels. The rebellion would set a pattern for future revolts: two successive ones were the 1930 Agri (Ararat) rebellion followed by Dersim in 1937. These rebellions were also suppressed brutally. The Dersim revolt and the state's conduct and tactics reverberate to this day.

The republican state was set on a policy of total assimilation. Its meager resources and unfavorable worldwide economic conditions in the 1930s worked against these goals. From 1937 until 1984, the beginning of the latest PKK-led revolt, Turkish Kurds appeared to be quiet. In reality, however, political activity continued unabated. Kurds made deals with the central government when it suited them to acquire resources for their regions or supported national parties that challenged the Kemalist status quo. Many Kurds, for instance, voted for the Democrat Party in the first free elections in the 1950s, and later in the 1970s they supported Islamist parties founded by Necmettin Erbakan, the founding father of Turkey's Islamist politics.

The Turkish military, the self-appointed guardians of the secular and nationalist republican system, was the one institution most apprehensive about Kurdish political mobilization. The frequent interventions by Turkey's military, though not directly aimed at Kurdish political activities, often targeted Kurds in their aftermath. Minutes of the 1960 coup governments reveal their fear of Kurdish activism; coup-makers discussed and implemented all kinds of measures, from the forced deportation of Kurds from eastern to western provinces, to their mass arrests, and to engineering the bureaucratic appointment process so as to prevent them from becoming teachers in their own provinces.[5]

The 12 March 1971 coup occurred amidst political radicalization by students, who like their brethren in Europe rebelled against political authority. The post-coup crackdowns designed to curb left-right violence also targeted growing feelings of nationalism among Kurds, especially after Baghdad concluded an autonomy agreement with Iraqi Kurdish leaders.[6] Kurdish students' sense of disillusionment with the failure of student revolts and with the Turkish left, which they accused of abandoning the Kurdish cause, convinced some Kurds to strike out on their own. Return to civilian rule in 1973 reignited the old divisions and violence. It was then that the PKK, led by Abdullah Öcalan, first made its appearance.[7]

It was the 1980 coup that turned out to be the decisive event for the Kurdish movement in Turkey. Though ostensibly targeted at the left, the generals were also concerned about what they perceived to be increasing Kurdish political mobilization in the south-eastern provinces. The departure to Syria of embryonic PKK cadres seeking to avoid waves of mass arrests of activists in the aftermath of the coup would transform the rebellion. Emboldened by Syrian President Hafez al-Assad's support and the deep alienation in the Kurdish provinces, the PKK after 1984 put together the single most durable, lethal, and challenging Kurdish insurrection the Turkish republic had faced since its inception. Years of counter-insurgency and scorched-earth tactics would do little to dent the organization and its ability to set the agenda for Kurds. If anything, the state's reliance on purely military means and increased repression served as lifeblood for the PKK, helping it to expand and win adherents.

The 1990s was a particularly violent decade, marked by the ascendancy of the PKK in selected regions and by an unforgiving counter-insurgency response culminating in thousands perishing in prisons or as victims of unknown assassins. By the end of the decade, Ankara threatened Syria militarily, forcing Öcalan to flee Damascus, only to be captured and put on trial. His capture did not end the insurrection. This is because much of the PKK leadership had already become ensconced in the Qandil mountain range in northern Iraq, and perhaps more importantly because of the re-emergence of organized Kurdish political activity. Nicole Watts demonstrates how new overtly pro-Kurdish political parties, despite continuous state harassment and bans, managed to reinvent themselves and challenge Ankara by contesting, and in some cases winning, local elections.[8] The failure of the counter-insurgency, the rising pressure from the European Union to which Turkey aspired to become a member, post-Cold War conditions seemingly more favorable to nationalist movements, the post-1991 existence of a Kurdish region in northern Iraq by a primarily US-defended no-fly zone, and greater solidarity among Kurds all helped contribute to a potentially new approach to Turkey's Kurds by Ankara. The election of the Justice and Development Party, AKP, in 2002 provided the needed impetus.

Changing attitudes, the AKP, and alternative approaches to the Kurdish question

Throughout the 1990s, with the counter-insurgency in full swing, Kurdish policy had become the exclusive province of the military establishment. The political parties, the state bureaucracy, the judiciary and the press, with the exception of a few journalists, projected a unified front with the military against Kurdish demands, and certainly when it came to the PKK and Kurdish politicians. This monolithic establishment blocked any venture, however rare, into the issue by civilian politicians. Dissent, even by established journalists and academics, was severely suppressed, sometimes through smear campaigns. If the aim was to curtail Kurdish activism, the strategy failed.

The Turkish military, the second largest in NATO, proved incapable of decisively defeating the PKK or exercising complete control over Kurdish provinces. The 1990s counter-insurgency campaign proved to be of limited success: it only rolled back the PKK from the heights it had achieved early on in the decade.[9] An unintended consequence of the counter-insurgency campaign was to displace large numbers of Kurds whose villages were destroyed. They not only resettled in Diyarbakir, the most important Kurdish city, but also all along the Mediterranean coast as well as in Istanbul. Unlike previous migrations, this one created the seeds of future problems by altering, sometimes radically, the ethnic composition of cities, such as Mersin and Adana, but also by making of Istanbul the largest Kurdish city in the world, with as many as 4 million inhabitants of Kurdish origin.

Though unified in appearance, the insurrection's tenacity gave rise to discordant voices within it. The original doubter had been Turgut Özal, who served both as prime minister and president. Against the military's objections, he sought to improve relations with the Kurdish authority in northern Iraq and was instrumental in getting the PKK to declare a unilateral ceasefire in 1993, which collapsed with the execution of thirty-three soldiers in May 1993.

Özal was in many ways an early iconoclast deemed untrustworthy by the military. However, even among the military brass and hardline establishment, there were individuals who, once freed from their official positions, articulated their doubts about government strategy. A former chief of the armed forces, Dogan Güres, now a member of parliament, admitted that he had experienced joy when the 1993 PKK ceasefire was announced; that the policy of denying Kurds individual (though not collective) rights was wrong, and Özal's "opening" to the Iraqi Kurds was a smart strategy.[10] Similarly, a hardliner on Syria who advocated forceful action against the Hafez al-Assad's regime for its support for the PKK, Sükrü Elekdag, a former ambassador and foreign ministry undersecretary, was very critical of the successive governments' inability to address some of the most basic of Kurdish demands, including broadcasting rights in Kurdish and less discriminatory treatment at the hands of state authorities.[11]

It was the AKP, however, that would initiate significant changes to Turkey's approach both to the PKK insurgency and to the Kurdish question. The new AKP leadership in the persons of both Erdoğan and then foreign minister Abdullah Gül had cut their teeth in earlier versions of Turkey's Islamic politics under Erbakan's leadership, before breaking with him to create the AKP. Erdoğan had been a successful mayor of Istanbul, elected on the Islamist Welfare Party (WP) ticket and Gül had been a minister and confidant of Welfare leader Erbakan, Turkey's first Islamist prime minister. The WP then and in its previous incarnations had benefited from both Kurdish protest as well as Kurdish conservative votes, and therefore its parliamentary group contained significant numbers of Kurdish members. Still, the WP's view of the Kurdish problem in Turkey was simplistic: that this was the outcome of secular Kemalist state formation that had prioritized Turkish ethnicity at the expense of Islamic brotherhood and unity. In 1991 Erdoğan, at the bequest of his party's leadership, had presented his report detailing solutions to the Kurdish problem. It was very critical of Turkish state policies. It not only argued that there had been flagrant denials of Kurdish human rights but also that governments' policies were counterproductive and strengthening the PKK.[12] His proposals, co-authored with Metin Metiner, currently an AKP MP, went further than anything contemplated at the time; some of the issues flagged are among ones currently under discussion, including the horny right to education in one's mother tongue. Erdoğan, therefore, was well acquainted with the issues by the time he assumed the prime ministry.

The 2003 American invasion of Iraq and overthrow of Saddam Hussein's regime would prove to be a critical event in the transformation of Turkey's Kurdish policy. Erdoğan and the AKP faced a very difficult test: within days after assuming power, the Bush administration began to lobby them heavily for permission to open a second front in the invasion of Iraq. This would entail thousands of American troops traversing Turkish territory. In exchange, the Turkish military would be given the right to establish a *cordon sanitaire* in northern Iraq against both the PKK and Iraqi Kurds. A resolution for the authorization of this agreement failed to pass in parliament on procedural grounds. In retrospect, the AKP, which had endorsed the American request, dodged a bullet. The insertion of Turkish troops into Iraq could have given rise to far too many unintended consequences, including conflict with both Iraqi Kurds and the PKK and a long-term costly involvement.

On the other hand, the Iraq war helped institutionalize and lead to the formal recognition of the Kurdistan Regional Government, KRG. Iraq became a federal state with the KRG its only recognized constituent state. In addition, the KRG won plaudits especially in the US as the one place in Iraq where Americans were warmly welcomed and also where the violence and civil war that would later wreck much of Iraq never took root. Paradoxically, the KRG's legitimation opened the possibility for Turkey to return to Özal's policy of rapprochement with Iraqi Kurds. Özal had envisaged it as a way to acknowledge Kurdish existence and thus send a message to Turkey's Kurds that Turkey could recognize Kurdish ethnicity in principle. At the onset, if Ankara appeared to hesitate at welcoming a recognized KRG, the AKP leadership understood that it had few options but to accept and make the best of the situation. This was further brought home by the excitement that the KRG's very existence was engendering among Turkish Kurds.

In an unexpected twist, the KRG emerged as one of Turkey's most important trading partners. Turkish companies began to invest in the KRG, and many others, Turkish and foreign, moved their Iraq operations to the relative quiet and calm of the KRG to avoid the violence consuming Baghdad. The KRG was quick to capitalize: to expand and deepen its relations with Turkey was deemed a strategic choice. Ankara represented potentially the region's most reliable partner, paradoxically perhaps even more important than Washington, which had a checkered history with the Iraqi Kurds.[13] These developments helped changed perceptions of the KRG in Turkey and provided opportunities for the Turkish government to engage with Masoud Barzani, the KRG president. Still, the military establishment tried to thwart the deepening of ties between Turkey and the KRG. In 2007 Yasar Büyükanit, chief of staff of the armed forces, personally and publicly intervened to prevent then Foreign Minister Gül from meeting the KRG Prime Minister Nechrivan Barzani.[14]

The real change toward Kurds in Turkey and Iraq occurred after the 2007 elections. The military, in its last ditch effort to check the consolidation of the AKP, tried to block Gül's ascension to the presidency with, among other measures, an ill-conceived midnight internet memorandum on 27 April 2007. The AKP called the military's bluff by scheduling early national elections. These elections, fought over the right to have Gül elected, culminated in a decisive AKP victory, and would spell the end of the military's hegemony over Turkish politics. After that date, the generals appeared to accept their new status and moved onto the sidelines of political decision-making. Unshackled from the meddling of officers, relations with Iraqi Kurds blossomed. Iraqi President Jalal Talabani visited Turkey; he had been prevented from being invited by Gül's predecessor, Necdet Sezer, an arch Kemalist and secularist, precisely because Talabani had been an Iraqi Kurdish leader in Iraqi Kurdistan. The Opening to Iraqi Kurds, as the process came to be known, represented the first step of the wider approach that Erdoğan planned to take at home toward reconciliation with Turkish Kurds.

Early on he had made use of the Turkish National Intelligence Organization, the TNIO, and its leader Emre Taner, to maintain ties with Iraqi Kurds and circumvent the military. Similarly, he used the TNIO under a new leader and close confidant, Hakan Fidan, to establish a channel to the PKK. This proved to be successful in leading to a unilateral PKK ceasefire that was also adhered to by the Turkish army. Surprisingly, when these secret talks were leaked, the public's response was muted, relieved at the prospect of a ceasefire and an end to casualties among conscripts. Implicitly, the public appeared to trust the government.

Turkish nationalists, both on the left and the right as well as Kemalists, were quite critical of the Opening, and have remained so to this day. The government with time was further emboldened to start negotiations with the imprisoned PKK leader Öcalan, perhaps the most reviled person in all of Turkey, and allowed him to communicate indirectly with his organization's leadership based in Qandil in northern Iraq.

Like all such endeavors, this Opening has had its many ups and downs. While the parties talk of a roadmap, the process remains murky. As is to be expected, both sides have sought to improve their own negotiating position. The PKK created civilian cadres called KCK, designed to institutionalize its de facto influence in the Kurdish-majority regions. It made use of occasional violence to demonstrate that it had control of both its paramilitary forces as well as civilians. The state used its judiciary to prevent the PKK from developing the KCK and other affiliated organizations by initiating mass trials and imprisoning, more often than not on questionable grounds, thousands of PKK/KCK supporters. State repression eased but by no means disappeared. As the government became more self-confident, it also took greater chances with the process by introducing to the public ideas and concepts that were previously deemed too sensitive. One issue on which both the government and the PKK seemed to agree was the marginalization of elected Kurdish political entities, including the most important political party, the Peace and Democracy Party, BDP. Its parliamentarians were primarily used to ferry messages between Öcalan and Qandil and serve as a conduit to the public at large. The BDP politicians, though elected figures, were never empowered to play a meaningful role in the peace process. Still, published accounts of the negotiations demonstrate their detailed nature, with the leading role being played by Öcalan in meetings held in his island prison with Kurdish parliamentarians and also with government bureaucrats.[15] The process culminated in a public meeting at the ornate Dolmabahce Palace in Istanbul, where the Interior Minister, the Deputy Prime Minister, and Kurdish MPs announced a roadmap.[16]

The governmental impetus

What prompted the AKP government and Erdoğan to assume such risks by seeking a negotiated solution to the problem? In effect, there were a number of motivating factors. First and foremost was the realization of the economic costs and potential economic damage that the Kurdish question represented. The Turkish economy grew very rapidly under AKP, benefiting from the maturation of reforms initiated in the 1980s that made it internationally much more competitive. The AKP's grand ambitions to develop Turkey into a commercial powerhouse and a crossroads for energy, transport routes, and capital required a stable environment. The PKK, incapable of defeating the Turkish state, had the option of ratcheting violence and undermining the stability which the AKP sought.

Even some in the Turkish military were coming to the conclusion that there was no military solution to the PKK problem; the organization had managed to reinvent itself after the capture of its leader. One of the more prominent chief of staffs, Ilker Basbug, already on record with his belief that a military solution was illusory,[17] tacitly gave his approval to the Opening by assuring the public that they had nothing to worry about because the Turkish military was hard at work, implying that the armed forces would be there to ensure peace and stability.[18]

A second reason why the resolution of the Kurdish problem was of paramount importance for the AKP was that it would help reduce the saliency of the military's role in politics. In the civil-military struggle, the military had traditionally made use of the insurgency as a means of interfering in politics and keeping politicians off balance. To be fair, given the complexity of the Kurdish issue, preceding governments had been quite content to offload it on the military. Prime Minister Tansu Çiller at one point toyed with the idea of introducing new ideas, but quickly relented under pressure and, in fact, gave the officers and internal security services a carte blanche in dealing with the Kurds with devastating consequences.

For the AKP, wrestling control of the Kurdish file from the military was an important way to reduce that institution's dominance over civil-military relations. In fact, military pronouncements and expressions of officers' preferences have since been reduced to almost nil. This is not say that the military has completely lost interest in this matter. The generals have serious qualms about the process, and especially with the prospect of devolution of powers to a Kurdish region. The then chief of staff, Necdet Özel, while admitting that he was uninformed of the roadmap's details, felt compelled to remind the public of the armed forces' red lines and that they would act if they were crossed.[19]

Third, Erdoğan and the AKP's ambitious foreign policy agenda, especially their desire to become an influential player in the Middle East and beyond, clashed with what others perceived as Turkey at war with its Kurdish minority. The insurrection and the concomitant human rights abuses constrained the "soft power" they were trying to project and undermined Turkey's relations with a variety of countries, including the European Union and the United States. For Erdoğan and his colleagues, if Turkey was going to aspire to a more central and important role in the world, it could not afford to be perceived to be fighting a civil war.

Finally, the Kurds already constituted an important segment of the AKP's base. Unlike other traditional parties, the AKP has drawn its votes from all corners of the country, including the Kurdish areas. The main opposition parties, the Republican People's Party, encumbered by a leadership unwilling to alienate its Kemalist core by opening its doors to Kurds, and the Nationalist Action Party, MHP, whose whole *raison d'être* is to oppose any recognition of Kurdish identity, receive very few votes from the Kurdish regions. For the AKP, holding on to its supporters among the conservative and more religious Kurdish voters is politically and ideologically critical as these voters are, in Hamit Bozarslan's words, "kurdified",[20] that is conscious and accepting of the Kurdish identity. Still, the conservative and Islamist Kurdish voter remains susceptible to either more extreme groups, such as the Kurdish Hezbollah movement, or to more traditional nationalist mobilization.

However, there has been a dramatic change in Kurdish political fortunes. The rise of the Syrian Kurds as a fighting force (see below) and the ceasefire and alliances buoyed Kurdish expectations. Sensing the change in the mood of the Kurdish public, the HDP abandoned Kurdish parties' past practice of running independent candidates for parliament for fear that as a party they would not cross the 10 per cent national threshold that prevents political parties from getting their elected members into parliament. In fact, in the June 2015 elections, the HDP received some 13.1 per cent of the vote and 80 seats. When the ruling AKP forced another set of elections in November of the same year, conducted in the midst of rising violence between the state and the PKK, the HDP again managed to cross the 10 per cent threshold with 10.7 per cent of the vote and 59 seats in parliament. The HDP's success in entering parliament, and especially the rise of its co-leader Selahattin Demirtas, has energized the Kurdish movement despite the return of violence.

The return of the conflict following Erdoğan's decision to abandon the ceasefire and negotiations in light of developments in Syria has caused untold damage in the Kurdish regions. The PKK decided to confront the state in cities, instead of its traditional rural locales, thereby putting civilians in the direct line of fire. This caused untold destruction as some cities such as Sur in Diyarbakir and Cizre were devastated, with the population forced to relocate.

International developments and the future of the Kurdish question

International developments, especially those on Turkey's borders, have had an inordinate impact on the evolution of Turkey's Kurdish problem. Just as in the 1980s, when the al-Assad regime decided to provide refuge and support for the PKK, developments in Syria are likely to shape the course of how Turkey deals with the Kurds. Similar to Iraq in the 1990s, with the embryonic Kurdish entity in northern Iraq that proved to be both a source of pride for Turkey's Kurds as well as a host for the PKK, the KRG today has helped by both relieving the pressure Ankara has been under, as well as providing the Kurds with the first taste of international legitimacy and recognition.

THE TRANSFORMATION OF TURKEY'S KURDISH QUESTION

The Syrian civil war and the rise of the Syrian PKK-affiliated Kurdish movement, the Democratic Union Party (PYD), has unnerved the Turkish authorities who dread the possibility that, in a post-Assad environment, Syrian Kurds could also win their autonomy like the Iraqi Kurds, thereby strengthening Turkish Kurds' strategic and negotiating positions. From the beginning, Ankara tried to enlist the help of Barzani and the KRG to frustrate the PYD's efforts to take charge of Syrian Kurdish communities. Barzani, who had his own reasons for wanting to impede the PYD's ascendancy in Syria, pushed hard for an alternative grouping, the Kurdistan National Council (KNC), to emerge as the dominant force among Syrian Kurds. The mainstream Syrian opposition's unwillingness to recognize the Syrian Kurds' aspirations and predicament, as well as the KNC's own military weakness in comparison with the PYD, doomed this effort.[21]

The balance was further upended when the Islamic State of Iraq and Syria (ISIS), also known as the Islamic State (IS), swept through Iraq's second largest city, Mosul, in June 2014, routed Iraqi Security Forces, and occupied significant swaths of both Iraqi and Syrian territories. It also acquired large stocks of American-supplied Iraqi army equipment. The US was forced to step into the breach when IS also defeated the Iraqi Kurdish peshmerga forces, sent to replace retreating Iraqis. For Washington, which had decided to remain on the sidelines of the Syrian civil war, the IS advance threatened two putative allies: the Iraqi state and the KRG. In the efforts of the Iraqi Prime Minister Nouri al-Maliki to centralize power, he had alienated both the Sunnis and the Kurds and disbanded the Sunni militias that had been so instrumental in combatting al-Qaeda earlier, thus creating the conditions for the IS takeover. The IS sweep served as a wake-up call leading to Maliki's demise and a new government in Baghdad.

From Turkey's perspective, the most dramatic change occurred in Syria. When IS decided to infiltrate the PYD-held Syrian Kurdish town of Kobanî, a fierce battle ensued. The PYD fighters, unlike their Iraqi brethren and Iraqi security forces, put up stiff resistance. In the eyes of the Kurds everywhere, the battle for Kobanî assumed epic proportions. Moreover, IS's determination to take the town marshaled large numbers of fighters and equipment which, in turn, provided the American military with a target-rich environment and an unexpected opportunity to inflict significant damage on IS. By contrast, Turkish leaders did not hide the fact that they would relish an IS victory dealing the PYD a heavy blow in Kobanî, the middle of the three-canton PYD attempt at building a post-Assad autonomous region.[22] Erdoğan repeatedly stated that he considered the PYD and IS as identical terrorist organizations.[23]

Despite Erdoğan's vehement opposition, the Obama administration decided not only to bomb IS forces besieging Kobanî, but also to resupply the PYD fighters from the air. In effect, the US had sided with the PYD, a PKK affiliate which itself is on the American terrorism list. The American intervention, which has also come with close coordination with PYD spotters on the ground, demonstrated the degree to which unexpected regional developments could trigger dramatic changes in the regional situation. Not surprisingly, the US involvement has buoyed Kurdish expectations, as they perceive their regional and international legitimacy has been enhanced. Both Turkey and the KRG have had to adjust to the new reality: the PYD, which has proven itself on the battlefield by regaining the whole of Kobanî, is now the single most important voice for Syrian Kurds.

Paradoxically, these developments have also strengthened the KRG's hand in relation to Turkey. Iraqi Kurds were quite critical of Turkish reluctance to help them against the June 2014 IS sweep.[24] Barzani had to bury the hatchet with the PYD after its forces helped the peshmerga clear places like Sinjar in Iraq, where IS had also defeated Iraqi Kurd forces. Since then, however, Barzani under Ankara's pressure has diminished his cooperation with the PYD and closed major crossings between the two sides. The other development that served as a warning clarion to Turkey was the quick response of Iran to the KRG's demand for assistance. In addition, demonstrations against the Turkish government's refusal to help Kobanî across the Kurdish regions in October 2014 not only culminated in scores of fatalities and injuries,[25] but also demonstrated the pent-up anger among Turkish Kurds and the potential for events getting out of hand with adverse repercussions on the "peace process." Under pressure, the Turkish government relented to the passage of 150 Iraqi Kurdish peshmerga into Kobanî to relieve the besieged forces. Once again, Iraqi Kurds have been pushed into the limelight by events; the US, which has prioritized the fight with IS, wants the KRG's peshmerga and a reconstituted Iraqi army to defeat the Islamist group. The US-PYD partnership continued, despite ferocious Turkish opposition, as strategic towns such as Manbij in Syria fell to PYD forces. Still, Washington has tried to contain the damage to US-Turkish relations by insisting that the PYD forces remain to the east of the Euphrates River. There is no question that the US is in an uncomfortable situation since it lists the PKK as a terrorist organization, while the links between the PKK and the PYD/PKK are obvious for everyone to see. The exigencies of the situation have Washington making a distinction between the PKK and the PYD, which is not on its terrorism list. In the end, the PYD is ideologically attached to the PKK and they share combatants. This, of course, will complicate the end game in Syria, as Ankara will object to any arrangement that solidifies the territorial gains made by the PYD.

Despite the absence of an end point in sight, the Syrian crisis has altered the Kurdish geopolitics for the region and for Turkey. Syrian Kurds are likely one day to achieve some of their demands; any Syrian state that emerges from this conflict is unlikely to be able to exercise a great deal of control over its periphery, and therefore will have make deals with varied constituencies, including the Kurds. For the first time, Ankara does not appear to be in complete control of the Kurdish issue.

The way ahead

For a while, it appeared as if the peace process would become the driver for Turkey. Procedurally the AKP had been extremely bold. It managed to ease Öcalan into the negotiations with limited, if any, political backlash, and has sustained a momentum of dialogue that has minimized armed clashes. The public were also relieved not to have their soldiers die in clashes with the PKK. Erdoğan had an opportunity not just to continue the peace process at home, but also to align himself with Syrian Kurds. Instead he has gambled everything on an all or nothing fight.

The Kurds, broadly speaking, have three overarching and interconnected demands: revisions to the constitution, complete cultural rights unencumbered by state intervention, and a modicum of administrative decentralization. The constitutional changes relate to the articles that identify Turkey's citizens as ethnically Turkish.[26] Although opposition to such change abounds, the constitution drafted in 1982 is the product of the last direct military regime and thus lacks legitimacy.

The cultural freedoms and the decentralization questions are intertwined. Kurds want to run as much of their affairs as possible, including the education system, and be able to teach their children in Kurdish as well as Turkish. However, Ankara is unlikely to agree to any formal decentralization plan that, as in Iraq, only encompasses the Kurdish regions. What is potentially possible is a gradual nationwide decentralization effort that does not discriminate between different regions but would provide Kurds with access to desired changes.

It is unlikely that any of these reforms will be discussed, or even contemplated, in the near future. Now that Erdoğan has assumed the presidency, he is intent on changing the constitution to introduce a formal presidential system whereby powers residing with the prime minister's office are transferred to him. The 15 July 2016 attempted coup has made these changes far easier to introduce. In his post-coup "war" against his former ally, the Gülen movement, he has succeeded in purging government cadres, generals and other military personnel and members of the judiciary, thereby ensuring that there are few if any sources of resistance to him. Erdoğan and his party's increasing authoritarian tendencies do not augur well for the future. On the Kurdish issue, the deliberate polarization and "take no prisoners" approach have served him well so far by solidifying his support with part of the electorate. The danger for him and the AKP is that in the absence of any hope of alternation of power, they will end up being the focus of all opposition.

Erdoğan may be counting on the power of the Turkish state, the general fatigue in Kurdish areas with the armed conflict, the concomitant fear of returning to the "bad old days", and the KRG's unwillingness to jeopardize its relations with Ankara to contain the PKK and Kurdish dissatisfaction.

His vision of concentrating powers in the presidential office at the expense of other institutions, be they the judiciary, parliament, or society, runs contrary to the spirit of what the resolution of the Kurdish problem had always been predicated upon: greater democratization of Turkish political space.[27] The peace process is handicapped by the fact that it is in the hands of two individuals, Erdoğan and Öcalan, who have little faith in democratic processes and actors. Of these two, Erdoğan held not only the initiative but also most of the cards; but international developments and the assertiveness of the Kurdish movement have evened out the playing field to some degree.

What is clear is that a return to the dynamics of the 1990s, that is a stalemated military conflict, is no longer an option. Kurdish expectations have been transformed both by the initiation of the peace process and by the developments in Iraq and Syria. Only a scorched-earth policy could defeat the PKK and the Kurdish movement—even then only temporarily—but that would come at a huge expense, politically, economically, and in terms of reputation. Will an Erdoğan who assumes all the powers he has coveted with a presidential system then return to the negotiating table? In the end this is what will determine the future of the conflict.

16

CONTRASTING TURKISH PARADIGMS TOWARD THE VOLATILE KURDISH QUESTION

DOMESTIC AND FOREIGN CONSIDERATIONS

Michael M. Gunter

Over the years, two overarching, seemingly contradictory themes involving change and continuity have characterized Turkey's policy toward the Kurds. During Ottoman times and even into the early Republican days in the early 1920s, the Kurds were granted a type of separate status befitting their unique ethnic identity.[1] However, around the time of the Sheikh Said Rebellion in 1925,[2] Kemalist Turkey abruptly canceled this policy and instead initiated one of denial, assimilation, and force.[3] Indeed, even in Turkish foreign policy, the Saadabad Treaty of 1937 with Iran and Iraq, as well as the Baghdad Pact of 1955 with those two states plus Great Britain and Pakistan, had in part the purpose of mutual cooperation in keeping the potentially volatile Kurdish issue quiet. The fear was that the Kurds would potentially challenge Turkey's territorial integrity and divide the state.

Only gradually, beginning in the 1970s and 1980s, when this position of denial, assimilation, and the fist had clearly failed, did Turkey cautiously and incrementally restart to reverse its policy and grant the Kurds some type of recognition.[4] Turgut Ozal's domestic and external proposals for Kurdish rights in the 1980s[5]—although followed by Suleyman Demirel, Tansu Ciller, Bulent Ecevit, and Ahmet Sezer's sterile return to what was essentially denialism—adumbrated Recep Tayyip Erdoğan's bold but ultimately unsuccessful Kurdish opening and subsequent peace process between the state and the Partiya Karkaren Kurdistane (PKK) or Kurdistan Workers Party[6] as well as the still efficacious de facto alliance with the Kurdistan Regional Government (KRG) in Iraq; these are the most recent manifestations of what was once again the state's changing policy.

However, behind this policy of change remains one of continuity, in which the state continues to see the Kurdish problem as one of security and maintenance of its territorial integrity, while the Kurds view it as one of achieving human rights and democracy. The sudden explosion of the Kurdish problem in Syria, due to the anarchy that the civil war has created there since 2011, has presented Turkey with a whole new dimension of the Kurdish security problem; at the same time, Turkey is suppos- edly trying to implement change in its Kurdish dealings. The 7 June 2015 and 1 November 2015 parliamentary elections in Turkey, in part, offered a referendum on Turkey's domestic and foreign policy toward the Kurds. However, the ultimate results seemed to be a victory for ultra-Turkish nationalism at the expense of helping to solve the Kurdish problem. Thus, the purpose of this chapter is to analyze Turkey's Kurdish policy in light of these two seemingly contradictory but related paradigms of change and continuity.

The continuity of security and its consequences

The present (1982) constitution instituted by the military after its successful coup in 1980 contained a number of specific provisions that sought to limit even speaking or writing in Kurdish. Its preamble, for example, declared: "The determination that no protection shall be afforded to thoughts or opinions contrary to Turkish national interests, the principle of the existence of Turkey as an indivisible entity." Two articles banned the spoken and written usage of the Kurdish language without specifically naming it.

Although restrictions on using the Kurdish language were eased following the Gulf War in 1991, Article 8 of the Anti-Terrorism Law that came into force in April 1991 made it possible to consider academics, intellectuals, and journalists speaking up peacefully for Kurdish rights to be engaging in terrorist acts. Similarly, under Article 312 of the Turkish Penal Code, mere verbal or written support for Kurdish rights could lead one to be charged with "provoking hatred or animosity between groups of different race, religion, region, or social class." Despite harmonization efforts by the European Union (EU), a new Article 301 took effect in June 2005 making it a crime to denigrate "Turkishness", a provision that made it possible for extreme nationalists and statists to accuse writers, scholars, and intellectuals such as Nobel Prize winner Orhan Pamuk of treason and subversion. Thus, although many partial reforms have occurred in recent years, as of this writing in 2015, the promised new, more democratic and civilian constitution has yet to be written.[7]

Erdoğan's reforms

In August 2005, Prime Minister Erdoğan declared that Turkey had a "Kurdish problem", had made "grave mistakes" in the past, and now needed "more democracy to
solve the problem."[8] Never before had a Turkish leader made so explicit a statement
regarding the Kurdish problem. As progressive Islamists, however, the AKP was
increasingly opposed by the reactionary Kemalist establishment, which included
Turkey's influential military, fearful of losing their long-held privileged positions.[9]

This situation eventually led to the crisis of 2007 over the election of the AKP's
Abdullah Gül as Turkey's new president. The AKP triumphed in this struggle by
winning an enormous electoral victory on 22 July 2007 (even slightly out-polling the
pro-Kurdish DTP in the south-east) and then electing Gül as president. Gradually
the AKP began to reduce the political influence of Turkey's military and secretive
Deep State,[10] which was opposed to Turkey's democratization and Kurdish rights.

Rise and fall of the Kurdish Opening

During the summer and fall of 2009, the continuing and often violent Kurdish problem in Turkey seemed on the verge of a solution when the ruling AKP government
of Prime Minister Recep Tayyip Erdoğan and President Abdullah Gül announced a
Kurdish Opening or Initiative (aka the Democratic Opening/Initiative). Stressing
the policy of change and reform, Gül declared that "the biggest problem of Turkey is
the Kurdish question" and that "there is an opportunity [to solve it] and it should not
be missed."[11] Erdoğan asked: "If Turkey had not spent its energy, budget, peace and
young people on [combating] terrorism, if Turkey had not spent the last 25 years in
conflict, where would we be today?"[12] Even the insurgent PKK, still led ultimately by
its imprisoned leader Abdullah Öcalan, itself briefly took Turkey's Kurdish Opening
seriously.[13] For a fleeting moment, optimism ran rampant.

However, it soon became evident that the AKP government had not thought
through its Kurdish Opening very well and then proved rather inept at trying to
implement it. Specific proposals were lacking. Furthermore, despite AKP appeals to
support its Kurdish Opening, all three of the parliamentary opposition parties
declined. Indeed, the Cumhuriet Halk Partisi (CHP) or Republican People's Party
(Kemalists or nationalists) accused the AKP of "separatism, bowing to the goals of
the terrorist PKK, violating the Constitution, causing fratricide and/or ethnic polari-
sation between Kurds and Turks, being an agent of foreign states, and even betraying
the country",[14] while the Milliyetci Hareket Partisi (MHP) or Nationalist Action
Party (Ultra Turkish nationalists) "declared the AKP to be dangerous and accused it
of treason and weakness."[15] Even the pro-Kurdish Demokratik Toplum Partisi (DTP)
or Democratic Society Party failed to be engaged because it declined to condemn the
PKK as the AKP government had demanded. Erdoğan too began to fear that any

perceived concessions to the Kurds would hurt his Turkish nationalist base and future presidential hopes.

Then on 11 December 2009 the Constitutional Court, after mulling over the issue for more than two years, suddenly banned the pro-Kurdish DTP[16] because of its close association with the PKK. Although the Baris ve Demokrasi Partisi (BDP) or Peace and Democracy Party quickly took the DTP's place—followed by the broader based Halklarin Demokratik Partisi (HDP) or People's Democratic Party in 2014—the state-ordered banning of the pro-Kurdish DTP could not have come at a worse time and seemed to put the kiss of death to the Kurdish Opening. In addition, more than 1,000 BDP and other Kurdish notables were placed under arrest for their supposed support of the PKK, yet another body blow to the Kurdish Opening. Soon the entire country was ablaze with the fury that had arisen, and the Kurdish Opening seemed closed.

Although the AKP won practically 50 percent of the popular vote or 326 seats, while the BDP and its allies won a record 36 seats in the parliamentary elections held on 12 June 2011, further problems soon arose and hopes for a renewed and more successful Kurdish Opening quickly foundered. The newly elected BDP MPs began to boycott parliament in protest over the jailing of five of their elected colleagues, while a sixth (the well-known Hatip Dicle) was stripped of his seat for "terrorism" offenses. Newly re-elected Prime Minister Erdoğan seemingly turned his back on an earlier promise to seek consensus on the drafting of a new constitution that would help solve the Kurdish problem, broke off contact with the BDP, and continued to declare that the Kurdish problem had been solved and only a PKK problem remained. Once again Turkey was falling back on its continuity policy of security in regard to the Kurds. However, how could the new AKP government begin to solve the Kurdish problem when it refused to deal with its main interlocutor?

Moreover, others took the security thesis even further and argued that the ultimate problem was the inherent ethnic Turkish inability to accept the fact that Turkey should be considered a multi-ethnic state in which the Kurds have similar constitutional rights as co-stakeholders with the Turks. Moreover, during 2011 and 2012, more leading intellectuals were rounded up for alleged affiliations with the KCK[17]/ PKK, whose proposals for democratic autonomy seemed to suggest an alternative government. Many of those arrested were also affiliated with the BDP.

These arrests pointed to serious problems. First, there was the nature of the crimes, which alleged no violence. Mere "association" was enough to be counted as a terrorist. In addition, the connections were tenuous. As Human Rights Watch noted, these arrests seemed aimed less at addressing terror than at attacking "legal pro-Kurdish political organizations."[18] Second, the arrests came at a time when Turkey was planning to develop a new constitution. The silencing of pro-Kurdish voices as constitutional debates went forward was counterproductive for Turkey's future. Finally, there was the way in which suspects were treated. Virtually all were subject to pre-trial detentions, effectively denying them freedom without any proof that they had committed a crime. Although precise figures are unavailable, Human Rights Watch declared that several thousand were on trial and another 605 in pre-trial detention on KCK/PKK-related charges.[19]

Despite this myriad of problems, contacts between the government and the PKK continued, with the result that in 2013 a formal ceasefire was proclaimed and negotiations of a sort began. However, the great optimism that these events aroused quickly receded and the peace process began to stall. It is to these current events that this chapter will now turn.

The interplay between static security and dynamic change

Peace can be a relative concept. Recep Tayyip Erdoğan is first and foremost an adept politician. His main purpose as Turkey entered its 2014-15 electoral cycle appeared to be to maintain and even expand his electoral mandate. In so doing, he had many opposing constituencies to appease and satisfy. If he went too far in satisfying the Kurds, he would surely alienate other, maybe even more important, elements of the electorate. As a result, he seems to have treated the mere agreement to begin the peace process as the goal itself, rather than as part of a process to address the root causes of the conflict. Once again the continuity policy of security had to be balanced against that of change. His so-called democratic package released on 30 September 2013 failed to implement any of the reforms the Kurds were looking for. Gone were the earlier hopes of a new, more democratic Turkish constitution. Instead, Erdoğan seemed more interested in women's headscarves.

Where then do we now stand? Should Turkey pursue the policy of security or change? The government seems uncertain. Thus, on the one hand, while urging Erdoğan to move faster and further, the Kurds also should remember that he has arguably done much more to begin trying to change Turkish policy and solve the Kurdish issue than all his predecessors combined. In addition, the Kurds should recall Erdoğan's bold declaration when the peace process began, that "if drinking poison hemlock is necessary, we can also drink it to bring peace and welfare to this country."[20]

However, from 30 June to 5 July 2013, the People's Congress of Kurdistan (Kongra-Gel), a PKK-affiliated body, held its ninth General Assembly and declared that the first stage of the peace process had been completed by the PKK withdrawals from Turkey.[21] Thus, it was now time for the Turkish state and government to take concrete steps and make the required legal arrangements for the second stage of the peace process by presenting a democratization package of legal reforms. Instead, the Turkish government was constructing new military posts and dams, increasing the number of village guards, and failing to ensure the connection between the PKK head Abdullah Öcalan and democratic circles. Thus, concluded the congress, the

Turkish government was raising doubts about the peace process and creating the risk of deadlock and failure.

In line with the gender equality principle, the Kongra-Gel assembly also elected Cemil Bayik and Bese Hozat as co-chairs of the Koma Civaken Kurdistan (KCK) or Kurdistan Communities Union to succeed Murat Karayilan; he, however, was supposedly appointed as the new leader of the Hezen Parastina Gel (HPG) or People's Defense Forces.[22] At the time there was much speculation about what these new appointments might mean for the peace process, with some thinking that Bayik would be more hawkish than the supposedly more moderate Karayilan.[23] However, it soon became clear that the reshuffling of leaders did not represent a policy change, but merely a procedural organizational restructuring. Öcalan, for example, was re-elected the *serok* or president of the KCK/PKK, and it was inconceivable that the switch of co-chairs between Karayilan and Bayik could have occurred without his approval. Thus, the leadership change probably did not signal a repudiation of the peace process.

By September 2013, however, there were more signs that "the peace process has become bogged down and neither party is prepared to risk an initiative."[24] Erdoğan accused the PKK of "not keeping its promises" and asserted that only 20 per cent of its guerrillas in Turkey had moved back over the border, most of them simply being children, invalids, and elderly people. Although the PKK had not released any official numbers, one of their spokesmen declared that "about 500" people had reached northern Iraq since the withdrawal process had started on 15 May 2013. This figure of 500 was close to that of 20 per cent cited by the prime minister. If so, this was good news for the peace process, as it was not easy for the PKK to evacuate Turkey without running into a fire fight with government troops. That no such conflict had occurred might also be viewed as a positive sign and a credit to both sides. Indeed, as already noted, as of mid-2015 nobody had been killed in an armed clash since the peace process had officially commenced in March 2013.

On the other hand, the new KCK co-chair Bayik had already announced that "if the government fails to take action by Sept. 1 [2013], the cease-fire between Turkey and the PKK will be broken."[25] The PKK claimed that it was living up to its part of the peace process by evacuating its militants from Turkey, but that the government was failing to reciprocate by presenting its promised democratization package of legal reforms. Thus, a few days later, the KCK Executive Council Presidency announced that the PKK had halted its withdrawal from Turkey, and accused Ankara of not living up to the agreement to implement democracy and a solution to the Kurdish problem.[26] Nevertheless, Bayik added that the PKK would continue the ceasefire.[27]

When the peace process began, the Kurds expected the government to take the following steps to facilitate matters: 1. Release from prison the approximately 5,000 KCK non-violent activists being held on terrorism charges. 2. Improve Öcalan's prison conditions to facilitate his ability to pursue peace. 3. Introduce mother-tongue education for the Kurds. 4. Reduce the 10 per cent electoral threshold for parliament that made it very difficult for pro-Kurdish parties to win seats in the Turkish parliament. 5. Expand the boundaries for civil liberties regarding organizing, assembly, and speech. 6. Delist the PKK from the terrorism list, since the government was now engaging it in a peace process.

Although a report in May 2014 indicated that Erdoğan had promised that Öcalan would be moved from his isolated island prison on Imrali to some form of more lenient house arrest, among other concessions, in return for Kurdish support for his presidential ambitions,[28] as of the end of May 2015 the government had not taken any of these steps. Instead, Erdoğan's democratization package announced on 30 September 2013 merely granted the following rights: 1. Established private schools for Kurdish-language education. 2. Restored the Kurdish village names that had been changed into Turkish. 3. Permitted the use of the letters X, Q, and W of the Kurdish alphabet on signposts and identification cards. 4. Granted freedom for political campaigning in Kurdish. 5. Abolished the student's daily vow of allegiance that began "I am a Turk." The Kurds were not satisfied with these provisions and also objected to their unilateral formulation, which negated their desire to commence equal negotiations with the government. The PKK wanted the government's mere dialogue with Öcalan to segue into real, in-depth negotiations in which specific proposals for a solution of the Kurdish problem were discussed. As Selahattin Demirtas, co-chair of the pro-Kurdish HDP, explained: "If you prepare the package without consulting us, we will not link it to the [peace] process. If we hear about this package for the first time from the mouth of the prime minister, then it will remain as your package."[29]

In addition, the PKK wanted Öcalan's prison conditions to be improved so that some of the HDP parliamentarians who wished to meet with him would not be arbitrarily vetoed by the government. The HDP, for example, stated that the government had prevented the delivery of letters from the PKK fighters in Qandil to Öcalan. Indeed, the death of Nelson Mandela in December 2013 reminded everyone how the South African peace process was forwarded successfully by the government releasing Mandela from prison, where he had been held on terrorism charges for some twenty-seven years.

Along these lines, Öcalan had three more requests: 1. The right to have external contacts in addition to his meetings with the BDP and the government. 2. Some sort of a neutral third-party observer or facilitator to monitor the negotiations as occurred in the earlier (2009-11) but secret Oslo talks between the government and PKK. Given the long-standing struggle and resulting level of mistrust between the two sides, the peace process would inevitably continue to founder without some neutral facilitator to bring them together and transparently serve as a witness and encourager. 3. The government should offer serious proposals and solutions. As Öcalan cautiously concluded: "While I maintain my belief in the [peace] process I expect the government to take a more positive initiative on negotiations."[30]

Instead, the government seemed to be flirting with the idea of shutting Öcalan and the PKK out of the peace process and instead somehow negotiating with Masoud Barzani, the president of the Kurdistan Regional Government (KRG) and head of the Kurdistan Democratic Party (KDP) in northern Iraq, who had become Turkey's de facto Kurdish ally in recent years. Indeed, in June 2014 Turkey actually announced that it would now recognize the KRG's independence if Iraq split up, which seemed increasingly possible after the Sunni Islamic extremist organization the Islamic State of Iraq and Syria (ISIS) captured Mosul and effectively divided Iraq into separate Sunni and Shia parts plus the KRG. Previously, Turkey's policy had been exactly the opposite: it would have gone to war to prevent KRG independence, which might have served as an unwanted model for Turkey's Kurds.[31]

Subsequently, on 16-17 November 2013 Erdoğan and Barzani met in Diyarbakir, Turkey. Here Erdoğan seemingly sought to leverage his energy and other economic and political dealings with Barzani to seek the Kurdish vote in the up-coming cycle of Turkish elections that began in 2014. (Erdoğan's AKP won the local elections on 30 March 2014, and on 10 August 2014 Erdoğan was chosen as the first popularly elected president in Turkish history.) The Turkish prime minister went so far as to encourage Barzani to establish a new, more moderate Kurdish party in Turkey with more Islamic characteristics than the secular and nationalist PKK.[32] By using the ancient technique of divide and rule, Erdoğan appeared to be seeking to split and weaken the Kurdish movement and make it more applicable to his wishes, not only with regard to the current peace process, but also in the many other avenues of Middle Eastern politics dealing with energy resources and the continuing civil war in Syria. In other words, Erdoğan was seeking to marry the seemingly contradictory policy of security continuity to changing reform. However, to the extent that Erdoğan was trying to use Barzani to marginalize the PKK, the Turkish-Kurdish peace process would fail because the PKK was the main Kurdish party in Turkey, not Barzani's Iraqi KDP or any other pro-Kurdish group in Turkey.

Parliamentary elections

As Turkey moved toward parliamentary elections on 7 June 2015, the peace process was becoming all the more problematic. In the spring of 2015, for example, Öcalan had called upon the PKK to hold an extraordinary congress to take a strategic and historic decision to abandon the armed struggle based on ten articles he suggested for implementing democratic politics. Chief among these proposals were: legal solutions for problems of gender, culture, and ecology; the development of a pluralistic understanding of the concept of identity, its definition, and recognition; the recognition of a democratic republic, common homeland and people with democratic criteria, within a pluralist democratic system with legal and constitutional guarantees; and a new Turkish constitution for the purpose of internalizing democratic transformation.[33]

However, the Turkish government seemed unwilling to respond, stressing only the PKK's willingness to disarm and that there was no longer a Kurdish problem, but ignoring the PKK's call for negotiations along the lines of Öcalan's ten articles mentioned above. In addition, the government proposed a new internal security bill that the PKK saw as a road to a more authoritarian system that would hinder the peace process.[34] Given that the AKP and Erdoğan have chosen to adopt a much more hostile attitude toward the Kurdish peace process than before—which is troubling since it was they who had initiated it in the first place—a strong showing for the AKP might end any realistic hopes for the peace process. On the other hand, a strong showing for the pro-HDP—now broadened to include conservative Kurdish voters who had previously supported the AKP as well as Turkish leftists and other elements opposed to the AKP—would be seen as approval for the peace process. Thus, the 7 June 2015 parliamentary election results and their aftermath might tell whether the peace process moved forward or died.

Foreign factors

The continuing civil war in Syria interjected the security continuity dimension as a further factor into the problems of the peace process. De facto Kurdish autonomy just across the Turkish border in Hasaka (Jazira) province played havoc with Turkey's fears regarding what it perceived as the PKK threat. The problem was even greater because the leading Kurdish party in Syria was the Partiya Yekitiya Demokrat (PYD) or Democrat Union Party, an affiliate of the PKK. In effect, this meant that even though the PKK was supposed to be withdrawing across the border into Iraq's Qandil Mountains, it had now extended its cross-border presence next to Turkey by several hundred miles in Syria. In addition, this new Syrian position granted the PKK a type of strategic depth that added to its influence.

At first, Turkey reacted to this situation by bitterly opposing the PYD politically and diplomatically and also covertly supporting armed Jihadist/Salafist groups such as Jabhat al-Nusra which was affiliated with al-Qaeda, and the even more extremist Islamic State in Iraq and Syria (ISIS), which even al-Qaeda had disowned.[35] These Salafists/Jihadists looked upon both the Assad regime and the secular Kurds as *Takfiri* or apostates. Bitter fighting broke out between them and the Syrian Kurds, largely led by the PKK-affiliated PYD. Soon Turkey found itself in the unenviable position of seemingly siding with al-Qaeda-affiliated Salafist/Jihadist fanatics against secular, even pro-Western Syrian Kurds. This became all the more apparent when Turkey disdained to join the US-led coalition against ISIS during the bitter fighting in Kobanî, Syria during September–October 2014.

Nevertheless, on 25 July 2013, amid reports that the PYD was about to declare Kurdish autonomy in Syria, Turkey sought to implement the change policy of Kurdish recognition and publicly invited Salih Muslim, co-chair of the PYD, to Istanbul for talks. Indeed one report claimed that the PYD had already produced a constitution for the Syrian Kurdish regions.[36] Under its provisions, Syria would become a democratic parliamentary federal system; western (Syrian) Kurdistan—aka Rojava, or the direction from where the sun sets—with Qamishli as its capital would be one of the federal or autonomous self-ruling regions making its own internal decisions. Kurdish and Arabic would be its official languages and self-ruling units would protect the Syrian borders from foreign intervention.

Then on 12 November 2013 the PYD moved yet another step toward some type of autonomy by declaring provisional self-rule in areas under its control and announced that it had formed a constituent assembly with a view toward creating a transitional government. However, both Turkey and the KRG responded negatively to what they perceived as change threatening their security. Barzani, for example, declared that "this is clearly a unilateral . . . act which disregards the other Kurdish parties."[37] Thus, it remained to be seen what the future held for Kurdish autonomy within what seemed to be the crumbling remains of the now failing Syrian state.

However, if the stalled Turkish-Kurdish peace process could be revived and brought to a successful conclusion, the Syrian Kurds might seek to become associated in some manner with Turkey. After all, the PYD of Salih Muslim is closely associated with the PKK and is by far the strongest Syrian Kurdish party. If its elder brother the PKK and elder statesman Abdullah Öcalan accept Turkey, the PYD and Salih Muslim might see fit to follow in their footsteps instead of risking life in a broken Syria. Turkey would not only continue to become more democratic and thus acceptable to Kurdish nationalists, but also offer the Kurds in Syria the 16th largest state economy in the world. After all, no matter what they do, the landlocked Kurds in Syria would obviously require good relations with Turkey to enjoy any chance for economic success.

Further, if Turkey joined the European Union (EU), as it has been formally seeking to do since 2005, the Syrian Kurds would suddenly become part of this most advanced economic bloc that also offers considerable political protection to its members. The PKK model, instead of Barzani's KDP/KRG, would have led ironically to a successful moderate future. Moreover, Turkish EU membership would also offer Barzani's KRG close ties with the EU given the de facto alliance between Turkey and the KRG. Even more, of course, the Kurds in Turkey would also enter the EU by definition.

A strong and democratic Turkey might offer the vast majority of Kurds in the world an incredibly bright future. For their part, the Kurds ironically would offer Turkey the Kemalist security it has always sought to the detriment of the Kurds, but now with the support and cooperation of the Kurds because it would now be to the benefit of the Kurds! What might have seemed counterfactual, just a decade ago, would have become reality. The seemingly contradictory policies of change and continuity would be harmonized.

Indeed, such a solution to Turkey's domestic and foreign Kurdish problems might fit in well with the grand geopolitical strategy of former Prime Minister Ahmet Davutoglu, which he terms strategic depth.[38] In his magisterial tome Davutoglu argues that because of Turkey's control of the Bosporus and its historical legacy as heir to the Ottoman Empire, it possesses a strategic depth or potential to become a trans-regional central power that once again can help unify and lead the Islamic world. In addition, supplementing these geopolitical attributes are such liberal elements as soft power, conflict resolution, and win/win solutions. Such an over-all geostrategic vision eschews Turkey's short-sighted, cold-war-induced hesitancy to pursue more imaginative roles and demands a more proactive foreign policy. It reflects Turkey's new-found self-confidence since the rise of the AKP. Thus, it follows that instead of fearing the Kurds who are fellow Muslims, Turkey should once again take their side and lead them as in former days. For their part, as argued above, the Kurds would have much to gain by associating themselves with a more democratic and inclusive Turkey.

The 7 June 2015 parliamentary elections potentially furthered and altered this situation as the AKP party lost the parliamentary majority it had held since 2002— although it remained by far the largest party—while the broadened pro-Kurdish HDP easily cleared the 10 per cent threshold for the first time.[39] The HDP accomplished this feat by gaining support from conservative Kurdish voters who had previously supported the AKP, but were now disenchanted with it for the stalled peace process and its failure to support the Syrian Kurds in Kobanî when ISIS attacked them in the fall of 2014, among other factors. In addition, the HDP gained support from some ethnic Turkish voters disenchanted with Erdoğan and the AKP's perceived authoritarianism; these people cast strategic or tactical votes against the AKP and for the HDP.[40]

This surge in support for the HDP constituted an historic opportunity to integrate pro-Kurdish activists into Turkish politics. On the other hand, the HDP's new inclusion of leftist Turkish support that included other minorities, women, and LGBTs ruled out an exclusive Kurdish nationalist agenda. The HDP's new, more inclusive winning strategy had been devised by Öcalan, but in the immediate aftermath nobody seemed to be mentioning this, or what the newly established parliamentary power of the young charismatic Selahattin Demirtas and his more inclusive HDP meant for the future of Kurdish politics and Öcalan's PKK in Turkey. Would the newly broadened HDP be able to rejuvenate the PKK peace process successfully with the now chastised AKP? On the other hand, how long would the new HDP alliance even hold, given its obvious links to the illegal PKK, still much despised by many Turks, some of whom had just cast strategic votes for it? (The supposedly social democratic CHP and ultra-nationalist MHP also gained more representation in parliament, and thus were part of the new mix too.) Therefore, the ultimate result of this new post-election political equation in Turkey was not a culmination of the long-standing Kurdish struggle, but simply the newest stage of a continuing process. Solutions for the Kurdish problem and peace process in Turkey remained a work in progress.

Collapse of the peace process

The collapse of the Turkish-Kurdish peace process[41] in July 2015 and renewed fighting seemingly pushed the situation back to square one. What caused this failure? Despite incredible progress toward a resolution, the two sides proved unable to bridge the enormous gap between them. On the one hand the government of Turkish president Recep Tayyip Erdoğan's Justice and Development Party (AKP) proved unwilling to conduct actual negotiations with Abdullah Öcalan, the imprisoned leader of the Kurdistan Workers' Party (PKK). Instead, the government believed that it could simply list the conditions for peace and have them accepted with minimal concessions. The old Kemalist penchant for maintaining a unitary ethnic Turkish state remained. Tellingly, for example, the government rejected a neutral third-party observer or facilitator who might have encouraged and recorded the talks while even making suggestions when the process reached impasses. The failure of the minimal Dolmabahce consensus—an attempt in March 2015 to establish a monitoring committee to oversee the failing peace process—and simmering Kurdish anger over the Turkish government's failure to support the Syrian Kurdish struggle in Kobanî that raged from September 2014 until January 2015 proved to be two of the final blows to the peace process.

On the other hand, the PKK's attempts to institute democratic autonomy or grass-roots, local governing structures of decentralization throughout much of south-eastern Anatolia seemed to the government to be Kurdish independence in disguise. Indeed, a month before the peace process even formally began in March 2013, the PKK formed the Patriotic Revolutionary Youth Movement (YDG-H). This new organization grew quickly into an armed, urban youth militia that enticed government security forces into street battles in numerous south-eastern cities. Thus a genuine resolution of the Kurdish issue proved beyond reach, despite the veneer of a peace process.

However, despite the current broken situation, the Turkish-Kurdish peace process has not returned to square one for a number of reasons. Compared to the days when the very word "Kurd" constituted a four-letter word in the Kemalist lexicon and denial of a Kurdish ethnic problem prevailed, the Kurdish issue has now been institutionalized within Turkish domestic politics and furthermore regionalized, indeed internationalized. Despite the current impasse, official Turkish talks with Öcalan, the PKK, and the legal pro-Kurdish People's Democratic Party (HDP) have given the

Kurdish issue in general and the PKK specifically a permanent legitimacy that would have been inconceivable even a decade ago. This has led to a situation where even such esteemed Turkish scholars as M. Hakan Yavuz and Nihat Ali Ozcan have recently suggested that Kurdish autonomy be considered as a solution: "for the first time, some Turks are thinking about separating from the Kurdish minority",[42] and that even "a Kurdish state seems to be inevitable, given the current political fragmentation throughout the Middle East."[43]

Former Turkish prime minister Ahmet Davutoglu's once touted policies of zero problems with neighbors and strategic depth have instead metastasized into ones of huge problems with neighbors and strategic quagmire. The opportunity spaces created by the Syrian civil war have helped give rise to the Islamic State of Iraq and Syria (ISIS) as well as the institutionalization of Rojava (western or Syrian Kurdistan) as a second de facto autonomous Kurdish state, and in this case one closely linked to the PKK. (The Kurdistan Regional Government (KRG) in Iraq, of course, is the other autonomous Kurdish state.) Within the horrific Syrian civil war raging just below Turkey's southern borders, ISIS and Rojava, two dynamic non-state actors, have created a dilemma of new realities that cannot be ignored or imagined away. Moreover, amidst all these new problems, including its early call for the demise of Bashar al-Assad's Syrian regime, Turkey has arguably come down on what seems the wrong or at least the losing side.

In a well-documented, misguided attempt to facilitate the overthrow of Assad and restore stability to its southern Syrian neighbor, Turkey has allowed jihadists from all over the world to transit its territory and cross into Syria to join ISIS.[44] By so doing, Turkey also hoped to reduce or even eliminate the threat it perceived in the rise of Rojava, which Turkey saw as a proto-PKK state that would transform its success against ISIS into a contiguous Kurdish-dominated territory along Turkey's southern border.

Thus, Turkey also sat by passively watching ISIS try to destroy the Syrian Kurds holed up just across the Turkish border in Kobanî during the vicious fighting for that city from September 2014 to January 2015. As Turkey perceived matters, support for the Syrian Kurds in Kobanî would be tantamount to aiding the PKK, a terrorist enemy that had been trying to dismember Turkey for more than thirty years. In addition, why should Turkey get involved when the United States, its superpower NATO ally, would not do more? It suited Turkey that ISIS and the Syrian Kurds were weakening each other by slugging it out while Turkey sat idle. Many Turks also felt betrayed that by giving the Syrian Kurds air support against ISIS, their American NATO ally was strengthening Kurdish attempts to seize Arab lands near the Turkish border and thus unify previously non-contiguous Syrian Kurdish cantons.

Subsequently, Turkey came to blame ISIS for deadly attacks that mostly killed only ethnic Kurdish citizens in such Turkish cities as Suruc (Kobanî's twin Turkish city) and Ankara in July and October 2015. These twin attacks furthered the Kurdish belief that the Turkish government could not or even did not want to protect them. Some actually claimed that Erdoğan had turned a blind eye to such attacks in order to further the perception of Turkey under siege and thus in a "wag the dog"-like fashion successfully win the snap election held on 1 November 2015. Such perceptions might have helped Erdoğan to reclaim power in the short run, but would certainly hinder his chances to restart the peace process in the long run.

In the summer of 2015, Turkey finally claimed to have entered the struggle against ISIS by allowing the United States to use the Turkish Incirlik airbase some 60 miles above the Syrian border to carry out bombing raids against ISIS. However, instead of Turkey striking ISIS, most of the Turkish air attacks hit the PKK bases in the Qandil Mountains along the border of the KRG and Iran, and even on occasion Syrian Kurdish forces in Rojava, leading some to conclude that Turkey was simply using ISIS as a foil to go after both the PKK and Democratic Union Party (PYD), its Syrian Kurdish partner. Indeed, at the end of August 2016, Turkish forces entered northern Syria and with their jihadist allies already there pushed ISIS out of the border city of Jarabulus and the Syrian Kurdish PYD east of the Euphrates River.

In the autumn of 2015, the Syrian crisis exploded in yet another destabilizing dimension when more than a million Syrian refugees began entering Europe from Turkey, where more than 2 million of them had already been severely taxing Turkey for some time. This sea of desperate humanity threatened the stability of the European Union (EU) and soon led the EU to offer Turkey $3.2 billion, progress toward visa liberalization, and a revitalization of Turkey's moribund EU accession process in return for Turkish help in stemming the refugee flood.

In Turkey, violence against the pro-Kurdish HDP had already begun in the lead-up to the 7 June 2015 elections and grew exponentially in the days heading toward the subsequent ones on 1 November 2015. Indeed, HDP leaders blamed their losses in the second election on the violent atmosphere that prevented mass rallies, as well as their party representatives from appearing in the mainstream mass media, particularly following the deadly bombing of the HDP rally in Ankara on 10 October 2015. Between July and 15 December 2015, violence claimed the lives of 194 security officials, at least 221 PKK insurgents, and as many as 151 civilians. Thousands of people across the region were also displaced.

The failed coup of July 2016 and its immediate aftermath

On the night of 15 July 2016, a failed coup occurred in Turkey, the aftermath of which has led to drastically changed country conditions, likely to make the overall situation in Turkey, including the Kurdish problem, much worse. At least 260 people were killed and more than 2,000 injured, according to Turkish government reports; the actual death toll was probably higher. However, Erdoğan himself declared to his supporters that the failed coup was a "gift from God."[45] This revealing confession meant that the failed coup gave him an excuse to further his own authoritarian ambitions, while purging his few remaining opponents. The future democratic course of Turkey itself seemed challenged.

For example, Amnesty International (AI) reported that the Turkish government had fired or suspended at least 50,000 people from various institutions, including judges, teachers, soldiers, police, and journalists.[46] The government was deeming "terrorists" anyone it did not like or agree with. AI also reported that it had credible evidence that post-coup detainees including generals were being beaten, tortured, and raped/sodomized either digitally or by having gun barrels stuck up their anal opening, a method of degrading opponents to which Muammar Qaddafi had reportedly been subjected with a bayonet just before he was killed in October 2011. Turkish police were keeping detainees in stress positions for up to two days at a time, beating them and denying them food, water, and medical treatment. The detainees were being held arbitrarily, denied access to lawyers and family, and not properly informed of the charges against them.

The Turkish government also declared a sweeping three-month state of emergency, which gave it the power to rule by decree and simply bypass the duly elected Turkish Parliament. Under one decree, suspects could be detained for as long as 30 days without charge and the government could listen in on all conversations they had with their attorneys. To make room for the thousands of post-coup detainees, Erdoğan then let thousands of supposedly non-violent criminals not connected to the attempted coup out of prison.

Thus, if conditions had become so bad for many ethnic Turks such as the military, judges, lawyers, journalists, and teachers, among others, what could hated and feared minorities such as the Kurds expect? As close friends of the Turkish Kurds concluded: "Kurds across the country are now threatened with suspension of their civil rights and freedoms by the widespread crackdown that Erdogan has launched in the wake of the attempted coup."[47]

This new state of emergency was in addition to the government-enforced curfews that had allowed its forces to roam freely against the civilian Kurdish population since the summer of 2015 when the Turkish-PKK ceasefire had broken down and heavy fighting resumed.[48] Indeed, over the past year Turkey's south-east has experienced a level of desolation virtually unknown outside active war zones such as parts of civil-war-torn Syria.[49] The historic Turkish city centers of Nusaybin, Cizre, and old Diyarbakir have been razed, leaving gaping holes in their former make-up. The entire city of Sirnak has been leveled, so that it resembles Homs or Aleppo. Some 2,000 people have died in the fighting.

On 11 September 2016, Turkey's interior ministry announced that it was taking direct control of 25 local government municipalities in the south-east, removing the elected pro-Kurdish People's Democratic Party (HDP) city mayors, and replacing them with government-appointed trustees. Ramazan Tunc, the main advisor to

Kamuran Yuksek, the co-president of the Democratic Regions Party (DBP), which was affiliated to the HDP, declared: "This isn't lawful. It's only possible because there is a state of emergency in Turkey, and what we have here are occupation forces taking over the democratically elected local governments in the Kurdish areas."[50]

On 12 September 2016, Mehmet Öcalan, the younger brother of imprisoned PKK leader Abdullah Öcalan and just back from visiting his elder brother, addressed a gathering at the DBP's Diyarbakir headquarters with a message from his elder brother. Quoting the PKK leader, Mehmet Öcalan said: "If the state was sincere, this many people would not have to die. Let the state send two of its men to Imrali and we can solve this problem within six months. This is a blind war: let the bloodshed and tears stop."[51] However, the Turkish government chose not to reply to Öcalan's call for the resumption of peace talks, simply repeating that it would continue to battle the PKK until it was defeated.

In September 2016, Turkey's education ministry also suspended 11,285 teachers for allegedly supporting Kurdish separatists.[52] Erdoğan claimed that the firing of the teachers and local mayors was part of the campaign against Kurdish terrorism. Figen Yuksekdag, co-chair of the HDP, replied: "There is a systematic embargo against us... that will raise the risk of a coup and civil war." These firings of teachers and mayors worried some in Turkey that such policies were fueling ethnic rivalries and renewing violence. Moreover, as prosecutors pressed on with PKK-related terrorism charges against pro-Kurdish HDP MPs, Erdoğan dropped some 1,500 charges against other opposition MPs for insulting him. These latest moves against the Kurds came at the same time as aggressive efforts against two other organizations on the government's official terrorism list: ISIS and the Gülenists, officially called the Fethullah Gülen Terrorist Organization (FETO) or parallel state, discussed below.

The detained teachers were all reportedly union members who had participated in a strike calling for a peaceful solution to the armed conflict between the government and the PKK. Sezgin Tanrikulu, a human rights lawyer and deputy leader of the main opposition party, the Republican People's Party (CHP), declared: "The dismissal of more than 11,000 teachers who had nothing to do with the coup attempt, and now the taking of teachers in custody in Diyarbakir, is a completely unlawful process against union-related activities."[53] Kemal Kilicdaroglu, the CHP leader who had earlier supported the introduction of emergency rule, now accused the government of using its powers to target opponents, rather than coup plotters. Human rights groups added that the crackdown on the PKK was increasingly targeting members of Kurdish civil society, including locally elected officials of the HDP, who continued to condemn PKK attacks. UN rights chief Prince Zeid Raad Al-Hussein, the current UN High Commissioner for Human Rights, declared: "We have received repeated and serious allegations of ongoing violations of international law as well as human rights concerns, including civilian deaths, extrajudicial killings and massive displacement."[54] In Istanbul's Galatasaray Square, Turkey's Saturday Mothers

(Comates Annelid) met for the 600th time since 1995 to demand an accounting for the thousands of people, mostly Kurds, who had been "disappeared" by security forces and the police over the years.[55]

Although Kurdish leaders in Turkey had tried to disassociate themselves from the attempted coup—after all, many of the military leaders now under arrest had been involved in the government's war against the PKK—Erdoğan still needed the PKK as an enemy to unite Turkey's nationalist vote behind him, as he had been doing since the pro-Kurdish HDP had cost him an absolute majority in parliamentary elections held on 7 June 2015. Thus, even though the HDP's co-chair Selahattin Demirtas had denounced the coup when it first occurred, Erdoğan chose not to thank and invite him to his presidential palace as he had the two leaders of the CHP and Nationalist Movement Party (MHP), the other two main parties in parliament who had also condemned the coup. This exclusion clearly intended to isolate the peaceful pro-Kurdish party and its leaders as enemies and supporters of terrorism.

Many Kurds in Turkey feared that the HDP's enforced exclusion from Erdoğan's post-coup rallies and other peaceful events would further disenfranchise and push the Kurds toward greater extremism, which they believed was Erdoğan's intention in order to secure Turkish nationalist support. Erdoğan's earlier attempt to criminalize the 1,128 Turkish and Kurdish academics who had signed a petition to the Turkish government in January 2016 asking that it end its renewed violence in the southeast,[56] and his successful campaign to strip HDP co-leader Selahattin Demirtas and other HDP MPs of their parliamentary immunity so they could be tried for trumped up charges of treason, had already served to marginalize the Kurds.[57]

The Gülenists

Fethullah Gülen is an important inter-faith Islamic scholar and imam who heads the Gülen or *Hizmet* (Service) Movement, which is an international network of universities, hospitals, charities, business associations, news outlets, and schools spread across more than 150 countries. He has lived in exile in the United States since 1999. Some dismiss him as a dangerous cult leader infiltrating existing state structures such as those of Turkey, while others hail him as an enlightened beacon of inter-faith ecumenicism. Apparently, he is both.[58]

For example, Gülenists who had successfully infiltrated the Turkish judiciary and police, among other state institutions, and were then allied with Erdoğan were apparently behind the sham Ergenekon and subsequent Sledgehammer trials (2008-11) that resulted in several hundred military, journalists, and opposition lawmakers, among other secularists, being sentenced to lengthy prison terms. These victims were only released in April 2016 and all verdicts annulled pending a re-trial after subsequent evidence showed that they had been convicted on blatant and even sloppy forgeries; these were written in fonts only invented after they were supposedly written, and riddled with anachronisms that betrayed their fraudulent nature, such as naming organizations that had not even come into existence at the time of the reputed crimes, among other inconsistencies.

Nevertheless, after neutralizing their common secular opponents, Gülen and Erdoğan became bitter political enemies. In December 2013, Gülen accused Erdoğan of corruption, while Erdoğan charged Gülen with trying to infiltrate state institutions and establish a parallel structure that would eventually overthrow him. Subsequently, Erdoğan accused Gülen of masterminding the failed coup and demanded that the United States extradite him. As of October 2016, the United States has refused on the grounds that there was no credible evidence indicating that Gülen was guilty. However, despite seemingly fantastic and probably exaggerated scenarios involving former CIA official Graham E. Fuller, among others, the sources cited above indicate that Gülen was probably guilty. On the other hand, although it is true that many in the US government had become frustrated with Erdoğan's behavior, it is unlikely that the United States was backing the failed coup. US vice president Joe Biden repeated this denial during his visit to Turkey on 24 August 2016.[59]

In addition to his activities discussed above, Fethullah Gülen has also given attention to the Kurdish problem in Turkey and across the border in the region of the Kurdistan Regional Government (KRG) in Iraq.[60] Until his break with Erdoğan in 2013, almost every town in south-eastern Turkey had a Gülen school, and many locals prized entry to them. In November 2008, the Gülen movement even opened a university in Erbil, the capital of the KRG. However, after the failed coup of 15 July 2016, these schools were closed down in Turkey, while the KRG took over their administration within its purview to appease Turkey.

Ironically, the Gülen movement shares many views in common with Erdoğan's Justice and Development Party (AKP) on how to deal with the Kurdish problem. For example, both use the rhetoric of a Golden Age at the time of the Ottoman Empire when both the Turks and the Kurds were united by their Islamic faith. In appealing to the Kurds, Gülen also stresses that he began life as a follower of the renowned Islamic mystic Said Nursi, an ethnic Kurd. On the other hand, the Gülen movement's deep roots in Turkish nationalism represent a powerful obstacle to overcome in any attempt to appeal to the Kurds. Thus, many Kurds are liable to see the Gülen movement as opium that is seeking to assimilate them, rather than help solve their problems as Kurds.

Gülen has supported two major conferences on the Kurdish issue to promote liberal and reformist perspectives: Lake Abant (Turkey) in 2008 and Erbil (KRG) in 2009. The second conference hosted more than 200 intellectuals of both Turkish and Kurdish origin. One of the themes of the later conference focused on Turkey's long-standing fear of the geographic term Kurdistan, perceiving it as an existential threat to Turkey's unity. Upon criticism by some Kurdish participants, Ali Bulac, a *Zaman* columnist, responded: "I am in the capital city of the Federation of the Kurdish Region in Iraq, and I'm not someone who minds stating this."[61]

The final declaration of the Abant Platform for this second conference on the Kurds termed the region "Kurdistan Regional Government." Only a week later, Turkish president Abdullah Gül paid a visit to Erbil and called the region "Kurdistan", becoming the first Turkish official to do so. Gülen has also taken a progressive stance on using the Kurdish language in education, calling on Turkey to take swift steps to train Kurdish language teachers, even before Erdoğan's government did so. Gülen further stated that Turkey should play a leading role in defending Kurds around the world. In 2011, Gülen established a private Kurdish TV channel, Dunya TV.

However, Gülen's attitude toward both the Kurdish Opening in 2009 and the subsequent ceasefire between the Turkish government and the PKK from March 2013 to July 2015 has been ambiguous.[62] He declared that "there is benefit in peace", but questioned whether the government really had a comprehensive plan or was being duped by the PKK, whose sincerity Gülen questioned. Thus, although not against the peace process in general, Gülen was skeptical of its success and critical of its methods.

Despite Gülen's ambiguous position toward the failed Turkish-PKK peace process, Erdoğan's claim that somehow the Gülenists are supporting the PKK is not based on reality. Indeed, the two have little in common other than their opposition to Erdoğan. Nevertheless, Erdoğan's claim that the Gülenists masterminded the failed coup and even support the PKK is believed by many in Turkey, and in the first instance is probably valid. However, Erdoğan's methods against all those not involved in the coup and the Kurds remain very disturbing. Nevertheless, public opinion polls indicate that his popularity has risen strongly in the coup's aftermath,[63] so it is possible, even likely, that the Turkish president will maintain his position and persist in his actions, to the long-term detriment of his country.

17.

THE KURDISTAN WORKERS' PARTY (PKK)

RADICAL DEMOCRACY AND THE RIGHT TO SELF-DETERMINATION BEYOND THE NATION-STATE[1]

Joost Jongerden

"Nothing is more precious than independence and freedom."
Mazlum Dogan, *Serxwebun*, 5 May 1982

"We threw the idea of an independent state into the dustbin a long time ago."
Hatip Dicle, *Cumhurriyet*, 1 February 2014

Introduction

The standard, modernist view has been that civilized societies have states, and primitive societies do not. According to anthropologist Pierre Clastres, this advocates "a doctrine which arbitrarily [ties] the state of civilisation to the civilisation of the State."[2] The idea that civilized societies have states makes an important claim: namely, that the state is the destiny of "civilized people" on its road to modernity, and those who have no state are not civilized. People without a state, it says, are thus the "not-civilized"; they are modernity's "other." And it is related to this idea of the state as both a symbol and a destiny of the civilized that it has become commonplace to consider state formation as the ultimate goal of political action.

Most of the Kurdish political movements that emerged in the 1960s and 1970s also framed their struggle in terms of an anti-colonialism that had the establishment of an independent state as its apogee. In its 1978 foundational program, the Kurdistan Workers' Party (Partiya Karkêren Kurdistane, PKK) similarly expressed the objective of establishing a single (united) independent state called "Kurdistan."[3] Over time, however, this changed. In 2005, the PKK announced that it considered the nation-state a hindrance on the road to freedom, and that its strategic objective was the establishment not of a state but of an interlinked network of councils as the basis of self-determination and a means for living together. "Drawing and dying for borders", argued Salih Muslim, chair of the PKK's sister party in Syria, the Democratic Union Party (Partiya Yekîtiya Demokrat, PYD), "is a European illness from the nineteenth and twentieth centuries." The council model of connectivity, he declared, is the model for the future.[4]

The aim of this chapter is to discuss and explain how the PKK developed a new understanding of the right to self-determination on the basis of a critique of the state and nation-state form. Outlining the PKK's imaginary of a new political architecture based on the praxis of "democratic autonomy" and "democratic confederalism" and the idea of active citizenship around which these revolve, I argue that democratic autonomy and confederalism are the cornerstones of a new political discourse, defined as a meta-language that instructs its members and followers how to live and act beyond the nation-state.[5] It needs to be emphasized that this chapter explores how the PKK thinks about self-determination and social relations, and not the way these ideas have been practiced. The chapter explores theoretical implications, not their realizations to date.

The chapter is structured as follows. First, I define what we need to understand by the PKK, followed by a discussion of the way in which the nation-state is taken for granted as a context or destiny of social action and practices. Then, I discuss the concepts of democratic autonomy and democratic confederalism. I first show how these concepts are embedded within a long political tradition of thought and linked to a rich history of practices, and then I discuss how the PKK's political outlook in the period of its inception was shaped around the objective of the establishment of an independent state and how, in the 2000s, the conception of the right to self-determination changed from a state-centered to a people- and connectivity-centered approach.

The PKK

Since this chapter concerns the political imaginary and architecture developed by the PKK and through which the PKK is developed, we should clarify how the PKK is to be understood. The PKK has been officially identified as a terrorist organization since it was placed on terrorist lists by the US in 1997 and the EU in 2002.[6] The terrorist labeling has been a subject of critique ever since.[7] More importantly here, the concept of terror or terrorism has very limited analytical value for the social sciences, since it is primarily a normative-political concept used to label and disqualify non-state actors.

The PKK has also been referred to as a "separatist" movement, or more specifically, because of its assumed nationalist character, it was considered separatist by those who defend the integrity of the states where the Kurds live: Turkey, Iraq, Iran, and Syria. As I have discussed elsewhere, however, the PKK is one or even the most important secular movement in the Middle East, and the liberation struggle it envisaged was not specifically implemented or framed in ethnic or nationalist discourses.[8] In fact, the process of party formation (1973-8) was influenced by the revolutionary left in Turkey. Not only did many of the PKK's founders have relations with the revolutionary left in Turkey, but its discourse was also influenced by this broad front. The militants considered themselves Marxists engaged in making a revolution, with Kurdistan as their focal area and with the intention of uniting the revolutionary left in Turkey. Today, indeed, the PKK expresses itself in a post-Marxist "radical democracy" discourse.[9] Finally, it would be wrong to depict the PKK as (just) a guerrilla/armed organization, or to characterize the PKK in (purely or even primarily) military (or similar) terms. Though resorting to violence, the PKK was and is a political organization, prompted to use violence in circumstances in which there was no alternative (legally permitted) avenue of genuine political expression.[10]

Reading PKK documents, one may distinguish between two political objectives that the movement has had since its inception. The first was a progressive realization of the right to self-determination; the second a transformation of Kurdish society through the elimination of relations of exploitation. Since the PKK envisaged the revolution in Kurdistan and Turkey as an intertwined process, it considered a reunification, or better, a non-chauvinist re-establishment of the left as important for the liberation struggle.[11] Militants active in the PKK do not refer to the movement as a military or insurgent movement primarily, as one such militant recently stated:

> Every single Kurdish movement is a revolt, but I don't mean the PKK is an insurrectionary movement. It isn't. The movements before the PKK were revolts, in terms of process, aims, and general emphasis, but the PKK is much more than this, so it shouldn't be called an insurrectionary movement. The PKK is a politically organised movement.[12]

When the Partiya Karkerên Kurdistane was established as a political party in 1978, it had a classic communist party type of organizational structure, with a general secretary as the leading party official and an executive committee responsible for direct operations. The highest executive institution was the central committee, and the party congress was the party's highest decision-making body. Over the years, however, the PKK transformed and grew more diverse.[13] What we refer to as the PKK today is actually a party-complex, a formation of parties and organizations comprising several parties (including the PKK as a party), a co-party that separately organizes women,[14] sister parties in Iraq (PÇDK) and Iran (PJAK), as well as Syria (PYD),[15] and guerrilla forces[16] related to these parties. Alongside this cluster of parties, the PKK established institutions through which the integration and coordination of political practices is facilitated. The most important of these today is the Association of Communities in Kurdistan (Koma Civakên Kurdistan, KCK),[17] which is basically a network of village, city, and regional councils, whose assembly is called the Kurdistan People's Congress, Kongra-Gel.[18] In short, the PKK today is a movement that has institutionalized itself in diverse areas and expresses itself in a radical democratic discourse.

Methodological nationalism

The way in which nation and state are assumed as self-evident, either as (quasi-)natural entities or given destinies, along with the framing of anti-colonial political movements as nationalist and their struggle in terms of nation-state building, brings to the fore an important problem in the political and social sciences: methodological nationalism. As a specific way of seeing the world,[19] methodological nationalism is the assumption that the nation-state is the natural social and political form of society.[20] This can take the form of approaches that 1) positively or explicitly affirm the nation-state as the basic unit of analysis, 2) follow this principle without being explicit or indicating any reflexive awareness, or 3) neglect and overlook the importance of nationalist doctrine for the modern world.[21]

The epistemology of the social sciences, it is argued, has been attached and shaped by the experience of the nation-state—which holds true both for academia and for the social and political imaginary in general. Wimmer and Schiller refer to this assumption as an "iron cage", since it confines and limits analytical capacities.[22] Nimni refers to the understanding of politics in the context of a world of nation-states as a hegemonic consensus that operates like an intellectual constraint and a powerful barrier against practices and ideas from which a new "political architecture" may arise.[23]

The naturalization of the nation-state has taken various forms in intellectual disciplines. Wimmer and Schiller distinguish between three variants of methodological nationalism in the social sciences.[24] First, the theoretical social sciences, from Bourdieu to Habermas and Luhman, it is argued, were captured by the apparent naturalness and givenness of a world divided by nation-states and (re)produced a systematic blindness to other forms of living.[25] Second, the more empirically oriented social sciences took nation-state discourses, loyalties, and agendas for granted, without problematizing them. Modernity was built on the premises of the nation-state as a separate unit, and the social sciences came to adopt this view fairly unquestioningly.[26] From the post-Second World War period of decolonization and after, the task of building nation-states was seen as an "evident corollary to the other tasks of modernisation, projecting as a model a vision of Western nation-state building" by Wimmer and Schiller, referring to modernization theorists such as Lerner and Rostow, to whom nation-building and state formation were natural bed-fellows (indeed, this combination became the only thinkable way of organizing society).[27] The idea of building a nation-state figures prominently in the work of anti-colonial thinker Franz Fanon.[28] Modern history thus became written as a history of nation-states.[29]

Third, and last, the territorialization of the social sciences and the reduction of its analytical focus to the borders of the nation-state meant taking nation-state borders as cutting off a particular part of the social world in a discrete entity, reproduced in the idea of "inside" and "outside." Anthony Smith refers to this when he defines methodological nationalism as an approach in social sciences in which "basic social data are always collected and evaluated in terms of entities called 'nation-states.'"[30] In anthropology, similarly, methodological nationalism was reproduced through the projection of the idea of the nation-state in the approach to the social world as divided into bounded and cultural specific units.[31] Here, the triumph of developmental evolution and consequent decline of (unprincipled) diffusionism in the analysis of societal change had long since led to the twentieth-century tendency for in-depth studies of single peoples as discrete entities (notably in the British tradition of social anthropology).

Analysis of the Kurdish issue has suffered from the same limitation and distortion of methodological nationalism. The self-evident manner in which research assumes the existing nation-state as the natural framework for investigation defines the construction of many studies on the Kurdish issue, with their framing of the states in which the Kurds live. First, although there are many reasons to specify the study of the Kurdish issue as in, for example, Turkey, this cannot be taken as self-evident and actually needs explanation; nor can it be assumed, similarly, that national independence is the natural and ultimate objective of political action for liberation. Through a discussion of the idea of radical democracy, with democratic confederalism and democratic autonomy as key-projects, and the related refashioning of the idea of the right to self-determination, the following considerations are offered as an attempt in the direction of de-naturalizing the conceptualization of the Kurdish issue as a state-oriented discourse.

Self-determination and the nation-state

In the period during which the PKK was formed, 1973-8, its political outlook was shaped around two main objectives: 1) the transformation of Kurdish society through the elimination of relations of exploitation, and 2) the unification of Kurdistan and the establishment of an independent state. At the time, the economy in northern Kurdistan (south-east Turkey) was based on agriculture; pockets of industry could be found in Batman (oil) and Antep (food, textiles, and furniture), but it was farming that dominated. Relations of exploitation were mainly defined by division of labor and hierarchy based on the distinctions between agricultural laborer, tenant farmer, and landowner. The large landowners, sometimes also both tribal and religious leaders, maintained close relations with the state and regarded peasants and villagers as their subjects. Essentially, social power relations were feudal in character. The PKK thought that a termination of relations of exploitation depended on ending the division of labor and hierarchy through land reform and its redistribution. In the party's programme, *The Road of Revolution in Kurdistan*, such societal transformation was considered to be dependent on a process of state-formation, the establishment of an "independent, united and democratic Kurdistan."[32] As Uzun puts it,

> In 1978, the PKK was founded as a Kurdish movement that adopted the legacy of the massacred revolutionaries of the Turkish Left. Based on Marxist-Leninist theory and the strategy of a long-term 'people's war', it aimed at achieving an 'independent Kurdistan.'[33]

After the formation of an independent state, a process of societal transformation could be initiated. The quest for independence was based on a Marxist-Leninist approach to the issue of self-determination, indeed, as specifically argued by Lenin:

> Consequently, if we want to grasp the meaning of self-determination of nations, not by juggling with legal definitions, or "inventing" abstract definitions, but by examining the historico-economic conditions of the national movements, we must inevitably reach the conclusion that the self-determination of nations means the political separation of these nations from alien national bodies, and the formation of an independent national state.[34]

In the case of Kurdistan, the issue was considered to be one not only of separation but also of colonialism and unification.[35] This is also why the Kurdistan Revolutionaries, the name used by the militants who established the PKK in 1978, discussed the issue of an independent and *united* Kurdistan. The treatment of this issue by Abdul Rahman Ghassemlou in his book *Kurdistan and the Kurds*, published by the Czechoslovakian Academy of Sciences in 1965, is typical of the way in which Kurdish political parties inspired by Marxism-Leninism started to look at the status of Kurdistan and the ultimate aim of liberation struggles from the 1960s onwards:

> Marxism-Leninism avows the right of self-determination to every nation, and this right for them has a concrete content. Lenin in his polemic with reformists and deviationists from Marxism showed clearly that the self-determination of nations means the political separation of these nations from alien national bodies and the formation of an independent national state. (...) Self-determination of nations in the programme of the Marxists cannot have any other meaning than political self-determination, political independence, and the formation of a national state. (...) [Lenin] censured anyone who denied the right, or regarded it otherwise than a right to separation. "A socialist who is a member of a domi-

nant nation", Lenin writes, "and thus not furthering the right of oppressed nations to separation during peace nor during war, is neither a socialist, nor an internationalist, but a chauvinist".[36]

The right to self-determination was looked upon as both an issue of separation and unification; a separation of Kurdistan from the various colonizing states and a unification of these parts into one state.[37] Moreover, a unification with other peoples in the Middle East was also considered as dependent on separation, since "brotherhood" cannot take place in a colonial relationship. Self-determination in the form of state formation was seen as part of a worldwide struggle for the liberation of oppressed nations, as expressed in the 1978 PKK manifesto:

> Given today's conditions, an independent state is the only true and correct way and therefore the only revolutionary thesis; other theses and roadmaps are reformist because they do not touch state-borders, and because they are reformist they are reactionary. Aiming to create a politically, economically, and in other ways independent country, the Kurdistan Liberation Movement, first in relation with the neighboring peoples, then peoples in the region and the world, will work in the interest of a world proletarian revolution.[38]

Summarizing, the right to self-determination generally was conceptualized in terms of separate state formation. This idea of self-determination became scrutinized in the 2000s, although it can be traced back to a critique of socialism as manifested ("real existing socialism") and the character of national liberation struggles as early as the 1980s.[39] As Abdullah Öcalan later stated in his court defense, "[T]he PKK, under the influence of real socialism, was for a long time unable to transcend the nation-statist paradigm."[40]

Öcalan historicized and problematized the issue of nation-state formation in respect to the PKK in his *Manifesto of a Democratic Civilisation*, a reflection on the party's history which localized the idea of self-determination as nation-state building in the context of a power struggle between the United States and the Soviet Union:

> The principal problem in the formation of the PKK is its ambiguity regarding the nation-statist ideology. In this respect, J. Stalin's thesis on the national question has been of particular influence. Stalin approached the national problem as that of establishing a state. This approach affected all socialist systems and national liberation movements. Lenin also accepted this right of nations to self-determination and its reduction to state formation, and this is the main cause for the ideological ambiguity of communist and socialist parties. The basic idea for the solution of the Kurdish issue when the PKK was established was the model of state formation developed by Stalin and approved by Lenin. Most of the liberation movements that peaked in that period (1950-70) aimed at the establishment of a state and considered this the only model. A separate state became the sacred principle of the socialist credo. To be a socialist and to give support for the establishment of a state by oppressed and colonised nations were considered one and the same. If you thought differ-

ently, you were not a socialist. In fact, the principle of the right to self-determination was put forward by the American President Wilson after the First World War and became related to the developing US hegemony. Lenin, who did not want to stay in the shadow of Wilson and wanted to gain the support of the colonial nations for the Soviet Union, further radicalised the principle and reduced it to the establishment of an independent state. A competition between the two systems thus began. The most obvious example was the support both tried to give to the national resistance initiated in Anatolia.[41]

In his work developed in the 2000s, but going back to the 1980s, Öcalan started to treat the relationship between self-determination and nation-state formation not as natural or self-evident but as historically contingent—emerging in the context of competition between the superpowers. He not only considers the nation-state as a particular historical construction, moreover, but also as a problematic one. The nation-state, he argues, is a center for the manufacture of subjects, one that attempts to inscribe a conceived culture onto the population.[42] As a result, the logic of the nation-state is that of a centralized assimilation-machine: it aims to transform cultures into culture, and languages into language. This production of a "*homo nationalis*" puts people and borders under surveillance, with fascism the highest stage of the nation-state.[43] Öcalan concludes that the nation-state does not liberate the subject from colonial status, but subjugates: "Contrary to what is thought, capitalism does not mean economic development but the systematic denial of economy. The nation-state goes against what is thought, not through democracy, freedom, and human rights, but in the denial of these values."[44]

This critique of the nation-state has brought the PKK to a rethinking of politics. At Newroz 2005, the PKK presented the declaration in which it explained its new model. Arguing that although at the beginning of the twentieth century the right to self-determination was interpreted as the right to form a state, the PKK, developing an alternative idea of politics, contended that democratization could not be established on the basis of a globalization of the nation-state model.[45]

Self-determination and democratic confederalism/autonomy

The PKK developed a new ideological and political outlook in the 2000s, based on the idea of "radical democracy" as developed in three intertwined projects—democratic republic, democratic autonomy, and democratic confederalism—that functioned as a "strategic dispositif", as ways in which Kurdish political demands were (re) defined and organized toward a people-oriented and emancipatory politics of connectivity.[46] The project for a democratic republic aimed at the disassociation of democracy from nationalism, of *demos* from *ethnos*. Concretely, this resulted in the proposal for a new constitution, one in which citizenship was not defined or even conceived in terms of ethnicity, but rather in terms of the civic republic and civil rights. In addition to separating nation and state, the idea of the democratic republic aimed at transcending the idea of a hierarchical and centralized state. Yet the idea of a democratic republic still centered upon the state. This is not the case with the ideas and projects of democratic autonomy and democratic confederalism.

"Democratic autonomy", according to the Kurdish MP Sebahat Tuncel, "refers to a status, a status of self-determination."[47] This directly refers to the capability of people to take decisions over their lives and determine their own future. Democratic confederalism can be characterized as a bottom-up system for self-administration, organized at the levels of village (*köy*), urban neighborhood (*mahalle*), district (*ilçe*), city (*kent*), and the region (*bölge*), which is referred to as "northern Kurdistan." According to one provincial party-leader in Diyarbakir:

> As a paradigm, democratic confederalism rejects centralism and the state and welcomes self-organisation of the people and their taking responsibility of their daily affairs and the places they live. Democratic confederalism is not oriented towards the taking over of state power, or focused on the state, but on developing alternative forms of power through self-organisation.[48]

An executive member of the Democratic Society Congress (Demokratik Toplum Kongresi, DTK), coordinating the projects of democratic autonomy and democratic confederalism in Turkey, refers to democratic confederalism and democratic autonomy as an alternative to the collapsed system of real existing socialism, which again has proved to be incapable of developing alternatives for capitalism. He refers to these projects as "a social model" which through the organization of councils, from the village level up, develops a democratic nation.[49]

The imprisoned PKK leader Abdullah Öcalan initiated a debate on democratic autonomy and democratic confederalism among the Kurds, inspired by the work of Murray Bookchin.[50] Bookchin, following Kropotkin, differentiates between two notions of politics, the Hellenic model and the Roman, which gave rise to two different conceptualizations of politics and understandings of government.[51] The first, the Hellenic model, stands for a participatory-democratic form of politics, with which Bookchin aligns himself; and the second, the Roman model, stands for a centralist and statist form, which he rejects.[52] The statist, centralized Roman model has a herd of subjects, but the Hellenic model an active citizenship.[53] Unfortunately, Bookchin argues, it is the Roman model that has become the dominant form in modern society, informing the American and French constitutionalists of the eighteenth century; the Athens model exists as a counter- and underground current, finding expression in the Paris Commune of 1871, the initial councils (soviets) that emerged in the spring-time of the revolution in Russia in 1917, and in the Spanish Revolution of 1936-9. Like Bookchin, Öcalan argues that statecraft must not be mistaken for politics; statecraft, Bookchin argues, has corroded the political domain and resulted in civic degradation.[54]

Bookchin projects his political imaginary for the recovery of humans as active citizens onto the idea of confederalism, defined as "the interlinking of communities with one another through recallable deputies mandated by municipal citizens' assemblies", which he regards as an "alternative to the nation-state."[55] Elsewhere, Bookchin defines confederalism as "a network of administrative councils whose members are elected from popular face-to-face democratic alliances, in the various villages, towns, and even neighborhoods of large cities."[56] According to Bookchin, confederalism reaches its fullest development in relation to a project of autonomy, "when placing local farms, factories, and other enterprises in local municipal hands" or "when a community (...) begins to manage its own economic resources in an interlinked way with other communities."[57] In this model, the economy is placed in the custody of the confederal councils, and thus "neither collectivised nor privatised, it is common."[58] As such, confederalism and autonomy are key notions in Bookchin's "radically new configuration of society."[59] In these projects of confederalism and autonomy, the means (defined as a network model of localized small-scale self-organization and self-administration) and the ends (defined as community-controlled economies) conflate. Thus combined, they can be considered an alternative politics, going beyond those of the nation-state. In conclusion, we might say that the principle underlying the paradigm shift is the development of a new political architecture, one that is based on a critique of the state and a connection to a praxis based on the self-governing abilities of people.

Discussion

This chapter has looked at the PKK's changing understanding of the right to self-determination. Self-determination is not conceptualized as the establishment of a state, but in terms of the right of people to make decisions, to take responsibility for the organization and regulation of their social, economic, political, and cultural affairs (democratic autonomy), and a bottom-up, council democracy for its administration (democratic confederalism). Here, I summarize and develop this with six points, related to the specific case of the PKK and also to wider analysis.

First, the PKK no longer defines the quest for independence in terms of state-building, which marks a radical break with the idea that the nation-state is a destiny: the teleological goal and end-point of political action. In the new political discourse, the PKK rejects the concept of the nation-state, defined as a spatially organized homogenous population which, as a political necessity, for its realization needs a strong, centralized state. Therefore, the construction of nation-states is not considered as liberating, but oppressive. It is this analysis that has led the PKK to reject the nation-state form and its pursuit as a desirable action or necessary objective of political action.

Second and relatedly, this changing understanding is based on the idea that we can distinguish the political realm from the statist realm and thus develop a politics that is not statist. The idea of the state, it is argued, is based on a separation of people from the political realm, and thus separates people from decision-making processes. If people assume decision-making powers, the argument goes, they can develop a form of government that is not statist. Senior PKK leaders Cemil Bayık and Duran Kalkan argue that this is a paradigm shift involving a move from state-building to society-building, and relatedly from taking power (*iktidar*, as in state or sovereign power) to developing societal self-governing capacities.[60] The councils established to this end are not envisaged as "lower" divisions of a central state, but rather the primary spaces for deliberation and decision-making.[61] This is what Arendt refers to as the empowerment of people in their capacity of citizens, and represents a form of government beyond the state.[62]

Third, the idea of allocating decision-making powers to local councils does not come with an inwardly oriented or parochial form of militant particularism. On the contrary, the concept of confederalism evokes a sense of connectedness, of village, neighborhood, city, and regional councils. This is a conceptualization of places and the people who live there, conceived not in terms of discrete and separate entities, but as related and connected to one another. Local self-government within the context of democratic confederalism is not based on separation from others, but on extending itself.[63] This then foregrounds the issue of how we relate to one another, including what Massey refers to as a "responsibility towards the wider relations on which we depend."[64] What this means in practice, of course, remains to be seen, since, to borrow the words of Marx about the meaning of the Paris Commune, it entails a "practical learning of extending relations."[65] Manifestly, any replacement of the state by a confederal system represents a thorough transformation of the very essence of the body politic. Yet it is impelled. The emphasis on responsibility and interconnectivity in the project of democratic autonomy and democratic confederalism has the potential to create inclusive geographies; democratic confederalism brings into focus the rights of people to take control over their own affairs as well as the way to relate to others, elsewhere.

Fourth and relatedly, the new paradigm of the PKK is not based on state-building and not concerned with the redrawing of borders. "Our idea of a democratic nation is not defined by flags and borders",[66] Öcalan argues, saying that "[t]he PKK does not derive the creation of a Kurdish nation-state from the right of self-determination of the peoples. However, we regard this right as the basis for the establishment of grass-roots democracies, without seeking new political borders."[67] Although the project of democratic confederalism does not aim at drawing new borders and the establishment of new political entities, this does not mean that the existing borders are accepted as a fact of life. "It is not realistic to demand the immediate abolition of the state",[68] Öcalan continues. "However, I do not mean to say that we have to take things as they are" and "it is possible to build confederate structures across all parts of Kurdistan without the need to question the existing borders."[69] In the course of events, the state is being transformed:

> At the end of this process, there should be a lean state as a political institution, which only observes functions in the fields of internal and external security and in the provision of social security. Such an idea of the state has nothing in common with the authoritarian character of the classic state, but would rather be regarded as a societal authority.[70]

Mustafa Karasu, another senior PKK leader, clarifies how a struggle that does not take borders as a point of reference may lead to a transcending of these borders:

> In bourgeois thinking, the right to self-determination is formulated in terms of establishing a state. But this is not the socialist understanding of self-determination. We think democratic confederalism is the best possible way of practicing self-determination. (...) Since democratic confederalism does not take the state as its main frame, it is also not about changing borders. On the contrary, it is a way of thinking and doing which is non-statist. The frame of reference in democratic confederalism is developing a system of people's democracy on the basis of self-organisation. As such, people develop their own institutions, councils. If people organise themselves from the bottom-up and establish relations with each other, with other councils, democratic confederalism renders borders as insignificant.[71]

The building of democratic confederalism across all parts of Kurdistan, or even the Middle East, does not question the borders as such, but as this occurs together with the development of confederal structures, these borders lose their meaning. Borders are rendered irrelevant, without being taken as the focus of the struggle.

Fifth, the development of a new paradigm also affected the PKK as a political party. At the start of this chapter, we argued that the PKK at the time of its establishment assumed a classical communist party type of organizational structure, but has been transformed into a party complex, characterized by a multiplicity of parties and organizations. This organizational transformation is related to the changing objective of the PKK. A party that wants to grab state-power or to become the state evokes organizational requirements that are different to those of a party that aims to create a network of practices through which self-government can be established.

Sixth, and finally, in respect of the issue of methodological nationalism in the social sciences, it is widely argued that everyday life is becoming cosmopolitan and should take globalism as its frame of reference.[72] Beck rightly criticizes "the core belief of the national gaze that politics and society can *only* be organised along the lines of the nation-states" and what he calls "zombie science" as a science of the unreal. "Methodological nationalism blinds social scientists to the nature and reality of the world they seek to understand."[73] The argument is that an appreciation of the contemporary global interconnectivity requires us to liberate ourselves from the container view of methodological nationalism. Such a freedom *from*, however—a negatively defined rejection of past limitations, a recognition of the breaking of the mould of yesterday's structure—may seem to leave us adrift in a formless ocean of constant motion without any meaningful direction. Such an alternative to methodological nationalism has been criticized as methodological placelessness, as the "challenge of maneuvering between the Scylla of methodological nationalism and the postmodern Charybdis of global flows and 'cosmopolitism without space.'"[74] The case discussed here, the project of radical democracy, does not introduce such a vision of opaque globalism to thinking beyond the nation-state, but draws our attention instead to a networked politics of connectivity. This networked politics is very much rooted— grounded in the local, in fact, embedded in the practices and actions of people and their communities—yet at the same time dynamic in connecting people to broader geographical (ultimately unlimited, global) terrains. In other words, thinking beyond methodological nationalism does not necessitate a thinking in global and abstract processes; it is conceivable as a global politics grounded in everyday life.

Conclusion

This analysis of the PKK project of radical democracy and a revision of its understanding of the right to self-determination shows us three things. First, it makes us aware of and question the operation of implicit and explicit methodological nationalism in analyses of liberation movements, and thence consider alternatives to state-oriented objectives. This radical democracy project takes as reference not the nation-state and its politics of submission, but self-government on the basis of active citizenship and connectivity. It revives a communal and federalist tradition against an authoritarian and centralist one. Second, it shows that a thinking beyond the nation-state does not necessarily mean thinking in amorphous global processes. The case for council democracy opens the possibilities for thinking in terms of local constructions of an ever-expanding politics, the grounded global. Third, this rethinking of politics has not involved the PKK abandoning claims to the right to self-determination, but rather its redefinition of this in terms of council democracy and self-administration—in short, a radical democracy of active citizenship. Returning to the words of Hatip Dicle cited at the beginning of this article: what is implied in his words is that the PKK threw the idea of a state in the dustbin *because* the party is attached to independence and freedom.

18.

THE PKK, THE KURDISH MOVEMENT, AND THE EMERGENCE OF KURDISH CULTURAL POLICIES IN TURKEY

Clémence Scalbert-Yücel

Since the end of the First World War and the early days of Kurdish nationalism, culture has played a key role in Kurdish politics. It was mobilized in the "work of national differentiation", to use Alain Dieckhoff's words,[1] or as a tool for the "invention of national identity", to use Anne-Marie Thiesse's.[2] In a very classical fashion, elements of culture were mobilized in order to build and put forward Kurdish particularisms; Kurdish nationalism fed on culture which, in return, it contributed to (re)defining.

The works of definition of a Kurdish national identity by Kurdish leaders and nationalists in the early twentieth century are now well studied.[3] These works are first at play in the early Kurdish journals published at the very end of the Ottoman Empire, which presented both political debates and literature and texts on national heroes and myths. The process of invention of a national identity continued intensively just after the First World War, in a very different context: that of the French and British mandates and the Turkish nation-state which worked actively, and often with violence, at both state and nation building. The context is also marked by the failure of Kurdish revolts in Turkey which led the nationalist elite based in the Levant to shift from military to cultural struggle.[4] The Kurdish nationalist elites, alarmed at the "threat" of destruction weighing upon the Kurdish people,[5] worked in connection with the French Orientalists in the Levant[6] at the construction of a national identity. The journal *Hawar*, published by the Bedir Khan brothers in the 1930s and 1940s in the Levant, was one of the fruits of this connection. It illustrates well the way in which elements of culture (as varied as language and oral tradition, but also classical literature, gender roles, religion, etc.) were used to build the specificity of the Kurds. It also marked how Kurdish culture has been defined for decades. The construction of the national identity and specificity continued until today; all Kurdish organizations produced some cultural works and articulated views on culture and national identity. Up until today, many studies in social sciences and history research have deconstructed these discourses of national identity and myths. Nationalism has been a prism through which Kurdish culture has been studied. Hamit Bozarslan analyzed Kurdish nationalism as a "doctrine of elaboration of Kurdishness",[7] and Martin Strohmeier studied key figures of Kurdish nationalism.[8] Other works focused on the role of homeland representation[9] or language[10] in national identity, on the construction of the myth of Newroz,[11] or on discourses of national identity in literature,[12] painting,[13] or music.[14]

The affirmation of the Kurdistan Workers' Party (Partiya Karkerên Kurdistane, PKK) as the hegemonic actor of the Kurdish political sphere brought an important change in the relationship between Kurdish politics and culture. Although culture continued to be used (while being simultaneously reformulated) as a tool to build the nation and the national identity, the Kurdish nationalist movement,[15] particularly from the 1990s onward, and later with pro-Kurdish local governments in Turkey's south-east from 1999, developed and put into practice cultural policies with "specific rationales", "practices", and "modes of organisation."[16] It is true that other organizations, like the Kurdistan Socialist Party with its subgroup Riya Azadî (Path to Freedom) and the Workers Vanguard Party of Kurdistan (Partiya Pêşenga Karkerên Kurdistan, PPKK), had started to develop cultural actions in the 1970s, prior to the PKK and without the breadth or the resources of the PKK. The PKK's size, capacity, hegemony, and longevity make it the first and single organization to have been able to develop and sustain a vision, practices, and organizations for culture. The liberalization of state policies (first under Turgut Özal in the early 1990s) that partially lifted the ban on the use of the Kurdish language[17] and recognized the existence of the Kurds offered conditions of possibility for such development.[18] If the movement's cultural policy was first largely "implicit" (since it was not necessarily formulated as such), it became more and more "explicit"[19] in particular with the establishment of the pro-Kurdish municipalities.

This chapter describes the ways in which the Kurdish movement's cultural policies took shape, around a specific rationale, formulated by Abdullah Öcalan, and through the building of cultural organizations, with the main aim of (re)constructing a Kurdish national identity. But the practices also fed the rationale, and it took some time for the ideology to be designed and stabilized. The policies' rationale indeed is not always strict and there are contradictions within Öcalan's thoughts themselves, which evolved through time. This critique is however only possible because the sphere of cultural production has grown bigger since the 1990s. The link between nationalism, politics, and culture is more criticized today by cultural producers themselves.[20] Indeed, although the PKK stressed the need for artists to support the struggle, it created some conditions of possibility for the emergence of a relatively independent Kurdish cultural and artistic scene today. The widening of the conditions of possibility was also due to the progressive softening of the legislation in Turkey in the 1990s, but more radically in the 2000s under the AKP government.[21] The inscription of public actors in the sphere of Kurdish culture under AKP rule does not lead to the end of state pressures on the cultural sphere. On the contrary, it makes culture and cultural policies a site of struggle between two different political blocs.

Abdullah Öcalan on art and culture

Abdullah Öcalan debated extensively the issues of art and culture. His vision and thesis on art were developed in interviews given for instance to Mehmet Ali Birand and Yalçın Küçük,[22] or under the pen name of Ali Welat in the culture and arts pages of the daily *Özgür Gündem* from 1993.[23] At that time, cultural organizations had already been established: ideological production and the practices of cultural institutions fed one another. The theses on art and culture that Öcalan developed in the early 1990s were actually very close to Marxist-Leninist ones and cannot be understood without taking into consideration the production of the New Man that the PKK was seeking.[24] The PKK aimed to transform the "Kurdish personality" by liberating it from alienation from both the Turkish state and society, and the Kurdish traditional social structures. Öcalan declared:

> Our revolution, initially ideological, political, and military in nature, is increasingly becoming a social one. That transforms peoples' lives a lot more and so produces major results and strong reactions. This is an uprising against the old social order – against the world of socialisation, relations, feelings, and impulses developed by the enemy. We are seeking to destroy this world.[25]

But this revolution was soon to take a cultural and artistic dimension, as he stressed in his interview with Yalçın Küçuk, published in 1993:

> I saw that politics and war were not enough to transform the human being. At that time, I also noticed that Kurdish musicians, writers or artists started to line up. I merged the two: this was closely related to the rise of the revolutionary movement. This started with Hunerkom.[26] Writers, painters appeared. Publications become more numerous. Pretty soon, it was like a flood.[27]

As the PKK was defined as the only organization to make possible the rebirth of society and the human being, the PKK was also the only organization that could renew, resurrect, and purify Kurdish art. There is however a tension between modernity and tradition within Öcalan's thoughts, as well as in his tastes: he has altogether encouraged the production of modern Kurdish music for propaganda (in particular after the PKK's second congress in 1982), listened to *dengbêj*, and fostered the formation of a symphonic orchestra as a mean of nationalization or nation-building.[28] In general, nonetheless, Öcalan had stressed the fact that past cultural and artistic productions must not be erased but should be produced anew; only that way could they be freed from their alienating character. The impossible love story between Mem and Zîn, told by Ahmedê Khanî, or the myth of the Blacksmith Kawa who is said to have liberated the Kurds from tyranny in the *Cherefname*, were reinterpreted by the PKK. This position is well expressed in the following words:

> PKK action as a whole is an artistic action. PKK action is the focus of the new art for Kurdistan, its source and includes almost all properties of arts in its body. In a Kurdistan without the PKK art is dead, and the remaining cannot be called art. The art of the Turkish Republic is an act of invasion. The art of Turkish Republic is an art of suffocation, assimilation and clearance of the existing traditions and activities of people in Kurdistan by the bourgeois. So art is dead. Therefore the emergence of the PKK is the resurrection of the art. It is the source of art, it is the foundation laid down.[29]

Following these ideas, the artist was to serve the revolution; to portray it; to put aside his or her own individuality and to take part, as a collective, in the revolution. But as shown in the above quote, Abdullah Öcalan's thinking, following again Marxist-Leninist lines, goes further. Aesthetics and revolution are one and cannot be separated: the PKK revolution is not only the focus of new art, but the PKK revolution is art in itself. Öcalan would imagine himself as an artist, filling the mountains with guerrilla fighters, while the writer Yaşar Kemal would have portrayed just one in *İnce Mehmet*. Öcalan declared to Yalçın Küçük:

> I wonder, am I becoming romantic? I don't know, but lately I have started to ask myself: 'Am I becoming a novelist?' I frequently use the word 'artistic' [...] Of course, boys and girls pop up in front of me. I work as no artist would. Sometimes I feel that I have passed into the Yeşilçam.[30] In some sense, I have become the main character.[31]

He would be both the main character and the director. But he could also become a novelist. He thought about the possibility of writing a novel in which he would feature at the center.[32] He and the PKK were the artist; the revolution its art. These were the main lines along which artistic practices were encouraged and cultural institutions established.

KURDISH CULTURAL POLICIES IN TURKEY

The Mesopotamia Cultural Center and the birth of a cultural policy

The first cultural institutions were established in Germany in the early 1980s with Hünerkom, the Union of Kurdistan's patriotic artists, and Koma Berxwedan, a music band whose name means Resistance that both narrated the PKK struggle and called on people to join it. The singers Hozan Seyitxan, Hozan Sefkan, and Mizgîn, who had created the band, were sent to Europe to develop the mobilization there. Music was given a definitive and central role in propaganda. Indeed, Koma Berxwedan provided the PKK with its political songs and military marches. Its singers were also guerrilla fighters, and both Sefkan and Mizgîn died as martyrs while fighting, in 1985 and 1992 respectively.[33] Later, when Med TV started broadcasting from Europe in 1995, stress was again put on songs praising the guerrilla fighters and on programs by singers like Hozan Seyitxan[34] and later Aram Tigran.

In Turkey, the first cultural institution to be established was the Mesopotamia Cultural Center (Navenda Çanda Mezopotamya, NÇM, in Kurdish; Mezopotamya Kültür Merkezi, MKM, in Turkish). It opened in Istanbul in 1991 just after the ban on the use of Kurdish in recording and print (law 2932) was lifted. The main center was (and still is) based in that city, but other branches were opened in Izmir (1994), Adana (1993), Mersin (1996), Diyarbakir (1993),[35] Urfa (only opened for a few months in 1997), and even in Erbil (1993–7). When the state of exception in Kurdistan was lifted in 2002, other branches were opened there. Today, NÇM and around sixty sister organizations have woven a strong network of cultural action throughout the Turkish territory.

The actions of the center were first organized into different branches (music, theater, folk dancing, art, and language). Each branch both trained students and artists and progressively developed professional theater or dance companies or music bands (*kom*).[36] NÇM also published a literary journal (*Rewşen*, later *Jiyana Rewşen*) which played a key role in the emergence of Kurdish writing in Turkey.[37] Another organization, the Kurdish Institute of Istanbul, was soon opened in 1992[38] in order to conduct academic research. Three sections were formed, dealing with language, history, and literature. Today, the institute still plays an important role in preparing Kurdish language and teaching materials, and raising awareness about mother-tongue issues.

Throughout the 1990s in Turkey, NÇM was the main actor to define and put into practice the movement's cultural policies, which were also discussed in the pages of its magazine *Rewşen* (1992-5). The leaflet presenting the organization underlined the fact that the center followed a specific political line and, provided support to people interested in art, but these people must in return support and protect the center.[39] Its goals were to protect the culture, art, history, and language of the peoples of Mesopotamia, which had been occupied, and to "recreate the national culture" that had been destroyed and assimilated.[40] Both the center and the work demanded some self-sacrifice.[41] The cultural struggle was portrayed in military terms: articles in *Rewşen* compared cultural institutions to "arsenals" and writers, musicians, or filmmakers to "warriors." Kurdish music bands (*kom*), inspired by the 1970s Turkish revolutionary bands and using Western music instruments, developed music perceived as modern and backing the armed struggle.[42] Music, dance, and theater plays were to serve the cause. The literature was to describe guerrilla and jail experiences. Apart from music, folklore, and theater courses, NÇM also provided young people with Kurdish language courses, at a time when it was completely forbidden to teach this language. Through language and art courses, the urbanized youth from Istanbul and other western cities got to familiarize themselves with their language, their culture. Therefore these cultural policies that were taking shape in the early 1990s had two main objectives: apart from the regeneration of the national culture, the cultural institutions also played a role in the politicization and mobilization on a large scale of a section of youth not mobilized in the political or military field.

Although after Öcalan's capture in 1999, and during the different periods of ceasefire, artists were no longer necessarily considered militants or warriors (this is well demonstrated for instance in the case of the musicians studied by Sinem Ezgi Sarıtaş), they still often supported the cause. However, it seems that the Kobanî war and Kobanî's events in the summer and autumn of 2014 regenerated (or maybe turned the spotlight on again) the early vision of art as developed by Öcalan. The song "I am Kobanî" by the Hasankeyf Orchestra presents similarities to the song produced in the 1980s and 1990s, as in the well-known song "They launched the fight on the mountains" by the band Koma Berxwedan:

Têkoşîn dan ser Çiya

Têkoşîn dan ser Çiya
Pêşve diçin tev wek şêra
Canê xwe feda dikin
Pêşmerge me, ew qehrman
PKKê rêberê me
Berxwedan jiyana me hey
ARGKê artêşa me hey

[...]

Reş û tavê diqetinin
Rojên xweş zû gêş tînin
Rizgarî ye ew pêk tînin

They launched the fight on the mountains

They launched the fight on the mountains
They move forward like lions
They sacrifice their life
Our fighters, the heroes,
The PKK is our guide
Resistance is our life, hey!
ARGK is our army, hey!

[...]

They tear apart the darkness
They bring beautiful and bright day
That is liberation [...]

Koma Berxwedan

Ez Kobanî me
'Di vê tariya kor û reş de
Ji goristana sar û bêdeng
Ez bang dikim navê mırovahi
Şiyar be

[...]

Li Kobanî şer û ceng e
Şer û cenge Berxwedane
Şerê hebûne û nebûnê
Tola Arîna û mîrxan e
Kobanî

Li Kobanî şer û cenge
Bijî berxwedana YPG/YPJ'ê.

I am Kobanî

In this darkness black and blind
From the cold and silent grave
I call the name of humanity
Wake up

[...]

The war and battle of Resistance
War for existence or disappearance

This is the revenge of Aryans and princes
Kobanî

There is war and battles in Kobanî
Long life to the resistance of YPG/YPJ!

(Hasankeyf Orchestra, 2014)

Now that the war is being waged again, be it in Syria by the People's Defence Units (Yekîneyên Parastina Gel, YPG) and Women's Defence Units (Yekîneyên Parastina Jinan, YPJ), or in Turkey or northern Iraq by the PKK, it is not uncommon to read, for instance, that the main work of art is the Kobanî resistance itself.[43]

A tight network of cultural institutions

Today, the goal of NÇM remains the propagation of Kurdish culture, still invisible in public institutions, as stated by interviewees. It defines itself as an "alternative", and as a Kurdish institution that inscribes itself in a wider project of counter-society.[44] It has several types of cultural actions, as in the early days. It provides evening and weekend classes to amateurs, and it produces and supports artists, whether music bands (although the *koms* are now often replaced by individual artists), theater companies (Jiyana Nû was created in Istanbul in 1992 and is reborn today), dance companies (Mezopotamya Dans) or cinema (with the Cinema Collective of Mesopotamia). Musicians and film-makers are organized and/or supported by production houses, Kom Müzik[45] and Yapım 13 respectively. Today, NÇM also plays the role of coordinator of the movement's cultural action throughout Turkey, for example by organizing every March all the Newroz celebrations of the pro-Kurdish municipalities.

Nowadays the NÇM network is only one part of a tight network of cultural institutions. This network has grown very dense in Kurdistan since the election of pro-Kurdish municipalities[46] after 1999 and the lifting of the state of exception. In March 2014's local election, the pro-Kurdish Peace and Democracy Party (Barış ve Demokrasi Partisi, BDP)[47] gained a hundred municipalities, including eleven cities. Since 2000, these municipalities have organized artistic and cultural festivals (and sometimes ecological events, as in Dersim or Van). The first festivals were organized in Diyarbakır,[48] considered the capital of Kurdistan, and later spread to all the other cities and towns of the region. Now that the metropolitan territory also includes rural areas, the cultural activities of the municipalities have spread to villages too. In the early 2000s, the festivals were first and foremost moments to rediscover the Kurdish culture and language that had been banned for decades, in a festive atmosphere in regions that have been devastated by years of war. After ten years of experience, the festivals became more specialized by sector: for example, the documentary film festival FilmAmed since 2012; the international festival for youth film since 2013 in Diyarbakir; the short movie festival Yilmaz Güney in Batman since 2011; the theater festival in Batman since 2010 and in Diyarbakir since 2012; and the Days of Kurdish Literature in Van in 2010.

The performance stages of the festivals are being filled by cultural professionals formed by and within the institutions of the Kurdish movement. The pro-Kurdish municipalities have indeed rebuilt their cultural infrastructures, often in relation to the NÇM's networks, whether temporarily (at the time of a festival) or permanently, with the long-term objective of training these professionals. For example, there was the reformation of the municipal theater company in Diyarbakir (Diyarbakır Büyükşehir Belediye Tiyatrosu, DBŞT) under the People's Democracy Party (Halkın Demokrasi Partisi, HADEP) in 1999. The company was founded in 1990 but dismantled by the Prosperity Party municipality in 1995.[49] The Folk Music Choir (Halk Müziği Korosu) had a similar fate. When the municipal staff regained their jobs on stage, a huge audience came to be enthralled by plays in the Kurdish language. Slowly, the Kurdish repertoire developed and the municipalities supported the translations of world theater into Kurdish for its own repertoire. *Hamlet* was translated into Kurdish by Kawa Nemir, and put on by DBŞT in co-production with the Amsterdam-based theater, RAST; it has been touring all over Turkey ever since. Other companies were then established within the fold of pro-Kurdish municipalities, and Batman for instance has become a second center in Kurdistan for Kurdish theater.[50] The Hasankeyf Orchestra was also founded there in 2012. It aims to build a symphonic orchestra using all the classical instruments, along with "Kurdish" ones. Although this orchestra is funded by the municipality, it is more than a local orchestra; it has a national vocation and aims to train musicians who will "bring Kurdish art to an international level."[51] And since all the municipalities are organized in a network, Batman has become the heart of musical creation for the movement as a whole. With such an orchestra, it is also "modern" national institutions that are created, reproducing what NÇM also did with the *kom*. Sarıtaş demonstrated how NÇM musicians were first trained by musicians from TRT or from the music conservatories, and how they have developed in science, training, and "occidental music."[52]

The web of municipalities also opened academies and conservatories. Like the orchestra, these institutions play a role beyond the local territory and influence, and play their part within cultural policies at the level of the Kurdish movement. The first pioneers, the conservatory Aram Tigran and the Cigerxwîn Academy, were established in Diyarbakir in 2010, by the metropolitan municipality and the district municipality of Yenişehir respectively, and take their names from a famous singer who was close to Öcalan and a famous Kurdish poet respectively. Later, the Martyr Nuda Culture Academy was opened in Van. The Middle East Cinema Academy

(Ortadoğu Sinema Akademisi) also aims to support Kurdish audio-visual productions.[53]

Looking in more detail at the academies, they offered in-depth "academic" training on the model of Turkish conservatories. The Cigerxwîn Academy offers training in cinema, theater, folk dancing, arts, music, and literature, in courses that last three years. Although the students must know Kurdish to register, training starts with a three-month language course. Students come from all over Turkey; they are provided with accommodation in the city and some pocket money. The goals of these institutions are to fight against "cultural genocide" and to work to produce an "alternative" culture, art, and literature. They train professionals who will move on to work in the theater, dance, music bands or a company of the network, or will become teachers in the NÇM network. The audio-visual training provides qualifications for the growing journalism sector of the Kurdish movement.

Within twenty-five years, many institutions have been opened, in several artistic fields, and are operating as a network in which the municipalities, along with NÇM, now play a key role. This network put into practice a specific vision of art and culture, which is today conceived as an alternative to national Turkish art in proposing a Kurdified vision of art. It also presents itself as a reformulated model of modernity, as an alternative to the Turkish model of modernity.[54] It aims to play a role in the world art scene and in the arena of art debates, as suggested by the staging and translation of world classics, or the use of international texts translated into Kurdish, as textbooks in the academies. Finally, it is important to stress that this network is so wide, and includes so many institutions and individuals from varied backgrounds, that far from being single-voiced, it aims to grow into boasting multiple voices. Indeed, since 2015 NÇM has been organizing the *İstanbul Kürt Kültür Sanat Günleri* (Istanbul's Days of Kurdish Culture and Art), which has given the stage to many artists, bands, and companies from Turkey and abroad, a genuinely plural scene that it helped to create.

The formation of a fragile independent scene

That movement was not of course the only instigator of cultural activities in the 1990s, nor the first. All political groups were involved in the cultural area, including for instance: in the diaspora, the work of the Paris Kurdish Institute; the productions of Kurdish refugees who had become writers in Sweden and opened publishing houses and published literary journals; or in Turkey, the activities of the foundation Kürt-Kav, close to the Kurdistan Socialist Party (PSK).[55] The PSK had actually opened the People's Cultural Association (Halk Kültur Derneği, HDK) in 1989, an association that attracted many young people but had to shut down when NÇM was established.[56] This shows how the PKK's work in the sphere of culture and art also reflected its need to retain and develop its hegemony in the Kurdish political sphere.

One must also mention the Nûbihar group, which has been publishing an eponymous journal in Kurdish since 1992 and founded the Nûbihar Association for Education and Culture in 2011. This Islamic Kurdish group has developed a strong readership and network of writers within Kurdistan and fostered the development of Kurdish literature of Muslim inspiration. Therefore all groups have played their part in the growth of literary, cultural, and artistic scenes. The PKK, however, due to the breadth of its movement and its powerful institutional structure, has certainly played a key role in shaping cultural policies and cultural operations, and hence the development of a Kurdish art scene in Turkey. It is sometimes difficult, however, for artists to maintain their autonomy; one such instance is the case of the poet Hüseyin Kaytan, who was founder of the theater company Jiyana Nû, but later joined the guerrillas and was completely ostracized for distancing himself from the movement.

NÇM has played the role, sometimes involuntarily, of incubator: it is in great part due to them that an independent Kurdish scene has emerged in Turkey. The theater company Seyr-ü Mesel was created in 2002 by ex-members of NÇM; the Destar company was established in 2008 by actors who were trained within NÇM.[57] *Jiyana Rewşen*, published by NÇM between 1996 and 2000, was the only Kurdish literary journal at the time; as such it made possible the development of a vibrant literary milieu that contributed to the rise of a Kurdish literary culture and the foundation of independent publishing houses in its wake (like Bajar or Lîs, for instance). Without the support of political parties or of public institutions, given their limited readership, these milieux and scenes would only survive with difficulty. Nowadays, however, they can sometimes get support from the municipalities or even from some state institutions.[58] But support has also come from independent agencies located outside the Kurdish state, or the state outside the polarized space. One of these was the foundation Anadolu Kültür, opened in Istanbul in 2002. The foundation's work is based on the fact that most cultural resources are located in the west of Turkey; it therefore aims to develop cultural programs and infrastructures across the whole country, through local partnerships so as to foster civil initiatives throughout the country. It also considers cultural initiatives as a means toward dialogue and conflict resolution, as indicated by its four main programs, entitled Arts and Cultural Dialogue in Anatolia; Cultural Diversity and Human Rights; Cultural Collaboration with Europe; and Art and Cultural Dialogue with Armenia. After its early days, Anadolu Kültür opened the Diyarbakir Cultural Centre (Diyarbakir Sanat Merkezi, DSM) in 2002, which has actively fostered the growth of the local creative and artistic scene, in collaboration with the municipality, local institutions and agencies. It has organized many meetings and training activities in all artistic disciplines, and has played a particularly strong role in the local literary scene, supporting many lectures and conferences, reading groups, translation activities, and the publication of a literary journal. The implantation of DSM both embedded it in the local scene and marked its progressive (and relative) depolarization.

The Kurdish scene today is very dynamic and plural, but remains fragile. Many legal obstacles regarding the use of Kurdish, for example, have been lifted and the state has started playing a role (though controversially) in Kurdish culture, as evidenced by: the permission for Kurdish plays to be performed on some public stages; the launching of TRT-6 (now TRT Kurdî), a state-owned TV channel broadcasting all kinds of programs in Kurdish (including artistic and literary ones), and providing employment opportunities for artists, writers, and musicians; the publication by the Ministry of Culture of a bilingual edition of the classical text *Mem û Zîn*; and the opening of Kurdish language and literature programs in some state universities. However, this involvement of the state in Kurdish cultural policies does not go hand in hand with support for the independent scene or milieu. It rather marks new forms of polarization. There is now a double policy: some tolerance, if not encouragement, of those involved in governmental operations, but obstacles, pressure, and various forms of censorship for others. Bans and trials are common. It is not uncommon that members of NÇM are accused of supporting terrorism. People recall the banning of the movie *Bakûr* (by Ertuğrul Mavioğlu and Çayan Demirel), a film that tells the life of PKK guerrilla fighters, during the 2015 Istanbul film festival.[59] But most obstacles are not legal: artists have difficulty finding stages where they can perform; they very rarely receive state subsidies; they may have difficulties in getting a visa; and are often under close scrutiny.[60]

Conclusion

Throughout its history, the PKK has known important shifts in organization, aims, and means, but also continuities. As the PKK grew bigger and stronger, it developed a body of texts that shaped its ideology. The PKK's cultural policies took shape within the practices, before being put in writing, writing that once again shaped the action. Throughout the years, practices and texts fed into one another. Early in the history of the party, the field of culture became a domain of political intervention: music was used for the diffusion of propaganda and for mobilization. Culture became a political tool, but at the same time it had to be redefined according to the Marxist-Leninist ideology of the PKK. Organizations were created that were tasked with developing cultural and artistic action, in line with the party. These organizations functioned as a network all over Turkey and Europe. The institutionalization of the movement's cultural actions went a step further with pro-Kurdish parties now at the head of municipalities in Kurdistan. This enabled the movement to develop more cultural institutions and organizations, and the cultural life in Kurdistan to bloom. Art and culture constituted a pillar of the struggle and inevitably fed it, but the prospering cultural institutions also made possible the emergence of independent artists and alternative activities. The redeployment of the PKK in the region, the wars it wages in Syria and Iraq, and the sieges of towns like Cizirê and Silvan reintroduce old discourses about the relationship between the party, war, art, and culture, stressing some elements of continuity. The clampdown on Kurdish opposition in the wake of the 15 July 2016 failed coup threatened this fragile Kurdish scene.

Beyond the elements of continuity, the history of the party and the movement it gathered around itself is marked by shifts and plurality, and is also dotted with contradictions. This is hardly surprising given the diversity of the party, its many different elements not always in agreement, and given the breadth of its actions that enable the emergence of an artistic scene, becoming progressively integrated within Turkish culture as a whole. The case of music is quite illustrative of this plurality and its inherent contradictions, since there is simultaneous demand for modern music for propaganda purposes, feudal traditions like the *dengbêj*, and national institutions like symphony orchestras. Further sociological studies of the movement's cultural policies are needed to reveal and analyze these shifts, this plurality, and their contradictions.

PART 3

THE KURDISH QUESTION AND SYRIA

19.

THE CURIOUS QUESTION OF THE PYD-PKK RELATIONSHIP

Zeynep Kaya and *Robert Lowe*

Recent work on the contemporary Kurdish nationalist movement in Syria has identi-fied a number of clear trends amidst the confusion of the civil war and the emergence of an autonomous Kurdish political entity.[1] One of the most pertinent questions to pursue is the relationship between the Democratic Union Party (Partiya Yekîtiya Demokrat, PYD) and the Kurdistan Workers' Party (Partiya Karkerên Kurdistane, PKK). It is clear that the future of the project in Rojava, of Kurdish politics in Turkey, and also of the states of Syria and Turkey will be significantly affected by the deep connections between these parties.

While the PYD is the current manifestation of an older strain of support for the PKK in Syria, until 2012 it was but one player of modest influence among many Kurdish parties in Syria. Since that summer, it has been extraordinarily successful in establishing itself as the dominant political and military force in most Kurdish areas of Syria, eclipsing the older Kurdish nationalist parties. It has set up an autonomous political administration according to a radical and experimental ideology. The PYD's position of power in Rojava, its intimate relationship to the PKK, its military success against Islamic State (IS), and its poor relationships with Turkey, the Kurdistan Regional Government (KRG), and the Syrian Arab opposition mean that it is now a highly significant player in the Syrian civil war, in Kurdish geopolitics, and in Middle East geopolitics.

Kurdish politics are often analyzed within the borders of the four sovereign states: Turkey, Iraq, Iran, and Syria, and hence the significance of trans-border relationships and influences can be neglected. However, interaction across state borders is a typical characteristic of Kurdish politics in the Middle East and has taken several forms, such as cooperation and conflict between Kurdish organizations and cross-border militant and recruitment activities of Kurdish parties in other states. The support which the PKK received from the Syrian regime in the past and the PKK's mobilization and recruitment activities among Syrian Kurds frame the PYD-PKK relationship today. This is an essential context for understanding recent developments in Kurdish parts of Syria where the PYD-PKK movement aspires to represent one people who happen to be divided by an arbitrary modern border. Many Kurds in Turkey and Syria who do not necessarily support these parties also view their society, culture, and politics as fully entwined.

Deep cross-border sociopolitical connections have long existed between Kurds in Syria and Turkey. These connections and the PKK's decades-long organization in both countries tie the PYD to the PKK's transnational activities in the Middle East. On the other hand, in order to increase its legitimacy among Syrian Kurds and in the eyes of the international community, the PYD feels the need to show itself as a genuine Syrian Kurdish party that is independent from the PKK. These factors force the PYD to focus mainly on Syrian Kurdish politics and downplay its links to the PKK. Indeed, the PYD-PKK connection is exposing the PYD to the complexity of national, transnational, and international interactions, creating vulnerabilities as well as opportunities for the party.

Excellent analyses of the PYD exist within wider studies of the Kurdish national movement in Syria[2] and in policy reports,[3] but research focusing specifically on the PYD is slim. The relationship between the PYD and its mother party is clearly intimate, but the complicated and varied contexts in which the parties operate suggest that it is not monolithic. This chapter aims to make a contribution to understanding the PYD by examining its relationship to the PKK, including the question of the PYD's denial of subservience, and then considering the related question of the PYD as a "Syrian Kurdish" party. It will also analyze how the PKK views the PYD and the influence of the link and the Rojava phenomenon on the PKK.

Problematizing the PYD-PKK bond

In the summer of 2012, the PYD took control of some towns in northern Syria which are predominantly Kurdish-inhabited. Over the following three years, the party expanded its territory and established a structure of autonomous government and associated institutions which it calls "Rojava" (west Kurdistan). For the reasons behind the rise of the PYD and analysis of the development of Rojava, see the following chapter in this volume, by Harriet Allsopp. The PYD is an offshoot of, and remains deeply connected to, the wider PKK movement. Examining the nature and extent of this connection is central to understanding the party's actions in Syria and its goals for the western Kurdistan project. It also has deep significance for the many other actors with interests in Rojava: the other Syrian Kurdish parties; the Syrian regime; the Syrian opposition groups; Turkey; the KRG; and the international community.

A number of scholars, analysts, and activists see the PYD as purely the manifestation of the PKK in Syria.[4] The numerous other Kurdish parties in Syria and their supporters, including the KRG in Iraq, also see no distinction between the two. For the Turkish authorities, the certainty that the parties are identical is a matter of deep political faith which drives Turkey's hostility to the PYD and Rojava and controls its policies toward the north of Syria.

And yet the PYD demurs. The party is very open, indeed proud, of its ties to the PKK, but it defines the relationship as an ideological alliance which is not institutionalized. For example, Salih Muslim, co-president of the PYD, confirms that the party follows the ideology of Abdullah Öcalan but describes the two parties as "brother organizations, which respect each other" and states that the PYD is independent in its practical policies and decision-making.[5] Another PYD official goes further: "PYD is completely distinct from the PKK. PKK lets the PYD choose what to do; if needed it will help, but not otherwise. PYD has its own leadership; it is a Syrian Kurdish party. The only commonality is the shared leftist ideology."[6] As for the PKK, its leaders often declare that the PYD is not directly controlled by the PKK, but rather emphasize that it is part of the Association of Communities in Kurdistan (Koma Civakên Kurdistan, KCK)[7], the umbrella organization for Kurdish parties in Turkey, Syria, Iran, and Iraq that follow Öcalan's ideology. To explore the curious question of the PYD-PKK relationship, it is first necessary to problematize the idea of the bond between the parties and to examine their history, institutional structures, ideology, resources, human capital, fighters, and funding.

Kurdish political parties in Syria date back to 1957 and were largely modeled on the Kurdish parties in Kurdistan-Iraq, especially the Kurdistan Democratic Party.[8] The PKK was founded in Turkey in 1978, and between 1980 and 1998 the Syrian regime allowed it to use Syrian and Lebanese territories as a base from which to conduct its armed campaign against the Turkish state. While in Syria, the PKK mobilized Syrian Kurds and some joined the movement as fighters. Syrian Kurds remain important members of the PKK to the present, including senior figures such as Bahoz Erdal, PKK military commander until 2004 and currently one of three men on the PKK's executive committee.

Following Syria's expulsion of the PKK in 1998 and the arrest of Abdullah Öcalan in 1999, the PKK decided to widen its activities and supported the establishment of sister parties in the other four parts of greater Kurdistan. This cross-border expansion is part of the development of the PKK from a single leftist political party into a larger party-complex comprising several parties and organizations.[9] The differing narratives of the PYD story begin in 2003 when the party was founded in Syria: being set up either by the PKK to maintain its support base in Syria[10] or by Kurds in Syria who happened to agree with PKK ideology as the best solution to their problems.[11]

The PYD operated largely separately from the numerous other Kurdish parties in Syria, marked out by its closeness to the PKK. Similarly to the other parties, it suffered from the attention of the Syrian authorities, often more severely, and a number of party members were jailed and died in detention. But the party had better discipline and clearer goals than its competitors, as well as the useful support of the experienced PKK, so that in 2012 when civil war engulfed Syria and the Assad regime's authority was weakened, it was ready to act.

For PKK supporters in Syria, the establishment of the PYD gave structure to their activities and the party derived legitimacy from the history of the PKK's struggle. The PYD's membership of the PKK party-complex is transparent: the party is a member of the KCK, in effect the executive body for all groups within the party-complex. The PYD states that every party in the KCK system has equal rights, although it should also be noted that the leadership of the KCK and the PKK is identical. The PYD has established political and social structures which mirror those of the PKK. The PYD set up the Western Kurdistan Democratic Society Movement (Tevgera Civaka Demokratîk a Rojava, TEV-DEM) in Syria, which includes numerous civil society organizations, e.g. the PKK runs the Democratic Society Congress (Kongreya Civaka Demokratîk, KCD) in Turkey. Similarly, the PYD established women's, youth, educational, and language organizations, such as the Star Union (for women), Youth Union, and Families of the Martyrs Foundation, which are modeled on the various elements of the PKK-complex in Turkey, as well as professional associations and local and village councils.

The PYD follows the ideology of the PKK and Öcalan apparently to the letter, inheriting the Marxist-Leninist influence on the early movement and, after 2000, the new idea of democratic autonomy which transcends the (defunct) nation-state and advocates decentralized organisation of political, social, and economic affairs by networks of local councils. It is argued that the nation-state must be rejected as a failure in favor of locally-organized self-government, and the benefits of this should be available to all peoples, not just Kurds. While neither party officially seeks independence or a united greater Kurdistan, the endgame of democratic autonomy involves the removal of existing national borders. The border between Turkey and Syria (in Kurdish terminology between northern Kurdistan and western Kurdistan) is therefore irrelevant to the purist's view of this theory. The ideology also builds on the older Kurdish nationalist view of Kurds in Turkey and Syria as one people, to confirm that the PYD and PKK are working toward the same ultimate goal.

PKK ideas about women's participation are also evident, so the PYD officially ensures co-representation of women in all positions in its organizations, and 40 per cent representation in the military. The PYD draws on the same well as the PKK for the symbolism and narrative of the movement, idealizing the charismatic leadership of Öcalan and the cult of martyrdom. The military structure of the PYD also emulates that of the PKK. Technically, the PKK is a political party and military activities are conducted by the People's Defence Forces (Hêzên Parastina Gel, HPG). Similarly in Syria, defense is conducted by the People's Protection Units (Yekîneyên Parastina Gel, YPG). The PYD claims that the YPG is not only answerable to it but also that it serves all the people of Rojava through its broader elected bodies which involve other parties and organizations. The PYD's control of territory has also enabled it to establish a civilian police force (Asayiş) which the PKK has not been able to do in Turkey.

The YPG has assumed domestic control of Rojava and has proved effective in fighting jihadist groups, including IS in 2014 and 2015. Part of the reason is that the PKK has supported the development of its military capability through supply of personnel and training from its veteran forces. It is also probable that the YPG receives arms from the PKK. The PKK's ability to assist was aided by ceasefires between it and Turkey and between PJAK and Iran. Syrian Kurds have noted an increasing presence in the YPG of fighters and commanders who are from Turkey and Iran.[12] The PYD is very open that ex-PKK fighters are serving with the YPG, but stresses that they have become YPG fighters who are answerable to the YPG command.[13] Moreover, Bilhan Tuncel states, "even many revolutionist, democratic, humanist internationalists all around the world join the YPG against radical religious groups who massacre people and brutally execute captives. The PKK's logistic and military support for YPG is a matter of duty and responsibility to the people of Syria, Kurdish or non-Kurdish."[14]

Harassment by the Syrian authorities forced PYD leaders into exile, and several, including Salih Muslim, were based with the PKK in Qandil in Kurdistan-Iraq until the change of circumstances brought about by the Syrian war allowed them to return to Syria to mobilize activities from 2011. The strongly authoritarian nature of the PKK is also evident in the PYD.[15] There is an inherent tension between the PYD's official positions on the practice of multi-party politics and tolerance and its actions on the ground. Similar to the PKK, the PYD is showing strong authoritarian tendencies, and its commitment to Kurdish unity and democracy is questionable. While the party insists that it is committed to pluralism, it has effectively imposed one-party rule in Rojava. For example, a PYD law announced in 2014 forbids the existence of political parties which do not recognize its administration.[16] As many of the other Kurdish parties do not recognize this, these are placed in a similar position of illegality to that under Ba'ath rule. There are numerous accusations of PYD harassment of political opponents, kidnapping, arbitrary arrest, restrictions on political activities, and the use of violence to quash domestic unrest.[17]

The PYD as a Syrian Kurdish party

The history of the parties, the extent of their operational links and support, their identical ideology and the development of the PYD party-complex as a near mirror-image of the PKK's all demonstrate the intimate connections between the parties and, further, suggest that the PYD is heavily influenced, if not controlled, by the PKK. The PYD's own insistence that it is an autonomous actor therefore requires explanation. There are two clear major reasons for this: the need for legitimacy and popularity among the Kurdish population of Syria; and the need for international support. Both are intimately connected to the question of whether the PYD is genuinely a Syrian Kurdish party dedicated to the interests of Kurds in Syria, or whether its overarching *raison d'être* is to support the goals of the PKK.

The historical focus of the PKK movement has been its struggle against the Turkish state. Kurds from other states were actively encouraged to join the organization, but to support it in the fight in Turkey, not to solve Kurdish problems in other states. In Syria, because of its alliance with the Ba'athist regime, the PKK not only failed to mobilize against the state's discrimination against Kurds, but even denied the existence of a specifically Syrian Kurdish people or problem. Öcalan notably endorsed the Syrian regime's denial of Syrian Kurdish aspirations and agreed that they were descendants of refugees from Turkey, undermining the legitimacy of the Kurdish nationalist movement in Syria.[18] The PKK viewed the Kurds in Syria primarily as a useful source of recruits for its fight in Turkey.

The Kurdish parties in Syria of the 1957 genealogy, although severely restricted and riven by factionalism, were broadly representative of the Kurdish political-cultural national movement and have only been eclipsed by the PYD since 2012. There is a strong tradition of hostility to the PKK and the PYD among Syrian Kurds who saw the movement diverting efforts from their own concerns in Syria and who broadly supported the 1957 parties. Further, until the Syrian war, the Kurdish movement in Syria had been non-violent, in stark contrast to the PKK. Therefore the PYD has always had a problem of legitimacy among the people it claims to represent, many of whom believe that the PYD and PKK prioritize their interests in Turkey above the interests of Syrian Kurds. The PYD has frequently given the impression that it believes the Turkish state is a greater threat than the Syrian state to Kurds in Syria. The strong authoritarian streak displayed by the PYD, which is so similar to that of the PKK, and the current accommodation with the regime, which continues the trend from the 1980s and 1990s, further undermine its legitimacy and expose the party to criticism of behaving like, or being, the PKK.

The PYD has therefore attempted to portray itself as a pluralist and democratic party, willing to cooperate with its rival Kurdish parties and involve them in the administration of Rojava, in the hope of improving its legitimacy among the large number of Kurds who are not natural supporters. The PYD agreed to a political deal with the many parties in the Kurdish National Council (KNC) by which representation throughout the structures of western Kurdistan and command of the YPG is shared equally between the two sides. In practice the PYD pays lip service to the deal, but officially it remains committed to power-sharing. As part of this, it is incumbent upon the party to downplay its ties to the PKK and to present itself as a movement dedicated specifically to serving the Kurds in Syria.

Connected to the PYD's need to present itself domestically as a Syrian Kurdish party willing to work with others is its need for international support. The PYD operates in a very tough neighborhood with only one sound ally (the PKK) and many enemies. It is well aware of the considerable potential it has for winning friends internationally, given the advantages it holds over other actors in Syria: being secular, comparatively democratic, popular, and disciplined. Most crucially of all, the YPG has become the most effective military force in Syria fighting against IS. Western powers prefer the KNC, KRG-linked parties to the PYD, hence strengthening its motive to promote power-sharing. And among the major reasons for international reluctance to back the PYD are its link to the PKK, considered a terrorist organization by the US and EU, and fears of upsetting Turkey. The PYD has also tried to persuade Turkey that it is distinct from the PKK, wary of the threat of Turkish invasion of northern Syria with the aim of attacking Rojava. Turkey was never likely to change its view, and the threat materialized in August 2016 when Turkish forces established a pocket of control inside Syrian territory, largely to stop the expansion of Kurdish-held territory, and increased its military engagement with the YPG. Since the fighting between IS and the YPG escalated in 2014, US support of the YPG has become crucial to the survival of Rojava and indeed the Kurdish population in Syria, who face catastrophic consequences should IS defeat the YPG.

There is a further possible explanation for the PYD's insistence that it is not merely a proxy for the PKK: that the different contexts in which the parties operate mean that the relationship is more subtle and flexible than often assumed and that the PYD's claim is not wholly inaccurate. This links to the increasing "Syrian Kurdish" nature of the PYD as its expansion and development of its own administrative and military functions within Syria have made it inherently more focused on Rojava. The PYD identifies closely with the PKK's struggle in northern Kurdistan, but the exceptional circumstances in western Kurdistan have given the party a more distinctive purpose and identity than it had prior to 2011. This is evident in Salih Muslim's description of the PYD as "Syrian patriots",[19] and the party stresses firmly that it does not seek separatism or the fragmentation of Syria.

It is clear that the PYD and PKK have considerably different operating contexts which produce different opportunities and constraints, in particular as the PYD is a party of government, something the PKK has never experienced. This has created a set of challenges for the PYD which are very different to those ever faced by the PKK. Further, the prospect of the PKK implementing democratic autonomy in any part of

Turkey is remote, and especially so since the resumption of violence between it and the Turkish state in 2015. While the PKK has returned to low-level guerrilla warfare and the prospects of political progress in Turkey recede, the PYD is attempting to implement democratic autonomy and run local government services and an army in a chaotic war zone in which there is an existential threat to the Kurdish population.

The internal dynamics of the PKK-PYD-YPG structures are fluid rather than monolithic, and there are factions within each. Some actors see local factors as paramount, especially those who have joined the PYD through expedience, while others take a broader and more ideological view. It is also worth noting that the PYD's commitment to limited and asymmetric plurality contrasts with the PKK, and also that the PYD did not employ violence between 2003 and 2012. It established its militia prior to 2011, but did not conduct military operations until the opportunity, or the necessity, of the civil war arose in 2012. The PYD argues that it poses no threat to Turkey, not least because Rojava would be unlikely to survive should Turkey choose to snuff it out. This raises the important question of whether, should developments force a choice, the PYD would put the interests of the PKK and the struggle in Turkey ahead of Syrian Kurdish interests, as happened in the 1990s. It is conceivable that the PYD-PKK bond, despite its great strength, could be tested by external pressures and internal tensions.

The developments in Syrian Kurdistan since 2012 indicate that the PYD has become a genuinely "Syrian Kurdish" political movement. The increased branding of the PYD as a separate party dedicated to serving the people of Rojava and the extraordinary conditions of war and political opportunity suggest a gentle and nuanced shift toward more autonomy from the PKK. The relationship remains ambiguous, quite probably deliberately so, and also because of the different strands of opinion within both parties. This ambiguity is also in keeping with the opacity of the PYD's political plans.

The trans-border PKK complex and the KCK

The PKK should be considered as a major actor with a trans-Kurdish implantation, and therefore as a structural pillar of the Kurdish political sphere well beyond Turkey.[20] The PKK and the PYD are part of the KCK, which presents itself as a non-state, non-military democratic, political, and social organization. The KCK was established in 2005 in line with the principles and organizational structures proposed in Öcalan's confederational model.[21] There are two further parties under the KCK umbrella: the Party of Free Life of Kurdistan (Partiya Jiyana Azad a Kurdistanê, PJAK), established in 2004 in Iran; and the Kurdistan Democratic Solution Party (Partî Çareserî Dîmukratî Kurdistan, PCDK), established in 2002 in Iraq. These four KCK parties, PKK, PYD, PJAK, and PCDK, conduct their affairs autonomously, but they need to do this in line with the principles adopted in the KCK charter. The fact that the leadership of the KCK is identical to the PKK's leadership implies that the PKK leadership has the ability to exert its power over other parties. Although the PKK remains a party with a focus on Turkey, through the KCK it acts like the center of a cross-border mechanism, as Bozarslan describes.

Despite the PKK dominance in the KCK, the relative autonomy of KCK parties from the PKK can be observed in practice. The organizational models and actions of each party vary from country to country, even from city to city within the same country. Parties in the KCK conduct their affairs based on the requirements of the country-specific and regional context, rather than being directed by the KCK in a top-down manner. Tuncel emphasizes that the KCK and Qandil do not take part in the PYD's or other parties' decision-making processes.[22] However, each party is expected to follow Öcalan's confederational system model in structuring their representative, administrative, and political systems; and there are certain models they follow in their military organization. Therefore, KCK leaders' claim that the PYD manages its affairs autonomously from the PKK might not be too far from reality.[23]

The different local political contexts facing each KCK party have led to significant variations between them. The case of PJAK is the most pertinent and valuable comparison to the PYD. While the Syrian authorities tolerated the existence of the PYD, Iran would allow no such presence by PJAK, which has operated from its base across the border in Kurdistan-Iraq while its leadership sits in Europe. The PYD was able to operate as a cultural-political nationalist party, similar to the other Kurdish parties in Syria, within the limited space permitted by the Ba'athist regime, and it did not take up arms until as a reaction deep into the chaos of the Syrian war. By contrast, PJAK was founded as an armed guerrilla movement and has conducted a sporadic campaign against Iran, but this has failed in the face of stiff Iranian response. Technically the fighting is conducted by the military organization the Force of Eastern Kurdistan (Hezi Rojhelati Kurdistan, HRK). Similar to the PYD's relationship to Kurdish society in Syria, PJAK has not been universally welcomed by Kurds in Iran who oppose its violent methods and its links to the PKK rather than the older Kurdish parties in Iran, and blame it for triggering increased repression by the Iranian state. PJAK would try to impose hegemony as the PKK has, but similarly to the PYD would have to find some compromise with the other Iranian Kurdish parties—the Democratic Party of Iranian Kurdistan and Komala—just as the PYD has done with the KNC parties. Following the PKK/PYD, PJAK has also dropped its emphasis on the traditional Kurdish nationalist agenda in favor of the ideology of democratic autonomy for all people in the region.

The PCDK, established in southern Kurdistan (Iraq) in 2002, has achieved the least traction of the PKK franchises, because Kurdistan-Iraq has already achieved autonomy and its well-established political movements are deeply opposed to the PKK. The KRG authorities have closed the party's headquarters and banned it from standing in parliamentary elections.[24] Orhan makes the point that while the PKK launches its attacks from Iraqi Kurdistan, it has a greater social base and more recruits from Syrian Kurdistan.[25]

PKK strategy in Rojava

The idea of a Kurdish fraternity underlies the PKK's support for the PYD. The PKK perceives Kurds as divided into four unnatural groups which have been suppressed and badly treated by regional regimes and their international allies. Therefore, supporting other Kurdish groups in Iran, Syria, and Iraq is a key goal for the PKK. The PKK insists that this fraternal support does not amount to control over the PYD.[26] The creation of PKK-affiliated parties in the other three parts of Kurdistan in the early 2000s reflects its increased interest in the Kurdish struggles in other states, rather than exploiting these purely for the benefit of the movement in Turkey. Alan Şemo states, "PKK and Qandil have always stated publicly that they respect the will and the decision of Rojava political parties and people. They are ready to help if required but do not impose any policy or decision on Syrian Kurds."[27] This rhetoric is in line with the KCK's overarching goal to implement Öcalan's democratic confederalism, a non-state structure governed by local administrations in a bottom-up model.

The PYD is also significant for the PKK for another reason. As a de facto party of government, the PYD is now putting PKK ideas into practice for the first time, and ahead of the mother party in Turkey. Therefore, PKK leaders strongly support the PYD and the Rojava experiment. In June 2015, Murat Karayılan, one of the four KCK leaders, commented on Turkey's plans to intervene in Syrian Kurdish territories and declared that "If they [Turkey] intervene in Rojava, we will do the same in Turkey, and the whole of Turkey will turn into a battlefield."[28] The PKK leadership, through the party's website, has often called for support for Rojava and said that the revolution in Rojava should be expanded to other parts of Kurdistan.[29]

PKK and KCK leaders strongly reject the claims of PYD authoritarianism in Rojava and emphasize the democratic character of the PYD rule. Cemil Bayık, one of the three members of the PKK's executive committee, stated that the PYD is not the sole ruler and that other Kurdish groups, and non-Kurds such as Assyrians and Arabs, are also part of the administration in the Rojava cantons.[30] Other Syrian Kurdish parties point to the undemocratic and oppressive policies and increasing dominance of the PYD in Kurdish politics in Syria.[31] Indeed, PKK and KCK leaders have huge interest in the success of the PYD and the Rojava experiment, because this will mean that the PKK's ideology and its model of governance are feasible and successful and, at least in theory, could be later rolled out across all four parts of Kurdistan, and indeed Turkey and the Middle East.

At an ideological level, the Rojava experiment implemented by the PYD has huge implications for Kurdish politics in Turkey. Rojava is a major concern for HDP politicians and Kurdish civil society organizations in Turkey and influences their discourse. Developments in Rojava have emboldened the PKK and Kurdish politicians in Turkey. The talks between the government and Öcalan in Turkey and the surrounding public discussion often referred to the Rojava experiment as an example of Öcalan's democratic federalism. In this process, the governing Justice and Development Party, although it constantly criticized the developments in Rojava and referred to Rojava only in the context of its criticism of the PKK and its activities, has tolerated discussions on decentralization in the public domain.

In addition to the ideological dimension, the PYD and Rojava are important strategically for the PKK and for its ability to maintain cross-border links in Syria. The PKK seeks to promote the PYD within Syria, because a strong PYD in Syria offers tactical and strategic advantages to the PKK. Until the emergence of autonomous Kurdish rule in Syria, the PKK's cross-border activities in Syria were substantially restricted, leaving Qandil in northern Iraq and the Iraqi-Turkish border as its main base of activity and sanctuary. Moreover, the success of the Rojava experiment and its possible recognition by outsiders and regional states would lead to the emergence of a PKK-friendly Kurdish political entity with a legitimate rule to govern for the first time in the Middle East. The creation and entrenchment of such a region means that the PKK can be present, maintain its organization, and continue to operate across Turkish-Syrian borders. This reality makes developments in Rojava hugely important for the PKK and its political aims, not only in Turkey but also in the wider region.

The battle for Kobanî is an excellent example of the importance of the PYD to the PKK and also to the Kurdish political parties in Turkey. During the fight between IS and the YPG, the PKK provided direct support to the town's defenders. Karayılan described the fight in Kobanî as one of the milestones in Kurdish history.[32] The successful defense of Kobanî has had huge implications for Kurdish communities in Turkey, especially among PKK sympathizers, as well as outside Turkey. Several Turkish Kurds wanted to cross the border to help YPG forces, and they protested when Turkey obstructed access from and to Kobanî. Turkey justified its actions by arguing that the PYD is purely the PKK, which it considers to be a terrorist organization as bad as IS.[33] Moreover, Syrian Kurdish autonomy and the PKK flags flying on the other side of the border created great anxiety for Turkey, which also made the prevention of cross-border links between PYD and PKK a key policy aim.

Despite Turkey's attempts at prevention, many Turkish citizens who were sympathetic to the Kurdish cause but were not involved in PKK's military operations joined the fight in Syria on the side of YPG forces against Islamist militants.[34] Funerals for Turkish citizens who lost their lives in the conflict, especially in Kobanî, have become a regular scene in many towns in eastern and south-eastern Turkey.[35] Moreover, outside the region, several members of diaspora Kurdish communities joined YPG forces to fight, and huge campaigns to raise money and support to help YPG forces and the people in Kobanî were organized among Kurdish diaspora communities in Europe.

Kurdish political parties in Turkey openly support Rojava and PYD control in the region.[36] Members of the People's Democratic Party (Halkların Demokratik Partisi, HDP), which made a major breakthrough in the Turkish parliament election in June 2015, lobbied for international support for the PYD and the defense of Kobanî. They criticized the Turkish government for blocking support to the YPG at the borders and for not supporting Rojava.[37] They have also made several declarations to argue for the legitimacy of Kurdish autonomous rule in Rojava.[38]

It is unsurprising that the PKK has provided unflinching and substantial support to its sister party in Syria. What is more notable is that the PKK's official position on its relationship to the PYD also consistently stresses the latter's autonomy. The pressures identified, which influence the PYD's insistence of its separateness, do not affect the PKK. Therefore the mother party's hold over its wider party complex is either sufficiently sophisticated to encourage such a public perception, or there is some truth in the claim. If, as argued in this chapter, the relationship is more nuanced than often assumed, and the PYD is indeed becoming more "Syrian Kurdish", this suggests that some very interesting and important dynamics could emerge.

There is no doubt about the depth and centrality of the PKK influence on the PYD and the Rojava experiment and also their shared ideology. However, the movements operate in different contexts and hence now in different ways. Most significantly, the PYD is effectively a party of government, experimenting with a revolutionary ideology, as well as providing critical military defense to a Kurdish population under a severe and immediate threat. Such conditions could create diverging needs and policies, presenting the PKK with a tension between its Turkey-centric goals and operational needs, and the success of its Syrian offshoot. In the 1990s, the PKK made a clear choice in favor of the former; it is conceivable it would do so again.

Conclusion

Analysis of the relationship between the PYD and PKK is crucial to understanding Kurdish politics in Turkey and Syria and indeed in the wider Middle East; the analysis in this chapter has thus identified evidence to support some of the major themes of this book. Cross-border links play such a critical role now on both movements that the inadequacies of state-centric research are confirmed. The sense that the early twentieth century is proving to be a "Kurdish moment" is firmly supported by the case in Rojava with the unprecedented and transformational establishment of autonomous Kurdish rule. But this experiment remains highly vulnerable and fragile. The PYD is aware of this and is careful not to overreach, while seeking improved international support and legitimacy.

Another consistent theme across the Kurdish movements is the levels of authoritarianism within the various political parties. The PYD also fits this trend as its PKK-infused character and determined opportunism on the ground, as well as its self-righteous belief in its ideology, have contributed to the strong strain of authoritarianism within the movement and its practices. Party hegemony is defined as the national interest, as demonstrated by the PYD's rigid certainty that its ideology and practice are correct. PYD hegemony is becoming increasingly visible in the general acceptance of the Rojava cantons idea, even by those deeply opposed to the PYD. Rojava is also proof that, whatever their shortcomings, Öcalan's ideas can be applied.

A further broader theme is that significant parts of Kurdish interests are now more than ever aligned with international interests. Despite international reservations about the PYD and the Rojava experiment, the party offers a vastly more palatable alternative to the violent jihadi groups, and the US military support of the Kurds at Kobanî marked a significant intervention. The nature of the PYD's relationship to the PKK has put the US in the delicate position of providing support to the PYD while continuing to back Turkey against the PKK. Interestingly, the PKK appears to be revealing signs of interest in working with the US, for instance by suggesting that the US play a role in restarting talks between the PKK and the Turkish government.[39] If true, this is a huge change for the PKK, an organization that always saw its ideological views as irreconcilable with those of the US, and perceived the US as an enemy in its struggle. The PKK's links to the PYD, with its increasing links to the US, can be considered as a factor in a possible closer US-PKK relationship.

The opportunity to establish and develop its own administration in Rojava has created the conditions for the PYD to become more "Syrian Kurdish." Yet at the same time, due to the desperate necessity of the existential conflict with IS, it is heavily reliant on PKK support. In order to increase its domestic and international recognition, and to make Rojava viable, the PYD has to work, or at least claim to work, with the other Kurdish parties. When the war ends, assuming the Kurdish population remains in Syria in large numbers, the PYD will probably need to make concessions to other Kurdish parties to present a united Kurdish front in negotiations with other actors. This requirement could be largely removed if it succeeds in entrenching its power base in Rojava and the Kurdish National Council parties are weakened even further. But successful leadership of the Kurdish population of Syria and negotiations for its future will require the PYD to commit to Syria, ahead of the PKK's struggle in Turkey. The PYD will also be required to make compromises to find a settlement with the majority of Syria which is not Kurdish; but to what extent they will agree to do so, and whether the PKK will allow this, is questionable.

20.

KURDISH POLITICAL PARTIES
AND THE SYRIAN UPRISING

Harriet Allsopp

This chapter examines the Kurdish political scene from the fifth year of the Syrian uprising. It considers two main questions. First, how was it possible for the Democratic Union Party (Partiya Yekîtiya Demokrat, PYD), a relative newcomer to Syrian Kurdish politics, to take control of Kurdish areas in Syria without serious interference? And second, what were the consequences of the rise of the PYD for the Kurdish political movement in Syria and beyond? It looks, in turn, at pre-uprising Kurdish politics and the Kurdish parties' entry into the Syrian uprising in March 2011; the rise of the PYD and the practical application of the PYD's "democratic autonomy" project; and finally, it analyzes the intensification of major fault lines and rivalries within Kurdish politics regionally and their consequences for the Syrian Kurdish political field.

The main Syrian Kurdish actors

In the interests of clarity, a complex and confusing array of more than twenty Kurdish political parties in Syria, and many more organizations that have similar political agendas, is divided into a number of groups:[1]

The "Syrian Kurdish political parties" of 1957

A title used quite loosely referring to Kurdish political parties that trace their origin to 1957 and the founding of the first Kurdish party in Syria. During the Syrian uprising, most grouped within the Kurdish National Council (KNC) in October 2011.[2] All were defined by Kurdish nationalist principles, but aims varied from minority rights to self-determination. Opinions on how to react and respond to the Syrian uprising also diverged.

The Partiya Yekîtiya Demokrat (PYD) et al

The main Kurdish party in Syria, distinct from and not included within the preceding bracket, formed in 2003. The PYD instigated the establishment of the autonomous Rojava administration and remained the driving political force within it. Although it asserts independence from the Partiya Karkerên Kurdistanê (PKK) in Turkey, it is connected both organizationally and ideologically to it through the Group of Communities in Kurdistan (Koma Civakên Kurdistan, KCK), and through the leadership of Abdullah Öcalan.[3] The PYD is also connected to other political, civil, and military organizations within Syria, such as the Western Kurdistan Democratic Society Movement (Tevgera Civaka Demokratik a Rojava, Tev-Dem), Yekitiya Star women's organization, the Union of Families of Martyrs, the Education and Language Institution, and the Revolutionary Youth Movement of Western Kurdistan. Together these organizations formed the People's Council of Western Kurdistan (PCWK) in December 2011,[4] superseded by Tev-Dem. The security services linked to the PYD are the People's Protection Units (including the Yekîneyên Parastina Gel, YPG; and Yekîneyên Parastina Jin, YPJ), and the Asayish (police).

Supreme Kurdish Committee (SKC)

These first two groupings joined to form the, now defunct, SKC in July 2012. Mediated by Masoud Barzani and the Kurdistan Democratic Party (KDP) Iraq, the SKC was an attempt to abate tensions between the KNC and the PCWK and to broker an agreement to manage jointly Kurdish areas. Despite equal representative powers, in practice authority remained strongly tilted toward the PYD and PCWK. Some parties within the KNC cooperated independently with the PYD, but the KNC ended its participation in the SKC because of its domination by the PYD.

Non-Party groups and individuals

Beneath the myriad of political parties lie several youth organizations[5] and independent Kurdish activists and intellectuals. The majority of these supported the wider aims of the Syrian uprising, whilst also projecting specifically Kurdish interest. The youth movement remains central to Kurdish issues in Syria, but is constrained by divisions within the political movement and domination by political parties.

Synopsis

There were high hopes for the Kurds when the Syrian uprising began. Syrian Kurdish politics was the most organized and visible opposition movement in Syria. After more than fifty years of illegal organization, the Syrian uprising offered the Kurds and their political parties a chance to obtain long-sought rights and to become recognized and legitimate political actors on the local, state, regional, and international levels. It was hailed as their historic moment to take center stage and seize the rewards of decades of struggle. The Kurds were characterized by outside observers as the "decisive minority" with the ability to mobilize en masse and the organizational capacity to turn the uprising into a revolution.[6] Nevertheless, the uprising also involved tremendous risk and it made explicit the intricate network of interest and relations within and beyond the Syrian Kurdish field and intensified its effect on Kurdish politics.

The response from the Kurdish street confirmed that the Kurdish youth widely supported the wider Syrian uprising and calls for the overthrow of the authoritarian Baʻath Party regime. After one year of the uprising, however, rather than falling in behind the Kurdish youth and the ethos of the original uprising, Kurdish political groups had established their own political positions, distinct from that of the regime and also from that of the nascent Syrian opposition movement. Two separate and competing umbrella organizations were established within the Kurdish political field: the Kurdish National Council, formed in October 2011; and the People's Council of Western Kurdistan, formed in December of the same year. These two alliances reflected a distrust of non-Kurdish opposition groups and their regional backers as well as historic and entrenched divisions within Kurdish politics regionally, between the PKK (the Kurdistan Workers' Party, native to Turkey) and Masoud Barzani's Kurdistan Democratic Party of Iraq. Political rivalries were widened and institutionalized within the Syrian field. External alliances and interference, ideological divisions, and disparities in military capabilities allowed the PYD to exert authority, take control of Kurdish areas, and build an armed force that would go on to play a major role in the fight against ISIS. With this, the parties of 1957, and much of the political and moral ethos of Kurdish nationalism that they represented, were marginalized. A new but precarious *modus vivendi* between the Kurdish blocs was established, leaving latent tensions smoldering and unresolved.

Pre-uprising Kurdish political parties

The first Kurdish political party in Syria (the Kurdish Democratic Party – Syria)[7] was formed in 1957. It was pioneered by Kurdish intellectuals and its agenda was defined by national identity, modernization, and development of the Kurdish psyche through educational and cultural endeavors. Military tactics had been abandoned after the failure of the Sheikh Said and Ararat revolts in Turkey. It was envisaged that national-ist education and modern social and political development would better protect the Kurdish people and identity from the worst effects of Arab nationalism and Ba'ath Party rule, under which discriminatory and oppressive policies targeted and criminal-ized Kurdish identity, culture, and organization in Syria. Traditional social and politi-cal structures and identities, however, continued to affect nationalist organization in Syria and the accommodation of both conservative traditional and progressive mod-ern outlooks within this party produced insurmountable conflicts of interest within the leadership. The political landscape quickly fragmented according to personal and semi-tribal relations and between intellectuals and local leaders. A plethora of parties resulted which were, nonetheless, defined by very similar political and national objec-tives and narratives.[8]

Without a unique history of armed nationalist struggle (such as that found amongst the Kurds of Iraq or Turkey) and as a result of the Ba'ath Party machinery of suppression, no strong leadership personalities emerged from within the Syrian Kurdish field. For support and legitimacy, many party leaders drew on connections to one or other of Barzani's KDP or Jalal Talabani's Patriotic Union of Kurdistan (PUK) and on local traditional social networks or loyal individuals and families.

This co-existence of weakened traditional social networks with modern political institutions allowed Kurdish political parties to serve as mediators in local conflicts, facilitators of cultural expression and agents promoting Kurdish nationalism. In a country in which any burgeoning civil society was destroyed or infiltrated by the ruling government, these Kurdish political parties managed to sustain some sem-blance of local civil society by carefully monitoring and adapting to the limitations set on them by the government. They were tolerated as long as they did not cross the regime's "red lines" around what behavior would be permitted. As a consequence, the parties rarely challenged the status quo and their suppression, instead opting to man-age it and, meanwhile, to retain benefits accruing from local leadership. Party leaders dominated the parties and gradually weakened their central modernist ethos without transforming them into organizations more recognizable as "political parties." Cultural development and progressive political agendas succumbed to personal rival-ries and interests, leaving an array of parties detached from Kurdish society. Attempts to remedy this situation simply added to the number of parties, rather than replacing those restricted by traditional social networks.

In contrast, the PYD grew from the PKK presence in Syria and was radically different from the parties of 1957 in ideology, method, socio-economic foundations, as well as in its understandings of Kurdish identity. PKK leader and ideologue Abdullah Öcalan was granted refuge in Syria in 1980, and his party trained and recruited within Syria without interference from the Ba'ath Party regime. Defined by its struggle against the Turkish state and social revolution, the PKK avoided issues indigenous to Syria.[9] Whilst other Kurdish parties remained subject to strict controls and activists faced arrests for organizing even simple local cultural events, the PKK established military training camps and became a dominant sub-state authority in many Kurdish areas of Syria. This implicit understanding between the PKK and the Assad regime contributed to the rift between the Syrian Kurdish parties and the PKK, and led many Syrian Kurds to regard the PKK as working against their interests.[10] With the expulsion of Öcalan from Syria in 1998 and the founding of the PYD in 2003 as a specifically Syrian political party, suspicion of the agenda of the PYD remained and latent tensions continued to divide the political field.[11] The PYD, however, inherited and exploited necessary legitimacy, leadership, armed power, and strategy from the PKK. It adopted its grand ideological narrative and its strategy for dealing with conflict situations and for mobilizing society.[12]

Kurdish nationalism in Syria had steadily risen through the 1990s and onwards. National identification was encouraged by the PKK's armed struggle against Turkey, the establishment of the no-fly zone over northern Iraq and the formation of the Kurdistan Regional Government there. After the year 2000, the opening of Syria to mobile communications technologies, satellite television, and the internet brought into the homes of Kurds in Syria news and images of the removal of Saddam Hussein, the official recognition of the Federal Kurdistan Region of Iraq, and the development of a thriving and prosperous prospective Kurdish state. Kurds in Syria were empowered through national identification. Political action became gradually more public, culminating in a spontaneous but short-lived "uprising" of the Kurds against the regime in March 2004.[13]

The intense surveillance that illegal political parties were subject to and the severe punishments that discussion of "revolution" or "opposition" entailed prevented the 1957 parties from developing strategies aimed at social mobilization and political change. This left most parties detached from Kurdish society and lacking any strategic plan for confronting their oppressors or for actively seizing opportunities as they arose. Ill-prepared for the uprising in 2004, the 1957 parties contributed to its pacification. Similarly unprepared for the 2011 Syrian uprising, they were slow to transform their politics. They struggled to move away from retrospective reaction to external events and adapt their institutions and policies in a manner that would enable them to lead the Kurdish population, govern ungoverned territories, and seize opportunities to advance Kurdish interests. In comparison, the PYD, drawing on the ideology and leadership experiences of the PKK and related organizations and with an armed group supported by the PKK in Qandil, had a strategy for both popular mobilization and for encroachment on and seizure of public and political space opened up by the retreat of the regime from northern Syria in July 2012.

The Syrian uprising

With the start of the Syrian uprising, Syrian Kurdish politics entered into new and unfamiliar territory. The regime retained a presence; the non-Kurdish opposition was divided, and various political groups became proxies for outside powers. Forming new strategic alliances and policy was far from straightforward. The majority of the 1957 parties' initial response to the uprising was to remain neutral, whilst independent youth movements supported the uprising and called for the fall of the regime. Although the rationale behind this muted reaction was based on the parties' overarching concern to protect the Kurdish people and regions from harm,[14] it served to deepen the rift between the parties and the people. Opportunities for Kurdish political groups to gain equal representation within the nascent non-Kurdish opposition movement or for their unique interests to be diligently addressed by joining it were limited by Turkish involvement. Within the first few months of the uprising, the 1957 parties had fixed on forming a representative Kurdish umbrella organization with two primary objectives: first, to unite the Kurdish voice and to represent Kurdish interests to the regime, the non-Kurdish opposition groups, and the international community; second, to balance the rising power of the PYD in Syria.

The formation of the Kurdish National Council (KNC) in October 2011 was unprecedented in the history of Kurdish politics in Syria. Whilst many previous attempts had been made to unite the Kurdish parties and their disparate voices, divisions between the left and right wings (based on categorizations of the Kurds in Syria and relations to the Syrian government) had triumphed. The KNC brought these two sides together and united their political agenda on Kurdish nationalist aims espoused by the more radical parties, which defined the Kurds as a national group living in their historic land and promoted visions of Kurdish self-rule in Syria. This political union, however, cemented divisions between the parties of 1957 and the PYD, which in turn formed a union of organizations named the People's Council of Western Kurdistan in December of the same year.[15]

As Kurdish political parties and youth groups jostled with each other in attempts to produce an authentic and united Kurdish voice, the PYD was expanding and extending its political, civil, and armed organizations. As a result, when regime forces withdrew from Kurdish areas, the PYD was ready to seize control of "liberated" territory. In what the PKK has called the "Rojava Revolution",[16] in July 2012 the PYD took over government buildings and local services, replacing them with their own institutions, and cordoned off Kurdish areas from other rebel and regime-controlled regions of Syria. Claims that the PYD colluded with the Assad regime became convenient explanations for the ease with which it took power and for the absence of resistance to it.[17]

The rapid seizure of power by the PYD left already embattled and weak Kurdish parties constrained once again. The influence of the PYD over political activity inside Syria increased, and rival political and military organization was suppressed or co-opted by it.[18] Even the KNC parties' own conceptualization of Kurdish nationalism thwarted efforts to advance their politics; avoiding internecine conflict became a justification for management of another unfavorable *modus vivendi*, this time with the PYD. Internally, many core aspects of the parties' pre-uprising identities remained unchanged, even if not unchallenged, despite the opportunities that the uprising generated. Notwithstanding their desire to advance their politics beyond the restraints that authoritarianism had imposed on them, Kurdish politics in Syria continued to grapple with issues that crippled it before the uprising. In the political vacuum that arose and amid calls for revolution, efforts to position the parties of 1957 as meaningful political actors in the new Syria were thwarted by their organizational fragmentation, inactivity, detachment from society, subservience to the KDP, PUK, and PKK, and their retreat from confrontation. Little change was made to party programs, despite the radical transformation of their political environment. Aside from statements of intent promoting a federal solution to the crisis in Syria, their policies toward the regime, the non-Kurdish opposition, the PYD, and on the future of Syrian Kurdish areas remained unclear.

Regionally, the turmoil in Syria and the ceasefires established between the PKK and Ankara (2013-15), and between the Free Life Party of Kurdistan (Partiya Jiyana Azad a Kurdistanê, PJAK) and Tehran (2011), allowed fighters based in Qandil to be assigned to work as members or leaders of YPG units, and arms supplies were directed to Syria, bolstering its capabilities.[19] The ability of the PYD to respond actively to the changing geopolitical situation in Syria and engage nationalist, disaffected, and disheartened youth through its civil and security apparatus gained it additional ground support and manpower from within Syrian Kurdish society. Meanwhile, the fluidity of its external relations and access to resources allowed it to form alliances and incorporate different factions within its administrative system. The Assad regime continued to deliver basic services and utilities to these areas, enabling the party to govern effectively with state-like power. The proliferation of jihadist groups on the borders of Kurdish regions encouraged other diverse groups, not ideologically or politically close to the PYD, to participate in its local governments and cooperate with YPG forces as a means of gaining security for their communities and access to services.[20] Some parties within the KNC also acquiesced to its rule,[21] fracturing this coalition and further inhibiting attempts to negotiate its position and role in the unfolding events. These diverse and strategic alliances, including informal pacts of non-aggression with local regime forces, further aided PYD entrenchment. By securing Kurdish territory, the developing PYD-led administration established itself as the only viable government and protection for Kurdish people and regions in Syria.

For the Assad regime, the pacification of Kurdish majority areas by the PYD indirectly served its interests. In the same manner that the influx of jihadist forces into the Syrian conflict supported, post factum, the regime's contention that the unrest in Syria was caused by "terrorists", the separation of the Kurds territorially and politically from the Syrian uprising deepened sectarian divisions within the Syrian opposition. Conflict ensued between Kurds and jihadist groups, between moderate rebel forces and extremists, and between Free Syrian Army brigades and the YPG. With multiple fronts within Syrian territory, the Assad regime avoided direct confrontation with Kurdish groups and concentrated forces in the strategic Damascus-Homs-Aleppo corridor.

PYD control and the new status quo

The PYD's connection to the PKK, its *modus vivendi* with the regime and its readiness to respond to opportunities enabled it to rise to power and dominate social, economic, and political organization in northern Syria. The PYD rapidly came to be characterized as the strongest Kurdish political party in Syria, despite its fundamental divergence from the historical ethos of the Syrian Kurdish nationalist movement. Correspondingly, the KNC's significance to Syrian Kurdish politics was diminished as its agency was constrained both by the PYD and by the policy choices of the parties within it and divisions between them. It remained focused on finding a solution to the Kurdish issue in Syria through alternative channels to that of the PYD, and developed a stance in opposition to the PYD.

By the end of 2016 the form of administration and the organizations involved had undergone several transformations, within which the agency of the PYD itself diminished and the administration as a system became self-sustaining, albeit bound by the same ideological and political vision of democratic autonomy and confederalism. Autonomy was first declared in November 2013, and PYD-controlled areas were divided into three separate administrative units, or cantons (Efrin, Kobanî, Jazira) on 21 January.[22] In March 2016 the declaration creating a Federation of Northern Syria, Rojava, was made by a range of political and religious organizations in cooperation with the PYD, within which different communities had the possibility of self-government. KNC parties, not recognizing the authority of the PYD or the system of government created by it, continued to operate outside it. The KNC considered unilateral and unlawful the PYD's declaration of autonomy, their "Social Contract",[23] and all the laws and promulgations that followed it. The KNC's rejection of the ideological doctrine and system of the PYD rendered illegal once again the majority of the political parties of 1957, which had operated illegally under the Syrian Ba'ath Party.[24]

The PYD's experimental democratic autonomy project advocated community-based local self-government,[25] producing democracy and freedom through a people unified in the pursuit of common goals, rather than by any centralized state power. According to PYD/PKK members, the period of political upheaval characterized as the "Arab Spring" demonstrated a failure of the nation-state system imposed upon the Middle East (predicted by Öcalan some twenty years ago),[26] and an opportunity to reform society and politics across the region. It was a rejection of the nation-state system as a model for the Middle East and an attempt to replace it with a confederation of peoples: a process of radical change including both society and institutions of state.[27] A myriad of institutions supporting the democratic autonomy project were established with ease in the political vacuum and country-wide turmoil in Syria. Implementation of its ideological narrative and government of Kurdish areas in accordance with the often abstract principles and political agenda set out in Öcalan's theories was more problematic, however, and the PYD was accused of human rights abuses, including arbitrary arrests and detentions, restrictions on freedoms of opinion and organization.[28] Whilst on the one hand ethnic and gender equalities were enshrined in policy, the attachment of the system to radical ideology and social revolution meant that diverse political agendas, such as those of the KNC parties, could not easily be accommodated within the PYD-led system. As a consequence, political and social organization by Kurds outside PYD control was disrupted and suppressed by militia and security services connected to the administration.[29] Numerous interviews confirmed that opponents of the PYD, particularly activists associated with the KNC, were excluded, imprisoned, or forced out of PYD-controlled areas through threats and violence.[30] Respondents within PYD-controlled areas described an emptying of the areas of opposition, with many political activists leaving for Turkey or the Kurdistan Region of Iraq.[31] Whilst attempts were made to redress the imbalance of power in the Kurdish political field through mediation by Masoud Barzani's KDP, the resulting Erbil power-sharing agreement of 2012 (through which the now redundant Supreme Kurdish Committee, SKC, was formed[32]) and the Dohuk Agreement of October 2014 were never implemented in practice.

The consequences of the PYD rise to power

In addition to polarizing Syrian-Kurdish domestic politics, the emergence of the PYD as a key actor in Syria highlighted a number of critical fault lines within the Kurdish political and nationalist movements and their effects on the practice of politics locally, regionally, and internationally. It intensified the clash between politics rooted in traditional networks and those based on ideological narratives. It precipitated competition between Kurdish parties over sources of legitimacy and security and raised questions about national sovereignty and regional interests.

Traditional, nationalist agenda vs utopian ideology

The Syrian uprising and the wider Arab Spring laid bare the continuing importance of long-suppressed sub-state loyalties and interests to the politics of the Middle East. The weakening of authoritarian political structures and ensuing conflicts invigorated the reliance on minority, tribal, and religious networks and pushed previously suppressed political interests and agendas to the fore. Within the politics of the 1957 genealogy of parties, sub-state semi-tribal loyalties historically served to preserve and support party politics and leaders, and Kurdish nationalism embraced tradition as national heritage. The constraints that illegality had imposed upon Kurdish political organization led to a reliance on traditional social networks for support, funding, legitimacy, and security. Geographical dimensions associated with these networks, as well as controls placed on the use of communications technologies, limited political organizations to the stretch of networks of personal loyalty. In the absence of a defined and overarching ideological doctrine in their politics and with only limited nationalist social projects, the ability of Kurdish parties of 1957 to develop mass or grass-roots support was impeded. The use of political parties and leadership to sustain traditional power relations, especially prior to the Syrian uprising, increased the parties' resemblance to personal cliques. With their entry into the Syrian conflict and the retreat of Syria's population to local and sectarian identities, bridging socio-economic divisions within Kurdish society in Syria became more complex.

The parties of 1957 lacked the incentive, capabilities, and resources to unite Kurdish society on a common political agenda. Kurdish political parties relied on a counter-nationalism to that of the Syrian Arab Ba'ath Party and the pursuit of Kurdish rights within the state, through nationalist rhetoric, democratic means, and lobbying, rather than through grand political narratives or the development of parallel institutional structures. They operated more as advocacy organizations than as recognizable political parties,[33] and ideological differences within this bloc were often a by-product of external influences and of attempts to negotiate their illegality in Syria. The retreat of the regime from northern Syria in July 2012 and the development of the PYD administration, however, forced the parties to redefine their struggle. Ethnic identity could not be actively suppressed by the regime, and its protection under PYD rule invalidated core components of the 1957 parties' social agendas and compounded the parties' struggle to gain mass support for the KNC. These rights remained vulnerable within the wider conflict in Syria, however, and allowed the parties to shift this focus toward the Syrian opposition, whilst within Kurdish society opposition to the PYD took priority.

In contrast, the PYD's strong ideological foundations and social project, as well as its links to the PKK, distinguished it clearly from other Kurdish parties in Syria. Öcalan's ideological framework dominated the politics of the PYD, its institutions, and strategy. The party's grand narrative and concentration on civil participation in the early months of the Syrian uprising gained it support at a time when many other Kurdish parties had disengaged from Kurdish society and their support bases were particularly weak.[34] The withdrawal of the regime allowed it to claim popular legitimacy from the realization of ethnic rights, and to concentrate efforts in the social field on its communalist narrative and on challenging the socio-economic and traditional loyalties that many other Kurdish parties relied on and affirmed.

PYD government of Kurdish areas was shaped by the party's attempt to implement Öcalan's theory of "democratic autonomy." In such a context, the Kurdish identity itself became secondary to notions of a pan-Middle Eastern identity and a confederation of autonomous peoples connected by structures of democratic decision-making and negotiation delinked from the state. This distanced the PYD further from the Kurdish nationalism espoused by other Kurdish parties and the political movement that had shaped Kurdish politics in Syria since the 1950s. Through the co-option of other political and social forces, symbols of martyrs and patriots, the charismatic leader and the greater good, the party encouraged wholesale abandonment, and loyalty, to complex and often intangible, transcendental, ideological narratives grounded in local participation. Its underlying ideology produced mechanisms of control and methods of creating and managing society akin to radical "socialist" and "populist" societies the world over. Somewhat paradoxically, the PYD relied on popular Kurdish national identity as the vehicle for this social revolution, for its expansionist socialist rhetoric, and for its legitimacy.

The nationalism and traditionally entrenched identity of the Kurdish parties of 1957 prevented them from directly confronting the PYD and from challenging its unilateral rule. Instead, their reliance on the KRG grew and the KNC was left with little choice but to compromise and manage a new, but nonetheless unfavorable, status quo by opposing the domination of the PYD and by retaining an active presence within the wider Syrian opposition. As the role of the PYD increased, the Kurdish experience in Syria became a model for PKK-linked organizations regionally and influenced the wider dynamics of the Kurdish issue. PJAK, in Iran, turned toward promoting active participation in Kurdish areas of Iran and a political dialogue with the government.[35] The core expansionist rhetoric of the PKK, PYD, and PJAK moved further from Kurdish nationalist agendas[36] grounded in a narrative of pan- and sub-state identity and repression (espoused by parties such as the KDP in Iraq and the majority of Syrian-Kurdish parties). It radicalized and widened the ideological gap between the PYD and the KNC and between the PKK and the KDP: between a social revolution and affirmation of traditional social networks.

The battle for legitimacy

Differences in nationalist rhetoric and ideological convictions, in turn, affected the ability of the parties within both the KNC and the PYD to gain legitimacy, albeit in different manners. The unique development of Kurdish politics in Syria had left political leaders without the historic claims to national leadership and military prowess necessary to gain domestic legitimacy. They lacked the demonstrable ability to protect and defend Kurdish territory and people against oppressors that Kurdish leaders in Iraq and Turkey gained through nationalist struggle. For the parties of 1957, reliance on traditional social networks alienated much of the population, in particular intellectuals and youth, and compounded the dearth in domestic legitimacy. A gradual decline in their support for civil society had also contributed to weakening their social base. For the PYD, the history of the PKK in Syria, its focus on Turkey (to the detriment of Syrian Kurdish issues), and its relations with the Assad dynasty had tarnished its reputation amongst Syrian Kurds. Its radical ideology and understandings of Kurdish identity were also rejected by much of the population favoring Kurdish nationalist discourse promoted by the KDP. As a consequence, legitimacy for all political parties in Syria was sought from external sources, notably Kurdish leaders in Iraq and Turkey.

The larger Syrian Kurdish parties (such as the KDP-S of Dr Abdul Hakim Bashar and the Kurdish Democratic Progressive Party of Abdul Hamid Darwish) had developed long-standing relations with the KDP and the PUK in the Kurdistan Region of Iraq. Their relatively larger support bases within Syria reflected the legitimacy imparted on them by these external Kurdish parties. Nonetheless, the support of Barzani and Talabani to Kurdish parties in Syria contributed to divisions within the political movement, its fragmentation and marginalization. Divisions within and between the KDP and PUK were mirrored within Syrian Kurdish politics. Party interests and political agendas, shaped by Iraqi sovereignty, dominated over those concerning Syria,[37] and as the PYD gained strength, diverging KDP and PUK policy toward this party limited KRG involvement in Syria.

After the start of the Syrian uprising, as Syria became a foreign policy priority, external legitimacy was sought, not only through Kurdish counterparts, but increasingly from the international community. Whilst international support for the Kurdistan Regional Government bolstered their Syrian Kurdish affiliates in the KNC, and direct communications with Western government officials were frequent, official recognition of the KNC parties as distinct actors with unique interests was unforthcoming. In the interests of preserving the unity of Syria and building a united Syrian opposition, KNC parties were instead encouraged to join the Syrian National Coalition as a prerequisite to sharing international support for the wider Syrian opposition.[38]

For the PYD, the legitimacy imparted on it by the PKK, its promotion of civil participation, and application of ethnic rights through its rule gained it grass-roots domestic support. The categorization of the PKK as a terrorist organization by Turkey, the USA, and other NATO members, however, left the PYD devoid of international legitimacy and without a platform for diplomatic engagement necessary to negotiate its future in Syria. The ISIS campaign in Iraq and Syria was a game changer for the PYD-led administration. By establishing US strategic military objectives distinct from the politics of wider Syrian conflict, the USA, the PYD, and YPG gained common interests and a basis for military cooperation against ISIS. The siege of Kobanî (September 2014 to January 2015) proved the YPG to be the USA's most reliable military asset in Syria, and secured it ongoing military aid and assistance. Yet, political factors hindered the organization's ability to gain and maintain outside support. Primarily, Turkey's fear of empowering the PKK through its proxies in Syria impacted significantly on US-Ankara relations and on the nature of support and requirements of the PYD/YPG. Accordingly, initial support was directed through the KRG and alongside the Dohuk power-sharing agreement between the PYD and KNC. Renegotiation of relations and military alliances were involved in major territorial advances against ISIS. Support to the YPG, outside recognized Syrian opposition groupings and against Turkey's interests, became a political minefield and involved substantial diplomatic maneuvering by the USA and adaptations by the PYD and YPG forces to meet its requirements.[39] Alliances with local Arab forces ensured that the YPG was able to maintain military assistance. The adaptability of the PYD-led administration to the political and military climate proved it capable of securing its longevity. Nevertheless, the attachment of US support to specific military objectives left unanswered critical questions about PYD international legitimacy post-ISIS, whilst Turkish military intervention in northern Syria in August 2016[40] underlined the vulnerability of the autonomy established there.

Within the PYD and related organizations, the delivery of military aid and support was interpreted as a victory in its quest for international legitimacy and a game changer for the Kurds' role in Syria.[41] Whilst the facilitation of aid to the YPG, despite its significance, did not represent any fundamental change in US or Turkish policy toward the PYD or PKK, within Syrian Kurdish society, regardless of opinions about PYD policy and methods of government, the siege of Kobanî, the YPG's central role in the battle against ISIS, and significant gains in territory provided the party with a definitive narrative of national resistance and heroism crucial for establishing endogenous legitimacy. Kobanî proved the PYD and the YPG to be protectors and leaders of the Kurds and ensured that their rule in Syria would remain uncontested by weaker parties and defended against outside powers.

Regional and international rivalry

Despite the criticism of the PYD and its methods of government by the KNC and by human rights organizations, the most organized attempts by the KNC to curtail its authority involved KDP mediation and KNC compromise. KNC parties were provided with little opportunity to develop alternatives to PYD rule in Syria. They were disempowered by the PYD itself, lacked the external backing necessary to challenge its rule, and were denied agency in their home affairs by relying on relations with Kurdish parties in the Kurdistan Region of Iraq. Patronage networks between Iraq and Syria were maintained during the crisis in Syria and the campaign against ISIS, but were subordinate to the KRG observance of Iraqi sovereignty, management of tense relations with the governments in Baghdad and Ankara, and internal opposition and instability in Iraq. The nuances of political relations between the KDP, PUK, and PKK, and military relations between the USA and Peshmerga and PKK/YPG forces, similarly prevented any decisive intervention by the KRG. As a result, pragmatic *realpolitik* limited the support available to Syrian Kurdish parties,[42] and the direct involvement of the KDP and PUK in Syrian Kurdish affairs increased.

The rise of the PYD in Syria was interpreted by many other political forces as PKK expansionism, and it polarized the politics of the Kurds regionally. After the PYD took control in Syria, the relations between the PYD and KDP deteriorated, and the battle for championship of the Kurdish cause was both extended beyond state borders and intensified. Relations between the PUK and PKK, in comparison, were more affable. KDP proxies in Syria were undermined, and divisions between KDP- and PUK-supported parties within the KNC resurfaced; the PYD reneged on power-sharing agreements brokered in Erbil, and even regions with close political and social links with the KDP witnessed an increase in PYD authority. A symbolic war of attrition between the KDP and PYD ensued; the former, utilizing its influence as a quasi-state power, dismissed the PYD declaration of autonomy. The border between the Kurdistan Region and PYD-held Syria became a stage where any political tensions between the two parties were played out. Border trenches and blocking the passage of politicians, Kurdish activists, and journalists between the two areas became symbolic of the regional rivalries within Kurdish politics.

Relations between the KDP and the PKK/PYD thawed considerably after the fall of Mosul to ISIS in June 2014. The ISIS threat to Erbil and Sinjar in August 2014, then Kobanî in October, provided an opportunity to test PKK/YPG and Peshmerga cooperation within Iraqi and Syrian territory. Faced with such a threat, the nationalist rhetoric of the PKK and PYD again increased, evoking common ground between fundamentally different political parties. This closing of ranks between the PKK/PYD and KRG, however, did not represent a bridging of political rifts or a coincidence of political agendas. Wider regional and international relations and power alignments involved in the Syrian conflict and the fight against ISIS added further complexities to Kurdish politics in Syria, which deepened PYD entrenchment in the areas and postponed the resolution of underlying conflicts within Kurdish politics.

International and regional interests in containing ISIS and influencing the conflict in Syria modified and complicated many pre-existing political alliances and rivalries. The KDP's relations with the USA and Ankara enabled it to emerge, particularly after the fall of Mosul, as an international player and decisive actor in Middle

Eastern affairs. YPG military cooperation with the USA against ISIS also increased its international role, whilst regionally PYD-PKK relations with the PUK and Gorran in Iraq arguably placed it closer to the sphere of Iranian influence, adding to political rivalries within the Kurdistan Region between the KDP and PUK, but also, in the face of ISIS, uniting unlikely partners. Within the Syrian field, the decisive intervention of Russia into the Syrian conflict in September 2015 and the development of its relations with the PYD[43] provided the PYD with a potential, if not predictable, source of political support post-ISIS and positioned it within increasing tensions between the USA and Russia over Syria.

The Syrian uprising brought Syrian Kurdish political organizations decisively onto the international and regional agenda. ISIS had exposed and heightened the centrality of the Kurds, regionally, to the campaign to roll back and degrade them. The agency of Syrian Kurdish parties (be it those within the KNC or the PYD) in their own politics remained constrained by outside powers and diverging interests. The PYD had stepped into the political vacuum left by the withdrawal of the regime from Kurdish areas and established itself as a decisive game player in the region, but its links to the PKK and lack of international recognition as a legitimate political actor left its future in Syria undetermined. The parties of the KNC continued to rely on external intervention to transform them from the illegal political organization that they were under the Ba'ath Party, and then under the PYD, to parties contributing to the future development of the Kurdish regions in Syria. The domination of trans-state political and ideological fault lines over local interests in Syria pushed parties of the KNC backstage, still waiting for opportunity.

The connection of Syrian Kurdish party legitimacy to external alliances established Kurdish areas of Syria as a territory in which regional rivalries were played out. These rivalries became amplified within the context of the Syrian uprising and influenced the conduct of various party actors, regional power relations, and diplomatic and military maneuverings. Whereas Syrian Kurdish parties were weakened by the involvement of the KDP, PUK, and PKK in their politics, the relative security of the Kurdish federal region in Iraq, the PKK ceasefire, then resumption of hostilities in Turkey, and the political vacuum within Syria allowed the Syrian Kurdish field to become an arena for regional contestation for leadership between the KDP and PKK, and for spheres of influence between regional powers as well as global ones.

Conclusion

Syrian-Kurdish politics was transformed by the Syrian uprising and by the military success of ISIS. At the time of writing, this story was not concluded. No obvious or realistic scenario that would enable observers to predict its outcome has presented itself. The continuation of the conflict in Syria postponed any resolution to the Kurdish question there, and whilst ISIS provided a unifying directive for the various

Kurdish political factions and an incentive for the fortification of Kurdish areas, the nature of the region and the complex local, regional, and international politics and interests left uncertain the future of the autonomy developed in northern Syria. The deep fissures and rivalries within the Kurdish political movement were widened and intensified in the Syrian field, suppressed only by imminent threats to shared Kurdish interests. Imagining any scenario (the fall or revival of the Assad regime, the degrading of ISIS, the division of Syria) left questions about the future of the Kurds in Syria. Nonetheless, both outward and inward perception of the Kurds regionally had been transformed by their critical role in confronting ISIS and the regional autonomy developed in Syria.

The rise of the PYD left other Kurdish political parties in Syria with a choice, about whether to acquiesce in PYD-led management of Kurdish regions or to rely on expected gains from loyalty to the KDP or PUK. Whilst the decisive emergence of the KNC parties onto the Syrian Kurdish political field was still elusive at the time of writing, dynamic shifts in the balance of power within Kurdish Syria were not inconceivable. The PYD had adopted more trappings of a recognizable political party than the parties of 1957 by assuming state-like power within Kurdish areas, by confronting ISIS, and by gaining endogenous legitimacy. Its connections to armed groups and various civil and administrative organizations and institutions within Syria, however, connected the system of government in northern Syria to an overarching ideological and political doctrine. Overriding questions of legitimacy and its sources, shifting alliances, and rival political doctrines remained central to Kurdish politics in Syria. Their pursuit, in such a turbulent political landscape, added to these politics layers of complexity reaching far beyond Syria's borders.

PART 4

THE KURDISH QUESTION AND IRAN

21.

THE KURDISH CONUNDRUM AND THE ISLAMIC REPUBLIC OF IRAN, 1979–2003

Nader Entessar

The purpose of this chapter is to analyze Kurd-state relations after the demise of the Pahlavi monarchy and the establishment of the Islamic Republic of Iran in 1979 through 2003. This is a crucial era because the developments in this period define the contours of minority-state relations for decades to come. In some ways, the Islamic Republic's centralizing government power and implementing authoritarian reforms to delineate the parameters of ethnic identity in Iran were the continuation of the policies that had been adopted during the reign of Reza Shah in the 1920s and 1930s. Reza Shah's policy of "authoritarian modernization" was based partly on forced migration of the country's nomadic tribes, eradication of the power of tribal chieftains, and adoption of sociopolitical and economic policies aimed at subsuming ethnic identities under the umbrella of a fully-integrated nation-state with the motto of "one country, one nation" as its defining characteristic.

Reza Shah's son and his successor, Mohammad Reza Shah, sought to continue his father's legacy with varying degrees of success, but at a cost of increasing resentment by the country's marginalized ethnic groups, especially the Kurds. Therefore, it was not surprising that, to a large extent, the Kurds enthusiastically supported the anti-monarchical upheaval and joined the revolutionary process against the Pahlavi monarchy from the outset. However, the revolutionary chaos intensified ethnic discontent and led to regional uprisings. As Rasmus Christian Elling has noted, a recurring source of ethnic discontent is that the new Islamic ruling elite "did not proceed to decentralize power and economic development as promised during the revolution."[1]

The Kurdish uprising against the new Iranian government began shortly after the establishment of the Islamic Republic in 1979 and continued with varying degrees of intensity for another six years. The whole notion of ethnic identity and ethnic demands outside the Islamic framework was anathema to the philosophy of Ayatollah Ruhollah Khomeini, the founder of the Islamic Republic. In Khomeini's words:

> Sometimes the word minorities is used to refer to people such as the Kurds, Lurs, Turks, Persians, Baluchis, and such. These people should not be called minorities, because this term assumes that there is a difference between these brothers. In Islam, such a difference has no place at all. There is no difference between Muslims who speak different languages, for instance, the Arabs or the Persians. It is very probable that such problems have been created by those who do not wish the Muslim countries to be united. ... They create the issues of nationalism, of pan-Arabism, pan-Turkism, and such isms, which are contrary to Islamic doctrines. Their plan is to destroy Islam and the Islamic philosophy.[2]

Ayatollah Khamenei's rejection of the concept of ethnic pluralism in the Muslim community was echoed shortly after the ratification of the Islamic Republic's constitution. Ironically, the new constitution recognized Iran's ethnic diversity. Article 15 of the constitution recognizes Persian as the official language of Iran and mandates that official texts and documents as well as educational materials and textbooks must be in Persian. However, the use of regional languages in the press and mass media is allowed, and teaching cultural and literary works in local languages is permissible so long as they are used along with Persian.[3] However, the Islamic Republic's constitution has no specific provisions dealing with broader sociopolitical rights of Muslim ethnic groups. The only recognition granted to the minorities in the constitution is for the religious minorities (Christians, Jews, and Zoroastrians). The constitution views the Kurds as an integral part of Iran's Islamic community and does not grant them any specific rights other than those that are granted to all members of Iranian society.

The Bazargan government, the Kurds, and the United States

After the establishment of the Islamic Republic, ethnic rebellions in parts of Iran alarmed the government of Prime Minister Mehdi Bazargan. The US government also shared Bazargan's apprehension about the implication of ethnic uprisings. As Mark Gasiorowski has observed, Washington wanted to promote political stability in post-revolutionary Iran and maintain the country's territorial integrity to serve as a barrier against the Soviet Union. The US also wanted to improve Washington's relations with Tehran by helping the Bazargan government to solidify its tenuous position among the contending forces in the nascent Islamic Republic. Finally, given the close relationship between the Iranian Kurdish groups and their counterparts in Iraq and Turkey, the US wanted to prevent the spillover effect of the Kurdish rebellion, fearing potential damage to US regional interests.[4] At Bazargan's request, the US provided Iran with some intelligence on ethnic uprisings and Iraq's invasion plans, beginning in May 1979 and culminating shortly before the takeover of the US Embassy in Tehran in November of that year.[5] Bazargan's colleagues, including those in the Liberation Movement of Iran that was headed by Barzargan, have vociferously challenged claims and assertions of US-Iranian intelligence cooperation.[6] However, the documents published after the takeover of the US Embassy in Tehran by the "Student Followers of the Line of Imam [Khomeini]" do indeed contain several materials on the CIA's activities to collect intelligence about Kurdish uprisings in Iran. What is debatable is the extent of the CIA's sharing of its intelligence information with the Bazargan government.

According to the *Documents From the US Espionage Den* (hereafter referred to as the Embassy documents), the CIA relied on several sources and individuals to monitor the Iranian Kurdish rebel activity in the early months of the existence of the Islamic Republic. Many of these sources most likely had already been known to the CIA as they had worked, directly or indirectly, with SAVAK, the Pahlavi regime's intelligence agency.[7] For example, Ali Homan Qazi, the son of Qazi Mohammad, the president of the short-lived Mahabad Republic of Kurdistan, was viewed by the CIA as an important source. Although the Shah's government executed Qazi Mohammad after the fall of the Mahabad Republic, it nevertheless added Ali Qazi to its payroll and supported him financially until the downfall of the monarchy.[8] Ali Qazi, whose cryptonym in the US Embassy documents was CATOMIC/19, was well connected with a number of Kurdish groups, especially the Kurdish Democratic Party of Iran (KDPI), which was then considered a "leftist" organization. He was also in touch with his brother-in-law Sardar Jaf, who "commanded 1,500 Kurdish guerrillas in the region west of Kermanshah and favoured a restoration of the monarchy."[9]

Another CIA asset and source on the Kurds was an Iranian Kurdish petroleum engineer who was identified in the Embassy documents only with the cryptonym SDTRANSIT/1 and who had been trained and paid by the CIA to provide intelligence on Kurdish and non-Kurdish leftist groups operating in Iran during the Bazargan era.[10] A KDPI member, identified as SDFICKLE/1 in the Embassy documents and who had been a SAVAK informant during the Pahlavi monarchy, served as an informed CIA source on the Kurdish activities. For a period of time, SDFICKLE/1 acted as a double agent against the Soviet Union. Up until mid-1979, he continued to meet with a Soviet intelligence officer in Germany, "reporting on these meetings to his former SAVAK case officer."[11] In June 1979, a CIA officer in Germany recruited SDFICKLE/1 to travel to Iranian Kurdistan and gather information on the Kurdish rebellion there. SDFICKLE/1 provided "useful information" about the activities of the various Kurdish groups in Iran, including those of the non-Kurdish Iranian leftist groups that were fighting with the Kurds in Iran. He also reported on the establishment of Kurdish organizations whose task was to assassinate Kurds who collaborated with the Islamic Republic's authorities.[12]

The Embassy documents identify several other figures that worked for and/or collected information for the US intelligence on Kurdish uprisings in Iran in the early phase of the Islamic Republic. However, not all informants or assets were Kurdish or Iranian personalities. One such individual was a Palestinian member of Fatah who had served as a paid CIA informant on several issues. Identified by the Embassy documents only by his cryptonym MJBARGE/1, he traveled to Iran in spring 1979 as part of a Palestine Liberation Organization delegation. In early September, MJBARGE/1 provided intelligence on the link between Iraqi President Saddam Hussein and Iranian Kurdish rebels and on how Saddam's regime was fueling Kurdish uprisings in Iran.[13] Again, it is difficult to ascertain how much of the information gathered by the US intelligence on Kurdish rebellion was conveyed to the Bazargan government, or if this information helped the Islamic Republic formulate strategies to combat Kurdish uprisings in the country. It is likely that the Islamic Republic had its own assets and sources of information, and it already had access to SAVAK's vast collection of intelligence data on the Kurds and other ethnic groups in the country.[14]

The constitutional struggle

The Kurdish struggle was fought on the political battlefront as well. The outline of the Islamic Republic's constitution had been formulated while Ayatollah Khomeini was living in exile in France. The proposed document was a mixture of the Iranian constitution of 1906 and the constitution of France's Fifth Republic. The draft of the Islamic Republic's proposed constitution was publicly unveiled by Bazargan's government on 18 June 1979. The initial Kurdish reaction to the draft of the proposed constitution was lukewarm, because it did not grant them rights of autonomy within the Iranian state. However, the then secular leftist KDPI was gratified that the document did not grant special privileges to the clergy, nor did it call for a political system dominated by the Shia Muslim clerics. Ayatollah Khomeini approved the draft constitution and asked that it be submitted for public vote. Bazargan, however, wanted the draft constitution to be debated by experts and various groups in the country and to have necessary modifications made to it before it was put before the public in a referendum. The KDPI joined a number of other voices in the country that demanded that a constituent assembly be elected to debate and revise the draft constitution.

As debates about the contours of the new constitution became intense, the Kurds insisted on including the right of ethnic autonomy in the constitution. To counter the increasing demands of ethnonationalists and fearing the unraveling of the foundation of the new regime, Ayatollah Khomeini delivered a major speech to a delegation of clerics from Mahabad in which he insisted that the debates over the draft constitution be conducted only within an Islamic framework. He also emphasized that the clergy had an obligation to prevent the inclusion of "non-Islamic concepts" into the document. From this point forward, it became increasingly clear that the gap between the emerging Islamic Republic of Iran and Kurdish aspirations was widening.[15] However, in an attempt to persuade the Kurds to participate in the Islamic Republic's first presidential election in 1980, Khomeini announced that he would consider asking the authorities to add an amendment to the constitution guaranteeing specific rights for Sunni Muslim minorities. This amendment would have allowed the Sunnis to have their own religious courts in areas where they constituted the majority of the population. The Kurdish leadership rejected this idea as insufficient. They wanted recognition as an ethnic, not religious, group. Besides, the Kurdish population consisted of both Sunni and Shia Muslims.

As the presidential election of 1980 approached, hopes for a negotiated settlement of the Kurdish issue diminished significantly. However, after the victory of Abolhassan Banisadr, whose candidacy the KDPI had not supported in the 1980 presidential election, the KDPI's Secretary General Abdolrahman Ghassemlou approached President Banisadr and presented him with a new plan for Kurdish autonomy. In his new proposal, Ghassemlou dropped the Kurdish demands to include the provinces of West Azerbaijan, Ilam, and Kermanshah as part of Kurdistan. Ghassemlou also offered to allow a majority popular vote to define the autonomous area of Kurdistan. Banisadr was positively inclined toward Ghassemlou's offer, but he insisted that the Kurds first lay down their arms and end their military confrontation with government forces before a political settlement could be reached. Ghassemlou, in turn, insisted that the Kurds would not disarm until their autonomy demands were met. Both sides parted company and new rounds of fighting broke out throughout Kurdistan.

In the midst of fresh fighting between the Kurds and the forces of the Islamic Republic, the KDPI held its 4th Congress in Mahabad in February 1980. At this meeting, the KDPI reaffirmed its support for the Iranian revolution and the country's territorial integrity while issuing autonomy demands that had already been rejected by the Iranian government. Nonetheless, the 4th Congress expressed its support for President Banisadr's program of granting more internal freedom to the country's ethnic groups.[16] For his part, Banisadr issued a perfunctory but conciliatory message expressing hope that peace would return to Kurdistan. Neither Banisadr nor the KDPI seemed to delve further into the notion of self-determination and autonomy that has bedeviled state-Kurdish relations from the outset and has led to violent clashes in Kurdistan for decades.

Self-determination and autonomy: fissures in state-Kurd relations and Kurdish factionalism

One of the most vexing problems regarding the realization of Kurdish self-determination has revolved around the meaning of the term "autonomy", which in Persian is referred to as *khodmokhtari*. The Persian term for autonomy carries a negative connotation; it equates autonomy with secession and/or total independence and conjures up the worst images of balkanization. Ayatollah Allame Nouri, a leading cleric with progressive views, suggested in late March 1980 that the Kurds refrain from using *khodmokhtari* in their publications and devise a new, "less threatening" term. The Kurds were amenable to using any term, including "Islamic autonomy" as suggested by Ayatollah Allame Nouri, as long as the government "recognized the concept of decentralization for itself and home rule for the Kurds and other ethnic minorities."[17] However, political developments in Iran, including President Banisadr's emerging power struggle with the increasingly assertive clerical establishment, the challenge posed to the government by the armed activities of several opposition forces, and the need for unity in the face-off with the United States over the holding of US hostages in the American Embassy in Tehran, relegated the discussion of Kurdish autonomy to a secondary concern for the government of the Islamic Republic. Nonetheless, the Kurds continued to redefine and rephrase the term "autonomy" for the next several years. During its 13th Congress, held on 3-7 July 2004, the KDPI decided to change its strategic slogan of "democracy for Iran, autonomy for Kurdistan" to "achieving Kurdish national rights within a democratic and federal Iran."

When Iraq invaded Iran on 22 September 1980 and occupied the province of Khuzestan, the Islamic Republic was faced with the prospect of a total war against an invading enemy. As a consequence, the loyalty of all Iranian citizens was demanded in defense of the motherland. The KDPI made a strategic error in seeking military and logistical support from the invading forces of Saddam Hussein. This was the proverbial straw that broke the camel's back, and Ghassemlou's declarations of support for Iran's territorial integrity began to ring hollow, at least in the calculus of the Iranian ruling elite. The KDPI also lost its luster as a leading organization for democracy and reform in Iran.

The KDPI has not been a monolithic entity. In fact, shortly after the establishment of the Islamic Republic in Iran, three factions developed within the KDPI. The dominant faction, led by Ghassemlou, favored a mixture of armed struggle and political negotiation vis-à-vis the Islamic Republic. The other two factions were associated with Karim Hessami and Ghani Bloorian, both of whom had developed close relations with the pro-Soviet Tudeh Party of Iran. Given the Tudeh Party's conciliatory posture toward the Islamic Republic until 1982, the Hessami and Bloorian factions of the KDPI favored negotiations and cooperation with the new government.[18] However, after the suppression of the Tudeh Party in 1982 and the subsequent arrest and execution of scores of Tudeh members, the Hessami and Bloorian factions of the KDPI adopted a policy of armed struggle against the Islamic Republic.[19] With the gradual improvement in Tehran-Moscow relations under Gorbachev's Soviet Union, the Hessami and Bloorian factions of the KDPI were marginalized in Kurdish politics in Iran.

The demise of the Hessami and Bloorian wings did not augur the end of factionalism in intra-Kurdish conflict in Iran. Despite Ghassemlou's strong and unwavering support for Kurdish autonomy demands throughout the 1980s, Ghassemlou's policy of negotiating with the Islamic Republic divided the KDPI into hostile subfactions. The non-Tudeh "left" in the KDPI accused Ghassemlou and the "Kurdish bourgeoisie" of betraying the Kurdish cause by abandoning KDPI's ideals in favor of a policy of reconciliation with the Islamic Republic.[20] Further fissures developed within the KDPI, and the seemingly unending schisms reached a turning point at the KDPI's 8th Congress in 1988, resulting in the expulsion of the fifteen prominent members of the party's executive committee. The left coalesced around the expelled members of the KDPI and established a new movement called the Kurdish Democratic Party of Iran—Revolutionary Leadership.[21] With its stridently Marxist orientation and its dogmatic sectarianism, this movement was unable to gain traction among the Kurdish population in Iran and eventually withered away.

On 13 July 1989, the KDPI's foundation was jolted when Ghassemlou was assassinated while meeting with the representatives of the Iranian government in a Vienna apartment. Two of Ghassemlou's Kurdish companions, Abdullah Ghaderi-Azar (the KDPI's second in command) and Mahmoud Fadhil Rasoul (a member of the Iraqi Patriotic Union of Kurdistan), were also assassinated at the same meeting. In addition, Mohammad Ja'far Sahrarudi, a representative of the Islamic Republic, was wounded in the jaw. The timing of Ghassemlou's assassination, when the KDPI was engaged in political negotiations with Tehran, raised many unanswered questions about the motives behind the attack. Sahrarudi, who returned to Iran to recuperate from his injury, gave a televised interview from his hospital bed in Tehran on 27 July 1989 in which he denounced the killers as terrorists and vowed to cooperate with the Vienna police.[22] The KDPI quickly issued an announcement condemning the Islamic Republic as the main culprit in the assassination, and the Iranian opposition groups abroad identified Sahrarudi as an intelligence operative who had orchestrated the assassination of Ghassemlou and the other Kurdish leaders. The Czechoslovakian-born widow of Ghassemlou, Nasrin (née Helen Krulich), charged that the meeting was a trap set by the Islamic Republic to kill her husband and thus weaken Kurdish opposition activities against the Iranian government.[23] The Vienna police also began to suspect the Iranian government's role in Ghassemlou's assassination, partly because of Sahrarudi's hasty departure from Vienna and the Iranian Embassy's refusal to allow officials in the Austrian criminal justice system to interview Amir Mansoor Bozorgian, an Iranian Kurd who acted as the interlocutor in arranging the meeting between Ghassemlou and the Iranian officials and was present during that fateful meeting.

Following Ghassemlou's murder, the KDPI appointed Sadeq Sharafkandi as its secretary general. In an eerily similar scenario to Ghassemlou's assassination, Sharafkandi, along with the KDPI's European and German representatives and four other Iranian dissident leaders, were gunned down in the Mykonos restaurant in Berlin on 17 September 1992, during the era of renewed Kurdish insurgency against the Islamic Republic. The Mykonos assassinations and the subsequent verdict handed down by a German court on 10 April 1997 further strained Kurdish-Iranian relations. The significance of the Mykonos verdict was that, for the first time, a foreign court had implicated the highest echelon of the Iranian government, including the Supreme Leader Ayatollah Ali Khamenei and the then president Ali Akbar Hashemi Rafsanjani, in ordering the assassination of the KDPI leader and the other dissidents. The loss of Ghassemlou and Sharafkandi dealt a major blow to the KDPI from which it has not yet recovered. Both Ghassemlou and Sharafkandi were adroit politicians who developed extensive contacts with a large cross section of Iranian society and had established effective political networks in Europe. There is no doubt that at the time of his assassination Ghassemlou was the most recognizable political leader with the widest appeal within the Kurdish and the broader Iranian population.

Last but not least, the Iran-Iraq War of 1980-88 and the US-led wars against Iraq provided opportunities and pitfalls for improving the Kurdish situation in Iran. It is beyond the scope of this chapter to discuss the implications of these wars for the Iranian Kurds.[24] Suffice it to say that the outlook for Kurdish autonomy demands as advocated by the KDPI and other Kurdish parties and organizations dimmed as a consequence of the aforementioned wars during the period of state-Kurdish relations covered in this chapter. Of course, the Kurdish condition will ebb and flow with changes in domestic political developments in Iran and changes in the country's regional and international politics.

The reform movement and the Kurds

The internal Kurdish factionalism in Iran coincided with major political changes in the country. The election of Mohammad Khatami as Iran's president in May 1997 and the defeat of the conservative forces in the February 2000 parliamentary elections generated hopeful but perhaps unrealistic expectations for significant political change in Iran. The Islamic Republic has failed to bring about genuine democracy and a meaningful participatory political system from its inception in 1979. However, through the expansion of the state's welfare and education structures, along with the expansion of information and communication technology, it has "overseen the incorporation of a large segment of the population, previously excluded, into a project of state-building."[25] The seemingly contradictory impulses in the Islamic Republic, including attempts to engage the vast segment of the country's population in electoral politics, engendered reformism in the late 1990s that "brought many previously excluded minority voters into an arena of nationwide politics."[26] At the same time, systemic discrimination, legal and otherwise, coupled with repeated episodes of repression against dissident voices and ethnic groups, has stifled attempts to reform the system even when reformists came to power.

Khatami, a mid-ranking reformist cleric, received close to 70 percent of the popular vote with a clear mandate to reform Iran's political system and allow the emergence of a genuinely pluralistic political culture in the country. As Khatami had stated, "we cannot expect any positive transformations anywhere [in Iran] unless the yearning for freedom is fulfilled. That is the freedom to think and the security to express new thinking."[27] Moreover, Khatami, from the beginning of his presidency, emphasized the notion of inclusiveness, or "Iran for all Iranians" as he called it, and the importance of the rule of law in enhancing the foundation of Iran's political system.[28] The Kurds, like many other Iranian citizens, welcomed Khatami's victory in the 1997 presidential election. The reform movement (the Second of Khordad Movement) that brought Khatami to power and provided him with political backing proved to be weak. In addition to limits that the Iranian constitution imposes on the authority of the office of presidency, Khatami and his supporters were challenged in all areas by their conservative opponents. When challenged, Khatami always conceded and backed off. The closing down of the reformist newspapers and organizations, as well as jailing of supporters of political reform, went unchallenged by Khatami throughout much of his two presidential terms, save occasional speeches he delivered denouncing violations of the rule of law by his opponents in the country's judiciary and security agencies.

In Kurdistan, the arrest of officials, some of whom had identified with Khatami's programs and had supported his presidency, intensified throughout Khatami's office. City council elections were nullified by conservative forces and the credentials of both pro-reform and independent Kurdish politicians and candidates were routinely rejected when they sought to run for various positions in the province of Kurdistan. In a crackdown on Kurdish officials, Abdullah Ramazanzadeh, the governor general of Kurdistan and a Khatami supporter who later served as the government spokesman, was summoned before the Special Court for Public Officials in April 2001 and was charged with the "dissemination of lies." Ramazanzadeh's "crimes" were his objections to the nullification of the votes of two constituencies in the Kurdish cities of Baneh and Saqqez. Specifically, Ramazanzadeh was charged with libeling the country's powerful Council of Guardians, which had ordered the nullification of the aforementioned constituency votes.[29]

Another significant factor that had kept the state-Kurd ties during Khatami's presidency tenuous was the presence of several prominent figures in the reform movement who had participated in the suppression of earlier Kurdish uprisings. Some Kurdish activists argued that today's reformers were yesterday's oppressors and thus they could not be trusted. The saga of Hamid Reza Jalaipour is a good case in point. Jalaipour, who became a significant architect of the Second of Khordad Movement and published cutting-edge critical commentaries on the country's sociopolitical system as the editor of the now defunct reformist daily *Asr-e Azadegan*, had spent ten years in Kurdistan fighting Kurdish autonomy demands. As a commander of a Revolutionary Guards unit, and later as governor of the cities of Naqdeh and Mahabad and Deputy Governor General for Political Affairs in Kurdistan, Jalaipour was directly or indirectly responsible for some of the worst revolutionary excesses in that region. When asked if he had any remorse about ordering the execution of fifty-nine Kurdish activists, he refused to offer an apology for his past actions. Instead, Jalaipour claimed that he could not be held responsible for actions undertaken when he was a revolutionary in his twenties and for actions that were necessary during wartime and were in the interest of saving the fledgling Islamic Republic.[30] Jalaipour later sought to disavow his statements by stating that he had been misquoted by the correspondent of *Asr-e Azadegan*, who happened to be an Iranian Kurd.[31] Jalaipour's predicament was illustrative of the obstacles that reformists encountered in articulating a coherent nationality policy in the Islamic Republic. It was not until 2005 that nationality issues were openly broached by candidates running in that year's presidential election.

The arrest of Abdullah Öcalan, founder and leader of the Kurdistan Workers' Party (PKK), on 15 February 1999 in Nairobi, Kenya by the Turkish security forces, affected the Kurds throughout the world. In Iran, major demonstrations took place in all major Kurdish cities as a reaction to Öcalan's arrest and against the Turkish government. These demonstrations later extended to Tehran and other Iranian cities. The Iranian security forces reacted harshly toward the demonstrators, thus exposing the limits of dissident activities in Khatami's Iran. The crackdown further dissipated Khatami's support among the Kurds. At the same time, some were fearful that abandoning the Second of Khordad Movement might bring about a worse situation for the Kurds than had existed under Khatami. These fears "would turn out to be prophetic, as the political divide within Khatami's government between reformists and conservatives widened."[32] This resulted, inter alia, in further repressive measures against the Kurds. The escalating repression forced all six Kurdish members of the Iranian parliament (*majlis*) to resign en masse.

The principal reformist candidate in the 2005 presidential election was Mostafa Moin. He made a special effort to woo voters from non-Persian nationalities and included the issue of Iran's multinational character as an important component of his presidential campaign. Moin criticized those who ignored Iran's multinational kaleidoscope and those who sought to divide the country on ethnic, linguistic, and religious bases. In this vein, Moin promised complete equality for all Iranians as guaranteed under the country's constitution. Recognizing the destabilizing potential of discrimination, Moin stated that his administration would be composed of all nationalities.[33] Echoing Khatami's campaign slogan, Moin also made "Iran for all Iranians" the centerpiece of his presidential campaign. Furthermore, several reformist writers and commentators opined that without recognizing the right of Iranian nationalities, democratic institutions would not take root in Iran. Also, many reformists welcomed Jalal Talabani's election as president of Iraq and viewed his accession to power in neighboring Iraq as the natural progression of the recognition of Kurdish rights in the region.[34] Alas, Moin's campaign was soundly defeated when he received negligible support in most of Iran's provinces. In Kurdistan, the disappointment with the Khatami administration had sourced Kurdish perception of the Second of Khordad Movement and official reformism in the country.

Conclusion

In this chapter, I focused on state-Kurd relations in the first two decades of the Islamic Republic of Iran. Many of the events that shaped the contours of the state's relations with the Kurds were unique to this period and were products of a specific historical period in contemporary Iranian history. That said, the Kurdish quest for identity and full and equal participation in Iran's sociopolitical life has remained fairly constant since the victory of the Iranian revolution of 1979 and the establishment of the Islamic Republic.[35] In fact, what it means to be an Iranian has experienced a continuing process of re-envisioning from the early years of the Iranian revolution.[36] We have already witnessed a partial understanding on the part of President Rouhani's administration that a heavy focus on the security-centered approach to Iranian nationality issues is not only counter-productive but in the long run may redound to the detriment of the country's sociopolitical cohesiveness and indeed its territorial integrity.[37]

Considering the above, one of the first domestic measures that Hassan Rouhani undertook after winning Iran's 2013 presidential election was to establish a special bureau in the office of president to handle the "ethnic issue." He appointed Ali Younesi, a cleric who had served, inter alia, as minister of intelligence during Khatami's reform era, as his special advisor and liaison in ethnic affairs. Younesi has taken some steps to reach out to various ethnic groups and has stated that his main task is to ensure the safety and equality of all ethnic groups, while moving away from securitizing ethnic issues. In fact, he has stated that looking at ethnic demands and grievances through a security lens is dangerous and counter-productive. As the experience of the Khatami era clearly demonstrated, the best of intentions do not necessarily translate into enduring policies.

22.

IDENTITIES AND ETHNIC HIERARCHY

THE KURDISH QUESTION IN IRAN SINCE 1979

Olivier Grojean

A conference in London on 20 February 2005 brought together seven organizations representing different "Iranian nationalities", including Baluchis, Kurds, Azeris, and Arabs. The conference delegates were assembled to promote the idea of a federalist Iran, founded on increased respect for minorities and true democracy, and it culminated in the founding of the *Congress* of *Nationalities* for a Federal Iran. Six months later, on 26 October, the American Enterprise Institute (AEI) held a meeting in Washington on the topic "The Unknown Iran: Another Case for Federalism?" to which Azeri, Turkmen, Kurdish, Baluchi, and Arab representatives were invited. The organizer, Michael Ledeen, pointedly observed during his opening remarks that the AEI's goal was not to "dismember Iran", but merely to inform the American public about the status of minorities in the country.

Other meetings could be cited to illustrate that—as a number of experts, and even the Iranian government itself, have argued—the West has played a key role in raising awareness, or at least signaling the unprecedented development, of independence and separatist movements in Iran since the mid-2000s. The George W. Bush administration promoted the idea of a "Greater Middle East" in an effort to reconfigure the region, and particularly to shape Iran in ways that were more consistent with American objectives. A 2007 presidential executive order commanded an increase in clandestine operations sponsored by the US among separatist groups in Iran in order to destabilize the Islamic Republic.[1] These are just a few of many examples that can be cited to show that foreigners either fomented or exploited unrest among Iranian minority groups, particularly the Kurds, in the 2000s. However, all these re-awakenings began well before the turn of the twenty-first century.

As an ancient, multi-ethnic, and multi-faith empire with Persian as the mother tongue of less than half its citizens, Iran is indeed unrivaled in terms of cultural diversity. The widespread idea that foreigners have exploited these groups, which represents a full-blown conspiracy theory in Iran, may very well be the proverbial tree that hides the forest, an observation supported by recent scientific studies of minorities in Iran.[2] From 1925 to 1979, the Pahlavi dynasty systematically campaigned to transform the ethnic mosaic of the Persian Empire into a centralized nation-state that did not accommodate identity-based rights. This effort was so successful that it was only after Reza Shah had abdicated and the Soviet and British occupied Iran in 1941 that the ill-fated and short-lived Kurdish Republic of Mahabad could be established in 1946. This separate Kurdish political entity was literally crushed only eleven months later,[3] and the Kurds would have to await the 1979 Revolution before they became (temporarily) empowered again, while the new Iranian regime was not yet completely established. The Kurds could only affirm their political and cultural rights for three or four years before a brutal crackdown.[4] The Islamic Republic does appear to be more tolerant toward other cultures or regional languages (Article 15 of the Constitution authorizes the use and teaching of "local" languages, for example), but it has in fact continued and expanded the unification project initiated under the Pahlavi dynasty, although presently on a nationalistic (i.e. Persian) and Islamic (i.e. Shia) basis. During the twentieth century, the large number of groups that comprise modern-day Iran became de facto minorities by becoming aware of their identities and voicing political and cultural demands, while also generally expressing genuine attachment to their Iranian national identity.

The Kurds offer a good example of these identity-centered "awakenings." Representing between 10 and 15 per cent of the Iranian population and speaking Kurdish as their mother tongue, though not Farsi, they live primarily in the provinces along the nation's north-western periphery: West Azerbaijan, Kurdistan, Kermanshah, and Elam. The vast majority of Kurds are Sunni Muslims, which makes them ineligible for many administrative functions, and their territory tends to suffer from under-investment. The Kurds are not only one of the largest Iranian minorities, but also, for nearly a century, one of the most active in terms of cultural and political demands, social movements, and guerrilla activities. Kurdish nationalism extends beyond Iranian borders, although Iranian Kurds generally reject secessionist ideas. Indeed, the Kurdish movement in Iran is closely tied to other movements that are demanding a redefinition of their relationships with the central government, more equitable resource distribution, some level of cultural independence (when coupled with demands for government investment) and political autonomy (decentralization, indigenization of the local administration, and changes in territorial borders).

IDENTITIES AND ETHNIC HIERARCHY

In terms of the theories of nationalism, Kurdish activism arguably resembles a "nationalism of reaction", in the face of a "modernizing" state seeking a cultural homogenization of the peoples that it controls and governs. Although probably valid, this argument does not enable a balanced understanding of the moments, situations, and specific configurations that can potentially allow the transformation of an environment of cultural friction between groups into political claims to the center; inter-individual conflicts into collective mobilization; or a peaceful movement into open, armed struggle. In fact, the system prioritizes some ethnic and religious identities over others, assigning each minority a rank inside a hierarchy, in turn generating peaceable, and occasionally violent, conflict.[5] Further, as Gilles Dorronsoro and I have argued elsewhere, it is possible to distinguish the ideal-typical ways by which hierarchies are transformed (somewhat adapted here to the post-revolutionary Iranian situation), which can facilitate the action of mobilizing actors. First, political transformation at the center can redefine the core identity and incite challengers to promote an alternative hierarchy; second, changes in the immediate environment multiply the phenomena of competition, mimicry, or cooperation at the periphery that can restructure the marginalized identities; and finally, exceptional events (local, national, and international) that break with routine temporality can trigger "moral shocks" or even completely redefine the ways in which individuals think and act. The present chapter explores these three pathways for interrogating identity-based hierarchies in order to analyze the Kurdish question in Iran since 1979, while envisioning the status of the Kurds within the broader perspective of the relationships between Iranian minorities and the state.

The denaturalization of group hierarchies by the center

The state is often at the heart of "conflicts of differentiation." Because of its power to categorize groups, redefine territorial boundaries, and create and implement public policy, governments have the power to recognize some groups while discriminating against others, in the process defining the relationships among various groups. As the guarantor of official history, governments similarly play a critical role in shaping the people's conceptual framework,[6] although this power is continually challenged. To some extent, there are obvious parallels with how the Kurdish question is represented in official Turkish historical accounts, such as maps and school textbooks.[7] Rapid transformations of the hierarchy can therefore take place at the center if the state or government seeks to transform the relative value of particular identities, whether this involves positive or negative consequences for the group in question. Indeed, a finding of the sociology of social movements is that both repression and official recognition have fundamentally uncertain effects on the processes of mobilization.

The Iranian Revolution in 1979 broke with the unifying, centralizing policies enforced by the Shah's regime, allowing minorities to express openly their specific cultural, linguistic, or religious demands. For example, more than 180 books about local Turkish cultures were published in Iran between 1979 and 1984, compared to only a handful in the previous ten years.[8] This is how, during this universalist, liberal phase of the revolution, the Kurdistan Democratic Party – Iran (the Partîya Demokrata Kurdistan – Iran, KDPI)[9] grew to be one of the leading political forces in Iranian Kurdistan. Attempting to control and organize protests since the fall of 1978, Abd al-Rahman Qasimlu's party found itself, after the Shah's departure on 16 January, in the position of co-managing majority-Kurdish regions with Komala,[10] and an influential figure put forward by the KDPI (who later became independent): Sheikh Ezaddin Hosseini. Committees were created in the cities along local ethno-political lines, including a Kurdish revolutionary committee in Mahabad, an Islamic group in Urumiyeh, and Kurdish and Sunni committees in Sanandaj, etc.[11] When negotiations with the Bazargan provisional government began on 14 February, the Kurds openly and hopefully demanded an autonomous Kurdistan inside redefined borders. The KDPI was subsequently granted legal status and on March 1, between 100,000 and 150,000 people attended Abd al-Rahman Qasimlu's first political rally in Mahabad.

This trend toward political openness gradually subsided. The Kurds were unprepared for this and rapidly became caught up in a series of incidents, many of which they caused themselves, such as the seizure of Iranian military installations by local KDPI forces. These incidents fueled tensions and culminated in the failure of the negotiations.[12] The Newroz (Kurdish New Year) crackdown in Sanandaj, and additional confrontations in Naqadeh and Merivan, led to a boycott of the referendum on the "Islamic" character of the Republic on 1 April. It became impossible for Qasimlu to participate in the Assembly of Experts that was created to draft a new constitution in August. On 17 August, Khomeini called for jihad against the Kurds, initiating a three-year state of war between the Kurdish movement and Iranian authorities, punctuated by sporadic attempts to negotiate. By the spring of 1984, the Iranian government had brought Kurdish territory under control, and Iranian peshmergas were forced to retreat into Iraq. Further attempts to negotiate gave way to confrontations, and the Iranian Kurds aligned themselves with Saddam Hussein against the Islamic Republic during the Iran-Iraq War (1980-88), while the Iraqi Kurds who sought refuge in Iran supported the Khomeini regime. Negotiations resumed only after the war ended, with the widely known conclusion: Qasimlu's assassination by Iranian special service agents in Vienna in July 1989, followed by the killing of his successor in Berlin in September 1992.

Challenges to the ethnic hierarchy—caused by the government's withdrawal at the outset of the Revolution, and its subsequent reassertion with violence by the new Iranian government—have directly contributed to the rise of mobilizations against the state. Some groups may also directly attack other groups when they feel threatened, however. The government unfailingly plays a key role in and exploits such inter-group conflicts. One example occurred during confrontations in Naqadeh in April 1979, where Azeri Shia held higher-ranking positions in the city than the local Sunni Kurds. On 7 April violence broke out between Kurdish and Azeri committees preparing for Qasimlu's second rally on 20 April in the wake of the accidental death of an Azeri at the hands of a Kurd.[13] On the day of the rally, Azeris fired into the crowd inside the stadium, interrupting Qasimlu. Fighting later broke out in Naqadeh between Azeris and Kurds as a consequence, lasting for three days, with four further days of violence in the neighboring villages. Kurdish sources reported over 350 fatalities, but violence in the ensuing months caused several hundred more fatalities, providing an opportunity for the government to send a large number of *Pâsdârân* to Azerbaijan and Kurdistan provinces to impose a semblance of calm in the region.

The above examples are based on a true revolution, in the sense of a radical change, of regime and political institutions. But a "simple" change of government can also provoke deep uncertainty (in terms of both hopes and fears) concerning the maintenance of the hierarchy, in turn inciting groups to mobilize. This was the case, for example, when Mohammad Khatami came to power in May 1997 and the conservatives lost the legislative elections in February 2000. Indeed, Khatami claimed to base his candidacy and presidency on inclusivity and on recognition of the many identities that contribute to Iranian-ness, under the slogan "Iran for all Iranians."[14] Kurds and other groups were suddenly allowed to express themselves in unprecedented ways, including newspapers and magazines, cultural and literary organizations, and the creation of a Kurdish faction in the Iranian parliament.[15] From the perspective of more traditional political organizations, it was also during this period that the KDPI abandoned armed conflict in favor of political struggle (in August 1996, but this change in policy was confirmed in the ensuing months), followed by the Komala in the early 2000s, although repression continues in Kurdistan to this day.[16] On the other hand, the return of the conservatives to power in 2005 with Mahmoud Ahmadinejad, after an electoral debate marked by the nationality question, coincided with the creation of the Kurdish United Front in Tehran in January 2006 (which united the Kurds in parliament), and facilitated an increase in armed conflict involving the Free Life Party of Kurdistan (Partiya Jiyana Azad a Kurdistan, PJAK), a party close to the Turkish Workers' Party of Kurdistan (Partiya Karkerên Kurdistane, PKK), which was officially founded in April 2004.

Important political changes at the center can thus help to challenge the hierarchy of identities and offer windows of opportunity for minority movements, or not, as the case may be. This explains why, following Ahmadinejad's highly contested re-election in 2009, the cities of the Iranian plateau such as Isfahan and Shiraz supported the Green Movement, while peripheral regions remained only minimally mobilized: there was no sign of a possible redefinition of the core identity. Based on the hypothesized emergence of "political sub-fields"[17] in the peripheral provinces of Iran (in other words, a fragmentation of the national political field), Gilles Riaux argues that minorities develop nowadays "an impressive distanciation from the national political arena, from which nothing further is expected."[18]

Changes in the peripheral environment, and the redefinition of minorities

Challenges to the identity hierarchy can also be explained by social, economic, and political changes that are increasingly independent of the center. It is this border that becomes, as it were, the "central issue", because it generates singular resources and constraints that can increase or decrease the status of certain identities.

Such boundaries can lie inside the country's borders, for example when administrative or territorial redistricting provokes uprisings or "localist" riots, as took place when a new province[19] was created in Ardebil in 1993, and more recently in Sabzevar in 2003 in response to plans to partition Khorasan province. Those plans included naming the neighboring city, Bojnurd, the capital of the new province.[20] These borders can also be external, and complications can arise when interactions with neighboring peoples become more frequent and intense. After the fall of the USSR, for example, Turcophone groups that occupied peripheral locations in the north of the country suddenly found that they were sharing borders with independent states like Azerbaijan, Turkmenistan, which triggered the much earlier, celebrated "awakening" of minority identities in the mid-2000s. In another case, the return of autonomist movements to Pakistani Baluchistan (which was more autonomous with respect to the central government, however) in the early 2000s had repercussions for Iranian Baluchis as well, some of whom founded Jundullah (Soldiers of Allah) and fought openly with government forces in 2005. Saddam Hussein's efforts to rally the Arabs of Khuzestan during the Iran-Iraq War, by contrast, failed dismally because the cross-border ethnic solidarity that he hoped to mobilize was secondary to Iranian national feelings.

Precisely because they involve internal or external border crossings, migrations can unleash periods during which identities become redefined. Internally, rural exodus transforms the relative value attributed to different identities, particularly when a local majority group suddenly finds itself a minority after moving to an urban setting. This occurred to Sunnis who migrated to Tehran, where there is not a single Sunni mosque (whereas numerous Sunni mosques were destroyed in other Iranian cities). The Sunnis residing in the capital can only pray or assemble at the mosque at the Pakistani embassy or in vacant lots. With respect to Kurds, as Farideh Koohi-Kamali has attempted to show, internal Kurdish migrations, particularly those in Kurdish regions in the 1960s and 1970s, increased solidarity among Kurds and contributed to the rise of a specific brand of Kurdish nationalism.[21] However, Martin van Bruinessen has argued that Iranian Kurdistan was far better integrated into other

Iranian regions than Koohi-Kamali contends,[22] largely because of internal migration toward other regions in Kurdistan and particularly toward Tehran, where large numbers of seasonal Kurdish migrants work in construction, but also to the oil-producing areas along the Gulf. As a result, as in Turkey, Kurdish migrants became by default an urban working class linked to their ethnic origins, particularly after mass displacements during the Iran-Iraq War.

Significant circulation and migration traversed external borders, in addition to Baluchistan, as mentioned earlier. The border between Iranian Kurdistan and Iraqi Kurdistan was particularly porous during the Iran-Iraq War, when refugees flowed in both directions: Iraqi Kurds toward Iran, and Iranian Kurds toward Iraq. The creation of an autonomous Kurdish entity in Iraq in 1991 did not immediately pave the way for a significant increase in political interaction between the two zones, however. Under pressure from both the Kurdistan Democratic Party (Partîya Demokrata Kurdistan, KDP) and the Kurdistan Patriotic Union (PUK, or the Yekîtîya Niştimanîya Kurdistan, YNK) who did not tolerate armed actions against Iran from their autonomous zone in Iraq, and under pressure from Iran itself, which stepped up incursions into Iraqi territory to destroy its Kurdish opposition (especially in 1993 and 1996), the KDPI and the Komala engaged in only a few small-scale raids between 1991 and 1996. The border remained open, however, and trade between Iran and Iraqi Kurdistan continued to grow, to the point that when the border was closed in 1996, Jalal Talabani, the leader of the PUK, agreed to allow the Iranian forces to cross the border and crush the KDPI camps on 28 and 29 July, contributing even more to the silencing of Iranian Kurdish organizations.[23]

The situation completely changed after the American intervention in Iraq in 2003, and especially since 2005, when the new Iraqi constitution granted Iraqi Kurdistan the status of a Federal State, thereby strengthening the KRG (Kurdistan Regional Government).[24] The KRG's newly important role and the comparatively peaceful situation in Iraqi Kurdistan allowed family visits, worker and student migrations, legal trade, the smuggling of manufactured goods, and the trans-border circulation of numerous political opponents and refugees (from Iran toward Iraq), while also making it possible for the two regions to attain an unprecedented level of integration.[25] This regional interdependence can be seen through the lens of "the complementarity of two antagonistic but juxtaposed economic systems, between, on one side, a liberal Iraqi Kurdistan with no desire to end smuggling, and on the other side, Iran, which, thanks to illegal trade, is able to circumvent the embargo of which it is a victim."[26] This has had particularly important implications for the political activities of the Iranian Kurdish opposition in Iraq.[27] Since 1993, KDPI peshmergas have descended from the mountains and established militarized camps in Koya, Djejnakan, and Degala. These peshmergas currently focus primarily on placing supporters seeking refuge inside Iraq in civilian camps that currently house more than 15,000 refugees.[28] KDPI activities are limited to more or less "long distance" political activities, particularly via the Tishk TV television channel, which has headquarters in Paris and broadcasts into Iranian Kurdish zones. Komala continues to maintain a highly militarized camp that primarily receives activists and sympathizers fleeing the Tehran regime, while also creating programming for its television channel, Rohjelat TV, with headquarters in Sweden.[29] This has prompted Leïla Porcher to claim that the term that best describes the present-day KDPI and Komala is "waiting": waiting for the eventual transformation of the Iranian regime's approach to activists and, for the refugees under their protection, waiting to migrate to Europe or elsewhere.[30]

These upheavals surrounding external borders have deeply influenced the PJAK's activities. The PJAK took advantage of zones controlled by the PKK on Mount Qandil in Iraq after 2004 and the space opened by cooling relations between the PKK and Iran to launch military operations against Iranian security forces through 2011. On the other hand, this renewed alliance between the PKK and the Iranian authorities after the beginning of civil war in Syria unquestionably explains the cease-fire declared by the PJAK in August 2011.[31] In short, the border is a mobilizing factor when it is more porous, but it can also precipitate the end of armed conflict when it is tightened.[32]

"Exceptional" events that rupture the hierarchy's established timeframe

Identities can ultimately be reshaped by "perturbing" events, which break the regulated temporality governing relationships between groups. This phenomenon is clearly visible in the biographical trajectories of many activists, who often report that triggering events determined their commitment to the cause. Although such "foundational events" should clearly be viewed with a certain skepticism, because they can easily reflect efforts to edit autobiographies retrospectively, it is impossible to disregard them completely, particularly when in view of the emotional aspect of such life-changing decisions.[33] The evidence suggests that the earliest activists of the future PJAK, annoyed by the lack of prospects offered by the KDPI and the Komala, were deeply influenced by the escape and subsequent arrest of Abdullah Öcalan, the PKK leader, in 1998-9.[34] In February 1999, tens of thousands of protesters gathered in Sanandaj, Mahabad, Bokan, Urmia, and Kermansha, as well as Kamiaran. A state of siege was announced in Sanandaj, Kamiaran, and Mahabad, which was followed by a crackdown that left thirty dead in Sanandaj. It was at this time that student groups began to become more organized, although informal student clubs had existed for ten years, following the massacre at Halabja and the assassination of the KDPI leaders. Although some of these groups were quickly disillusioned by the Öcalan trial and his "betrayal" of the Kurdish movement,[35] others, who probably came under PKK influence earlier and had scrutinized Kurdish autonomy in Iraq, were driven into zones controlled by the PKK in Iraqi Kurdistan as early as 1999.[36] Helped by the numerous PKK guerrillas of Iranian origin, they gradually developed a real party that became a sister organization to Öcalan's organization.

Indeed, after 1999, and then in 2001, the PKK lost government support due to Turko-Syrian and Turko-Iranian alliances, at a time of increasing talk of an American intervention in Iraq. In parallel, the early 2000s represented a crucial period in terms of redefined political objectives and methods for continuing the Öcalan party's struggle. The prospect of independence or autonomy for Turkey's Kurdish regions had lost relevance, and after 2003 demands focused on the idea of a "Democratic Confederation of the Middle East" and later on "democratic confederalism." It was within this context that the Party for a Democratic Solution for Kurdistan (Parti Çareseri Demokrati Kurdistan, PÇDK) was established in Iraq in April 2002, the PYD in September 2003 in Syria, and the PJAK in April 2004 in Iran.[37] Although these parties were formed over a period of two years, it was clearly essentially for technical reasons, because as early as September 2002 there was talk of establishing three sister PKK organizations: the PÇDK in Iraq, a certain "Selahaddin Eyyubi Movement" in Syria, and finally a provisional "Kurdistan Movement for Freedom and Fraternity" in Iran.[38]

It is therefore clear that a group of autonomous individuals—not highly organized, but deeply affected by foundational international and regional events—came under the wing of an experienced organization, and began to act collectively in an organized way, leading to armed struggle against Iran as early as 2004. More in-depth analysis will be required to establish, for example, whether the Kurdish students who initiated these mobilizations possessed local or "peripheral" resources (which is likely), or whether they had strong cultural capital instead that might have enabled them to become part of more "central", established networks.[39] It is evident that joining a larger organization cannot take place without conflict, as was the case with the PYD in Syria.[40] In 2005, a group called the "PJAK Reorganization Committee" seceded and moved to Iraqi Kurdistan under the name Kurdistan Democratic Union. In the same year, a group of members of this group in turn seceded to create an ephemeral organization called the "Kurdish alliance."[41] Most PJAK members nevertheless remained within the sister organization of the PKK, enabling a sustained armed struggle that ended only in 2011.

Without actually giving rise to a fully-fledged political party or a guerrilla fighting force, various other events, often violent, contributed to the emergence of relatively spontaneous movements in Iranian Kurdistan in the 1990s and 2000s that proved to be more or less long lasting. These "riots" reveal unequal power struggles between two groups, or rather between a group and the state, which is the guarantor of the established hierarchy. These violent riots are usually reactive, and they can be unleashed when an incident challenges the hierarchy or, on the contrary, when it makes the hierarchy more visible, increasing its presence in daily life. This sometimes occurs during "forbidden" inter-group marriages, when "privileged" access to certain sites is called into question (which occurred at the Al-Aqsa Mosque in Jerusalem, in the case of the Palestinians). Riots can also be triggered, as described earlier, when the land of reference of a group becomes subject to territorial redefinition. Finally, violence can break out when domination becomes so intolerable that a group is overwhelmed by a collective feeling of indignation, such as the riots in July–August 2005 in Mahabad, Baneh, Bukan, Divandareh, Oshnaviyeh, Piranshahr, Sanandaj, Saqqez, and Sardasht, after the death of the young Kurdish man in Mahabad whose body was dragged behind a security forces jeep.

This type of riot occurred again in early May 2015, when news began to circulate that a member of the Iranian intelligence services had attempted to rape a young woman named Farinaz Khosrawani, who then allegedly jumped from the fourth floor of the hotel where she worked and died on impact. Protests were held on 7 May in Mahabad, where the events had taken place, but also in Sardasht, Sanandaj, Marivan, Oshnaviyeh, and Saghez, as well as in Kurdistan in Iraq, Turkey, and Syria. The hotel in Mahabad was sacked and burned by the protesters, and hundreds of arrests and interrogation summons followed. The subsequent crackdown left dozens more wounded. A few days later, the deputy governor of Western Azerbaijan province offered a rival version of the facts, according to which the young woman apparently had a tryst with the suspect and attempted to flee after the hotel manager had told her mother about it. She then fell and was killed after attempting to escape through the window. Muhtadi's Komala contradicted this version of events by reasserting the accusation of attempted rape shortly afterwards, supported by his own arguments. On 14 May, a general strike was announced in Mahabad, Sanandaj, Sardasht, Bokan, Shino, Piranshar, Ashnaviyeh, and Urmiye, and the strikers demanded that the individuals responsible for Khosrawani's death be brought to justice and that the protesters currently under arrest be freed. Protests were held in various European capitals as well, and on the same day, the Free and Democratic Society of Eastern Kurdistan (Komalgay Demokratîk û Azadiya Rojhilatê Kurdistanê, KODAR, a political organization created by the PJAK in 2014) called for the democratization of the Iranian regime, asserting that if no action was taken, it would fight for the unilateral creation of a self-governed Rojhelat, on the model of Syrian cantons. On 15 May, under circumstances that remain unclear, violent confrontations with government security forces erupted, leaving at least one fatality. Tensions rapidly fell, however, and were followed by more ordinary forms of repression, including routine intimidation, summons, arrests, and regular executions of individuals convicted of pro-Kurdish activities.

Clearly, without necessarily challenging the government in the medium or long term or serving as an instrument for preserving the status quo (which is profoundly inegalitarian), the many riots among nearly every minority over the past thirty-five years provide irrefutable evidence that certain outrageous events are simply unacceptable to the groups concerned. For the protesters, not reacting would be tantamount to accepting renewed devaluation of their identity. Stigmatized by the regime, each violent episode could potentially have engendered broader and longer-lasting mobilization if it had received stronger support and back-up from political organizations, as the inevitable crackdowns after each riot provoked attempts by armed groups to avenge the population.[42] But this Clausewitzian logic is not automatic, and it is simultaneously dependent on the political configurations at work and on the conjunction of diverse specific factors.

Conclusion

As this chapter has argued, the movements to protest against the prevailing ethnic and religious hierarchy in Iran typically pursue a range of processes that sometimes overlap. Extraordinary events that accentuate or, on the contrary, weaken the hierarchy among ethnic or religious groups—such as publicly avowed human rights violations, for example—can initially be perceived as "turning points", constituting moments in which actors' identities become reconfigured, both by and through mobilization. Economic, social, and political changes on the periphery can also often engender the reconfiguration of identity-based systems and can easily help facilitate the rise of protest movements. This can ultimately give rise to hope when the government appears to become open to redefining the hierarchy, as occurred during the Iranian Revolution, but also again with the rise to power of the reformers in 1997.

From this perspective, Hassan Rouhani's election in 2013 clearly failed to generate the same expectations and hopes as Khatami's election, as though the earlier failure of the reformers had led minorities to become somewhat disillusioned about the prospects for regime change from within. The peripheral regions also appear no longer to feel as concerned by the policies of the center as they once were. In late July 2015, after the signature of the historic Iranian nuclear agreement, and two months after the riots in Mahabad, Hassan Rouhani traveled to Sanandaj for the first time to promote ethnic and religious equality in Iran. He promised new investments in Kurdistan province, especially dams and roads, and he announced the creation of university programs in Kurdish literature and Kurdish-language news programming in the official press agency, IRNA. He also confirmed that Iran supported its own Kurds in the same way that it defended Iraqi Kurds by fighting the Islamic State alongside the peshmergas. This was followed in September by the appointment of the first-ever Sunni (and Kurdish) ambassador to represent Iran abroad.

These various indications of a new opening are to some extent consistent with the 2013 electoral campaign, but it nevertheless elicited only muted enthusiasm among the Kurds. At the same time, the KDPI was reoccupying areas along the Iranian border, amid increasingly frequent clashes between Revolutionary Guards and PJAK guerrilla fighters. To certain observers, President Rouhani is merely copying a strategy adopted by Turkey between the late 2000s and the June 2015 legislative elections:

promoting minimal cultural reforms as a means of depoliticizing the Kurds' demands, while simultaneously circumventing the various Kurdish Iranian political organizations by relying on the Iraqi KDP and especially the PUK. Given the Iranian institutional context, it would probably be unrealistic to expect major reforms regarding Kurdish demands or, more broadly, the demands of the country's other ethnic and religious minorities. At the same time, it will be difficult for Tehran to avoid addressing crucial questions that undermine its internal stability and that have extensive regional and international ramifications.

23.

FELLOW ARYANS AND MUSLIM BROTHERS

IRANIAN NARRATIVES ON THE KURDS

Walter Posch

Multicultural and harmonious Iran

In this chapter we try to explain the relationship of the Iranian Kurds with Iran as seen from the central government's perspective. Doing so means taking two aspects into account, both being state-centric and ideological at the same time: one is Iran acting as a multi-ethnic nation state; the other one is the regime trying to implement its eclectic ideology. In either case, scholars and intellectuals from the Islamic Republic employ certain narratives. Narratives that are ideologically and politically relevant[1] like these are necessary for shaping and expressing political identities, helping formulate and maintain worldviews, political discourses, and ideology, and therefore serve—or challenge—political power. Most importantly, narratives simplify complex situations into a clear chain of events and thus help to shape the present.

In order to understand the narratives employed, we have to analyze (1) Iranian national identity and ethnicity, and (2) the relationship between Iran and its Kurds, both of which should help us (3) to explain how the Islamic Republic reacts to Kurdish nationalism, which Tehran sees as a threat. As our focus is on narratives rather than on the minutiae of contemporary developments, we have (a) consulted literature produced in Iran by Iranian scholars, some of them affiliated or at least related to security institutions of the country; and (b) eschewed going into details of current affairs: for these we rely on the articles of Stansfield and Ahmadzadeh, and Bayat.[2]

We may start our reflection with the main narrative on Iran's ethnic situation as promoted by Iranian elites, who contrary to some of their neighbors always recognized the country's ethnic and linguistic diversity. The Supreme Leader Ayatollah Ali Khamenei himself depicts Iran as a multicultural and multi-ethnic entity:

> I want everybody to know this: that the Islamic system understands multi-ethnicity (*tannavo'-e aqvâm*) in our great and vast country as an opportunity. Different traditions and different habits and customs and various mentalities and contrasts are opportunities, so the many elements of this nation can complement each other.[3]

Such a statement on behalf of Iran's highest authority is easily understandable. However, there are good reasons to take the official positive depiction of harmonious conviviality of Iran's ethnic groups with a pinch of salt. An "ethnic challenge" for Iran must exist, as this is the only reason to explain why the prestigious Centre for Strategic Research devotes much scholarly attention to ethnicity. For instance, this center issued in 2012 the third edition of Seyyed Reza Salehi-Amiri's over-600-page volume on *The Management of Ethnic Enmity in Iran* which proves the importance that the Iranian leadership devotes to this question, which is related to Iranian national identity.[4]

Iranian national identity: three narratives

Iran still bears many inclusive primordial features more typical of empires than of modern exclusive nation states.[5] The country's multi-ethnicity is firmly rooted in the geographic and historic character of *Iranzamin*, the heart of *Persophonia*, i.e. the area of the rule (*qalamrou*) of the Persian language, encompassing the confines of the modern nation-state.[6] The Persian center is almost like a citadel: separated by high mountain ranges and two seas, Iran has often been referred to as a fortress or an island: a place apart from its neighbors, not unlike the insular position of Britain vis-à-vis continental Europe.[7] Thus, Iran's geographic dimension is inseparable from the country's imperial legacy, which in turn is multi-ethnic by definition. Yet this concept of multi-ethnicity is not equally inclusive, as will be shown in the next section.

Modern Iran has basically two major narratives for integrating ethnic groups in the greater Iranian identity: to focus on common language and ethnic roots, and to stress Islamic brotherhood. Both narratives serve different ideologies and have been further diversified. These narratives have been applied sometimes in contradiction to one another, but more often in cooperation. They include such divergent narratives as the nationalist narrative on Persianness and Aryanness, a traditional Islamic narrative, a combined nationalist-Islamist and a pan-Islamist narrative.

With Iran ceasing to be an empire and becoming a nation state in the twentieth century, the relationship between multi-ethnicity and Iranianness had to be redefined.[8] Starting with the constitutional revolution of 1906, a monolingual vision of constructing Iran as a modern nation state was pursued. These efforts peaked under the rule of Reza Khan and Mohammad Reza Shah. During the two Pahlavis, Persian was promoted to the detriment of local languages, often in combination with racist Aryan propaganda. The equation Aryan (*âriyâi*)=Iranian was in itself a tool for national integration for the Kurds, Baluch, Gilak, Lur, Mazandaranis, and others. Even Turkish speakers like the Azeris were ascribed to the common Aryan version of Iranian heritage and thus integrated, albeit with a detour: their Aryan roots were quickly rediscovered;common Iranian genetic roots thus trumped the Azeris' Turkish mother tongue.[9] Aryanness, Persianness, or extremist Persian nationalism/chauvinism[10] in language and origin were combined with the dictatorship of the Shah[11] and became the sole defining element of Iranian identity, underpinning secular Iranian nationalism with a racist tone for which the term Pahlavism has been coined.[12] In political reality, the Pahlavist narrative on Iranian national identity had to discriminate between non-Persians and sidelined Islamic political discourses.

Islam in general and political Islam in particular have largely been seen as a clear opposite to secular nationalism. At first sight, this assessment can easily be confirmed. Stressing the brotherhood of all Muslims was easier for the Islamic Republic than for the Pahlavis. This attitude made it possible to give public recognition to the country's multilingual reality: Article 15 of the Iranian constitution, whilst referring to Persian as the official language, explicitly allows "the use of regional (*mahalli*) and tribal (*qoumi*)languages in the press and mass media, for teaching their literature in schools ... in addition to Persian."[13] And according to Article 19, "all people of Iran, whatever ethnic group or tribe they belong to, enjoy equal rights; and color, race, language, and the like do not bestow any privilege."[14] Even so, more than forty years after the Islamic revolution, there are still no schools for languages other than Persian, and the nature of the relationship between "ethnicity" or "ethnic minority" (*qoum, qoumiyat)* and the "nation" (*mellat*) remains complicated (see below).

It is important to understand that nationalism and political Islam are not necessarily enemies; in political reality they go well together. It was not only the outbreak of the war against Iraq which allowed nationalism to return a few years after the revolution with a vengeance, albeit in an Islamic revolutionary guise.[15] Already as early as the 1940s and 1950s, a group of radical Islamists calling themselves the *Fedâyân-e Eslâm* mixed pan-Islamic tenets with fervent nationalism. Their ideological legacy reverberates to this day in the security establishment and on the political fringes of the Islamic Republic's body politic (the hezbollahis).[16] These fringe groups had their heyday when many of them came to political power under Ahmadinejhad, who quasi-officially married Aryanism with Islamism and under whose presidencies ethnic tensions increased.[17]

In theory the ideology of the Islamic Republic of Iran promotes pan-Islamism. The underlying idea is that Iran should become the leader of the Islamic world, thus the Supreme Leader claims to be the Commander of the Faithful. But Iran's Islamism is supra-confessional in theory only; in reality it is perceived as Shia. Aware that Sunni Muslims would not accept this claim, some ideologues have argued that intra-confessional *fatvâs* issued by Khamenei and a thorough explanation of the meaning of *velâyat-e faqih* would be enough to convince the rest of the Islamic world to accept Iran's leadership.[18] The realities are however far from this, but Iran tried on occasion to make use of the influence of Iranian Sunnis abroad. This led to contradictory results with regard to the Deobandi-inspired Sunni clergy in Sistan and Baluchistan: domestically Tehran tries to control and to curtail their activities inside the country; whereas on the international level Tehran attempts to "play the Sunni card", i.e. they tolerate and support the foreign activities of Iranian Sunni organizations in countries with Sunni majorities, such as the Central Asian Republics.[19] In short, Sunni Islam is viewed as an opportunity on the international stage, but a serious domestic challenge.

None of the three main narratives on Iranian identity—Aryan, Islamic, and pan-Islamist—is inclusive enough to offer a common framework of reference to all groups in Iran.

An Iranian conundrum: ethnicity, minority, and nation

Iranian terminology in the context of ethnicity is tricky, since the Persian and European terms are not at all congruent. The terms "ethnic group" or "ethnicity" (*qoum, qoumiyat*) have achieved their current meaning only recently, as dictionaries would still list "nation" and "tribe" for *qoum*. Likewise, one has to take into consideration that "nation" (*mellat*) also means people (*khalq*) and sometimes society (*jâme'e*)—no wonder Persian authors would often get confused themselves.[20] Yet generally speaking *qoum* resonates positively and non-discriminatorily in Iranian common and scholarly parlance. It is also clearly preferred to "ethnic minority" as employed by Western scholars.[21] One reason is that the term "minority" (*aqalliyat*) is usually employed to denote religious minorities, and some of them, like the Armenians or Assyrians, are also ethnic ones. Another aspect is the fact that the "majority-minority" dichotomy does not sufficiently address the reality of the 85 percent of Persian speakers who are not necessarily of Persian descent, to which one can add bilingualism, the thorny question of what is a mere dialect of Persian or what is a language, and related to all these aspects, the role of Persian as a cultural marker of Iranianness.[22] Hence some Iranian authors go so far as to reject the concept of "ethnic minority" as unfeasible for Iran.[23]

Salehi-Amiri tries to overcome the problem by distinguishing multi-ethnicity (*tanavvo'-e qoumi*) from multiculturalism (*takassor-e farhangi*). For both of these, he insists on the necessity of formulating cohesive strategies (alas, without further elaboration). The "dominating spirit of the constitution of the Islamic Republic is the explanation for the acceptance of the strategy of 'unity in multiculturalism.'" This strategy (if that term is applicable at all) seems to be explained as a "possibility of a multitude (*takassor*) of different sub-cultures (*khordeh-farhanghâ*) and ethnic groups (*aqvâm*) in a common legal framework (*chârchûb-e moshtarak-e mejâz*) and the recognition of multi-ethnicity and multi-culturalism."[24]

And this approach turns into the common identification of "Iranian" for all Iranians. Thereby "a sort of common-Iranian, super-ethnic cultural *koiné*" is postulated, which "is the main fundament of Iranianness today."[25] Iranianness can therefore be understood as the result of an "integration of local cultures and organic incorporation of their relevant elements" from which "the Iranian identity" emerges.[26] In this sense, multi-ethnicity and multiculturalism have to be understood as national identity per se. On the surface of things, one could read Salehi-Amiri's and Amanolahi's "cultural" approach as an adaptation of another concept: the *Kulturnation*. According to this the Iranian nation would be a "largely passive cultural community" (*Kulturnation*) rather than an "active political nation" or *Staatsnation*.[27] Understanding national and ethnic identities in a cultural sense could indeed be a possible way to deal with Iranian multi-ethnicity. However, such an understanding is misleading, because national identities are political concepts by definition, the more so in an ideological country like the Islamic Republic.

Furthermore, the "local cultures" in question—meaning Iran's ethnic groups—are not regarded as equal, as Ludwig Paul's analysis of Friday prayer sermons from the 1980s to the 1990s has shown: On top of this understanding of Iranianness with almost no difference are the Shia, i.e. Persians and Azeris,[28] followed by the Sunnis and the non-Muslim recognized minorities at the bottom. Nomadic tribes, taking an intermediate position between Sunnis and Shia and Bahais, are not counted at all. "It is obvious", concludes Paul, "that the various groups constituting the Iranian nation are not attributed the same degree of 'Iranianness.'"[29]

Iranian experts and decision-makers are more aware than anyone else of this problem. Their definition of the issue takes as their point of departure a very Western understanding of ethnicity, namely Anthony D. Smith's *National Identity*[30], which they try to adapt to Iranian circumstances:

> According to the constitution[31] the ethnic minorities can be classified in three groups: 1) ethnic groups (*goruh-e qoumi*) that distinguish themselves strictly from the viewpoint of ethnicity and form a group on their own without the peculiarities of confession (*mazhab*) or religion (*din*), such as the Azeris; 2) the group of ethnic-confessional minorities (*aqal-liyat—e qoumi-mazhabi*), like the Kurds and the Baluch; and 3) the group of religious minorities, like the Armenians and others.[32]

This concept in itself has two major flaws. Firstly, it does not address all groups in Iran, such as Shia Kurds or those groups—Sunni and Shia alike—whose languages are generally subsumed as Persian dialects, such as Taleshi, Gilak, and Mazandaranis, let alone Azeri and Persian Sunnis. Secondly, it tries again to combine Islamic religious terminology with an ethnic secular one; the Shia Azeris are an "ethnic-group" whilst the Kurds and Baluch are ethnic-confessional minorities. In other words, to their great displeasure Iran's Sunnis are pushed toward the category of non-Muslims, which is a clear contradiction of revolutionary Iran's pan-Islamist ideology. Hence, even if the political leadership gives multi-ethnicity in Iran a positive spin, and despite all the scholarship devoted to a positive cultural reading, the topic remains highly politicized in a negative way.

Political role and securitization of qoumiyat

It is in politics that the discriminatory side of Iran's inclusive Iranian identity becomes most evident, because the official recognition of multi-ethnicity within Iran's body politic also limits the political role of ethnicity in Iran. According to Abbas Vali, "the ethnic community [i.e. the *qoum*] and its history are local", therefore "they lack political and discursive autonomy" and "have no political rights vis-à-vis the sovereign."[33] Political sovereignty as described in the constitution of the Islamic Republic of Iran contains two different and inherently contradictory concepts: a divine one, namely the rule of the jurisprudent (*velâyat-e faqih*, i.e. the Supreme Leader); and a popular-democratic one ("the people"). Both principles are in different ways problematic when it comes to addressing minority rights.

The popular-democratic principle—whose most vociferous adherents can be found within the reformist political camp—stresses citizenship (*hoquq-e shahrvandi*), i.e. the rights of the "people" or the "nation" vis-à-vis the Supreme Leader. During the two Khatami presidencies, the debate on civil society, reform, and citizenship did indeed include questions of language rights. Yet key terms such as "people" and "nation" are defined as Persian and the relevant political discourse has been and is conducted in Persian and hence ignores local cultures and minority rights, or at best, pays only lip service to them. The reason for this is simple: since the reformist discourse aims to strengthen the republican, i.e. constitutional, rights of citizenship, it could not chart new waters beyond what has been laid down in the constitution; it thus confines the expression of ethnicity to the general formula of "observance of citizens' rights."[34] Following this logic, language rights would be dealt with in the framework of citizens' rights, which is similar to how Turkish liberals tried to address their own Kurdish issue.[35]

The concept of *velâyat-e faqih* on the other hand neither recognizes any form of nationalism (*melli-garayi*) or ethnicity-based politics (*qoumiyat-garayi*), nor does it draw a strict line between Sunnis and Shia. Instead, it stresses the unity and brotherhood of all Muslims, the *ummah*. Even so, for Iran's Sunni population the *velâyat-e faqih* is perceived as a foreign concept in three ways:

- as a Shia concept, pan-Islamic undertones notwithstanding;

- of Persian identity, even if the current Supreme Leader is an ethnic Azeri;

- as the embodiment of Tehrani centralism.

Hence the institution of *velâyat-e faqih* does not help to integrate Iran's Sunnis into Iran's body politic, even when the office holder, Supreme Leader Khamenei, tries his best to do so. On the contrary, by its very Shia nature *velâyat-e faqih* embodies discrimination against Iranian Sunnis and "distrust of the Sunnis in the upper echelons of the clerical state and such institutions as the armed forces", still an ongoing reality.[36] The result is discrimination, as can be seen in mere economic facts: Iran's poorest provinces are also the ones where the majority of the population adheres to the Sunni confession of Islam. This is not to say that there is an active policy of depriving Iran's Sunnis, predominately Kurds, Baluch, and Turkmens. But since local Sunni elites have not the same access to economic decision-making processes and investment planning as the Shia, deprivation of Sunni provinces is quasi-institutionalized.

Hence, neither concept offers much for cultural or confessional divergent ethnicities. As a result, the inclusive concept of Iranianness comes with partial exclusion; therefore, inclusion and exclusion can be regarded as two sides of the same coin of Iranian multi-ethnicity. Furthermore, the conditions of inclusion as well as the realities of exclusion have to politicize ethnicity in Iran, making the ethnic question one of the most important problems of the Islamic Republic. What makes things worse is the securitization of the ethnic question in Iran.

In spite of all the virtues of Iranian multiculturalism and recognition of multi-ethnicity at the highest political level and within the wider political and academic community, the core issue for Iranian decision-makers is the management of diversity in favor of the ultimate aim of the Iranian nation-state, that is Iran's national unity:

> Starting [with the insight] that national harmony and unity results from the conviviality of the ethnic groups (*aqvâm*) one has to undertake an effort to formulate the content and form of ethnic policies (*siyâsathâ-ye qoumi*) in a way that would not disturb the principle of the harmony of the society (nation).[37]

The timid formulation according to which "ethnic policies" should not disturb ethnic harmonies points to the heart of the problem and explains, for instance, why there are still no local languages taught in schools, recent developments in Kurdistan notwithstanding.[38] It becomes even clearer when one looks at the long list of threats to national harmony or unity recorded by Salehi-Amiri, which includes almost all civic rights: such as the right of free association, an increase of political, societal and cultural demands, organizing new political groups, cultural and religious/confessional societies, a demand to obtain higher positions in the administration, increase of publication in local languages, incompetence in speaking Persian, strengthening of extremist (*efrâti*)[39] ethnic and confessional feelings among experts, intellectuals and ethnic political parties, protests and harsh critiques of officials, strengthening of the ethnic identity and weakening of the national identity. Addressing these points by say easing restrictions on cultural demands, investments, or anti-discriminatory measures would only lead to even more demands.[40] Hence, the same Iranian authors employ two contradictory narratives: one on multicultural peaceful conviviality of all ethnic groups in Iran, and the other on national harmony and unity. This logic reveals great distrust on behalf of at least parts of the Iranian administration toward any kind of political activities by ethnic groups, and confirms Abbas Vali's argument that ethnic groups are not entitled to be political actors on their own. Rather, a management of Iran's ethnicities is envisioned, whereby among the "managers" (*modirân*), state institutions of the security apparatus are given a prominent role to play.[41] This point is a further confirmation of the securitization of Iran's ethnic diversity, although it must be stressed that unlike the Kurdish issue in Turkey, securitization is not an official doctrine and the regime is well aware of the risks of securitization.

But securitization of ethnicity has deep roots in the Islamic Republic: Iran's Turkmens, Baluch, and Kurds were among the first to revolt, and consequently had to experience the Islamic regime's security-centered approach at the beginning of the revolution in the early 1980s. The political importance of these fights must not be underestimated, since leading figures of the Islamic Republic were either fighting there, or they held positions in the provincial administration at the height of the fights; these include IRGC commanders Mohsen Rezai, Yahya Rahim-Safavi and Mohammad Jaafari, who had their first combat experience in Kurdistan, and also Qasim Soleimani, the commander of the Qods Branch of the IRGC. Soleymani was in Kurdistan and Western Azerbaijan at the same time as a certain Mahmoud Ahmadinejhad, later to become president of the Islamic Republic of Iran; together with Esfandiar Rahim Mashai, they belonged to a clique of Orumiyeh, headed by governor Alireza Sheykh-Attar, who would later make a career in Iran's diplomatic corps and who is also a renowned expert on the Kurdish issue.

Iran and its Kurds: securitization, social policy, and poverty

Common wisdom has it that Kurds were not the most rebellious ethnic group in Iran, as nationalist feelings among Iranian Kurds (*kurdayeti*) were rather underdeveloped, at least in comparison to Iraq. Furthermore, Kurdish elites were said to have been better integrated into Iran's body politic than elsewhere in the region.[42] But the new regime faced its most important security challenge in Kurdistan. Tehran succeeded quickly in quelling Kurdish ethnic unrest and driving out all secular and left-wing political groups of the Kurds, most notably the KDP-I, Komalah, and Khebat. Several deals with religious and traditional leaders of the different Kurdish communities in the early 1980s drove a wedge between leadership of the nationalist Kurdish parties and the ordinary Kurdish population in the country; and a set of security arrangements with the leaders of Iraqi Kurdish organizations denied Iraqi-Kurdish territory as a base for operations for their fighters, the peshmerga.[43] The assassination of Abdolrahman Qasemlou, the KDP-I's charismatic leader, in 1989 in Vienna[44] and the murder of his successor, Sadeq Sharafkandi, in 1994 in Berlin[45] were seen as the regime's *coup de grâce* for the KDP-I in peculiar, and Iran's Kurdish movement in general. As seen from Tehran's perspective, there were good reasons to believe that these murders could have "solved" Iran's Kurdish issue, hezbollahi-style.

After the neutralization of the KDP-I and Komalah in the early 1990s, the Iranian authorities focused on the regional aspects of the Kurdish issue. Kurdish politics were conducted as part of a wider political equation in the region, rather than as a domestic issue. There was a clear priority to prevent any nationalist spill-over effects from the emerging zone of Kurdish self-rule in northern Iraq, where Iran competed with Turkey for influence. Even so, Tehran and Ankara's interests converged in the sense that they wanted to stabilize the Iraqi Kurds, enough to enable them to counterbalance Saddam Hussein's central government in Baghdad, but keeping them weak enough to stop them separating from Iraq or developing irredentist capacities toward Iran and Turkey. During the 1990s, this policy of "omni-balancing" went considerably well for Iran, as it also took the role of outside actors into consideration, namely the US.[46] Yet Kurdistan remained a major challenge for the Islamist regime, mainly due to ideological and social domestic reasons and changed international circumstances, such as the 2003 US intervention in Iraq.

One of the main problems of Iran's Kurdish provinces is home-made and relates to the discriminatory nature of the Persian-Shia state: poverty. Even Iranian officials had to admit to the high rates of poverty in Kurdistan and West Azerbaijan, for which they usually hold responsible the previous regime, the long Iran-Iraq war, and of course foreign imperialist intervention.[47] Although at least some of these arguments are valuable, officials hardly ever mention the obvious correlation between poverty and confessional affiliation. Rather, Iranian officials would point to the measures undertaken by the government to remedy the situation: for instance, investment and development programs, such as road-building projects conducted by the provincial authorities and the Ministry of Agriculture Jihad.[48] Another important point of the government's investment and development programs was the opening of border markets with Iraq: the border markets of Tamarchin of Piranshahr and Kileh of Sardasht are some of the most profitable in the country.[49] In Ministry of Agriculture JihadKurdish cities are lauded as being among the best supported concerning social welfare and benefits, including the possibility of taking insurance. The refinery in

Mahabad and a big sugar factory near Bukan should further help reduce poverty.[50] Other social services are provided too: for the families of war veterans, public housing, factories etc. Education too has improved since Peyam-e Noor University and Islamic Azad University have opened branches in many Kurdish cities.[51] However, cultural life in Kurdistan is poorly developed: cinemas, galleries, theaters, etc. are hard to find, although the cultural scene definitely benefited from Khatami's liberalization.[52] From an analytical perspective, it would be wrong to argue that Iranian authorities are not investing in the Kurdish provinces, but results are sobering as the contribution of Kurdistan's economy to the national economy remains very low, or almost non-existent,[53] and even Iranian sources admit reluctantly to mismanagement by officials in the provinces.[54]

Furthermore, most investment and job creation programs are run by "the sacred institution of the Guardians of the Islamic Revolution", and therefore are part of the securitization of the Kurdish provinces. Among these are construction and urbanization projects in Kurdistan province, conducted by the enterprises belonging to the IRGC. They also employ local Sunnis throughout the country "as an example of Islamic unity."[55] But for Iran's Islamic authorities, the securitization of Iran's ethnic question in general and the Kurdish issue in peculiar is neither the only nor the preferred way to deal with the problem. Yet it became the dominating paradigm, and remains so until this day. Kurdish political activists would criticize the security-based approach as counterproductive, and had it softened under Khatami. The Supreme Leader too complains about a security-centered approach and the ongoing militarization of the Kurdish provinces; if a third of the means for these efforts had been spent on cultural issues, then, he is convinced, better results could have resulted.[56] The following excerpt from a speech by the Supreme Leader shows in a nutshell the Iranian dilemma: on the one hand, Khameneh invokes Kurdistan's identity as part of Iran's *Kulturnation*, which he tries to promote as a main narrative on the Iranian Kurds; and at the same time he voices concerns about a security-centered approach:

> This province is in my view a cultural province (*ostân-e farhangi*). I have repeatedly said that there are some who try to make this province a securitized and militarized province. Thus they turn the truth upside down. This is something the Islamic Republic didn't do and quite naturally cannot do. Who did this? The enemies of the Islamic Republic have propagated that the Islamic Republic neither likes nor accepts the Kurdish people (*qoum-e Kord*) or Sunni confession (*mazhab-e ahl-e tasannon*). This was a lie and is the opposite from reality![57]

The importance of culture and learning are leitmotivs in Khamenei's speeches. In this vein, Iranian security experts made use of modern Western scholarship. For instance, the research office of the provincial government (*ostândâri*) of West Azerbaijan had Kurdish and Western scholarly literature on the Kurds translated into Persian, analyzed, and the result compiled and published in a very limited edition to be distributed to Iranian decision-makers responsible for domestic and international aspects of the Kurdish issue.[58] In combination with the experience of the previous regime's security apparatus and new revolutionary zeal, the authorities would begin to formulate a new narrative aiming to bind the Iranian Kurds to the Islamic Republic. Elements of this narrative are intended to appeal to Kurds and Iranians likewise, and fall within the framework we have established in the previous section on Iranian identity: they are (a) historic-linguistic, i.e. an Iranian argument; and (b) an Islamist one. They are worth analyzing as they help understand the regime's ideological nature and the tensions between the Kurds and the regime.

Fellow Aryans and Muslim Brothers

The establishment of the Islamic Republic of Iran was based on outwardly pan-Islamist but essentially Shia tenets. This had to lead to a double rupture with the non-Shia parts of the Kurdish elites: for the pious Sunnis, the concept of *velâyat-e faqih* has not much appeal, as one could see in the lackluster enthusiasm to join the *basij*[59] and the secularist Marxism-inspired Kurdish modernizers opposed the religious-based regime from the beginning. And both groups would only partially accept the secular, pan-Iranian narrative depicting them as fellow Aryans serving Iran.

The historic-linguistic argument used to explain the relationship between Iran and its Kurds is still valid though, and not only among secularists. It combines the "Pan-Iranian" narrative with a certain reading of history where Kurds play a central role as Iranians. This political and historic narrative stresses the natural bond of the Kurds with Iran. For instance, throughout history Kurds have played an important role as border guards, and they were trustworthy supporters of Iran [60]:

> because throughout their ancient history the Kurds of *Iranzamin* have shown a lot of sacrifices for the defence and security of the territorial integrity of greater Iran [fulfilling] their role as experienced border guards (*marzdârâni rashid*) and fighters.[61]

Apparently there is some recognition that Iran's Kurds are not separatists, unlike those of other countries. In this context the Aryan narrative of the 1930s is employed, which we showed had reappeared during the heyday of the Islamic Revolution. Accordingly, common historic experience is invoked, going back to pre-Islamic times, but also to common ethnic roots (race, *nezhâd*).[62] Because "even before the Persians became Iranians the Kurds were Iranians", therefore one intellectual argues that "separating the Kurds of Iran from Iran is impossible and tantamount to suffocation", whereas Kurds "separating from Iraq, Turkey and Syria is possible and tantamount to the Kurds taking a fresh breath" and finally joining Iran.[63] How strong this narrative is can be seen in the Basiji magazine *Okhovvat*. Even Iran's pan-Islamists feel the need to stress that the Kurds belong "to the purest Iranian races and peoples"[64] as they are part "of the most ancient peoples of Aryan origin."[65] According to some Iranian nationalists, it is the Kurds' Aryan origins that bind them to Iran:

> The Kurdish people belong to the ethnic groups of Aryan origin. Additionally to Iran they also live in other regions of the Middle East and the Caucasus. According to historic documents they were one of the most important tribes [*eyâlât*, recte *îlât*] from the emergence of Greater Iran, of which the current landscape (*sarzamin*) is only a small part until the battle of Chalderan [in 1514]. The Kurdistan area was from 612 BC until the fifteenth century AD, that is, about 2000 years, an inseparable part of Iran.[66]

Hence, Pan-Kurdism is part of Pan-Iranianism, according to the phrase "wherever the Kurds are, there is Iran." This is so far interesting, as it was first formulated by those Kurdish intellectuals of the KDP-I who were shot in the Mykonos affair,[67] and it is still one of the main arguments of this banned party. The reading of Pan-Kurdism as part of Pan-Iranism provides another justification for Iranian support of the Kurdistan Regional Government based on racist rather than strategic arguments, because the "brothers of the same Iranian blood (*barâdarân-e ham khun*)", that is the Kurds of the KRG, should be supported against "non-Iranian enemies" in order to have "a puffer against the historic competitors of the Aryans."[68]

Thus, stressing the Kurds' Aryanness/Iranianness not only claims them for Iran, but it should also work as an ideological underpinning of Iranian foreign policy. It is not a surprise to see that Jafarzadeh's, Mir-Sanjari's, and Gharibi's articles were published in 2008, 2010, and 2011 respectively, that is under Ahmadinejhad who promoted the project of "Persophonia."[69] But these claims are phoney, as there are certainly many more important reasons than being "Aryan" determining and shaping Tehran's relationship to the KRG. The same can be said about the Aryan or pan-Iranian argument in general, which has lost much of its rhetorical potency. For instance, when President Khatami visited Kurdistan, he once again embraced the Aryan/Iranian narrative, claiming that "nobody has the right to claim to be more Iranian than the Kurds"; but at the same time a core demand of the Kurds' language instruction in Kurdish has been ignored.[70] This was due to the fact that reformists were not able to develop another more inclusive frame of reference for the relationship between Iran and its Kurds. Even worse, a certain "orientalist" (in the Saidian sense) reading of the Kurds became the main interpretation within reformist circles, coexisting with securitization.[71]

Another factor aggravating the relationship between the Kurds and the state is of course the Sunni confession. The fact that the majority of Kurds follow Sunnism is passed over with a simple argument: Sunnism in the case of the Kurds is seen as less a problem since they follow the Shafiite confession of Sunnism, which "has a great closeness to the confession of the majority of the Iranian nation – Shiism."[72] Yet the confessional differences are recognized and understood as a threat, especially in the provinces (*ostân*) of Kurdistan and Western Azerbaijan. However, more important for Iran's pan-Islamist vocation is the potential Iranian Islamists' hope that Kurdistan could offer to support Islamic unity under Iranian leadership. In this task, the role of the clergy (*ruhâniyat*) of Kurdistan is clearly defined:

> In fulfilment of their very special task which is the publication and spreading of the noble Islam, the Sunni clergy in the region shall exercise this duty and function in such a beautiful way that in the execution of this very duty they fulfil one [special] function [namely] the safeguarding of the unity of Islam.[73]

This unity will be achieved by reverting to Imam Shafii, whose *feqh*, as Iranian authors always stress, is closest to Shiism, and who had paid his respect to one of the Shia imams, Zeyn el'Abedin; this is a not so hidden argument to tell Iran's Sunni Kurds to submit to Shia Iran. Even more, Sunni-Shafii Kurds, just like the Shias, have a great love for the imams, as can be seen by the names of the twelve imams given to their children, panegyric poetry lauding them, the presence of so many saintly tombs (*emâmzâdeh*), etc.[74] The cultural proximity is thought to have a positive impact on inter-confessional relations in Iran and the wider Islamic world. The key institution to promote Islamic unity is the Great Islamic Centre for the West of the Country (*markaz-e bozorg-e eslâmi-e gharb-e keshvar*), which was created in the early 1980s. This center is headed by Ayatollah Muhammad Hoseyni Shahrudi, the Supreme Leader's deputy in Kurdistan. Its main task is promoting the "approximation" (*taqrib*) of the confessions.[75] It does so mainly by publications, training of the Sunni clergy, including opening a branch of the University of Islamic Confessions , issuing declarations and *fatva*s, and channeling them toward the principle of Islamic unity.[76]

Hence, Islamic brotherhood with Iran's Sunnis remains firmly under Shia control. This concept is clearly paternalistic, because the Shia state institutions are in the lead in defining the "function" of the Sunni clergy to promote "approximation" of the confessions. It is therefore important to understand that the Iranian term "Islamic unity" (*vahdat-e eslâmi*) has less to do with ecumenical questions, but relates to national security, because "defending Islam is defending the Islamic Republic of Iran and this is related to Islamic unity." Supreme Leader Khamenei formulates it this way: "I pay great importance to national unity, because security emerges from unity; when there is no unity, then national security is threatened."[77] The Kurdish Sunni clergy's task as seen from the regime's perspective is to maintain Muslim brotherhood in the country. However, basing state control over Iran's Sunnis on the clergy might turn out to be the wrong investment, in face of new challenges.

It is highly ironic that one of the biggest and certainly the most pertinent threat for both Islamic unity and the Islamic Republic itself is political Islam. Radical Sunni, i.e. Wahhabi and Salafi groups, are often said to have been supported by the US and other powers[78] who allegedly promote "Bahaism and Wahhabism."[79] Radical Sunni propaganda must have got some traction among Iranian Kurds, and theological debates and different interpretations of the *feqh* very often get heated and are viewed as threats to Islamic unity, i.e. they are treated as threats to national security.[80] A main point of grievance must be the accusation that Shias would distort the Quran.[81] Salafism especially seems to have become a formidable counter-movement against the Islamic Republic's authorities, and traditional Kurdish society likewise. During the 2000s throughout Kurdistan, and recently also in the Kurdish parts of Khorasan, pious Salafist communities (*jemaat*) emerged: organized in "ideal cities", they follow the principle of "denunciation and self-exile" (*takfir va hejrat*). Outwardly they stay out of politics, for instance they do not participate in elections. Yet they chart new waters beyond the failure of radical Sunnism, such as Ansar al-Islam in Iraqi Kurdistan and the Kurdish secular parties and organizations on one side, and the Shia Islamic Republic on the other.[82] This development is reminiscent of other Sunni regions, for instance in Pakistan and Baluchistan with the Deobandis, or among the Turkish Kurds with the Hizbullah Cemaati. Thus the question remains whether and if so when the Kurdish Salafiya decide to go political, by say creating political organizations of their own.

The Iranian security analysts we have consulted do not pay special attention to the Salafist communities, and Western scholarship on them is with the notable exception of Dudoignon almost non-existent. We are therefore in no position to answer the pertinent question of whether and in which way they are connected to radical Sunnis of the jihadi branch abroad, notably the Islamic State, and if and how they are already in contact with Central Asian, Afghan, and Pakistani fundamentalists. The challenge of the Salafis and similar Sunni movements will certainly increase, although it is not clear whether they will follow the regional trend of mixing radical Islamist views with national identity. In any case, Kurdish groups in general find little attraction in Iranian narratives intended to bind them to Iran, but may pick on one or the other argument; but this is not the case with the Salafists, who for theological reasons cannot find any common ground with Tehran. Even so, Iranian security elites view Kurdish nationalism (*kurdayeti*) as a bigger threat anyway. Therefore we have to conclude that among Iranian Kurds, neither the Aryan narrative on Kurdish-Iranian brotherhood nor the narrative on common Muslim brotherhood dominates, whereas Kurdish nationalism does.

The KRG's impact on Kurdish nationalism: Kurdayeti, the threat of Kurdish nationalism

Whenever Iranian officials admit the existence of threats to national security in Kurdish populated provinces (i.e. Kurdistan and West Azerbaijan, less so Kermanshah, which has a Shia-Kurdish majority), then they would address these threats in Islamic terminology and invoke strengthening Islamic unity as a solution to everything. This is regardless of whether these threats are classified as hard security threats (*tahdid-e sakht*) or soft (*tahdid-e narm*), as both are taken equally seriously.[83] Iranian experts admit that Western powers were able to implement secularism (*sekulârism, lâ'ism*), socialism and liberalism, Marxism, communism, the left in general, and other ideologies among Iran's Kurds.[84] According to one estimate, more than fifty political groups are active among the Kurds of Iran.[85]

It is not only Western influence; after all, Iranian analysts are of course well aware of the importance of Kurdish nationalism (*kurdayeti*) with or without Marxist leanings.[86] One way to deal with it is to deny its significance and argue that Kurdish nationalism (*qoum-garâyi, kurdayeti*) in multi-ethnic regions like Kurdistan does not make any sense, and the increase of "national sentiment in the population is due to the lack of real understanding of the human nature."[87] As a consequence, Kurdish opposition groups have no real concerns; they are not at all home-grown, but result from foreign interventions.[88] Foreigners would intervene in Iran's Kurdish-inhabited provinces because of their strategic position and the great enmity that intervening powers, both Eastern and Western, have against revolutionary Iran.[89] Thus, the ideologies that local Kurdish political groups embrace are foreign in origin and supported only by parties and individuals who outwardly defend the rights of the Kurdish people, often by promoting the "false" Western notion of human rights (*hoquq-e bashar*), "but on the other hand they have no sincere relationship with the history, mentality, religion and values of the Kurds."[90] Furthermore, whether it is the KDP-I, Komalah, or Khebat, their reputation has been tarnished because during the Iran-Iraq war they were supported by Saddam Hussein and therefore kept their silence about his crimes against the Kurdish people. Hence Iran's Kurds understood their real intentions[91] and are well aware of the fact that "the work (*amalkard*) of the defenders of *kurdayeti* results in the brutality and treason of the Kurdish people."[92]

This said *kurdayeti* remains a threat which has to be taken seriously, because it is efficiently supported by Western media outlets, mostly satellite TV and radio. These outlets are generally accused of sowing discord between Kurds and other Iranians, and between Sunni and Shias. But they also promote the superiority of Western culture and Western cultural values, which in turns strengthens the ideological position of the opposition groups, especially when it comes to secularism.[93] Most Iranian Kurdish opposition groups have their own TV stations, such as the KDP-I's "Tishk TV" in Paris, Kurd-Channel in London, the Komalah's Rojhelat TV, the PJAK's Newroz TV, and the communist Komalah TV in Sweden; but also Zagros TV belonging to the KRG.[94] Iranian officials are indeed aware of their efficiency, because they broadcast in local (*mahalli*) languages.[95]

One of the greatest concerns for Tehran is the increasing demand for self-rule or autonomy (*khod-mokhtâri, khod-gerdâni*) and federalism among Iranian Kurds, for which Iraqi federalism serves as a role model. Iranian experts understand the Kurdish wish for autonomy as a first step toward full independence, which is regarded as the true ideal of the Kurds.[96] They evaluate this ideal from an Iranian national security perspective and hint at the fact that most if not all Kurdish movements aspiring to Kurdish independence were either foreign-sponsored or have allowed foreigners to intervene in regional affairs. This, so their argument goes, turned out as a major miscalculation on behalf of the Kurds, because throughout the twentieth century Kurdish nationalists have been dropped according to their supporting powers' own strategic calculation: the short-lived Republic of Mahabad of 1945-6 is the most telling example.[97] This narrative equates autonomy with separatism and connects it to foreign intervention, and finally it threatens promoters of autonomy/independence with the same fate as the proponents of Mahabad, whose most prominent members were executed. But vague ideas about autonomy and federalism have already got traction in Iran: in 2005 Hasanzadeh, the KDP-I's secretary general, met with representatives of the KRG, congratulating them for the federalism they had achieved.[98] During the first Khatami years, federalism and its possible introduction in Iran have been hotly debated.[99] Azeri intellectuals especially devoted much attention to it, some of them even concluding that only federalism would be able to secure the conviviality of Iran's ethnic groups and thus guarantee the survival of Iran.[100] As seen from Tehran's perspective, Iran's Kurds could become go-betweens connecting the political reality of Iranian Kurdistan with the intellectuals of Iranian Azerbaijan. Pooling forces, Iranian Kurds and Azeris would be strong enough to pressurize Tehran for significant political concessions. To the best of our knowledge, nothing tangible happened and a potential Azeri-Kurdish alliance would not come into being. Given the known resentments between the two groups, it might have been a hard sell anyway.

This said, Tehran has reasons to be concerned. After the fall of Saddam Hussein in 2003 and with the new Iraqi constitution of 2005 which made Iraq a federal country, the KRG became an important point of reference for all Kurds, boosting Kurdish self-confidence beyond the borders of Iraq.[101] Changes in the Iraqi constitution put the existence of the KRG on a solid legal basis and gave them a fair share of Iraqi oil revenues. According to one Iranian estimate, Kurdistan has after Iran and Qatar the seventh greatest proven reserves in natural gas. Therefore Hasan Bouzhmehrani and Mehdi Pour-Eslami concluded that the KRG can use these funds to conduct a policy of domestic stabilization and projection of soft power to all Kurdish regions, including those in Iran.[102] This would ultimately change the relationship between Tehran and Erbil. For decades the Iraqi Kurdish parties relied on military and political support from Iran. Therefore the Iranian authorities dealt with them mostly via the security apparatus and were ill-prepared for the new situation, although it did not take long for Tehran to understand what was at stake.

What makes the KRG such a formidable challenge is Erbil's promotion of *kurdayeti* Kurdish nationalism and combining it with Western principles such as human rights, democracy, freedom of expression, including in the media, its dealings with international organizations, and attracting international capital and promoting free economy.[103] The point here is not whether the KRG is already a beacon of liberal democracy and free enterprise: the KRG's own shortcomings in these fields did not go unnoticed by the Iranian Kurds; but it is with Erbil's potential that Iranian concern lies. As soon as the independence of Kurdistan became a political option, even if only in theory, Tehran warned the KRG and Mas'ud Barzani not to declare independence or to overplay the "Kurdish card."[104]

Perhaps even better than the KRG government itself, Tehran is aware of the important impact that cultural activities in Iraqi Kurdistan have for Iran. Iranian observers quote the high numbers of Kurdish newspapers in Erbil, the high numbers of Kurdish internet sites, and the existence of seven state universities, including an American University; all of them attract Kurds from Iran and Turkey too.[105] The KRG also actively supports festivals and meetings of Iranian Kurds, where the role of Mahabad and its leader Qazi Mohammad were honored. The Kurdish nationalist symbolism attached to him is a concern for many in Tehran, because the flag of the ill-fated Republic of Mahabad (red-white-green with sun) became the banner for all Kurds. Via the KRG, this banner created by Iranian Kurds achieved international recognition.[106] Tehran also views the Kurdistan regional government's cultural activities with distrust. Erbil introduced a series of permanent cultural events, from literature to history to music events, where Iranian Kurds are prominently present. Among them Iranian Kurdish music ensembles were perceived as a national security threat for the Islamic Republic of Iran, because they use art to promote pan-Kurdish propaganda, and their concerts are widely covered and broadcast to Iran.[107] But the Iranians also observe the limits of Iraqi-Kurdish soft power. The KRG's influence among the mostly Shia Kurds in Eylam and Kermanshah is much less significant; the same can be said about the Kurds of Khorasan.[108] Even so, the KRG remains a mixed blessing for Iran: as an important political partner, but at the same time as a rallying point for Iran's own Kurds.

The Kurdish vote

There are other ways to tackle Kurdish nationalism or *kurdayeti*, such as greater inclusion of Kurds in Iran's body politic. This was tried immediately after the revolution restrictions were eased and a Kurdish Sunni even became governor. This changed after hostilities between Kurdish groups and the government broke out. As a consequence, there were almost no Kurds employed in the local administrations. This situation was remedied only under Khatami when most district governors and administrators were Kurds.[109] Back then, the authorities undertook some kind of "devolution" by staffing the local and regional administration by up to 80 per cent with the local Kurdish population. Easing censorship resulted in a wave of publications on Kurdish issues in Kurdish and Persian, which influenced the younger generation of Kurdish intellectuals.[110] But international developments, namely the stabilization of the Kurdistan regional government in Iraq and the re-emergence of the PKK as an important trans-national Kurdish force, would pose a serious challenge for the way the Islamic Republic of Iran "handles" its Kurds.

In the 2000s Iran's Kurds got increasingly restless as they showed their dissatisfaction with current affairs.[111] Inspired by the new self-confidence emanating from the Kurdistan region, Iranian Kurds started relentlessly articulating well-known demands: among them support for Kurdish language and culture, an end to ethnic discrimination (*tabyiz-e qoumiyati*), an end to economic deprivation, and regional development figured most prominently.[112] Frustration runs high in Kurdistan, as regular mass protests show: in 2005 several government buildings were destroyed in Mahabad,[113] and similar incidents continued to take place throughout the two Ahmadinejhad presidencies and under Rouhani, the last time being in the same town in summer 2015.

But riots are not the preferred tool of political contestation: Iranian Kurds also use the ballot box. Abstention and participation in elections are powerful ways of political messaging. Khatami and after him Rouhani were able to rally the Kurdish vote, whereas Ahmadinejhad had almost no support in Iran's border provinces.[114] As a consequence, the Kurdish vote is tied to the reformist camp, which is a mixed blessing: the reformists take the Kurdish vote for granted, whereas appealing to the Kurdish vote for fundamentalist and neo-fundamentalist candidates such as Ahmadinejhad or Jalili is not attractive at all. It is still debated whether the fact that opposition parties KDP-I and Komalah encouraged the Kurds to participate in the 1997 elections[115] was key to Khatami's success in the Kurdish provinces, or not. However, the most important political act was the formation of a "Kurdish caucus" (*fraksyun-e Kord*) in the Iranian parliament. In this caucus, Kurds of several provinces would pool sources and get organized to promote Kurdish interests, such as the appointment of Kurdish Sunni governors and administrators. The caucus also voiced its opinion in international politics, as letters to Kofi Annan and the European parliament show, after which the situation of the Kurds in Iraq and Turkey was debated.[116] Iranian political factions and caucuses are very loose, and many initiatives seem to be on behalf of individual Kurdish deputies rather than the caucus. Even so, the creation of the caucus and its tolerance of the reformists were severely criticized and interpreted as "a soft security threat Iraqi Kurdistan poses against the Islamic Republic of Iran."[117] There is certainly a correlation between the increased prestige and international weight of the KRG and the formation of the Kurdish caucus in the Iranian parliament.

But for the time being, it is hard to gauge the real impact of the caucus on bilateral relations between Tehran and Erbil. In any case, the Kurdish caucus continues its activities, although concerns about an ethnic caucus in parliament still exist with the wider public. This is the reason why Kurdish deputies like Seyyed Ehsan Alavi stress that their activities remain firmly grounded in Iranian law and in the framework of parliamentary regulations.[118] He too criticizes the security-based approach toward

Kurdistan. It is however unlikely that this would change any time soon, because a changing strategic environment and the re-emergence of the PKK from 2003 onwards posed new challenges for Iran's security forces.

Return of the guerrillas: PKK/PJAK and KDP-I

Iran's relations with the PKK passed through several phases. During the 1980s and 1990s contacts were mostly sporadic and subject to the broader picture of Iranian Turkish relations.[119] Back then, Tehran viewed the PKK as a nuisance rather than a threat, even when in the aftermath of the detention of Abdullah Öcalan in 1999, protest in the Kurdish regions of Iran broke out. Tehran's nonchalance is understandable, because the protests were rather a spontaneous and disorganized outburst of sympathy for a fellow Kurd, and not at all organized and managed by the PKK's underground structures, which at that point were almost non-existent in Iran. The creation of the Party of a Free Life (PJAK) and its corresponding militia (HRK/ YRK) in 2003 changed the course of events.

PJAK is part of the Community of Societies of Kurdistan, or KCK as the new PKK is called.[120] Initially the Iranian security establishment misjudged the PJAK for two reasons: firstly, because party leader Abdurrahman Hajji Ahmadi lives far away in Germany and is in no position to direct military operations personally; and secondly, because they were used to dealing with the intellectual and educated cadres of KDP-I, Komalah, and Khebat, many of whom hailed from the traditionally politically active old local Kurdish elites. PJAK however politicized the downtrodden and poorer layers of society and recruited its fighters exclusively from them.[121] As a result, the Iranian security establishment which was used to knowing almost all activists and sympathizers of banned Kurdish organizations by name was caught by surprise and offered a classic interpretation: PJAK would simply be a tool for Western intelligence, pursuing counter-revolutionary and anti-Iranian aims.[122]

The PJAK's force, HRK, was trained by the PKK's main force, the HPG, and was initially used as a security detail for the organization's headquarters in the Qandil Mountains in Iraq.[123] Yet before long they made incursions into Iranian territory and, copying tactics the HPG applies against Turkey, they too attacked border posts mostly in the Sardasht region. In return Iranian artillery shelled some of the PKK camps on the other side of the border. But in 2008 the conflict took a new turn when a team of PJAK bombers was detained in Tehran. This came as a shock for Iran's intelligence services, because they were just boasting of having prevented terrorist attacks in the greater Tehran area since the creation of the Ministry of Intelligence in 1984.[124] But 2008–10 marked an increase in PKK/PJAK guerrilla attacks in the border provinces and bomb attempts in the metropolitan areas. It remains unclear to this day whether it was sheer luck or a well-planned operation when in 2011 a high-ranking commander of the PKK, probably Murat Karayılan, fell into the hands of

Iranian security forces. Tehran stopped its attempt at a ceasefire agreement on its own terms with the PKK leadership, which in turn ordered PJAK to leave the country. As seen from an Iranian perspective, the ensuing diplomatic brawl with Turkey was a cheap price to pay compared to the improvement of its own security.[125]

Whether formally signed or not, the security agreement between the PKK leadership and the Iranians held, to the chagrin of PJAK and HRK. The situation started to change by early 2013 when PJAK increased its activities in Iran.[126] In May–June the next year PJAK held its fourth regular party congress and reorganized its guerrillas: HRK was transformed to the Eastern Kurdistan Units (YRK) and the Women's Defence Forces (HPJ) were established. At the same congress a Persian adaption of the KCK manifesto was published under the name of "Manifesto of the Democratic and Free Society of Eastern Kurdistan – KODAR."[127] This paper was rejected by other Kurdish opposition groups, such as KDP-I or Komalah, both organizations having suffered time and again from the PKK/PJAK intolerance and overbearing demeanor toward them. The idea would be to establish "democratic autonomy" in Iran's Kurdish areas under the name of KODAR, which would be politically dominated by PJAK. This development is reminiscent of PKK's plans to establish autonomous self-rule in Syria and Turkey. Illusionary as it seems, it must still be taken seriously since KODAR is one of the few texts that actually tries to formulate a political alternative for the Kurds of Iran, underpinned by an assertive guerrilla movement.

The dramatic events around the siege of the Syrian Kurdish town of Kobanî in autumn 2014 politicized not only Iran's Kurds but many secularists and leftists in Iran too. Just as in Europe, Iranian media also covered the defenders of Kobanî: the People's Defence Units (YPG) and the Women's Protection Units (YPJ). The latter especially resonated positively with the secular layers of society.[128] And since YPG and YPJ belong to the PKK, the mother organization of PJAK, much of the prestige reflected on the PJAK and YRK, who at a certain point in time, probably in early summer 2014, had to send their fighters far away from Iran to locations in Iraq and Syria. Upon their return in early 2015, they tried to benefit from violent protests in Sanandaj and Mahabad in April, which Tehran answered by once again shelling PKK camps in Qandil. It is unclear whether the clashes between the PKK's main force HPG and the peshmerga of the KDP-I in May 2015, which occurred because the HPG denied the peshmergas free passage through Qandil into Iran, are directly related to the YRK's preparations to infiltrate Iran.[129] In any case, ever since summer 2015 minor clashes take place between Iranian forces and YRK fighters. Finally in mid-2015 the KDP-I joined the mix and infiltrated Iran once again, this time unmolested from HPG or YRK. Apparently the KDP-I are trying to mend fences with the PKK, as they have offered support for Rojava, that is Syrian Kurdistan.[130] This means that at least two Kurdish groups, KDP-I and PJAK, picked up arms against the Iranian authorities. As a result, one has to expect further securitization of Iran's Kurdish regions, something that bodes badly for the new president's reform agenda.

Conclusion: last chance Rouhani?

The election of moderate president Hassan Rouhani brought an experienced member of Iran's security establishment to power. Rouhani's government consists mostly of technocrats who try to improve Iran's economy and strengthen the rule of law. This also includes economic devolution and investment in the most impoverished Sunni provinces of Iran. But he has also embraced a reformist political language and stresses the rights of the citizen (*hoquq-e shahrvand*). A paper issued by the vice-presidency addresses the ethnic and confessional issues head on: article 3/21 reconfirms the constitution's promise of equality, and formulates a clause of non-discrimination regarding "cultural, ethnic, confessional and linguistic identities"; article 3/22 confirms the duty of the government to cooperate with Iranian radio and television to ensure the use of "local and ethnic languages alongside the Persian language and under preservation of national unity and the common Iranian identity"; article 3/23 allows the use of languages in associations "according to the law"; and 3/24 obliges the government to safeguard the cultural heritage of all ethnic groups. Article 3/129 reads like a confirmation that political and legal practice in Iran on confessions and ethnic groups needs improvement.[131] Regardless of what Rouhani has already achieved in this field, the awareness of the untenable ethnic and confessional discrimination in Iran of which (among others) Sunni Kurds are primary victims is widespread. This explains why two presidential candidates of the 2013 elections, both coming from the Revolutionary Guards, would address these topics head on: former commander of the IRGC Mohsen Rezai campaigned in favor of teaching local languages, and the former head of Iran's police Mohammad Baqer Qalibaf promised to promote Sunnis to higher positions, if elected.[132]

Hence, awareness is there, and Rouhani has already taken important steps. Perhaps inspired by the example of Turkey where chairs for teaching Kurdish have begun at some universities, the University of Sanandaj was allowed to teach some lessons in Kurdish language and literature in 2015.[133] Most likely voices like Salehi-Amiri's are right when they warn that any partial fulfilment of demands would lead to more demands: for instance, in early 2015 Kurdish intellectuals demanded language instruction in high schools in Saqez.[134] This speaks to those security-minded Iranian nationalists in the administration who fear that instruction in local languages will ultimately threaten Iran's national unity. Yet President Rouhani is not one to give in easily and he doesn't miss an occasion to stress the importance of the charter on citizenship rights. On 31 May 2016, for instance, Rouhani reconfirmed his government's anti-discriminatory stance concerning Iran's Sunnis and the right of language instruction. At a meeting in Mahabad, he stated: "all people of Iran, be they Shia or Sunni, are equal in their citizenship rights (*hoquq-e shahrvandani*)" and he confirmed that he is not satisfied that Iran has only one Kurdish-Sunni diplomat. At the same time he stresses his function as president of the Islamic Republic and as head of the

Higher National Security Council, indicating that Iran's security apparatus supports his stance, which is more than likely, given former generals' Rezai and Qalibaf positive stance on the topic.[135]

Even so, Rouhani is between a rock and a hard place. To begin with, his main card to play, economic development, does not bode well; and demands and hopes of the wider public and in the ethnic provinces are dashed. The combination of social and ethnic frustration in turn is the best recruiter for organizations like the PJAK. Furthermore, as seen from a central Iranian perspective, where Ahmadinejhad and his followers hold their votes, recent developments are seen as sign of weakness: Iran allows Kurdish language instruction at the university, and in return the security situation in the province deteriorates and emboldens further demands. One thing is clear: to invoke the narratives of common Aryan Iranian roots and common Muslim brotherhood will not be enough to address Kurdish grievances in a proper way and to help to find a common multi-ethnic and multicultural framework for all Iranians.

The problem may lie even deeper: Rouhani's approach to tackling the ethnic question in Iran as the reformists did, namely by formulating it as part of citizens' rights, may fail simply due to the inherent contradictions in the Iranian constitution, political practice, administrative incapacities, and ongoing securitization. This said, if a more inclusive Islamic Republic based on the rule of law is aspired to, then there is simply no other alternative to Rouhani's way, whose government might well be the Islamist regime's last chance anyway. The question is now whether Rouhani and his advisors will be able to create a new inclusive common Kurdish-Iranian narrative drawing on the existing narratives and underpinning them with rule of law and prosperity. If not, it will be unlikely that the younger generation of Iranian Kurds will have enough political patience and willingness to set all their hopes on Rouhani's reforms; then radical movements like PJAK or the Salafists, emboldened by regional events, would radicalize the younger generation further. This would be extremely risky; as the old Kurdish saying goes, states get weak and sick, but they just don't die.

PART 5

THE KURDISH QUESTION AND IRAQ

24.

THE KURDISH EXPERIENCE IN POST-SADDAM IRAQ

Gareth Stansfield

For the Kurds of Iraq, as for many peoples and communities across the Middle East and Islamic world, 11 September 2001 would constitute a watershed in their political situation. The next decade would see the Kurds emerge from relative obscurity, existing in an anomalous de facto entity with no legal basis, to being a core part of the new Iraq.[1] Their political leaders would make a swift transition from being relatively weak and highly defensive parochial figures with curricula vitae that, in 2001, displayed excellent records in internal war-fighting but a far more chequered record in governance and administration, to being the most mature and experienced members of the post-Ba'ath political elite that emerged in the months and years following March 2003. The scene was therefore set for the Kurds to consolidate their fragmented entity and to make the transition from being an anomaly on the map of the region, existing because of a series of events that had given the Kurds geopolitical space which they could exploit, to being a codified and legal reality in the form of a constitutionally defined and approved Kurdistan Region of Iraq.[2] Challenges would lie ahead, and often of a very serious nature. Whether it was ensuring that the Kurdish political front remained unified in the face of significant inter-party tensions, or finding compromises with their Iraqi partners in managing the affairs of the new state, or dealing with the pressures imposed by their Turkish and Iranian neighbors, or coping with the demands brought about by their own internal political and economic weaknesses in the 2013–16 period, the Kurdish existence in the post-2003 environment was certainly not straightforward. They had to struggle to negotiate their position in the new state; the Kurdistan Democratic Party (KDP) and the Patriotic Union of

Kurdistan (PUK) had to find a way by which they could manage their enduring antipathy in a theater in which other actors would exploit any obvious division; and they had to cope with a range of significant security challenges, including a near-death experience at the hands of the Islamic State of Iraq and al-Sham (ISIS) in the summer of 2014.[3]

By 2016, the Kurds of Iraq had somehow navigated the very stormy waters of Iraqi political developments; but even after twenty-five years of a seemingly upward trajectory, the future looked uncertain. Politically and economically, the elites had to confront uncomfortable truths. They had been in power since 1991, yet there was little evidence to suggest that the KDP in particular would easily relinquish control over the most significant governmental institutions, including the Kurdistan Regional Government (KRG) and the Kurdistan Regional Presidency (KRP). Politically, the Region was ostensibly unified, but in reality the KDP and the PUK remained the de facto local hegemons in Erbil and Dohuk, and Suleimani and Kirkuk respectively, and while they managed to hold together a working relationship that gave some semblance of unity to the Region, their decades-old competition for the accolade of being leader of the Kurdish nationalist movement in Iraq remained as energized and focused as ever before.[4] In the economic realm, the KDP-led initiative to develop an oil and gas sector independent of the government of Iraq had started well, with an increasingly vibrant sector being established from nothing, but which had run into serious problems caused by Baghdad's contesting the KRG's right to export oil independently, and by the collapse in world oil prices in 2015.[5] The result was an economic stand-off between Erbil and Baghdad that saw the economy of the KRI collapse and serious discontent emerge from within Kurdish society aimed at their leaders.[6] Finally, while the Kurdish leadership had perennially flirted with the idea of secession, it had never actually come close to doing anything about it. While the referenda plans were well supported by a society that had held the notion of independence as an unattainable dream, President Barzani now found himself in a position of having to deliver this referendum, and also then to manage the expectation of independence, or also lose the confidence of a population already increasingly skeptical of the motives of their political leaders.[7]

By the middle of 2016, all these pressures were now converging and creating a perfect and dangerous political, economic, and social storm. At the level of the political leadership, there were ferocious arguments over the continuation of Massoud Barzani as president of the Region, which remained unresolved as the KDP, PUK, and Gorran engaged in a heated war of words.[8] At the same time, the economy had been devastated and the KRG found itself in several billion dollars' worth of debt, unable to pay public sector salaries for months on end.[9] This appalling economic situation had then been further deepened by the influx of refugees from Syria and Iraq, caused by the expansion of the Islamic State. The numbers of refugees and internally displaced peoples (IDPs) who took refuge in the KRI were astonishingly high. By early 2015, some 1.5 million had fled IS and sought sanctuary in the KRI, which constituted a 28 per cent increase in the KRI's population, with more arriving throughout the year and into the next.[10] Meanwhile, President Barzani announced his intention to hold a series of referenda sometime toward the end of the year, firstly to define the territorial extent of the Kurdistan Region (with particular reference to those parts of the once-disputed territories retaken by the peshmerga forces following the rise of IS in 2014, and including Kirkuk, Khanaqin, Sinjar, and eastern parts of Nineveh govenorate), and then to vote perhaps on sovereignty (which could then be used to negotiate a new, perhaps confederal relationship with Baghdad), or maybe on outright independence.[11] Would the Kurds come through this storm by finding a way through their political differences, building a new oil and gas sector to repair their economy, expanding the territorial extent of their Region, and declaring their independence? Or would any one of these challenges cause the integrity of the Kurdistan Region to be undermined? Or would the leadership simply chart a course through these turbulent waters that would then see them continue on their incremental journey of further entrenchment of their autonomy, while attempting to square the circle of democratizing while also preserving older, more authoritarian, power structures? Whatever scenario comes to pass, 2016 will probably be viewed as a watershed year in the history of the Kurds of Iraq. This chapter presents an overview of this critical period, between 2003 (and with reference to some events in preceding years) and 2016.

Protecting the Region

Even though Kurdish elites were well aware of the US turning its attention once again to Saddam's regime following the events of 11 September 2001, political elites and society at large had concerns about attempting to target the regime of Saddam Hussein.[12] Indeed, anecdotal evidence suggested that broader Kurdish public opinion was in fact against the US taking military action against the Ba'ath regime.[13] Many in the leaderships of both the KDP and PUK had become wary of external, and always US-led, plans to remove Saddam Hussein from power, and both parties had suffered considerably in previous years when they threw their support into US-led and sponsored plans, only to see Saddam exact a terrible revenge upon them. These lessons were keenly felt and remembered. In 1975, the US withdrew their support from the KDP when regional developments made a dependency on the Kurds redundant.[14] In more recent memory, the Kurds remembered all too clearly the encouragement given by President George H. W. Bush to rise up against Saddam's regime in 1991, only to see their *rapareen* not supported, and then be ferociously crushed by Saddam's Republican Guard, while Western forces did nothing to stop them at first, only being deployed to assist the Kurds when the scale of the humanitarian tragedy of the Kurdish exodus to the mountains, in the depths of a bitter winter, become televised to Western audiences.[15] Even later, in 1995, the US failed to honor their commitment to support a coup against the regime that had, at the very last minute, resulted in the initiative failing; Saddam's forces had then entered the KRI in 1996, destroying the military units of the opposition Iraqi National Congress (INC), and routing the PUK from Erbil.[16] And so it was understandable that the Kurdish people remained not just wary but fearful of any US military assault, with people genuinely believing that the US could not be trusted to protect them if they supported a regime change policy, and that Saddam would unleash further ethnic cleansing upon them, as he had done through the Anfal campaign in the 1980s, and maybe resort to launching devastating chemical attacks on the Kurds as he had done in Halabja just fifteen years before.[17]

Some in the Kurdish leaderships of the KDP and PUK, which by now were acting with a degree of unity in their foreign policy, looked beyond the immediate threat of the military action to remove Saddam, and began to consider with some concern what a post-Saddam Iraq would mean for them.[18] Particularly among those leaders who had engaged with the US in the period following 9/11, the determination that appeared to be growing in Washington, DC to remove Saddam from power was convincing. They realized that they would need to find some way either to obtain guarantees about their status in the post-Saddam setting, or to be strong enough at least to protect what they had achieved, in the form of the KRI's institutions and autonomy.

Autonomy and federalism

The Kurdish leadership's understanding of the concept of federalism had been maturing at least since the 1970s, when Mulla Mustafa Barzani was engaged in negotiating the March Agreement of 1970 that led to the failed Autonomy Law of 1975.[19] By the 1990s, the Kurds had begun to view their autonomy as being a permanent feature on the map of Iraq and understood that, to preserve this status, post-Saddam Iraq would need to change from being a unitary to a federal state. Their determination to see this change happen was illustrated by their insistence in the founding meeting of the INC in Vienna in 1992—as the umbrella organization of all Iraqi opposition groups—that federalism would be recognized as being the future model for the organization of the state.[20] Kurdish thinkers in the political party elites had also begun to consider new possibilities for Iraq as a whole. Some of them had become increasingly familiar with concepts such as power-sharing, consociational arrangements, and different federal options, including federacy and confederacy, and brought this new knowledge of the range of possibilities to the fore as the probability of war became more likely after 2001.[21]

While the Kurds were at first worried about the seriousness and reliability of US intentions, this soon evaporated as 2002 progressed and the US rapidly moved from the planning stage to seeing their immense military organization deploy and position to such a level that not going ahead with the invasion would be unthinkable. They also felt increasingly comfortable in believing that the US would accommodate the KRI, and the federal and autonomous aspirations of the Kurds, in the planning for "the day after" regime change. After all, surely the US, as a federal state with significant powers devolved to its constituent parts, would see the logic of also rebuilding Iraq in its own image, so the Kurds' rationale tended to go. The Kurds would also hear, from various parts of the US administration, voices that would assuage their fears, and take these voices as fact, whereas those views that ran counter to their view of how Iraq should be, and instead foresaw a situation whereby the KRI would be disestablished and the unitary state re-imposed from Baghdad, were dismissed as being unrepresentative. This pattern, of choosing to believe what they wanted to believe, would remain a common feature, and weakness, of Kurdish leaders in the years following 2003.

Negotiating the constitution

The Kurds' early confidence in their view of how post-regime-change Iraq would develop seemed to be well-placed in the immediate period following Saddam's demise. Having committed their peshmerga forces to assist, or perhaps to take advantage of, the coalition's assault and to stream southwards from Erbil and Suleimani to Kirkuk, Tikrit, and ultimately Baghdad, the Kurds from the beginning were the first and only Iraqi actors to have a territorial base in Iraq, to be able to deploy significant numbers of military forces, and to have had an enduring relationship with Western governmental and intelligence services spanning back over many years. And the first attempt by the coalition to bring order to Iraq in these early days also seemed to benefit the Kurds. General Jay Garner, a retired US army general tasked with heading the Office for Reconstruction and Humanitarian Assistance (ORHA), already had good relations with the Kurdish leadership stemming from his leadership of Operation Provide Comfort, the international mission to protect the Kurds of Iraq, in 1991.[22] However, the Kurds' hope ended abruptly when Garner was quickly withdrawn, the ORHA disbanded, and a new Coalition Provisional Authority (CPA) established under the leadership of US ambassador Paul L. Bremer III. With sovereign authority for Iraq vested in his office, Bremer quickly set about institutionalizing this sovereignty within the offices of the CPA, making any notion of Iraqi involvement in government, at least in this immediate post-Saddam period, of an advisory rather than executive nature.[23] While this was possible within the context of the government of Iraq-controlled Iraq, this model did not acknowledge the specificity of political life and the de facto autonomy of the Kurdistan Region. Yet, at first, Bremer and his team seemed to ignore the reality of the Kurds' situation. Indeed, when Bremer first presented Barzani and Talabani with a CPA draft of a paper on the general principles of federalism for Iraq, with specific reference to the Kurds, the powers and competences of the KRI would have been heavily depleted, with no responsibility for security, the management of natural resources and the economy, and the control of borders: all of which would be the responsibility of Baghdad. Furthermore, the symbol of Kurdish autonomy, the peshmerga, would be disbanded or integrated into the Iraqi army.[24]

The Kurds pushed back strongly against this policy. Ultimately, they were in a relatively strong position: it would be extremely problematic in PR terms for the US to oppose what was by now an institutionalized autonomous political system headed by allies that had stood side by side with the regime-change initiative, and militarily the US would find the job of securing the Kurdistan Region, along with the rest of Iraq, perhaps a region unnecessarily too far. The Kurdistan Region from then on was treated to a degree as being separate to the rest of Iraq, but it still sat uncomfortably in how the CPA operated and how Western administrators engaged with its leaders. The CPA, for example, did not operate a distinct Kurdistan Region office, but instead had the Kurdistan Region incorporated into a "CPA North" jurisdiction, which included Kirkuk and Mosul as well. And, perhaps more worryingly for the Kurds, the CPA was viewed by them to have a strong bias against them, which the Kurdish leadership linked to the pre-eminence of the State Department in the staffing of the CPA, and thus made the Kurdish leaders suspicious of the actions and motives of the occupying powers, as well as their Iraqi counterparts who had quickly fallen into a pattern of communally-focused political interests.

The Kurds then focused their attention on the drafting of the permanent constitution. Based on the interim Transitional Administrative Law (TAL) of 2004 as a starting point, the constitution of 2005 recognized the KRI as a federal region replete with a range of powers and competences.[25] The constitution enshrined the role of the peshmerga while also blocking the deployment of Iraqi Security Forces (ISF) without the prior permission of the Kurdistan parliament; it gave the KRG control over future oil fields, while also specifying the sharing of responsibility for the operations of existing oil fields, which meant that Kirkuk would be shared if it were to be integrated in the KRI in the future.[26] With this in mind, the constitution's Article 140 outlined a three-stage process by which the question of the "disputed territories" (those lands to the south of the KRI still claimed by the Kurds) would be resolved, and with a timeframe set to conclude the matter by the end of 2007.[27] That the process outlined in Article 140 was never implemented increasingly caused problems for the leadership of the Kurds. Having supported the constitution largely because of the inclusion of this article, Baghdad's simply ignoring it would make the Kurds even more determined to take matters into their own hands.[28]

The Kurds and the sectarian civil war

Meanwhile, in the rest of Iraq, the goodwill that had existed in the immediate aftermath of deposing the Ba'ath regime had quickly evaporated. Iraqis of varying identities had begun to organize armed resistance against what were by now seen not as liberating forces, but occupiers. Across non-Kurdish Iraq, from Basra to Mosul, insurgent forces began to take an increasingly significant toll on the US-led multi-national forces (MNF-I).[29] The targeting also included embassies as well, as Iraq descended into what was, in this first iteration of violence, a reaction against outside powers. In what would prove to be the first outing of Arab Sunni jihadist violence, the Jordanian embassy was targeted, and the UN mission in Baghdad was destroyed, with many killed, in a vehicle-borne improvised explosive device (VBIED) attack (otherwise known as a suicide car or truck bomb) by the increasingly effective Al-Qaeda Iraq (AQI) organization of Abu Musab al-Zarqawi.

These attacks quickly escalated as the focus of the insurgent groups moved away from targeting the occupiers to targeting each other. Early on in the post-regime-change period, Western military observers were very much of the opinion that "Iraqis will not fight Iraqis." Yet this was what was now happening. Baghdad becoming increasingly tense and divided between its Sunni and Shia neighborhoods. With AQI on the one hand and the Shia militias of the Jaish al-Mahdi and the Badr organization on the other, the situation quickly began to unravel; by 2006, Iraq's mixed cities, and especially Baghdad, were convulsed in what was sectarian conflict and communal "cleansing", with each side targeting the other in what was becoming an orgy of destruction, violence, and death.[30] The trigger for a fully-fledged Sunni-Shia sectarian civil war came in February 2006. Being home to the Askariyya shrine and thus a place of profound religious significance for Shia, Samarra is halfway between Baghdad and Mosul and thus located in an area of Sunni predominance. It was therefore an easy and alluring target for Zarqawi's AQI. Its destruction was the event that turned the already violent conflict in Iraq into a civil war that would destroy any remnant of secular national identity and put together those forces that would become such a prominent feature in the current period, including the Islamic State and the various Shia militias.

But the Kurds had little involvement, or even interest, in this struggle. Or, more accurately, they had little interest in being involved in this struggle. Indeed, there seemed to be among Kurdish leaders a view that an Arab civil war in Iraq was perhaps even in their interests, as it would divert the attention of Baghdad away from challenging the Kurds in the disputed territories and opposing their plans to develop an independent oil and gas sector. An Arab civil war also made the Kurdish leadership look more mature, balanced, and stable compared to their counterparts in Iraq, and allowed the Kurds to engage even more fully with the MNF-I, and particularly the special forces element, in targeting AQI cells operating in the Arab triangle that lay to the south of the Kurdistan Region. The heightened sectarianism that overwhelmed Iraq from 2006 onwards also had a further, regional, effect that would strengthen Kurdish resolve. The polarization of regional Middle East political life into sectarian camps had increased since 2003, and the decline into violence in Iraq caused a rift in the relationship between Ankara and Baghdad: a rift into which the KRI, and especially the KDP element of it, neatly fitted.[31]

Disenchantment with Baghdad, rapprochement with Ankara

Even so, soon after successfully negotiating a constitution, the result of which was largely satisfactory for the Kurds, the relationship between the Kurdish leadership and their partners in the government of Iraq deteriorated after the elections of 2005. The Kurds, ebullient in their success, looked with urgency toward the implementation of Article 140 and the resolution of the emotive question of the status of the disputed territories. Yet they found no partner in the government of Iraq who would assist them in implementing this article. Furthermore, the prime minister, Ibrahim al-Ja'afari, seemed to have adopted a peculiarly anti-Kurdish position, perhaps as a means to bolster his own domestic popularity among Shia supporters, many of whom had begun to see the Kurds as being overly demanding in the constitutional negotiations, and who viewed the Kurds' federal demands as being nothing more than the first step toward their secession from the state.

This deterioration in Erbil's relationship with Baghdad was mirrored by Ankara's engagement with Baghdad becoming more troubled. The change in the relationship, and its effects, were remarkable and would have ramifications that continued for the next decade, and perhaps beyond.[32] Throughout the 1990s and into the 2000s, the position of Turkey toward the Kurds of Iraq had varied between begrudging acceptance to outright hostility; and under Prime Minister Recep Tayyip Erdoğan, the relationship was usually more toward the latter.[33] This animosity had deep historic and social roots in Turkey, but the overarching fear was of a successful Kurdistan Region of Iraq becoming an example for other Kurds to emulate, and particularly those in Turkey. Furthermore, if the Kurdistan Region of Iraq made the transition from being an autonomous entity within Iraq to being an independent Republic of South Kurdistan, the impact this event would have on the Kurds of Turkey was considered to be unacceptably dangerous. And so throughout the 1990s the Turkish state had employed a policy of ensuring that they constrained the ability of the Kurds of Iraq to prosper economically, or to strengthen themselves politically. Turkey also engaged in the game of intra-Kurdish rivalries, at times working closely with Barzani's KDP and using this alliance to pressure and sometimes attack the PKK bases that had been established in the Qandil Mountains in the northernmost part of the Kurdistan Region of Iraq. Already in the 1990s, Turkey's relationship with Barzani could be seen to be important. When the PUK launched what would prove to be their final attack against the KDP in 1997, Operation Vengeance Storm, and nearly captured the KDP stronghold of Saryrash next to the headquarters of the KDP in the town of Salahadin, it was Turkey that came to Barzani's aid, launching airstrikes against the PUK and forcing them to withdraw.[34] Still, while maintaining Barzani and the KDP was important for Turkey, so too was limiting the extent of the Kurdistan Region's success; for a four-year period following the fall of Saddam's regime, the policy of Erdoğan's Turkey remained fixed on this two-track approach.[35]

But limiting the upward trajectory of the Kurdistan Region proved to be difficult for Erdoğan, for two reasons. First, the Kurds' new-found constitutionally mandated legal status in Iraq legitimized them not only in Iraq, but also in the wider international community. The Kurdistan Region was now able to engage, albeit as a sub-state region, with international actors, and the leadership of the KRG did this was energy and enthusiasm. They also had a great opportunity to shine in the post-2005 period. With the rest of Iraq falling into the mires of sectarian civil war, the Kurds presented themselves as the success story of Western interventionism: of being "The Other Iraq", which had embraced democracy, peace, and expected prosperity.[36] It was a powerful message delivered at a moment in time when US and Western audiences craved news that their involvement in Iraq had not been a total disaster.

The second reason why Ankara found it difficult to contain the Kurdistan Region was that the government of Turkey's partner of choice in the form of the government of Iraq proved to be increasingly unresponsive to building a strong bilateral relationship. What seemed to have been Erdoğan's strategy at this time was to pursue a policy of bringing Barzani and the KDP under the patronage of Ankara, while also tightly controlling the ability of the KRG to strengthen their economic ties to, and through, Turkey. At the same time, Ankara was forcefully pushing to work directly with Baghdad concerning any issue to do with Iraq, including those pertaining to the Kurdistan Region, so as to ensure that Erbil remained subordinate to Baghdad; thereby they hoped to constrain the Kurds within the framework of the Iraqi state. Erdoğan's problem, however, was that the Iraqi state had become colored by the politics of sectarianism, particularly since the 2005 election which saw the Sunni Arabs largely boycott proceedings; the state had now become the preserve of the Shia, with Kurdish support provided by the PUK. As Erdoğan hailed from the Muslim Brotherhood-associated Justice and Development Party (AKP), and was thus tied to region-wide Sunni political organization with strong links to Arab Gulf states, and with Turkey having a distinctly cool relationship with Iran, it was perhaps to be expected that Baghdad showed little interest in Ankara's advances. For Erdoğan, faced with an institutionalized Kurdistan Region that now enjoyed enhanced international legitimacy, and with Baghdad not willing to engage, the way forward was increasingly clear: to make a transition from constraining the Kurdistan Region to embracing it. The shift also reflected the AKP's own foreign policy priorities which, in 2007 at least, prioritized economic development even above security concerns.[37] Key to this was securing cheaper energy, and particularly gas supplies, and breaking Turkey's dependence on the unsustainably expensive imports coming from Russia and Iran.[38] Considering the options available to Ankara, the Kurdistan Region of Iraq and its proven but as yet unexploited oil and gas reserves provided an unparalleled opportunity to rebalance its energy imports. This would now be achieved not by coercing and threatening the Kurds, but instead by enhancing the links created mainly by KDP diplomats in the 1990s and building strong and durable relations with the Kurdistan Region, and especially the KDP, in order to ensure that Turkish interests would be well represented in the oil and gas sector developments that the leaders of the Kurdistan Region had been actively and openly discussing.[39]

Building an oil and gas sector

Kurdish leaders had been conditioned by their experiences in the 1990s and before to ensure that they would be in control of their revenue streams in the future. Their view of oil revenue, or more accurately how such revenue was used, was not at all positive. While they believed that vast seas of oil sat under "their" territory (meaning the giant Kirkuk field), they would complain how their oil wealth had never been theirs to control and, far from seeing it invested by Baghdad into the Kurdistan Region for the benefit of those who lived there, the Kurds would instead see their wealth used to purchase weapons and to fund operations such as the Anfal campaign, the aim of which was to depopulate and ethnically cleanse the rural areas of the Kurdistan Region.[40] In the 1990s, the Kurds were no longer targeted in such systematic ways, but between 1991 and 1997 they received little if anything in the form of revenue support from Baghdad. From 1997, the UN oil for food program established by Security Council Resolution 986 allowed the government of Iraq to sell significant amounts of oil, with the Kurdistan Region then being allocated 17 per cent of the revenue: a figure that would then continue to be used in the post-Saddam period as well.[41] But again, the Kurds were not in control of their own resources and a strong culture of dependency had taken hold of the Kurdistan Region, a culture that many leadership figures saw as essential to change.[42] Of course, control of an oil and gas sector would also give those members of the leadership with authority over the sector's decisions new positions that could be used potentially to accrue immense amounts of private wealth, an accusation which was regularly leveled at the KRG leadership in the post-2014 period.[43] But, as the Kurds emerged into the light of the post-Saddam environment, the mood was to build this sector, to control it and be independent of Baghdad, and ultimately to see the Kurdistan Region undergo an economic transformation as an oil-exporting entity.

Of course, the oil sector of Kirkuk was very well established before the 2003 period, having been discovered by the Iraq Petroleum Company (IPC) in 1927. Yet Kirkuk had not been taken into the Kurdistan Region of 1991, and remained formally outside the jurisdiction of the KRG after 2003. However, the KRG had been making some headway in developing an independent oil sector even in the 1990s when they developed the Taq-Taq field to the south of Koya for local use. Interestingly, when considering Turkey's engagement with the Kurdistan Region, it was Turkish investment and companies that partnered the KRG in the development of the Taq-Taq field, with Genel Enerji signing a production-sharing contract in July 2002, before regime change had happened.[44]

The manner in which the Kurds also sought to enshrine their rights to develop their own oil and gas sector in the Transitional Administrative Law (TAL) negotiations of 2004 and the constitution negotiations of 2005 suggest that considerable thought had been given to moving ahead with these early initiatives. Several articles of the constitution—namely 110, 111, 112, 114, and 115—set out a series of provisions that gave the federal (i.e. regional) authority power to negotiate international treaties and agreements, and a distinction is made, in Article 112, between "present" and "future" fields, with the Kurds' understanding being that the central government's jurisdiction covers "present" fields, and the federal authority's jurisdiction covers any new resources that may be developed.[45] The problem has been, however, that the constitution is more of an indicative framework onto which more detailed plans need to be added. As such, the meanings of much of the constitution, and especially the articles related to the competences and authorities of governorates and regions, is open to interpretation. From the perspective of the KRG, however, the constitution was clear: they had the rights and the responsibilities to push ahead with building their own oil and gas sector.[46]

With the constitutional provisions in place, the Kurds now needed someone to develop a strategy to make their plans a reality. This figure was Abdullah Abdulrahman Abdullah, later to be known as Ashti Hawrami. As someone who had worked as an engineer for the Iraqi National Oil Company, and then the British National Oil Company in the North Sea in the 1970s, and then headed consulting companies in the UK (one of which did highly detailed work surveying the Kirkuk fields), Hawrami was exactly who the Kurdish leadership needed to energize their plans and build the sector. His entry into Kurdish political life is unclear, with some members of the PUK noting that he made contact with them in the first instance, and then handed him on to their KDP counterparts; but his association with the KDP leaders, and his impact thereafter, is obvious. He divided the Kurdistan Region into a mosaic of exploration blocks and put into place production-sharing contracts that were designed to attract international oil companies (IOCs) not only to the Kurdistan Region, but away from the rest of Iraq—such was the generosity of the terms being offered by the Kurds, and the tardiness in the Baghdad-governed sector. His plan succeeded. From 2007 onwards, Hawrami's strategy began to bear fruit as medium-sized IOCs entered the KRI, including US companies in the form of Hunt Oil. Larger discoveries were being found too, with Heritage Oil finding the large Miran gas field in May 2009, and Gulf Keystone discovering the Shaikhan oil field in 2010. By then, the KRG had signed contracts with a range of IOCs and had begun producing gas for local power generation. It was producing oil from the northern-most dome of the Kirkuk structure, Khurmala, and the KRI had attained the position in the hydrocarbons sector of being one of the most exciting new prospects on the global energy map.

By now, there was consternation in Baghdad as the government of Iraq viewed the KRG's oil and gas strategy as being contrary to the constitution, and ultimately illegal. Prime Minister Nouri al-Maliki and his Minister of Oil Hussain al-Shahristani demanded that Erbil submit all the contracts signed with IOCs to Baghdad for their review and approval—which the KRG refused to do. As the KRG continued to grow their oil and gas sector, with production for export booming and more companies entering the north, the war of words between Erbil and Baghdad became more heated, but there was little to stop the Kurds from carrying on regardless. And when, in November 2011, the world's largest non-state oil company, ExxonMobil, signed contracts for six exploration blocks, with some of them being in, or at least very close to, the disputed territories, the scene was set for a rapid deterioration in the relationship between Erbil and Baghdad, and between President Barzani and Prime Minister Maliki.

Barzani versus Maliki

It is an interesting exercise to look back to the period before the rise of the Islamic State in 2014, and after the ending of the sectarian civil war, largely brought about by the surge of US forces and the supporting of Sunni Arab tribes against the latest variant of AQI, the Islamic State of Iraq (ISI), in 2010. Many formative developments were happening in Iraq in this period, most of which lie outside the scope of this chapter but still warrant some mention, to allow the role and actions of the Kurds to be better understood.

By 2010, the insurgency had largely been quelled and many observers believed Iraq to be making the transition to relative peace and stability at last. However, while the levels of violence declined during this time, the underlying political tensions between the leaderships of the Shia, Sunnis, and Kurds were very much heightened, and it was during the period 2010–12 that the final building blocks of the eruption of ISIS were laid. Key among all the participants in this period was Prime Minister Nouri al-Maliki, who had replaced the highly unpopular Ibrahim al-Ja'afari. The Kurds in particular saw the new prime minister as being a weak figure whom they could cow and control. However, Maliki recognized his relative weak position and set about building new patronage structures and making himself into a populist leader. To achieve this, he first confronted his main Shia rival, the ever-recalcitrant Muqtada al-Sadr, and ordered the Iraqi Security Forces (ISF) to launch a surprise attack against the Jaish al-Mahdi in Basra in 2008.[47] With Muqtada defeated, Maliki turned his attention to the north. Tensions with the KRI President Massoud Barzani had grown since Maliki's assumption of the premiership, over the status of Kirkuk and the unwillingness of Maliki to discuss implementing Article 140 in time to meet the constitutionally-mandated deadline of the end of 2007. The Kurds responded forcefully, threatening to withdraw from the government of Iraq and thus destabilize the government itself.[48] From Maliki's perspective, as an Iraqi nationalist leader who had little experience of dealing with the Kurds, it was impossible for him to embrace the implementation of Article 140, and not least because it would have almost certainly seen Kirkuk vote to merge with the Kurdistan Region. This was an eventuality that Maliki would have deemed unacceptable, and it would also have fundamentally weakened his strategy of being a strong leader of an Arab-dominated Iraq. Compounding this Arab-Kurd vision of Maliki was the KRG's oil and gas strategy. As has been outlined earlier, the KRG had been rapidly building its own sector, signing PSAs with IOCs, and making grand declarations of future intent—all of which had been vociferously opposed by Maliki and his Minister of Oil Hussein al-Shahristani.

The scene was therefore set for the enmity between Barzani and Maliki to grow. Both leaders increasingly appealed to nationalist sentiments, Kurdish and Iraqi, and both moved their military forces against each other in the disputed territories. Meanwhile, Maliki began to show his sectarian colors against the Sunni Arab community.[49] The elections of 2010 saw Maliki lose marginally to the Sunni-associated Iraqiyya block of Iyad Allawi, only to be kept in power by Western powers too nervous to allow for a change of government during the final few years before the agreed withdrawal of US forces, planned to take place at the end of 2011; this prompted Maliki to be even more forceful and the Sunnis to be more reactionary.[50] Following the exiting of US forces at the end of 2011, Maliki pursued even more sectarian-colored policies. He ordered the arrest of Vice President Tariq al-Hashemi on terrorism charges, and also sought the arrest of the popular Anbar politician Rafi al-Issawi. Demonstrations took place across Sunni Arab Iraq, and also in Baghdad (which by now was Shia dominated), and these demonstrations were put down with increasingly violent and deadly force by ISF units answering directly to Maliki. But Maliki was playing with fire. Within the Sunni community, remnant ISI units still existed, as did powerful formations of former regime elements (from the Ba'ath period), and there was a huge swathe of disaffected and marginalized tribal figures who had worked with the US forces against AQI, only to see the promises made to them evaporate. These groups began to reorganize under the banner of ISI and its new leader, Abu Bakr al-Baghdadi, in response to the deprivations inflicted on them by Maliki.

The Kurds were also feeling Maliki's wrath. He was so angered by their continued promotion of their oil and gas sector that he began to withhold the transfer of funds from Baghdad to Erbil, thus inhibiting the ability of the KRG to govern while also damaging the economy of the KRI itself.[51] But the impact of this policy was merely to make the Kurds' leaders even more determined to generate sources of revenue that were independent of Baghdad. By the beginning of 2014, the rhetoric from both

Barzani and Maliki had become highly inflammatory, and it is interesting to imagine what would have happened if ISIS had not appeared in Mosul in June. Before then, the biggest concern of the Kurdish leadership was the presence to the west of Kirkuk and the south of Erbil of the ISF Dijla Operations Command: a military force which the Kurdish leadership was convinced would be used by Maliki against the Kurds once again. Would Maliki have ordered Erbil to be retaken, and attacked Barzani and the KDP peshmerga in Erbil as he had attacked Muqtada and the Jaish al-Mahdi in Basra? Or would Barzani, desperate to generate more oil revenue and also to shore up his leadership credentials, have ordered the Kurdish occupation of Kirkuk? What would have been the reaction of the PUK leadership and their peshmerga force to either eventuality? This last question leads on to several issues that will be addressed toward the end of this chapter, concerning the cohesion of the political system in the Kurdistan Region in the period following the rise and then containing of IS. But, of the two possibilities of Maliki-led and Barzani-led aggression, both could have happened, and both were arguably more possible than what actually did happen in the summer of June 2014, as the next iteration of the Sunni Arab insurgency, namely ISIS, built on its earlier successes in Anbar and surprised itself and shocked the world by its swift conquest of Iraq's major northern city of Mosul.

The rise of the Islamic State and the Kurds' near death experience

The territorial extent of the Islamic State, since 2014, has established itself over a core territory stretching from east of Aleppo, to Raqqa and Deir az-Zur in Syria, to Fallujah, the environs of western Kirkuk, and to Mosul in Iraq. Although its spread has become a new reality on the map of the Middle East, the organization of the Islamic State and its antecedents has not. Indeed, before the Islamic State was announced as ISIS in the pronouncement of its leader Abu Bakr al-Baghdadi on 29 June 2014 in the Great Mosque of al-Nuri in Mosul that established the Caliphate, its precursors were well known to Iraqi, Kurdish, and Western intelligence services as they had followed, analyzed, and fought the several incarnations of the Sunni insurgency in Iraq since 2003.[52] The lineage of the Islamic State went back to the al-Qaeda Iraq of Abu Musab al-Zarqawi, and before then to a range of dangerous violent jihadist groups, including the Kurdish Ansar al-Islam; former regime groups were also very well known within Kurdish intelligence circles, so the rise of ISIS from 2012 onwards was scarcely a surprise to in-country observers.[53]

The Kurdish intelligence services also had a ringside seat in following the growth of ISIS in Mosul. As their own security concern was focused on the deployment of ISF forces near their boundary in the disputed territories, they took considerable interest in following the deployment of ISF units across Nineveh, Salahadin, Kirkuk, and Diyala provinces, and would have been well aware of the level of morale, expertise, and postures of the main brigades, not least because they already had some highly placed officers within these units. The KDP intelligence service, the Parastin, would also have been benefiting from the close relationship that had developed between their party's leadership and the Governor of Nineveh, Atheel al-Nujaifi. Previously an ardent enemy of Barzani, Nujaifi's relations with Barzani proved the age-old adage that "my enemy's enemy is my friend."[54] With both of them in open conflict with Maliki, they found a common cause on which to build a local alliance that further strengthened the engagement between Turkey, the KDP, and Sunni Arab organizations and tribes. This coalescence of interest would crystallize further in the years following the fall of Mosul and might well prove to be influential in determining a post-Islamic State ordering.

The origins of Islamic State as an organization can be traced back to the 1990s, as Iraqi society become more Islamic in its orientation: driven to a degree, but not wholly, by Saddam's "Return to Faith" campaign (*al-Hamlah al-Imaniyya*), and with there being a rise across the country and region of violent radical jihadist groups.[55] Of interest during the late 1990s were the activities of one Abu Musab al-Zarqawi, who engaged with al-Qaeda in Afghanistan and earned himself some notoriety back in his homeland of Jordan. The Kurdistan Region, too, had its fair share of radical Islamist groups. The previously well-established Islamic Movement of Kurdistan (IMK) could not satisfy the aspirations of many of its younger fighters returning from Afghanistan, so a new group formed under Mulla Ali Bapir called the Islamic Group of Kurdistan (IGK). This group then saw its more radical members hive off to form Jund al-Islam, which led to the dangerous Ansar al-Islam, which then merged with various Arab groups to form Ansar al-Sunnah.[56] Of course, these organizational developments are of interest and show a near linear progression from the 1990s to the present. But by 2010, the Sunni Arab insurgency in Iraq, whether nationalist or jihadist, had been broken by the combined efforts of Iraqi militias defeating AQI/ISI, and the strategies pursued by the US military forces during the surge campaign. What allowed these organizations to regroup was the emergence of new leaders in ISI, and in particular Abu Bakr al-Baghdadi and his lieutenants, who were willing to learn not only from the mistakes made by ISI during the civil war, but also from how their opponents had defeated them. But they needed a supportive environment in which to operate, and this was provided by the government of Iraq's marginalizing and intimidating the broader Sunni Arab community. Very quickly, from 2012 onwards, ISI transformed itself from the remnants of the failed insurgency to the spearhead of something very new, ambitious, and capable.

By 2012, ISI had made the transition into being ISIS, and was operating with relative impunity across the Sunni-dominated governorates. Yet even the taking of Fallujah to the west of Baghdad at the beginning of 2013 did little to awaken the government of Iraq to the danger that was growing. Meanwhile, Governor Nujaifi in Mosul was sending urgent reports of ISIS activities on the outskirts of Mosul to Baghdad and to his allies in Erbil, noting how their black-market activities were becoming very extensive, and his ability to limit their spread was negligible. On 6 June, following the killing of an ISIS commander by the ISF, an ISIS force of some 1,500 personnel had begun to attack military positions on the outskirts of the city. These attacks, when they happened, were largely dismissed by those aware of them, due to the size of the ISF presence in bases around the city. However, by 9 June this ISF force was shown to be devoid of leadership and ultimately hollow, as the officers largely fled the city, and their leaderless units, made up of recruits largely from the Shia south, began to flee, fearing not only their treatment at the hands of ISIS, but the wrath of a local population that viewed the ISF units as being Maliki's Shia tools of oppression in a proud Sunni city.[57]

ISIS and their allies from former regime groupings such as Jaish al-Rijal al-Tarika al-Naqshabandiyya (JRTN) and Jama'at Ansar al-Islam quickly took Mosul and then moved eastwards, pushing into Arab-dominated Kirkuk, and thus threatening to capture the ISF Dijla operations command base with its significant stores of weapons, and then move on to the city of Kirkuk itself. Countering this move, the Kurdish leadership from both KDP and PUK deployed the peshmerga forces into the disputed territories, taking control of Kirkuk and its oil fields, and moving into areas of Nineveh and Diyala governorates they had previously claimed as part of the disputed territories. In taking Mosul, ISIS had also given the Kurds the opportunity to seize most of the disputed territories, including Kirkuk, which they had sought through the Article 140 process. For the Kurdish leadership, Article 140 had now been implemented through some form of *force majeure* logic, and they were not minded to view their territorial expansion as being of a temporary nature.[58]

However, although the Kurds had protected their border against the new threat for the time being, ISIS did not stop moving. With alarming speed, ISIS forces raced south, capturing Tikrit on 11 June and surrounding the oil refinery at Baiji, thereby depriving northern Iraq of refined petroleum products. Tal Afar then fell to the JRTN on 15 June. By the end of the month, Anbar governorate was in ISIS's hands, allowing them to move unhindered between Iraq and Syria in a territory that ISIS, on 29 June, declared as the Caliphate and the organization 'The Islamic State'.

Now known as Caliph Ibrahim by his followers, Abu Bakr surprised his northern neighbors by unleashing a wave of attacks on the Kurdistan Region from the beginning of August. Targeting Christian and Yezidi targets in Nineveh province, IS fighters then assaulted the town of Gwer in the south of Erbil governorate on 5 August, and captured Makhmour. The peshmerga forces had largely evacuated from the front, and with few forces available to stop Erbil from being invaded, President Barzani appealed for assistance to PUK forces, to the YPG and PKK, and also to his archrival in Baghdad, Nouri al-Maliki. To their credit, they all came to the defense of Erbil, with Maliki organizing Iranian airstrikes at very short notice, and PUK, YPG, and PKK fighters all deploying against IS. Most importantly, Western air power was also brought to bear on the marauding IS fighters on 7 August.

Security, political, and economic concerns: the perfect storm

The Kurdistan Region had survived its near death experience, but many questions then remained unanswered. How the Kurds would manage their new defensive line against a dangerous and aggressive enemy was unclear, as was any understanding of how the Iraqi state would now work, effectively dissected by the Islamic State. The Kurdish hierarchy also had to show real leadership at a time when they had failed to provide the most basic element of security and defense against an enemy that, by their own admission, they knew in advance. The economy remained in a terrible state, and with the rise of IS there were few indications as to how the KRG could resurrect its fortunes while re-equipping the badly mauled peshmerga, providing for some 1.5 million refugees who had fled to the Region, and managing what was still a contested oil and gas initiative.[59]

In addition to the security crisis brought about by the advance of IS, the Kurdistan Region was thrown into a political crisis at the end of July.[60] President Barzani's term of office, which had already been extended by three years in July 2013, was due to end at the end of the month, yet no plans had been set in place for him to be replaced, or to continue in the role. Gorran in particular adopted a stringently anti-Barzani position in negotiations, while also recognizing, privately, that there were no other candidates from any political party who could possibly replace Barzani. The PUK moved to a slightly more conciliatory position in public, noting that while they had no personal problem with Barzani remaining as president, the competences of the office should be diluted as they feared what others in that position, with such extensive powers, might do—perhaps as a veiled reference to Massoud's son, Masrour. The negotiations then focused on whether the president should be elected by a popular vote, or by a parliamentary vote, with the KDP pushing for the former, and the PUK/Gorran for the latter. The months ran on throughout 2015, with the Kurdish parties resorting to attacking each other in their media outlets; when the Gorran speaker of parliament, Dr Yousif Mohammed, was blocked from entering parliament by KDP forces on 12 October, parliament was effectively suspended. This political crisis remains unresolved in 2016, with President Barzani remaining in office, although without a formal mandate, and with parliament not meeting. For the Kurdish population at large, the matter looked to be one of elites arguing over power while at their gates loomed an existential threat in the form of IS, and in their homes a dire economic situation got worse by the day. Squabbles over the presidency, at this moment in time, only served to drive a wedge between the elites and the society over which they governed.

Economically, the Kurdistan Region had been in a perilous state before the rise of IS, caused by an effective economic embargo imposed on the region by the Maliki government, and also by the excessive size of the public sector in the Kurdistan Region. Corruption, too, was also rumored to be playing a very significant role in the

Kurdistan Region. The KRG leadership, for its part, increasingly pointed to the effect of nearly 2 million refugees, and the need to pay the peshmerga forces, as additional reasons for the KRI's economic plight. However, the generally-held opinion among Kurds at this time was that their economic woes had been brought about by the economic embargo imposed by Baghdad, which prevented the KRG from paying salaries, and mismanagement by the Kurdistan leadership, whether by accident or through corruption, over a period of many years. More so than at any other time in the history of the Kurdistan Region, there was now a divide between the political elites and the population at large. Most worryingly for all, the questions that had brought about the divide (concerning the presidency, the economy, or security) had no answers, or at least the leadership could give no answers. It was in this setting that President Barzani made clear his intention to take matters into his own hands: to hold a referendum on the territorial extent of the Kurdistan Region, and then one on its status—of being in or out of Iraq, as part of a confederacy of states within Iraq, or as an independent sovereign Republic of Kurdistan.

The Kurdistan Region at a threshold: toward independence, autonomy, or muddling through?

Massoud Barzani's stance toward Iraq has rarely suggested that he is an ardent Iraqi nationalist, proud to see the Kurds as loyal Iraqis alongside the Sunni and Shia Arabs; and his disagreements with Prime Minister Maliki only seemed to harden his view. Following ISIS's taking of Mosul, the war of words between Barzani and Maliki heightened considerably, with Maliki accusing the Kurdish leader of being complicit in the fall of Mosul, and Barzani responding with scathing attacks against the integrity of the Iraqi prime minister. Barzani was also more confident in his position, seeing the collapse of the ISF forces that he thought could have been used by Maliki against the peshmerga. And so, perhaps sensing a degree of popular support as Iraq looked to be imploding in an orgy of sectarian violence, Barzani announced his desire to hold a referendum on independence in July 2014. This, of course, faltered as the Kurds were left exposed to the IS onslaught in August, but the possibility of holding a referendum never disappeared. The next outing for the referendum idea came at the height of the dispute over the presidency of the Kurdistan Region, in October 2015. Perhaps Massoud's timing was not his best: while it was logical to suggest that a referendum should at least be held in the disputed territories in order to approbate them formally into the Kurdistan Region, the notion that the Kurds could then move toward independence was viewed by some as using nationalist sentiment to refocus popular attention onto something other than economic problems. He again spoke publicly about a "statehood referendum" on 3 February, and throughout 2016, making clear his commitment to the idea. The question to be asked, then, is what are the trajectories for the Kurdistan Region? To secede from Iraq and form the Republic of Kurdistan? To renegotiate their position in Iraq as a confederal state? Or to muddle through and remain in Iraq, under the terms of the constitution?

At the time of writing, in 2016, it is not entirely clear which of these trajectories are being followed. Indeed, a case could be made that all of them are equally in effect. The pressure to secede is intense, and not just from the very significant numbers who would genuinely wish to see an independent Republic of Kurdistan happen sooner rather than later. Massoud Barzani has put an inordinate amount of pressure on himself by stating publicly on many occasions that there will be referenda. If he then attempted to retreat from this position, his credibility as a leader would surely be called into question. There are also many reports suggesting that Turkey would be minded to see Barzani declare independence, through whatever means he can, in order to consolidate Ankara's hold further over the political trajectory of the Kurds of Iraq and finally to secure access to the valuable gas reserves that exist in the region. Such reports are as contradictory as they are interesting, and not least because it is very difficult to decipher the national interests of states such as Turkey, and Iran as well, when it comes to the Kurdish question. Different parts of the state have different agendas toward the Kurds and questions of national security, and one important part saying something supportive (such as President Erdoğan's office) does not necessarily mean that another important part (such as the General Military Command) would agree. There is also the question of the reaction of Baghdad to Kurdish independence. Some reports and analysts suggest that the Shia parties are minded to say "good riddance" to the Kurds, having viewed them as unreliable allies (as they were slow to take military action against ISIS), and complaining bitterly about Iraq's economic embargo against them, while they export as much oil as they can. Quite simply, many Shia now do not understand the logic of maintaining the Kurds in Iraq; and without them having the opportunity to exploit political divisions between Shia and Sunni parties, there is a view in Baghdad that an Iraq without Kurds would be a much more balanced place. It is perhaps an unfair view, as many times Kurdish leaders, and especially Jalal Talabani, have brought their Arab counterparts to compromise, but it is one that is increasingly held. This support would evaporate if the Kurds were to attempt to include Kirkuk within their new state. As in the 1970s, Kirkuk remains a key stumbling block for any Iraqi government, and now for the Shia militias; a Kurdish takeover of the city is perhaps one of the few events that could happen which would see Shia and Sunnis unite against a common enemy. As the Kurdish leadership cannot contemplate a Kurdistan without Kirkuk, confrontation clearly remains a distinct probability.

If the option to secede looks complex, then the option to "muddle through" is even more so, and not least because the current "muddling through" dynamics, whether political, security, or economic, are not sustainable. Already, Kurdistan has accrued vast amounts of debt (estimates range between $16 billion and $30 billion) and the KRG has no real idea how to stop this debt increasing, let alone reduce it. The Kurdish population, too, seems to be increasingly angered by the lack of initiative shown by their political masters; and so, while change may be viewed as disruptive, a lack of change would be more so.

The interim position would be to find a way to renegotiate the Kurdistan Region's position in Iraq, and this is perhaps where Massoud Barzani has been heading: in his later statements on the referendum, he has talked about a "non-binding" vote on sovereignty. In effect, such a referendum would pose the question, "Should the Kurds be sovereign?" If the answer is Yes, then that would effectively transfer sovereignty over the Kurdistan Region from Baghdad to Erbil, and the Kurds would then, in this scenario, seek to renegotiate a new constitution for Iraq that would be confederal, rather than federal, in design. Such an Iraq would be constituted by sovereign units (such as the Kurdistan Region, and maybe a Jazira Region covering the west, and a Basra Region, along with a Holy Cities Region, for example) coming together to form Iraq, rather than having a central state devolve powers down to the region as is meant to happen now. But this is a complicated scenario to imagine, not least because it requires the Kurds to have partners across Iraq and in the international community who would be willing to reboot the whole Iraq political system, which would in effect mean acknowledging that the efforts made during the entire period since 2003 have been in vain.

25.

ARABIZATION AS GENOCIDE

THE CASE OF THE DISPUTED TERRITORIES IN IRAQ

Mohammed Ihsan

Arabization as a means of destroying the Kurdish social fabric has been a recurrent strategy of the various regimes that have succeeded in the Middle East. In different degrees of oppression that did not exclude overt violence, countries like Turkey, Iraq, Syria, and Iran among others have pursued policies to "unite" their territories in order to guarantee their "political unity." In some cases these policies, which have been adopted for years, have led to dramatic demographic changes in the territories targeted. Such policies include examples of forced displacement and multiple killings. In the long run, the consequences of these policies have been particularly significant because they have affected the cultural and social fabric of the population involved. So the word genocide acquires new meanings, and terms like "languacide" or "culturecide" are appropriately included. These terms have now become common in the study of this phenomenon.

The Kurdish case is particularly interesting in this respect. The division of the Kurds into four countries—Iran, Iraq, Syria, and Turkey—offers a unique opportunity to analyze and evaluate different attempts to "arabize" or "Turkify" their territories. It is not within the scope of this chapter to offer a comparison between the four cases; however, it is important to understand that the process of exclusion, that which here we will call "arabization" in Iraq, is not an isolated case, but is part of a pattern that can be found in different contexts. For example, the policies adopted by Turkey since the coming to power of Mustafa Kamal Atatürk have been particularly harsh. Article 88 of the Turkish constitution of 2001 stipulates that "the people of Turkey, regardless of religion and race, are Turks with regards to Turkish citizenship." [1] Article 3 of the same constitution stipulates that "the Turkish state, with its territory and nation, is an indivisible entity. Its language is Turkish."[2] The issue of laws which negate the presence of any minority in the country, accompanied with implementation by force, have caused the emergence of insurgent groups such as the PKK and endless political and military confrontation. This is in addition to the damage suffered by the Kurds in Turkey who had to abandon their land, their culture, and their language in the name of an ideology that denies the presence of minorities in its territory and fails to transform them into participant citizens of a multilingual and multicultural society.

In Iraq, something similar happened. Since its creation in 1921, the multicultural and multilingual Iraqi society has been ruled under pan-Arab ideologies imposed by external factors which have undermined and totally compromised any peaceful coexistence among the different ethnic groups living in the area. The new country was conceived and run without any constitutional recognition of non-Arab identities. This pattern was followed by King Faisal I (1921-33), who failed to recognize the diversity of the Iraqi population and could only promote Arab nationalism and culture. Later, the brief presence of Abd al-Karim Qasim's government, overthrown by the Ba'ath Party in 1968, also failed in the task of promoting coexistence through the political recognition of the minorities. In this context, Kurds, Turkomans, Assyrians, and others were deprived of their democratic, national, and cultural rights.[3]

It was in the 1960s with the coming to power of the Ba'ath Party that arabization became a tool to change the demography of Kurdistan. This phenomenon was at first implemented in a very subtle way and saw an intensification starting from 1979 when Saddam Hussein came to power; it continued until his fall in 2003. The arabization process is very interesting, especially if seen in the context of other forms of genocide carried out against the Kurds during the regime, such as the persecution of the Faylee Kurds, the abduction and murder of 8,000 Barzanis, the Anfal campaign, and Halabja. It constitutes a starting point, a type of blueprint for the other genocides at a time when the regime was sure it could act with impunity. This explains why, in comparison with other crimes, this particular act of arabization spanned a long period of time.[4] In addition, in order to implement this crime, the regime used educational and judicial systems as well as the police and security forces to implement its policies. The final aim was to ban Kurdish culture and history. This policy soon turned into an ethnic cleansing operation, which means that there is a direct link between arabization and genocide. This policy was adopted by the Ba'ath regime and by the Arab nationalists with the purpose of eliminating the Kurdish presence in the territory. Genocide has been used as a means for arabization in order to guarantee the dictator's exclusive control of the land and the fulfilment of pan-Arab ideology.[5] The arabization was carried out in two ways: the first was through forced deportation; the second took advantage of the Iran-Iraq war and the

Anfal Operation

indiscriminate use of the Iraqi army against civilians. The forced deportations were likely to be made more acceptable to Iraqi society by the expropriation of land by the government, which was then in turn given to the Arab settlers from central and southern Iraq.

Disputed areas

The areas most affected by the arabization have become "disputed areas", a term used by the Iraqi Federal Government for territories which are claimed as Kurdish. The disputed territories include territories inside the governorates of Kirkuk (all parts), Nineva (Mosul), Diyala, Wasit (Kut), Sahaladin, Erbil, and Dohuk. It would be too long and beyond the scope of this chapter to analyze all the territories mentioned. All the districts including Mosul, Sinjar, Tel'afar, Shaikan, Khaneqin, Moqdadiya, Makhmoue, Faida, and Baladroz have experienced policies of discrimination which were implemented consistently over a long period of time, a strategy that shows the increase in scale and scope of the arabization policies: for example, telegram no.

21347 from the Committee of North Affairs, dated 18 August 1974, ensuring that Kurdish properties were confiscated. Ten years later the RCC (Revolutionary Command Council) with decision no. 710 established the forced evacuation of the properties confiscated, a decision reiterated later. Only four years later, in 1994, with decision no. 9420 dated 17 October, the RCC ordered the destruction of the villages of Gamesh Tapa and Kazana and the deportation of their inhabitants. This constituted a common pattern in all the districts included in the disputed territories.[6]

The case of Kirkuk constitutes the most crucial example, for two main reasons. The first is the presence of oil in the area, which makes it a very sensitive area for the stability of the region, provoking the opposition of other regional players like Turkey. The second reason is that Kirkuk has never been just simply about oil. Kirkuk, more than any other area, symbolizes the forced displacement, the destruction of Kurdish homes, the occupation of their land by Arab settlers and the consequent destruction of the Kurdish way of life.[7] Despite the decreased number of Kurds living in the city, the governor of Kirkuk addressed a letter dated 16 November 1996 to the Commander of the Northern Bureau expressing his preoccupation with regard to the number of Kurds still living in the area. He attested to the fact that the Kurdish population of the city constituted 60 per cent of the overall population. The letter also explains how entire quarters, such as Karama in Iskan and Shorja, had become completely Kurdish.[8] In addition, Kirkuk, with its multi-ethnic population comprising Kurds, Arabs, Turkomans, and Assyrians, represented a unique opportunity to implement policies of power-sharing never introduced before in the Middle East. This caused an intensification of the arabization policy in the area, with a resulting mass deportation and prohibition of employment of Kurds by Arabs. As a consequence, the demography of the city changed considerably due to the various decrees and decisions imposed by the government.

Petroleum plays a decisive role in determining the future development of the Kurdistan region in general and the Kirkuk governorate in particular. During the colonial period in Iraq, the British-mandated government made special efforts to retain the Kirkuk region for strategic and economic purposes. The governorate is rich in natural minerals, fertile land, much-needed rural crops, forests, and important oil reserves. Oil was first produced from the Kirkuk fields in 1927 in Baba Gurgur (well K172) and Ain Zala; these wells soon became an essential resource for the Iraqi state. The oil was exported through the main northern pipeline system (Banias and Tripoli in Syria and Lebanon respectively) on the Mediterranean coast, to Turkey through the Iraqi-Turkish line, to the Terminal Port at Cihan, and to Basra southward through the strategic line at Haditha. From this southern port of Basra, the petroleum was exported through two sea terminals: the deep terminal of Al-Bakir and the terminal of Khor Al-Amaya. Another option for transporting petroleum was via the Iraqi line across Saudi Arabia to the Red Sea terminal.[9]

In the early 1970s the export capacity of the main pipeline system reached around 72 million tons per year (about 475 million barrels per year). However, the absence of scientific plans limited export capacity of the pipeline system, and the contamination of oil due to water infiltration in the oil fields damaged the productivity of the wells in Kirkuk. The central government built production plants to exploit and produce liquefied gas from the oil and further extracted sulfur from the gas for industrial purposes and export. A pipeline was also constructed to transport the liquid gas from Kirkuk to Baghdad.[10]

Kirkuk became the base for the Iraq Petroleum Company (IPC), which initially included an ethnically mixed labor force, representative of the diverse composition of the governorate: Kurds, Arabs, Turkomans, and Christians (Chaldean, Assyrian, and Armenian). However, with the conclusion of the 50-50 profit-sharing agreement between the IPC and the Iraqi government in 1952, the IPC's largely British staff was gradually replaced by trained Iraqis. This change was part of the larger movement for Iraqi independence, and after the assumption of Ba'athist power in 1963 it became linked to the state's arabization processes. The ethnically mixed IPC workforce were transferred outside the Kirkuk governorate and replaced by large numbers of Arab settler populations. In one single decision the central government transferred 2,500 Kurdish employees from the company and other establishments to outside the governorate. With the nationalization of the IPC and the oil industry in 1972, followed by the Yom Kippur War and the OPEC crisis, the role of petroleum in Iraqi politics and economic life gained increasing significance. The central government used its petroleum revenues to finance state-led development and social welfare programs, while neglecting other sectors.

Kirkuk is about more than petroleum. Kurdish history and honor are deeply involved in the way that confiscation of assets from the original families, without any compensation, is viewed. For Kurds, Kirkuk symbolizes decades of forced displacement, the destruction of their homes, and the occupation of their lands by Arab settlers. The human rights abuses linked to the arabization process have only underlined the historical, territorial, and symbolic value of this territory to the Kurdistan region and its population.

Changes in administrative units and internal borders[11]

From 1929 to 1987 the administrative units of the Kirkuk governorate underwent changes that detached some districts while adding others. In 1929 the governorate included:

1. The district of Kirkuk, including the sub-districts of Kirkuk, Daqoq, and Alton Kopri.

2. The district of Chamchamal, including the sub-district of Chamchamal.

3. The district of Kifri (Salahiya), including the towns of Kifri, Toz Khormato, Qere Tape, Sherwana Castle, Shibicha.

4. The district of Gil, including the sub-districts of Gil and Sangaw.

In 1936 the administrative units of the governorate changed to include:

1. The district of Kirkuk, including the sub-districts of Kirkuk, Alton Kopri, and Milha.

2. The district of Chamchamal, including the sub-districts of Aghjalar, Shwan, and Sangaw.

3. The district of Kifri, including the towns of Toz Khormato, Qere Tepe, and Sherwana Castle.

4. The district of Gil, including the sub-districts of Qader Karam and Daqoq.

In 1948 the administrative units changed again and included:

1. The district of Kirkuk, including the sub-districts of Qara Hassan (Laylan), Alton Kopri (Pirde), Milha, and Shwan.

2. The district of Kifri, including the sub-districts of Kifri, Bebaz, Qere Tepe and Sherwan.

3. The district of Toz, including the sub-districts of Toz, Daqoq, and Qader Karam.

In 1957 the Kirkuk governorate underwent additional changes in its administrative units and internal borders. According to the 1957 census the governorate included:

1. The district of Kirkuk, including the sub-districts of Haweeja, Shwan, Alton Kopri, and Qara Hassan.

2. The district of Kifri, including the sub-districts of Bebaz, Sherwana, and Qara Tepe.

3. The district of Chamchamal including the sub-district of Aghjalar and Sangaw.

4. The district of Toz including the sub-districts of Qader Karam, and Daqoq.

The most important administrative changes occurred after 1975. The central government (1) annexed the two districts of Chamchamal and Kalar from the Kirkuk governorate and attached them to the governorate of Sulaimani; (2) annexed the district of Toz Khormato and attached it to the governorate of Salahadin; and (3) annexed the district of Kifri and attached it to the governorate of Diyala (republican decrees nos. 608 and 42 dated 15 December 1975 and 1 January 1976 respectively). The governorate also gained new, Arab-populated territories. The district of Zab was annexed from the Mosul governorate and attached to the governorate of Kirkuk (republican decree no. 111 on 16 November 1987).

In January 1976 the Iraqi central government changed the name of the Kirkuk governorate to Tameem, meaning nationalization (republican decree no. 41). At that time, the governorate measured 10,319 sq. km and had a population of 492,615, which increased to 752,743 in 1997 and then 1,280,000 by 2007.

District	Sub-district	Center	Number of villages	Total number of villages
Kirkuk	Center of Kirkuk	Kirkuk	101	
	Qara Hassan	Laylan	56	
	Alton Kopri	Alton Kopri	61	
	Haweeja	Haweeja	226	
	Shwan	Redan	76	420
	Bebaz	Bawa Nor	68	
Kifri	Qere Tepe	Qere Tepe	105	
	Sherwana	Sherwana	145	318
Chamchamal	Chamchamal	Chamchamal	64	64
	Aghjalar	Aghjalar	62	
	Sangaw	Goptepe	76	
Toz	Toz	Toz	79	
	Daqoq	Daqoq	62	
	Qader Karam	Qader Karam	93	372
Total			1,274	1,274

Table 25.1 Administrative units of the Kirkuk governorate, 1957.
Source: Ministry of Extra-Regional Affairs, KRG, 2014.

Demographic changes

The population of Kirkuk includes three main ethnic groups: Kurds, Arabs, and Turkomans. Prior to the central government's arabization campaign that commenced in the early 1960s, the Kurds constituted more than 64 per cent of the total population of the Kirkuk governorate and 53 per cent of the population of the Kirkuk district. By 1977 they represented 37 per cent while Arabs represented 44 per cent and Turkomans represented 16 per cent. The Christian population declined from about 9 per cent to less than 2 per cent.

Years	1977	1987	1997
Arabs	218,755		544,596
Kurds	184,875		155,861
Faili Kurds	388		1,105
Turkomans	80,347		50,099
Armenians	581		116
Syrian, Chaldean	4,050		758
Others	180		205
Unknown	3,439		3
Total	492,615	601,219	752,743

Table 25.2 Distribution of the population in the governorate of Kirkuk between 1977 and 1997. Source: Ministry of Extra-Regional Affairs, KRG, 2014.

Year	Arabs	Kurds	Turkomans	Christians	English
1958	1	38	16	40	3
1960	1	43	16	35	2
1963	2	33	20	41	1
1965	5	29	23	40	1
1968	9	28	27	32	1
1972	25	20	25	28	
1978	51	9	22	16	
1982	62	5	20	11	
1988	69	3	21	19	
1995	70	2	19	7	
2000	73	1	19	6	
2003	69.45	5.8	19.98	4.75	

Table 25.3 Percentage of workers at North Oil Company in Kirkuk between 1958 and 2003. Source: Ministry of Extra-Regional Affairs, KRG, 2014.

The previous charts and graphs reveal a negative relationship between the level of Kurdish and Christian workers and Arab employees developing over time. That is, as Kurdish and Christian employees decreased, Arab workers increased; at the same time Turkoman manpower remained nearly static. No major population shifts occurred in Kirkuk between 1996 and 2003. However, after the fall of Saddam Hussein and the Ba'athist regime in April 2003, demographic changes in the population occurred in both directions: a return of Kurdish families to Kirkuk (224,544 persons) and an exit of Arab families from Kirkuk (about 5,986 out of a total of 52,973). The only data available today on the population of Kirkuk (population 705,014) are based on the food supply forms of 30 April 2007. However, due to the recent events in the area and the rise of ISIS (Islamic State), this figure is likely to have changed considerably. In the residential Kurdish quarters of Raheem Awa, Iskan, Imam Qasim, Rizgari and Shorfja, the number of Kurds is estimated to be 263,012. Added to this, the number of Kurds in the mixed quarters is estimated at 163,700, while the total number of Kurds in the city of Kirkuk is 426,712, or 60 per cent of the total population.

In a letter dated 8 November 1996, just a few years before the fall of the regime, addressed to the chairman of the North Committee of the Revolutionary Command Council (RCC), the governor of Kirkuk complained that the Kurds formed about 60 per cent of the population. He added: "there are whole Arab quarters which have become solely Kurdish, such as Karama in Iskan and the police quarter in Shorja." In this letter he also stated that "trade and economic matters in the city are still in Kurdish hands, so are the contractors and artisans and public facilities and services."[12]

Status in December 2016

At present the governorate of Kirkuk consists of three districts: Kirkuk, Haweeja, and Dibis, and the sub-districts of Toz Khormato, Daqoq, Al-Riyadh, Alton Kopri, and Sengaw. The districts of Chamchamal, Kifry, Kalar, and Toz Khormato that were part of the Kirkuk governorate prior to administrative changes in 1976 have become part of Sulaimani, Diyala, and Salahadin governorates.

The district of Kirkuk

The district of Kirkuk was created by a royal decree in 1937. After the abolition of the districts of Shawn, Sara Hassan, Yacht, and al-Rabies, its land mass was 3,122 sq. km. According to the 1987 census, the population of the district was 418,694. The district of Kirkuk is a commercial, agricultural, and industrial center, and is rich in natural resources (sulfur, gas and oil). The discovery of oil reserves in 1927 amounted to 25,583 million barrels in 584 wells. Some of the wells in the Bay Hassan field are situated within the administrative borders of the Erbil governorate.

As part of the Kirkuk governorate, the district was subjected to a vicious ethnic cleansing campaign by the Iraqi government against Kurdish and Turkoman populations. The Iraqi central government issued various decrees and decisions that forcibly caused demographic changes which altered the ethnic composition of the city.

The district of Haweeja (Milha-Khwelin)

Haweeja district was created in 1961 and is traditionally an Arab-populated region of Kirkuk (republican decree no. 387). It has an area of 1,965 sq. km, after the abolition of al-Zab and al-Abbasi sub-districts and their attachment to the district center in 1987. According to the 1977 census, Haweeja's population was 52,179, mainly Arab, with only 4 per cent of the population being Kurdish. Haweeja district has one sub-district, Al-Riyadh.

Al-Riyadh

This sub-district was created in 1961 (republican decree no. 328). The area covers 1,311 sq. km and the population is 28,884 according to the 1987 census.

The district of Dibis (Dobiz)

Dibis was established in 1987 after the abolition of the al-Quds district (republican decree no. 321). According to the 1977 census, its population was 37,815, of which the Kurds represented about 52 per cent (19,721), Arabs 38 per cent (14,356), Turkomans about 9 per cent (3,240), and Assyrians less than 1 per cent, or 122 persons. In 1987, the total population increased by only about 2,000. The district of Dibis has two sub-districts, as follows.

Alton Kopri

This sub-district was created in 1945 (royal decree no. 564). It has an area of 335 sq. km and a population of 7,512 according to the 1987 census.

Sergeran

Sergeran belonged to the Makhmour-Kandinawa/Erbil governorate in 1957, but was attached to the Dibis district in the Kirkuk governorate in 2000 (republican decree no. 245). According to a memo issued by the mayor of Sergeran municipality in early 2007, the sub-district has a population of 15,000. Like other areas of Kirkuk, Sergeran was subjected to a deportation campaign and expropriation of land from Kurdish farmers to Arab settlers brought from the southern governorates of Diwaniya (Qadisiya). So far, 2,690 cases have been examined in the sub-district, requiring land to be returned to its original owners. Prior to the 1975 administrative changes Kirkuk included other districts, as follows.

The district of Chamchamal (in the Sulaimani governorate)

Chamchamal was annexed from the Kirkuk governorate and attached to the Sulaimani governorate in 1975 (republican decree no. 608). After the abolition of the two sub-districts of Aghjala and Sangaw in 1987, its area totaled 2,379 sq. km. According to the 1987 census, the population was 70,552 persons. Chamchamal's economy is dependent upon agriculture: wheat, barley, sunflower, vegetables, potatoes, and oil seeds. The district has a natural gas field (not in production) and two drilled wells containing a reserve equal to 279.6 million barrels of crude oil.

The district of Kalar (in the Sulaimani governorate)

Kalar was annexed from the Kirkuk governorate (Tameem) and attached to the governorate of Sulaimani in 1975 (republican decree no. 258). It has an area of 2,111 sq. km, a decrease from 3,332 sq. km after the abolition of the districts of Bebaz and Tilako and their attachment to the center of the district in 1987 (republican decrees no. 321 and 911 dated 11 June 1987 and 16 November 1987 respectively). According to the census of 1977, the population of Kalar was 52,773; in 1987 it was 82,400. The economy of this district is based on agriculture with production of wheat, barley, vegetables, bulbs, oil seeds, and the breeding of sheep and cows. Kalar is also the seat of the Jaf tribe and boasts the stone-built Sherwana castle.

The district of Kifry

Currently part of the Diyala governorate, but according to TAL and Article 58AB of the Iraqi constitution it is legally part of Sulaimani governorate.

The district of Toz Khormato (in the Salahadin governorate)

Toz Khormato was established in 1952 by a royal decree. It was annexed from the Kirkuk governorate (Tameem) and attached to the governorate of Salahadin (Tikrit) in 1976 (republican decree no. 41), with the exception of Daqoq district. After the abolition of the district of Nojol and its annexation to the center of the district, the area was 1,542 sq. km. Nojol is situated in the east of Toz Khormato bordering the governorate of Sulaimani. The population in 1977 was 75,737. According to the 1987 census, the population was 51,998. The economy is agriculture-based, with the main crops including wheat, barley, oil seeds, sunflower, cotton, vegetables, and fodder. Toz Khormato had two sub-districts: Amirly and Sulaiman Beg.

Amirly

This sub-district was established in 1969 (republican decree no. 439) and has an area of 739 sq. km. According to the 1977 census, the population was 15,104 and increased to 22,522 in 1987; this until its occupation by ISIS. In 2016 after a large battle between ISIS and Iraqi forces Amirly was liberated again, but it is still a war zone because its population did not manage to return to their homes.

Sulaiman Beg

Sulaiman Beg was established in 1969 (republican decree no. 440) and has an area of 288 sq. km. According to the 1977 census, the population was 7,719 and increased to 11,733 in 1987.

Negotiating with Baghdad: the disputed territories versus peace and stability

After 2003 and the fall of the regime, the new Iraqi constitution offered the opportunity to solve the issue of the disputed territories through legal means. Article 140 established that all these areas should go through three main steps: (1) Normalization providing for the return of Kurds and other ethnic minorities displaced by arabization. (2) A census in order to determine the demographic composition of the population. (3) A referendum with the purpose of determining the status of the disputed territories.[13] By agreeing to include article 140 into the constitution, the Iraqi government for the first time recognized arabization as a genocide against the Kurds. This would have meant a step forward with regard to the building of a new Iraq on a different basis. The three steps also signaled the willingness of the Iraqi government to acknowledge the mistakes of the past by using the law in defense of the citizen. That same year (2005) a commission was created to implement article 58 of the TAL (Transitional Administrative Law) which would become article 140 of the constitution. Unfortunately, the deliberations of this high committee were very short-lived, in part due to the lack of funding, but in reality because neither the US nor the Iraqi government were interested in resolving the issue. Both sides thought that by this time the issue would be solved, but in reality it has remained the main source of insecurity and instability for all Iraq in general and Kurdistan in particular. The result was that none of the steps provided for in the constitution, with the exception of the normalization process, have been implemented. The normalization process was so badly managed and caused so many tensions that it almost caused a civil war, which it was supposed to avoid. Regarding the sensitive issue of the census, the federal government refused to conduct a new census, knowing that the last data were collected in 1957. Of course on this basis the idea of a referendum is not viable, since it is impossible to have a clear idea of the composition of the population in the disputed areas without clear census data.[14]

The numbers are important to establish the Kurdish claim over these territories: the size of Iraq today is 437,509 sq. km. The size of the KRG today is 5,328 sq. km, while the size of the disputed areas between Baghdad and Erbil is 45,050 sq. km. This means that 48 per cent of the KRG's land is still disputed between Baghdad and Erbil. However, the issue does not limit itself to a claim for the annexation of territories. It has been a lasting omission of the American administration that the dispute was not resolved before their withdrawal. It is increasingly evident that the issue of the disputed territories between the KRG and the federal government in Baghdad has implications for the peaceful coexistence of the different ethnic groups present in the country. The implementation of article 140 would have created an opportunity for Iraq and the Kurds to start a new era of peace and stability, with the opportunity finally to solve political problems through legal means without resulting to conflict and war. The federal government in Baghdad, however, was not prepared or willing to enter into such a discussion. This approach was backed by the US and other external powers who preferred a unified Iraq to keep peace and stability in the area. Iraq with the eight years of Maliki's government went back to the cycle of dictatorships that has characterized its modern history. Thus, an opportunity was lost to rebuild the country on common ground.

This lack of vision was due mainly to the fact that Maliki's government did not accept the idea of federalism or any other political solution to the problem of the different voices present in the country, and opted for a systematic exclusion of entire sectors of the society on religious grounds. An "elite bargain" was struck that compromised forever any possibility of a government inclusive of the minorities.[15] This position was clearly evident from the beginning: for example, the rhetoric used by the candidates during the 2005 elections revealed how the political system based on a wider national representation instead of on local representatives made possible the mobilization of voters in favor of political parties and not of individual candidates. In this way the candidates did not have the opportunity to talk about programs involving the creation of jobs, security, and other important issues. Forced by the electoral system, the candidates had to play the sectarian card because it was the only one that distinguished them from one another.[16] This had two effects: first, that in the following years Iraq saw a long sectarian war between Sunnis and Shia; and second, that the country could not embark on the path of reconciliation which could have led to a process of democratization of the country. This is why it is so important to solve the issue of the disputed territories.

For both Shia and Sunnis, the idea of society is strongly linked to religion; and this isolates them from the vision that the Kurds have of society, which must be democratic and, most importantly, secular. This is not just an ideological statement, but an idea that entails a different way of dealing with the past, the present, and the future of an entire community. It reflects the ability of a given society to overcome its past and to build a new future. In Iraq, the religious divide between Shia and Sunnis prevented society from undertaking the necessary steps toward reconciliation. The intransigent religious separation of the two sects did not help the birth of a new political system based on respect for minorities, and it led to the gradual polarization and militarization of the two parties, leaving little space for a productive democratic atmosphere or confrontation. Unlike the Kurds, Shia and Sunnis do not share an identity. They do not even share a political ideal that would unite them in the post-war nation-building. From the beginning, the roadmap agreed upon in Baghdad was very difficult to implement. In 2005, during Dr Ayad Allawi's rule, Baghdad established a committee to normalize only Kirkuk, leaving aside all the other areas. This meant that the committee started as a failure, with absolutely no progress thereafter. For this reason nothing was achieved after one year: no money was allocated, no one managed to lead the committee.

During Maliki's term (2006) another committee was established to implement article 140, and its directive roadmap was to sort out the fate of the 45,050 sq. km of the disputed areas. Its purpose was to encourage people who had been deported to return to their homes, and to encourage the new settlers to return to their original homeland. In addition the committee aimed to bring back those who were expelled from their jobs, and had a directive to tackle the issue of the administrative border between these territories. A voting list was also prepared in order to determine who had the right to participate in the referendum, and in which areas the referendum should take place.

Despite all the efforts, the committee kept facing obstruction from the federal government. In 2006, Maliki issued article 22, setting three specific dates: it stipulated that (1) normalization in the disputed territories should be completed by 31 March 2007; (2) a census should be completed by July 2007; and (3) a referendum be conducted by 15 November 2007. Since then, nothing has been achieved or implemented. In 2010, the second term of Maliki's rule, Baghdad simply ignored the target date and bypassed the implementation of the article. After eight years of the Maliki-led government, we can observe that very little has been achieved despite the hard work and the US$1 billion that was spent on the implementation of article 140. In 2011, the federal government changed the plan totally. Instead of concentrating on the disputed territories, they enlarged the concept of those areas, in order to cover all of Iraq excluding the Kurdistan region. This meant that roughly more than 50 per cent of the committee's budget was spent on Basra, Nasriya, Amara, and Diwaniya, but not Kurdistan.

In this situation, any reconstruction effort was hindered by the impossibility of a real understanding by the Americans of the situation on the ground. There was the additional unlikelihood of the Iraqi ruling class engaging in a process of revision. This is despite the fact that this effort was partly supported by the Allied presence. All of this made impossible the implementation of most of the articles introduced first in the TAL and then in the 2005 constitution regarding transitional justice and reconciliation.

The events since June 2014, with the rise of ISIS which has engulfed Iraq and the whole of the Middle East, have completely changed the situation. With Kurdistan in control of the disputed areas, and defying the federal government in Baghdad and the West, Masoud Barzani said in an interview: "We waited for ten years for Baghdad to solve article 140. Now it has been accomplished, because the Iraqi army pulled out and our peshmerga forces had to step in, so now the problem is solved. There will be no more conversation about it."[17] Masoud Barzani asked MPs "to promptly create[18] an independent electoral commission to begin preparations for holding a referendum", adding that "The time has come for us to determine our future."[19] All this had the purpose of guaranteeing that the Kurds' requests do not aggravate the situation in a country that is already unstable, and that they are willing to collaborate on a legislative level with all the parties concerned. The dispute over the implementation of article 140 of the 2005 constitution claimed by the Kurds as their constitutional right is not resolved, particularly in the current fluid situation. It is true to say that while the peshmerga forces control the previous disputed areas, there are some resulting downsides to this position. The current demographic composition of Kirkuk could compromise this historic gain and draw the Kurdish region into the religious and sectarian dispute that is now destroying Iraq. Despite the provision of reassurance immediately after the annexation from the Kurdish authorities that all minorities' rights would be respected, Arab and Turkoman communities living in these areas have voiced their fear about this possibility. Immediately after the peshmerga took control of the city, the Iraqi Turkoman Front in Kirkuk announced through its leader, Arshad Salihi, the mobilization of the militia in the city if Kirkuk was not returned to the central government.[20] The size of the oil fields in the newly Kurdish-controlled areas also raised concerns, not only in Baghdad, and has increased the security challenges that Kurdish forces have to face. Only a few days after these events, a twin bomb exploded in the area of Toz Kharmato causing thirty-one fatalities. Even though there is a lack of claimed responsibility for this incident, the perception of the people living in the area is that the Kurdish claim over this land could now trigger a new, deadly sectarian war. But after the expected end of the war with ISIS and the loss of more than a thousand peshmerga martyrs, it would be very hard for the Kurds to leave their lands again to strangers.

A glimpse of the future

It is very difficult, given the war with ISIS, to foresee what the future has in store for the region. In the last year it became evident that the KRG is increasingly under pressure to collaborate with the international community in the fight against ISIS.

Some observers commented that this could be a way to independence, especially considering that the KRG is seen now as a credible interlocutor by many Western powers. However, the claim to independence is still a very sensitive issue and it should not be a priority of the KRG at this moment. The relationships with Baghdad are extremely strenuous and the negotiations over the budget are only one example of the difficulties. The refusal from Baghdad to deal with this issue demonstrates that the federal government's position toward the Kurds and their claims has not changed. Despite calls from the United States and other Western powers on Baghdad to form a government of national unity including Sunnis, Shia, and Kurds, the federal government has been unable to do so. One of the main obstacles, after thirteen years of the supposed "new Iraq", is the lack of trust between the different groups in Baghdad. It also demonstrates that democracy, equality, and citizenship cannot be imposed from above. Consolidating ties with Europe and the US means that the Kurdish region is obtaining international support and the recognition of its right to defend itself against terrorism as well as to self-determination, a concept that Masoud Barzani has expressed very well in the letter he addressed to the Iraqi people. By claiming self-determination for the Kurds in the context of the current crisis, Masoud Barzani interprets the Kurdish historical right to self-determination claimed by Mustafa Barzani in 1931 and later in 1944, which aimed at founding a Kurdish province including the cities of Kirkuk, Khaneekeen, Sulalmani, Erbil, and the Mosul towns (Dohuk, Zakho, Akra, Sinjar, and Sheikan). At the same time, he reminds the Iraqi Kurds that their slogan was "Democracy for Iraq and self-determination for Kurdistan", reminding politicians that no agreement will be reached without these conditions having been fulfilled.[21]

In light of the subsequent demographic changes and recent events in the region, the defense of the Kurdish claims over the disputed territories needs to be revisited in order not to repeat the same mistakes committed in the past. The Kurds have to respect the fundamental rights of the non-Kurdish population living in the area without the use of military force. In other words, annexation does not have to resemble the arabization process implemented by the Ba'ath Party and Saddam's regime. It is very important to show, not only to the population living in the disputed territories but also to the neighboring countries, that in the last twenty-five years Kurdistan has been a source of stability and good governance in the area. The way in which the Kurds will deal with the disputed territories in the current situation is an extremely sensitive subject. The Kurds have to face reality and accept that the implementation of article 140 has to be partial. In order to stay in the negotiations, they should give up some of the areas which are historically Kurdish. Article 140 provides for the restitution of lands to the Kurds, a process that implies the displacement and resettlement of the Arab population now living in some of the areas. Giving up the claims to Arab-majority towns, for example those in which Arab residents are not the consequence of arabization, would be a first step to easing the negotiations with Baghdad.

Some of the Arab population residing in areas like Hawija in Kirkuk province, for example, would resent a forced incorporation into the Kurdish region, and this could cause social unrest in the future. A forced integration would be disastrous for the Arabs and for the Kurds, because most of them living in Hawija, Rabia, and even Mandali, Badra, and Jassan in Wasit province, which are part of the disputed territories, were settled in those areas even before the beginning of the arabization process in 1968. Therefore, the KRG cannot legally ask those Arabs to leave the area, since article 140 states that leaving and returning is optional. If the Kurds pursue the same policy that was pursued against them in the past, they would put themselves in a dangerous situation and they might lose some Kurdish territories as a result. This is why any referendum on whether to incorporate areas into the Kurdistan Region should be held locally. Holding a referendum at a sub-district level has the advantage of guaranteeing a Kurdish administrative presence in the area. With the exemption of Kirkuk, holding a referendum at a provincial level would be to the Kurds' advantage. It is a fact that the Kurds are not the majority in Nineva, Diyala, Salahaddin, and Wasit provinces. This requires a huge effort on the Kurds' part, because they cannot identify the voters on recent censuses, and have to use the 1957 one, since Maliki canceled every voting list for the voters prepared by the Iraqi authorities in charge of organizing the referendum.

Even if we manage today to put an end to the Islamic State by military force, the issue of the disputed territories still needs to be solved; otherwise different forces similar to ISIS will emerge. If there is a lack of clear vision for the future and a wrong implementation of future policy, then these difficulties will translate into geographical pockets of instability. Neither the KRG nor Iraq will manage to maintain the security of this area. It is time for the current government in Baghdad to think seriously about how to implement article 140. If this article is not implemented, it will remain the mother of all other issues and could be the source of other longer and bloody conflicts in the area.

26.

THE DEVELOPMENT OF KURDISTAN'S HIGHER EDUCATION SECTOR

A GENDER PERSPECTIVE

Katherine Ranharter

Education is a fundamental human right and it is decisive to the
development of individuals (men and women) and societies.[1]

The importance of education in general and of gender equality within education in
particular has long been acknowledged internationally.[2] Its formative function for
individuals and society alike are thereby of particular importance in societies which
are in the process of undergoing a transformation, such as the Kurdistan Region of
Iraq, which went from oppression by the Ba'ath regime and internal conflict to self-
rule and autonomous dealing.

    As part of this process, the Kurdistan Region experienced a period of expansion
and development in the previous decade, which is now again at threat of crumbling,
as a result of a failing economy, the war on ISIS, and internal political disputes. In
2003, the fall of Saddam Hussein, together with the amalgamation of the two main
political parties and previous rival entities in the Kurdistan Region, provided the
basis for a period of relatively peaceful living, independent governance, and financial
growth. After years of suppression by the Ba'ath regime and the aftermath of internal
and external warfare, the new millennium saw the expansion of the financial market,

the development of infrastructure, and the building of international recognition. To encourage these trends further, as well as increasing independence from Baghdad, the decision-makers of the Region supported the rapid development of specific sectors, one of which was the sector of higher education.

The higher education sector, which fell victim to the wars and to Saddam Hussein's campaign against Kurdish culture, was chosen as one of the areas to underpin the ongoing development of the Region and its progress toward international recognition. The resulting investment by the KRG in the higher education sector initially arguably led to an unparalleled boom in educational facilities and study places. This development was then halted dramatically in 2014, when economic and political problems—which had been brewing under the surface—emerged with the appearance of ISIS in the Region.

The aim of this chapter is to examine critically the development of the sector since the fall of Saddam Hussein, from boom to stagnation, by focusing particularly on the role of gender equality and the part that women have played in the most recent developments within the higher education sector. This will be done firstly by examining the political factors surrounding the dramatic developments of the previous decade; then moving on to analyze the possibility of access to higher education for women and girls of different parts of society; finally, before reaching the conclusion, quality and gender inclusion within the sector will be looked at in detail. Specific attention will be paid to the correlation between the politics of the Region and developments in higher education by addressing the following questions. What lies behind the rapid boom and the consequential stagnation of development of the higher education sector? Is gender equality supported as part of the changes of the sector, and if so by whom, for which reasons, and to what effect? What impact does this support have on the development of gender equality and the standing of women within society? And are wider gender considerations taking place, or are women merely seen as globalized capital? It would take more than one chapter of a book to respond to these questions in the detail they deserve, but as this area is part of an under-researched terrain, it is the aim of this study to act as a starting point of discussion and to lead as an example for future research in the areas of the Kurdistan Region, and gender and education after conflict more generally. The chapter is based on the analysis of primary and secondary sources describing the phenomenon, as well as field research conducted in the Region on several occasions over the past four years, as part of which a substantial number of interviews were conducted in 2012 with students and lecturers working in the Region as well as with decision-makers at various levels.[3]

Kurdistan's higher education sector

The initial development phase of Kurdistan's higher education sector after 2003 can safely be described as a boom: a "boom" being considered to be a period of sudden growth and development, which in the case of the higher education system in the Kurdistan Region meant an unparalleled numerical expansion of institutions of higher education, in addition to a considerable financial injection into the sector to promote its growth from both quantitative and qualitative perspectives. There was only one university operating in the Region in 1992. By comparison, in 2015 there were thirty state and state-recognized private education institutions[4] accommodating approximately 100,000 students,[5] just under half of whom are women.[6] Furthermore, the KRG laid special emphasis on training local youth outside the country. As part of this initiative, PhD candidates were provided with a salary and allowances from the state throughout their study. Also, since 2010, thousands of Master's and PhD students were sent abroad every year to internationally renowned universities in Europe, Asia, North America, Australia, or a neighboring country. They were supported with a full scholarship, including fees and living expenses for themselves and their immediate family, via the HCDP (the Human Capacity Development Program in Higher Education).[7] While this scheme was described as very successful by students involved before 2014, the recent financial crisis has seen the KRG being unable to pay overseas students for months, with some not having received scholarship payments since early 2014, and the situation only starting to ameliorate in autumn 2016.[8]

Considering the current number of institutions in detail, it can be seen that the KRG has put a strong emphasis on building a physical infrastructure within the education sector, which is internationally competitive when considering the Region's size and population. Norway, with approximately the same number of people as the Kurdistan Region, namely 5.2 million,[9] currently boasts just over forty universities and higher education institutions.[10] The number of higher education institutions present in the Region is thirty-two; but while 47 per cent of 25–34 year-olds attain tertiary education in Norway,[11] only approximately 3 per cent of people in the Kurdistan Region access higher education. Of universities and higher institutions currently operating in the Kurdistan Region, only four were established before 2003 and the majority were established after 2006. While expansion of the education sector is certainly of value, as will be seen as part of the analysis below, the rapid growth experienced in the Kurdistan Region is not entirely beneficial. The arguably hurried establishment of a high number of institutions, in conjunction with the comparably low percentage of the population accessing higher education, raises the question whether the quality of higher education, both in its admission and outcome, was at the forefront of the unprecedented numerical expansion of the sector.[12] This question is of particular importance when looking at the role of women and gender within the sector.

Before looking at the situation of women and gender in more detail, it is of vital importance to understand the background to the very rapid expansion in Kurdistan's higher education sector for the Region, and its leaders, as this will demonstrate some of the reasons why quantitative—rather than qualitative—development may have (at least initially) been primarily at the forefront of decision-makers' minds as part of the expansion of the sector. We must also look at recent developments, which are currently overshadowing the significance of education and which risk taking away some of the advances fought for in the previous decade. This will in turn serve the understanding of women's situation and gender involvement in the sector as well as the wider Region. It is thereby necessary to look at the Region's past, the aims of the current political parties, and the dynamics of the Kurdistan Region's economy. The combination of these three factors has led to an expansion of higher education institutions at a rate which is arguably disproportionate to the timescale involved and which hampers the potential possible to be achieved through tertiary education at various levels.

Firstly, as in other regions undergoing a transformation process after an era of conflict, the policy decisions of the Region can be seen to be closely entangled with its history and past. This was shaped by occupation and oppression, with the different regimes, from the Arab Caliphate, to the Mongols, the Ottomans, and the modern Iraqi government destroying and reforming the Kurds' way of life.[13] It was accompanied by a suppression of the Kurds' intellectual and cultural heritage, especially in more recent times. The trend peaked in a proactive "arabization" process by the Saddam regime throughout the 1980s. As explained by Wölte, children were not allowed to use the Kurdish language in school, and any intellectual and academic exchange relating to the Kurdish issue was suppressed.[14] With regard to the situation of women, the percentage of women at university was comparably high under the rule of Saddam, especially in specialized courses. By the end of the 1970s, 51 per cent of Baghdad University's new medical students were female. The course of "English translation" even achieved 75 per cent female participation.[15] Furthermore, in the 1970s and 1980s women were actively supported to join the labor force, and their involvement peaked during the Iran-Iraq wars, in order to replace men at the frontline.[16] While this tactical inclusion of women in higher education and the labor force during Saddam cannot be directly connected to today's situation of women in higher education, it might have become one of the reasons why there has from the outset been a near equal number of enrolments by men and women at university level in the Region. So while the difficult years under Ba'ath Party rule might not have been disadvantageous to female enrolment, they certainly have been to intellectual development within the Kurdistan Region as a whole, and the focus on boom in the higher education sector after the fall of Saddam can be seen in terms of a policy to make good the lost years, to promote Kurdish academia, and thereby also make Kurdistan visible to the world.

This leads to the second reason. From a political perspective, an increasingly educated population at university level ensures that the demands of the Region's continuous economic development[17] are met, as well as the needs for well-educated future leaders. The focus on an enhanced higher education sector also ensures international interaction and recognition. This is arguably of particular importance to Kurdistan's decision-makers wishing to showcase the Region's strength, to reinforce their autonomy, and to pave the way for possible independence. These efforts could be seen to have borne fruit, as the Kurdistan Region was frequently referred to in public as "the success story of Iraq."[18] For example, the UK Higher Education International Unit of the Illuminate Consulting Group praised Kurdistan's flourishing higher education sector as far back as 2009.[19] With regard to women's inclusion in the sector, the education and employment of qualified women—at least in quantitative terms——is often considered an indicator of a country's identification with Western values, which are seen as equivalent to being "developed," and consequently recognized as a competitive player within the international community. As expressed by Abu-Lughod inter alia, women's standing within society is part of an "ideological terrain" which reflects society's wider cultural position and beliefs.[20] Women's behavior, their rights and duties, thereby serves as a mark to the outside world of the local culture. As noted by Al-Ali, in the case of the Middle East women are used as a personification of the standing toward the West.[21] In the case of the Kurdistan Region, there is a strong sensation of an approximation toward the West, at least from the ruling political parties. With regard to women's role as a symbol of this approximation, it was an often heard opinion among people interviewed that the government is seen as particularly favoring women with certain features, such as women who are perceived to be educated, wearing Western-style clothing, or returning from the West to their system.[22] As such, the development of the higher education sector in general, including women's participation in particular, can partly be seen as a move aimed at international recognition.

Thirdly, as noted above, the Kurdistan Region needs an increased number of graduates to guarantee continuous economic development and a successful deployment of its people. Kurdistan's economy, as with the rest of Iraq, is largely based on the oil industry. According to the 2011 national budget, 95 per cent of state income is from oil revenues. Since there is little other industry, oil revenues are currently largely invested in the public sector, which amounts to approximately 60 per cent of full-time employment countrywide.[23] Since there is currently no other major industry, the Region's human resources are necessarily directed elsewhere: partly to the higher education sector, which has until now been only partly successful. Despite the obvious importance of higher education as a source of additional industry, presently only approximately 3 per cent of the population are accessing tertiary education. While this comparably small percentage might simply be a consequence of the Region's disadvantaged standing in the decades before 2003, the current increase in number of institutions present in the Region has not correlated with an equal increase in people accessing these institutions. Furthermore, while women currently comprise nearly half of students at higher education institutions, their path to a consequential inclusion in the workforce is still often made difficult by social attitudes and other challenges, which result in fewer women becoming part of the workforce than accessing higher education.[24] Considering that, as part of its process of disengaging from the decision-makers in Baghdad and Iraq as a whole, the Kurdistan Region has basically eliminated Arabic as a working language and job opportunities for Arabs from other parts of the country, in conjunction with a general need to build an independent economic basis for a region which had never been self-ruled in modern times; this means that the Region's own intellectual resources will be of vital importance to realize its previously declared "success story" in the future. This strategy will arguably be of even greater importance now, considering the Kurdistan Region's current frail situation, with problems reaching from the political sphere to the economic one, which have already had an adverse effect on the operation of Kurdistan's universities.[25]

In order to achieve the above-named goals, the government has expanded the higher education sector, which—if done to a high qualitative standard—bears the possibility of achieving all of the above. But until now, thirteen years after the reforms started, it seems that quantity rather than quality has primarily been at the forefront of development. This is especially exemplified when looking more closely at the situation of women's and gender inclusion within the sector.

Women's inclusion: from access to equality?

As noted above, women currently comprise nearly half of the Region's overall undergraduate and postgraduate students, and this development is generally seen as being supported by the decision-makers in the Region. Government representatives are very vocal in supporting women in areas requiring graduates, including in decision-making posts[26] and as employees in the public sector.[27] As part of its "Vision for the Future," which is to be realized until 2020, the KRG has as one of their policy priorities to enable equal opportunities for women in all areas, including the education sector.[28] It is actions like these that have led to the belief amongst some members of the public (as explained by two middle-aged employees in Erbil) that the government is favoring qualified women over housewives and that educated women receive undue support.

While this might be the experience of some individuals, research shows that practical support from the government to women hoping to access the higher education sector is limited. The KRG has generally refrained from introducing positive discrimination in favor of women, and particularly those from less advantaged backgrounds, wishing to enter university. The Region's officials have put in place several structures supporting the opportunity of all to attend institutions of higher education. However, as shown below, these are not sufficient to ensure true equality of access.

Public university education is provided free of charge, and a limited number of dormitory places are made available at no cost to students who live far from the university.[29] At the same time, individual universities have established different systems of financial aid to help students with particular needs.[30] Furthermore, Master's students and PhD candidates are expressly supported by the regional government and, according to former minister Dr Dlawer Ala'Aldeen, up to 30 per cent of postgraduate scholarships were awarded to women; he referred to this achievement as "a cultural revolution."[31] This extensive financial support for students in general should mean that everybody can access institutions of higher education solely on their merits, regardless of financial background, class, religion, or gender. However, the reality is different. Only approximately 3 per cent of the population are currently in higher education, and as will be explained in more detail below, the lack of prerequisite support means that access is far more easily achieved for certain parts of the population, often youngsters from an urban background with financial family backing. As in other areas, such as politics or the economy,[32] the KRG freely supports full inclusion in their talks[33] and public statements. The official website of the Ministry of Higher Education and Scientific Research states:

> The University seeks to prevent discrimination on the grounds of race, colour, ethnic origin, nationality, religious belief, gender, sexual orientation, disability, age, marital status, family circumstance, citizenship, social and economic status, or any other individual differences.[34]

Furthermore, ministerial regulations were issued in support of equal opportunities and gender equality.[35] However, until now it has not built the necessary foundations to ensure that all applicants and especially women benefit equally from the new opportunities. There are no provisions for positive discrimination or quotas in the higher education sector for women in general, and for women of different social backgrounds in particular. While such policies are arguably not necessary or even desirable, as the percentage of women in higher education is close to 50 per cent, a problem presents itself when considering support for different groups within society. While some students from less advantaged families might be able to access higher education through their abilities alone, the majority will struggle to meet the same standards as their more advantaged peers (assuming that the quality of their schooling and family support is a different one), without adjusted standards of acceptance in the short run and equal prerequisites in the long run.

For example, children, and especially girls, from different social backgrounds are not provided with equal opportunities to follow a path leading to higher education. This begins at primary school. Experience shows that especially in rural areas, girls are under-represented in school enrolments. Social impediments still often prevent them from completing education. These include a lack of appropriate facilities close to their homes, the journey to school, the low quality of teaching, and especially their families' negative attitudes towards the schooling of girls. Such impediments make it difficult or impossible for girls to complete their education.[36] In addition to issues of access, it has become apparent through field research that there is a great discrepancy between the quality of schooling in the city and in the country, as well as between public and private education.[37] Especially before 2014, the KRG was working towards ameliorating this situation by building more schools and improving the curriculum structure.[38] Despite these efforts, there is still a shortage of school and university infrastructure, which—in connection with a lack of modern facilities—leads to great challenges within the system, as argued by Mhamad.[39] There are currently still 6,000 schools in the Region which operate on two or three shifts, and overcrowded classrooms do not provide children with the opportunity to learn and develop.[40] The situation is continuously worsening, with teachers taking to the streets and some boycotting school as a result of reduced and delayed salaries for teachers.[41] The concentration on numerical expansion and the consequential persistent variations in quality within the school system result in unequal access to the higher education system, which is based on merit derived from results achieved at school.

The resulting lack of fully inclusive access to higher education has wide-reaching consequences for the women unable to access the facilities, as well as society as a whole. While higher education is only one part of the education system, it is arguably the one that educates future leaders and thereby lays the foundation for future reform. It has already been claimed by Bertha von Suttner that education lies at the core of achieving equality between women and men.[42] As later taken up by scholars such as Tuyizere, it is argued that education's process of fostering understanding and providing equal opportunities has the ability to contribute to an increased equitable relationship between the genders.[43] This is supported by Kabeer and Hartwig, who maintain that increased participation by women within the education system and the knowledge accompanying this involvement will influence women's personal development as well as their position in society, and will provide more equal power relations between the genders.[44] The likely exclusion from higher education of women from less advantaged parts of society results in social marginalization and a lifelong lack of opportunities for them and their families. From a gender perspective, Kabeer notes that an increased presence of women at all levels within the educational structure can ameliorate their individual situations within society through a change in power relations.[45] Furthermore, since the majority of economically active women in the Region are employed in the public sector or in jobs which at the minimum require a high school diploma, receiving a university qualification is likely to enhance the possibility of improving personal economic standing.

But this can only happen if, as a starting point, the entire population, namely women and men from all parts of society, have an equal chance of accessing education.

In the Kurdistan Region where, as a result of a prevailingly unequal education system, young people find themselves in an inhomogeneous situation when it comes to accessing higher education, this is currently not present. In the case of women, the lack of prerequisite state support often means that society's attitudes and support matter more than any theoretical possibilities through government. Families have to be willing to release female students from household chores, to permit them to marry later in life, as well as to spend most of the day outside the house often mingling with the opposite sex. Several people in the Region—from a doctor, to a student, to a housewife—explained that many in Kurdish society increasingly prefer women's role to be housewife and mother. While they might be happy to have other women access higher education and jobs, they do not extend this tolerance to the women in their own families. There is a lack of regulations to compensate for the existing social disparities. This situation was to a certain degree ameliorated in the years following the fall of Saddam, which was marked by financial stability and economic growth at 12 per cent between 2009 and 2011, pushing young women into higher education as a result of the demand for skilled labour, and also bringing many into the labour market;[46] but this development is likely to backtrack again following the current financial problems, with individuals' priorities changing according to their financial and physical security. At the same time, there is the prevailing opinion that there is too little support for mothers and housewives from the government's side.[47] This results in both those staying at home and those continuing in education feeling unfairly treated, with many female students feeling pressure to comply with social standards of becoming "a good wife and mother,"[48] which effectively precluded them from using their degree as part of a career.[49] Such comments were supported by Ferda Cemiloğlu, a Kurdish entrepreneur and head of the Management Committee of the Kurdish Women Entrepreneurs Association in 2011. She noted the negative impact on the Region of many highly educated women choosing not to take up a profession after the completion of their studies, with currently less than 5 per cent of business owners being women in the Region.[50] Consequently, many women become housewives after marriage, or if they decide to work, they enter the civil service.[51] At the same time, housewives are feeling that they are being left alone from official sides.[52] The results of this forked support for women in higher education and as professionals, from society as well as government, have already been noted by academics, who describe the situation of women in the Kurdistan Region currently as highly contradictory. But while it is a general stance that "backward" culture, local practices and religion, i.e. society, are the root cause that makes women's rights hard to realize in practice,[53] this author argues that it is just as much the government's too superficial support which leads to inequalities in society, and all the effects this then has. As a result of the existing social pattern in the Region and the patriarchal thought structure, inequalities affect women—and in particular women from less advantaged backgrounds—more than men. It follows that while gender equality might be present in the higher education sector, social equality is lacking. Equal opportunity is not available to all segments of the population, and especially not to all women.

The resulting prevalent inequalities in the education sector not only have consequences for individuals, but also for wider national development. As explained by Tuyizere, an inclusive education provides a higher number of people with the ability to work and feed their families, which consequently also boosts the Region's economy.[54] Furthermore, the way an education system operates, whether it is gender-inclusive or not, is greatly influential on wider behavior within society, which can go as far as ameliorating or inflaming conflict, argue Leach and Dume.[55] This point is also taken up by Eifler and Seifert, who claim that the provision of all levels of education, including tertiary education, is of vital importance for long-term change at a time of conflict transformation.[56] While the fact that social or gender equality is currently lacking in the Kurdistan Region's higher education sector is certainly detrimental in this regard, it has to be noted that the existing sexual equality at least partly opens up the possibility to promote gender equity within society in the long run. But to date the lack of inclusive representation in the higher education sector leads to a loss of human resources for the Region as a whole. This is reflected in the current employment sector, where female economic inactivity reaches over 80 per cent.[57] Academics such as Abu-Lughod argue that once women's inclusion in education is achieved, the entire Region will advance as a consequence of having a fully educated population.[58] In the Kurdish case, this would likely lead to further economic advances, as currently only 3 per cent of the population hold a bachelor's degree or higher.[59] From a political point of view, enhanced presence of women would increasingly affect current decision-making. By not actively supporting the entry of all segments of the population, and especially women, into higher education, the KRG is arguably pursuing a hidden curriculum at present. It implicitly backs the existing patriarchal structure and supports differentiation between those in power and the rest.[60] It can consequently be said that the system currently accepts, if not supports, inequalities, although this might change with future development of the higher education sector, led by the higher number of institutions and growing student population.[61]

Numbers alone are not enough: quality and gender inclusion

Quality of teaching and the general message propagated by the institutions are vital for development; as Klaus Seitz cynically observes, education and schooling are "the primary vehicle through which society produces and legitimates inequality."[62] While education has the potential to overcome conflict on a variety of levels, it can equally be used to support social differences and inequalities.[63] Speaking in gender terms, if a patriarchal structure and ideas are retained within the higher education system, numerical equality will not lead to gender equality. So what is the situation for the students currently studying at Kurdistan's universities? Is gender included in the curriculum? Has the KRG considered gender as part of the expansion? Is the KRG's general support of women's inclusion merely directed toward advances in the Region, or is it also considering the specific benefits for women?

Academics have repeatedly observed that women are used as a development resource, such as to increase the number of women in the workforce or in decision-making positions, specifically to support particular advances of a region in times of need, but without considering the impact on the women individually and without inherently changing the existing patriarchal structure.[64] One indicator of this phenomenon is the lack of specific gendered measures, such as quotas and positive discrimination, but more importantly also measures which might facilitate access on a broader level, such as part-time jobs and studies, childcare provisions, adult education focused on mothers, or an enhanced public transport system. In the case of the Kurdistan Region, the first type of supportive measures, i.e. quotas and positive discrimination, are present in certain areas (namely access to parliamentary positions and government employment),although not in the higher education sector. The second set of measures, which can be described as more in-depth measures, are greatly lacking. [65]

While the resources directed toward women are often welcomed regardless of their imperfections, a lack of gender consideration leads to them being integrated into a patriarchal system that increases the potential for exploitation, such as a double burden of work and social chores, a lack of freedom of choice, and an increased pressure to conform to a lifestyle that does not fit the circumstances.[66] The continuous existence of a patriarchal system leads to a "hidden curriculum," as described by Shapiro, which is also still present in many educational institutions, and which advantages some more than others.[67] From a gender perspective, it is argued that the hidden curriculum in most formal education systems supports in some form a hegemonic or authoritative concept of manliness, in contrast to a positive concept of gender equality.[68] As argued by Abu-Lughod inter alia, it is not sufficient merely to provide women and girls with the opportunity to access education; there is an undisputed need for high quality education, which is often lacking.[69]

The general standard of education within the Kurdistan Region is still often criticized from both within and outside the Region. For instance, several scholars at the International Conference on Kurdish Studies at the University of Exeter in September 2012, as well as lecturers at the University of Kurdistan Hawler in April 2012, considered that many of the Region's universities were working within an outdated system and with a weak structure. There is also criticism from students of the influence of one of the leading political parties within the university structure, as a consequence of which a certain percentage of students gain admission not necessarily on merit, but because of family or party connections.[70] Furthermore, there is a problem of quality assurance on a broader level,[71] and as argued by Mhamad there is a great divide between universities and the job market in Kurdistan. Universities are arguably incapable of suiting society's needs, and graduates are not suitably trained to have a positive impact on the economy.[72] As a result of the need for improvement of quality over a range of areas, gender considerations are often not at the forefront.

An overall need for improvement in quality within the sector has also been acknowledged by the government itself. As noted by former Minister for Higher Education and Scientific Research, Professor Dlawer Abdul Aziz Ala'Aldeen, the lack of a long-term action plan for higher education over many years, as well as a lack of international experience, has resulted in problems within the teaching structure, the admission procedure, and the capacity of the system. Furthermore, the quality of teaching and style of learning, especially in PhD and Master's programs, is still seen as requiring improvement.[73] The various challenges were met with reform.[74] Even though there is a desire to improve the quality of higher education in general, specific gender considerations as part of such an improvement seem to be lacking from the government's side. Gender is not explicitly part of the reform agenda: not for the students or for the staff.

As revealed by the concluding report on "Female Iraqi Academics in Iraqi Kurdistan", female postgraduate students, researchers, and lecturers are increasing, but they are still sidelined when it comes to representing the Region internationally, accessing decision-making posts or publishing.[75] While there is no legal discrimination, an arcane and incoherent system, in conjunction with social attitudes and lack of gender consideration with regard to domestic responsibilities, results in practical discrimination.[76] Also on a general level, quality assurance in higher education institutions is under current circumstances no longer in the forefront. While there are still some attempts by the government to improve the situation of the higher education system,[77] other matters have taken over on a priority level.[78]

Individual actions taken by the universities present a slightly different picture. Various universities include the principle of equal opportunity without discrimination in their mission statements.[79] At a more practical level, various gender research centers and workshops have been initiated at a number of universities. For instance, the British Council, as part of the British Council's Development Projects in Higher Education, funded a Gender and Violence Studies Centre in conjunction with the University of Sulaimani.[80] In addition the Salahaddin University, Hawler has been active in encouraging gender research by signing an agreement with the School of Oriental and African Studies of the University of London for a joint research, supervision, and student exchange program in "gender studies and women empowerment in the decision-making processes for the Kurdistan Region."[81] Similarly, the American University of Iraq, Sulaimani is working on developing a gender studies and research program;[82] and the University of Kurdistan Hawler aims to support their female students by initiating a women empowerment program.[83]

While the initiatives taken by the different universities reflect the importance of gender inclusion, their wider impact is unclear when considering the development of gender equality more broadly. According to Opotow, Gerson, and Woodside, a gender-inclusive education which includes critical reflection by pupils and students is considered beneficial for both individuals and society. Highlighting the differences between women and men, as well as the resulting suppressive structures and their implications for society and individuals, can help support enhanced gender inclusion.[84] In the Kurdistan Region, the universities' initiatives are only accessible to a small percentage of people in higher education, who themselves only comprise a minimal percentage of the population as a whole. Of this small percentage of students in the higher education sector, the majority accessing these programs are women, while it is agreed by the general population that the driving force for gender development within society is men. One young female student interviewed as part of the field research emphasized this point by explaining that while the actions for women at university are good, they merely reach "those who do not need it anyway." It would be advantageous to concentrate on reaching women from less educated backgrounds, as well as men.[85]

At the same time the existing initiatives are only taken on at some of the universities, and on a very individual basis. As noted above, the government has failed to put a wider strategy into place for the full inclusion of gender considerations and a proactive gender development program at all institutions of higher education and throughout all disciplines. One result of the lack of gender consideration across the disciplines is that even on campus, existing social prejudices concerning gender inclusion can still be observed. As explained by a male student: "It is not possible to do everything you want at uni. If a girl stands up for herself as part of a discussion or by taking up an official position, she is threatened to lose her reputation. Most guys' mentality is still against women, even at uni."[86]

It follows that while positive developments in gender inclusion within the higher education sector are present in the Kurdistan Region through individual initiatives, gender inclusion is not part of a wider strategy by the KRG. This leads to the assumption that there is no specific interest in the impact of higher education on women or on gender equality in society as a whole. Instead, government actions suggest that women are considered a "resource for globalizing capital," a superficial example of translating Western values or gaining a currently needed increased workforce, rather than encouraging a group intrinsically worth investment.[87] Despite the general improvements that have undoubtedly taken place, the lack of a wider gender inclusive strategy by the government is arguably shortsighted, as only an organized and in-depth gender inclusion will lead to the economic and political advances aimed for by the KRG.

Conclusion

The KRG's general interest and investment in its higher education sector post 2003 is undeniable. The establishment of over twenty-five new public and private higher education institutions in the Region in the last decade is only one example of this support, together with investments in international scholarships and reforms which address raising the quality of the university structure.

The expansion of the higher education sector provided the KRG with one of the foundations to achieve their goals of international recognition, economic growth, and independence. As part of this, improvements have been achieved by the KRG and the widening of the higher education system has been realized to a certain extent. Compared to the situation ten or twenty years ago, the government has worked hard and invested greatly in expanding the higher education sector and raising its quality as quickly as possible. But the process is now again in danger of collapsing. The current financial crisis is taking away some of the advances fought for in the previous decade. Private schools are closing down, teachers are on strike, university students sent abroad for scholarships go unpaid and are left in limbo. If not resolved soon, the consequence will be an inadequately educated young population (with the under twenties comprising over half the population) and a potential brain drain from the Region. The future has thus become increasingly unclear again.

While women and girls have not been left behind in the initial process, improved support is still required, especially in the current circumstances. As seen previously in Iraq and other parts of the world, situations of conflict and financial difficulties often have a dramatic effect on women and gender equality, with women and girls becoming restricted in their choices, being forced to stay at home, and being the first to be forced out of the workforce if jobs go unpaid and the unemployment rate is rising. As part of aiming for the three targets stated, the KRG has recognized the importance of including women in the equation. Gender equality is laid down as a foundation of university education, and KRG representatives never tire of pointing out that nearly 50 per cent of university students are female and that up to 30 per cent of postgraduate scholarships are awarded to women. However, in-depth work to ensure gender equality within the system has until now been lacking from the government's side, and it does not seem that the government has the intention or even the strength to improve this situation foreseeably.

It should nevertheless be appreciated that the KRG has started to develop a system which could eventually lead to the inclusion of a substantial percentage of both men and women, from all parts of society. For instance, there are no fees for higher education, a scholarship system is generally in place, and more universities are being built. At the same time it should be noted that there are currently no special provisions to support women from all segments of society, and an overall strategy for gender inclusion by the government is lacking.

As discussed throughout the chapter, the lack of full gender inclusion in the sector leads to a loss for individuals, for society, and for the Region as a whole. Specifically, the absence of advanced support to include youngsters, and especially girls, from less advantaged backgrounds into higher education results in a decrease in economic opportunities, including a sacrifice of human capital for the Region, which counteracts parts of the main aims for the initiation of the higher education boom. This is not helped by a lack of a clear gender strategy within the university's structures and teaching. While the individual institutions are partly achieving their own targets in this regard, it is currently unlikely to have a broader impact or reach the wider population, as a result of problems of access.

It may therefore be concluded that gender considerations currently do not seem to be at the forefront of the KRG's strategy for higher education. This leads to the assumption that women's inclusion in the higher education sector is motivated by the potential increase of human resources and the symbolism for the Region and its society, rather than by the wider benefits for the women themselves. The consequential lack of progress toward the formulation and implementation of a gender strategy has resulted in people being left behind and in the Region's potential for development not being realized to its fullest extent.

27.

WATER AND DEVELOPMENT IN IRAQI KURDISTAN

Greg Shapland

Geography has not been kind to the Kurdistan Region of Iraq (KRI), by depriving it of its own access to the sea. In another sense, however, geography has been a good deal kinder, by endowing the region with what are, by regional standards, generous supplies of water. Moreover, those water supplies are much less vulnerable to the actions of upstream states than are those in the rest of Iraq. At the same time, the Kurdistan Region has been developing rapidly and its population growing. More-over, it currently has to cope with over a million internally-displaced people (IDPs) from elsewhere in Iraq and refugees from Syria: a 28 per cent increase in its popula-tion.[1] And climate change adds significant uncertainties to the picture. So manag-ing the water resources available to it in order to meet all the demands on them will be a major challenge for the Kurdistan Regional Government (KRG).

How much water is available?

First, it is important to note that comprehensive, detailed, and consistent data on the water resources of Iraqi Kurdistan are not publicly available. However, there appears to be enough information to establish orders of magnitude and draw some sound, albeit general, conclusions.

Unlike many parts of the Middle East, Iraqi Kurdistan receives a good deal of precipitation (snow as well as rain), especially in its more mountainous areas. Some of this precipitation is retained as soil moisture (making agriculture without irrigation possible in many areas, especially in winter). Or it emerges as springs or runs off into rivers, providing surface water which can be used for a variety of economic purposes, as well as sustaining the natural environment. Or it is retained as groundwater, to be abstracted by means of wells.

As far as surface water is concerned, the principal sources are the Tigris and its tributaries: from upstream to downstream, the Feesh Khabour; the Greater Zab; the Lesser Zab; the Uzaym (Adhaim); and the Diyala (see Map 24.1). Of these five, only the Uzaym rises within the Kurdistan Region of Iraq.

From the point at which it enters Iraq to a point just upstream of the Mosul Dam, a distance of 138 km, the main stem of the Tigris forms the boundary between the Governorate of Dohuk in the Kurdistan Region and the Governorate of Ninawa.[2] (In the reservoir behind the Mosul Dam, the boundary follows what was the line of the main stem of the river before it was submerged.) This gives the KRI access to the waters of the Tigris.

The average natural flow of the Tigris as it enters Iraq was, for the 1946-87 period, 16.7 bcm/a (billion cubic metres per annum).[3] Note that this is an average flow and there is considerable variation from year to year: the flow in a high year can be almost twice the average, and in a low year barely half the average.

However, it is the tributaries of the Tigris joining it in Iraq which constitute the main source of surface water for the Kurdistan Region. The average flows of these tributaries are given in Table 27.1.

River	Feesh Khabour	Greater Zab	Lesser Zab	Adhaim	Diyala
Average flow in bcm/a	2	12.7	7.8	0.8	4.6

Table 27.1: Average flows of main tributaries of the Tigris joining the river in Iraq[4]

Again, note that these are average flows. The variations in flow of these tributaries of the Tigris generally mirror those of the Tigris itself.

Iran has dammed the Sirwan and al-Wand rivers, which are tributaries of the Diyala. But the two most important tributaries in terms of volume of flow, the Greater Zab and Lesser Zab, have not been dammed by the KRI's upstream neighbors. As an indication of the importance of the two Zabs to the national Iraqi water budget as well as that of Iraqi Kurdistan, these two rivers contribute over half of the average flow of the Tigris at Baghdad.

As well as variability of flow between years, there is also variability between seasons. For the whole of the Tigris basin, high flow is from February to June (inclusive), with a peak in spring as the winter snows melt. Low flow is from July to January (inclusive). Dams on the Tigris and its tributaries have reduced this seasonal variability of flow and hence the risk of flooding. The groundwater resources available to the Kurdistan Region of Iraq seem to have been less well studied than the surface waters. But of the three main groundwater basins shared with Iran and Turkey, only one (the Halabja-Khurmal Basin, shared with Iran) is being utilized at anything near its capacity within Iraqi Kurdistan.[5]

This is reassuring for the KRG's economic and water planners. However, there is a good deal of uncertainty in this situation. First, there is uncertainty about the extent to which these shared aquifers are replenished by underground flow from Turkey and Iran.[6] The more they are replenished in this way (rather than from within the KRI), the greater the vulnerability of Iraqi Kurdistan's groundwater resources, given the uncertainty about what abstractions these countries might make in future from the aquifers.

Moreover, the tendency of international oil companies working in the KRI to drill wells for the local population as a goodwill gesture has greatly increased the abstraction of groundwater. In the absence of any centralized planning of such activity, there is a clearly a risk of over-abstraction.[7] The quality of the water (surface and ground) available in the KRI is generally high. However, given the rapid urban and economic development of the Region and the lack of comprehensive waste-water treatment facilities, water quality is likely to be declining rather than improving. For example, Rudaw (a KRI-based news website) reported in May 2014 that all of Erbil's human waste is dumped into the Greater Zab.[8]

Water infrastructure in the KRI

Two dams were built on the Iraqi part of the Lesser Zab in the 1960s: the Dukan and the Dibis. The Dukan Dam was built to help regulate the flow of the Tigris, but also to generate hydropower and provide water for irrigation. The Dibis Dam regulates discharge to the Kirkuk Irrigation Project in the northern part of Kirkuk Governorate—not, of course, part of the Kurdistan Region as presently defined, but an area with a Kurdish majority and quite likely, therefore, to remain under Kurdish control in any permanent settlement of its status.

The Greater Zab has not yet been dammed. A dam at the Bekhme (Bakhma) site has been planned since the 1940s and construction finally began in 1988. The aim of the project was to generate hydropower and supply water for irrigation to northern Iraq. The outbreak of the Gulf War in 1990 led to construction being suspended. At the time of writing, the dam remains unfinished. And such a major infrastructure project will have to wait until the financial situation of the government in Baghdad (or the KRG) has recovered from the shock of the fall in oil prices in 2014. Construction of the Mandawa (Mundwa) Dam, downstream from Bekhme, has not yet started. Its purpose is to regulate the outflow from Bekhme.

What is the present level of demand and how is it likely to grow?

In most parts of the KRI, rainfall is sufficient for agriculture without irrigation, at least in winter. Rain-fed agriculture is the norm in the upland parts of the KRI. In the three Governorates making up the KRG, only 11 per cent of cultivable land is irrigated.[9] In many cases this is on a small scale, but there are also a number of more substantial projects. Even with only 11 per cent of the cultivable land being irrigated, agriculture uses 90 per cent of the region's water supply.[10] (This is not an exceptionally high figure in Middle East terms, but looks high for an area with rainfall levels well above the average for the region.) The percentage of water used in agriculture may even increase if the KRG acts to meet the demand for irrigation for summer crop production. Such demand is especially strong in the lowlands, where average annual rainfall is less than 600 mm.[11] In the absence of data on the percentage of rain-fed cultivated land which would benefit from irrigation, it is impossible to say how great this increased demand might be. But it would certainly be possible to irrigate more efficiently, and greater efficiency could free up water to enable such demand to be met.

Additional water for irrigation could also be made available by treating urban waste-water. There is certainly ample scope to do so (see above, section 1).

However, the installation of more efficient irrigation equipment, waste-water treatment plant, and distribution networks for treated water would need capital investment. With the KRG budget in continuous crisis, this investment would (for the foreseeable future) have to come from the private sector.

Supplying refugees and IDPs

As of February 2015, there were 1.5 million Iraqi IDPs and Syrian refugees in the KRI. This constitutes a 28 per cent increase in the KRI's population since early 2012.[12] These numbers could, of course, fall in the future. But there is also a possibility that they will rise.

Although the number of people living in the KRI has increased by over a quarter as a result of the influx of IDPs and refugees, the strain on the Region's water budget has not increased to the same extent. (This is because the IDPs and refugees are using water for drinking, personal hygiene, and cooking but not for water-consuming economic activities such as industry or irrigated agriculture.) But the same World Bank report estimates that there was an 11 per cent increase in demand for water for refugees and IDPs between October 2012 and September 2014. In absolute terms, this translates into an additional estimated total water demand of 17.1 mcm/a: an increase in demand of a size and suddenness with which governmental authorities rarely have to deal.

Government of Iraq and KRG water policy

Iraq's National Development Plan, 2013-17, stipulates the "continued implementation" of large dams, naming Bekhme, Mandawa, Taq-Taq, and Khazar-Comel (in Dohuk Province).[13] All are in KRI. However, their implementation has been delayed by Iraq's security and financial crises. When they are eventually built, these dams will have a total storage capacity of 22 bcm, as compared to 150-200 mcm for the small dams for which the Plan provides elsewhere in Iraq. From these statistics alone, it is clear that the Kurdistan Region will be central to any attempt to increase levels of water availability for Iraq as a whole, or even simply to maintain them at present levels. One should be aware that the water budget for Iraq as a whole is facing a severe challenge. Reduced usable flow in the Euphrates and the main stem of the Tigris (as a result of abstractions and pollution by Turkey and Syria and climate change) will mean reduced agricultural output (because less water will be available for irrigation). At least 696,000 hectares of agricultural land might have to be abandoned in Iraq as a consequence of projects in Turkey on the Euphrates and Tigris. This would represent the loss of 37 per cent of the area (1.9 million hectares) which has been cultivated in "recent years" (though the total potential arable area in Iraq is 4 million hectares).[14]

So the Kurdistan Region will become more important as a source of food for Iraq and hence more important to the country's "food security." At the same time, one should bear in mind the likelihood that Iraq will provide food security for its people mainly by using foreign exchange (earned by exporting oil and gas) to import food from the rest of the world.

Moreover, one should not imagine that planning the use of the Region's water resources will be a straightforward business, given that the available supply is not precisely known. According to the KRG's Ministry of Planning:

> we do not have adequate estimates of our groundwater resources. In fact, we do not have a full study of our water resources, so we face a very high risk of mismanaging our water supplies and especially of depleting our groundwater. We will correct this situation in our quest to provide water security for the residents and businesses of our Region.[15] More specifically, the KRG Regional Development Strategy (RDS) notes the following water-related challenges:

- Limited water resources available for agriculture, in addition to insufficient storage

- capacities existing at present, in comparison with actual needs.

- Unregulated use of water in certain fields, in addition to water wastage by the three

- major sectors of agriculture, industry, and households.

- Poor involvement of water consumers into [sic] water management procedures and lack of water conservation guidance.

- Failure to rationalize field irrigation procedures, especially flood irrigation.

With irrigation using 90 per cent of the water consumed in the KRI, it is important for the KRG to confront this last challenge. Flood (surface) irrigation is a very inefficient method of irrigation, as a lot of water is lost to evaporation. According to the US Geological Survey, drip (or trickle) irrigation can achieve the same results with a saving of water of up to 25 per cent.[16]

There is, however, no financial incentive for farmers to introduce more efficient irrigation systems, because water taxes are based on land area rather than consumption. As a result, the KRG Ministry of Planning estimates that individual water usage within the Kurdistan Region is approximately four times higher than the World Bank standard. This level of water usage has been sustained by the abstraction of groundwater, causing those supplies to dwindle. To counter the over-abstraction of groundwater, the KRG plans to build more dams.[17] Given the present financial constraints, however, it is almost inevitable that these projects will be delayed.

According to the Invest In Group, the KRG is planning other measures to address the pressure on water resources. These measures include the installation of water meters, new laws to promote more binding regulations, and the creation of multiple water treatment plants.[18]

There is clearly parliamentary recognition of the need to take action. In March 2015, the media reported that the Kurdistan parliament was working on legislation aimed at rationalizing the use of surface and groundwater resources in the region.

Upstream neighbors

Turkey and Syria are upstream of the KRI on the main stem of the Tigris; Turkey is upstream of the KRI on three of the main tributaries of the Tigris which join the river in Iraq, namely the Feesh Khabour, the Greater Zab, and the Lesser Zab. For its part, Iran is upstream of the KRI on some of the tributaries of the Diyala.

As far as the main stem of the Tigris is concerned, there are both general and specific agreements between Iraq and its upstream neighbors. The most important agreement between Iraq and Turkey is the 1946 Treaty of Friendship and Good Neighbourliness. The provisions of the Treaty relating to the Tigris include the following language: "the resolving of all issues such as ... the utilization of water for industrial and agricultural purposes ... have [sic] to be on the basis of complete equality."

Iraq has a much more specific agreement with Syria, namely, the 2002 Agreement on the Creation of a Pumping Station in Syria on the Tigris. This specified the volume of water which the pumping station could abstract from the river.

In 1980, Iraq and Turkey signed the Protocol for Technical and Economic Cooperation. Syria joined its fellow riparians of the Tigris and Euphrates and signed the Protocol in 1983. (Iran, also a riparian of the Tigris, was not involved in this initiative.) The Protocol mandated the establishment of a joint technical committee to discuss the question of regional waters, including the two main rivers shared by the three riparians. The committee met a number of times but, in the absence of agreement on the basis for assessing the three countries' respective water needs, failed to make substantive progress.

There are no specific water agreements governing any of the four main tributaries which join the Tigris in Iraq: the Feesh Khabour, Greater Zab, Lesser Zab, and Diyala (and its tributaries).[19]

In 1975, Iran and Iraq signed an agreement on the use of shared watercourses, in which the signatory parties agreed on the division of a number of shared Tigris tributaries.[20] The agreement provided for a mechanism for the division of the waters of the tributaries of the Tigris shared by Iran and Iraq. However, this mechanism does not seem to have been established. And the agreement appears to have been forgotten: it does not seem to have been cited even by Iraq, which has a grievance against Iran in respect of the Diyala and its tributaries.

In sum, the legal framework governing the exploitation of the Tigris and its tributaries is patchy and incomplete. In theory, all states in the basin are bound by the provisions of the 1997 UN Convention on the Non-Navigational Uses of International Watercourses, since it entered into force in 2014. The Convention requires all states using the waters of an international watercourse to do so in an "equitable and reasonable" manner.

However, Turkey has been notably hostile to the Convention and is not likely to be constrained by its provisions; and Turkey would probably insist in any case that its use of the Tigris was indeed equitable and reasonable. For its part, Iran voted in favor of the Convention in 1997. But in failing to provide Iraq with details of its projects on the tributaries of the Diyala, Iran has ignored one of the key provisions of the Convention, namely Article 9: Regular exchange of data and information.

Turkey constructed three major dams on the Tigris (the Karalkizi, Diçle, and Batman dams) between 1985 and 1999. The Karalkizi Dam is hydropower only: while it may have affected the pattern of flow of the Tigris in Iraq (the "regime" of the river), it will not have affected the overall volume available to Iraq averaged over a year. The Diçle and Batman dams store water for irrigation as well as hydropower.

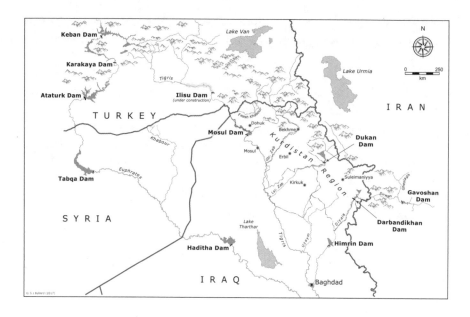

Water in Iraq and Kurdistan

Turkey is continuing to build dams on the Tigris, of which the Ilisu and Silvan are the largest. Once these dams are in operation, Turkey's net abstractions from the Tigris for irrigation will reach 5 bcm/a.

As already noted, the Greater Zab is the most important of the Tigris tributaries in Iraq in terms of flow: its average annual flow is roughly that of the other three "Iraqi" tributaries combined. It would therefore be a serious matter for Iraq (including the KRI) if Turkey were to abstract large quantities of water from the Greater Zab. However, while Turkey has plans to build two dams on the river, these will be for hydropower only: the terrain is discouraging for irrigation, which is in any case not much needed in this area of relatively high precipitation. So these dams would affect the seasonal pattern of flow of the Greater Zab (perhaps to the advantage of Iraq and the KRI), but not its overall annual flow.

Abdulsattar Majeed, the KRG's Minister of Agriculture and Water Resources, summed up the position of the KRG vis-à-vis Turkey's activities upstream by declaring in April 2015 that the KRG had no disputes with Turkey over water.[21] By contrast, KRG officials have publicly complained of Iranian actions which have reduced and will reduce still more the flow of the Diyala into Iraq. The Gheshlagh (Qeshlagh, or Vahdat) and Gavoshan dams have already been built on tributaries of the Diyala. As well as generating hydropower, both dams provide water for irrigation and for the cities of Sanandaj and Kermanshah respectively.

Moreover, according to Rudaw, the Garan dam, on a tributary of the Sirwan river in Iran's Kurdistan Province, poses a danger to the flow of water into the reservoir behind the Darbandikhan dam on the Diyala in the KRI. Rudaw quoted Rahman Khani, Director of the Darbandikhan dam, as having said that 70 per cent of the flow of the Diyala at Darbandikhan comes from Iran. Iranian projects on the headwaters of the Diyala would therefore have a considerable impact on the amount of water in the Darbandikhan reservoir.[22] One academic source suggests that the impact of such works has already been significant, with an average reduction in flow of the river of between 2004 and 2013 of nearly 24 per cent in February and about 77 per cent in September.[23]

However, Khani was not able to say how severe the impact of Iranian projects would be, as Iran had consistently refused to share information about the projects with either the KRG or the government in Baghdad. And the same Rudaw article quoted Akram Mohammed Anwar, Director of Kurdistan Region Dams, as accusing Iran of turning a deaf ear to Kurdish concerns—even when those concerns have been raised in Tehran by the visiting Iraqi (as opposed to KRG) Minister of Water Resources.

Given the importance of the relationship between Baghdad and Erbil on the one hand and Tehran on the other (especially since the ISIL offensive of summer 2014), neither the Iraqi government nor the KRG is likely to make more energetic moves to dissuade Iran from pursuing its projects on the headwaters of the Diyala. The Iraqi authorities in both Baghdad and Erbil will have to continue to adapt to lower volumes of water in the Diyala.

The downstream neighbor

The KRI's downstream neighbor is, of course, the rest of Iraq. So far, nothing the KRG has done with the water resources in the territory it controls has been to the detriment of the rest of Iraq. Quite the reverse: for decades, the KRI has stored and supplied water for irrigation projects outside the KRG and provided hydropower too.

There is no reason why this arrangement should not continue. Even though population growth and economic development in the KRI will produce more consumers of water (households, businesses, and modern farms), greater efficiency in water use should enable their needs to be met without depriving consumers outside the KRI. For this to be possible, however, substantial capital investment will be needed, with a good deal of the funding needing to come from the government in Baghdad.

What impact will climate change have?

There is inevitably a good deal of uncertainty about the impact of climate change on the water resources of the KRI. However, regional climate models suggest higher temperatures and substantial decreases in the average annual flow of the Tigris (and

Euphrates) by the end of the century, ranging from 19 to 58 per cent. This would naturally apply to the water resources of the KRI, which falls within the Tigris basin.[24]

The projected reductions in river discharge will decrease the hydropower potential of the basin and so adversely affect the production of electricity. In irrigated agriculture, water loss through evapotranspiration will continue to increase in the future, as a result of higher temperatures.None of this extra pressure on water resources means that disputes between the KRI and its neighbors (whether upstream or downstream) over water will inevitably arise. With advanced water-management techniques and political leaderships prepared to promote cooperation, it ought to be possible to avoid such disputes.

The economic and political outlook

Given the high level of water availability relative to the population, the unlikelihood of its neighbors depriving it of a large proportion of its water supply, and the scope for conservation and recycling, water should not be a serious obstacle to the economic development of Iraqi Kurdistan. Nor need it be the cause of disputes between the KRI and its neighbors. However, a good outcome will require enlightened political leadership on the part of all interested parties as well as the investment of substantial sums of money. Similarly, water by itself would not be an impediment to independence, should the leadership of Iraqi Kurdistan choose that course. Moreover, it would not be an effective weapon for neighbors hostile to such a step to use against an independent Iraqi Kurdistan.

28.

PEACE EDUCATION IN THE KURDISH REGION OF IRAQ

EVOLUTION AND LIMITATIONS

Kelsey Shanks

Peace education in the formal education sector refers to the process of promoting the knowledge and skills needed for students to interpret the world around them and react to potential conflicts in a peaceful and non-violent manner. Such programs can be introduced through a stand-alone subject, integrated throughout the whole curriculum, or more effectively, through a combination of the two. The Kurdish Regional Government (KRG) Ministry of Education, various United Nations agencies, and additional international actors have all engaged with the notion of peace education in the Kurdistan Region of Iraq (KRI) under various project titles. These different interventions have each tackled the knowledge, skills, and pedagogy associated with peace education within KRI state schools. Yet, this research suggests that despite concerted efforts, the local context, scope of the subject, and confusion over terminology have resulted in limited sustainable impact within the KRI education sector. This chapter does not attempt to evaluate the impact of peace education programs on students' attitudes and behaviors; instead it seeks to investigate the evolution of the subject and highlight barriers to the subject's integration into the mainstream curriculum.

The information presented is drawn from open qualitative interviews with Ministry of Education officials, UN agency staff engaged with peace education, a sample of school directors and social science teachers in Erbil, Duhok, and

Suleimaniya, and academics specializing in relevant education themes. Interviews were conducted face-to-face across the KRI between 2014 and 2015. The first section will provide a brief introduction to the context in the KRI and the education environment post-2003. The following section is dedicated to providing a clear conceptual understanding of peace education and the relevant terminology. Despite ministerial, donor, and academic engagement with the concept, it is evident that peace education remains an often-misunderstood term. The third section moves on to depict the evolution of peace education components in the KRI. This section will map interventions that have had the potential to influence the integration of peace education into the Kurdistan Region's curriculum and explore their successes and restraints. The final section will unpack the various limitations and barriers to integrating peace education within the KRI.

Context

Throughout the end of the twentieth century and the beginning of the twenty-first, Iraq and the Kurdistan Region of Iraq were subjected to a myriad of external and internal influences that have shaped their current position. What is now the Kurdish Region of Iraq gained autonomy from Saddam's Iraq in 1991, with a regional government being established the following year.[1] By the end of the first Gulf War, the majority of Kurdish-populated areas of northern Iraq became effectively outside Baghdad's control, separated by a no-fly zone and the unofficial boundary known as the Green Line. This resulted in the Iraqi Kurdistan Region of Iraq achieving relative autonomy from Saddam's Iraq and limiting the continued influence of the Ba'ath Party's systematic Arabization policies within those areas.

In addition to the population movements and outright violence of the arabization era, the narrative of oppression pays significant attention to the denial of educational rights.[2] Education became a deliberate vehicle through which the Ba'ath Party sought to implement arabization in the Region. In accordance with the planned systematic assimilation of the north's non-Arab population, study in non-Arabic languages was prohibited. All civil servants, including teachers, were obliged to join the Ba'ath Party and were subjected to ideological testing and surveillance.[3] The regime controlled the teaching of all subjects, using history, geography, and civics to enforce Ba'athist ideology. They forbade reference to Iraq's multicultural make-up, and as such ethnic historical narratives were omitted from the curriculum.[4] The establishment of the Kurdistan Regional Government led to the formation of the regional Ministry of Education, which was able to safeguard education in areas under its control from such manipulations.

Despite achieving greater control of education within the Region, the Kurdish governance did not alleviate the population's exposure to conflict. The rivalry between the Kurdistan Democratic Party (KDP) and the Patriotic Union of Kurdistan (PUK) resulted in a de facto partition of the Region.[5] The KDP retained control of Duhok and Erbil, while PUK administered Suleimaniya. This tenuous power-sharing agreement collapsed in 1994 and led to a civil war which is known in Kurdish as "*brakuzhi*" meaning "brother killing brother." The violent conflict between the KDP and the PUK was finally brought to an end in 1998 with the Washington Agreement. Yet the legacy of civil war and conflict between the two parties has shaped contemporary Iraqi-Kurdish politics.[6] The 2003 invasion of Iraq extended the era of instability; and conflict with Baghdad continued over the definition of the KRI southern border with Iraq and the distribution of oil revenues from the Region. The KRG claimed that areas with high Kurdish populations remained beyond the Green Line and unjustly continued to fall under central Baghdad's control. Most notably, the oil-rich governorate of Kirkuk, regarded as the Kurdish Jerusalem, has taken center stage in the disputed territories narrative. Consequently the KRI continued to feel the impact of instability created by the ongoing tensions with the Baghdad government.

In 2014 the power dynamic in the Region changed dramatically once more with the fall of neighboring Mosul to the extremist terror group Islamic State (IS). The need to foster peace and stability in Iraq was amplified by the destabilization of the country and resulting mass population movements. This conflict has changed many national and local peace dynamics irrevocably, and the sectarian nature of the conflict has pushed the political debate over political representation and participation to the forefront of the peace-building discussion. The expansion of IS control has led to massive internal displacement, and Iraq is now contending with one of the largest internally displaced populations in the world. Millions of Iraqis have been forced to flee the ongoing violence; the Kurdistan Region of Iraq has become refuge to almost a million Iraqi IDPs of all ethnic backgrounds. Unfortunately, the wider sectarian-based conflict and the strain on host communities has led to growing ethnically-defined tensions across the Region.

The combination of UN sanctions, international embargos, and the impact of ongoing conflict has severely damaged the KRI's education infrastructure. The devastating legacy of neglect is still felt by schools across the Region today. This, coupled with the 2016 KRI economic crisis and IS-induced displacement emergency, has resulted in huge challenges to providing appropriate levels of education in the fragile socio-economic and political environment. Equally, the cumulative effects of sustained deprivation and decades of social and political instability have long-term implications for the Region's population. As the Kurdistan Regional Government is working to counter these consequences, the rest of the world is looking to KRI and Iraqi youth as the generation that need to ensure a new era of stability and peace. In this respect it is essential that youth be provided with the skills, not just for successful economic integration, but also to play an active part in shaping society in accordance with the principles of peace, equity, and social justice. Education policy-makers today must avoid focusing solely on the repair of damaged educational infrastructure; they must also ensure that education stakeholders and schools are empowered to support wider societal priorities. Education provides space to reinforce KRI's push for societal change, such as urging peaceful coexistence, protecting the rights of marginalized groups, and championing gender equality.

Locating peace education

Peace education as understood by UNICEF refers to the process of promoting the knowledge, skills, attitudes, and values needed to bring about the behavior changes that will enable children, youth, and adults to prevent conflict and violence, both overt and structural; to resolve conflict peacefully; and to create the conditions conducive to peace, whether at an intrapersonal, interpersonal, intergroup, national, or international level.[7] Consequently, many concepts have become synonymous with peace education, such as conflict resolution, human rights education, citizenship, civics, and life skills. In this respect peace education has become an umbrella term for education associated with the problem of violence and strategies for peace. Within this field, programming can aim to reach adults, children, and communities alike, through a variety of media such as structured learning, seminars and workshops, collaborative community projects, or even through art and drama. However, this chapter is concerned specifically with the implementation of peace education programs through formal education curricula.

The design of a formal peace education curriculum does not have an intrinsically linear development; instead it is more comparable to a web of concepts, values, and skills that interconnect to help build peace through influencing peaceful behavior.[8] Yet, despite the vast potential of peace education, a review of the literature highlights an absence of common understandings and consensus over what constitutes the subject. Unfortunately, this spiral of activities has created confusion over terminology and the jurisdiction of agencies working in the field of peace education, preventing a clear strategic framework for its implementation. Traditional discourse surrounding peace education acknowledges that a broad spectrum of subjects fall under its umbrella: students of peace education should be knowledgeable about history, diversity, human rights, civics, democracy, and the environment. Based on the knowledge of such components, students can start, with the help of trained educators, to acquire the necessary skills in order to be able to put theory into action through active decision-making, analytical thinking, and methods of non-violent conflict resolution.

By definition, peace education should be contextually specific and reflective of issues present in students' everyday lives. Therefore, in practice, it can vary from interpersonal conflict resolution applied in schools, to educating against perceptions of real enemies and the process of making peace. Thus, within the education sector, two distinct streams of peace education can be identified.

Firstly, we have what we will refer to as "Peace Education for Societal Change." This stream is engagement that seeks to cultivate a peaceful outlook in general, peace education that mobilizes pupils and teachers to take part in a campaign for a peaceful society. As such, it encourages students to carry the banner for an alternative vision of society that counters the beliefs, attitudes, and actions which have previously led to negative societal impacts.[9] In this respect, peace education can be seen as a type of socialization process for a better future.

The second stream of peace education can be called "Peace Education for Reconciliation" and deals more specifically with the emotive issues of engaging with peace in the aftermath of violence. This stream seeks to promote a peaceful disposition toward a particular ethnic in the context of previous inter-group conflict.[10] Such programs aim to aid the legitimization of each collective historical narrative, promoting the critical examination of all contributions to conflict and allowing room for empathy for others' suffering to promote engagement with non-violent activities and a shared peaceful future.[11]

Both forms of peace education have the common objective of fostering change in order to create more peaceful environments in which equality, justice, tolerance, human rights, and environmental quality prevail. For example, multicultural education can be adopted to promote both streams of peace education, yet while the first deals with different collective narratives in general, the latter must also engage with the challenges of emotive and painful historical events which impact on the conceptualization of group identity. In this respect, the sociopolitical context in which the peace education curriculum is applied has significant influence in terms of programming. Some argue that in post-conflict settings it is essential to interact with both approaches to peace education, while others recognize that the latter often evokes an ideological battleground that can hamper its practical implementation.[12]

While the general stream is often implicit in many of the international communities' education interventions at the country level, the latter reconciliation approach requires engagement with issues of political significance that often prove too controversial. Therefore, this more sensitive aim requires broader negotiation in the school setting. Formal curricula may not be the most effective entry point in this respect, but ensuring that all curriculum subjects are conflict-sensitive and provide a balanced and impartial description of history, geography and religion is a step toward these aims. Infusion of the principles of peace education across the curriculum can serve to lay the foundations for wider political and societal engagement with issues of reconciliation and the legitimization of narratives. Within the Kurdistan Region of Iraq, a history of violent interethnic conflict and political fragility makes both components useful tools for building a peaceful future in the Region.

The KRG states that more than 50 per cent of the 5 million population are under twenty years old, and national academics have long highlighted the need for generational reform and advancement.[13] Peace education can serve to play a supportive role in reinforcing such long-term societal changes. Youth and children growing up in the KRI require support to negotiate both the current conflict and cross-generational historical traumas in a peaceful manner. It is necessary for education stakeholders to harness the potential of schools in a systematic manner. In order for peace education to address the issues faced in KRI, it is vital that actors understand the conflict context. For any peace-building intervention to be effective, it must be driven by a theory of change that is based on sound understanding of the situation. Peace education for societal change can serve to advance general peaceful behaviors in a community, but contextual education for reconciliation programming is ultimately more powerful in the wake of interethnic conflict.

The roots of the conflict in the Region can be traced to many complex and integrated issues of local, national, regional, and international origins. Many local organizations are endeavoring to unpack conflict triggers in order to address them in peace-building efforts within the KRI. In this respect the successful accommodation of diversity has been highlighted as a significant challenge in the KRI. Although the majority of the Region's population is Kurdish, it is also traditionally home to Assyrian, Chaldean, Turkmen, Yezidi, and Arab communities. This ethnic diversity reflects the significant religious and linguistic diversity in KRI. The majority of Kurds, Turkmen, and Arabs within the KRI are reported to be of the Sunni Muslim tradition, while the Region also has populations of Assyrian Christian, Shia Muslim, Yezidi, Mandean, and Sahbak faiths.[14] Linguistically the KRI states that Kurdish and Arabic are official languages, with both Sorani and Kurmanji Kurdish dialects widely spoken.[15] But the education system also has schools using Turkish and Assyrian as the medium of instruction.

Interethnic relations are not without historical instances of conflict, and tensions can be found between communities. Within the KRI, minority groups speak of acceptance and governmental support; whereas in the surrounding disputed territories, accusations of attempted assimilation by Kurdish groups are present and territorial disputes damage already fraught Arab-Kurd relations.[16]

The occupation of neighboring land by IS has intensified the need for efforts to strengthen the accommodation of diversity and promote healthy intergroup relations in the KRI. These events have not only amplified identity indicators and sensitized intergroup relations, but also increased the population diversity within the KRI through the influx of a million IDPs.

In this respect, peace education can be employed to address three areas of identity-driven tension in the KRI: first, the promotion of equal democratic rights for all identity groups; second, addressing the legacy of identity issues created by the previous regime; and third, tackling the heightened role of religious identity post-2003. Peace education can provide a channel through which to promote intergroup dialogue and foster understanding of the need for peaceful coexistence amongst communities. As such, education can provide the opportunity to foster narratives of the "past and visions for the future" and allow students to locate themselves and their communities within the context of present conflicts and contestation.[17]

Peace education programs in the KRI

The KRG Ministry of Education has focused significant efforts on improving education standards.[18] The reforms include extending compulsory education from six to nine years, modernizing learning objectives, and attempts to move KRI education toward international standards of good practice. During this process, particular emphasis has been placed on the development of human rights and citizenship education. Attention to such subjects would demonstrate the KRG's recognition and commitment to education's role in helping to build a peaceful, just society. As key components of peace education, citizenship and human rights education can emphasize the need to protect disadvantaged and vulnerable groups and promote the celebration of diversity. In addition, many NGOs and UN agencies have initiated programs within the formal education structure to support the KRG Ministry of Education in its pursuit of peace education objectives. This section will seek to map the interventions that have fallen under the peace education conceptual remit and present the evolution of the subject in KRI curricula. As such, the section will explore whether actors have chosen to employ "societal change" or "reconciliation" agenda and unpack the targeted subject areas.

Peace education knowledge: the evolution of existing curriculum subjects

The KRG Ministry of Education has taken significant steps to improve education standards in the Region and takes pride in the advancements of curriculum development. The subjects of civics, human rights, and citizenship all have formal teaching time devoted to them and cover a range of topics from justice to environmental responsibility (see Figure 28.1: Peace education curriculum subjects). Civics and human rights are stand-alone subjects within the school timetable, while citizenship makes up one third of the social studies curriculum. In terms of teacher training, teaching resources, and textbook development, each subject has received varying degrees of support and development. Each of the curriculum interventions to enhance knowledge of peace education subjects has been strongly grounded in a broad approach to peace-building for societal change.

Civics: The Ministry of Education introduced Civic Education for grades 3, 4, 5, and 6 in 2003. Textbooks were developed in collaboration with the Ministry of Human Rights, Macmillan Publishers, and the Foundation for Democracy. The textbooks were subsequently revised twice, each time to make them more culturally appropriate to the KRI context. The resulting changes were primarily to imagery and the characters used, while key topics and themes remained the same. Over the subsequent ten years the Ministry of Education estimate that they have trained 13,000 teachers and 330 supervisors in the subject.

In 2006 the United States Institute for Peace engaged in developing a "Rights of the Citizen" curriculum in Iraq. The project sought to help students understand the principles behind the new Iraqi state and constitution and build a sense of national community based on elements of Iraqi culture that would be familiar to students. USIP worked primarily in Baghdad, but simultaneously liaised with the KRG Ministry of Education to implement the project in the north. However, due to the existing subject of civics, KRG Ministry officials requested that rather than provide a new alternative curriculum, USIP help enhance the existing teaching of civic education through the development of a teacher's guide on teaching national and civic education from the 4th to the 9th grade.

Human Rights: Human rights education was introduced as early as 2001 in KRG schools and continues to be taught in grades 5, 7, and 10. The project was a collaborative effort between the Ministry of Education, the Ministry of Human Rights, and the Norwegian People's Aid (NPA). The Ministry of Education developed textbooks and financed the training of 830 teachers in the subject. The Ministry's independent financing of the program has generated a strong sense of ownership over this subject. This is reflected in the pride with which the developments are presented. In 2013 the Ministry developed additional animations to support classroom activities for grades 7 and 10. Similar resources for grade 10 were also in development.

Citizenship: Citizenship education is taught as one third of the subject of social studies (which also includes history and geography) in grades 4 through to 9. Textbooks are provided, but there are no teacher's guides for the subject. The subject has a strong element of environmental responsibility and emphasis on life skills.

Civics	Human Rights	Citizenship (part of Social Studies)	Democracy
Grades 3, 4, 5 & 6	Grades 5,7 & 10	Grades 4 -9	Grade 10
Privacy	Belonging	Environment	Democracy
Justice	Needs	Communication	
Power and Authority	Stages of human rights	Problem Solving	
Responsibility	Differences	Life Skills	
	Rights	Decision Making	
	Responsibilities		

Peace Education Infused into other subjects	
Social Studies	Grades 4-9
Religious Education	Grades 1-12
Science of Religion	Grades 10-12

Figure 28.1: Peace education curriculum subjects

Subject	Actor	Teacher Training	Teachers Resources
Civics	Ministry of Education	Teachers Trained: 3,000 Supervisors: 330	Teachers Guide: Grades 4-9
	United States Institute of Peace	Teachers Trained: 62	Teachers Guide
Human Rights	Ministry of Education Ministry of Human Rights	Teachers Trained: 830	Resources: TV animations
Citizenship	Ministry of Education	Teachers Trained:	None

Figure 28.2: Peace education teacher training and resources

The wider curriculum: In addition, the principles of peace have theoretically been infused into a range of curriculum subjects such as Islamic education, which promotes tolerance and Islamic principles of peace; science of religion, which covers the teaching of regionally specific religions such as Kaka'I, Yezidi, and Shabak; and finally social studies, which includes the sensitive subjects of geography and history.

Peace education skills: UN agencies and the development of Life Skills

In 2010-12, the UNESCO Office in Iraq collaborated with Beirut offices of Economic and Social Commission for Western Asia (ESCWA) and the UN Population Fund (UNFPA), the objective being to raise awareness of civic values and life skills in schools, the community, and youth centers across Iraq, including the KRI. The project developed a series of six core modules and targeted education providers, as well as the direct engagement of Iraqi youth (aged twelve to nineteen) to ensure wide support for the establishment of violence-free learning environments. Within the framework of the ESCWA-UNESCO-UNFPA project, civic values were conceptually defined as including the following concepts: human rights, citizenship, national identity, toler-ance, and gender equality. Civic Values were defined as enhancing the culture of acceptance among adolescents and would ensure their sense of belonging to the State of Iraq, thus combating sectarianism and communal divide. As for life skills, they were defined for the purpose of the project as encompassing interpersonal communication skills, negotiation/refusal skills, empathy, cooperation and teamwork, advocacy skills, decision-making and problem-solving skills, critical thinking, skills for increasing internal focus of control, managing feelings, as well as stress management skills. Unfortunately, this project had more success within Federal Iraq, due to an emphasis on belonging to the Iraqi State. The failure to contextualize the project to the KRI reality of Kurdish nationalism saw it fail to be adopted widely within KRI.

Subject	Originator	Teacher training	Teacher's resources
Life Skills	UNESCO	Life Skills training of trainers package for secondary schools; Trainers trained: 6 Teachers trained: 56	
	UNFPA		Forthcoming UNFPA Life Skills for basic education
	UNFPA ESCWA	Training guide	Vocational Life Skills teacher/ student activity book

Figure 28.3: UN interventions in Life Skills

Peace Education				
MoE infusion into curriculum Peace education as part of other subjects Religious Education Social Studies	MoE curriculum subjects: Human Rights Civics Citizenship	2006 MoE & USIP revision of Civics textbooks and teacher's guide	2011 MoE and UNICEF child-friendly schools standards	Youth Life Skills and Citizenship program; MoE UNESCO UNFPA ESCWA

Figure 28.4: Peace education in the KRI

Limitations to the integration of peace education

Despite these efforts, the general perception from interviewees across the spectrum of education providers was that peace education, as a curriculum pursuit, remains largely missing from KRI schools. The inclusion of subjects that fall under the peace education umbrella remains unreflective of the technical support, financial investment, and time spent on cultivating such subjects. This can be put down, in part, to the status of the Region's education system post-2003 as that of "reconstruction" with it subsequently being in a "crisis" situation post-June 2014. This has led to the education system suffering persistent underfunding; schools often operate in shifts with limited classroom time for core subjects, resulting in the neglect of non-examination classes such as citizenship. However, a number of problematic issues beyond that of capacity were raised in relation to the failure to integrate peace education into the school system post-2003. These issues can be viewed as obstacles inherent in the system, as opposed to resource-based.

Conflict sensitivity: In order for formal education to be harnessed for the purposes of peace-building, it needs to be conflict-sensitive. One of the stated obstacles to achieving the successful integration of peace education interventions in the Kurdish Region of Iraq is the absence of conflict sensitivity within the wider curriculum and throughout the structural management of the education system as a whole. Unfortunately, it was reported that some subjects retain conflict-insensitive elements and work in opposition to peace education principles. Anecdotal evidence presented during data collection suggested that various elements of the wider curriculum serve to contradict the message of peace education in schools: for example, the use of shari'a-based inheritance laws in mathematics questions, which serve to enforce

429

gender inequality; and the continually contested historical interpretations failing to reflect the Region's diversity.

Furthermore, the use of Islamic education as an advancer of peace was called into question by regional academics.[19] Although the curriculum contains many valuable messages of equality and peace, it also retains some conflicting elements. The subject's very role in a public institution has been questioned, as it currently falls under the heading of "instruction in faith" rather than "instruction about faith." It was suggested that rather than fostering tolerance, Islamic education in the KRI is a "propagandistic tool to spread absolutist values and a worldview that lacks usefulness in the education of students in the values of diversity, tolerance, and openness to others."[20] The absolutist nature of the subject also influences the delivery of religious science, which teaches about other faiths in the Region. Other religions are taught from an Islamic perspective, often resulting in the dismissal of practices as "witchcraft". This subject is criticized also for being deprioritized and often completely neglected. Incidentally, in non-Islamic schools it appears to be missing entirely from the curriculum.

Furthermore, Kirmanj's analysis of the history and social studies textbooks suggests that a repetitive use of "the other" serves to divide Kurdish students from their Arab and minority-ethnicity neighbors, an accusation that was supported by school-level interviews in all three KRI governorates.[21] There are a number of ways in which the education system is deemed to be insensitive to the wider community conflicts. Shanks also highlights the structural inequalities between linguistically-defined schools across the northern Iraqi region, where both Iraqi regional ministries have influence.[22] If the education system contradicts the messages introduced through specific peace education subject areas, or whole school ethos campaigns, it will limit the effectiveness of interventions. Even teachers who champion the promotion of peace education systematically are hindered by the contradictory messages within the school system.

Subjects and buzzwords: The structural organization of the curriculum was also considered an obstacle to peace education's integration by many interviewees. Attention was drawn to the fact that each subject heading (human rights, citizenshp, social studies, etc.) is designed independently and without connection to the others. This has resulted in the repetition of topics and no coherent links between the key concepts presented. The curriculum subjects lack focus or coordinated learning objectives. In addition, the assigned delivery of subjects has created an imbalance between the grades. Rather than spreading topics and objectives equally across the grades, they are bunched in certain stages. For example, grade 10 has the responsibility for a number of complex subjects: human rights, democracy, and also the study of Kurdish Genocide.[23] Educators complained that this overload of topics has led to each one being delivered in very narrow terms with no room for real exploration of themes.

There is a linear development to a child's education: students progress through basic and secondary education following a prescribed curriculum. In this respect, even subjects without inherently linear progression within them can be taught through the systematic building of knowledge and skills throughout the school life cycle of a child. However, the implementation of these disjointed and unconnected projects reportedly fails to harness this potential. Projects do not consider what has gone before, what may come after, or even what already exists in the curriculum. In this respect opportunities have been missed to strengthen a child's learning. Equally, the mixed delivery of different subjects under the sphere of peace education is not time-effective. Given the nature of school shifts and limited classroom time in KRI schools, better organization and coordination of subjects falling within this concept would be more beneficial to students' overall learning outcomes. Adding extra subjects rather than linking to existing ones has been detrimental to the acceptance of the concept and the ability of the teacher to find the time to teach it.

The confusion over subjects and their topical remits is reflective of the discourse surrounding peace-building in general. The debate around peace-building's utility has been hindered by imprecision, ideological dissimilarities, and competing organizational mandates.[24] The absence of clarity over terminology within the education community further exaggerates this division. Concepts relating to peace education, such as human rights, citizenship, cohesion, resilience, and life skills remain blurred, lacking clear divisions, connections, and understanding. Furthermore, education stakeholders in the KRI come from both local and international communities. The UN and international agencies' support for education has resulted in the education community having influence from diverse cultures, languages, and systems of communication. Frequently, changing buzzwords and terminology relating to peace education at the international policy level has led to a high level of confusion in the field and overlapping project objectives. In order to access funding and international aid resources, those working on education within the KRI ministry and international agencies are expected to understand the ever-changing vocabulary surrounding peace education, contextualize how it relates to peace education in KRI, and then act upon it accordingly.

Consequently, mixed terminology has hindered a clear understanding of the corresponding aims of many subjects that fall under the peace education banner. International stakeholders have proposed separate projects under differing terminology which amount to the same thing, confusing ministerial understanding rather than building capacity. It was suggested that efforts to advance curricula in the KRI have resulted in duplicated projects by different stakeholders that have wasted resources. This is illustrated by the United States Institute for Peace engagement in developing a Rights of the Citizen curriculum. The project did not acknowledge the KRI Ministry of Education's existing subject of civics until ministry officials requested that rather than provide a new alternative curriculum, USIP help enhance the existing teaching of civic education. Rather than projects promoting peace education knowledge and skills working in harmony, a variety of concepts are competing to achieve the same aims.

Furthermore, the design of the UNESCO-led project illustrates the obstacle of uncoordinated subjects further; outputs for the project were divided between UN agencies, so that resources were developed for vocational schools, secondary education, and civil society youth groups. The project failed to engage with the existing KRI curriculum at each level when developing its life skills package. Education stakeholders suggested that a more integrated approach would have provided stronger results and ensured uptake of the project in the KRI. By failing to provide a joint strategic framework, there was little for the KRG ministry to implement. The fragmented nature of projects led to a confusing number of resources within the ministry without clear definition of their purpose and therefore hampered the government's further application of programs. As a consequence, this project has so far failed to impact on strategy in the KRI. The opportunity to work within the existing ministry frameworks and build education sector capacity from within was missed. Instead the project merely added another layer to deliver.

Unfortunately, there was inadequate continuous and transparent coordination between the UN agencies and with the ministry, which resulted in duplicated work and overlapping agendas even within the project. UN agencies have different mandates, programming approaches, timeframes, and concepts of the end-state, which can constitute a great barrier to coordination. They make it difficult for different agencies to align toward a common objective or to develop joint operations. Each agency often views their own approach as the best approach, and believes that all other agencies should align with them. Lack of coordination between agencies hindering peace-building objectives was highlighted by Campbell and Hartnett in 2005. They suggest that each agency consider itself to be a sovereign entity. An agency will therefore only participate in coordination efforts that help it to meet its own particular objectives and mission. Even coordination efforts that are statutorily mandated require some degree of voluntary participation.

The building of civic values, the advancement of life skills, citizenship, civics, and human rights education can each fall under the remit of peace education and can each be strengthened by fostered links with one another. However, projects have been addressed in isolation from one another, and also from the reality of the classroom, adding to an already confused series of subjects being delivered. The provision of resource books, teacher's guides, and training are all helpful to a certain point, but without a strategic program for implementation they fail to secure the subjects' objectives, adding instead to confusion and the varied quality of delivery of the subjects across the Region.

Inappropriate teaching resources: The chosen topics to be taught also require closer scrutiny. Interviewees suggested that there was a failure to engage the education stakeholders adequately with issues of specific importance in the KRI, such as gender, ethnic diversity, and the rights of marginalized communities and refugees. There is general consensus that peace-building requires consideration of local norms and values, and cannot be purely influenced by international best practice or externally identified concepts of peace. Unfortunately, perceptions presented in interviews suggested that peace education in KRG often fails to meet these criteria. The peace education subjects that have been developed all remain centered around generic liberal peace topics, reflecting the reluctance of the international community and the Ministry of Education to address meaningfully any sensitive issues that might be deemed political. There is a distinct lack of space within the curriculum for engagement with peace-building for reconciliation. Interviewees reported missed opportunities to contextualize subjects in the realities of history and current events in the Region. Subjects were reportedly taught in the abstract, without reference to any topic that might be deemed sensitive. Furthermore, the final report was presented with unsubstantiated claims of UN agencies failing to act on information that highlighted the need to tackle sensitive issues such as gender and FGM. Buried reports and disengagement from important subjects were perceived to be prohibiting evocative subjects from being addressed through peace education. The balance between working within a ministry and obtaining local ownership and tackling unpopular issues of significance was not being met.

When context-specific subjects are included, a reported lack of follow-through from policy to practice has resulted in little impact at the classroom level. For example, interviewees suggested that some topics that are deemed to promote ethnic diversity are available within the curriculum but do not get implemented at the school level. For example, the inclusion of topics relating to minority communities are often relegated to the last period of the week and therefore not actually taught. In addition, some of the generic peace education topics that are taught have been criticized for the inappropriate nature of the subject matter in relation to the age of the child, with textbooks and topics often superseding the students' level of understanding.[25] This was particularly true in reference to the ministry-developed primary level subjects, which often fail to make connections that are relevant to the students' own experience.[26] Equally, despite the new emphasis on Human Rights in the 2009 curriculum reform, this subject lacks useful resource materials. The observations of this research confirmed the findings of Osler in 2013 that the Human Rights textbooks are "clinical and uninteresting, containing long extracts from international instruments, such as the Universal Declaration of Human Rights, but with little or no guidance as to what they mean or how they might be made accessible to teachers and relevant to students."[27] The emphasis appears to be on knowledge, not on developing human rights dispositions or values.[28]

Lack of sustainability and inadequately trained teachers: The findings suggested that perceptions prevail that many teachers remain untrained in the basic principles of modern pedagogy and continue to use teacher-centric classroom delivery. This observation was prevalent amongst education observers consulted from the ministry to the classroom. There was a general acknowledgement that teacher training needs to be deemed a priority. Each of the subjects introduced to promote peace education is in principle dependent on the active engagement of children so that they are provided with the opportunity to think critically. Subjects used in the promotion of peace education should also use role-play, games, and collaborative learning projects to implement negotiation and working together. If teachers are not trained in child-centered teaching pedagogies, then civics, citizenship, and human rights education will fail to deliver important subject-specific messages.

Equally, despite the Ministry of Education's teacher training programs, it is a common assumption that teachers within these subjects have little in the way of subject-specific training. Teachers are drawn from the history and geography specialisms. It is essential that the teacher clearly understands the concepts and ideals that they are delivering, given that teachers must become "peace role models"; a teacher who preaches human rights without demonstrating what is being taught devalues the subject and prevents the learning outcomes from being achieved. Furthermore, if teachers are not subject-specialists, it becomes easier to de-prioritize these subjects in favor of more traditional lessons, which was a common claim heard in consultations.

Sinclair suggests that training teachers in experimental pedagogy for peace education is an over-ambitious aim as training programs face a number of inherent obstacles.[29] She suggests that there are often unrealistic timeframes for training programs; short-term investment from external stakeholders results in training that is often brief in duration and lacks any follow-up support after completion. Consequently, pedagogical changes are not sustainable, as teachers return to the traditional teaching methods that are more familiar and socially expected of them. Local traditions and cultural norms cannot easily be changed through a one-off training program that offers no long-term professional development support. As one teacher commented, "I had the training and the willingness to continue teaching peace, but it came to a stop; no support, no monitoring, all those who were trained gradually forgot the training and returned to traditional teaching."[30] International donor funding cycles are seen to prevent real investment in teacher training as a tool for peace-building for a number of interconnected reasons. One of the major challenges for peace education is the timeline. Conflict transformation takes place over long periods of time, and peace education by its very nature is a long-term process. However, stakeholders are often forced to design programs which fit within the two- or three-year funding cycles.

Furthermore, teacher training in conflict-affected regions like Iraq and the Kurdistan Region of Iraq often focuses on a country's capital city or easily accessible regions, creating pockets of exclusion and engaging only a sample of easily reached teachers. This is often due to security concerns and serves to prevent the national roll-out of training programs. In the KRI, this obstacle was illustrated by encounters with teachers who have received frequent training by various agencies post-2003, while others outside the easy-to-access areas remain untrained in their subject specialism. One teacher remarked on the fact that she was not the one who required the training, "but I am the one who repeatedly gets offered it, because our school is here."

Conclusions and ways forward

The formal education curriculum has the potential to impact the next generation of children in the Kurdistan Region of Iraq and promote behavior conducive to peace. The classroom provides a space to encourage key aspects of peaceful behavior, while also allowing emotive subjects to be presented in a safe and representative manner. The umbrella of peace education encompasses, and is synonymous with, a variety of concepts seeking to achieve this aim: conflict resolution, human rights education, citizenship, civics and life skills. The peace education initiatives implemented in the KRI have had the potential to provide solid foundations for peace education in the Region's schools. But unfortunately, the limitations listed in the previous sections, combined with the overall capacity gaps, have to some extent undermined these achievements.

The breadth of the concept has led to confused terminology and an increasing use of buzzwords in the education arena. Failure to conceptualize the interdependent nature of the subjects adequately under the heading of peace education and the increasingly isolated way in which each subject area is addressed has led to duplication of efforts. This confusion has also allowed teachers to concentrate on the generic soft topic areas, ignoring the more sensitive and political areas needed to address conflict triggers effectively. Furthermore, the efforts of external educators have failed to engage productively with existing education structures, serving to move the delivery of peace education even further away from an integrated program of delivery. This not only wastes the allocation of resources, but also wastes the already limited classroom time in KRI schools. These conceptual issues, coupled with a lack of sustainable funding, have limited the systematic integration of peace education in the Kurdistan Region of Iraq. This is a great shame, considering the acceptance of the subject by the Ministry of Education and the political will for its inclusion. The international community's efforts have not fully succeeded in advancing the use of education for peacebuilding and building ministry capacity in this area.

29.

THE IRAQI KURDISH RESPONSE TO THE "ISLAMIC STATE"

POLITICAL LEVERAGE IN TIMES OF CRISIS

Benjamin Isakhan

In June 2014 the Sunni Arab fundamentalist terrorist organization of the Islamic State of Iraq and Syria (ISIS) expanded rapidly across parts of central and northern Iraq.[1] They captured significant cities such as Mosul and Tikrit, adding them to their existing strongholds in a number of restive Sunni-majority towns and cities in Iraq (including Ramadi and Fallujah, which they had held since January 2014) and in Syria (such as Raqqa, which they controlled from March 2013). In a matter of days, ISIS had bulldozed key parts of the border between Iraq and Syria and declared their new "Islamic State." Having seized such large swathes of territory, they began to impose their strict fundamentalist vision: they set up makeshift shari'a law courts in which "infidels" (non-Muslims, those who refused to endorse their ideology publicly and even those accused of petty crimes like drinking alcohol) were tried and, in many cases, executed; women were forced into marriages and then raped; girls as young as fourteen were sold as sex slaves, while boys as young as twelve were indoctrinated and armed before being used as child soldiers; and minority groups like Christians and Yezidis faced cruel and deadly persecution, ranging from public crucifixion to being slaughtered and dumped in mass graves.[2] With every victory, ISIS increased in strength, money, military equipment, and prestige among their fellow militant Sunni jihadists. They also increased in confidence, threatening to topple the Shia-dominated government of Iraqi Prime Minister Nouri Al-Maliki and the Alawite (a sub-sect of Shia Islam) leaders of the regime of President Bashar al-Assad in Syria.

Not surprisingly, a great deal of academic debate, political analysis, and media discussion has already begun to document the various causes and consequences of the deadly ISIS advance.[3] This chapter joins with other research in focusing specifically on the Iraqi Kurdish response to the rapid and devastating advance of ISIS.[4] Of course, the Iraqi Kurdish response to the ISIS advance has been a multifaceted, complex, and evolving one that includes military strategy, pragmatic politics, and aspirations of independence. Leaving aside the fact that the ISIS advance has granted the Iraqi Kurds unprecedented access to Iraq's rich oil reserves and the fact that the initial Kurdish reaction was to ramp up their rhetoric toward complete secession from Iraq, this chapter focuses on two further dimensions of the Iraqi Kurdish response. Firstly, it documents the Iraqi Kurdish seizure of the so-called "disputed territories," especially Kirkuk, and their stated intent to hold a referendum on the future of these regions (effectively to force a resolution to Article 140 of the constitution). Secondly, the chapter documents the Iraqi Kurdish use of the ISIS advance as leverage to enhance Kurdish relations dramatically with the US and Europe via direct military support (including airstrikes and weapons supply) and to become the key launchpad in the fight against ISIS planned for 2015. The chapter concludes by briefly assessing the efficacy and wisdom of the Kurdish strategy of leveraging the ISIS onslaught to advance their own interests.

The 'golden opportunity': the Kurds seize the disputed territories

Within days of the ISIS conquest of Mosul, Shoresh Haji, a Kurdish member of parliament, referred to the events as a "golden opportunity to bring Kurdish lands in the disputed territories back under Kurdish control."[5] In fact, in a move that he must have quickly regretted, Iraqi Prime Minister Nouri Al-Maliki had his personal secretary Hamid Al-Musawi telephone the leader of the Kurdistan Democratic Party (KDP) and President of the Kurdish Region (KR), Masoud Barzani, formally to request that the peshmerga secure the disputed territories before ISIS seized more of Iraq: "it would be a good thing if you moved in."[6] Barzani gave the order and the first of 30,000 peshmerga took control of major roads and checkpoints, then villages and towns, followed by major cities across the so-called "disputed territories" (which are now often referred to as the "liberated territories" by Kurdish officials and news sources). The peshmerga confronted ISIS several times, as well as other small pockets of local resistance, but mostly they took the territory peacefully. Within a matter of days the Kurds had expanded their existing territory by about 40 percent, including the oil-rich city of Kirkuk.

THE IRAQI KURDISH RESPONSE TO THE "ISLAMIC STATE"

In seizing Kirkuk and the disputed territories, the Kurds had effectively forced a decision to be finally made on the future status of these regions. The debate between Baghdad and Erbil over the disputed territories goes back to the problems embedded in the Iraqi constitution, a document hastily drafted and ratified under US tutelage in 2005.[7] Leaving aside other complex problems left unresolved by the constitution, a key issue of intense negotiations has been the status of the KR (comprised of the three provinces of Erbil, Sulaimani, and Dohuk) and the disputed territories. In terms of the status of the KR, from the very beginning of the post-Saddam era the Kurds had made it very clear that their involvement in a new and democratic Iraq was contingent on Sunni and Shia Arab acceptance of a loose federal structure in which the KR would retain the autonomy it had worked so hard to build from 1991.[8] This was in fact a dramatic toning down of some of the early post-invasion rhetoric which called for complete Kurdish secession from Iraq.[9] By 2005 the Kurds had estimated, quite correctly, that they had more to gain from being autonomous within Iraq rather than seceding, and pressured the new government toward such an end.[10] While Kurdish autonomy was initially a sensitive and controversial issue, the obstinacy of the Kurds meant that the other factions had little choice but to accept their position.[11]

While the constitution does guarantee the autonomy of the KR, it does not effectively resolve the contentious nature of the disputed territories. This term refers to a large swathe of land that lies between the official territory of the KR and the rest of Iraq, stretching across five additional Iraqi provinces from the eastern border with Iran through to the western border with Syria. The centerpiece is the entire oil-rich province of Kirkuk, home to a key city of the same name which the Kurds have long coveted in the belief that it is the rightful capital of a larger Kurdistan. Kirkuk is sometimes referred to as the "Kurdish Jerusalem": a term believed to have been coined by famed Kurdish guerrilla fighter and PUK leader Jalal Talabani, to invoke both the city's cultural significance to the Kurds and the long struggle by various groups to control it. Under the rule of Saddam Hussein, the Ba'ath Party attempted to "arabize" Kirkuk and other disputed territories in the 1970s and 1980s by driving the Kurds out and replacing them with Arab Iraqis from the south.[12] Following the ousting of the Ba'ath by the US-led coalition in 2003, the Kurds pushed hard for a reversal of this arabization which became enshrined in Article 140 of the Iraqi constitution. The central premise is that Arabs who were brought to Kirkuk under the arabization program are to return to their homes in the south with financial compensation from the Iraqi government, and that Kurdish families who were forced out could then reclaim their property. In addition, Article 140 stipulates that the Iraqi government was to hold a referendum across the disputed territories by 31 December 2007 to determine whether they would come under the jurisdiction of the central government in Baghdad or under the KR based in Erbil.[13] Although the referendum was initially planned for 15 November 2007, it has been mired in the sluggish bureaucracy and clever politicking of Baghdad; many Iraqi politicians know that a final decision on the disputed territories would likely go the way of the Kurds, weakening the central government and serving as another step on the long road to Kurdish independence. Naturally, the Kurds have been frustrated by the constant delays over Article 140 and have viewed the stalling as a deliberate attempt to undermine and antagonize them.

Given this complex history, it is little wonder that the Kurds seized their "golden opportunity" to capture the disputed territories. Initially, Kurdish President and KDP leader Masoud Barzani argued that the Kurdish control of the disputed territories had in fact rendered Article 140 invalid and that it was no longer necessary to reverse the arabization process nor to hold a referendum in the disputed territories. On 27 June he stated that "Article 140 of the constitution has been implemented and completed for us, and we will not talk about it any more... We have been patient for 10 years with the federal government to solve the problems of these (disputed) areas. Now, this (issue)...is achieved."[14]

Not surprisingly, such rhetoric met with a sharp response from Baghdad. Indeed, shortly after the ISIS advance and the Kurdish seizure of the disputed territories, Maliki accused Barzani of conspiring with ISIS to divide Iraq and that their moves represented a flagrant challenge to the unity of the Iraqi state.[15] He was explicit that the Kurdish intervention in Kirkuk was "unacceptable" and that the disputed territories "will return (to Iraq) as well as the weapons which were seized by the Kurdish Peshmerga forces after controlling Kirkuk... I warn the Kurdish people that these behaviours will put them in a maze with no way [out]."[16] Such dangerous rhetoric was echoed by figures within Maliki's State of Law Coalition such as Sheikh Adnan Al-Shahmani, who is an MP, a member of the Parliamentary Security and Defence Committee, and also the leader of the Shia militia known as Al-Risaliyoun ("Upholders of the Message"). He claimed that the Kurdish seizure of Kirkuk and Barzani's desire to resolve Article 140 of the constitution independently of Baghdad was a "declaration of war and a transcendence of the Constitution." He then vowed that the Iraqi government would "make it a mission to resolve the Kirkuk crisis after settling the situation in Mosul, and ... abolish Barzani to the mountains."[17]

Lashing out at such statements, the Kurds accused Baghdad of being hysterical and called for the resignation of Maliki, threatening to boycott all cabinet meetings and to defer indefinitely any involvement in the formation of a new government.[18] They did, however, gradually tone down their rhetoric on Article 140. The Kurds were concerned that if the annexation of the disputed territories did not have the support of Baghdad, it could lead to dissent across the disputed territories, to a civil war with the central government, and a loss of legitimacy and prestige on the international stage. Many prominent Kurds therefore shifted from arguing that Article 140 was now invalid, to instead asserting that they would not leave the disputed territories until the long-awaited referendum had been held. As Muhama Khalil, the Kurdish head of the Economic Committee in the Iraqi parliament, put it: "People in Kirkuk and Singar [sic] should be the decision makers about their destiny... The people in Kirkuk called for our help after the Iraqi Army fled. Now we are not leaving until they hold a referendum."[19]

The seizure of the disputed territories and the threat of a referendum in these areas gave the Kurds considerable leverage over the process to form a new government in Baghdad during August and September 2014. Under enormous international pressure, a series of complex political negotiations rapidly unfolded toward the creation of a more inclusive government constituted by representatives of all of Iraq's key ethno-religious political factions. The Kurds made several key demands. Although there are too many to list here, it is hardly surprising that one of their priorities was to seek written guarantees that the status of the disputed territories (Article 140) would be resolved within one year of the formation of the new Iraqi government, by finally holding a referendum.[20] In September the Iraqi parliament voted to approve the new unity government, led by the veteran Shia politician Haider Al-Abadi: a key player in both the Dawa party and the State of Law Coalition, both of which remain headed by ousted Prime Minister Maliki. Although the new government is generally perceived to be more legitimate and inclusive than the authoritarian and sectarian regime of Maliki,[21] its formation included the rotation of several familiar faces, including Maliki who became one of three Iraqi vice presidents. Nonetheless, the Kurds did win a significant victory by not only securing written agreements on referenda to be held across the disputed territories, but also by having five ministers appointed to the new government, including Finance Minister Hoshyar Zebari, as well as Rowsch Shaways becoming Deputy Prime Minister, and prominent PUK member Fouad Massoum appointed the new President of Iraq.

A key litmus test of Erbil-Baghdad relations will therefore depend on whether the Abadi government honors their agreement and exactly how and when they hold the referenda to determine whether the disputed territories formally come under Kurdish control or not. Holding such referenda will certainly be a remarkably challenging endeavor in the face of the ongoing fight against ISIS. Much will also depend on the Kurds. It remains to be seen how they would react if the Abadi government does not honor its agreement, and whether they would withdraw peacefully if the referenda are held on time and certain parts of the disputed territories vote against Kurdish rule. Paradoxically, now that the disputed territories are under their control, the Kurds may themselves choose to delay the process for fear that it might not go their way; or, more likely, that it will not be honored by Baghdad or perceived as legitimate in the eyes of the international community. They could also use ISIS as an excuse to delay it for the foreseeable future—as Baghdad used the violence in Kirkuk to delay the referendum over the last decade.

Also critical is how exactly the Kurds govern the disputed territories until the matter is resolved. It ought to be remembered that the Kurds did not have a wide public mandate nor seek the consent of local populations in seizing the disputed territories. In addition, in taking Kirkuk and the disputed territories, the Kurds have dramatically expanded their rule over significant minorities. While the KR is home to minority ethno-religious groups such as the Yezidis and many different Christian groups, these are generally smaller communities of the Region and do not have a strong tradition of militant resistance. Kirkuk and the other disputed territories, however, are constituted by a complex and fragile cultural mosaic with histories of both peaceful coexistence and periods of conflict. The Kurds have insisted that they are committed to peaceful coexistence and inclusive government, and their record in the KR and in Kurdish governed cities such as Kirkuk support this claim. As Safeen Dizayee, a KR spokesman, has said:

> When Kirkuk and the disputed areas become part of the K.R.G., whether they are Turkmen, Chaldean, Assyrian or Arab, they will be represented in Parliament and the government... Our draft constitution identifies the rights of these communities far more than the federal constitution.[22]

Nonetheless, there will be resistance to Kurdish rule among various communities. If the Kurds are perceived to have effectively annexed the disputed territories (for example without a referendum), or if they are seen to have deliberately delayed the referendum, they are likely to antagonize certain groups. Two key pockets of resistance have already become evident: the Shia Turkmen and Sunni Arab populations, both of which have little if any allegiance to the Kurds and are more likely to want the disputed territories returned to Baghdad. In late August 2014, three car bombs exploded in Kirkuk killing more than twenty people. The attack appeared to be the work of ISIS and targeted Kurdish forces. In the wake of the attack, there was a spate of execution-style killings mostly targeting Sunni Arabs and Turkmen and widely believed to be the work of the peshmerga by way of retaliation. One Sunni citizen of Kirkuk stated that "We Sunnis are regarded with suspicion and treated as if we are all members of the Islamic State."[23] Such graphic examples aside, the Kurds have also been employing more subtle tactics which may antagonize local populations across the disputed territories, including erecting billboards of Kurdish peshmerga martyrs and Kurdish flags. As one resident put it, "The Kurds are trying to make everything in Kirkuk Kurdish."[24] How the KRG manage the territories and how they develop an inclusive system that appeases local Arab and Turkmen demands and loyalties will affect their ability to consolidate their territory.

From defeat to launchpad: the peshmerga receive unprecedented foreign military support

In early August 2014, ISIS fighters suddenly and spectacularly defeated the peshmerga on several fronts. In addition to seizing several small towns and villages across the disputed territories and other areas of northern Iraq, ISIS won three significant victories over the peshmerga. The first occurred on 3 August when ISIS stormed Sinjar, a pocket of Kurdish-controlled territory on the western border with Syria with a significant Yezidi community. This led to a mass humanitarian disaster as ISIS immediately executed hundreds of Yezidis and thousands more were forced to flee up Mount Sinjar without material possessions, weapons, or supplies. The second ISIS victory came on 6 August when they took several Kurdish-controlled towns about 50 km from Erbil and then surged toward Erbil itself, leading to fears that they would conquer the seat of KRG power. The final blow came the following day (7 August) when the peshmerga lost the Mosul dam to ISIS, the largest dam in Iraq and a crucial piece of Iraqi infrastructure. ISIS threatened to burst open the dam, potentially flooding areas inhabited by millions of Iraqis as far away as Baghdad and stifling any advance by their opponents from the south.

These rapid defeats humiliated the Kurds and exposed the fact that the peshmerga were not as militarily sophisticated (as well trained, organized, or as heavily armed) as had so often been assumed, and certainly less so than their foes in ISIS. Although the peshmerga does include many well-trained units with up-to-date weaponry, the bulk of its force is made up of passionate but poorly trained volunteers who wear ill-fitting and mismatched uniforms and often fight with weapons they inherited from their fathers and grandfathers; some carry Kalashnikovs from the 1970s. These rag-tag units were suddenly patrolling a 1,000 km jagged border and attempting to defend it against the sophisticated tactics and advanced weaponry of ISIS, with little more than light weapons such as machine guns, grenade launchers, and mortars.[25] While they do have some tanks, armored personnel carriers, and rocket launchers, much of this equipment was captured decades ago in bitter battles with Saddam's regime. Lieutenant General Hegmadem Osmat who commanded a sizeable peshmerga battalion stationed west of Erbil near the ISIS frontline described the ISIS advance: "They had more modern weapons than us, they came with tanks, and RPGs, and heavy artillery... For every mortar we shot at them, they would shoot a dozen back."[26]

The relatively poor training of the peshmerga and their lack of sophisticated weaponry are indicative of the fact that throughout the nine long years of military occupation, the US funded and trained the peshmerga only a fraction of the extent that they did the Iraqi Security Forces (ISF). Indeed, when the Kurds seized the disputed territories, they were amazed to find that the ISF were in possession of brand new weapons that had recently been supplied by the US to the ISF but not to the peshmerga. As Masoud Barzani's son and the Kurdish Intelligence Chief put it, "The Iraqi Army has the best equipment: M-16s, night-vision goggles, Humvees... We never got any of that... The Americans never gave us anything, and they've blocked us from acquiring new weapons on our own."[27] What is being referred to here is a decades-old US policy sometimes referred to as the "One Iraq" policy, which insists that the different factions in Iraq must work together toward a cohesive and united future. In other words, the US officially oppose Kurdish independence, in part because they desperately want to protect the legacy of the 2003 war in Iraq and the decade-long project (which cost billions of dollars and thousands of American lives) to turn Iraq into a united, prosperous, and democratic nation.[28] They also believe that Kurdish independence would inflame the region and antagonize neighboring states with their own Kurdish populations, such as Turkey, Iran, and Syria. Key to the "One Iraq" policy has been to prevent any direct sales of weapons or military equipment to the Kurds: all of which had to be overseen and approved by Baghdad.[29] This has meant that many deals brokered by the Kurds have been caught up in the bureaucratic red tape and complex politicking of Baghdad, with weapons and equipment rarely ending up in the hands of the peshmerga.

Fearing a mass humanitarian tragedy in Sinjar, the flooding of large swathes of Iraq from the Mosul dam, and the fall of Erbil, the US needed a dramatic re-think of their "One Iraq" policy, or at least their position on the direct supply of weapons and military equipment to the Kurds. Although the Obama administration had thus far been reticent in engaging ISIS in either Syria or Iraq, they knew that the collapse of the Kurdish autonomous enclave would be disastrous for the region and for US interests there. A group of 129 US military advisors were rushed into Erbil to consult with the peshermega and advise the US government about how they could best assist in the Kurdish struggle against ISIS. They also sent in an unknown number of US Special Forces operatives to advise and assist on the ground; along with several European states, they quickly and directly supplied ammunition, weapons systems, surveillance equipment, and other light arms to the Kurds.[30]

In addition to the direct supply of weapons, training, and military equipment to the peshmerga, what tipped the balance back in favor of the Kurds in the fight against ISIS was the decision by the US and its key allies to conduct a series of airstrikes across northern Iraq. On 7 August Obama stated that the US would use airstrikes to assist the civilians trapped by the sudden advance of ISIS across the disputed territories. Although the speech was mostly framed in terms of preventing "a potential act of genocide" against the Yezidis, one of the key thrusts of his speech was to protect the Kurdish capital of Erbil. As President Obama put it:

> To stop the advance on Erbil, I've directed our military to take targeted strikes against ISIL terrorist convoys should they move toward the city. We intend to stay vigilant, and take action if these terrorist forces threaten our personnel or facilities anywhere in Iraq, including our consulate in Erbil and our embassy in Baghdad. We're also providing urgent assistance to Iraqi government and Kurdish forces so they can more effectively wage the fight against ISIL.[31]

The airstrikes began on 8 August 2014 on various ISIS targets across northern Iraq, as well as dropping urgently needed supplies of food and water to the stranded Yezidis. By 14 August, the combination of US airstrikes and Kurdish ground operations had broken the siege on Mount Sinjar, allowing thousands of Yezidi refugees to escape. On

16 August, US airstrikes also hit ISIS targets around the Mosul dam, allowing the peshmerga to retake it. About 200 commandoes from the ISF's Counter Terrorism Unit played a crucial role in the operation, marking the first time that the peshmerga and ISF had fought side by side against a common enemy.[32] By the end of August, the peshmerga were in control of the vast majority of the territory that had been seized in the ISIS encroachment, heralding a major victory for the Kurdish-US alliance.

Using these successes as leverage, the Kurds made it a key condition of being part of the political negotiations to form a new Iraqi government in August and September 2014 that the peshmerga be recognized as a legitimate part of the ISF, with direct funding from Baghdad and the right to buy their own weapons from external parties without Baghdad's approval. With little choice, given the ISIS onslaught and enormous international pressure to resolve differences quickly and amicably, the Shia Arab-dominated government agreed. Content that a new and inclusive government was in place in Baghdad, in mid-September Obama outlined his four-pronged plan to "degrade and ultimately destroy" ISIS, in collaboration with a broad coalition of over sixty countries in total: to continue conducting airstrikes; to draw on the US counter-terrorism capabilities to thwart ISIS attacks; to provide humanitarian assistance to innocent civilians; and to continue to fund, arm, train, and advise various forces on the ground who could fight against ISIS on behalf of the US. In terms of the latter, Obama stated that he would "send an additional 475 service members to Iraq" to support the "Iraqi and Kurdish forces with training, intelligence and equipment."[33]

Although this strategy to "degrade and ultimately destroy" ISIS is, at the time of writing, still very much in its early stages, it has had its share of dramatic successes and epic failures, with ISIS remaining a credible and catastrophic force in the Middle East and across the world. Among the many significant victories have been the efforts of the Iraqi Kurds to defeat ISIS on several fronts and to successfully defend much of the territory from subsequent ISIS attacks through late 2014 and into 2015. For example, in late December 2014, the peshmerga and Yezidi volunteers backed by some 53 coalition airstrikes accomplished a remarkable feat, managing in under 48 hours to claw back approximately 3,000 sq. km from ISIS—a large swathe of territory stretching from the KR to Mount Sinjar.[34] To celebrate the victory, Barzani visited Mount Sinjar and vowed to defeat ISIS and free the city of Sinjar itself. However, because of the awkward and isolated geography of Sinjar city as well as its proximity to ISIS strongholds in Syria, and perhaps fearing the costs of a protracted asymmetric urban confrontation with ISIS, by as late as April 2015 the peshmerga had still not taken Sinjar city from ISIS.[35] In terms of defending their territory: in November 2014 the peshmerga repelled an ISIS advance on the Mosul dam;[36] in late January 2015 they defeated a multi-pronged attack on Kirkuk by hundreds of ISIS militants;[37] and in mid-February 2015 they thwarted ISIS as they repeated their August 2014 assault on Kurdish towns some 50 km to the south-west of Erbil.[38] Although each of these victories was hard won and came at the cost of dozens of Kurdish lives, they continued to demonstrate the capacity of the Kurds, despite grave conditions and lack of adequate equipment, to defeat ISIS in the territories they controlled.

The success of Kurdish operations, their involvement in the new Iraqi government, and their valiant efforts against ISIS have seen their relations with the US and the international coalition evolve dramatically. They are routinely viewed in Washington as a stabilizing force in the region and as a key ally in the fight against ISIS. They are also widely seen as preferable to the many Iranian-backed Shia militias who are now deeply embedded within the ISF and in many instances waging their own autonomous campaigns. The ferocious and blood-thirsty reputation of the worst of these militias, along with their blatantly sectarian agenda, are cause for grave concern among those involved in the international effort to oust ISIS. For all these reasons, the KR has now become the key launchpad for the major international plan to retake Mosul and other key Iraqi territory from ISIS in 2015. The KR also has great strategic value, with several heavily fortified bases, close proximity to Mosul, a long and relatively secure border with ISIS, and land access to key allies such as Turkey: all of which will allow the campaign against ISIS to strike on several simultaneous fronts.[39]

Demonstrating the peshmerga's commitment to the effort to retake Mosul, in mid-January 2015 a force of 5,000 conducted a large-scale maneuver backed by coalition airstrikes in which they took roughly 300 sq. km of territory surrounding Mosul. They advanced on Mosul from three sides and then launched a barrage of missiles at ISIS targets within the city.[40] Nonetheless, there is some confusion and/or disagreement about whether the Kurds will actually be involved in the fight to retake Mosul city. There are several reasons for Kurdish reluctance. The first is the fact that liberating a large city such as Mosul from ISIS would be an extremely long and dangerous affair (as can be seen in the protracted and bloody campaign in Tikrit conducted by the ISF and Shia militias in March 2015). A second key concern for the Kurds is that whoever retakes Mosul risks further aggravating existing tensions within Iraq. For example, if the Kurds capture Mosul it would likely be perceived as a Kurdish land grab and therefore part of a larger Arab-Kurdish territorial dispute. Similarly, if Shia militias and the ISF (which were widely resented in Mosul prior to the ISIS advance) take the city, then they risk further antagonizing the Sunni-Shia divide in Iraq.[41] A predominant view seems to be that any effort to retake Mosul needs to be led and sustained by moderate Sunni Arabs, both within Mosul and from across Iraq.[42] But the question remains as to whether such Sunni Arabs have the capacity to conduct the operation, the extent to which they would want to collaborate with Kurdish or Shia forces, and should they succeed, what their short- or long-term allegiances would be to the broader Iraqi state and its people. Considering all these complex variables, it is no wonder that there is little clarity on how exactly the coalition and its allies plan to retake Mosul. Indicative of this is the fact that, as late as March 2015, Barzani expressed concern not only about who exactly would liberate Mosul and the Kurdish role in the operation, but also revealed that he had "not heard any serious proposal from Baghdad about the liberation of Mosul. They are not consulting on this matter with us."[43]

Despite such issues, it seems likely that the Kurds will play a significant role in the effort to retake Mosul from ISIS, most likely by moving into the eastern part of the city (where many Kurds lived before the ISIS conquest). Toward this end, the United States and many of its coalition partners have directly supplied or plan to supply Kurdish forces with military equipment, small arms, ammunition, non-lethal military gear, and training support. But it is clear that from very early on in the campaign against ISIS, the United States had been supplying the Kurds directly with small- and medium-sized arms (this has been relatively modest), amounting to a few thousand boxes of ammunition, rifles, and rocket launchers.[44] In early November 2014, Obama asked Congress for $1.6 bn to train and arm 9 Iraq army and 3 peshmerga brigades, as well as to develop a training site and up-to-date airbase at Bashur within the KR; but by March 2015 Congress was still undecided as to whether to pass new legislation that would allow them to bypass Baghdad and supply additional heavy weaponry directly to the Kurds.[45] Although other coalition partners have supplied the Kurds with some heavier artillery (such as Germany who provided MILAN missiles which have proved highly effective against ISIS),[46] the weapons supplied thus far fall well short of what the Kurds claim they will need to turn the tide against ISIS. To their great frustration and despite repeated pleas, the Kurds have not received the requested tanks, helicopters, heavy armaments and artillery, Humvees, and armored personnel carriers.[47]

The Kurds are also gravely concerned about their capacity to confront and defeat ISIS in complex asymmetric urban environments, which they will urgently need to do if they are to play a role in liberating Sinjar or Mosul or even defend their own cities.[48] Although the Kurds waged many successful campaigns in the 1970s and 1980s, they did so largely using guerrilla tactics in rural environments, descending from their strongholds in the rugged mountain terrain that stretches across their territory. To up-skill the Kurds in urban warfare and anti-terror tactics, expert trainers from across the world have also arrived in the KR, including those from Turkey, Germany, the UK, Italy, the Netherlands, along with smaller groups from countries across Scandinavia, Eastern Europe, and Central Asia.[49] The Pentagon has devised its own program to train the peshmerga which started in January 2015.[50] Nonetheless, as with the lack of supply of heavy weapons, the Kurds feel that they need a great deal more training and have formally requested additional programs from their allies.

The US airstrikes to defend Erbil and put parts of the disputed territories back in Kurdish hands, as well as the plan for the KR to be the lauchpad for the next phase of the fight against ISIS, has caught the ire of Baghdad, itself facing a creeping ISIS encroachment. Iraqi officials have repeatedly urged the US to conduct airstrikes on ISIS positions around Baghdad, as well as to protect oil and energy infrastructure vital to Iraq's economic survival. They have argued that protecting Erbil while allowing Baghdad to slide closer toward an ISIS takeover (or at least a prolonged ISIS siege) would guarantee the end of Iraq. The ISF and Shia militias have been operating largely without US airstrikes in and around Baghdad and in their efforts to take on ISIS in neighboring provinces. It is only when they surge further north and appear to struggle to oust ISIS on their own that the ISF have benefited from US airstrikes (such as in their effort to retake Tikrit).[51] However, the issue that most concerns Baghdad is the direct supply of weapons, training, and military equipment to the Kurds. As well as greatly enhancing their military capacity and their unilateral relations with various foreign states, it will also dramatically increase the ability of the Kurds to push for potential secession.

Conclusion

There can be no doubting the fact that the Iraqi Kurds have been savvy in leveraging the ISIS advance and the Kurdish seizure of the disputed territories to force a final resolution of Article 140 of the constitution, to get additional powers and autonomy from Baghdad, and to gain unprecedented military support, training, and equipment from the US and its coalition partners. On the one hand, this strategy has not only dramatically improved Kurdish standing in Iraq, the region, and among the international community, but also significantly improved the prospects of achieving the long-held Kurdish aspiration of independence, even if there remain many key obstacles to its fruition. On the other hand, the Iraqi Kurds are playing a very dangerous game. The rapid annexation of Kirkuk and the disputed territories without a public mandate, any Kurdish-led delays on the promised referenda, and the attempt to "Kurdishize" the towns and cities across the territories could lead to local dissent and violence as well as a loss of prestige on the international stage. By using the current crisis and their control of the disputed territories as leverage to further their own interests, the Iraqi Kurds are increasingly perceived in Baghdad as self-interested cynical opportunists. The animosity between Baghdad and Erbil may well escalate when the ISIS threat subsides and the Kurds continue to control the disputed territories and have increased access to weapons and training supplied by their foreign allies. Finally, the Iraqi Kurds must consider the fact that the support of the US and the international coalition is born of convenience; the US remains committed to its "One Iraq" policy and, although it may provide weapons, training, and equipment to the Kurds in the short term, such support is very unlikely to outlive the ISIS threat. In other words, the current strategy of the Iraqi Kurds could see a situation in which, given a defeat of ISIS, the Kurds would be left with a revolt in the disputed territories, escalating tensions with Baghdad, and the withdrawal of all US and international support: all of which raises serious concerns about the future of Iraq-Kurdish relations and poses significant challenges for the geopolitics of the region.

30

IN PURSUIT OF FRIENDS

THE KURDISTAN REGION'S FOREIGN AFFAIRS AND DIPLOMACY

Renad Mansour

There is an old Kurdish proverb that states, "If you do not knock at anyone's door, no one will knock at your door." For Iraq's Kurds, who faced an involuntary attachment to an Arab central government in Baghdad and a set of neighboring states that historically expressed suspicions towards irredentism, knocking at doors abroad and searching for international support was for some time perceived to be a necessary lifeline. Asked about this reality, the Kurdistan Region Government (KRG) Department of Foreign Relations (DFR)'s head, Falah Mustafa, once told the author, "We are tired of brothers; what we want are friends."[1] To him, "brothers" meant the same neighboring actors that had oppressed the Kurds throughout the twentieth century. For much of the Kurdistan Region's leadership, engaging in foreign affairs and diplomacy was not only perceived as a strategic choice, but also as a way to survive as a sub-state in a precarious neighborhood.

However, to complicate this predicament, in international relations a sub-state like the Kurdistan Region often struggles to open doors vis-à-vis *de jure* or recognized juridical states. According to the English school of international relations, the art of diplomacy and foreign affairs has been exclusively state-centric since the establishment of the modern Westphalian system. Watson writes that "recognition of independence, where it exists, both in practice and of rights, is a prerequisite of diplomacy."[2] Staunch resistance to opening a "Pandora's box" of alternative diplomacies ultimately led the 1971 Vienna Conference on Diplomatic Intercourse and Immunities to define diplomacy as an inter-state endeavor.[3] As such, a "diplomat" is one who represents his or her *de jure* state government. Under these circumstances, sub-state or non-state actors face difficulties with membership.

Despite the exclusivity of this club, the Kurdistan Region persistently engaged in foreign affairs and diplomacy and consequently tested state-centric assumptions. For its leadership, effectively communicating to the outside world was a top priority. Mustafa believed that "we need to communicate to the outside world to let them know where Kurdistan is, how stable it is, how secure it is, how welcoming it is, and to promote its culture, history, tourism, people, business opportunities, and investment. Communication is important because without it people do not take us at face value and accept what we say, they need to verify."[4] This need, according to Mustafa, was based on his perception that representing a sub-state constantly entailed having to justify its seat at the table. In post-2003 Iraq, the foreign relations portfolio trumped domestic issues. As will be discussed, the government's official website, for instance, featured diplomatic meetings and international events rather than domestic issues.

For the longest time, even those who opposed internal political dynamics and formed an opposition to the ruling elite nonetheless shied away from jeopardizing the diplomatic program. Nawshirwan Mustafa, who led an opposition called Gorran, or Change, against the ruling Kurdistan Democratic Party (KDP) and Patriotic Union of Kurdistan (PUK), adamantly declared that his priority was internal KRG governance and administration, not foreign relations.[5] As will be discussed, the decline of the Kurdistan Region's economy after 2013, when the central government in Baghdad stopped sharing its revenues with Erbil, made many question the state-building process and whether diplomacy could achieve statehood. In any case, the leadership continued to rely on foreign affairs and diplomacy, notwithstanding growing opposition.

This chapter analyzes this fascination with foreign relations and diplomacy in the post-2003 Iraq context and asks: What drove the Kurdistan Region's pursuit of relations with *de jure* states and international organizations? To provide background, I begin with a brief overview of the development of diplomacy and foreign relations since the creation of Iraq. Then, to answer the question, I argue that the pursuit is aimed at overcoming an unfavorable union and finding alternatives to Baghdad's sphere of influence, developing the capacities of statehood, and bolstering the sub-state's domestic and international legitimacy. Put differently, Kurdistan Region's leadership viewed diplomacy as a temporary solution to overcome problems associated with the international system's unwillingness to offer juridical recognition. Linking it together, this chapter concludes with an analysis of how foreign affairs and diplomacy changed the character of the leaders, who became confident statespeople.

KURDISTAN REGION'S FOREIGN AFFAIRS AND DIPLOMACY

The development of foreign affairs

A brief look into how the Kurdistan Region's foreign affairs and diplomacy progressed in the twentieth century provides useful insights, particularly to understanding its impact on the character of the leadership. Different leaders during different eras, since the creation of the Iraqi state, have made claims to represent the Kurdistan Region on the international stage. This process has matured over the years.

During the initial period, foreign affairs and diplomatic endeavors were divided into two groups. The "Westernized" Kurdish elite, such as Sheriff Pasha, enjoyed access to European capitals and practised Westphalian diplomacy. However, they were too far removed to claim representation over the population. Local tribal leaders, such as Shaikh Mahmud Barzinji, the Bedr Khan brothers, or Sayid Taha, practised largely ad hoc foreign relations and ultimately became a disappointment to British political officers who were stationed in the region. The inability of both groups to satisfy the British mandatory power, among other reasons, ultimately led to the incorporation of the Mosul vilayet into Iraq. From this point on, generations of Kurdish leaders would have to engage in foreign affairs from the position of sub-state representatives.

The nationalist movement was institutionalized to some extent under Mullah Mustafa Barzani, who was the first to employ quasi-diplomats, namely Kurdish students studying in Europe and the US. Then, in the early 1970s, Barzani enjoyed a covert US-Iran-Israel partnership bent on countering the rise of the Ba'ath Party in Iraq. However, in 1975, this brief partnership came to an end when Washington betrayed Barzani to broker the Algiers Agreement between Iran and Iraq. The covert and unstable nature of the foreign relations harmed the movement and ultimately led to the infamous betrayal in Algiers.

Following this, various competing political parties emerged and began to engage in independent relations with foreign actors. At this point, for *de jure* states, practising foreign affairs with the sub-state was still taboo. As such, the Kurds found themselves primarily reaching out to international organizations, journalists, academics, and individual foreign political figures who sympathized with their cause. However, the leadership's relations with *de jure* states remained precarious; as a result, it could not acquire protection from foreign governments when Saddam Hussein's Ba'ath regime launched genocidal offensives, namely the al-Anfal campaign, against them in the mid-1980s.

The year 1991 presented a benchmark: for the first time the international community, led by a US-French-UK-brokered no-fly zone, publicly committed to protecting Iraq's Kurds from Saddam's reach. Foreign relations and diplomacy became less covert as foreign capitals began engaging with leaderships and representatives abroad of the political party, namely Masoud Barzani's Kurdistan Democratic Party (KDP) and Jalal Talabani's Patriotic Union of Kurdistan (PUK). However, progress was impeded by internal fighting, problems with institutionalization under the Kurdistan Regional Government (KRG), and an uncertain future with the rest of the country.

Following the 2003 US-led invasion of Iraq, the Kurds emerged on the world stage as a partner and success story. They took advantage of a "re-marriage" with a weakened Arab Iraq to ensure that the KRG could engage in its own bilateral relations. In 2006, the leadership established the Department of Foreign Relations (DFR) to institutionalize the sub-state's foreign relations and move away from party politics. Although this process has been slow, and the political parties continue to dominate the sub-state's foreign affairs, the international community, including heads of state and international organizations, now openly engage with Kurdistan Region. The remainder of this chapter will examine the primary drivers behind the leadership's foreign affairs and diplomacy in post-2003 Iraq.

Alternatives to an untrustworthy central government

As discussed, the leadership believed that external actors could serve as a lifeline to circumvent an unwilling marriage to Arab Iraq. This perception was driven by a mistrust of the central government and opportunism that sought to increase autonomy vis-à-vis a weak and conflict-ridden post-2003 Baghdad. Despite its emergence as a de facto state that enjoyed many of the trappings of statehood, however, the Kurdistan Region continued to rely on the central government for a large majority (nearly 95 per cent) of its budget.[6] The leadership wanted to use foreign affairs and diplomacy to attract economic and political *de jure* state partners and ultimately to move away from Baghdad's sphere of influence.

The most evident case of the alternatives policy was the Erbil-Ankara relationship. Driven by the ruling KDP, the sub-state built a strong working relationship with Erdoğan's Justice and Development Party (AKP), along with other political parties in Turkey, to overcome reliance on Baghdad.[7] They also developed relations with the Turkish intelligence organization (Milli Istihbarat Teskilati) and Turkish military officials.[8] As such, this relationship was formed primarily from economic considerations; it nonetheless required diplomatic outreach, particularly in the early days following 2003, when Ankara refused to speak directly with the Kurdistan Region and demanded that negotiations include Iraqi or international *de jure* state officials.

Given these realities, the sub-state leadership's diplomatic goal was to appeal to Turkey's interests. To do this, the negotiation team, led by Nechirvan Barzani, Safeeen Dizayee, and Ashti Hawrami, among others, focused on two key issues critical for their negotiating counterparts. First, they were aware of Turkey's growing need for natural resources and frustration with an inefficient Baghdad. As such, they positioned the KRG as an effective oil and gas exporter that could better serve Turkey's needs. Second, the negotiators were also aware of Ankara's increased anxiety toward

Iran's sphere of influence in post-2003 Iraq and consequently argued that they could serve as an important ally to influence Baghdad's political scene.

To establish direct or bilateral ties with Turkey, the sub-state's leadership wanted to alleviate anxieties associated with the historic fear of irredentism. The single biggest issue and domestic concern for Turkey was its own Kurdish population and the efforts of the Kurdistan Workers' Party (PKK). Rather than playing to ethno-national ties and working for a "Greater Kurdistan", which would include parts of Turkey, the sub-state's leadership consistently stressed a non-irredentist policy to mitigate anxieties over being associated with a Kurdistan and reassured the *de jure* state that its project was merely confined to the borders of Iraq. More critically, the KDP leadership began working with Ankara to tackle the PKK threat. For example, in May 2008, Nechirvan Barzani invited Turkish intelligence liaisons in Erbil to review arrival records to monitor whether the PKK was flying via Erbil.[9] Moreover, following 2011, the sub-state pursued Turkey's interests in the Syrian civil war. It worked to limit PKK influence in Syria by delegitimizing the PKK-linked Democratic Union Party (PYD) and working to find alternative representation models and Kurdish leaders in Syria. The leadership wanted to allay some of the risk for Turkey, which was alarmed with the re-emergence of the PKK on its border with Syria.

Despite a relationship that began with mistrust, ten years after the 2003 US-led invasion, Erbil and Ankara signed an oil and gas agreement whereby Erbil would begin selling directly to Ankara.[10] According to the energy deal, the Kurdistan Region agreed to transport 420,000 barrels per day of crude oil to Turkey via a newly built pipeline.[11] The agreement was the product of several years of diplomatic negotiation in which the sub-state's diplomats had to mitigate risk and build trust with Ankara. The KRG agreed to export 2 million bpd of oil and 10 billion cubic meters of gas per year to Turkey, via pipelines.[12]

Although the relationship suffered periodical setbacks, Ankara, for the first time, was bilaterally negotiating with the Region's diplomats. By 2013, the sub-state became Turkey's third largest export market.[13]

However, the economic crisis beginning in early 2014, when then Iraqi Prime Minister Nouri al-Maliki decided to cut Erbil off from Baghdad's revenues, showed the vulnerabilities in the Kurdistan Region's alternatives policy. The global decline in the price of oil and the emergence of the so-called Islamic State, which led to an IDP/refugee crisis and an ongoing war, further damaged the sub-state's economic independence. Although the projections of exports were eventually hurt, the KRG's Ministry of Natural Resources (MNR) nonetheless reported that the KRG exported 452,145 bpd in January 2016. These exports went to Turkey via the Kirkuk-Ceyhan oil pipeline, not the newly built independent pipeline.[14]

Despite the uncertain future with this policy, the leadership is nonetheless committed to finding alternative sources to circumvent dependence on the central government. However, rather than becoming dependent on one side and risking betrayal, as in 1975, the leadership uses diplomacy to *manage* dependencies. For instance, when the Islamic State emerged on its borders and Turkey was slow to act, it relied on its relationship with Iran to acquire quick support to fend off the salafi-jihadi group. Or, when a ship carrying the KRG's oil was facing difficulties offloading to Turkey or the US, the leadership relied on its relationship with Israel to find a market for its product. KRG diplomats exhibited agential power in moulding relations with several strategic allies, even when the allies had strained relations with each other. Throughout this process, Washington and Tel Aviv were mired in a dispute with Tehran over its nuclear programme, among other political differences. Despite their rivalries, the US, Turkey, Iran, and Israel were the KRG's greatest supporters and state-builders. The leadership decided to keep all doors open and to build multiple dependencies. A traumatic memory of isolation and the 1975 betrayal drove the policy of non-enmity. For the leadership, diplomacy would facilitate multiple dependencies to overcome the precarious position of being a sub-state linked to an antagonistic central government.

Building a "legitimate" state

Apart from finding alternatives to Baghdad's sphere of influence, the leadership also wanted to use diplomacy to develop the capacities of statehood. One of the most important of these capacities is the ability to wield coercion: both externally to defend its borders, and internally to control and administer the use of legitimate violence in society. Max Weber famously defines a state as an entity that holds a monopoly on "*legitimate* violence." Without juridical recognition, then, the Kurdistan Region's leadership relied on diplomacy as a means of wielding coercion for two purposes: to ensure an effective international alliance structure that could maintain the KRG's monopoly, and to help it build on its security institutions.

In August 2014, President Barack Obama's decision to re-intervene in Iraq surprised many because it ran counter to his policies of withdrawal and non-interference in Iraq (and Syria) despite the emergence of the Islamic State, which was taking over major cities such as Mosul and crossing so-called "red lines" linked to reports on the use of chemical weapons. Several *de jure* states, such as Turkey and the Gulf States, had previously pleaded with Washington to engage against the Islamic State, to no avail. However, at this point, Islamic State fighters began threatening Erbil, and as such, the sub-state's leadership used diplomacy to ensure that their capital would not fall.

The summer of the fall of Mosul, the Kurdistan Region intensified its diplomatic engagements in Washington DC. The leadership wanted to ensure that they could muster protection with the looming external Islamic State threat. DFR Head Falah Mustafa and President Barzani's chief of staff, Fuad Hussein, frequently traveled to foreign capitals to relay the imminent threat. According to Fuad Hussein, who boasted that he was now a regular feature in the US State Department, President

Barzani made "a lot of phone calls to Washington" to explain to US Vice President Joe Biden how in August IS had taken over Makhmour and surrounding areas close to Erbil. Ultimately, within days, Obama decided to re-engage in Iraq; the US Air Force supported the peshmerga's campaign to reclaim territories in Makhmour and Gwer. Hussein concluded that "Barzani built an extensive network of relations with the international community and we have seen its results."[15] To the leadership, this was a clear signal of Washington's support for the peshmerga's sovereignty to protect the external borders of the Kurdistan Region.

The leadership also viewed diplomacy as an opportunity to develop the Kurdistan Region's own capabilities. Part of this was convincing foreign capitals to send arms and provide military training for the sub-state. During the Islamic State crisis in the summer of 2014, the top priority of all the sub-state's diplomats was to negotiate weapon transfer agreements with foreign governments. Even in negotiations with Baghdad, a senior Kurdish diplomat claimed, "our top priority is to arm the peshmerga."[16] This extended to foreign governments, where the leadership searched for political allies. For instance, an "arm the peshmerga" campaign, led by senior officials such as US senators John McCain and Joni Ernst, among others, emerged to help develop the peshmerga's capacity. Ernst, who had met with the Kurdistan Region's representatives and leadership a number of times, told a senate hearing that the US should support the peshmerga because "they're willing to fight. In close combat. And it is truly unmatched by any other group in that region."[17] These comments were in part a product of the sub-state's outreach efforts with individuals that it deemed influential in foreign capitals.

If the governments seemed slow or unresponsive, then the leadership resorted to public diplomacy, namely the media, to reach out to the population, which could then pressure its respective government. For instance, President Barzani told the BBC that "the weapons they [IS] possess are more advanced than what the peshmerga have. What we are asking our friends to do is to provide support and to cooperate with us in providing the necessary weapons that would enable us to defeat these terrorist groups."[18] As such, this "arm the peshmerga" campaign was not only active in governments, but became well known among foreign publics.

For the leadership, training the peshmerga was another important state-building step that it could address through diplomacy. Italy, for instance, opened a consulate in Erbil in December 2015 and agreed to expand its military training program less than one month later.[19] Similar to acquiring weapons, then, the leadership wanted to use diplomacy to train its security apparatus.

The strategy proved to some extent successful, although the leadership continued to push for more support. Immediately after the summer of 2014, the US and some Europeans, such as the UK, Germany, the Netherlands, and Italy, sent trainers to focus on the use of Milan and heavy armaments. In November 2014, for instance, the US issued some 350 million USD to support three Kurdish brigades. The package included 219 mortars and 720 tactical vehicles.[20] Eventually, training bases were created at Binaslawa and Atrush.[21] The US Consul General in Erbil, Matthias Mitman, stated that Washington was training some 4,000 fully equipped peshmerga.[22]

Beyond material support and training to help with state-building, the leadership also sought to legitimize its security forces—in line with Weber's definition of *legitimate* violence. Through diplomacy, the representatives wanted to convince foreign capitals that the peshmerga was not another paramilitary or militia in Iraq, but a legitimate security force. This strategy worked and many foreign capitals recognized the Kurdistan Region's peshmerga as a legitimate entity, unlike, for example, the Kurdistan Workers' Party (PKK) in Turkey. The recognition was best showcased in the case of Kobanî, where the US and its allies agreed for the Kurdistan Region's peshmerga to march from Iraq through Turkey to Syria in order to fight the Islamic State. At this point, the peshmerga was not only mandated to fight in its territories, but was also authorized to invade another *de jure* state to fight in a civil war. As such, diplomacy was crucial to convincing counterparts of the legitimacy of the peshmerga.

Apart from the security apparatus, the leadership wanted to use diplomacy to build other state capabilities, namely infrastructure. Diplomatic relations often crossed over to investment opportunities and partnerships, particularly once the foreign diplomat had left office. For instance, Jay Garner, Director of the Office for Reconstruction and Humanitarian Assistance in 2003, left the US military to pursue business interests in the Kurdistan Region. The KRG leadership also developed strong business relations with Zalmay Khalilzad, the US Ambassador to Iraq 2005-7. He then became president of Gryphon Partners and worked to connect businesses and investors to the Kurdistan Region. Diplomacy, for the leadership, was a tool to attracting investment and building the sub-state.

The oil and gas industry also benefited from foreign relations. At times, the two were closely linked. The Kurdistan Region's leadership employed "energy diplomacy" to benefit from its relations with another state, to attract that state's companies, or to use its relations with an oil and gas company to engage with its state. For example, in May 2015, a delegation including Russia's Deputy Foreign Minister Mikhail Bogdanov, Deputy Energy Minister Yuri Sentyurin, and Gazprom's Chairman Alexander Dyukov visited Nerchirvan Barzani.[23] Gazprom had a strong relationship with the Russian government, and for the KRG the oil company could be used to build trust and bring *de jure* state negotiators to the table as well as develop the oil and gas sector.

Oil and gas companies, through energy diplomacy, could help the Kurdistan Region build infrastructure independent from the central government. Benefitting from its increased foreign relations with Turkey, the KRG signed a Production Sharing Contract (PSC) with the Turkey-based Genel Energy, which explored and exported oil and gas from the Region. Part of the agreement, however, was to also build a 25-mile pipeline from Duhok to Fishkabur, Turkey.[24] This would be the first pipeline entirely within the sub-state's boundaries and the first opportunity to export oil without Baghdad's interference. The leadership ensured that PSCs also included capacity-building initiatives beyond the oil and gas sector. According to the KRG Ministry of Natural Resources (MNR), after signing a PSC:

> oil companies pay a capacity building bonus, which is an upfront payment towards funding large social programmes including infrastructure development. The bonus goes towards funding projects such as hospitals, housing, schools and universities, water treatment plants, humanitarian aid, security, as well as towards vocational, technical and higher education programmes to help develop Kurdistan's workforce. [25]

In short, then, foreign relations with states could lead to better relations with those states' companies, which could then help build critical infrastructure and develop the sub-state's capacities.

Acting like statespeople

Thus far, this chapter has argued that the Kurdistan Region's leadership relied on foreign relations both to distance itself from Baghdad and to build legitimate state institutions and infrastructure; this was part of its attempt to circumvent impediments caused by the sub-state status. To further this process, the leadership perceived diplomacy to be a symbolic expression of international standing and, to some extent, statehood. The idea was: if you cannot be a state, then at least act like a statesperson to circumvent the sub-state status.

Acting like a statesperson was most evident in the sub-state's diplomatic communication. More specifically, to enmesh the sub-state and *de jure* state line, the leadership chose to conform to and embrace principles of protocol. The representatives thought that using protocol would let international actors know that they were professionals worthy of being included in the club. Dindar Zebari, for instance, believed that "presentation also is important as a key factor of taking the dialogue seriously."[26] Prior to 2006, the Kurdistan Region had no international consuls or consulate-generals. Its representatives were initially inexperienced and untrained in how to act vis-à-vis the emerging diplomatic corps. They sought to tell diplomatic counterparts that the KRG was interested in joining the club of diplomacy, despite the sub-state status. Their message was to some extent successful. Sir Terence Clark, former UK Ambassador to Iraq, met regularly with KRG representative Bayan Sami Abdul Rahman and concluded that "she carried herself as if she was an ambassador. She seemed to be recognised in diplomatic circles in London as if she were representing a state."[27]

This act, in an effort to join the club, included abiding by certain etiquette, table manners, dress codes, and so forth. In the DFR, Falah Mustafa administered a strict dress code. A former employee in the DFR claimed that Mustafa scolded him once for forgetting to button his suit jacket when standing up to greet a delegation from the UK.[28] The leadership also viewed table manners as an important communication tactic. When invited to a diplomatic dinner, KDP foreign relations head Hawrami believed he was "not there to eat."[29] DFR official Hoshang Mohamed recalled that "the first course offered to the DFR diplomats after its establishment in 2006 was in protocol and etiquette, including which fork and knife to use when." Mohamed, who attended the course, stated that diplomats were trained to eat an olive with their fingers to avoid a potential disaster if the fork threw the olive across the table.[30] For the leadership, this etiquette represented another opportunity to communicate non-verbally its desire to conform to the diplomatic club.

Foreign affairs and nation-building

As discussed, the Kurdistan Region's history of isolation meant that its foreign relations remained largely covert or unofficial throughout much of the twentieth century. However, following 1991, and even more so after 2003, the leadership became international diplomats who constantly met with heads of states and other senior officials. This change in international standing facilitated a sense of pride for the sub-state's leaders, who regularly boasted of their government's new-found relevance in foreign affairs.

This sense of pride was most evident on the KRG's main government website, www.cabinet.gov.krd, which primarily featured press releases of the leadership's meetings with foreign officials and participation in international conferences. On the website, the KRG prioritized this aspect over domestic issues, which tend to be more common features on the US (www.whitehouse.gov) or UK (www.gov.uk) government websites. A former KRG employee criticized the government for choosing to publish on its website the Nepalese ambassador's visit to the Region as the top news story on the day of the KRG's September 2013 provincial elections.[31] Publishing the visit rather than the elections signified the importance the KRG placed on diplomatic communication. The emphasis on its new-found standing was used to prove the sub-state's international legitimacy, status notwithstanding, to both local and international audiences.

The final pillar of effective statehood is when the population and international actors perceive the governmental entity as legitimate. This legitimacy comes from successful nation-building or the construction of an "imagined community." Writing on the European context, Linz argues that state-building historically preceded nation-building and that "in spite of the saliency of the idea of the nation, the reality of statehood, old or new, is still dominant."[32] For the Region's leadership, efforts required constructing a nation out of the nascent state-building project to legitimize the sub-state government to both its domestic constituency as well as the international community.

According to Lecours, sub-states with stronger nationalist movements employ stronger diplomacies.[33] The 2005 unofficial referendum on independence demonstrated that the Region's population was overwhelmingly secessionist. Scholars of nationalism have traditionally focused exclusively on domestic political, social, and economic transformations to explain nation-building.[34] According to these scholars, the leadership constructs an imagined community to convince the domestic audience to come together as a nation. The Kurdistan Region's leadership used foreign affairs as a tool to incite nationalist sentiment and to achieve legitimacy among the local population. It used successes in diplomacy to argue that a KRG nation was more conducive to moving beyond a history of isolation. To an extent, then, domestic political, social, and economic transformations contributed to the nation-building programmes.

However, while these influences remain important aspects of nation-building, history shows that nations are constructed or destroyed through geopolitics and international affairs, including the break-up of empires after wars, invasions, and annexations. In a period of transformation, diplomacy and the negotiation of statehood can also facilitate the reconstruction of nationhood. The Kurdistan Region's international affairs program was in the first instance facilitated by *de jure* states: primarily the US. Yet, international empowerment took on a life of its own. The leadership believed its external outreach was an important part of building its imagined community. Although representatives subdued the ethno-national instinct, they used relations with *de jure* states and international organizations to build their nation, which was confined to Iraqi Kurdistan. Through diplomatic channels, the sub-state's representatives wished to gain recognition for their government and their people. Rather than just convincing the domestic population, therefore, they also wished to persuade *de jure* states that had the authority to recognize Iraqi Kurdistan. The leadership believed that this would facilitate nation-building.

Growing confidence following international engagements

A form of superiority shaped the sub-state's leaders, particularly in the post-1991 context. As discussed with the website content, they did not shy away from expressing their confidence. The leadership often boasted about how influential its government had become in powerful circles in Washington, London, and elsewhere. As it became more influential and as its international standing increased, the representatives became more confident.

The confidence was particularly evident vis-à-vis other sub-state or non-state actors. As the Kurdistan Region's leaders increased their international profile and high-level meetings with senior *de jure* state diplomats, they became less inclined to deal with unrecognized entity. "Partners of choice" referred to *de jure* state counterparts. Previously, the leaders actively participated in events convened by the Unrepresented Nations and Peoples Organization (UNPO). However, as the sub-state grew in international standing, it stopped sending representatives to these meetings because of a growing perception that such events were less important than meetings with state officials and major international agencies.

The sense of superiority extended to the "Greater Kurdistan" question. The sub-state's leaders asserted that when Kurds from all countries spoke of "Kurdistan", they usually meant Iraqi Kurdistan. They were confident in the belief that their sub-state was now "Kurdistan." In meetings, it was common for Kurds from Syria to refer to their area as Rojava (Western Kurdistan), for Kurds from Turkey to refer to their area as Bakur (Northern Kurdistan), and Kurds from Iran to refer to their area as Rojhelat (Eastern Kurdistan). However, the Iraqi Kurd delegation more frequently referred to their sub-state as "Kurdistan" rather than "Bashur" or Southern Kurdistan. When questioned, the Kurdistan Region's diplomats often replied that the extent of their state-building warranted this labeling.[35]

A setback in state-building

After 2013, the promise of the Kurdistan Region as the "new Dubai" or the "Other Iraq" suffered setbacks. The economy declined in the first instance because Iraqi Prime Minister Nouri al-Maliki decided to stop paying Erbil the revenues that the constitution mandated. Shortly after, the Islamic State's takeover of Iraqi cities led to a humanitarian problem that saw swarms of IDPs seek refuge in the region. The leadership was also now tasked with defending its land against the Islamic State. The collapse in the price of oil, which was more than halved, hurt the emerging oil and gas exporter. Further contributing to this loss of control in nation-building was President Masoud Barzani's decision to remain in power despite the end of his term. As such, the underlying tensions in the Kurdistan Region's rentier economy were exposed and the sub-state government was no longer able to pay its employees, including the peshmerga.

This failure in state-building led many citizens to protest against the leadership, which found it more difficult to hide behind nationalist rhetoric based on a diplomatic pursuit of recognition. In Erbil in October 2016, for instance, famous writer and poet Farhad Pirbal decided to strip his clothes to protest against not receiving his salary. He called on everyone to protest against Prime Minister Barzani.[36] Moreover, when President Barzani called for a referendum on independence, leaders from the PUK and Gorran, for the first time, decided to stand against the move. The economic and political legitimacy crisis of the Barzanis, therefore, has led many to question the diplomatic process of using foreign affairs to build a state and nation.

Despite this, however, the Kurdistan Region's leadership continues to rely on the same diplomatic tactics to remain relevant in Western capitals. This is done to ensure that counterparts in Washington, London, and elsewhere can continue to support the KRG state-building process. Its sub-state status means that it will continue to use such tactics.

Conclusion

The Kurdistan Region faced an international system that remained hostile to the emergence of new *de jure* states. Despite changes as it became an important ally for many international actors, its representatives still felt the need to employ diplomatic tactics aimed at overcoming the gap between state and sub-state. The leadership viewed gaining independence as the final step of a long process. To them, it was not conducive to declare statehood without international support. As such, the leadership emphasized foreign affairs as the ticket to statehood and eventual independence.

More critically, as we have discussed, employing a foreign affairs program also served as a temporary means to overcoming the gap between *de jure* states and the sub-state. It was a key facilitator of both state-building and the search for alternatives to dependence on the central government. It also gave the leaders a sense of confidence. Many boasted that US President Obama or other influential figures were inviting the Kurdistan Region's President Barzani to Washington on a number of occasions—whereas certain *de jure* state leaders were finding it difficult to access Washington.

The year 2014 was critical for KRG. With soured relations vis-à-vis Baghdad, its economy and state-building project began to decline. Many began questioning the so-called "new Dubai" thesis and the sense of confidence that the leadership employed. However, it was also the year that the Erbil-Washington relationship was tested vis-à-vis the emergence of the Islamic State. For the leadership, August 2014 marked a defining moment when they witnessed Obama commit to a policy of supporting and protecting Iraq's Kurds from the Islamic State—a departure from the memory of 1975. This decision was in part due to the Region's diplomatic tactics, which this chapter has analyzed. Following 2014, the Kurdish question became a household issue in many foreign capitals.

However, the sub-state status means that the leadership must continue to engage in foreign affairs to gain a seat, which is not always guaranteed. For instance, in January 2015, President Barzani expressed anger at not being invited to an anti-Islamic State meeting of coalition partners in London.[37] For the Kurdistan Region leadership, its status remains precarious and dependent on a strong foreign relations portfolio, which is the key to remaining relevant on the international stage.

31.

A PARADIGM SHIFT IN US–KURDISTAN REGION RELATIONS POST-2014

THE EVOLUTION TO A STRATEGIC PARTNERSHIP

Mohammed Shareef

"I do think the Kurds used that time that was given by our troop sacrifices in Iraq. They used that time well, and the Kurdish region is functional the way we would like to see it. It is tolerant of other sects and other religions in a way that we would like to see elsewhere. So we do think it's important to make sure that that space is protected."

Barack Obama, 44th president of the United States, 8 August 2014[1]

US strategy toward the Kurdistan Region of Iraq has seen various transitions since the end of the First World War. With the steady rise of the United States as a major player in the Middle East, the perception of the Kurds in US foreign policy gradually changed. However, as a result of the US-led invasion of Iraq in 2003, the nature and mechanisms of interaction changed considerably, especially after 2005. After 15 October 2005, namely after the ratification of the Iraqi constitution in a general referendum by the Iraqi people, US-Kurdistan Region relations evolved into an institutionalized relationship based on mutual respect and interests through an official but undeclared US Kurdish policy. The public ratification of the constitution allowed for the Kurdistan Region to be officially recognized as a formal semi-autonomous entity, stipulated clearly within the framework and articles of the permanent Iraqi constitution. As a result, this development gave the Kurdistan Region the necessary legality, and subsequently the US greater freedom in its interactions with this sub-state entity and its capital Erbil. This new form of interaction dramatically changed the nature of the relationship between the world's only superpower and a mini (non-state) entity situated in a hostile Middle East. The methods and means of the relationship were unusual, almost on a par between two independent states; although the Kurdistan Region exhibits certain characteristics of a sovereign state, it is certainly not yet, at least, fully independent. With the ratification of the Iraqi constitution, Kurdistan was no longer seen as a de facto entity by the Americans with no legal status, but *de jure* rather with recognition and status (albeit) within the framework and confines of Iraq.

Though a clear change of strategy was visible, there was no actual change in policy. It was not the intention of the US to breach the sovereignty of Baghdad over its Kurdish north or to antagonize Arab Iraq, either by implication or by matter of fact actions. Nevertheless, Iraq's sustained turmoil at so many levels since 2003, including Baghdad's incompetence at tackling its internal affairs, its lack of stability and security, and Kurdistan's determination to sidestep Arab Iraq made this US objective ever more elusive and unattainable.

Since the initiation of diplomatic relations between Iraq and the US on 30 March 1931, the United States has perceived its relations and interests with Arab Iraq far superior to its sympathies for Kurdish nationalist aspirations. The US policy position has been one of finding a political solution within Iraq's national boundaries. It is US policy that the Iraqi government and the Kurds be able to come promptly to a mutually satisfactory agreement. The US does not contemplate a policy toward the Kurds that could allow for an independent state. Its policy toward the Kurds is always one in which the Kurds are part of a greater Arab Iraq, with Baghdad as its capital.[2] The United States were initially reluctant, stemming from their idealistic approach to a new Iraq in the post-2003 invasion environment, but eventually allowed for ethnic federalism in the Transitional Administrative Law for Iraq written under Paul Bremer's auspices in the early days of the occupation. This was only after they were finally forced to reconsider their previous non-accommodating position after strong Kurdish protest and consequent to their more realistic assessment of the facts on the ground in Iraq. Following the ratification of the permanent Iraqi constitution (and even shortly before), senior Bush administration officials also made a point of visiting Erbil to emphasize the importance of federalism in Iraq and the new status of the Kurds. Masoud Barzani had been elected several months earlier, in June 2005, by the Kurdistan parliament to be president of the Kurdistan Region, and was invited officially to the White House to a warm welcome from President George W. Bush on 25 October 2005. This was the first time in the history of the Kurdish liberation movement that a Kurdish leader had been received by a US president at the White House. It was hailed as a milestone in Kurdish-American relations

Essentially, US Iraq policy at the sub-national level (that is, toward the Kurds) has transitioned through five major phases. Phase one, 1918-23, represented America's implicit "rhetorical support" for Kurdish self-determination, after Woodrow Wilson's famous Fourteen Points speech until the signing of the Treaty of Lausanne. Phase two, 1961-71, was characterized by "contacts": essentially unilateral Kurdish attempts to gain US support, but to no avail. Phase three, 1972-5, was a "covert relationship" demonstrated in secret US support through its CIA intelligence agency. And phase four, 1991-2004, was an "overt relationship" following the mass exodus of the Kurds, consequent on the failed Kurdish uprising. Finally phase five, from 2005 till the present, evolved into an "overt institutionalized relationship."[3] And within this institutionalized framework, it further evolved into a strategic partnership from 3 August 2014 onwards, mostly as a result of the real and palpable threat from Islamic extremism embodied in the Islamic State of Iraq and Syria (ISIS); also because of Arab Iraq's weaknesses and incompetence; but more importantly from the strategic and military role that the Kurdistan Region came to play in the fight against Islamic radicalism in the Middle East.

It is often said that the success story that is Kurdistan has American fingerprints on it. This may be true. However, the American contribution, though instrumental, was accidental, not intentional. The US helped create the Kurdish autonomous entity inadvertently after Saddam's defeat in Kuwait in 1991. After the UN's Security Council passed resolution 688 on 5 April 1991 demanding an immediate end to the repression of the civilian Kurdish population, Operation Provide Comfort was launched the following day to deal with the humanitarian crisis, ensuing from the mass exodus of the Kurds stranded on the borders of Turkey and Iran. What later happened in terms of an emerging Kurdish entity was never planned nor envisaged in Washington. The whole operation was a humanitarian one and nothing more; in fact, the humanitarian intervention itself was not an American-led initiative; it was based on a proposal by UK Prime Minister John Major and French President François Mitterand: they were the ones who forced it upon the Americans. It was only after James Baker's fact-finding mission to the Turkish-Iraqi border that he was able to go back to President Bush senior and ask for something be done. It was a reluctant intervention; nobody in the decision-making process in the US during 1991-2, which set up Operation Provide Comfort, the Safe Haven, and eventually the no-fly zone, thought that this US-led intervention would create what exists today in Kurdistan. The US had no idea that it would evolve into the Kurdistan Regional Government, the Iraqi Kurdistan Parliament, a flag, a (draft) constitution, and the peshmerga. Jay Garner, the commanding general of the operation, described Operation Provide Comfort as humanitarian in nature but not totally lacking a political element either. The political element pushed primarily by John Major was that at least Britain and the

US should keep the Kurds from dying, as Bush senior had rhetorically encouraged a mass rebellion that was left to collapse in an intolerant public and politically damaging atmosphere.[4] And it was at this stage that the fourth phase of US-Kurdish interaction catapulted an "overt relationship", ending eventually with the US-led invasion of Iraq in 2003 and subsequently evolving into the "overt institutionalized relationship."

When President Obama came to office in January 2009, it was a personal priority of his to disengage or at least reduce US involvement in the Middle East—a luxury he later realized the US could not afford. As soon as Obama came to office he wanted to distance the US from Iraq. He held to a campaign pledge to end US involvement in the country. He did not feel that the United States should have been involved in Iraq at all. Obama was against the Iraq war even as an Illinois senator as early as 2002 before the US invasion of Iraq. The US military departure from Iraq in December 2011 was essentially part of a larger Obama administration strategy to distance itself from the greater Middle East. The Obama administration started to put greater emphasis on Asia in 2011. The greater Middle East, it was believed, had come to dominate and distort American foreign and defense policy, and a course correction was called for. The Obama administration's vehicle for this correction was the announcement of a "pivot" or "rebalancing" toward Asia. A fresh recognition that China was not just rising but becoming more assertive gave the pivot some urgency.[5]

The United States' intention to distance, disengage, and detach itself from the Middle East was premature, as later became apparent. Although the US is the second largest oil producer after Saudi Arabia at 10.59 million barrels per day (mbd), it is still burdened with the top spot as the highest oil consumer at the global level, which in 2015 was on average 19.51 mbd. This means that American energy security is still largely dependent on the Middle East, especially considering that fracking on US territory has a very long way to go before their oil interests in the region decline as a consequence of energy-sufficiency. And in addition to oil, the US has other pressing national interests in the region which would make it difficult for them to disengage any time soon: primarily the security of Israel and their continued regional hegemony. Adding to Kurdistan Region's strategic value to the United States, in addition to their role in the global fight against Islamic extremism comes the potentially important role they could play in the global energy market. According to Kurdistan's Ministry of Natural Resources, actual oil production was 650,000 bpd by the end of 2015, with a forecast of 2 mbd by the end of 2019.[6] If this forecast proves accurate, the international community with the US at its helm will have a stake in a viable and stable oil-producing Kurdistan, contributing substantially toward steady and even possibly cheaper oil prices on the world market. Today, Iraqi Kurdistan is estimated to have around 45 billion barrels of oil and 110 trillion cubic feet of gas, making it the tenth largest hydrocarbon reserve in the world.[7]

In light of Obama's actions, essentially the withdrawal of US troops from Iraq, indications from the Obama administration that its priorities lay elsewhere and the lack of attention paid to Syria's civil war in 2011 created the impression that American influence was waning. Former CIA director David Petraeus stated: "Our withdrawal from Iraq in late 2011 contributed to a perception that the US was pulling back from the Middle East." This perception complicated the United States' ability to shape developments in the region and thus to further its interests. These perceptions also shook many US allies, and for a period at least made it harder to persuade them to support American approaches. According to Petraeus: "Neither the Iranians nor Daesh are ten feet tall, but the perception in the region for the past few years has been that of the US on the wane, and our adversaries on the rise. I hope that we can begin to reverse that now."[8]

There was a reason for this. Principally, the foreign policy establishment under the Obama administration, as under the Clinton administration, was led by career professionals and practitioners, primarily pragmatists, not ideologues. Obama's first ambassador to Iraq, Christopher Hill, was appointed with no experience of Iraq or elsewhere in the Arab world or the Middle East. The Obama administration was primarily focused on furthering US national interests, preserving American power, and dealing with problems as they came up. The Obama administration's approach caused some even to question whether they had a strategy at all or merely responded to events. "American policy is very weak", observed Fuad Hussein, chief of staff to the president of the Kurdistan Region in Iraq. "It is not clear to us how they have defined their interests in Iraq", Hussein stated. "They are picking events and reacting on the basis of events. That is the policy."[9] Essentially, after the US military withdrawal in 2011, they placed stability before democracy, and prior to their departure they attempted to strengthen Prime Minister Nouri al-Maliki's ability to maintain control and the unity of the country through a strengthened Iraqi military. To do this, at the beginning of the Obama presidency, Washington focused on securing its long-term strategic relationship with Maliki by both engaging and appeasing him, so that they could more easily withdraw US forces: this became more visible after Maliki's second term, starting on 11 November 2010. This strategy turned out to become a recipe for disaster.

In fact, it was apparent that the United States placed greater priority on a successful Arab Iraq over Kurdistan. One of the major objectives of Saddam's overthrow in the US-led Operation Iraqi Freedom was to create out of Iraq a model for the rest of the Middle East. The Bush administration wanted a new democratically governed Iraq to serve as an example to the rest of the region. The intention was to create a domino effect to facilitate the end of repressive and undemocratic regimes in the Middle East. This never materialized in Arab Iraq, however; the Kurdish north was totally different and a remarkable success story, although certainly not without its own flaws. The Obama administration's continuation of this policy and its prioritization of Arab Iraq over Kurdistan was a mistake they were soon to realize and a reality that strategically elevated and amplified Kurdistan's status in US Middle East policy considerations in the wake of Arab Iraq's ineptitude.

However, one must ask: Why did Arab Iraq fail? The reason was basically the unexpected aftermath of the war. A sustained insurgency was not anticipated. The Ba'athists, in coordination with the jihadists, had managed to launch a damaging military campaign in Iraq. Moreover, the US's mishandling in the transfer of authority to the Iraqis after Saddam's overthrow was a mistake, based on unfounded and unrealistic assumptions of a post-Saddam Iraq. It opened up the perception that the US was not a liberator, but an occupier in the eyes of the average Iraqi. It offended the personal dignity and national pride of many Iraqis, creating opportunities exploitable by hard-core Ba'athists, sectarian extremists, foreign jihadists, Iraqi nationalists, tribal members, and Iraq's ill-intentioned neighbors, severely destabilizing Iraq, from which it has not yet recovered nor will recover any time soon.

Making matters worse, America mismanaged and mishandled the Kurds; the US had inadvertently put both major Kurdish parties and allies, the Kurdistan Democratic Party (KDP) and Patriotic Union of Kurdistan (PUK), on the terrorist list soon after the 11 September 2001 al-Qaeda attacks on America. Both Kurdish parties were caught up in the broad provisions of the US Patriot Act, which was passed by the US Congress and signed into law by President George W. Bush on 26 October 2001. The law allowed the KDP and PUK to be unintentionally labeled as terrorists. The law effectively provides that a Tier III terrorist organization is any group of two or more people engaged in any armed resistance deemed unlawful by their government, no matter how repressive or corrupt that government may be.[10] Consequently, both the KDP and PUK fell under the provisions of this act (designed purely to serve immigration law purposes), barring admission to the United States for members of practically any movement that has ever supported resistance to an established government.

This led President Barzani to cancel a visit to the United States. Barzani's refusal to accept the invitation to visit Washington in May 2014 was a clear diplomatic statement to register protest on the US position. It was also a show of new-found confidence and strength and a recognition of Kurdistan's place as an emerging and potentially significant power in the Middle East. It also demonstrated that Barzani felt more established as a leader, in other words more powerful and independent internally with no major rivals inside Kurdistan. Additionally, it showed a lack of confidence in the Obama administration's ability and determination to help resolve the Kurdistan Regional Government's (KRG) outstanding issues with Baghdad, namely: Kurdistan's independent oil sales and the funding of the peshmerga terminated since 2006, and more crucially the freezing of the Kurdistan Region's share of the national budget since February 2014. The moment the invitation was sent in January 2014, Falah Mustafa (Head of KRG's Foreign Relations Department) informed Robert Beecroft (American ambassador to Baghdad) that Barzani's visit would not proceed until the KDP and PUK were removed from the terrorist list. In an earlier visit in April 2012, President Barzani had already requested the Obama administration to remove the PUK and KDP from the Tier III designation during a meeting at the White House, but little had been done to this end.

Before this incident, however, the Kurdish leadership was not so assertive in their diplomatic interactions with the United States. They often opted for appeasement. The KRG was worried about American pressure. During the writing of the Transitional Administrative Law in 2004, Peter Galbraith (a former US ambassador and an advisor to the Kurdish leadership) advised the Kurdish negotiators in Baghdad that the United States needed the Kurds at least as much as the Kurds needed the Americans. He told them that the Bush administration might not like the Kurds insisting on their rights, but it would still respect them for doing so.[11] Nawshirwan Mustafa (Coordinator General of the Gorran movement) also recalls that after Saddam was toppled, the Kurdish leadership chose to pursue its special party interests, and in order to please the United States it failed to make the most of the opportunities available to advance the Kurdish cause in Iraq. Najmaldin Karim (Governor of Kirkuk) also believed that in the immediate aftermath of Saddam's overthrow the Kurdish leadership lacked assertiveness and aggression; Karim compared the Kurds to the Sunni Arabs, who were comparable in numbers, but more vocal in their requests to the US. The Kurds, he argued, were suffering from "the battered child syndrome", neglecting to capitalize on their new-found authority, influence, and status.

Barzani's visit was eventually rescheduled for May 2015, and was successfully made. The postponement did not lead to a souring of US-KRG relations, as the US primarily sees the pro-American KRG as a valuable asset in a hostile and predominantly anti-American Middle East, and thus could not afford to lose an ally in such a region.[12] In late November 2013, Senator John McCain and four others co-sponsored and introduced Senate Amendment number 2421, known as the McCain Amendment, which removed the PUK and KDP from being treated as Tier III terrorist groups under the Patriot Act. Senator McCain led efforts in the Senate to end the sanctions on the Kurdish parties, and introduced a stand-alone bill on the matter, with the Obama administration's support.

Also, during a testimony at a Congressional Committee hearing, Brett McGurk, who at the time was the State Department's deputy assistant secretary for Iraq and Iran, acknowledged that the two parties should be removed from the blacklist. On 5 February 2014, McGurk told the hearing on behalf of the administration that he thought it was imperative to do so. He also said that the administration was 100 per cent supportive of the legislative fix to the problem. He made clear, however, that President Obama could not rectify the anomaly with a stroke of the pen. It would require action in Congress to amend the Patriot Act. He said that the administration looked forward to working with the relevant committees in Congress to get that done.[13] Eventually, on 13 December 2014, the US Congress passed the National Defense Authorisation Act (NDAA) with a provision removing the KDP and PUK from the list of designated organizations under US immigration laws.[14]

One of the major articles of US policy at the (Arab Iraq) national level and based on the Strategic Framework Agreement signed in the last days of the Bush administration in November 2008 was the "Defense and Security Cooperation", which included US assistance at various levels, including military equipment. When Iraqi Prime Minister Maliki met President Obama during a visit to Washington on 1 November 2013, the main purpose of the visit was to request US support amid escalating security concerns in Iraq, primarily the ever-rising Sunni unrest in the country. The US was also concerned with the rising terrorist activities of the Islamic State in Iraq and the Levant (ISIL) which had not yet captured huge swathes of Iraq's territory, and to this end agreed to consider Iraqi requests for intelligence assistance, training, and weaponry. The US wanted a stable, strong, and unified Iraq, and if this required US military hardware, it would show no reluctance to oblige. America had essentially put all its eggs in one basket (that is, Arab Iraq), which it would eventually come to regret, and it was a consequence of this miscalculation that America would come to value a strategic military partnership with the Kurds.

The United States believed that establishing a military base in the Kurdistan Region would send the wrong messages—a decision they would later reconsider. The Kurds, they thought, would use the opportunity to declare independence, which they did not support. The United States did not want to encourage Kurdish independence, nor did they want to be drawn into defending their existence if and when it was declared. With US military on Kurdish territory, they knew that after the declaration of Kurdish independence they might be forced to intervene militarily against hostile regional states. The United States was unwilling to be involved in protecting a Kurdish entity, as the Kurdistan Region (they believed at the time) had no particular strategic importance in US foreign policy calculations, nor would there be any public support or tolerance inside America for US bloodshed and financial costs for such an enterprise. Ironically, during the lengthy and often stalled negotiations between Baghdad and Washington in the summer of 2008 to authorize a mandate for US military presence after the expiration of UNSCR 1790 on 31 December 2008, President Barzani tried to encourage the establishment of a US military base in the Kurdistan Region. Barzani visited Washington in October 2008, and during a talk at the Center for Strategic and International Studies he welcomed the possibility of basing US forces in Kurdistan.[15] The White House did not respond to the offer, deeming the stationing of US forces in the Kurdistan Region as too risky and easy to misinterpret.

However, the United States was forced to rethink and reconsider its disengagement from Iraq after the ISIS invasion and occupation of Iraq's third major city, Mosul, on 10 June 2014. After the fall of Mosul, the US became ever more concerned with Iraq's future prospects as a unified and viable entity. To this end, Secretary of State John Kerry visited Erbil on 24 June 2014 to have a "heart to heart with Kurdish officials." According to a senior US official, they were to make it clear that the Obama administration believed it was in "nobody's interest to have a kind of al-Qaeda on steroids" on its southern border. The only way to prevent this happening, the Obama administration believed, was to make sure that a moderate Sunni component was able to clear any territory seized by ISIS, and to do that the Kurds need to remain part of the Iraqi government. Baghdad-Erbil relations were already in turmoil, peaking with Maliki's suspension of Kurdistan's share of the national budget. The US believed that if the Kurds decided to withdraw from the Baghdad political process, this would accelerate a lot of the negative trends in Iraq and the wider region. Kerry urged the Kurds to back the formation of a new, inclusive government in Baghdad. Masoud Barzani told Kerry that it could no longer be business as usual: "We are facing a new reality and a new Iraq." And while he did not reject Kerry's request that the Kurds be part of a new, inclusive government in Baghdad, Barzani insisted that this would have to be on Erbil's terms.

But the actual last straw that drew the United States directly back into Iraq and the growing conflict was the Islamic State's aggression on the Yezidi Kurds, killing hundreds of its men and abducting and raping hundreds of its women and girls. This was after ISIS made a major incursion into Kurdistan, capturing huge swathes of Iraqi Kurdish territory on 3 August 2014. ISIS had overrun Kurdish forces in the western Iraqi Kurdish towns of Sinjar and Makhmour, and surged as far as the town of Gwer, only 31 miles from the Kurdish capital city of Erbil. In addition to the tragic and immense human cost it had inflicted, it also put at risk the US consulate personnel and American citizens living in Kurdistan, mostly in Erbil, and more importantly the whole relatively successful Kurdish entity in northern Iraq.

As a result, Kurdish aspirations for independence heavily reported in the media suddenly seemed crushed in the aftermath of this tragedy. But this unfortunate turn-around, mostly the result of the ISIS incursion, unexpectedly provided the Kurds with both an unprecedented opportunity and also major hurdles. On the one hand, plans for an independence referendum were abruptly put on hold; on the other hand, however, the cold Western reception to Kurdish calls for independence (mostly in early June 2014) were neutralized and replaced by serious Western concern for the protection of the Kurdistan Region. Almost overnight, NATO and the EU found on their eastern border a radical Islamic expansionist caliphate determined to destroy the West, and locally challenging US hegemony in the region. After the Kurdish defeat in Sinjar, the West realized that they could not afford nor would it be in their interest to lose Kurdistan: a pro-Western, largely democratic, predominantly secular, and economically prosperous entity in the Middle East. To this end, major Western powers took steps to halt and repel ISIS advances by promptly providing humanitarian assistance, air attacks, and weapons to the Kurds. President Obama had to date been intentionally passive and disengaged from the Middle East, especially so since the US withdrawal from Iraq in December 2011, but was now greatly alarmed. Obama described the situation:

When you have a unique circumstance in which genocide is threatened, and a country is willing to have us in there, you have a strong international consensus that these people need to be protected and we have a capacity to do so, then we have an obligation to do so. But given the island of decency the Kurds have built, we also have to ask not just how do we push back on ISIL, but also how do we preserve the space for the best impulses inside of Iraq; that very much is on my mind, that has been on my mind throughout.[16]

Consequently, for the first time since the US withdrawal on 18 December 2011, on 8 August 2014 US Navy McDonnell Douglas F/A-18 Hornet fighters bombed an ISIS artillery unit outside Erbil, and four US fighters later bombed ISIS military convoys, some of them advancing on Erbil and besieging Kurdish forces defending Erbil. Furthermore, in April 2015 the United States established a new Joint Coalition Coordination Center (JCCC) near Erbil, the capital of the Kurdistan Region, to coordinate efforts in countering the Islamic State. The US Central Command (CENTCOM) stated: "The new center will also set the conditions to relocate the Ninewa Operations Center from Baghdad to northern Iraq to coordinate future operations in Ninewa and Mosul."[17] CENTCOM was essentially stating that the new military center reaffirmed Washington's commitment to support security forces (primarily the peshmerga) in northern Iraq in order to defeat ISIS. By June 2015, the US had deployed an additional 450 troops to Iraq, increasing the US troop presence in Iraq incrementally to at least 4,850; most were military advisors and trainers to assist, train, and advise Iraqi security forces, including peshmerga and Sunni tribal forces, in order to degrade and defeat ISIS. The Kurdish forces (peshmerga) in effect became the West's "boots on the ground" and the West's first line of defense against a fanatical Islamic army, subsequently elevating the status of the Kurds from merely a relatively useless friend and a potential headache to a strategic and vital military partner against a global war on Islamic extremism. At a practical level as intelligence and military partners, the Kurds are the most reliable units on the ground. Previously, the Kurds seemed to have no particular strategic importance in US national interest calculations in the Middle East. The US did appreciate the value of a special relationship with the Kurds at the bipartisan level, however, so they then worked backwards, rather than having a US strategic interest in Iraqi Kurdistan per se: a principle which had no relevance in international relations.[18]

Jen Psaki (US State Department spokesperson) on 9 February 2015 stated that more than 3 million lbs of equipment in over sixty cargo flights had been sent to the Kurds. This included more than 15,000 hand grenades, nearly 40 million rounds of light and heavy machine gun ammunition, 18,000 assault rifles, and 45,000 mortar rounds. Psaki said that most of the 1,000 US airstrikes in Iraq have been in support of the Kurdish peshmerga and that Washington had equipped them with the necessary arms. Nevertheless, though appreciative, the Kurds were not totally pleased with the level of support provided. Moreover, America was determined to make the delivery through Baghdad, adding to Kurdistan's despair. Rear Admiral John Kirby, the spokesperson for the US Department of Defense, stated: "Right now, for the United States, our role is principally in helping transport, logistically get the stuff to the Kurdish forces. There's been no decision to directly arm the Kurds from American stockpiles." Psaki also added: "Our policy remains that all arms transfers must be coordinated via the sovereign central Government of Iraq. This is a legal requirement under US law."

However, in a further development contrary to the Obama administration's official policy and highlighting the ascendancy of the Kurds in Washington, there came legislation H.R.1654 proposed on 26 March 2015 by congressman Ed Royce (Republican, California), chairman of the House Foreign Affairs Committee, and Eliot Engel (Democrat, New York). It called on Washington to tender Iraqi Kurds as a "reliable and stable partner of the United States."[19] The most striking feature of the bill, similar to the failed H.R.5747 proposal introduced in 2014, was its recognition of "Iraqi Kurds" as a partner of the US. "Our critical partner in the fight against ISIS is in great need of heavy weapons and armored vehicles", the proposed bill said. "We haven't gotten Iraqi Kurdish 'Peshmerga' forces what they need. Even so, they have proven to be the most effective ground force currently fighting ISIS."

As a result, the House Armed Services Committee of the US Congress proposed clauses in the annual National Defense Authorisation Act (NDAA) 2016 defense budget that included direct military assistance to Kurds and Iraqi Sunni forces, despite opposition from the Obama administration. According to the defense bill, of 715 million USD allocated to the Iraqi government, 179 million USD had to go directly to the Kurdish peshmerga and Sunni tribal forces battling the Islamic State (ISIS). The bill "would require that the Kurdish Peshmerga, the Sunni tribal security forces with a national security mission, and the Iraqi Sunni National Guard be deemed a country." Doing so "would allow these security forces to directly receive assistance from the United States."

Moreover, US senator and 2016 Republican presidential candidate hopeful Rand Paul called for direct arms supplies to Iraq's Kurds, and even went further by stating that the Kurds should have their own homeland. He said: "I would draw new lines for Kurdistan and I would promise them a country."[20]

The Obama administration ultimately opposed the measure, saying that bypassing Baghdad would undermine Iraq's territorial integrity. US Secretaries of Defense and State personally wrote letters to the Senate urging against the provision. Secretary of State John Kerry argued that Iraq's fragile territorial and political unity would be in jeopardy if the amendment passed. Secretary of Defense Ashton Carter reasoned that arming the Kurds would trigger the revenge of the Shia militias to unleash attacks on US personnel and interests in Iraq.[21]

Although bipartisan legislation was sponsored by both Republicans and Democrats to support the Kurds, the Republicans were more proactive when it came to Iraq. There were two major reasons for this: firstly, to register Republican party dissatisfaction with the Obama administration's handling of the ISIS issue and US Middle East policy in general; secondly, to maintain balance among Iraq's major components so as not to weaken one side at the expense of the other, especially as Iran had extended its hegemony into Iraq through the Shia-led government in Baghdad. Additionally, the different responses inside Iraq to the bill demonstrated that Iraq was fragmented and that all three major components (Kurds, Sunni Arabs, and Shia Arabs) were pursuing different agendas. The very fact that the Kurds and Sunni Arabs chose to boycott the vote in the Iraqi Council of Representatives against the bill only reinforced this point. The Kurds aspired to independence, the Sunnis to devolution, essentially semi-autonomous federal regions, and the Shia to a strong and centralized Iraq.[22] The Obama administration expressed its rejection of the bill in its pro-Kurdish form as it implied the break-up of Iraq and breached the sovereignty of Baghdad over the state of Iraq. On 16 June 2015, the Senate voted 54-45 against the measure. The majority of Democrats, following the White House's lead, voted against the amendment. This meant that a watered down and amended bill was eventually sent to the White House for approval. If passed, the amendment would have given the President the option of sending US military equipment, including anti-tank weaponry, body armor, and communications directly to the KRG for three years. In a statement released after the vote, Senator Joni Ernst (Republican, Iowa) said that she remained committed to supporting Iraqi Kurds, whom she described as key partners in defeating ISIS: "The United States simply cannot afford any delays in arming our Kurdish partner on the ground at such a critical moment."[23] However, this was not the end of direct US assistance to the Kurds. Remarkably, the Kurdish acting Peshmerga Minister Karim Sinjari and US acting Assistant Secretary of Defense Elissa Slotkin signed a memorandum of understanding in the presence of Masoud Barzani in Erbil on 12 July 2016.[24] In this unprecedented memorandum that came after intense lobbying lasting two years, the United States committed to direct military and financial support to the value of 415 million USD to the peshmerga forces on the frontlines in the war against the Islamic State, with particular focus on the liberation of Mosul from ISIS that commenced on 17 October 2016.[25]

Characterizing the ascendancy of the Kurds and evolving US-Kurdish relations, US involvement with the Kurds did not restrict itself to Iraq alone. As a result of the escalation and the real threat of ISIS, the US was also obliged to support the Kurdish People's Protection Units (YPG) in Syria for two primary reasons: firstly, because the YPG's offensive had been successful and was narrowly focused on fighting ISIS, rather than focusing first on regime forces; and secondly, in the public relations war, public sympathy in the West tended to view the Kurds as the most forward-thinking rebel group in the battle against Islamic extremism.[26] To endorse this sentiment, Brett McGurk, the US Special Presidential Envoy for the Global Coalition to Counter ISIS, made a visit to Syrian Kurdistan (Rojava) 30–31 January 2016 on the first anniversary of the liberation of the northern Syrian Kurdish town of Kobanî from ISIS. This was the first official visit by a senior US official to liberated Syrian Kurdish territory to discuss the fight against ISIS. US ties with the Syrian Kurds have grown deeper despite the concerns of NATO ally Turkey.[27] On 8 February 2016 US State Department spokesperson John Kirby stressed and reiterated that the United States did not recognize the PYD as a terrorist organization, much to the dissatisfaction of its NATO ally Turkey.[28]

But this was no easy balancing act for the US, as the Democratic Union Party (PYD) and its military wing the YPG had strong connections to the Kurdistan Workers' Party (PKK), designated by US, EU, and Turkey as a terrorist group. This was hugely problematic for America, as Ankara was deeply concerned with the group's advance and sympathetic treatment in the international media. But despite these concerns, the US appeared to be committed to maintaining its air support for the Syrian Kurds, both near the Euphrates in the west and the outskirts of Raqqa in the south. The question for the US was whether aiding an enemy of the Turkish state would impinge dramatically on their relationship with a NATO ally. To some extent the immediacy of degrading and defeating ISIS trumped concerns of longer-term tension with Ankara. There were also numerous efforts by both the US and European partners to engage the PYD in discussions with a wider pan-Syrian opposition to help prevent this, but these attempts were largely unsuccessful. The PYD resisted cooperating with the Syrian opposition, although it has made clear that it did not seek to establish an independent state. Instead, it sought to reach agreement with neighboring Turkey, viewing Ankara as the main hindrance to the group's wider acceptance in the international community. Ankara remains wary of the PYD's gains and has built much of its Syria policy around preventing the empowerment of the Syrian Kurds. The American military's first strategy suggests continued support for the YPG, particularly since they have proved themselves capable of taking and defending territory. On 30 October 2015 the US decided to send up to fifty special operations forces to Syria in a new military offensive against ISIS. The task of the American forces is to join YPG Kurdish forces to help choke off supply lines to Islamic State militants in their Syrian de facto capital Raqqa.[29]

With regard to US policy toward Iranian Kurds, there seems to be little progress and interest. Mustafa Hejri, secretary general of the Democratic Party of Iranian Kurdistan (KDPI), made an unofficial visit to Washington in June 2015. His visit to the US was on his own initiative and largely received by congressional members. Essentially, no one from the Obama administration met him. Hejri's visit was greatly linked with the events that were happening in the Middle East: the war with ISIS and talks between Western countries and Iran about their nuclear program. His major purpose was to convey Kurdish concerns and views to the Americans about potential negative aspects of the deal for the Kurds.[30]

Hejri's focus mostly, especially to the Americans, was that the US deal with Iran was potentially good if Iran is ultimately prevented from obtaining a nuclear bomb, in effect a good development for regional and world peace. However, the nuclear deal was detrimental to the Kurds: the lifting of economic sanctions would strengthen Iran by letting it freely sell its oil. This development would potentially allow Iran to gain access to revenues more easily and allow Iran to meddle in the affairs of the region. According to Hejri, Iran's hand will be more open to "export their revolution" in the region and assist allies such as Bashar Assad's regime in Syria, Hezbollah in Lebanon, and the Houthis in Yemen. These actions would consequently further Iran's policies and would cause more tension and wars in the region. Another reason for his visit was ISIS: Hejri wanted to tell the Americans, contrary to what the Obama administration thought, that Iran and the US did not share the common goal of fighting ISIS. According to Hejri, Iran did not want to fight ISIS, and was actually one of the key actors that wanted to make ISIS stronger. This assertion was allegedly based on intelligence the KDPI had received from credible sources within the Islamic Republic of Iran. The fall of Mosul and Ramadi were evidence of Iran's policies to strengthen ISIS, according to Hejri.[31]

The rise of the so-called Islamic State is essentially a consequence of three interacting and interlinked factors. The first is competition for regional hegemony among Turkey, Iran, and Arab nations, especially Saudi Arabia. The second is the spillover of the civil war in Syria. And the third is Sunni grievances in Iraq and the souring of Sunni-Shia relations in Baghdad. The United States wants to return stability to Iraq and the Middle East: the rise of ISIS is deemed an obstruction to this policy objective, and the unity of Iraq is perceived to serve this purpose.

Although this strategic US-Kurdish partnership is a significant evolution, in reality however the Kurds are still vulnerable; their status has not totally changed as regards the international context of the Middle East. When needed, as a pawn they gain value; when redundant, they are insignificant; but overall they remain an asset and an ally to the US in a hostile region. The place of the Iraqi Kurds in US foreign policy ends up being renegotiated all the time. It is an ongoing subject of negotiation based on three major factors: partly on what is happening in Baghdad; partly on regional alliances; partly on how the US sees its long-term role in Iraq and the Gulf.[32] Nevertheless, the Kurdistan Region is gradually emerging and establishing itself with the West as an increasingly valuable and strategic partner in an ever increasingly inhospitable, antagonistic, and unfriendly Middle East.

Since the overthrow of Saddam Hussein in 2003, the Kurds have stressed three major requisites to stay within the confines of the national borders of the Iraqi state: firstly, democratic rule, manifested in the full implementation of the nationally ratified permanent Iraqi constitution and broad national consensus in Baghdad; secondly, a peaceful Iraq without violence and civil war; thirdly, equal Arab-Kurd partnership in the governance of Iraq. Bayan Sami Abdul Rahman, the Kurdistan

Regional Government's High Representative to the United States, has repeatedly stated that if Iraq reverts to dictatorship, or is plagued by civil strife, or if the Kurds are not treated as equal partners, then the Kurds will ultimately secede. All these conditions have now been realized.

Nechirvan Barzani, the Prime Minister of the Kurdistan Region, stated very clearly after the ISIS incursion that there were essentially two phases in Iraq's post-Saddam history: "before Mosul and after Mosul."[33] For the Kurds, it was clearly a historical opportunity. In an interview with CNN's Christiane Amanpour in June 2014, Masoud Barzani, President of the Kurdistan Region, said that it was time for the Kurdish people to practise their right to self-determination: "The time is here for the Kurdistan people to determine their future and the decision of the people is what we are going to uphold." He declared that an official referendum would be held and that the people would decide, regardless of any regional or international opposition.[34] In July 2014 he told the Kurdish parliament, "The time has come to decide our fate, and we should not wait for other people to decide it for us."[35]

Many prerequisites for Kurdistan's independence already exist, and although the Kurdish leadership have wisely chosen to debate and argue for the right to self-determination, they have decided not to pursue it right now. The Kurdish leadership, however, must be clear in Washington about the Kurdish people's desire for independence. They should also state clearly that as pragmatic leaders they have no intention of declaring independence right now, but as democratic leaders this is inevitable since this is what Kurdish people really want. During President Barzani's meeting with President Obama and Vice President Biden in May 2015, the issue of Kurdistan's right to self-determination was highlighted by Barzani, to which Biden responded by saying: "Mr President, we will see an independent Kurdistan in our lifetime."[36]

If Kurdistan gains independence, US-Iraq relations will continue as normal. The United States would not want to alienate or antagonize Arab Iraq. However, what will happen inside Iraq is likely to cause American concern. The secession of Kurdistan will most probably lead to greater unrest among the Arab Sunni population, increase Sunni-Shia tension, and amplify the influence of the Shia political groups and the Islamic Republic of Iran. However, US interests in Arab Iraq will remain largely unchanged. US Iraq policy is more one of continuity than of change, as US interests regarding Iraq are defined by the same fundamental concerns: the same fundamental questions and issues almost always lead to the same fundamental answers.[37] With regard to US interests in Iraq, there are five major areas of concern that have dominated US–Iraq relations since 1979 and beyond: a secure supply of oil, concerns about Iraqi sponsorship of terrorism, the proliferation of WMD, the containment of Iran, and Iraq's role in the Arab-Israeli dispute.[38]

US policy toward both Arab Iraq and Kurdistan is far more consistent than is often assumed. The only difference with the Obama presidency has been his style of leadership and the importance he personally placed on the various issues in the US

foreign policy agenda. An instinct for pragmatic government, realism, political caution, and a renewed emphasis on diplomacy as a tool of US national security policy
have characterized his style of leadership. The Obama approach has been relatively
non-ideological in practice, but informed by an overarching sense of the United
States' role in the world in the twenty-first century, which was implemented largely
in a non-hawkish manner.

At the National Defense University in Washington on 9 April 2015, Joe Biden
stated: "We want what Iraqis want: a united, federal and democratic Iraq that is
defined by its own constitution, where power is shared among all Iraqi communities,
where a sovereign government exercises command and control over the forces in the
field." Officially, the US still wants a united Iraq with a strong Baghdad as its capital.
However, America privately acknowledges that Iraq is in crisis. Washington is now
psychologically accepting that Iraq has the potential of breaking up.[39] John Brennan,
CIA director, publicly stated on 10 September 2015: "I think the Middle East is
going to be seeing change over the coming decade or two that is going to make it look
unlike it did."[40] For this reason, it would only make sense for the US to play a role in
negotiating the imminent secession between Erbil and Baghdad.

Essentially, a policy is a vision, a view, and a goal. And US foreign policy toward
Iraq has been for the most part consistent in its goals. What has happened is that different issues have gained heightened attention at different times. Various American
goals in Iraq have been amplified or reduced in relative importance based on the
geopolitical context of the era. What could also be argued is that different strategies
have been pursued, adopted, and then adjusted to achieve these goals. In essence what
has changed are the strategies (what to do?) and tactics (how to do it?) when it has
come to issues of US foreign policy relating to Iraq, and not US policy per se. Basically,
it has been only the nature of the relationship not the objectives that have changed.

Consequently, in light of the current upheaval in the Middle East, it is only natural to expect change. The old order in the Middle East is quickly disappearing and the
Arab Spring is evolving at considerable speed. The transition is still in its early phases,
and what will follow (and when) is uncertain. Some borders, however, are likely to be
redrawn, and some new states may even emerge as a result.[41] Most of the states in the
Middle East were artificially created at the beginning of the twentieth century with
complete disregard to the ethnic and sectarian make-up of the region. Hence the only
way to ensure and restore stability to the region is to readjust some of these borders
based on facts on the ground.

And within this framework a political solution in Baghdad with respect to Sunni
grievances will be necessary. The same goes for Syria, whether Bashar al-Assad remains
in power or not. If Sunni grievances are not addressed, ISIS will find an audience and
sympathizers among the Sunni populations in both countries. Only the moderate
Sunni population in Iraq will be able to uproot and marginalize this group, and this
can only be done if the majority of Sunnis do not feel that this radical group has a role

to play in defending them. As for Syria, effective Western support for the moderate Syrian opposition and an end to the Ba'ath regime in Damascus will lead to the eventual demise of the group.

32.

RE-CLAIMING HALABJA

Nicole F. Watts

For the 16 March 2014 commemoration to honor the estimated 5,000 victims of the 1988 chemical bombing of Halabja, civic leaders placed an enormous banner next to the graveyard where local people gathered to remember those who died.[1] Like posters and other banners hung around the town, it featured the Kurdish national colors of red, green, yellow, and white, along with an image of an apple, emblematic of the smell of bitter apples associated with toxic nerve gasses. Written across the top of this particular banner, though, was a more unusual declaration that made reference to that week's decision to designate Halabja—until that point a city and an administrative district within the Iraqi Kurdish province of Sulaimani—its own province. It read: *Xwênî (5000) şehîd, kiraye merekebî wajukirdinî be parêzga bûnî Hełebce*, or, as rendered in English on the banner, "The blood of 5,000 martyrs became the Ink of Signing Halabja into a province." Such prominent linkage of the victims of the chemical gassing, on the one side, to the campaign to make Halabja the Kurdistan region's fourth official province, on the other, offers a striking example of the sometimes paradoxical nature of politics and activism in Halabja. Although some might debate exactly who bears responsibility for the 1988 bombing, carried out by the Iraqi air force in the final months of the Iran-Iraq war, it is clear that the thousands of people who died that day did not do so to make Halabja a province. How, then, are we to understand such a declaration? Why would activists think it appropriate to link such an enormous calamity—often depicted as the signal event of a Kurdish genocide—to the much more prosaic decision to declare Halabja the Kurdistan region's fourth official province? Why would local people depict their family members' deaths as paving the way for a change in Halabja's administrative status?

The chapter takes up these questions as a means of exploring state-society relations in Halabja and the Kurdistan region of Iraq. I suggest that the banner and Halabjan activism more generally are indicative of Halabjans' efforts to re-claim their city and its inhabitants, living and deceased, not only from an Iraqi Ba'athist past but also from a Kurdish-party-dominated present. The banner can be read as a declaration of ownership—"they are our martyrs"—and an enunciation of a localized collective memory[2] that challenges Kurdish authorities' hegemony over narratives of nationhood and suffering. The campaign to make Halabja a province constituted a crucial part of this effort. Not only would Halabja-as-province shift material and political resources into local hands, it would also facilitate re-mapping Halabja over a new territorial and symbolic domain. This new domain incorporates but de-centers Halabjan martyrdom and signals a locally empowered and defined present/future that flies in the face of both earlier efforts to destroy the town and more recent efforts to universalize it on behalf of the Kurdish cause.

Attending to the politics of Halabjan activism pushes us to re-think Kurdish political dynamics around the region and to take into account the way that localized, ground-up politics are shaping nationalizing projects directed from above. This is particularly important in the context of a historical moment in which several key Kurdish national(ist) groups exert increasing influence over territory and governance processes across the region,[3] as well as over the frames of meaning that come to dominate internal and external perceptions of these dynamics. The province campaign and other Halabjan activisms do not reject the legitimacy of the Kurdistan Regional Government (KRG) or the broader project of Kurdish self-determination, but they do aim at a transformation in power dynamics so as to grant local people more control over these processes. As Eidson has reiterated,[4] pluralizing the notion of collective memory by incorporating processes of local historical memory production does not have to mean creating clear-cut binaries that exist in mutually exclusive and oppositional ways: rather, different communities—local people, urban elites, national party leaderships, etc.—coexist under "various encompassing principles and various ways of being encompassed and constituted." This, he argues, "means that struggles and processes of individuation or transformation occur not in opposition to overarching categories, such as society or even the nation, but within them."[5]

Studying Halabjan activism encourages us to deepen the level of analysis from the macro- to the micro-level, and it pushes us to reconsider the agency of local actors, not necessarily at the expense of national dynamics, but to nuance, pluralize, and complicate them. In Iraqi Kurdistan, party elites have sought to establish a "right of enunciation" for Halabja and "to organise both ethical statements and a professional class that speaks for the victims",[6] and the successful province campaign and other

Halabjan protest events provide us with opportunities to listen to these voices speaking for themselves and in interaction with elites.

This chapter is organized into four main parts. The first discusses Halabja's critical place in the Kurdish national mythos, looking at its representative and functionalist roles, as well as the way its status as a martyred city has abstracted and universalized its identity. The second part contrasts this generalizability of the Halabjan experience with an "Other Halabja" that is localized, distinctive, and rebellious. The third part highlights some of the tensions of this dualism in Halabja itself and some of the institutional avenues for the articulation of local interests. The last part offers a brief analysis of the 2014 commemoration ceremony and the campaign to make Halabja a province as a way of exploring Halabjan efforts to re-claim their city and offer new versions of Halabjan collective identity.

Halabja abstracted: the martyr in the national and international narratives

For most people who follow Kurdish affairs, Halabja—an Iraqi Kurdish town of about 100,000 people about 8 miles from the Iranian border—is best known as the site of the worst single chemical attack on civilians of the twenieth century. Iraqi warplanes bombed the city with toxic nerve gasses on 16 March 1988, killing between 3,200 and 5,000 men, women, and children.[7] At least another 10,000 people are believed to have died later from the effects of the gasses. Halabja has since become a—perhaps the—central motif of a Kurdish national narrative steeped in tragedy and betrayal. In her study on "cyberKurds", Shailoh Phillips writes that there are several thousand internet sites dedicated solely to commemorating the attack on Halabja, and that viewing the graphic images of suffering on these sites helps produce a shared collective memory.[8] In art, film, literature, and politics, Halabja is discursive shorthand for the many atrocities carried out against Kurds at the hands of central states.[9] Those killed in the attack are referred to, like other civilians and soldiers who die in the context of the Kurdish national struggle, as martyrs sacrificed in the defense of the Kurdish cause.[10] The attack constituted a profound national trauma, setting in motion "a continuum of fear" concerning the possibility of similar chemical attacks and an "unmovable conviction"[11] that no central government could ever be trusted.

The horror that was Halabja has thus become iconic, and universalized as the perennial Kurdish experience (for there were many other chemical attacks, though none on so large a scale, and many other slaughters, both in Iraqi Kurdistan and elsewhere). In the process it has also become abstracted and anonymous. While the reference to Halabja is widely understood, historicized, and localized, Halabja is an enigma. A 2011 survey carried out by the Kurdish Institute for Victimology and Fighting Genocide bemoaned the lack of knowledge about Halabja among schoolchildren older than nine years old, reporting that 57 percent had "very little" knowledge of what had happened there,[12] let alone what life was like in the city. The degree to which the town itself has become an abstraction is eloquently captured in Samira Makhmalbaf's film *Blackboards*, in which, as scholar Dimitris Eleftheriotis writes, "The detachment of the signifier of 'Halabja' from its historical and material referent is powerfully and tragically emphasised by the inability of the old men in *Blackboards* to recognise their birthplace when they eventually reach it."[13]

The abstracted Halabja-as-martyr serves both external and internal functions for state- and nation-building. The attack is widely used to legitimate the need for Kurdish self-determination[14] and became, as journalist Kevin McKiernan noted wryly, "Exhibit A in the litany of horrors" perpetrated by the Ba'ath regime and used by American officials to try to justify the 2003 invasion of Iraq.[15] Halabja is a linchpin in efforts to bring about international recognition of a Kurdish genocide, and figured prominently in Dutch, Swedish, and British decisions formally to recognize a Kurdish genocide.[16] To remember Halabja, so the message goes, is to understand that Kurds will never be safe without their own state. It has been generalized as a symbol in international campaigns to prevent the spread of chemical weapons; in December of 2012 the Hague City Council approved a decision to create a Halabja monument in the city in the garden of the Organisation for the Prohibition of Chemical Weapons.[17] Though the monument took the form of the "Silent Witness"—the image of the fallen Omar Khawar and his young son photographed by Ramazan Öztürk—the very fame and ubiquity of the image, depicted in statue form both in front of the Monument of Martyrs and in one of Halabja's main roundabouts as well as in countless other photographs and statues throughout the region and the world, speaks to the simultaneously human and yet anonymized Halabja.

Halabja-as-martyr also constituted a key component of the KRG's internal efforts to reconstruct the idea of the Kurdish nation and bind its Kurdish subjects together after decades of Kurd-on-Kurd conflict. The historic memory of the attack serves as a unifying trope for a Kurdish polity deeply divided by war and competition between the Kurdistan Democratic Party (KDP) and the Patriotic Union of Kurdistan (PUK),[18] traditionally the two dominant—and rival—parties in the region. In this light the Kurdish parliament's designation of Halabja as "peace capital" of Kurdistan on 30 September 2014[19] can be seen as representing not only a symbolic rebuttal of its status as "chemical city" and victim of Ba'athist violence but also representing a move to use the city (abstracted) to create an alternatively nationalized capital space, because the actual KRG capital of Erbil is still very much seen as KDP territory.

The other Halabja

Although it has been represented as typifying a national if not transnational Kurdish experience, actual Halabja has a distinctive political history that is highly localized and in some ways quite exceptional. Neither the KDP nor the PUK have been able to secure their authority there, and the city and its environs for many years served as a base for Islamist groups. In the mid-1990s it became the headquarters of the Islamist Movement of Kurdistan (IMK), the third largest party in the Kurdistan region in that period and allied with the KDP against the PUK.[20] Halabja in those years was nominally under KDP control, the only KDP territory in the otherwise PUK-controlled Sulaimani governorate in the civil war of the 1990s, but to all intents and purposes it was governed by the IMK. It was handed over to the PUK as part of the KDP-PUK ceasefire, which governed alongside Islamist parties until 2002, when a faction of the IMK merged with the radical Jund al-Islam to form Ansar Al-Islam, which was active in the region and influential in Halabja itself. After a number of violent clashes, Ansar al-Islam was finally ousted in 2003 in the run-up to the US-led invasion of Iraq, at which point the city was integrated into the Sulaimani governorate and placed under the administrative authority of the PUK.

Official PUK control did not translate into widespread electoral support. Halabjan votes tend to be divided among a number of different parties, and no party has ever ranked first there in two consecutive elections.[21] In the September 2013 regional parliamentary elections, the opposition Gorran party edged out the PUK in Halabja, but in the April 2014 provincial and Iraqi government elections, the PUK came out on top. In both elections the combined support for the two major Islamic parties—the Kurdistan Islamic Union and the Kurdistan Islamic Group—amounted to more votes than for either Gorran or the PUK.

Halabja on the street: activist Halabja

An image of an "other" and rebellious Halabja also emerges from its recent history of protest and street politics. One of the earliest and most important examples was the 2006 protest at the Halabja Monument of Martyrs, organized by local students who argued that Kurdish officials had lost their right to lead the commemoration ceremony by failing to deliver on promises to the city.[22] The demonstration resulted in the looting and burning of the monument and the death of a seventeen-year-old Halabjan youth at the hands of Kurdish security forces. The destruction of a monument by the families of the very people it was designed to honor, and the death of the young man, horrified many Kurds and attracted widespread international attention, but it was one of the first clear signals of the tension between local people and Kurdish authorities over the status of Halabja and the nature of governance there.

If Halabja itself has been used—monumentalized—as a nationally martyred mnemonic space that transcends party allegiances, the Halabja Monument of Martyrs can be seen as a kind of monument within a monument: an epitomization of this generalized and abstracted representation of the attack, as well as the highly politicized use of its memory. Located just outside the city on the main road from Sulaimani, the monument opened in September 2003 with a ceremony attended by then US secretary of state Colin Powell, US administrator Paul Bremer, and Kurdish party leaders Masoud Barzani and Jalal Talabani.[23] Most contemporary monuments involve lengthy deliberation processes over the site and content of the memorial,[24] but the Halabjan monument was commissioned by the PUK with almost no community input. It was built in a grand architectural style and houses life-sized mannequins of victims depicted in various stages of death.

Contrasts between word and deed, between promises and local conditions, and between historic and local memories, crystallized in Halabja in the space of the monument and the annual ceremonies. The glaring contrast between the pomp and circumstance of the officially organized commemoration events and the impoverished conditions in the city came to epitomize local complaints that political leaders and the parties were exploiting Halabja's suffering for personal and political gain. Local residents expressed anger and frustration over what some viewed as the hypocrisy of public pronouncements of sorrow versus the corruption and nepotism that meant aid often never reached Halabja and projects went unfinished. Activists repeatedly pointed to the fact that the monument was built just outside the city, meaning that visitors and dignitaries could attend commemorations without ever entering the town itself, suggesting perhaps that officials cared more about the dead than the living, and more about appearances than actual projects.[25]

Demonstrations, marches, and public criticism of the Kurdistan Regional Government (KRG) have subsequently been regular features of Halabjan political life. Later commemoration ceremonies were often disrupted by protesters, and prominent political leaders were taken to task for failing to deliver on pledges of support for the city (in 2011, for instance, one man threw his prosthetic leg at the prime minister and called him a liar).[26] Halabja played an important role in the anti-government demonstrations that swept Sulaimani province in early 2011, and two policemen were killed there in otherwise largely non-violent protests.[27] Smaller-scale protest actions were common: university graduates protested preferential hiring practices by burning their diplomas; teachers protested their unpaid salaries;[28] and veterans protested cuts in their disability allowances.

This other, more mutinous Halabja has fueled a kind of tension between Halabja abstracted as victim (on the one side) and Halabja localized as suspect and even traitor (on the other). This dualism crystallized in 2014-15 when local and foreign media outlets began reporting that more than a hundred young people from the city had joined the Islamic State group (ISIS) in Syria, and that several key ISIS military commanders were from Halabja.[29] In the words of one Iraqi Kurdish news outlet, the city "once better known as being synonymous with the spirit of Kurdish resistance and nationhood" was now gaining "an unenviable reputation as being the primary source of Kurds abandoning the secularism of their people to serve Islamic State."[30]

Local voices: grievances and mobilization

There is little doubt, though, that the vast majority of Halabja's inhabitants, like other Kurds in Iraqi Kurdistan, support Kurdish self-determination, if not outright independence. It was to emphasize this perspective that Halabjan civic leaders and party representatives gathered in a "carnival for independence" in the summer of 2014 to send a message calling for the "establishment of an independent Kurdish state and democracy for the Kurdish people."[31] Rather than constituting a rejection of Kurdish nationalism, Halabja's protest politics are instead indicative of a disjuncture between Halabja abstracted-as-martyr, on the one hand, and a localized and lived Halabja, on the other. Over time, the tensions between these two Halabjas have produced a struggle between local people and Kurdish authorities for control over Halabja's material, political, and symbolic capital.

As I have written elsewhere,[32] Halabjan protest and criticism of the KRG have stemmed from several sources. There have been widespread complaints about the lack of services and infrastructure in the town, and the slow pace of redevelopment. Despite millions of dollars pledged in aid by both international donors and the KRG, Halabja in 2006 and as late as 2010 was still a city in ruins. If, as Verdery writes bluntly, the dead "can be a site of political profit",[33] then living Halabja seemed to have little to show for it. Most of the roads were unpaved, building projects were unfinished, and poor infrastructure meant problems with drinking water and erratic electricity supplies. Medical and education demands far outstripped existing facilities. Though by 2014 services and infrastructure had improved substantially—the (public) University of Halabja opened in August of 2011, and there were new health clinics, kindergartens and schools, as well as big improvements to roads, communications, agriculture, sewage, and water projects—overall improvements in the quality of life could not hide the fact that the material benefits of Kurdish autonomy were benefitting some people much more than others. Local bitterness also stemmed from perceptions that, despite official discourses of mourning, the party leadership, especially the PUK, bore some portion of responsibility for the 1988 chemical bombing because their peshmerga entered the town in coordination with Iranian forces at a time when the Ba'ath regime had threatened chemical reprisals for such actions.[34] This localized historical memory of Kurdish party culpability in the attack contrasted with an official historic memory that focused solely on Ba'athist terror. Other, and more widespread, complaints about the KRG also revolved around the top-down nature of governance, endemic problems of corruption and nepotism, and the degree to which party affiliation determined promotions, contracts, and other kinds of professional and political opportunities.[35]

The 2009 emergence of the Gorran party, or Movement for Change, through a schism within the PUK, served to bring many of these concerns into the open, and provided opposition groups with new resources and opportunities. Even before then, though, small but determined groups in Halabja had begun to translate societal frustrations into visible and more potent forms of discontent. The 2006 protest at the Halabja Monument of Martyrs, and the subsequent detention of three dozen students accused of illegal protest and of destroying the monument, mobilized non-governmental organizations, opposition media, and local activists, leading to the eventual release of the students and to more sustained campaigns to pressure authorities to address Halabja's demands.[36] Non-governmental organizations and civil society organizations in the Kurdistan region have typically been closely connected to political parties, giving them very little autonomy. The years following the monument protest and the formation of Gorran saw broader changes in communication, technology, and organizational life across the Kurdistan region: opposition and independent media outlets such as Awêne news, KNN television, and Nalia radio and television publicized and fomented criticism of the ruling parties and the KRG; tens of thousands of Kurds, especially young people, began discussing and debating the nature of KRG rule on Facebook and other social media sites; and some civil society groups and non-governmental organizations—once nearly all aligned with one of the ruling parties—began to work more autonomously. Cumulatively, this allowed alternative and localized voices to begin to contribute to conversations about the nature of KRG governance and how the project of self-determination was unfolding.

Halabja's particular propensity for mounting and sustaining campaigns—and extracting concessions from Kurdish authorities—is in part due to the fact that Halabja possesses an important reservoir of what Pierre Bourdieu refers to as symbolic capital:[37] put very roughly, status and resources derived from perceptions of special status or honor. Halabja's symbolic capital comes from its status as a martyred city that is seen as having paid a special sort of price in the Kurdish struggle for independence.[38] Many of the conflicts between activists and authorities in Halabja can be seen as a struggle for control over this symbolic capital,[39] and many of the concessions Halabja has won can be attributed to the fact that it is very difficult (if not impossible) for Kurdish authorities to be seen as publicly rejecting Halabjan demands or going against what is perceived of as the will of the city.

It takes people and organizational efforts, however, to harness such symbolic resources and channel them into protests and sustained campaigns, and between 2006 and 2016 Halabja itself became something of a center of NGO and pressure group activism. This is partially because, due to its symbolic status, it attracted more international interest and support than other places. NGOs and government-affiliated institutes such as Mercy Corp, Relief International, the German-based Wadi, the Switzerland Green Cross, and the National Endowment for Democracy (funded by the US Congress) have been among the many entities that have sent the city money, training, and expertise. But the prominence of Halabjan activism also lies in the way such external support intersected with local people organizing themselves to speak on behalf of Halabjan interests and concerns. The Society for the Chemical Weapons

Victims of Halabja (sometimes referred to as the Halabja Chemical Victims Association) was founded in 1992 to advocate on behalf of victims and victims' families, and though sometimes locally criticized for not doing enough, it has long called on the government to provide better medical care and more funds for new housing for victims' families.[40]

In the months following the 2006 Monument protest, more than a dozen local associations came together to found a kind of local assembly that could pressure the government to do more, and activists led follow-up groups trying to hold politicians to their promises.[41] Groups such as the Youth Activities Development Center in Halabja and Denge Nwê radio (sometimes spelled Dangi Nwê)[42] began training youth and airing conversations on a range of subjects, including highly sensitive topics such as divorce, female genital mutilation, and mental illness. They also held workshops on police-community relations, corruption, and civil society. Such activities served to bring Halabjan grievances and concerns into the public arena, and to keep them there. In October 2006 the Democracy and Human Rights Development Center, a Sulaimani-based NGO that was active in Halabja, distributed a questionnaire for distribution in Halabja asking people for their opinion of the government and its work in the city.[43] These generally negative responses were published in the opposition press and used as the basis for further NGO activities. The 2011 protests in Sulaimani province and Halabja built on this earlier activism and took it further, facilitating the formation of relationships and providing activists with organizational models they subsequently used to broaden grass-roots societal engagement. Many of their efforts can be seen as projects designed to build a Halabja that acknowledged but moved beyond the horrors of the past. The Spi (Spey) Org for the Gassed Areas initiated community empowerment projects including English courses, literacy programs, and driver training.[44] Some of their projects—local oral history projects, a program for the best documentary film, training journalists in TV production—also became part of the production of a locally historicized Halabja. A questionnaire distributed between December 2012 and February 2013 to 2,500 Halabja residents by Denge Nwê and the Spi Org is illuminating not necessarily for its responses, which indicated some but not overwhelming dissatisfaction with governmental and party policies, but for the nature of the questions themselves, which highlight the kinds of priorities the organizers thought were important for the city. These included questions about the performance of the KRG, the nature of the commemoration ceremony, services and infrastructure, the activities of NGOs, and the way Halabja had been represented and remembered in the international arena.[45]

Reclaiming Halabja: localization

Amidst this sphere of activism, demands for local control over the 16 March commemoration ceremony and to make Halabja a province stand out as fundamental efforts to assert localized control over the symbolic, territorial, and administrative status of the city and its people. The 2014 commemoration banner linking the victims of the 1988 chemical gassing with Halabja's new status as a province was contingent on the successful outcome of both these campaigns.

Local commemoration and the Halabja Monument of Martyrs

Sites of memory and "martyrological commemorations"[46] require continual re-affirmation and "endless recycling of their meaning"[47] to remain relevant. Especially in transitional periods, such places and events can become objects of contention and dispute, either co-opted or glorified by groups seeking ways to extend their influence, or conversely disavowed and even abandoned.[48] Competition for control over these concrete manifestations of historic and collective memory often takes place between competing elites, but it may also take place between elites and ordinary people. Tamir Sorek documents such struggles among Palestinian citizens of Israel who, he argues, strategically mobilized a localized rather than nationalized martyrology as a defensive stance against the Israeli state.[49] The 16 March commemoration and the Halabja Monument of Martyrs have produced similar contestations but for different reasons: local martyrology as an offensive stance against a nationalized martyrology dominated by Kurdish elites.

Commemoration events and commemorative landscapes serve not only to remember the suffering of victims of past aggression, but also to reaffirm boundaries between "them" and "us."[50] Regionally, Halabja as icon has served to demarcate Kurdish boundaries from a host of "others": from Baghdad and from Iraq's Arab communities, from Turks and Ankara, from the Iranian state, and from the Syrian regime. As such boundary-making and -maintaining devices, its commemorations have often been contentious events that brought local Kurdish populations into conflict with authorities and non-Kurdish groups.[51] But in Halabja itself they have also served as boundary-makers between Kurdish authorities and local people, as evidenced by the 2006 protest and the many disruptions of Halabjan commemorative events there. With activists threatening disruption again if they were not locally run, in early 2014 the Sulaimani governor's office granted permission for local civic leaders to organize the commemoration ceremony by themselves.[52] The 2014 commemoration ceremony, coming in conjunction as it did with the formal declaration of Halabja as province, became a platform for a proclamation of the relevance and power of a localized Halabja. Several changes to the event highlight this shift away from Halabja abstracted and toward Halabja localized and historicized. First, civic leaders used space differently. Normally the commemoration had been held at the Monument of Martyrs itself. In 2014, activists encouraged local people to gather in front of the municipality in the center of Halabja and at the edge of the main market, and from there to march to the cemetery of martyrs where the main commemoration ceremony was held. Shaho Homa Faraj, head of the media planning committee for the anniversary, said:

> The monument would kill the sense of feeling, because in a corner of it you put all the politicians, and everyone else would be outside. There was a sense of separation, and people would stay outside. It feels more real to have it at the cemetery, which has been and is the symbol of the martyrdom of Halabja. For people to visit their martyrs they go to the cemetery; they don't go to the monument. That's where the real graves are. So we thought there would be a real connection to the past for the martyrs' families.[53]

This formal commemoration at the ceremony took place on the morning of 16 March, attended by tens of thousands of Halabjans of all ages. Dressed in colorful and formal attire, they walked the congested streets past Ali Bag Park, past the governor's office and the girls' high school, and then down the narrower road toward the cemetery. Some held banners in remembrance of those who had died in 1988, and celebrating the designation of Halabja as a province. People gathered around the mass graves at the entrance to the cemetery as well as closer to the podium. A young man sold commemoration T-shirts, and children played on the fences and down on the ground under their parents' feet in an atmosphere that was halfway between a remembrance service and a massive town party.

This shift from a highly contentious site on the outskirts of town to a central, locally memorialized space placed the victims themselves, the families, and the lived town of Halabja at the physical and symbolic center of the commemoration. The Monument was not ignored, however. In the late afternoon, thousands of these same people came to gather informally there. Families chatted outside, queued to go inside the monument, and children played on the rusting Iraqi army tanks parked around. This gathering inside and outside the monument served as an acknowledgment of its national and greater symbolic relevance, and, at the same time, as a visible demonstration of local spatial control of the site.

The content of the commemoration ceremony and day also served to localize the event by (literally) taking it out of the mouths of officials and into the community itself. Local organizers decided the event would be non-partisan: speeches were restricted to a short note from the governor, a few words from a representative of the martyrs' families, and a brief message from the head of the municipality to announce that President Barzani had signed the province agreement. Party leaders were not permitted to give speeches. There was also an emphasis on activities designed to engage community input. Shaho Homa Faraj said: "We wanted to do the least amount of activities around the podium and take it outside."[54] They organized a festival, a fine arts program, panel discussions, and several football games in the newly built Halabja sports center and stadium. Such activities also served to demonstrate Halabja's local capacity to bridge party, tribe, and religious differences, to unite as a community, and to pull off such an event successfully successfully.[55]

The campaign to make Halabja a province

Local activists also used the commemoration as a platform for celebrating Halabja's new administrative designation as province. While the commemoration ceremony and planning can be seen as a kind of ground-up re-claiming of Halabja, the designation of Halabja as province constituted a more formal project of re-mapping: by demarcating a set of new territorial boundaries, Halabja was expanded from city and district to something much larger, re-situating it within the administrative and symbolic map of the Kurdistan region. On 13 March 2014 Kurdish President Masoud Barzani had signed a declaration establishing Halabja as an administrative province, effective from 16 March, the day of the anniversary. Becoming a province involved designating administrative headquarters in Halabja, the allocation of Iraqi federal and KRG funds directly to a new Halabja governorate, appointing a governor and two deputy governors, the creation of a 25-person provincial council, the establishment of a new civil service, and much more extensive governance powers. Included in the new province were seven districts, giving the new province a population of about 337,000.[56]

Establishing Halabja as a province made it the fourth official province in the Kurdistan region and the nineteenth in Iraq; the announcement of its new status in the spring of 2014 brought widespread messages of support from across the Kurdish political spectrum. Such public pronouncements notwithstanding, the decision was not a foregone conclusion; proposals and promises to make Halabja a province date back to the late 1960s when the Iraqi government proposed making it, Duhok, and Najaf provinces. Although the latter two were duly designated provinces, Halabja was not. In the late 1990s the proposal resurfaced, and in 1999 the Kurdistan National Assembly approved a motion to make Halabja a province. However, the delicate balance of power between the PUK and the KDP at the time blocked its implementation. Making Halabja a province was one of the protesters' formal demands in the 2006 demonstration at the monument, but in the top-down, party-dominated context of KRG politics, devolving power to a new localized entity ran against the grain. Because Halabja and its resources, symbolic and otherwise, had been part of Sulaimani province—dominated historically by the PUK, and after 2009 also by Gorran—removing Halabja from its jurisdiction constituted a significant blow to these parties. Resistance to the new province also came from residents in communities that Kurdish authorities intended to include within the new Halabjan borders. In particular, some residents of Sharazoor and Said Sadiq argued that they—not Halabja—were more suited to be the center of a new province, and that Halabja's "tribal and political" identity made it less suitable than they to be the headquarters for a new province.[57] Even sympathetic observers agreed that the ramshackle conditions of Halabja itself and the lack of infrastructure made turning it into an administrative capital particularly challenging. The success of the province campaign in the face of these obstacles is rooted in part in Halabja's symbolic capital, which meant that no politician wanted to be seen as publicly resisting what they had come to view as the popular will of the residents of the city. But the translation of this popular support into such a significant administrative change can be linked more specifically to efforts from above and below. From above, President Barzani and the KDP took an active role in promoting Halabja's new designation.[58] Though he had in fact expressed support for the plan for several years, the timing of his decision to sign off on the plan brought cynical commentary in the independent and opposition media, where a number of analysts depicted his support as an election ploy designed to bring more support for the KDP from Halabjan voters and to weaken the PUK and Gorran.[59]

Perhaps just as important, certainly for making the issue relevant to the KDP, were campaigns from below by many different Halabjan activists. In 2011 a small group of students and local activists began a petition drive to collect signatures in support of making Halabja a province. After collecting 22,000 signatures they presented the petitions to President Barzani, to other top Kurdish officials, and to the Iraqi government in Baghdad. A local group was formed to promote the campaign, and the KRG duly created a small committee to explore the possibilities for a transition.[60] In March 2013, during his commemoration speech, President Barzani announced his intention to promote Halabja to province, and in June 2013 the KRG Council of Ministers declared that it would proceed with plans for the conversion. The request was sent to the Iraqi government, and in December 2014 the Iraqi Cabinet headed by then Prime Minister Nouri al-Maliki announced that it had approved the request. Legally, however, the decision still required Iraqi parliamentary approval, which stalled in the months following, largely due to wider disputes between the KRG and Baghdad concerning the creation of additional provinces in disputed areas.[61] Undeterred by the potential political fallout, local activists held a number of demonstrations in the spring of 2014 calling for the KRG to make good on its promises and sign off on the final decision. On 2 March 2014 thousands of people took to the city's streets calling for Halabja to be made a province. Observers called it one of the largest peaceful demonstrations in Halabja's history,[62] and protesters said that if the formal decision was not forthcoming they would prevent politicians from speaking at the commemoration ceremony. Activists then decided to "occupy" the space in front of the municipality building by erecting a huge tent there that could become a kind of province-campaign capital. Activist Naseh Abdul Rahim Rashid remembered: "We said, 'This tent can be for one of two things: We can make it a place for a huge demonstration [against the KRG] on the 16th of March, or it can be a place for a huge celebration.' We said to the government: 'It's up to you which one it is!'"[63]

Caught between Baghdad from above and threats of demonstrations from Halabja from below, government officials finally decided to push on ahead, arguing that, legally, the final decision to make Halabja a province rested with the KRG and did not need to await Baghdad's approval.[64] The Kurdistan Council of Ministers signed the parliament decision on 13 March 2014, and on the anniversary day of the chemical attack President Barzani signed the decision into law. It took nearly another year, but on 8 February 2015 the Kurdistan parliament met in Halabja in an extraordinary session to approve the motion providing a legal framework for the change.[65]

Local activists and politicians used several main rationales to promote the province campaign, and, taken collectively, they highlight how Halabjans tried to position the city as both within and somehow distinct from the Kurdish national project. The first rationale is a nationalist one, the logic being that since former Iraqi President Saddam Hussein tried to destroy Halabja, both literally and figuratively erasing it from the map, the KRG and the community would go to the other extreme and upgrade Halabja's status by expanding its territorial and administrative presence on the Kurdish and Iraqi map. In binary terms this can be understood as genocide versus recognition. Fazil Basharati, former member of the Kurdish parliament and deputy of the KDP's Halabja branch, said: "The Ba'ath had tried to get rid of Halabja in the past, so we were going in the other direction. They wanted to kill Halabja; we wanted to revive it."[66] Activist Nawshirwan Mohammad, head of the local province campaign, elaborated:

> Halabja is symbol of the oppression against the Kurds, and we want to promote that symbol for all Kurds. It's important to show Halabja is a province and not just a small district. The sound of it is bigger than a district, so it carries more weight. Symbolically the genocide is bigger and has more legitimacy when you put it this way. When we have an independent Kurdistan we'll be able to say that one of our *provinces* has suffered this.[67]

Activists also used a second frame that can be termed a localist-legal frame. This justifies Halabja's designation as a province on two grounds: first by alluding to earlier legal proposals and decisions to make it a province, beginning with Ottoman discussions in the 1880s to the Kurdistan parliament's unfulfilled resolution proclaiming it a province in 1999; and second, by reference to what is depicted as Halabja's illustrious past. This localist-legal frame reaches to the first decades of the twentieth century, before the years of Ba'athist destruction that reduced much of the city to rubble, to present Halabja as a center of trade, poetry, and culture. "Halabja does not only start with 16 March 1988", said Dwalar Haider, a long-time civic activist and active campaigner for the provincial status. "Before that it was a center of education and intellectual people; we had many religious schools, and it was a cultural center."[68] This narrative of local distinctiveness puts great emphasis on poets like Abdullah Goran, sometimes called the father of modern Kurdish literature, who was born in Halabja in 1904; and on prominent personages such as Adela Khanun, sometimes referred to as "Queen Adela" and "the first female mayor in the history of Kurdistan", effectively ruler from 1909 until her death in 1924,[69] and widely credited with transforming the town architecturally, culturally, and politically.The third frame that activists used is a good governance rationale which speaks to the broader push for more transparent and accountable governance within Iraqi Kurdistan. In some ways this good governance rationale can be seen as a recapitulation of a longer-term struggle for political influence between Halabja and Sulaimani, as they suggest Halabja will be better run and more prosperous if it is locally governed, with budgets controlled at the ground level and not run through Sulaimani's administrative offices. Sayit Mahmud, an activist involved with the campaign, said: "It will help the city revive again and develop in terms of the economy and other sectors. I believe that will happen because now we don't have to go back to Sulaimani and other places to ask what should be done in this area. Now we will be the ones making the decisions."[70] Turning Halabja into an administrative capital is also depicted as a move likely to bring jobs, people, and new supporting infrastructure to the city (and, indeed, some of the infrastructure projects completed between 2010 and 2014 were viewed as necessary building blocks for any future provincial status).

Conclusion

Local efforts to control the commemoration ceremony and to make Halabja an administrative province are part of a longer-term and broader effort by local people to take charge of Halabja's symbolic, material, and political resources. The 2014 commemoration ceremony and the linkage of the declaration of provincial status with the sacrifices made by earlier generations of Halabjans can be seen as efforts to redirect the uses of Halabjan martyrdom toward a present and future that is not merely about Kurdish self-determination but, within this, about *Halabjan* self-determination. Both the campaign for designating Halabja a province and the 2014 commemoration illustrated efforts to produce a differently bordered and differently imagined Halabja that might determine its own identity and run its own affairs. The success of these efforts represented a significant surrendering of material, political, and symbolic resources on the part of the KRG and the ruling parties, particularly the Patriotic Union of Kurdistan (PUK) and Gorran. De-partifying the commemoration ceremony, shifting the formal ceremonies from the Monument of Martyrs to the city and cemetery, referencing Halabja's distinctive history and contributions to cultural and economic life all constitute efforts at localizing Halabja, its suffering, and its special status. At the same time, both these projects maintain Halabja's centrality to the Kurdish national mission, even offering it up as a kind of Kurdish civic vanguard. [71]

Local moves toward re-claiming Halabja highlight the ongoing relevance of localized, sub-national, and even alter-national identities within a dynamic process of Kurdish state- and nation-building in the Middle East. Halabja does not simply represent a catastrophic moment in Kurdish history or stand as a warning of "never again", though its symbolic resonance in this capacity has been and remains important. The choices and activities of its people have forced Kurdish authorities to cede symbolic and administrative turf. In so doing, they have pushed them—and us—to acknowledge the relevance not only of Halabja's past but also its present and its future.

33.

MEDIA, POLITICAL CULTURE, AND THE SHADOWS OF THE MILITIA WAR IN IRAQI KURDISTAN

Andrea Fischer-Tahir

On 18 May 2010, the weekly *Awêne* published a column entitled "Don't Misuse the Movement", in which the editor-in-chief strongly criticized the leadership of the Kurdistan Democratic Party (KDP), the Patriotic Union of Kurdistan (PUK), and the Change Movement (Gorran). He accused the first two groups of defamation and the latter of attempting to gain control of the civil protest campaign, "We Will Not Remain Silent." The campaign was launched after a student who also worked as a journalist had been kidnapped in Erbil and found dead on 5 May 2010. The column made several allusions to the Kurdish militia war of the 1990s and accused all three groups of exploiting the campaign to settle old scores. At this point it concluded: "If there was justice, all of you would get life imprisonment or be hanged for murder. The people have gone silent on your crimes. So you should put an end to that chapter, too."

I will take this discourse fragment as the starting point for discussing the media in the Kurdistan Region of Iraq. As described elsewhere,[1] the establishment of a "Kurdish quasi-state"[2] triggered the birth of a diverse media landscape, building on the media founded in the 1960s or earlier in the interests of the liberation movement.[3] In 2000, the KDP and PUK began to broadcast on satellite channels; other parties followed suit. More than a hundred websites emerged, primarily to circulate political information und negotiate public opinion.[4] In 2010, there were about 800 media agencies operating throughout the Kurdistan Region and about 5,000 men and women were registered as journalists.[5] Most of the media were controlled by political groups either in power or in opposition. *Awêne* was founded in 2006 as an

497

"independent political weekly"[6] and, partly assisted by international NGOs, became a leading newspaper. In the course of the mass protests of 2011, *Awêne* increased its support for Gorran. This makes it an ideal case to exemplify some of the key features of Kurdish (print) media. What kind of media emerged in terms of property and control, and how are these regulated by the KRG? Where do the political and journalistic fields and their respective discourses overlap? How do translocal flows of knowledge shape professional performance and self-image?

The above quotation touches on issues of political culture and memory, and hints at the militia war of 1994-8. This conflict between the PUK and KDP, but also between the PUK and the Kurdistan Islamic Movement, and between the KDP and Kurdistan Workers' Party (PKK), was waged with the primary aim of securing political dominance, the appropriation and control of international aid and border taxes, and informal trade with the Iraqi regime. The war arose from multi-layered political and social conflicts in a post-war society. The uncertain juridical and political status of the Kurdish Region led to a deepening of contradictions between competing groups, while interventions by Turkey and Iran, and eventually by the Iraqi regime, contributed to permanent instability. The militia war claimed approximately 5,000 lives and rendered almost 100,000 people internally displaced persons.[7]

In my observation throughout the late 1990s and early 2000s, the militia war as a propagandistic narrative source more or less disappeared from the KDP and PUK media after the overthrow of the Iraqi regime in 2003. In order to coexist peacefully and stand united vis-à-vis other political groups in Iraq, the ruling parties pursued a strategy that Paul Connerton called "prescriptive forgetting."[8] This strategy was adopted by other symbol handlers—politicians, grass-roots activists, journalists, artists, and social scientists—all of whom perceived the militia war as a highly sensitive issue. Yet, the memory was still alive, in the everyday conversations of relatives, colleagues, and friends. Also a number of private media commemorated the war from time to time by announcing the anniversary of specific events. These references to the past, however, were often merely an opportunity for a statement on political injustice or corruption. One such example is our newspaper column.

In order to understand this discourse fragment, I will first of all reconstruct the modes of production to which it owes its existence. I will then examine author, text, and audience, making use of media analysis approaches developed in cultural studies. In particular, I draw on Stuart Hall's model of encoding/decoding,[9] which allows awareness of media production relations and the frameworks and structures of knowledge and meaning. The chapter is based in particular on focus group discussions conducted in 2009 and 2010 in Sulaimani, Erbil, and Rania, on qualitative content analysis of print media from the same period, especially *Awêne*, *Kurdistan-î Nwê* (PUK), and *Xebat* (KDP), and on interviews with journalists. From a perspective of social anthropology, I want to discuss contemporary Kurdish journalism as a "professional intellectual activity",[10] and exemplify the "widely diffused idea" that the term newspaper refers both to a "globally practiced model" and a "localised cultural practice."[11]

The literature on the political field in the Kurdistan Region is increasing. Several works analyze its structuration and multiple conflicts; here the focus tends to be on the big players as actors in national, regional, or even global settings.[12] Other work explores contentious state-society relations, supplementing the top-down perspective on power with a bottom-up approach.[13] Whereas the former ascribes agency to those "in power", the latter tends to neglect that modes of political protest are shaped by power relations and interests that are more complex. Therefore, I discuss journalistic performance from a micro-perspective, arguing that actors of protest also use their power not only to legitimize their practice but because they claim moral and political authority, too.

Kurdish political journalism

In terms of property and control, the Kurdish media can be understood, firstly, as run by parties and party-like groups; notably the most influential KDP, PUK, Change, the Islamic Union in Kurdistan-Iraq, and the Islamic Group in Kurdistan-Iraq—the five parties that coalesced to form the KRG following elections in 2013. Likewise included in this category are the Kurdistan Islamic Movement, the Kurdistan Communist Party, the Worker-Communist Party, and other smaller entities. The second category contains the private media controlled by influential politicians that give more space to varied opinions, such as the Rudaw network (Nechirvan Barzani) and the media group Khak (Hero Ibrahim Ahmed). The third category embraces media with no obvious political affiliation, founded through private investment. Examples are the weeklies *Hawlatî* and *Awêne,* the journal *Livîn,* and Nalî TV. The fourth category refers to media financially backed by local and international NGOs; these tend to be low-budget weeklies, periodicals, local radio channels, and websites. Although the third and fourth media categories frequently claim to be "independent" (*serbexo*), as a rule they adhere to the agenda of the actor group behind them. Over time they have aligned themselves in many instances with one or other of the major competitors in Iraqi Kurdish politics.[14]

The KRG partly regulates its media politics independently of Baghdad and since 1992 has issued respective decrees and laws. The Kurdistan Journalists Syndicate registers those working professionally in the media field. It played a decisive role in pushing parliament and government to approve the Law on Journalism in 2007. Despite its reference to print media only, the law "constitutes considerable progress in terms of freedom of expression and press freedom, notably since it decriminalises press offences."[15] The syndicate also claims to safeguard the social welfare of its members when it comes to financial assistance in the case of illness, retirement, or distribution of land plots.[16]

Media production in the KRG has always been shaped by the logic of political conflict and war, as well as by translocal flows of knowledge. The media of the liberation movement were heavily influenced by Marxist-Leninist ideas on the function of mass media in a revolutionary or anti-colonial context, whereas university education in Baghdad was confined for the most part to Egyptian textbooks. The end of the 1990s saw technical colleges and universities in Sulaimani, Erbil, and Duhok establish departments for media and communication studies, and an opening up to academic assistance from various countries. In addition, the London-based Institute for War and Peace Reporting (IWPR), Dutch Press Now, or the German Media in Cooperation and Transition offered courses on basic coverage skills, story writing, television and radio production, on the "ethics of journalism", the idea of "investigative journalism", and last but not least, how to structure media agencies to meet the needs of a market economy. They also provided long-term supervision of the work of individual journalists or collectives. This was not a simple "East-West" encounter, because many of the instructors were Kurdish returnees from the diaspora, or local journalists and former participants of similar training courses. In addition, Kurdish journalists—hired as stringers, correspondents, fixers, photo journalists, or translators—acquired journalistic routine through international media agencies such as Reuters, BBC, or AFP, or from foreign journalists traveling through the region. But at the same time, these local actors contributed to the world's understanding of Kurdistan and Iraq by means of their translated words and the knowledge they generated in the field with their "embodied skills."[17]

The appropriation of new ideas and techniques has led to significant change in the representational modes at "program" level in Kurdish media. Moreover, interviews with Kurdish journalists indicate that there is more than one notion of "journalism" (*rojnamegerî*) circulating in the field. While some actors tend to define journalism as a professional activity that must adhere to "international standards", others refer to a "specific Kurdish journalism" as a "weapon in the struggle for Kurdish independence" and thus in sharp contrast to both "commercial Western journalism" and the journalism of "Arabs, Turks and Iranians." A third group, however, sees its journalistic performance as "social commitment" to "help and advance people and society." At times I found all three notions in one and the same media agency, regardless of the category it belonged to in terms of property and control, and its overall political agenda. It can therefore be assumed that ideas on journalism are not fashioned solely by the self-image of a particular media organization. Instead, these imaginations spring from the combined experience of social origins, education, working practice, and discourses within or overlapping with the journalistic field and beyond. Although the media landscape in Kurdistan is an almost perfect reflection of the political field, with its many parties, party-like movements, clientelist networks, and with grass-roots groups, the socio-cultural diversification of representational practice transcends the boundaries of political belonging; as do the appropriated terms and arguments to justify and interpret individual practice. Thus, Kurdish journalists tend to describe their work and their own prospects in association with notions of "professionalism" (*profeşonalitî*), "standard" (*standard*), "quality" (*kwalitî*), "flexibility" (*fileksibiltî*), and "career" (*karîr*). In general, organizations of the UN, the US aid apparatus, as well as NGOs were the prime movers in Kurdistan when it came to diffusing ideas of life-long learning, individual agency, professional flexibility, and market orientation, a process corresponding to the neoliberalization of the political economy since the re-integration of Kurdistan into the Iraqi oil-economy after 2003. The transfer of "neoliberal techniques"[18] has contributed to empowering the media. At the same time, the need to attract readers in order to survive financially and the interest in gaining public attention has also led to sensational journalism. Kurdish feminists argue that the latter is practiced specifically "at the expense of women", whose physical appearance is not only exploited under the "advertising" (*rêklam*) rubric. Media stories on violence against women, such as prostitution, honor killings, or female genital mutilation, often work with pornographic representations of women.[19]

As a result of the growing influence of *Hawlatî*, *Awêne*, and *Livîn*, senior media officials in the KDP and PUK have expressed their suspicion that international media NGOs are "spies" who support "extremists" against the government.[20] Yet the influence of the private media led to a decision to issue the "Law on the right to information" in 2013. Theoretically the law demands greater transparency from state institutions. Adjustments to the regulations limiting freedom of the media and of opinion are still in progress. Hence the 1969 Iraqi Penal Code remained the legal source of reference to accuse journalists of "breaching the peace." In addition, on numerous occasions political arbitrage hits those who are not protected by powerful parties.

Contesting authoritarian rule

Although television, radio, and social media are relevant sources of information, newspapers show no evidence of biting the dust. My observation is that whenever the latest big man statements or scandals involving well-known figures are published, more people seem to be "informed" about the content of specific newspapers than have actually read them. One of the leading newspapers in the market is *Awêne*: twenty pages of political rubrics such as domestic (*Kurdistan*), international ("world", *cîhan*), Iraqi (*Iraq*) and local (*lokal*), in addition to economy, culture, social affairs, etc. When the first issue of *Awêne* appeared in January 2006, the staff consisted mostly of men and women who had previously worked for *Hawlatî*;[21] they had left the paper because of decision-making problems with the owner, a Sulaimani businessman. *Awêne* is issued by a collectively administered corporation invested in by journalists, writers, and business people. The company also issues *Awêne Sports*, manages a website, and owns a publishing house. In 2009-10, *Awêne* had a run of 9,000 copies and was sold primarily in the Sulaimani and Erbil governorates.[22] It employed more than fifteen reporters, most of whom were freelance and male. Only one of the five editors was a woman.[23] It is striking that the percentage of women is higher in the media affiliated with the ruling parties; women explain this with more regular working hours and salaries that are both higher and more secure, whereas "working for private and opposition media can sometimes leave you without proper protection."[24]

In the time when the discourse fragment I will discuss later on was published, *Awêne*'s managing director was Asos Hardi, an intellectual of origin in Sulaimani's old social elite. The editor-in-chief was Shwan Muhamad, born in 1964 in Sulaimani, and in the 1980s a peshmerga of the Communist Party; from 1994 to 2000 he was director of the Communist TV channel Azadî, but then he left for *Hawlatî*. Since 2003 he has worked with AFP, and along with Asos Hardi assisted international NGOs as a co-trainer for local journalists. Both men represented themselves as strong advocates of "performing journalism according to international standards" and preferred a notion of journalism as "watchdog." Individually and as a newspaper, they faced several charges and accusations.[25]

This should suffice as the background for an abridged version of one of Shwan Muhamad's texts from the regular column "Window" (*pencere*):

Don't Misuse the Movement!

The popular movement that emerged after the murder of Sardasht Osman in Kurdistan is on the way to serving the interests of the political parties that are even trying to get rid of it. This popular movement, backed especially by journalists (*rojnamenûsan*) and intellectuals (*roşinbîran*), involves daily demonstrations inside and outside Kurdistan and the writing of dozens of essays, and also the support of thousands of young people carrying flags. [This movement] is not only meant as a condemnation of Sardasht Osman's murder but is the reaction of journalists and the like-minded to a situation [...] in which people are constantly humiliated, injured, threatened and beaten [...]. The aim of this movement is clear: we will not remain silent about the murder of Sardasht Osman, Soran Mama Hama and Abdul Sattar Tahir. [...] The intention behind suspecting the movement of acting in the interests of a certain political side is as clear as daylight. You with your old hostilities and depraved history of violence and killing, you seek to wage a war at the expense of Sardasht Osman. [...] But you will fail. It is true that Kurdish memory is tired (*zakîre-î xeļk-î Kurdistan zakîreyek-î hilake*) but neither the killings nor the wounds of the disgraceful fratricide (*şeŗ-î birakujî*) are forgotten, nor the killings of 1991 that targeted independent and patriotic people (*xaļkan-î bêlayen-î nîştimanî*) in Sulaimani, Duhok and Erbil [...] Even less have we forgotten the years of civil war (*şeŗ-î nawxo*), the May '94 (*Ayar-î 94*), and – even more unpatriotic (*na nîştimanîtir*) – the bringing in of the Iranian Pasdaran and the Turkish Gendarmeri (*pelkêşkirdin-î pasdar-î Iran-u gendarme-î Turkiya*), and the 31 August [1996] (*31-î Ab*). If there was justice, all of you would get life imprisonment or be hanged for murder. [...] The people have gone silent on your crimes. So you should put an end to that chapter, too. [...] At the time when peace in Kurdistan was made, not one of the three leaders of the KDP, PUK and Gorran was strong enough to offer an apology to the people and to the victims. We therefore ask you to put a shawl on the past, as the Kurds say, and be silent about it (*peroyek bew mêjuweda biden we bêdeng-î lêbiden*). [...] This movement is one of discontented youth (*gencan-î narazîye*) crying out with one voice: we deserve a better life.[26]

At first glance, this text appears to defend "We Will Not Remain Silent" (*Bê deng nabin*), the campaign that emerged after the murder of Sardasht Osman. As a student of the English Department of Salahuddin University, Osman had published in numerous private newspapers and on websites. Several media laid his assassination at the doorstep of the KDP security head, Masroor Barzani. It is widely assumed that the student was killed because of a satirical poem entitled "I'm in love with Barzani's daughter" (*Min 'aşiqe-î kiçeke-î Barzanîm*[27]) on www.kurdistanpost in December 2009, a website representing itself as "independent."[28] The case of Sardasht Osman[29] tells us much about journalism and political culture in the Kurdistan Region. Firstly, as elsewhere, anyone can use media space to publish their ideas; if indeed it ever existed, the image of "journalism" as a clearly defined profession has become blurred as a result of technological development and social change. Secondly, although there is a certain degree of freedom of opinion, there are so-called red lines. For example, if someone in power is personally targeted in an article on corruption, a political comment, or a rumor about moral standards, the author risks being charged or becoming a victim of threats, violent attacks, or even murder. Thirdly, this case points to the male domination of media and public discourse. In a discussion with feminists in Sulaimani, one of whom was a member of the PUK, another supported the Change Movement, and the third worked for an international NGO whose local branch supported Gorran indirectly, the women recalled "the gender ignorance" in Osman's piece and the debate that followed his murder. Their argument was that "This is a male power game, men at the bottom against the government. But in this game why exploit the name of Barzani's youngest daughter, who has no rights anyway?"[30]

The then editor-in-chief of *Awêne*, Shwan Muhamad, was not concerned with details about Sardasht Osman, or indeed with journalist Soran Mama Hama[31] or politician and writer Abdul Sattar Tahir[32], both of whom wrote for *Livîn* and were killed in 2008. Instead, his column is a comment on authoritarian politics, party competition, and physical violence in the political field, which undermines any independent movement. The author refers also, as he clarified in an interview, to the killing of members of the Communist Party and the leftist Toilers Party (Zahmatkeshan) after the uprising in 1991. But he refers in particular to the militia war of the 1990s. In doing so, he terms the war as either *şeṛ-î birakujî* (fratricide) or *şeṛ-î nawxo* (interior war). He alludes to the first clashes between PUK and KDP in May 1994 with *Ayar-î 94*. The collaboration between PUK and Iran is addressed as *pelkêşkirdin-î pasdar-î Iran*, which literally means: pulling the arm of the Iranian Pasdaran. With *31-î Ab* he recalls the KDP's "invitation" to Iraqi troops on 31 August 1996.

As for the militia war, there are various names in Kurdistan: apart from the two above-mentioned versions, it is referred to as the "KDP-PUK war" in PUK-controlled areas, whereas people in Bahdinan frequently speak of the "PUK-KDP war" and the "KDP-PKK war", all names with a specific signification depending on the respective war experience and political preference, and thus dense statements or codes. And so are "May 94", "31 August", and "bringing in/pulling the arm of the Pasdaran" as used in the column. I take these dense statements or codes as an expression for the fact that narrating the militia war is highly fragmented and less formalized. It is striking how Shwan Muhamad calls for "silencing" the past in the interests of all concerned, the people and the dominant parties: we the people were generous enough to forget your crimes; so you as those responsible for the war should be silent, too.

In the light of other reports, interviews, and columns by the same author, this text shows the deep frustration of a journalist and former communist. In a talk about it, he admitted that he was very angry when writing it. However, he also expressed his concern about the climate in Kurdistan:

> The political parties still work with the logic of interior war. Yes, conditions have changed. Saddam is gone, the parties have financial means and enjoy international relations. They cannot wage war but they are still undemocratic. Each one strives for dominance, whereas independent people are either suspected of acting in the interests of the enemy or the parties try to make you one of them. Not everyone in the party, but certain elements and leaders.[33]

The last sentences of this statement leave room for consensus even with parts of the ruling parties and are in line with a statement he made a year earlier:

> We Kurds always insist on the difference between a mountain here and another one there. But we are one country and one nation. We all have so much in common: security as a public good belongs to all of us, human rights belong to all of us, and democracy belongs to all of us.[34]

Shwan Muhamad's utterances suggest an imagination of power relations as a binary of criminally corrupt elements inside the parties on the one hand, and critical journalists and like-minded intellectuals as the real Kurdish patriots with the moral right to speak for the people, on the other hand—an interpretation common among journalists who work for supposedly independent media. This proves what Nicole Watts summarized as the consensual principles of Kurdish political acting: according to a belief in the self-determination of Iraqi Kurds, faith in the Kurds as a nation and in Kurdish nationalism, legitimacy of a freely elected Kurdish government, and finally the aspiration to avoid another militia war.[35] Nonetheless, the newspaper column as well as the campaigns that followed the murder of Sardasht Osman, whether "We will not remain silent" or the campaign launched by the Gorran TV channel KNN,[36] indicate additional moments in Kurdish political practice. Not only do the crimes of "those above" become transformed into symbolic capital of the actors of protest; it is also the martyr-dom of the journalists that serves as a legitimization to speak in the name of "the peo-ple." This echoes a basic principle of political culture since the liberation struggle: the more martyrs we have, the more legitimate our struggle and authority.[37]

Contesting contestations of authority

I had the column discussed in several focus groups.[38] One such discussion took place in October 2010 in a café in Erbil, frequented predominantly by educated middle-class locals and foreigners. The group consisted of four men and one woman between twenty-one and twenty-seven years of age: one of them had worked for *Awêne* and later for Rudaw; the rest were students at the Kurdistan University Erbil and worked part-time for private media or those of the KDP. All of them were well informed about current debates and declared that *Awêne* was one of their favorite newspapers. One of the men even remembered reading the said column when it was published several months ago. The group's first reaction to the question of how they understood the text was as follows:

> A: It's against the people who are trying to manipulate something. And who's interested in manipulating something? Gorran wants to incorporate the thing, the campaign [...].

> B: I think he [the author] is the one who wants to manipulate the movement. [...] He says, Gorran, this is not your campaign. It's mine. He wants to make himself the owner of the campaign. [...]

> C: Yes, that may be but it's also a beautiful message, because in this country the parties control everything. I mean they control every aspect of our lives. So I think it's an impor-tant point here. If you launch a campaign, maybe like this one, against social and political injustice, against the abuse of human rights, then certain people who are against equality and freedom will come and control you.

> [...]

> D: This column was written when relations between KDP and Gorran were very tense. Every day the KDP launched propaganda against Kak Nawshirwan [Mustafa Amin]. Every day there was a negative headline about him in *Xebat* or on Zagros TV, [in English] *Nawshirwan as the bloody evil*, because for the KDP, Nawshirwan was behind the cam-paign for Sardasht Osman. [...] And this article is a reply to both the KDP and Nawshirwan: we belong to none of you.

Following Stuart Hall we find three ways of reading: A and D tend to accept the message of the author or the "dominant code", and refer to the context of the column as a political comment. B, on the other hand, who presented himself as a sympathizer of the KDP, unmasked the particularistic interest of the author, exemplifying an "oppositional way of reading." C, finally, shows a "negotiated way of reading": although the author claims authority, he makes an important point. Later on, the discussion turned to the militia war as addressed in the column. Then one of the young men said:

> C: You see the Ba'ath was an Arab government. That means they were different from you. The crimes of the Ba'ath, well, that's your enemy with an evil fascist ideology. But you're Kurds! And in the fratricide you killed other Kurds, and at times you did so just because a *tasbih* was yellow. So they [the Kurdish leaders] must be brought to justice just like the Ba'ath regime.

This statement begins with a common interpretation of the war: that Kurds killed Kurds is the greatest crime. To exemplify how brutal the war was, the speaker mentions people who were killed because their prayer beads were in the "wrong" color: in this case yellow, as the KDP flag. The young man is talking about a time when he himself was a child living in the collective town of Baziyan near Sulaimani. He is nevertheless familiar with narratives about those who were attacked, humiliated, or killed at PUK checkpoints because their shirts or something they carried were yellow, or at KDP checkpoints for wearing something green. He draws a more radical conclusion than Shwan Muhamad does: not if there was justice but there must be justice.

The column was also the starting point for a discussion held in October 2010 at the Humanities faculty of the University of Sulaimani, which involved five men and one woman aged between twenty-three and thirty-seven. The participants were in agreement that the column's argument was justified insofar as it rejected the aggressive tactics of the big parties, including Gorran, and addressed the "injustice we have had for fifteen years." On the other hand, they called to mind that "things are more complicated":

> H: Yes, we all saw how KNN [Gorran TV] arrived and made the Sardasht Osman affair their own affair. But it's not all bad with KNN and the Gorran movement. Remember! Whenever there was a protest against the government before Gorran, the government claimed: There's a foreign hand behind this, the Iranians, the Arabs, and so on. Now it's us.

> K: It's us. It's ourselves.

> H: It's us. And that's better.

In the course of the discussion, some participants criticized those journalists who claim to speak for the people. There was a consensual view that the author neglected that Sardasht Osman was first and foremost a student. The author's argument was interpreted as an attempt to control the political protest. Also allusions to the militia war were debated. Several participants showed approval of the radical tone of the column, but reminded others that "fratricide merely serves as a metaphor." Others expressed the hope that someday there would be justice for the victims and an opportunity to conduct academic research on the subject. Not today, however, because:

> H: You can't have justice as long as these guys are still in power. And that's the difference with the Ba'ath regime and the whole business of transitional justice in Baghdad.

One participant then declared:

> M: I think it's better not to talk [about the war] because if I were to say who did something to me when I was in prison, my brother would kill them and then there'd be even more violence. [...] You'd cause a lot of social problems. Men would be killed or a woman divorced, and so on. And if you investigate the civil war, if you ask questions, people say you're spying on me.

M (37), coming from a family with strong religious ties, was involved in the Islamic Movement at a young age and imprisoned by PUK security forces during the war. Today he is a secularist who has published numerous essays on issues such as democratization, political culture, and violence. His utterance not only refers to his personal drama, but also addresses the social contradictions resulting from the violent past and the difficulties of dealing with neighbors remembered as perpetrators, the various political affiliations across families and kin groups, and the desire for revenge. Shwan Muhamad, like M, argues in favor of silencing the war.

Aftermath and conclusion

Since 2010, demonstrations by relatives of those who disappeared or were killed during the militia war have taken place in Erbil and Sulaimani, primarily with demands for information on the fate of the lost ones.[39] These events were covered by NGO-backed media, private media, or those of the Communist Party. This as well as the growing civil unrest and increasing influence of Gorran and respective shifts in the modes of ruling Kurdistan constituted the background to setting some social aspects of the war heritage on the agenda. In October 2012, the government announced that the 117 disappeared belonging to the PUK and the 150 seen as belonging to the KDP, the Islamic Movement, and the PKK "are dead."[40] So far, individual parties, in typical clientelist fashion, have awarded pensions to the bereaved of those they now consider their martyrs. The Kurdistan parliament set up a commission to discuss compensation to former prisoners and pensions for the bereaved,[41] and in February 2014 the government's directorate for political prisoners announced the decision to compensate former militia war prisoners.[42] A media debate on the occasion of the twentieth anniversary of the war, which I personally expected for 2014, did not take place: mainly because of new conflicts. After elections in September 2013, for more than nine months the parties did not come to an agreement on a future government, which caused feelings of fear among many people. In that time, but also already during the election campaigns, the militia war as a propagandistic metaphor saw a come-back. In addition, the political climate was very tense because of ongoing disintegration of the PUK. Eventually, the so-called Islamic State took control of Mosul and a new war started. Under such circumstances, speaking about inner-Kurdish conflicts in terms of justice was not deemed appropriate; nor has is it been to the present day. Instead, war against the IS served the authoritarian Kurdish government to hold the population compliant, despite ongoing human rights violations, increasing social contradictions, or the failure to pay salaries and pensions over many months. At the same time, established Kurdish leftists, for example, hesitate to call for new public unrest due to a "Kurdayeti-reflex"—when Kurdistan is threatened by outer enemies, Kurds must stand together[43]—a feature of political culture rooting in interpretations of Kurdistan as an internal colony. However, the younger generation of "like-minded people" (as Shwan Muhamad would call them) seems to prefer writing their hope for change on the screen of visions set by the PYD/PKK since the battle for Kobanî.

Reporters without Borders concluded from their field study that the Kurdistan "region's media are inseparably connected to its politics, hence the difficulty journalists are running into as they attempt to exert their independence."[44] Likewise other work interprets power relations as the authorities/the government vs. oppositional and independent media.[45] However, "independence" barely means to be free of political or other interest groups. It sometimes springs from the semantics of "international standards of proper journalism", or it belongs to the "proposal lyrics" addressing foreign donors. In other cases the designation "independent" simply serves to protect oneself, or it serves as a metaphoric distinction from a political system that had come under question. As the example discussed here in detail has shown, "independent" actors are not free from the desire to exert power and claim authority. It would also be a mistake to believe that the label "independent" goes hand in hand with such principles as "grass-roots democratic" behavior. NGO-backed media agencies as well as private media tend to adopt the "personalistic nature"[46] of political organization still evident in parties and "civil society" groups. Nevertheless, the diversification and openness of the Kurdish media landscape affords the requisite structure to negotiate the political issues of the past, the present, and the future.

34.

EXPERIENCES OF HONOR-BASED VIOLENCE, AND MOVING TOWARD ACTION IN IRAQI KURDISTAN

Nazand Begikhani and *Gill Hague*

This chapter discusses the distressing subject of violence and killings which are carried out in the name of "honor." It is based on a two-year major piece of research on "honor"-based crimes inside Kurdish communities in Iraqi Kurdistan Region and in the UK, the first of its kind, which broke new ground regarding this issue. While entirely independent, the study was funded by the Kurdistan Regional Government (KRG) and conducted by the Centre for Gender and Violence Research, University of Bristol, Roehampton University, and Kurdish Women's Rights Watch (based in Iraqi Kurdistan and the UK). The study was led by the University of Bristol under the direction of Professor Gill Hague, with Dr Nazand Begikhani leading the research in Iraqi Kurdistan and Dr Aisha Gill conducting the research in the UK. The findings and the arguments presented here refer specifically to the section of the study conducted in Iraqi Kurdistan Region, and have been updated on the basis of Dr Begikhani's continuing fieldwork in Iraqi Kurdistan Region.

The chapter presents a discussion of "honor"-based violence (HBV), followed briefly by the study aims and methods, with longer sections on our findings and recommendations. Using a gender perspective, it places particular emphasis on the ideas and plans for action on honor-based violence which emerged from the research. The study and this chapter are based on activism and attempts to enable social change for women.

Honor-based violence has existed throughout history and occurs in societies across the world from Europe to Africa, and from South and East Asia to Latin

America.[1] Although this paper is about Kurdish communities, the application of an "honor code" to women's conduct, and sexual behavior in particular, is in no way limited to Kurdish societies, nor is it specific to Islamic cultures. Indeed, the practice is not confined to any particular type of society, community, religion, culture, or social class/stratum.[2]

What is honor-based violence: parameters and contexts?

Honor-based violence covers a wide range of abuses which include physical violence, assaults and killings committed in the name of honor, curtailment of liberty and/or basic rights (including access to education), coerced suicide (including enforced self-immolation), and starvation and poisoning as punitive measures. If a woman has been raped, it is not uncommon for her to be forced into marriage with the man who committed the assault(s). Honor crimes can include abandonment, removal of children, female genital mutilation, denial of sexual autonomy, forced virginity testing, forced hymen repair, forced abortion, and the imprisonment, abuse or murder of partners who are deemed inappropriate.[3]

The most extreme form of honor-based violence—killing in the name of honor— is very widespread. The United Nations estimates that 5,000 women are killed in the name of honor each year, mainly in the Middle East and Asia. However, it is impossible to determine the exact number of women who are killed annually, or how widespread honor crimes are, as reports to the police are sporadic, not least because both male and female family members often try to cover up honor crimes. Many victims disappear, never to be found.[4]

Crimes committed in the name of honor are usually differentiated from other forms of gendered violence in that they most frequently occur within a framework of family and community structures that permit and perpetuate these abuses. Honor-based violence tends to involve premeditated acts that, due to family/social value systems and norms, are seen as necessary to restore honor in a (real or perceived) situation in which the family's, as well as the community's, honor is deemed to have been threatened or damaged.[5] It often results in the control of women's sexual and social choices by male relatives, and thus can be legitimized by the perception that women should obey strict codes of behavior regulated by (usually senior) male family members, and should be punished if they do not.[6]

While there is a tendency in the West to see honor killings and other forms of HBV as related to specific cultural traditions strongly defined as non-Western,[7] the reality, as we noted above, is that these crimes are not confined to any particular religion, culture, type of society or social stratum.[8] Bourdieu argues that "honor" is not a specific aspect of cultural practice, but rather emerges from a constellation of interpersonal exchanges.[9] Thus, even though honor crimes are found in many different societies, each unique social and cultural context should be individually evaluated to determine how and why these practices have arisen. As Pope stresses, the forms that honor crimes take change not only from country to country, but also from local area to area.[10] This is because different meanings are attributed to the notion of honor in different contexts, and these meanings also change and evolve over time.[11]

Nonetheless, despite these complexities, both the mainstream media and individual politicians and professionals across Western countries continue to attribute HBV solely to particular geographical regions, cultural factors, and faiths. However, many feminists have developed arguments that all fundamentalist religious movements globally (including, for example, Christian ones) have a strong tendency to use the control of women's bodies symbolically to assert a broad agenda of authoritarian political and cultural control.[12] Thus, understanding why HBV occurs requires looking beyond simple descriptive labels or cultural stereotypes and, instead, examining the meanings ascribed to the term "honor" in different communities.

In overall terms, the literature highlights that honor codes and associated views about the subordinate position of women are embedded in broad and persuasive social structures and ways of thinking which revolve around strongly gendered values and norms that legitimize control of women's sexual and bodily conducts. The result is the imposition of restrictions on the lives and activities of women, and some implicated men, with any perceived "deviation" from these controls being likely to attract some form of retribution or punishment.[13]

While honor-based killings may not be prevalent everywhere, some idea of honor has existed in almost all human societies.[14] In many societies, throughout history and presently, male "honor" is viewed as depending on an individual's public reputation and, thus, is something that can be actively achieved. Female "honor", on the other hand, is determined not by active achievement, but by the avoidance of certain behaviors, and especially by sexual discretion. Men acquire "honor" by virtue of their character, family, position, and public behavior, but they can easily lose it because of supposedly dis-"honorable" behaviour by "their" womenfolk, which is also likely to be seen to reflect badly on the wider family and community.[15]

Public attention is frequently brought to bear on honor-based violence when the details of a particularly shocking crime are broadcast in the media, often in a sensationalized way. It is then particularly common for the wider community involved to become unjustly stigmatized as a likely site of further such violence.[16] This has certainly been the case for Kurdish communities over the last two decades.[17] However, it is neither appropriate nor accurate to victimize particular communities. On the other hand, this does not absolve societies from addressing the context-specific manifestations of honor-based violence that occur in their own localities in order to lead to social development and to challenge harmful social practices.

One specific trigger behind this research was the murder by stoning of a teenage Yazidi girl, Du'a Khalil, in Iraqi Kurdistan. Du'a was stoned to death in 2007 in the Ba'shiqah administrative sub-district of the Mosul governorate. Du'a's case sparked national and international reactions when the scene was filmed by mobile phone cameras and the distressing footage broadcast across the world. Amateur footage also showed that police officers stood by and failed to intervene.[18] After worldwide reaction, four men were finally convicted of this murder in 2010 and sentenced to death.

In 2007, partly as a response to the atrocity surrounded Du'a Khalil'a case, the then prime minister of Iraqi Kurdistan Region established various initiatives on honor-based violence. The international, collaborative research reported here was then commissioned to provide evidence to facilitate the development of effective strategies to be implemented by the KRG, relevant agencies, and also women's rights organizations.

Aims and methods

The main objectives of our research were to assess the nature of honor-based violence, including honor killings, in Iraqi Kurdistan and the Kurdish diaspora in the UK; to evaluate the impact of these practices on Kurdish women; and both to assess the development to date of strategies and policies to address the issue, and to provide data and recommendations to support interventions, initiatives, and social action.

A total of 120 semi-structured interviews were carried out in Iraqi Kurdistan Region with government officials, police, women's NGOs, and other agencies, together with twelve in-depth interviews with survivors/family members, and further informal interviews with victims of burnings. Detailed case studies of the prosecution of honor killing cases were also carried out, with some of these involving multiple interviews with family members and the professionals involved. Participant observation methods were also used, including observing several prosecution cases. Furthermore, throughout the project, a comprehensive media monitoring exercise was carried out and the data collected were subjected to a simple form of content analysis. We relied on content analysis of a number of media outlets, including women's publications, official and independent newspapers, satellite TV and radio programs.

The Kurdish "honor" code

Within the specific parameters of Kurdistan Region, our findings demonstrated the importance of developing an understanding of what is meant by honor in this very particular context, and how this concept is used to justify violence against women. In Kurdish society, the collective (that is, family, clan, local community and/or the wider nation of Kurdistan) frequently provides codes against which honor and dishonor are measured, and these codes tend to place a particularly heavy burden of responsibility on women. Despite some positive changes in recent years, especially in the cities, women in Iraqi Kurdistan are still usually expected to be chaste prior to marriage, obedient, subservient, docile, modest, and to comply with the demands of male members of their family. According to our respondents, highly restrictive expectations are often created in relation to dress, physical and social mobility, education, relationships with the opposite sex, and matters of choice in love, marriage, and divorce.

Dishonor, *a'r*, and shame, *a'ib*, are caused when women breach a variety of social and sexual boundaries, such as going out of the home frequently, forming romantic relationships, being seen in male company, or losing their virginity before marriage. Maintaining and restoring honor requires removing the *a'r* through the act of cleansing or purifying, *ghasl*, the collective's honor. Women interviewed during this study reported that they had been perceived as "bad", dishonorable, or shameful. They had, variously, undergone mental and physical abuse, torture, confinement, coercion, forced marriage, mutilation and/or disfigurement (including, in a small number of cases, the cutting off of their ears and noses), genital mutilation, forced divorce, rape as punishment, forced abortion, and public dishonoring. We also identified the new issue of honor crimes through cyber-abuse, where women in Kurdistan had been dishonored and shamed through the use of the internet. Some women also reported that their movements had been entirely controlled and that they had been deprived of schooling and educational opportunities.

Other interviewees discussed cases in which women had been forced to commit suicide, including via self-immolation. In fact, the team investigated a series of cases of burnings of women, both those conducted deliberately by perpetrators, and also those identified as self-inflicted or accidental (although no one else in the very busy, full households concerned was ever burned in these accidents, and it seemed that no one else was ever present to help). Our findings revealed that both men and women may face murder if they are deemed to have damaged their family or community's honor, especially via undertaking love affairs or even engaging in minor contacts with a member of the opposite sex.

The research interviews showed that the frequent enforcement of honor codes places such a high tariff on deviation that it can act to generate practices of concealment and hiding; these may add fuel to familial codes involving the constant observation of young women, and to social policing, including gossip and rumor. Confining and silencing women within the home in Kurdistan, and rendering them fearful of the dangers of entering public spaces (physically and through words), could be seen in case studies in the research to have diminished their strength, vitality, and skills. According to our interviewees and the sparsely available statistics, the overwhelming majority of women subjected to honor-based violence in Kurdistan Region are the young (aged fourteen to thirty years).[19]

> The climate created by honor crimes undermines the physical, emotional, and psychological well-being of women and can result in emotional distress, hopelessness, self-harming, and suicidal thoughts and actions. Our interviewees confirmed that the effects on men can

also be destructive, and children, both male and female, in our study had suffered loss, death of parents, and violence. The practice and expectation of honor-based violence were described as also including damaging role models that are likely to be emulated by some children and young people. The study thus suggests that it is not only women who suffer during honor violence, but society as a whole.

Combating honor-based violence in Iraqi Kurdistan

While accurate figures concerning honor-based violence are not available, our research found that there is evidence that the phenomenon remains widespread in Iraqi Kurdistan. Our informants illustrated how the practice had been generally accepted in the past as inevitable, and as part of normal life. However, it was widely suggested that things are beginning to change, albeit very slowly. The practice previously seen as "honorable" is now open to being characterized as "dishonorable" and sometimes degrading for the perpetrators in a way which was not the case in the past. Honor-based violence policies and initiatives have begun to be developed by official authorities, local communities, media groups, faith leaders, and especially women's rights groups.

Creating space to allow concerns to be heard has not been easy. Kurdistan's involvement in the recent Iraq war was complex, following as it did the attempted genocides of the Kurdish population. After the mass exodus in 1991, Iraqi Kurds elected a parliament and formed a government, but this move was followed soon after by the fratricidal war between the two main political parties, the Kurdistan Democratic Party (KDP) and the Patriotic Union of Kurdistan (PUK). Nevertheless, with the end of the Iraqi regime in 2003 and the reunification of the KRG in 2006, a more favorable environment has been created, with civil society functioning and at peace, for the formation of campaigns and more active women's organizations. This development was facilitated by several factors, including the departure of the Ba'athist regime, growing awareness of human rights, including women's rights, the work of international organizations, and the return of exiled women from the diaspora.[20]

Today, there are more than fifty women's organizations, many working on violence against women. We collected research evidence that these organizations are involved in raising public awareness, training other agencies on women's issues, campaigning, providing outreach services, and offering protection to victims/potential victims of violence. Women's NGOs provide legal services, lawyers and/or mediation services, and counseling centers. The most significant service that women's rights groups offer abused women, and those at risk of murder, has been refuge. In Sulaimani, *Zhinan* Kurdistan Women's Union and ASUDA for Combating Violence Against Women have been running two women's shelters since 1999, and a very small number of other refuges exist. These positive services are very few, however, in the wider context of the Region, and are all critically overburdened and vulnerable to attack.

Although some commentators have claimed that there has not been enough cooperation and solidarity between women's NGOs, they have continued throughout often difficult and sometimes hostile conditions to provide services and have formed some functioning networks, for example *Nawandi Hawbashi Zhinan* (Women's Joint/Cooperative Centre), established in 1997, including eighteen women's and civil rights groups, the Women's Network, established in 2005 with twenty-two organizations, and Jiyan Group, established in summer 2012 regrouping fourteen organizations.

The importance of international NGOs, and of UN as well as foreign government agencies, cannot be ignored in relation to the task of raising awareness and providing helpful resources to support work on violence against women and honor-based violence. For instance, the research team observed constructive seminars and training courses provided by agencies like the Global Justice Centre, International Human Rights Law Institute, the US Regional Reconstruction Team, and WADI. Many of these bodies have also been involved in running awareness-raising programs and providing materials and logistical support to local women's organizations. However, there remains an extreme shortage of training, refuge spaces, and women's support services overall.

Government responses

Until recently, honor-based violence was not integrated into government political agendas, not only in the Iraqi Kurdistan Region, but around the world. However, the KRG has engaged in a variety of activities in recent years. In 2007, it initiated the High Commission to Monitor Violence against Women and also established government Directorates to Combat Violence Against Women. In 2011, the Regional Government established the High Council for Women's Affairs, followed in 2012 by the creation of the Women's Rights Monitoring Board (WRMB). While the Directorates have started to collect data and statistics as well as to develop focused responses, the High Council for Women's Affairs started to set up strategies to combat violence against women. The WRMB, led by the PM, has also started to monitor women's rights violations in the Region and to address violence against women overall, as well as HBV issues, at the very highest level of the government. The findings of this study show, though, that responses by official bodies in the Region continue usually to be poor. Within the criminal justice system, for example, the police, and also legal representatives, in Kurdistan often do little and blame each other for the lack of rigorous investigation and poor judicial practice that impact many cases. As a result, conviction rates in honor-based violence cases are low and many alleged murderers escape prosecution altogether.

Against a history of war and killings, the government of Iraqi Kurdistan is working within a transitional context. The use of violence and also of informal and tribal justice remains common. However, if the rule of law is to prevail, our study found that there must be a clear commitment to subordinate informal structures and customary legal processes to the nation's laws. In strengthening the rule of law, as was witnessed in the testimony of some interviewees, it is necessary to recognize that the judiciary and police at times come under threat from conflicting political interests in the Region and within powerful tribal and community networks, when pursuing the perpetrators of honor crimes.

The study found that the government and relevant agencies have made a start in working to combat honor-based violence. Kurdish law-makers and the KRG have made several notable legal amendments to the criminal codes aimed at removing the leniency with which perpetrators of such crimes were treated in the past. In the extreme case of killings, various legal articles have been introduced since 2000, removing provisions which had previously allowed drastic reductions in the penalties faced by those who had killed, if they had done so in the name of honor. In June 2011, the Kurdistan parliament passed the Combating Domestic Violence Law. These actions, and other new legal remedies, have set a positive precedent, although unfortunately our study has revealed that the improvements have not been implemented reliably, or to any significant level.

An action plan

Despite these difficulties, however, there is the beginning of political will to address honor-based violence in Iraqi Kurdistan as part of global efforts to tackle the issue.[21] The first need in the Region is for the further development and embedding of this political will to take the issue forward. An Action Plan was developed from our study to contribute to this process, building on the gendered analysis which we developed.

Action plans are meant to be achievable within realistic time limits. However, cultural change itself is complex, and often involves a lengthy process fraught with conflict and contradictions. Thus, the Action Plan we developed puts forward pointers only to drive future developments. It recommends that a coordinated multi-pronged approach be adopted and identifies five main issues that require intense focus in Iraqi Kurdistan.

1. Legal and strategic policy development

The first issue involves legal, strategic, and policy developments and reforms within the Kurdistan National Assembly (in terms of the strengthening and bringing together of previously scattered legal statutes). Continuing the task of removing lenience in the prosecution of honor crimes and developing consistent and robust justice policies is needed if the Region is to move forward in preventing honor-based violence. The study recommendations for the criminal justice system, the police, and the judiciary aim to improve the detection and prosecution of offenders, alongside a stronger government response. The issue of customary law versus formal law is a particularly important one in the context of honor crime, as noted, and the research identified a pressing need for clear commitments that customary and traditional legal systems are made secondary to the official legislature and formal law.

2. Reforming the education system

Education is the key in combating HBV, hence reforming the education curriculum is essential. Such reform should start from the schooling of children onwards and contribute to a coordinated effort taking on issues of HBV and gender-based violence. The reform would be expected to include the development of gender equality education, sex education, and citizenship education, but in a culturally and socially sensitive context, drawing on experiences of other countries.

3. Services for victims

There remains a huge lack of enough services for victims. Thus, the second area of work centers on setting up more support and protection services, including shelters for victims and their families. At the moment, the very small number of such services means that victims are most commonly left unsupported. If there is a commitment to address honor crimes in the Region, then the provision of supportive services is of key importance. In the militarized context of Iraqi Kurdistan, this also includes providing better security, protection, and support for shelters, developed in collaboration with the women's organizations concerned.

4. Training on honor-based violence for professionals

The fourth area addresses the need for training programs for relevant professionals to increase skills and improve attitudes to honor-based violence. Those who deal with informal customary law, cultural systems, and tribal justice need to be trained on women's rights, honor-based violence, and gender equality. All relevant professionals need to be trained in how to work with cases. The training needs to be secular in approach but culturally and religiously aware, to include contextual understandings that honor-based violence is usually a form of gender-based violence and to raise awareness about the deeply damaging nature of the practice to women, girls, and the whole society.

5. Public awareness-raising

The fifth area involves the development of comprehensive awareness-raising programs for the public to be rolled out across communities, towns, and rural areas. Such awareness-raising programmes would be expected to take place in villages and to use popular culture in the form of songs and drama (learning from similar programs developed in other countries).

6. Multi-stranded strategies

More widely, the government should encourage multi-agency strategies on HBV and an improved system of cooperation and forum-building between women's community projects and the government, the police, and other agencies to enable more effective joint working.

Conclusion

In conclusion, despite current difficulties in the threatened climate of this part of the Middle East, the showcasing and exposure of honor-based violence and discussion of causes and remedies are accumulating in Iraqi Kurdistan Region. The commissioning and carrying out of this study is part of a welcome trajectory toward attempting to tackle the issue and demonstrates that Iraqi Kurdistan is taking a key part in developing good practice. However, honor crimes remain endemic and embedded in Kurdistan Region, and are part of a broad spectrum of violence against women legitimized by the widespread continuation of male control over Kurdish families and all aspects of community life. The genocide that the Kurdish people have experienced in recent years, consecutive wars, including the Iraq wars and the militarization of the Region, have contributed to the continued practice of both honor- and gender-based violence.

Unsurprisingly, given the painful history of the Kurds, and the fact that the KRG has only been established relatively recently, progress in Iraqi Kurdistan has been slow overall. There is an urgent need for the legal provisions concerning honor-based violence, which are currently scattered across various legal instruments, to be consolidated and for robust legal, policing, and prosecution procedures to be developed to signal that honor-based violence is no longer socially or legally acceptable or accepted. To be effective, the KRG and Kurdistan National Assembly must initiate and take part in a coordinated, integrated response involving a range of agencies. In particular, there is a pressing need in Iraqi Kurdistan for safe refuges, witness protection programs, and wider safety, security, and support measures. It is also important that attention is paid to changing the cultural attitudes that underpin honor-based violence. Public education and awareness-raising, with the involvement of local people, are keys in this respect, complemented by training for all professionals involved in addressing honor-based violence.

As a final word, honor-based violence is not only a manifestation of gender inequality, but actively works to reinforce it. States across the world have duties under international law to protect and support women's rights, including by taking steps to tackle violence against women. However, many continue to fail to do so. It is vital that honor-based violence, including honor killings, remains on the international human rights agenda and is viewed as a form of gender-based violence. Progress may be slow, but an encouraging beginning has been made in the Iraqi Kurdistan Region. However, there is still a strong need to stimulate social change, justice, and action on violence against women in general, and honor-based violence in particular.

35

THE KURDISTAN REGION OF IRAQ AND THE FEDERAL CONSTITUTION

A PERIMETER PLINTH OF STATE TERRITORIAL INTEGRITY OR A STEPPING STONE TO SECESSION?

Francis Owtram

Deeply divided societies and the "paradox of federalism"

This chapter describes and analyzes the place of the Kurdistan Region of Iraq (KRI) in the Iraqi federal constitution of 2005.[1] It argues that in the short to medium term the KRI will remain part of Iraq, but in the longer term the impact of events since August 2014 have increased the likelihood of the secession of the KRI and the declaration of an independent state. It places this analysis of Iraq's constitutional issues in a broader theoretical context: that of state formation and change in the international system, the potential of federalism in the Middle East to manage deep social divisions, and insights of Realism adapted to intra-state group conflict. The deep divisions just alluded to partly originate from the consequences of the correspondence and straight lines drawn on the 1916 Sykes-Picot map which was enclosed with the Asia Minor Agreement signed between Britain and France, 16 May 1916. This ushered in the Sykes-Picot era, when the Middle East was divided by drawing "a line from the 'e' in Acre to the last 'k' in Kirkuk."[2] It is thus deemed imperative to embed the analysis of this chapter in the historical trajectory of the region inhabited by the

Kurds of Iraq from the end of the First World War. This trajectory has encompassed uprisings in 1923, 1932, and 1943, the signing of an autonomy agreement in 1970 subsequently reneged on by Baghdad, the de facto autonomous area created within the no-fly zone 1991-2003, and since 2005 its current federal incarnation—classified in one analysis as "a recognized unrecognized state."[3]

In advancing this analysis, the chapter adopts the combined theoretical approach advocated by Hinnebusch[4] in which he posits that the "Middle East's unique features defy analysis based on any one conceptual approach to international relations ... [such that it is necessary to] ... deploy a combination of several to capture its complex reality." Theories can be conceived of as the different lens used on a camera: a different lens can be utilized according to the subject matter under investigation. Some topics might be more usefully analyzed by one theory than another, and using a different theoretical lens will bring into sharp relief different aspects of the same phenomenon.[5] In this chapter, empirical material is ordered by concepts derived from theories of federalism, specifically the "paradox of federalism", that is the potential of federalism both to constrain secession and to induce it. In the image of the subtitle of this chapter, the stone of the constitution is potentially both a perimeter plinth on which to base the boundaries of Iraqi state territorial integrity, and a stepping stone to be thrown down by the Kurds to "cross the Rubicon" to the apparently green pastures of independence. Of course, to what extent the signatories of the constitution see it as being "set in stone" will also influence the outcome of this instance of the paradox. This conceptualization from federalism studies is combined with the insights of the "ethnic security dilemma" derived from the Realist theory of inter-state behavior adapted to an intra-state context.[6] Underlying this is the theoretical foundation of structuralist interpretations of the formation of the state system of the Middle East.

The chapter first reviews the relevant literature on federalism with a particular focus on the notion of the "paradox of federalism."[7] In doing so it builds on and updates the analysis presented in earlier research.[8] In investigating federalism in Iraq, Erk and Swendon's contention is endorsed, namely that the empirical evidence from single case studies allows the building of theoretical models and has the potential to be generalized and contribute to the unearthing of wider patterns.[9] It advances this analysis by examining the provisions of the Iraqi constitution in two domains: armed forces and security, and hydrocarbons. The chapter concludes with a consideration of the prospects of the KRI in a federal Iraq. Firstly, the historical context of the current situation is briefly reviewed.

Mountain lands divided: the Kurds' ancestral homeland in the Middle East

For many centuries the Ottoman Empire was a major expansionary power (in 1514 it defeated the Persian Safavid Empire in the battle of Chaldiran, gaining the lands of contemporary northern Iraq) which advanced to the gates of Vienna in 1529. As with all empires, it went through a rise and fall. The more dynamic European capitalist powers, principally Britain and France, began to encroach on the Ottoman Empire in the nineteenth century, imposing onerous treaties known as capitulations due to its indebtedness and leading to the initiation of various programs of internal reform by the Turks.[10] From the late eighteenth century, Turkey became known as the "Sick Man of Europe": in British foreign policy terms, the "Eastern Question" concerned how to manage the decline and eventual demise of the Ottoman Empire without allowing its imperial rivals to gain territory and influence that would impart a strategic advantage, particularly in terms of threatening Britain's route to its territories in India.

The Ottoman Empire's decision to enter the First World War on the side of the Central Powers sealed its fate. British planning for a post-war world started with the Sykes-Picot correspondence for the division of the Arab territories. The Kurds—who had inhabited the mountains of the Taurus mountain range for millennia and who possessed their own language and cultural identity—were incorporated into Iraq as a territorially concentrated minority after the war. They were also divided between Turkey, Syria, and Iran.[11] At this moment of change in the international and regional system, the Kurds found themselves contained and incongruous within the boundaries and structures of the Iraqi and other successor states. Referring to such incongruity, Halliday contends that if an ethnic group finds itself in such a position, then another opportunity to obtain independence may not present itself until another moment of large-scale change in the international system: the group will find itself in a position of "post-colonial sequestration", that is, possessed legally by another.[12] Thus, the Kurds found themselves under the jurisdiction of Arab and Turkish governments in Baghdad, Damascus, and Ankara. Iraq was declared independent (but with a treaty with the UK making it subject to British advice) as a constitutional monarchy in 1932. Following the bloody overthrow of the monarchy in 1958, a republic was established.[13] Under the Ba'ath Party regime led by Saddam Hussein, nearly every macro-method of "ethnic conflict regulation" (as categorized by McGarry and Edwards under the sub-section "methods for eliminating difference") was used against the Kurds: genocide, forced mass population transfers, integration, and assimilation.[14] McGarry and O'Leary identify two broad choices in responding to national and religious diversity: integration or accommodation.[15] Integrationists envisage "a strong, centralised and ethically impartial Iraqi state ... necessary for multiple reasons." Identifying accommodation with consociation, they highlight the distinction between corporate consociationalism (where representation is based on pre-conceived ideas of community allegiance) and liberal consociationalism (where elections are used as a means of ascribing allegiance). Iraqi federalism embodied liberal consociationalist principles to try to manage the divisions between Iraq's different groups. However, Eduardo Abu Ltaif's recent study found that of Lijphart's required liberal consociational factors advocated, two were missing (grand coalition and mutual veto) and the other two (proportionality and autonomy) were insufficiently strong in the Iraqi constitution to maintain stability.[16] The following analysis narrates how these consociational deficits came about and gives a sense of the obstacles to implementing the necessary consociational measures.

After regime change: federalism and the management of intra-state conflict

Such was the Kurds' experience of repression under a centralized Iraqi state that they were very open to the possibilities of federalism. The establishment of federalism in Iraq has been the result of an external intervention in Iraq: the invasion by the US and allies in 2003, which led to the demise of the genocidal regime of Saddam Hussein. Regime change in Iraq had been a key part of the neo-conservative agenda of the George W. Bush presidency, and the events of 9/11 set in motion interventions in Afghanistan and Iraq under the doctrine of pre-emptive defence envisaged by the 2001 National Security Strategy.

Prior to this, the 1991 Gulf War and resulting northern no-fly zone had been followed by the Iraqi Kurdish civil war of the mid-1990s, which was resolved by the 1998 Washington Agreement. Under this agreement the Kurdish political parties (KDP and PUK) agreed to bury their differences and work toward the overthrow of Saddam Hussein. All of this had led to the obtaining of de facto autonomy in the three northern predominantly Kurdish provinces of Dohuk, Erbil, and Sulaimaniyah.

A further reason for Kurdish support of federalism was that the United States had no policy of supporting Kurdish independence. US policy toward the Kurds was configured in relation to its policy toward Arab Iraq and Turkey, which placed Iraqi territorial integrity high on the agenda.[17] Turkey was deeply suspicious of any granting of autonomy or federal rights to the KRI, because of the example it would set to the Kurds in Turkey. It was a long step for the Turkish government to overcome the denial of Kurdish identity on which the Atatürk state was built. Post-Ottoman Turkey adopted and continues to pursue a highly integrationist approach in a diametrically opposed philosophy to federalism which involves power-sharing and self-rule.

Federalism: definition, origins, and pattern

This section briefly reviews key concepts in the theory and practice of federalism necessary to assess the place of the Iraqi Kurds in the constitution of Iraq.[18] The term federalism and its associated cognate definitions (federation, confederation, federacy) is derived from the Latin *foedus*, meaning an alliance amongst individuals and communities allowing the promotion of specific and common interest. Riker defined federalism as requiring two levels of government that rule the same land and people; each level of government must have at least one area where it is autonomous, and there is some constitutional guarantee of the autonomy of each government in its specified area.[19] A federated unit may have all the features of government: a legislature, executive, and judiciary, and indeed a population that looks to it for government. It is a political unit that displays all aspects of organization, and is not far away in function from a sovereign state.

Another salient consideration is the matter of federal origins, which pertains to the nature of the agreement to create the federal union. Is the federalism a "holding together" of units that have long existed in union, or a "coming together" of previously sovereign entities? Iraq may be seen as exhibiting both features: it has long existed as a sovereign state, but it can be argued that the Kurdistan Region had enjoyed a form of de facto autonomy since the creation of the no-fly zone. Thus, the decision to enter the federal union conformed to a "coming together" federal origin as well. In this regard it is particularly important to be aware of the KRI's historical trajectory as an unrecognized state from the 1970 Iraqi-Kurdish Autonomy Agreement onwards, when considering federal origins.[20]

From this starting point, it is useful to identify the great variety in types of federal polity. A federation may be symmetrical or asymmetrical; asymmetrical federalism refers to a case where one of the sub-units in the federal union has formally considerably more autonomy than other sub-units.[21] Liam Anderson contends that one of the problems with Iraqi federalism has been that it is insufficiently asymmetrical: the asymmetrical recognition of the Kurdistan Region contained in the Transitional Administrative Law was not incorporated into the 2005 constitution.[22] This could yet have implications for the outcome of the paradox of federalism in Iraq.

The paradox of federalism

Simply put, in the case of fragile polities such as Iraq, there are those who argue that federalism will lead to the country's break-up as opposed to those who contend it is the only way to maintain the country's territorial integrity. Both statements are potentially right: this is the "paradox of federalism." Thus, Danilovich and Owtram note that the "paradox of federalism consists in federalism's potential to both prevent and induce succession."[23] While federal structures may in the short term alleviate societal tensions, they may in the longer term lower the costs of secession: federalism allows the creation of governmental structures and experience in governance. Thus, the paradox: federalism is potentially both secession constraining and secession inducing. That said, secession is not seen as desirable by many existing recognized states. The world is composed of over 2,500 ethnic groups, but only 190 sovereign states; and the recognized sovereign states have a default preference for the maintenance of state territorial integrity, rather than the creation of new sovereign states. The international community has a "low appetite" for secession: to allow the principle of easy secession would potentially destabilize many of these recognized states with an attendant possibility of conflict. Hence, federalism has been regarded as an important means of maintaining state territorial integrity.

Establishing federalism in Iraq

Federalism in Iraq was introduced in 2003 by an occupying power following invasion and removal of a brutal integrationist regime that in some ways was an "inevitable" response to the fissiparous tendencies of the artificial state constructed by the British to allow exploitation of oil.[24] The Middle East state system created by the British and French, based on the Sykes-Picot map, drew arbitrary lines dividing tribes, ethnic groups, and co-religionists. The Mandate for Iraq was based on the Ottoman *vilayet* of Baghdad, Basra, and Mosul and placed together Sunni, Shia, and Kurd under an imported Hashemite monarch, in a state dominated by the same Sunni elite which held sway under Ottoman rule. Approximately 75–80 percent of Iraqi citizens are Arab, and 15-20 percent are Kurd. Of the Muslim population, approximately 35 percent are Sunni, and 65 percent Shia. There is also a mosaic of other religions, sects, and ethnic groups who have inhabited the lands of Mesopotamia for millennia, including Yazidis, Assyrian Christians, and Turkmen.[25]

For the US officials and individuals involved, negotiating a new federal constitution between the representatives of these groups was an exercise in the art of the possible, with many issues sometimes left deliberately ambiguous, contradictory, or put to one side for later resolution and agreement. The result was the 2005 constitution and its articles concerning numerous contentious issues.[26] Many in the Sunni community effectively boycotted the process and thus disenfranchised themselves, a massive deficit for the legitimacy of the 2005 constitution.

Furthermore, certain constitutional provisions have not been implemented or they are cherry-picked by Baghdad and Erbil according to their preference. A blow to the constitution was the non-implementation of Article 140, which aimed to deal with the disputed territories, Kirkuk in particular. Amongst all the stipulations of constitutional law, one key point needs to be borne in mind for the future prospects of Iraqi federalism: the need for negotiation and compromise.[27] However, the very ambiguity that was necessary to achieve the signatures of the different parties involved means that the thorny issues left untouched are probably more difficult to resolve. We turn now to the two mini-case studies which illustrate some of the more contentious aspects of the constitution: KRI security and the peshmerga; and the exploitation of hydrocarbons and their associated revenues.

KRI security and the peshmerga

The retention of an armed force could be portrayed as a clear indication of intent to secede. The Kurds have long relied on their fighters, the peshmerga (those who face death), to protect them from various threats; indeed, their revered status within Kurdish society mean that they constitute part of Kurdish identity: men and women fight alongside each other as equals and of the same military prowess. Kurds are also cognizant that when Baghdad has been weak, it has made concessions to the Kurds; but when strong, it has sought to reassert itself against them with brutal intent. Thus, the Kurds would never disband the peshmerga units. An independent fighting force may appear contrary to Article 9, which states: "The formation of military militias outside the framework of the armed forces is prohibited." However, if the peshmerga is seen as a "regional security force", or "guards of the region" according to Article 21, then clearly it is not in breach of the constitution. The Kurdistan Regional Government attempted to integrate the peshmerga into federal structures, but the Maliki government rebuffed these proposals and sought to reduce their numbers and withhold funding.[28] After US withdrawal from Iraq at the end of 2011 and the loss of an overarching and mediating power, the Iraqi state intensified its process of recrimination and collapse in which each ethnic group had to assess its relative strength and the intentions of other communities: a clear case of the "security dilemma and ethnic conflict."

The security dilemma and ethnic conflict in Iraq

At this point the insights of Realist IR theory can be deployed to explain the calculations that may operate between different intra-state groups in a collapsing empire or state. Realist IR theory argues that in a condition of anarchy (defined as the absence of an overarching authority) security becomes the first concern of states as a matter of existential survival. In Realist IR theory the "security dilemma" is a concept aiming to explain inter-state behavior: that a state preparing to defend itself may be perceived as offensive to other states who may engage in building up their military capabilities, thus actually resulting in decreasing security. Posen applies the notion of the security dilemma developed from inter-state behavior to the situation between different ethnic groups within a collapsing empire or collapsing state: what he coined as the "security dilemma and ethnic conflict."[29]

Groups finding themselves in a collapsing state in a condition of anarchy must assess the relative threat of other groups and their capacity to act, which may be a function of their group cohesion as armaments may be rather rudimentary. In a collapsing state, offensive operations are elevated above defensive measures. If an ethnic group has members in isolated pockets separated from the main group, these will be difficult to defend if attacked. Groups assess their power relative to other groups and whether it is likely to remain at that level or decrease. If it is felt that the group occupies a strong position which may weaken, then there is an incentive to take offensive measures quickly. Furthermore, if there is a history of bitter conflict and competition it is more likely that groups will perceive each other as offensive threats.[30]

The Islamic State occupation of Mosul and assault on Erbil

The occupation by IS of Iraq's second biggest city, Mosul, the subsequent declaration of the Caliphate and taking of control of large swathes of Iraq sent shock waves throughout the Middle East and worldwide. This manifestation of the "intra-state security dilemma" here is that ethnic groups act based on what history suggests their neighbors would do. In this regard, the attempted assault and occupation of Erbil by IS in 2014 was no surprise to peshmerga commanders: for them this was the same evil of the Sunni Ba'athist officers repackaged in another radical Islamist form meting out extreme brutality as part of its strategy to occupy and control populations.[31] Assyrian Christians fled for their lives to the Kurdistan Region or outside Iraq to Europe and North America. IS reserved a particular hatred for the Shia who were summarily executed if captured. The ancient religion practised by the Yazidi Kurds was also held in contempt by IS: they attempted genocide against the Yazidis in Sinjar who fled to their eponymous mountain refuge, where they found protection from a force dispatched by Syrian Kurds as the peshmerga of the KRG had been withdrawn to defend Erbil; the Yazidi women who were caught by IS were taken as sex slaves or raped and killed. As the IS convoys came to within 20 miles of Erbil in August 2014, and families arranged to get their young girls out of the city, US airstrikes were initiated against the IS forces to ward off this imminent threat to its consulate and the capital of the Kurdistan Region.

However, when it came to other forms of military support, the Americans have insisted on supplying arms to the KRG via the federal capital, Baghdad, as required by US law; the arms never arrived via this route, and the best hope that the peshmerga had of obtaining modern armaments was of capturing materiel from the Islamic State military forces. This they did, and supported by coalition airstrikes they progressively pushed IS back and created facts on the ground pertaining to the disputed territories: at the time of writing, the Kurds occupy 90 percent of the territories they dispute with Baghdad and are unlikely to give them up, including the Ninevah Plain near Mosul.

Sectarianism and Sunni support of IS

Under the sectarian approach of the Maliki government (2006-14), the Sunni community felt itself to be progressively excluded. Arguably, until the Sunni community feel their interests are taken into account, some elements of it may see IS as their militia and defender against Shia death squads.[32] That said, it is important to avoid oversimplifying a complex picture: Rasha Al Aqeedi gives an insightful analysis into the social basis of IS support and attitudes of Muslawis to IS. In August 2014 IS fighters seized the depots of the divisions (30,000 soldiers) of the Iraqi army who laid down their weapons, took off their Iraqi army uniforms, and handed over Mosul and its inhabitants to 200 IS fighters. This was an Iraqi army which had had $26 billion invested in it in equipment and training by the United States.[33] At that point the Kurdish peshmerga seemed to be the only effective "boots on the ground"; subsequently the Iraqi army regrouped and retook Fallujah and Tikrit with the help of the Popular Mobilization Units (PMU) which included Shia militias. Denise Natali points out that it will be a "long road to Mosul" and emphasizes the importance of doing the necessary preparatory work.[34] The initial operations in October 2016 to clear villages on the approach to the city clearly demonstrated that it would be no easy task to retake Mosul from ISIS. Furthermore, much would need to be done to prevent Islamic State from merely going undercover and morphing into another group at a later opportune moment.[35] An even greater challenge will be to craft a post-IS deal which enables the different communities to live together, one of the most challenging of which will be federal relationships to allow the sharing of wealth from oil and gas.

Federalism, hydrocarbons and the KRI: challenges of revenue sharing

The Kurdistan Region of Iraq was described by Tony Haywood, Chief Executive of Genel, as "one of the last great oil and gas frontiers."[36] The provisions of the constitution relating to oil and gas are central to issues of Iraqi federalism.[37] The oil reserves of Iraq—the superfields in Basra, the Kirkuk massive dome, the reserves in the undisputed governorates of the Kurdistan Region, and even some discoveries in the Anbar province inhabited by Sunnis—do currently yield billions of dollars in revenues and could potentially make even more.

The constitution contains several articles relating to oil and gas. McGarry and O'Leary argue that the constitution clarifies that natural resources are not an exclusive competence of the federal government. Article 111 declares that "oil and gas are owned by all the people of Iraq" and is deliberately not a sub-clause of the preceding Article 110 detailing the exclusive powers of the federal government. They also contend that Article 111 should be interpreted in line with Article 115, which states that all competencies not specifically allocated to the federal government belong to the regions. Also, Article 111 should be placed in the context of Article 121 which allows the regions to nullify measures outside the exclusive competences of the central government.

Furthermore, Article 112 states that the federal government will with the producing regional government and governorates manage the oil and gas taken from present fields; the federal government with the producing regional government will also develop the necessary strategic policies to develop the oil and gas wealth to the greatest use for the Iraqi people. This is also to be read in conjunction with Articles 115 and 121 which achieve regional legal supremacy. There is nothing to stop the federal and regional government from instituting cooperative measures of working together, and this was envisaged in the draft federal oil legislation.[38] Unfortunately, cooperative measures between Baghdad and Erbil have been in short supply.

Under the constitution, the KRG should receive a proportion of the revenue from Iraq's oil sales pro rata according to its population: in theory 17 percent of the revenue, although in practice a maximum of only 11 percent has ever been received. Furthermore, the KRG has not received their share from the budget since March 2015 (payments after the December 2014 agreement with Baghdad), due to an ongoing dispute with Baghdad. Tax collection and current oil sales are not transparent enough to enable an assessment of what percentage of the KRG budget deficit is covered by local resources.[39] Currently, the KRG is unable to pay salaries to its employees, who constitute 80 percent of the population. This inability to pay its employees includes the peshmerga fighting on the front line, who tried to make ends meet by driving taxis until the US stepped in to pay their salaries. The populace is asking where the money has gone and are quick to blame this on the corruption of the political elite. No doubt this is a factor, but there is also a more significant underlying structural issue: that 80 percent of the population is on the KRG payroll with sometimes unspecified jobs, an aspect of the *rentier* state social contract inherited from earlier regimes.[40] This was sustainable with oil at $100 a barrel, but at under $30-45 a barrel it is not; this combined with the war with ISIS and the strain of hosting 1.5 million IDPs means that the KRG is technically insolvent and unable to pay wages, leading to strikes by disgruntled workers.[41] In Kirkuk, Kurdish employees of the federal government are paid, but those employed by the KRG are not.[42] The population asks why they should suffer from austerity measures (salaries cut in half) when it was the responsibility of the political elite to diversify the tax base and institute necessary reforms during the good times of economic boom.[43] It brings into question again the system of dynastic republicanism[44] operating in the Kurdistan Region, dissatisfaction with which is the force behind the rise of the Gorran (change) party as well as providing fertile recruiting ground for IS to attract Kurds to its ranks. In Iraqi Kurdistan up to 600 Kurds have joined the ranks of ISIS, lured by the propaganda of people like Khattab al-Kurdi, who emphasize themes such as the conflict between the KDP and PUK and their corrupt activities.[45]

Not surprisingly, ordinary people in the Kurdistan Region of Iraq question why, with all the oil revenue being generated, they do not have reliable electricity, water, food for their families, and essentially no security of life, livelihood, or liberty. Evidence can be found that the elites of Iraq, including those of the KDP and PUK, have considerably enriched themselves, siphoning off money to offshore accounts in opaque financial transactions. As Natali puts it, they have all benefited from the constitutional stalemate which she sees as the most likely outcome, rather than statehood for the KRI.[46] Additionally, in contrast to the view that Iraq now lends itself to a tripartite division into autonomous Shia, Sunni, and Kurdish areas, Natali contends that "Iraq has become an amalgam of hyper-localized entities seeking self-rule and self-protection, while remaining dependent on Baghdad and prone to proxy conflicts ... Among the Kurds, divisions run deep over claims to territories and their resources."[47] Both Natali and Abu Latif find that the necessary consociational measures are presently missing. It is also questionable whether in the longer term the US is willing or able to play the role it has in supporting federalism in Iraq. Since the revolutions of 2011 in the Middle East and ensuing civil wars, it is undoubtedly the case that Iraq has been in the throes of a period of change in the regional and international system. According to Halliday's analysis, this may present opportunities for the Kurds to move from their position of "post-colonial sequestration." In these circumstances, we can now conclude on these developments for the KRI and the federal constitution: is it a perimeter plinth or a stepping stone?

Conclusion: The Kurdistan Region of Iraq and the federal constitution: a perimeter plinth of state territorial integrity or a stepping stone to secession?

This chapter has considered the prospects for federalism in Iraq and the place of the Kurdistan Region within it. In February 2016, the KRG President, Masoud Barzani, called for an end to the Sykes-Picot era and announced preparations for a referendum on independence for the Kurdistan Region of Iraq.[48] Harvey and Stansfield caution that the "Kurdish example is in fact a useful case study in not taking nationalist rhetoric focused upon independence at face value."[49] Using the organizing concept of the "paradox of federalism", this chapter has reviewed the empirical evidence in the case of the federal constitution and the Kurdistan Region of Iraq and we now return to the chapter's key question: is the constitution secession constraining or secession inducing? In a previous work written in 2013 I concluded:

> In connection with the paradox of federalism this chapter finds that in the short to medium term the current federal system provides the different political elites a framework within which they benefit from a political stalemate which enable them to develop their financial interests. In the longer term a deal will need to be done to resolve key issues, possibly in a form of asymmetrical federalism. The federalization of natural resources will be one of the toughest areas to negotiate but regional geopolitics and the Kurdistan Region's dependence on the central government for its revenue will likely maintain the Kurdistan Region's placed in a federal Iraq.[50]

For asymmetric federalism, it would be vital for the negotiating partners not to act as if the constitution was in fact "set in stone"; there would have to be willingness to negotiate and compromise, but this seems to be in ever shorter supply, and each round of war and conflict reduces the essential commodity for any negotiation: trust. Furthermore, in a changed international system, it is not clear whether the US will be able or willing to play the role of banging the heads together of the conflicting parties to achieve consensus.

The obstacles to KRI independence still exist in the short to medium term. In the longer term, however, and particularly since the Islamic State threatened Erbil in 2014 (a manifestation of the intra-state security dilemma), the needle in the barometer of probability has moved in my view toward the Kurdistan Region of Iraq seceding at some point from Iraq. Whether it will be under the current leadership(s) is another matter. Unless they can achieve economic reform and address issues of good governance, it is not inconceivable that they could be swept away, just like other republican dynasties in the Middle East.

ANNEX TO CHAPTER 27
KRG POLICY PRIORITIES FOR
WATER AND SANITATION

(Extract from "Kurdistan Region of Iraq 2020: a Vision for the Future," http://www.mop.krg.org/resources/MoP%20Files/Newsletter/kurdistan_region_of_iraq_2020_new.pdf)

Our focus through 2017 for improving water and sanitation services to residents of our Region will include the following policy priorities:

- Completing a full hydrological study of the Kurdistan Region. Such a study would assess both the quantity and quality of all natural water sources, including rivers, groundwater supplies, and aquifers to better understand groundwater potential, and would analyze water inputs, uses, storage, and flows. It would quantify rainfall and snowfall trends and patterns; runoff of this rainfall and snowfall into streams and groundwater; recharge rates into groundwater; evaporation rates from agricultural lands, irrigation channels, and other lands; and wastewater return flow, among other important categories. We expect that this study will provide the baseline on which we will determine all future management and investment decisions.

- Completing an integrated water resources management plan. Building on the hydrological study and on our work on management of the Great Zab river basin, we will make strong progress on the development of an integrated water resources management plan for the Region. This plan will help us develop and manage all our water resources to make sure we have the right quality and quantity of water for the health of the people and for agriculture, industry, and all other parts of our economy, while at the same time helping us sustain our ecosystems and environment. It will also help us design well-planned programs to attract local and international investment in the water sector. As part of designing and fulfilling this plan, we will strengthen connections among water-related institutions in the Kurdistan Region, and between those institutions and international institutions. We will disseminate public information to increase public awareness about water use and treatment so all residents of the Kurdistan Region can help safeguard this precious resource.

• Increasing access to clean water. We will continue our efforts to provide universal access to clean water, focusing on increasing access to drinkable water in rural areas and improving the quality of drinking water in both cities and villages. Our strategy for improving water access will entail five elements:

(1) estimating the amount of water leakage in the existing water transportation infrastructure and supporting investments to eliminate it;

(2) investing in water storage facilities to address seasonal fluctuations;

(3) upgrading water treatment infrastructure to international standards;

(4) expanding opportunities for private participation in water provision; and

(5) reforming the water tariff system to reduce waste and provide for cost recovery.

• Upgrading sewerage systems. To protect our environment and public health, the expansion of water access must be accompanied by investments in sewerage. We will develop a Regionwide sewerage plan to invest in treatment plants and infrastructure, make water and sanitation infrastructure an integral part of city planning, help residents of low density areas install and maintain septic tanks and expand infrastructure for refuse collection and treatment, create facilities to treat industrial waste, and introduce a system of municipal taxes and user fees to pay for sanitation services. So that we may not only protect the environment and public health, but also aid our economy, we intend that water treated by the new sewerage treatment plants will be recycled for agricultural purposes.

NOTES

INTRODUCTION

1. Richard N. Haass, "The Irony of American Strategy: Putting the Middle East in Proper Perspective", *Foreign Affairs* 92:3 (2013) p. 66.

2. William Hague, "We Can't Now Turn Our Backs on the Chaos in the Middle East", *Daily Telegraph*, 26 April 2016, http://www.telegraph.co.uk/opinion/2016/04/25/we-cant-now-turn-our-backs-on-the-chaos-in-the-middle-east/

3. For an excellent analysis of the failings of the Arab state system, see Kenneth Pollack, "Fight or Flight: American's Choice in the Middle East", *Foreign Affairs* (March/April 2016), https://www.foreignaffairs.com/articles/middle-east/2016-02-16/fight-or-flight

4. The literature on the Arab-Israeli dispute and the plight of the Palestinians is voluminous and beyond the scope of a book on the Kurds to delve into in great detail. Two books which provide balanced entry points into these subjects are Avi Shlaim, *The Iron Wall: Israel and the Arab World* (London: Penguin, 2000); and Alan Dowty, *Israel/Palestine* (Cambridge: Polity Press, 2005).

5. See Ali Ansari, *Confronting Iran* (London: Hurst & Co., 2006). For an account of the rise of sectarianism in Middle East political life, see Frederic Wehrey, *Sectarian Politics in the Gulf: From the Iraq War to the Arab Uprisings* (New York: Columbia University Press, 2014).

6. Pollack, "Fight or Flight." For a detailed account of the skewing effects of oil economies on Arab Gulf societies, see Kristian Coates Ulrichsen, *Insecure Gulf: The End of Certainty and the Transition to the Post-Oil Era* (London: Hurst & Co., 2011).

7. The classic references on the role of the military in Arab states include J. C. Hurewitz, *Middle East Politics: The Military Dimension* (London: Praeger, 1969); Mohammed Tarbush, *The Role of the Military in Politics: A Case Study of Iraq to 1941* (London: KPI, 1985); and Barry Rubin and Thomas Kearney (eds), *Armed Forces in the Middle East: Politics and Strategy* (London: Frank Cass, 2002). See also Gareth Stansfield, "Political Life and the Military," in Youssef Chouieri (ed.), *A Companion to the History of the Middle East* (London: Blackwell, 2005) pp. 355-71.

8. Gareth Stansfield, "The Unravelling of the Post-First World War State System? The

Kurdistan Region of Iraq and the Transformation of the Middle East," *International Affairs* 89:2 (2013) pp. 259-82.

9.   Western academic literature on the Kurds and Kurdistan is relatively sparse before the 1990s. Notable and valuable works include Arshak Safrastian, *Kurds and Kurdistan* (London: Harvill Press, 1948); Abdul Rahman Ghassemlou, *Kurdistan and the Kurds* (Prague: Czechoslovak Academy of Sciences, 1965); Edmund Ghareeb, *The Kurdish Question in Iraq* (Syracuse, NY: Syracuse University Press, 1981); Sa'ad Jawad, *Iraq and the Kurdish Question 1958–1970* (London: Ithaca Press, 1981). Thanks to intrepid journalists, the literature on the Kurds between the end of the Second World War and the 1990s is rich with several detailed accounts, particularly of the rebellion of the Kurds of Iraq against successive Iraqi regimes. Notable examples include William Douglas, *Strange Lands and Friendly People* (New York: Harper & Brothers, 1951); David Adamson, *The Kurdish War* (London: George Allen & Unwin, 1964); Dana Adams Schmidt, *Journey Among Brave Men* (Boston: Little, Brown & Co., 1964); Chris Kutschera, *Le Mouvement National Kurde* (Paris: Flammarion, 1979); John Bulloch and Harvey Morris, *No Friends but the Mountains: The Tragic History of the Kurds* (London: Viking, 1992); Jonathan Randall, *After Such Knowledge, What Forgiveness?* (New York: Farrar, Straus and Giroux, 1997).

10.   For a detailed account of US and Iran diplomacy concerning the Kurds of Iraq, see Bryan Gibson, *Sold Out? US Foreign Policy, Iraq, the Kurds, and the Cold War* (New York: Palgrave Macmillan, 2015).

11.   For accounts of the Kurdish *rapareen*, see Michael Gunter, *The Kurdish Predicament in Iraq: A Political Analysis* (New York: St Martin's Press, 1999); Gareth Stansfield, *Iraqi Kurdistan: Political Development and Emergent Democracy* (London: RoutledgeCurzon, 2003); Ofra Bengio, *The Kurds of Iraq: Building a State Within a State* (Boulder, CO: Lynne Rienner, 2012). For accounts of the Shi'i *intifadah*, see Faleh Jaber, "Why the Uprisings Failed," *Middle East Research and Information Project Middle East Report* 176: 22 (May/June 1992), http://www.merip.org/mer/mer176

12.   For a detailed account of the Iran-Iraq War, see Pierre Razoux, *The Iran-Iraq War* (Cambridge, MA: Harvard University Press, 2015).

13.   For more information concerning the treatment of the Kurds in post-revolutionary Iran, see Nader Entessar, *Kurdish Politics in the Middle East* (Lanham, MD: Lexington Books, 2010); David Romano, *The Kurdish Nationalist Movement: Opportunity, Mobilization and Identity* (Cambridge: Cambridge University Press, 2006); and Gareth Stansfield, "Kurds, Persian Nationalism, and Shi'i Rule: Surviving Dominant Nationhood in Iran", in David Romano and Mehmet Gurses (eds), *Conflict, Democratization, and the Kurds in the Middle East: Turkey, Iran, Iraq, and Syria* (New York: Palgrave Macmillan, 2014). For accounts of the *Anfal* campaign and the use of chemical weapons against the Kurds of Iraq, see Human Rights Watch, *Genocide in Iraq: The Anfal Campaign Against the Kurds* (New York: Human Rights Watch,

1993); Joost Hiltermann, *A Poisonous Affair: America, Iraq, and the Gassing of Halabja* (Cambridge: Cambridge University Press, 2007); and Mohammed Ihsan, *Nation Building in Kurdistan: Memory, Genocide and Human Rights* (London: Routledge, 2016).

14. See Sabri Ates, *The Ottoman Iranian Borderlands: Making a Boundary, 1843–1914* (Cambridge: Cambridge University Press, 2013); Janet Klein, *The Margins of Empire: Kurdish Militias in the Ottoman Tribal Zone* (Stanford, CA: Stanford University Press, 2011).

15. For the history of Sheikh Mahmoud's activities in post-First World War Kurdistan, see Saad Eskander, "Britain's Policy in Southern Kurdistan: The Formation and the Termination of the First Kurdish Government, 1918–1919," *British Journal of Middle Eastern Studies* 27:2 (November 2000) pp. 139-63.

16. See Archie Roosevelt, Jr, "The Kurdish Republic of Mahabad", *Middle East Journal* 1:3 (July 1947) pp. 247-69; William Eagleton, Jr, *The Kurdish Republic of 1946* (London: Oxford University Press, 1963).

17. See Douglas Little, "The United States and the Kurds: A Cold War Story," *Journal of Cold War Studies* 12: 4 (2010) pp. 62-99; Stansfield, *Iraqi Kurdistan*.

18. See David McDowall, *A Modern History of the Kurds* (London: I. B. Tauris, 1997); Charles Tripp, *A History of Iraq*, 3rd edn (Cambridge: Cambridge University Press, 2007).

19. Rex Zedalis, *Oil and Gas in the Disputed Kurdish Territories* (London: Routledge, 2012); Stansfield, "The Unravelling"; Gareth Stansfield, "Kurdistan Rising: To Acknowledge or Ignore the Unravelling of Iraq," *Brookings Middle East Memo*, no. 33 (July 2014), http://www.brookings.edu/~/media/research/files/papers/2014/07/kurdistan-iraq-isis-0731/kurdistan-iraq-isis-stansfield-0731.pdf

20. For a critical assessment of the KRI economy, see Denise Natali, "The Kurdish Quasi-State: Leveraging Political Limbo," *Washington Quarterly* 38: 2 (Summer 2015) pp. 145-64.

21. Gareth Stansfield, "The Islamic State, the Kurdistan Region, and the Future of Iraq: Assessing UK Policy Options," *International Affairs* 90:6 (2014) pp. 1329-50.

22. Robert Olson, "The Kurdish Rebellions of Sheikh Said (1925), Mt. Ararat (1930), and Dersim (1937–8): Their Impact on the Development of the Turkish Air Force and on Kurdish and Turkish Nationalism," *Die Welt des Islams* 40:1 (March 2000) pp. 67-94.

23. For an analysis of the political progression of the Kurdish movement in Turkey, see Cengiz Gunes, *The Kurdish National Movement in Turkey* (London: Routledge, 2012).

24. Güneş Murat Tezcür, "The Ebb and Flow of Armed Conflict in Turkey: An Elusive Peace," in David Romano and Mehmet Gurses (eds), *Conflict, Democratization, and*

the Kurds in the Middle East: Turkey, Iran, Iraq, and Syria (New York: Palgrave Macmillan, 2014) pp. 171-88, reference at p. 172.

25. For detailed work on the Kurdish movement in Turkey, and with particular reference to the role played by the PKK, see Paul White, *Primitive Rebels or Revolutionary Modernizers* (London: Zed Books, 2000); Ali Kemal Özcan, *Turkey's Kurds: A Theoretical Analysis of the PKK and Abdullah Ocalan* (London: Routledge, 2006); Gunes, *The Kurdish National Movement*; Aliza Marcus, *Blood and Belief: The PKK and the Kurdish Fight for Independence* (New York: New York University Press, 2007); Cengiz Gunes and Welat Zeydanlioglu (eds), *The Kurdish Question in Turkey: New Perspectives on Violence, Representation, and Reconciliation* (London: Routledge, 2014).

26. Michael Gunter, 'The Continuing Kurdish Problem in Turkey After Öcalan's Capture,' *Third World Quarterly* 21:5, pp. 849-69.

27. The former prime minister of Turkey, Ahmet Davutoğlu, was the architect of the "zero problems" policy. For his own presentation of the policy, see Ahmet Davutoğlu, "Principles of Turkish Foreign Policy and Regional Political Structuring," Turkey Policy Brief Series (Paris: International Policy and Leadership Institute, 2012). http://www.ankara.veleposlanistvo.si/fileadmin/user_upload/dkp_16_van/docs/Principles_of_Turkish_Foreign_Policy_and_Regional_Political_Structuring_by_Ahmet_Davutoglu.pdf

28. Mohammed Shareef, *The United States, Iraq and the Kurds: Shock, Awe and Aftermath* (London: Routledge, 2014) p. 167.

29. For an assessment of the impact of the results of the June 2015 elections, see Ersin Kalaycıoğlu, "The Conundrum of Coalition Politics in Turkey, *Turkish Studies* 17:1, pp. 31-8.

30. While receiving less attention than the situation in Iraq and Turkey, there has been an increase in the number of publications on the Kurds of Syria. The most notable of these include: Harriet Montgomery (Allsopp), *The Kurds of Syria: An Existence Denied* (Berlin: European Centre for Kurdish Studies, 2005); Jordi Tejel, *Syria's Kurds: History, Politics and Society* (London: Routledge, 2009); Robert Lowe, "The *Serhildan* and the Kurdish National Story in Syria," in Robert Lowe and Gareth Stansfield (eds), *The Kurdish Policy Imperative* (London: Royal Institute of International Affairs, 2010) pp. 161-79; Harriet Allsopp, *The Kurds of Syria: Political Parties and Identity in the Middle East* (London: I. B. Tauris, 2014); Michael Gunter, *Out of Nowhere: The Kurds of Syria in Peace and War* (London: Hurst & Co., 2014).

31. Lowe, "The *Serhildan*."

32. The concept of "democratic autonomy", which in effect outlines a political system structured around a network of localized and autonomous administrative units. The concept is outlined in some detail in the anonymously written TATORT Kurdistan, *Democratic Autonomy in North Kurdistan: The Council Movement, Gender Liberation,*

and Ecology – in Practice: A Reconnaissance into Southeastern Turkey (Porsgrun, Norway: New Compass Press, 2013).

33. Abdullah Öcalan, *Prison Writings II: The PKK and the Kurdish Question in the 21ˢᵗ Century* (London: Pluto Press, 2011) p. 82.

1. NEW PERSPECTIVES ON WRITING THE HISTORY OF THE KURDS IN IRAQ, SYRIA AND TURKEY

1. This chapter is a part of a larger research project entitled *States, Minorities and Conflicts in the Middle East: A Comparative Study of the Durability of States and Regimes and Dissident Movements in Egypt, Iraq, and Turkey, 1948–2003*. I am grateful to the Swiss National Science Foundation, which provided the grant to support this four-year research project launched in 2010. However, the views expressed herein are my own, and do not necessarily reflect those of the Foundation.

2. Djene Bajalan and Sara Z. Karimi, "The Kurds and their history," *Iranian Studies* 47:5 (2014 pp. 679-81.

3. Ibid., p. 680.

4. Issam Nassar, "Reflections on Writing the History of Palestinian Identity," *Palestine-Israel Journal* 8:4 (2002) p. 24.

5. Monika Baar, *Historians and Nationalism: East-Central Europe in the Nineteenth Century* (Oxford: Oxford University Press, 2010).

6. Stefan Berger and Chris Lorenz (eds), *The Contested Nation: Ethnicity, Class, Religion and Gender in National Histories* (New York: Palgrave Macmillan, 2008) p. 552; Mark Mazower, *Dark Continent: Europe's Twentieth Century* (London: Penguin, 1998).

7. National history is understood here as a specific form of historical representation which aims at the formation of a nation state, or seeks to influence the existing self-definitions or a national consciousness. Stefan Berger, "National Historiographies in Transnational Perspective: Europe in the nineteenth and twentieth centuries," *Storia della Storiografia* 50 (2006) p. 14.

8. Dipesh Chakrabarty, *Provincializing Europe: Postcolonial and Historical Difference* (Princeton, NJ: Princeton University Press, 2000); Partha Chatterjee, *The Present History of West Bengal* (New Delhi: Oxford University Press, 1997); Ranajit Guha, *Elementary Aspects of Peasant Insurgency in Colonial India* (New Delhi: Oxford University Press, 1983).

9. Berger and Lorenz (eds), *The Contested Nation*, p. 2.

10. Ibid., pp. 11-12.

11. Joep Leersen, "Nation and ethnicity," in Berger and Lorenz (eds), *The Contested Nation*, p. 103.

12. Will Kimlycka and Eva Pföstl (eds), *Multiculturalism and Minority Rights in the Arab World* (Oxford: Oxford University Press, 2014).

13. There are, of course, some exceptions. See Ahmad Abdalla, *The Student Movement and National Politics in Egypt, 1923–1973* (London: Saqi Books, 1985); Hanna Batatu, *The Old Social Classes and the Revolutionary Movements in Iraq: A Study of Iraq's Old Landed and Commercial Classes and of its Communists, Ba'thists and Free Officers* (Princeton, NJ: Princeton University Press, 1978); Abdallah Hanna, *Al-qadiyya al-zira'iyya wa-l-harakat al-fallahiyya fi Suriyya wa-Lubnan, 1820–1920*, Vols 1 and 2 (Beirut: Al-Farabi, 1975/8); Abdallah Hanna, "The attitudes of the Syrian Communist Party and the Arab Socialist Party towards the peasant movement in Syria in the 1950s," in Gérard D. Khoury and Nadine Méouchy (eds), *Etats et sociétés en quête d'avenir (1945–2005): Dynamiques et enjeux* (Paris: Geuthner, 2007) pp. 327-36.

14. Hamit Bozarslan, "Quelques remarques sur le discours historiographique kurde en Turquie: 1919–1980," *Asien, Afrika, Lateinamerika* 29 (2001) pp. 47-71.

15. Hamit Bozarslan, "Some Remarks on Kurdish Historiographical Discourse in Turkey, 1919–1980," in Abbas Vali (ed.), *Essays on the Origins of Kurdish Nationalism* (Costa Mesa, CA: Mazda, 2003) pp. 16-17.

16. Malmîsanij, *Kürt Teavün ve Terakki Cemiyeti ve Gazetesi*, 2nd edn (Istanbul: Avesta, 1999).

17. Jordi Tejel, *Le mouvement kurde de Turquie en exil. Continuités et discontinuités du nationalisme kurde sous le mandat français en Syrie et au Liban, 1925–1946* (Bern: Peter Lang, 2007).

18. Elsewhere, though, I have argued that the opposite was also true. Turkish authorities were also obliged to take into consideration the dissenting discourses elaborated by Kurdish intellectuals who were in exile in Syria and Lebanon after the establishment of the Turkish Republic. In that respect, Kurdish intellectuals who organized around the Khoybun Committee (1927-43) became "legitimate" representatives of the Kurdish opposition to the Kemalists, in part due to the relative freedom of action in the Levant under the French Mandate. As such, the Kemalist intelligentsia were forced to respond to the Kurdish nationalist discourse too: Jordi Tejel, "The Shared Political Production of *the East* as a *Resistant* Territory and Cultural Sphere in the Kemalist Era, 1923–1938," *European Journal of Turkish Studies* 10 (2009) http://ejts.revues.org/4064

19. Mohammad Amin Zaki Beg, *Kürdistan tarihi* (Istanbul: Komal, 1977); Mohammad Amin Zaki Beg, *Kürd ve Kürdistan Ünlüleri* (Spanga: Apec, 1998).

20. Kamal M. Ahmad, *Kurdistan during the First World War*, English trans. by Ali Maher Ibrahim (London: Saqi Books, 1994).

21. Thomas Bois, *Connaissance des Kurdes* (Beirut: Khayats, 1965); Cecil J. Edmonds, *Kurds, Turks and Arabs: Politics, Travel and Research in North-Eastern Iraq, 1919–*

1925 (London: Oxford University Press, 1957); William Eagleton, *The Kurdish Republic of 1946* (London: Oxford University Press, 1963).

22. David Adamson, *The Kurdish War* (New York: Praeger, 1964); Edgar O'Ballance, *The Kurdish Revolt, 1961–1970* (Hamden: Archon, 1973).

23. Chris Kutschera, *Le Mouvement National Kurde* (Paris: Flammarion, 1979); Jonathan C. Randal, *After Such Knowledge, What Forgiveness? My Encounters with Kurdistan* (New York: Farrar, Straus and Giroux, 1997); Susan Meiselas, *Kurdistan: In the Shadow of History* (Random House / University of Chicago Press, 2005).

24. Hamit Bozarslan, *La Question Kurde* : *Etats et minorités au Moyen-Orient* (Paris: Presses de Sciences Po, 1997); Nelida Fuccaro, *The Other Kurds: Yazidis in Colonial Iraq* (London and New York: I. B. Tauris, 1999); Hans-Lukas Kieser, *Der verspasse Friede. Mission, Ethnie und Stadt in den Ostprovinzen det Türkei, 1839–1938* (Zurich: Chronos, 2000); Robert Olson, *The Emergence of Kurdish Nationalism and the Sheikh Said Rebellion, 1880–1915* (Austin: University of Texas Press, 1989).

25. Martin van Bruinessen, *Agha, Shaikh and State: On the Social and Political Organization of Kurdistan* (Utrecht: University of Utrecht, 1978).

26. David McDowall, *A Modern History of the Kurds* (London: I. B. Tauris, 1996).

27. Hamit Bozarslan, "Research Guide: Kurdish Studies," *Middle East Review of International Affairs* 4:2 (2000) https://groups.google.com/forum/#!topic/cl.nahost.kurdistan/JTFgiPaMPpg

28. François Hartog, "Le témoin et l'historien," *Gradhiva* 27 (2000) pp. 1-14.

29. Zinar Silopi (Kadri Cemil Pasha), *Doza Kurdistan:* Kürt Milletinin 60 Yillik Esaretten Kurtulush Savashi Hatiralari (Ankara: Öz-Ge, 1991); Ekrem Cemil Pasha, *Muhtasar Hayatim* (Brussels: Institut kurde de Bruxelles, 1991); Nuri Dersimi, *Dersim ve Kürt Milli Mücadelesine: Dair Hatiratim* (Ankara: Öz-Ge, 1992); Nuri Dersimi, *Kürdistan tarihinde Dersim* (Cologne: Mezopotamien Verlag, 1999).

30. Musa Anter, *Hatiralarim* (Istanbul: Doz Basim, 1990); Naci Kutlay, *Anilarim* (Istanbul: Avesta, 1998).

31. Kemal Burkay, *Anilar: Belgeler*, Vols 1 and 2 (Stockholm: Roja Nû, 2001, 2009); Nawshirwan Mustafa, *Jian: Be tementirîn rojnamey kurdî 1926–1938* (Sulemani: Zargata, 2002); Nawshirwan Mustafa, *Edeb û Tarixî Kurdî* (Sulemani: Zargata, 2012).

32. http://www.univsul.org/E_D_Direje.aspx?Jimare=251&Besh=12

33. Andrea Fischer-Tahir, "Searching for Sense: The Concept of Genocide as Part of Knowledge Production in Iraqi Kurdistan," in Jordi Tejel, Peter Sluglett, Riccardo Bocco, and Hamit Bozarslan (eds), *Writing the Modern History of Iraq: Historiographical and Political Challenges* (Singapore: World Scientific, 2012), pp. 227-43.

34. Respectively, http://www.bitlisname.com/Haber/konferans_1914_bitlis_ayaklan-masi/306/; http://www.hrantdink.org/?Detail=584&Activities=3&Lang=en

35. http://www.ismailbesikcivakfi.org/default.asp?sayfa=haber&id=98#. VG8y-DvMGUc

36. Sabri Atesh, *The Ottoman-Iranian Borderlands: Making a Boundary, 1843–1914* (Cambridge: Cambridge University Press, 2013); Hakan Ozoglu, *Kurdish Notables and the Ottoman State: Evolving identities, competing loyalties, and shifting boundaries* (Albany, NY: SUNY, 2004).

37. Ugur Ü. Üngör, *Young Turk Social Engineering: Mass Violence and the Nation State in Eastern Turkey, 1913–1950*, PhD dissertation, Amsterdam, 2009; Yektan Türkyilmaz, *Rethinking Genocide: Violence and Victimhood in Eastern Anatolia, 1913–1915*, PhD dissertation, Duke University, NC, 2011; Seda Altug, *Sectarianism in the Syrian Jazira: Community, Land and Violence in the Memories of World War I and the French Mandate, 1915–1939*, PhD dissertation, Utrecht University, 2011.

38. Janet Klein, *The Margins of Empire: Kurdish Militias in the Ottoman Tribal Zone* (Palo Alto, CA: Stanford University Press, 2011); Joost Jongerden and Jelle Verheij (eds), *Social Relations in Ottoman Diyarbekir, 1870–1915* (Leiden: Brill, 2012); Nilay Özok-Gündogan, "Ruling the Periphery, Governing the Land: The Making of the Modern Ottoman State in Kurdistan, 1840–1970," *Comparative Studies of South Asia, Africa and the Middle East* 34:1 (2014) pp. 160-75.

39. Jordi Tejel, "Repenser les nationalismes minoritaires: le nationalisme kurde en Irak et en Syrie durant la période des mandats, entre tradition et modernité," *A contrario* 11 (2009) pp. 151-73; Jordi Tejel, "Les territoires de marge de la Syrie mandataire: le mouvement autonomiste de la Haute Jazîra, paradoxes et ambiguïtés d'une intégration nationale inachevée (1936–1939)," *Revue des Mondes Musulmans et de la Méditerranée* 126 (2009) pp. 205-22.

40. Seda Altug and Benjamin T. White, "Frontières et pouvoir d'Etat: La frontière turco-syrienne dans les années 1920 et 1930," *Vingtième siècle* 3:103 (2009) pp. 91-104; Nelida Fuccaro, "Ethnicity and the City: the Kurdish Quarter of Damascus between Ottoman and French Rule, c.1724–1946," *Urban History* 30:2 (2003) pp. 206-24; Benjamin T. White, "The Kurds of Damascus in the 1930s: Development of a Politics of Ethnicity,» *Middle Eastern Studies* 46:6 (2010) pp. 901-17.

41. Fuccaro, "Ethnicity and the City"; Jordi Tejel, "Urban Mobilization in Iraqi Kurdistan during the British Mandate: Sulaimaniya, 1918-1930," *Middle Eastern Studies* 44:4 (2008) p. 537-52.

42. Marc Bloch, *Apologie pour l'histoire ou métier d'historien* (Paris: Armand Colin, 1949).

43. Barrington Moore, *Social Origins of Dictatorship and Democracy: Lord and Peasant in the Making of Modern World* (Boston, MA: Beacon Press, 1966).

44. Stefan Berger, "Comparative history," in Stefan Berger, Heiko Feldner, and Kevin Passmore (eds), *Writing History* (London: Arnold, 2003) pp. 166-8.

45. Anthony G. Hopkins (ed.), *Globalization in World History* (New York: Norton,

2002); Anthony G. Hopkins, *Global History: Interactions between the Local and the Universal* (New York: Palgrave, 2006).

46. Christopher A. Bayly, *The Birth of the Modern World 1780–1914: Global Connections and Comparisons* (Oxford: Blackwell, 2004).

47. Jennifer Helgren and Colleen A. Vasconcellos (eds), *Girlhood: A Global History* (New Brunswick, NJ: Rutgers University Press, 2010) p. 2.

48. David Fitzgerald and Roger Waldinger, "Transnationalism in question," *American Journal of Sociology* 109:5 (2004) pp. 1177-95.

49. Isabel Hofmeyr, "AHR Conversations: On Transnational History," *American Historical Review* 111:5 (2006) pp. 1444-64.

50. Pierre-Yves Saunier, "Globalisation," in Akira Iriye and Pierre-Yves Saunier (eds), *The Palgrave Dictionary of Transnational History* (New York: Palgrave, 2009) p. 462.

51. Gareth Austin, "Commercial Agriculture and the Ending of Slave-trading and Slavery in West Africa, 1787–c.1930," in Robin Law, Suzanne Schwarz, and Silke Strickrodt (eds), *Commercial Agriculture, the Slave Trade and Slavery in Atlantic Africa* (Oxford: James Currey, 2013) pp. 243-65; Gopalan Balachandran, *Globalizing Labour? Indian Seafarers and World Shipping, c. 1870–1950* (Delhi and Oxford: Oxford University Press, 2012).

52. Samuel Moyn and Andrew Sartori (eds), *Global Intellectual History* (New York: Columbia University Press, 2013).

53. Daniel Laqua, "Transnational intellectual cooperation, the League of Nations, and the problem of order," *Journal of Global History* 6:2 (2011) pp. 223-47.

54. Christina Norwig, "A First European Generation? The Myth of Youth and European Integration in the Fifties," *Diplomatic History* 38:2 (2014) pp. 251-60; Sean Guillory, "Culture Clash in the Socialist Paradise: Soviet Patronage and African Students' Urbanity in the Soviet Union, 1960–1965," *Diplomatic History* 28:2 (2014) pp. 271-81.

55. Vera Eccarius-Kelly, "Political movements and leverage points: Kurdish activism in the European diaspora," *Journal of Muslim Minority Affairs* 22:1 (2002) pp. 91-118; Nicole F. Watts, "Institutionalizing Virtual Kurdistan West: Transnational Networks and Ethnic Contention in International Affairs," in Joel S. Migdal, *Boundaries and Belonging. States and Societies in the Struggle to Shape Identities and Local Practices* (Cambridge: Cambridge University Press, 2004) pp. 121-47.

56. There are some small pieces though that can be used as a basis for further research. Omar Sheikhmous, "Kurdish cultural and political activities abroad," Paper presented in Berlin, 17-22 December 1989; Jordi Tejel, "Etudiants émigrés et activisme en Europe: le cas de la KSSE (1958–1975)," in Hamit Bozarslan and Clémence Scalbert-Yücel (eds), *Joyce Blau: l'éternelle chez les Kurdes* (Paris: IKP, 2013) pp. 43-61.

57. Afshin Matin-Asgari, *Iranian Student Opposition to the Shah* (Costa Mesa, CA:

Mazda, 2002); Matthew Shannon, "'Contacts with the opposition': American foreign relations, the Iranian student movement, and the global sixties," *The Sixties* 4:1 (2011) pp. 1-29.

58. University of Exeter and the Public Library in Lausanne hold many records concerning the KSSE.

59. Raphaël Dallaire, *Fief montagnard, régence humanitaire: L'endiguement des déplacés internes kurdes dans le 'havre de sécurité' du Nord de l'Irak, 1991–1992*, Global Migration Research Paper 10 (2015).

60. Leyla Neyzi, "Oral History and Memory Studies in Turkey," in Celia Kerslake, Kerem Öktem, and Philip Robins (eds), *Turkey's Engagement with Modernity: Conflict and Change in the Twentieth Century* (New York: Palgrave Macmillan, 2010) pp. 443-59.

61. Atesh, *The Ottoman-Iranian Borderlands*; Sabri Atesh, "In the Name of the Caliph and the Nation: The Sheikh Ubeidulllah Rebellion of 1880–1881," *Iranian Studies* 47:5 (2014) pp. 735-98.

62. Orit Bashkin, *The Other Iraq: Pluralism, Intellectuals and Culture in Hashemite Iraq, 1921–1958* (Palo Alto, CA: Stanford University Press, 2009); idem, *New Babylonians: A History of Jews in Modern Iraq* (Palo Alto, CA: Stanford University Press, 2012).

63. http://www.aborne.org/the-network.html

64. http://kurdishstudiesnetwork.net/

2. SOCIAL MOVEMENT THEORY AND POLITICAL MOBILIZATION IN KURDISTAN

1. Ralph H. Turner and Lewis M. Killian, *Collective Behavior* (Englewood Cliffs, NJ: Prentice Hall, 1987) p. 223.

2. For instance, see Wil Pansters, "Social Movements and Discourse: The Case of the University Reform Movement in 1961 in Puebla, Mexico", *Bulletin of Latin American Research* 9:1 (1990), pp. 79-101.

3. Mario Diani and Doug McAdam (eds), *Social Movements and Networks: Relational Approaches to Collective Action* (Oxford: Oxford University Press, 2003).

4. Andrew G. Walder, "Political Sociology and Social Movements", *Annual Review of Sociology* 35 (2009), pp.393-412.

5. John D. McCarthy and Mayer N. Zald, "Resource Mobilization and Social Movements: A Partial Theory", *American Journal of Sociology* 82:6 (1977), pp. 1212-41.

6. Robert D. Benford and David A. Snow, "Framing Processes and Social Movements: An Overview and Assessment", *Annual Review of Sociology* 26 (2000), pp. 611-39.

7. Doug McAdam, John D. McCarthy, and Mayer N. Zald (eds), *Comparative Perspectives*

on Social Movements: Political Opportunities, Mobilizing Structures, and Cultural Framings (New York: Cambridge University Press, 1996).

8. Steven M. Buechler, "New Social Movement Theories," *Sociological Quarterly* 36:3 (1995), pp. 441-64.

9. For a good example of this, see Susan Eckstein (ed.), *Power and Popular Protest: Latin American Social Movements* (Berkeley, CA: University of California Press, 1989), and particularly ch. 4 by Timothy Wickham-Crowley, "Winners, Losers, and Also-Rans: Toward a Comparative Sociology of Latin American Guerrilla Movements."

10. For a good recent overview of the current field, see Donatella Della Porta and Mario Diani (eds), *The Oxford Handbook of Social Movements* (Oxford: Oxford University Press, 2015).

11. David Romano, *The Kurdish Nationalist Movement: Opportunity, Mobilization and Identity* (Cambridge: Cambridge University Press, 2006). The book was based on a doctoral dissertation of the same name submitted to the University of Toronto in 2002. In recognition of the fact that a number of different and often competing versions of Kurdish nationalism or politicized Kurdish ethnicity existed and continue to co-exist and compete in the Middle East, the title of the work should probably have been *The Kurdish Nationalist Movements* rather than ... *Movement*.

12. Theda Skocpol, *States and Social Revolutions* (London: Cambridge University Press, 1979).

13. Romano, *The Kurdish Nationalist Movement*, pp. 61-2.

14. Ibid., pp. 69–70. The book's rational choice argument regarding the PKK's rise relied heavily on the logic of Popkin's analysis of the Communist rise in Vietnam, as presented in Michael Taylor, *Rationality and Revolution* (New York: Cambridge University Press, 1988).

15. Romano, *The Kurdish Nationalist Movement*, ch. 3. The Turkish state's suppression of other Kurdish and leftist movements and Syria's provision of sanctuary to PKK militants also, of course, played a role.

16. Especially because the possibilities for upward advancement in Turkey were good for Kurds who assimilated to Turkish culture and did not make an issue of their distinctive Kurdishness, identities and goals of the Kurdish movements in Turkey need explaining.

17. These were taken from McAdam, McCarthy, and Zald (eds), *Comparative Perspectives on Social Movements*.

18. Romano, *The Kurdish Nationalist Movement*, pp. 99-100.

19. Ibid., p. 161.

20. Ibid., p.176-8. In this excerpt I cite Crawford Young, "Patterns of Social Conflict: State, Class and Ethnicity", *Daedalus* 111:2 (Spring 1982) p. 91; Bert Klandermans, Hanspeter Kriesi, and Sidney Tarrow (eds), "From Structure to Action: Comparing social movement research across cultures", *International Social Movement Research*

(London: Jai Press, 1988) pp. 4, 361; and Kate Nash, *Contemporary Political Sociology: Globalization, Politics, and Power* (Oxford: Blackwell Publishers, 2000) p. 139.

21. Romano, *The Kurdish Nationalist Movement*, ch. 6 and 7.

22. In the case of the PKK, the need to "remake identities" was taken so seriously that the movement spoke and published about creating "new men and women" fit for the post-revolutionary society that would emerge.

23. Not all of these studies relied upon or were even necessarily aware of 2006's aforementioned *The Kurdish Nationalist Movement* on social movement theories and the Kurds, of course. Early ones in particular, such as Azad Gündoğan's MA thesis, came to the same conclusion (of applying social movement theories to the Kurds) in much the same way: by looking at developments in social movement theories and simply wondering how this might help shed light on other topics to which the theories had yet to be applied.

24. David Romano, *Kürt Dirilişi: Olanak, Mobilizasyon ve Kimlik* (Istanbul: Vate, 2010).

25. For example, Nicole Watts, *Activists in Office: Kurdish Politics and Protest in Turkey* (Seattle: University of Washington Press, 2010) pp. 5, 180; and Cengiz Gunes, *The Kurdish National Movement in Turkey: From Protest to Resistance* (New York: Routledge, 2012) pp. 16-19.

26. Jordi Tejel, *Syria's Kurds: History, Politics and Society* (New York: Routledge, 2009) p. 13. The final reference is to Nelida Fuccaro, "Minorities and Ethnic Mobilisation: The Kurds in Northern Iraq and Syria", in N. Meouchy and P. Sluggett (eds), *The British and French Mandates in Comparative Perspectives (Leiden:* Brill, 2004) pp. 579-95.

27. Tejel, *Syria's Kurds*, p. 89.

28. Tejel, *Syria's Kurds*.

29. Watts, *Activists in Office*, p. 4.

30. Watts, p. 9 cites Doug McAdam, Sidney Tarrow, and Charles Tilly, *Dynamics of Contention* (Cambridge: Cambridge University Press, 2001), p. 8.

31. Gunes, *The Kurdish National Movement in Turkey: From Protest to Resistance* (New York: Routledge, 2012), p. 4.

32. Gunes cites Stuart Hall, "Introduction: Who Needs 'Identity'?" in Stuart Hall and Paul du Gray (eds), *Questions of Cultural Identity* (London: Sage Publications, 1996), p. 3 for more on this concept.

33. Gunes, *The Kurdish National Movement in Turkey*, p. 5.

34. Aysegül Aydin and Cem Emrence, *Zones of Rebellion: Kurdish Insurgents and the Turkish State* (New York: Cornell University Press, 2015), inside front book jacket.

35. Ibid., p. 129.

36. Ibid., p. 130.

37. The movement bears no relation to the more well-known Lebanese Shia Hezbullah group.

38. In 2015 the author had a chance to read a draft manuscript of Gürbüz's book.

39. Properly fitting the pieces together in this case must mean more than an additive approach to various social movement theory insights on the Kurds, however. Rather, the pieces need to be seen as mutually constitutive of each other and forming a whole (or system) greater than the sum of its parts. In this sense, there should be room for more "macro-level" social movement theory work that seeks to investigate how various factors at different levels of analysis interrelate and affect each other.

3. RELIGION AMONG THE KURDS

1. For a recent collection of papers on these various groups, including Christian ones, see Khanna Omarkhali (ed.), *Religious Minorities in Kurdistan* (Berlin: De Gruyter, 2014). On the Yazidis, see e.g. Nelida Fuccaro, *The Other Kurds: Yazidis in Colonial Iraq* (London: I. B. Tauris, 1999); Christine Allison, *The Yezidi Oral Tradition in Iraqi Kurdistan* (London: Curzon, 2001); Philip Kreyenbroek, *Yezidism: Its Background, Observances, and Textual Tradition* (Lewiston, NY: Edwin Mellen, 1995); Birgül Açıkyıldız, *The Yezidis* (London: I. B. Tauris, 2010). On the Ahl-e Haqq, next to the classical studies by Minorsky, see e.g. Nuri Yasin al-Hirzani, *al-kake'iyye: Dirasa anthrubulujiyya li'l-haya al-'ijtima'iyya* (Erbil, 2007). On the (Kurdish) Alevis, see for example the papers collected in Paul White and Joost Jongerden (eds), *Turkey's Alevi Enigma: A Comprehensive Overview* (Leiden: Brill, 2003). On the Shabak, see Amal Vinogradov, "Ethnicity, cultural discontinuity, and power brokers in Northern Iraq: The case of the Shabak," *American Ethnologist* 1 (1974) pp. 207-18; Michiel Leezenberg, "Between Assimilation and Deportation: History of the Shabak and the Kakais in Northern Iraq," in B. Kellner-Heinkele and K. Kehl-Bodrogi (eds), *Syncretistic Religious Communities in the Near East* (Leiden: Brill, 1997).

2. For a notable exception, see for example Martin van Bruinessen and Joyce Blau (eds), "Islam des Kurdes," *Les annales de l'autre Islam* 5 (Paris: INALCO, 1998). See also the papers collected in Van Bruinessen's *Mullas, Sufis, and Heretics: The Role of Religion in Kurdish Society* (Istanbul: ISIS Press, 2000).

3. Thus, I will also avoid discussion of how, especially in more secular nationalist circles, the Yezidi faith has come to be construed as a branch or offshoot of Zoroastrianism, and as such the Kurds' original, pre-Islamic religion.

4. I have described his process of vernacularization in more detail in "Elî Teremaxî and the vernacularisation of madrasa learning in Kurdistan," *Iranian Studies* 47:5, pp. 713-33. See also Zeynelabidin Zinar, *Xwendina medresê* (Stockholm, 1993).

5. I. Weismann and F. Zachs (eds), "Foreword," *Ottoman Reform and Muslim Regeneration: Studies in Honor of Butrus Abu-Manneh* (London: I. B. Tauris, 2005) p. 10. Cf. e.g. Albert Hourani, "Sufism and Modern Islam: Mawlana Khalid and the Naqshbandi order," in his *The Emergence of the Modern Middle East* (London: Palgrave Macmillan, 1981) pp. 75-89; Butrus Abu-Manneh, *Studies on Islam and the Ottoman Empire in the 19th century (1826–1876)* (Istanbul: Isis Press, 2001).

6. Martin van Bruinessen, *Agha, Shaikh, and State: The Social and Political Structures of Kurdistan* (London: Zed Books, 1992) esp. pp. 224-34. In fairness, it should be noted that van Bruinessen also mentions the Khalidiyya Naqshbandi's distinct and decentralized organizational structure as a prime cause of their rapid expansion.

7. Yitzak Nakash, *The Shi'ites of Iraq* (Princeton, NJ: Princeton University Press, 1994) esp. pp. 25-48.

8. Butrus Abu-Manneh, "The Naqshbandiyya-Mujaddidiyya in the Ottoman lands in the early 19th century," *Die Welt des Islams* XXII (1982) pp. 1-36.

9. Abu-Manneh, "The Naqshbandiyya-Mujaddidiyya in the Ottoman lands," pp. 34-5.

10. The *Ehmedî* has been reprinted regularly, and is still available in most bookstores in Iraqi and Iranian Kurdistan. The text of the *Eqîdetname*, based on an 1877 manuscript, was published by Muhammad Mala Karim in 1981 as *Aqîday kurdiy Mawlânâ Khâlidî Naqshbandi* (*Govârî korî zanyârî 'irâq-dastay kurde* 8: 199-222); this edition was reprinted in Kemal Re'ûf Muhammad, *Eqîdey 'imân – 'eqîdey kurdî* (Erbil, 2004).

11. Cf. my "Between local rivalries and transnational networks: Mawlana Khalid as a linguistic pioneer," paper presented at the international conference on Mawlânâ Khalid Naqshbandi, Sulaimaniya, 2009.

12. Serif Mardin, "The Nakshibendi order of Turkey," in M. Marty and S. Appleby (eds), *Fundamentalisms and the State* (Chicago: Chicago University Press, 1993) p. 205; quoted in Hakan Yavuz, *Islamic Political Identity in Turkey* (Oxford: Oxford University Press, 2003), pp. 138, 298.

13. Van Bruinessen, *Agha, Shaikh, and State*, p. 234.

14. On the Qadiris in Kurdistan, see especially Martin van Bruinessen, "The Qadiriyya and the lineages of Qadiri shaykhs in Kurdistan," *Journal of Sufi Studies* 1 (1999); cf. van Bruinessen, *Agha, Shaikh, and State*, ch. 4, esp. pp. 216-40.

15. In contemporary Turkey, a recent version of this story is available in several different languages; in English it is *Confessions of a British Spy* (Hakikat kitabevi, n.d.), http://www.hakikatkitabevi.net/book.php?bookCode=018, accessed 7 February 2015.

16. Clandestinely, however, Kurdish-language *madrasa* education continued for decades, even if on a much smaller scale; cf. Leezenberg, "Elî Teremaxî and the Vernacularization of Medrese Learning in Kurdistan," *Iranian Studies* 47:5 (3 September 2014), pp. 713-33.

17. Yavuz, *Islamic Political Identity in Turkey*, ch. 7.

18. Rohat Alakom, "Said Nursi entre l'identité kurde et l'identité musulmane," *Les annales de l'autre Islam* 5 (1998), pp. 317-31.

19. Said Nursî, *Divan-ı harbi örfi* (Istanbul: Tenvir Nesriyat, 1992) pp. 59-61, quoted in Alakom, "Said Nursi," pp. 321-3. Alakom also notes how in later editions of Nursî's work the references to Kurdistan, Kurds, Kurdish identity, and Kurdish national awakening

have tacitly been changed to more neutral terms like "eastern Anatolia" and "citizens," or even omitted altogether.

20. See Yavuz, *Islamic Political Identity in Turkey*, in particular ch. 6.

21. Abdurrahim Alkis, speaking at the Nûbihar symposium "Ziman û dîn û nasname," Diyarbakır, September 2013.

22. On Kaftaro, see Annabelle Böttcher, *Syrische Religionspolitik unter Assad* (Freiburg im Breisgau: Arnold-Bergsträsser-Institut, 1998); Leif Stenberg, "Préserver le charisma: Les consequences de la mort d'Ahmad Kaftaro sur la mosquée-complexe Abu al-Nur," *Maghreb-Mashrek* 198:4 (2008), pp. 65-73. On al-Butî, see Andreas Christmann, "Islamic scholar and religious leader: A portrait of Shaykh Muhammad Sa'îd Ramadân al-Bûtî," *Islam and Christian–Muslim Relations* 9 (1998) pp. 149-69; the appendix to this article reproduces a debate between al-Buti and a young salafist from *al-lâmadhhabiyya*. See also al-Butî's own memoirs of his father, *Hadha Wâlidi* (Damascus, 1995), Turkish translation *Babam Molla Ramazan al-Bûtî* (Istanbul, 2007).

23. On the Afghan jihad and its links to the al-Azhar network, the Muslim Brotherhood, and the Jamaat-i Islami, see Olivier Roy, *Islam and Resistance in Afghanistan* (Cambridge: Cambridge University Press, 1989); on the Salafi-Jihadi "movement" (which was never unified or centrally led), see in particular Gilles Kepel, *Jihad: Expansion et déclin de l'islamisme* (Paris: Gallimard, 2000).

24. There is as yet no fully-fledged academic study on the background and activities of the Kurdish Hizbullah, only a number of journalistic sources; but see Gilles Dorronsoro, *La nébuleuse Hizbullah* (Istanbul, 2004). On KH's re-emergence in the early twenty-first century, see Mustafa Gürbüz, "Revitalization of Kurdish Islamic Sphere and Revival of Hizbullah in Turkey," in F. Bilgin and A. Sarıhan (eds), *Understanding Turkey's Kurdish Question* (London: Lexington Books, 2013), pp. 167-78.

25. Fehim Tastekin, "Could an alternative Kurdish party succeed in Turkey?" *Al-Monitor*, 27 June 2016, http://www.al-monitor.com/pulse/originals/2016/06/turkey-kurds-kurdish-parties-splitting-hdp-hudapar.html, accessed 30 October 2016.

26. "How Cizre became a combat zone," *Al-Monitor*, 15 January 2015, http://www.al-monitor.com/pulse/security/2015/01/turkey-syria-kurds-kobane-cizre.html#, accessed 7 February 2015.

27. There is little information on IS activities inside Turkey, and even less that is reliable. One CHP representative claimed that four quarters in Gaziantep were in IS hands: "CHP'li vekil: Gaziantep'te 4 mahalle IŞİD'in elinde," *BirGün*, 21 August 2016, http://www.birgun.net/haber-detay/chp-li-vekil-gaziantep-te-4-mahalle-isid-in-elinde-125079.html, accessed 3 November 2016. For an English-language overview, see Aaron Stein, "The Islamic State in Turkey: A Deep Dive into a Dark Place," *War on the Rocks*, 6 April 2016, https://warontherocks.com/2016/04/the-islamic-state-in-turkey-a-deep-dive-into-a-dark-place/, accessed 3 November 2016.

28. Interview, London, June 2000. On IMIK, see my "Political Islam among the Kurds," in

F. Abdul-Jabar and H. Dawod (eds), *The Kurds: Nationalism and Politics* (London: Saqi Books, 2006) pp. 203-27, esp. pp. 216-23.

29. Krekar's memoirs appeared in Norwegian as *Med egne ord* (Oslo: Aschehoug, 2000).

30. Interviews with Ali Bapir, May 2009, May 2011. For Komalî's perspective on the 1980s "Islamic revolt" in Iraqi Kurdistan, see for example Sherîf Werzêr and Muhammad Zerzî (eds), *Jewleyek le qewlayî khâkî nîshtîmanda* (Sulaimaniya, 2009).

31. Olivier Roy, *The Failure of Political Islam* (Cambridge, MA: Harvard University Press, 1994); *Globalized Islam: The Search for a New Ummah* (London: Hurst & Co., 2004). A similar analysis of contemporary global Islam as driven by ethics rather than politics can be found in Faisal Devji, *Landscapes of the Jihad* (London: Hurst & Co., 2005). For a recent overview of the different forms of Salafism, see the papers collected in R. Meijer (ed.), *Global Salafism* (London: Hurst & Co., 2009).

32. Roy's attempt at dissolving all "post-Islamist" religiosity into purely political and "nihilist" motives appears to proceed from an a priori assumption that politics is essentially secular, and that conversely all religions are in essence apolitical. Considerations of space preclude a fuller discussion of these points, however.

33. http://icsr.info/2015/01/foreign-fighter-total-syriairaq-now-exceeds-20000-surpasses-afghanistan-conflict-1980s/, accessed 7 February 2015. One should be cautious about these figures, of course, many of which are no more than rough estimates based on sources of varying reliability. Moreover, not all foreigners are actively involved in fighting; particularly the higher educated ones may also serve as medical doctors, engineers, judges, and of course publicity workers using various digital media; there are indications that other foreigners, being unfamiliar with either language, terrain, or military tactics, are simply used as cannon fodder in the guise of suicide bombers.

34. Hugh Thomas, *The Spanish Civil War*, 4th edn (Harmondsworth: Penguin, 2001), p. 941.

35. An exception may be the Naqshbandi Army, allegedly led by Ba'athist and former Iraqi Vice President Izzat al-Duri, which is claimed to incorporate members of Arab, Kurdish, and Turkomen tribes. Reportedly, this militia was formed in 2006, in order to resist the American occupation and to protect Naqshbandis from the actions of al-Qaeda in Iraq; but it was claimed to have joined with IS in the summer of 2014 for the conquest of Mosul. This alliance, however, seems more tactically than ideologically driven. Cf. http://web.stanford.edu/group/mappingmilitants/cgi-bin/groups/view/75, accessed 7 February 2015.

36. On this topic, cf. my "Iraq, IS and the Kurds: Redefining political, religious, and sexual boundaries," keynote lecture, ACMES convention, University of Amsterdam, January 2015.

4. POLITICS OF MEMORY

1.   Ellen L. Fleischmann, "Selective Memory, Gender and Nationalism: Palestinian Women Leaders of the Mandate Period," *History Workshop Journal* 47 (Spring 1999) pp. 141-58.

2.   Anthony Smith, "Nations and Their Pasts," *Nations and Nationalism* 2:3 (1996), p. 359.

3.   Ibid., p. 359.

4.   Ibid., p. 361.

5.   Ibid.

6.   Anthony Smith, "Gastronomy or Geology," *Nations and Nationalism* 1:1 (1995) p. 16.

7.   Anne Galloway, "Collective remembering and the importance of forgetting: a critical design challenge," at http://purselipsquarejaw.org/papers/galloway_chi2006.pdf, last accessed 8 July 2014.

8.   Şerefhan Bitlisi, *Şerefname*, trans. M. E. Bozarslan (Istanbul: Hasat, 1990).

9.   Ferdowsi, *Shahnameh*, trans. Dick Davis (New York: Penguin, 2006).

10. A short book is devoted to the story by Shirzad Alkadhi, *The Legend of Kawa* (Pittsburg: RoseDog Books, 2011).

11. Kurdiye Bitlisi, "Dehak Efsanesi," *Jin* 1 (November 1918) pp. 6-9. At the end of the article, the date is given as 25 October 1918.

12. Ibid., p. 9.

13. Kurdiye Bitlisi, "Kürtler Münasebetiyle," *Jin* 3 (20 Teşrin-i Sani 1334) p. 5.

14. Martin van Bruinessen, *Agha, Shaikh, and State: The Social and Political Structures of Kurdistan* (London: Zed Books, 1992) p. 267.

15. Amir Hassanpour, *Nationalism and Language in Kurdistan 1918-1985* (San Francisco, CA: Mellon Research University Press, 1992) p. 53.

16. Ahmed-i Hani, *Mem u Zin*, trans. M. E. Bozarslan (Istanbul: Koral, 1975), p. 56.

17. Although Michael Chyet does not comment on the nationalist nature of the epic, he points out that this aspect only gained traction in the last part of the twentieth century. See "'And a Thornbush Sprang up Between Them': Studies on 'Mem u Zin, a Kurdish Romance,'" PhD dissertation (University of California, Berkeley, 1991) p. 62.

18. Süleymaniyeli Tevfik, "'Jin' Mecmuası Vasıtasıyle Kurdiye Bitlisi Kardeşime," *Jin* 28 (Teşrin-i Sani 1334) p. 4.

19. Sherko Kirmanj, "Kurdish History Textbooks: Building a Nation-State within a Nation-State," *Middle East Journal* 68:3 (Summer 2014) pp. 367-84, esp. p. 372.

20. Ibid., p. 373.

21. Abdullah Öcalan, *Prison Writings: The PKK and the Kurdish Question in the 21st Century*, trans. and ed. by Klaus Happel (New York: Transmedia Publishing, 2011) pp. xii-xiii.

22. Abdullah Öcalan, *Kürdistan Devriminin Yolu (Manifesto)* (Cologne: Waşanen Serxwebun, 24, 1978) pp. 30-32.

23. Cengiz Güneş, "Explaining the PKK's Mobilization of the Kurds in Turkey: Hegemony, Myth and Violence," *Ethnopolitics* 12:3 (October 2012) pp. 247-67, esp. p. 263.

24. Sherko Kirmanj, "Kurdish Integration in Iraq: The Paradoxes of Nation Formation and Nation Building," in Ofra Bengio (ed.), *Kurdish Awakening: Nation Building in a Fragmented Homeland* (Austin: University of Texas Press, 2014) pp. 87-8.

5. "BEING IN TIME"

1.   Gabriel Martinez-Gros, *Ibn Khaldûn et les sept vies de l'Islam* (Arles: Actes-Sud, 2006) pp. 143-4.

2.   Kenneth Thompson, *Beliefs and Ideology* (London: Open Press, 1986) p. 29.

3.   For the documents, cf. Paul White, *Primitive Rebels or Revolutionary Modernizers? The Kurdish National Movement in Turkey* (London: Zed Books, 2000).

4.   A. Vali (dir.) *Essays on the Origins of Kurdish Nationalism* (Costa Mesa, CA: Mazda, 2003).

5.   Jean Leca, "Nationalisme et universalisme", *Pouvoirs* 57 (1991) pp. 31-42.

6.   Taline Ter Minassian, *Colporteurs du Komintern: l'Union soviétique et les minorités au Moyen-Orient* (Paris: Sciences-Po, 1997).

7.   Cf. for documents, W. Jwadieh, *The Kurdish Nationalist Movement: Its Origins and Development* (Syracuse, NY: Syracuse University Press, 1960) p. 169.

8.   Cf. Joost Jongerden and Jelle Velheij (eds), *Social Relations in Ottoman Diyarbékir, 1870–1915* (Leiden and Boston: Brill, 2012).

9.   Quoted in Mehmet Bayrak, *Kürtler ve Ulusal Demokratik Mücadeleleri. Gizli Belgeler, Arastirmlar, Notlar* (Ankara: Özge Yayinlari, 1993) p. 110.

10. Cf. Hamit Bozarslan, *Entre le nationalisme et la 'umma : l'islam kurde au tournant du siècle* (Amsterdam: MERA Occasional Papers, 1992).

11. Cf. for the acts, Khoybun, *Les massacres des Kurdes en Turquie* (Cairo: Khoybun, 1927) p. 35.

12. For Azadi, cf. Martin van Bruinessen, *Agha, Sheikh and State, The Social and Political Structures of Kurdistan* (London: Zed Books, 1992); and Robert Olson, *The Emergence of Kurdish Nationalism and the Sheikh Said Rebellion (1880–1925)* (Austin, TX: University of Texas Press, 1989).

13. Cf. H. H. Serdî, *Görüş ve Anılarım, 1907–1985* (Istanbul: Med Yayınları, 1985).

14. Cf. Jordi Tejel Gorgas, «La Ligue nationale kurde Khoybun. Mythes et réalités de la première organisation nationaliste kurde", *Etudes Kurdes* (special edition, 2007).

15. Cf. Khoybun, *Les massacres des Kurdes en Turquie*, p. 9.

16. Cf. Hamit Bozarslan, "Correspondance entre le général Rondot et les frères Bederkhanî," *Etudes kurdes* 3 (2001) pp. 73-4.

17. Cf. William Eagleton, *The Kurdish Republic of Mahabad* (Oxford: Oxford University Press, 1946); Abbas Vali, *The Kurds and the State in Modern Iran: The Making of Kurdish Identity* (London: I. B. Tauris, 2011).

18. Abdurrahman Ghasemlou, *Kurdistan and the Kurds* (Prague: Czechoslovak Academy of Sciences, 1965).

19. For an interesting account of the left-wing movements in Iranian Kurdistan, see Selahettin Ali Arik, *Dr. Sivan. Sait Elçi-Süleyman Muini ve Kürt Trajedesi (1960–1975)* (Istanbul: Peri Yayınları, 2011) p. 336-56.

20. Cf. K. Cemil Paşa, *Doza Kurdistan. Kürt Milletinin 60 Yıllık Esaretten Kurtuluş Savaşı Hatıraları* (Ankara: öz-Ge, 1991) p. 181.

21. I. Ch. Vanly, *Le Kurdistan irakien entité nationale: Etude de la Révolution de 1961* (Neuchatel: Editions de la Baconnière, 1970).

22. Cf. Metin Yüksel, "I Cry Out so that You Wake Up: Cegerxwin's Poetics and Politics of Awakening", *Middle Eastern Studies* 4:50 (2013) pp. 1-18.

23. Cf. Hamit Bozarslan, "49'ların Anıları Üzerine Tarihsel-Sosyolojik Okuma Notları ve Bazı Hipotezler", *Tarih ve Toplum* 16 (2013) pp. 127-43.

24. Cf. Hamit Bozarslan, "Türkiye'de Kürt Sol Hareketi", *Modern Türkiye'de Siyasi Düşünce*, vol. 8 (Istanbul: Iletisim, 2007) pp. 1167-1207; and "Between integration, autonomization and radicalization: Hamit Bozarslan on the Kurdish Movement and the Turkish Left", interview with Marlies Casier and Olivier Grojean, *European Journal of Turkish Studies* 14 (2013, internet edition).

25. Cf. Komal Yayınları, *DDKO Dâvâ Dosyası*, vol. 1 (Ankara: Komal Yayınları, 1975) pp. 489-630.

26. Ali Arık, *Dr. Sivan*, p. 98.

27. Franz Fanon, *Pour la révolution africaine: Ecrits politiques* (Paris: La Découverte, 2006) p. 111.

28. Cf. for a selection of documents, E. A. Türkmen and A. Özmen (eds), *Kürdistan Sosyalist Solu Kitabi. 60'lardan 2000'lere Seçme Metinler* (Ankara: Dipnot, 2014).

29. For this concept, cf. Clifford Geertz, "Ideology as a Cultural System", in David Apter (ed.), *Ideology and Discontent* (New York: Free Press, 1964) p. 65; and Maxime Rodinson, *Marxisme et le monde musulman* (Paris: Seuil, 1972) p. 311.

30. Cf. KDP, *Irak Kürdistan Demokratik Partisi Yeni Stratejisi* (İstanbul: Üçüncü Dünya Yayınları, 1978); KDP, *The Road of the Kurdish Liberation Movement* (London: Calvert North Star Press, 1977).

31. Hamit Bozarslan, "Revisiting the Middle East's 1979", *Economy and Society* 41:4 (2012) pp. 558-67.

32. Bernard Rougier, *Everyday Jihad: The Rise of Militant Islam among the Palestinians in Lebanon* (Cambridge, MA: Harvard University Press, 2009).

33. Cf. Hamit Bozarslan, "The Kurds and Middle Eastern 'state of violence', 1980s and 2010s", *Kurdish Studies* 2 (2014) pp. 4-13.

34. Cf. Nicole Watts, *Activists in Office: Kurdish Ethnic Politics, Political Resources, and Repression in Turkey* (Seattle, WA: Washington University Press, 2009).

35. Anthony Giddens, *The Nation-State and Violence* (Berkeley and Los Angeles, CA: University of California Press, 1987) pp. 46-7.

6. SEPARATED BUT CONNECTED

1. For the dual role of tribes and tribalism in Kurdish society, see Eli Amarilyo, "The dual relationship between Kurdish tribalism and nationalism", in Ofra Bengio (ed.), *Kurdish Awakening: Nation Building in a Fragmented Homeland* (Austin, TX: Texas University Press, 2014) pp. 63-79.

2. According to Ferhad Pirbal, a famous Kurdish artist and historian, it was the Seljuk Sultan Sanjar who in 1150 established an autonomous region for the Kurds and called it Kurd Ustani, namely the Kurdish state. *Kurdishglobe*, 13 August 2008, http://www.kurdish-globe.net/displayPrintableArticle.jsp?id=8F45BFF7E739694E09A76D76AB92C3F8

3. See for example Şeref Han, *Şerefname: Kürt Tarihi*, vol. 18 (Istanbul: Yöntem Yayınları, 1975) pp. 14, 209.

4. Hakan Özoğlu, *Kurdish Notables and the Ottoman State* (New York: SUNY, 2004) p. 35.

5. Özoğlu, *Kurdish Notables*, p. 18. It was established on 17 December 1918.

6. In 1927. Mustafa Kemal Atatürk, *Nutuk* (Istanbul: Alfa, 2009) p. 9. As a rule, Turkish sources use the term Kürt and not Kurdistan when mentioning this society. See for example Milliyet, http://blog.milliyet.com.tr/kurt-teali-cemiyeti/Blog/?BlogNo=335981; WowTurkey, http://wowturkey.com/forum/viewtopic.php?t=93708

7. Abbas Vali, *Kurds and the State in Iran: The Making of Kurdish Identity* (London: I. B. Tauris, 2011) pp. 19-20.

8. David McDowall, *A Modern History of the Kurds* (London: I. B. Tauris, 2004) p. 237.

9. Vali, *Kurds and the State*, p. 20.

10. McDowall, *A Modern History of the Kurds*, p. 237. Philips suggests that the party was founded in 1944. David L. Philips, *The Kurdish Spring: A New Map of the Middle East* (New Brunswick, NJ: Transaction Publishers, 2015) p. 88.

11. See for example the celebration held in Sweden in January 2014, http://www.dailymotion.com/video/x1a1ldt_sal-yadi-damezrandni-komari-kurdistan-le-swed-2014-01-18-www-serqela-org_music. In the Kurdistan Region in Iraq (KRI), they commemorate its establishment while stressing the continuity between that experience and their own in Iraq. For Masoud Barzani's 66th anniversary speech, see http://www.daily-motion.com/video/x1a1ldt_sal-yadi-damezrandni-komari-kurdistan-le-swed-2014-01-18-www-serqela-org_music

12. The map appears in http://www.akakurdistan.com/kurds/map/map.html. Özoğlu noted that the Lurs do not seem to consider themselves Kurds, even though Sherefhan does include them within the boundaries of what he described as Kurdistan. Özoğlu, *Kurdish Notables*, p. 42. The KRG's attempt to link with the Lurs was attested to in the celebration of the 66th anniversary of Komari Kurdistan, where Lurs folk dancers participated in the celebration. Personal information.

13. Zimane Kurdi 1 (Xweseriya Demokratik, K. Cizire, no place, no date) p. 141.

14. See for example http://www.xoybun.com/. https://www.youtube.com/watch?v=g1_iZY1Ppg4; Vali, *Kurds and the State*, p. 43; Özlem Belcim Galip, *Imagining Kurdistan: Identity, Culture and Society* (London: I. B. Tauris, 2015) pp. 109-11, 137-42.

15. See Michael Gunter, *Out of Nowhere: The Kurds of Syria in Peace and War* (London: Hurst & Co., 2014) pp. 3, 7.

16. Interestingly, the term South Kurdish Confederation was used by the British in 1918 when they attempted to install a pro-British government, headed by Shaykh Mahmud Barzinji, in parts of Kurdistan. Wadie Jwaideh, *The Kurdish National Movement: Its Origin and Development* (Syracuse, NY: Syracuse University Press, 2006) pp. 160-70.

17. Thus, for example, the Kurdish conference held in July 2013 in Diyarbakir, the central city of that region in Turkey, carried the following title: "North (Bakur) Kurdistan unity and solution conference", *Kurdpress*, 11 July 2013, http://kurdpress.com/En/NSite/FullStory/News/?Id=4803#Title=Diyarbakir conference announces demands from government.

18. *Jiyan* (newspaper, 1926-36), Mustafa Shawqi, *Kurdistan*, year 1, no. 1. I am grateful to Ceng Sagnic for providing me with this source.

19. Haber7.com, quoting Yeni Safak, 23 October 2013, http://www.haber7.com/ortadogu/haber/1087312-barzani-kuzey-iraki-yasakladi, accessed 27 October 2013.

20. Abdullah Öcalan, *The Road Map to Negotiations* (Cologne: International Initiative Edition, 2012) pp. 87-9.

21. *Hurriyet Daily News*, 8 April 2013, http://www.hurriyetdailynews.com/pkk-leader-reiterates-kurdish-confederation-as-stateless-solution-.aspx?pageID=238&nid=44479

22. The leader of the PYD, Salih Muslim, expressed the same ideas in an interview with the author, 9 December 2012.

23. KurdishMedia.com, 15 March 2009, http://www.kurdmedia.com/article.aspx?id=15549

24. The best source for following this constant crisscrossing in the sixteenth century is Şeref Han, *Şerefname: Kürt Tarihi* (Istanbul: Yöntem Yayınları, 1975). See for example the chapter on the Ardalans, pp. 108-12.

25. For example the big Jaf tribe was part Turkish and part Persian. E. B. Soane, *To Mesopotamia and Kurdistan in Disguise* (London: John Murray, 2nd edn 1926) p. 217.

26. Joyce Blau, *Le Problème Kurde* (Brussels: Publications du Centre pour l'Etude des Problèmes du Monde Musulman Contemporain, 1963) p. 29.

27. Soane, *To Mesopotamia and Kurdistan*, pp. 215-20.

28. McDowall, *A Modern History*, p. 216.

29. Ibid., p. 217.

30. Michael Gunter, "Khoybun", in *Historical Dictionary of the Kurds* (Lanham, MD: Scarecrow Press, 2003).

31. McDowall, *A Modern History*, p. 205.

32. Vali, *Kurds and the State*, pp. 78, 169.

33. Gunter, *Out of Nowhere*, p. 16.

34. McDowall, *A Modern History*, p. 408.

35. In summer 2014 the KDPT was allowed to reorganize, but there was a big controversy in Turkey regarding the term Kurdistan in its title. See *Al-Monitor*, 7 July 2014, http://www.al-monitor.com/pulse/iw/originals/2014/07/turkey-daloglu-t-kdp-kurdistan-supreme-court-kardas.html

36. See for example Martin van Bruinessen, "The Kurds in Movement: Migrations, mobilizations, communications and the globalization of the Kurdish question", Working Paper 14, Islamic Area Studies Project, Tokyo, Japan, 1999.

37. According to United Nation sources, the number of refugees reached 226,934 by 2014. Aljazeera, 18 March 2014, http//:www.aljazeera.com/indepth/opinion/2014/03/iraqi-kurds-yesterday-victims-s.201431865247574237-htm/

38. Muhammad Talab Hilal, "Dirasa ʿan muhafazat al-Jazira min al-nawahi al-qawmiyya wal-ijtimaʿiyya wal-siyasiyya", in Jawad Mella, *Al-Siyasa al-Isti ʿmariyya lihizb al-Ba ʾth al-Suri fi Gharb Kurdistan* (London: Western Kurdistan Association Publications, 2004) pp. 98-100.

39. Ibid., pp. 80, 82-3.

40. Ibid., p. 76.

41. Ibid., pp. 79-89.

42. Ibid., pp. 72, 76.

43. Gunter, *Out of Nowhere*, p. 41.

44. Gunter, *Out of Nowhere*, pp. 40-45.

45. Ismet G. Imset, *The PKK: A Report on Separatist Violence in Turkey* (Ankara: Turkish Daily News Publications, 1992) p. 179.

46. Harriet Allsopp, *The Kurds of Syria: Political Parties and Identity in the Middle East* (London: I. B. Tauris, 2014) p. 91.

47. These numbers are mentioned in textbooks as well, e.g. *Babetin Komalayeti*, no. 4 (Turkey, 2013, or Kurdish year, 2713) p. 40.

48. Gülistan Gürbey, "Peaceful settlement through autonomy?" in Gülistan Gürbey and Ferhad Ibrahim (eds), *The Kurdish Conflict in Turkey: Obstacles and Chances for Peace and Democracy* (New York: St Martin's Press, 2000) p. 60.

49. Quoted from a conference on "Remembering the Halabja genocide", GUE GNl, 16 March 2012, https://www.google.co.il/url?url=https://peaceinkurdistancampaign.files.word-press.com/2012/03/summary-of-halabja-conference-in-epoc&rct=j&frm=1&q=&esrc=s&sa=U&ei=aEyqVKmbD9HsaPy8gJAN&ved=0CBoQFjAC&sig2=YBzClqq8J77BIA0ynVgp_Q&usg=AFQjCNE0oA6K56fycEvgNYbJZ8XJrnrWoA

50. Aljazeera, 18 March 2014, http://www.aljazeera.com/indepth/opinion/2014/03/iraqi-kurds-yesterday-victims-s-201431865247574237.htm/

51. For a collection of such songs, see https://www.youtube.com/watch?v=54P6LTQ2fSU; http://www.kurdvid.com/sivan-perwer-helebce-video_31917ab74.html; https://www.youtube.com/watch?v=1mv5BCERBjk

52. Aliza Marcus, *Blood and Belief: The PKK and the Kurdish Fight for Independence* (New York: NYU Press, 2007) p. 2.

53. Jordi Tejel, "Toward a generational rupture within the Kurdish movement in Syria?" in Ofra Bengio (ed.), *Kurdish Awakening: Nation Building in a Fragmented Homeland* (Austin, TX: Texas University Press, 2014) p. 223.

54. *Al-Hayat*, 7 February 2015, http://www.alhayat.com/Articles/7243606; *Nefel*, 16 May 2016, http://www.nefel.com/articles/article_detail.asp?RubricNr=1&ArticleNr=8701

55. *World Bulletin*, 29 December 2014, http://www.worldbulletin.net/haber/151825/barzani-my-plan-is-to-change-the-sykes-picot-agreement

56. *Foxnews*, 18 August 2014, http://www.foxnews.com/world/2014/08/18/expendables-kurdistan-old-soldiers-flock-to-battefront-to-fight-isis/

57. *Ekurd Daily*, 31 October 2014, http://ekurd.net/mismas/articles/misc2014/10/syriakurd1628.htm

58. Rudaw, 28 January 2015, http://rudaw.net/english/opinion/28012015

59. *Ekurd Daily*, 17 March 2015, http://ekurd.net/kurdish-pkk-leader-sets-out-6-conditions-for-laying-down-arms-2015-03-17

60. *Open Democracy*, 27 July 2015, https://www.opendemocracy.net/evren-balta/how-turkish-elections-changed-foreign-policy-of-turkey

61. Quoted in *Mideast Mirror*, 6 September 2016, https://webmail.tau.ac.il/horde/imp/message.php?mailbox=aW1wc2VhcmNoAHdVVkRNanBSb1lSWDE4eUpWY0dFUVlB&uid=142006&thismailbox=SU5CT1g. At the time of writing, the fighting is still ongoing.

62. Rudaw, 22 October 2014, http://rudaw.net/english/kurdistan/221020141

63. *Al-Hayat*, 14 February 2015.

64. At the same time this increased the rivalry between the KRG and the PKK.

65. The KRG offered support for rebuilding Kobanî. Waarmedia, 14 February 2015, http://waarmedia.com/english/krg-to-help-rebuild-kobane/

66. Allsopp, *The Kurds of Syria*, p. 222.

67. McDowall, *A Modern History*, p. 455.

68. For a discussion, see, Osten Wahlbeck, *Kurdish Diasporas: A Comparative Study of Kurdish Refugee Communities* (London: Macmillan Press, 1999). The most important Kurdish diaspora is in Europe (850,000) and the US (*c.*35,000), but there are also other small Kurdish communities in countries such as Russia, Australia, and Israel.

69. A small number of Kurdish male members of the Ottoman aristocracy or political dissidents found their way to the West in the second part of the nineteenth century. Amir Hassanpour, *Nationalism and Language in Kurdistan 1918-1985* (San Francisco, CA: Mellen University Press, 1992) p. 217.

70. Ibid., pp. 171-5.

71. Ibid., pp. 171-5.

72. Mücahit Bilci, "Black Turks, white Turks; on the three requirements of Turkish citizenship", *Insight Turkey* 11:3 (2009) p. 31.

73. Jawad Mella, *Kurdistan and the Kurds: A Divided Homeland and a Nation without State* (London: Western Kurdistan Association Publications, 2005) p. 245.

74. Kurdistan Commentary, 19 April 2009, http://kurdistancommentary.wordpress.com/2009/04/19/the-state-of-kurdish-media/

75. Benedict Anderson, *Imagined Communities: Reflections on the Origin and Spread of Nationalism* (London: Verso, 1991) pp. 26-46.

7. FACT AND FICTION IN MODERN KURDISH NARRATIVE DISCOURSE

1. Ian Watt's ideas about the individualism and the rise of the novel can be seen in his seminal work: *The Rise of the Novel: Studies in Defoe, Richardson and Fielding* (London: Hogarth Press, 1995). Michel Foucault's concept of "the will to knowledge" can be found in most of his works, especially in *The History of Sexuality, Vol. I: An Introduction*, trans. Robert Hurley (New York: Vintage Books, 1990).

2. David Lodge, *Consciousness and the Novel: Connected Essays* (Cambridge, MA: Harvard University Press, 2002) p. x.

3. Jeremy Hawthorn, *Studying the Novel*, 6th edn (London and New York: Bloomsbury Academic, 2010) p. 232.

4. Ibid., p. 4.

5. The existing criticism on early Kurdish fiction does not in any sense stray far from traditional literary criticism, in which one looks for the immediate intentions of the author. A collection of traditional critics can be found in Hama Sharif Azad (ed.), *Jamil Saibiy Shakarnus* [The masterpiece writer Jamil Saib] (Hawler: Mukiryani, 2012).

6. For a detailed review of the rise and development of the Kurdish novel, see Hashem Ahmadzadeh, *Nation and Novel: A Study of Persian and Kurdish Narrative Discourse* (Uppsala: Acta Universitatis Uppsaliensis, 2003).

7. Natali Denise, *The Kurds and the State: Evolving National Identity in Iraq, Turkey and Iran* (Syracuse, NY: Syracuse University Press, 2005) p. 25.

8. Hawthorn, *Studying the Novel*, p. 38.

9. For a more detailed study of the thematic and stylistic features of the Kurdish novel and its changes, see "Stylistic and thematic changes in the Kurdish novel," in *Borders and the Changing Boundaries of Knowledge*, Inga Brandell, Marie Carlson, and Önver A. Çetrez (eds), Swedish Research Institute in Istanbul, *Transactions*, Vol. 22 (Stockholm, 2015) pp. 219-39.

10. For a study of the traces of statelessness in the Kurdish novel, see Hashem Ahmadzadeh, "Longings for State in the Kurdish Narrative Discourse," in Annika Rabo and Bo Utas (eds), *The Role of the State in West Asia* (Istanbul: Swedish Institute, 2005) pp. 63-76.

11. Elaine Showalter, *A Literature of Their Own: From Charlotte Bronte to Doris Lessing* (London: Virago, 1999).

12. David McDowall, *A Modern History of the Kurds* (London: I. B. Tauris, 1997) p. 9.

13. Ibid., p. 117.

14. Wadie Jwaideh, *The Kurdish Nationalist Movement: Its Origins and Development* (Syracuse, NY: Syracuse University Press, 2006) p. 131.

15. Ahmad Khwaja, *Chim di: Shorshakani Shekh Mahmud* (Hawler: Aras, 2013) p. 213.

16. Khwaja, 2013, pp. 130-31.

17. Jamal Baban, "Peshaki," in Jamil Saib, *La Khawma* (Hawler: Aras, 2008) p. 28.

18. Ibid., p. 67.

19. Ibid., p. 72.

20. Ibid., p. 76.

21. Ibid., p. 78.

22. Ibid., p. 48.

23. Ibid., p. 59.

24. Rafiq Hilmi, *Yaddasht: Kurdistani Eraq u Shorshakani Shekh Mahmud* [The notes: Iraqi Kurdistan and Sheikh Mahmud's revolutions], Vol. 1 (Baghdad: Maarif, 1956) p. 67.

25. Ibid., p. 64.

26. There is a rich selection of non-fiction material about this period, both by foreign and Kurdish authors, such as Amin Zaki Bag, Rafiq Hilmi, Piramerd, and Rasul Hawar. The notes of the British officers in the region, e.g. E. B. Soane and J. C. Edmonds, are also valuable sources about Sheikh Mahmud's period from a colonial point of view.

27. Saib, *La Khawma*, p. 58.

28. Ahmad Khwaja, *Chim Di: Shorishakani Shekh Mahmudi Mazin* (Hawler: Aras, 2013) pp. 79-80.

29. Saib, *La Khawma*, p. 81.

30. M. R. Hawar, *Shekh Mahmudi Qaraman u Dawlatakay Khwaruy Kurdistan* [The Leader Sheikh Mahmud and Southern State of Kurdistan], Vol. 1 (London: Jaf Press, 1990) p. 206.

31. Kamran Subhan, "Ahmad Mukhtar Jaf: She'reki terorkirw" [Ahmad Mukhtar Jaf: An assassinated poem], *Bas*, No. 230, 17/3/2015, p. 9.

32. Ahmad Mukhtar Jaf, *Masalay Wizhdan: Chon Bum ba Khanadan* [The Question of Conscience: How I became Noble], introduced and analyzed by Ihsan Foad (Hawler: Aras) p. 15.

33. Gerard Delanty and Patrick O'Mahony, *Nationalism and Social Theory* (London: Sage, 2002) p. 15.

34. Jaf, *Masalay Wizhdan*, p. 16.

35. Ibid., p. 54.

36. Ibid., p. 26.

37. Ibid., p. 9.

38. Ibid,, p. 47.

39. Ibid., p. 21.

40. Ibid., pp. 22-3.

41. It was a common and relatively well paid job in front of the governmental offices, especially the courts, where a relatively educated man wrote petitions for the plaintiffs.

42. Jaf, *Masalay Wizhdan*, p. 32.

43. Ibid., p. 34.

44. Delanty and O'Mahony, *Nationalism and Social Theory*, p. 15.

45. Jaf, *Masalay Wizhdan*, pp. 38-9.

46. Hawthorn, *Studying the Novel*, p. 5.

47. Ibid., p. 34.

48. Piramerd translated *Kamachezhan* from Turkish into Kurdish. In the introduction to the translation he talks about how he became familiar with the book prior to leaving Istanbul to return to Silemani in 1925. He read early parts of the book which had been published in a Turkish newspaper in installments, and then translated the whole book in 1942. See Piramerd, *Kamanchazhan* [The Violinist] (Hawler: Aras, 2012) pp. 7-8. According to Omed Ashna, in 1970, when a new edition of this novel was published, it became clear that the novel originally belonged to the Danish writer Hans Christen Andersen. Earlier it was assumed, even by the translator himself, that it was originally a German work. See Omed Ashna, *Piramerd u Pedachunawayaki Nwey Zhiyan u Barhamakani* [Piramerd and a research about his life and work] (Hawler: Aras, 2001) p. 61.

49. Martin van Bruinessen, "From Adela Khanum to Leyla Zana: Women as Political Leaders in Kurdish History," in Shahrezad Mojab (ed.), *Women of a non-State Nation: The Kurds* (Costa Mesa, CA: Mazda, 2001) p. 97.

50. C. J. Edmonds, *Kurds, Turks and Arabs: Politics, Travel and Research in North-Eastern Iraq, 1919–1925* (London: Oxford University Press, 1957) pp. 149, 341.

8. POLITICAL AND EVERYDAY RELIGION IN KURDISTAN

1. As an ethnographer who largely carries out presence-based research, I have less ability to speak to the subject of Kurds and religion in Iran than elsewhere.

2. Martin Van Bruinessen, "Kurdish Society, Ethnicity, Nationalism and Refugee Problems", in Philip G. Kreyenbroek, and Stefan Sperl (eds), *The Kurds: A Contemporary Overview*, (Abingdon: Routledge, 1992) pp. 26-52.

3. Khanna Omarkhali, "Introduction", in Omarkhali, Khanna (ed.), *Religious Minorities in Kurdistan: Beyond the Mainstream* (Wiesbaden: Harrassowitz Verlag, 2014).

4. Kurdistanica, "Religion in Kurdistan", in *KURDISTANICA: The Encyclopaedia of Kurdistan*, 2008, http://www.kurdistanica.com/; Martin Van Bruinessen, "The Qadiriyya and the Lineages of Qadiri Shaykhs in Kurdistan", in Martin Van Bruinessen, *Mullas, Sufis and Heretics: The Role of Religion in Kurdish Society* (Istanbul: Isis Press, 2000) pp. 213-29; Omarkhali, Khanna, "Introduction"; Philip G. Kreyenbroek, *Yezidism: Its Background, Observances and Textual Tradition*, Vol. 62, Texts and Studies in Religion (Lampeter, UK: Edwin Mellen Press, 1995); Christine Allison, *The Yezidi Oral Tradition in Iraqi Kurdistan* (London: Curzon, 2001); Martin Van Bruinessen and Joyce Blau, *Islam des Kurdes* (Paris:

ERISM, 1998); David Wilmshurst, *The Ecclesiastical Organisation of the Church of the East, 1318-1913* (Leuven: Peeters, 2000).

5. Human Rights Watch, *World Report 2015: Events of 2014* (Bristol: Policy Press, 2015), p. 553.

6. United Nations High Commissioner for Refugees (UNHCR), Official General Report on Northern Iraq, 2000, p. 55.

7. Oso Sabio, *Rojava: An Alternative to Imperialism, Nationalism, and Islamism in the Middle East. An Introduction* (Raleigh, NC: LULU Press, 2015).

8. Fred Abrahams, Nadim Houry, and Tom Porteous, *Under Kurdish Rule: Abuses in PYD-Run Enclaves of Syria*, Human Rights Watch, 2014.

9. Diane E. King, "My Field Site is Soaked with Blood", *Society for Applied Anthropology Newsletter* 20:1 (2009), pp. 32-4.

10. Janet Klein, *The Margins of Empire: Kurdish Militias in the Ottoman Tribal Zone* (Palo Alto, CA: Stanford University Press, 2011).

11. Huda Ahmed writes, "In December 2003, the governing council established by the CPA proposed Resolution 137, which would have fully repealed the 1959 code and placed decisions about family matters in hands of religious authorities. Though this measure was canceled after women's rights advocates raised objections, a similar provision appeared in the 2005 constitution as Article 41, which gives Iraqis the right to choose what personal status rules they want to follow based on their 'religions, sects, beliefs, or choices.' Article 41, however, is currently suspended after women's advocates, NGOs, members of parliament, legal professionals, and the judiciary protested against the provision, viewing it as a way to increase sectarian divisions and impose undue restrictions on women. Until the dispute over Article 41 is resolved, the unified system based on the 1959 code remains in effect. In practice, a woman's ability to defend her rights often depends on decisions by her family, tribal authorities, or the officials of her religious sect, as personal status disputes are commonly settled without recourse to a civil court." Huda Ahmed, "Iraq", in Sanja Kelly and Julia Breslin (eds) *Women's Rights in the Middle East and North Africa: Progress Amid Resistance* (Lanham, MD: Rowman & Littlefield Publishers, 2010) pp. 167-8.

12. Institute for International Law and Human Rights, "Iraq's Minorities and Other Vulnerable Groups: Legal Framework, Documentation and Human Rights" (Baghdad: Institute for International Law and Human Rights, 2013) p. 41.

13. Ronald Sempill Stafford, *The Tragedy of the Assyrians* (Piscataway, NJ: Gorgias Press, 2006 [1935]) p. 21.

14. Martin Van Bruinessen, "The Qadiriyya and the Lineages of Qadiri Shaykhs in Kurdistan", in Martin Van Bruinessen, *Mullas, Sufis and Heretics: The Role of Religion in Kurdish Society* (Istanbul: Isis Press, 2000) p. 213.

15. Diane E. King, *Kurdistan on the Global Stage: Kinship, Land, and Community in Iraq* (New Brunswick, NJ: Rutgers University Press, 2014).

9. THE SHIFTING BORDERS OF CONFLICT, DIFFERENCE, AND OPPRESSION

1. This chapter originated with a paper read in the symposium "Cultural Change in Iran and Iraniate Societies," Vienna, September 2013. My thanks to the organizers, and also to "Samira," Dr Mohammed Ihsan, Dr Shukriya Rasul, Halima Barzani, and Nafeesa Haji for assistance with fieldwork, information, translation, and transcription. The text presented here was cited but not transcribed in Christine Allison, "Old and New Oral Traditions in Badinan»", in P. G. Kreyenbroek, and F. C. Allison (eds), *Kurdish Culture and Identity* (London: Curzon, 1996) pp. 42-4.

2. Kurdish cultural work in the USSR, the principal source of Kurmanji (Northern Kurdish) literature until the 1990s, was state-supported; in the homelands Kurdish cultural production was by its very nature an act of political contestation.

3. Cf. Başgöz, I., 'Folklore Studies and Nationalism in Turkey', *Journal of the Folklore Institute* 9:2/3 (1972) pp. 162-76; A. Öztürkmen 'Folklore on Trial: Pertev Naili Boratav and the Denationalization of Turkish Folklore', *Journal of Folklore Research* 42:2 (2005) pp. 185-216; Yüksel, M., 'Dengbêj, Mullah, Intelligentsia: The Survival and Revival of the Kurdish Kurmanji Language in the Middle East, 1925-1960', PhD thesis, University of Chicago, 2011; Hamelink, W., 'The Sung Home: Narrative, morality and the Kurdish Nation', PhD thesis, University of Leiden, 2014.

4. I omit the USSR only for reasons of space.

5. See R. Bauman and C. L. Briggs, *Voices of Modernity: Language Ideologies and the Politics of Inequality* (Cambridge: Cambridge University Press, 2003), pp. 163-96 on Herder, linguistic ideology, and modernity.

6. *Sämtliche Werke* 18, p. 347, cited in Bauman and Briggs, *Voices of Modernity*, p. 193.

7. In *Folk Songs* (1778), quoted by J. Storey, *Inventing Popular Culture: From Folklore to Globalization* (Oxford: Blackwell, 2003) p. 4.

8. Storey cites William Motherwell (1827) and Francis James Child (1857); Storey, *Inventing Popular Culture*, p. 5.

9. Bauman and Briggs, *Voices of Modernity*, p. 177.

10. Storey, *Inventing Popular Culture*, p. 14.

11. R. Dorson, *The British Folklorists: A History* (Abingdon: Routledge, 1968), pp. 196, 206. Both are cited in Storey, *Inventing Popular Culture*, pp. 6-7.

12. Storey, *Inventing Popular Culture*, pp. 5-6.

13. Ibid., pp. 13-15; Bauman and Briggs, *Voices of Modernity*, pp. 193-5.

14. For example, Gayatri Chakravorty Spivak, Edward Said, and Partha Chatterjee.

15. For Herder and those who followed him, this was urbanization and the industrial revolution.

16. The Soviet Union was the source of broadcasts received by Kurds elsewhere, and numerous Iraqi Kurdish scholars were educated there.

17. E.g. Celil, O and Celil, C. *Zargotina K'urda/Kurdskij Folklor*, Moscow: Nauk, 1978. For a discussion of folklore and its role in Soviet Kurdish literature, see Christine Allison,

"Memory and the Kurmanji novel: Contemporary Turkey and Soviet Armenia", in C. Allison, and P. G. Kreyenbroek (eds) *Remembering the Past in Iranian Societies* (Wiesbaden: Harrasowitz Verlag, 2013) pp. 189-218.

18. Başgöz, "Folklore Studies and Nationalism in Turkey", pp. 163-4.

19. Başgöz, "Folklore Studies and Nationalism in Turkey", p. 165. Gökalp published folklore in the form of tales for children, to influence the younger generation, see A. Çakir, "The Representation of the *Dengbêj* Tradition in Kurdish Contemporary Popular Discourse", MA thesis, University of Exeter, 2011.

20. Çakir, "The Representation of the *Dengbêj* Tradition in Kurdish Contemporary Popular Discourse".

21. Ibid., p. 20; see also M. Hakan Özoğlu, *Kurdish Notables and the Ottoman State: Evolving Identities, Competing Loyalties, and Shifting Boundaries* (Albany, NY: State University of New York Press, 2004) and M. Strohmeier, *Crucial Images in the Presentation of a Kurdish National Identity: Heroes and Patriots, Traitors and Foes* (Leiden: Brill, 2003), for the evolution of these ideas through other periodicals.

22. Strohmeier, *Crucial Images in the Presentation of a Kurdish National Identity*, p. 152.

23. For his activity within the *Türk Ocakları* or "Turkish Hearths" movement and its influence on the Young Turk government and Mustafa Kemal, see Öztürkmen, "Folklore on Trial", p. 183.

24. The Turkish Language Society and the Turkish Historical Society, both established in 1932. See Ugur Ü. Üngör, *The Making of Modern Turkey: Nation and State in Eastern Anatolia, 1913-1950* (Oxford: Oxford University Press, 2011) pp. 229-30 for the discourse glorifying Turkishness.

25. For Gökalp's theories, see U. Heyd, *Foundations of Turkish Nationalism: The Life and Teachings of Ziya Gökalp* (London: Luzac and Harvill Press, 1950) pp. 104-48.

26. E.g. Zeydanlioğlu, W., "Turkey's Kurdish language policy", *International Journal of the Sociology of Language* 217 (2012) pp. 99-125.

27. Directed by Fuat Köprülü, see Başgöz, "Folklore Studies and Nationalism in Turkey", p. 169.

28. From 1928 to 1931, he taught comparative religion, religious history, and folk traditions of the Caucasus (Birkalan 2001: 42).

29. Birkalan 2001: 42.

30. Başgöz, "Folklore Studies and Nationalism in Turkey", p. 171.

31. For People's House activity in Diyarbakir during the early Republic, see Üngör, *The Making of Modern Turkey*, pp. 232-40.

32. Accusations included: belittling Namık Kemal by planning to include folk poets in his commemoration, his emphasis on resistance against the state in ancient Turkish legends especially Koroğlu, his correction of a student's comments on Ziya Gökalp, and his citation in class of *kızılbaş* (i.e. Alevi) poets (Özturkmen, "Folklore on Trial", pp. 200-201; H. Birkalan, "Pertev Naili Boratav, Turkish Politics and the University Events", *Turkish Studies Association Bulletin* 25:1 (2001) pp. 55-7).

33. For the Iranian equivalent of the Turkish "Sun Language Theory", see A. Hassanpour,

Nationalism and Language in Kurdistan, 1918-1985 (San Francisco, CA: Mellen Research University Press, 1992) pp. 125-30.

34. The Kurds' existence was acknowledged, though by 1960 Kurdish was still being classified as a "dialect" of Persian.

35. Enjavi dates, background presided over by Fuat Köprülü.

36. "*Ganjinayi farhange mardom*", 1973-7. A large archive was amassed in this way.

37. The possibility of folklore being "superstition" had also exercised the writers of *Jîn* (Çakir, "The Representation of the *Dengbêj* Tradition in Kurdish Contemporary Popular Discourse", p. 20).

38. M. Omidsalar, "Persia" in W. M. Clements, (ed.), *The Greenwood Encyclopaedia of Folklore and Folklife*, Vol. 2, (Westport and London: Greenwood Press, 2006) p. 425.

39. Gareth Stansfield and Hashem Ahmadzadeh, 'The Political, Cultural and Military Re-awakening of the Kurdish Nationalist Movement in Iran', *Middle East Journal* 64:1 (2010) pp. 22-6.

40. Çakir, "The Representation of the *Dengbêj* Tradition in Kurdish Contemporary Popular Discourse", p. 22.

41. See Jordi Tejel, "Les constructions de l'identité kurde sous l'influence de la 'connexion kurdo-française' au Levant (1930-1946)»", *European Journal of Turkish Studies* (2006).

42. *L'Âme des Kurdes à la lumière de leur folklore* (Paris: Cahiers de l'Est).

43. E. Davis, *Memories of State: Politics, History and Collective Identity in Modern Iraq* (Berkeley, CA: University of California Press, 2005) p. 38.

44. Ibid., p. 21

45. Ibid., p. 21.

46. Ibid., p. 311 n.4.

47. For example, Dr Shukriya Rasul and the literary scholar Dr Maruf Khaznadar.

48. *Hawar* and other early nationalist productions remained little known in Turkey, at least until the 1960s.

49. Öztürkmen, "Folklore on Trial", pp. 187-9.

50. The content reflected the politics of the editorial board (Çakir, "The Representation of the *Dengbêj* Tradition in Kurdish Contemporary Popular Discourse", p. 24). See Ibid., p. 27 n.79 for *Azadî*, a Marxist magazine produced in 1979.

51. Ibid., p. 12.

52. Saritaş, B. S. E., "Articulation of Kurdish Identity through Politicized Music of *Koms*", Master's thesis, Middle East Technical University, Istanbul, 2010, p. 110.

53. See Y. Kanakis, "Dancing the future of Hakkari's past, according to 9-year-old Ayfer", in C. Allison and P. G. Kreyenbroek (eds) *Remembering the Past in Iranian Societies* (Wiesbaden: Harrasowitz Verlag, 2013) pp. 113-24, for details of this cultural diglossia.

54. Saritaş, "Articulation of Kurdish Identity through Politicized Music of *Koms*", p. 107.

55. Cengiz Güneş, *The Kurdish National Movement in Turkey: From Protest to Resistance* (Abingdon: Routledge, 2012) p. 113.

56. Güneş, *The Kurdish National Movement in Turkey*, p. 113.

57. See Nicole Watts, *Activists in Office: Kurdish Politics and Protest in Turkey* (Seattle: University of Washington Press, 2010) pp. 157-8 on Newroz in Diyarbakir.

58. See M. Yeğen, 'The Kurdish Question in Turkish State Discourse', *Journal of Contemporary History* 34: 4 (1999) pp. 555-68; Aykan, Y., 'Unacknowledged Memory: The nineteenth-century Ottoman Empire and the ambivalence of national memory in the Turkish Republic', in Allison, C. and P. G. Kreyenbroek (eds) *Remembering the Past in Iranian Societies* (Wiesbaden: Harrasowitz Verlag, 2013) pp. 78-94.

59. For these events, see David McDowall, *A Modern History of the Kurds* (London: I. B. Tauris, 1994) pp. 368-96.

60. See J. Sheyholislami, J., *Kurdish Identity, Discourse and New Media (London: Palgrave, 2011)* for a full account.

61. Morad, personal communication from a PhD thesis in preparation, 2015.

62. Especially the "Rojava cantons" in Syria, Kurdish organizations in the diaspora, and PJAK's constituency in Iran.

63. Saritaş, "Articulation of Kurdish Identity through Politicized Music of *Koms*", p. 65; Ibid., p. 66.

64. Ibid., p. 106.

65. See Ibid., p. 111 and Kanakis, "Dancing the future of Hakkari's past, according to 9-year-old Ayfer", for young people who have learned "Kurdish culture" from the movement. See also John Hutchinson on cultural nationalism: Hutchinson, J. and A. D. Smith (eds), *Nationalism: A Reader* (Oxford: Oxford University Press, 1994) p. 128.

66. Hamelink 2014: 66-7.

67. Although grateful for their new-found public respect, not all *dengbêj* are happy to be co-opted into the Kurdish cause: Ibid., pp. 165-6.

68. Jaba's publication of 1860 and his manuscript collection, now held at the State Library in St Petersburg, reflect his collaboration with the scholar Mehmud Bayazidi.

69. E.g. Morad on Iraqi Kurdistan (PhD thesis in preparation).

70. Hamelink, "The Sung Home", p. 72.

71. Ibid.

72. M. Mills, "What('s) Theory?", *Journal of Folklore Research* 45:1, (2008) pp. 15-16.

73. Based on my own experience (cf. Christine Allison ,*The Yezidi Oral Tradition in Iraqi Kurdistan*, (London: Curzon, 2001) p. 38.

74. Paredes' call to a more engaged folkloristics was taken up by very few and he was later erased from folklore genealogies (Briggs 2008: 98).

75. For a sensitive discussion, see M. Mills, "'Are You Writing Our Book Yet?" War, Culture, Structural Violence, and Oral Historical Representation', in C. Allison and P. G. Kreyenbroek (eds) *Remembering the Past in Iranian Societies* (Wiesbaden: Harrasowitz Verlag, 2013) pp. 165-76.

76. Briggs 2008: 91-6.

77. Bauman and Briggs' notion of entextualization enables the study of both literary and folkloric discourse by collapsing the distinction between "oral" versus "literary." For an interrogation of Benedict Anderson's work, see Christine Allison, « From Benedict Anderson

to Mustafa Kemal: Reading, Writing and Imagining the Kurdish Nation", in Bozarslan, Hamit and Clémence Scalbert-Yücel (eds), *Joyce Blau: l'éternelle chez les Kurdes* (Paris: IKP, 2013) pp.101-34.

78. Briggs 2008: 101.

79. R. Bauman, "The Philology of the Vernacular", *Journal of Folklore Research* 45:1 (2008) p. 30; Barber, K., *The Anthropology of Texts, Persons and Publics: Oral and Written Culture in Africa and Beyond* (Cambridge: Cambridge University Press, 2007) p. 22.

80. A pseudonym.

81. For details surrounding the events of the Treaty of Algiers, see McDowall, *A Modern History of the Kurds*, pp. 337-40.

82. The BBC documentary "Saddam's Road to Hell" (2007, available on YouTube) dates the massacre to August 1993.

83. This may mean that it was easy for the state to imprison the men, or in the context of the current demand, that it would be easy to take the women to the prisons now.

84. The polyvalent word *xerîbî* denotes strangeness, bereftness, estrangement, and exile. Amy de la Bretèque unfailingly translates this as "exile"; my translation varies with context.

85. Amy de la Bretèque cites Alexandra Pillen's observation that Kurmanji-speaking women from Turkey use a limited vocal range when they describe traumatic experiences (oral presentation, 2012, cited in E. Amy de la Bretèque, *Paroles Melodisées: Récits épiques et lamentations chez les Yézidis d'Arménie* (Paris: Garnier, 2013) p. 112.

86. The terminology varies; see Hamelink, "The Sung Home", p. 72.

87. Amy de la Bretèque, *Paroles Melodisées*, pp. 107-12.

88. See D. E. King, "The Personal is Patrilineal: *Namus* as Sovereignty", *Identities* 15:3 (2008) pp. 317-42 for a discussion of *namûs*.

89. For Anfal widows' discourse, see K. Mlodoch, "Fragmented Memory, Competing Narratives", in Jordi Tejel, Peter Sluglett, Riccardo Bocco, and Hamit Bozarslan (eds), *Writing the Modern History of Iraq. Historiographical and Political Challenges* (Singapore: World Scientific, 2012) pp. 205-26.

90. Amy de la Bretèque, *Paroles Mélodisées*, pp. 104-7.

91. Bauman, R. "The Philology of the Vernacular", p. 31.

92. Amy de la Bretèque's description of Yezidi funeral songs in Armenia includes songs performed by men and accompanied by the *duduk*, a double-reed wind instrument regarded as ancient and folkloric. Men and women considered the entire repertoire an important part of Yezidi duties of honoring the dead.

93. Interview, Qush Tepe, 27 July 1992.

94. A. Kleinman, V. Das and M. M. Lock, (eds), *Social Suffering*, (Berkeley, CA: University of California Press, 1997) p. 84.

95. D. Fassin and R. Rechtman, *The Empire of Trauma: An Inquiry into the Condition of Victimhood*, trans. R. Gomme (Princeton, NJ: Princeton University Press, 2009).

96. Andrea Fischer-Tahir, *Brave Men, Pretty Women? Gender and Symbolic Violence in Iraqi Kurdish Urban Society* (Berlin: Europäisches Zentrum für Kurdische Studien, 2009).

97. A campaign of disappearances and deportations by the Ba'ath government against the Kurds; McDowall, *A Modern History of the Kurds*, pp. 357-60 has details.

98. See BBC documentary "Saddam's Road to Hell," available on YouTube.

99. See Mlodoch, "Fragmented Memory, Competing Narratives".

100. Nicole Watts, "The Role of Symbolic Capital in Protest: State-Society Relations and the Destruction of the Halabja Monument in Northern Iraq", *Comparative Studies of South Asia, Africa and the Middle East* 32:1 (2012) pp. 70-85.

101. The women occupied an "unspeakable and unhearable ... zone"; Kleinman, Das and Lock, (eds), *Social Suffering*, p. 88.

10. KURDISH MUSIC IN ARMENIA

1. Also spelt Êzdî in Armenian Yezidi publications, and as Yazidis in some English publications. In Kûrmancî Kurdish the name is spelt Êzîdî, and ئێزیدی or یەزیدی in Kurdish Iraq and أزدي in Arabic.

2. Martin van Bruinessen, "Kurdish society, ethnicity, nationalism and refugee problems", in Philip G. Kreyenbroek, and Stefan Sperl (eds), *The Kurds: A Contemporary Overview* (Abingdon: Routledge, 1992) p. 38; Philip G. Kreyenbroek and Khalil Jindy Rashow, *God and Sheikh Adi Are Perfect: Sacred Poems and Religious Narratives from the Yezidi Tradition* (Wiesbaden: Harrassowitz Verlag, 2005), p. 5.

3. Eşo, Wezîrê, "Diroka Kurdê Sovyeta Kevin" [Kurdish History in the Former Soviet Union), *NÛDEM* 31 (1999) p. 18.

4. Kreyenbroek and Rashow, *God and Sheikh Adi Are Perfect*, p. 5.

5. Omerxalî, Xanna, *Yezidisyatî* ["Yezidism"], Istanbul: Mezopotamya Centre, Avesta Publications (written in Kurdish Kûrmancî), 2007, p. 15.

6. Kreyenbroek and Rashow, *God and Sheikh Adi Are Perfect*, p. 5.

7. Stephen Blum, "Introduction, Kurdish Music", in Sadie, Stanley and John Tyrell (eds), *The New Grove Dictionary of Music and Musicians* (Oxford: Oxford University Press, 2001). Komitas did not differentiate between Yezidi music and other Kurds' music during his research.

8. Poladian, Sirvart, 'Komitas Vardapet and his Contribution to Ethnomusicology', *Ethnomusicology* 16:1 (1972) p. 84.

9. Çaçanî, Karliyn, *The Culture of the Kurds from the View Point of Armenian Writers*, Yerevan: Institute of Oriental Studies (in Armenian), 2004, pp. 231-4.

10. Çaçanî, *The Culture of Kurds*, p. 247; Eşo, "Diroka Kurdê Sovyeta Kevin", p. 36.

11. O. Celil and C. Celil, *Zargotina K'urda/Kurdskij Folklor* (Moscow: Nauk, 1978) p. 36.

12. Victoria Arakelova, "Bayt'ā Gilāvīyē — A Lament for a Noble Woman. Or Evidence for Polygamy among the Yezidis", *Iran and the Caucasus*, 3 (1999) p. 135.

13. Celîl and Celîl, *Zargotina K'urda*, pp. 490-503.

14. Ibid., pp. 36-37.

15. Roudenko, Margarita, *The Kurdish Ritual Poetry (Funeral Lamentation)*, Moscow: Nauka

Publications, published in Russian by the USSR Academy of Science, the Institute of Oriental Studies, 1982, p. 6.

16. Celîl and Celîl, *Zargotina K'urda*, p. 36.

17. Cewarî, Nûra, "Sazbendiya kurdên Ermenistanê" ["Music of the Armenian Kurds"], *NÛDEM* 31 (1999), pp. 49-55 (collected articles written in Kurdish Kûrmancî) p. 49.

18. Zagros, Nahro, 'Music of a Confused Society', *Hetq*, Investigative Journalists of Armenia, 2006, p. 11, http://archive.hetq.am/eng/culture/0605-nahro.html

19. Wehr, Hans, *A Dictionary of Modern Written Arabic*, 4th edn, J. M. Cowan (ed.) (Urbana, IL: Spoken Language Services, 1994) p. 160.

20. Celîl, Cemîla, *Kilam û Miqamêd Cimeta Kurda* (Kurdish Maqam and Folk Music), (Stockholm: ROJA NU publications, 1982) pp. 5-6.

21. Shexani, Naif, ["A Concept of the World in Music"] (Arbil: Publications of the Ministry of Culture and Youth of the Kurdish Government of Iraq, 2010), p. 101.

22. Berdal Aral, "The Idea of Human Rights as Perceived in the Ottoman Empire", *Human Rights Quarterly*, 26:2 (2004) p. 467.

23. Habib Hassan Touma, *The Music of the Arabs* (Winona, MN: Hal Leonard Books, 2003) p. 38.

24. Celîl, *Kilam û Miqamêd Cimeta Kurda*, pp. 5-6.

25. Selah Hirurî, ["A Number of Historical Songs in Kurdish History"] (Duhok, Kurdistan: Sipirez Publications, 2004), p. 14.

26. Cemîla Celîl, "Kurdish Folk Songs of the Yerevan Region", trans. from Russian into Kurdish Soranî by Izedin Mistefa Resul, Sulaymany (Iraq: Publications of Kurdish Heritage Institute of the Ministry of Culture, 2004) p. 10.

27. See "Musical instruments" later in this chapter for further and more detailed discussion of the physical and aesthetic nature of the musical instrumentation.

28. Celîl, "Kurdish Folk Songs of the Yerevan Region", p. 8.

29. Celîl, *Kilam û Miqamêd Cimeta Kurda*, p. 9.

30. Ibid.

31. Celîl, "Kurdish Folk Songs of the Yerevan Region", p. 10.

32. Cewarî, "Sazbendiya kurdên Ermenistanê", p. 50.

33. Celîl and Celîl, *Zargotina K'urda/Kurdskij Folklor*, pp. 25-40.

34. Eşo, "Diroka Kurdê Sovyeta Kevin", p. 36.

35. Ali Askhr Nesrullah Poor, ["Kurdish Musical Instruments"], trans. from Farsi to Kurdish Bahdini by Masoud Mohhamed Guli Duhok (Kurdistan: Spirez Publications, Iraqi Kurdistan, 2005) p. 51.

36. Cewarî, "Sazbendiya kurdên Ermenistanê", p. 51.

37. Poor, ["Kurdish Musical Instruments"], p. 90.

38. Martin Stokes (ed.), *Ethnicity, Identity and Music: The Musical Construction of Place* (London: Bloomsbury, 1997) p. 5.

11. THE SHEIKH UBEIDULLAH REBELLION OF 1880

1. For an account of the literature, see Sabri Ateş, "In the name of the caliph and the nation: The Sheikh Ubeidullah Rebellion of 1880-81," *Iranian Studies* 47:5 (2014) pp. 735-98.
2. See Abbas Vali, *Kurds and State in Iran: The Making of Kurdish Identity* (London: I. B. Tauris, 2011) p. 1; and Amir Hassanpour, "The Making of Kurdish Identity: Pre-20th Century Historical and Literary Sources," in *Essays on the Origins of Kurdish Nationalism*, Abbas Vali (ed.) (Costa Mesa, CA: Mazda, 2003) p. 148.
3. Martin van Bruinessen, "The Sadate Nehri or Gilanizade of Central Kurdistan," in *Mullas, Sufis and Heretics: The Role of Religion in Kurdish Society* (Istanbul: Isis Press, 2000).
4. For such fears see BOA.MVL 227/21, 8 June 1851 Tezkere-i Seraskeri (General Staff, Memoranda).
5. Ali Akbar Qaragozlu, "Eftetah-e Naseri: Ruzname-e Guzaresh-e Ettefaqiyye," in Iraj Afshar, *Daftar-e Tarikh: Majmu`e-ye Asnad va Manabe`-ye Tarikhi*, Vol. 4 (Tehran: Bonyad-e Mowqufat-e Mahmud Afshar, 1389/2011) pp. 107-58.
6. Martin van Bruinessen, *Agha Shaikh and State: The Social and Political Structures of Kurdistan* (London: Zed Books, 1992) p. 229.
7. BOA.Y.E.E 35/112, 1298.R.7/13 May, 1875, *Sealed Report by Necib Ali* (hereafter Necib Ali's report).
8. Ibid.
9. Both Ottoman and Iranian documents mention such pleas.
10. Ahmed Muhtar Paşa, *Anadolu'da Rus Muharebesi*, I, Enver Yaşarbaş (ed.) (Istanbul: Petek Yayınlari, 1985) pp. 23-7, 44-5.
11. BOA.HR.SYS 726/45, Tehran Embassy to the Ottoman Ministry of Foreign Affairs (hereafter OMFA) 6 July 1878.
12. BOA.Y.A.HUS 162/36, this file includes many of the sheikh's letters to the sultan and other Ottoman authorities.
13. PRO.FO 78/2911, Trotter General Consul of Kurdistan to Sir A. H. Layard, British Ambassador to Istanbul, Erzurum, 5, 12 September 1879, Abbot to T. Thomson British Minister at Tehran, 25 September 1879.
14. BOA.Y.A.HUS, 162/36, 27 October 1879.
15. PRO.FO 78/2991, Erzeroum, 15 July 1879, Major Henry Trotter, Consul of Kurdistan to Marquis Salisbury, Secretary of State for Foreign Affairs. For a similar interpretation, see Hakan Özoğlu, *International Journal of Middle Eastern Studies* 33 (2001) p. 390.
16. Speer, *Hakim Sahib*, pp. 82-3.
17. For the first Ottoman responses to the outbreak of the rebellion, see BOA.Y.A.RES 10/3, 16 or Y.A.RES., 8/7, 11-13 October 1880.
18. Muhammad Rahim Nusrat Makoi, *Tarikh-i Enqelab-i Azerbaijan va Khawanin-i Maku*, p. 18.
19. Qurians, *Qiyam-i*, pp. 95-6; and BOA.Y.A.RES 10/3, Ottoman Deputy Consul of Urumieh's Report.
20. At the time of the revolt too it was claimed that Cochran and Colonel Clayton, British

Vice Consul of Kurdistan, had encouraged the sheikh to rebel. Speer, *Hakim Sahib*, pp. 83-4. For Ottoman Embassy of Tehran's response, see BOA.HR.SYS 726/110, To OMFA, 24 Teşrin-i Evvel 1880. For Abbot's own account of the first steps of the revolt, see PRO. FO 60/431, Abbot to British Minister at Tehran, 10 December 1880, or to Lord Aberdeen, 30 December 1880.

21. Speer, *Hakim Sahib*, p. 90.

22. BOA.HR.SYS 726/110, Tehran Embassy Telegram no. 60, 3 TS, 1880 / 3 November 1880.

23. Speer, *Hakim Sahib*, pp. 93-4.

24. According to Qurians, all in all they had 300-400 Martini rifles: Qurians, *Qiyam-i*, pp. 37-8. Also BOA.HR.SYS 107/3, and HR.SYS 726/109, Tehran Embassy to the Ottoman Ministry of Foreign Affairs, 6 TE (October), 1880.

25. BOA.Y.PRK EŞA 2/71, 1297/ 9 October 1880.

26. Qurians, *Qiyam-i*, p. 43.

27. Qurians, *Qiyam-i*, p. 57.

28. BOA.Y.PRK HR 5/31, Samih Pasha to Ottoman Ministry of Defense 28 November 1880, and 4th Army Mushir Nafiz Pasha to OMD, 1298.M.6/08 December 1880.

29. Qurians reports these atrocities in detail.

30. Qurians, *Qiyam-i*, p. 64. See also BOA.Y.A.RES 10/3 Consul General of Tabriz to the Ottoman Ministry of Interior as reported by the Ottoman Consul of Urumieh, 20 January 1881.

31. PRO.FO. 60/431, Abbot to R. Thomson, 30 December 1880.

32. BBA.Y.A.RES 10/3, p.15, 20 January 1881. For a similar account, see Speer, *Hakim Sahib*, p. 98.

33. BBA.Y.A.RES 9/23, Ottoman Council of Ministers Resolution, 2 January 1880.

34. BOA.Y.A.RES 10/3, Said Pasha to the Palace 18.Ra 98-7 Mart 97/19 February 1881.

35. *Gozidah-'i Asnad-i*, vol. 6, pp. 576-80, 583.

36. BOA.Y.A.HUS 167/38, Form [Said Pasha-Grand Vizier] to the Palace, 24 March 1881.

37. Ibid.

38. BOA.Y.PRK.A 3 / 4, Ahmed Ratib Bey to the Sultan, 3 January 1881, Sheikh to Government of Van, 14 December 1880.

39. BOA.Y.PRK.A 3/4, Ottoman Council of Ministers, 23 January 1881.

40. BOA, Y PRK MYD 1/85, Ahmed Ratib Bey [Rewanduz] to the Sultan, 20-24 February 1881.

41. BOA.Y.PRK.ASK, 7/34, From Nafiz Pasha to OMD, 31 May 1881.

42. BOA.HR.SYS 723/20 Tehran Embassy to OMoF, 24 June 1881.

43. *Guzidah-i Asnad*, Vol. 6, p. 597.

44. Reverend S. G. Wilson, *Persian Life and Customs: With Scenes and Incidents of Residence and Travel in the Land of the Lion and the Sun* (Edinburgh: Oliphant Anderson and Ferrier, 1896) pp.118-19; and PRO.FO. 60/441, Abbot to Thomson, 7 June 1881.

45. Wilson, *Persian Life and Customs*, p. 121; and PRO.FO. 60/441, Abbot to Thomson, 3 August 1881.

46. For the interrogation of Abdullah, see BOA.Y.PRK.KOM 3/65, Commission of Inquiry Minutes, 20 August 1882. For the interrogation of Mehmed Said Effendi, see BOA.Y.PRK. KOM 3/66, 21 August 1882.

47. BOA.Y.PRK.UM 18/39, Report from Ferik Musa Pasha, 18 December 1882.

48. BOA.Y.YRK.AZJ 6/118 [Undated].

49. BOA.Y.PRK.AZJ 4/96, Sheikh Ubeidullah to Sultan Abdülhamid, 12 October 1881.

50. BOA.Y.A.HUS 172/32, Memoranda and cover letters of the OMoF, 11-14-16 February 1882.

51. PRO.FO. 60/441, Abbot to Earl Granville Tabriz, 1 October 1881.

52. BOA.HR.SYS 726/110, Ottoman Tehran Embassy to Ottoman Minister of Foreign Affairs, 25, 26, 27, 28 TE [October] 1880.

53. BOA.Y.PRK.ASK 5/2, 4th Army Mushir Samih Pasha to Ottoman Ministry of Defense, 22 November 1880.

54. BBA, Y PRK A 3/4, Proceedings of the Ottoman Council of Ministers, 21 Safer 97-11 KS 96/23 January 1881.

55. BOA.Y.PRK.EŞA 7/23, IMFA to OMFA [dated 1298-1882].

56. A. D. Smith, "War and ethnicity: the role of warfare in the formation, self-images and cohesion of ethnic communities," in *Nationalism: Critical Concepts in Political Science*, Vol. 5 (London: Routledge, 2002) p. 1623.

12. JOURNALISM BEYOND BORDERS

1. This chapter is a revised version of the very first paper I wrote as a graduate student at Princeton University, and also my first paper on Kurdish history. It was fun to revisit this paper, which I submitted to Professor Şükrü Hanioğlu for our seminar on late-Ottoman history in November 1994, and to see that I was able to keep largely intact much of what I wrote then, with revisions only in framing the topic and using some secondary sources more critically. I subsequently developed my understanding of the Kurdish press and its role in early Kurdish nationalism in my MA thesis (Princeton, 1996), which further developed parts of my 1994 paper. During this process I became so fascinated with the Hamidiye Light Cavalry that I chose it as the topic for my PhD thesis (Princeton, 2002) and my book, *The Margins of Empire: Kurdish Militias in the Ottoman Tribal Zone* (Stanford, CA: Stanford University Press, 2011).

2. Extant copies of the 31 issues published between 1898 and 1902 have been published by M. Emîn Bozarslan. In his two-volume collection, he has reprinted the journals, transliterated the articles, and provided translations of some articles into modern Turkish: M. Emîn Bozarslan, *Kurdistan (1898-1902)* (Uppsala: Weşanxana Deng, 1991). Numbers 10, 12, and 17-19 are missing from this collection. Malmîsanij has located issues 17 and 18 and reprinted them along with commentary in his *Abdurrahman Bedirhan ve İlk Kürt Gazetesi, Kurdistan, Sayı 17 ve 18* (Sweden: n.p., 1992).

3. Mikdad Midhat Bedirkhan, *Kurdistan* 1 (9 Nisan 1314 / 22 April 1898) p. 1; in Bozarslan's collection, Vol. 1, original at end of volume, transliteration of Kurdish article on p. 112.

4. Amir Hassanpour, *Nationalism and Language in Kurdistan 1918-1985* (San Francisco, CA: Mellon Research University Press, 1992) pp. 79, 458.

5. See M. Şükrü Hanioğlu, *The Young Turks in Opposition* (New York: Oxford University Press, 1995) pp. 132, 169-70, 184, 188,190, 192, 197-8 and footnotes on these pages. See also "Ahrar-ı Osmaniye Kongresi," *Kurdistan* 31; in Bozarslan's collection, Vol. 2, original at end of volume, transliteration from Ottoman on pp. 560-64.

6. Hanioğlu, *The Young Turks in Opposition*, p. 71.

7. David Kushner, *The Rise of Turkish Nationalism 1876-1908* (London: Frank Cass, 1977) p. 6.

8. Ibid.

9. Hanioğlu, *The Young Turks in Opposition*, p. 213.

10. Hanioğlu also cites an article that appeared in *Serbesti* (18 February 1909) called "Bir Ermeni Kilisesinde Bedirhanpaşazade Abdurrahman Beyefendi'nin İrad Etdikleri Nutk-i Beliğ," in which Abdurrahman Bedirkhan was quoted for his comments on Armenian and Kurdish relations *after* the Young Turk Revolution of 1908 (*The Young Turks in Opposition*, p. 351, n. 251). He did continue to work with the CUP, at least loosely, as he contributed to Abdullah Cevdet's İctihad in 1904; see Hanioğlu, *Doktor Abdullah Cevdet ve Dönemi*, (Istanbul: Üçdal, 1981) p. 54, but he may also have been disillusioned with the CUP after the Congress of 1902, when a split in the movement occurred. See ahead.

11. Hanioğlu, *The Young Turks in Opposition*, pp. 117, 170.

12. Ibid., p. 299, n. 96. There are at least two articles about *Kurdistan* in *Osmanlı*, an official CUP paper founded in 1897.

13. Hanioğlu, *The Young Turks in Opposition*, p. 184.

14. *Kurdistan* 26 (1 Kânûn-i Evvel / 14 December 1900); in Bozarslan's collection, Vol. 2, original at end of volume, transliteration of Ottoman article on p. 466.

15. Letter #2 in *Kurdistan* 4 (21 Mayıs 1314 / 3 June 1898) p. 1; in Bozarslan's collection, Vol. 1, original at end of volume, transliteration of Ottoman original on p. 146.

16. Letter #3 in *Kurdistan* 4 (21 Mayıs 1314 / 3 June 1898) p. 2, in Bozarslan's collection, Vol. 1, original at end of volume, transliteration of Ottoman original on p. 147.

17. See, for example, the letter from "Diyarbekir Notable, Ş.M." in *Kurdistan* 13 (20 Mart 1315 / 1 April 1899) p. 1; in Bozarslan's collection, Vol. 1, original at end of volume, translation of Kurdish letter into Latin orthography on p. 259.

18. For a discussion of literacy in Kurdistan, see Hassanpour, *Nationalism and Language in Kurdistan*, esp. pp. 77-81.

19. There is evidence that CUP centers in such places as Adana and Diyarbakir, two of the cities from which letters were sent to *Kurdistan*, distributed banned publications (see Hanioğlu, *The Young Turks in Opposition*, p. 120).

20. Hanioğlu, *The Young Turks in Opposition*, p. 106. Hanioğlu notes that several CUP journals were commonly read aloud in coffee-houses and other beverage-drinking establishments.

21. It should be noted, however, that letters to the editor were sometimes fabrications of the

editors themselves, many of whom wrote their own "puffs" and praise for their journals (personal communication from Hanioğlu, spring 1996).

22. Signed Li Şamê N. H., "Teqrîz: Ji Şamê Hatîye," *Kurdistan* 3 (7 Mayıs 1314 / 20 May 1899) p. 3; in Bozarslan's collection, Vol. 1, original at end, transliteration on p. 136.

23. "Kürdlere," *Kurdistan* 25 (18 Eylül 1316 / 1 October 1900); in Bozarslan's collection, Vol. 2, original at end of volume, transliteration of Ottoman article on p. 440.

24. Abdurrahman Bedir Khan was a staunch opponent of foreign intervention in Ottoman affairs. At the Congress of Ottoman Opposition he sided with the group who looked upon Great Power intervention with extreme disfavor. While others in this faction had their own reasons for embracing this view, Abdurrahman Bedirkhan's stemmed primarily from his fear that Europe would one day succeed in separating Armenia from the Ottoman Empire, which most Kurds opposed. In fact, it seems as if Abdurrahman Bedirkhan had worked to improve Kurdish-Armenian relations to stave off European intervention for some time. Ahmad notes that he had made similar comments to those quoted here as early as the mid-1890s when he met with the chairperson of the Armenian Revolutionary Federation (*Dashnaktsutiun*) in Geneva, where the two discussed prospects for collaboration between Kurds and Armenians (p. 163, n. 65). An editorial letter in *Kurdistan* even threatened that if Sultan Abdülhamid II did nothing to mend oppressive conditions in the region, the Kurds would have no choice but to ally with the Armenians and create their own rule of justice (Letter from Diyarbekir Eşrafından Ş. M., *Kurdistan* 13 (20 Mart 1315 / 1 April 1899) pp. 1-2; in Bozarslan's collection, Vol. 1, original at end, transliteration on pp. 259-60). Abdurrahman Bedirkhan and other Kurdish figures also published articles in the Armenian press.

25. "Kürdlere," *Kurdistan* 25 (18 Eylül 1316 / 1 October 1900); in Bozarslan's collection, Vol. 2, original at end of volume, transliteration from Ottoman on p. 442.

26. "Hamidiye Süvari Alaylar," *Kurdistan* 28 (1 Eylül 1317 / 14 September 1901); in Bozarslan's collection, Vol. 2, original at end of volume, transliteration from Ottoman on pp. 499-500.

27. "Kürdler ve Ermeniler," *Kurdistan* 26 (1 Kânûn-i Evvel / 14 December 1900); in Bozarslan's collection, Vol. 2, original at end of volume, transliteration from Ottoman on p. 462. The Hamidiye and its involvement in the Armenian massacres of 1894-6 added to the reasons why Armenians continued to join the anti-Hamidian opposition, sometimes within the CUP and sometimes outside its auspices; see Kamal Madhar Ahmad, *Kurdistan During the First World War* (London: Saqi Books, 1994) pp. 152-3.

28. *Kurdistan*. 6 (28 Eylül 1314 / 10 October 1898) pp. 2-3; in Bozarslan's collection, Vol. 1, original at end, transliteration of Kurdish article on p. 179.

29. *Kurdistan* 27 (Şubat-ı Evvel [*sic*: Kânûn-i Sânî] 1316 / 10 February 1901) p. 1; in Bozarslan's collection, Vol. 2, original at end, transliteration of Kurdish article on pp. 471-2.

30. Abdurrahman Bedirkhan, "Kurdistan ve Kürdler," *Kurdistan* 24 (19 Ağustos 1316 / 1 September 1900); in Bozarslan's collection, Vol. 2, original at end of volume, transliteration from Ottoman on p. 425.

31. Ibid.; in Bozarslan's collection, Vol. 2, original at end of volume, transliteration from Ottoman on p. 427.

32. Belated because the poet had died in 1897.

33. This poet received special attention in the press as someone who was acknowledged elsewhere as being "very conscious of his Kurdish nationality": Victor Minorsky, "Kurds," in *First Encyclopedia of Islam 1913-1936*, Vol. 4 (New York: Brill, 1987) p. 1154. According to Hassanpour (*Nationalism and Language in Kurdistan*, pp. 90-94) for Haci Qadirê Koyî, language cultivation and national sovereignty went hand in hand. He recognized the importance of developing a press for these goals in one of his poems: "A hundred epistles and odes are not worth a penny (any more)/ Newspapers and magazines have (now) become valuable and respected" (p. 221). Joyce Blau notes that this poet's principal work was "The book of my people," a work devoted to outlining the problems of the Kurds: Joyce Blau (ed.), *Mémoire du Kurdistan* (Paris: Editions Findakly, 1984), p. 123.

34. *Kurdistan* started a trend in printing *Mem û Zîn* in serial form in the Kurdish press. Later Kurdish newspapers and journals have also printed parts of the Kurdish epic, including *Rojî Kurd, Diyarî Kurdistan, Zarî Kirmancî, Rûnakî, Hawar, Gelawêj*, and *Dengî Gêtî Taze*. See Hassanpour, *Nationalism and Language in Kurdistan*, p. 88.

35. For a study of the epic poem, see Michael Chyet, "'And a thornbush sprang up between them': Studies on Mem U Zin, a Kurdish Romance," PhD dissertation, University of California at Berkeley, 2 vols., 1991. See also Hassanpour, *Nationalism and Language in Kurdistan*, pp. 83-90.

36. Hassanpour, *Nationalism and Language in Kurdistan*, p. 87.

37. Ismet Cheriff Vanly, *Survey of the National Question of Turkish Kurdistan with Historical Background* (N.p.: Hevra, 1971) p. 16, Vanly's translation.

38. *Kurdistan* 2 (23 Nisan 1314 / 5 May 1898) p. 4; in Bozarslan's collection, Vol. 1, original at end, transliteration on pp. 126-7.

39. In issues 8, 9, and 11, brief recounts of the histories of the Botan *mîr*s appeared; and in issues 13 and 14, articles on Bedirkhan Bey. Bozarslan surmises ("Introduction," Vol. 1, p. 74) that it is highly likely that pieces on the Bedirkhan family also appeared in issues 10 and 12, which are missing from his collection. For now this question must remain unanswered.

40. See, for example, Wright and Breath in *Missionary Herald* 42 (1846), in Arshak Safrastian, *Kurds and Kurdistan* (London: Harvill Press, 1948) pp. 54-5; and Osman Bey (aka Major Frederick Millingen), *Wild Life Among the Koords* (London: Hurst and Blackett, 1870) pp. 212-13.

41. Martin van Bruinessen notes that certain documents found in the Ottoman archives "suggest another reason for the revolt. There were plans for administrative reorganization, according to which Botan was to be split and divided between the two *eyalets* [provinces] of Diyarbakir and Mosul. Bedir Khan vehemently protested these plans, which, he thought, were designed to break his power." Van Bruinessen, *Agha, Shaikh and State: The Social and Political Structures of Kurdistan* (London: Zed Books, 1991) pp. 202-3, n. 107.

He cites Nazmi Sevgen's series of publications on the Kurds: "Kürtler," *Belgelerle Türk Tarihi*, esp. nos. 11-19 (1968-9).

42. "Bedirhan Bey," *Kurdistan* 14 (7 Nisan 1315, 19 April 1899); in Bozarslan's collection, Vol. 1, original at end of volume, transliteration from Ottoman article on p. 282.

43. "Welat-Weten," *Kurdistan* 9 (3 Kânûn-i Evvel 1314 / 15 December 1898); in Bozarslan's collection, Vol. 1, original at end of volume, transliteration of Kurdish article on p. 227.

44. *Kurdistan* 6 (28 Eylül 1314 / 10 October 1898); p. 3, in Bozarslan's collection, Vol. 1, original at end, transliteration of Kurdish article on p. 179.

45. *Kurdistan* 2 (23 Nisan 1314 / 5 May 1898) p. 1; in Bozarslan's collection, Vol. 1, original at end, transliteration on p. 122.

46. Van Bruinessen, *Agha, Shaikh and State*, pp. 6-7.

13. MOBILIZATION OF KURDS IN TURKEY DURING THE 1980s AND 1990s

1. Article 2 of the "Law regarding publications in languages other than Turkish" (Law no. 2932, enacted on 19 October 1983) prohibited the expression and dissemination of thought in languages other than those that were the first language of the states recognized by Turkey, effectively banning the Kurdish language; Derya Bayır, *Minorities and Nationalism in Turkish Law* (London: Routledge, 2013) p.103.

2. These include the TKSP (Socialist Party of Turkish Kurdistan), which was established in 1974 but changed its name to the Socialist Party of Kurdistan (PSK in Kurdish acronym) during its 3rd party congress in 1992, the PKK (Kurdistan Workers' Party) which was formally established on 27 November 1978 but had existed as a small political cell since 1973, Rizgarî (Liberation, 1976), KUK (Kurdistan National Liberationists, 1978), Kawa (1978), Ala Rizgarî (Flag of Liberation, 1979) and Tekoşin (Struggle, 1979). Rizgarî, Ala Rizgarî, Tekoşin, Kawa, were able to exist only as small groups publishing pamphlets and magazines, while others (such as the TKSP) proved to be more durable; but since the military coup in Turkey in September 1980, most of its activities have been taking place mainly in Europe.

3. For a more detailed discussion of the PKK's mobilization of the Kurds in Turkey during the 1980s and 1990s, see Cengiz Gunes, "Explaining the PKK's Mobilization of the Kurds in Turkey: Hegemony, Myth and Violence," *Ethnopolitics* 12:3 (2013) pp. 247-67.

4. Two examples of these are Omer Taspinar, *Kurdish Nationalism and Political Islam in Turkey: Kemalist Identity in Transition* (London: Routledge, 2005); and Demet Yalcin Mousseau, "An inquiry into the linkage among the nationalizing policies, democratization and ethno-nationalist conflicts: the Kurdish case in Turkey," *Nationalities Papers* 40:1 (2012) pp. 45-62.

5. David Romano, *The Kurdish Nationalist Movement: Opportunity, Mobilisation and Identity* (Cambridge: Cambridge University Press, 2006) p. 73.

6. Güneş M. Tezcür, "Violence and nationalist mobilisation: the onset of the Kurdish insurgency in Turkey," *Nationalities Papers* 43:2 (2015) pp. 248-66.

7.   Ibid., p. 249.

8.   Ibid.

9.   See also ftn. 20. "Newroz" is the popular Kurmanji Kurdish spelling, but there are other spellings used, including *Nawroz* in the Kurdistan Region of Iraq, and *Nevruz* in Turkish. The spelling of the word has been contested, but the popularly attended celebrations orga- nized by the Kurdish in Turkey use "Newroz," and the official celebrations organized by the state use "Nevruz." Lerna Yanik, "'Nevruz' or 'Newroz'? Deconstructing 'the inven- tion' of a contested tradition in Turkey," *Middle Eastern Studies* 46:2 (March 2006) pp. 285-302.

10. The concept of hegemony is drawn from Marxist theorist Antonio Gramsci and refers to "ethical, moral and political leadership." Aletta Norval, *Aversive Democracy: Inheritance and Originality in the Democratic Tradition* (Cambridge: Cambridge University Press, 2007) p. 46.

11. Ahmet H. Akkaya, "The 'Palestinian Dream' in the Kurdish Context," *Kurdish Studies* 3:1 (2015) pp. 47-63.

12. Abdullah Öcalan, *Kürdistan Devriminin Yolu – Manifesto* [The Path of Kurdistan Revolution - Manifesto] (Cologne: Weşanên Serxwebûn, 1992) p. 198.

13. PKK, *Politik Rapor: Merkez Komitesi Tarafından PKK 1. Konferansına Sunulmuştur* [Political Report: Submitted by the Central Committee to the PKK First Conference] (Cologne: Weşanên Serxwebûn, 1982) p. 162.

14. Abdullah Öcalan, *3. Kongre Konuşmaları* [Discussions of the Third Congress] (Cologne: Weşanên Serxwebûn, 1993) pp. 143-4.

15. The village guard system was established in the mid-1980s; some took part in it volun- tarily, but many people were coerced into becoming village guards. It functioned as a Kurdish pro-state paramilitary force, and they frequently took part in military operations against the PKK guerrillas.

16. Abdullah Öcalan, *Kürdistanda Halk Savaşı ve Gerilla* [People's War and Guerrilla in Kurdistan] (Cologne: Weşanên Serxwebûn, 1993) pp. 301-22.

17. *Serxwebûn* (September 1991) pp. 1- 2.

18. The program of the ERNK was drafted in the early 1980s and appeared as one of the PKK's key political texts in 1982: PKK, *Kürdistan Ulusal Kurtuluş Problemi ve Çözüm Yolu: Kürdistan Ulusal Kurtuluş Cephesi Program Taslağı* (Cologne: Weşanên Serxwebûn, 1984 2nd edn).

19. For a more detailed discussion of the PKK's reactivation of the myth of Newroz to con- struct a contemporary myth of resistance, see Cengiz Gunes, *The Kurdish National Movement in Turkey: From Protest to Resistance* (London: Routledge, 2012) pp. 31-7, 101-23.

20. It is generally accepted that Newroz has been celebrated for nearly 3,000 years in the Near and Middle East. It has a strong connection with Zoroastrianism and Persian mythology; however, there are various other ancient festivals celebrated by ancient societies, includ- ing the Hittites and the Babylonians, to which its origins are also traced. Delal Aydın offers an extended discussion of the construction of Newroz as a myth of origin. She draws

attention to the various discussions in the Kurdish journal *Jîn* during 1918-19, which highlighted the lack of a national holiday for Kurds; and it was within this framework that the legend of Kawa was constructed as a Kurdish national figure. However, initially the celebration of a national holiday was proposed for 31 August as opposed to 21 March. Further attempts were made in the 1930s to construct the legend of Kawa as the myth of origin by the leader of the Ararat Rebellion, Ihsan Nuri. Nuri associated the legend of Kawa with the festival of Tolhildan rather than Newroz, because Newroz had already acquired a national character in Iran, strongly associated with the Persian legend of Jamshid. See Delal Aydın, "Mobilizing the Kurds in Turkey: Newroz as a Myth," in Cengiz Gunes and Welat Zeydanlıoğlu, *The Kurdish Question in Turkey: New Perspectives on Violence, Representation and Reconciliation* (London: Routledge, 2014) pp. 68-89.

21. Aletta Norval uses Wittgenstein's discussion on "aspect dawning" and "aspect change" to provide an account of the way in which political grammars are challenged and the changes that take place in them: "Aspect dawning and change occurs when one realizes that a new kind of characterization of an object or situation may be given, and we see it in those terms." Norval, *Aversive Democracy*, 113.

22. The headline "Diyarbakir Cezaevinde Katliam" [Massacre in Diyarbakir prison] was used by *Serxwebûn* to announce the death of Mazlum Dogan (*Serxwebûn*, June 1982, pp.10-11).

23. *Serxwebûn*, March 1983, p. 9.

24. *Serxwebûn*, December 1982, p. 4.

25. *Berxwedan*, Special Issue, June 1994, p. 4.

26. *Serxwebûn*, March 1986, p. 24.

27. See for example *Serxwebûn*, 15 April 1994.

28. *Serxwebûn*, 15 April 1994, pp. 16-19.

29. *Serxwebûn*, April 1994, p. 19.

30. *Berxwedan*, Special Issue, March 1994.

31. Norval, *Aversive Democracy*, p. 179, emphasis in original.

32. *Berxwedan*, 31 March 1994, pp. 15-16.

14. TURKEY'S KURDISH PROBLEMS, THE KURDS' TURKISH PROBLEMS

1. Erik Meyersonn, "How Turkey's social conservatives won the day for HDP", 8 June 2015, http://erikmeyersson.com/2015/06/08/how-turkeys-social-conservatives-won-the-day-for-hdp/, last accessed 14 June 2015.

2. "Ruling AKP regains majority", 2 November 2015, http://www.bbc.com/news/world-europe-34694420, last accessed 22 January 2016.

3. Amnesty International, "Turkey: end abusive operations under indefinite curfews", https://www.amnesty.org/en/documents/eur44/3230/2016/en/, last accessed 22 January 2016.

4. "28 mayors replaced with trustees by Turkish government", *Hurriyet Daily News*, 11 September 2016, http://www.hurriyetdailynews.com/turkish-interior-ministry-appoints-

trustees-to-28-municipalities-over-pkk--feto-links.aspx?pageID=238&nID=103784& NewsCatID=341, last accessed 8 October 2016.

5. Pinar Tremblay, "Why is AKP losing the Kurds?" *Al-Monitor*, 31 May 2015, http://www. al-monitor.com/pulse/originals/2015/05/turkey-elections-akp-losing-kurdish-support. html, last accessed 24 June 2015.

6. Tozun Bahcheli and Sid Noel, "The Justice and Development Party and the Kurdish question", in Maries Casier and Joost Jongerden (eds), *Nationalism and Politics in Turkey: political Islam, Kemalism and the Kurdish issue* (London and New York: Routledge, 2011) pp.101-20; Umit Cizre, "The emergence of the government's perspective on the Kurdish issue", pp.1-12 and Cengiz Candar, "The Kurdish question: the reasons and fortunes of the 'opening,'" pp.13-19, both *Insight Turkey* 11:4 (Fall 2009); Hugh Pope, "Turkey and the democratic opening for the Kurds", in Fevzo Bilgin and Ali Sarihan (eds), *Understanding Turkey's Kurdish Question* (Lanham and Plymouth: Lexington Books, 2013) pp.117-40.

7. Henri J. Barkey and Graham E. Fuller, *Turkey's Kurdish question* (Lanham, MD: Rowman and Littlefield, 1998); Kemal Kirisci and Gareth Winrow, *The Kurdish Question and Turkey: an example of a trans-state ethnic conflict* (London and Portland: Frank Cass, 1997); Andrew Mango, *Turkey and the War on Terror: for forty years we fought alone* (London and New York: Routledge, 2005); David McDowall, *A Modern History of the Kurds* (London: I. B. Tauris, 1997) pp.418-44; Ali Sarihan, "The two periods of the PKK conflict: 1884-1999 and 2004-2010", in Bilgin and Sarihan (eds), *Understanding Turkey's Kurdish Question*, pp. 89-102; Gunes Murat Tezcur, "The ebb and flow of armed conflict in Turkey: an elusive peace", in David Romano and Mehmet Gurses (eds), *Conflict, Democratization and the Kurds in the Middle East* (New York: Palgrave Macmillan, 2014) pp.171-88.

8. Tulin Daloglu, "Erdogan's many positions on the Kurdish issue", *Al-Monitor,* 23 April 2013, http://www.al-monitor.com/pulse/originals/2013/04/erdogan-kurdish-issue-flip-flop-turkey-peace.html, last accessed 6 June 2013; see also "Erdogan changes his mind on Kurdish issue again: timeline", *Hurriyet Daily News*, 17 March 2015, http://www.hurri-yetdailynews.com/erdogan-changes-mind-on-kurdish-issue-again-timeline.aspx?pageID =238&nID=79818&NewsCatID=338, last accessed 17 June 2015.

9. Michael M. Gunter, *Out of Nowhere: the Kurds of Syria in peace and war* (London: Hurst & Co., 2014) pp. 61-7.

10. *Turkey: the PKK and a Kurdish settlement*, Europe Report 219, International Crisis Group, 11 September 2012, p. 1.

11. Jenna Krajeski, "After the hunger strike", *New Yorker*, 29 November 2012, http://www. newyorker.com/online/blogs/newsdesk/2012/11/after-the-kurdish-hunger-strike-in-turkish-prisons.html, last accessed 6 June 2013.

12. For the full text, see http://www.ekurd.net/mismas/articles/misc2013/3/turkey4603. htm, last accessed 6 June 2013.

13. Yilmaz, Ensaroglu, "Turkey's Kurdish question and the peace process", *Insight Turkey* 15:2 (Spring 2013) pp. 7-17; Michael M. Gunter, "The Turkish-Kurdish peace process stalled

in neutral", *Insight Turkey* 16:1 (Winter 2014) pp. 19-26; Hugh Pope in Bilgin and Sarihan (eds), *Understanding Turkey's Kurdish Question*; Ana Villellas, "New peace talks in Turkey: opportunities and challenges in conflict resolution", *Insight Turkey* 15:2 (Spring 2013) pp. 19-26.

14. *Turkey and the PKK: Saving the Peace Process,* Europe Report 234, International Crisis Group, 6 November 2014, p. 6.

15. Patrick Markey and Isobel Coles, "Insight: hopes, suspicions over peace in Kurdish rebel hideout", Reuters, 27 March 2013, http://www.reuters.com/article/2013/03/27/us-iraq-turkey-pkk-insight-idUSBRE92Q0J520130327, last accessed 19 June 2103; Tim Arango, "Rebel keeps Kurds' guns close at hand in peace talks with Turkey", *New York Times*, 11 April 2013, http://www.nytimes.com/2013/04/12/world/middleeast/rebel-kurd-karay-ilan-defiant-in-turkish-talks.html?pagewanted=all&_r=0, last accessed 19 June 2013.

16. "Ahmet Turk blames Ankara government, warns the peace talks will fail", *Kurdpress*, 11 June 2013, http://www.kurdpress.com/En/NSite/FullStory/News/?Id=4733#Title=%0A%09%09%09%09%09%09%09%09Ahmet Turk blames Ankara government, warns the peace talks will fail%0A%09%09%09%09%09%09%09%09, last accessed 19 June 2013.

17. "Kurdish conference ends with list of demands from gov't", *Today's Zaman*, 17 June 2013, http://www.todayszaman.com/news-318516-kurdish-conference-ends-with-list-of-demands-from-govt.html, last accessed 17 June 2013.

18. Gunes Murat Tezcur, "Prospects for resolution of the Kurdish question: a realist perspective", *Insight Turkey* 15:2 (Spring 2013) pp. 69-84.

19. "Bayik says PKK won't lay down arms unless gov't takes concrete steps", *Today's Zaman*, 31 March 2015, http://www.todayszaman.com/anasayfa_bayik-says-pkk-wont-lay-down-arms-unless-govt-takes-concrete-steps_376828.html, last accessed 25 June 2015.

20. Johanna Nykanen, "Identity, narrative and frames: assessing Turkey's Kurdish initiatives", *Insight Turkey* 15:2 (Spring 2013) pp. 85-101.

21. *Turkey and the PKK: Saving the Peace Process,* Europe Report 234, International Crisis Group, 6 November 2014, pp. 36-7.

22. Mahmut Bozarslan, "What caused the clashes in Diyarbakir?" *Al-Monitor*, 15 June 2015, http://www.al-monitor.com/pulse/originals/2015/06/turkey-diyarbakir-remains-tense-after-clashes-between-kurds.html?utm_source=Al-Monitor+Newsletter+%5BEnglish%5D&utm_campaign=26b00ca343-June_16_2015&utm_medium=email&utm_term=0_28264b27a0-26b00ca343-102324909, last accessed 17 June 2015.

23. For insights into Turkey's evolving policy toward the Syrian crisis, see "Turkey's role in a shifting Syria", Atlantic Council, 13 May 2015, http://www.atlanticcouncil.org/blogs/menasource/turkey-s-role-in-a-shifting-syria, last accessed 18 June 2015; "Turkey's evolving Syria strategy", *Foreign Affairs*, 9 February 2015, http://www.foreignaffairs.com/articles/143023/aaron-stein/turkeys-evolving-syria-strategy, last accessed 5 March 2015: "The origins of Turkey's buffer zone in Syria", 11 December 2014, http://warontherocks.com/2014/12/the-origins-of-turkeys-buffer-zone-in-syria/, last accessed 9 February 2015, all by Aaron Stein. See also Ozlem Tur, "Turkey and the Syrian crisis: deepening regional and domestic challenges", *Orient* 1 (2015) pp. 23-8.

24. For a useful compilation of allegations, suspicions, and evidence, see David. L Phillips, "Research Paper: ISIS-Turkey Links", 9 November 2015, http://www.huffingtonpost. com/david-l-phillips/research-paper-isis-turke_b_6128950.html, last accessed 7 February 2015.

25. "Erdogan: I don't understand why Kobane is so strategic for the US", *Today's Zaman*, 22 October 2015, http://www.todayszaman.com/national_erdogan-i-dont-understand-why-kobani-is-so-strategic-for-us_362331.html, last accessed 6 March 2015.

26. "Turkish President says troubled by Kurdish advance in Syrian Kurdistan", 14 June 2015, http://ekurd.net/turkish-president-says-troubled-by-kurdish-advance-in-syrian-kurdistan-2015-06-14, last accessed 16 June 2015.

27. "Turkey warns US and coalition against demographic change in Syria", *Hurriyet Daily News*, 16 June 2015, http://www.hurriyetdailynews.com/turkey-warns-us-and-coalition-against-demographic-change-in-syria.aspx?pageID=238&nID=84055&NewsCa tID=338, last accessed 17 June 2015.

28. "PKK, ISIL are the same, says Erdoğan", *Today's Zaman*, 4 October 2014, http://www. todayszaman.com/national_pkk-isil-are-the-same-says-erdogan_360766.html, last accessed 5 March 2015.

29. For a statement of Turkey's position by President Erdoğan's foreign policy advisor, see Ibrahim Kalin, "What Turkey wants in the war on Islamic State", *Wall Street Journal*, 21 October 2014, http://www.wsj.com/articles/ibrahim-kalin-what-turkey-wants-in-the-war-on-isis-1413758083, last accessed 5 March 2015. See also "Fighting ISIL not a priority for Turkey: US spy chief", *Hurriyet Daily News*, 27 February 2015, http://www. hurriyetdailynews.com/fighting-isil-not-a-priority-for-turkey-us-spy-chief.aspx?pageID =238&nID=78946&NewsCatID=359, last accessed 5 March 2015.

30. Nihat Ali Ozcan and H. Erdem Gurkaynak, "Who are these armed people on the mountains?" February 2012, www.tepev.org.tr, last accessed 17 May 2012.

31. "Flight of Icarus? The PYD's precarious rise in Syria", Middle East Report 151, International Crisis Group, 8 May 2014; Michael M. Gunter, *Out of Nowhere: the Kurds of Syria in peace and war* (London: Hurst & Co., 2014).

32. For analyses of Syria's Kurdish politics, see Denise Natali, "Syria's Kurdish Quagmire", 3 May 2012, www.ekurd.net/mismas/articles/misc2012/5/syriakurd486.htm, last accessed 3 May 2012; Jordi Tejel, *Syria's Kurds: history, politics and society* (London and New York: Routledge, 2009); *Syria's Kurds: A Struggle Within a Struggle*, Middle East Report 136, International Crisis Group, 22 January 2013; *Who Is the Syrian Kurdish Opposition?: The Development of Kurdish Parties, 1956-2011*, KurdWatch, Report 8, December 2011.

33. Sevil Erkus, "Erdoğan vows to prevent Kurdish state in northern Syria, as Iran warns Turkey", *Hurriyet Daily News*, 27 June 2015, http://www.hurriyetdailynews.com/erdogan-vows-to-prevent-kurdish-state-in-northern-syria-as-iran-warns-turkey.aspx?pageID =238&nID=84630&NewsCatID=338, last accessed 27 June 2015.

34. For details, see www.kurdwatch.org.

35. "Turkey objects to PYD as date for Syria talks remains unclear", *Hurriyet Daily News*, 21 January 2016, last accessed 23 January 2016.

36. Serkan Demirtas, "Syria supporting PKK, says intelligence report", *Hurriyet Daily News*, 23 March 2012, www.hurriyetdailynews.com/report-syria-supporting-pkk. aspx?pageID=238&nid=16699, last accessed 27 February 2013; Cengiz Candar, "Turkey claims Iran providing logistical support for PKK", *Al-Monitor*, 30 December 2012, www. al-monitor.com/pulse/originals/2012/al-monitor/iran-turkey-shiite-sunni-pkk.html, last accessed 22 January 2013; Oytun Orhan, "Syria's PKK game", *Today's Zaman*, 14 February 2012, www.todayszaman.com, last accessed 27 February 2013.

37. Sevil Kucukkosum, "PYD leader meets Turkish officials", *Hurriyet Daily News*, 3 June 2013, http://www.hurriyetdailynews.com/pyd-leader-meets-turkish-officials.aspx?page ID=238&nID=48066&NewsCatID=352, last accessed 20 June 2013.

38. Gokhan Bacik, "Turkey and Russia's proxy war and the Kurds", 21 January 2016, http:// www.gmfus.org/publications/turkey-and-russias-proxy-war-and-the-kurds, last accessed 22 January 2016.

39. Amed Dicle, "Will Turkey's Jarablus win lead to showdown with Kurds?" *Al-Monitor*, 25 August 2016, http://www.al-monitor.com/pulse/originals/2016/08/turkey-syria-jarab-lus-main-target-kurds-isis.html?utm_source=Boomtrain&utm_medium=manual&utm_ campaign=20160826&bt_email=william.h.park@kcl.ac.uk&bt_ts=1472229405057, last accessed 8 October 2016.

40. "Syrian Kurdish PYD leader says Turkey must get rid of its 'Kurdophobia,'", 17 June 2015, http://ekurd.net/syrian-kurdish-pyd-leader-says-turkey-must-get-rid-of-its-kurdopho-bia-2015-06-17, last accessed 18 June 2015.

41. "Iraqi Kurdish leader Barzani urges support for peace process in Diyarbakir rally with Turkish PM", *Hurriyet Daily News*, 16 November 2013, http://www.hurriyetdailynews. com/iraqi-kurdish-leader-barzani-urges-support-for-peace-process-in-diyarbakir-rally-with-turkish-pm.aspx?PageID=238&NID=58028&NewsCatID=338, last accessed 20 June 2015.

42. See Bill Park, *Turkey-Kurdish Regional Government relations after the US withdrawal from Iraq: putting the Kurds on the map*, Strategic Studies Institute, US Army War College, March 2014, pp. 8-14.

43. Ibid., pp. 22-31; Ali Balci, *"Energized" neighbourliness: relations between Turkey and the Kurdish Regional Government*, Analysis 9, Foundation for Political, Economic and Social Research (SETA), September 2014; Nicholas Borroz, "Turkey's energy strategy: Kurdistan over Iraq", *Turkish Policy Quarterly* 13:2 (Summer 2014) pp. 103-10.

44. Charles Kennedy, "KRG announces plans to build second oil pipeline to Turkey", 31 October 2013, http://oilprice.com/Latest-Energy-News/World-News/KRG-Announces-Plans-to-Build-Second-Oil-Pipeline-to-Turkey.html, last accessed 27 June 2015.

45. "Turkey, KRG agree 50-year energy deal", *Anadolu Agency*, 4 June 2014, http://www. aa.com.tr/en/rss/340164--turkey-krg-agree-50-year-energy-deal.

46. Khalid Al Ansary and Bruce Stanley, "Cash strapped Iraqi Kurds to start gas exports to Turkey in 2016", 13 January 2016, http://www.bloomberg.com/news/arti-cles/2016-01-13/cash-strapped-iraqi-kurds-to-start-gas-exports-to-turkey-in-2016, last accessed 22 January 2016.

47. "Turkey gives loan to Kurdistan Regional Government", *Daily Sabah*, 25 February 2015, http://www.dailysabah.com/money/2015/02/25/turkey-gives-loan-to-kurdistan-regional-government, last accessed 24 June 2015.

48. "US says oil firms should respect Baghdad government", 21 August, 2012, www.ekurd. net/mismas/articles/misc2012/8/govt2064.htm; "Nuland on Iraq oil deals", Turkish Radio and Television Corporation (TRT), 9 January 2013, www.trt-world.com/trt-world/en/newsDetail.aspx?HaberKodu=3d31f4cf-fe09-4026-a320-7f4c9ae9390c.

49. For more detail on this, see Bill Park, *Turkey's Policy Towards Northern Iraq: Problems and Perspectives;* Adelphi Paper 374, London: International Institute for Strategic Studies, May 2005; Asa Lundgren, *The Unwelcome Neighbour: Turkey's Kurdish policy* (London and New York, I. B. Tauris, 2007).

50. Gareth Jenkins, "A military analysis of Turkey's incursion into northern Iraq", *Terrorism Monitor* 65, 7 March 2008, www.jamestown.org/programs/gta/single/?tx_ttnews%5Btt_news%5D=4774&tx_ttnews%5BbackPid%5D=167&no_cache=1, last accessed 18 February 2013.

51. Kemal Avci, "Erdoğan advisor blames Maliki, says Iraq 'practically divided,'" Rudaw, 18 June 2014, http://rudaw.net/english/interview/18062014, last accessed 22 June 2014. See also Bill Park, "Turkey's dual relationship with Iraq: Ankara, Baghdad and Erbil", *Orient* 1 (2015) pp. 55-6.

52. Hevidar Ahmed, "Senior Kurdistan official: IS was at Erbil's gates, Turkey did not help", Rudaw, 16 September 2014, http://rudaw.net/english/interview/16092014; Dorian Jones, "Islamic state tests Turkey-Iraqi Kurd ties", *Voice of America News*, 12 September 2014, http://www.voanews.com/content/islamic-state-tests-turkey-iraqi-kurd-tie/2447851.html, both last accessed 22 September 2014.

53. *Syria's Kurds: a struggle within a struggle*, Middle East Report 136, International Crisis Group, 22 January 2013.

54. Fehim Tastekin, "Kurdish rivalry delays victory in Sinjar", *Al-Monitor*, 3 February 2015, http://www.al-monitor.com/pulse/originals/2015/02/turkey-syria-iraq-kurdish-rivalry-yezidi-lan.html?utm_source=Al-Monitor+Newsletter+%5BEnglish%5D&utm_campaign=654f8c1564-February_4_2015&utm_medium=email&utm_term=0_28264b27a0-654f8c1564-102324909, last accessed 24 June 2015.

55. *The Kurdish National Council in Syria*, Carnegie Middle East Center, 15 February 2012, www.carnegie-mec.org/publications/?fa=48502, last accessed 25 January 2013.

56. "Syrian Kurds sign power-sharing deal to draw more support", 23 October 2014, http://www.ekurd.net/mismas/articles/misc2014/10/syriakurd1576.htm; "TEV-DEM council member speaks about Duhok agreement", 26 October 2014, http://www.ekurd.net/mismas/articles/misc2014/10/syriakurd1599.htm, both last accessed 24 June 2015.

57. Fehim Tastekin, "KRG trench divides Syrian, Iraqi Kurds", *Al-Monitor*, 21 April 2014, http://www.al-monitor.com/pulse/contents/authors/fehim-tastekin.html?b=65, last accessed 24 June 2015; Wladirmir van Wildenburg, "Border arrests reveal disunity, conflict among Syrian Kurds", *Al-Monitor*, 21 May 2013, http://www.al-monitor.com/pulse/originals/2013/05/pyd-arrests-syrian-kurds.html, last accessed 5 June 2013.

58. Interview with senior PYD figure, London, 25 March 2015.

59. See for example Vager Sadullah, "PKK and KDP: there's drama between Kurdistan's two best frenemies", 12 February 2015, http://ekurd.net/pkk-and-kdp-theres-drama-between-kurdistans-two-best-frenemies-2015-02-12, last accessed 25 June 2015.

60. A point made very strongly by a senior PYD official in an interview in London, 25 March 2015.

61. Bill Park, "Turkey's isolated stance: an ally no more, or just the usual turbulence?", *International Affairs* 91:3 (May 2015) pp. 581-600.

15. THE TRANSFORMATION OF TURKEY'S KURDISH QUESTION

1. Stansfield Gareth, "The Unravelling of the Post-First World War State System? The Kurdistan Region of Iraq and the Transformation of the Middle East," *International Affairs* 89:2 (2013).

2. Janet Klein, *The Margins of Empire: Kurdish Militias in the Ottoman Tribal Zone* (Stanford, CA: Stanford University Press, 2011) pp. 4-12.

3. Michael A. Reynolds, *Shattering Empires* (Cambridge: Cambridge University Press, 2011) pp. 46-81.

4. Martin van Bruinessen, *Agha, Shaikh and the State* (London: Zed Books, 1992) pp. 281-3.

5. Cemil Kocak (ed.), *27 Mayis Bakanlar Kurulu Tutanaklari* v. 1 & 2 (Istanbul: Yapi Kredi Yayinlari, 2010) pp. 62-4.

6. Taspinar Omer, *Kurdish Nationalism and Political Islam in Turkey* (New York and London: Routledge, 2005) p. 93.

7. Marcus Aliza, *Blood and Belief* (New York: New York University Press, 2007) pp. 33-51.

8. Nicole Watts, *Activists in Office: Kurdish Politics and Protest in Turkey* (Seattle: University of Washington Press, 2010).

9. Henri J. Barkey, "Turkey and the PKK: A Pyrrhic Victory?" in Robert Art and Louise Richardson (eds), *Democracy and Counterterrorism Lessons from the Past* (Washington, DC: USIP Press, 2007).

10. Hasan Cemal, *Kürtler* (Istanbul: Dogan Kitapçilik, 2003) pp. 60, 67, 157.

11. Sükrü Elekdag, "Kürt Sorunu," *Milliyet*, 16 August 1999.

12. Belma Akçura, *Devletin Kürt Filmi* (Ankara: Ayraç Kitabevi Yayinlari, 2008) pp. 243-7.

13. Shwan Zulal, "Survival Strategies and Diplomatic Tools: The Kurdistan Region's Foreign Policy Outlook," *Insight Turkey* 14:3 (2012) pp. 148, 156.

14. Yasemin Çongar, "Kusatilmislik ve 'dinamik güçler," *Milliyet*, 19 February 2007.

15. Öcalan, *Demokratik Kurtulus ve Özgür Yasami Insa* (Imrali tutanaklari) (Neuss, Germany: Mezopotamya Yayinevi, 2015).

16. "Dolmabahçe anlaşması", *Cumhuriyet*, 28 February 2015, http://www.cumhuriyet.com.tr/haber/turkiye/224047/Dolmabahce_anlasmasi.html

17. Murat Yetkin, "Türk Devletinin PKK ile Imtihani: Üçüncü Asama," *Radikal*, 2 January 2015.

18. Fikret Bila, "Org. Basbug: Siyaset ve Terör Agalarından Kurtulmak Lazım," *Milliyet*, 22 September 2009.

19. "Necdet Özel: Kirmizi Çizgiler Asilirsa Geregini Yapariz," *Radikal*, 30 August 2014.

20. Hamit Bozarslan, "Les Kurdes et l'Option Étatique," *Politique Étrangère* 2 (2014) p. 21.

21. Bill Park, "Turkey, the US and the KRG: Moving Parts and the Geopolitical Realities," *Insight Turkey* 14:3 (2012) p. 116.

22. Rusen Çakir, "(IS)ID'in Türkiye'ye Ettigi ve Edebilecegi Kötülükler," *Vatan*, 8 October 2014.

23. "Cumhurbaskani Erdogan: 'PYD bizim icin PKK ile estir,'" *Hürriyet*, 20 October 2014.

24. "Türkiye'den Güçlü Tavir Bekliyorduk," *Vatan*, 13 October 2014.

25. "6-7 Ekim bilançosu 50 ölü", *Hürriyet*, 6 November 2014, http://www.hurriyet.com.tr/6-7-ekim-in-aci-bilancosu-50-olu-27525777

26. Henri J. Barkey and Direnç Kadioglu, "The Turkish Constitution and the Kurdish Question," Carnegie Endowment for International Peace, 1 August 2011.

27. Nuray Mert, "Ya asıl sorun 'Kürtlerin iktidarla ittifakı' değilse? Ya kavgaya tutuşurlarsa?" *Diken*, 5 January 2015. http://www.diken.com.tr/ya-asil-sorun-kurtlerin-iktidar-ile-ittifaki-degilse-ya-kavgaya-tutusurlarsa/

16. CONTRASTING TURKISH PARADIGMS TOWARD THE VOLATILE KURDISH PROBLEM

1. On why Kurdish nationalism presented such a minimal threat in Ottoman times, see Hakan Ozoglu, *Kurdish Notables and the Ottoman State: Evolving Identities, Competing Loyalties, and Shifting Boundaries* (Albany, NY: State University of New York, 2004) p. 117; Denise Natali, *The Kurds and the State: Evolving National Identity in Iraq, Turkey, and Iran* (Syracuse, NY: Syracuse University Press, 2005) p. 24.

2. For background, see Robert Olson, *The Emergence of Kurdish Nationalism and the Sheikh Said Rebellion, 1880-1925* (Austin, TX: University of Texas Press, 1989); Martin van Bruinessen, *Agha, Shaikh and State: The Social and Political Structures of Kurdistan* (London and New Jersey: Zed Books, 1992) pp. 265-305.

3. For background, see Jacob M. Landau (ed.), *Ataturk and the Modernization of Turkey* (Boulder, CO: Westview Press, 1984); Feroz Ahmad, *The Making of Modern Turkey* (London and New York: Routledge, 1993). On the primitive state of the Kurdish national identity and language during the 1920s and 1930s, see Martin Strohmeier, *Crucial Images in the Presentation of a Kurdish National Identity: Heroes and Patriots, Traitors and Foes* (Leiden and Boston: Brill, 2003).

4. M. Hakan Yavuz, "Five Stages of the Construction of Kurdish Nationalism in Turkey", *Nationalism and Ethnic Politics* 7 (Autumn 2001) pp. 1-24; Hamit Bozarslan, "Kurdish Nationalism in Turkey: From Tacit Contract to Rebellion (1919-1925)", in Abbas Vali

(ed.), *Essays on the Origins of Kurdish Nationalism* (Costa Mesa, CA: Mazda, 2003) pp. 163-90.

5. For an analysis of Ozal's proposals, see Michael M. Gunter, "Turgut Ozal and the Kurdish Question", in Marlies Casier and Joost Jongerden (eds), *Nationalism and Politics in Turkey: Political Islam, Kemalism and the Kurdish Issue* (London and New York: Routledge, 2011) pp. 85-100.

6. For background on the PKK, see Aliza Marcus, *Blood and Belief: The PKK and the Kurdish Fight for Independence* (New York and London: New York University Press, 2007).

7. For background, see Michael M. Gunter, "Turkey: The Politics of a New Democratic Constitution", *Middle East Policy* 19 (Spring 2012) pp. 119-25.

8. Cited in "The Sun Also Rises in the South East", Briefing (Ankara), 15 August 2005.

9. For background, see Michael M. Gunter and M. Hakan Yavuz, "Turkish Paradox: Progressive Islamists versus Reactionary Secularists", *Critique: Critical Middle Eastern Studies* 16 (Fall 2007) pp. 289-301.

10. On Turkey's Deep State, see Michael M. Gunter, "Turkey, Kemalism and the 'Deep State,'" in David Romano and Mehmet Gurses (eds), *Conflict, Democratization and the Kurds in the Middle East: Turkey, Iran, Iraq, and Syria* (New York: Palgrave Macmillan, 2014) pp. 17-39.

11. Cited in "Gul: Kurdish Problem is the Most Important Problem of Turkey", *Today's Zaman*, 11 May 2009.

12. Cited in *Today's Zaman*, 12 August 2009.

13. Author's contacts with Kurdish sources in Europe and the Middle East. For background, see Michael M. Gunter, *The Kurds Ascending: The Evolving Solution to the Kurdish Problem in Iraq and Turkey* (New York: Palgrave Macmillan, 2nd edn 2011) pp. 155-88.

14. *Hurriyet*, issues of 18 November 2009, 2 December 2009, 9 December 2009, and 14 December 2009, as cited in Menderes Cinar, "The Militarization of Secular Opposition in Turkey", *Insight Turkey* 12 (Spring 2010) p. 119.

15. Odul Celep, "Turkey's Radical Right and the Kurdish Issue: The MHP's Reaction to the 'Democratic Opening,'" *Insight Turkey* 12 (Spring 2010) p. 136.

16. For more on the legal, pro-Kurdish political parties in Turkey, see Nicole F. Watts, *Activists in Office: Kurdish Politics and Protest in Turkey* (Seattle and London: University of Washington Press, 2010).

17. The Koma Civaken Kurdistan (KCK) or Kurdistan Communities Union is an umbrella organization that supposedly includes the PKK. In practice, however, the two are the same.

18. Human Rights Watch, "Turkey Arrests Expose Flawed Justice System", 1 November 2011, http://www.hrw.org/news/2011/11/01/turkey-arrests-expose, last accessed 13 November 2011.

19. Ibid.

20. "Turkey's Erdoğan Calls for More Support for Peace Move", *Today's Zaman*, 26 February 2013, http://www.todayszaman.com/news-308165-turkey's-Erdogan, last accessed 1 March 2013.

21. The following data were taken from "Kongra-Gel Held its 9th General Assembly", Firatnews.com, 10 July 2013, http://en.firatnews.com/news/news/kongra-gel, last accessed 11 July 2013.

22. In reality, Karayilan had long held this position. As already noted, the KCK is an umbrella organization that supposedly includes the PKK. In practice, however, the two are the same.

23. Amberin Zaman, "Kurdish Rebel Group in Turkey Re-Focuses on Syria", *Al-Monitor*, 17 July 2013, http://www.al-monitor.com/pulse/originals/2013/07/pkk-leadership-change. . . , last accessed 19 July 2013.

24. This citation and the following information are largely taken from Guillaume Perrier, "Uneasy Truce Holds as Kurdish Guerrilla Forces Withdraw from Turkey", *Guardian*, 3 September 2013, https://www.theguardian.com/world/2013/sep/03/kurdistan-turkey-erdogan-truce-peace-limbo, last accessed 5 September 2013.

25. This citation and the following data were garnered from "PKK Plans 100 Protests a Day, Expecting Action from Gov't", *Today's Zaman*, 25 August 2013, http://www.mesop. de/2013/08/25/pkk-plans-100-protests, last accessed 25 August 2013.

26. "PKK Stops Further Withdrawing from Turkey", MESOP, 10 September 2013, http:// www.mesop.de/2013/09/10/pkk-stops-further, last accessed 10 September 2013.

27. Chase Winter, "Turkey's Strained Kurdish Peace Process", foreignpolicy.com, 11 December 2013, http://www.foreignpolicy.com/posts/2013/12/11, last accessed 13 December 2013.

28. "Disillusioned and Divided", *Economist*, 24 May 2014, p. 45.

29. Cited in Kadri Gursel, "Time Running Out for Turkey-PKK Peace Process", *Al-Monitor*, 4 November 2013, http://www.al-monitor.com/pulse/originals/2013/11/akp-stall-kurd-peace-process.html, last accessed 11 November 2013.

30. Cited in "Öcalan: This Process Has Three Components", *Kurdish Info*, 8 December 2013, http://www.kurdishinfo.com/ocalan-process-three-components, last accessed 14 December 2013.

31. "Celik Signals Turkey to Welcome Independent Kurdish State in Iraq", *Today's Zaman*, 29 June 2014, http://www.mesop.de/2014/06/29/mesop-news-celik-signals, last accessed 30 June 2014.

32. Ulas Doga Eralp, "Turkey's Rapprochement with Iraqi Kurdistan: An Obstacle to Kurdish Peace Process?" *Eurasiareview*, 28 November 2013, http://www.mesop.de/2013/11/28/ turkeys-rapprochement, last accessed 28 November 2013.

33. Kurdistan National Congress (KNK), "The Peace Process in Turkey-Kurdistan Has Reached a Serious Stage", 9 March 2015. KNK homepage: www.kongrakurdistan.net, last accessed 15 April 2015.

34. Selahattin Demirtas, "The Middle East, the Kurdish Peace Process in Turkey, and Radical Democracy", *Turkish Political Quarterly* 13 (Winter 2015) p. 30, in www.turkishpolicy. com, last accessed 15 April 2015.

35. See, for example, David L. Phillips, "Research Paper: ISIS-Turkey List", *Huffington Post*, 9 November 2014, http://www.huffingtonpost.com/david-l-phillips/research-paper-isis-

turke_b_6128950.html, which cites numerous sources. In addition, see Amberin Zaman, "Syrian Kurdish Leader: Ankara Supporting Jihadists", *Al-Monitor*, 23 September 2013, www.al-monitor.com/pulse/security/2013/09/pyd-leader-salih-muslim-turkey-support-jihadists-syria.html, last accessed 5 October 2013.

36. "PYD Announces Constitution for Kurdish Regions", *Kurdpress*, 22 July 2013, http://www.mesop.de/2013/07/22/pyd-announces, last accessed 22 July 2013.

37. "PYD 'Playing a Dangerous Game': PYD Has Authority Only on Regions 'Given by the al-Assad Regime': Iraqi Kurdish Leader Barzani", Anadolu Agency, 14 November 2013, http://www.mesop.de/2013/11/14/pyd-playing -a-dangerous-game, last accessed 14 November 2013.

38. Ahmet Cavutoglu, *Strategik Derinlik: Turkiye'nin Uluslararasi Konumu* [Strategic Depth: Turkey's International Position] (Istanbul: Kure Yayinlari, 2001). Although this 560-plus-page book has not been translated into English, see Behlul Ozkan, "Turkey, Davutoglu and the Idea of Pan-Islamism", *Survival: Global Politics and Strategy* 56 (August-September 2014) pp. 119-40; and Alexander Murinson, "The Strategic Depth Doctrine of Turkish Foreign Policy", *Middle Eastern Studies* 42 (November 2006) pp. 945-64 for good analyses.

39. For background, see Tim Arango and Ceylan Yeginsu, "Governing Party Loses Majority in Turkish Vote", *New York Times*, 8 June 2015, p. 1; and Burcu Ozcelik, "What the HDP Success Means for Turkey", *Sada* (Carnegie Endowment for International Peace), 11 June 2015, http://carnegieendowment.org/sada/2015/06/11/what-hdp-success, last accessed 12 June 2015.

40. Specific grievances against the AKP included the Gezi Park protests in June 2013 that revealed wide-spread resentments, corruption scandals involving Erdoğan and his government in December 2013, Erdoğan's super-presidential proposals perceived by many as dangerously authoritarian, Erdoğan's new 1,100-room presidential palace, the perceived failure of the AKP's complicated Syrian policy, and the resulting 2 million Syrian refugees straining the Turkish infrastructure, and maybe most significantly the slowing Turkish economy, among others.

41. For background, see Michael M. Gunter, "Reopening Turkey's Closed Kurdish Opening", *Middle East Policy* 20 (Summer 2013) pp. 88-98; and Michael M. Gunter, "The Turkish-Kurdish Peace Process Stalled in Neutral", *Insight Turkey* 16 (Winter 2014) pp. 19-26.

42. M. Hakan Yavuz and Nihat Ali Ozcan, "Turkish Democracy and the Kurdish Question", *Middle East Policy* 22:4 (Winter 2015) p. 76.

43. Ibid., p. 78.

44. See ftn. 35.

45. Cited in "After the Coup, the Counter-coup", *Economist*, 23 July 2016, p. 14.

46. A subsequent report increased the figure to 80,000 civil servants suspended from their jobs and more than 20,000 arrested. Mustafa Akyol, "Turkey's Great Purge", *New York Times*, 23 August 2016, http://www.nytimes.com/2016/08/24/opinion/turkey's-great-purge.html, accessed 25 August 2016. The following discussion is based largely on Amnesty International, "Turkey: Independent Monitors Must Be Allowed to Access Detainees

amid Torture Allegations", 24 July 2016, http://www.amnesty.org/en/latest/
news/2016/07/turkey...", accessed 26 July 2016; Merrit Kennedy, "Amnesty International:
After Turkey's Failed Coup, Some Detainees are Tortured, Raped", National Public Radio
(NPR),25July2016,http://www.npr.org/sections/thetwo-way/2016/07/25/487254277/
amnesty-nternational-after ...", accessed 29 July 2016; "Amnesty International Reports
'Credible Evidence' Turkey Torturing Post-coup Detainees", *Haaretz*, 29 July 2016, http://
www.haaretz.com/middle-east-news/turkey/1.733018, accessed 29 July 2016; Jason
Hanna and Tim Hume, "Turkey Detainees Tortured, Raped after Failed Coup, Rights
Group Says", CNN, 27 July 2016, http://www.cnn.com/2016/07/26/europe/turkey-
coup-attempt-aftermath/, accessed 29 July 2016; William Reed, "Turkish Police Torture,
Rape Own Soldiers, Officers, Judges", Clarion Project, 25 July 2016, https://www.clari-
onproject.org/analysis/turkish-police-rape-own-soldiers-officers-judges, accessed 29 July
2016; Elizabeth Redden, "Turkey's Fraying International Ties", *Inside Higher Ed*, 29 July
2016, https://www.insidehighered.com/news/2016/07/29/how-crackdown-turkey-
affecting-international-academic-collaboration, accessed 29 July 2016; and interviews
with various sources who asked to be anonymous given the fluid, dangerous situation prevailing in Turkey.

47. Peace in Kurdistan Campaign, "Neither Coup nor State of Emergency: Turkey Needs
Peace and Democracy", 25 July 2016, https://peaceinkurdistancampaign.
com/2016/07/25/neither-coup-nor-state-of emergency...", accessed 29 July 2016.

48. For an analysis, see Michael M. Gunter, "The Kurdish Issue in Turkey: Back to Square
One?" *Turkish Policy Quarterly* 14 (Winter 2016) pp. 77-86. The entire issue of this journal contains many other articles related to the failure of the ceasefire.

49. The following discussion was largely taken from Tom Stevenson, "Loss and Depression
in Turkey's Kurdish Southeast", DW, 28 September 2016, http://www.dw.com/en/loss-
and-depression-in-turkeys-kurdish-southeast/a-19557734, accessed 28 September 2016.

50. Cited in ibid.

51. Cited in ibid.

52. The following discussion and citation are taken from Emre Peker, "Turkey's Post-Coup
Crackdown Hits Kurds", *Wall Street Journal*, 26 September 2016, http://www.wsj.com/
articles/turkeys-post-coup-crackdown-hits-kurds-1474934122, accessed 28 September
2016.

53. This citation and following discussion were taken from Dorian Jones, "Kurdish Teachers'
Arrests Heighten Concerns about Turkey's Emergency Rule", *Voice of America*, 26
September 2016, http://www.voanews.com/a/arrests-kurdish-teachers-turkey-emer-
gency-rule/3525498.html, accessed 28 September 2016.

54. Cited in "The Return of Turkey's 'Dirty War' against the Kurds", DW, 16 September 2016,
http://www.dw.com/en/the-return-of-turkeys-dirty-war-against-the-kurds//a-19557637,
accessed 28 September 2016.

55. "Turkey's Saturday Mothers Meet for 600th Time Demanding Justice for Forcibly
Disappeared", DW, 25 September 2016, http://www.dw.com/en/turkeys-saturday-moth-

ers-meet-for-600th-time-demanding-justice-for   forcibly-disappeared/a-35884103, accessed 28 September 2016.

56. "Turkish President Vows 'Treasonous' Academics Will Pay the Price", *Hurriyet Daily News*, 20 January 2016, http://www.hurriyetdailynews.com/turkish-president-vows-trea-sonous-academics-will-pay-the-price.aspx?pageID. . . , accessed 5 March 2016.

57. Ceylan Yeginsu, "Turkish Parliament Approves Stripping Lawmakers of their Immunity", *New York Times*, 20 May 2016, http://www.nytimes.com/2016/05/21/world/europe/turkey-parliament-immunity-kurds.html, accessed 26 September 2016.

58. The following discussion is largely based on the eye-opening analyses by Michael A. Reynolds, "Damaging Democracy: The U.S., Fethullah Gülen, and Turkey's Upheaval", Foreign Policy Research Institute, www.fpri.org/article/2016/09/damaging-democracy-u-s-fethullah-gulen-turkeys-upheaval/, accessed 3 October 2016; and Asli Aydintasbas, "The Good, The Bad, and The Gulenists: The Role of the Gulen Movement in Turkey's Coup Attempt", European Council on Foreign Relations, September 2016, www.ecfr.eu/page/-/ECFR_188_-_The_Good_The_Bad_And_The_Gulenists.pdf, accessed 25 September 2016. For further background, see M. Hakan Yavuz, *Towards an Islamic Enlightenment: The Gülen Movement* (New York: Oxford University Press, 2013).

59. "US Had No Foreknowledge of Turkey Coup Attempt: Biden", Press TV, 24 August 2016, http://www.presstv.ir/Detail/2016/08/24/4815/Biden-US-Turkey-coup-yildirim, accessed 26 August 2016.

60. The following discussion is largely based on Mustafa Gurbuz, "Turkey's Kurdish Question and the Hizmet Movement", Rethink Paper 22, Rethink Institute, Washington, DC, March 2015, www.rethinkinstitute.org/wp-content/uploads/2015/03/Gurbuz-Turkey's-Kurdish-Question-and-Hizmet.pdf, accessed 30 August 2016; and Mustafa Gurbuz, "Recognition of Kurdish Identity and the Hizmet Movement", Gülen Movement, http://www.gulenmovement.us/recognition-of-kurdish-identity-and-the-hizmet-movement.html, accessed 30 August 2016.

61. Cited in Gurbuz, "Turkey's Kurdish Movement and the Hizmet Movement", p. 9.

62. The following discussion is largely taken from Mustafa Akyol, "Is Gülen Movement against Peace with PKK?" *Al-Monitor*, 22 May 2013, http://www.al-monitor.com/pulse/originals/2013/05/gulen-movement-peace-process-pkk.html, accessed 30 August 2016.

63. Christopher de Bellaigue, "Welcome to Demokrasi: How Erdogan Got More Popular Than Ever", *Guardian*, 30 August 2016, https://www.theguardian.com/world/2016/aug/30/welcome-to-demokrasi-how-erdogan-got-more-popular-than-ever, accessed 29 September 2016; Onur Ant, "Erdoğan's Approval Rating Soars in Turkey Following Coup Attempt", Bloomberg, 10 August 2016, http://www.bloomberg.com/news/articles/2016-08-11/erdogan-s-approval-rating-soars-in-turkey-following-coup-attempt, accessed 29 September 2016.

17. THE KURDISTAN WORKERS' PARTY (PKK)

1. This contribution is based on a body of work on the PKK developed in collaboration with Ahmet Hamdi Akkaya and Joost Jongerden, "The PKK in the 2000s: continuity through breaks," in Marlies Casier and Joost Jongerden (eds), *Nationalisms and Politics in Turkey: Political Islam, Kemalism and the Kurdish Issue* (London: Routledge, 2011); Ahmet Hamdi Akkaya and Joost Jongerden, "Reassembling the Political: The PKK and the Project of Radical Democracy", *European Journal of Turkish Studies* 12 (2012); Ahmet Hamdi Akkaya and Joost Jongerden, "Confederalism and Autonomy in Turkey: The Kurdistan Workers' Party and the Reinvention of Democracy", in Cengiz Gunes and Welat Zeydanlioglu (eds), *The Kurdish Question in Turkey: New Perspectives on Violence, Representation and Reconciliation* (Abingdon: Routledge, 2013); Joost Jongerden and Ahmet Hamdi Akkaya, "The Kurdistan Workers' Party and a New Left in Turkey: An Analysis of the Revolutionary Movement in Turkey through the PKK's Memorial Text on Haki Karer", *European Journal of Turkish Studies* 14 (2012); Joost Jongerden and Ahmet Hamdi Akkaya, "Democratic Confederalism as a Kurdish Spring: the PKK and the quest for radical democracy", in Mohammed Ahmet and Michael Gunter (eds), *The Kurdish Spring: Geopolitical Changes and the Kurds* (Costa Mesa, CA: Mazda, 2013a); Joost Jongerden and Ahmet Hamdi Akkaya, *PKK Üzerine Yazilar* (Istanbul: Vate Yayinlari, 2013b).
2. Pierre Clastres, *Society against the State, Essays in Political Anthropology* (New York: Zone Books, 1989) p. 190.
3. PKK, *Kürdistan Devriminin Yolu*, 1978.
4. Salih Muslim, speaking at the Flemish Parliament in Brussels, 18 September 2014.
5. Nigel Thrift, *Knowing Capitalism* (London: Sage, 2005) p. 24.
6. The first country that listed the PKK as a terrorist organization was the UK. "With a thirty-year history of 'terrorism' in Ulster / Northern Ireland, the UK responded quickly to the changed environment following the 9/11 attacks in the US, and, as of 28th March 2001, the PKK found itself officially listed as a terrorist organization alongside eighteen other foreign organizations active in the United Kingdom." Marlies Casier, "Designated Terrorists: The Kurdistan Workers' Party and its Struggle to (Re)Gain Political Legitimacy", *Mediterranean Politics* 15:3 (2010) p. 9.
7. In Europe, critique came not only from Kurdish organizations and the left, but also from within the EU institutions. In 2008, the Luxembourg-based Court of First Instance ruled that decisions made by EU governments in 2002 and 2004 to list the PKK as a terrorist organization were illegal under EU law. In 2016, over a hundred members of the European Parliament demanded the removal of the PKK from the EU list of terrorist organizations.
8. Jongerden and Akkaya, ""Born from the Left", 2011.
9. See Mustafa Karasu, *Radikal Demokrasi* (Neus: Wesanen Mezopotamya, 2009).
10. Hamit Bozarslan, *Violence in the Middle East, the political struggle to self-sacrifice* (Princeton,

NJ: Markus Wiener Publishers, 2004) p. 23; Jongerden and Akkaya, "Born from the Left", 2011, pp. 168-9.

11. Jongerden and Akkaya, "The Kurdistan Workers' Party", 2012, p. 10.

12. Interview with PKK militant, E. D., 8 June 2014.

13. See Akkaya and Jongerden, "The PKK in the 2000s", 2011; "Reassembling the Political", 2012.

14. Women's organizations in the PKK have a long history. The first Union of Women guerrillas was formed in 1995, followed by the first women's party in 1999. The name of the women's party has changed several times—currently operating as the Party of Free Women in Kurdistan (Partiya Azadiya Jin a Kurdistan, PAJK). The PAJK functions as the ideological center for women's groups organized autonomously, with the Community of Assertive Women (Koma Jinen Bilind, KJB) as front organization and the Free Women Units (YJA-STAR) as the organization of women guerrillas.

15. Iraq: Kurdistan Democratic Solution Party (Partiya Çareseriya Demokratik a Kurdistan, PÇDK), formed in 2002; Iran: Free Life Party of Kurdistan (Partiya Jiyana Azad a Kurdistan, PJAK), established in April, 2003; Syria: Democratic Union Party (Partiya Yekîtiya Demokrat, PYD), established in 2003.

16. The guerrilla forces are organized mainly into three bodies: the People's Defense Forces (Hêzên Parastina Gel, HPG), which constitutes the military organization of the party-movement; the Force of Eastern Kurdistan (Hezi Rojhelati Kurdistan, HRK), which is working parallel to the political goals of the PJAK; and YJA-Star.

17. The Association of Associations in Kurdistan (Koma Komalan Kurdistan, KKK) was established in 2005 and in 2007 renamed as Association of Communities in Kurdistan (Koma Civakên Kurdistan, KCK). It is both a concept embodying the idea of democratic confederalism as developed by Öcalan and a societal organization presented as an alternative to the nation-state that Öcalan sees as a model for the resolution of the problems of the Middle East. In the PKK party complex, the KCK can be considered the executive body, with all parties and organizations coordinated through it.

18. Kongra-Gel is the people's front within the PKK complex, to some extent taking over the functions of the ERNK, which was abolished in 2000. It can be considered the legislative body. Jongerden and Akkaya, "Democratic Confederalism", 2013a, pp. 165-7.

19. Christian Berndt, "Territorialized Key Words and Methodological Nationalism: Cultural Constructions of Institutional Change in Germany", *European Urban and Regional Studies* 10:4 (2003) pp. 283-95.

20. Andreas Wimmer and Nina Glick Schiller, "Methodological Nationalism and Beyond: Nation-state Building, Migration and the Social Sciences", *Global Networks* 2:4 (2002) p. 301.

21. Ibid., p. 327.

22. Ibid., p. 302.

23. Ephraim Nimni, "The Conceptual Challenge of Non-Territorial Autonomy", in Ephraim Nimni, Alexander Osipov, and David Smith (eds), *The Challenge of Non-Territorial Autonomy* (Oxford: Peter Lang, 2013) p. 6.

24. Wimmer and Schiller, "Methodological Nationalism", 2002, pp. 304-5.

25. Ibid., p. 304.

26. Ulrich Beck and Elisabeth Beck-Gernsheim, "Global Generations and the Trap of Methodological Nationalism for a Cosmopolitan Turn in the Sociology of Youth and Generation", *European Sociological Review* 25:1 (2009) p. 34.

27. Wimmer and Schiller, "Methodological Nationalism", 2002, pp. 304-5.

28. Frantz Fanon, *The Wretched of the Earth* (New York: Grove Press, 1963) pp. 206-48.

29. Of course there were exceptions, such as the work of Eric Wolf and Immanuel Wallerstein (see Wimmer and Schiller, "Methodological Nationalism", 2002, p. 305).

30. Anthony Smith, "Nationalism and Classical Social Theory", *British Journal of Sociology* 34:1 (1983).

31. Wimmer and Schiller, "Methodological Nationalism", 2002, p. 305.

32. PKK, *Kürdistan Devriminin Yolu,* 1978, p. 127.

33. Adem Uzun, *Living Freedom: The Evolution of the Kurdish Conflict in Turkey and the Efforts to Resolve It* (Berlin: Berghof Foundation, 2014) p. 3.

34. Vladimir Lenin, *The Rights of Nations to Self-determination*, 1914, https://www.marxists.org/archive/lenin/works/1914/self-det/ch01.htm

35. Ismail Besikci, *International Colony Kurdistan* (London: Taderon Press, 2004); Abdul Rahman Ghassemlou, *Kurdistan and the Kurds* (Prague: Czechoslovak Academy of Sciences, 1965) p. 247.

36. Ibid., p. 246.

37. Ibid., p. 247.

38. PKK, *Kürdistan Devriminin Yolu*, 1978, p. 128.

39. In an interview, Duran Kalkan stated that in the establishment process of the PKK in the 1970s, it had oriented itself on the struggle of national liberation movements and the socialism of the day, but that the failure of these movements to bring what they had promised required critical examination: "The PKK examined all national liberation movements. They fought huge battles, gave millions of martyrs and won their wars, but what they got was little. (...) They were not able to realise their objectives. (...) This asked for a re-examination. This was crucial for the emergence of a paradigm shift' (Duran Kalkan, personal communication, 30 October 2014). Cemil Bayık traces the origins of the new paradigm to a meeting of the central committee of the PKK in 1984. At this meeting Öcalan claimed that what was referred to as 'real existing socialism' in fact did not have much to do with socialism. This was based, among other things, on a critique of the state. While socialism promised the dissolution of the state and its replacement by an association of free citizens in which the free development of each is the condition for the free development of all, the state in countries that had declared themselves socialist had only become increasingly powerful. 'The new paradigm [of the PKK] did not emerge abruptly, but evolved from this critique.'" Cemil Bayık, personal communication, 30 October 2014.

40. Abdullah Öcalan, *Prison Writings III: The Road Map to Negotiations* (Cologne: International Initiative Freedom for Abdullah Öcalan – Peace in Kurdistan, 2012b) p. 89.

41. Abdullah Öcalan, *Demokratik Uygarlık Manifestosu: Kültürel Soykırım Kıskacında Kürtleri Savunmak* (Neuss: Mezopotamya Yayınları, 2012a) pp. 271-2.

42. Abdullah Öcalan, *Demokratik Uygarlık Manifestosu: Ortaduğu'da Uygarlik Krizi ve demokratik Uygarlık Çözümü* (Neuss: Mezopotamya Yayınları, 2010) p. 196.

43. Etienne Balibar, *The Nation Form* (London: Verso, 2002) p. 93; Öcalan, *Demokratik Uygarlık Manifestosu*, 2010, pp. 195-6.

44. Öcalan, *Demokratik Uygarlık Manifestosu*, 2010, p. 193.

45. Uzun, *Living Freedom*, 2014, p. 22.

46. Akkaya and Jongerden, "Reassembling the Political", 2012, p. 22.

47. Personal communication, 12 November 2011.

48. Personal communication, 10 July 2011.

49. Personal communication, 12 July 2011.

50. Janet Biehl, "Bookchin, Öcalan, and the Dialectics of Democracy", in *Challenging Capitalist Modernity: Alternative Concepts and the Kurdish Quest,* 3-5 February 2012, Hamburg, p. 10; Abdullah Öcalan, *Prison Notes June 18, 2008.*

51. Kropotkin argued that: "Throughout the history of our civilization, two traditions, two opposing tendencies have confronted each other: the Roman and the Popular; the imperial and the federalist; the authoritarian and the libertarian." Peter Kropotkin, *The State: Its Historical Role* (London: Freedom Press, 1947 / 1897) p. 60.

52. Damian White, *Bookchin: A Critical Appraisal* (London: Pluto Press, 2008) p. 159.

53. Kropotkin, *The State*, 1947; Murray Bookchin, "Libertarian Municipalism: An Overview", *Green Perspectives* 24 (1991) p. 11.

54. Murray Bookchin, *The Next Revolution: Popular Assemblies and the Promise of Direct Democracy* (London: Verso, 2014).

55. Bookchin, "Libertarian Municipalism", p. 7.

56. Murray Bookchin, "The Meaning of Confederalism", *Green Perspectives* 20 (1990) p. 11.

57. Ibid.

58. Ibid., p. 10.

59. Ibid., p. 4.

60. Personal communications, 30 October 2014.

61. Joost Jongerden, *Demokrasiyi Radikalleştirmek: Güç, Politika, İnsanlar ve PKK* [Radicalizing Democracy: Power, Politics, People and the PKK] (Istanbul: Research Turkey, 2015), http://researchturkey.org/tr/radicalising-democracy-power-politics-people-and-the-pkk/, accessed 26 October 2015.

62. Hannah Arendt, *On Revolution* (London: Penguin Press, 1990 / 1963) p. 253.

63. In this respect, democratic confederalism revives the imaginary of the Paris Commune of 1871; see Kristin Ross, *Communal Luxury, the Political Imaginary of the Paris Commune* (London: Verso, 2015).

64. Doreen Massey, "Geographies of Responsibility", *Geogr. Ann.* 86:1 (2004) p. 17.

65. Ross, *Communal Luxury*, 2015, p. 90.

66. Abdullah Öcalan, *War and Peace in Kurdistan* (Cologne: International Initiative Peace in Kurdistan-Freedom for Abdullah Öcalan, 2014) p. 39.

67. Ibid., p. 31.
68. Ibid., p. 31.
69. Ibid., p. 33.
70. Ibid., pp. 31-2.
71. Karasu, *Radikal Demokrasi*, 2009, pp. 208-10, 217-19.
72. Ulrich Beck, "The Cosmopolitan Condition: Why Methodological Nationalism Fails", *Theory, Culture and Society* 24:7-8 (2007a); Beck and Beck-Gernsheim, "Global Generations", 2009, p. 25.
73. Ulrich Beck, *Cosmopolitanism* (2007b), http://www.ulrichbeck.net-build.net/index.php?page=cosmopolitan, accessed 28 July 2015.
74. Ludger Pries, "Configurations of geographic and societal spaces: a sociological proposal between 'methodological nationalism' and the 'spaces of flows.'" *Global Networks* 5:2 (2005) p. 185.

18. THE PKK, THE KURDISH MOVEMENT, AND THE EMERGENCE OF KURDISH CULTURAL POLICIES IN TURKEY

1. Alain Dieckhoff, "Nationalism Revisited," in Alain Dieckhoff and Christian Jaffrelot, *Revisiting Nationalism: theories and process* (London: Hurst & Co., 2005) pp. 62-77.
2. Anne-Marie Thiesse, *La création des identités nationales. Europe XVIII-XIXème* (Paris: Le Seuil, 2001).
3. For instance, Celilê Celîl, *Jiyana Rewşenbirî û Siyasî ya Kurdan (di Dawiya Sedsala 19'a û Destpêka Sedsala 20'a de)* (Uppsala: Weşanên Jina Nû, 1985); Hakan Özoglu, *Kurdish Notables and the Ottoman State. Evolving Identities, Competing Loyalties, and Shifting Boundaries* (Albany, NY: State University of New York Press, SUNY Series in Middle-East Studies, 2004).
4. Jordi Tejel Gorgas, *Le mouvement kurde en exil. Continuités et discontinuités du nationalisme kurde sous le mandat français en Syrie et au Liban (1925-1946)* (Bern: Peter Lang, 2007).
5. See for example Prince Sureya Bedr Khan, *The Case of Kurdistan against Turkey* (Stockholm: Sara, 1995 / 1928).
6. Jordi Tejel Gorgas, "Les constructions de l'identité kurde sous l'influence de la 'connexion kurdo-française' au Levant (1930-1946)", *European Journal of Turkish Studies* 5 (2006), http://ejts.revues.org/751, paragraphe 35, last accessed 15 July 2015.
7. Hamit Bozarslan, *La question kurde. États et minorités au Moyen-Orient* (Paris: Presses de Science Politique, 1997).
8. Martin Strohmeier, *Crucial Images in the Presentation of a Kurdish National Identity. Heroes and Patriots, Traitors and Foes* (Leiden, Boston: Brill, 2003).
9. Maria T. O'Shea, *Trapped Between the Map and the Reality. Geography and Perception of Kurdistan* (London: Routledge, 2004).
10. Amir Hassanpour, *Nationalism and Language in Kurdistan 1918-1985* (San Francisco, CA: Mellon Research University Press, 1992).

11. Delal Aydin, "Mobilising the Kurds in Turkey. Newroz as a myth," in Cengiz Gunes and Welat Zeydanlioğlu (eds), *The Kurdish Question in Turkey: New Perspectives on Violence, Representation, and Reconciliation* (London: Routledge, 2014) pp. 68-84; Aykan, Bahar, "Whose Tradition, Whose Identity? The politics of constructing 'Nevruz' as intangible heritage in Turkey", *European Journal of Turkish Studies* 19 (2014), http://ejts.revues. org/5000, last accessed 17 October 2015.

12. For instance, Hashem Ahmadzadeh, *Nation and Novel. A Study of Persian and Kurdish Narrative Discourse* (Uppsala: Acta Universitalis Upsaliensis, Studia Iranica Upsaliensi 6, 2003); Clémence Scalbert-Yücel, "Le monde rural dans la poésie contemporaine kurmandji en Turquie," *Etudes rurales* 186 (2011) pp. 181-96.

13. Clémence Scalbert-Yücel, "Mémoire spontanée et travail de mémoire - Exil et diaspora: Le processus de création chez six peintres kurdes en Europe," *Etudes Kurdes* 5 (2003) pp. 7-23.

14. Siynem Ezgi Sarıtaş, "Articulation of Kurdish identity through politicised music of Koms," (Ankara: ODTÜ, unpublished MA dissertation, 2010).

15. Nicole Watts defines a movement as "an interactive field of actors sustaining a public, collective challenge to authorities based on common purposes and social solidarities." The Kurdish national movement is an ethno-political movement that "seeks to impress ethnically defined interest on the state agenda." Nicole Watts, *Activists in Office. Kurdish politics and protest in Turkey* (Seattle, WA: University of Washington Press, 2000) p. 21. The term "Kurdish movement" is however often considered as composed of the PKK and related associations and its followers, thereby concealing opposition and political diversity within the ethno-political movement. Here I also limit the understanding of the Kurdish movement to the movement around the PKK, constituting a wide array of individual and organizations.

16. Vincent Dubois, "Cultural Policy Regimes in Western Europe," *International Encyclopedia of the Social and Behavioral Sciences*, 2nd edn (Amsterdam: Elsevier, 2014), available at https://halshs.archives-ouvertes.fr/halshs-00836422/document, last accessed 13 September 2015.

17. Clémence Scalbert-Yücel, "The 'liberalization' of Turkish policy towards the Kurdish language: the influence of external actors", in Robert Lowe and Gareth Stansfield (eds), *The Kurdish Policy Imperative* (London: Royal Institute of International Affairs, 2010) pp. 116-29.

18. Clémence Scalbert-Yücel, "Emergence and equivocal autonomization of a Kurdish literary field in Turkey," *Nationalities Papers* 40:3 (2012) pp. 357-72.

19. Jeremy Ahearne, "Cultural Policy Explicit and Implicit: A Distinction and Some Uses," *International Journal of Cultural Policy* 15:2 (2009) pp. 141-53.

20. See for instance Marlene Schäfers, "Being sick of politics: The production of *dengbêjî* as Kurdish cultural heritage in contemporary Turkey," *European Journal of Turkish Studies* 20 (2015), http://ejts.revues.org/5200, last accessed 1 October 2015.

21. Clémence Scalbert-Yücel, "Common Ground or Battlefield? Deconstructing the Politics of Recognition in Turkey", *Nationalism and Ethnic Politics* 22:1 (2016) pp. 71-93. One

notes, however, a renewed pressure on the sphere of Kurdish cultural producers since the failed coup, with the arrests of Kurdish language writers, the shutdown on Kurdish language schools or TV channels, and of theaters and cultural centers.

22. Mehmet Ali Birand, *Apo ve PKK* (Istanbul: Milliyet Yayinlari, 1992); Yalçin Küçük, *Kürt Bahçesinde Sözleşi* (Ankara: Basak, 1993).

23. Books on the topic were published only after Öcalan's incarceration in 1999. See *Tarih Günümüzde Gizli ve Biz Tarihin Baslangıcında Gizliyiz* (Istanbul: Aram, 2000); and *Kültür ve Sanat Devrimi üzerine* (Istanbul: Aram, 2008).

24. On this issue see Olivier Grojean, "The Production of the New Man within the PKK," *European Journal of Turkish Studies* 8 (2008, English translation 2014), http:// ejts.revues.org/4925, last accessed 13 October 2015.

25. Abdullah Öcalan, "Wie leben? (Teil V) Erobert das Leben! Aus dem Buch *Wie leben* von Abdullah Öcalan," *Kurdistan Report* 86, p. 35, translated and quoted in Olivier Grojean, "The Production of the New Man within the PKK", *European Journal of Turkish Studies* 8 (2008, English translation 2014), http://ejts.revues.org/4925, paragraph 12.

26. Note from the author: Hünerkom, the Union of Kurdistan's patriotic artists, was funded in Germany in 1983. See the following section.

27. Öcalan in Yalçin Küçük, *Kürt Bahçesinde Sözlesi* (Ankara: Basak, 1993) pp. 379-80.

28. In the middle of the 1990s, the symphony orchestra of Halabja was founded in Germany. Some recall odd evening parties in which PKK militants were selling the *Serxwebûn* journal in bow ties.

29. Öcalan, *Kültür ve Sanat Devrimi üzerine*, 2008, p. 11; translation from Sarıtaş, "Articulation of Kurdish identity", 2010, p. 65.

30. This was the name of a street in Beyoğlu where the cinema industry was located during its heyday between the 1950s and 1970s. The term is used to refer to the Turkish film industry.

31. Öcalan in Yalçin Küçük, *Kürt Bahçesinde Sözlesi* (Ankara: Basak, 1993) p. 378.

32. Ibid., p. 382.

33. See http://www.mirbotan.com/sanatci-hayati-and-biyografi/223293-kadin-sanatci-devrimci-mizgin-gurbet-aydin.html, last accessed 22 October 2015.

34. See http://www.mirbotan.com/sanatci-hayati-and-biyografi/47736-seyitxan-biyografi-hayati-roportaj.html, last accessed 22 October 2015.

35. The Diyarbakir branch was closed and reopened many times.

36. On bands and their musicians, see Sarıtaş, "Articulation of Kurdish identity", 2010.

37. Clémence Scalbert-Yücel, *Langue, littérature et engagement. Le champ littéraire kurde en Turquie 1980-2010* (Paris: Petra, 2014) pp. 273-82.

38. The institute is closely related to NÇM; see *NÇM Tanıtım Bröşürü* (Istanbul: NÇM, n.d.) p. 66.

39. Ibid., p. 59.

40. Ibid., p. 58.

41. Ibid. p. 5.

42. Sarıtaş, "Articulation of Kurdish identity", 2010.

43. See for instance the special issue of the magazine *Sancı Kültür Sanat Edebiyat Dergisi* 2 (2015) on the issue of "Destruction and the art of foundation: Kobanî."

44. Interviews with the head of NÇM, February 2015.

45. Kom Müzik was established in 1997 in the neighborhood of Unkapani, Istanbul, and produced NÇM bands and singers.

46. Different pro-Kurdish parties that include an ethno-national dimension to their agenda succeeded one other following numerous bans.

47. It has since been replaced by the Party of the Democratic Regions (Demokratik Bölgeler Partisi, DBP) at the regional level, and the Democratic Party of the People (Halkların Demokratik Partisi, HDP) at the national level.

48. On Diyarbakir's festival, see Clémence Scalbert-Yücel, "Common Ground or Battlefield? Deconstructing the Politics of Recognition in Turkey", *Nationalism and Ethnic Politics* 22:1 (2016) pp. 71-93.

49. These arenas are threatened again with the appointment by the government of administrators in pro-Kurdish municipalities in September 2016: they have decided to close the Batman City Theater, and DBŞT actors have seen their work turned into municipal police work.

50. Jonas Ramuz, *Action publique de la culture et résistances. La ville de Batman, Kurdistan (Turquie)* (Paris: EHESS, unpublished MA dissertation, 2014).

51. See http://orkestraheskif.org/hs/, last accessed 17 October 2015.

52. Sarıtaş, "Articulation of Kurdish identity", 2010, p. 74.

53. To these institutions could be added the house of *dengbêj* in Diyarbakir and Van, and the network of Kurdish courses called Kurdî-Der.

54. Interviews, Istanbul, February 2015. See also Nicole Watts, *Activists in Office*, ch. 6.

55. See Clémence Scalbert-Yücel, *Langue, littérature et engagement*, 2014.

56. See Sarıtaş, "Articulation of Kurdish identity", 2010, pp. 70-71.

57. For more details on these companies, see Elif Baş, "The Rise of Kurdish theatre in Istanbul," *Theatre Survey* 56:3 (2015) pp. 314-35.

58. In 2009 Lemi Bilgin, the general director of state theaters, declared that Kurdish plays could be staged in forty-four state theaters in twelve cities. See ibid., p. 331.

59. On that movie and censorship in Turkish cinema, see Esin Berktaş, "Why was *Bakur: A Guerrilla Documentary* not screened in the festival?" 15 July 2015, https://tr.boell.org/de/node/2687, accessed 10 October 2015.

60. For more details, see Siyahbant, *Siyahbant Research Reports – 2013. Part II: Freedom of Expression in the Arts and Censorship in Kurdish Region, Diyarbakir, Batman*, https://www.indexoncensorship.org/2014/02/freedom-of-expression-in-the-arts-and-censorship-in-kurdish-region-diyarbakir-batman/, last accessed 17 October 2015. See also Baş, "The Rise of Kurdish theatre in Istanbul", 2015.

19. THE CURIOUS QUESTION OF THE PYD-PKK RELATIONSHIP

1. Harriet Allsopp, *The Kurds of Syria: Political Parties and Identity in the Middle East* (London: I. B. Tauris, 2014); Robert Lowe, "The emergence of Western Kurdistan and the future of Syria", in David Romano and Mehmet Gürses (eds), *Conflict, Democratization and the Kurds in the Middle East* (New York: Palgrave Macmillan, 2014) pp. 225-46; Michael Gunter, "The Kurdish Spring", *Third World Quarterly* 34:3 (2013) pp. 441-57; Eva Savelsberg and Jordi Tejel, "The Syrian Kurds in transition to somewhere", in Michael Gunter and Mohammed M. A. Ahmed (eds), *The Kurdish Spring: Geopolitical Changes and the Kurds* (Costa Mesa, CA: Mazda, 2013).

2. Allsopp, *The Kurds of Syria*; Jordi Tejel, *Syria's Kurds: History, Politics and Society* (New York: Routledge, 2008).

3. International Crisis Group, "Flight of Icarus? The PYD's precarious rise in Syria", *Middle East Report* 151 (2014); International Crisis Group, "Syria's Kurds: A struggle within a struggle", *Middle East Report* 126 (2013).

4. Eva Savelsberg, "The Syrian-Kurdish movements", in David Romano and Mehmet Gürses (eds), *Conflict, Democratization and the Kurds in the Middle East* (New York: Palgrave Macmillan, 2014) pp. 85-107; Tejel, *Syria's Kurds*; International Crisis Group, "Flight of Icarus?"; *Kurdwatch*, European Center for Kurdish Studies, Berlin. www.kurdwatch.com/

5. Author interview with Salih Muslim, London, December 2013.

6. Author interview with Alan Şemo, Foreign Affairs Representative, PYD, London, August 2012.

7. "Bayık Independent'e konuştu" [Bayık spoke to the *Independent*], Hürriyet, http://www.hurriyet.com.tr/dunya/27561606.asp, last accessed 14 August 2014.

8. See Allsopp, *The Kurds of Syria* for the evolution of the parties of the 1957 genealogy.

9. See Joost Jongerden's Chapter 17 in this volume.

10. Mehmet Orhan, "Transborder violence: The PKK in Turkey, Syria and Iraq", *Dynamics of Asymmetric Conflict* 7:1 (2014) pp. 30-48, p. 33; International Crisis Group, "Flight of Icarus?"; Michael Gunter, *Out of Nowhere: The Kurds of Syria in Peace and War* (London: Hurst & Co., 2013) p. 450.

11. "Leading cadres (of Syrian Kurds who had supported the PKK in the 1990s) declared the establishment of the PYD without any involvement of the PKK or any other political party." Email to the author from Alan Şemo, Foreign Affairs Representative, PYD, August 2015. "The PYD was generated by Syrian Kurds who believed that a struggle in cooperation with the PKK would serve best in achieving their national and political aims and reaching a democratic and peaceful solution to their problems." Author interview with Bilhan Tuncel, writer, politician, and expert on Kurdish politics in Turkey, October 2015, UK.

12. Allsopp, *The Kurds of Syria*; International Crisis Group, "Flight of Icarus?"

13. Email from Alan Şemo, August 2015.

14. Author interview with Bilhan Tuncel, expert on Kurdish politics in Turkey, writer, and politician.

15. Savelsberg, "The Syrian-Kurdish movements."
16. Wladimir van Wildenberg, "Rival Kurdish parties battle for power in Syria", *Al-Monitor*, www.al-monitor.com/pulse/originals/2014/05/kurdistan-kdp-pyd-erbil-barzani-ocalan-syria.html, last accessed 24 September 2015.
17. *Kurdwatch*; International Crisis Group, "Flight of Icarus?"
18. Tejel, *Syria's Kurds*, p. 78.
19. Shiraz Adel Yadidi, interview with Salih Muslim, Sulaimani, 25 September 2011, in *PYD Information File*, Peace in Kurdistan, November 2012.
20. Hamit Bozarslan, "The Kurds and Middle Eastern 'State of Violence': The 1980s and 2010s", *Kurdish Studies* 2:1 (2014) pp. 48-91.
21. Yıldıray Oğur, "10 soruda KCK?" [KCK in 10 questions], *Taraf*, http://arsiv.taraf.com.tr/yazilar/yildiray-ogur/10-soruda-kck/18032/; Abdullah Öcalan, *Democratic Confederalism*, trans. by International Initiative (London: Transmedia Publishing, 2011).
22. Author interview with Bilhan Tuncel.
23. Email to author from Güney Yıldız, BBC journalist, September 2015.
24. International Crisis Group, "Syria's Kurds", p. 19.
25. Mehmet Orhan, "Transborder violence: The PKK in Turkey, Syria and Iraq", *Dynamics of Asymmetric Conflict* 7:1 (2014) pp. 30-48, p. 40.
26. Bilhan Tuncel emphasizes that the "PKK's ideological influence on the PYD is different from the mentality of the Cold War era, which saw ideological affiliation as a form of imposition. The PKK leaders in Qandil instead have no organic influence on PYD decision-making mechanisms." Author interview.
27. Author interview with Alan Şemo.
28. "Çatışmasızlığa son veren üçgen" [The triangle that ended the ceasefire], *Anadolu Ajansı*, http://www.aa.com.tr/tr/haberler/590099--catismasizliga-son-veren-ucgen-hdp-pkk-kck, last accessed 24 September 2015.
29. PKK's website, http://www.pkkonline.com/en/index.php?sys=article&artID=210, last accessed 25 September 2015.
30. Ruşen Çakır's interview with Cemil Bayık, http://www.rusencakir.com/Cemil-Bayik-ile-soylesi--Tam-metin/2439, last accessed 24 September 2015.
31. The PKK is also often criticized by other Kurdish parties in Turkey for preventing their activities. See for example the speech by Ramazan Moray from Rights and Freedoms Party (Hak ve Özgürlükler Partisi, Hak-Par) at a meeting in Diyarbakır in 2014, "PKK ve PYD'ye tepkiler sürüyor" [Reactions to PKK and PYD continues], *Doğruhaber Gazetesi*, http://www.dogruhaber.com.tr/mobil/Haber.php?id=130433, last accessed 25 September 2015.
32. "Kobanî son dakika! Murat Karayılan: PYD ilerliyor" [Kobanî last minute! Murat Karayilan: PYD moving forward], *Internethaber*, http://www.internethaber.com/kobani-son-dakika-murat-karayilan-pyd-ilerliyor-741555h.htm, last accessed 16 November 2015.
33. "Erdoğan'dan IŞİD ve PKK açıklaması" [Erdoğan's ISIS and PKK declaration], http://www.zaman.com.tr/gundem_erdogandan-isid-ve-pkk-aciklamasi_2247277.html, last accessed 16 November 2015.

34. Güneş M. Tezcür and Sabri Çiftçi, "Radical Turks: Why Turkish citizens are joining ISIS?" *Foreign Affairs*, Council on Foreign Relations, 2014.

35. Author fieldwork visit in Turkey, July 2015.

36. Most recently, Figen Yüksekdağ, co-president of HDP, said that her party counts on PYD and YPG in their fight against IS: "Figen Yüksekdağ: Sırtımızı YPJ'ye YPG'ye ve PYD'ye yaslıyoruz" [We lean on YPJ, YPG and PYD], *Hürriyet*, http://www.hurriyet.com.tr/sondakika/29587681.asp, last accessed 16 November 2015.

37. "HDP'li Baluken: Türkiye, Rojava modeline destek vermeli" [HDP's Baluken: Turkey should support the Rojava model], *Radikal*, http://www.radikal.com.tr/politika/hdpli_baluken_turkiye_rojava_modeline_destek_verilmeli-138342, last accessed 16 November 2015.

38. "Yüksekdağ: Rojava sınırında tank değil barış sesleri yükselmeli" [Yüksekdağ: We should hear the sound of peace not tanks at the Rojava border], *Evrensel*, http://www.evrensel.net/haber/256318/yuksekdag-rojava-sinirinda-tank-degil-baris-sesleri-yukselmeli, last accessed 16 November 2015.

39. "PKK Türkiye'yle çatışmaları durdurmak için ABD ile gizlice görüşüyor" [PKK is holding secret talks with the US to end the conflict with Turkey], BBC Türkce, http://www.bbc.com/turkce/haberler/2015/08/150816_daily_telegraph_pkk_abd, last accessed 16 November 2015.

20. KURDISH POLITICAL PARTIES AND THE SYRIAN UPRISING

1. These divisions are not mutually exclusive or discrete, and as is shown in what follows, political loyalties and allegiances overlap and transcend these categories. These are artificial divisions intended as tools for explaining the political field in Syria three years into the Syrian uprising.

2. Parties included within the KNC were: Partîya Dêmokrata Pêşverû a Kurdî li Sûriyê (Abdul Hamid Darwish), Partîya Yekîtî ya Dêmokrat a Kurd li Sûriyê (Sheikh Ali), Partîya Dêmokrat a Kurdî li Sûriyê (Nusradin Ibrahim), Partîya Dêmokrat a Kurdî li Sûriyê (el-Partî) (Dr Abdul Hakim Bashar), Partîya Dêmokrat a Kurdî li Sûriyê (Abdul Rahman Aluji), Partîya Welatperêz a Dêmokrat a Kurdî li Sûriyê (Tahir Safouk), Partîya Yekîtî ya Kurd li Sûriyê (Ismail Hemi), Partîya Azadî ya Kurd li Suryê (Mustafa Juma'a), Partîya Azadî ya Kurd li Suryê (Mustafa Oso), Partîya Çep a Kurdî li Sûriyê – Congress (Muhammad Musa), Partîya Çep a Kurdî li Sûriyê – Central Committee (Salih Gido), Partîya Dêmokrat a Kurdî ya Sûrî (el-Sûrî) (Jamal Sheikh Baqi), Partîya Wekhevî Dêmokrat a Kurdî li Sûriyê (Aziz Daoud), Partîya Yekîtî ya Kurdistani li Sûriyê (Omar Daoud), Partîya Rêkeftina Dêmokrat a Kurdistani - Sûriyê (Nash'at Muhammad), Partîya Dêmokrata Pêşverû a Kurdî li Sûriyê (Faisal Yusef).

3. Although this party denied direct organizational connections to the PKK, its decision-making is connected to the web of political, civil, and military organizations of the KCK, which also includes the PKK, PJAK, as well as their armed wings, and which is led by Kongra-Gel and Abdullah Öcalan.

4. Formed on 16 December 2011.

5. Organizations such as Tevgera Cewanen Kurd, SAWA, and Avahî.

6. Omar Hossino and Ilhan Tanir, "The Decisive Minority: The Critical Role of Syria's Kurds in the Anti-Assad Revolution", Henry Jackson Society, USA, March 2012, http://henryjacksonsociety.org/wp-content/uploads/2012/03/The-Decisive-Minority.pdf, last accessed 25 November 2015.

7. The exact and original party name continues to be subject to debate, reflecting conflicts within this party over the inclusion or exclusion of the word "Kurdistan" in the party name. See Harriet Allsopp, *The Kurds in Syria, Political Parties and Identity in the Middle East* (London, I. B. Tauris, 2014) pp. 75-6.

8. For more detail on this subject, refer to Allsopp, *The Kurds in Syria*.

9. Thousands of Syrian Kurds were killed fighting with the PKK against the Turkish state.

10. Author interviews 2002–16.

11. Despite this ready support base, the PYD is not believed to have been particularly strong prior to the uprising. Author interviews, 2002–14; International Crisis Group (ICG), "The Flight of Icarus?" *Middle East Report* 151, Erbil/Brussels, 2014, http://www.crisisgroup.org/~/media/Files/Middle%20East%20North%20Africa/Iraq%20Syria%20Lebanon/Syria/151-flight-of-icarus-the-pyd-s-precarious-rise-in-syria.pdf, last accessed 25 November 2015.

12. Author interviews 2002-14; ICG, "The Flight of Icarus?" p. i.

13. Known as the "Qamishli Uprising," protests spread to all Kurdish areas and lasted about two weeks. For more information see Allsopp, *The Kurds in Syria*; Jordi Tejel, *Syria's Kurds, History, Politics and Society* (London: Routledge, 2009).

14. The parties' leadership feared that full involvement of the Kurds would provoke the regime to launch a targeted attack on Kurdish areas, to label the uprising as sectarian, and to use this rationale to subvert the nascent movement. They also feared that the Arab opposition would not support the Kurds should they come under attack from the regime.

15. The PCWK became defunct with the PYD declaration of autonomy and the development of the Rojava Administration, based on a democratic confederalism of diverse peoples. The PCWK was effectively replaced by Tev-Dem, which was not defined by the Kurdish ethnicity and territory.

16. PKK, n.d.

17. The nature of any relationship between the PYD and the Assad regime remains an area of contention and precise details are unavailable. It is possible, however, to identify many examples of unofficial non-confrontation and coexistence based on mutual benefit and convenience, for example in Qamishli and Ashrafiya (Aleppo), and even cooperation against other mutually hostile forces (for example in Hasaka in August 2014). However, the YPG and regime force have also come into conflict on several occasions.

18. ICG, "The Flight of Icarus?" p. 6-7.

19. Particularly after the start of the PKK ceasefire and peace process with Turkey, and the PJAK-Iran ceasefire of 2011, additional PKK guerrillas and arms were redirected to Syria.

20. Many local leaders of minority groups, such as Assyrians, Syriac, and some Arab tribes, opted to participate in PYD government.

21. Abdul Hamid Darwish's Kurdish Democratic Progressive Party (Partîya Dêmokrata Pêşverû a Kurdî li Sûriyê); Sheikh Ali's Kurdish Democratic Union Party (Partîya Yekîtî ya Dêmokrat a Kurd li Sûriyê); and Jamal Sheikh Baqi's Syrian Kurdish Democratic Party (Partîya Dêmokrat a Kurdî ya Sûrî, el-Sûrî).

22. Each canton was governed through a presidential system involving twenty-two ministries.

23. Text of the PYD Social Contract of 29 January 2014 can be found on http://www.kongrakurdistan.net/en/the-social-contract-of-rojava/, last accessed 10 November 2014.

24. The law on formation and operation of political parties was passed on 17 April 2014. The PYD law on political parties forbade the formation of new parties that did not recognize the rule of the PYD-led government and required pre-existing parties to register or face legal prosecution. "Illegal" political organization would be punishable by legal prosecution, fines, prison sentences, and the closure of unlicensed organizations. By the end of August 2014, only eight other political parties had been licensed, none of these being KNC parties. For translation, see KurdWatch, 30 September 2014; see also Azad Jemkari, "PYD launches 'law of political parties' in northern Syria", ARA News, 28 April 2014, www.aranews.org/en/home/kurdish-region/1309-pyd-launch-law-of-political -parties-in-northern-syria.html, last accessed 28 April 2014.

25. ICG, "The Flight of Icarus?" p. 6.

26. Ibid., p. 12.

27. PYD, n.d.

28. Human Rights Watch, "Under Kurdish Rule: Abuses in PYD-run Enclaves of Syria" (USA: HRW, 2014), http://www.hrw.org/sites/default/files/reports/syria0614_kurds_ForUpload.pdf, last accessed 25 November 2015; author interviews with Syrian Kurds.

29. Offices of the KDP-S and Yekîtî parties were targeted and members of the political leadership expelled from Syrian Kurdish areas; interviews and news reports.

30. Interviews with Kurds from Efrin, May 2014. In April 2014 several members of the Kurdistan Democratic Party of Syria, a union of four Kurdish Syrian parties formed in the Kurdistan Region, were tried in the "People's Court" which issued judgments against five KDPS members in Efrin, sentencing them to between twenty and ten years on charges related to terrorism (ARA News, 3 April 2014). In other reports, members of the party as well as journalists working for the Erbil-based Rudaw were expelled from Syria or refused entry by the PYD and ordered to remain in the Kurdistan Region. Indeed, Human Rights Watch devoted 106 pages to the question of human rights violations under the PYD (HRW, 2014).

31. Author interviews. Activists and politicians connected to other Syrian Kurdish parties reported being monitored, followed, and threatened by the PYD or its security services.

32. Text available on KurdWatch, 1 July 2012.

33. Most realist Western conceptualizations and understandings of political parties place the pursuit of power and electoral competition central to their definition.

34. See Allsopp, *The Kurds in Syria*.

35. Rudaw, "Iranian Kurdish Group Shifts Policy, seeking Democratic Autonomy", 6 May 2014, http://rudaw.net/english/middleeast/iran/06052014, last accessed 7 May 2014.

36. Rudaw, "Senior PKK Leader says Group no longer Seeks a Kurdish State", 7 May 2014, www.rudaw.net/mobile/english/middleeast/turkey/07052014, last accessed 7 May 2014.

37. Prior to the Syrian uprising and formation of the KNC, the major rift within the Syrian Kurdish politics, reflecting that between the KDP and the PUK, concerned whether the Kurds were defined as a national group or a minority ethnic group in Syria. With the re-alignment of Kurdish politics toward the definition of the Kurds as a national group living within their historic territory during the Syrian uprising, this rift has shifted to the relations of parties within the KNC to the PYD. Parties close to the PUK opted to cooperate with PYD rule in Syria. Notably, Hamid Darwish's Progressive Party (Taqadummi).

38. In August 2013, KNC leaders signed a formal agreement to join the SNC, whilst continuing to work toward specifically Kurdish aims and a federal political structure, opposed by the SNC.

39. In October 2014, several demands were made of the PYD as a prerequisite for considering international military support: a severing of connections to the PKK; the incorporation of the YPG under the FSA; and a declaration of opposition to the Assad regime.

40. Operation Euphrates Shield.

41. See for example the statements of Aldar Xalil, member of the executive council of Tev-Dem, interviewed by Rudaw, "Tev-Dem Rep: Kobane has upset their plans", 25 October 2014, https://rojavareport.wordpress.com/2014/10/25/tev-dem-rep-kobane-has-upset-their-plans/, last accessed 27 October 2014.

42. Suggestions that the KDP create a second military force within Rojava were opposed by the PUK, following the PYD; Mala Bakhtiyar suggested that armed forces belonging to other parties should join the PYD. ANF News, "Mala Bakhtiyar: Ditch decision the KDP's alone", 7 May 2014, http://en.firatnews.com/news/news/mala-bakhtiyar-ditch-decision-the-kdp-s-alone.htm, last accessed 20 May 2014.

43. See for example Wladimir van Wilgenberg, "Russia's intervention in Syria and the Kurdish question", *The Diplomat* (online), 9 March 2016, http://thediplomat.com/2016/03/russias-intervention-in-syria-and-the-kurdish-question/, last accessed 14 October 2016.

21. THE KURDISH CONUNDRUM AND THE ISLAMIC REPUBLIC OF IRAN, 1979–2003

1. Rasmus Christian Elling, *Minorities in Iran: Nationalism and Ethnicity after Khomeini* (New York: Palgrave Macmillan, 2013) p. 55.

2. Quoted in David Menashri, "Khomeini's Policy Toward Ethnic and Religious Minorities", in Milton J. Esman (ed.), *Ethnicity, Pluralism, and the State in the Middle East* (Ithaca, NY: Cornell University Press, 1988) p. 217.

3. *Matn-e Kamel-e Qanoon-e Assassi-e Jomhouri-e Islami Iran* [The Complete Text of the Constitution of the Islamic Republic of Iran] (Tehran: Hamid Publications, 1983) p. 28. See also Atabaki Touraj, "Contesting Marginality: Ethnicity and Construction of New Histories in the Islamic Republic of Iran", in Kamran Scot Aghaie and Afshin Marashi (eds), *Rethinking Iranian Nationalism and Modernity* (Austin, TX: University of Texas Press, 2014) p. 224.

4. Mark Gasiorowski, "US Covert Operations toward Iran, February-November 1979: Was the CIA Trying to Overthrow the Islamic Regiome?", *Middle Eastern Studies* 51:1 (January 2015) p. 126.

5. Mark Gasiorowski, "US Intelligence Assistance to Iran, May-October 1979", *Middle East Journal* 66:4 (Autumn 2012) pp. 613-27.

6. Asghar Bazargani, "Etteham-e Iran Doostan-e Sia be Bazargan" [Charges of the CIA Friends of Iran Against Bazargan], Jonbesh-e Rah-e Sabz (Jeres), http://www.rahesabz. net/story/65613/, last accessed 25 January 2014.

7. For a detailed analysis of SAVAK's activities in and cultivation of Kurdish assets, see Erfan Qaneei Fard, *Tond Bad-e Havades: Gogtogo ba Issa Pejman, Maamoor-e Vijeh Shah va Nemayandeh-e SAVAK dar Kurdestan-e Araq* [The Storm of Events: An Interview with Colonel Issa Pejman, the Shah's Special Representative and SAVAK's Intelligence Officer in the Iraqi Kurdistan] (Tehran: Elm Publisher, 2012).

8. Parviz Sabeti, one of the most powerful and feared figures in the last two decades of the Pahlavi monarchy and the head of SAVAK's influential Third Division, which was in charge of internal security, provides some information about how SAVAK cultivated key Kurdish figures and played them off against each other. According to Sabeti, Ali Qazi, who had left Iran for Berlin before the Iranian revolution of 1979, maintained his contact with SAVAK throughout his residency in Germany. In the only, albeit wide-ranging, interview that Sabeti has given since he left Iran, he explains how SAVAK had penetrated almost all the Iranian opposition groups and how it recruited many Kurdish sources. See Erfan Qaneei Fard, *Dar Damgah-e Hadese: Goftogo-I ba Parviz Sabeti, Mdir-e Amniyat-e Dakheli-e SAVAK* [In the Net of Events: An Interview with Parviz Sabeti, the Head of SAVAK's Division of Internal Security] (Los Angeles: Ketab Corporations, 2012) pp. 535-53.

9. Gasiorowski, "US Covert Operations toward Iran", p. 127.

10. *Espionage Documents*, vol. 32, pp. 65-96.

11. Gasiorowski, "US Covert Operations toward Iran", p. 128.

12. *Espionage Documents*, vol. 32, pp. 97-110.

13. *Espionage Documents*, vol. 44, pp. 37-8.

14. For a collection of SAVAK documents on the KDPI, see *Chap dar Iran be Ravayat-e Asnad-e SAVAk: Hezb-e Demokrart-e Kurdestan* [The Left in Iran According to SAVAK Documents: The Kurdish Democratic Party], vol. 1 (Tehran: Center for Research on Historical Documents, Ministry of Intelligence, 1999).

15. For details of constitutional debates on Kurdish ethnic rights, see Nader Entessar, *Kurdish Politics in the Middle East* (Lanham, MD: Lexington Books, 2010) pp. 34-47. See also

Nader Entessar, "The Kurdish National Movement in Iran Since the Islamic Revolution of 1979", in Mohammed M. A. Ahmed and Michael M. Gunter (eds), *The Evolution of Kurdish Nationalism* (Costa Mesa, CA: Mazda, 2007) pp. 260-75.

16. "Barnameh va Assasnameh-e Hezb-e Demokrat-e Kurdestan-e Iran" [The Platform and Constitution of the Kurdish Democratic Party of Iran], 4th Congress of the KDPI, 19-23 February 1980.

17. Sepehr Zabih, *Iran Since the Revolution* (Baltimore, MD: Johns Hopkins University Press, 1982) p. 89.

18. Younes Parsa Benab, *Tarikh-e Sad Saleh-e Ahzab Siyasi-e Iran* [A One Hundred Year History of Iranian Political Parties and Organizations], vol. 2 (Washington, DC: Ravandi Publishing House, 2006) pp. 403-5.

19. Nozar Alaolmolki, "The New Iranian Left", *Middle East Journal* 41:2 (Spring 1987) p. 230.

20. Nasser Mohajer, "Ensheab dar Hezb-e Demokrat-e Kurdestan-e Iran" [A Division in the Kurdish Democratic Party of Iran], *Aghazi No* 7 (Summer 1988) pp. 25-9.

21. Ibid., p. 27. See also Nader Entessar, "The Kurdish Mosaic of Discord," *Third World Quarterly* 11:4 (October 1989) pp. 83-100.

22. *Kayhan*, 28 July 1989.

23. *Iran Times*, 28 July 1989. In a six-part interview with the *Voice of America*'s Persian TV (5-9 September 2008), Nasrin Ghassemlou provided detailed information as to why and how the Islamic Republic organized her husband's assassination.

24. For details, see Nader Entessar, *Kurdish Politics in the Middle East*, ch. 3 and 5; Nader Entessar, "The Kurdish Factor in Iran-Iraq Relations", in Middle East Institute, *The Iranian Revolution at 30*, Viewpoints special edn (Washington, DC: Middle East Institute, 2009) pp. 143-5: and Nader Entessar, "The Impact of the Iraq War on the Future of the Kurds in Iran", in Mohammed M. A. Ahmed and Michael M. Gunter (eds), *The Kurdish Question and the 2003 Iraqi War* (Costa Mesa, CA: Mazda, 2005) pp. 174-91.

25. Elling, *Minorities in Iran*, p. 203.

26. Ibid.

27. Mohammad Khatami, *Islam, Liberty and Development* (Binghamton: Institute of Global Cultural Studies, 1998) p. 4.

28. For details, see Seyyed Mohammad Khatami, *Tose-e Siyasi, Tose-e Eqtesadi va Amniyat* [Political Development, Economic Development and Security] (Tehran: Tarh-e No, 2000) pp. 55-97.

29. Islamic Republic News Agency (IRNA), 9 April 2001.

30. *Asr-e Azadegan*, 6 March 2000. See also Hamid Reza Jalaipour, *Kurdestan: Ellat-e Tadavom-e Bohran-e An Pas Az Enghelab-e Eslami* [Kurdistan: Causes for the Perpetuation of its Crisis after the Islamic Revolution] (Tehran: Foreign Ministry Press, 1993). For a critical analysis of the role of the Kurds in Khatami's reform movement, see Khaled Tavakoli, "Kurdestan va Vaqa'ye Dovom-e Khordad" [Kurdistan and the Events of the Second of Khordad], *Goft-O-Gu* 40 (August–September 2004) pp. 35-44.

31. Mohammad Ali Zakariaee, *Konferans-e Berlin: Khedmay ya Khiyanat* [The Berlin Conference: Service or Treason] (Tehran: Tarh-e No, 2000) p. 211.

32. Iran Human Rights Documentation Center (IHRDC), *On the Margins: Arrest, Imprisonment and Execution of Kurdish Activists in Iran Today* (New Haven, CT: IHRDC, April 2012), p. 10. See also Nader Entessar, "Human Rights and the Kurdish Question in the Middle East", in Mahmood Monshipouri (ed.), *Human Rights in the Middle East: Frameworks, Goals, and Strategies* (New York: Palgrave Macmillan, 2011) pp. 99-103.

33. Emrouz, http://www.emrouz.info/ShowItem.aspx?ID=1226&p=1, last accessed 13 April 2005.

34. Ataollah Mohajerani, "Entekhab-e Talabani" [Talabani's Election], Emrouz, http://www.emrouz.info/ShowItem.aspx?ID=1117&p=1, last accessed 7 April 2005.

35. Nader Entessar, "The Kurds in Iran: The Quest for Identity", in Ofra Bengio (ed.), *Kurdish Awakening: Nation Building in a Fragmented Homeland* (Austin: University of Texas Press, 2014) pp. 233-51.

36. Elling, *Minorities in Iran*, pp. 161-202.

37. Nader Entessar, "Between a Rock and a Hard Place: The Kurdish Dilemma in Iran", in David Romano and Mehmet Gurses (eds), *Conflict, Democratization, and the Kurds in the Middle East* (New York: Palgrave Macmillan, 2014) pp. 211-24.

22. IDENTITIES AND ETHNIC HIERARCHY

1. Selig S. Harrison, "The US Meddles Aggressively in Iran", *Le Monde Diplomatique*, English edn (October 2007) pp. 1, 7.

2. For recent studies, see Rasmus C. Elling, *Minorities in Iran. Nationalism and Ethnicity after Khomeini* (New York: Palgrave Macmillan, 2014); Saleh Alam, *Ethnic Identity and the State in Iran* (New York: Palgrave Macmillan, 2013).

3. Abbas Vali, *Kurds and the State in Iran. The making of Kurdish Identity* (London: I. B. Tauris, 2011).

4. Chris, Kutschera, *Le défi kurde ou le rêve fou de l'indépendance* (Paris: Bayard, 1997) pp. 157-221.

5. Gilles Dorronsoro and Olivier Grojean, "Identity, Hierarchy and Mobilization," in idem (eds), *Identity, Conflicts and Politics in Turkey, Iran and Pakistan* (London: Hurst, New York: Oxford University Press, 2017).

6. Pierre Bourdieu, *Sur l'Etat* (Paris: Seuil, 2011).

7. Etienne Copeaux, *Espaces et temps de la nation turque. Analyse d'une historiographie nationaliste, 1931-1993* (Paris: CNRS Éditions, 1997); Etienne Copeaux, *Une vision turque du monde à travers les cartes, de 1931 à nos jours* (Paris: CNRS Éditions, 2000).

8. Bilgehan A. Gökdağ and Rıza, Heyet, "İran Türklerinde Kimlik Meselesi", *Bilig* 30, pp. 76-9, quoted in Gilles Riaux, "The Origins of the Protest Movement against Ethnic Hierarchy. The Azerbaijani Cause in Iran", in Dorronsoro and Grojean (eds), *Identity, Conflicts and Politics in Turkey, Iran and Pakistan*.

9. The PDK in Iran was founded in September 1945 and proclaimed the Kurdish Republic

of Mahabad in 1946. Since the 1960s, it has been torn between Barzani's Iraqi PDK and a brand of Soviet-influenced socialism.

10. The Revolutionary Organization of the Toilers of Iranian Kurdistan (Komalaye Shoreshgeri Zahmat Keshane Kurdistane Iran, or more simply Komala) is a Maoist organization founded by Kurdish university students in 1969. It operated in secret until the Revolution.

11. Kutschera, *Le défi kurde ou le rêve fou de l'indépendance*, p. 158.

12. Hashem Ahmadzadeh and Gareth Stansfield, "The Political, Military, and Cultural Reawakening of the Kurdish National Movement in Iran", *Middle East Journal* 64:1 (2010) pp. 17-18.

13. Chirine Mohséni, "The Instrumentalization of Ethnic Conflict by the State: the Azeri-Kurdish Conflict in Iran", in Dorronsoro and Grojean (eds), *Identity, Conflicts and Politics in Turkey, Iran and Pakistan*. The information contained here was taken from that chapter.

14. Nader Entessar, "Between a Rock and a Hard Place: The Kurdish Dilemma in Iran", in David Romano and Mehmet Gurses (eds), *Conflict, Democratization, and the Kurds in the Middle East. Turkey, Iraq, Iran and Syria* (New York: Palgrave Macmillan, 2014) p. 215.

15. Gareth Stansfield, "Kurds, Persian Nationalism, and Shi'i Rule: Surviving Persian Dominant Nationhood in Iran", in Romano and Gurses (eds) *Conflict, Democratization, and the Kurds in the Middle East*, p. 76.

16. Khatami did not in fact have the support of the Ayatollah Ali Khamenei of the Council of the Revolutionary Guards and of the judiciary power. See Ali Ansari, *Iran, Islam and Democracy: The Politics of Managing Change* (London: Chatham House, 2006).

17. Gilles Dorronsoro and Nicole Watts, "Toward Kurdish Distinctiveness in Electoral Politics. The 1977 Local Elections in Diyarbakir", *International Journal of Middle East Studies* 41:3 (2009) pp. 457-78.

18. Gilles Riaux, 'Téhéran et ses provinces. L'hypothèse de l'émergence de sous-champs politiques dans les regions périphériques de la République islamique", *Outre-Terre* 28 (2011) pp. 319-28.

19. H. E. Chehabi, "Ardabil becomes a Province: Center-Periphery relations in Iran", *International Journal of Middle-East Studies* 29 (1997) pp. 235-53.

20. Christian Bromberger, "Ethnic and Regional Ferment in Iran: The Gilan Example", in Dorronsoro and Grojean (eds), *Identity, Conflicts and Politics in Turkey, Iran and Pakistan*.

21. Farideh Koohi-Kamali, *The Political Development of the Kurds in Iran. Pastoral Nationalism* (New York: Palgrave Macmillan, 2003).

22. Martin van Bruinessen, "Book Review of *The Political Development of the Kurds in Iran: Pastoral Nationalism*, Farideh Koohi-Kamali", *Middle Eastern Studies* 41:1 (2005) pp. 153-5.

23. Kutschera, *Le défi kurde ou le rêve fou de l'indépendance*, pp. 219-21.

24. Olivier Grojean and Merve Özdemirkiran, "Ce que le Kurdistan d'Iraq fait au 'grand' Kurdistan. Enjeux et modalités de la constitution d'un espace transfrontalier", *Les Dossiers du CERI* 4 (2014), http://www.sciencespo.fr/ceri/fr/content/dossiersduceri/

ce-que-le-kurdistan-d-irak-fait-au-grand-kurdistan-enjeux-et-modalites-de-la-constitu-tion-d-un-espace-transfrontalier

25. Even if the two regions already experienced very high levels of integration, during the Mahabad Republic in 1946 and the 1960s and 1970s.

26. Cyril Roussel, "Circulations à la frontière entre Kurdes d'Iraq et Kurdes d'Iran. Clandestinité économique et politique au Moyen-Orient", *EchoGéo* 25 (2013) p. 4, https://echogeo.revues.org/13550?lang=en

27. The two parties split numerous times during the 1980s, 1990s, and 2000s. There are currently three tendencies within the KDPI, and no fewer than five currents of the Komala. See Ahmadzadeh and Stansfield, "The Political, Military, and Cultural Reawakening of the Kurdish National Movement in Iran", p. 23.

28. Ibid., pp. 24-5.

29. Observations of the Komala training camp led by Abdulla Mohtadi, near Suleymaniye, June 2014.

30. Leïla Porcher, "How to oppose Islamic Republic of Iran? Everyday political practices of Kurdish Iranian militants in Iraq", unpublished presentation at the workshop "The Development of Relations between States and the Kurdish Areas: What Impact on Local Modes of Governance?" Erbil, Institut français du Proche-Orient (IFPO), 2 June 2014. Because they have no nationality, the Iranian Kurds cannot legally work or obtain a driver's license; they also lack the right to own land or leave Iraqi Kurdistan.

31. According to Jordi Tejel and Eva Savelsberg, the Iraqi president and leader of the PUK, Jalal Talabani, encouraged the PJAK to initiate a unilateral ceasefire, and in exchange, Iran supposedly agreed to allow the Party of Democratic Union (Partiya Yekîtiya Demokrat, PYD, the PKK's sister organization in Syria) to arm itself in Syria. See Eva Savelsberg and Jordi Tejel, "The Syrian Kurds in 'Transition to Somewhere,'" in Mohammed M. A. Ahmed and Michael M. Gunter (eds), *The Kurdish Spring. Geopolitical Changes and the Kurds* (Costa Mesa, CA: Mazda, 2013), pp. 208-9. A large number of PJAK fighters reportedly went to Syria to join the PYD.

32. Border security was ensured more by the mother organization, the PKK, more than by Iranian security forces.

33. Marc Bessin, "Le trouble de l'événement: la place des émotions dans les bifurcations", in Marc Bessin, Claire Bidart, and Michel Grosseti (eds), *Bifurcations. Les sciences sociales face aux ruptures et à l'événement* (Paris: La Découverte, 2010), pp. 306-28.

34. Interview with an Iranian Kurdish PKK official based in Iran in 1998 and 1999, Berlin, July 2004.

35. Chris Kutschera, "Kurdistan d'Iran: Le Réveil des Kurdes", *Le Nouvel Observateur* 2085 (21-27 October 2004), http://www.chris-kutschera.com/reveil.htm, published in an abbreviated version in English under the title "Iran: a Kurdish Awakening", *Middle East Magazine* (January 2005), http://www.chris-kutschera.com/A/Kurds-Iran.htm

36. Based on an interview with Akif Zagros and Gulistan Dugan, members of the PJAK leadership council, Brandon argues that "the group began in Iran around 1997 as an entirely

peaceful student-based human rights movement." See James Brandon, "Iran's Kurdish Threat: PJAK", *Terrorism Monitor* 4:12 (2006).

37. Olivier Grojean, "Un champ d'action régionalisé? Le PKK et ses organisations sœurs au Moyen-Orient", *Les Dossiers du CERI* 4 (2014), http://www.sciencespo.fr/ceri/fr/content/dossiersduceri/un-champ-d-action-regionalise-le-pkk-et-ses-organisations-soeurs-au-moyen-orient?d05

38. Murat Unlu, "New PKK organizations in Turkey, Iraq, Iran and Syria to unify Kurds", *Turkish Daily News*, 3 September 2002.

39. Cf. Gilles Dorronsoro and Olivier Grojean, "Engagement militant et phénomènes de radicalisation chez les Kurdes de Turquie", *European Journal of Turkish Studies* (2004), pp. 8-9, https://ejts.revues.org/198

40. Jordi Tejel, *Syria's Kurds. History, Politics and Society* (Oxford and New York: Routledge, 2009), p. 79.

41. Ahmadzadeh and Stansfield, "The Political, Military, and Cultural Reawakening of the Kurdish National Movement in Iran", p. 25.

42. The first of the PJAK's armed actions allegedly took place in 2004 in the region of Meriwan after security forces killed ten protesters. See Brandon, "Iran's Kurdish Threat: PJAK".

23. FELLOW ARYANS AND MUSLIM BROTHERS

1. An in-depth reflection on narratives and ideology would carry us too far away from our topic. For the purpose of this article we refer to the following authors: Phillip L. Hammack and Andrew Pilecki, "Narrative as Root Metaphor for Political Psychology", *Political Psychology* 33:1 (2012) pp. 75-103; Shaul R. Shenhav, "Concise narratives: a structural analysis of political discourse", *Discourse Studies* 7:3 (2005) pp. 315-35; Shaul R. Shenhav, "Political Narrative and Political Reality", *International Political Science Review* 27:3 (2006) pp. 245-62; Terry Eagleton, *Ideology: An Introduction* (London: Verso, 1991).

2. Gareth Stansfield and Hashem Ahmadzadeh, "The Political, Cultural and Military Re-awakening of the Kurdish Nationalist Movement in Iran," *Middle East Journal* 64:1 (2010) pp. 11-27; Kaweh Bayat, "Iran and the 'Kurdish Question'", *Middle East Report* 247 (2008) pp. 28-35.

3. Mamosta Rahman Gharibi, "Kordestân forsathâ va tahdidhâ-ye farâvari-ye vahdat-e eslâmi" [Kurdistan: wider chances and threats for Islamic unity], *Okhovvat* 4:13 (2011) pp. 106-32, here p. 126.

4. Seyyed Reza Salehi-Amiri was President Rouhani's deputy when the latter was head of the CSR; in 2013 he was appointed caretaker for the Sports and Youth Ministry, and has headed the Iranian National Library since 2014.

5. Cf. the chapter on "Empire, nationalités et nation en Iran," in Xavier Planhol, *Les Nations du Prophète. Manuel géographique de politique musulman* (Paris, 1993) pp. 495-591.

6. Bert Fragner, *Die Persophonie, Regionalität, Identität und Sprachkontakt in der Geschichte Asiens*, 5 ANOR (Berlin, 1999).

7.   Bernard Hourcade, "Le recomposition des identités et des territoires en Iran islamique," *Annales de Géographie* 638/639, pp. 511-30, here p. 513.

8.   Planhol, *Les Nations du Prophète*, pp. 495-501; and following him Hourcade, "Le recomposition des identités et des territoires en Iran islamique," pp. 512-14.

9.   This racist detour is not entirely incorrect, cf. Planhol, *Les Nations du Prophète*, pp. 509-12; on the Azeris in Iran, see Gilles Riaux, *Ethnicité et nationalisme en Iran. La cause azerbaïdjanaise* (Paris, 2012); and Seyyed Reza Salehi-Amiri, *Modiriyat-e monâze'ât-e qoumi dar Irân* [The management of ethnic enmity in Iran] (Tehran, 2012) pp. 361-420.

10. Salehi-Amiri, *Modiriyat-e monâze'ât-e qoumi dar Irân*, p. 248.

11. Alirezâ Sarrafi, "Negâhi be vâqiyyat-e tanavvo,"-e qoumi va melli-ye Irân: chashmaandâzi az Irân-e federâl," *Dilmâj* 16 (2006) pp. 6-21, here pp. 11, 12.

12. Salehi-Amiri, *Modiriyat-e monâze'ât-e qoumi dar Irân*, p. 420.

13. On the conflation of terms regarding *qoumi*, see below.

14. Salehi-Amiri, *Modiriyat-e monâze'ât-e qoumi dar Irân*, p. 453.

15. Ludwig Paul, "Iranian Nation and Iranian-Islamic Revolutionary Ideology," *Die Welt des Islams*, New Series 39:2 (1999) pp. 183-217, here pp. 212-15.

16. On the hezbollahis and their role within the political landscape of Iran, see Walter Posch, "The end of a beautiful friendship: Mahmoud Ahmadinejad and the Principalists," in Houshang E. Chehabi, Farhad Khosrokhavar, and Clement Therme (eds), *Iran and the Challenges of the Twenty-First Century. Essays in Honour of Mohammad-Reza Djalili* (Costa Mesa, CA: Mazda, 2013) pp. 50-78; and idem, "Islamistische Gewalt in der Islamischen Republik Iran", in Jasmina Rupp and Walter Feichtinger (eds), *Der Ruf des Dschihad. Theorie, Fallstudien und Wege aus der Radikalität* (Vienna, 2016) pp. 267-318.

17. Stephane A. Dudoignon, "Inter-Confessional Relations in Iran: Conflicts and Transfers in the Aftermath of 9/11", in Chehabi, Khosrokhavar, and Therme (eds), *Iran and the Challenges of the Twenty-First Century*, pp. 96-110, here p. 105; see also Navid Fozi, "Neo-Iranian Nationalism: Pre-Islamic Grandeur and Shiite Eschatology in President Mahmoud Ahmadinejad's Rhetoric", *Middle East Journal* 70:2 (2016) pp. 227-48.

18. Walter Posch, *The Third World, Global Islam and Pragmatism. The Making of Iranian Foreign Policy*, SWP Research Paper (Berlin, 2013) p. 12.

19. Dudoignon, "Inter-Confessional Relations in Iran", pp. 108-9.

20. Cf. Sarrafi, "Negâhi be vâqiyyat-e tanavvo,-e qoumi va melli-ye Irân", pp. 6-8, 13-16.

21. Cf. Hourcade, "Le recomposition des identités et des territoires en Iran islamique", p. 515.

22. For Persian as a language of culture and an *art de vivre*, see Hourcade, "Le recomposition des identités et des territoires en Iran islamique", p. 516; and Fragner, *Die Persophonie, Regionalität, Identität und Sprachkontakt, passim*.

23. Amanolahi, Sekandar: "A note on ethnicity and ethnic groups in Iran", *Iran and the Caucasus* 9:1 (2005) pp. 37-41, here pp. 37, 39.

24. Salehi-Amiri, *Modiriyat-e monâze'ât-e qoumi dar Irân*, pp. 423-5, 452, 562.

25. Amanolahi, "A note on ethnicity", p. 41.

26. Ibid., p. 39.

27. Paul, "Iranian Nation and Iranian-Islamic Revolutionary Ideology", p. 206; Anthony D. Smith, *National Identity* (Reno, Las Vegas, 1991) p. 8.

28. On Iran's bi-national Azeri-Persian character, see Planhol, *Les Nations du Prophète*, pp. 501-9.

29. Paul, "Iranian Nation and Iranian-Islamic Revolutionary Ideology", pp. 203-4.

30. See Salehi-Amiri, *Modiriyat-e monâze'ât-e qoumi dar Irân*, pp. 63-70.

31. The previous elaborations do not necessarily lead to this conclusion, which in my view are a very far stretch from what the drafters of the constitution had in mind anyway.

32. Salehi-Ameri, *Modiriyat-e monâze'ât-e qoumi dar Irân*, p. 454.

33. Abbas Vali, "The Kurds and their 'Others': Fragmented Identity and Fragmented Politics", in Faleh Jabar and Hosham Dawod (eds), *The Kurds, Nationalism and Politics* (London: Saqi Books, 2006) pp. 49-78, here p. 68.

34. Salehi-Amiri, *Modiriyat-e monâze'ât-e qoumi dar Irân*, p. 452.

35. Baskin Oran, *Türk Dış Politikası. Kurtuluş Savaşından Bugüne. Olgular, Belgeler, Yorumlar*, vol. III: 2001-2012 (Istanbul, 2013) pp. 740-49.

36. Bayat, "Iran and the 'Kurdish Question,'" p. 35.

37. Salehi-Amiri, *Modiriyat-e monâze'ât-e qoumi dar Irân*, p. 452.

38. The formulation is unclear: whether these policies are conducted on behalf of or by the ethnic groups themselves.

39. The term *efrâti* extremism is used in a threefold way in Iran's highly polemic political language: 1) to denote the *salafi* and *vahhâbi* schools and movements of Sunni Islam, in this sense directed against the Sunnis of Iran; 2) to discredit the belief and practices of certain Sufi and Alavi communities (Ahl-e Haqq, Ali-Elâhi etc.), here used alternatively to *ghâliye* or *ghulât*; and finally 3) as a political term for the most extremist hezbollahi groups.

40. Salehi-Amiri, *Modiriyat-e monâze'ât-e qoumi dar Irân*, pp. 566-7.

41. Ibid., p. 72.

42. Planhol, *Les Nations du Prophète*, pp. 546-7; Hassan Bouzhmehrani, and Mehdi Pour-Eslami, "Tahdidhâ-ye narm-e khodmokhtâri-ye eqlim-e Kordestân-e 'Erâq va ta'sir-e ân bar Kordhâ-ye Irân", [The soft threats of Kurdistan in Iraq and its impact on the Kurds of Iran], *Jâme-shenâsi-ye Jehân-e Eslâm* 2:1 (2014) pp. 87-110, here p. 89; Denise Natali, *The Kurds and the State. Evolving Identity in Iraq, Turkey, and Iran* (Syracuse University Press, 2006) pp. 149-55.

43. Natali, *The Kurds and the State*, pp. 140-49.

44. Thomas Riegler, *Im Fadenkreuz: Österreich und der Nahostterrorismus 1973 bis 1985* (Vienna, 2011) pp. 459-64.

45. For a readable literary account on this episode, see Roya Hakakian, *Assassins of the Turquoise Palace* (New York: Grove Atlantic, 2011); we assume that Hakakian's account owes much to the following report: Iranian Human Rights Centre (ed.), *Murder at Mykonos: Anatomy of a Political Assassination* (New Haven, CT, 2007).

46. Robert Olson, *Turkey's Relations with Iran, Syria, Israel and Russia, 1991-2000. The Kurdish and Islamist Questions* (Syracuse University Press, 2001) pp. 1-10, 74.

47. Hasan Jafarzadeh, "Touse'eh-ye motavâzen-e Âzarbâyjân-e Gharbi bar bastar-e hamgarâyi

va amniyat", [Balanced development in Western Azerbaijan regarding conviviality and security], *Okhovvat* 1:3 (2008) pp. 99-105, here pp. 101-2.

48. Ibid., p. 104; Khaled Tavvakoli, "Kordestân va vâqe'e-ye dovvom-e Khordâd",. [Kurdistan and the second Khordad issue], *Goftogu* 40 (2004) pp. 38-9.

49. Jafarzadeh, "Touse'eh-ye motavâzen-e Âzarbâyjân-e Gharbi bar bastar-e hamgarâyi va amniyat", pp. 103-4.

50. Ibid., p. 104.

51. Ibid., pp. 104-5.

52. Tavvakoli, "Kordestân va vâqe'e-ye dovvom-e Khordâd", pp. 40-1.

53. Ibid., p. 38.

54. Gharibi, "Kordestân forsathâ va tahdidhâ-ye farâvari-ye vahdat-e eslâmi", p. 122.

55. Ibid., p. 127.

56. Ibid., p. 122.

57. Ibid., p. 129.

58. Alireza Sheikh-Attar, *Kordhâ va qodrathâ-ye manteqehi va gheyr-e manteqehi* [The Kurds and the regional and international powers] (Tehran, 2003) p. 14.

59. Dudoignon, "Inter-Confessional Relations in Iran", p. 105.

60. Gharibi, "Kordestân forsathâ va tahdidhâ-ye farâvari-ye vahdat-e eslâmi", p. 113.

61. Mir Mehrdad Mir-Sanjari, "Har ja ke Kord ast, Iran ast", [Wherever a Kurd is, is Iran], *Tabnak,* 26 August 2010.

62. Amiri-Salehi, *Modiriyat-e monâze'ât-e qoumi dar Irân*, pp. 243-4.

63. Malek Hoseyn Baratzadeh, "Hambastegi-ye nezhâdi-ye Kordhâ bâ Irân va esteqlâl-talabi-ye Kordhâ az Torkiye, Erâq va Suriye", [The racial connection of the Kurds with Iran and the Kurdish wish of independence from Turkey, Iraq and Syria], http://www.malekhos-sein.blogfa.com/post/28

64. Jafarzadeh, "Touse'eh-ye motavâzen-e Âzarbâyjân-e Gharbi bar bastar-e hamgarâyi va amniyat", p. 102.

65. Gharibi, "Kordestân forsathâ va tahdidhâ-ye farâvari-ye vahdat-e eslâmi", p. 112.

66. Mir-Sanjari, "Har ja ke Kord ast, Iran ast."

67. Hakakian, *Assassins of the Turquoise Palace*, p. 15.

68. Mir-Sanjari, "Har ja ke Kord ast, Iran ast."

69. Dudoignon, "Inter-Confessional Relations in Iran", pp. 108, 109.

70. Bayat, "Iran and the 'Kurdish Question,'" p. 35.

71. Tavvakoli, "Kordestân va vâqe'e-ye dovvom-e Khordâd", p. 41.

72. Jafarzadeh, "Touse'eh-ye motavâzen-e Âzarbâyjân-e Gharbi bar bastar-e hamgarâyi va amniyat", p. 102; Gharibi, "Kordestân forsathâ va tahdidhâ-ye farâvari-ye vahdat-e eslâmi", pp. 124-5.

73. Gharibi, "Kordestân forsathâ va tahdidhâ-ye farâvari-ye vahdat-e eslâmi", p. 124.

74. Gharibi, "Kordestân forsathâ va tahdidhâ-ye farâvari-ye vahdat-e eslâmi", p. 125; on the importance of the *emâmzâdeh*s as a typical Iranian cultural phenomenon, see Planhol, *Les Nations du Prophète*, pp. 505-8.

75. On the Iranian institutions involved in ecumenical projects, see Buchta Wilfried, "The

Failed Pan-Islamic Program of the Islamic Republic: Views of the Liberal Reformers of the Religioius Semi-Opposition", in Nikki R. Keddie and Rudi Matthee, *Iran and the Surrounding World: Interaction in Culture and Cultural Politics* (Washington, DC, 2003) pp. 281-304; and idem, "Tehran's Ecumenical Society (*majma' al-taqrib*): a Veritable Ecumenical Revival or a Trojan Horse of Iran", in Rainer Brunner and Werner Ende, *The Twelver Shia in Modern Times. Religious Culture & Political History* (Leiden, Boston, Berlin: Brill, 2001) pp. 333-53.

76. Gharibi, "Kordestân forsathâ va tahdidhâ-ye farâvari-ye vahdat-e eslâmi", p. 128.

77. Ibid., p. 108

78. Ibid., p. 119.

79. Jafarzadeh, "Touse'eh-ye motavâzen-e Âzarbâyjân-e Gharbi bar bastar-e hamgarâyi va amniyat", p. 102.

80. Gharibi, "Kordestân forsathâ va tahdidhâ-ye farâvari-ye vahdat-e eslâmi", p. 122.

81. Ibid., p. 123.

82. Dudoignon, "Inter-Confessional Relations in Iran", pp. 104-5.

83. Gharibi, "Kordestân forsathâ va tahdidhâ-ye farâvari-ye vahdat-e eslâmi", p. 114.

84. Jafarzadeh, "Touse'eh-ye motavâzen-e Âzarbâyjân-e Gharbi bar bastar-e hamgarâyi va amniyat", p. 100; Gharibi, "Kordestân forsathâ va tahdidhâ-ye farâvari-ye vahdat-e eslâmi", p. 121.

85. Gharibi, "Kordestân forsathâ va tahdidhâ-ye farâvari-ye vahdat-e eslâmi", p. 121.

86. Salehi-Amiri, *Modiriyat-e monâze'*ât-e qoumi dar Irân, p. 252; and Reza Afruz, "Hobâbhâ-ye siyâsi dar Kordestân-e Iran", [Political bubbles in Iranian Kurdistan], *Bâztâb*, 6 October 2005.

87. Gharibi, "Kordestân forsathâ va tahdidhâ-ye farâvari-ye vahdat-e eslâmi", pp. 115-16.

88. Ibid., p. 119.

89. Ibid., p. 112.

90. Jafarzadeh, "Touse'eh-ye motavâzen-e Âzarbâyjân-e Gharbi bar bastar-e hamgarâyi va amniyat", p. 101.

91. Ibid., pp. 102-3.

92. Afruz, "Hobâbhâ-ye siyâsi dar Kordestân-e Iran."

93. Gharibi, "Kordestân forsathâ va tahdidhâ-ye farâvari-ye vahdat-e eslâmi", pp. 116-17.

94. Stansfield and Ahmadzadeh, "The Political, Cultural and Military Re-awakening of the Kurdish Nationalist Movement in Iran", p. 24; Bouzhmehrani and Pour-Eslami, "Tahdidhâ-ye narm-e khodmokhtâri-ye eqlim-e Kordestân-e 'Erâq va ta'sir-e ân bar Kordhâ-ye Irân"pp. 100-1.

95. Gharibi, "Kordestân forsathâ va tahdidhâ-ye farâvari-ye vahdat-e eslâmi", p. 116.

96. Bouzhmehrani and Pour-Eslami, "Tahdidhâ-ye narm-e khodmokhtâri-ye eqlim-e Kordestân-e 'Erâq va ta'sir-e ân bar Kordhâ-ye Irân", p. 97.

97. Bouzhmehrani and Pour-Eslami, "Tahdidhâ-ye narm-e khodmokhtâri-ye eqlim-e Kordestân-e 'Erâq va ta'sir-e ân bar Kordhâ-ye Irân", p. 97.

98. Ibid., p. 103.

99. Aydin Sadeqi, "Fedrâlism va tarhi-ye "amali az ân barâ-ye Irân", [Federalism and its application for Iran], *Dilmâj* 16 (2006) pp. 22-41, here pp. 33-9.

100. Kamran Keshtiban, "Federâlism: tanhâ rahyâft-e momken dar hamgarâyi-e melli", [Federalism: the only possible solution for national convivality], *Dilmâj* 16 (2006) pp. 42-9.

101. Bouzhmehrani and Pour-Eslami, "Tahdidhâ-ye narm-e khodmokhtâri-ye eqlim-e Kordestân-e 'Erâq va ta'sir-e ân bar Kordhâ-ye Irân", p. 100.

102. Ibid., p. 100.

103. Bouzhmehrani and Pour-Eslami, "Tahdidhâ-ye narm-e khodmokhtâri-ye eqlim-e Kordestân-e 'Erâq va ta'sir-e ân bar Kordhâ-ye Irân", p. 101.

104. Mohammad Hadi, "Rahbarân-e Kord-e "Erâq va estefâdeh az kârt-e Akrâd-e hamsâyeh, bakhsh-e nakhost: Mas"ud Bârezâni" [The Kurdish leaders of Iraq and their utilization of neighboring Kurds: Part 1, Mas'ud Barzani], *Bâztâb*, 20 November 2006.

105. Bouzhmehrani and Pour-Eslami, "Tahdidhâ-ye narm-e khodmokhtâri-ye eqlim-e Kordestân-e 'Erâq va ta'sir-e ân bar Kordhâ-ye Irân", p. 100.

106. Ibid., p. 104.

107. Ibid., p. 103.

108. Ibid., p. 103.

109. M. S. Majidpour, "Negâhi be shâkheshâ-ye touse'e dar Kordestan", *Goft-e-gu* 40 (2005) p. 86; Salehi-Amiri, *Modiriyat-e monâze'ât-e qoumi dar Irân*, p. 253; Tavvakoli, "Kordestân va vâqe'e-ye dovvom-e Khordâd", p. 42.

110. Bayat, "Iran and the 'Kurdish Question,'" p. 35; Tavvakoli, "Kordestân va vâqe'e-ye dovvom-e Khordâd", p. 42.

111. Afruz, "Hobâbhâ-ye siyâsi dar Kordestân-e Iran."

112. Bouzhmehrani and Pour-Eslami, "Tahdidhâ-ye narm-e khodmokhtâri-ye eqlim-e Kordestân-e 'Erâq va ta'sir-e ân bar Kordhâ-ye Irân", p. 105.

113. Ibid., p. 103.

114. This is not the place to go into the details of the Iranians' voting patterns; for in-depth analysis on the topic, see the following site maintained and managed by Bernard Hourcade: http://www.irancarto.cnrs.fr.

115. Tavvakoli, "Kordestân va vâqe'e-ye dovvom-e Khordâd", p. 41.

116. Ibid., pp. 41-2.

117. Bouzhmehrani and Pour-Eslami, "Tahdidhâ-ye narm-e khodmokhtâri-ye eqlim-e Kordestân-e 'Erâq va ta'sir-e ân bar Kordhâ-ye Irân", p. 105.

118. Seyyed Hasan Alavi, "Tashkil-e frâksyun-e nemâyandegân-e Kord-e majles-e dahom" [Formation of the caucus of the Kurdish deputies in the 10th majles], *Mehr News*, 3 May 2016.

119. Olson, *Turkey's Relations with Iran, Syria, Israel and Russia*, pp. 44-104.

120. For an in-depth analysis of KCK, see Walter Posch, "Die neue PKK. Zwischen Extremismus, politischer Gewalt und strategischen Herausforderungen, Teil 1", Österreichische Militärische Zeitschrift 2 (2016) pp. 139-55; idem, "Die neue PKK, Teil 2," Österreichische Militärische Zeitschrift 3 (2016) pp. 295-311; and idem, "The changing faces of the PKK",

in Wolfgang Taucher, Matthias Vogl, and Peter Webinger, *The Kurds. History, Religion, Language, Politics* (Vienna: Ministry of the Interior BMI, 2015) pp. 87-110.

121. Cf. E. Qane'ifard, "Shenâkhtnâme-ye ferqe-ye teruristi-ye PKK va PJAK", *Fararu*, 19 May 2011, and his rant on the uneducated PJAK fighters.

122. Mojtabâ Sadeqi and Mohsen Zeyrak, "PJAK mikhvâst jâddeh-sâff-kon-e Âmrikâ bâshad", [PJAK wants to clear the way for the USA], *Bultannews*, 1 September 2011.

123. Qane'ifard, "Shenâkhtnâme-ye ferqe-ye teruristi-ye PKK va PJAK"; Posch, "Die neue PKK, Teil 1", pp. 296-303; idem, "Changing Faces", pp. 102-7.

124. On Iran's security apparatus, see Posch, "Der Sicherheitsapparat der Islamischen Republik Iran", *Handbuch der Iranistik* (Berlin, 2016).

125. Bayram Sinkaya, "Rationalisation of Turkey-Iranian Relations: Prospects and Limits", *Insight Turkey* 14 (2012) pp. 137-56.

126. "Enqelâb-e Eslâmi va royâhâ-ye fântezi-e goruhakhâ-ye zedd-e enqelâb", [The Islamic Revolution facing the fantasies of counter-revolutionary groups], *Bultan*, 18 February 2013.

127. Posch, "Changing Faces", p. 87-9. I could not retrieve the text of the Kodar constitution on the internet, not even on their homepage, http://www.kodar.info/farsi. I am grateful to Sherween Taheri, Hamburg, for having provided me with a paper copy.

128. See for instance "Akkâs-e Zan-e Irâni dar pâdgân-e zanân-e Kord", [Iranian female photographer in the camp of Kurdish women] *Entekhab*, 5 May 2015.

129. Posch, "Die neue PKK, Teil 2", p. 305.

130. See the KDP-I's internet site www.pdki.org; information refers to the year 2015 mostly.

131. The following points all come from the Vice-presidency for Legal Affairs, *Manshur-e hoquq-e shahrvandi, matn-e pish-nevis-e gheyr-e rasmi* [Manifesto of citizens' rights, unofficial draft paper] (Tehran, 2013) p. 5 and *passim*.

132. Walter Posch, "Mäßigung statt Neuanfang: Iran nach den Präsidentschaftswahlen 2013", *SWP-Aktuell* 39 (Berlin, 2013) p. 3.

133. "Tadris-e zabân va adabiyât-e Kordi dar dâneshgâh-e Kordestân", [Instruction in Kurdish and language instruction at the University of Kurdistan], *Asr-e Iran*, 16 September 2015.

134. Sedâ-ye Mo'allem, "Tâbu-ye amuzesh-e zabân-e Kordi dar madâres-e Saqez shekasteh shod", [The taboo of Kurdish language instruction in the schools of Saqez has been broken], www.sedayemoallem.ir, 10 April 2015.

135. "Hich Kas Haqq Nadârad Tabyiz-e beyn-e mazâheb va aqvâm qâel bâshad", [Nobody has the right to discriminate among the confessions and ethnic groups], IRINN, 31 May 2016, w.irinn.ir/news/print/161998/; this article is the source for Umid Niyash, "Rouhani defends Iranian ethnics' right of mother tongue teaching", *Trend*, 31 May 2016, http://en.trend.az/iran/politics/2540073.html. However, Niyash's statement that Rouhani has promised language instruction in Turkish and the opening of centers for learning Azeri Turkish in Tebriz and Ardabil is nowhere to be found in the heavily edited statement of Rouhani's.

24. THE KURDISH EXPERIENCE IN POST-SADDAM IRAQ

1. For accounts of the Kurds' experience in Iraq in the 1990s, see Michael Gunter, *The Kurdish Predicament in Iraq: A Political Analysis* (London: Macmillan, 1999); Gareth Stansfield, *Iraqi Kurdistan: Political Development and Emergent Democracy* (London: Routledge, 2003); and Ofra Bengio, *The Kurds of Iraq: Building a State within a State* (Boulder, CO: Lynne Rienner, 2012).

2. See Haidar Ala Hamoudi, *Negotiating in Civil Conflict: Constitutional Construction and Imperfect Bargaining in Iraq* (Chicago, IL: University of Chicago Press, 2014) pp. 53-4.

3. Gareth Stansfield, "The Islamic State, the Kurdistan Region, and the Future of Iraq", *International Affairs* 90:6 (November 2014) pp. 1329-50.

4. Winston Harris, "Chaos in Iraq: Are the Kurds Truly Set to Win?" *Small Wars Journal* (28 August 2014).

5. See Raad Alkadiri, "Oil and Federalism in Iraq", *International Affairs* 86:6 (November 2010) pp. 1315-28; Robin Mills, "Under the Mountains: Kurdish Oil and Regional Politics", Oxford Institute for Energy Studies Paper: WPM 63 (Oxford: OIES, 2016).

6. Gareth Stansfield, "Kurdistan Rising: To Acknowledge or Ignore the Unraveling of Iraq", Brookings Institution Middle East Memo 33 (Washington, DC: Brookings Institution, July 2014).

7. Ibrahim Marashi, "The Kurdish Referendum and Barzani's Political Survival", Al-Jazeera, 4 February 2016, http://www.aljazeera.com/indepth/opinion/2016/02/kurdish-refer-endum-barzani-political-survival-iraq-160204111835869.html

8. Loveday Morris, "As their power grows, Iraq's Kurds are fighting among themselves", *Washington Post*, 12 October 2015, https://www.washingtonpost.com/world/middle_east/as-their-power-grows-iraqs-kurds-are-fighting-among-themselves/2015/10/12/2f86ef74-70d4-11e5-ba14-318f8e87a2fc_story.html

9. See Stansfield, "Kurdistan Rising"; Mark DeWeaver, "Iraqi Kurdistan Economic Report 2016: Kurdistan's Great Recession", in *Kurdistan Region of Iraq Report*, Macropolis Report, 8 January 2016, http://www.marcopolis.net/iraqi-kurdistan-economic-report-2016-kurd-istan-s-great-recession.htm; Isabel Coles, "Protests intensify in Iraqi Kurdistan amid economic crisis", Reuters, 9 February 2016, http://www.reuters.com/article/us-mideast-crisis-iraq-protests-idUSKCN0VI11X

10. Sibel Kulaksiz, *The Kurdistan Region of Iraq: Assessing the Economic and Social Impact of the Syrian Conflict and ISIS* (Washington, DC: World Bank, 2015).

11. Isabel Coles, "Iraqi Kurdish leader calls for non-binding independence referendum", Reuters, 2 February 2016, http://www.reuters.com/article/us-iraq-kurds-idUSKCN0VB2EY

12. Ofra Bengio notes that "[a]s early as November 2001 Barham Salih, head of the PUK government, was summoned to Washington to meet with Secretary of Defense Donald Rumsfeld . . . [there was also] a secret meeting between Barzani, Talabani, and President George W. Bush in April 2002 that would have important implications for future Kurdish-US relations." Bengio, *The Kurds of Iraq*, p. 266.

13. During this period, I spoke often with friends in the Kurdistan Region—including those affiliated with political parties, and those who were not—and there was a commonly-held nervousness about the West planning to take military action against Saddam, with many viewing themselves as being on the frontline in such a conflict, facing a very dangerous enemy, and with uncertain international support.

14. See Henry Kissinger, *White House Years* (Boston: Little, Brown, 1979) p. 1265; Bengio, *The Kurds of Iraq*, pp. 142-6; Bryan Gibson, *Sold Out? US Foreign Policy, Iraq, the Kurds, and the Cold War* (New York: Palgrave, 2015).

15. Human Rights Watch, *Endless Torment: The 1991 Uprising in Iraq and its Aftermath* (New York: Human Rights Watch, 1992).

16. Robert Baer, *See No Evil: The True Story of a Ground Soldier in the CIA's War on Terrorism* (New York: Crown, 2002); Gareth Stansfield, *Iraq: People, History Politics*, 2nd edn (Cambridge: Polity Press, 2016).

17. For an account of the Anfal campaign of ethnic cleansing and genocide, see Mohammed Ihsan, *Nation Building in Kurdistan: Memory, Genocide and Human Rights* (London: Routledge, 2016). For an account of the attack on Halabja in 1988, see Joost Hiltermann, *A Poisonous Affair: America, Iraq, and the Gassing of Halabja* (Cambridge: Cambridge University Press, 2007).

18. The KDP and PUK had overcome the vicissitudes of the civil war of the 1990s and embarked upon an internal peace process from 1998. The UK and then US became involved in the process, leading to the signing of the Washington Agreement in 1999 that gave a roadmap for the normalization relations between the two parties and the coordination of the activities of the KRGs of Erbil and Suleimani. See Gareth Stansfield, "Governing Kurdistan: The Strengths of Division", in Brendan O'Leary, John McGarry, and Khaled Salih (eds), *The Future of Kurdistan in Iraq* (Philadelphia, PA: University of Pennsylvania Press, 2005) pp. 195-218.

19. David McDowall, *A Modern History of the Kurds*, 3rd edn (London: I. B. Tauris, 2004).

20. Hamid al-Bayati, *From Dictatorship to Democracy: An Insider's Account of the Iraqi Opposition to Saddam* (Philadelphia, PA: University of Pennsylvania Press, 2011); Khalil Osman, *Sectarianism in Iraq: The Making of State and Nation Since 1920* (London: Routledge, 2015).

21. I resided in the Kurdistan Region of Iraq between 1997 and 2001 and met regularly with the leaderships of the KDP and PUK. As a PhD student in political science, and working on concepts of power-sharing, federalism, and consociationalism, I had many long discussions with prominent figures in both parties on these subjects, including the late Sami Abdul Rahman, Nechirvan Barzani, and Hoshyar Zebari of the KDP, and Dr Barham Salih, Kosrat Rasoul, and Sadi Pire of the PUK. Already, by the end of the 1990s, the level of critical thinking toward these concepts that existed in the elites of these parties was very advanced indeed. See Stansfield, *Iraqi Kurdistan*, 2003 for a full listing of these interviews.

22. Don Eberly, *Liberate and Leave: Fatal Flaws in the Early Strategy for Postwar Iraq* (Minneapolis, MN: Zenith Press, 2009).

23. For accounts of the formation and subsequent record of the CPA, see Larry Diamond, *Squandered Victory: The American Occupation and the Bungled Effort to Bring Democracy to Iraq* (New York: Times Books, 2005); Ali Allawi, *The Occupation of Iraq: Winning the War, Losing the Peace* (New Haven, CT: Yale University Press, 2007). For Bremer's personal account, see L. Paul Bremer III, *My Year in Iraq: The Struggle to Bring a Future of Hope* (New York: Simon & Schuster, 2006).

24. Peter Galbraith, *The End of Iraq: How American Incompetence Created a War Without End* (New York: Simon & Schuster, 2006).

25. See Stansfield, *Iraq: People, History Politics*, 2016, pp. 189-90 for details concerning the constitutional referendum of 15 October 2005.

26. Ibid., pp. 168-9.

27. For an analysis of Article 140 and the disputed territories, see Liam Anderson and Gareth Stansfield, *Crisis in Kirkuk: The Ethnopolitics of Conflict and Compromise* (Philadelphia, PA: University of Pennsylvania Press, 2009); Stefan Wolff, "Governing (in) Kirkuk: Resolving the Status of a Disputed Territory in Post-American Iraq", *International Affairs* 86:6 (November 2010) pp. 1361-80; Peter Bartu, "Wrestling with the Integrity of a Nation: The Disputed Internal Boundaries in Iraq", *International Affairs* 86:6 (November 2010) pp. 1329-44.

28. For an insightful account of the impact of the constitutional negotiations on Iraq's societal integrity, see Salam Karam, "The Constitution as Unfinished Business: The Making and Un-Making of the Power Relations in Iraq, 2003-2010", unpublished PhD dissertation, Department of Politics and International Studies, School of Oriental and African Studies, University of London, 2016.

29. For accounts of the commencement of the Sunni and Shia insurgencies, leading to the sectarian civil war that started in earnest in 2006, see Toby Dodge, *Iraq's Future: The Aftermath of Regime Change*, Adelphi Paper 372 (London: IISS/Routledge, 2005); Ahmed Hashim, *Insurgency and Counter-Insurgency in Iraq* (London: Hurst & Co., 2006); Nicholas Krohley, *The Death of the Mehdi Army: The Rise, Fall, and Revival of Iraq's Most Powerful Militia* (London, Hurst & Co., 2015).

30. See Eric Herring and Glen Rangwala, *Iraq in Fragments: The Occupation and its Legacy* (Ithaca, NY: Cornell University Press, 2006); Gareth Stansfield, "Accepting Realities in Iraq", Middle East Programme Briefing Paper MEP BP 07/02 (May) (London: Chatham House, 2007).

31. From being dismissed in earlier decades as being of importance in the politics of the region, sectarianism as a defining element of Middle East international relations has become accepted as a norm in the early twenty-first century. Much has been written on this theme, but two books stand out as being particularly insightful. Vali Nasr's 2006 work on *The Shia Revival* was one of the first to predict what would prove to be an accurate contestation between Sunnis and Shia. Frederic Wehrey's 2014 work on *Sectarian Politics in the Gulf* then details how these conflicts subsequently unfolded. Vali Nasr, *The Shia Revival: How Conflicts Within Islam Will Shape the Future* (New York: W. W. Norton, 2006);

Frederic Wehrey, *Sectarian Politics in the Gulf: From the Iraq War to the Arab Uprisings* (New York: Columbia University Press, 2014).

32. See Soner Cagaptay, Christina Bache Fidan, and Ege Cansu Sacikara, "Turkey and the KRG: An Undeclared Economic Commonwealth", Policy Analysis Policywatch 2387 (Washington, DC: Washington Institute for Near East Policy, 16 March 2016), http://www.washingtoninstitute.org/policy-analysis/view/turkey-and-the-krg-an-undeclared-economic-commonwealth

33. Başik İnce, *Citizenship and Identity in Turkey: From Atatürk's Republic to the Present Day* (London: I. B. Tauris, 2012); Stansfield, *Kurdistan Rising*, 2014.

34. Stansfield, *Iraqi Kurdistan*, 2003.

35. For an analysis of the contradictions inherent in this two-track approach, see Bill Park, "Iraq Futures, Turkish Options", *European Security* 17:1 (2008) pp. 85-104.

36. See Liz Sly, "Kurdistan: The Other Iraq", *Washington Post*, 28 May 2011, https://www.washingtonpost.com/lifestyle/travel/kurdistan-the-other-iraq/2011/05/24/AGSJAnCH_story.html

37. Balci Ali, "'Energized' Neighborliness: Relations Between Turkey and the Kurdish Regional Government", SETA Analysis no. 9 (Istanbul: SETA, September 2014) p. 11.

38. See Emre Tunçalp, "Turkey's Natural Gas Strategy: Balancing Geopolitical Goals and Market Realities", *Turkish Policy Quarterly*, 13 December 2015, http://turkishpolicy.com/article/774/turkeys-natural-gas-strategy-balancing-geopolitical-goals-market-realities

39. For a recent assessment of Turkey-KRG relations, see F. Stephen Larrabee, "Turkey and the Changing Dynamics of the Kurdish Issue", *Survival* 58:2 (2016) pp. 67-73.

40. Ihsan, *Nation Building in Kurdistan*. I personally recall many such conversations with members of the leaderships of the KDP and PUK during the 1990s, directly equating the use of "their" oil wealth derived from Kirkuk to procure weapons and munitions that would ultimately be used against not only the peshmerga, but also civilians.

41. The most comprehensive and detailed account of the economic problems faced by the KRI during the 1990s remains Helena Cook, *The Safe Haven in Northern Iraq: International Responsibility for Iraqi Kurdistan* (Colchester and London: University of Essex/Kurdistan Human Rights Project, 1995); and Sarah Graham Brown, *Sanctioning Saddam: The Politics of Intervention in Iraq* (London: I. B. Tauris, 1999).

42. Denise Natali, *The Kurdish Quasi-State: Development and Dependency in Post-Gulf War Iraq* (Syracuse, NY: Syracuse University Press, 2010).

43. See, for example, Triska Hamid, "Corruption and cronyism hinder Kurdistan", *Financial Times*, 5 September 2012, http://www.ft.com/cms/s/0/ea716668-f759-11e1-8c9d-00144feabdc0.html#axzz46g24k0bt

44. Robin Mills, "Under the Mountains: Kurdish Oil and Regional Politics", Oxford Institute for Energy Studies Paper WPM 63, January 2016, pp. 8-9.

45. For an extensive and detailed discussion of the various oil-related articles of the constitution of Iraq, and the manner in which they have been interpreted, see Rex Zedalis, *Oil*

and Gas in the Disputed Kurdish Territories: Jurisprudence, Regional Minorities and Natural Resources in a Federal System (London: Routledge, 2012).

46. See Rex Zedalis, The Legal Dimensions of Oil and Gas in Iraq: Current Reality and Future Prospects (Cambridge: Cambridge University Press, 2009).

47. For a detailed description of Maliki's targeting of the Jaish al-Mahdi in 2008, see Richard Iron, "The Charge of the Knights", RUSI Journal 158:1 (2013) pp. 54-62.

48. For an influential policy-related analysis of the status of the disputed territories at this time, see International Crisis Group, Oil for Soil: Toward a Grand Bargain on Iraq and the Kurds, Middle East Report 80 (Brussels: ICG, 28 October 2008).

49. For a comprehensive analysis of the rise of sectarian politics in Iraq, see Harith al-Qarawee, Iraq's Sectarian Crisis: A Legacy of Exclusion (Beirut: Carnegie Middle East Center, 2014), http://carnegieendowment.org/files/iraq_sectarian_crisis.pdf

50. This point, about Maliki losing the 2010 election to Allawi, but remaining as prime minister largely due to US support, cannot be overstressed and should be recognized as being a critical event in the subsequent rise of the Islamic State. While alternative histories are not worth pursuing too far, it is interesting to imagine what would have happened in Iraq if Allawi's victory had been honored. It is not too outlandish to speculate that the marginalization of the Sunnis would have stopped, thus removing a key formative pillar of the resurgent Islamic State of Iraq (ISI) that would then go on to form ISIS.

51. See Yaniv Voller, "Kurdish Oil Politics in Iraq: Contested Sovereignty and Unilateralism", Middle East Policy 20:1 (2013) pp. 68-82.

52. See Adam Withnall, "Iraq crisis: Isis declares its territories a new Islamic state with 'restoration of caliphate' in Middle East", Independent, 30 June 2014, http://www.independent.co.uk/news/world/middle-east/isis-declares-new-islamic-state-in-middle-east-with-abu-bakr-al-baghdadi-as-emir-removing-iraq-and-9571374.html

53. The literature on Islamic State has grown prodigiously since 2014. Some of the most insightful of what are still relatively early attempts to make sense of IS include Patrick Cockburn, The Rise of Islamic State: ISIS and the New Sunni Revolution (London: Verso, 2014); Charles Lister, The Syrian Jihad: Al-Qaeda, the Islamic State and the Evolution of an Insurgency (London: Hurst & Co., 2015); Michael Weiss and Hassan Hassan, ISIS: Inside the Army of Terror (New York: Regan Arts, 2015); Jessica Stern and J. M. Berger, ISIS: The State of Terror (London: HarperCollins, 2015).

54. Wladimir van Wilgenburg, "Breaking from Baghdad: Kurdish Autonomy vs. Maliki's Manipulation", World Affairs 75:4 (2012).

55. See Amatzia Baram, "From Militant Secularism to Islamism: The Iraqi Ba'th Regime 1968-2003", Occasional Paper of the History and Public Policy Program (Washington, DC: Wilson Center, October 2011).

56. Gareth Stansfield, "Finding a Dangerous Equilibrium: Internal Politics in Iraqi Kurdistan – Tribes, Religion, and Ethnicity Reconsidered", in Faleh Jabar and Hosham Dawood (eds), The Kurds: Nationalism and Politics (London: Saqi Books, 2006).

57. For accounts of the fall of Mosul, see Weiss and Hassan, ISIS: Inside the Army of Terror; and Stern and Berger, ISIS: The State of Terror. See also Tallha Abdulrazaq and Gareth

Stansfield, "The Day After: What to Expect in Post-Islamic State Mosul", *RUSI Journal* 161:3 (2016).

58. See Gareth Stansfield, "The Islamic State, the Kurdistan Region, and the Future of Iraq: An Assessment of UK Policy Options", *International Affairs* 90:6 (2014) pp. 1329-50.

59. See World Bank, *The Kurdistan Region of Iraq: Assessing the Economic and Social Impact of the Syrian Conflict and ISIS* (Washington, DC: World Bank, 2015).

60. See Gareth Stansfield, "The Struggle for the Presidency in the Kurdistan Region of Iraq", *RUSI Commentary*, 2 June 2015; Nussaibah Younis, "Iraqi Kurdistan Needs a Referendum to Resolve its Political Crisis", Atlantic Council MENASource, 23 October 2015.

25. ARABIZATION AS GENOCIDE

1. Constitution of the Republic of Turkey, https://global.tbmm.gov.tr/docs/constitution_en.pdf, last accessed 15 October 2015.

2. Ibid.

3. Mohammed Ihsan, *Nation-building in Kurdistan: Memory, Genocide and Human Rights* (Abingdon: Routledge, 2016).

4. Ibid.

5. Toby Dodge, *Iraq: from War to a New Authoritarianism* (Abingdon: Routledge, 2012).

6. The documents mentioned have been gathered by the author in his role as Minister of Extra-Regional Affairs for the Kurdistan Regional Government. A translation can be found in his book *Nation Building in Kurdistan: Memory, Genocide and Human Rights* (Abingdon: Routledge, 2016).

7. For an analysis of the significance of Kirkuk in the negotiations over the disputed territories, see Liam Anderson and Gareth Stansfield, *Crisis in Kirkuk: the ethnopolitics of conflict and compromise* (Philadelphia, PA: University of Pennsylvania Press, 2009); and Henry D. Astarjian, *The Struggle for Kirkuk: the rise of Hussein, oil and the death of tolerance in Iraq* (Santa Barbara, CA: Praeger Security International, 2007).

8. See ftn. 6.

9. Ihsan, *Nation Building in Kurdistan*.

10. Ibid.

11. All the data regarding the status of the disputed territories have been published in the *Report on the Administrative Changes in Kirkuk and the Disputed Regions* published by the Minister of Extra-Regional Affairs of the Kurdish Regional Government in 2014, http://drmohammedihsan.com/Books.aspx

12. This letter is part of the documentation gathered by the author during his investigations carried out in his role of Minister of Extra-Regional Affairs. A translation of this letter can be found in the Appendix of his book *Nation Building in Kurdistan*.

13. The full text of the 2005 Iraqi constitution is available at http://www.iraqinationality.gov.iq/attach/iraqi_constitution.pdf, last accessed 15 October 2015.

14. Ihsan, *Nation Building in Kurdistan*.

15. Toby Dodge, *Iraq from War to New Authoritarianism* (London: International Institute for Strategic Studies, 2012).

16. Ibid.

17. "Iraq's Kurds Rule Out Giving Up Kirkuk", Aljazeera, http://www.aljazeera.com/news/middleeast/2014/06/iraq-kurds-rule-out-retreating-from-kirkuk-20146271440878594.html, last accessed 7 July 2015.

18. The commission was created just a few weeks after this interview.

19. "Iraq's Kurds Rule Out Giving Up Kirkuk."

20. Aljazeera, "Kurdish-Turkmen tension on the rise in Kirkuk", Aljazeera, 18 June 2014, http://www.aljazeera.com/news/middleeast/2014/06/kurdish-turkmen-tension-rise-kirkuk-2014617122142958412.html, last accessed 7 July 2014.

21. Interview with Masoud Barzani, http://www.al-monitor.com/pulse/originals/2014/07/iraq-kurdistan-region-barzani-interview-crisis-independence.html, last accessed 2 March 2015.

26. THE DEVELOPMENT OF KURDISTAN'S HIGHER EDUCATION SECTOR

1. UNESCO Iraq Office, "Literacy Network for Iraq, Gender and Education for All", http://www.lifeforiraq.org/en/content/gender-and-education-all, last accessed 9 January 2013.

2. See "World Declaration on Education for All 1990", Article 3(3) in UNESCO, *The Dakar Framework for Action*, p. 75; International Covenant on Economic, Social and Cultural Rights (1966), Article 13(1); Convention on the Elimination of All Forms of Discrimination Against Women (1979), Article 10.

3. It should thereby be noted that the author took into consideration the more recent developments as part of the analysis, but that any interview observations are primarily based on a time prior to the current economic and political turmoil, as seen by the general population, and opinions might thus have changed since the initial interviews were conducted.

4. Ministry of Higher Education and Scientific Research, "Universities in Kurdistan", http://www.mhe-krg.org/node/23, last accessed 13 January 2016.

5. O. Moss, "Laying the Foundations" (2013), http://www.the-report.net/iraq/kurdistan-region-sep2013/666-education-laying-the-foundations, last accessed 14 March 2014.

6. Ministry of Higher Education and Scientific Research, "Higher Education in Kurdistan Region", http://www.mhe-krg.org/node/105, last accessed 14 March 2014.

7. Ministry of Higher Education and Scientific Research, "KRG Scholarship Program Human Capacity Development", http://www.mhe-krg.org/index.php?q=node/249, last accessed 14 March 2014.

8. Rudaw, "KRG resumes payment to its students in foreign universities" (2016), http://rudaw.net/english/kurdistan/060920163?keyword=higher%20education, last accessed 10 October 2016.

9. Kurdistan Regional Government, "The Kurdistan Region in Brief", http://cabinet.gov.krd/p/p.aspx?l=12&p=210, last accessed 13 January 2016; Statistics Norway, "Population,

1 January 2016, estimated", https://www.ssb.no/en/befolkning/statistikker/folkemengde, last accessed 13 January 2016.

10. Complete University Guide, "Studying in Norway", http://www.thecompleteuniversityguide.co.uk/international/europe/norway/, last accessed 13 January 2016.

11. OECD, "Education at a Glance 2013 Norway", http://www.oecd.org/edu/Norway_EAG2013%20Country%20Note.pdf, last accessed 13 January 2016.

12. See Ekurd, "Iraqi parliamentary education committee reveals fake universities in Kurdistan", Ekurd.net (2015), http://ekurd.net/education-committee-reveals-fake-universities-in-kurdistan-2015-07-11, last accessed 10 October 2016.

13. Jaafar Hussein Khidir, "The Kurds and Kurdistan and Recent Political Development of IKR", Universität Wien dissertation (2002), p. 63.

14. Sonja Wölte, *Human Rights Violations against Women during War and Conflict*, Geneva: Women's International League for Peace and Freedom, Report of a Roundtable Discussion parallel to the UN Commission on Human Rights (1997) p. 19.

15. Valentine Moghadam, *Modernizing Women: gender and social change in the Middle East*, 2nd edn (Boulder, CO: Lynne Rienner, 2003) p.60.

16. Nadje Al-Ali, "Reconstructing gender: Iraqi women between dictatorship, war, sanctions and occupation", *Third World Quarterly* 26:4-5 (2005) pp. 745-6.

17. Dlawer Ala'Aldeen, "Studying for Master's degree in Kurdistan Region, Reforming the Master's Degree in the Kurdistan Region: Enhancing Capacity and Quality", Ministry of Higher Education and Scientific Research, http://www.mhe-krg.org/node/117, last accessed 11 March 2014.

18. See for example Luke Harding, "Revisiting Kurdistan: 'If there is a success story in Iraq, it's here,'" *Guardian* (2014), http://www.theguardian.com/world/2014/jul/16/arrived-in-kurdistan-with-chemical-weapon-suit-iraq-saddam-hussein, last accessed 17 May 2015.

19. Illuminate Consulting Group, *UK Higher Education engagement with Iraq*, Research Series/4, UK Higher Education International Unit (2009) p. 22.

20. Lila Abu-Lughod (ed.) *Remaking Women, Feminism and Modernity in the Middle East* (Princeton, NJ: Princeton University Press, 1998) p. 3.

21. Al-Ali in James Simon, "Kurdistan, Women in Iraq", video (2009), http://www.youtube.com/watch?v=x4POLH2O208, last accessed 13 January 2016.

22. Interviews in Sulaimani, 9 August 2012, 1 June 2012; and in Erbil, 20 April 212, 25 April 2012.

23. UNDP – Iraq, "Women's Economic Empowerment, Integrating Women into the Iraqi Economy" (UNDP, 2012) p. 10.

24. For a comprehensive analysis of women's situation in Kurdistan's labor force, see Ranharter, *Gender Equality and Development after Violent Conflicts: The Kurdistan Region of Iraq* (London: Palgrave Macmillan, 2015).

25. *Ekurd Daily*, "Universities in Iraqi Kurdistan warn education could be suspended over late salaries", 7 September 2016, http://ekurd.net/universities-kurdistan-salaries-2016-09-07, last accessed 10 October 2016.

26. Kurdistan Region Presidency, "President Barzani Congratulates Women on International

Women's Day", 2014, http://www.krp.org/english/articledisplay.aspx?id=y1bXnwLtkPE, last accessed 7 December 2014.

27. Invest in Group, "Overview: Kurdistan Region of Iraq, Human Capital", http://www. investingroup.org/publications/kurdistan/overview/human-capital, last accessed 8 December 2014.

28. Ross Anthony, Michael Hansen, Krishna Kumar, Howard Shatz, and Georges Vernez, "Building the Future, Summary of Four Studies to Develop the Private Sector, Education, Health Care and Data for Decisionmaking for the Kurdistan Region-Iraq", Ministry of Planning Kurdistan Regional Government (Santa Monica, CA: RAND Corporation, 2012) p. xii.

29. Ministry of Higher Education and Scientific Research, Higher Education.

30. See for example University of Duhok, "Financial Aid", http://www.uod.ac/en/financial-aid, last accessed 14 March 2014; University of Sulaimani, "Study", http://www.univsul. org/E_U_Xwendin.aspx, last accessed 14 March 2014.

31. Alexandra Pironti, "Kurdistan Building New Army in Fight for Education", Rudaw (2013), http://rudaw.net/english/kurdistan/281120131, last accessed 14 March 2014.

32. See Ranharter, *Gender Equality and Development*.

33. Pironti, "Kurdistan Building New Army."

34. Ministry of Higher Education and Scientific Research, "Equal Opportunities", http://www.mhe-krg.org/node/27, last accessed 14 March 2014.

35. Dlawer Ala'Aldeen, "A determined push for higher education progress in Kurdistan", *University World News* (2012), http://www.universityworldnews.com/article. php?story=20120615064310850, last accessed 14 March 2014.

36. See UNICEF, *Girls' Education in Iraq*, 2010; and interviews in Erbil on 8 April, 12 July, 21 July 2012.

37. For a full discussion, see Katherine Ranharter, "Gender Equality and Development After Violent Conflict: The Effects of Gender Policies in the Kurdistan Region of Iraq", PhD thesis, University of Exeter, 2013, pp. 266-8.

38. Anthony, Hansen, Kumar, Shatz, and Vernez, "Building the Future", pp.11-17.

39. Aras Ahmed Mhamad, "The education crisis facing Iraqi Kurdistan", *The World Weekly* (2016), http://www.theworldweekly.com/reader/view/magazine/2016-03-31/the-education-crisis-facing-iraqi-kurdistan/7315, last accessed 10 October 2016.

40. Ibid.

41. Rudaw, "Kurdistan demo organizers call for minister to resign, lifting austerity measures", 2016, http://rudaw.net/english/kurdistan/270920165?keyword=higher%20education, last accessed 10 October 2016; Rudaw, "As schools open in Kurdistan minister hears teachers' grievances, urging patience", 2016, http://rudaw.net/english/kurdistan/011020 0161?keyword=education, last accessed 10 October 2016.

42. Sandra Hedinger, *Frauen über Kried und Frieden* (Frankfurt am Main: Campus, 2000) p. 95.

43. Alice Tuyizere, *Peace, Gender and Development, The Role of Religion and Culture* (Kampala: Makerere University, Fountain Publishers, 2007) p. 194.

44. Naila Kabeer, "Gender Equality and Women's Empowerment: A Critical Analysis of the Third Millennium Development Goal", *Gender and Development* 13:1 (2005) p. 17; Elisabeth Hartwig, *Rural African Women as Subjects of Social and Political Change, A Case Study of Women in Northwestern Cameroon* (Münster: LIT Verlag, 2005) p. 144.

45. Kabeer, "Gender Equality", p. 17.

46. Pishtiwan Jamal, "Female business owners less than 5% in Iraqi Kurdistan", *Ekurd.net*, 14 May 2015, http://ekurd.net/female-business-owners-less-than-5-in-iraqi-kurdistan-2015-05-14, last accessed 10 October 2016.

47. Interviews in Sulaimani on 28 May 2012, and Erbil on 13 April 2012.

48. Interviews in Erbil on 24 and 29 June 2012.

49. Interviews in Erbil on 24 and 29 June 2012, and in Sulaimani on 8 August 2012.

50. As noted by Jamal, not only society, but also government is to blame for the small number of businesswomen in the Region, as it is much harder for them to secure government financial support to start their business ventures. See Jamal, "Female business owners less than 5% in Iraqi Kurdistan."

51. Solin Hacador, "The Big Success of Women Entrepreneurs is a Kurdish Princess", *Kurdistan Tribune* (2011), http://kurdistantribune.com/2011/big-success-of-women-entrepreneurs-kurdish-princess/, last accessed 14 March 2014.

52. Interviews in Sulaimani on 28 May and 4 June 2012, and in Erbil on 16 April and 2 July 2012.

53. Nadje Al-Ali and Nicola Pratt, "Between Nationalism and Women's Rights: The Kurdish Women's Movement in Iraq", *Middle East Journal of Culture and Communication* 4 (2011) p. 345.

54. Tuyizere, *Peace, Gender and Development*, p. 194.

55. Fiona Leach and Mairead Dume (eds), *Education, Conflict and Reconciliation, International Perspectives* (Bern: Peter Lang, 2007) p. 22.

56. Christine Eifler and Ruth Seifert, *Gender Dynamics and Post-Conflict Reconstruction* (Frankfurt am Main: Peter Lang GmbH, 2009) p. 85.

57. Kurdistan Region Statistics Office, *Labour Force*, Fact Sheet 3 (Erbil: Kurdistan Region Statistics Office, 2012b).

58. Abu-Lughod, *Remaking Women*, p. 102.

59. Kurdistan Region Statistics Office, *Education*, Fact Sheet 2 (Erbil: Kurdistan Region Statistics Office, 2012a) p. 3.

60. For a full discussion of women and gender in decision-making, see Ranharter, *Gender Equality*, ch. 3.

61. For more on education as a generator and legitimizer of inequalities, see Klaus Seitz, *Bildung und Konflikt, Die Rolle von Bildung bei der Entstehung, Prävention und Bewältigung gesellschaftlicher Krisen – Konsequenzen für die Entwicklungszusammenarbeit* (Rossdorf: TZ-Verlagsgesellschaft, 2004).

62. Ibid., p.82.

63. Ibid., pp.48-9.

64. Lakshmi Lingam in Isabella Bakker and Rachel Silvey, *Beyond States and Markets, the Challenge of Social Reproduction* (Abingdon: Routledge, 2008) p. 72.

65. See Ranharter, *Gender Equality*, chs 3 and 4.

66. Sylvia Chant and Caroline Sweetman, "Fixing women or fixing the world? 'Smart economics', efficiency approaches, and gender equality in development", *Gender and Development* 20:3 (2012) pp. 519-21.

67. Svi Shapiro, *Educating Youth for a World beyond Violence, A Pedagogy for Peace* (New York: Palgrave Macmillan, 2010) p. 83.

68. Davies in Seitz, *Bildung und Konflikt,* p.53

69. Lila Abu-Lughod, "Dialects of Women's Empowerment: The International Circuitry of the Arab Human Development Report 2005", *International Journal of Middle East Studies* 41 (2009) p. 87.

70. Interviews in Erbil on 9 April 2012, in Sulaimani on 10 August 2012, and in Vienna on 5 November and 4 December 2012

71. *Ekurd Daily*, "Iraqi parliamentary education committee reveals fake universities in Kurdistan", 11 July 2015, http://ekurd.net/education-committee-reveals-fake-universities-in-kurdistan-2015-07-11, last accessed 10 October 2016.

72. Mhamad, "The education crisis facing Iraqi Kurdistan."

73. Ala'Aldeen, "Studying for Master's degree in Kurdistan Region."

74. Ministry of Higher Education and Scientific Research, "A Roadmap to Quality, Reforming the System of Higher Education and Scientific Research in the Kurdistan Region of Iraq, A Report on the Main Achievements, From 1st November 2009 to 1st September 2010" (Erbil: Kurdistan Regional Government, 2010).

75. Al-Ali, "Reconstructing Gender", p. 2.

76. Ibid, pp.4–7.

77. Matthew Reisz, "Iraqi Kurdistan looks to national ranking to improve", *Times Higher Education* (2016), https://www.timeshighereducation.com/news/iraqi-kurdistan-looks-national-ranking-improve, last accessed 10 October 2016.

78. Mhamad, "The education crisis facing Iraqi Kurdistan."

79. Hawler Medical University, "Vision and Mission", Hawler Medical University, http://hmu.edu.iq/About/VisionandMission.aspx, last accessed 14 March 2014; University of Duhok, "Mission, Vision and Core Values", http://www.uod.ac/en/mission, last accessed 14 March 2014.

80. Matthew Reisz, "Iraqi Kurdish scholars put gender theory to the test", *Times Higher Education* (2011), http://www.timeshighereducation.co.uk/story.asp?storycode=417730, last accessed 14 March 2014.

81. SUH, "London's SOAS Signs Agreement with SUH" (2012), http://www.suh-edu.com/index.php?option=com_content&view=article&id=484%3Alondons-soas-signs-agreement-with-suh&catid=1%3Alatest-news&Itemid=162&lang=en, last accessed 14 March 2014.

82. M. Abboud, "The Role of Higher Education in Exploring Gender in Iraq: Inaccurate

Numbers Challenge Efforts to Address Women's Issues in the KRG", American University of Iraq – Sulaimani (2013), http://auis.edu.iq/node/1158, last accessed 15 March 2014.

83. University of Kurdistan, Hawler, "UKH Leads Women Empowerment in Higher Education", http://www.ukh.ac/detailsArticls.php?ZID=1&CID=106&AID=602, last accessed 8 December 2012.

84. Susan Opotow, Janet Gerson, and Sarah Woodside, "From Moral Exclusion to Moral Inclusion: Theory for Teaching Peace", *Theory into Practice* 44:4 (2005) p. 309.

85. Interview in Sulaimani on 10 August 2012.

86. Interview in Erbil on 9 April 2012

87. Lingam in Bakker and Silvey, *Beyond States*, p. 72.

27. WATER AND DEVELOPMENT IN IRAQI KURDISTAN

1. World Bank, *Kurdistan Region of Iraq: Economic and Social Impact Assessment of the Syrian Conflict and the ISIS Crisis* (Washington DC: 2015) p. 2. The report cites figures supplied by the KRG Ministry of Planning.

2. F. Lorenz and E. J. Erickson, *Strategic Water: Iraq and Security Planning in the Euphrates-Tigris Basin* (Quantico, VA: Marine Corps University Press, 2014) p. 144.

3. J. M. Trondalen, *The Euphrates River and the Tigris River: Water Resources Management – An Independent Technical Study* (Geneva: Compass Foundation, 2005) p, 22. The study uses flow figures for the 1946-87 period, because this preceded Turkey's filling of reservoirs behind its dams on the Tigris.

4. UN-ESCWA and BGR, *Inventory of Shared Water Resources in Western Asia* (Beirut: 2013) p. 128.

5. Ibid., p. 551.

6. Ibid., p. 549.

7. Rudaw (Kurdish-language news website), "Despite Abundant Water, Kurdistan Prone to Future Shortages", 17 May 2014, last accessed 27 April 2015.

8. Ibid.

9. Figure derived from R.H.M. Rashid, "The Use of Water for Sustainable Rural Development: A Case Study in the Kurdistan Regional Government", abstract of doctoral thesis, Cluj-Napoca, 2014, Table 3.11, p. 33. Rashid is citing 2010 figures from the KRG Ministry of Agriculture and Water Resources data.

10. Ibid., p. 60.

11. Ibid., p. 50.

12. World Bank, *Kurdistan Region of Iraq*, p. 2.

13. Ministry of Planning, *National Development Plan, 2013-2017* (Baghdad: Government of Iraq: 2013) p. 35.

14. I. E. Issa, N. A. Al-Ansari, G. Sherway, and S. Knutsson, "Expected Future of Water Resources in Tigris-Euphrates Rivers Basin, Iraq", *Journal of Water Resource and Protection* 6:5 (April 2014).

15. KRG Ministry of Planning, *Kurdistan Region of Iraq 2020: a Vision for the Future*, 2013, p. 21.

16. US Geological Survey Water School website, *Irrigation Techniques*, 2014, http://water.usgs.gov/edu/wuir.html, last accessed 26 April 2015.

17. Rudaw, "Despite Abundant Water."

18. Invest In Group website, *Kurdistan Region – Review*, last accessed 26 April 2015.

19. UN-ESCWA and BGR, *Inventory of Shared Water Resources*, p. 143.

20. For the text of the agreement, see http://www.ucdp.uu.se/gpdatabase/peace/Iran-Iraq%20 19751226b.pdf

21. Hawlati, Kurdish-language website, 16 April 2015, translated into English by BBC Monitoring.

22. Rudaw, "Iranian Dam Projects Beginning of a Water War with Kurdistan", 3 December 2013, last accessed 27 April 2015.

23. F. A. M. Al-Faraj and M. Scholz, "Impact of upstream anthropogenic river regulation on downstream water availability in transboundary river watersheds", *International Journal of Water Resources Development* 31:1 (2015).

24. D. Bozkurt, O. L. Sen, S. Hagemann, "Projected river discharge in the Euphrates-Tigris Basin from a hydrological discharge model forced with RCM and GCM outputs", *Climate Research* 62 (2015) pp. 131-47.

28. PEACE EDUCATION IN THE KURDISH REGION OF IRAQ

1. G. Stansfield, *Iraqi Kurdistan: Political Development and Emergent Democracy* (London: Routledge, 2003).

2. Kerkuklu, 2007; Al-Hirmizi, 2005

3. Velloso de Santisteban, 2005: 63

4. Kerkuklu, 2007: 11

5. McDowall, 2003

6. Stansfield, *Iraqi Kurdistan*.

7. S. Fountain, 'Peace education in UNICEF', Working paper, Education Section Program Division, New York: UNICEF, 1999, p. 1.

8. INEE, *Peace Education Handbook*, 2008, www.inee.com/peaceeducation, accessed 10 September 2013.

9. I. Harris, 'Conceptual underpinnings of peace education', in Salomon, G. and B. Nevo (eds), *Peace Education: The Concept, Principles, and Practices Around the World* (New York: Lawrence Erlbaum, 2012) pp. 15-26.

10. G. Salomon and B. Nevo (eds), *Peace Education: The Concept, Principles, and Practices Around the World* (New York: Lawrence Erlbaum, 2012).

11. Ibid.

12. Ibid.

13. KRG, 2015.

14. Nazand Begikhani, Aisha Gill and Gill Hague, with Kawther Ibraheem, 'Honour-based

Violence (HBV) and Honour-based Killings in Iraqi Kurdistan and in the Kurdish Diaspora in the UK', Erbil: Kurdistan Regional Government (and University of Bristol and University of Roehampton, UK), 2010.

15. Kurmanji is spoken in Duhok, while Sorani is used in Erbil.

16. Shanks, 2015

17. Paulson, 2011

18. Audrey Osler and Chalank Yahya, "Challenges and complexity in human rights education: Teachers' understandings of democratic participation and gender equity in post-conflict Kurdistan-Iraq", *Education Inquiry* 4:1 (2013) pp. 189-210.

19. S. Kirmanj, "KRG's Islamic Education Textbooks and the Question of Peaceful Coexistence in Kurdistan Region", Working paper presented at University of Duhok, Education and Peace building conference, 2014.

20. Ibid.

21. Kirmanj, "KRG's Islamic Education Textbooks and the Question of Peaceful Coexistence in Kurdistan Region."

22. Shanks, 2015.

23. Rahman and Abdullah, 'The prospects for the development of civic education system educational curricula in the Kurdistan Region – Iraq', Working paper presented at University of Duhok, Education and Peace building conference, 2014.

24. D. Smith, 'Towards a strategic framework for peacebuilding: getting their act together', Overview report of the Joint Utstein Study of Peacebuilding, 2004; E. McCandless and S. Doe, 'Strengthening Peacebuilding efforts in Liberia: a discussion document for UNMIL and the UNCT', 15 April 2007, O/DSRSG for Recovery and Governance (Liberia: UNMIL); M. Barnett, H. Kim, M. O'Donnell, and L. Sitea, L., 'Peacebuilding: What's in a Name?' *Global Governance* 13:1 (2007).

25. Rahman and Abdullah, "The prospects for the development of civic education system educational curricula in the Kurdistan Region – Iraq."

26. However, this is not across the board, and topics such as Justice, Ownership, and the Environment are deemed successful, as is the new development of animations for Human Rights education.

27. Osler and Yahya, "Challenges and complexity in human rights education."

28. Rahman and Abdullah, "The prospects for the development of civic education system educational curricula in the Kurdistan Region – Iraq."

29. Interview, 2015.

30. Ibid.

29. THE IRAQI KURDISH RESPONSE TO THE "ISLAMIC STATE"

1. This chapter, written in December 2014 and updated in April 2015, reflects a very specific and rapidly evolving sequence of events triggered by the expansion of ISIS across western and central Iraq. It documents the Iraqi Kurdish response to these events and the very specific ways they used them as leverage with Baghdad and the US-led international

coalition to further their own ambitions. No doubt the situation for ISIS, the Kurds, Baghdad, and the international coalition will have changed dramatically by the time of publication.

2. B. Isakhan, "The Iraq Legacies and the Roots of the 'Islamic State,'" in B. Isakhan (ed.), *The Legacy of Iraq: From the 2003 War to the 'Islamic State'* (Edinburgh: Edinburgh University Press; New York: Oxford University Press, 2015)

3. B. Isakhan (ed.), *The Legacy of Iraq: From the 2003 War to the 'Islamic State'* (Edinburgh: Edinburgh University Press; New York: Oxford University Press, ; B. Isakhan, "The Road to the 'Islamic State': State-Society Relations after the US Withdrawal from Iraq", in B. Isakhan, S. Mako, and F. Dawood (eds), *State and Society in Iraq: Citizenship under Occupation, Dictatorship and Democratization* (London: I. B. Tauris, 2016); J. Stern and J. M. Berger, *ISIS: The State of Terror* (New York: HarperCollins, 2015); M. Weiss and H. Hassan, *ISIS: Inside the Army of Terror* (New York: Simon & Schuster).

4. G. Stansfield, "The Islamic State, the Kurdistan Region and the Future of Iraq: Assessing UK Policy Options", *International Affairs* 90:6 pp.1329-50.

5. Haji, cited in T. Goudsouzian and L. Fatah, "Fall of Mosul: What's at Stake for the Kurds?" Aljazeera, 12 June 2014.

6. Al-Musawi, cited in D. Filkins, "The Fight of Their Lives", *New Yorker*, 29 September 2014.

7. B. Isakhan, *Democracy in Iraq: History, Politics, Discourse* (London: Ashgate,

8. G. Stansfield, *Iraqi Kurdistan: Political Development and Emergent Democracy* (London: RoutledgeCurzon).

9. B. Isakhan, "Succeeding and Seceding in Iraq: The Case for a Shiite State", in D. Kingsbury and C. Laoutides and (eds), *Territorial Separatism and Global Politics* (London: Routledge; P. Sluglett, "Common Sense, or a Step Pregnant with Enormous Consequences: Some Thoughts on the Possible Secession of Iraqi Kurdistan", in D. H. Doyle (ed.), *Secession as an International Phenomenon: From America's Civil War to Contemporary Separatist Movements* (Athens, GA: University of Georgia Press) pp. 319-37.

10. P. Sluglett, "Kurdistan: A Suspended Secession from Iraq", in A. Pavkovic and R. Peter (eds), *The Ashgate Research Companion to Secession* (London: Ashgate,)

11. A. Dawisha, *Iraq: A Political History from Independence to Occupation* (Princeton, NJ: Princeton University Press); G. Stansfield, *Iraq: People, History, Politics* (Cambridge: Polity Press) p. 2.

12. M. Farouk-Sluglett and P. Sluglett, *Iraq Since 1958: From Revolution to Dictatorship* (London: I. B. Tauris)pp. 187-90.

13. L. Anderson and G. Stansfield, *Crisis in Kirkuk: The Ethnopolitics of Conflict and Compromise* (Philadelphia, PA: University of Pennsylvania Press).

14. Barzani cited in *E-Kurd.net*, "Article 140 of Iraqi constitution completed for us and will not talk about it anymore", 2014

15. *Middle East Monitor*, "Maliki's Coalition: Kurdish annexation of Kirkuk is a declaration of war", 2014.

16. Maliki cited in *ARANews*, "Al-Maliki to Barzani: areas dominated by Kurds will return", 4 July

17. Shahmani, cited in *Middle East Monitor*, "Maliki's Coalition", 2014.

18. J. Ditz, "Kurds Boycott Cabinet After Maliki Blocks Cargo Flights", Anti-war.com, 2014

19. Khalil, cited in M. Chulov and F. Hawramy, "Fears grow in Baghdad that US is abandoning the city to its fate", *Guardian*, 17 August 2014.

20. N. Mahmoud, "Talks on New Iraqi Government Snag over Disputed Kurdish Territories", Rudaw 2014

21. B. Isakhan, "Shattering the Shia: A Maliki Political Strategy in Post-Saddam Iraq", in B. Isakhan (ed.), *The Legacy of Iraq: From the 2003 War to the 'Islamic State'* (Edinburgh: Edinburgh University Press; New York: Oxford University Press, 2015d)

22. Dizayee, cited in J. Krajeski and S. A. Meyersept, "Litmus Test for Kurdistan", *New York Times*, 2014

23. Ibid.

24. Ibid.

25. Pollack, "Iraq: Understanding the ISIS Offensive Against the Kurds", Brookings Institution, 11 August 2014.

26. Osmat, cited in S. Frenkel, "Kurdish Forces Seek More U.S. Help In Fight Against ISIS", Buzzfeed, 2014

27. Barzani, cited in Filkins, "The Fight of Their Lives", 2014.

28. B. Isakhan, "The Iraq Legacies: Intervention, Occupation, Withdrawal and Beyond", in B. Isakhan (ed.), *The Legacy of Iraq: From the 2003 War to the 'Islamic State'* (Edinburgh: Edinburgh University Press; New York: Oxford University Press).

29. D. Natali, *Kurdish Quasi-State: Development and Dependency in Post-Gulf War Iraq* (Syracuse, NY: Syracuse University Press,

30. Frenkel, "Kurdish Forces Seek More U.S. Help", 2014; H. Pamuk, "Kurds Push to Drive ISIS from Mosul Dam as US Air Support Pounds Militants", *Business Insider*, 18 August 2014.

31. B. Obama, "President Obama Makes a Statement on Iraq", White House, 2014

32. H. Cooper and Gordon, "Iraqi Kurds Expand Autonomy as ISIS Reorders the Landscape", *New York Times*, 29 August 2014.

33. B. Obama, "Statement by the President on ISIL", White House, 10 September 2014.

34. F. Hawramy, "Kurdish Sinjar offensive too late for some Yazidis", *Al-Monitor*, 26 December 2014.

35. S. Kittleson, "Yazidi wary amid stalled Sinjar offensive", *Al-Monitor*, 12 April 2015.

36. A. Sarhan, "Kurdish Peshmerga foil ISIS attack near Mosul Dam", *Iraqi News*, 26 November 2014.

37. K. Fahim, "Islamic Militants Surprise Kurds in Iraq, Killing a Commander in a Day of Attacks", *New York Times*, 2015; Salih, "Kurds and ISIL battle over Kirkuk", Aljazeera, 5 February 2015.

38. T. Lister, "ISIS launches major assault on Kurdish front in Iraq", CNN, 18 February 2015.

39. M. Knights, "Iraqi Kurdistan: The Middle East's next 'Little Sparta'?" Aljazeera, 2014

40. J. Moore and S. Al-Salhy, "Kurdish land-grab stuns Baghdad", *Newsweek*, 2015

41. Ibid.

42. S. Atran and Stonemarch, "The Kurds' Heroic Stand Against ISIS", *New York Times*, 16 March 2015.

43. Barzani, cited in A. Zaman, "PM Barzani: Shiite militias should be regulated", *Al-Monitor*, 24 March 2015.

44. C. Caryl, "Want to Hurt the Islamic State? Here's How", *Foreign Policy*, 6 February 2015.

45. J. Pecquet, "Will Congress Arm Iraqi Kurds?" *Al-Monitor*, 2015

46. Salih, "Kurds and ISIL battle over Kirkuk", 2015.

47. Cooper and Gordon, "Iraqi Kurds Expand Autonomy", 2014; S. Pelley, "Iraq's Kurds praise U.S. support, want more against ISIS", CBS News, 9 September 2014.

48. K. Hlavaty, "With eye on Mosul, coalition advisers train Peshmerga", *Al-Monitor*, 2015

49. G. Charbel, "Barzani: The region's new borders will be drawn in blood", *Al-Monitor*, 15 February 2015; A. Smale, "German soldiers may help train forces in Iraq", *New York Times*, 17 December 2014.

50. Caryl, "Want to Hurt the Islamic State?" 2015.

51. M. Chulov and F. Hawramy, "Iraqi Kurds strengthen their positions while Isis advances on Baghdad", *Guardian*, 2014

30. IN PURSUIT OF FRIENDS

1. Interview with Falah Mustafa in Cambridge, October 2013.

2. Adam Watson, *Diplomacy: The Dialogue Between States* (New York: McGraw Hill, 1983) p. 24.

3. Noe Cornago, *Plural Diplomacies: Normative Predicaments and Functional Imperatives* (Leiden: Martinus Nijhoff Publishers, 2013) pp. 3-4.

4. Interview with Falah Mustafa in Erbil, May 2013.

5. Hill, Senior Advisor to Misenheimer's Meetings.

6. See Denise Natali, *The Kurds and the State: Evolving National Identity in Iraq, Turkey, and Iran* (Syracuse, NY: Syracuse University Press, 2005).

7. Gareth Stansfield, "UK Government Policy on the Kurdistan Region of Iraq", speech to the HOC Foreign Affairs Committee, 6 May 2014, http://www.parliamentlive.tv/Main/Player.aspx?meetingId=15383, last accessed 6 May 2014.

8. Ibid.

9. Ryan Crocker, "KRG Upbeat on Talks with Turkey", DoS, 10 May 2008, http://cable-gatesearch.net/cable.php?id=08BAGHDAD1451&, last accessed 5 April 2014.

10. Al-Hurra, "Turkiya wa-Kurdistan al-'Iraq tawqa'an 'aquda lil-naft wal-ghaz" [Turkey and Iraqi Kurdistan Sign a Contract for Oil and Gas]", 29 November 2013, http://www.alhurra.com/content/Iraqi-kurds-and-turkey-seal-oil-deal/238077.html, last accessed 4 September 2015.

11. KRG, "Kurdistan Oil and Gas Factsheet", *The Review: Kurdistan Region of Iraq* (Erbil: Invest In Group, 2013) p. 34.

12. Hemeyra Pamuk and Orhan Coskun, "Exclusive - Turkey, Iraqi Kurdistan clinch major energy pipeline deals", 6 November 2013, http://uk.reuters.com/article/2013/11/06/uk-turkey-iraq-kurdistan-idUKBRE9A50HN20131106, last accessed 4 September 2015.

13. Sonar Cagaptay, Christina Bache Fidan, and Ege Cansu Sacikara, "Turkey and the KRG: An Undeclared Economic Commonwealth", Washington Institute for Near East Policy, 16 March 2015, http://www.washingtoninstitute.org/policy-analysis/view/turkey-and-the-krg-an-undeclared-economic-commonwealth, last accessed 23 September 2015.

14. KRG MNR, "Monthly Export Report: January 2016", 4 February 2016, http://mnr.krg.org/images/monthlyreports/EXPORTs/MNR_Monthly_Export_Report_January_2016.pdf, last accessed 24 February 2016.

15. Hevidar Ahmed, "Senior Kurdistan Official: IS Was at Erbil's Gates; Turkey Did Not Help", 16 September 2014, http://rudaw.net/english/interview/16092014, last accessed 19 January 2015.

16. Suadad al-Salhy, "Our Priority is to arm the Peshmerga", Al Jazeera, 28 October 2014, http://www.aljazeera.com/news/middleeast/2014/10/priority-arm-pesh-merga-20141027764994436.html, last accessed 8 April 2016.

17. Joni Ernst, "U.S. Policy in Iraq and Syria", Senate Armed Services Committee, CSPAN, 21 May 2015, http://www.c-span.org/video/?326186-1/hearing-us-policy-iraq-syria, last accessed 8 April 2016.

18. Caroline Wyatt, "Iraqi Kurdish Leader Barzani Seeks Weapons to Fight IS", 10 August 2014, http://www.bbc.co.uk/news/world-middle-east-28730618, last accessed 19 January 2015.

19. http://www.kurdistan24.net/en/news/435ad4dc-6b60-4b1d-8592-557cc1b20ca0/Italy-expands-military-training-in-Kurdistan

20. Ibid.

21. Michael Knights, "U.S. Support to Peshmerga: Too Little, Too Late?" Al Jazeera, 29 March 2015, http://www.aljazeera.com/indepth/opinion/2015/03/support-peshmerga-late-150327084137906.html, last accessed 8 April 2016.

22. Rudaw, "U.S. Consul General: We are Training 4,000 Peshmerga with Full Set of Equipment, Arms", 14 February 2016, http://rudaw.net/english/interview/14022016, last accessed 8 April 2016.

23. KRG, "Kazbrum [GazProm] ta'alinu 'an ziyadat istathmarataha fi iqlim Kurdistan" [Gazprom announces an increase in investment in the Kurdistan Region]", 18 May 2015, http://cabinet.gov.krd/a/d.aspx?s=040000&l=14&a=53334, last accessed 10 June 2015.

24. Genel Energy, "Operations: Kurdistan Region", <http://www.genelenergy.com/opera-tions/kurdistan-region-of-iraq.aspx, last accessed 10 June 2015.

25. KRG MNR, "Capacity Building", http://mnr.krg.org/index.php/en/the-ministry/capac-ity-building, last accessed 10 June 2015.

26. Interview with Dindar Zebari in Erbil, January 2014.

27. Telephone interview with Sir Terence Clark, July 2015.

28. Interview with Anonymous in Erbil, May 2013.

29. Interview with Hemin Hawrami in Erbil, January 2014.

30. Interview with Hoshang Mohamed in Erbil, January 2014.

31. Interview with Anonymous in Erbil, January 2014.

32. Juan Linz, "State Building and Nation Building", *European Review* 1 (1993) p. 358.

33. André Lecours, "Paradiplomacy: Reflections on the Foreign Policy and International Relations of Regions", *International Negotiations* 7 (2002) p. 101.

34. See Benedict Anderson, *Imagined Communities: Reflections on the Origin and Spread of Nationalism* (London: Verso, 2006); Eric Hobsbawm, *Nations and Nationalism Since 1780: Programme, Myth, Reality* (Cambridge, Cambridge University Press, 1990); Anthony Smith, *The Ethnic Origins of Nations* (Oxford: Basil Blackwell, 1986).

35. As part of an Iraq Institute for Strategic Studies project entitled "Governing Diversity: the Kurds in the new Middle East" the author convened conferences that brought together Kurds from all four states between December 2013 and August 2015.

36. The film can be found at https://www.youtube.com/watch?v=_Yg-XxFk2UA, last accessed 12 March 2017.

37. Awan News, "Al-Barzani yahajumu muwatamir landan bi-sabab 'adamu da'wat al-iqlim alayahu wa-yawakidu: la yahaqa lay kana tamthalina" [Barzani criticizes the London conference because of the failure to invite the Region and confirms: "Nobody Legally Represented us"]", 23 January 2015, http://tinyurl.com/naxtged, last accessed 18 August 2015.

31. A PARADIGM SHIFT IN US-KURDISTAN REGION RELATIONS POST-2014

1. Barack Obama, quoted in Thomas Friedman, "Obama on the World: President Obama Talks to Thomas L. Friedman about Iraq, Putin and Israel", *New York Times*, 9 August 2014, http://www.nytimes.com/2014/08/09/opinion/president-obama-thomas-l-friedman-iraq-and-world-affairs.html, last accessed 25 October 2015.

2. Lokman Meho, *The Kurdish Question in US Foreign Policy: A Documentary Sourcebook* (Westport, CT: Praeger Publishers, 2004) p. 445.

3. Marianna Charountaki, *The Kurds and US Foreign Policy: International Relations in the Middle East since 1945* (Oxford: Routledge, 2011) pp. 256-7.

4. Ibid., p. 149.

5. Richard N. Haass, "The Irony of American Strategy: Putting the Middle East in Proper Perspective", *Foreign Affairs* 92:3 (2013) p. 59.

6. Mohammed Shareef, "China's Dual Diplomacy: Arab Iraq and the Kurdistan Region", in Niv Horesh (ed.), *Toward Well-Oiled Relations: China's Presence in the Middle East Following the Arab Spring* (New York: Palgrave Macmillan, 2016) p. 84.

7. Mohammed Shareef, "Kurdistan: Political Stability and Widespread Security", *Equilibri* 13 (published by Fondazione Eni Enrico Mattei in cooperation with il Mulino, the premier Italian university publisher).

8. David Petraeus, quoted in Liz Sly, "Petraeus: The Islamic State isn't our biggest problem in Iraq", *Washington Post*, 20 March 2015, https://www.washingtonpost.com/news/

worldviews/wp/2015/03/20/petraeus-the-islamic-state-isnt-our-biggest-problem-in-iraq, last accessed 24 November 2015.

9.   Fuad Hussein, quoted in Michael R. Gordon, "Failed Efforts and Challenges of America's Last Months in Iraq", *New York Times*, 23 September 2012, p. A1.

10. Kurdistan Regional Government, "Iraq: Representation in the United States", 2014, http://new.krg.us/statement-of-krg-us-on-tier-iii-designation-of-kdp-and-puk/, last accessed 17 August 2015.

11. Peter Galbraith, *The End of Iraq: How American Incompetence Created a War Without End* (New York: Simon & Schuster, 2006) pp. 162-3.

12. Renad Mansour, *How the Kurds Helped Draw the United States Back to Iraq* (Beirut: Carnegie Middle East Center, , http://carnegie-mec.org/2015/06/29/how-kurds-helped-draw-united-states-back-to-iraq/ib65, last accessed 7 January 2016.

13. Brett McGurk, quoted in Harvey Morris, "White House Pledges Support for Measures to Remove Kurdistan Parties from Terrorism List", Rudaw, 12 February 2014, http://rudaw.net/mobile/english/kurdistan/120220141, last accessed 28 September 2015.

14. "Two leading Iraqi Kurdish parties are taken off US terrorism list", ,http://www.middle-asteye.net/news/two-leading-iraqi-kurdish-parties-are-taken-us-terrorism-list-1048291370, last accessed 17 June 2015.

15. Masoud Barzani, "The Kurdistan Region and the Future of Iraq" (Washington, DC: Center for Strategic and International Studies, , http://csis.org/event/ kurdistan-region-and-future-iraq, last accessed 15 July 2015.

16. Barack Obama, quoted in Thomas Friedman, "Obama on the World."

17. Yerevan Saeed, "US establishes new military center in Kurdistan region", Rudaw, 4 September, http://rudaw.net/mobile/english/kurdistan/040920156?ctl00_phMain Container_phMain_ControlComments1_gvCommentsChangePage=5, last accessed 23 October 2015.

18. Shareef, *The United States, Iraq and the Kurds: Shock, Awe and Aftermath* (London: Routledge, 2014) p. 173.

19. Foreign Affairs Committee Press Release, "Chairman Royce, Ranking Member Engel Introduce Legislation to Authorize the Supply of Weapons Directly to Kurdish 'Peshmerga,'" (26 March 2015), http://foreignaffairs.house.gov/press-release/chairman-royce-ranking-member-engel-introduce-legislation-authorize-supply-weapons, last accessed 17 June 2015.

20. Rand Paul, quoted in Matthew Boyle, "Exclusive – Rand Paul: Arm the Kurds to Battle ISIS and Radical Islam, Give Them Kurdistan", Breitbart, 10 March 2015, http://www.breitbart.com/big-government/2015/03/10/exclusive-rand-paul-arm-the-kurds-to-battle-isis-and-radical-islam-give-them-kurdistan/, last accessed 19 April 2015.

21. Yerevan Saeed, "US Senate votes down bill to directly arm Kurds", Rudaw, 17 June 2015, http://rudaw.net/mobile/english/kurdistan/17062015, last accessed 23 August 2015.

22. Mohammed A. Salih, "US military aid bills highlight Iraq's deep divisions", Al Jazeera, 15 May 2015, http://www.aljazeera.com/news/2015/05/150509084945317.html, last accessed 27 May 2015.

23. Akbar Shahid Ahmed and Christine Conetta, "Congress Voted Against Directly Arming Iraq's Kurds. Here's What That Means for the ISIS Fight", *Huffington Post*, 29 June 2015, http://www.huffingtonpost.com/2015/06/29/congress-arm-kurds_n_7647068.html, last accessed 6 January 2016.

24. "US to Provide Direct Military and Financial Support to Peshmerga", 12 July 2016, http://rudaw.net/english/kurdistan/120720161, last accessed 9 October 2016.

25. Eric Lipton, "Iraqi Kurds Build Washington Lobbying Machine to Fund War Against ISIS", *New York Times*, 7 May 2016, http://www.nytimes.com/2016/05/07/us/politics/iraqi-kurds-build-washington-lobbying-machine-against-isis.html?_r=1, last accessed 10 October 2016.

26. Michael Stephens and Aaron Stein, "The YPG: America's new best friend?" Aljazeera, 28 June 2015, http://www.aljazeera.com/indepth/opinion/2015/06/ypg-america-friend-isil-kurds-syria-150627073034776.html, last accessed 20 November 2015.

27. "U.S. Envoy Makes First Visit to Syrian Kurdish Areas", NRT TV, 9 December 2015, http://www.nrttv.com/EN/Details.aspx?Jimare=5149, last accessed 2 February 2016.

28. "PYD not a terrorist organization, US repeats", *Hurriyet Daily News*, 9 February 2016, http://www.hurriyetdailynews.com/pyd-not-a-terrorist-organization-us-repeats.aspx?PageID=238&NID=94925&NewsCatID=358, last accessed 10 February 2016.

29. Ibid.

30. Mustafa Hejri, quoted in Yerevan Saeed, "KDPI leader: Iran wants to strengthen ISIS to further own hegemony", Rudaw, 15 June 2015, http://rudaw.net/english/interview/15062015, last accessed 20 September 2015.

31. Ibid.

32. Shareef, *The United States, Iraq and the Kurds*, p. 173.

33. Nechirvan Barzani, quoted in "Iraq conflict: Kurds 'will not help retake Mosul,'" BBC News, 17 June 2014, http://www.bbc.co.uk/news/world-middle-east-27883997, last accessed 17 October 2015.

34. Masoud Barzani, quoted in Amanpour, "Iraqi Kurdistan leader Massoud Barzani says 'the time is here' for self-determination", CNN, 23 June 2014, http://amanpour.blogs.cnn.com/2014/06/23/exclusive-iraqi-kurdish-leader-says-the-time-is-here-for-self-determination, last accessed 17 November 2015.

35. Masoud Barzani, "Ever Closer to Independence", *The Economist*, 19 February 2015, http://www.economist.com/news/international/21644167-iraqs-kurds-are-independent-all-name-they-must-play-their-cards-cleverly-if-they, last accessed 20 June 2015.

36. Barack Obama and Jo Biden, quoted in Darbaz Kosrat Rasul Ali, Rudaw, 17 May 2015, https://www.youtube.com/watch?v=LWKbynYgEV4, last accessed 26 November 2015.

37. Shareef, *The United States, Iraq and the Kurds*, p. 119.

38. Ibid., p. 198.

39. Joe Biden, quoted in Dave Boyer, "Forget what he said in 2006: Joe Biden speaks out for a unified Iraq", *Washington Times*, 9 April 2015, http://www.washingtontimes.com/news/2015/apr/9/joe-bidens-iraq-unity-speech-contradicts-2006-supp/?page=all, last accessed 20 June 2015.

40. "U.S. Intelligence Chiefs Say Iraq, Syria May Not Survive As States", Radio Free Europe/ Radio Liberty, 11 September 2015, http://www.rferl.org/content/iraq-syria-us-intelli-gence-doubt-survival-as-states/27240681.html, last accessed 7 February 2016.
41. Haass, "The Irony of American Strategy", p. 66.

32. RE-CLAIMING HALABJA

1. Author's note: this chapter is based on research carried out in Halabja and the Kurdistan region of Iraq between 2009 and 2014. I wish to thank my friend and research assistant Peshawa Ahmad for his extraordinary generosity and hard work. Unless otherwise noted, translations from Sorani Kurdish are by him. I also wish to thank everyone I interviewed for their time and thoughts, and the editors and fellow authors in this volume for their support and feedback. Any mistakes or errors of interpretation are my own.
2. Jeffrey K. Olick, "Collective Memory: The Two Cultures," *Sociological Theory* 17:3 (1999) pp. 333-48; Tamir Sorek, *Palestinian Commemoration in Israel: Calendars, Monuments, and Martyrs* (Stanford, CA: Stanford University Press, 2015); John Eidson, "Which Past for Whom? Local Memory in a German Community during the Era of Nation Building," *Ethos* 28:4 (2000) pp. 575-607.
3. See David L. Phillips, *The Kurdish Spring: A New Map of the Middle East* (New Brunswick, NJ: Transaction Publishers, 2015); Gareth Stansfield, "The Unravelling of the Post-First World War State System? The Kurdistan Region of Iraq and the Transformation of the Middle East," *International Affairs* 89: 2 (2013) pp. 259-82; Nicole F. Watts, "Redefining the Kurdish Nation," in *Rethinking Nation and Nationalism*, POMEPS Study Series 14 (May 2015), ed. Marc Lynch, http://pomeps.org/2015/03/04/redefining-the-kurdish-nation/, last accessed 15 November 2015.
4. John Eidson, "Which Past for Whom? Local Memory in a German Community during the Era of Nation Building", *Ethos* 28:4 (2000) pp. 575-607; and "Between Heritage and Countermemory: Varieties of Historical Representation in a West German Community", *American Ethnologist* 32:4 (2005) pp. 556-75.
5. Ibid., p. 578.
6. Stephen Legg, "*Sites of counter-memory: the refusal to forget and the nationalist struggle in colonial Delhi,*" *Historical Geography* 33 (2005) p. 185.
7. Joost R. Hiltermann, *A Poisonous Affair: America, Iraq, and the Gassing of Halabja* (Cambridge: Cambridge University Press, 2007); and "The 1988 Anfal Campaign in Iraqi Kurdistan," 2008, http://www.massviolence.org/IMG/article_PDF/ The-1988-Anfal-Campaign-in-Iraqi-Kurdistan.pdf, last accessed 12 November 2015; Ofra Bengio, *The Kurds of Iraq: Building a State Within a State* (Boulder, CO: Lynne Rienner, 2012) pp. 181-3; David McDowall, *A Modern History of the Kurds* (London: I. B. Tauris, 1997) p. 358; Jonathan C. Randal, *After Such Knowledge, What Forgiveness? My Encounters with Kurdistan* (Boulder, CO: Westview Press, 1999) p. 233; Human Rights Watch, "Genocide in Iraq: The Anfal Campaign Against the Kurds," July 1993.

8. Shailoh Phillips, "Cyberkurds and Cyberkinetics: Pilgrimage in an Age of Virtual Mobility", *Etnofoor* 20:1 (2007) p. 23.

9. See, for example, poetry by Choman Hardi, Hamid Qaladizayi, Kamal Mirawdel, and Buland al Haydari's poem "So That We Will Not Forget" (*Li-kay la nansa*). For a thoughtful analysis of Halabja's impact on al Haydari's work, see Hilla Peled-Shapira, "Was Halabja a Turning Point for the Poet Buland al-Haydari?" *Kurdish Studies* 2:1 (2014) pp. 14-33. Film and documentary examples include *Jiyan* (2002), Saîd Kakeyî's *Waiting for Hiwa* (2003), *Halabja: The Lost Children* (2011), *Halabja: Life after Death* (2014), and films by Bahman Ghobadi and Samira Makhmalbaf. For written accounts of the attack on Halabja, see Michael J Kelly, *Ghosts of Halabja: Saddam Hussein and the Kurdish Genocide* (Westport, CT: Praeger Security International, 2008); Christiane Bird, *A Thousand Sighs, A Thousand Revolts: Journeys in Kurdistan* (New York: Ballantine, 2004), pp. 214-27; Randal, *After Such Knowledge*, pp.232-4; Sheri. J. Laizer, *Martyrs, Traitors, and Patriots: Kurdistan after the Gulf War* (London: Zed Books, 1996), among others.

10. For an important discussion of the concept of martyrdom in Kurdish history, politics, and literature, see Mariwan Kanie, "Martyrdom between nation and religion: political love, poetry and self-sacrificing in Kurdish nationalism," unpublished PhD dissertation, University of Amsterdam, 2010, as well as work by Andrea Fischer-Tahir on narratives of genocide in "Searching for Sense: The Concept of Genocide as Part of Knowledge Production in Iraqi Kurdistan," in Riccardo Bocco, Hamit Bozarslan, Peter Sluglett, and Jordi Tejel (eds), *Writing the History of Iraq: Historiographical and Political Challenges* (London: World Scientific Publishing and Imperial College Press, 2012) pp. 227-46.

11. Hiltermann, *A Poisonous Affair*, pp. 225-6.

12. "The next generation of Kurds know little about their history," *Kurdish Globe*, 27 March 2011.

13. Dimitris Eleftheriotis, *Cinematic Journeys: Film and Movement* (Edinburgh: Edinburgh University Press, 2010), p. 152.

14. See, for instance, its depiction in Dexter Filkins, "The Fight of their Lives," *New Yorker*, 29 September 2014, http://www.newyorker.com/magazine/2014/09/29/fight-lives, last accessed 12 November 2015.

15. Kevin McKiernan, *The Kurds: A People in Search of their Homeland* (New York: St Martin's Press, 2006) p. 276.

16. For a transcript of the British parliamentary discussion, see http://www.publications.parliament.uk/pa/cm201213/cmhansrd/cm130228/debtext/130228-0002.htm#13022853000002, last accessed 1 May 2015.

17. For the Kurdish Genocide Committee's press release on the decision, posted on Facebook, see https://www.facebook.com/KurdishGenocideComitteeHalabjaCommemoration/posts/554963964624723, last accessed 30 May 2015. Also see Unrepresented Nations and Peoples Organization, "Iraqi Kurdistan: Halabja Genocide Monument in The Hague," 12 December 2012, http://unpo.org/article/15260, last accessed 14 November 2015.

18. Segall notes the Kurdish use of what she calls "the Halabja lament" and the ways in which memories of the attack have been used to push for political reconciliation. See Kimberly

Wedeven Segall, *Performing Democracy in Iraq and South Africa: Gender, Media, and Resistance* (New York: Syracuse University Press, 2013) pp. 21-6.

19. For more on the origins of political divisions between the PUK and the KDP, see Gareth Stansfield, "From civil war to calculated compromise: The unification of the Kurdistan Regional Government in Iraq," in Robert Lowe and Gareth Stansfield (eds), *The Kurdish Policy Imperative* (London: Chatham House, 2010) pp. 130-44.

20. See "Kurdistan Parliament in One Year," https://www.perleman.org/uploads/pdf/Kurdistan-Parliament-in-one-year.pdf, last accessed 12 November 2015.

21. Human Rights Watch, "Ansar al-Islam in Iraqi Kurdistan," 5 February 2003, https://www.hrw.org/report/2003/02/05/ansar-al-islam-iraqi-kurdistan, last accessed 10 November 2015.

22. Mihreban Selam, "Halabja Changes the Ranking Again," *Awêne*, 7 May 2014, http://www.awene.com/article/2014/05/07/32026, last accessed 11 November 2015.

23. Nicole F. Watts, "The Role of Symbolic Capital in Protest: State-Society Relations and the Destruction of the Halabja Martyrs Monument in the Kurdistan Region of Iraq," *Comparative Studies on South Asia, Africa, and the Middle East* 32:1 (2012) pp. 70-85; Hiltermann, *A Poisonous Affair*; Patrick Cockburn, "Hundreds protest as Kurds remember Halabja gas attack," *Independent*, 17 March 2006, http://www.independent.co.uk/news/world/middle-east/hundreds-protest-as-kurds-remember-halabja-gas-attack-5335673.html, last accessed 12 November 2015.

24. See, for instance, the US Dept of State Archive 2001-9, "Remarks at Halabja Mass Grave Site Ceremony," 15 September 2003, http://2001-2009.state.gov/secretary/former/powell/remarks/2003/24100.htm, last accessed 11 November 2015.

25. See Craig Evan Pollack, "Intentions of Burial: Mourning, Politics, and Memorials Following the Massacre at Srebrenicak," *Death Studies* 2 (2003) pp. 125-42; Katharyne Mitchell, "Monuments, Memorials, and the Politics of Memory," *Urban Geography* 24:5 (2003) pp. 442-59; Tamir Sorek, *Palestinian Commemoration in Israel: Calendars, Monuments, and Martyrs* (Stanford, CA: Stanford University Press, 2015).

26. Watts, "The Role of Symbolic Capital in Protest."

27. Tiare Rath, "Halabjans Suffer Neglect and Exploitation", Institute for War and Peace Reporting, 8 November 2015, https://iwpr.net/global-voices/halabjans-suffer-neglect-and-exploitation, last accessed 9 November 2015.

28. Kurdistan Regional Government Cabinet, "Investigative committee releases report on protests in Kurdistan," 2 May 2011, http://cabinet.gov.krd/a/d.aspx?l=12&s=02010100&r=223&a=39829&s=010000, last accessed 3 November 2015; also *Kurdish Globe*, 27 March 2011.

29. See, for example, KNN news, "University Graduates Burn Certificates in Iraqi Kurdistan," 10 April 2014, http://knnc.net/en/full-story-26627-28-False#.VUUNCZNV48I, last accessed 9 November 2015.

30. Abigail Hauslohner, "ISIS recruits Kurdish youths, creating a potential new risk in a peaceful part of Iraq," *Washington Post*, 23 June 2014, https://www.washingtonpost.com/world/isis-recruits-kurdish-youth-creating-a-potential-new-risk-in-a-peaceful-part-of-

iraq/2014/06/23/2961ea2e-defd-4123-8e31-c908f583c5de_story.html#, last accessed 10 November 2015; Leyla Fadel, "Kurdish Officials Worry About Kurds Joining the Islamic State," National Public Radio, 16 December 2014, http://www.npr.org/sections/parallels/2014/12/16/370978024/kurdish-officials-worry-about-kurds-joining-the-islamic-state, last accessed 12 November 2015; Jenna Krajeski, "How the War with ISIS has Exposed Kurdistan's Internal Divisions," *The Nation*, 6 April 2015, http://www.the-nation.com/article/celebrated-its-stability-iraqi-kurdistan-actually-plagued-corruption-nepotism-and-int/, last accessed 8 November 2015.

31. "From the Chemical Tragedy to Supplement the Extremism with Fighters: shock in Halabja: our youth enrolled in ISIS," *Shafaq News*, 16 December 2014, http://english.shafaaq.com/stories/12484-from-the-chemical-tragedy-to-supplement-the-extremism-with-fighters-shock-in-halabja-our-youth-enrolled-in-isis.html, last accessed 10 November 2015.

32. Kurdistan Parliament news, 27 Augusr 2014, http://www.perlemanikurdistan.com/Default.aspx?page=article&id=20239&l=1, last accessed 1 November 2015.

33. Watts, "The Role of Symbolic Capital in Protest", pp. 70-85.

34. Katherine Verdery, *The Political Lives of Dead Bodies: Reburial and Postsocialist Change* (New York: Columbia University Press, 1999), p. 33.

35. See, for instance, Hiltermann, *A Poisonous Affair*, pp. 120-24; Watts, "The Role of Symbolic Capital in Protest."

36. See, for instance, Krajeski, "How the War with ISIS has Exposed Kurdistan's Internal Divisions"; Jay Loschky, "In Iraqi Kurdistan, Satisfaction with Infrastructure Crumbles," Gallup polling, 7 September 2012, http://www.gallup.com/poll/157298/iraqi-kurdis-tan-satisfaction-infrastructure-crumbles.aspx, last accessed 8 November 2015; also Amnesty International, "Days of Rage: Protest and Repression in Iraq," http://www.europarl.europa.eu/meetdocs/2009_2014/documents/d-iq/dv/d-iq20120925_08_/d-iq20120925_08_en.pdf, last accessed 6 November 2015.

37. Watts, "The Role of Symbolic Capital in Protest."

38. Pierre Bourdieu, "Rethinking the State: Genesis and Structure of the Bureaucratic Field," *Sociological Theory* 12:1 (1990) pp. 1-18.

39. Watts, "The Role of Symbolic Capital in Protest."

40. For other applications of symbolic capital to contestation over memory and monuments, see Benjamin Forest and Juliet Johnson, "Unraveling the Threads of History: Soviet-Era Monuments and Post-Soviet National Identity in Moscow," *Annals of the Association of American Geographers* 92 (2002) pp. 524-47.

41. Luqman Abdul Qadir, interview with author, 25 March 2010, Halabja; also see Sahand Nadir, "Kurdistan Region (Iraq): Victims of chemical weapons feel abandoned by the authorities," *Kurdish Globe*, 5 December 2006, http://ekurd.net/mismas/articles/misc2006/12/kurdlocal283.htm, last accessed 2 November 2015; Azeez Mahmood and Mariwan Hama-Saeed, "Locals commemorating twentieth anniversary of chemical attacks recall past broken promises," Institute for War and Peace Reporting, 15 March 2008,

http://www.kurdishaspect.com/doc031508IWPR.html, last accessed 12 November 2015.

42. Watts, "The Role of Symbolic Capital in Protest", pp. 83-4.

43. Denge Nwê radio began broadcasting in 2005, with a particular focus on youth and women's issues. It is supported by the German-based non-governmental organization WADI. See the WADI website, http://en.wadi-online.de/index.php?option=com_content&view=article&id=24&Itemid=25, last accessed 12 November 2015.

44. DHRD Monthly Report, 16 October 2006.

45. Dlawar Haider, interview with author, 17 March 2014, Halabja.

46. Denge Nwê/Spi Organization for the Gassed Areas, "Halabja Survey Results - Final," 6 March 2013.

47. Sorek, *Palestinian Commemoration in Israel*.

48. Pierre Nora, "Between Memory and History: Les Lieux de Mémoire," *Representations* 26 (1989) pp. 26-34.

49. See Forest and Johnson, "Unraveling the Threads of History"; Tamir Sorek, "Cautious Commemoration: Localism, Communalism, and Nationalism in Palestinian Memorial Monuments in Israel", *Comparative Studies in Society and History* 50:2 (2008).

50. Sorek, "Cautious Commemoration"; *Palestinian Commemoration in Israel*.

51. Sara McDowell and Máire Braniff, *Commemoration as Conflict: Space, Memory and Identity in Peace Processes* (Basingstoke: Palgrave Macmillan, 2014), http://www.palgrave-connect.com/pc/doifinder/10.1057/9781137314857.0001, last accessed 12 November 2015.

52. A commemoration in Istanbul in 2003 organized by the pro-Kurdish Democratic People's Party, for instance, resulted in the detention of 26 people. See Agence France Presse, "Turkish police detain 26 people at Halabja commemoration," 16 March 2003. Within Iraq, commemorations in Kirkuk in 2004—the first-ever officially recognized—were criticized by some Arab and Turkoman residents who complained that they had been organized by Kurds there without any consultation with other groups. See Ibrahim Khalil, "Other ethnic groups say Kurds' Halabja ceremony provocative," Deutsche Presse-Agentur, 16 March 2004.

53. Shaho Homa Faraj, interview with author, 18 March 2014, Halabja.

54. Ibid.

55. Ibid.

56. Shaho Homa Faraj, Ariwan Salah, and Ardalan Kakayih, interviews with author, 18 March 2014, Halabja.

57. Aras Ahmed Mhamad, "Halabja to Become 19th Province in Iraq," KNN news, 2 January 2014, http://knnc.net/en/full-story-14836-28-False, last accessed 13 November 2015.

58. See Mihreban Selam, "Halabja's Provincial Bid Caught Up in Objections from Surrounding Towns," *Awêne*, 8 June 2013, http://awene.com/article/2013/06/08/22623, last accessed 13 November 2015.

59. This was described by, among others, Faizil Basharati, interview with author, 20 March 2014.

60. See, for instance, "Former Parliamentarian: 'Making Halabja a Province is Unlawful,'" *Awêne*, 13 March 2013, http://awene.com/article/2014/03/13/30498, last accessed 13 November 2015.

61. This, along with much of the other information in this section, comes from the author's interviews conducted (individually) in Halabja with the following: Hasan Abdulla, 17 March 2014; Naseh Abdul Rahim Rashid, 17 March 2014; Nowshirwan Mohammad, 18 March 2014; Faizil Basharati, 20 March 2014; and Worya Hama Karim, 21 March 2014, as well as from *Awêne* and other news reports. See, for instance, Mihrewan Selam, "Campaign Launched to Make Halabja a Province," 25 February 2014, http://awene.com/article/2014/02/25/30091; and "Follow-up Campaign Launched in Halabja's Bid for Provincial Status," 24 May 2013, http://awene.com/article/2013/05/24/22144, last accessed 13 November 2015.

62. Mohamed Zangeneh, "Iraq: Kurdistan president repeats call for Halabja to become province," *Asharq al-Awsat*, 8 March 2014, http://english.aawsat.com/2014/03/article55329797/iraq-kurdistan-president-repeats-call-for-halabja-to-become-province, last accessed 11 November 2015; also "Iraqi cabinet votes to convert Halabja to a province," *Shafaq*, 31 December 2013, http://english.shafaaq.com/politics/8421--iraqi-cabinet-votes-to-convert-halabja-to-a-province-.html, last accessed 14 November 2015.

63. Osamah Golpy, "Halabja: City of Peace becomes Kurdistan's fourth province," Rudaw, 2 August 2015, http://rudaw.net/english/kurdistan/08022015, last accessed 13 November 2015.

64. Naseh Abdul Rahim Rashid, interview with author, 17 March 2014, Halabja.

65. Zangeneh, "Iraq: Kurdistan president repeats call for Halabja to become province."

66. "Kurdish parliament in final step to name Halabja as fourth province," Rudaw, 5 February 2015, http://rudaw.net/english/kurdistan/050220152, last accessed 14 November 2015.

67. Faizil Basharati, interview with author, 20 March 2014, Halabja.

68. Nowshirwan Mohammad, interview with author, 18 March 2014, Halabja.

69. Dlawar Haider, interview with author, 17 March 2014, Halabja.

70. Martin van Bruinessen, "From Adela Khanun to Leyla Zana: Women as Political Leaders in Kurdish History," in Shahrzad Mojab (ed.), *Women of a Non-State Nation: The Kurds* (Costa Mesa, CA: Mazda, 2001) pp. 95-112.

71. Sayit Mahmud, interview with author, 18 March 2014, Halabja.

72. This is evidenced by local demonstrations in 2014 and 2015 calling on Kurds to protect their own, to remain unified, and to keep independence on the agenda. See Osamah Golpy, "Halabja Rally: No Peshmerga deployment outside Kurdistan", Rudaw, 3 January 2015, http://rudaw.net/english/kurdistan/030120151, last accessed 14 November 2015.

33. MEDIA, POLITICAL CULTURE, AND THE SHADOWS OF THE MILITIA WAR IN IRAQI KURDISTAN

1. Jaffer Sheyholislami, *Kurdish Identity, Discourse, and the New Media* (New York: Palgrave Macmillan, 2011); Reporters without Borders, *Between Freedom and Abuses: the Media Paradox in Iraqi Kurdistan* (Paris, 2010).

2. Denise Natali, *The Kurdish Quasi-State. Development and Dependency in Post-Gulf War Iraq* (New York: Syracuse University Press, 2010).

3. See Amir Hassanpour, *Nationalism and Language in Kurdistan, 1918–1985* (San Francisco, CA: Mellen Research University Press, 1992).

4. According to the Kurdish Ministry of Communication and Transportation, since 2013, 2 million people have regular access to the internet, while 26 companies secure internet provision. See http://pukmedia.com/en/EN_Direje.aspx?Jimare=3500, last accessed 10 October 2014.

5. Interview with Ferhad Awni, Journalist Syndicate, Erbil, 13 October 2010.

6. Interview with Shwan Muhamad, editor-in-chief *Awêne*, Sulaimani, 19 September 2009.

7. On the militia war, see Michael M. Gunter, *The Kurdish Predicament in Iraq. A Political Analysis* (London: Macmillan, 1999); Michiel Leezenberg, "Urbanization, privatization, and patronage: The political economy of Iraqi Kurdistan", in Faleh A. Jabar and Hosham Dawod (eds), *The Kurds. Nationalism and Politics* (London: Saqi Books, 2006) pp. 151-79.

8. Paul Connerton, "Seven types of forgetting", *Memory Studies* 1:1 (2008) pp. 59-71.

9. Stuart Hall, 'ENCODING/DECODING', in *Culture, Media, Language: Working Papers in Cultural Studies, 1972-79* (London: Hutchinson, 1980) pp. 128-38. See also, John Fiske, *Media Matters and Political Change* (Minneapolis/London: University of Minnesota Press, 1994).

10. Dominik Boyer and Ulf Hannerz, "Introduction. Worlds of journalism", *Ethnography* 7:1 (2006) pp. 5-17, here p. 6.

11. Per Ståhlberg, "On the journalist beat in India: Encounters with the near familiar," *Ethnography* 7:1 (2006) pp. 47-67, here p. 65.

12. Gareth Stansfield, *Iraqi Kurdistan. Political Development and Emergent Democracy* (London/New York: RoutledgeCurzon, 2003); Brendan O'Leary, John McGarry, and Khalid Salih (eds) *The Future of Kurdistan in Iraq* (Philadelphia, PA: University of Pennsylvania Press, 2005); David Romano, "Iraqi Kurdistan: challenges of autonomy in the wake of US withdrawal", *International Affairs* 86:6 (2010) pp. 1343-5; Aziz Mahir, *The Kurds of Iraq: Ethnonationalismus and National Identity* (London: I. B. Tauris, 2011).

13. Nicole Watts, "Democratization and Self-determination in Kurdistan Region of Iraq", in David Romano and Mehmet Gurses (eds): *Conflict, Democratization and the Kurds in the Middle East. Turkey, Iran, Iraq, and Syria* (New York: Palgrave Macmillan, 2014) pp. 141-68, here p. 150.

14. Reporters without Borders, *Between Freedom and Abuses*, p. 9 makes a slightly different distinction: media of the ruling parties, media indirectly affiliated with them, media of

the opposition, and media claiming to be independent, which is very much reflecting the self-representation of the actors. Watts, "Democratization and Self-determination", p. 156f addresses "oppositional and independent media" and thus suggests a distinction between those on the one side, and the media of the ruling parties on the other.

15. Reporters without Borders, *Between Freedom and Abuses*, p. 10.

16. Interview with Ferhad Awni, see ftn. 5.

17. See also Amahl Bishara, "Local hands, international news: Palestine journalists and the international media", *Ethnography* 7:1 (2006) pp. 19-46.

18. James Ferguson, "The uses of neoliberalism", *Antipode* 41:1 (2009) pp. 166-84.

19. Runak Faraj, "The women's question and the role of the media in Iraqi Kurdistan", paper presented at the 4th Bedirkhan Conference, 21-24 April 2007, Berlin; Interview with Sara Qadir, *Awêne*, Sulaimani, 4 October 2010.

20. Interview with Ferhad Awni, see ftn. 5; interview with Nejed Surme, editor-in-chief of *Xebat*, Erbil, 12 October 2009; interview with Stran Ebdullah, editor-in-chief of *Kurdistan-î Nwê*, 15 September 2009.

21. *Hawlatî* appeared first in November 2000; due to a lack of financial sustainability, both the newspaper and website were shut down in February 2016.

22. Interview with Shwan Muhamad, editor-in-chief of *Awêne*, Sulaimani, 19 September 2009. According to Zuhair al-Jezairy, editor-in-chief of the news agency Aswat al-Iraq, in 2009 the Iraqi newspaper with the highest circulation (20,000 copies) was the state-owned *al-Sabah* (The Morning). Interview with him, Sulaimani, 7 October 2009.

23. Interviews with Shwan Muhamad, see ftn. 6; also interview 21 October 2010.

24. Interviews with Hero Ceza und Kwestan Abdul-Qadir Koste, *Kurdistan-î Nwê*, Sulaimani, 3 October 2009; with Ala Latif, *Hawlatî*, Sulaimani, 5 October 2009; with Shanaz Ebdurrahman, *Awêne*, 6 October 2010.

25. Interviews with Shwan Muhamad, 19 September 2009; talk with Asos Herdi, Sulaimani, 1 October 2010. When I visited Kurdistan in January 2013, Shwan Muhamad had already left *Awêne* and had founded his own news website *Spee* (www.speemedia.com, last accessed 11 October 2016).

26. *Awêne*, 18 May 2010.

27. http://www.niqash.org/articles/?id=2673&lang=ku, last accessed 10 October 2014.

28. http://www.ekurd.net/mismas/articles/misc2010/5/state3816.htm, last accessed 10 October 2014.

29. Reporters without Borders, *Between Freedom and Abuses*, p. 20.

30. Interviews with Runak Faraj, Koral Nuri, and Shilan Nuri, Sulaimani, 24 October 2010.

31. Reporters without Borders, *Between Freedom and Abuses*, p. 18.

32. http://www.ekurd.net/mismas/articles/misc2008/3/kirkukkurdistan339.htm, last accessed 14 October 2014; http://www.amnesty.org/en/appeals-for-action/investigate-attacks-journalists-kurdistan-region-iraq, last accessed 10 October 2014.

33. Interview with Shwan Muhamad, 21 October 2010.

34. Interview with Shwan Muhamad, 19 September 2009.

35. Watts, "Democratization and Self-determination", p. 151.

36. See also Reporters without Borders, *Between Freedom and Abuses*, p. 19.

37. See Fischer-Tahir, *"Wir gaben viele Märtyrer": Widerstand und kollektive Identitätsbildung in Irakisch-Kurdistan* (Münster: Unrast, 2003); Nicole Watts, "The role of symbolic capital in political protest: State-society relations and the destruction of the Halabja Martyrs Monument in the Kurdistan Region of Iraq", *Comparative Studies of South Asia, Africa and the Middle East* 32:1 (2012) pp. 70-85.

38. Discussions were held in Kurdish language; transcription and translation by the author.

39. *Niqash*, 18 May 2011; *Sbeiy*, 16 June 2011; *Niqash*, 23 February 2012; *Rega-i Kurdistan*, 8 October 2012.

40. *Awêne*, 7 October 2012.

41. Interview with attorney Karzan Fazil Tawfiq, Sulaimani, 27 January 2014.

42. *Awêne*, 19 February 2014.

43. Talk with the long-standing left-wing activist Wazira Jalal, sister of prominent Komala martyr Shahid Aram, Jiyani Nwê, Sulaimani, 6 March 2016.

44. Reporters without Borders, *Between Freedom and Abuses*, p. 2.

45. Watts, "Democratization and Self-determination", p. 156f.

46. Lawrence Rosen, *Bargaining for Reality: The Reconstruction of Social Relations in the Muslim Community* (Chicago: University of Chicago Press, 1984).

34. EXPERIENCES OF HONOR-BASED VIOLENCE, AND MOVING TOWARD ACTION IN IRAQI KURDISTAN

1. Lama Abu Odeh, "Crimes of honour and the construction of gender in Arab societies", in M. Yamani (ed.), *Feminism and Islam* (New York: New York University Press, 1996) pp. 141-94.

2. Nazand Begikhani, "Honour-based violence: the case of Iraqi Kurdistan", in L. Welchman and S. Hossain (eds), *Honour: Crimes, paradigms and violence against women* (London: Zed Books, 2005) pp. 209-29; Aisha Gill, "Patriarchal violence in the name of 'honour,'", *International Journal of Criminal Justice Sciences* 1:1 (2003) pp. 1-12.

3. Welchman and Hossain, *Honour*; United Nations Assistance Mission for Iraq (UNAMI), United Nations Commission on Human Rights Agency (UNAMI), and ASUDA, *Eliminating violence against women: perspectives on honour-related violence in the Iraqi Kurdistan Region* (Suleymaniya Governorate, Suleymaniya, Iraqi Kurdistan: UNAMI, UNHR and ASUDA, 2009).

4. Moira Dustin, *Gender equality, cultural diversity, European comparisons and lessons* (London: London School of Economics, Gender Institute and the Nuffield Foundation, 2006).

5. Begikhani, "Honour-based violence"; Aisha Gill, "Reconfiguring 'honour'-based violence as a form of gendered violence", in M. Idriss and T. Abbas (eds), *Honour, Violence, Women and Islam* (London: Routledge-Cavendish, 2010) pp. 218-32.

6. Welchman and Hossain, *Honour*.

7. Nicola Piper, "Gender and migration: A paper prepared for the policy analysis and research

programme of the global commission on international migration", (Geneva: Global Commission on International Migration, UNFPA, 2004).

8. Sherry Ortner, "The Virgin and the State", *Feminist Studies* 4:3 (October 1978) pp. 19-35; Shahrzad Mojab and Nahla Abdo, *Violence in the Name of Honour: Theoretical and political challenges* (Istanbul: Istanbul Bilgi University Press, 2004).

9. Pierre Bourdieu, *Outline of a Theory of Practice* (Cambridge: Cambridge University Press, 1977).

10. Nicole Pope, "'Honour' Killing: Instruments of patriarchal control", in Shahrzad Mojab and Nahla Abdo (eds), *Violence in the Name of Honour: Theoretical and political challenges* (Istanbul: Bilgi University Press, 2004).

11. Nazand Begikhani, Aisha Gill, and Gill Hague, *Honour-Based Violence: Experiences and counter-strategies in Iraqi Kurdistan and the UK Kurdish Diaspora* (London: Ashgate, 2015).

12. Pnina Werbner, "Veiled Interventions in Pure Space: Shame and Embodied Struggles among Muslims in Britain and France", Special Issue on "Authority and Islam", *Theory, Culture and Society* 24:2 (2007) pp. 161-86; Nira Yuval-Davis, "Interview with Professor Nira Yuval-Davis: After gender and nation", *Studies of Ethnicity and Nationalism* 9:1 (2009) pp. 128-38.

13. Begikhani, "Honour-based violence."

14. Unni Wikan, *In Honour of Fadime: Murder and shame* (Chicago: University of Chicago Press, 2008).

15. Begikhani, Gill and Hague, *Honour-Based Violence*.

16. Veena Meeto and Heidi Mirza, "There is nothing honourable about honour killings: Gender, violence and the limits of multiculturalism", *Women's Studies International Forum* 30:3 (2007) pp. 187-200.

17. Nazand Begikhani, Aisha Gill, and Gill Hague, with Kawther Ibraheem, *Honour-based Violence (HBV) and Honour-based Killings in Iraqi Kurdistan and in the Kurdish Diaspora in the UK* (Erbil: Kurdistan Regional Government (and University of Bristol and University of Roehampton, UK) 2010.

18. Nazand Begikhani, "Du'a's murder compared to other honour-related killings", *Aso daily paper*, Sulaimani: Khandan, 3 May 2007.

19. See Barewabarayti baduwadachuni tundutiji u dij ba afratan [Directorate to follow up violence against women, DFVAW], "Barudokhi komalayati afratan la haremi Kurdistan la sali 2009, lagal barawurdkariyak sabarat ba asti tundutikyakan la newan hardu Sali 2008-2009, la 1/1/2009 ta 31/12/2009, Hawler, Slemani, Duhok" [Report on social situation of women in Kurdistan in 2009, with a comparison with 2008 violence cases, in Erbil, Sulaimani, and Duhok (Erbil, Iraqi Kurdistan: Wazarati nawkho, hikumati haremi, 2009).

20. See Begikhani, "Honour-based violence."

21. United Nations Commission on Human Rights (UNHR), "Working towards the elimination of crimes against women committed in the name of honour. 57th session of the United Nations Commission on Human Rights", report no. 0246790 (New York: United Nations, 2002).

35. THE KURDISTAN REGION OF IRAQ AND THE FEDERAL CONSTITUTION

1. Some of the structure of this chapter, including the case studies, follows that of a research and publication project with my former colleague at the University of Kurdistan Hewler, Alex Danilovich. See Alex Danilovich, *Iraqi Federalism and the Kurds: Learning to Live Together* (Farnham: Ashgate, 2014), which includes a co-authored chapter and my chapter on federalization of natural resources. See also ftn. 8.

2. Tarek Osman, "Why border lines drawn with a ruler in WW1 still rock the Middle East", BBC News, 14 December , http://www.bbc.co.uk/news/world-middle-east-25299553

3. James Harvey and Gareth Stansfield, "Theorizing Unrecognized States", in Nina Caspersen and Gareth Stansfield (eds), *Unrecognized States in the International System* (London: Routledge, 2011) p. 19.

4. Raymond Hinnebusch, *International Politics of the Middle East* (Manchester: Manchester University Press, 2003) p. 1.

5. A similar analogy is used in John Bayliss, Patricia Owen, and Steve Smith, 'Introduction' to their *The Globalization of World Politics* (Oxford: Oxford University Press, 2013) p. 3.

6. Barry Posen, "The Security Dilemma and Ethnic Conflict", *Survival* 35:1 (1993) pp. 27-47.

7. See Jan Erk and Lawrence Anderson, "The Paradox of Federalism: Does Self-Rule Accommodate or Exacerbate Ethnic Divisions", in Jan Erk and Lawrence Anderson, *The Paradox of Federalism* (London: Routledge, 2010) p. 2.

8. See Francis Owtram, "The Foreign Policies of Unrecognized States", in Nina Caspersen and Gareth Stansfield (eds), *Unrecognized States in the International System* (London: Routledge, 2011) pp. 128-43; Francis Owtram, "The Kurdistan Region of Iraq: Ethnic Conflict and the Survival of Dynastic Republicanism in a De Facto State", in Johannes Artens (ed.), *De Facto States and Ethnic Conflicts* P@X online bulletin (Centre for Social Studies, University of Coimbra, September 2012), vol. 21, pp. 13-15; Francis Owtram, "The Federalization of Natural Resources", in Alex Danilovich, *Iraqi Federalism and the Kurds: Learning to Live Together* (Farnham: Ashgate, 2014) pp. 113-39; Francis Owtram, "Oil, the Kurds and the Drive for Independence: An Ace in the Hole or Joker in the Pack?" in Alex Danilovich (ed.), *Iraqi Kurdistan in Middle East Politics* (London: Routledge, 2016); Alex Danilovich and Francis Owtram, "Federalism as a Tool to Manage Conflicts and Associated Risks", in Danilovich, *Iraqi Federalism and the Kurds*; Herish Khalil Mohammed and Francis Owtram, "Paradiplomacy of Regional Governments in International Relations: Foreign Relations of the Kurdistan Regional Government (2003-2010)", *Iran and the Caucasus* 18 (2014) pp. 65-84.

9. Jan Erk and Wilfried Swenden (eds), *New Directions in Federalism Studies* (London: Routledge, 2003) p. 1.

10. Paul Cammack, David Pool, and William Tordoff, *Third World Politics: A Comparative Introduction*, (Basingstoke: MacMillan, 1994) pp. 41-5.

11. Denise Natali, *The Kurds and the State* (Syracuse, NY: Syracuse University Press, 2005) pp. 26-47.

12. Fred Halliday, "Tibet, Palestine and the Politics of Failure", Open Democracy News Analysis (2008), https://www.opendemocracy.net/article/tibet-palestine-and-the-politics-of-failure, last accessed, 5 April 2016.

13. See Charles Tripp, *A History of Iraq* (Cambridge: Cambridge University Press, 2007).

14. Cited in Beverley Milton-Edwards, *Politics of the Middle East* (Cambridge: Polity Press, 2006) p. 229.

15. John McGarry and Brendan O'Leary, "Iraq's Constitution of 2005: Liberal Consociation as Political Prescription", in Sujit Choudhry (ed.), *Constitutional Design for Divided Societies: Integration or Accommodation?* (Oxford: Oxford University Press, 2008) pp. 342-4.

16. Eduardo Abu Ltaif, "The Limitations of the Consociational Arrangements in Iraq", *Ethnopolitics Papers* 36 (September 2015), https://www.psa.ac.uk/sites/default/files/page-files/AbuLTaif_EP_No38.pdf, last accessed 24 October 2016.

17. See Mohammed Shareef, *The United States, Iraq and the Kurds: Shock, Awe and Aftermath* (London: Routledge, 2014) pp. 135-83.

18. This section is drawn from Danilovich and Owtram, "Federalism as a Tool."

19. William Riker, *Federalism: Origins, Operation and Significance* (Boston, MA: Little, Brown and Company, 1964).

20. See James Harvey and Gareth Stansfield, "Theorizing Unrecognized States: Sovereignty, Secessionism and Political Economy", in Nina Caspersen and Gareth Stansfield (eds), *Unrecognized States in the International System* (London: Routledge, 2011) p. 19.

21. John McGarry, "Asymmetrical Federalism and the Plurinational State", 3rd International Conference on Federalism, Brussels, 2005, cited in Liam Anderson, "Reintegrating Unrecognized States", in Caspersen and Stansfield, *Unrecognized States*, p. 196

22. Liam Anderson, "Internationalizing Iraq's Constitutional Dilemma", in Robert Lowe and Gareth Stansfield, *The Kurdish Policy Imperative* (London: RIIA, 2012).

23. Danilovich and Owtram, "Federalism as a Tool."

24. On attempts to build Iraqi identity, see Sherko Kirmanj, *Identity and Nation in Iraq* (Boulder, CO and London: Lynne Rienner, 2013).

25. See http://worldpopulationreview.com/countries/iraq-population/ last accessed 24 October 2016.

26. For the official Arabic version of the constitution and an unoText of the constitution in English, see http://zaidalali.com/resources/constitution-of-iraq/, last accessed 5 April 2016.

27. Liam Anderson and Gareth Stansfield, Crisis in *Kirkuk: the Ethnopolitics of Conflict and Compromise* (Philadelphia, PA: University of Pennsylvannia Press, 2009) p. 8. See also the ESRC-funded project, "Understanding and Managing Intra-state Territorial Competition: Iraq's Disputed Territories in Comparative Perspective", http://www.disputedterritories.org/ last accessed 24 October 2016.

28. Danilovich, *Iraqi Federalism and the Kurds*, p. 65.

29. Posen, "The Security Dilemma."

30. This summary is drawn from Shahrzad Sabet, "An Overview of Barry Posen's 'The Security Dilemma and Ethnic Conflict,'" isites.harvard.edu/fs/docs/icb.topic265244.files/Shahrzad, last accessed 5 April 2016.

31. See Denise Natali, "The Islamic State's Baathist Roots", *Al-Monitor*, April 2015, http://www.al-monitor.com/pulse/originals/2015/04/baathists-behind-the-islamic-state.html, last accessed 5 April 2016.

32. See Rasha Al Aqeeda, "Iraq and Ruin: The Once and Future Mosul", *American Interest*, 26 September 2016, http://www.the-american-interest.com/2016/09/26/the-once-and-future-mosul/ last accessed 21 April 2016.

33. Peter van Buren, "Dude, Where's My Humvee? Iraq Losing Equipment to Islamic State at Staggering Rate", Reuters, 2 June 2015, http://blogs.reuters.com/great-debate/2015/06/02/dude-wheres-my-humvee-iraqi-equipment-losses-to-islamic-state-are-out-of-control/ last accessed 5 April 2016.

34. Denise Natali, "Long Road to Mosul", *War on the Rocks*, February 2016, http://warontherocks.com/2016/02/the-long-road-to-mosul/ last accessed 5 April 2016.

35. See Patrick Ryan and Patrick B Johnston, "After the Battle for Mosul, Prepare for the Islamic State to Go Underground", *War on the Rocks*, October 2016, http://warontherocks.com/2016/10/after-the-battle-for-mosul-get-ready-for-the-islamic-state-to-go-underground/ last accessed 24 October 2016.

36. Kari Lundgren and Brian Swint, "Hayward to Spark Oil Fight in Iraqi 'Last Great Frontier,'" Bloomberg, 8 September 2011, http://www.bloomberg.com/news/articles/2011-09-08/tony-hayward-to-spark-oil-fight-in-iraqi-last-great-frontier- last accessed 5 April 2016.

37. See Owtram, "Federalization of Natural Resources"; Rex Zedalis, *Oil and Gas in the Disputed Kurdish Territories: Jurisprudence, Regional Minorities and Natural Resources in a Federal System* (London: Routledge, 2012).

38. John McGarry and Brendan O'Leary, "Iraq's Constitution of 2005", in Sujit Choudry (ed.), *Constitutional Design for Divided Societies: Integration or Accommodation?* (Oxford: Oxford University Press, 2007) pp. 115-16.

39. Informal communication with residents of the Kurdistan Region of Iraq. The KRG Ministry of Natural Resources monthly export report lists revenue generated from oil exports via Turkey. See this report for March 2016: http://mnr.krg.org/images/monthlyreports/EXPORTs/MNR_Monthly_Export_Report_March_2016.pdf

40. See Guancomo Luciani, "Oil in the International Political Economy of the Middle East", in Louis Fawcett (ed.), *International Relations of the Middle East* (Oxford: Oxford University Press, 2009).

41. Campbell MacDiarmid, "The World's Staunchest Ally Against ISIS is Fighting on Empty", *Maclean's*, 29 February 2016, http://www.macleans.ca/news/world/the-worlds-staunchest-ally-against-isis-is-fighting-on-empty/, last accessed 21 march 2017.

42. Denise Natali on @DNataliDC.

43. Mohammed A. Salih, "Kurdistan's Economy is on its Knees", *Newsweek*, 23 March 2016, http://newsweekme.com/kurdistans-economy-is-on-its-knees/ last accessed 5 April 2016.

44. See Owtram, "The Kurdistan Region of Iraq."

45. *National Geographic*, "Kurds of the Caliphate", https://www.youtube.com/watch?v=Q2X7eP6d0ME, last accessed 24 October 2016.

46. Denise Natali, "Stalemate, not Statehood, for Iraqi Kurdistan", *Lawfare*, https://www.lawfareblog.com/stalemate-not-statehood-iraqi-kurdistan, last accessed 5 April 2016.

47. Denise Natali, "The Myth of a Tripartite Iraq", *Al-Monitor*, 18 June 2016, http://www.al-monitor.com/pulse/originals/2016/06/iraq-myth-tripartite-sunni-shia-kurd-stability-isis.html, last accessed 24 October 2016.

48. "Kurds to vote on independence from Iraq in 2016", January,http://www.alaraby.co.uk/english/news/2016/1/7/kurds-to-vote-on-independence-from-iraq-in-2016

49. Harvey and Stansfield, "Theorizing Unrecognized States."

50. Owtram, "Federalization of Natural Resources", p. 135.

BIBLIOGRAPHY

Abboud, M., 'The Role of Higher Education in Exploring Gender in Iraq: Inaccurate Numbers Challenge Efforts to Address Women's Issues in the KRG', American University of Iraq – Sulaimani, 2013, http://auis.edu.iq/node/1158, last accessed 15 March 2014.

Abdalla, Ahmad, *The Student Movement and National Politics in Egypt, 1923–1973*, London: Saqi Books, 1985.

Abdul Qadir, Luqman, Interview with author, 25 March 2010, Halabja.

Abu Odeh, Lama, 'Crimes of honour and the construction of gender in Arab societies', in Yamani, M. (ed.), *Feminism and Islam*, New York: New York University Press, 1996, pp. 141-94.

Abrahams, Fred, Nadim Houry, and Tom Porteous, *Under Kurdish Rule: Abuses in PYD-Run Enclaves of Syria*, Human Rights Watch, 2014.

Abu-Lughod, Lila, 'Dialects of Women's Empowerment: The International Circuitry of the Arab Human Development Report 2005', *International Journal of Middle East Studies* 41 (2009), pp. 83-103.

———(ed.), *Remaking Women, Feminism and Modernity in the Middle East*, Princeton, NJ: Princeton University Press, 1998.

Adamson, David, *The Kurdish War*, New York: Praeger, 1964.

Afruz Reza, 'Hobâbhâ-ye siyâsi dar Kordestân-e Iran' ['Political Bubbles in Iranian Kurdistan'], *Bâztâb*, 6 October 2005.

Ahmad, Kamal M., *Kurdistan during the First World War*, English trans. by Ali Maher Ibrahim, London: Saqi Books, 1994.

Ahmadzadeh, H. and Gareth Stansfield,'The Political, Cultural, and Military Re-Awakening of the Kurdish Nationalist Movement in Iran', *Middle East Journal* 64:1 (2010), pp. 11-27.

Ahmed, Akbar Shahid and Christine Conetta, 'Congress Voted Against Directly Arming Iraq's Kurds. Here's What That Means for the ISIS Fight', *Huffington Post*, 29 June 2015, http://www.huffingtonpost.com/2015/06/29/congress-arm-kurds_n_7647068.html, last accessed 6 January 2016.

Ahmed, Hevidar, 'Senior Kurdistan official: IS was at Erbil's gates, Turkey did not help', Rudaw, 16 September 2014, http://rudaw.net/english/interview/16092014

Ahmed, Huda, 'Iraq', in Kelly, Sanja and Julia Breslin (eds) *Women's Rights in the Middle*

East and North Africa: Progress Amid Resistance, Lanham, MD: Rowman & Littlefield Publishers, 2010, pp. 157-92.

Ahmetbeyzade, Cihan, 'Kurdish Nationalism in Turkey and the Role of Peasant Kurdish Women', in Mayer, Tamar (ed.), *Gender Ironies of Nationalism: Sexing the Nation*, Abingdon: Routledge, 2000, pp. 187-209.

Akar, B., 'Designing and developing core modules for life skills and civic values in Iraq and Iraqi Krudistan', Working paper presented at University of Duhok, Education and Peace building conference, 2014.

Akkaya, Ahmet H., 'The 'Palestinian Dream' in the Kurdish Context', *Kurdish Studies*, 3:1 (2015), pp. 47-63.

Akkaya, Ahmet Hamdi and Joost Jongerden, 'The PKK in the 2000s: continuity through breaks', in Casier, Marlies and Joost Jongerden (eds), *Nationalisms and Politics in Turkey: Political Islam, Kemalism and the Kurdish Issue*, Abingdon: Routledge, 2011.

————'Reassembling the Political: The PKK and the Project of Radical Democracy', *European Journal of Turkish Studies* 12 (2012).

———— 'Confederalism and Autonomy in Turkey: The Kurdistan Workers' Party and the Reinvention of Democracy', in Gunes , Cengiz and Welat Zeydanlioglu (eds), *The Kurdish Question in Turkey: New Perspectives on Violence, Representation and Reconciliation*, Abingdon: Routledge, 2013.

Ala'Aldeen, D., 'Studying for Master's degree in Kurdistan Region, Reforming the Master's Degree in the Kurdistan Region: Enhancing Capacity and Quality', Ministry of Higher Education and Scientific Research, http://www.mhe-krg.org/node/117, last accessed 11 March 2014.

———— 'A determined push for higher education progress in Kurdistan', *University World News*, 2012, http://www.universityworldnews.com/article. php?story=20120615064310850, last accessed 14 March 2014.

Al-Ali, Nadje, 'Reconstructing Gender: Iraqi women between dictatorship, war, sanctions and occupation', *Third World Quarterly* 26: 4-5 (2005), p. 742.

Al-Ali, N. and N. Pratt, *What Kind of Liberation? Women and the Occupation of Iraq*, Berkeley, CA: University of California Press, 2008.

————Al-Ali, Nadje and Pratt, Nicola, 'Between Nationalism and Women's Rights: The Kurdish Women's Movement in Iraq', *Middle East Journal of Culture and Communication* 4 (2011), pp. 337-53.

Al-Ali, Nadje, Muzhda Muhammed, Hataw Kareem, Dlaram Salih, and Kawther Akreyi, *Female Iraqi Academics in Iraqi Kurdistan: Roles, Challenges & Capacities*, Final Research Report, DelPHE Iraq, 2012.

BIBLIOGRAPHY

Al Ansary, Khalid and Stanley, Bruce, 'Cash strapped Iraqi Kurds to start gas exports to Turkey in 2016', 13 January 2016, http://www.bloomberg.com/news/articles/2016-01-13/cash-strapped-iraqi-kurds-to-start-gas-exports-to-turkey-in-2016, last accessed 22 January 2016

Al-Faraj, F. A. M. and M. Scholz, 'Impact of upstream anthropogenic river regulation on downstream water availability in transboundary river watersheds', *International Journal of Water Resources Development* 31:1 (2015).

Alavi, Seyyed Hasan, 'Tashkil-e frâksyun-e nemâyandegân-e Kord-e majles-e dahom' ['Formation of the caucus of the Kurdish deputies in the 10th majles'], *Mehr News*, 3 May 2016.

Albright, Madeline K., Cohen, William S., 'Preventing Genocide: A Blueprint for Policymakers', 2008, www.http//www.ushmm.org.

Ali, Darbaz Kosrat Rasul, Rudaw, 17 May 2015, https://www.youtube.com/watch?v=LWKbynYgEV4, last accessed 26 November 2015.

Alis, Ahmet, 'The Process of the Politicisation of the Kurdish Identity in Turkey: The Kurds and the Turkish Labor Party (1961–1971)', MA thesis, Boğaziçi University, 2009.

Al-Jazeera, 'Kurdish-Turkmen Tension on the Rise in Kirkuk', 18 June 2014, http://www.aljazeera.com/news/middleeast/2014/06/kurdish-turkmen-tension-rise-kirkuk-2014617122142958412.html

Al-Jazeera, 'Iraq's Kurds Rule Out Giving Up Kirkuk', 28 June 2014, http://www.al-jazeera.com/news/middleeast/2014/06/iraq-kurds-rule-out-retreating-from-kirkuk-20146271440878594.html

Allison, Christine 'Old and New Oral Traditions in Badinan', in Kreyenbroek, P. G. and F. C. Allison (eds), *Kurdish Culture and Identity*, London: Curzon, 1996, pp. 29-47.

——— *The Yezidi Oral Tradition in Iraqi Kurdistan*, London: Curzon, 2001.

———'From Benedict Anderson to Mustafa Kemal: Reading, Writing and Imagining the Kurdish Nation', in Bozarslan, Hamit and Clémence Scalbert-Yücel (eds), *Joyce Blau: l'éternelle chez les Kurdes*, Paris: IKP, 2013, pp.101-34.

——— 'Memory and the Kurmanji novel: Contemporary Turkey and Soviet Armenia', in Allison, C. and P. G. Kreyenbroek (eds) *Remembering the Past in Iranian Societies*, Wiesbaden: Harrasowitz Verlag, 2013, pp. 189-218.

Allison, C. and P. G. Kreyenbroek (eds) *Remembering the Past in Iranian Societies*, Wiesbaden: Harrasowitz Verlag, 2013.

Allsopp, Harriet, *The Kurds in Syria, Political Parties and Identity in the Middle East*, London: I. B. Tauris, 2014.

———'The Kurdish Autonomy Bid in Syria: Challenges and Reactions', in Gunter, Michael and Mohammed M. A. Ahmed, (eds), *The Kurdish Spring: Geopolitical Changes and the Kurds*, Costa Mesa, CA: Mazda, 2013.

Al-Marashi, Ibrahim, *Iraq's Armed Forces: An Analytical History*, London: Routledge, 2009.

Al-Shukri, Ali Yousif, *International Criminal Law in a Changing World*, Cairo: Dar Enzak, 2009.

Altuğ, Seda, *Sectarianism in the Syrian Jazira: Community, Land and Violence in the Memories of World War I and the French Mandate, 1915–1939*, PhD dissertation, Utrecht University, 2011.

———— and Benjamin T. White, 'Frontières et pouvoir d'Etat: La frontière turco-syrienne dans les années 1920 et 1930', *Vingtième siècle* 3:103 (2009), pp. 91-104.

Alwardi Ali, *Social Glimpses of Modern Iraqi History: The Ottomans, Safavids and Mamluks*, Saarbruken: Lambert Academic Publishing, 2010.

Amanolahi, Sekandar, 'A note on ethnicity and ethnic groups in Iran', *Iran and the Caucasus* 9:1 (2005), pp. 37-41.

Amanpour, Christiane, 'Iraqi Kurdistan leader Massoud Barzani says "the time is here" for self-determination', CNN, 23 June 2014, http://amanpour.blogs.cnn.com/2014/06/23/exclusive-iraqi-kurdish-leader-says-the-time-is-here-for-self-determination, last accessed 17 November 2015.

Amel, Ahmed, 'Genocide Prevention', in Igwara, O. (ed.), *Ethnic Hatred: Ethnic Genocide in Rwanda*, London: ASEN Publications, 1995.

Amin Zaki Beg, Mohammed, *Kürdistan tarihi*, Istanbul: Komal, 1977.

————*Kürd ve Kürdistan Ünlüleri*, Spanga: Apec, 1998.

Amnesty International, 'Days of Rage: Protest and Repression in Iraq', http://www.europarl.europa.eu/meetdocs/2009_2014/documents/d-iq/dv/d-iq20120925_08_/d-iq20120925_08_en.pdf, last accessed 6 November 2015.

Amnesty International, 'Turkey: end abusive operations under indefinite curfews', 20 January 2016, https://www.amnesty.org/en/documents/eur44/3230/2016/en/

Amy de la Bretèque, E., *Paroles Melodisées: Récits épiques et lamentations chez les Yézidis d'Arménie,* Paris: Garnier, 2013.

Anadolu Ajansı, 'Çatışmasızlığa son veren üçgen' ['The triangle that ended the ceasefire'], http://www.aa.com.tr/tr/haberler/590099--catismasizliga-son-veren-ucgen-hdp-pkk-kck, last accessed 24 September 2015

Anderson, L. and G. Stansfield, *Crisis in Kirkuk: The Ethnopolitics of Conflict and Compromise*, Philadelphia, PA: University of Pennsylvania Press, 2009.

ANF News, 'Mala Bakhtiyar: Ditch decision the KDP's alone', 7 May 2014, http://en.firatnews.com/news/news/mala-bakhtiyar-ditch-decision-the-kdp-s-alone.htm, last accessed 20 May 2014.

———— 'PYD prosecutes rival Kurdish politicians in Syria's Efrin', 3 April 2014, www.aranews.org/en/home/kurdish-region/1326-pyd-prosecute-rival-politicians-in-syria-s-efrin.html, last accessed 7 May 2014.

BIBLIOGRAPHY

Anter, Musa, *Hatıralarım*, Istanbul: Doz Basim, 1990.

Anthony, R., M. Hansen, K. Kumar, H. Shatz, and G. Vernez, *Building the Future, Summary of Four Studies to Develop the Private Sector, Education, Health Care and Data for Decisionmaking for the Kurdistan Region - Iraq*, Ministry of Planning Kurdistan Regional Government, Santa Monica, CA: RAND Corporation, 2012.

Arakelova, Victoria, 'Bayt'ā Gilāvīyē — A Lament for a Noble Woman. Or Evidence for Polygamy among the Yezidis', *Iran and the Caucasus,* 3 (1999), pp. 135-42.

Aral, Berdal, 'The Idea of Human Rights as Perceived in the Ottoman Empire', *Human Rights Quarterly*, 26:2 (2004), pp. 454-82.

ARANews, 'Al-Maliki to Barzani: areas dominated by Kurds will return', 4 July 2014.

Arango, Tim, 'Rebel keeps Kurds' guns close at hand in peace talks with Turkey', *New York Times,* 11 April 2013, http://www.nytimes.com/2013/04/12/world/middleeast/rebel-kurd-karayilan-defiant-in-turkish-talks.html?pagewanted=all&_r=0

Arendt, Hannah, *On Revolution*, London: Penguin, 1990 / 1963.

Arzt, Donna, *Refugees into Citizens*, New York: Council of Foreign Relations, 1997.

Asr-e Iran, 'Tadris-e zabân va adabiyât-e Kordi dar dâneshgâh-e Kordestân' ['Instruction of Kurdish and language instruction at the University of Kurdistan'], Asr-e Iran, 16 September 2015.

Astarjian, Henry, *The Struggle for Kirkuk: The Rise of Hussein, Oil, and the Death of Tolerance in Iraq*, Santa Barbara, CA: Praeger Security International, 2007.

Ateş, Sabri, *The Ottoman-Iranian Borderlands. Making a Boundary, 1843–1914*, Cambridge: Cambridge University Press, 2013.

——— 'In the Name of the Caliph and the Nation: The Sheikh Ubeidullah Rebellion of 1880–1881', *Iranian Studies* 47:5 (2014), pp. 735-98.

Atran, S. and D. M. Stonemarch, 'The Kurds' Heroic Stand Against ISIS', *New York Times*, 16 March 2015.

Austin, Gareth, 'Commercial Agriculture and the Ending of Slave-trading and Slavery in West Africa, 1787–c.1930', in Law, Robin, Suzanne Schwarz, and Silke Strickrodt (eds), *Commercial Agriculture, the Slave Trade and Slavery in Atlantic Africa*, Oxford: James Currey, 2013, pp. 243-65.

Avci, Kemal, 'Erdoğan advisor blames Maliki, says Iraq "practically divided"', Rudaw, 18 June 2014, http://rudaw.net/english/interview/18062014

Aydin, Aysegül and Cem Emrence, *Zones of Rebellion: Kurdish Insurgents and the Turkish State*, Ithaca, NY: Cornell University Press.

Aydın, Delal, 'Mobilizing the Kurds in Turkey: Newroz as a Myth', in Gunes, Cengiz and Welat Zeydanlıoğlu, *The Kurdish Question in Turkey: New Perspectives on Violence, Representation and Reconciliation*, London: Routledge, 2014, pp. 68-89.

Aykan, Y. Unacknowledged Memory: The nineteenth-century Ottoman Empire and the ambivalence of national memory in the Turkish Republic', in Allison, C. and P. G. Kreyenbroek (eds) *Remembering the Past in Iranian Societies*, Wiesbaden: Harrasowitz Verlag, 2013, pp. 78-94.

Azeez, Mahmood and Mariwan Hama-Saeed, 'Locals commemorating twentieth anniversary of chemical attacks recall past broken promises', Institute for War and Peace Reporting, 15 March 2008, http://www.kurdishaspect.com/doc031508IWPR.html, last accessed 12 November 2015.

Baar, Monika, *Historians and Nationalism: East-Central Europe in the Nineteenth Century*, Oxford: Oxford University Press, 2010.

Bahcheli, Tozun and Sid Noel, 'The Justice and Development Party and the Kurdish question', in Casier, Maries and Joost Jongerden (eds), *Nationalism and Politics in Turkey: political Islam, Kemalism and the Kurdish issue*, Abingdon: Routledge, 2011, pp.101-20.

Bacik, Gokhan, 'Turkey and Russia's prox war and the Kurds', 21 January 2016, http://www.gmfus.org/publications/turkey-and-russias-proxy-war-and-kurds

Bajalan, Djene and Sara Z. Karimi, 'The Kurds and their history', *Iranian Studies* 47:5 (2014), pp. 679-81.

Bakker, Isabella and Rachel Silvey, *Beyond States and Markets, the Challenge of Social Reproduction*, Abingdon: Routledge, 2008.

Balachandran, Gopalan, *Globalizing Labour? Indian Seafarers and World Shipping, c.1870–1950*, Delhi and Oxford: Oxford University Press, 2012.

Balci, Ali, *'Energized' neighbourliness: relations between Turkey and the Kurdish Regional Government*, Analysis 9, Foundation for Political, Economic and Social Research (SETA), September 2014.

Balibar, Etienne, *The Nation Form*, London: Verso, 2002.

Ball, Howard, *Prosecuting War Crimes and Genocide: The 20th Century Experience*, Lawrence, KA: University Press of Kansas, 1999.

Baratzadeh, Malek Hoseyn, 'Hambastegi-ye nezhâdi-ye Kordhâ bâ Irân va esteqlâl-talabi-ye Kordhâ az Torkiye, Erâq va Suriye' ['The racial connection of the Kurds with Iran and the Kurdish wish of independence from Turkey, Iraq and Syria'], http://www.malekhossein.blogfa.com/post/28

Barber, K., *The Anthropology of Texts, Persons and Publics: Oral and Written Culture in Africa and Beyond*, Cambridge: Cambridge University Press, 2007.

Barewabarayti baduwadachuni tundutiji u dij ba afratan [Directorate to follow up violence against women, DFVAW], 'Barudokhi komalayati afratan la haremi Kurdistan la sali 2009, lagal barawurdkariyak sabarat ba asti tundutikyakan la newan hardu Sali 2008-2009, la 1/1/2009 ta 31/12/2009, Hawler, Slemani, Duhok' ['Report on social situation of women in Kurdistan in 2009, with a comparison with 2008 violence cases, in Erbil, Sulaimani and Duhok'], Erbil, Iraqi Kurdistan: Wazarati nawkho, hikumati haremi, 2009.

Barkey Henri J. and Graham E. Fuller (eds), *Turkey's Kurdish Question,* Lanham, MD: Rowman and Littlefield, 1998.

Barnett, Michael, *Eyewitness to a Genocide: The United Nations and Rwanda*, Ithaca, NY: Cornell University Press, 2002.

Barnett, M., H. Kim, M. O'Donnell, and L. Sitea, L., 'Peacebuilding: What's in a Name?' Global Governance 13:1 (2007).

Bar-Siman-Tov, Yacob, *From Conflict Resolution to Reconciliation*, Oxford: Oxford University Press, 2004.

Barzani, Masoud, 'Ever Closer to Independence', *The Economist*, 19 February 2015, http://www.economist.com/news/international/21644167-iraqs-kurds-are-independent-all-name-they-must-play-their-cards-cleverly-if-they, last accessed 20 June 2015.

Başgöz, I., 'Folklore Studies and Nationalism in Turkey', *Journal of the Folklore Institute* 9:2/3 (1972), pp. 162-76.

Basharati, Faizil, Interview with author, 20 March 2014, Halabja.

Bashkin, Orit, *The Other Iraq: Pluralism, Intellectuals and Culture in Hashemite Iraq, 1921–1958*, Palo Alto, CA: Stanford University Press, 2009.

———*New Babylonians: A History of Jews in Modern Iraq*, Palo Alto, CA: Stanford University Press, 2012.

Batatu, Hanna, *The Old Social Classes and the Revolutionary Movements in Iraq: A Study of Iraq's Old Landed and Commercial Classes and of its Communists, Ba'thists and Free Officers*, Princeton, NJ: Princeton University Press, 1978.

Bauman, R. 'The Philology of the Vernacular', *Journal of Folklore Research* 45:1 (2008), pp. 29-36.

Bauman, R and C. L. Briggs, 'Poetics and Performance as critical perspectives on language and social life', *Annual Review of Anthropology* (1990), pp. 59-88.

——— *Voices of Modernity: Language Ideologies and the Politics of Inequality*, Cambridge: Cambridge University Press, 2003.

Bauman, R. and J. Sherzer, *Explorations in the Ethnography of Speaking*, Cambridge: Cambridge University Press, 1974, 2nd edn 1989.

Bayat, Kaweh, 'Iran and the "Kurdish Question"', *Middle East Report* 247 (2008), pp. 28-35.

Bayır, Derya, *Minorities and Nationalism in Turkish Law*, London: Routledge, 2013.

Bayly, Christopher A., *The Birth of the Modern World 1780–1914: Global Connections and Comparisons*, Oxford: Blackwell, 2004.

BBC News, 'Iraq conflict: Kurds "will not help retake Mosul"', 17 June 2014. http://www.bbc.co.uk/news/world-middle-east-27883997, last accessed 17 October 2015.

BIBLIOGRAPHY

BBC Türkce, 'PKK Türkiye'yle çatışmaları durdurmak için ABD ile gizlice görüşüyor' ['PKK is holding secret talks with the US to end the conflict with Turkey'], http://www.bbc.com/turkce/haberler/2015/08/150816_daily_telegraph_pkk_abd, last accessed 16 November 2015.

Beck, Ulrich, 'The Cosmopolitan Condition: Why Methodological Nationalism Fails', *Theory, Culture and Society* 24:7-8 (2007), pp. 286-90.

———*Cosmopolitanism*, 2007, http://www.ulrichbeck.net-build.net/index.php?page=cosmopolitan, accessed 28 July 2015.

Beck, Ulrich and Elisabeth Beck-Gernsheim, 'Global Generations and the Trap of Methodological Nationalism for a Cosmopolitan Turn in the Sociology of Youth and Generation', *European Sociological Review* 25:1 (2009), pp. 25-36.

Begikhani, Nazand, 'Honour-based violence: the case of Iraqi Kurdistan', in Welchman, L. and S. Hossain (eds), *Honour: Crimes, Paradigms and Violence Against Women*, London: Zed Books, 2005, pp. 209-29.

———'Du'a's murder compared to other honour-related killings', Aso daily paper, Sulaimani: Khandan, 3 May 2007.

Begikhani, Nazand, Aisha Gill and Gill Hague, with Kawther Ibraheem, 'Honour-based Violence (HBV) and Honour-based Killings in Iraqi Kurdistan and in the Kurdish Diaspora in the UK', Erbil: Kurdistan Regional Government (and University of Bristol and University of Roehampton, UK), 2010.

———*Honour-Based Violence: Experiences and Counter-Strategies in Iraqi Kurdistan and the UK Kurdish Diaspora*, London: Ashgate, 2015.

Bell-Fialkoff, Andrew, 'A Brief History of Ethnic Cleansing', *Foreign Affairs* 72 (1993), pp. 110-21.

Bengio, Ofra, *The Kurds of Iraq: Building a State Within a State*, Boulder, CO: Lynne Rienner, 2012.

Berger, Stefan, 'Comparative history', in Berger, Stefan, Heiko Feldner, and Kevin Passmore (eds), *Writing History*, London: Arnold, 2003, pp. 166-8.

———'National historiographies in transnational perspective: Europe in the nineteenth and twentieth centuries', *Storia della Storiografia* 50 (2006), pp. 3-26.

———and Chris Lorenz (eds), *The Contested Nation: Ethnicity, Class, Religion and Gender in National Histories*, New York: Palgrave Macmillan, 2008.

Berndt, Christian, 'Territorialized Key Words and Methodological Nationalism: Cultural Constructions of Institutional Change in Germany', *European Urban and Regional Studies* 10:4 (2003), pp. 283-95.

Besikci, Ismail, *International Colony Kurdistan*, London: Taderon Press, 2004.

Biehl, Janet, 'Bookchin, Öcalan, and the Dialectics of Democracy', in *Challenging Capitalist Modernity: Alternative Concepts and the Kurdish Quest*, 3-5 February 2012, Hamburg.

Bilgin, Fevzo and Ali Sarihan (eds), *Understanding Turkey's Kurdish Question,* Lanham, MD: Lexington Books, 2013.

Bird, Christiane, *A Thousand Sighs, A Thousand Revolts: Journeys in Kurdistan*, New York: Ballantine, 2004.

Birkalan, H., 'Pertev Naili Boratav, Turkish Politics and the University Events', *Turkish Studies Association Bulletin* 25:1 (2001), pp. 39-60.

Bloch, Marc, *Apologie pour l'histoire ou métier d'historien*, Paris: Armand Colin, 1949.

Bloxham, Donald, *The Great Game of Genocide: Imperialism, Nationalism and the Destruction of the Ottoman Armenians*, Oxford: Oxford University Press, 2005.

Bois, Thomas, *Connaissance des Kurdes*, Beirut: Khayats, 1965.

Bookchin, Murray, 'The Meaning of Confederalism', *Green Perspectives* 20 (1990).

––––––– 'Libertarian Municipalism: An Overview', *Green Perspectives* 24 (1991).

––––––– *The Next Revolution: Popular Assemblies and the Promise of Direct Democracy*, London: Verso, 2014.

Borroz, Nicholas, 'Turkey's energy strategy: Kurdistan over Iraq', *Turkish Policy Quarterly* 13:2 (2014), pp. 103-10.

Bourdieu, Pierre, *Outline of a Theory of Practice*, Cambridge: Cambridge University Press, 1977.

––––––– 'Rethinking the State: Genesis and Structure of the Bureaucratic Field', *Sociological Theory* 12:1 (1990), pp. 1-18.

Bouzhmehrani, Hassan and Mehdi Pour-Eslami, 'Tahdidhâ-ye narm-e khodmokhtâri-ye eqlim-e Kordestân-e 'Erâq va ta'sir-e ân bar Kordhâ-ye Irân' ['The soft threats of Kurdistan in Iraq and its impact on the Kurds of Iran'], *Jâme-shenâsi-ye Jehân-e Eslâm* 2:1 (2014), pp. 87-110.

Boyer, Dave, 'Forget what he said in 2006: Joe Biden speaks out for a unified Iraq', *Washington Times*, 9 April 2015, http://www.washingtontimes.com/news/2015/apr/9/joe-bidens-iraq-unity-speech-contradicts-2006-supp/?page=all, last accessed 20 June 2015.

Boyle, Matthew, 'Exclusive — Rand Paul: Arm the Kurds to Battle ISIS and Radical Islam, Give Them Kurdistan', Breitbart, 10 March 2015, http://www.breitbart.com/big-government/2015/03/10/exclusive-rand-paul-arm-the-kurds-to-battle-isis-and-radical-islam-give-them-kurdistan/, last accessed 19 April 2015.

Bozarslan, Hamit, *La question kurde. Etats et minorités au Moyen-Orient*, Paris: Presses de Sciences Po, 1997.

––––––– 'Research Guide: Kurdish Studies', *Middle East Review of International Affairs* 4:2 (2000), https://groups.google.com/forum/#!topic/cl.nahost.kurdistan/JTFgi-PaMPpg

––––––– 'Quelques remarques sur le discours historiographique kurde en Turquie: 1919–

1980', *Asien, Afrika, Lateinamerika* 29 (2001), pp. 47-71.

——— 'Some Remarks on Kurdish Historiographical Discourse in Turkey, 1919–1980', in Vali, Abbas (ed.), *Essays on the Origins of Kurdish Nationalism*, Costa Mesa, CA: Mazda, 2003, pp. 14-39.

——— *Violence in the Middle East,* Princeton, NJ: Markus Wiener Publishers, 2004.

——— 'The Kurds and Middle Eastern "State of Violence": The 1980s and 2010s', *Kurdish Studies* 2:1 (2014), pp. 48-91.

Bozarslan, H. and C. Scalbert-Yucel (eds), *Joyce Blau: l'éternelle chez les Kurdes*, Paris: Karthala, 2013.

Bozarslan, Mahmut, 'What caused the clashes in Diyarbakir?', *Al-Monitor*, 15 June 2015, http://www.al-monitor.com/pulse/originals/2015/06/turkey-diyarbakir-remains-tense-after-clashes-between-kurds.html?utm_source=Al-Monitor+Newsletter+%5BEnglish%5D&utm_campaign=26b00ca343-June_16_2015&utm_medium=email&utm_term=0_28264b27a0-26b00ca343-102324909

Bozkurt, D., O. L.Sen, S. Hagemann, 'Projected river discharge in the Euphrates-Tigris Basin from a hydrological discharge model forced with RCM and GCM outputs,' *Climate Research* 62 (2015), pp. 131-47.

Brifcani, Mostafa, *Barzani: The Leader of the Kurdish National Movement*, Egypt: Al-Aharam Press, 1996.

Bruinessen, Martin van, 'Kurdish society, ethnicity, nationalism and refugee problems', in Kreyenbroek, Philip G. and Stefan Sperl (eds), *The Kurds: A Contemporary Overview*, Abingdon: Routledge, 1992.

Buchta, Wilfried, 'The Failed Pan-Islamic Program of the Islamic Republic: Views of the Liberal Reformers of the Religioius Semi-Opposition', in Keddie, Nikki R. and Rudi Matthee, *Iran and the Surrounding World: Interaction in Culture and Cultural Politics*, Seattle: University of Washington Press, 2003, pp. 281-304.

——— 'Tehran's Ecumenical Society (*majma' al-taqrib*): a Veritable Ecumenical Revival or a Trojan Horse of Iran', in Brunner, Rainer and Werner Ende, *The Twelver Shia in Modern Times. Religious Culture & Political History*, Leiden: Brill, 2001, pp. 333-53.

Bulloch, John, Morris, Henry, *No Friends But the Mountains: The Tragic History of the Kurds*, London: Penguin, 1991.

Bultan, 'Enqelâb-e Eslâmi va royâhâ-ye fântezi-e goruhakhâ-ye zedd-e enqelâb' [The Islamic Revolution facing the fantasies of counter-revolutionary groups], 18 February 2013.

Burkay, Kemal, *Anılar. Belgeler*, Vols 1 and 2, Stockholm: Roja Nû, 2001, 2009.

Burkhalter, Holly J., 'The Question of Genocide: The Clinton Administration and Rwanda', *World Policy Journal* (Winter 1994-5), pp. 44-54.

BIBLIOGRAPHY

Çaçanî, Karliyn, *The Culture of the Kurds from the View Point of Armenian Writers*, Yerevan: Institute of Oriental Studies (in Armenian), 2004.

Çakir, A., 'The Representation of the *Dengbêj* Tradition in Kurdish Contemporary Popular Discourse', MA thesis, University of Exeter, 2011.

Çakır, Ruşen, interview with Cemil Bayık, http://www.rusencakir.com/Cemil-Bayik-ile-soylesi--Tam-metin/2439, last accessed 24 September 2015.

Cameron David, 'Making Federalism Work', in Bouillon, Markus, David Malone, and Ben Roswell (eds), *Iraq: Preventing a New Generation of Conflict*, Boulder, CO: Lynne Rienner, 2007.

Candar, Cengiz, 'The Kurdish question: the reasons and fortunes of the "opening"', *Insight Turkey* 11:4 (2009), pp. 13-19.

———'Turkey claims Iran providing logistical support for PKK', *Al-Monitor,* 30 December 2012, www.al-monitor.com/pulse/originals/2012/al-monitor/iran-turkey-shiite-sunni-pkk.html

Carnegie Middle East Center, 'The Kurdish National Council in Syria', 15 February 2012, www.carnegie-mec.org/publications/?fa=48502

Caryl, C., 'Want to Hurt the Islamic State? Here's How,' *Foreign Policy,* 6 February 2015.

Casier, Marlies, 'Designated Terrorists: The Kurdistan Workers' Party and its Struggle to (Re)Gain Political Legitimacy', *Mediterranean Politics* 15:3 (2010), pp. 393-413.

Casier, Marlies and Joost Jongerden (eds), *Nationalism and Politics in Turkey: Political Islam, Kemalism and the Kurdish Issue*, Abingdon: Routledge, 2011.

Celîl, Cemîla, *Kilam û Miqamêd Cimeta Kurda* (Kurdish Maqam and Folk Music), Stockholm: ROJA NU publications, 1982.

———'Kurdish Folk Songs of the Yerevan Region', trans. from Russian into Kurdish Soranî by Izedin Mistefa Resul, Sulaymany, Iraq: Publications of Kurdish Heritage Institute of the Ministry of Culture, 2004.

Celîl, Ordixan, *Zargotina K'urda*, Moscow: Naûka publications, 1978.

———*Rêdaksîya sereke ya edebîyata rohilatê*, Moscow: Department of Eastern Literature, 1978.

Celil, O and Celil, C. *Zargotina K'urda/Kurdskij Folklor*, Moscow: Nauk, 1978.

Cemil Pasha, Ekrem, *Muhtasar Hayatım*, Brussels: Institut kurde de Bruxelles, 1991.

Ceren, Belge, 'State Building and the Limits of Legibility: Kinship Networks and Kurdish Resistance in Turkey,' *International Journal of Middle East Studies* 43:1 (2011), pp. 95-114.

Cewarî, Nûra, 'Sazbendiya kurdên Ermenistanê' [Music of the Armenian Kurds], *NÛDEM* 31 (1999), pp. 49-55 (collected articles written in Kurdish Kûrmancî).

Chakrabarty, Dipesh, *Provincializing Europe: Postcolonial and Historical Difference*, Princeton, NJ: Princeton University Press, 2000.

BIBLIOGRAPHY

Chalk, Frank, 'Genocide in the Twentieth Century: Definitions of Genocide and their Implications for Prediction and Prevention', *Holocaust and Genocide Studies* 4:2 (1989), pp. 149-60.

Chalk, Frank and Kurt Jonassohn (eds), *The History and Sociology of Genocide: Analyses and Case Studies*, New Haven, CT: Yale University Press, 1990.

Chant, Sylvia and Caroline Sweetman, 'Fixing women or fixing the world? 'Smart economics', efficiency approaches, and gender equality in development', *Gender and Development* 20:3 (2012), pp. 517-29.

Charountaki, Marianna, *The Kurds and US Foreign Policy: International Relations in the Middle East since 1945*, Oxford: Routledge, 2011.

Charbel, G., 'Barzani: The region's new borders will be drawn in blood', *Al-Monitor*, 15 February 2015.

Chatterjee, Partha, *The Present History of West Bengal,* New Delhi: Oxford University Press, 1997.

Charny, Israel W., *How Can We Commit the Unthinkable? Genocide: The Human Cancer*, Boulder, CO: Westview Press, 1982.

———— (ed.) *Towards the Understanding and Prevention of Genocide*, Boulder, CO: Westview Press, 1984.

Chirot, Daniel and McCauley, Clark, *Why Not Kill Them All? The Logic of Mass Political Murder*, Princeton, NJ: Princeton University Press, 2006.

Chulov, M. and F. Hawramy, 'Fears grow in Baghdad that US is abandoning the city to its fate', *The Guardian*, 17 August 2014.

———— 'Iraqi Kurds strengthen their positions while Isis advances on Baghdad.' *The Guardian*, 26 June 2014.

CIA, *The Pike Report*, Nottingham: Spokesman Books, 1977.

Çicek, Cuma, 'Ulus, din, Sinif: Türkiyede Kürt Mutabakatinin Insasi,' *Iletisim* (2015).

Ciment, James, *The Kurds, State and Minority in Turkey, Iraq and Iran*, New York: Facts on File, 1996.

Cizre, Umit, 'The emergence of the government's perspective on the Kurdish issue', *Insight Turkey* 11:4 (2009), pp. 1-12.

Clastres, Pierre, *Society against the State, Essays in Political Anthropology*, New York: Zone Books, 1989.

Clements, W. M. (ed.), *The Greenwood Encyclopaedia of Folklore and Folklife*, Vol. 2, Westport and London: Greenwood Press, 2006.

Complete University Guide, 'Studying in Norway', 2016, http://www.thecompleteuniversityguide.co.uk/international/europe/norway/, last accessed 13 January 2016.

Constitution of the Republic of Turkey, https://global.tbmm.gov.tr/docs/constitution_en.pdf

Convention on the Elimination of All Forms of Discrimination Against Women, 1979, Article 10.

Cooper, H. and M. R.Gordon, 'Iraqi Kurds Expand Autonomy as ISIS Reorders the Landscape', *New York Times*, 29 August 2014.

Couch, Christopher M., 'Aghas, Sheiks, and Daesh in Iraq: Kurdish robust action in turmoil,' MA thesis, Naval Postgraduate School, 2016.

Dadrian, Vahakn N., 'A Typology of Genocide', *International Review of Modern Sociology* 5 (1975), pp. 201-12.

Dallaire, Raphaël, *Fief montagnard, régence humanitaire: L'endiguement des déplacés internes kurdes dans le 'havre de sécurité' du Nord de l'Irak, 1991–1992*, Global Migration Research Paper 10 (2015).

Daloglu, Tulin, 'Erdoğan's many positions on the Kurdish issue', *Al-Monitor*, 23 April 2013, http://www.al-monitor.com/pulse/originals/2013/04/erdogan-kurdish-issue-flip-flop-turkey-peace.html

Danilovic, Alex, *Iraqi Federalism and the Kurds*, London: Ashgate, 2014.

Davis, E., *Memories of State: Politics, History and Collective Identity in Modern Iraq*, Berkeley, CA: University of California Press, 2005.

Dawisha, A., *Iraq: A Political History from Independence to Occupation*, Princeton, NJ: Princeton University Press, 2009.

Demirtas, Serkan, 'Syria supporting PKK, says intelligence report', *Hurriyet Daily News*, 23 March 2012, www.hurriyetdailynews.com/report-syria-supporting-pkk.aspx?pageID=238&nid=16699

Denge Nwê/Spi Organization for the Gassed Areas, 'Halabja Survey Results - Final', 6 March 2013.

Dersimi, Nuri, *Dersim ve Kürt Milli Mücadelesine: Dair Hatıratım*, Ankara: Öz-Ge, 1992.

———*Kürdistan tarihinde Dersim*, Cologne: Mezopotamien Verlag, 1999.

DHRD Monthly Report, 16 October 2006.

Ditz, J., 'Kurds Boycott Cabinet After Maliki Blocks Cargo Flights', Anti-war.com, 10 July 2014.

Doğruhaber Gazetesi, 'PKK ve PYD'ye tepkiler sürüyor' ['Reactions to PKK and PYD continues'], http://www.dogruhaber.com.tr/mobil/Haber.php?id=130433, last accessed 25 September 2015.

Dorson, R., *The British Folklorists: A History*, Abingdon: Routledge, 1968.

Dryaz, Massoud Sharifi, 'De la résistance microscopique à l'action collective organisée: engagement et désengagement des militants dans l'espace kurde,' PhD thesis, L'École des hautes études en sciences sociales, Paris, 2015.

Dudoignon, Stéphane A., 'Inter-Confessional Relations in Iran: Conflicts and Transfers in the Aftermath of 9/11', in Chehabi, Houshang E., Farhad Khosrokhavar, and

Clement Therme,(eds), *Iran and the Challenges of the Twenty-First Century. Essays in Honour of Mohammad-Reza Djalili,* Costa Mesa, CA: Mazda, 2013, pp. 96-110.

Dundes, A., *Interpreting Folklore.* Bloomington, IN: Indiana University Press, 1980.

Dustin, Moira, 'Gender Equality, Cultural Diversity: European Comparisons and Lessons', London: London School of Economics, Gender Institute and the Nuffield Foundation, 2006.

Eagleton, Terry, *Ideology an Introduction,* London: Verso, 1991.

Eagleton, William, *The Kurdish Republic of 1946,* London: Oxford University Press, 1963.

Eccarius-Kelly, Vera, 'Political movements and leverage points: Kurdish activism in the European diaspora', *Journal of Muslim Minority Affairs* 22:1 (2002), pp. 91-118.

The Economist, 'Turkey and the Kurds: Ethnic Cleansing', *The Economist,* 17 December 1994, pp. 52-3.

Edmonds, Cecil J., *Kurds, Turks and Arabs: Politics, Travel and Research in North-Eastern Iraq, 1919–1925,* London: Oxford University Press, 1957.

Eidson, John, 'Which Past for Whom? Local Memory in a German Community during the Era of Nation Building', *Ethos* 28:4 (2000), pp. 575-607.

———'Between Heritage and Countermemory: Varieties of Historical Representation in a West German Community', *American Ethnologist* 32:4 (2005), pp. 556-75.

Eifler, Christine and Ruth Seifert, *Gender Dynamics and Post-Conflict Reconstruction,* Frankfurt am Main: Peter Lang GmbH, 2009.

Ekici, D., 'Imagination: The Making of Kurdish National Identity in the Kurdish Journalistic Discourse (1898-1914)', PhD thesis, University of Exeter, 2015.

E-Kurd.net, 'Article 140 of Iraqi constitution completed for us and will not talk about it anymore', 27 June 2014.

———'Iraqi parliamentary education committee reveals fake universities in Kurdistan', Ekurd.net, 2015, http://ekurd.net/education-committee-reveals-fake-universities-in-kurdistan-2015-07-11, last accessed 10 October 2016.

———'Universities in Iraqi Kurdistan warn education could be suspended over late salaries', Ekurd.net, 2016, http://ekurd.net/universities-kurdistan-salaries-2016-09-07, last accessed 10 October 2016.

Eleftheriotis, Dimitris, *Cinematic Journeys: Film and Movement,* Edinburgh: Edinburgh University Press, 2010.

Entekhab 'Akkâs-e Zan-e Irâni dar pâdgân-e zanân-e Kord' [Iranian female photographer in the camp of Kurdish women], Entekhab, 5 May 2015.

Ercan, Harun, 'Dynamics of Mobilisation and Radicalization of the Kurdish Movement in the 1970s in Turkey,' MA thesis, Koç University, Comparative Studies in History and Society, 2010.

BIBLIOGRAPHY

Eşo, Wezîrê, 'Diroka Kurdê Sovyeta Kevin' [Kurdish History in the Former Soviet Union), *NÛDEM* 31 (1999), pp. 6-31 (collected articles written in Kurdish Kûrmancî).

——— ['If we write in the language of our enemies, we will destroy our nation'], interview in Erbil, Iraq, *Kowar Magazine* 6 (2006) (in Kurdish Soranî), pp. 32-7.

Ersanli, Busra, Gunay Goksu Ozdogan, and Nesrin Ucarlar (eds), *Türkiye Siyasetinde Kürtler: Direniş, Hak Arayışı, Katılım* 3rd edn, Istanbul: Iletisim Yayinlari, 2016.

Evrensel, 'Yüksekdağ: Rojava sınırında tank değil barış sesleri yükselmeli' ['Yüksekdağ: We should hear the sound of peace not tanks at the Rojava border'], http://www.evrensel.net/haber/256318/yuksekdag-rojava-sinirinda-tank-degil-baris-sesleri-yukselmeli, last accessed 16 November 2015.

Erkus, Sevil, 'Erdoğan vows to prevent Kurdish state in northern Syria, as Iran warns Turkey', *Hurriyet Daily News*, 27 June 2015, http://www.hurriyetdailynews.com/erdogan-vows-to-prevent-kurdish-state-in-northern-syria-as-iran-warns-turkey.aspx?pageID=238&nID=84630&NewsCatID=338

Fahim, K., 'Islamic Militants Surprise Kurds in Iraq, Killing a Commander in a Day of Attacks', *New York Times*, 30 January 2015.

Fanon, Franz, *The Wretched of the Earth*, New York: Grove Press, 1963, pp. 206-48.

Faraj, Shaho Homa and Ariwan Salah and Ardalan Kakayih, collective interview with author, 18 March 2014, Halabja.

Farouk-Sluglett, M. and P. Sluglett, *Iraq Since 1958: From Revolution to Dictatorship*, London: I. B. Tauris, 2003 [1987].

Fassin, D. and R. Rechtman, *The Empire of Trauma: An Inquiry into the Condition of Victimhood*, trans. R. Gomme, Princeton, NJ: Princeton University Press, 2009.

Field, Henry, *The Anthropology of Iraq: Kurdistan*, Chicago: Field Museum of Natural History, 1951.

Filkins, D., 'The Fight of Their Lives', *New Yorker,* 29 September 2014. http://www.newyorker.com/magazine/2014/09/29/fight-lives

Fischer-Tahir, Andrea, *Brave Men, Pretty Women? Gender and Symbolic Violence in Iraqi Kurdish Urban Society*, Berlin: Europäisches Zentrum für Kurdische Studien, 2009.

——— 'Searching for Sense: The Concept of Genocide as Part of Knowledge Production in Iraqi Kurdistan', in Tejel, Jordi, Peter Sluglett, Riccardo Bocco, and Hamit Bozarslan (eds), *Writing the Modern History of Iraq. Historiographical and Political Challenges*, Singapore: World Scientific, 2012, pp. 227-43.

Fitzgerald, David and Roger Waldinger, 'Transnationalism in question', *American Journal of Sociology* 109:5 (2004), pp. 1177-95.

Foreign Affairs Committee Press Release, 'Chairman Royce, Ranking Membe Engel Introduce Legislation to Authorize the Supply of Weapons Directly to Kurdish "Peshmerga"', 26 March 2015, http://foreignaffairs.house.gov/press-release/chairman-royce-ranking-member-engel-introduce-legislation-authorize-supply-weapons, last accessed 17 June 2015.

Forest, Benjamin and Juliet Johnson, 'Unraveling the Threads of History: Soviet-Era Monuments and Post-Soviet National Identity in Moscow', *Annals of the Association of American Geographers* 92 (2002), pp. 524-47.

Fountain, S., 'Peace education in UNICEF', Working paper, Education Section Program Division, New York: UNICEF, 1999.

Fourth Geneva Convention, 1949, http://www.icrc.org

Fozi, Navid, 'Neo-Iranian Nationalism: Pre-Islamic Grandeur and Shiiite Eschatology in President Mahmoud Ahmadinejad's Rhetoric', *Middle East Journal* 70:2 (2016), pp. 227-48.

Fragner, Bert, *Die Persophonie, Regionalität, Identität und Sprachkontakt in der Geschichte Asiens*, 5 ANOR, Berlin, 1999.

Frazer, M., 'Iraqi Kurdistan youth struggle despite economic growth', Press TV, 2011, http://www.presstv.com/detail/182589.html

Frenkel, S., 'Kurdish Forces Seek More U.S. Help in Fight Against ISIS', Buzzfeed, 26 August 2014.

Friedman, Thomas, 'Obama on the World: President Obama Talks to Thomas L. Friedman about Iraq, Putin and Israel', *New York Times*, 9 August 2014, http://www.nytimes.com/2014/08/09/opinion/president-obama-thomas-l-friedman-iraq-and-world-affairs.html, last accessed 25 October 2015.

Fuccaro, Nelida, *The Other Kurds: Yazidis in Colonial Iraq*, London and New York: I. B. Tauris, 1999.

——— 'Ethnicity and the City: the Kurdish Quarter of Damascus between Ottoman and French Rule, c.1724–1946', *Urban History* 30:2 (2003), pp. 206-24.

——— 'Minorities and Ethnic Mobilisation: The Kurds in Northern Iraq and Syria', in Meouchy, N. and P. Sluggett (eds), *The British and French Mandates in Comparative Perspectives,* Leiden: Brill, 2004, pp. 579-95.

Galbraith, Peter, *The End of Iraq: How America Created a War without End*, London: Simon & Schuster, 2007.

Gharibi, Mamosta Rahman, 'Kordestân forsathâ va tahdidhâ-ye farâvari-ye vahdat-e eslâmi' [Kurdistan: wider chances and threats for Islamic unity], *Okhovvat* 4:13 (2011), pp. 106-32.

Ghassemlou, Abdul Rahman, *Kurdistan and the Kurds*, Prague: Czechoslovak Academy of Sciences, 1965.

Gill, Aisha, 'Patriarchal violence in the name of 'honour'', *International Journal of Criminal Justice Sciences* 1:1 (2003), pp. 1-12.

——— 'Reconfiguring 'honour'-based violence as a form of gendered violence', in Idriss, M.

and T. Abbas (eds), *Honour, Violence, Women and Islam*, Abingdon: Routledge, 2010, pp. 218-32.

Gordon, Michael R., 'Failed Efforts and Challenges of America's Last Months in Iraq', *New York Times*, 23 September 2012.

Goudsouzian, T. and L. Fatah, 'Fall of Mosul: What's at Stake for the Kurds?' Al-Jazeera, 12 June 2014.

Government of Iraq, Ministry of Planning, 'National Plan 2013-2017', http://www.mop.gov.iq/mop/resources/IT/pdf/456.pdf

Guest, John S., 'Yezīdīs', in Bowker, John (ed.), *The Oxford Dictionary of World Religions*, Oxford: Oxford University Press, 2002.

Guha, Ranajit, *Elementary Aspects of Peasant Insurgency in Colonial India*, New Delhi: Oxford University Press, 1983.

Guillory, Sean, 'Culture Clash in the Socialist Paradise: Soviet Patronage and African Students' Urbanity in the Soviet Union, 1960–1965', *Diplomatic History* 28:2 (2014), pp. 271-81.

Gündoğan, Azat Zana, 'The Kurdish Political Mobilisation in the 1960s: The Case of the 'Eastern Meetings', MA thesis, Middle East Technical University, 2005.

Güneş, Cengiz, *The Kurdish National Movement in Turkey: From Protest to Resistance*, Abingdon: Routledge, 2012.

——— 'Explaining the PKK's Mobilization of the Kurds in Turkey: Hegemony, Myth and Violence', *Ethnopolitics* 12:3 (2013), pp.247-67.

Gunter, Michael, *The Kurds of Iraq, Tragedy and Hope*, London: Macmillan, 1992.

——— *The Kurdish Predicament in Iraq, A Political Analysis*, London: Macmillan, 1999.

——— 'The Kurdish Spring', *Third World Quarterly* 34:3 (2013), pp. 441-57.

——— 'The Turkish-Kurdish peace process stalled in neutral', *Insight Turkey* 16:1 (2014), pp. 19-26.

——— *Out of Nowhere: The Kurds of Syria in Peace and War*, London: Hurst, 2013.

Gürbüz, Mustafa, *Rival Kurdish Movements in Turkey: Transforming Ethnic Conflict*, Amsterdam: Amsterdam University Press, 2016.

Haass, Richard N., 'The Irony of American Strategy: Putting the Middle East in Proper Perspective', *Foreign Affairs* 92:3 (2013), p. 59.

Hacador, S., 'The Big Success of Women Entrepreneurs is a Kurdish Princess', *Kurdistan Tribune*, 2011, http://kurdistantribune.com/2011/big-success-of-women-entrepreneurs-kurdish-princess/, last accessed 14 March 2014.

Hadi, Mohammad: 'Rahbarân-e Kord-e 'Erâq va estefâdeh az kârt-e Akrâd-e hamsâyeh, bakhsh-e nakhost: Mas'ud Bârezâni' [,The Kurdish leaders of Iraq and their utilization of neighboring Kurds, Part 1, Mas'ud Barzani'], *Bâztâb*, 20 November 2006.

BIBLIOGRAPHY

Haider, Dlawar, Interview with author, 17 March 2014, Halabja.

Hakakian, Roya, *Assassins of the Turquoise Palace*, New York: Grove Press, 2011.

Hakan Özoğlu, M., *Kurdish Notables and the Ottoman State: Evolving Identities, Competing Loyalties, and Shifting Boundaries*, Albany, NY: State University of New York Press, 2004.

Hamelink, W., 'The Sung Home: Narrative, morality and the Kurdish Nation', PhD thesis, University of Leiden, 2014.

Hammack, Phillip L. and Pilecki, Andrew, 'Narrative as Root Metaphor for Political Psychology', *Political Psychology* 33:1 (2012), pp. 75-103.

Hanna, Abdallah, *Al-qadiyya al-zira'iyya wa-l-harakat al-fallahiyya fi Suriyya wa-Lubnan, 1820–1920*, Vols 1 and 2, Beirut: Al-Farabi, 1975/8.

——— 'The attitudes of the Syrian Communist Party and the Arab Socialist Party towards the peasant movement in Syria in the 1950s', in Khoury, Gérard D. and Nadine Méouchy (eds), *Etats et sociétés en quête d'avenir (1945–2005): Dynamiques et enjeux*, Paris: Geuthner, 2007, pp. 327-36.

Harding, Luke, 'Revisiting Kurdistan: 'If there is a success story in Iraq, it's here', *The Guardian*, 16 July 2014, http://www.theguardian.com/world/2014/jul/16/arrived-in-kurdistan-with-chemical-weapon-suit-iraq-saddam-hussein, last accessed 17 May 2015.

Harris, I., 'A Select Bibliography for Peace Education', *Peace and Change* 34 (2009) pp. 571-6, doi: 10.1111/j.1468-0130.2009.00601.x

——— 'Conceptual underpinnings of peace education', in Salomon, G. and B. Nevo (eds), *Peace Education: The Concept, Principles, and Practices Around the World*, New York: Lawrence Erlbaum, 2012, pp. 15-26.

Hartog, François, 'Le témoin et l'historien', *Gradhiva* 27 (2000), pp. 1-14.

Hartwig, Elisabeth, *Rural African Women as Subjects of Social and Political Change, A Case Study of Women in Northwestern Cameroon*, Münster: LIT Verlag, 2005.

Hasan, Arfam *The Kurds: A Historical and Political Study*, London: Oxford University Press, 1966.

Hassanpour, A., *Nationalism and Language in Kurdistan, 1918-1985*, San Francisco, CA: Mellen Research University Press, 1992.

Hawler Medical University, 'Vision and Mission', http://hmu.edu.iq/About/VisionandMission.aspx, last accessed 14 March 2014.

Hawramy, F., 'Kurdish Sinjar offensive too late for some Yazidis', *Al-Monitor*, 26 December 2014.

Hedinger, Sandra, *Frauen über Kried und Frieden*, Frankfurt am Main: Campus, 2000.

Helgren, Jennifer and Colleen A. Vasconcellos (eds), *Girlhood: A Global History*, New Brunswick, NJ: Rutgers University Press, 2010.

BIBLIOGRAPHY

Heyd, U., *Foundations of Turkish Nationalism: The Life and Teachings of Ziya Gökalp*, London: Luzac and Harvill Press, 1950.

Hiltermann, Joost R., 'The 1988 Anfal Campaign in Iraqi Kurdistan', 2008, http://www.massviolence.org/IMG/article_PDF/The-1988-Anfal-Campaign-in-Iraqi-Kurdistan.pdf, last accessed 12 November 2015.

——— *A Poisonous Affair: America, Iraq, and the Gassing of Halabja*, Cambridge: Cambridge University Press, 2007.

Hirurî, Selah, ['A Number of Historical Songs in Kurdish History'], Duhok, Kurdistan: Sipirez Publications, 2004.

Hirsch, Herbet, *Genocide and the Politics of Memory, Studying Death to Preserve Life*, Chapel Hill, NC: University of North Carolina Press, 1995.

Hirschon, Renee (ed.), *Crossing the Aegean: An Appraisal of the 1923 Compulsory Population Exchange Between Greece and Turkey*, Oxford: Berghahn, 2003.

Hlavaty, K., 'With eye on Mosul, coalition advisers train Peshmerga', *Al-Monitor*, 27 February 2015.

Hobsbawn, E. J., *Nations and Nationalism Since 1780*, Cambridge: Cambridge University Press, 1991.

Hofmeyr, Isabel, 'AHR Conversations: On Transnational History', *American Historical Review* 111: 5 (2006), pp. 1444-64.

Hopkins, Anthony G. (ed.), *Globalization in World History*, New York: Norton, 2002.

——— *Global History. Interactions between the Local and the Universal*, New York: Palgrave, 2006.

Hornik, Richard, 'With A Little Help from Friends', *The Times*, 11 June 1990, p. 34.

Horowitz, Irving Louis, 'Genocide and the Reconstruction of Social Theory: Observations on the Exclusivity of Collective Death', *Armenian Review* 37 (1984), pp. 1-21.

——— *Taking Lives: Genocide and State Power*, Piscataway, NJ: Transaction Publishers, 1997.

Hossino, Omar and Ilhan Tanir, 'The Decisive Minority: The Critical Role of Syria's Kurds in the Anti-Assad Revolution', Henry Jackson Society, USA, March 2012, http://henryjacksonsociety.org/wp-content/uploads/2012/03/The-Decisive-Minority.pdf, last accessed 25 November 2015.

Hourcade, Bernard, 'Le recomposition des identités et des territoires en Iran islamique', *Annales de Géographie*, 113ᵉ Année, 638/639, pp. 511-30.

——— http://www.irancarto.cnrs.fr

Hovannisian, R. G. (ed.), *Genocide in Perspective*, Piscataway, NJ: Transaction Publishers, 1993.

Human Rights Watch, 'Genocide in Iraq: The Anfal Campaign Against the Kurds', 1993.

Human Rights Watch, 'Judging Dujail: The First Trial before the Iraqi High Tribunal', 18:9 (1999).

Human Rights Watch, 'Ansar al-Islam in Iraqi Kurdistan', 5 February 2003, https://www.hrw.org/report/2003/02/05/ansar-al-islam-iraqi-kurdistan

Human Rights Watch, 'Iraq: State of the Evidence', 2004.

Human Rights Watch, 'Under Kurdish Rule: Abuses in PYD-run Enclaves of Syria', 2014, http://www.hrw.org/sites/default/files/reports/syria0614_kurds_ForUpload.pdf

Human Rights Watch, *World Report 2015: Events of 2014*, Bristol: Policy Press, 2015.

Hürriyet, 'Bayık Independent'e konuştu' ['Bayık spoke to the *Independent'*], http://www.hurriyet.com.tr/dunya/27561606.asp

Hürriyet, 'Figen Yüksekdağ: Sırtımızı YPJ'ye YPG'ye ve PYD'ye yaslıyoruz' ['We lean on YPJ, YPG and PYD'], http://www.hurriyet.com.tr/sondakika/29587681.asp, last accessed 16 November 2015.

Hürriyet, 'Figen Yüksekdağ: Sırtımızı YPJ'ye YPG'ye ve PYD'ye yaslıyoruz' ['We lean on YPJ, YPG and PYD'], http://www.hurriyet.com.tr/sondakika/29587681.asp

Hutchinson, J. and A. D. Smith (eds), *Nationalism: A Reader*, Oxford: Oxford University Press, 1994.

ICC, 'Rome Statute of the International Criminal Court', 1998, http://www.icc-cpi.int/nr/rdonlyres/ea9aeff7-5752-4f84-be94-0a655eb30e16/0/rome_statute_english.pdf

———— Statute, 2000, www.http://www.icc-cpi

———— 'Elements of Crimes', 2011, http://www.refworld.org/docid/4ff5dd7d2.html

ICJ, Annual Report, 1998, 'Application of the Convention on the Prevention and Punishment of the Crime of Genocide 15 (Bosnia and Herzegovina v. Yugoslavia).'

ICTR, International Criminal Tribunal for Rwanda, http://www.unictr.org/

ICTY, 'Statute of the International Criminal Tribunal for the Former Yugoslavia', 2009, http://www.icty.org/sections/LegalLibrary/StatuteoftheTribunal

Idriss, Mohammad and Tahir Abbas (eds), *Honour, Violence, Women and Islam*, Abingdon: Routledge, 2010.

Ihsan, Mohammed, *Kurdistan and War Dilemma,* London: Dar Al Hikma, 2000.

————Interviewed by Rudaw TV, 16 June 2014, https://www.youtube.com/watch?v=VK9BJ_njckQ

———— *Nation Building in Kurdistan: Memory, Genocide and Human Rights*, London: Routledge, 2016.

IHT, 'Statute of the Iraqi Special Tribunal', 2003, http://www.ibanet.org/Committees/WCC_IHT.aspx

Illuminate Consulting Group, 'UK Higher Education Engagement With Iraq', Research Series/4, UK Higher Education International Unit, 2009.

BIBLIOGRAPHY

INEE, *Peace Education Handbook*, 2008, www.inee.com/peaceeducation, accessed 10 September 2013.

Institute for International Law and Human Rights, 'Iraq's Minorities and Other Vulnerable Groups: Legal Framework, Documentation and Human Rights', Baghdad: Institute for International Law and Human Rights, 2013.

International Covenant on Economic, Social and Cultural Rights 1966, Article 13 (1).

International Crisis Group (ICG), 'Turkey: The PKK and a Kurdish Settlement', Europe Report 219, (2012).

———'Syria's Kurds: A Struggle Within a Struggle', Middle East Report 136 (2013).

——— 'Flight of Icarus?', Middle East Report 151 (2014), https://www.crisisgroup.org/middle-east-north-africa/eastern-mediterranean/syria/flight-icarus-pyd-s-precarious-rise-syria

——— 'Turkey and the PKK: Saving the Peace Process', Europe Report 234 (2014), https://www.crisisgroup.org/europe-central-asia/western-europemediterranean/turkey/turkey-and-pkk-saving-peace-process

———'Arming Iraq's Kurds: Fighting IS, Inviting Conflict', Middle East Report 158 (2015).

Internethaber, 'Kobanî son dakika! Murat Karayılan: PYD ilerliyor' [Kobanî last minute! Murat Karayilan: PYD moving forward], http://www.internethaber.com/kobani-son-dakika-murat-karayilan-pyd-ilerliyor-741555h.htm, last accessed 16 November 2015.

Invest in Group, 'Overview: Kurdistan Region of Iraq, Human Capital', http://www.investingroup.org/publications/kurdistan/overview/human-capital/, last accessed 8 December 2014.

———'Kurdistan Region – Review', http://www.investingroup.org/review/178/ (no date), website visited 26 April 2015.

Iranian Human Rights Documentation Center, 'Murder at Mykonos: Anatomy of A Political Assassination', New Haven, CT: Iranian Human Rights Documentation Center, 2007, http://www.iranhrdc.org/english/publications/reports/3150-murder-at-mykonos-anatomy-of-a-political-assassination.html

IRINN, 'Hich Kas Haqq Nadârad Tabyiz-e beyn-e mazâheb va aqvâm qâel bâshad' [Nobody has the right to discriminate among the confessions and ethnic groups], IRINN, 31 May 2016, w.irinn.ir/news/print/161998/

Isakhan, B., *Democracy in Iraq: History, Politics, Discourse*, London: Ashgate, 2012.

——— 'The Iraq Legacies and the Roots of the "Islamic State"', in Isakhan, B., (ed.), *The Legacy of Iraq: From the 2003 War to the 'Islamic State'*, Edinburgh: Edinburgh University Press, 2015, pp. 223-35.

——— 'The Iraq Legacies: Intervention, Occupation, Withdrawal and Beyond', in Isakhan,

B., (ed.), *The Legacy of Iraq: From the 2003 War to the 'Islamic State',* Edinburgh: Edinburgh University Press, 2015, pp. 1-18.

——— (ed.), *The Legacy of Iraq: From the 2003 War to the 'Islamic State',* Edinburgh: Edinburgh University Press, 2015.

——— 'Shattering the Shia: A Maliki Political Strategy in Post-Saddam Iraq,' in Isakhan, B., (ed.), *The Legacy of Iraq: From the 2003 War to the 'Islamic State',* Edinburgh: Edinburgh University Press, 2015, pp. 67-81.

——— 'Succeeding and Seceding in Iraq: The Case for a Shiite State,' in Kingsbury, D. and C. Laoutides (eds), *Territorial Separatism and Global Politics.* London: Routledge, 2015.

——— 'The Road to the "Islamic State": State-Society Relations after the US Withdrawal from Iraq,' in Isakhan, B., S. Mako and F. Dawood (eds), *State and Society in Iraq: Citizenship under Occupation, Dictatorship and Democratization.* London: I. B. Tauris, 2016.

Issa, I. E., N. A. Al-Ansari, G. Sherwany, and S. Knutsson, 'Expected Future of Water Resources in Tigris-Euphrates Rivers Basin, Iraq,' *Journal of Water Resource and Protection* 6:5 (April 2014).

Jaba, A., *Recueil de notices et de récits kurdes servant à la connaissance de la langue,* St Petersburg, 1860.

Jabbour, Khayrazad Kari, 'Peace education in the Lebanese Curriculum,' *Anadolu Journal of Educational Sciences International* 3:2 (2013).

Jafarzadeh, Hasan, 'Touse'eh-ye motavâzen-e Âzarbâyjân-e Gharbi bar bastar-e hamgarâyi va amniyat' ['Balanced development in Western Azerbaijan regarding convivality and security'], *Okhovvat* 1:3 (2008), pp. 99-105.

Jamal, Pishtiwan, 'Female business owners less than 5% in Iraqi Kurdistan,' Ekurd.net, 2015, http://ekurd.net/female-business-owners-less-than-5-in-iraqi-kurdistan-2015-05-14, last accessed 10 October 2016.

Jemkari, Azad, 'PYD launches 'law of political parties' in northern Syria,' ARA News, 28 April 2014, www.aranews.org/en/home/kurdish-region/1309-pyd-launch-law-of-political -parties-in-northern-syria.html, last accessed 28 April 2014.

Jenkins, Gareth, 'A military analysis of Turkey's incursion into northern Iraq,' *Terrorism Monitor* 6:5 (2008), www.jamestown.org/programs/gta/single/?tx_ttnews%5Btt_news%5D=4774&tx_ttnews%5BbackPid%5D=167&no_cache=1

Jones, Adam, *Genocide: A Comprehensive Introduction,* London: Routledge, 2006.

Jones, Dorian, 'Islamic state tests Turkey-Iraqi Kurd ties,' *Voice of America News,* 12 September 2014, http://www.voanews.com/content/islamic-state-tests-turkey-iraqi-kurd-tie/2447851.html

Jongerden, Joost, *Demokrasiyi Radikalleştirmek: Güç, Politika, İnsanlar ve PKK* ['Radicalizing Democracy: Power, Politics, People and the PKK'], Istanbul: Research Turkey, 2015, http://researchturkey.org/tr/radicalising-democracy-power-politics-people-and-the-pkk/, accessed 26 October 2015.

Jongerden, Joost and Ahmet Hamdi Akkaya, 'Born from the Left: The Making of the PKK', in Casier, Marlies and Joost Jongerden (eds), *Nationalisms and Politics in Turkey: Political Islam, Kemalism and the Kurdish Issue*, London: Routledge, 2011.

——— 'The Kurdistan Workers' Party and a New Left in Turkey: An Analysis of the Revolutionary Movement in Turkey through the PKK's Memorial Text on Haki Karer', *European Journal of Turkish Studies* 14 (2012).

——— 'Democratic Confederalism as a Kurdish Spring: the PKK and the quest for radical democracy', in Mohammed Ahmet and Michael Gunter (eds), *The Kurdish Spring: Geopolitical Changes and the Kurds*, Costa Mesa, CA: Mazda, 2013.

——— *PKK Üzerine Yazilar*, Istanbul: Vate Yayinlari, 2013.

Jongerden, Joost and Jelle Verheij (eds), *Social Relations in Ottoman Diyarbekir, 1870–1915*, Leiden: Brill, 2012.

Kabeer, N., 'Gender Equality and Women's Empowerment: A Critical Analysis of the Third Millennium Development Goal', *Gender and Development* 13:1 (2005), pp. 13-24.

Kalin, Ibrahim, 'What Turkey wants in the war on Islamic State', *Wall Street Journal*, 21 October 2014, http://www.wsj.com/articles/ibrahim-kalin-what-turkey-wants-in-the-war-on-isis-1413758083

Kanakis, Y., 'Dancing the future of Hakkari's past, according to 9-year-old Ayfer', in Allison, C. and P. G. Kreyenbroek (eds) *Remembering the Past in Iranian Societies*, Wiesbaden: Harrasowitz Verlag, 2013, pp. 113-24.

Kanie, Mariwan, 'Martyrdom between nation and religion: political love, poetry and self-sacrificing in Kurdish nationalism', unpublished PhD dissertation, University of Amsterdam, 2010.

Karasu, Mustafa, *Radikal Demokrasi*, Neus: Wesanen Mezopotamya, 2009.

Karim, Worya Hama, Interview with author, 21 March 2014, Halabja.

Kavak, Seref, 'The Democratic Society Party as a 'Party for Turkey': Official and Grassroots Politics of a Changing Identity 2005–2009', MA Thesis, Boğaziçi University, 2010.

Kelly, Michael J., *Ghosts of Halabja: Saddam Hussein and the Kurdish Genocide*, Westport, CT: Praeger Security International, 2008.

Kennedy, Charles, 'KRG announces plans to build second oil pipeline to Turkey', 31 October 2013, http://oilprice.com/Latest-Energy-News/World-News/KRG-Announces-Plans-to-Build-Second-Oil-Pipeline-to-Turkey.html

Keshtiban, Kamran, 'Federâlism: tanhâ rahyâft-e momken dar hamgarâyi-e melli' ['Federalism: the only possible solution for national convivality'], *Dilmâj* 16 (2006), pp. 42-9.

BIBLIOGRAPHY

Khasro, Guran, *Kurdistan Through History*, Stockholm, 1992.

Khidir, Jaafar Hussein, 'The Kurds and Kurdistan and Recent Political Development of IKR', Universität Wien dissertation, 2002.

Kieser, Hans-Lukas, *Der verspasse Friede. Mission, Ethnie und Stadt in den Ostprovinzen det Türkei, 1839–1938*, Zurich: Chronos, 2000.

Kimlycka, Will and Eva Pföstl (eds), *Multiculturalism and Minority Rights in the Arab World*, Oxford: Oxford University Press, 2014.

King, D. E., 'The Personal is Patrilineal: *Namus* as Sovereignty', *Identities* 15:3 (2008), pp. 317-42.

King, Diane E., 'My Field Site is Soaked with Blood', *Society for Applied Anthropology Newsletter* 20:1 (2009), pp. 32-4.

King, Diane E., *Kurdistan on the Global Stage: Kinship, Land, and Community in Iraq*, New Brunswick, NJ: Rutgers University Press, 2014.

Kinnane Derek, *The Kurds and Kurdistan*, London: Oxford University Press, 1924.

Kirisci, Kemal and Gareth Winrow, *The Kurdish Question and Turkey: An Example of a Trans-state Ethnic conflict*, London: Frank Cass, 1997.

Kirmanj, S., 'KRG's Islamic Education Textbooks and the Question of Peaceful Coexistence in Kurdistan Region', Working paper presented at University of Duhok, Education and Peace building conference, 2014.

Kissinger, Henry, *Years of Renewal*, London: Weidenfeld and Nicolson, 1999.

Kittleson, S., 'Yazidi wary amid stalled Sinjar offensive', Al-Monitor, 12 April 2015.

Klein, Janet, *The Margins of Empire: Kurdish Militias in the Ottoman Tribal Zone*, Palo Alto, CA: Stanford University Press, 2011.

Kleinman, A., V. Das and M. M. Lock, (eds), *Social Suffering*, Berkeley, CA: University of California Press, 1997.

Knights, M., 'Iraqi Kurdistan: The Middle East's next "Little Sparta"?' Al-Jazeera, 23 November 2014.

Krajeski, Jenna, 'After the Hunger Strike', *New Yorker*, 29 November 2012, http://www.newyorker.com/online/blogs/newsdesk/2012/11/after-the-kurdish-hunger-strike-in-turkish-prisons.html

Krajeski, Jenna, 'How the War with ISIS has Exposed Kurdistan's Internal Divisions', *The Nation*, 6 April 2015, http://www.thenation.com/article/celebrated-its-stability-iraqi-kurdistan-actually-plagued-corruption-nepotism-and-int/, last accessed 8 November 2015.

Krajeski, J. and S. Meyersept, 'A Litmus Test for Kurdistan', *New York Times*, 30 September 2014.

Kreyenbroek, Philip G. and Khalil Jindy Rashow, *God and Sheikh Adi Are Perfect: Sacred Poems and Religious Narratives from the Yezidi Tradition*, Wiesbaden: Harrassowitz Verlag, 2005.

BIBLIOGRAPHY

Kreyenbroek, Philip G., *Yezidism: Its Background, Observances and Textual Tradition*, Vol. 62, Texts and Studies in Religion, Lampeter, UK: Edwin Mellen Press, 1995.

KRG Ministry of Planning, 'Kurdistan Region of Iraq 2020: A Vision for the Future', September 2013, http://www.mop.krg.org/resources/MoP%20Files/Newsletter/kurdistan_region_of_iraq_2020_new.pdf)

Kropotkin, Peter, *The State: Its Historical Role*, London: Freedom Press, 1947 / 1897.

Kucukkosum, Sevil, 'PYD leader meets Turkish officials', *Hurriyet Daily News*, 3 June 2013, http://www.hurriyetdailynews.com/pyd-leader-meets-turkish-officials.aspx?pageID=238&nID=48066&NewsCatID=352

Kuper, Leo, *Genocide: Its Political Use in the Twentieth Century*, Harmondsworth: Penguin, 1981.

——*International Action against Genocide*, New Haven, CT: Yale University Press, 1982.

——'The Prevention of Genocide: Cultural and Structural Indicators of Genocidal Threat', *Ethnic and Racial Studies* 12:2 (1989), pp. 157-74.

——'The Genocidal State: An Overview', in Van den Berghe, P. (ed.), *State, Violence and Ethnicity*, Colorado: University Press of Colorado, 1990.

——'Reflections on the Prevention of Genocide', in Fein , H. (ed.), *Genocide Watch*, New Haven, CT: Yale University Press, 1992.

——(ed.), *The Prevention of Genocide*, New Haven, CT: Yale University Press, 1985.

Kurdish Regional Government, 'Report on the Administrative Changes in Kirkuk and the Disputed Regions', 2014, http://drmohammedihsan.com/Books.aspx

Kurdistan Regional Government, 'Iraq: Representation in the United States' 2014, http://new.krg.us/statement-of-krg-us-on-tier-iii-designation-of-kdp-and-puk/, last accessed 17 August 2015.

Kurdistan Region Presidency, 'President Barzani Congratulates Women on International Women's Day', 2014, http://www.krp.org/english/articledisplay.aspx?id=y1bXnwLtkPE, last accessed 7 December 2014.

Kurdistan Region Statistics Office, *Education*, Fact Sheet 2, Erbil: Kurdistan Region Statistics Office, 2012a.

——*Labour Force*, Fact Sheet 3, Erbil: Kurdistan Region Statistics Office, 2012b.

Kurdistan Regional Government, 'The Kurdistan Region in Brief', http://cabinet.gov.krd/p/p.aspx?l=12&p=210, last accessed 13 January 2016.

Kurdistanica, 'Religion in Kurdistan', in *KURDISTANICA: The Encyclopaedia of Kurdistan*, 2008, http://www.kurdistanica.com/

KurdWatch, 'Who is the Syrian Kurdish Opposition? The Development of Kurdish Parties, 1956-2011', Report 8, December 2011.

——'Cooperation agreement between the People's Council of West Kurdistan and the Kurdish National Council', 1 July 2012, www.kurdwatch.org/pdf/kurdwatch_D027_en_ar.

pdf, last accessed 11 September 2012.

——— 'Law on political parties for the cantons of Jazirah, Kabani and Afrin', 30 September 2014, http://www.kurdwatch.org/pdf/KurdWatch_D034_en_ar.pdf, last accessed 25 November 2015.

Kutlay, Naci, Anılarım, Istanbul: Avesta, 1998.

Kutschera, Chris, *Le mouvement national kurde*, Paris: Flammarion, 1979.

Laqua, Daniel, 'Transnational intellectual cooperation, the League of Nations, and the problem of order', *Journal of Global History* 6:2 (2011), pp. 223-47.

Laizer, Sheri J., *Martyrs, Traitors, and Patriots: Kurdistan after the Gulf War*, London: Zed Books, 1996.

Leach, Fiona and Mairead Dume (eds), *Education, Conflict and Reconciliation, International Perspectives*, Bern: Peter Lang, 2007.

Leersen, Joep, 'Nation and ethnicity', in Berger, Stefan and Chris Lorenz (eds), *The Contested Nation: Ethnicity, Class, Religion and Gender in National Histories*, New York: Palgrave Macmillan, 2008, pp. 75-103.

Legg, Stephen, 'Sites of counter-memory: the refusal to forget and the nationalist struggle in colonial Delhi', *Historical Geography* 33 (2005).

Lemkin, Raphael, *Axis Rule in Occupied Europe: Laws of Occupation, Analysis of Government, Proposals for Redress*, Washington, DC: Carnegie Endowment for International Peace, Division of International Law, 1944.

——— *Key Writings of Raphael Lemkin on Genocide*, 1944, http:// www.preventgenocide. org/lemkin.online, accessed 22 March 2013.

Levine, Daniel H. and Linda S. Bishai, 'Civic Education and Peace-building: Examples from Iraq and Sudan', US Institute of Peace, 2010.

Lipton, Eric, 'Iraqi Kurds Build Washington Lobbying Machine to Fund War against ISIS', *New York Times*, 7 May 2016, http://www.nytimes.com/2016/05/07/us/politics/iraqi-kurds-build-washington-lobbying-machine-against-isis.html?_r=1, last accessed 10 October 2016.

Lister, T., 'ISIS launches major assault on Kurdish front in Iraq', CNN, 28 February 2015.

Lorenz, F. and E. J.Erickson, *Strategic Water: Iraq and Security Planning in the Euphrates-Tigris Basin*, Quantico, VA: Marine Corps University Press, 2014.

Loschky, Jay, 'In Iraqi Kurdistan, Satisfaction with Infrastructure Crumbles', Gallup polling, 7 September 2012, http://www.gallup.com/poll/157298/iraqi-kurdistan-satisfaction-infrastructure-crumbles.aspx, last accessed 8 November 2015.

Lowe, Robert, 'The emergence of Western Kurdistan and the future of Syria', in Romano, David and Mehmet Gürses (eds), *Conflict, Democratization and the Kurds in the Middle East*, New York: Palgrave Macmillan, 2014, pp. 225-46.

——— 'The *Serhildan* and the Kurdish national story in Syria', in Lowe, Robert and Gareth

Stansfield (eds), *The Kurdish Policy Imperative*, London: Royal Institute of International Affairs, 2010, pp. 161-8.

Lundgren, Asa, *The Unwelcome Neighbour: Turkey's Kurdish Policy,* London: I. B. Tauris, 2007.

Machel, Graça, 'Impact of Armed Conflict on Children', UN General Assembly, 1996.

Mahmoud, N., 'Talks on New Iraqi Government Snag over Disputed Kurdish Territories', Rudaw, 7 September 2014.

Mahmud, Sayit, Interview with author, 18 March 2014, Halabja.

Majad, Abdul Arif, *The Kurdish Question in Iraq: 1958-1975*, Beirut: Al Mada, 1975.

Malmîsanij, *Kürt Teavün ve Terakki Cemiyeti ve Gazetesi*, 2nd edn, Istanbul: Avesta, 1999.

Mango, Andrew, *Turkey and the War on Terror: For Forty Years We Fought Alone,* Abingdon: Routledge, 2005

Mann, Michael, 'The Dark Side of Democracy: The Modern Tradition of Ethnic and Political Cleansing', *New Left Review* 235 (1999), pp. 18-45.

———*The Dark Side of Democracy: Explaining Ethnic Cleansing*, Cambridge: Cambridge University Press, 2005.

Mansour, Renad, 'How the Kurds Helped Draw the United States Back to Iraq', Beirut: Carnegie Middle East Center, 2015, http://carnegie-mec.org/2015/06/29/how-kurds-helped-draw-united-states-back-to-iraq/ib65, last accessed 7 January 2016.

Mansousi Al-Sawi, Mohammed, *Makalatfi Al Kanon al dawli*, Cairo: Al Ahram, 2004.

Mardini, Ramzy, 'The Revival of the Shi'a Militancy in Iraq', *CTS Sentinel* (2011), https://www.ctc.usma.edu/posts/the-revival-of-shia-militancy-in-iraq

Markey, Patrick and Isobel Coles, 'Insight: hopes, suspicions over peace in Kurdish rebel hideout', Reuters, 27 March 2013, http://www.reuters.com/article/2013/03/27/us-iraq-turkey-pkk-insight-idUSBRE92Q0J520130327

Marrus, Michael, *The Holocaust in History*, London: Weidenfeld and Nicolson, 1987.

——— (ed.), *The Unwanted: European Refugees in the Twentieth Century*, Oxford: Oxford University Press. 1985.

Massey, Doreen, 'Geographies of Responsibility', *Geogr. Ann.* 86:1 (2004), pp. 5-18.

Matin-Asgari, Afshin, *Iranian Student Opposition to the Shah*, Costa Mesa, CA: Mazda, 2002.

Mazower, Mark, *Dark Continent: Europe's Twentieth Century*, London: Penguin, 1998.

McCandless, E. and S. Doe, 'Strengthening Peacebuilding efforts in Liberia: a discussion document for UNMIL and the UNCT', 15 April 2007, O/DSRSG for Recovery and Governance (Liberia: UNMIL).

McDowall, David, *The Kurds, A Nation Denied*, London: Minority Group Publication, 1992.

———*A Modern History of the Kurds*, London: I. B. Tauris, 1994.

McDowell, Sara and Máire Braniff, *Commemoration As Conflict: Space, Memory and Identity in Peace Processes*, Basingstoke: Palgrave Macmillan, 2014.

McKiernan, Kevin, *The Kurds: A People in Search of Their Homeland*, New York: St Martin's Press, 2006.

Meeto, Veena and Heidi Mirza, 'There is nothing honourable about honour killings: Gender, violence and the limits of multiculturalism', *Women's Studies International Forum* 30:3 (2007), pp. 187-200.

Meho, Lokman, *The Kurdish Question in US Foreign Policy: A Documentary Sourcebook*, Westport, CT: Praeger Publishers, 2004, p. 445.

Meiselas, Susan, *Kurdistan: In the Shadow of History*, Random House / University of Chicago Press, 2005.

Meyersonn, Erik, 'How Turkey's social conservatives won the day for HDP', 8 June 2015, http://erikmeyersson.com/2015/06/08/how-turkeys-social-conservatives-won-the-day-for-hdp/

Mhamad, Aras Ahmed, 'The education crisis facing Iraqi Kurdistan', *The World Weekly*, 2016, http://www.theworldweekly.com/reader/view/magazine/2016-03-31/the-education-crisis-facing-iraqi-kurdistan/7315, last accessed 10 October 2016.

Middle East Eye, 'Two leading Iraqi Kurdish parties are taken off US terrorism list', 2015, http://www.middleeasteye.net/news/two-leading-iraqi-kurdish-parties-are-taken-us-terrorism-list-1048291370, last accessed 17 June 2015.

Middle East Monitor, 'Maliki's Coalition: Kurdish annexation of Kirkuk is a declaration of war', 30 June 2014.

Mills, M., 'What('s) Theory?', *Journal of Folklore Research* 45:1, (2008), pp. 19-28. '"Are You Writing Our Book Yet?" War, Culture, Structural Violence, and Oral Historical Representation', in Allison, C. and P. G. Kreyenbroek (eds) *Remembering the Past in Iranian Societies*, Wiesbaden: Harrasowitz Verlag, 2013, pp. 165-76.

Ministry of Higher Education and Scientific Research, 'Universities in Kurdistan', http://www.mhe-krg.org/node/23, last accessed 13 January 2016.

———'A Roadmap to Quality, Reforming the System of Higher Education and Scientific Research in the Kurdistan Region of Iraq, A Report on the Main Achievements, From 1st November 2009 to 1st September 2010', Erbil: Kurdistan Regional Government, 2010.

———'Equal Opportunities', http://www.mhe-krg.org/node/27, last accessed 14 March 2014.

———'Higher Education in Kurdistan Region', http://www.mhe-krg.org/node/105, last accessed 14 March 2014.

———'KRG Scholarship Program Human Capacity Development', http://www.mhe-krg.org/index.php?q=node/249, last accessed 14 March 2014.

Mir-Sanjari, Mir Mehrdad, 'Har ja ke Kord ast, Iran ast' [,Wherever a Kurd is, is Iran'],

Tabnak, 26 August 2010.

Mitchell, Katharyne, 'Monuments, Memorials, and the Politics of Memory', *Urban Geography* 24:5 (2003), pp. 442-59.

Mlodoch, K., 'Fragmented Memory, Competing Narratives', in Tejel, Jordi, Peter Sluglett, Riccardo Bocco, and Hamit Bozarslan (eds), *Writing the Modern History of Iraq. Historiographical and Political Challenges*, Singapore: World Scientific, 2012, pp. 205-26.

Moghadam, V., *Modernizing Women: gender and social change in the Middle East*, 2nd edn, Boulder, CO: Lynne Rienner, 2003.

Mohammad, Nowshirwan, Interview with author, 18 March 2014, Halabja.

Mojab, Shahrzad and Nahla Abdo, *Violence in the Name of Honour: Theoretical and political challenges*, Istanbul: Istanbul Bilgi University Press, 2004.

Moore, Barrington, *Social Origins of Dictatorship and Democracy: Lord and Peasant in the Making of Modern World*, Boston, MA: Beacon Press, 1966.

Moore, J., and S. Al-Salhy, 'Kurdish land-grab stuns Baghdad', *Newsweek*, 21 January 2015.

Morris, Harvey, 'White House Pledges Support for Measures to Remove Kurdistan Parties from Terrorism List', Rudaw, 12 February 2014, http://rudaw.net/mobile/english/kurdistan/120220141, last accessed 28 September 2015.

Moss, O., 'Laying the Foundations', 2013, http://www.the-report.net/iraq/kurdistan-region-sep2013/666-education-laying-the-foundations, last accessed 14 March 2014.

Moyn, Samuel and Andrew Sartori (eds), *Global Intellectual History*, New York: Columbia University Press, 2013.

Mustafa, Nawshirwan, *Jian: Be tementirîn rojnamey kurdî 1926–1938*, Sulemani: Zargata, 2002.

———*Edeb û Tarixî Kurdî*, Sulemani: Zargata, 2012.

Nassar, Issam, 'Reflections on Writing the History of Palestinian Identity', *Palestine-Israel Journal* 8:4 (2002), pp. 24-37.

Natali, Denise, 'Syria's Kurdish Quagmire', 3 May 2012, www.ekurd.net/mismas/articles/misc2012/5/syriakurd486.htm

——— *The Kurds and the State: Evolving Identity in Iraq, Turkey, and Iran*, Syracuse, NY: Syracuse University Press, 2006.

———*Kurdish Quasi-State: Development and Dependency in Post-Gulf War Iraq*, Syracuse, NY: Syracuse University Press, 2010.

Neyzi, Leyla, 'Oral History and Memory Studies in Turkey', in Kerslake, Celia, Kerem Öktem, and Philip Robins (eds), *Turkey's Engagement with Modernity: Conflict and Change in the Twentieth Century*, New York: Palgrave Macmillan, 2010, pp. 443-59.

Nimni, Ephraim, 'The Conceptual Challenge of Non-Territorial Autonomy', in Nimni, Ephraim, Alexander Osipov and David Smith (eds), *The Challenge of Non-*

BIBLIOGRAPHY

Territorial Autonomy, Oxford: Peter Lang, 2013.

Niyash, Umid, 'Rouhani defends Iranian ethnics' right of mother tongue teaching', *Trend*, 31 May 2016, http://en.trend.az/iran/politics/2540073.html

Nora, Pierre, 'Between Memory and History: Les Lieux de Mémoire', *Representations* 26 (1989), pp. 26-34.

Norval, Aletta, *Aversive Democracy: Inheritance and Originality in the Democratic Tradition*, Cambridge: Cambridge University Press, 2007.

Norwig, Christina, 'A First European Generation? The Myth of Youth and European Integration in the Fifties', *Diplomatic History* 38:2 (2014), pp. 251-60.

NRT TV, 'U.S. Envoy Makes First Visit to Syrian Kurdish Areas', 9 December 2015, http://www.nrttv.com/EN/Details.aspx?Jimare=5149, last accessed 2 February 2016.

Nykanen, Johanna, 'Identity, narrative and frames: assessing Turkey's Kurdish initiatives', *Insight Turkey* 15:2 (2013), pp. 85-101.

O'Ballance, Edgar, *The Kurdish revolt, 1961–1970*, Hamden: Archon, 1973.

——— *The Kurdish Struggle*, New York: St Martin's Press, 1996.

Obama, Barack, 'President Obama Makes a Statement on Iraq', White House, 7 August 2014.

——— 'Statement by the President on ISIL', White House, 10 September 2014.

O'Connor, Francis Patrick, 'Armed Social Movements and Insurgency: The PKK and its communities of support,' MA thesis, European University Institute, 2014.

——— 'Radical political participation and the internal Kurdish diaspora in Turkey', *Kurdish Studies* 3:2 (2015), pp. 151-71.

O'Connor, Francis Patrick and Leonidas Oikonomakis, 'Preconflict Mobilization Strategies and Urban-Rural Transition: The Cases of the PKK and the FLN/EZLN,' *Mobilization: An International Quarterly* 20:3 (September 2015), pp. 379-99.

Öcalan, Abdullah, *Kürdistan Devriminin Yolu – Manifesto* [The Path of Kurdistan Revolution - Manifesto], Cologne: Weşanên Serxwebûn, 1992.

———*3. Kongre Konuşmaları* [Discussions of the Third Congress], Cologne: Weşanên Serxwebûn, 1993.

——— *Kürdistanda Halk Savaşı ve Gerilla* (People's War and Guerrilla in Kurdistan), Cologne: Weşanên Serxwebûn, 1993.

———*Prison Notes,* 18 June 2008.

———*Demokratik Uygarlık Manifestosu: Ortaduğu'da Uygarlik Krizi ve demokratik Uygarlık Çözümü*, Neuss: Mezopotamya Yayınları, 2010.

———*Democratic Confederalism*, trans. by International Initiative. London: Transmedia Publishing, 2011.

———*Demokratik Uygarlık Manifestosu: Kültürel Soykırım Kıskacında Kürtleri Savunmak*, Neuss: Mezopotamya Yayınları, 2012a.

———— *Prison Writings III: The Road Map to Negotiations*, Cologne: International Initiative Freedom for Öcalan — Peace in Kurdistan, 2012b.

———— *War and Peace in Kurdistan*, Cologne: International Initiative Freedom for Abdullah Öcalan — Peace in Kurdistan, 2014.

OECD, 'Education at a Glance 2013 Norway', http://www.oecd.org/edu/Norway_EAG2013%20Country%20Note.pdf, last accessed 13 January 2016.

Olick, Jeffrey K., 'Collective Memory: The Two Cultures', *Sociological Theory* 17:3 (1999), pp. 333-48.

Olson, Robert, *The Emergence of Kurdish Nationalism and the Sheikh Said Rebellion, 1880–1915*, Austin: University Texas Press, 1989.

————*The Kurdish National Movement in the 1990s*, Lexington, KY: University of Kentucky Press, 1996.

———— *The Kurdish Question and Turkish–Iranian Relation*, Costa Mesa, CA: Mazda, 1998.

———— *Turkey's Relations with Iran, Syria, Israel and Russia, 1991-2000: The Kurdish and Islamist Questions*, Syracuse, NY: Syracuse University Press, 2001, pp. 1-10, 74.

Omarkhali, Khanna, 'Introduction', in Omarkhali, Khanna (ed.), *Religious Minorities in Kurdistan: Beyond the Mainstream*, Wiesbaden: Harrassowitz Verlag, 2014.

Omerxalî, Xanna, *Yezidisyatî* ['Yezidism'], Istanbul: Mezopotamya Centre, Avesta Publications (written in Kurdish Kûrmancî), 2007.

Omidsalar, M., 'Persia' in Clements, W. M. (ed.), *The Greenwood Encyclopaedia of Folklore and Folklife*, Vol. 2, Westport and London: Greenwood Press, 2006, pp. 413-29.

Omissi, David E., *Air Power and Colonial Control: The Royal Air Forces, 1919-1939*, Manchester: Manchester University Press, 1990.

Opotow, S., Gerson, J., and S. Woodside, 'From Moral Exclusion to Moral Inclusion: Theory for Teaching Peace', *Theory into Practice* 44:4 (2005), pp. 303-18.

Oran, Baskin, *Türk Dış Politikası. Kurtuluş Savaşından Bugüne. Olgular, Belgeler, Yorumlar*, Vol. III 2001-2012, İstanbul, 2013, pp. 740-49.

Orhan, Mehmet, 'Transborder violence: The PKK in Turkey, Syria and Iraq', *Dynamics of Asymmetric Conflict* 7:1 (2014), pp. 30-48.

Orhan, Oytun, 'Syria's PKK Game', *Today's Zaman*, 14 February 2012.

Ortner, S., 'The Virgin and the State', *Feminist Studies* 4:3 (1978), pp. 19-35.

Osler, Audrey (ed.), *Teachers, Human Rights and Diversity: Educating Citizens in Multicultural Societies*, London: Trentham Books, 2005.

Osler, Audrey and Chalank Yahya, 'Challenges and complexity in human rights education: Teachers' understandings of democratic participation and gender equity in post-conflict Kurdistan-Iraq', *Education Inquiry* 4:1 (2013), pp. 189-210.

Ozcan, Nihat Ali and H. Erdem Gurkaynak, 'Who are these armed people on the mountains?'

February 2012, www.tepev.org.tr

Özoğlu, Hakan, *Kurdish Notables and the Ottoman State: Evolving Identities, Competing Loyalties, and Shifting Boundaries*, Albany, NY: SUNY, 2004.

Özok-Gündogan, Nilay, 'Ruling the Periphery, Governing the Land: The Making of the Modern Ottoman State in Kurdistan, 1840–1970', *Comparative Studies of South Asia, Africa and the Middle East* 34:1 (2014), pp. 160-75.

Öztürkmen A. 'Folklore on Trial: Pertev Naili Boratav and the Denationalization of Turkish Folklore', *Journal of Folklore Research* 42:2 (2005), pp. 185-216.

Palmer, Alison, 'Colonial and Modern Genocide: Explanations and Categories', *Ethnic and Racial Studies* 21:1 (1999), pp. 89-115.

Palumbo, Michael, *The Palestinian Catastrophe: The 1948 Expulsion of a People from their Homeland*, London: Faber, 1989.

Pamuk, H., 'Kurds Push to Drive ISIS from Mosul Dam as US Air Support Pounds Militants', *Business Insider,* 18 August 2014.

Pappé, Ilan, *The Ethnic Cleansing of Palestine*, Oxford: Oneworld, 2006.

Paredes, A., *With his Pistol in his Hand: A Border Ballad and its Hero,* Austin, TX: University of Texas Press, 1958.

Park, Bill, 'Turkey's Policy Towards Northern Iraq: Problems and Perspectives', Adelphi Paper 374, London: International Institute for Strategic Studies, May 2005.

———*Turkey-Kurdish Regional Government Relations After the US Withdrawal from Iraq: Putting the Kurds on the Map*, Strategic Studies Institute, US Army War College, March 2014.

———'Turkey's dual relationship with Iraq: Ankara, Baghdad and Erbil', *Orient* 1 (2015), pp. 53-7.

———'Turkey's isolated stance: an ally no more, or just the usual turbulence?', *International Affairs* 91:3 (2015), pp. 581-600.

Paul, Ludwig, 'Iranian Nation and Iranian-Islamic Revolutionary Ideology', *Die Welt des Islams*, New Series 39:2 (1999), pp. 183-217.

Pecquet, J., 'Will Congress Arm Iraqi Kurds?', Al-Monitor, 24 March 2015.

Peled-Shapira, Hilla, 'Was Halabja a Turning Point for the Poet Buland al-Haydari?' *Kurdish Studies* 2:1 (2014), pp. 14-33.

Pelley, S., 'Iraq's Kurds praise U.S. support, want more against ISIS', CBS News, 9 September 2014.

Phillips, David. L, 'Research Paper: ISIS-Turkey Links', 9 November 2015, http://www.huffingtonpost.com/david-l-phillips/research-paper-isis-turke_b_6128950.html

———*The Kurdish Spring: A New Map of the Middle East*, New Brunswick, NJ: Transaction Publishers, 2015.

Phillips, Shailoh, 'Cyberkurds and Cyberkinetics: Pilgrimage in an Age of Virtual Mobility', *Etnofoor* 20:1 (2007).

Piper, N., 'Gender and migration: A paper prepared for the policy analysis and research programme of the global commission on international migration', Geneva: Global Commission on International Migration, UNFPA, 2005.

Pironti, A., 'Kurdistan Building New Army in Fight for Education', Rudaw (2013), http://rudaw.net/english/kurdistan/281120131, last accessed 14 March 2014.

PKK, Kürdistan Devriminin Yolu, 1978.

———*Politik Rapor: Merkez Komitesi Tarafından PKK 1. Konferansına Sunulmuştur* [Political Report: Submitted by the Central Committee to the PKK First Conference], Cologne: Weşanên Serxwebûn, 1982.

———*Kürdistan Ulusal Kurtuluş Problemi ve Çözüm Yolu: Kürdistan Ulusal Kurtuluş Cephesi*

Program Taslağı, Cologne: Weşanên Serxwebûn, 1984 2ⁿᵈ edn.

———'PKK 11ᵗʰ Congress, Declaration of the Central Committee of the PKK', n.d., http://www.pkkonline.com/en/index.php?sys=article&artID=211, last accessed 5 May 2014.

Planhol, Xavier de, *Les Nations du Prophète: Manuel géographique de politique musulman*, Paris: Fayard, 1993.

Poladian, Sirvart, 'Komitas Vardapet and his Contribution to Ethnomusicology', *Ethnomusicology* 16:1 (1972), pp. 82-97.

Pollack, Craig Evan, 'Intentions of Burial: Mourning, Politics, and Memorials Following the Massacre at Srebrenicak', *Death Studies* 2 (2003), pp. 125-42.

Pollack, K. M., 'Iraq: Understanding the ISIS Offensive Against the Kurds', Brookings Institution, 11 August 2014.

Poor, Ali Askhr Nesrullah, ['Kurdish Musical Instruments'], trans. from Farsi to Kurdish Bahdini by Masoud Mohhamed Guli Duhok, Kurdistan: Spirez Publications, Iraqi Kurdistan, 2005.

Pope, Hugh, 'Turkey and the democratic opening for the Kurds', in Bilgin, Fevzo and Ali Sarihan (eds), *Understanding Turkey's Kurdish Question,* Lanham, MD: Lexington Books, 2013, pp. 117-40.

Pope, Nicole, '"Honour" Killing: Instruments of patriarchal control', in Mojab, S. and N. Abdo (eds), *Violence in the Name of Honour: Theoretical and Political Challenges*, Istanbul: Bilgi University Press, 2004.

Posch, Walter, 'The end of a beautiful friendship: Mahmoud Ahmadinejad and the Principalists', in Chehabi, Houshang E., Farhad Khosrokhavar and Clement Therme (eds), *Iran and the Challenges of the Twenty-First Century. Essays in Honour of Mohammad-Reza Djalili*, Costa Mesa, CA: Mazda, 2013, pp. 50-78.

——— 'Islamistische Gewalt in der Islamischen Republik Iran', in Rupp, Jasmina and Walter Feichtinger (eds), *Der Ruf des Dschihad: Theorie, Fallstudien und Wege aus der Radikalität*, Vienna, 2016, pp. 267-318.

——— 'The Third World, Global Islam and Pragmatism: The Making of Iranian Foreign Policy', SWP Research Paper, Berlin, 2013.

——— 'Mäßigung statt Neuanfang: Iran nach den Präsidentschaftswahlen 2013', SWP-Aktuell 39, Berlin, 2013.

——— 'The changing faces of the PKK', in Taucher, Wolfgang, Matthias Vogl and Peter Webinger, *The Kurds. History, Religion, Language, Politics*, Vienna: Ministry of the Interior BMI, 2015, pp. 87-110.

——— 'Die neue PKK: Zwischen Extremismus, politischer Gewalt und strategischen Herausforderungen, Teil 1', Österreichische Militärische Zeitschrift 2 (2016), pp. 139-55.

——— 'Die neue PKK. Zwischen Extremismus, politischer Gewalt und strategischen Herausforderungen, Teil 2', Österreichische Militärische Zeitschrift 3 (2016), pp. 295-311.

——— 'Der Sicherheitsapparat der Islamischen Republik Iran', in *Handbuch der Iranistik*, Berlin, 2016.

Pries, Ludger, 'Configurations of geographic and societal spaces: a sociological proposal between "methodological nationalism" and the "spaces of flows"', *Global Networks* 5:2 (2005), pp. 167-90.

PYD, 'Social Contract', 29 January 2014, http://www.kongrakurdistan.net/en/the-social-contract-of-rojava/, last accessed 10 November 2014.

——— 'The Project of Democratic Self-Governance in Western Kurdistan', n.d., http://www.pydrojava.net/en/index.php?option=com_content&view=section&layout=blog&id=7&Itemid=54, last accessed 10 October 2014.

Radikal, 'HDP'li Baluken: Türkiye, Rojava modeline destek vermeil' ['HDP's Baluken: Turkey should support the Rojava model'], http://www.radikal.com.tr/politika/hdpli_baluken_turkiye_rojava_modeline_destek_verilmeli-138342, last accessed 16 November 2015.

Radio Free Europe/Radio Liberty, , 'U.S. Intelligence Chiefs Say Iraq, Syria May Not Survive as States', 11 September 2015, http://www.rferl.org/content/iraq-syria-us-intelligence-doubt-survival-as-states/27240681.html, last accessed 7 February 2016.

Rahman and Abdullah, 'The prospects for the development of civic education system educational curricula in the Kurdistan Region – Iraq', Working paper presented at University of Duhok, Education and Peace building conference, 2014.

Randal, Jonathan C., *After Such Knowledge, What Forgiveness? My Encounters with Kurdistan*, New York: Farrar, Straus and Giroux, 1997.

BIBLIOGRAPHY

Ranharter, K., 'Gender Equality and Development After Violent Conflict: The Effects of Gender Policies in the Kurdistan Region of Iraq', University of Exeter, PhD thesis, 2013.

───── *Gender Equality and Development After Violent Conflicts: The Kurdistan Region of Iraq*, London: Palgrave Macmillan, 2015.

Rashid, Naseh Abdul Rahim, Interview with author, 17 March 2014, Halabja.

Rashid, R. H. M., 'The Use of Water for Sustainable Rural Development: A Case Study in the Kurdistan Regional Government', abstract of doctoral thesis, Cluj-Napoca, 2014, http://www.usamvcluj.ro/en/files/teze/en/2014/razhen.pdf

Reisz, Matthew, 'Iraqi Kurdish scholars put gender theory to the test', *Times Higher Education*, 13 October 2011, http://www.timeshighereducation.co.uk/story.asp?storycode=417730, last accessed 14 March 2014.

───── 'Iraqi Kurdistan looks to national ranking to improve', *Times Higher Education*, 31 January 2016, https://www.timeshighereducation.com/news/iraqi-kurdistan-looks-national-ranking-improve, last accessed 10 October 2016.

Riaux, Gilles, *Ethnicité et nationalisme en Iran: La cause azerbaïdjanaise*, Paris: Karthala, 2012.

Riegler, Thomas, *Im Fadenkreuz: Österreich und der Nahostterrorismus 1973 bis 1985*, Vienna, 2011, pp. 459-64.

Romano, David, *The Kurdish Nationalist Movement: Opportunity, Mobilisation and Identity*, Cambridge: Cambridge University Press, 2006.

Romano, David and Mehmet Gurses (eds), *Conflict, Democratization and the Kurds in the Middle East*, New York: Palgrave Macmillan, 2014.

Ross, Kristin, *Communal Luxury, the Political Imaginary of the Paris Commune*, London: Verso, 2015.

Roudenko, Margarita, *The Kurdish Ritual Poetry (Funeral Lamentation)*, Moscow: Nauka Publications, published in Russian by the USSR Academy of Science, the Institute of Oriental Studies, 1982.

Roudi, F., 'Youth Population and Employment in the Middle East and North Africa: Opportunity or Challenge?' Population Reference Bureau, 2011.

Rudaw, 'Iranian Kurdish Group Shifts Policy, seeking Democratic Autonomy', 6 May 2014, http://rudaw.net/english/middleeast/iran/06052014, last accessed 7 May 2014.

───── 'Senior PKK Leader says Group no longer Seeks a Kurdish State', 7 May 2014, www.rudaw.net/mobile/english/middleeast/turkey/07052014, last accessed 7 May 2014.

───── 'Tev-Dem Rep: Kobane has upset their plans', 25 October 2014, https://rojavareport.wordpress.com/2014/10/25/tev-dem-rep-kobane-has-upset-their-plans/, last accessed 27 October 2014.

——— 'US to Provide Direct Military and Financial Support to Peshmerga', 2016, http://rudaw.net/english/kurdistan/120720161, last accessed 9 October 2016.

——— 'As schools open in Kurdistan minister hears teachers' grievances, urging patience', 1 October 2016, http://rudaw.net/english/kurdistan/011020161?keyword=education, last accessed 10 October 2016.

——— 'KRG resumes payment to its students in foreign universities', 6 September 2016, http://rudaw.net/english/kurdistan/060920163?keyword=higher%20education, last accessed 10 October 2016.

——— 'Kurdistan demo organizers call for minister to resign, lifting austerity measures', 27 September 2016, http://rudaw.net/english/kurdistan/270920165?keyword=higher%20education, last accessed 10 October 2016.

Rummel, R. J., *Lethal Politics: Soviet Genocides and Mass Murder 1900-1987*, Piscataway, NJ: Transaction Publishers, 1990.

——— *Genocide and Mass Murder*, Honolulu: University of Hawaii, 1993.

——— 'Power, Genocide, and Mass Murder', *Journal of Peace Research* 31:1 (1994), pp. 1-10.

——— *Death by Government*, Piscataway, NJ: Transaction Publishers, 1997.

Sabio, Oso, *Rojava: An Alternative to Imperialism, Nationalism, and Islamism in the Middle East (An Introduction)*, Raleigh, NC: LULU Press, 2015.

Sadeqi, Aydin, 'Fedrâlism va tarhi-ye 'amali az ân barâ-ye Irân' ['Federalism and its application for Iran'], *Dilmâj* 16 (2006), pp. 22-41.

Sadeqi, Mojtabâ and Zeyrak, Mohsen, 'PJAK mikhvâst jâddeh-sâff-kon-e Âmrikâ bâshad' ['PJAK wants to clear the way for the USA'], *Bultan*, 1 September 2011.

Sadullah, Vager, 'PKK and KDP: there's drama between Kurdistan's two best frenemies', 12 February 2015, http://ekurd.net/pkk-and-kdp-theres-drama-between-kurdistans-two-best-frenemies-2015-02-12

Saeed, Seevan, 'The Kurdish National Movement in Turkey: From the PKK to the KCK', PhD thesis, University of Exeter, 2014.

Saeed, Yerevan, 'KDPI leader: Iran wants to strengthen ISIS to further own hegemony', Rudaw, 15 June 2015, http://rudaw.net/english/interview/15062015, last accessed 20 September 2015.

——— 'US Senate votes down bill to directly arm Kurds', Rudaw, 17 June 2015, http://rudaw.net/mobile/english/kurdistan/17062015, last accessed 23 August 2015.

——— 'US establishes new military center in Kurdistan region', Rudaw, 4 September 2015, http://rudaw.net/mobile/english/kurdistan/040920156?ctl00_phMainContainer_phMain_ControlComments1_gvCommentsChangePage=5, last accessed 23 October 2015.

Sagrma, A'. J., ['A Foundation Page of Kurdish Music'], Sulaimani, Kurdistan: Institute of Kurdish Heritage of the Kurdish Cultural Ministry, 2003.

BIBLIOGRAPHY

Salahaddin University, Hawler, 'London's SOAS Signs Agreement with SUH', 2012, http://www.suh-edu.com/index.php?option=com_content&view=article&id=484%3Alondons-soas-signs-agreement-with-suh&catid=1%3Alatest-news&Itemid=162&lang=en, last accessed 14 Mar. 2014.

Salehi-Amiri, Seyyed Reza, *Modiriyat-e monâze'ât-e qoumi dar Irân* ['Management of ethnic enmity in Iran'], Tehran, 2012.

Salih, Khaled, 'Anfal: The Kurdish Genocide in Iraq', *Digest of Middle East Studies* 4:2 (1995), pp. 24-39.

Salih, Mohammed A., 'Kurds and ISIL battle over Kirkuk', Al-Jazeera, 5 February 2015.

———'US military aid bills highlight Iraq's deep divisions', Al-Jazeera, 15 May 2015, http://www.aljazeera.com/news/2015/05/150509084945317.html, last accessed 27 May 2015.

Salomon, G., 'The Nature of Peace Education: Not All Programs Are Equal', in Salomon, G. and B. Nevo (eds), *Peace Education: The Concept, Principles, and Practices Around the World*, New York: Lawrence Erlbaum, 2002, pp. 3-14.

———'Does Peace Education Make a Difference in the Context of an Intractable Conflict?', *Peace and Conflict: Journal of Peace Psychology* 10:3 (2004), p. 257.

Salomon, G. and B. Nevo (eds), *Peace Education: The Concept, Principles, and Practices Around the World*, New York: Lawrence Erlbaum, 2012.

Sarafian, A., 'United States Official Documents on the Armenian Genocide', *Armenian Review* (1993).

Sarhan, A., 'Kurdish Peshmerga foil ISIS attack near Mosul Dam', *Iraqi News*, 26 November 2014.

Sarihan, Ali, 'The two periods of the PKK conflict: 1884-1999 and 2004-2010', in Bilgin, Fevzo and Ali Sarihan (eds), *Understanding Turkey's Kurdish Question*, Lanham, MD: Lexington Books, 2013, pp. 89-102.

Saritaş, B. S. E., 'Articulation of Kurdish Identity through Politicized Music of *Koms*', Master's thesis, Middle East Technical University, Istanbul, 2010.

Sarrafi, Alirezâ, 'Negâhi be vâqiyyat-e tanavvo'-e qoumi va melli-ye Irân: chashmaandâzi az Irân-e federâl', *Dilmâj* 16 (2006), pp. 6-21.

Sarvastain, G., *Kurds and Kurdistan*, London: Harvill Press, 1978.

Sassoon, Joseph, *Saddam Hussain's Ba'ath Party: Inside an Authoritarian Regime*, Cambridge: Cambridge University Press, 2012.

Saunier, Pierre-Yves, 'Globalisation', in Iriye, Akira and Pierre-Yves Saunier (eds), *The Palgrave Dictionary of Transnational History*, New York: Palgrave, 2009, pp. 456-62.

Savelsberg, Eva, 'The Syrian-Kurdish movements', in Romano, David and Mehmet Gürses (eds), *Conflict, Democratization and the Kurds in the Middle East*, New York: Palgrave Macmillan, 2014, pp. 85-107.

———and Tejel, Jordi, 'The Syrian Kurds in Transition to Somewhere', in Gunter, Michael and Mohammed M. A. Ahmed, (eds), *The Kurdish Spring: Geopolitical Changes and the Kurds*, Costa Mesa, CA: Mazda, 2013.

Security Council, Resolution 935, 1994, http://www.refworld.org/docid/3b00f16034.html

Sedâ-ye Mo'Allem, 'Tâbu-ye amuzesh-e zabân-e Kordi dar madâres-e Saqez shekasteh shod' ['The taboo of Kurdish language instruction in the schools of Saqez has been broken']. www.sedayemoallem.ir, 10 April 2015.

Segall, Kimberly Wedeven, *Performing Democracy in Iraq and South Africa: Gender, Media, and Resistance*, New York: Syracuse University Press, 2013.

Seitz, K., *Bildung und Konflikt, Die Rolle von Bildung bei der Entstehung, Prävention und Bewältigung gesellschaftlicher Krisen – Konsequenzen für die Entwicklungszusammenarbeit*, Rossdorf: TZ-Verlagsgesellschaft, 2004.

Shannon, Matthew, '"Contacts with the opposition": American foreign relations, the Iranian student movement, and the global sixties', *The Sixties* 4:1 (2011), pp. 1-29.

Shapiro, Svi, *Educating Youth for a World Beyond Violence: A Pedagogy for Peace*, New York: Palgrave Macmillan, 2010.

Shareef, Mohammed, 'Kurdistan: Political Stability and Widespread Security', *Equilibri* 13:3 (2009), p. 443.

——— *The United States, Iraq and the Kurds: Shock, Awe and Aftermath*, London: Routledge, 2014, p. 173.

———'China's Dual Diplomacy: Arab Iraq and the Kurdistan Region', in Horesh Niv (ed.), *Toward Well-Oiled Relations:China's Presence in the Middle East Following the Arab Spring*, New York: Palgrave Macmillan, 2016, pp. 69-93.

Shareef Atlim Mohammed Mahir, Wahid, Abdul, *The Encyclopaedia of International Humanitarian Law*, Cairo: International Red Cross Committee, 2002.

Sheikh-Attar, Alireza, *Kordhâ va qodrathâ-ye manteqehi va gheyr-e manteqehi* ['The Kurds and the regional and international powers'], Tehran, 2003.

Sheikhmous, Omar, 'Kurdish cultural and political activities abroad', Paper presented in Berlin, 17-22 December 1989.

Shenhav, Shaul R., 'Concise narratives: a structural analysis of political discourse', *Discourse Studies* 7:3 (2005), pp. 315-35.

———'Political Narrative and Political Reality', *International Political Science Review* 27:3 (2006), pp. 245-62.

Shexani, Naif, ['A Concept of the World in Music'], Arbil: Publications of the Ministry of Culture and Youth of the Kurdish Government of Iraq, 2010.

Sheyholislami, J., Kurdish Identity, Discourse and New Media, London: Palgrave, 2011.

Silopi, Zinar (Kadri Cemil Pasha), *Doza Kurdistan. Kürt Milletinin 60 Yıllık Esaretten Kurtuluş Savaşı Hatıraları*, Ankara: Öz-Ge, 1991.

BIBLIOGRAPHY

Şimşek, Sefa, 'New Social Movements in Turkey Since 1980', *Turkish Studies* 5:2 (2004), pp.111-39.

Simon, Thomas W., 'Defining Genocide', *Wisconsin International Law Journal* 15:1 (1996), pp. 243-56.

Simon, James, 'Kurdistan, Women in Iraq', 2009, http://www.youtube.com/watch?v=x4POLH2O208, last accessed 13 January 2016.

Sinkaya, Bayram, 'Rationalisation of Turkey-Iranian Relations: Prospects and Limits', *Insight Turkey* 14 (2012), pp. 137-56.

Sluglett, P., 'Common Sense, or a Step Pregnant with Enormous Consequences: Some Thoughts on the Possible Secession of Iraqi Kurdistan', in Doyle, D. H. (ed.), *Secession as an International Phenomenon: From America's Civil War to Contemporary Separatist Movements*, Athens, GA: University of Georgia Press, 2010, pp. 319-37.

———— 'Kurdistan: A Suspended Secession from Iraq', in Pavkovic, A. and R. Peter (eds), *The Ashgate Research Companion to Secession*, London: Ashgate, 2011, pp. 539-41.

Sly, Liz, 'Petraeus: The Islamic State isn't our biggest problem in Iraq', *Washington Post*, 20 March 2015, https://www.washingtonpost.com/news/worldviews/wp/2015/03/20/petraeus-the-islamic-state-isnt-our-biggest-problem-in-iraq, last accessed 24 November 2015.

Smale, A.,'German soldiers may help train forces in Iraq', *New York Times*, 17 December 2014.

Smith, Anthony D., 'Nationalism and Classical Social Theory', *British Journal of Sociology* 34:1 (1983).

————*National Identity*, Reno, NV: University of Nevada Press, 1991.

Smith, A., and C. S. Ellison, 'Youth, education, and peacebuilding: Engaging youth in planning education for social transformation', Northern Ireland: UNESCO Centre, University of Ulster, 2012.

Smith, D., 'Towards a strategic framework for peacebuilding: getting their act together', Overview report of the Joint Utstein Study of Peacebuilding, 2004.

Soane, E. B., *Mesopotamia and Kurdistan in Disguise*, London: John Murray, 1912.

Sorek, Tamir, 'Cautious Commemoration: Localism, Communalism, and Nationalism in Palestinian Memorial Monuments in Israel', *Comparative Studies in Society and History* 50:2 (2008).

————*Palestinian Commemoration in Israel: Calendars, Monuments, and Martyrs*, Stanford, CA: Stanford University Press, 2015.

Sornsin, Kristin M., 'Out of the Mountains into Politics: The Kurdish Nationalist Movement of Iraq', MA Thesis, Central European University, 2008.

Spencer, Philip, *Genocide Since 1945*, London and New York: Routledge, 2012.

Stafford, Ronald Sempill, *The Tragedy of the Assyrians*, Piscataway, NJ: Gorgias Press, 2006 [1935].

BIBLIOGRAPHY

Stansfield, G., *Iraqi Kurdistan: Political Development and Emergent Democracy*, London: Routledge, 2003.

——— *Iraq: People, History, Politics*, Cambridge: Polity, 2007.

———'From civil war to calculated compromise: The unification of the Kurdistan Regional Government in Iraq', in Lowe, Robert and Gareth Stansfield (eds), *The Kurdish Policy Imperative*, London: Chatham House, 2010, pp. 130-44.

'The Unravelling of the Post-First World War State System? The Kurdistan Region of Iraq and the Transformation of the Middle East', International Affairs 89:2 (2013), pp. 259-82.

———'The Islamic State, the Kurdistan Region and the Future of Iraq: Assessing UK Policy Options', *International Affairs* 90:6 (2014), pp. 1329-50.

Stansfield, Gareth and Liam Anderson, *Crisis in Kirkuk: the Ethnopolitics of Conflict and Compromise*, Philadelphia, PA: University of Pennsylvania Press, 2009.

Stansfield, Gareth and Hashem Ahmadzadeh, 'The Political, Cultural and Military Re-awakening of the Kurdish Nationalist Movement in Iran', *Middle East Journal* 64:1 (2010), pp. 11-27.

Stanton, G., 'Building an Anti-Genocide Regime', in Totten, S. (ed.), *The Prevention and Intervention of Genocide: A Critical Bibliographic Review*, Piscataway, NJ: Transaction Publishers, 2008.

Statistics Norway, 'Population, 1 January 2016, estimated', https://www.ssb.no/en/befolkning/statistikker/folkemengde, last accessed 13 January 2016.

Stein, Aaron, 'The Origins of Turkey's Buffer Zone in Syria', 11 December 2014, http://warontherocks.com/2014/12/the-origins-of-turkeys-buffer-zone-in-syria/

———'Turkey's Evolving Syria Strategy', *Foreign Affairs*, 9 February 2015, http://www.foreignaffairs.com/articles/143023/aaron-stein/turkeys-evolving-syria-strategy

———'Turkey's role in a shifting Syria', Atlantic Council, 13 May 2015, http://www.atlanticcouncil.org/blogs/menasource/turkey-s-role-in-a-shifting-syria

Stephens, Michael and Aaron Stein, 'The YPG: America's new best friend?' Al-Jazeera, 28 June 2015, http://www.aljazeera.com/indepth/opinion/2015/06/ypg-america-friend-isil-kurds-syria-150627073034776.html, last accessed 20 November 2015.

Stern, J. and J. M. Berger, *ISIS: The State of Terror*, New York: HarperCollins, 2015.

Stokes, Martin (ed.), *Ethnicity, Identity and Music: The Musical Construction of Place*, London: Bloomsbury, 1997.

Storey, J., *Inventing Popular Culture: From Folklore to Globalization*, Oxford: Blackwell, 2003.

Strohmeier, M., Crucial Images in the Presentation of a Kurdish National Identity: Heroes and Patriots, Traitors and Foes, Leiden: Brill, 2003.

Talabani, J., *Kurdistan wa al Hraka Al kawmiya*, Beirut: Dar Al Talia, 1971.

Taspinar, Omer, *Kurdish Nationalism and Political Islam in Turkey: Kemalist Identity in*

Transition, London: Routledge, 2005.

Tastekin, Fehim, 'KRG Trench Divides Syrian, Iraqi Kurds', Al-Monitor, 21 April 2014, http://www.al-monitor.com/pulse/contents/authors/fehim-tastekin.html?b=65

———— 'Kurdish Rivalry Delays Victory in Sinjar', Al-Monitor, 3 February 2015, http://www.al-monitor.com/pulse/originals/2015/02/turkey-syria-iraq-kurdish-rivalry-yezidi-lan.html?utm_source=Al-Monitor+Newsletter+%5BEnglish%5D&utm_campaign=654f8c1564-February_4_2015&utm_medium=email&utm_term=0_28264b27a0-654f8c1564-102324909

Tavvakoli, Khaled, 'Kordestân va vâqe'e-ye dovvom-e Khordâd' ['Kurdistan and the 2nd Khordad issue'], *Goftogu* 40 (2004), pp. 35-43.

Teitelbaum, Michael, 'Forced Migration: The Tragedy of Mass Expulsions', in Glazer, N. (ed.), *Clamor at the Gates: The New American Immigration*, San Francisco, CA: Institute for Contemporary Studies, 1985.

Tejel, Jordi, 'Les constructions de l'identité kurde sous l'influence de la «connexion kurdo-française» au Levant (1930-1946)', *European Journal of Turkish Studies* (2006).

———— *Le mouvement kurde de Turquie en exil. Continuités et discontinuités du nationalisme kurde sous le mandat français en Syrie et au Liban, 1925–1946*, Bern: Peter Lang, 2007.

———— *Syria's Kurds, History, Politics and Society*, London: Routledge, 2008.

———— 'Urban Mobilization in Iraqi Kurdistan during the British Mandate: Sulaimaniya, 1918–1930', *Middle Eastern Studies* 44:4 (2008), p. 537-52.

———— 'The Shared Political Production of *the East* as a *Resistant* Territory and Cultural Sphere in the Kemalist Era, 1923–1938', *European Journal of Turkish Studies* 10 (2009), http://ejts.revues.org/4064

———— 'Repenser les nationalismes minoritaires: le nationalisme kurde en Irak et en Syrie durant la période des mandats, entre tradition et modernité', *A contrario* 11 (2009), pp. 151-73.

———— 'Les territoires de marge de la Syrie mandataire: le mouvement autonomiste de la Haute Jazîra, paradoxes et ambiguïtés d'une intégration nationale inachevée (1936–1939)', *Revue des Mondes Musulmans et de la Méditerranée* 126 (2009), pp. 205-22.

———— 'Etudiants émigrés et activisme en Europe: le cas de la KSSE (1958–1975)', in Bozarslan, Hamit and Clémence Scalbert-Yücel (eds), *Joyce Blau: l'éternelle chez les Kurdes*, Paris: IKP, 2013, pp. 43-61.

Tejel, Jordi, Peter Sluglett, Riccardo Bocco, and Hamit Bozarslan (eds), *Writing the Modern History of Iraq. Historiographical and Political Challenges*, Singapore: World Scientific, 2012.

Tezcur, Gunes Murat, 'When Democratization Radicalizes: The Kurdish nationalist movement in Turkey', *Journal of Peace Research* 47:6 (2010), pp. 775-89.

BIBLIOGRAPHY

———'Prospects for Resolution of the Kurdish Question: a Realist Perspective', *Insight Turkey* 15:2 (2013), pp. 69-84.

——— 'The Ebb and Flow of Armed Conflict in Turkey: An Elusive Peace', in Romano, David and Mehmet Gurses (eds), *Conflict, Democratization and the Kurds in the Middle East,* New York: Palgrave Macmillan, 2014, pp. 171-88.

———'Violence and Nationalist Mobilisation: The Onset of the Kurdish Insurgency in Turkey', *Nationalities Papers* 43:2 (2015), pp. 248-66.

Tezcür, Güneş M. and Sabri Çiftçi, 'Radical Turks: Why Turkish citizens are joining ISIS?' *Foreign Affairs*, Council on Foreign Relations, 2014.

Thrift, Nigel, *Knowing Capitalism*, London: Sage, 2005.

Toktamis, Kumru, 'From Mobilisation to Nationhood,' MA thesis, New School for Social Research, 2007.

Touma, Habib Hassan, *The Music of the Arabs*, Winona, MN: Hal Leonard Books, 2003.

Tremblay, Pinar, 'Why is AKP Losing the Kurds?' Al-Monitor, 31 May 2015, http://www.al-monitor.com/pulse/originals/2015/05/turkey-elections-akp-losing-kurdish-support.html

Tripp, Charles, *A Modern History of Iraq*, Cambridge: Cambridge University Press, 2000.

Trondalen, J. M., 'The Euphrates River and the Tigris River: Water Resources Management – An Independent Technical Study', Compass Foundation, 2005.

Tur, Ozlem, 'Turkey and the Syrian crisis: deepening regional and domestic challenges', *Orient* 1 (2015), pp. 23-8.

Turgut, L., *Mündliche Literatur der Kurden in den Regionen Botan und Hekari*, Berlin: Logos Verlag, 2009.

Türkyilmaz, Yektan, *Rethinking Genocide: Violence and Victimhood in Eastern Anatolia, 1913–1915*, PhD dissertation, Duke University, NC, 2011.

Tuyizere, Alice, *Peace, Gender and Development: The Role of Religion and Culture*, Kampala: Makerere University, Fountain Publishers, 2007.

Ubaidi, S., *Kiraaton Siyasia wa Nafsiya lil Iraq bahda al Takher*, Beirut: Arab Scientific Publisher, 2007.

UNDP, Iraq, *Women's Economic Empowerment, Integrating Women Into the Iraqi Economy*, UNDP, 2012.

UNESCO, 'Trans-disciplinary Project: Towards a Culture of Peace', 1998, http://www.unesco.org/cpp/uk/projects/infoe.html

UNESCO, World Education Forum, The Dakar Framework for Action, *Education for All: Meeting our Collective Commitments*, ED-2000/WS/27, Dakar, Senegal, 2000.

UNESCO Iraq Office, 'Literacy Network for Iraq, Gender and Education for All', http://www.lifeforiraq.org/en/content/gender-and-education-all, last accessed 9 January 2013.

BIBLIOGRAPHY

UNESCO, UNFPA, ESCWA, 'Civic Values and Life Skills, Iraq – Selected Documents consulted', 2012.

UNESCO, UNHCR, INEE, Inter-Agency Peace Education Program, Skills for Constructive Living: Overview of the Program, Community Course Booklet, Facilitators' and Trainers' Training Guide, Teacher Activity Book, France, 2005.

UNESCWA, 'Policy paper on current approaches to integrating civic values and life skills into formal and non-formal education in Iraq', 2012.

Üngör, Ugur Ü., *Young Turk Social Engineering: Mass Violence and the Nation State in Eastern Turkey, 1913–1950*, PhD dissertation, Amsterdam, 2009.

——— *The Making of Modern Turkey: Nation and State in Eastern Anatolia, 1913-1950*, Oxford: Oxford University Press, 2011.

UNICEF, 'Promoting the Rights of Children in IRAQ: Rekindling Hope in a Time of Crisis: A Situation Analysis', UNICEF, Iraq support Center in Amman, Jordan, 2007.

UNICEF, *Girls' Education in Iraq*, 2010.

United Nations Assistance Mission for Iraq (UNAMI), United Nations Commission on Human Rights Agency (UNAMI) and ASUDA, *Eliminating violence against women: perspectives on honour-related violence in the Iraqi Kurdistan Region*, Suleymaniya Governorate, Suleymaniya, Iraqi Kurdistan: UNAMI, UNHR and ASUDA, 2009.

——— 'Women in Iraq' Factsheet, 2013, http://unami.unmissions.org/LinkClick.aspx?file ticket=xqx9gxy7Isk%3D&tabid=2790&language=en-US

United Nations Charter, 1945, http://www.un.org

United Nations Commission on Human Rights (UNHR), 'Working towards the elimination of crimes against women committed in the name of honour. 57th session of the United Nations Commission on Human Rights', report no. 0246790, New York: United Nations, 2002.

United Nations General Assembly, Convention for the Prevention and Punishment of the Crime of Genocide: Resolution 260, 1948, http://www.ohchr.org

United Nations General Assembly, *Universal Declaration of Human Rights, Department of State publication, 3381*. Washington, DC: US Government Printing Office, 1949.

United Nations High Commissioner for Refugees (UNHCR), Official General Report on Northern Iraq, 2000.

United Nations International Law Commission, *ILC Report*, New York: UN Publications, 1991.

——— *ILC Report A/51/10*, New York: UN Publications, 1996.

United Nations Security Council, 'Report of the Specialists Appointed by the Secretary General to Investigate Allegation by the Islamic Republic of Iran Concerning the Use of Chemical Weapons, no. S/16433', 1984, http://www.securitycouncilreport.org/

atf/cf/%7B65BFCF9B-6D27-4E9C-8CD3-CF6E4FF96FF9%7D/Disarm%20
S16433.pdf

———Resolution 688, 1991, http://www.casi.org.uk/info/undocs/scres/1991/688e.pdf

University of Duhok, 'Financial Aid', http://www.uod.ac/en/financialaid, last accessed 14
March 2014.

——— 'Mission, Vision and Core Values', http://www.uod.ac/en/mission, last accessed 14
March 2014.

University of Kurdistan, Hawler, 'UKH Leads Women Empowerment in Higher Education', http://www.ukh.ac/detailsArticls.php?ZID=1&CID=106&AID=602, last
accessed 8 December 2012.

University of Sulaimani, 'Study', http://www.univsul.org/E_U_Xwendin.aspx, last accessed
14 March 2014.

US Department of State, Dispatch 1:8, 1990, p. 205.

———Iran and Iraq Human Rights Reports 2011, New York: Nova Publishers, 2012.

US Geological Survey, Water Science School, 'Irrigation Techniques', 2014, https://water.
usgs.gov/edu/irmethods.html

Uslu, Emrullah, 'The Transformation of Kurdish Political Identity in Turkey: Impact of
Modernisation, Democratisation and Globalisation,' PhD Thesis, University of
Utah, 2009.

Uzun, Adem, Living Freedom: The Evolution of the Kurdish Conflict in Turkey and the Efforts
to Resolve It, Berlin: Berghof Foundation, 2014.

Vali, Abbas, 'The Kurds and Their "Others": Fragmented Identity and Fragmented Politics', in
Jabar, Faleh and Hosham Dawod (eds), The Kurds, Nationalism and Politics, London: Saqi Books, 2006, pp. 49-78.

Van Bruinessen, Martin, Agha, Shaikh and State: On the Social and Political Organization of
Kurdistan, Utrecht: University of Utrecht, 1978.

Van Bruinessen, Martin, 'Kurdish Society, Ethnicity, Nationalism and Refugee Problems',
in Kreyenbroek, Philip G. and Stefan Sperl (eds), The Kurds: A Contemporary
Overview, Abingdon: Routledge, 1992, pp. 26-52.

Van Bruinessen, Martin, 'Mullas, Sufis and Heretics: The Role of Religion in Kurdish Society', Istanbul: Isis Press, 2000.

Van Bruinessen, Martin, 'The Qadiriyya and the Lineages of Qadiri Shaykhs in Kurdistan', in
Van Bruinessen, Martin, Mullas, Sufis and Heretics: The Role of Religion in Kurdish
Society, Istanbul: Isis Press, 2000, pp. 213-29.

Van Bruinessen, Martin, 'From Adela Khanun to Leyla Zana: Women as Political Leaders
in Kurdish History', in Mojab, Shahrzad (ed.), Women of a Non-State Nation: The
Kurds, Costa Mesa, CA: Mazda, 2001, pp. 95-112.

Van Bruinessen, Martin, and Joyce Blau, Islam des Kurdes, Paris: ERISM, 1998.

BIBLIOGRAPHY

Van den Berge, Wietse, 'Syrian Kurdish Political Activism: A Social Movement Theory Perspective,' *Middle East: Topics and Arguments* 4 (2015), pp. 160-69.

Van der Stoel, Max, *Reports on the Situation in Iraq*, 1993/74'E/CN.4/1994/58, 16; E/CN.4/1995/56, 15 February 1995, p. 14; 4 March 1996, 5; 14 November 1997 (A/C.3/52/7), 4; 23 November 1998; and the annual report, GENEVA, Press Release HR/CN/892, 31 March 1999.

Van Esveld, B., 'The Anfal Trial and the Iraqi High Tribunal', Report of the International Centre for International Justice, 2009, www.ictj.org

Van Wildenburg, Wladirmir, 'Border arrests reveal disunity, conflict among Syrian Kurds', Al-Monitor, 21 May 2013, http://www.al-monitor.com/pulse/originals/2013/05/pyd-arrests-syrian-kurds.html

———'Rival Kurdish parties battle for power in Syria, Al-Monitor, www.al-monitor.com/pulse/originals/2014/05/kurdistan-kdp-pyd-erbil-barzani-ocalan-syria.html, last accessed 24 September 2015.

Verdery, Katherine, *The Political Lives of Dead Bodies: Reburial and Postsocialist Change*, New York: Columbia University Press, 1999.

Vetesen, Arne Johan, 'Genocide: A Case of Responsibility for Bystanders', *Philosophy and Social Criticism* 27 (2001), pp. 1-33.

Vice-presidency for Legal Affairs, *Manshur-e hoquq-e shahrvandi, matn-e pish-nevis-e gheyr-e rasmi* ['Manifesto of citizens' rights: unofficial draft paper'], Tehran, 2013, p. 5.

Villelas, Ana, 'New Peace Talks in Turkey: Opportunities and Challenges in Conflict Resolution', *Insight Turkey* 15:2 (2013), pp. 19-26.

Vriens, L., 'Children, war, and peace: a review of fifty years of research from the perspective of a balanced concept of peace education', in Raviv, A., L. Oppenheimer and D. Bar-Tal (eds), *How Children Understand War and Peace*, San Francisco, CA: Jossey-Bass, 1999, pp. 27-58.

Wadie, Jwaideh, *The Kurdish Nationalist Movement: Its Origin and Development*, Syracuse University Press, 1960.

Wallimann, Isidor, Dobkowski, Michale (ed.), *Genocide and the Modern Age: Etiology and Case Studies of Mass Death*, London: Greenwood, 1987.

Watts, Nicole F., 'Institutionalizing Virtual Kurdistan West: Transnational Networks and Ethnic Contention in International Affairs', in Migdal, Joel S., *Boundaries and Belonging. States and Societies in the Struggle to Shape Identities and Local Practices*, Cambridge: Cambridge University Press, 2004, pp. 121-47.

———'Activists in Office: Pro-Kurdish Contentious Politics in Turkey,' *Ethnopolitics* 5:2 (2006), pp. 125-44.

———*Activists in Office: Kurdish Politics and Protest in Turkey*, Seattle: University of Washington Press, 2010.

———— 'The Role of Symbolic Capital in Protest: State-Society Relations and the Destruction of the Halabja Monument in Northern Iraq', *Comparative Studies of South Asia, Africa and the Middle East* 32:1 (2012), pp. 70-85.

———— 'Redefining the Kurdish Nation', in Lynch, Marc (ed.), *Rethinking Nation and Nationalism*, POMEPS Study Series 14 (May 2015), http://pomeps.org/2015/03/04/redefining-the-kurdish-nation/, last accessed 15 November 2015.

Wehr, Hans, *A Dictionary of Modern Written Arabic*, 4th edn, J. M. Cowan (ed.), Urbana, IL: Spoken Language Services, 1994.

Weiss, M. and H. Hassan, *ISIS: Inside the Army of Terror*. New York: Simon & Schuster, 2015.

Welchman, Lynn and Sara Hossain, (eds), *Honour: Crimes, Paradigms and Violence Against Women*, London: Zed Books, 2005.

Weller, M., 'When Saddam is brought to court', *The Times*, 3 September 1990, p. 92.

Werbner, Pnina, 'Veiled Interventions in Pure Space: Shame and embodied struggles among Muslims in Britain and France', Special Issue on 'Authority and Islam', *Theory, Culture and Society* 24:2 (2007), pp. 161-86.

Whitaker, Ben., Revised and Updated Report on the Question of the Prevention and Punishment of the Crime of Genocide, no. E/CN.4/Sub.2/1985:6, 1985.

White, Benjamin T., 'The Kurds of Damascus in the 1930s: Development of a Politics of Ethnicity', *Middle Eastern Studies* 46:6 (2010), pp. 901-17.

White, Damian, *Bookchin: A Critical Appraisal*, London: Pluto Press, 2008.

Wikan, Unni, *In* Honour *of Fadime: Murder and Shame*, Chicago: University of Chicago Press, 2008.

Wilgenberg, Wladimir van, 'Russia's intervention in Syria and the Kurdish question', *The Diplomat* (online), 9 March 2016, http://thediplomat.com/2016/03/russias-intervention-in-syria-and-the-kurdish-question/, last accessed 14 October 2016.

Willett, Edward, *The Iran-Iraq War, War and Conflict in the Middle East*, New York: Rosen Publishing Group, 2004.

Wilmshurst, David, *The Ecclesiastical Organisation of the Church of the East, 1318-1913*, Leuven: Peeters, 2000.

Wimmer, Andreas and Nina Glick Schiller, 'Methodological Nationalism and Beyond: Nation-state Building, Migration and the Social Sciences', *Global Networks* 2:4 (2002).

Wölte, Sonja, *Human Rights Violations against Women During War and Conflict*, Geneva: Women's International League for Peace and Freedom, Report of a Roundtable Discussion parallel to the UN Commission on Human Rights, 1997.

World Bank, 'Kurdistan Region of Iraq: Economic and Social Impact Assessment of the Syrian Conflict and the ISIS Crisis', Washington, DC: World Bank, 2015, https://openknowledge.worldbank.org/handle/10986/21597 License: CC BY 3.0 IGO

BIBLIOGRAPHY

Yalcin Mousseau, Demet, 'An Inquiry into the linkage among the nationalizing policies, democratization and ethno-nationalist conflicts: the Kurdish case in Turkey', *Nationalities Papers* 40:1 (2012), pp. 45-62.

Yamani, Mai (ed.), *Feminism and Islam*, New York: New York University Press, 1996, pp. 141-94.

Yanik, Lerna, '"Nevruz" or "Newroz"? Deconstructing "the Invention" of a Contested Tradition in Turkey', *Middle Eastern Studies* 46:2 (March 2006), pp. 285-302.

Yeğen, M., 'The Kurdish Question in Turkish State Discourse', *Journal of Contemporary History* 34:4 (1999), pp. 555-68.

Yeleser, Selin, 'A Turning Point in the Formation of the Kurdish Left in Turkey: The Revolutionary Eastern Cultural Hearths (1969–1971),' MA Thesis, Boğaziçi University, 2011.

Yilmaz, Ensaroglu, 'Turkey's Kurdish Question and the Peace Process', *Insight Turkey* 15:2 (2013), pp. 7-17.

Yüksel, M., 'Dengbêj, Mullah, Intelligentsia: The Survival and Revival of the Kurdish Kurmanji Language in the Middle East, 1925-1960', PhD thesis, University of Chicago, 2011.

Yuval-Davis, Nira, 'Interview with Professor Nira Yuval-Davis: After gender and nation', *Studies of Ethnicity and Nationalism* 9:1 (2009), pp. 128-38.

Zaman, 'Erdoğan'dan IŞİD ve PKK açıklaması' ['Erdoğan's ISIS and PKK declaration'], http://www.zaman.com.tr/gundem_erdogandan-isid-ve-pkk-aciklamasi_2247277.html,

Zaman, A., 'PM Barzani: Shiite militias should be regulated', Al-Monitor, 24 March 2015.

Zeydanlioğlu, W., 'Turkey's Kurdish language policy', *International Journal of the Sociology of Language* 217 (2012), pp. 99-125.

Zolberg, Aristide R., Astri Suhrke, and Sergio Aguayo, 'International Factors in the Formation of Refugee Movements', *International Migration Review*, 20:2 (1986), pp. 151-70.

———*Escape from Violence: Conflict and the Refugee Crisis in the Developing World*, Oxford: Oxford University Press, 1989.

ABOUT THE CONTRIBUTORS

Hashem Ahmadzadeh received his doctorate on Middle East Studies from Uppsala University. His dissertation, 'Nation and Novel: A Study of Persian and Kurdish Narrative Discourse', was published by Uppsala University the same year. Besides conducting research about various aspects of Kurdish culture and literature, he has been teaching at the University of Exeter, the University of Uppsala and the French–Lebanese University in Kurdistan.

Christine Allison holds the Ibrahim Ahmed Chair of Kurdish Studies at the University of Exeter. She studied Classics and French at Oxford followed by a doctorate on the oral traditions of the Yezidis of Iraq at the School of Oriental and African Studies (SOAS), University of London. After a lectureship at INALCO, Paris, she joined Exeter's Centre for Kurdish Studies in 2007. She writes on folklore, memory, orality and religious minorities of the Middle East.

Harriet Allsopp is an academic scholar whose research has focused on Kurdish political organization, nationalisms and channels of representation and dissent in Syria. She holds a PhD in Politics from Birkbeck College, University of London and is the author of *The Kurds of Syria: Political Parties and Identity in the Middle East* (I. B. Tauris, 2014).

Sabri Ateş is an associate professor at Southern Methodist University's Department of History in Dallas, Texas. He is the author of *Tunalı Hilmi Bey: Osmanlıdan Cumhuriyet'e Bir Aydın* (Istanbul: Iletişim Yayınları, 2009), and *Ottoman-Iranian Borderlands: Making a Boundary* (Cambridge: Cambridge University Press, 2013). At present he is working on a new book project entitled 'Sheikh Abdulqadir Nehri and the Pursuit of an Independent Kurdistan'.

Henri Barkey is Director of the Middle East Program at the Woodrow Wilson Center, Washington, DC. He is also the Cohen Professor of International Relations at Lehigh University.

Nazand Begikhani is a senior research fellow at the University of Bristol. She has over twenty years' experience in research, writing, advocacy for women's rights and consultancy. She has published a number of articles and books on gender, identity, violence and honour crimes, including *Honour-based Violence: Experiences and Counter Strategies in Iraqi Kurdistan and the UK Kurdish Diaspora* (with Gill & Hague, Farnham: Ashgate, 2015). She was awarded the UK Emma Humphrey's Memorial Prize (2000) and the Kurdistan Gender Equality Prize (2015) for her writing and activism against gender-based violence. She is also an award-winning poet with eight poetry collections.

Ofra Bengio is Senior Research Associate and Head of Kurdish Studies Program at the Moshe Dayan Center, Tel Aviv University. She is the author of several books and over a hundred essays and articles on the history of the Middle East, with special emphasis on the Kurds.

Hamit Bozarslan received a doctorate in history in 1992 and in political sciences in 1994. Since 1999, he teaches at the Ecole des hautes études en sciences sociales (EHESS) in Paris. He is the author of *Révolution et état de violence Moyen-Orient 2011-2015* (Paris: Éditions du CNRS, 2015), *Une histoire de la violence au Moyen-Orient* (Paris: Éditions La Découverte, 2008), and *La question kurde: Etats et minorités au Moyen-Orient* (Paris: Presses de Sciences Po, 1997).

Nader Entessar is Professor and Chair of the Department of Political Science and Criminal Justice at the University of South Alabama. He is the author of many books, articles and book chapters on the Middle East, including *Kurdish Ethnonationalism* (Boulder, CO: Lynne Rienner, 1992) and *Kurdish Politics in the Middle East* (Lanham, MA: Lexington Books, 2009). He is also the co-author, with Kaveh Afrasiabi, of *Iran Nuclear Negotiations: Accord and Detente Since the Geneva Agreement of 2013* (Lanham, MA: Rowman and Littledfield, 2015) and of a forthcoming book on the Iran nuclear accord and the remaking of the Middle East.

Andrea Fischer-Tahir has a doctorate in anthropology. She has experience of extensive field research in Iraqi Kurdistan and has published on political history, memory, gender, and media. She has worked at Koye University, Kurdistan; the Zentrum Moderner Orient in Berlin; and Philipps University, Marburg. Recently, she edited *Disciplinary Spaces: Spatial Control, Forced Assimilation, and Narratives of Progress Since the Nineteenth Century* (Berlin: Transcript Verlag, 2017).

Olivier Grojean is Assistant Professor of Political Science at the University Paris 1 Panthéon-Sorbonne. His research focuses on political commitment, political parties, radicalization and violence in Turkey, Kurdistan and the Middle East. His most recent book, edited with Gilles Dorronsoro, *Identity and Politics in Turkey, Iran and Pakistan*, will be published in 2017 (Hurst/Oxford University Press).

ABOUT THE CONTRIBUTORS

Cengiz Gunes is Associate Lecturer at The Open University. His main research interests are in the areas of peace and conflict studies, the Kurds in the Middle East, the international relations of the Middle East and Turkish politics. He is author of *The Kurdish National Movement in Turkey: From Protest to Resistance* (Abingdon: Routledge, 2012).

Michael M. Gunter is Professor of Political Science at Tennessee Technological University. He also is the Secretary-General of the EU Turkey Civic Commission (EUTCC), headquartered in Brussels. He is the author or editor of many scholarly books on Kurds and the Kurdish question. His most recent books are *Out of Nowhere: The Kurds of Syria in Peace and War* (London: Hurst, 2014); and *The Kurds: A Modern History* (Princeton, NJ: Markus Wiener Publishers, 2017).

Gill Hague is Emeritus Professor of Violence Against Women Studies, University of Bristol. She has worked on violence against women for forty-five years and was a founder of the Centre for Gender and Violence Research, now one of the largest activist-based research centres in the world for this subject. Gill has produced more than 120 publications on gender violence, working internationally on the issue in countries including South Africa, India, Mexico, Uganda and Iraqi Kurdistan.

Mohammed Ihsan was minister for Extra Regional Affairs, Kurdistan Regional Government, from 2005 to 2011, and variously Minister for Human Rights, President of the General Board for Disputed Areas in Iraq, International Investigator for Genocide crimes in Iraq (2001 to 2005), and Kurdistan Representative to Federal Government in Iraq (2007 to 2012). He holds a doctorate in International Law from the University of London and a second doctorate (Exon) in Political Science from the University of Exeter. He is Senior Research Fellow in Defence Studies Department at King's College London and Honorary Research Follow at University of Exeter. He has authored various articles and books on Kurdistan and Iraq. In the last few years most of his research has been devoted to the Kurdish question and the Middle East, as well as investigations into genocide and war crimes.

Benjamin Isakhan is Associate Professor of Politics and Policy Studies and Founding Director of POLIS, a research network for Politics and International Relations at the Alfred Deakin Institute for Citizenship and Globalization, Deakin University, Australia. He is also Adjunct Senior Research Associate, Department of Politics and International Relations at the University of Johannesburg, South Africa.

Joost Jongerden is an assistant professor at the Rural Sociology Group and the Center for Space, Place and Society at Wageningen University and has a special appointment as Professor at the Asian Platform for Global Sustainability &

Transcultural Studies at Kyoto University in Japan. His main interest is the relation between people, place and power.

Zeynep Kaya is a research fellow at the Middle East Centre and research officer at the Centre for Women, Peace and Security at the London School of Economics and Political Science. She received her doctorate from the LSE and works on Kurdish politics in the Middle East and gender and displacement in Iraq.

Diane King is Associate Professor of Anthropology at the University of Kentucky. Her work focuses on kinship, gender, the state, migration and religion in the Middle East, with a particular focus on Kurdistan, where she was one of the few anthropologists to undertake residential participant observation research in the 1990s. Her most recent book is *Kurdistan on the Global Stage: Kinship, Land, and Community in Iraq* (New Brunswick, NJ: Rutgers University Press, 2014).

Janet Klein is an associate professor of History at the University of Akron, and received her doctorate from Princeton University in 2002. Her work explores the construction of minorities in the late-Ottoman period. She is the author of *The Margins of Empire: Kurdish Militias in the Ottoman Tribal Zone* (Stanford, CA: Stanford University Press, 2011) and numerous articles.

Michiel Leezenberg teaches in the Philosophy Department and in the Islam in the Modern World program at the University of Amsterdam. He has spent considerable time doing field research in Kurdistan, and has published widely on the politics, society, economics and intellectual history of the region.

Robert Lowe is the Deputy Director of the Middle East Centre at the London School of Economics. He is also the Executive Director of the British Society for Middle Eastern Studies. Robert worked for the Middle East and North Africa Programme at Chatham House from 2001-2010. He held a Research Fellowship from The Leverhulme Trust from 2008 to 2010.

Renad Mansour is an academy fellow at Chatham House. He is also a guest lecturer at the London School of Economics, where he teaches on the international relations of the Middle East. He has held positions as lecturer and supervisor at the faculty of politics at the University of Cambridge. Mansour was also an El-Erian fellow at the Carnegie Middle East Center.

Francis Owtram is an honorary research fellow at the University of Exeter and a Gulf History Specialist at the British Library. He previously lectured in the Department of Politics and International Relations at the University of Kurdistan Hewler, Erbil,

Iraq. His research interests include unrecognized states, federalism, global political economy and foreign policy with special reference to Iraq and Oman.

Hakan Özoğlu is Professor of History and the Director of Middle Eastern Studies at the University of Central Florida. His publications include *Kurdish Notables and the Ottoman State: Evolving Identities Competing Loyalties and Shifting Boundaries* (Albany, NY: SUNY Press, 2004), and *Caliphate to Secular State: Power Struggle in the Early Turkish Republic* (Santa Barbara, CA: Praeger, 2011). He is the recipient of a 2017-18 Fulbright Core Fellowship.

Bill Park is a Senior Lecturer in the Defence Studies Department, King's College, London. He is a council member for the British Institute at Ankara (BIAA), an editorial board member for the journal *Mediterranean Politics*, and sits on the international advisory panel for the journal Turkish Studies. He is also Visiting Scholar at TOBB-ET University in Ankara.

Walter Posch studied Turkish and Ottoman History and Iranian Studies in Vienna, Istanbul and Bamberg/Germany. He worked as a Middle East analyst focusing on Iran, Turkey, Iraq, the Kurdish Issue and political Islam for the National Defense Academy of the Austrian Army (2000-2004, and 2015-), at the European Union Institute for Security Studies (EUISS 2004-2009) and at the German Institute for International Affairs (SWP 2010-2014).

Katherine Ranharter is a PhD candidate at the University of Exeter. Her main research interests comprise Kurdish and Iraqi politics, gender, conflict and society. She is the author of *Gender Equality and Development After Violent Conflict: The Kurdistan Region of Iraq* (London: Palgrave Macmillan, 2015).

David Romano holds the Thomas G. Strong Chair in Middle East Politics at Missouri State University. He is the author of *The Kurdish Nationalist Movement* (Cambridge: Cambridge University Press, 2006) and the co-editor of *Conflict, Democratization and the Kurdish Issue in the Middle East* (London: Palgrave Macmillan, 2014). He writes a weekly political column for *Rudaw*, an Iraqi Kurdish newspaper.

Clémence Scalbert-Yücel has a doctorate in geography from La Sorbonne University Paris IV and a BA in Kurdish language and civilisation from the Institut National des Langues et Civilisations Orientales. She is Senior Lecturer at the Institute of Arab and İslamic Studies at the University of Exeter where she teaches ethnopolitics and Kurdish Studies. She is the author of several works on language policies, Kurdish literature and heritage including *Langue, Littérature et engagement: Le champ* *littéraire kurde en Turquie - 1980-2010* (Paris, Petra, 2014). She is a member of the editorial board of the *European Journal of Turkish Studies*.

Kelsey Shanks is a Middle East researcher focused on youth, education and conflict. She has both practical and academic experience of working on youth related issues in fragile environments; with significant experience in Iraq and Somalia. She has served as a peace-building education advisor to UNICEF Iraq and as education technical advisor to UNAMI Political Affairs. She has held research positions at the University of Ulster's UNESCO center, the University of York's Postwar Reconstruction and Development Unit (PRDU) and the Institute of Arab and Islamic Studies at the University of Exeter. Her publications focus on the relationship between youth and conflict: with specific interest in the politicization of identity through formal education structures and educations potential role in building peace.

Greg Shapland is a writer on politics, security and resources in the Middle East and North Africa. He was Head of Research Analysts in the FCO from 2010-13 and is now affiliated to Chatham House and the Universities of Sussex and Exeter. He is the author of *Rivers of Discord: International Water Disputes in the Middle East* (London: Hurst, 2007).

Mohammed Shareef is a lecturer in Politics and International Relations of the Middle East at the University of Exeter, and previously a lecturer in International Relations at the University of Sulaimani in Kurdistan. Shareef completed his doctorate in International Relations at the University of Durham and has an MSc in International Relations from the University of Bristol. His research interests include US foreign policy in the Middle East. He is the author of, amongst others, *The United States, Iraq and the Kurds: Shock, Awe and Aftermath* (Abingdon: Routledge, 2014).

Gareth Stansfield is Professor of Middle East Politics at the University of Exeter. He is also a Senior Associate Fellow of the Royal United Services Institute (RUSI), and a Global Fellow of the Wilson Center, Washington, DC. He has worked extensively on the politics of Iraq and Kurdistan for twenty years, with research projects including the development of the Kurdistan Region of Iraq in the 1990s, the state-building process in post-regime change Iraq, and the conflict management of Kirkuk and other disputed territories.

Jordi Tejel is a research professor at the Graduate Institute of International and Development Studies, Geneva. His main research interests include state–society relations, border issues, nationalism and state-building in the Middle East. His most recent books include *Syria's Kurds: History, Politics and Society* (Abingdon: Routledge, 2009); (ed. with Peter Sluglett, Riccardo Bocco, and Hamit Bozarslan, *Writing the History of Iraq: Historiographical and Political Challenges* (Hackensack,

ABOUT THE CONTRIBUTORS

NJ: World Scientific Press, 2012); and *La question kurde: passé et présent* (Paris: L'Harmattan, 2014).

Nicole F. Watts is a professor in the Department of Political Science at San Francisco State University. Her publications include *Activists in Office: Kurdish Politics and Protest in Turkey* (Seattle, WA: University of Washington Press, 2010) and many articles on dissent and campaigns for political change in the Kurdistan region of Iraq; especially in Halabja, the focus of her current book.

Nahro Zagros is Vice President of Soran University, Kurdistan, Iraq. He did his doctorate in ethnomusicology at the University of York. His research interests include cultural anthropology, musicology, Yezidism and Kurdistan's socio-political affairs within the wider Middle-Eastern context.